THE OXFORD INTERNATIONAL LAW LIBRARY

THE OXFORD INTERNATIONAL LAW LIBRARY

This series features works on substantial topics in international law which provide authoritative statements of the chosen areas. Taken together they map out the whole of international law in a set of scholarly reference works and treatises intended to be of use to scholars, practitioners, and students.

Multinational Enterprises and the Law

Second Edition

PETER T MUCHLINSKI

LLB (Lond), LLM (Cantab), Barrister,
Professor in International Commercial Law,
The School of Oriental and African Studies,
University of London

OXFORD
UNIVERSITY PRESS

OXFORD

UNIVERSITY PRESS

Great Clarendon Street, Oxford OX2 6DP

Oxford University Press is a department of the University of Oxford.
It furthers the University's objective of excellence in research, scholarship,
and education by publishing worldwide in

Oxford New York

Auckland Cape Town Dar es Salaam Hong Kong Karachi
Kuala Lumpur Madrid Melbourne Mexico City Nairobi
New Delhi Shanghai Taipei Toronto

With offices in

Argentina Austria Brazil Chile Czech Republic France Greece
Guatemala Hungary Italy Japan Poland Portugal Singapore
South Korea Switzerland Thailand Turkey Ukraine Vietnam

Oxford is a registered trade mark of Oxford University Press
in the UK and in certain other countries

Published in the United States
by Oxford University Press Inc., New York

British Library Cataloguing in Publication Data

Data available

Library of Congress Cataloging in Publication Data

Muchlinski, Peter.
Multinational enterprises and the law / Peter T. Muchlinski. — 2nd ed.
  p. cm. — (The Oxford international law library)
Includes bibliographical references and index.
  ISBN 978–0–19–928256–2 (hardback : alk. paper) — ISBN 978–0–19–922796–9
(pbk. : alk. paper)   1. International business enterprises—Law and legislation.
2. International business enterprises.   I. Title.
  K1322.M83 2007
  346'.065—dc22   2007010207

Typeset by Newgen Imaging Systems (P) Ltd., Chennai, India
Printed in Great Britain
on acid-free paper by
Antony Rowe Ltd., Chippenham, Wiltshire

ISBN 978–0–19–928256–2 (Hbk.)
ISBN 978–0–19–922796–9 (Pbk.)

1 3 5 7 9 10 8 6 4 2

Preface and Acknowledgments
to the Second Edition

The subject of regulating multinational enterprises (MNEs) has grown apace since the publication of the first edition in 1995. I was once asked whether focusing on 'multinationals' was not a little '*passé*'. The need for so much new material in this edition suggests that the question can be answered 'not yet'! Since 1995 we have witnessed the founding and operation of the World Trade Organization (WTO), the rise of many new regional economic groupings, the growth of new economic powers such as India and China and, with all of this, the continued rise of a globally integrated economy. All have had legal consequences upon the economic regulation of MNEs and the foreign direct investment (FDI) carried out by such firms. These effects will be discussed both at the conceptual level in Part I and at the level of national regulation in Part II.

Of particular note are two major developments, which have necessitated significant changes from the first edition. The first is the development of a social dimension to MNE regulation. Since 1995, the role of MNEs in the protection of fundamental rights has become a central issue. These rights include labour rights, human rights, and environmental protection rights. The result has been a growth of concern over 'international corporate social responsibility' (ICSR) which focuses on the role of MNEs in the process of upholding fundamental rights and furthering sustainable development. Accordingly, a new Part III has been added with specialist chapters on all three of the above mentioned themes. Equally, the discussion of regulatory policy in chapter 3 highlights ICSR as a factor in the development of policy responses to MNEs.

The second major development since 1995 has been the rapid rise in international investment arbitration during the first years of the 21st century. This has generated a mass of new arbitral decisions all of which have an important contribution to make towards the interpretation of international investment agreements. This is especially so in the case of bilateral investment agreements (BITs) of which there are now nearly 3000 in existence. These developments are analysed in Part IV. The mass of new decisions has resulted in the need for an additional chapter, chapter 16, dealing with the issues of non-discrimination, fair and equitable treatment, and full protection and security. Furthermore, chapter 15 has been comprehensively rewritten to take account of the new decisions on takings of property, with particular stress upon the issue of regulatory takings. These substantive chapters are followed by a fully revised chapter 17 on the codification of international standards, which includes a discussion of the failure of the Multilateral Agreement on Investment and of the adoption of investment rules in the WTO, and the final chapter, chapter 18, on the procedural aspects of international dispute settlement.

I would like to express my thanks, first of all, to Sarah Hibbin and Feja Lesniewski for their invaluable help in tracking down materials, and making sure that I did not miss anything of note, and to Dr Alan McKenna of Kent Law School for his indispensable assistance in updating the tables. In addition my thanks go out to Michael Likosky, who commented on Part III, Alice Palmer, who offered valuable comments on chapter 14, Olga Martin-Ortega, for her comments on chapter 13, Christoph Schreuer, for his guidance on the new arbitrations and their contents, and to all those who have discussed my ideas with me over the past few years. I would like to mention in particular Karl Sauvant, with whom I had the pleasure to work on the UNCTAD Series on Issues in International Investment Agreements and various editions of the *World Investment Report*, a major exercise in making sure I learnt properly the ins and outs of international investment rules. Also at UNCTAD my thanks go to Victoria Aranda, Anna Joubin-Bret, Argyrios Fatouros, Torbjorn Fredriksson, Kalman Kalotay, Pedro Roffe, Elisabeth Tuerk, Joerg Weber, and James Zhan for their stimulating input, over the past nine years, into our mutual learning process on MNEs and FDI, and to M Sornarajah with whom I worked happily on numerous joint projects and whose own work in this field has been a source of stimulation.

I would have found learning about the social dimension of MNE regulation much harder but for exchanges with a number of Australian based colleagues. In particular Sarah Joseph has given me great help, and food for thought, both through her presentations and published work. I also thank Tom Campbell and David Kinley, who invited me to participate in conferences in Australia in 2001, where I presented the first drafts of what were to become chapter 13 and inputs into chapter 3. Thanks are due too to Menno Kamminga and Sam Zia Zariffi whose workshop in Rotterdam in 1999 allowed me to meet and to discuss these issues with some of the leading scholars in the field.

More recently I have had the benefit of exchanging ideas with colleagues on the Committee on the International Law on Foreign Investment of the International Law Association. There are too many to mention by name, so my thanks to you all. Special mention should be made of Federico Ortino and Gillian Triggs, who made me think differently about investor obligations as well as rights, and Myfanwy Badge whose work on corporate liability has ensured that I have been fully up to date with developments in that sphere. I have also had the benefit of learning from my research students, three of whom have since published their doctoral work and are all cited where relevant. They are Drs Amazu Asouzu, Amanda Perry-Kessaris and Rory Sullivan. I look forward to my current, and future, research students contributing in a similar manner to future editions!

Further thanks are due to the editors and staff at the various journals from which I have had permission to reproduce sections of my earlier published work. These are: the International Lawyer, International Affairs, the International and Comparative Law Quarterly, the Company Lawyer, Non-State Actors and International Law and the Connecticut Law Review. I also thank Cambridge University Press, for permission to use extracts from a forthcoming book chapter in chapter 13. In addition I thank the International Law Association (ILA) and Christoph Schreuer, as Chair of the ILA Committee on the International Law on Foreign Investment, for permission to draw upon the First Report of the Committee, which I had the pleasure to write as Rapporteur to the Committee. Full acknowledgments and specific references are given at appropriate points in the text.

Finally I would like to express my thanks for the financial support offered for this project from the School of Oriental and African Studies and to Kent Law School for giving me the opportunity to come to grips with WTO Law over the past five years, an indispensable input into the new edition.

I have endeavoured to state the law accurately as at 1 October 2006.

Peter T Muchlinski
The School of Oriental and African Studies
1 October 2006

Preface and Acknowledgments
to the First Edition

This book seeks to give a comprehensive introduction to the regulation of multi-national enterprises (MNEs) as the principal vehicles for foreign direct investment (FDI).[1] The question of how states should respond to MNEs was first placed on the post-war political agenda in the late 1960s. Although there are numerous historical instances of concern over 'international combines' the contemporary debate on MNEs has acquired a far greater political importance, for reasons that will be explored in chapter 1. This has resulted in systematic policy responses to such enterprises. It is the purpose of this book to trace the evolution of these responses since the 1960s and to highlight the considerable changes in approach towards MNE regulation over the last 30 years. As such the book constitutes a study of evolution and change in international business regulation. Naturally, a book of this size cannot act as an encyclopaedia of the law relating to MNEs and FDI. It can do no more than familiarize the reader with the principal issues and methods of MNE regulation that human endeavour has so far created. The book suggests some possible future developments in this area, but, as a result of the uncertainty that global economic and political change has generated in recent years, this aspect of the work is approached with some caution. The primary focus of the book is legal. In particular, Part II sets out a relatively detailed account of the principal techniques of MNE regulation used by home and host states, while Part III considers the emerging responses of international law to this type of business association. However, the book would lack coherence if it were restricted to a description of legal sources without relating them to the existing knowledge, possessed by other social sciences, of MNEs and their activities. Indeed, if one were to look at legal sources alone the MNE would not exist: all one would find is a series of national companies whose principal shareholder happens to be a foreign company, and/or a network of interlocking contracts between entities of different nationalities. No hint of the complex systems of international managerial control, through which the operations of the multinational group are conducted, would be discovered. Furthermore, in the absence of an interdisciplinary framework, the aims and objectives of the various legal responses to MNEs could not be properly understood.

---

[1] Foreign direct investment is defined as follows by Professor JH Dunning: '(1) The investment is made *outside* the home country of the investing company, but *inside* the investing company. Control over the use of the resources transferred remains with the *investor*. (2) It consists of a 'package of assets and intermediate products, such as capital, technology, management skills, access to markets, and entrepreneurship.' See JH Dunning *Multinational Enterprises and the Global Economy* (Wokingham: Addison Wesley, 1993) 5. Exhibit 1.2.

Their meaning, let alone their efficacy, could not be determined. Therefore Part I of this book is devoted to relating the knowledge of other disciplines about MNEs to the concerns of lawyers. Thereby, it is hoped to build a bridge between law and other disciplines involved in the study of MNEs, from which a valuable mutual discourse could ensue.

A book that seeks to offer an introduction to so wide-ranging a topic could not have been written without the help of others. In particular, I would like to acknowledge the assistance, over the past 10 years, of my external examiners on the London University LLM course 'Multinational Enterprises and the Law' from which this book has evolved. They are, in chronological order, Professor Tom Hadden of the Queens University of Belfast, Dr Tony Carty of Glasgow University and Professor Sol Picciotto, formerly of the University of Warwick, now of the University of Lancaster. Each has provided me with important and constructive comments upon my course and upon the ideas that I have been developing. Furthermore, each has, in turn, provided me with the opportunity to test certain thoughts and draft chapters upon audiences at their respective home universities, or at conferences organized by them. The feedback from these expositions has proved to be very valuable. In addition I would like to express my thanks to Professor William E Butler of University College London for giving me the opportunity to present earlier drafts of chapters 15 and 17 at successive sessions of the Anglo-Soviet Symposium on Public International Law in 1990 and 1991. Again the feedback was of great value.

Furthermore, special thanks must be given to Tom Hadden for reading and commenting upon the drafts of chapters 1 to 5 and chapter 9. Thanks is also due to the following colleagues at LSE who have allowed me to benefit from their expertise in comments offered upon drafts of individual chapters: Professor Rosalyn Higgins QC, who read and commented upon the international legal aspects of the book; Professor Lord Wedderburn of Charlton QC, who gave me considerable assistance and important reflections upon chapter 13; Professor Anthony Hopwood, who offered me the benefit of his expertise in international accounting by reviewing chapter 10; Professor Tom Nossiter, who read and commented upon an earlier draft of chapter 4; and Judith Freedman, who offered a valuable critique of an earlier draft of chapter 9. Naturally, I remain solely responsible for any errors that remain.

Thanks are also due to the numerous research assistants who have helped me over the years to track down materials and references. Foremost among them is my research student Amazu Asouzu, who has offered invaluable help in reading the entire draft of the manuscript, commenting critically upon my ideas, and updating and completing references. Others who have given much help include: Ruth Gordon, Elizabeth Small, Richard Pailthorpe, Matthew Logan, Tee Golvala, Deshpal Singh Panesar, and Nicholas White. I would further like to thank all my students on the 'Multinationals' course who have, over the years, discussed my thoughts in class, given me important materials and subsequently corresponded with me over developments in their respective home jurisdictions. Indeed, I would like to acknowledge my debt to the LSE for providing me with a stimulating academic environment in which to bring this project to a successful conclusion. I would like to offer further thanks to the LSE Research Fund, which has supplied much of the funding for research assistance, and to the Nuffield Foundation, whose generous grant ensured that I could benefit from research assistance above and beyond the limits of in-house funding, and which allowed me to defray many of the costs of preparing the manuscript. A final word of acknowldgment is also due to my former employer and former colleagues at the University of Kent at Canterbury, where the first seeds for a book on the regulation of multinationals were sown, and where the first prototype for my course on multinationals was approved and tested.

I have endeavoured to state the law accurately as at 1 July 1994.

Peter T Muchlinski
London School of Economics and Political Science
1 July 1994

Contents

II. ECONOMIC REGULATION BY HOME AND HOST COUNTRIES

III. THE SOCIAL DIMENSION

Table of Cases

DECISIONS OF THE EUROPEAN COURT AND COMMISSION

The European Court of Justice and the Court of First Instance

DECISIONS OF INTERNATIONAL COURTS AND TRIBUNALS

International Centre for the Settlement of Investment Disputes (Decisions and Awards of ICSID Tribunals including NAFTA cases under the Additional Facility procedure)

WTO Dispute Settlement Body (Including GATT 1947 Panel Reports)

Table of Statutes

Table of EC Materials

Table of Treaties

Table of Official Publications of Governments and International Organizations

INTERNATIONAL ORGANIZATIONS

Andean Common Market (ANCOM)

Commission on Intellectual Property Rights

International Bank for Reconstruction and Development (IBRD or World Bank)

World Bank

United Nations Conference on Trade and Development (UNCTAD)

General

Abbreviations

African Journal of International and Comparative Law	RADIC
Alberta Law Review	Alta.L.Rev.
All England Law Reports	All ER
All India Reporter	AIR
American Journal of Comparative Law	Am.Jo.Comp.L
American Journal of Economics and Sociology	Am.J.Econ. & Soc.
American Journal of International Law	AJIL
American Society of International Law Proceedings	ASIL Proc
American University Journal of International Law and Policy	Am.U.J.Int'l L & Pol'y
Annuaire Français du Droit International	AFDI
Arbitration International	Arb.Int'l
Arbitration Journal	Arb.J
Atlantic Reporter	A
Australian Law Journal	ALJ
Australian Law Journal Reports	AJLR
British Journal of Industrial Relations	Brit.Jo.Ind.Rel.
British Journal of International Studies	Brit.J.Int.Stud.
British Yearbook of International Law	BYIL
Bulletin for International Fiscal Documentation	BIFD
Bundesgerichthofszeitung	BGHZ
Business History Review	Bus.Hist.Rev.
Business Lawyer	Bus.Law
Butterworths Company Law Cases	BCLC
California Appeal Cases Third Series	Cal.App.3d
Canadian Bar Review	Can.Bar.Rev.
Canadian Business Law Journal	Can.Bus.LJ
Columbia Journal of Transnational Law	Col.J.Transnat.L
Columbia Journal of World Business	Col.Jo.World Bus
Columbia Law Review	Col.LR
Command Paper	Cmnd or Cmd
Common Market Law Reports	CMLR
Common Market Law Review	CMLRev.
Company Lawyer	Co.Law
Connecticut Journal of International Law	Conn.J.Int'l.L
Connecticut Law Review	Conn. LR
Cornell International Law Journal	Cornell Int.L.Jo.
Criminal Appeal Reports	Cr.App.R

Delaware Journal of Corporate Law — Del.J.Corp.L
Dominion Law Reports Third Series — DLR 3d
Duke Law Journal — Duke LJ

Economic Journal — Econ.Jo.
European Business Law Review — EBLR
European Competition Law Review — ECLR
European Court Reports — ECR
European Journal of International Law — EJIL
European Law Review — ELR

Federal Register — Fed.Reg.
Federal Reporter Second Series — F 2d
Federal Supplement — F Supp
Fordam Law Review — Fordam L.Rev.

George Washington Journal of International Law and Economics — Geo.Washington Jo. Int'l Law & Econ.
Georgia Journal of International Law — Ga JIL

Harvard International Law Journal — Harv.ILJ
Harvard Law Review — Harv.LR
Hastings International and Comparative Law Review — Hastings Int'l & Comp.L.Rev.
Her Majesty's Stationery Office — HMSO

ICSID Review-Foreign Investment Law Journal — ICSID Rev-FILJ
Indian Journal of International Law — Ind.ILJ
Industrial Law Journal — ILJ
International Business Lawyer — Int'l Bus. Lawyer
International Company and Commercial Law Review — ICCLR
International and Comparative Law Quarterly — ICLQ
International Court of Justice Reports — ICJ Reports
International Journal of Accounting — Int.J.Acctg
International Journal of the Sociology of Law — Int'l.Jo.Soc.L
International Labour Review — Int'l.Lab.Rev.
International Law Reports — ILR
International Legal Materials — ILM
International Organization — Int.Org.
International Review of Industrial Property and Copyright Law — IIC
Iran-United States Claims Tribunal Reports — Iran-US CTR
Israel Law Review — Israel LR

Journal du Droit International — JDI
Journal of Business Law — JBL

Journal of Corporation Law	J.Corp L
Journal of Industrial Relations	Jo.Ind.Rel.
Journal of International Arbitration	Jo.Int'l.Arb.
Journal of International Business Studies	J.Int.Bus.Stud.
Journal of International Economic Law	JIEL
Journal of International Law and Economics	Jo.Int.Law & Econ.
Journal of Maritime Law and Commerce	Jo.Mart.L.& Comm.
Journal of Political Economy	Jo.Pol.Econ.
Journal of World Investment (now Journal of World Investment and Trade)	JWI (JWIT)
Journal of World Trade Law (now Journal of World Trade)	JWTL (JWT)
Law and Contemporary Problems	Law and Cont.Prob.
Law and Policy in International Business	Law & Pol.Int'l Bus.
Law Quarterly Review	LQR
Law Reports Appeal Cases	AC
Law Reports Chancery Division	Ch
Law Reports Queens (Kings) Bench	QB (KB)
Lawyer of the Americas	Law.Am
Lloyd's Law Reports	Lloyd's Rep
McGill Law Journal	McGill LJ
Melbourne Journal of International Law	Melbourne Jo Int'l.L
Michigan Law Review	Mich.L.Rev.
Modern Law Review	MLR
Neue Juristische Wochenschrift	NJW
New York Law Journal	NYLJ
New York Reporter Second Series	NY 2d
New York Supplement Second Series	NYS 2d
New York University Journal of International Law and Policy	NYUJ Int'l Law and Pol.
New York University Law Review	NYULR
New York University Law Quarterly Review	NYULQR
New Zealand Company Law Cases	NZCLC
North Carolina Journal of International and Commercial Regulation	NCJ Int'l & Com.Reg.
North Eastern Reporter Second Series	NE 2d
Northern Reporter	NR
Northwestern Journal of International Law and Business	NW J.Int'l Law & Bus.
Official Journal of the European Communities	OJ
Official Journal of the European Communities Special Edition	OJ Sp.Ed.
Oxford Bulletin of Economics and Statistics	Oxford.Bull.Econ. & Stat.

Pacific Reporter Second series	P 2d
Political Science Quarterly	Pol.Sci.Q
Proceedings of the Hague Academy of International Law	Hague Recueil
Property and Conveyancing Reports	P & CR
Quarterly Journal of Economics	Q.Jo.Econ.
Rutgers Law Review	Rutgers LR
South Eastern Reporter Second Series	SE 2d
South Western Reporter Second Series	SW 2d
Southern Reporter Second Series	SO 2d
Tax Cases	TC
Tax Law Review	Tax L Rev
Tax Notes International	Tax Notes Int'l
Texas International Law Journal	Texas ILJ
Thomas Jefferson Law Review	Thomas Jefferson L. Rev.
Trade Mark Review	TMR
Trade Regulation Reports	Trade Reg.Rep
Transactions of the Grotius Society	Trans.Grot.Soc
UNCTAD Review	UNCTAD Rev
United Kingdom Statutory Instrument	SI
United Kingdom Treaty Series	UKTS
United Nations Treaty Series	UNTS
United States Code	USC
Uniter States Law Week	USLW
United States Supreme Court Reports	US or S Ct
United States Treaty Series	UST
University of British Columbia Law Review	U.Brit.Col.LR
University of Chicago Law Review	U.Chi.L.Rev.
University of Miami Inter-American Law Review	U.Miami Inter-Am.L.Rev.
University of Miami Law Review	U.Miami L.Rev.
University of New South Wales Law Journal	UNSWLJ
University of Toronto Law Journal	U of Toronto LJ
Vanderbilt Journal of Transnational Law	Vanderbilt Jo.Transnat.Law
Virginia Journal of International Law	Va.J.Int'l.L
Weekly Law Reports	WLR
Yale Law Journal	Yale LJ
Yearbook of Commercial Arbitration	YB Comm.Arb.
Yearbook of the International Law Commission	YBILC

PART I

THE CONCEPTUAL FRAMEWORK

1

Getting to Know Multinational Enterprises

Multinational enterprises (MNEs) are perhaps the most talked about forms of business association in the contemporary 'globalizing' world and economy.[1] It is often said that the major MNEs have a turnover larger than many nation states, that they are powerful enough to set their own rules and to sidestep national regulation. They appear to be a power unto themselves.[2] This is by no means a new concern. Similar worries have been expressed at various points in modern history. The current debate has echoes in the past. It is possible to say that the origins of contemporary concern over MNEs arise from a number of factors present in the 1960s and 1970s. These centred on the rise of American MNEs in particular,[3] documented instances of sensational abuses of power by such firms, most notably in the overthrow of the elected Marxist government of Salvador Allende in Chile in 1973,[4] a trend of scepticism, if not outright hostility, towards Western capitalism among left-wing circles in Western countries, and opposition from the communist Eastern Bloc countries and China as an aspect of the Cold War.[5] These were matched by new developments in economic theory, which, for the first time,

---

[1] The terms 'globalizing' and 'globalization' are used with caution in this work. They are shorthand for some very complex, and not very well understood, transnational economic developments. The role of 'globalization' as an ideological and methodological issue in the development of regulatory policy towards MNEs will be considered in ch 3.

[2] See RS Barnet and RE Muller *Global Reach: The Power of Multinational Corporations* (New York: Simon and Schuster, 1974). For a more recent version of this argument see, for example, David Korten *When Corporations Rule the World* (West Hartford, Conn: Kumarian Press, 1995), Naomi Kline *No Logo* (London: Flamingo, 2000).

[3] For statistical data on the rise of US MNEs see Raymond Vernon *Sovereignty at Bay* (London: Pelican 1971) 40–41 (oil), 48–49 (non-oil extractive industries), 68–71 (manufacturing). According to Tugendhat the book value of US foreign direct investment rose from $7200m to $70 763m between 1946 and 1969: Christopher Tugendhat *The Multinationals* (London: Pelican, 1971) at 45. For concerns over US MNE power in Europe see Jean Servan-Schreiber *The American Challenge* (English edn, Harmondsworth: Penguin, 1968). For Japanese concerns see MY Yoshino 'Japan as Host to the International Corporation' in C. Kindleburger (ed) *The International Corporation* (Cambridge, Mass: MIT Press, 1970) from 345 especially 358–59.

[4] See Anthony Sampson *The Sovereign State: The Secret History of ITT* (London: Coronet, 1973) ch 11; See T Moran *Multinational Corporations and the Politics of Dependence: Copper in Chile* (Princeton University Press, 1977) 252–53; US Congress Senate Subcommittee on Multinationals: *Hearings on Multinational Corporations and US Foreign Policy* 93rd Congress 2nd Session (US Govt Printing Office 1974).

[5] To these may be added the widespread opposition to the Vietnam War which served further to vilify the US and the Western economic and political system that it led.

distinguished between cross-border trade and investment flows,[6] and in economic history, which documented the rise of modern MNEs.[7]

The 1960s and early 1970s were also the period when the newly independent states of the southern hemisphere coalesced into an international pressure group within the United Nations (UN), the so-called 'Group of 77' and demanded the introduction, through multilateral action, of a New International Economic Order as a means of ensuring economic independence. In this context the MNE could be seen as an agent of economic dependency exploiting the host developing country.[8] In response, the UN was encouraged to develop a comprehensive policy of MNE regulation to assist developing countries who felt powerless to act unilaterally, and who feared the more sinister effects of corporate power as witnessed by sensational cases of its abuse. The UN Secretary General was persuaded to set up a Group of Eminent Persons to study the role of MNEs in development and international relations. The Group reported on 24 May 1974.[9] The Group's report helped to lay down not only immediate UN policy in the field of MNEs, but also what could be described as the 'conventional framework' of issues generated by MNEs in their relations with developing countries.[10]

For now, in this introductory chapter it is essential to get to know what MNEs are. This requires, first, some discussion of definitions, if only because lawyers need some definitions of complex entities to determine what is being regulated! Secondly, the patterns of MNE growth over time and space will need to be considered. Thirdly, the main explanations of MNE growth, and the role of legal factors in this process, will be considered. That will lay the ground for chapter 2, which will introduce the MNE from the inside and compare business and legal forms of MNE organization, leading to the foundations of a theory of control. Finally, in this introductory part of the book, chapter 3 will deal with the development of MNE regulation, focusing on the economic costs and benefits of MNE activity for home and host countries, and the development of regulatory agendas. This

---

[6] See DK Fieldhouse 'The Multinational: A Critique of a Concept' in A Teichova et al (eds) *Multinational Enterprise in Historical Perspective* (Cambridge: Cambridge University Press, 1986) from 9 especially 13.

[7] Of importance here is the pioneering work of the Harvard University Comparative Multinational Enterprise Project, coordinated by Raymond Vernon in the late 1960s and early 1970s. See R Vernon *Sovereignty at Bay* above n 3; Mira Wilkins *The Emergence of Multinational Enterprise: American Business Abroad from the Colonial Era to 1914* (Harvard, 1970) and *The Maturing of Multinational Enterprise American Business Abroad from 1914 to 1970* (Harvard, 1974); Lawrence Franko *The European Multinationals* (Harper & Row, 1976); and the collection of papers in 48 Business History Review (Autumn 1974).

[8] The principal UN General Assembly Resolutions on the New International Economic Order are: Res 3201 (S–VI) of 9 May 1974 *The Declaration on the Establishment of a New International Economic Order*; Res. 3202 (S–VI) of 16 May 1974 *The Programme of Action on the Establishment of a New International Economic Order* both reproduced in 13 ILM 715–66 (1974). These were followed by Res 3281 (XXIX) of 15 January 1975 *The Charter of Economic Rights and Duties of States* reproduced in 14 ILM 251–65 (1975).

[9] UN Doc E/5500/Add l (Part I) 24 May 1974. The report is reproduced in 13 ILM 800 (1974).

[10] The Eminent Persons Report is discussed further in ch 3 at 119–21.

chapter will consider not only narrow economic analyses, but will extend to ideological issues and the interests of the various actors in the 'globalizing' international economic system, as currently understood.

(1) Problems of Definition

The first use of the term 'multinational' in relation to a corporation has been attributed to David E Lilienthal who, in April 1960, gave a paper to the Carnegie Institute of Technology on 'Management and Corporations 1985' which was later published under the title 'The Multinational Corporation'(MNC). Lilienthal defined MNCs as, 'corporations ... which have their home in one country but which operate and live under the laws and customs of other countries as well'.[11] This definition sees the MNC as a uninational enterprise with foreign operations. The approach is orientated towards the experience of US firms. Firms of multiple national origin, such as the Anglo-Dutch corporations Unilever or Royal Dutch Shell, are not considered. The existence of such firms alongside uninational MNCs has prompted a distinction to be made between these two groups of international business associations. Unfortunately, usage has not always been uniformly applied and some terminological confusion has resulted. This is particularly apparent when one compares the distinctions drawn by economists when defining the MNE with those that have entered into United Nations usage.

Economists have favoured a simple all-embracing formula defining as a 'multinational enterprise' any corporation which 'owns (in whole or in part), controls and manages income generating assets in more than one country'.[12] This definition distinguishes between an enterprise that engages in *direct investment*, which gives the enterprise not only a financial stake in the foreign venture but also managerial control, from one that engages in *portfolio investment*, which gives the investing enterprise only a financial stake in the foreign venture without any managerial control.[13] Thus the MNE is a firm that engages in *direct investment outside its home country*, that is, in *foreign direct investment* (FDI). The term 'enterprise' is favoured over 'corporation' as it avoids restricting the object of study to incorporated business entities and to corporate groups based on parent/subsidiary relations alone. International production can take numerous legal forms.[14] From an economic perspective the legal form is not crucial to the classification of an enterprise as 'multinational'.

[11] Quoted in DK Fieldhouse above n 6 at 10.

[12] Neil Hood and Stephen Young *The Economics of the Multinational Enterprise* (Longman, 1979) at 3. See too JH Dunning *Multinational Enterprises and the Global Economy* (Addison Wesley, 1993) 3–4.

[13] On the relationship between foreign portfolio investment and FDI see 'Special Feature: Foreign Portfolio and Direct Investment' 8 Transnational Corporations 7 (N. 1, 1999) and UNCTAD *World Investment Report 1997* (New York and Geneva: United Nations, 1997) ch III.

[14] On which see ch 2.

By contrast, the United Nations (UN) moved away from this simple formula towards a distinction between 'multinational corporations' (MNCs) and 'transnational corporations' (TNCs). In its report, the UN Group of Eminent Persons adopted the simple economist's definition of MNCs as 'enterprises which own or control production or service facilities outside the country in which they are based. Such enterprises are not always incorporated or private; they can also be co-operatives or state-owned entities'.[15] However, during discussions of the report at the Fifty-Seventh Session of ECOSOC in 1974, several representatives argued in favour of the term '*transnational corporation*'. This term, it was said, better expressed the essential feature of operation across national borders than did the term 'multinational'. That term should be reserved for enterprises which were jointly owned and controlled by entities from several countries. Latin American representatives pointed out that the term 'multinational' was being used by the Andean Group countries to refer to corporations jointly set up under Andean Group rules.[16] Such enterprises were not intended to come under UN scrutiny. They were different from uninational corporations operating across national borders.[17]

In response to such opinions, the ECOSOC adopted the term 'transnational corporation' for the purposes of the UN programme on MNEs.[18] Henceforth, what economists call 'multinationals' would be known as 'transnationals' in UN parlance. Thus UN terminology originally distinguished between enterprises owned and controlled by entities or persons from one country but operating across national borders – the '*transnational*' – and those owned and controlled by entities or persons from more than one country – the '*multinational*'. However, in practice, this distinction appears no longer to be made in UN publications and reports. The term TNC can be used to cover all types of cross-border business associations that engage in direct investment as opposed to portfolio investment or cross-border trade.

By contrast, the politically and economically more homogeneous group of states belonging to the OECD arrived, in 1976, at an agreed definition of the MNE for the purposes of the OECD Guidelines on Multinational Enterprises. According to the current version of the OECD Guidelines, multinational enterprises:

usually comprise companies or other entities established in more than one country and so linked that they may co-ordinate their operations in various ways. While one or more of these entities may be able to exercise a significant influence over the activities of others, their degree of autonomy within the enterprise may vary widely from one multinational enterprise to another. Ownership may be private, state or mixed.[19]

---

[15] See report of the UN Group of Eminent Persons *The Impact of Multinational Corporations on Development and on International Relations* above n 9 at 25.

[16] See further ch 2 at 75–76.

[17] See UN Commission on Transnational Corporations *Transnational Corporations in World Development: A Re-Examination* (New York: United Nations, 1978 UN Sales No E.78.II.A.5.) Annex I at 159.   [18] ibid.

[19] OECD *Guidelines for Multinational Enterprises* (Paris: OECD, 2000) or <http://www.oecd.org/dataoecd/56/36/192248.pdf> Guideline I 'Concepts and Principles' para 3. For the old version of this

The crucial characteristic of a MNE is, according to this definition, the ability to coordinate activities between enterprises in more than one country. Other factors are not decisive. The definition is, therefore, broad enough to encompass both equity and non-equity based direct investment, regardless of the legal form, or ownership, of the undertakings. The old version of this definition, which stressed control even more strongly by way of reference to the ability of one company to control the activities of another company located in another country, had been substantially adopted in the final version of the proposed text of the shelved United Nations Draft Code of Conduct on Transnational Enterprises.[20]

The above definitions should be seen as no more than broad conceptual guidelines as to which kinds of firms are MNEs and which are not. Inevitably, a certain degree of arbitrariness is involved, as exemplified in particular by the old terminological debates in the UN. Much depends on the purpose for which the definition is being devised and on the available evidence of international business activities. However one wishes to define *the* MNE, a task which may not be possible with any degree of accuracy, from a regulator's perspective the major consideration remains whether certain types of international business associations are, through the nature of their activities, so distinct from uninational enterprises that they require separate regulation.

In this respect it may be helpful to show how MNEs differ from uninational enterprises that share certain of their features.[21] The first of these is the multilocation domestic enterprise. MNEs may share the following similarities with this type of enterprise: first, they own income generating assets in more than one location and use these in combination with local resources to produce goods or services. Secondly, both types of enterprise enjoy the competitive advantages of a larger economic unit when compared with single plant enterprises. However, the crucial difference between a MNE and the multilocation domestic enterprise is that the former operates its assets and controls their use across national borders, whereas the latter remains within them. Furthermore, unlike the multiplant domestic company, a MNE will organize itself into divisions whose managerial reach crosses national frontiers, and through which the national identity of the various operating companies in the group disappears, even though such identity continues on a formal level through the requirement of incorporation under the laws of the various states in which the MNE operates.[22] The second close relation of a MNE is the domestic firm that exports part of its output. It is similar to a MNE in that it sells part of its output across national borders. However, a MNE differs in that it trades across borders in factor inputs as well as finished products,

paragraph see *OECD Guidelines 1991 Review* (Paris: OECD, 1992) at 104; also reproduced in *The OECD Guidelines for Multinational Enterprises* (Paris: OECD, 1994, 1997).

[20] See UN Doc E/1990/94 12 June 1990 para 1 at 5. See further ch 17 for further discussion of the OECD Guidelines and Draft UN Code of Conduct for TNCs.

[21] See JH Dunning *International Production and the Multinational Enterprise* (London: Allen & Unwin, 1981) 7 on which the following account is based. See too Hood and Young above n 12 at 5–9.

[22] On which see further ch 2.

and between affiliates of the group as well as with unconnected third parties. This raises the possibility of controlling trade within a MNE to the advantage of the group as a whole, and represents one of the major competitive advantages possessed by MNEs over domestic firms.[23] The third close relation of a MNE is the domestic firm that exports part of its factor inputs, for example, technical know-how and managerial skills. This is done by means of licensing foreign firms to develop markets abroad. MNEs can also export such knowledge, but with the difference that they usually maintain control over that knowledge by selling it only to affiliates. As will be more fully explained below, the choice between serving the foreign market by employing a foreign licensee, or by setting up a foreign sales and/or production subsidiary, lies at the heart of understanding the reasons behind the growth of MNEs.

By way of summary the following general features of MNEs should be stressed: although in many respects they resemble various types of uninational companies, MNEs differ in their capacity to locate productive facilities across national borders, to exploit local factor inputs thereby, to trade across frontiers in factor inputs between affiliates, to exploit their know-how in foreign markets without losing control over it, and to organize their managerial structure globally according to the most suitable mix of divisional lines of authority. These factors permit MNEs to affect the international allocation of productive resources, and thereby to create distinct problems in the development of economic policy in the states where they operate. Consequently, MNEs can and should be treated as a distinct type of business enterprise for the purposes of economic regulation.

(2) The Principal Phases of MNE Growth

It is difficult to place a precise date on the evolution of MNEs. It is arguable that the history of the evolution of MNEs should begin with the great European colonial trading companies established in the 16th and 17th centuries.[24] Indeed, the view has been put that the chartered trading companies of the 16th to 18th centuries may vary only in the degree, but not in the kind, of productive integration across

---

[23] See further below at n 28 at 28–31.

[24] For the charters of the major English trading companies see: CT Carr *Select Charters of Trading Corporations* (Selden Society, 1913). See, for a discussion of the sovereign immunities of the East India Company, *Nabob of the Carnatic v East India Co* (1791) 1 Ves Jr 70; *The Ex-Rajah of Coorg v East India Co* (1860) 29 Beav 300; FA Mann *Studies in International Law* (Oxford: Oxford University Press, 1973) 200–203, MJ Farelly 'Recent Questions of International Law: The British Government and the Chartered Companies in Africa' 10 LQR 254 (1894). See further McNulty 'Predecessors of the Multinational Corporation' Col.Jo.World Bus. (May–June 1972) 73; Havrylyshyn 'The Internationalisation of Firms' 5 JWTL 72 (1971); Michael B Likosky *The Silicon Empire: Law Culture and Commerce* (Aldershot: Ashgate, 2005) at 61–68. On the East India Company see Philip Lawson *The East India Company: a History* (London: Longman Group, third impression 1997).

borders to be found in a modern MNE.[25] However, the majority of economists and business historians place the emergence of the modern MNE in the second half of the 19th century. Thus, American MNEs began to appear in the middle of the 19th century.[26] Similarly, the first truly multinational European firms appeared in the mid- to late 19th century.[27] This period saw the development of the modern technologies, manufacturing and management processes which created the possibility of a genuine international division of production by firms.[28]

The evolution of modern MNEs has hitherto been divided into three historical periods, interrupted by the First and Second World Wars of the 20th century.[29] The impact of the two world wars on the growth of MNEs, and the evolution of foreign direct investment (FDI), was highly significant, disrupting patterns of trade and investment and, in particular, ensuring the end of Germany's challenge to become the leading home country for MNEs, a role to be taken up by the US after 1945. Thus, the first period begins with the emergence of the earliest internationally integrated, privately owned manufacturing firms, in about the middle of the 19th century, and ends in 1914 with the outbreak of the First World War. The second period begins in 1918 and ends with the outbreak of the Second World War in 1939. The third period begins in 1945 and encompasses the rise of foreign direct investment by MNEs to current levels.

[25] See Ann M Carlos and Stephen Nicholas 'Giants of an Earlier Capitalism: The Chartered Trading Companies as Modern Multinationals' 62 Bus.Hist.Rev. 398 (1988) and 'Managing the Manager: An Application of the Principal Agent Model to the Hudson's Bay Company' 45 Oxf. Econ. Papers 243 (1993).

[26] Mira Wilkins *The Emergence of Multinational Enterprise: American Business Abroad From the Colonial Era to 1914* (Harvard: Harvard University Press, 1970).   [27] See Franko above n 7.

[28] On which see further AD Chandler *Scale and Scope: The Dynamics of Industrial Capitalism* (Belknap/Harvard University Press, 1990). See too JH Dunning *Multinational Enterprises and the Global Economy* (Wokingham: Addison Wesley, 1993) ch 5. For an overview of the historical literature on the growth of MNEs see Mira Wilkins 'The History of the Multinational Enterprise' in Alan M Rugman and Thomas L Brewer (eds) *The Oxford Handbook of International Business* (Oxford: Oxford University Press, 2000) 3. For a general account of the history of MNEs see Geoffrey Jones *The Evolution of International Business: an Introduction* (London: Routledge, 1996) and *Multinationals and Global Capitalism: from the Nineteenth to the Twenty First Century* (Oxford: Oxford University Press, 2005).

[29] See Dunning *Multinational Enterprises* above n 28, Peter T Muchlinski *Multinational Enterprises and the Law* (Oxford: Blackwell Publishers, revised paperback edn, 1999) at 20–32. By contrast John Cantwell takes a longer view and divides the history of the growth of MNEs into four periods: merchant capitalism (1600–1770), industrial capitalism (1770–1890), finance capitalism (1890–1945), and global capitalism (1945–onwards): 'The Changing Form of Multinational Enterprise Expansion in the Twentieth Century' in Alice Teichova, Maurice Levy-Leboyer and Helga Nussbaum (eds) *Historical Studies in International Corporate Business* (Cambridge: Cambridge University Press, 1989) 15. Geoffrey Jones used five periods which he admits are arbitrary and overlapping: origins (before 1880), growth (1880–1930), alternatives to multinational enterprise (1930s and 1940s), resurgence (1950–1980), and global business (1980 to present): *Evolution of International Business* above n 28 at 25–59. His more recent book identifies four main phases: the global economy (1820s to 1914); globalization challenged and reversed (1914–50); restoring a global economy (1950–80); and the new global economy (1980 to present): *Multinationals and Global Capitalism* above n 28 ch 2. This is closer to the approach of this work, although, for reasons given in the text, the author feels that the new global economy really established itself during the 1990s.

Clearly, the period after 1945 has to be further subdivided. It is a period in which significant qualitative changes have taken place in the evolution of global business organization and in regional and multilateral regulatory developments. Thus the third period should be modified to take into account the rise of more highly integrated global economic activities after around 1990, when the widespread liberalization of national economies during the 1980s allowed for an increase in market access opportunities, the growth of global securities markets, global financial services and a rise in services based FDI in particular, coupled with the establishment of major new regional and multilateral agencies for the institutionalization of such a liberal economic order, culminating in the founding of the WTO in 1995.

(a) The First Period: 1850–1914

During this period MNEs, as understood in contemporary economic thought, first began to emerge as part of the newly developing modern industrial economy. British investment was particularly prominent in this period. British investments were to be found in railways, ranching, timber, and mining. The geographical destination for these investments was primarily North America, including both the US and Canada, Australia, and Argentina. Such investments often took the form of 'free-standing' companies.[30] Typically, these companies were incorporated in the UK and comprised of a British board of directors and company secretariat which would oversee the overall operation of the company. However, their major operating assets were located and managed overseas. These companies would have no British based operations or assets. Thus they were not MNEs in the sense of contemporary definitions. The principal reason for this form of company was access to the London capital market as a means of financing overseas business projects.

In the 1890s the first market-orientated foreign investments were undertaken by British MNEs. However, there is little agreement among business historians as to how much British investment of this period could be attributed to direct investment undertaken by MNEs. Estimates vary from between 10 per cent[31] to as high as 40–50 per cent.[32] In the same period, European MNEs began to

---

[30] See Mira Wilkins 'Defining a Firm: History and Theory' in Peter Hertner and Geoffrey Jones *Multinationals: Theory and History* (Aldershot: Gower, 1986) 80 esp at 84–87; Geoffrey Jones 'Origins, Management and Performance' in G Jones (ed) *British Multinationals: Origins, Management and Performance* (Gower Business History Series, 1986) from 1 especially 3–4. See further Mira Wilkins and Harm Schroter (eds) *The Free Standing Company in the World Economy 1830–1996* (Oxford: Oxford University Press, 1998).

[31] J Stopford 'The Origins of British-Based Multinational Manufacturing Enterprises' 48 Business History Review 303 (1974). Stopford's figures have been doubted: see G Jones 'The Expansion of British Multinational Manufacturing 1890–1939' in T Inoue and A Okochi (eds) *Overseas Business Activities: Proceedings of the Ninth Fuji Conference* (1984) at 126.

[32] See Svedberg 'The Portfolio-Direct Composition of Private Foreign Investment in 1914 Revisited' 88 Economic Journal 763 (1978); I Stone 'British Direct and Portfolio Investment in Latin America Before 1914' 37 Journal of Economic History 690 (1977).

appear.[33] In particular, German firms became dominant in chemicals, artificial textiles, and electrical goods.[34] From among other European countries, notable early MNEs included, from Sweden, the Nobel Company and SKF,[35] and from Holland, the electrical corporation, Philips, the foodstuffs manufacturer Margarine Uni (later merged with Lever Bros of the UK to form Unilever), and Royal-Dutch Shell, which was formed by Anglo-Dutch oil interests in 1907.[36] However, it was not until after the Second World War that European firms established their most significant multinational operations. Thus, for example, French firms did not make their strongest impact as foreign direct investors until the 1950s, even though by 1914 France was the second largest foreign investor from Europe after the UK.[37]

The pre-1914 period also saw the growth of the first US MNEs.[38] Arguably, the American Singer Sewing Machine Company can be regarded as the first true manufacturing MNE.[39] It was the first successful international American manufacturing business.[40] Other US firms embarked upon a strategy of international production in fields as diverse as metal products, telegraphy, telephones, phonographs, light bulbs, railway braking systems, chemicals, oil, cars, and office equipment. The strongest period of growth for US enterprises abroad occurred between 1893 and 1914, at a time when the US domestic market was in recession, making foreign markets more attractive, and when a combination of stock market conditions and new antitrust laws encouraged mergers of firms into giant corporations with interests both in home and foreign markets.[41] The principal locations for

[33] See Franko above n 7. See the criticism of Franko's study in Hertner and Jones above n 30 at 7. See further the contributions to Hertner and Jones in chs 6 to 10; Mira Wilkins 'European Multinationals in the United States 1875–1914' in A Teichova et al (eds) *Multinational Enterprise in Historical Perspective* (Cambridge: Cambridge University Press, 1986) 55 and Mira Wilkins *The History of Foreign Investment in the United States to 1914* (Cambridge, Mass: Harvard University Press, 1989).

[34] See Peter Hertner 'German Multinational Enterprise Before 1914: Some Case Studies' in Hertner and Jones (eds) above n 30 ch 7 113.

[35] See C Tugendhat *The Multinationals* (London: Pelican, 1973) at 33 and 147; and see E Hornell and J Vahlne *Multinationals: The Swedish Case* (Croom Helm, 1986) 4–6.

[36] Franko above n 7 at 52.

[37] This was mainly portfolio investment: J Savary *French Multinationals* (Frances Pinter/IRM, 1984) 1–2. However, there is no comprehensive study of the evolution of French MNEs during this period and the information appears to be rather speculative. Thus the proportion of French foreign direct investment in 1914 may in fact be higher than reported by Savary who, relying on the work of Franko (above n 7), notes that by 1914 only one French firm had industrial subsidiaries abroad. See further P Hertner and G Jones above n 30 contributions by Fridenson: 'The Growth of Multinational Activities in the French Motor Industry 1890–1979' 157 and Broder: 'The Multinationalisation of the French Electrical Industry 1880–1914: Dependence and its Causes' 169.

[38] See M Wilkins (1970) above n 7.

[39] This claim is made by Christopher Tugendhat in *The Multinationals* above n 3 at 33.

[40] See Wilkins above n 38 at 37–45. Samuel Colt had set up a factory for the manufacture of his revolvers in the UK in 1852. However, the investment failed and was sold off in 1857. According to Wilkins this appears to have been the first foreign branch plant of any American company: ibid at 30.

[41] See further Wilkins above n 38 at 70–109; Chandler above n 28 at 71–79.

US foreign investments up to 1914 remained in Canada and Mexico. Investments in raw materials and agriculture were made in the rest of Latin America, while in Europe considerable investments were undertaken in selling, assembly, processing, and manufacturing. However, despite such rapid overseas expansion, by 1914, the US still received more foreign investment than it exported, and the size of foreign direct investment relative to total US investment was small – some 7 per cent of US gross national product in 1914. Nevertheless, such facts should not diminish the significance of this trend. As Mira Wilkins points out, the percentage of US outward direct investment to the total US GNP has always remained at about 7 per cent, even in the mid-1960s at the height of US dominance in relation to such investment.[42] The significant fact is that US firms were willing to expand abroad and did so during this period.

The overall pattern of foreign direct investment in the 40 years prior to the First World War makes this period stand out as one of MNE growth second only to the period since the Second World War.[43] The overall pattern of investments was, however, different from that experienced in the post-Second World War period. In particular, about three-fifths of foreign investment capital was directed to today's developing countries, which were, at the time, the African and Asian colonies of the principal European powers, and the newly independent capital-importing countries of Latin America. The distribution of investment across industry sectors has been estimated at about 55 per cent in primary products, 20 per cent in railways, 15 per cent in manufacture, 10 per cent in trade and distribution with the remainder in public utilities and financial services.[44] Therefore, the pattern of foreign direct investment in this period represented a system geared primarily towards the supply of raw materials and agricultural produce from the South to meet the needs of manufacturers and growing populations in the industrialized North.

(b) The Second Period: 1918–1939

The second period, between 1918 and the outbreak of the Second World War in 1939, is characterized by the continued development of MNEs but, by comparison with the late 19th and early 20th centuries, at a slower rate due to the general instability in the world economy during this period. This led to the pursuit of highly nationalistic economic policies by states as a means of protecting themselves against the resulting world depression. Such policies, in turn, led to an increased incidence of national cartels in key industries and to the erection of high tariff barriers to trade, as compared with the period up to 1914. The investment

---

[42] ibid at 201–02.
[43] See J Dunning 'Changes in the Level and Structure of International Production: The Last One Hundred Years' in M Casson (ed) *The Growth of International Business* (London: George Allen & Unwin, 1983) 85–91. For an updated analysis see Dunning above n 28.   [44] ibid.

environment after the First World War had undergone changes that were on the whole inimical to the expansion of foreign direct investment by firms. First, the Bolshevik Revolution took the Soviet Union outside the capitalist economic system. Although Western firms did operate in the USSR in the 1920s, as joint ventures with Soviet state enterprises under Lenin's New Economic Plan, these were liquidated by Stalin.[45] So by 1930, a major region of the world was closed off to private foreign investment. Similarly, the break-up of the Austro-Hungarian and Ottoman empires created changes in political boundaries that made the free movement of investments more difficult.[46] Secondly, the collapse of international capital markets in the late 1920s and early 1930s brought with it economic chaos with high inflation followed by deflation and the growth of exchange controls.[47] This led to the Great Depression in the 1930s and to a massive decline in world trade. Thirdly, in response to these economic problems, and in view of continuing fear of another war, many states turned to increasingly nationalistic economic policies. In particular, Italy and Germany adopted fascist economic policies, with their emphasis on national control over manufacturing and raw materials, and on the acquisition of foreign territory for political and economic expansion.[48]

A significant feature of the economic nationalism of the inter-war years was the growth of greater integration between firms of the same nationality.[49] These national combines subsequently entered into international cartels with their foreign competitors.[50] For example, the German combine IG Farben entered into agreements with its Swiss competitors represented by the Interest Association and with ICI of the United Kingdom. The Swedish Match combine achieved market control through the related technique of obtaining a national production monopoly in host countries and taking over local competitors.[51] In the electro-technical industry, market-sharing agreements were concluded between German and US firms.[52] Further international cartels were set up between European (including British) firms in the steel, oil and rayon markets.[53]

---

[45] See J Wilczynski *The Multinationals and East-West Relations* (London: Macmillan 1976) 108 n 11.

[46] P Jacquemot *La Firme Multinationale: Une Introduction Economique* (Paris: Collection Gestion, Economica, 1990) 25. See, for example, Kernbauer and Weber 'Multinational Banking in the Danube Basin: The Business Strategy of the Viennese Banks After the Collapse of the Hapsburg Monarchy' in Teichova et al (eds) above n 6 at 185. [47] Tugendhat above n 3 at 39.

[48] See, on Germany, Overy 'German Multinationals and the Nazi State in Occupied Europe' in Teichova et al (eds) above n 6 at 299. On Italy see Denis Mack Smith *Mussolini* (Granada, 1983) 133–42, 219–20.

[49] For example IG Farben, and Osram in Germany: Overy ibid. Chandler above n 28 at 564–84. In Sweden, the Swedish Match combine: Franko above n 7 at 95–96. In the UK ICI: L Hannah *The Rise of the Corporate Economy* (2nd edn, Methuen 1983) 38. See further WJ Reader *Imperial Chemical Industries: A History* (1970) vol I 439–66; Chandler above n 28 at 356–66.

[50] See further Jones (1996) above n 28 at 123–27 and Jones (2005) ibid at 57–60, 90–92, 122–23.

[51] Franko above n 7 95–96.

[52] See H Schroter 'A Typical Factor of German International Market Strategy: Agreements Between US and German Electrotechnical Industries up to 1939' in Teichova et al (eds) above n 6 at 160.

[53] See Tugendhat above n 3 at 41–44. For further examples of international cartels of this period, see E Hexner *International Cartels* (London: Pitman, 1946).

American firms could not cartelize their operations in the same way as European firms because of certain differences between European and American business conditions. According to Franko, these were, first, the existence of strong antitrust laws in the US which would have rendered cartels between US firms illegal. It was not until the years following the Second World War that similar competition laws became established in European economies. Secondly, European businessmen had more opportunities to cartelize their operations due to geographical proximity and to the existence of stable and interrelated business elites by comparison with the US.[54] However, legal controls within the US did not stop US firms from joining overseas cartels. So, for example, in 1928 a cartel was formed between Shell, Anglo-Persian (now BP), and Standard Oil of New Jersey to protect their non-US interests. In 1933, US companies entered the Second International Steel Cartel with British, Chinese, Polish, and Austrian companies.[55] American companies did get a concession from their government, in the Webb-Pomerene Act of 1918, which permitted US firms to enter into cartels aimed at collective export sales and to join overseas cartels provided that these had no adverse effect on competition within the US.[56] Otherwise American firms would have been disadvantaged in world markets.

During this period, the use of international cartels and direct investments by firms are best seen as complementary business strategies, and not as mutually exclusive alternatives. Thus, while cartels delayed the integration of international production by MNEs, they also protected this process by enabling participating firms to undertake direct investments in regions reserved for their exclusive operation under the terms of the cartel agreement, thereby rendering the cost of the direct investment bearable by reducing the risk of damaging competition.[57] The patterns of direct investment reflected the division of world markets into spheres of influence. Thus, Canada and Latin America continued to be the most significant destinations for US direct investment, accounting for some two-thirds of the total. Similarly, during the 1930s, British firms showed a preference for investment in the Empire, particularly Australia, South Africa, and India.[58] This is explicable in part by the fact that such markets were often allocated to British firms under international trading agreements, although it should be noted that some 39.2 per cent of British direct investments were made in Europe during this period.[59] Continental European firms remained dominant in Europe, their direct investments in Europe accounting for 61 per cent of all direct investments by European firms.[60]

[54] Franko above n 7 at 97–98.   [55] Tugendhat above n 53.
[56] Webb-Pomerene Act s 2. See further *US v United States Alkali Export Association Inc* 86 F Supp 59 (1949).
[57] See Nussbaum 'International Cartels and Multinational Enterprises' in Teichova et al (eds) above n 6 at 131 esp at 138–39.   [58] G Jones in T Inoue and A Okochi (eds) above n 31 at 144.
[59] ibid.   [60] Dunning above n 43 at 92.

The existence of agreed and imposed restrictions on competition did affect the pattern of direct investment in the inter-war period. It was not until the 1930s that the value of direct investments exceeded the pre-war figure.[61] By 1938, the overall stock of foreign direct investment had risen by at least 50 per cent over 1914 levels.[62] According to Professor Dunning, during this period US direct investment continued to grow, rising to 27.7 per cent of world capital stock in 1938, second only to the UK which held some 39.8 per cent.[63] Despite the above mentioned difficulties, firms from both countries set up subsidiaries in European host states.[64] German firms also engaged in direct investments overseas in an attempt to reconstruct their pre-war international manufacturing networks.[65]

(c) The Third Period: 1945–1990

The third period begins in 1945 and continues to around 1990. During this period MNEs acquired unprecedented importance in international production. The growth of MNEs in this period can be divided into two phases.[66] The first is that of the rapid growth of American MNEs from the end of the Second World War to about 1960, a period in which such firms were without any appreciable international competition from countries other than Britain. The second phase, from 1960 to 1990, is characterized by the relative decline of US MNE dominance, the revival of competition from European MNEs following the reconstruction of European industry after the Second World War, and the rise of new competition from Japanese MNEs. The period is further characterized by the rise of new MNEs in certain newly industrializing countries of the southern hemisphere and, more recently, by the opening up of new markets for MNEs in China, the former Soviet Union, and in the formerly socialist countries of Eastern Europe.

(i) The Period of American Dominance: 1945–1960

The Second World War had devastated much of the industry of Europe and Japan. The main European belligerents experienced the forced divestiture of their overseas assets. The overseas affiliates of German companies were expropriated as enemy property for the second time in a century. Similarly, British companies experienced the loss of their mainland European subsidiaries. It has been estimated that more than 40 per cent of total British overseas assets were lost due to

---

[61] ibid at 92–93.   [62] ibid at 92 n 12 and Table 5.1 at 87.   [63] ibid.

[64] On US firms in the inter-war period see Mira Wilkins *The Maturing of Multinational Enterprise: American Business Abroad From 1914 to 1970* (Cambridge, Mass: Harvard University Press, 1974); on British firms see G Jones (ed) above n 30.

[65] See eg V Schroter 'Participation in Market Control Through Foreign Investment: IG Farbenindustrie AG in the United States' in Teichova et al (eds) above n 6 at 171.

[66] Dunning above n 43 at 93–94; Dunning above n 28 at 125–33.

destruction, expropriation, nationalization, or sale between 1939 and 1956.[67] The companies of other European powers had ceased trading as independent entities during the war, having been integrated into the German war effort.[68]

By contrast US companies emerged from the war in a strong position. They had escaped the massive destruction and seizure of assets experienced in Europe. They had also been strengthened by the stimulus of war production. This had ensured highly profitable markets and had spurred the companies to the development, testing and introduction of new products and processes.[69] US firms were at that time better resourced and geared for the development of new technologies, and for the discovery of new products and markets, than their British or European competitors.[70] Thus US firms were in a unique position to expand into overseas markets whether through exports or direct investment.

Numerous external factors stimulated the rapid expansion of direct investment by US firms in this period.[71] First, the introduction of Marshall Aid in 1948 provided the capital basis for the reconstruction of Europe's shattered economy, which in turn opened up new opportunities for direct investment by US firms. Secondly, the new international financial and trading system established after the war through the International Monetary Fund (IMF), World Bank (IBRD), and General Agreement on Tariffs and Trade (GATT) ensured the supremacy of the US dollar as the standard currency for international transactions and favoured the gradual liberalization of the international economy through the removal of tariff barriers to trade. The removal of such restrictions allowed for the setting up of integrated production plants in more than one country. The resulting decrease in the cost of cross-border intrafirm transfers of materials, semi-finished products, and finished goods was essential to the success of such a strategy.

Thirdly, the US Government offered tax concessions to firms investing abroad, permitting them to credit tax paid overseas against US tax liability and to defer the repatriation of profits free of tax liability, in effect giving such firms interest free loan capital for re-investment abroad.[72] The US Government also tackled the remaining international cartels through antitrust prosecutions brought during the 1940s and 1950s.[73] Fourthly, improvements in the speed and reliability of international communications and transport after the war ensured better control over the activities of overseas subsidiaries than had hitherto been possible.

Fifthly, European governments were enthusiastic recipients of direct investment by US firms as a means of encouraging fuller employment and higher standards of living. The establishment of the EC in 1957 is said to have acted as a further

---

[67] D Shepherd, A Silberston and R Strange *British Manufacturing Investment Overseas* (London: Methuen, 1985) 13. [68] See Overy above n 48.

[69] R Vernon *Sovereignty at Bay* above n 3 at 91. [70] ibid 94–101.

[71] See Hood and Young above n 12 11–12; Tugendhat above n 3 ch 2 'The American Invasion'; Vernon above n 69 at 91–101.

[72] Such tax privileges have since been narrowed down. See further ch 7 below.

[73] On which see ch 4 at 133–35.

stimulus to US direct investment.[74] While the existence of the EC undoubtedly facilitated the extension of integrated cross-border production within the Community, it is doubtful whether the founding of the Community was a decisive factor in increasing US direct investment. Such investment would probably have occurred in any case given the size and attractions of the national markets within the various Member States, although the plants established by US firms might have been less specialized and less closely linked.[75]

In this period US firms accounted for some two-thirds of the increase in total direct investment and in the number of new subsidiaries since 1938.[76] By 1960 the US is estimated to have held some $32.8 billion of accumulated foreign direct investment, representing 49.2 per cent of the total world stock. The UK was the second largest direct investor, with a total stock of $10.8 billion representing 16.2 per cent of the total. France was the third largest with a stock of $4.1 billion giving 6.1 per cent of the total. As yet Japan was a very small scale foreign direct investor with a share of 0.7 per cent of the total, while Germany held 1.2 per cent.[77]

At the same time as US firms dominated the world economy, European firms began to reappear and grow.[78] In the early 1950s the Allied administration of Germany deconcentrated the industrial combines of the Nazi era. Firms such as Bayer and Hoechst were reconstituted from IG Farben. They began to buy back confiscated foreign plants in Latin America as a first step towards full international competitiveness. Other German companies, for example, Siemens, AEG, and Daimler-Benz rebuilt their international sales networks. Italy also emerged at this time as a source of foreign direct investment. Between 1946 and 1955 Fiat and Olivetti led the way, setting up foreign manufacturing plants in Europe and Latin America. France began to make a significant impact on export markets in this period, particularly in the motor and tyre industries, which would eventually lead to a rapid increase in the establishment of foreign manufacturing plants during the 1960s and 1970s.[79]

The pattern of direct investment was beginning to display new characteristics. First, while in 1914 some two-thirds of foreign direct investment was directed towards developing countries, by 1960 this had fallen to about 40 per cent. The traditional pattern of investments by firms from Northern industrialized countries in raw material and agricultural ventures in the southern hemisphere, characteristic of the period prior to 1914, began to be superseded by a new pattern of investment in technologically advanced manufacturing and service industries by firms from industrially advanced countries within other industrialized countries. This reflects a growth in market orientated investment, as opposed to supply

---

[74] See eg Tugendhat above n 3 who attributes the shift of investment by US firms from the UK to mainland Europe to the formation of the EC.   [75] Vernon above n 3 at 93.

[76] Dunning above n 43 at 93–94.   [77] ibid Table 5.1 at 87.

[78] See Franko above n 7 at 98–104, on which the following paragraphs are based.

[79] See J Savary above n 37 at 2; CA Michalet and M Delapierre *La Multinationalisation des Entreprises Françaises* (ed Gauthier-Villars, 1973) 18–29.

orientated investment typical of the earlier colonial era. Secondly, the measure of direct investment in manufacturing had risen as the proportion taken up by agricultural and public utility investments was in decline, while mining and raw materials investments continued at levels similar to those of earlier periods.[80]

(ii) The Period of Renewed International Competition: 1960–1990

Since 1960 the share of US and UK direct investment stock had been steadily falling while that of Germany, Japan, and Switzerland had been rising.[81] American dominance peaked in the mid-1970s, when some 50 per cent of foreign direct investment outflows came from the US. By 1985 this figure had fallen to some 25 per cent. Western Europe took over as the major source region for foreign direct investment, accounting for some 50 per cent of the total.[82] Direct investment to developing countries declined further over this period. According to Dunning, of an estimated $293 billion invested by the seven leading home countries in 1978, 26.5 per cent was in developing countries. This was slightly higher than the 1971 figure, but below that recorded in 1960.[83] According to the OECD, by 1989 the total figure had declined to 19 per cent.[84]

The period since 1960 marks the emergence of Japan as a major foreign investor. Prior to that period Japanese foreign investment was negligible.[85] Until 1959 Japanese outward direct investment was restricted due to a preoccupation with domestic reconstruction and strict governmental controls under its exchange control laws.[86] The small amount of direct investment that occurred before 1960 was centred on the textiles industry, with some investment in iron and steel production, and in mining. Latin American countries, in particular Mexico, Argentina, and Brazil, were the favoured locations. During the early 1960s Japanese firms began to make investments in the neighbouring countries of Taiwan, Thailand, Hong Kong, and Singapore.[87] Japanese direct investments grew rapidly in the early 1970s when

---

[80] Dunning above n 43 at 94.   [81] ibid at 96.

[82] UNCTC *Transnational Corporations in World Development: Trends and Prospects* (New York: United Nations, 1988 UN Doc ST/CTC/89) at 74 and Table V.2 at 77.

[83] Dunning above n 43 at 96–97.

[84] See OECD *International Direct Investment – Policies and Trends in the 1980s* (Paris: OECD, 1992). The UNCTC estimated that in 1985 the figure was 23 per cent: UNCTC *Transnational Corporations in World Development: Trends and Prospects* (New York: United Nations, Doc ST/CTC/ 89 1988) at 80.

[85] See further Mira Wilkins 'Japanese Multinational Enterprise Before 1914' 60 Bus.Hist.Rev. 199 (1986).

[86] See Yoshino 'The Multinational Spread of Japanese Manufacturing Investment since World War II' 48 Bus. Hist. Rev. 357 at 360–61 (1974). On the emergence of Japanese MNEs, see further MY Yoshino *Japan's Multinational Enterprises* (Cambridge, Mass: Harvard University Press, 1976); T Ozawa *Multinationalism, Japanese Style: The Political Economy of Outward Dependency* (Princeton: Princeton University Press, 1979); L Franko *The Threat of Japanese Multinationals – How the West Can Respond* (Wiley/IRM Series on Multinationals, 1983); T Ozawa 'Japan in a New Phase of Multinationalism and Industrial Upgrading: Functional Integration and Trade Growth' 25 JWT (No 1 February 1991) 43; D Eleanor Westney 'Japan' in Rugman and Brewer above n 28 at 623.

[87] Ozawa ibid at 13–14.

the government liberalized, and then removed, restrictions on the export of capital as a means of stemming the appreciation of the Yen.[88] Not only did Japanese firms continue to invest in the newly industrializing countries of Asia, they also began to make their first significant investments in industrially advanced countries.[89] An important motive for investment in local production plants was the avoidance of US restrictions on imports of Japanese goods. Similar motivations also lay behind Japanese direct investments in Europe since the early 1970s.[90] Such defensive investments in manufacturing plants in developed countries became an increasingly significant feature of Japanese investment patterns in Western Europe and the US since the late 1970s, as have efforts at industrial collaboration with European and American firms.[91] Apart from the above mentioned investments in manufacturing plants in neighbouring Asian countries, much Japanese investment occurred in the raw materials sector. Japan is a resource scarce country. Consequently its firms have invested heavily in overseas resource extraction ventures, on the basis of a 'develop and import' policy.[92] This policy was particularly significant in the Middle Eastern oil industry during the 1970s, allowing Japan to weather the effects of increased oil prices following the actions of OPEC in 1973.[93]

Japanese investment in developing countries declined during the 1980s. In 1986 the share stood at 33 per cent of all Japanese investment.[94] In line with other major home countries, Japan redirected investment away from developing countries towards developed countries and, in particular, to the United States, where increases occurred in both manufacturing and services investments.[95] The sectoral composition of Japanese direct investment also underwent change. The largest proportion of Japanese outward investment was now in the services sector, reflecting the strength of Japanese firms in financial services and trade. The bulk had been made in the developed countries, following the liberalization of international capital markets in the late 1980s.[96]

Apart from the rise of Japanese MNEs, the period from 1960 to 1990 is characterized by a reversal of the role played by the US from that of the leading home country for outward investment to that of the leading host country. Between 1975 and 1986 the inward stock of foreign direct investment in the US multiplied 7.5 times.[97] Most of this investment came from West European firms. Japan was the third largest investor followed by Canada.[98] The principal reasons behind this

[88] ibid at 16.   [89] Yoshino above n 3 48 Bus.Hist.Rev. at 373.

[90] See Franko above n 86 at 71.

[91] See further Louis Turner *Industrial Collaboration with Japan* (RIIA/RKP Chatham House Papers No 34, 1987); M Mason and D Encarnation (Eds) *Does Ownership Matter: Japanese Multinationals in Europe* (Oxford: Clarendon Press, 1994).

[92] See Ozawa (1979) above n 86 ch 5.   [93] ibid at 140–53.

[94] UNCTC 1988 above n 84 at 77.

[95] See Fujita 'FDI between Japan and the United States' The CTC Reporter No 29 (Spring 1990) 31.   [96] ibid at 87.

[97] UNCTC 1988 above n 84 at 74.

[98] See E Graham and P Krugman *Foreign Direct Investment in the United States* (Institute for International Economics, Washington DC, 1989) 34 Table 2.2. By 1990 the figures were as follows: UK

growth during the 1980s were the relatively good prospects for the US economy at a time when the global economy as a whole had been slowing down, the rapid depreciation of the dollar since 1985, making investment in the US relatively cheap, particularly through the purchase of existing US assets, and the liberalization of US financial markets, which encouraged the inflow of foreign firms in that sector. In addition, as noted above, Japanese firms increased their presence in response to the rise of protectionist measures and sentiment against imports from Japan, as did efforts at industrial collaboration.[99] However, by the early 1990s, Japanese investment slowed down in response to the weakness of the US economy.[100]

At the same time US firms reduced their outward investments, preferring to expand their domestic operations at the expense of foreign expansion. Having reached their peak in 1975, US outward investments declined relative to those from other home countries. In the 1980–83 period US outward investment turned down sharply, in response to sluggish world economic conditions. In particular, US firms financed the expansion of their domestic operations by borrowing funds from their overseas affiliates, thereby reversing the flow of capital funds within the firm. By this means US MNEs were able to take advantage of cheaper capital available in Eurodollar markets, relative to US financial markets, for their domestic investments.[101]

Between 1975 and 1985 Western Europe replaced the US as the major source for outward direct investment, having been hitherto the major host region. As the US became the principal host to foreign direct investment, Western Europe's share declined, reflecting slower growth prospects in the region. More limited investment prospects combined with high levels of saving by European MNEs, provided the incentive and the assets for their expansion into the US market. The major investors came from the UK and Germany. Apart from investment in the US, there were numerous cross-border mergers and acquisitions within Europe, aimed at obtaining greater scale economies in preparation for the Single European Market after 1992.[102]

Turning to the developing countries, it has already been noted that investment flows into these countries continued to decline. Up to 1975 much of this decline could be explained by the wave of nationalizations during the 1960s and early 1970s in the natural resource industries, particularly oil. However, the decline

---

26.8 per cent; Japan 20.7 per cent; Netherlands 15.9 per cent; Canada 6.9 per cent: see E Graham and P Krugman *Foreign Direct Investment in the United States* (Institute for International Economics, Washington DC, 2nd edn, 1991) at 43. Figures up to 1992 are presented by the authors in ibid (3rd edn, 1995) Table 2.2 at 44. These show little change from 1990.

[99] UNCTC 1988 above n 84 at 75.

[100] *Financial Times* 16 June 1992 4: 'Multinationals Switch Focus of Investment'. On the slow down in the US economy see Graham and Krugman (1991) above n 98 at 21–23, ibid 3rd edn, 1995 at 20–21.

[101] OECD *Recent Trends in International Direct Investment* (Paris: OECD, 1987) 11.

[102] UNCTC 1988 above n 84 at 79–80.

during the 1980s is explicable on the basis of increasingly limited business opportunities for MNEs in developing countries.[103] On the other hand, the period since 1980 saw the rise of MNEs from developing countries.[104] Though their investments represented less than 3 per cent of the world's total stock of outward direct investment in 1985, several of these corporations owned assets of over $1 billion and represented a significant, if not dominant force in their national economies. They were located mainly in Korea, Brazil, Mexico, and the oil exporting countries. The most significant sector was the oil industry, where state-owned national oil corporations were formed after the nationalizations of the late 1960s and early 1970s. These companies have since expanded their activities in petroleum refining and distribution beyond the borders of their home states.[105] In manufacturing, corporations from the Republic of Korea were particularly significant.[106]

Finally, since the late 1970s, there was a marked improvement in access for MNEs to the formerly socialist states of Eastern Europe, and to China and the former Soviet Union. During the 1980s all these economies revised their policies on inward direct investment, moving away from their traditional prohibitions on direct investment by foreign firms. The entry of foreign firms as partners in joint ventures with domestic enterprises was permitted, followed, in some cases, by the passing of laws permitting investment by wholly owned subsidiaries of foreign firms.[107] Some of these countries established free economic zones as a further incentive to foreign investors.[108] As regards outward investment, firms from these countries also began to operate abroad, primarily as state-owned sales and trading companies, although some direct investments in financial services and manufacturing had been made.[109]

(d) The Fourth Period: 1990 onwards

The present period can be distinguished from its preceding period by certain important qualitative changes in the patterns of FDI, the adoption of truly global

---

[103] ibid 80.

[104] See Sanjaya Lall et al *The New Multinationals: The Spread of Third World Enterprises* (Wiley/IRM Series on Multinationals, 1983); Louis T Wells *Third World Multinationals* (MIT Press, 1983); Jones (2005) above n 28 at 245–49.

[105] Eg the Kuwait Petroleum Company, which owned refining facilities in the US and distribution facilities in the UK operating under the 'Q8' trade name; see: L Turner *Oil Companies in the International System* (RIAA/George Allen & Unwin, 1983) 237–39. Similarly Petroleos de Venezuela owned 50 per cent of the stock in the German company Ruhr Oel GmbH and two oil companies in the US Citgo Petroleum Corp and Nynas Petroleum; see UNCTC 1988 above n 84 at 38.

[106] Eg Samsung had 39 offices in 29 countries by 1980; it opened a production plant in the US in 1984 and it planned to establish 15 overseas factories by 1990: UNCTC ibid at 39 and Box II.2.

[107] See further ch 6.

[108] Tolentino 'Overall Trends of Foreign Direct Investment' *The CTC Reporter* No 29 (Spring 1990) 28.

[109] See further C McMillan *Multinationals from the Second World* (London: Macmillan, 1987); G Hamilton (ed) *Red Multinationals or Red Herrings?* (Frances Pinter, 1986); J Wilczynski *The Multinationals and East-West Relations* (London: Macmillan, 1976) ch 6 'Joint Ventures' at 104–108

production chains by MNEs and their associates, a marked shift from raw materials and manufacturing towards services based FDI, and the development of major regional trade and investment liberalization regimes, alongside the establishment of the WTO.

Turning to patterns of FDI, the period began with a sharp downturn in FDI. This can be attributed to the recession in the US in 1990–91, which led to a reduction of outward FDI from Japan and the UK.[110] By 1992 it was becoming clear that the downturn affected the developed economies most of all. The share of developing country inward FDI flows continued to grow, accounting for some 25 per cent of all inflows, much in excess of their share between 1986–1991. The bulk of this went to the 10 leading developing host countries.[111] The downturn ended in 1993 and the major capital-exporting states began to re-emerge into their prominent positions, while the leading developing host countries continued to attract increased investment, with China becoming the major developing host country by 1995.[112] By the mid-1990s, the share of FDI to Sub-Saharan Africa had declined rapidly due to decreased demand for raw materials and the relative inability of these countries to attract manufacturing or services investment.[113] This problem has continued and Africa remains in need of much greater investment.[114] Inflows into Central and Eastern Europe rose steadily over this period but were 'lumpy' in that the amount of inflow depended on the extent of foreign participation in the privatization process.[115] Inflows into East Asia continued to grow even in the face of the financial crisis of 1997, emphasizing the long-term market and technology driven nature of FDI into the region.[116]

In the first years of the 21st century FDI again fell, due to a rapid slowdown in merger and acquisition activity,[117] but has since recovered.[118] By 2003 China

and ch 8 'Socialist-Owned Multinationals'. For a comparison of the old 'red multinationals' with the new emerging MNEs from the former Eastern Bloc see Vladimir Andreff 'The Newly Emerging TNCs From Economies in Transition: A Comparison with Third World FDI' in 12 Transnational Corporations 73 (No 2, 2003).

[110] See UNCTAD *World Investment Report 1992* (New York: United Nations, 1992) at 11–17.

[111] UNCTAD *World Investment Report 1993* (New York: United Nations, 1993) at 16–18. These were, in descending order, Singapore, Mexico, China, Brazil, Malaysia, Hong Kong, Argentina, Thailand, Egypt, and Taiwan.

[112] See UNCTAD *World Investment Report 1994* (New York and Geneva: United Nations, 1994) at 9–18; *World Investment Report 1995* (New York and Geneva: United Nations, 1995) at 12.

[113] UNCTAD *World Investment Report 1996* (New York and Geneva: United Nations, 1996) at 56–71. Africa's share of inward FDI to developing countries was 3.8 per cent in 1996, the lowest since the early 1980s. On average Africa's inflows had more than halved from 11 per cent in 1986–90 to 5 per cent in 1991–96.

[114] See further UNCTAD *Foreign Direct Investment in Africa* (New York and Geneva: United Nations, 1995); *Foreign Direct Investment in Africa: Performance and Potential* (New York and Geneva: United Nations, 1999).

[115] ibid at 96–99.

[116] UNCTAD *World Investment Report 1997* (New York and Geneva: United Nations, 1997) at 208–209. See further UNCTAD *The Financial Crisis in Asia and Foreign Direct Investment* (New York and Geneva: United Nations, 1998).

[117] UNCTAD *World Investment Report 2003* (New York and Geneva: United Nations, 2003) at 15–19.

[118] UNCTAD *World Investment Report 2005* (New York and Geneva: United Nations, 2005) at 3–15.

emerged as the world's leading host country.[119] At the same time new sources of FDI have emerged from Brazil, Russia, India, and China, the so-called 'BRICs'. These countries are becoming increasingly important new players in the world economy and have the capacity to transform the focus of economic power in the coming years. That said, MNEs from the BRICs tend to be smaller than those from traditional Western home countries or Japan, and they are not yet truly global actors. Their existence brings with it the need for their home countries to reorientate their policies away from a purely inward FDI orientation and take into account the interrelationship between inward and outward FDI promotion.[120]

These shifting patterns of investment, with the inclusion of the major developing and transitional economies alongside the 'Triad' of Western Europe, North America, and Japan has led to increasingly global chains of production led by MNEs.[121] These may involve internal chains located among affiliates operating in different countries, or they may involve sets of linked subcontractors. These structures allow for the flow of materials, semi-finished goods, final products and information, across the chain. Key to their success are the various service functions provided at different points of the chain allowing for integration and coordination of global production processes. The effect of such structures is to create global production networks between firms, affiliates, subcontractors and even rival firms in the course of strategic alliances, which are different from the less integrated single firm chains characteristic of earlier periods of international production. This does not mean that modern production systems are somehow decoupled from a specific location. To the contrary, the effects of such chains are essentially local as their components are embedded in the particular place that offers the correct mix of locational advantages which make it a suitable site for the economic function performed there.[122] Indeed, production chains tend to

---

[119] ibid at xiii.

[120] See further Karl P Sauvant 'New Sources of FDI: The BRICs. Outward FDI from Brazil, Russia, China and India' 5 JWIT 639 (2005), Nagesh Kumar *India's Emerging Multinationals* (London: Routledge, 2007), and see, on MNEs from developing countries more generally, UNCTAD *World Investment Report 2006* (New York and Geneva: United Nations, 2006).

[121] See Peter Dicken *Global Shift: Reshaping the Global Economic Map of the 21st Century* (London: Sage Publications, 4th edn, 2003) ch 2 on which this paragraph draws. See further Manuel Castells *The Information Age: Economy Society and Culture, Volume I: The Rise of the Network Society* (Oxford: Blackwell Publishing, 2nd edn, 2000) ch 3. How far this process has gone is still a matter of considerable uncertainty and debate. Research undertaken in 2002 by Professor Alan Rugman for the UK Economic and Social Research Council (ESRC) suggests that the majority of the world's top 500 MNEs are regional players, focusing on their home region, and that they are not very good at managing global operations. Only a handful such as Nestlé or Unilever can bee seen as truly global with investments across all of the 'Triad' countries: 'UK Competitiveness and the Performance of Multinational Companies' (Swindon: ESRC, Final Report, 2005) and press release 'Strategies and Performance of the World's Biggest 500 Multinationals Expose the Myth of Globalization' 2 September 2002 at <http://www.esrcsocietytoday.ac.uk/ESRCInfoCentre/PO/releases/2002/september/stratergies.aspx>. See also Alan Rugman and Alain Verbeke 'Regional transnationals and Triad strategy' 13 Transnational Corporations 1 (No 3, 2004). See further Paul N Doremus, William W Keller, Louis W Pauly and Simon Reich *The Myth of the Global Corporation* (Princeton University Press, 1998).

[122] Dicken above n 121 at 20–21. See also Michael Storper *The Regional World* (New York: The Guilford Press, 1997) Part IV 'Globalization and Territorial Specificity'.

cluster around locations that offer these advantages. Thus, MNEs are shaping a new international division of labour that sees new countries and locations becoming a part of the productive global economy. This has significant regulatory consequences that will be examined further in subsequent chapters.

A third feature of the contemporary period is the emphasis on services over raw materials and manufacturing investment. The share of services in the national products of most countries has been steadily rising in recent years, reaching 72 per cent of GDP in developed, 52 per cent in developing, and 57 per cent in the Central and East European economies in 2001.[123] This is explicable on the basis that most non-information based services are by their nature non-storable and so have to be produced at the place of consumption, and by reason of the wave of liberalization in services sectors that has gathered momentum during the 1990s.[124] As yet services are less transnationalized than manufacturing. However, as information technologies allow for more services to become tradable, this has given rise to the 'offshoring' of certain information based activities.[125] This can occur through captive means, by the setting up of an affiliate in another country, or by outsourcing the service to a third party provider. The former will occur where the outsourced service is too valuable to allow an outsider to have control over it, while the latter will occur for more standardized and separable activities. The most well known example of this process is the offshoring of software development and call centre services to India.[126]

Finally, the contemporary period has seen the rise of regional trade and investment integration agreements and the establishment of the WTO. Together these create a new regulatory environment for MNEs and FDI. At the regional level, many countries are following the examples of the European Union (EU) and the North American Free Trade Agreement (NAFTA) and are developing more liberalized trading arrangements through bilateral or regional Free Trade Agreements (FTAs), or working towards a fully fledged Common Market by way of a Regional Economic Integration Organization (REIO).[127] Many FTAs now contain chapters on the liberalization of investment and by their very nature REIOs will seek to create rights of free movement of capital and establishment for inter-regional investors.[128] Thus, investor rights are being recognized at the regional and bilateral

---

[123] UNCTAD *World Investment Report 2004* (New York and Geneva: United Nations, 2004) at 97.

[124] ibid. See Additya Mattoo and Sacha Wunsch-Vincent 'Pre-Empting Protectionism in Services: The GATS and Outsourcing' 7 JIEL 765 (2004).   [125] ibid ch 4 on which this account draws.

[126] See ibid at 169–73 for a detailed analysis. See also 'The new geography of the IT industry' *The Economist* 19 July 2003 47. By comparison this is one area where China lags behind India, at least for the time being: 'Watch out India: Special Report: Outsourcing in China' *The Economist* 6 May 2006 at 79.

[127] Examples include the Andean Community, MERCOSUR, CAFTA in Latin America, CARICOM in the Caribbean, the African Economic Union and regional organizations such as COMESA in Africa, and ASEAN in South East Asia. For a full list of economic integration agreements from 1945 to 2005 see UNCTAD *Investment Provisions in Economic Integration Agreements* (New York and Geneva: United Nations, 2006) at 147.

[128] See ibid for detailed analysis of the relevant provisions.

levels in an ever increasing number of international arrangements, leading to an entrenchment of those rights as a matter of international legal obligation. Furthermore, the establishment of the WTO has created certain expectations as to the nature of the regulatory environment in which investors operate. For the first time, the WTO agreements have introduced multilateral disciplines on investment related issues regarding services, intellectual property rights, and trade related investment measures.[129] In addition, the control of state discretion as regards trade policy under the GATT has a direct effect on investment conditions in the regulating country, given the close relationship between trade and investment activity. Thus the contribution of the WTO to the development of a permissive and protective legal and regulatory environment for MNEs and their investments should not be underestimated, even though detailed rules for investment have so far failed to materialize.[130]

(3) Explanations for the Growth of MNEs

Having traced the principal phases in the growth of MNEs over time and space, this section will summarize the major explanations for MNE growth developed by economists. The next section will relate these to legal phenomena. The economic literature on the growth of MNEs is extensive.[131] Of importance for present purposes is the extraction, from that literature, of the major trends of economic analysis as a prelude to a discussion of the role of legal factors in the growth of MNEs. Such an exercise is of value in that economists have identified numerous factors in the growth of MNEs that have implications for legal policy responses of the kind to be considered later in this work. Thus the remainder of the present chapter seeks to link the findings of economists to the concerns of lawyers. To that extent it offers a response – albeit a very cursory one – to the call made by John Dunning for the adoption of a greater interdisciplinary stance in the study of the nature and causes of international production.[132] The first theoretical developments, in the 1960s, involved the adaptation of the classical theory of the firm and the theory of imperfect or 'monopolistic' competition into the theory of MNE 'ownership-' or 'firm-specific advantage'. In his landmark PhD in1960 Stephen Hymer was the first to suggest that firms invested overseas so as to gain higher profits from a

---

[129] See further chs 6 and 11.   [130] See ch 17.

[131] See further Dunning above n 28 especially chs 3 and 4 and John H Dunning 'The Key Literature on [International Business] Activities: 1960–2000' in Rugman and Brewer (eds) above n 28 at 36; Jones (2005) above n 28 ch 1. For a valuable, although now somewhat dated, introduction to the principal economic theories of the MNE and foreign direct investment, see Hood and Young above n 12. See also Richard E Caves *Multinational Enterprise and Economic Analysis* (Cambridge: Cambridge University Press, 2nd edn, 1996); Christos Pitelis and Roger Sugden *Nature of the Transnational Firm* (London: Routledge, 2nd edn, 2000).

[132] See JH Dunning *Explaining International Production* (London: Unwin Hyman 1988) ch 12.

competitive advantage owned by them.[133] To do so they had to organize an integrated international operation so as to retain control over their advantage, and to avoid the uncertainties of operating at arm's length in an open market.

Hymer's pioneering work gave rise to subsequent refinements of the 'monopolistic' theory of multinational enterprise, notably by his former supervisor, Charles Kindleberger. According to Kindleberger, MNEs possess competitive advantages in goods markets, through their ability to differentiate branded products, in factor markets, through their possession of superior management skills (which, when combined with advantages in goods markets or large scale production, increase returns), in their possession of patents and trade secrets, in the economies of scale employed in production and in their access to capital.[134] Thus a MNE is most likely to emerge in industries where one or more of the following features exist: competition in branded products; the need for highly efficient management and large scale production; research into, and development of, productive technology and products for which there is a global market, and resulting large scale capital requirements. Consequently, MNEs are prevalent in branded products industries such as pharmaceuticals, food and beverages and cosmetics, in concentrated industries such as automobiles, chemicals, electrical goods, farm machinery, or office equipment, and in highly capital intensive industries such as oil.

The 'monopolistic' theory of multinational enterprise was followed by an adaptation of the theory of international trade and location theory into the theory of 'location-specific' advantages. The starting point for 'location-specific' analysis of foreign investment is the classical economic model of international trade.[135] This model assumes that countries will specialize in the production of goods that require a high input of factors with which they are especially well endowed, and that such goods will be exported in exchange for others requiring inputs of factors with which the country concerned is poorly endowed. The model assumes that both labour and capital are internationally immobile and that in all respects the international market is perfectly competitive. The principal significance of the classical model for analysing foreign direct investment lies in its recognition that different countries enjoy different endowments of productive resources. However, it contains a number of weaknesses that render it incapable of explaining why firms choose to produce abroad rather than trade through exports. Most importantly, the assumption of perfect competition in international markets cannot be sustained. Firms are not equally endowed with competitive assets, or with knowledge of global markets. Nor is the world economy immune from barriers to free

---

[133] Stephen Hymer *The International Operations of National Firms* 1960 PhD thesis, MIT (published in 1976 by MIT Press).

[134] CP Kindleberger *American Business Abroad: Six Lectures on Direct Investment* (Yale University Press, 1969) at 14–27.

[135] Commonly referred to as the Heckscher-Ohlin Model. See JH Dunning above n 132 at 22–23. See further James R Markusen 'International Trade Theory and International Business' in Rugman and Brewer (eds) above n 28 at 69.

trade. Indeed, the reverse appears to be closer to the truth, notwithstanding post-war attempts at trade liberalization. Finally, neither labour nor, more especially, capital can be assumed to be internationally immobile. The MNE is the very antithesis of this assumption.

Yet it would be wrong to consider that there is no relationship between the economic analysis of trade and direct investment. Direct investment theory must accept that since trade and investment are complementary and, in some cases, interchangeable methods of international production the two strands of economic thought must meet. They do so by pointing to situations in which unequal resource endowments between countries cause market failure which traders or investors possessing superior competitive endowments can exploit to the detriment of other market actors. The transition from trade to investment can then be explained by reference to the transaction costs associated with arm's length sales as compared with the long-term savings in cost that can be achieved through going multinational.[136] This, too, depends upon an understanding of the relationship between the firm and the location in which it has a market.

A significant early attempt to explain the location of direct investment by MNEs along such lines was the 'product cycle' thesis, developed by Raymond Vernon. This was the first comprehensive attempt to integrate firm and location-specific factors of MNE investment within a long-run time perspective. It explained the move to foreign locations by US MNEs in terms of the gradual loss of competitive advantage experienced by a firm during the life cycle of its product. According to Vernon's theory, as the product matures, demand in the domestic market becomes saturated. This necessitates the seeking out of new opportunities for profit in foreign markets which, in turn, may prompt the firm to invest in local production for such markets. Furthermore, as the life cycle of the product nears its end, the only way to remain competitive may be to reduce production costs still further. Consequently, location in low cost production areas may be necessary. This explains why locations in less developed countries may be used.[137]

The second stage of theoretical development, in the 1970s, involved the refinement of earlier work and led to greater concentration on the replacement of

---

[136] See further JH Dunning above n 132 ch 2. On the application of the transaction cost approach as an explanation of the growth of British MNEs, see Nicholas 'British Multinational Investment before 1939' (1982) Journal of European Economic History 605; Nicholas 'The Theory of Multinational Enterprise as a Transactional Mode' in Hertner and Jones (eds) above n 30 at 64.

[137] See 'International Investment and International Trade in the Product Cycle' 80 Q.Jo.Econ. 190 (1966). This original version of the 'product cycle' thesis is further developed by Vernon in his book *Sovereignty at Bay* above n 3. The 'product cycle' thesis began to lose its relevance by the mid-1970s as Vernon himself admitted: see R Vernon 'The Location of Economic Activity' in J Dunning (ed) *Economic Analysis and the Multinational Enterprise* (Allen & Unwin, 1974) 89; 'The Product Cycle Hypothesis in a New International Environment' 41 Oxford Bull.Econ. & Stat. 255 (1979); *Sovereignty at Bay* at 109. While the 'product cycle' thesis works as an explanation for the expansion of US MNEs abroad, and may still explain the entry of new US firms into international production, it is of limited relevance in explaining the behaviour of established MNEs or MNEs from other home states.

markets for intermediate products by the internationally coordinated division of production within the MNE. This has become known as the theory of 'internalization'. The classic concept of 'internalization' was developed in the 1930s by Ronald Coase to explain the growth of domestic multiplant firms.[138] Put simply, where the firm encounters high 'transaction costs' (the costs associated with the supply of a market through arm's length deals between seller and buyer) in procuring supplies and distributing final products through the open market, it may be able to reduce those costs by carrying out such transactions within the firm, that is, by 'internalizing' those transactions. Thereby the uncertainties of the market are replaced by the common administration of the supplier and consumer of the traded product through the vertically integrated hierarchy of the firm. Similar internalization advantages can be gained by producers at the same level of production coming together in a horizontally integrated firm through merger or takeover.[139]

The British economists Peter Buckley and Mark Casson refined the theory of 'internalization' into a theory of MNE growth.[140] They assert that 'internalization of markets across national boundaries generates MNEs'.[141] According to Buckley and Casson, an integrated MNE will generate flows of goods associated with production between affiliates across borders. Furthermore, transborder flows of intermediate products will take place. These include flows of semi-processed materials and, most importantly, types of knowledge and expertise embodied in patents or human capital associated with the firm's marketing, R&D, labour training, management, and financial activities. The MNE will undertake such transfers so as to avoid the costs and inefficiencies of effecting such transactions at arm's length with outside suppliers and distributors, and so as to protect its 'firm-specific' advantage in productive knowledge.[142] Furthermore, the internalization of markets for intermediate products will occur where governments intervene in international markets through tariffs or restrictions on capital movements or where there exist discrepancies between countries in rates of income and profit taxation. These interventions depend to a large degree on the valuation of internationally traded intermediate goods. In external markets the arm's length prices involved are readily available. Should the firm internalize the market the prices of the intermediate

---

[138] Ronald Coase 'The Nature of the Firm' 4 Economica (New Series) 386 (1937). More recently the writings of Oliver Williamson have elaborated on this concept; see *Markets and Hierarchies: Analysis and Antitrust Implications* (New York: Free Press, 1975); *The Economic Institutions of Capitalism: Firms, Markets, Relational Contracting* (New York: Free Press, 1985); *Economic Organisation: Firms Markets and Policy Control* (Harvester Wheatsheaf, 1986) especially 158–62 on MNEs.

[139] See further Jean-Francois Hennart *A Theory of Multinational Enterprise* (Ann Arbor: University of Michigan Press, 1982) and 'Theories of the Multinational Enterprise' in Rugman and Brewer (eds) above n 28 at 127.

[140] PJ Buckley and M Casson *The Future of the Multinational Enterprise* (London: Macmillan, 1976, revised 2nd edn with new introduction, 1991) at 2. (References are to the 1991 edition.)

[141] ibid at 33.

[142] ibid at 37–38. See also Caves above n 131 ch 1; Kindleberger above n 134 at 17 for a discussion of the licensing/direct investment choice, which implies a 'transaction cost' approach.

goods can be more readily controlled and so liability to taxes and tariffs may be reduced through transfer pricing techniques.[143]

Of the various markets in intermediate products the market in productive knowledge is considered to carry the strongest incentive for internalization. This is because, first, knowledge provides a 'monopolistic' advantage best exploited by the firm itself rather than through licensing; secondly, the production of knowledge requires long-term R&D and this entails lengthy appraisal and effective short-term synchronization of efforts which may be impossible at arm's length; thirdly, flows of knowledge are difficult to value and so provide an excellent basis for reductions in tax liability through transfer pricing. Buckley and Casson conclude:

There is a special reason for believing that internalisation of the knowledge market will generate a high degree of multinationality among firms. Because knowledge is a public good[144] which is easily transmitted across national boundaries its exploitation is logically an international operation; thus unless comparative advantage or other factors restrict production to a single country, internalisation of knowledge will require each firm to operate a network of plants on a world-wide basis.[145]

From this conclusion Buckley and Casson argue that the pattern of growth of MNEs since the Second World War 'is a by-product of the internalization of markets in knowledge'.[146] This reflects the profitability of controlling and coordinating R&D across borders, which, they maintain, is at the heart of the successful and expanding MNE.[147]

This explanation of post-war growth of MNEs is related by Buckley and Casson to factors that have increased the potential profitability of R&D. These include the stimulation of demand for high technology goods by governments, in response to their military requirements; increased numbers of high income consumers who purchase sophisticated consumer goods; and, possibly, social factors

---

[143] On which see further ch 7.

[144] Defined by the authors as '[a good] which can be sold many times over, because the supply to one person does not reduce the supply available to others' ibid at 38.

[145] ibid at 45.

[146] ibid at 59. By comparison, prior to the Second World War, 'multinationality was a by-product of the internalisation of intermediate product markets in multistage production processes', particularly in the primary products industries such as food, minerals and oil: ibid at 59–60.

[147] See further ibid at 56–59. Buckley and Casson thus locate the MNE's advantage not merely in the possession of a unique asset, but, rather, in the process of creating and exploiting that asset through the internalization of the relevant factor markets. They write that the MNE's principal advantages are:

The rewards for past investment in (i) R & D facilities which create an advantage in technological fields, (ii) the creation of an integrated team of skills, the rent from which is greater than the sum of the rewards to individuals, and therefore accruing to 'the firm' and within which individuals, as such, are dispensable, (iii) the creation of an information transmission network which allows the benefits of (i) & (ii) to be transmitted at low cost within the organisation but also protects such information, including knowledge of market conditions, from outsiders.

ibid at 69. See further Sylvia Ostry 'Technology Productivity and the Multinational Enterprise' 29 Jo.Int'l.Bus.Stud. 85 (1998).

which have increased preferences for novelty and continued improvements in product quality.[148] The shift towards the internalization of markets in knowledge may also help to explain why MNEs have tended to invest more in developed countries since the Second World War. The cost of adapting such knowledge to different market conditions and the absence of sufficient reserves of skilled labour, capital for R&D and affluent consumers make developing countries less attractive as locations for investments based on high technology knowledge.[149]

The third stage of theoretical development, in the late 1970s and 1980s, marks the adoption of an 'eclectic' approach in explaining international production. This most recent contribution is attributable to the work of John Dunning.[150] The 'eclectic paradigm' does not offer a single, all-embracing, explanation of international production through MNEs. Indeed, as Dunning points out, 'it is not possible to formulate a single operationally testable theory that can explain all forms of foreign-owned production'.[151] Such an explanation is highly unlikely, given the range of companies and industries involved. On the other hand Dunning accepts that, 'it is possible to formulate a general paradigm of MNE activity, which sets out a conceptual framework and seeks to identify clusters of variables relevant to all kinds of foreign-owned output.'[152] The 'eclectic paradigm' rests on the acceptance that, by themselves, the various theories put forward to explain international production by MNEs cannot claim to offer a complete explanation, but that they each identify relevant and interrelated phenomena which, when viewed together, can lead towards a better understanding of the causes of international production by MNEs.

The 'eclectic paradigm' is based on the complementary nature of theories based on firm or ownership-specific, location-specific, and internalization factors, referred to as O, L, and I factors. It posits that the level and structure of a firm's foreign productive activities will rest on four conditions.[153] First, there is the extent to which the firm possesses sustainable ownership (O) advantages as compared to firms of other nationalities serving the same markets. Secondly, assuming that such O advantages exist, the enterprise must assess how far its interest lies with its internal exploitation of its O advantages rather than with selling them, or licensing their use, to other firms. These are the internalization (I) advantages of the firm. They may reflect the superior organizational efficiency of the firm and/or its ability to exercise monopoly power over the assets under its governance. Thirdly, assuming the above two conditions are satisfied, the extent to which the global interests of the firm are served by creating or using its O advantages in a foreign location needs to be considered. The resources to do this are unevenly spread out. Those countries which have them will possess a locational (L) advantage over

[148] ibid at 60.   [149] ibid at 61.
[150] See JH Dunning *International Production and the Multinational Enterprise* (George Allen & Unwin, 1981) *Explaining International Production* above n 132, and *Multinational Enterprises and the Global Economy* above n 28 ch 4.   [151] Dunning above n 28 at 68.
[152] ibid.   [153] See Dunning ibid at 79–80 on which this summary draws.

those that do not. Fourthly, given the configuration of the ownership, location and internalization (OLI) advantages facing a particular firm, the extent to which a firm believes that foreign production is consistent with its long-term management strategy will have to be determined.[154] Dunning goes on to predict that where a country's firms possess significant O advantages, where they have significant incentives to internalize their use, and where they have significant incentives to exploit these in a foreign location, the more likely they are to engage in foreign production. Equally, countries are likely to attract foreign investment by MNEs when the reverse conditions apply.[155]

More recently, Dunning has adapted the OLI model to take account of the rise in transnational strategic alliances between firms.[156] In essence such alliances enhance each participant's O advantages and extend I advantages across the participants. The OLI model can thus be modified to complement the hierarchical analysis of internalization in traditional single group enterprise structures and to take account of joint cooperative activity between firms. In addition L advantages need to be considered in relation to their capacity to influence the extent and structure of localized centres of excellence into which strategic alliances may choose to locate.[157] More broadly, Dunning suggests that as the spatial distribution of FDI undertaken by MNEs is increasingly influenced by the characteristics of investment locations that can enhance the strategic assets of the MNE, then location may itself become an aspect of the O advantages of the firm. As Dunning points out: '[w]ith the gradual geographical dispersion of created assets, and as firms become more multinational by deepening or widening their cross-border value chains, then, both from the viewpoint of harnessing new competitive advantages and more efficiently deploying their home-based assets, the structure and content of the location portfolio of firms becomes more critical to their global competitive positions.'[158]

To understand this point more fully, it is necessary to distinguish four different types of international investment: natural resource seeking, market seeking,

---

[154] ibid.   [155] ibid.

[156] According to Yoshino and Srinivasa Rangan a strategic alliance, 'links specific facets of the businesses of two or more firms. At its core, this link is a trading partnership that enhances the effectiveness of the competitive strategies of the participating firms by providing for the mutually beneficial trade of technologies, skills, or products based upon them. An alliance can take a variety of forms, ranging from an arm's length contract to a joint venture'. They see three necessary and sufficient characteristics of a strategic alliance: the firms involved pursue agreed goals but remain independent; they share the benefits of the alliance and control over the performance of assigned tasks; they contribute on a continuing basis in one or more key strategic areas such as technology products and so forth. Michael Y Yoshino and U Srinivasa Rangan *Strategic Alliances: An Entrepreneurial Approach to Globalization* (Harvard: Harvard Business School Press, 1995) at 4–5. See also Andrew C Inkpen 'Strategic Alliances' in Rugman and Brewer (eds) above n 28 at 402.

[157] See John H Dunning *Alliance Capitalism and Global Business* (London and New York: Routledge, 1997) ch 3.

[158] See John H Dunning 'Location and the Multinational Enterprise: A Neglected Factor?' 29 J.Int'l.Bus.Stud. 45 (1998).

efficiency seeking, and strategic asset seeking investment.[159] The first is strongly based on locational factors as the distribution of natural resources is uneven across countries and regions. However, as will be shown in the next section, other locational factors such as infrastructure development and regulatory conditions may affect the firm's decision to invest. Market seeking investment aims to supply a significant foreign market through local production or service provision that replaces importation. The investment may grow over time and in turn begin to export to third markets where the location offers strategic trade advantages to the MNE. It may also change in nature and composition as the product cycle thesis predicts. Efficiency seeking FDI aims to enhance the competitiveness of the firm by allowing for a more cost effective cross-border integration of production. It has the effect of increasing intrafirm trade as it involves a rationalization of the MNEs operations and increased specialization at the affiliate level. In the contemporary investment climate, the key efficiency enhancing locational advantages appear to be knowledge driven, rather than the low wage advantages that earlier theories identified.[160] Finally, strategic asset seeking investment enhances competitiveness by accessing the knowledge based assets of the investment location. This can be done by establishing new plants, or by acquisition of, or alliance with, local firms. The key factor is for the MNE to tap into the local innovation system and thereby enhance its technological efficiency. This may lead to the establishment of R&D facilities outside the home country.

The effects of such investment choices by MNEs have tended towards the creation of FDI 'clusters' around locations offering the correct mix of locational advantages for the enhancement of firm competitiveness. The major practical effect of this process has been the increasing global integration of production between localized innovation clusters allowing for possible spillovers of knowledge across borders between such clusters.[161] In addition, this has given rise to policy developments that concentrate on the enhancement of the attractiveness of a location as an innovation cluster, whether through incentives and performance requirements or through wider support policies such as infrastructure improvement and training and skills enhancement.[162] Furthermore, such developments have led to changes in the business organization of MNEs allowing for more flexible forms of organization, of which strategic alliances are but one example.[163]

---

[159] See Alan Rugman and Alain Verbeke 'Location Competitiveness and the Multinational Enterprise' in Rugman and Brewer (eds) above n 28 at 150 at 158–60 on which this paragraph draws.

[160] See Rugman and Verbeke above n 159. This is not to say that low wages are irrelevant in investment decisions. Much depends on the nature of the industry involved. More mature low technology industries will still see wage differentials as an important locational factor.

[161] See Rugman and Verbeke ibid at 171–72. See too Dicken above n 121 ch 8: Saskia Sassen 'The Locational and Institutional Embeddedness of the Global Economy' in George A Berman, Matthias Herdegen and Peter L Lindseth *Transatlantic Regulatory Co-operation: Legal Problems and Political Prospects* (Oxford: Oxford University Press, 2000) 47. Sassen notes that this process also creates centres of command and control around the main financial centres of the world.

[162] See further ch 11.   [163] See further ch 2.

This requires some rethinking of what a MNE is. In particular it may no longer be possible to understand the future development of such firms by reference to the existing theories, which concentrate on the initial decision, by a distinct firm, to enter a foreign market through direct investment. Rather, it will be necessary to see the MNE as an entity that has helped to establish the contemporary model of integrated international production and is now being reshaped by that very system. Indeed, it may be better to view the MNE as a productive system, which can take a multiplicity of forms ranging from a highly integrated hierarchy of jointly held entities to a loose network of coordinated economic collaborators acting on behalf of a lead firm or as equal collaborators. This makes identification of the precise boundary of the firm harder in some cases, and requires an understanding of how productive networks of firms behave. In addition it requires examination of flexible approaches to business organization, a greater recognition of the role of entrepreneurship in MNEs, and closer study of cooperative business structures.[164] Furthermore, the role of legal factors in shaping and reshaping MNEs should be considered.

(4) The Role of Legal Factors in the Growth of MNEs

As noted above, the first attempts to explain the growth of the MNE concentrated on its 'ownership-specific' advantages. The potential MNE should possess some unique competitive advantage which is capable of international exploitation. The foregoing discussion suggested that the evolution of MNEs is attributable in large part to the possession of technological advantage and large firm size. The two are closely related. Large size may be important to successful innovation because of high research and development (R&D) costs which can only be borne by a larger enterprise.[165] Furthermore, firm size is closely connected to the protection of technological advantage. As seen above, this is a factor also taken up by later theories based on the concept of 'internalization'.

In relation to 'ownership-' or 'firm-specific' factors the most significant function of capitalist legal systems is to facilitate the creation and exploitation of such advantages by firms, including the MNE. Of particular importance are, first, the protection of the firm's innovations and brands as proprietary rights and, secondly, the creation of structures conducive to the growth of large corporations. The first task can be met by a system of intellectual property rights protection, coupled with an effective system of contract law which can regulate the use of the firm's property in the hands of a licensee, while the second can be met by a system of company law that allows for the creation of a large joint stock fund and the ownership

---

[164] See Mark Casson with Peter Buckley 'Models of Multinational Enterprise: A New Research Agenda' in Mark Casson (ed) *Economics of International Business: A New Research Agenda* (Cheltenham: Edward Elgar, 2000) 1.   [165] Hood and Young above n 12 at 49.

of shares by one company in another, without restriction as to the nationality of
the shareholding company.

A system of patent law ensures the protection of the firm's competitive advantages by granting to the firm a monopoly for the exploitation of that advantage for
a specified period of time. This legal right assists in the creation of a more certain
environment for the extraction of a full return on the firm's investment in innovation. Patent rights will complement the firm's protection of its innovation through
the market power it enjoys as a result of its integrated international network and
from the difficulty of recreating advanced industrial technology.[166] Given the
existence of such organizational and technological factors in the protection of
competitive advantages, it has been argued that patent law is not used to protect
those advantages, at least where MNEs are involved.[167] Therefore, the contemporary significance of patent law as a means of protecting the firm-specific advantages of MNEs is open to debate. This is exacerbated by the use in certain countries
of technology transfer laws which establish controls over the manner in which
the foreign firm may sell and apply its technology in the host state. On the other
hand, the major capital exporting states continue to insist on the legal protection
of intellectual property rights owned by their MNEs and this policy has been given
greater weight by the WTO Agreement on Trade Related Aspects of Intellectual
Property Rights (TRIPs Agreement).[168]

Furthermore, the role of patent law as an historical incentive for the growth of
direct investment cannot be doubted. For example, in Canada in 1872 non-
Canadians were permitted for the first time to hold Canadian patents. An increase
in direct investment through subsidiaries of US companies resulted. Historical
evidence on individual firms suggests that patent protection played a crucial role
in encouraging direct investments in the Canadian agricultural implements, electrical engineering, and automobile industries.[169] There is also evidence to suggest
that patent legislation was instrumental in the encouragement of inward direct
investment in France, Germany, and England.[170]

To the extent that size is a contributing factor to multinationality, legal conditions that permit the growth of large corporations can be seen as instrumental in
the growth of MNEs. The availability of the joint stock limited liability company
is, in the words of Leslie Hannah, 'a necessary precondition for the widespread
adoption of modern industrial organisation'.[171] It facilitates the creation of a large

---

[166] See SP Magee 'Information and the Multinational Corporation: An Appropriability Theory
of Direct Investment' in JN Bhagwati (ed) *The New International Economic Order* (MIT Press,
1977) 317.

[167] See Sanjaya Lall 'The Patent System and the Transfer of Technology to Less-Developed
Countries' 10 JWTL 1 at 8–10 (1976).

[168] These issues will be pursued further in chs 6 and 11 below.

[169] These points were made by my former colleague Greg Marchildon, in my LLM seminar at
LSE in November 1988.   [170] See Dunning above n 43 at 107.

[171] L Hannah 'Mergers Cartels and Concentration: Legal Factors in US and European
Experience' in N Horn and J Kocka (eds) *Law and the Formation of Big Enterprises in the 19th and
Early 20th Centuries* (Gottingen, 1979) 306.

investment fund for the conduct of the business carried on by the company, which is legally separate from the private property of the company's members, who are protected from personal liability for the debts of the company up to the limits of their respective contributions to the capital of the company.

Modern company law has evolved in a manner especially conducive to the growth of large scale businesses. In particular, the acceptance of the holding company concept made mergers and acquisitions much simpler, and permitted the growth of corporate groups.[172] In the US, New Jersey was the first state to authorize one corporation to hold shares in another under legislation passed in 1888. Other states subsequently followed suit.[173] In the UK a company was permitted to hold subsidiaries if their aims accorded with the aims of the parent as stated in its articles of association.[174] In Germany, the limited liability company provided an instrument for the accumulation and centralization of capital. In particular, the establishment of the supervisory board as the directing organ of the company permitted control of the enterprise by representatives of the investment banks which held widespread controlling interests in German corporations in the late 19th century.[175]

However, while the existence of the corporate legal form has been a necessary element in the growth of large corporate groups it is not a sufficient element.[176] Economic factors have been the primary stimulants to the development of large corporations. Thus there were discernible uniformities in the growth, during the late 19th and early 20th centuries, of large enterprises in the various industrializing countries.[177] Equally, in the US and UK rising share prices in the late 19th century may have stimulated the earliest mergers between firms.[178] Furthermore, in Germany, the early development of integrated corporate groups may have resulted from the relative economic underdevelopment of the country.[179] Therefore, the role of legal factors in the growth of large enterprises should be seen as one of having influenced the form that these enterprises would take but not one that caused their evolution.

Finally, considerable speculation has arisen over the role of competition laws in the evolution of corporate group structures. It has been argued that the passage of competition laws acts as a stimulant to merger activity by blocking off the possibility of increasing monopoly power through the conclusion of cartel agreements

---

[172] Hannah ibid at 308; Chandler above n 28 at 73.

[173] See J Willard Hurst *The Legitimacy of the Business Corporation in the US 1780–1970* (Virginia University Press, 1970) at 69.

[174] Hannah above n 171 at 308.

[175] See Reich in Horn and Kocka (eds) above n 171 at 262–71; Hopt ibid at 227–41; Horn ibid at 123–89. (These papers are published in German but contain English summaries.)

[176] Hannah above n 171 at 308.

[177] See further A Chandler and H Daems (eds) *Managerial Hierarchies: Comparative Perspectives on the Rise of the Modern Industrial Enterprise* (Cambridge, Mass: Harvard University Press, 1980) and Chandler above n 28 on patterns in the US, UK, and Germany.

[178] Hannah above n 171 at 309–310.

[179] See Kocka and Siegrist in Horn and Kocka (eds) above n 171 at 55–122. (In German with English summary.)

between competing firms. While there is some evidence of a coincidence between the passage of such laws and an increase in merger activity,[180] no conclusive correlation between these factors has been established.[181] Indeed, the fact that firms will enter cartels, even if they are illegal under the laws of the countries in which the participating firms operate, should make such a correlation hard to establish. Furthermore, as noted earlier, cartels and mergers may be seen as complementary and not alternative strategies.[182] Therefore, it may not be possible to prove that competition law considerations act as decisive factors in the growth of large national and multinational corporations, given that economic factors will determine the extent to which a firm will collude with others to control a market or internalize that market through internal expansion or the takeover of competitors.

The foregoing discussion has related legal phenomena to theories of MNE growth based on firm size and technological advantage. However, not all explanations of MNE growth concentrate on these two factors. For example, it has been argued that a firm may have to go multinational so as to coordinate and neutralize the threat posed by its competitor's decision to go multinational.[183] Other theories have concentrated on the competitive advantage enjoyed by MNEs in international capital markets as an explanation of MNE growth.[184] Another possible explanation of multinationality, related to the financial aspects of the foreign activities of firms, is that certain companies invest abroad not to achieve economies of scale and production but to diversify investment and, thereby, reduce risk.[185] These explanations are related to competitive conditions in international capital and products markets and do not, as such, imply any significant role for legal factors as devices for the protection of firm-specific advantage.

However, there may be significant legal issues related to the regulation of the particular industry or country in which the firm operates, that contribute to the overall patterns of competition in relation to which the MNE functions. For

---

[180] See Hannah above n 171 at 311–14 on the US merger boom of the 1890s coinciding with the Sherman Act; L Hannah *The Rise of the Corporate Economy* (Methuen, 2nd ed, 1983) at 147–49 on the increase in UK mergers after the passage in 1956 of the Restrictive Trade Practices Act. See further Brian Cheffins 'Mergers and Corporate Ownership Structure: The United States and Germany at the Turn of the 20th Century' 51 Am. Jo. Comp. L. 473 (2003).

[181] See Hannah ibid; WR Cornish 'Legal Control Over Cartels and Monopolisation 1880–1914: A Comparison' in Horn and Kocka (eds) above n 171 at 280–305.

[182] Hannah ibid at 312; Kocka and Siegrist above n 179 at 62 et seq.

[183] Caves above n 131 at 93; FT Knickerbocker *Oligopolistic Reaction and the Multinational Enterprise* (Harvard University Press, 1973). See also K Cowling and R Sugden *Transnational Monopoly Capitalism* (Brighton: Wheatsheaf Books, 1987) at 16–22, who see such defensive behaviour as a response to competitive 'attack' coming from the firm that goes multinational first.

[184] See eg R Aliber 'A Theory of Direct Foreign Investment' in Charles Kindleberger (ed) *The International Corporation* (Cambridge, Mass: MIT Press, 1970) 17 and 'The Multinational Enterprise in a Multiple Currency World' in JH Dunning (ed) *The Multinational Enterprise* (London: George Allen & Unwin, 1971) 49. For a critique of Aliber's theory, see Hood and Young above n 12 at 51; P Buckley and M Casson *The Future of the Multinational Enterprise* (London, Macmillan, 2nd ed, 1991) at 71.

[185] See Kopits 'Multinational Conglomerate Diversification' 32 Econ.Int. 99 (1979). See also Caves above n 131 at 21.

example, Hood and Young argue[186] that if a firm has privileged access to raw materials or minerals this counts as a firm-specific advantage although, in general, a requirement for raw materials is a country-specific factor influencing the location of extractive, processing, or production activities. The retention of control over the raw materials concerned hinges initially on the possession of extractive technology. This advantage is then enhanced by the market power obtained by the firm in controlling access to the raw material and by vertical integration into production and distribution.[187] This can explain, for example, the dominance of the oil industry by the 'oil majors'[188] or the reasons for multinationality in the copper industry.[189] However, the possession of access to raw materials may not be a permanent source of advantage. External political pressures for greater host country control over natural resources and/or drops in demand for the finished products based on the raw material due to substitution or conservation have caused vertical disintegration in raw materials industries. Thus, the possession of raw materials is a firm-specific asset strongly conditioned by locational factors, including home and host state legal regulation, and technological factors, which connote the earlier discussion on legal protection of ownership advantages. Furthermore, the role of legal factors as elements in the MNE/host state bargaining process should not be overlooked.[190]

It follows from the earlier discussion of economic theory that the choice of whether a firm should make a direct investment depends on whether the costs of doing so can be offset in the long run against the benefits. This, in turn, depends on the interaction of O and I advantages with local conditions in prospective host locations. Relevant local factors include inter alia: whether the size and growth potential of the host's market is sufficient to justify the cost of opening a local production unit; whether the host state provides a gateway to other markets through exports; whether the local workforce is capable of working in the new plant; whether wages are at a level that makes local production profitable; whether there are any public subsidies that can offset the cost of the investment; whether the host state will set up barriers to protect the local production unit against outside competition. If these factors point to long-term profitability the firm will undertake a direct investment through a subsidiary. Thus, an economic transition from market to firm in the supply of the host state market will take place.

---

[186] Above n 12 at 53.

[187] See eg TAB Corley 'Strategic Factors in the Growth of a Multinational Enterprise: The Burmah Oil Company 1886–1928' in M Casson (ed) *The Growth of International Business* (London: George Allen & Unwin, 1983) 214.

[188] These are the largest oil companies: Exxon/Mobil, Texaco, Gulf/Chevron, Royal Dutch Shell, and BP.

[189] See Theodore Moran *Multinational Corporations and the Politics of Copper in Chile* (Princeton: 1977).

[190] See Peter T Muchlinski 'Law and the Analysis of the International Oil Industry' in J Rees and P Odell (eds) *The International Oil Industry: An Interdisciplinary Perspective* (London: Macmillan, 1987) 142. See further ch 3 below.

There can be little doubt that legal factors form an important category of locational factors, designed to facilitate the achievement of state economic goals whether these consist of protecting indigenous firms from foreign competition, of allowing foreign firms to enter the economy under strict controls, or by providing positive incentives to investors in an attempt to improve the host state's advantages as a location for MNEs. In theory, therefore, the state may use its political power to alter its locational advantages through law and thereby influence the investment decisions of MNEs.[191] The process may be illustrated by analysing the ways in which a firm might supply its products to customers in the host state. It is useful, first, to consider the issue in purely economic terms and then to examine how different legal regimes might affect the firm's choices. It is assumed that commercial conditions in the host state make it an attractive market for the foreign firm. Firms will not normally invest in the host state where this is not the case.

The simplest way to supply customers in the host state is for the firm to export its goods to the host market. This alternative will be chosen where the transaction costs of direct sales to end customers under an international sales contract are low enough not to affect the profitability of the transaction to the firm. However, the supply of the host market through direct sales will become unattractive where the volume of exports to the host is such that the transaction costs of exporting are getting too high. The transaction costs involved would include costs of negotiating individual contracts, and the costs of monitoring compliance. Some relief from negotiation costs could be obtained by selling in the export market through an agent. However, this too can involve transaction costs, particularly in relation to monitoring the agent's compliance with the terms of the agency agreement. Thus, the firm may have to consider whether it should move to licensing local production or to making a direct investment.

In order for licensing to be chosen the host country must be endowed with a sufficient level of industrial organization and labour skills to offer suitable potential licensees for the exploitation of the foreign firm's assets. In the absence of a suitable licensee, the firm has only the choice between high cost exporting and direct investment. On the other hand, where a suitable licensee does exist, the firm must consider the cost of entering a licensing agreement over those of a direct investment in a subsidiary.[192] Of prime importance is the question of whether the licensee can be trusted to use the firm's O advantages in a manner that will not undermine their commercial worth. This is particularly significant in relation to unique technology or know-how, whose commercial value lies in its proper use and in the retention of its confidential character. A licensee may not be sufficiently

---

[191] See further World Bank *World Development Report 2005: A Better Investment Climate for Everyone* (Washington DC: The World Bank, 2005) especially ch 5. See also OECD *Policy Framework for Investment* (Paris: OECD, 2006) and *Policy Framework for Investment: A Review of Good Practices* (Paris: OECD, 2006).

[192] See, for analysis of the economic considerations, Caves above n 131 at 167–72 and see also ch 11 at 437–39.

capable or trustworthy, even under a strict contractual regime governed by terms favourable to the licensor, to be entrusted with the exploitation of the technology in question. In such a case, the higher cost option of establishing a local subsidiary, or the takeover of the potential licensee by the licensor, may be the only commercially effective way of protecting the foreign firm's O advantages.

How does state intervention through law affect these choices? The export option will only remain open so long as the host state does not pursue protectionist policies that seek to reduce the presence of foreign products in the local market. However, assuming that the host state wishes to preserve the consumption of the goods or services offered by the foreign firm, it may prefer that those products are locally produced. The host state may seek this objective by imposing high tariff barriers to trade, thereby cutting out the possibility of serving the market through exports from the home country. The foreign firm then has a choice between jumping the tariff barrier and setting up local production, whether through a licensee or a production subsidiary, or not investing at all. The firm may be forced to jump the tariff barrier and go multinational if the host market is too large to be ignored, or if competitors are undertaking the expense of licensing or direct investment. Indeed, 'tariff jumping' has proved to be a significant historical reason for firms setting up production subsidiaries in host countries.[193]

Alternatively, the host state may use its regulatory power to require that the foreign firm supply the market through the licensing of a local firm or through an equity joint venture with a local firm or state entity. Here the foreign firm must decide whether the costs of compliance are outweighed by the costs of not investing at all. The market conditions in the host country, as related to the position of the firm in the global market, and to that of its competitors, will be taken into account. If it can afford to do so, the firm may decline the opportunity to invest.[194] If not it will have to sustain the cost of complying with the law and enter into the required licensing agreement or joint venture.

On the other hand, the host state may be dependent on the foreign firm to transfer its technology and know-how to the host state. In these circumstances, the host state may relinquish its power to restrict entry and establishment and may offer investment incentives to induce the MNE to invest. This raises questions relevant to the location-specific advantages of host states concerning differences between their respective regulatory environments. A MNE may choose to invest in state A rather than state B if the law of state A offers fewer regulatory constraints

---

[193] See eg the case of British MNEs in the inter-war years: Geoffrey Jones in Inoue and Okochi (eds) above n 30. For the effect of tariff barriers to trade on US MNEs see Mira Wilkins (1970) above n 7 especially 78–109. The industrialization of Canada and Australia through inward direct investment owes much to the use of tariff barriers to trade: see Caves above n 131 at 34–36 and references there cited.

[194] For example when, in 1973, India introduced a foreign ownership limit of 40 per cent in Indian subsidiaries of foreign firms IBM and Coca-Cola decided to leave the Indian market rather than compromise its policy of investing abroad only through wholly owned subsidiaries. See further ch 5 at 186–87.

than the law of state B. Thus, for example, differences in, inter alia, disclosure requirements,[195] levels of taxation,[196] competition controls,[197] or principles of corporate liability[198] can influence the decision of a MNE to locate in A rather than B.

From the foregoing discussion it is clear that legal factors will have a role to play in determining the locational characteristics of the host state. However, it would be wrong to assume that they are of prime significance. Much MNE investment goes to countries with rather unstable and erratic legal orders. Ultimately, MNEs invest in a country because of its economic attractions, which, when combined with the O and I advantages of the firm, should serve to generate profit. If not, investment by the MNE is unlikely. In addition, not all MNEs will respond to the legal environment of the host country in the same way. Firms from home countries in which legal approaches to regulation and dispute settlement are not culturally significant may place less value on the nature of the legal environment when deciding whether or not to invest.[199] Indeed, it appears that the need for a transparent, stable and predictable legal system, with impartial and effective legal dispute settlement mechanisms, is of greatest importance to US and other Western MNEs, which are used to a legalistic approach to business, and to intergovernmental organizations, such as the World Bank, which use quality of the legal system as a factor in determining whether to support projects with funding.[200] Equally, the ability to create stability and reduce investment risk through political and other, more informal, channels may be sufficient to offset any concerns in this regard. However, it is preferable for the host country to ensure that its legal system is sound so as to avoid the possible loss of investment that might be influenced by legal conditions in cases where the economic advantages of investment may be marginal.

The legal aspects of internalization advantages in MNE growth raise perhaps the most contentious issues. The ability of a MNE to take advantage of differences in regulatory environments between states is seen as one of its internalization advantages. The resulting potential for the ineffectiveness of national regulation over the activities of MNEs has led certain states to apply their laws extraterritorially to non-resident units of MNEs operating within their jurisdiction. The

---

[195] See ch 9.   [196] See ch 7.   [197] See ch 10.   [198] See ch 8.

[199] See further Amanda Perry *Legal Systems as a Determinant of FDI: Lessons from Sri Lanka* (The Hague: Kluwer Law International, 2001) and Amanda Perry-Kessaris 'Finding and Facing Facts About Legal Systems and Foreign Direct Investment in South Asia' 23 Leg. Stud. 649 (2003).

[200] Legal stability and 'good governance' are key elements of the so-called 'Washington Consensus' on market-led development strategy. Whether it is possible to determine when a legal system fits these criteria, and whether investors actually care, is still open to discussion: see Perry-Kessaris above n 199 and Lawrence Tshuma 'The Political Economy of the World Bank's Legal Framework for Economic Development' in Julio Faundez, Mary E Footer and Joseph J Norton (eds) *Governance, Development and Globalization* (London: Blackstone Press, 2000) 7 also in 8 Social and Legal Studies (No 1, 1999). On 'good governance' see further Julio Faundez (ed) *Good Government and Law* (London: MacMillan, 1997).

consequence has been to encourage conflict over the exercise of such jurisdiction between the regulating state and the state in which the targeted unit of the MNE operates.[201] The conflict caused by uncoordinated unilateral state policies has led to attempts at greater international cooperation in regulatory matters and at the evolution of an international consensus over the standards to be applied to the regulation of MNEs.[202] The supranational incorporation of MNEs has also been considered.[203] The development of a genuine international law of foreign direct investment would serve to reduce the internalization advantages enjoyed by MNEs as a result of diversity in national regulations, through the harmonization of state policies. However, such harmonization may not produce desirable results as regards the welfare of individual states. It may not, therefore, be politically feasible.[204] In addition, attempts at harmonization may be undermined through 'creative compliance' by firms, allowing for a formal compliance with regulatory rules that they do not wish to observe, while at the same time by-passing their regulatory effect.[205]

Further issues arise out of the relationship between O advantages and I advantages. In particular, the possession of a monopolistic advantage by a MNE suggests the need to control any abuse of that advantage through competition law. However, proponents of theories based on the concept of internalization will argue that the replacement of the market in intermediate goods with the hierarchy of the firm is an efficient outcome and the resulting competitive advantage to the firm should not be interfered with. The argument runs that the law should encourage such efficiency gains by not opposing the creation of internalization advantages. In the case of MNEs such advantages can be created, either, by mergers between suppliers and consumers of intermediate products, involving the takeover of a domestic firm by a foreign firm, or by the establishment of a subsidiary of a foreign firm in the host state. In the former case, the foreign nationality of the purchaser should not bar the takeover while, in the latter case, the potential threat posed by the new investment to the long-term survival or development of domestic competitors should not prevent entry. This approach is taken by countries which espouse an 'open door' to foreign inward investment.[206]

On the other hand, states may react by seeking to unbundle the internalization advantages of MNEs. According to Hood and Young,[207] a major difficulty with Buckley and Casson's above mentioned thesis is that the long-run political or other costs of internalization may eventually make it prohibitively expensive, especially

---

[201] See ch 4.   [202] See further Part IV.

[203] See C Wilfred Jenks 'Multinational Entities in the Law of Nations' in Wolfgang Friedmann (ed) *Transnational Law in a Changing Society: Essays in Honour of Phillip C. Jessup* (New York: Columbia University Press, 1972) 70 and see further ch 2 at 72–76.   [204] See further ch 3.

[205] See Doreen McBarnet 'Transnational Transactions, Legal Work, Cross-Border Commerce and Global Regulation' in Michael Likosky (ed) *Transnational Legal Processes: Globalisation and Power Disparities* (London: Butterworths, Lexis-Nexis, 2002) 98.

[206] See, for example, the UK's policy on foreign takeovers discussed in ch 10.

[207] Above n 12 at 57.

where host nations adopt discriminatory policies towards MNEs. For example, in the late 1960s and early 1970s, the wave of major nationalizations by the OPEC countries of upstream oil production facilities owned and controlled by the major oil companies effectively de-internalized those activities and replaced them with arm's length dealings between the newly formed national oil production companies that took over the nationalized assets and the oil majors: internalization gave way to interdependence between independent companies.[208]

Apart from forced divestiture a host state could compel the sharing of firm-specific advantages with local firms through compulsory joint ventures, technology transfer licences, and performance requirements. Again, the choice will be influenced by the host state's view of the welfare effects of inward direct investment.[209] However, in an environment geared towards investment promotion and economic deregulation, the exploitation, by the MNE, of its knowledge advantages within its internalized structures is more likely to be accepted and host states may refrain from regulation that interferes with this choice. Furthermore, as more open networks of enterprises combine to develop new products and processes, the state may choose to promote such cooperative linkages and to encourage joint ventures and other knowledge sharing systems to develop. Such an approach would be permissive rather than mandatory in that the aim would be to offer the right legal environment to encourage commercially based decisions to cooperate. On the other hand, the state may need to guard against the anti-competitive abuse of such cooperative relationships and ensure that, where necessary, the competition authorities will intervene and prevent such abuses from arising or sanction abuses that have already occurred.[210]

Finally, in relation to internalization issues, the legal response to the internalization of labour markets, identified by Cowling and Sugden as a significant competitive advantage of the MNE,[211] should be considered. Cowling and Sugden argue inter alia that firms become multinational in order to take advantage of lower labour costs that result from the firm's enhanced ability to 'divide and rule': 'by producing in various countries firms divide their workforce, thereby reduce labour's bargaining power, and consequently obtain lower labour costs.'[212] The ability to reduce labour costs in this way may be at least a contributory reason for the existence of some multinationals.[213] The advantage enjoyed by the MNE over domestic firms as an exploiter of labour will depend to a significant degree on the legal conditions regarding labour relations that are imposed on it by host states. The responses of countries vary from protection of trade union rights and collective bargaining to outright repression. Thus countries may differ in the extent to

---

[208] See further P Odell and J Rees (eds) *The International Oil Industry* (London: Macmillan, 1987) especially papers by Penrose at 9; Zakariah at 107; Peter T Muchlinski at 142.

[209] See further ch 3.   [210] See further ch 10 at 394–97.   [211] Above n 183.

[212] ibid at 62.

[213] See further Roger Sugden 'The Importance of Distributional Considerations' in Pitelis and Sugden (eds) above n 131.

which their laws will preserve the comparative advantage of MNEs over labour. The diversity of legal responses to the protection of labour rights represents, in itself, a barrier to effective cross-border trade union organization. To that extent legal factors may assist in the preservation of the MNEs advantages in this field.[214]

A final, overarching, factor in the legal response to the growth of MNEs concerns the conceptualization of how global production chains should be regulated. Here Francis Snyder's concept of 'global legal pluralism' is helpful.[215] He sees this process as encompassing a range of structural sites which include 'a variety of institutions, norms and dispute resolution processes located and produced at different structured sites around the world'.[216] He contemplates non-state,[217] state, supranational, and multilateral law creating entities within his definition of 'sites'. Secondly, Snyder sees the relations between these sites as being varied in both structure and process. Thus sites may be, 'autonomous and even independent, part of the same or different regimes, part of a single system of multi-level governance, or otherwise interconnected'.[218] The important thing is that these sites interact with global economic networks to create the global playing field on which regulation occurs. Thus: '[g]lobal legal pluralism does more ... than simply provide the rules of the game; it also constitutes the game itself, including the players.'[219] This approach allows us to see the process of global regulation in a diversified context. In particular it shows how territorial, regional, international, and informal sources of legal rules and practices act as an input into legal globalization. Furthermore, it allows us to consider the power relations between the principal players and the sites of global legal pluralism by stressing the interactions between them. Though Snyder does not go so far as to say that the network of legal rules and practices that governs a given global production chain will reflect the structure of authority and power in that chain,[220] there is nonetheless the capacity to use his approach as a vehicle for the study of power relations in the process of global legal governance.[221]

---

[214] See further ch 12.

[215] See Francis Snyder 'Governing Economic Globalisation: Global Legal Pluralism and EU Law' in Francis Snyder (ed) *Regional and Global Regulation of International Trade* (Oxford: Hart Publishing, 2002) 1. See too by the same author 'Global Economic Networks and Global Legal Pluralism' in George A Bermann, Matthias Herdegen and Peter L Lindseth (eds) *Transatlantic Regulatory Co-operation: Legal Problems and Prospects* (Oxford: Oxford University Press, 2000) 99 and 'Governing Economic Globalisation: Global Legal Pluralism and European Law' 5 ELJ 334 (1999). This passage is taken from Peter T Muchlinski 'Globalisation and Legal Research' 37 Int'l. Law 221 at 236–37 (2003).   [216] Snyder (2002) ibid at 10.

[217] This includes informal systems of business regulation through commercial customs and practices, the application of firm and industry based codes of conduct, and the internal disciplinary procedures of MNEs. See further Jean Philippe Robe 'Multinational Enterprises: The Constitution of a Pluralistic Legal Order' in Gunther Teubner (ed) *Global Law Without a State* (Aldershot: Datrmouth Publishing, 1997) 45 and Peter T Muchlinski ' "Global Bukowina" Examined: Viewing the Multinational Enterprise as a Transnational Law Making Community' ibid 79; Roy Goode 'Usage and its Reception in Transnational Commercial Law' 46 ICLQ 1 (1997).   [218] ibid at 11.

[219] ibid.   [220] ibid at 45.   [221] These themes will be further discussed in ch 3.

Concluding Remarks

The present chapter has sought to offer definitions of MNEs, trace their evolution over time and space, summarize the leading explanations as to why the growth of such firms has occurred, and to identify the most significant legal factors that may have contributed, and continue to contribute to that growth. This is by no means a final or complete analysis. The reasons for the growth of MNEs are open to considerable debate, as reflected by the emergence of an 'eclectic' paradigm, rather than a single dominant theory of international production. Our understanding of the contribution of legal factors to the growth of MNEs is even less advanced than economic theory. Nonetheless, as this chapter has sought to show, the study of such factors can evolve within the same general framework as used by the 'eclectic' paradigm. On the other hand, the 'eclectic' paradigm's concentration on firm, location, and internalization factors in the growth of MNEs cannot offer a complete explanation of the origins of legal responses to MNE activities. This approach must be supplemented by reference to the relationship between the business organization and legal forms of multinational enterprise and by an understanding of the debate on the effects of MNE operations on national economies and resulting approaches to regulation, for which approaches based on legal pluralism offer the best conceptual framework. These further considerations will form the basis of the next two chapters.

2

Business and Legal Forms of Multinational Enterprise: Towards a Theory of Control

This chapter deals with the relationship between the business organization and legal form of MNEs. It will consider, first, the principal types of business organization and control structures commonly found in modern MNEs. Secondly, the main kinds of legal forms adopted by MNEs will be described. Thirdly, it will end with an assessment of the interrelationship between these two elements. This will seek to provide answers to a crucial matter in the regulation of MNEs, namely, where does control over the activities of the enterprise lie, and do the legal forms into which MNEs are expected to fit adequately reflect the allocation of decision-making power in the firm. As will be seen below, legal forms may not coincide with the business organization of the firm. This may lead to a mismatch between the firm's control structures and the legal structures through which the firm is sought to be regulated, to the detriment of effective regulation. The chapter proceeds on the basis of two assumptions: first, that the business form of the enterprise tends to reflect the market strategy taken by it, in accordance with the 'strategy and structure' thesis of Alfred Chandler[1] and, secondly, that the legal form adopted will aim at the most cost effective accommodation between the corporation's business needs and the regulatory requirements to which it is subject.[2] Here, a significant factor will be the degree of freedom, as to the choice of legal form, given to the MNE in its various operating jurisdictions.

(1) MNEs as Transnational Business Organizations

This section outlines the main phases of organizational development undertaken by MNEs.[3] In particular it contrasts the traditional 'hierarchical' model of

---

[1] See further AD Chandler *Strategy and Structure: Chapters in the History of the American Industrial Enterprise* (Cambridge, Mass: MIT Press, 1962); *The Visible Hand: The Managerial Revolution in American Business* (Harvard: Belknap, 1977); *Scale and Scope: The Dynamics of Industrial Capitalism* (Harvard: Belknap, 1990).

[2] On which see further Ray Vernon and Louis T Wells *The Economic Environment of International Business* (Prentice-Hall, 4th edn, 1986) ch 2.

[3] See D Eleanor Westney and Srilata Zaheer 'The Multinational Enterprise as an Organization' in Alan M Rugman and Thomas L Brewer (eds) *The Oxford Handbook of International Business* (Oxford: Oxford University Press, 2000) 349. For historical analysis of developments in MNE organization see

international business organization with the more recent, flatter 'heterarchical' model. It is not suggested that all MNEs will follow a change from hierarchy to heterarchy. Rather, it is necessary to understand the choices open to firms when determining their organizational structure and to realize that this choice will depend on many variables. As noted in the introduction the most important of these is nature of the market that the firm serves and the mix of functions required to do so successfully.[4] In addition, the organizational skill of senior management will be influential.[5] This will dictate the firm's ability to adapt to change, and the level of involvement of line management and the workforce in such decisions. Furthermore, the internal political culture of the firm may be significant.[6] The temptation to 'build empires' and, thereby, to create unwieldy and unresponsive management structures, is as likely in the private as the public sector. The responsive corporation will guard against this. Finally, external factors, such as host government policy, which may require the use of certain forms of business organization, will affect such decisions.[7]

In common with other large multilocation enterprises, MNEs have outgrown the simple managerial structure of the small entrepreneurial corporation.[8] Corporate growth demands a greater specialization and division of labour within the firm. At first, growth may be piecemeal with new subsidiary corporations being formed as the need for new functions arises, and as new products or services are developed. Eventually, however, a major rationalization may take place, with a reorganization of the company along divisional lines of control based on managerial functions, products, and areas of operation.[9] This process of 'divisionalization' has been defined as follows:

Divisionalisation is the process by which the structure of a group of companies is changed from the traditional relationship of parent company and subsidiary company to one where all the operating functions of several, or possibly all of the wholly-owned subsidiaries are performed within one corporate entity, and the discrete functions are organised within separate divisions of that company. The previous structure in which each function had a separate formal and legal corporate existence is dispensed with.[10]

Within the MNE such reorganization may involve a restructuring of the global functions of the group. The principal lines of control will differ according to the

Geoffrey Jones *Multinational Enterprises and Global Capitalism: From the Nineteenth to the Twenty-first Century* (Oxford: Oxford University Press, 2005) chs 6 and 7.

   [4] See 'A Survey of the Company' *The Economist* 21 January 2006.

   [5] See, on the influence of managerial attitudes to international business, Howard Perlmutter 'The Tortuous Evolution of the Multinational Corporation' 5 Col.Jo.World Bus. 9 (1969).

   [6] See CK Prahalad 'Strategic Choices in Diversified MNCs' 54 Harv.Bus.Rev. 67 (1976).

   [7] See Yves L Doz and CK Prahalad 'How MNCs Cope with Host Government Intervention' Harv.Bus.Rev. March–April 1980 at 149.   [8] See generally the works of Chandler above n 1.

   [9] See further Mira Wilkins *The Maturing of Multinational Enterprise: American Business Abroad From 1914 to 1970* (Cambridge, Mass: Harvard University Press, 1974) ch 15; Lawrence Franko *The European Multinationals* (London: Harper, 1976) ch 8.

   [10] Deloitte, Haskins, and Sells *Corporate Structure – Subsidiaries or Divisions?* (August 1983) cited in Robert I Tricker *Corporate Governance* (Aldershot: Gower, 1984) at 145.

type of firm and the kinds of markets in which it operates. They will also evolve over time. Thus it is not uncommon for a firm to have begun on its path to multinational organization with an export department, which is then superseded by an international division responsible for all the firm's overseas activities, including exports and direct investments, which, in its turn, may be replaced by a global divisionalization of the firm.[11]

Space prevents a detailed analysis of the different models of global divisionalization. This has been done elsewhere.[12] However, certain valid generalizations can be usefully made. For example, a company, such as an oil company, which locates, extracts, processes, transports, and distributes raw materials, will tend to organize around global functional divisions. On the other hand, a company with an undiversified line of products or services, operating in more than one country or region, will tend to organize around a global area divisional structure, while a company with a highly diversified line of products or services will tend to organize around global product or service divisions.[13] If such a diversified company also operates in many different geographical markets it may adopt a matrix structure in which lines of management based on product and area divisions cross. In such cases the management of the firm may become a complex process with competition and conflict emerging between the various lines of command.[14]

Ultimately, divisional structures should represent the most effective communication system between the decision-making centres of the firm and the market[s] in which it operates. In a mature MNE, the size and complexity of the managerial structure could itself become a hindrance to such communication, especially if this process becomes politicized by reason of internal conflicts.[15] In response to this problem MNEs have begun to experiment with more decentralized forms of organization. According to Dunning, the global firm must bear in mind two types of balancing act in this process.[16] The first is that between the international integration of production within the firm and the responsiveness of individual

---

[11] See further, on evolutionary patterns of MNE structural growth following Chandler's 'strategy and structure' thesis: John Stopford and Louis Wells Jr *Managing the Multinational Enterprise* (New York: Basic Books, 1972) Part I. For a different, but complementary, approach based on conflicts in decision-making: MZ Brooke and H Lee Remmers *The Strategy of the Multinational Enterprise* (Pitman, 2nd edn, 1978) ch 2. European MNEs began not with an international division but with a 'mother-daughter' structure in which heads of foreign subsidiaries reported directly to the head of the parent company: Westney and Zaheer above n 3 at 352 citing Lawrence Franko above n 9.

[12] See Westney and Zaheer above n 3 at 370–75; D Channon and M Jalland *Multinational Strategic Planning* (London: Macmillan Press, 1978) chs 2 and 3; S Robock and K Simmonds *International Business and Multinational Enterprises* (Irwin, 4th edn, 1989) ch 11; JH Dunning *Multinational Enterprises and the Global Economy* (Wokingham: Addison Wesley, 1993) ch 8.

[13] Dunning ibid at 217.

[14] See further Christopher A Bartlett and Sumantra Ghoshal *Managing Across Borders: The Transnational Solution* (Harvard Business Press, 1989, paperback edn, 2001) 31–32. See too the example of the Dutch electrical company, Philips: 'The Matrix Master' in *The Economist* above n 4 at 4.

[15] See Westney and Zaheer above n 3 at 357–58.

[16] Above n 12 at 218–19, on which this paragraph draws. See also Stephen B Tallman and George S Yip 'Strategy and the Multinational Enterprise' in Rugman and Brewer (eds) above n 3 at 317.

affiliates to the needs of the national economies within which they operate.[17] This may require greater input from local managers in corporate decision-making and greater exchange of information among affiliates.[18] The second is that of obtaining the advantages of geographical and product based organizational structures while avoiding their weaknesses. This may lead to a shift of emphasis away from a hierarchical, vertical, control structure, to a 'heterarchical' network of cooperative and lateral relationships.[19]

The trend towards 'heterarchy' may lead firms to spread certain functions geographically across the enterprise. Thus R&D need not remain tied to the parent company, as has been the trend in past years.[20] Similarly, certain divisional head offices could be relocated outside the home state. Furthermore, the firm itself could be reorganized into smaller, self-standing units of decision-takers who will come together in a mix that fits the business tasks that the firm faces, without creating permanent organizational structures. The role of the head office will then be transformed from that of the ultimate policy-maker and directing 'brain', to that of coordinator and identifier of new business opportunities and the creator of task force networks within the firm. This function may extend beyond the firm to outside bodies possessing the required business and/or technological expertise to realize a business project. Thus, not only will hierarchical structures within the firm be subject to greater organizational flexibility, but the organizational boundaries between individual firms themselves will begin to blur, as increased numbers of strategic alliances are formed.[21]

This new approach to corporate organization has been followed in recent years by several leading MNEs. For example, both BP and General Electric have moved towards a more flexible and innovation driven structure.[22] IBM has also modified

---

[17] On which see further Yves Doz *Strategic Management in Multinational Companies* (London: Pergamon Press, 1986).

[18] See further Julian Birkinshaw *Entrepreneurship in the Global Firm* (London: Sage Publications, 2000) who shows that decentralized entrepreneurial activity on the part of subsidiary managers is increasingly significant in modern MNEs and 'Strategy and Management in MNE Subsidiaries' in Rugman and Brewer (eds) above n 3 at 380.

[19] See further Ghoshal and Bartlett above n 14 and 'The Multinational Corporation as a Differentiated Organisational Network' 15 Academy of Management Review 603 (1990); Yves Doz and CK Prahalad 'Managing DMNCs: A Search for a New Paradigm' 12 Strategic Management Journal 145 (1991); Gunnar Hedlund 'The Hypermodern MNC: A Heterarchy?' 25 Human Resource Management 9 (1986); Gunnar Hedlund and Bruce Kogut 'Managing MNCs: the End of the Missionary Era' in Gunnar Hedlund (ed) *TNCs and Organisational Issues* (UN Library on Transnational Corporations/Routledge, 1992); R Van Tulder and G Junne *European Multinationals in Core Technologies* (Wiley/IRM, 1988) ch 3.

[20] See Nagesh Kumar 'Intellectual Property Protection, Market Orientation and Location of Overseas R&D Activities by Multinational Enterprises' 24 World Development 673 (1996).

[21] For an extensive account of this thesis see Robert Reich *The Work of Nations: Preparing Ourselves for 21st Century Capitalism* (New York: Simon and Schuster, 1991). See too Bartlett and Ghoshal above n 14; K Ohmae *Triad Power: The Coming Shape of Global Competition* (Free Press, 1985) and ibid *The Borderless World* (Fontana, 1991); Michael Z. Brooke 'Multinational Corporate Structures: The Next Stage' Futures April 1979 at 111; Dunning above n 12 at ch 9.

[22] See Christopher A Bartlett, Sumantra Ghoshal, and Julian Birkinshaw *Transnational Management: Text Cases and Readings in Cross-border Management* (Boston: McGaw Hill Irwin, 4th edn, 2004) ch 8 Cases 8–1 and 8–2 at 774–813.

its traditional hierarchical structure to be more responsive to innovation and client needs. It has reorganized as a more open entity around three core business segments: systems and financing, software, and services.[23] In addition, information technology based companies, such as Cisco Systems, may use a 'front-end/back-end' structure.[24] This integrates the back-end production systems, which typically contribute a large number of different products that go to create the final products, and the front-end retail and marketing organization that deals with customers. This allows for the integration of R&D and production and the customer focus and retail functions without the need for a complex matrix organization. However, this system depends on close coordination between the front and back ends of the enterprise to ensure market responsiveness.

A further factor moving MNEs towards the reconstruction of their internal organization is the availability of electronic communication and information technologies. This may permit a greater disaggregation of value chains across locations, the emergence of 'virtual' MNEs and to increase the competitive potential of small and medium sized firms across borders.[25] A familiar example of how IT has changed business organization is the 'just in time' stock ordering process which has reduced the need for the distributor to build up a large inventory of stock and, instead, to respond to customer orders by requesting supplies directly from the production line. Such advantages can be complemented by the global sourcing of inputs on a 'just in time' basis as pioneered by the Japanese car industry after 1980.[26] Equally the kinds of open, collaborative, transnational organizations outlined above would be impossible to manage without good IT connections.[27] A major opportunity offered by IT is the reduction of owned and controlled subsidiaries, allowing for a saving in overall costs. For example, Nortel Networks, a Canadian IT internet network builder, sold off 15 manufacturing plants in 1998 to its existing suppliers of components and signed new long-term supply agreements with them. This allows the firm the flexibility to outsource supply to locations nearer to the customer.[28] Furthermore, IT will have a positive effect on the ability of the firm to transfer technological innovation through its production network, and to speed up the process of technology diffusion across borders.[29]

The trend towards more open heterarchical organizations indicates what the future of all MNE organizations might look like.[30] However, decentralization and

---

[23] See IBM *Annual Report 2005* Chairman's Letter at 6 and Management Discussion at 17–21 available at <http://www.ibm.com/annualreport>.

[24] See Westney and Zaheer above n 3 at 374 on which this account draws.   [25] ibid at 368.

[26] See Geoffrey Jones *The Evolution of International Business: An Introduction* (London: Routledge, 1996) at 138–39.

[27] See further 'E-Management' Survey *The Economist* 18 November 2000.   [28] ibid at 47.

[29] See John Cantwell 'Innovation and Information Technology in the MNE' in Rugman and Brewer (eds) above n 3 at 431.

[30] A flatter 'cell' structure for emerging enterprises from developing countries may make the transition to global activity attainable for such firms in certain industries and regions: see John A Mathews *Dragon Multinational: A New Model for Global Growth* (Oxford: Oxford University Press, 2002). This study examines Acer, the Taiwanese IT company; the Hong Leong hotel group of Singapore; Ispat

'networking' takes time to put in place and it may encounter resistance from entrenched interests in the firm, especially where it may lead to reorganizations involving job losses. In addition, flatter organizations offer less in the way of pro- motion opportunities. Thus the human resistance to change may be a factor to take into consideration.[31] Nevertheless, the trend towards 'networking' and 'het- erarchy' must be considered as a significant modification to the conventional notion of the MNE as a unitary pyramid of decision-takers, one which has import- ant implications for discussions of legal regulation and liability, given the chan- ging structures of control that may be involved.

Finally, before going on to the legal forms of multinational enterprise, it is necessary to consider the degree of centralized control that the head office of a MNE might exercise over local affiliates. While each firm will determine the degree of centralization/decentralization required in accordance with its percep- tion of the most cost effective and efficient strategy, empirical studies have shown up certain common patterns among MNEs.[32] The findings have concentrated on two sets of factors: first, the general influences on the locus of decision-taking and, secondly, the degree of influence commonly exercised by the parent in relation to particular types of decisions.

As to the first, after an extensive review of significant empirical studies, the OECD offers the following conclusions:

... a foreign subsidiary may be seen as having relatively little autonomy if it belongs to a large multinational group established in many foreign countries; if it manufactures fairly standardised products; if the activities of the members are largely integrated, with import- ant interflows of products between them (this holds true especially for the investment and finance function); if it has been created to serve a market larger than the country in which it is established; or if the parent company holds a large portion of the equity. On the other hand, a subsidiary may be seen as more autonomous if it was acquired to serve mainly the local market; if it belongs to a small group; if it has interchange of products with the rest of the group and is operating in an activity slightly different from that of other members (the opposite holds true for the marketing function); if an important part of its common shares is held by local investors; and if the whole concern pursues a growth strategy.[33]

International in steel; Cemex of Mexico in cement; and Li and Fung from Hong Kong in contract manufacturing.

[31]   See *The Economist* Survey 2006 above n 4 at 1–5 and 14.

[32]   See further OECD *Structure and Organisation of Multinational Enterprises* (Paris: OECD, 1987); Dunning above n 12 at 222–32; Richard E Caves *Multinational Enterprise and Economic Analysis* (Cambridge: Cambridge University Press, 2nd edn, 1996) at 63–69; Birkinshaw above n 18; Martinez and Jarillo 'The Evolution of Research on Co-ordination Mechanisms in Multinational Corporations' 20 Jo.Int'l.Bus.Stud. 489 (1989). On control over decision-making in UK sub- sidiaries of foreign-owned firms, see M Steuer et al *The Impact of Foreign Direct Investment on the United Kingdom* (Department of Trade and Industry, 1973) ch 7; S Young, N Hood and J Hamill *Decision-making in Foreign Owned Multinational Subsidiaries in the UK* ILO Working Paper No 35 (Geneva: ILO, 1985).

[33]   OECD ibid at 35. Birkinshaw notes that where a subsidiary is acting as part of a global supply chain, offering standardized global products, it is highly unlikely to be autonomous in its market-oriented

To these factors may be added: the nationality and resulting business culture of the parent (for example there is some evidence to suggest that US firms tend to be more centralized than non-US firms); the age of the subsidiary, in that centralization may decrease over time; the method of entry into the host state, in that a new establishment may be more closely controlled than an acquired local company; the industrial sector in which the firm operates, in that some industries will be more globally integrated and centralized than others; the performance of the subsidiary, in that poor performance increases central control; and the tendency of geographically organized MNEs to be less centralized than functional, product, or matrix-organized firms.[34] As to the second, Dunning points out that centralized decisions are more likely in areas that are: 'perceived as being culture free, in those which offer substantial economies of common governance, and those which are likely to be more efficiently implemented by the parent firm.' He cites R&D, capital expenditure plans, and dividend policy as examples. By contrast, decisions confined to the affiliate, or matters needing sensitivity to local environments and relationships, such as personnel and labour relations or sales promotion, are likely to be made on a decentralized basis.[35]

Following from the above, for the purposes of discussing control and regulation of MNEs, a distinction will have to be made, first, between hierarchically and heterarchically integrated MNEs and, secondly, between integrated MNEs and 'transnational networks' involving free-standing firms. Furthermore, the actual degree of control exercised by a parent over its affiliates will vary in accordance with a significant range of factors. This makes the prediction of parent company control for regulatory purposes dependent on specific market and organizational conditions, requiring often difficult economic and commercial analysis. This may lead to the use of presumptions of control as a device for the formulation of legal structures for MNEs, and for the activation of substantive regulations against non-resident units of the MNE. It is an issue that will recur in a number of areas discussed in this work.

(2) Legal Forms of Multinational Enterprise

This section offers an attempt at a comprehensive classification and analysis of the principal types of legal structures employed by MNEs in the course of their operations. The legal structure used will be the product of a number of factors, including the nature of the business activity in question and the transaction costs

---

functions. This can be contrasted with an earlier period of investment by MNEs where market seeking investment was likely to be locally targeted and the subsidiary given a degree of freedom to adapt a standard product to local requirements: in Rugman and Brewer above n 18 at 390–92.

[34] Dunning above n 12 at Table 8.1 at 225 using Young, Hood and Hamill above n 32 as source.
[35] Dunning ibid at 226.

involved,[36] the extent to which the law will require the use of a particular structure, the principal national characteristics of the firm and those of the legal cultures from which, and within which, it operates. The underlying aim is to create a legal structure that will offer the fewest regulatory burdens while permitting the maximum operational flexibility that is permissible under the law of the state in which the legal structure resides. The resulting legal structure may or may not correspond to the business structure of the enterprise concerned. Much depends on particular circumstances and on the extent that the hand of management may be involved in an attempt to reduce regulatory burdens.

The classification used divides MNE legal structures into those based on contract, equity based corporate groups, joint ventures between independent firms, informal alliances, publicly owned MNEs, and supranational forms of international business.[37] The first three are the most common forms of legal organization open to privately owned and operated firms, the fourth emerges from the observable tendency of MNEs to adopt business alliances that have no clear legal form but which may generate legal liabilities, the fifth considers the distinct legal features of state-owned MNEs while the last considers examples of existing forms of supranational business entities developed by regional organizations of states and briefly contrasts the privately owned MNE with the so-called 'public international corporation', a creature of the public sector and international treaty which may perform business functions similar to those carried out by MNEs.

(a) Contractual Forms

As noted in chapter 1, the OECD definition of multinational enterprise is not limited to equity based groups, but extends to any company or other entity that can exert a significant influence over another or at least to be so linked as to coordinate their operations.[38] Furthermore, as noted in chapter 1, the supply of foreign markets may be achieved through business forms that fall short of setting up an owned and controlled subsidiary in the host state. The legally binding contract offers various options in this respect, ranging from simple one-off export sales to complex and permanent international consortia. Discrete export sales can be disregarded for the purposes of this work, given the incidental and arm's length nature of such transactions. However, in other cases where international business is carried on by means of contract, there may emerge a relationship of control and dominance by one party which creates a degree of business integration that would

---

[36] See ch 1.
[37] The classification emerges from the following sources: RE Tindall *Multinational Enterprises* (Dobbs Ferry: Oceana, 1975) ch 4; CM Schmitthoff 'The Multinational Enterprise in the United Kingdom' in HR Hahlo, J Graham Smith and RW Wright *Nationalism and the Multinational Enterprise* (Sijthoff/Oceana, 1977) 22–38 and Appendices at 343–65 and Leo D'Arcy, Carole Murray, and Barbara Cleave *Schmitthoff's Export Trade* (London: Sweet & Maxwell,10th edn, 2000) Part 8; CD Wallace *Legal Control of the Multinational Enterprise* (Martinus Nijhoff, 1983) 13–16; RI Tricker above n 10 at 149–50.   [38] See n 8 above.

come within the OECD definition of a MNE. Thus it is appropriate to consider such 'controlled' contractual relations as a legal form of multinational enterprise. Such enterprises may lie beyond the normal distinction between corporation and contract, forming a distinct type of business association that applies both corporate and contractual methods of organization. Günter Teubner has described such associations as 'network organisations'.[39] Contractual linkages can be divided between those aimed at distribution and those aimed at production.

(i) Distribution Agreements

The simplest form of such relations arises where a producer in the home state enters into a distribution agreement with a distributor in the host state.[40] In return for sole or exclusive selling rights in the host state and, possibly, other territories, the distributor will be obliged to purchase the producer's products and to use its best efforts to sell them. This may involve the transfer of intellectual property rights, such as trade marks and know-how, so that the seller can maintain the identity and quality of the product. This offers a useful route into a foreign market for the producer without the need for the expenditure associated with the establishment of a sales subsidiary.

A similar effect may be achieved through the establishment of a distribution franchise. This differs from a simple distribution agreement in that the producer in the home state (the franchisor) transfers to the local distributor (the franchisee) a complete business format, including relevant intellectual property rights and know-how, in return for the capital contribution needed to establish the outlet from the franchisee. The degree of control exercised by the franchisor over the franchisee is considerably greater than that which normally occurs in an ordinary distribution agreement, where the distributor is usually free to sell goods as it sees fit after purchase of stocks from the producer. This is because, under a franchise, the franchisor seeks to expand its products and brand image abroad in a uniform business format, which helps to develop its presence as an international business.[41] This method of internationalization has been used, in particular, by retail chains offering specialized goods, such as, for example, computer hardware and software, cosmetics or wedding attire, for which there is a uniform international demand but where the manufacturer or retailer (which may be the same entity) lacks, or does not wish to commit, the capital to set up subsidiaries or branches in every foreign sales location.

---

[39] See Günter Teubner 'The Many-Headed Hydra: Networks as Higher-Order Collective Actors' in J McCahery, S Picciotto, and C Scott (eds) *Corporate Control and Accountability* (Oxford: Clarendon Press, 1993) 41. See further G Teubner 'Unitas Multiplex: Corporate Governance in Group Enterprises' in D Sugarman and G Teubner (eds) *Regulating Corporate Groups in Europe* (Baden-Baden: Nomos, 1990) 67–104; G Teubner 'Beyond Contract and Organisation? The External Liability of Franchising Systems in German Law' in C Joerges (ed) *Franchising and the Law: Theoretical and Comparative Approaches in Europe and the United States* (Baden-Baden: Nomos, 1992) 105.   [40] See further *Schmitthoff's Export Trade* above n 37 at 647–54.

[41] See further JN Adams and KV Prichard Jones *Franchising: Practice and Precedents in Business Format Franchising* (Haywards Heath: Tottel Publishing 5th edn, 2004).

(ii) Production Agreements

Should overseas demand for a product manufactured in the home state be such as to make overseas production desirable, a number of contractual options present themselves. First, the producer (the licensor) may license a local manufacturer (the licensee) to produce the product in the host state. This will involve the transfer of patented technology and know-how to the local manufacturer, who will be bound to use the technology in a manner that protects the licensor's competitive advantage in the technology. The licence may form part of a wider production franchise package where, in return for the capital contribution of the local producer, the patented technology is accompanied by a business format and by close franchisor control over the acts of the franchisee.

Such arrangements may raise questions as to whether any anti-competitive effects are created by restrictive clauses in the licensing agreement or franchise. In developing states a further question arises regarding the benefits of the technology transfer to the local economy. These matters will be considered in chapter 11. It should be noted that licensing is an option open only where a suitable local producer can be found, and where the risk of damaging interference by third parties in the patented technology and secret know-how is small. If these difficulties exist, the producer in the home state may have little alternative but to set up a manufacturing subsidiary in the host state.

The most advanced contractual form of MNE is the international consortium. This is defined as 'an organisation which is created when two or more companies co-operate so as to act as a single entity for a specific and limited purpose'.[42] At their most complex international consortia can act as integrated international production enterprises, hardly distinguishable in economic terms from equity based international groups. Indeed the legal form may take that of an incorporated joint venture company or partnership. Such forms are most often used for specific, large-scale construction or engineering projects that require the skills and resources of companies from more than one state for their successful realization. Examples include the discovery, in 1970, of the North Sea oil fields by a multinational consortium of four companies led by Phillips Petroleum, the joint development and production of Concorde by Sud Aviation of France and the British Aircraft Company of the UK[43] and, in its original form as a French Groupement d'Intérêt Economique (GIE), Airbus Industrie.[44]

---

[42] See *Schmitthoff's Export Trade* (London: Sweet and Maxwell, 9th edn, 1990) at 343.

[43] Examples taken from Tindall above n 37 at 75.

[44] Airbus Industrie was originally composed of four original participating companies from Germany (Deutsche Airbus, 37.9 per cent), France (Aerospatiale, 37.9 per cent), the UK (British Aerospace, now BAE Systems, 20 per cent), and Spain (CASA, 4.2 per cent). Each participant manufactures parts of the aircraft in its home country. Those parts are then transported by Airbus's own aircraft to the production lines at Toulouse and Hamburg for final assembly. The legal form of the consortium was that of a French Groupement d'Intérêt Economique (GIE), which offered the advantages of joint partnership and legal personality, but without the regulatory or fiscal burdens of full incorporation. Given that Airbus developed into a large-scale multinational manufacturing enterprise, it

(iii) Public Private Partnerships

More recently complex construction contracts involving MNEs have been drawn up using public private partnership (PPP) structures. Typically, such contracts will be on a BOO (Build Own Operate), BOT (Build Own Transfer), or BOOT (Build Own Operate and Transfer) basis, giving a concession to the foreign private contractors for a specified period of years whereupon ownership vests in the public or private sector of the host country.[45] The private parties will secure finance and bring in the relevant technology and know-how, while local partners will usually supply the workforce and supporting infrastructure needed by the project. Finance is provided by way of 'project finance'. This may be by way of 'non-recourse' finance, where the lender looks only to the project's assets and revenue stream for repayment or by 'limited recourse' finance which allows the lender to look to the totality of the project sponsors' assets for repayment.[46] The main benefit of a PPP approach is that the state retains strategic control over the project, obtains the assets at the end of the contract period while at the same time attracting new capital and accelerating the process of construction. Such an approach has been widely used in public utility infrastructure projects in developing countries, utilizing global project finance available through the World Bank and other inter-governmental bodies.[47] As will be seen in chapter 14, such arrangements have been criticized for their potential to interfere with the human and environmental rights of local communities. PPPs have been seen as potentially anti-democratic arrangements as the public nature of the project function is not accompanied by the same degree of public accountability as would surround a

---

was felt that its original legal form would no longer be adequate to deal with the resulting problems of accountability (in that the GIE did not have to produce financial results) and unlimited liability that were a consequence of using the French GIE form. In particular the US had been pressing Airbus for greater openness about government subsidies. In addition, management at Airbus wanted more freedom to outsource production beyond the parent companies. Airbus became a French public limited company on 1 January 2001. The parents were reduced to two: BAE Systems (20 per cent interest) and the European Aeronautic, Defence and Space Company (EADS, 80 per cent interest) as a result of, first, the takeover by Deutsche Aerospace, the parent of Deutsche Airbus, of CASA followed by the merger of Deutsche Aerospace and Aerospatiale. See 'A Short History of Airbus' at <http://www.airbus.com/en/corporate/people/Airbus_short_history.html> and see further I McIntyre *Dogfight: the Transatlantic Battle over Airbus* (Praeger, 1992) ch 5. BAE Systems has decided to sell its stake 'BAE Endorses Sale Price of its Airbus Stake' *Financial Times* 7 September 2006 at 19. 'BAE Agrees Sale of Stake in Ailing Airbus' *The Guardian* 7 September 2006 at 25.

[45] *Schmitthoff's Export Trade* above n 37 at 512.

[46] See UNIDO *BOT Guidelines* (Vienna: United Nations, 1996) 4–5 and ch 9; David A Levy 'BOT and Public Procurement: A Conceptual Framework' 7 Ind.Int'l & Comp.L.Rev. 95 (1996); William M Stelwagon 'Financing Private Energy Projects in the Third World' 37 Catholic Law 45 (1996); Nagla Nassar 'Project Finance, Public Utilities and Public Concerns: A Practitioner's Perspective' 23 Fordham Int'l L.J. 60 (2000).

[47] See further ch 14 at 551–52, 561–62 Michael Likosky (ed) *Privatising Development: Transnational Law Infrastructure and Human Rights* (Leiden: Martinus Nijhoff Publishers, 2005); Michael Warner and Rory Sullivan *Putting Partnerships to Work* (Sheffield: Greenleaf Publishing, 2004); Oxfam *Exploring the Links between International Business and Poverty Reduction: A Case Study of Unilever in Indonesia* (Oxford: Oxfam, December 2005) at <http://publications.oxfam.org.uk/oxfam/display.asp?ISBN=0855985666>.

purely publicly run project. However, there is evidence that such arrangements can work and are on the whole consistent with fundamental rights observance.[48] In particular, specialized community participation and monitoring mechanisms can be put into place including the involvement of civil society groups and other relevant non-governmental organizations (NGOs) as participants in the PPP.[49]

(b) Equity Based Corporate Groups

The most commonly held image of a MNE is that of a closely controlled group of companies linked by shares held by the parent company and its intermediate holding companies. While this is an acceptable starting point, it fails to describe the considerable variations of structure that can be developed through the use of the parent/subsidiary relationship. In particular, there exist noticeable differences between groups from different countries and regions. The group structure adopted is a product of the business and legal environment from which the firm has grown. It is therefore legitimate to classify group structures along national or regional lines. This approach will be adopted below, where some of the most common and distinctive structures will be described. However, the resulting classification should not be treated as immutable. As noted in section (1) of this chapter, the process of group organization is a dynamic one and, as firms become more global in their operations and business culture, new group forms will develop. These will result in changes in group legal structures. Therefore, this section will end with some thoughts on the likely legal consequences of such changes.

(i) The Anglo-American 'Pyramid' Group

This type of structure consists of a parent company which owns and controls a network of wholly or majority-owned subsidiaries, which may themselves be intermediate holding companies for sub-groups of closely held subsidiaries. The resulting structure is that of a 'pyramid' with the parent company at its apex. As noted above, when the 'pyramid' crosses borders, this represents the 'classic' conception of the MNE which underlies much of the thinking on MNE regulation.

Although the 'pyramid' structure of ownership and control is widely used throughout the major capital-exporting states other than Japan (which will be considered below), it is especially typical of US and UK held MNEs of the mid-20th century.[50] For example the US auto manufacturer, Ford, has traditionally

---

[48] See further the essays in Warner and Sullivan above n 47. There remains the risk that PPPs will be attacked because they are perceived as an example of foreign greed and indifference to the local community: see Monte Reel 'Turning the Taps Back to the States: Privatization of Utilities Fall Out of Favour in Latin America' *Washington Post Foreign Service* 27 March 2006 A10 available at <http://www.washingtonpost.com>.   [49] For discussion see ch 14.
[50] On the other hand, according to Tom Hadden, in Canada and Australia 'it is more common for major groups to be structured in a more complex manner, with interlocking webs of majority and minority holdings which make it more difficult to assess accurately the profitability and solvency

operated through 100 per cent owned overseas subsidiaries. In Europe, Ford of Europe replicated this structure across the continent after having combined its then separate UK and German companies in 1967.[51] Where necessary, Ford will hold less than 100 per cent. For example, at 31 December 2005, its ownership interest in Mazda was 33.9 per cent.[52] Similarly, IBM was organized as a closely held US group coordinating its global activities through IBM World Trade Corporation, which acted as the holding company for IBM's wholly owned regional holding companies, which in turn acted as holding companies for regional and national sub-groups of wholly owned subsidiaries.[53] Such structures were typical not only for manufacturing but also natural resources companies.[54]

In common with US MNEs, British MNEs tended to organize along extended lines of closely held parent/subsidiary relationships. In a study of the legal and business organization of three British corporate groups up to 1979, namely, Bowater, Reckitt and Colman, and the Rank Organization,[55] Tom Hadden observed the large size and complexity of the groups. At that time, Bowater had some 420 companies of which almost 200 were registered in the UK alone, some held at three levels of remove from the ultimate parent;[56] the Rank group contained some 220 companies excluding those jointly held by Rank-Xerox;[57] while

either of the group as a whole or of its constituent companies or to identify those who are formally responsible for their operations': 'The Regulation of Corporate Groups in Australia' in 15 UNSWLJ 61 at 64 (1992). On Canada, see T Hadden, R Forbes, and R Simmonds *Canadian Business Organisations Law* (Toronto: Butterworths, 1986) ch 9.

[51] See Ford Motor Company *The Making of Ford in Europe* (Public Affairs Doc No 2.5/589).

[52] Ford Motor Company Inc *Annual Report 2005* 71 at <http://www.ford.com/en/company/ investorInformation/companyReports/annualReports/2005annualReport/2005_pdfs.htm>.

[53] See HG Angello 'Multinational Corporate Groups' 125 Hague Receuil (1968 III) 447 at 503–504; T Hadden *The Control of Corporate Groups* (London: IALS, 1983) 73–76. However, as noted above, more decentralization of managerial functions has taken place and is likely to continue in the future.

[54] See, for example, the corporate organization of Cape Asbestos plc in its South African operations up to 1979, discussed in ch 4 at 148 and ch 8 at 323. See further Geoffrey Jones above n 26 at 82–91.

[55] Hadden ibid. The fourth company studied was IBM (UK) Ltd. A more recent example is the Irish group Guinness plc. It operated through two core companies, United Distillers, the group's spirits company, and Guinness Brewing Worldwide, which brewed Guinness stout throughout the world. It also owned Cruzcampo, making Guinness Spain's largest brewer: see *Guinness plc Fact File* (1992). In 1997 Guinness and Grand Metropolitan merged to form Diageo, the world's leading drinks group. Diageo is organized around area and functional subsidiaries: see *Annual Report 2005* 148 at <http://www.diageo.com/NR/rdonlyres/56E989BF-A832–4338-9C00–3B74C15CEAAD/0/ Annualreport2005.pdf>.

[56] This group has undergone considerable changes since the time of the Hadden study. In 1984 Bowater plc demerged and the paper and pulp business, its founding function, was taken over by a newly founded US company Bowater Inc. See Bowater Inc 'History at a Glance' <http://www. bowater.com/en/history.shtml>. On 1 June 1995 Bowater plc changed its name to Rexam plc and made consumer packaging its core business. Since 1995 it has divested itself of over 100 businesses and has made acquisitions only in this core field; see 'History' at <http://www.rexam.com/index.asp?pageid= 30&animation=off&year=2003&company=Rexam#2003Rexam> and Rexam plc *Corporate Profile* (July 2006) at <http://www.rexam.com/files/pdf/corporate_profile.pdf>.

[57] For a recent list of principal subsidiary and associated undertakings of the Rank Group plc, see *Annual Report and Accounts 2005* at 90 at <http://www.rank.com/rnk/investor/fininfo/reports/2006/>.

Reckitt and Colman contained some 170 companies.[58] The major reason given for this proliferation was the expansion of these companies by way of acquisition. It led to different patterns of overseas sub-groups. Some were organized around an intermediate holding company in a particular country, such as, for example, Reckitt and Colman Australia or Bowaters of Canada, while other groups were operated through subsidiaries of the principal British operating company for the given line of business. By contrast the fourth company in the study, IBM (UK), had a simple corporate structure involving a single UK holding company and four operating subsidiaries.[59] Furthermore, Hadden found that some firms were using 'agent only' companies as a means of reducing the administrative burdens of full disclosure. These duties were avoided by the transfer of a subsidiary's assets to its holding company, leaving the subsidiary to trade as the agent of the holding company, obliged only to produce a formal balance sheet in which its capital would be typically offset by a loan to the holding company.[60] None of these groups has remained unchanged with major restructuring taking place in all but the Rank Group, reflecting the relative incompatibility between large conglomerate group structures and the need for flexible and focused organization in an increasingly integrated global economy.[61]

(ii) European Transnational Mergers

A number of large MNEs have been created through what Channon and Jalland call 'transnational merger'.[62] These structures represent a border between corporate groups headed by one parent and joint ventures between independent companies. In some cases such entities started as joint ventures and then developed an integrated international structure. In other cases the legal characteristics of the joint venture form have remained. Transnational mergers have occurred in both the private and public sectors of industry. This type of MNE is especially common in Europe, where the integration of national companies across borders into larger enterprises, offering new economies of scale and scope, is a well established phenomenon.

According to Schmitthoff four factors influence the choice of legal and managerial structure in the transnational merger.[63] First, the national stock exchange

---

[58]   Hadden above n 53 at 9 and Appendices.

[59]   ibid 11. Reckitt and Colman merged in 1999 with Benckiser NV to create Reckitt Benckiser plc: see 'Our History' at <http://www.reckittbenckiser.com/about/history.cfm>. The principal subsidiaries are listed in the *Annual Report 2004* at 49: <http://www.reckittbenckiser.com/documentlib/normal/annualreport2004.pdf>.

[60]   ibid at 13. See further O Osunbor 'The Agent-Only Subsidiary Company and the Control of Multinational Groups' 38 ICLQ 377 (1989); Tricker above n 10 at 66–67.

[61]   See details in preceding notes.

[62]   Above n 12 at 45. Although the emphasis is on European transnational mergers such mergers of course also occur outside Europe. See, for example, the 1998 merger of the German and US car makers Daimler-Benz and Chrysler which resulted in a single parent company DaimlerChrysler AG located in Stuttgart Germany: see *Annual Management Report 2005* at <http://www.daimlerchrysler.com/Projects/c2c/channel/documents/829818_DC_GB05_E_Kapitel_03_management_report.pdf>.

[63]   See Schmitthoff in Hahlo, Smith, and Wright above n 37 at 32–33.

quotation of each participating company must not be affected. The usual solution is the creation of a twin holding company located in each home state, based on joint shareholding by the founding parent companies, and the transfer of operating activities to subsidiaries that may be jointly or separately owned and controlled by the holding companies. An example is the Anglo-Dutch oil company Royal Dutch Shell. Until its unification on 20 July 2005, this firm consisted of a Dutch parent (Royal Dutch Petroleum Co) and a British parent (Shell Transport and Trading Co) who owned and controlled Dutch and British holding companies in a ratio of 60/40 per cent with Royal Dutch holding the majority share. The national holding companies shared a unified management board. Each national holding company in turn owned and controlled its nationally based operating subsidiaries as separate sub-groups. After unification, a new single parent company was established, Royal Dutch Shell plc.[64] It is headquartered in The Hague but incorporated in the UK and listed on the London Stock Exchange. The share exchange transaction has preserved the 60/40 split between Dutch and UK shareholders.[65] However, there is now a unified board of management under one chief executive, following the Anglo-American model of corporate governance. In addition, an internal restructuring of the group subsidiaries has taken place. Royal Dutch was merged into a subsidiary Shell Petroleum NV and the remaining minority shareholders of Royal Dutch would be bought out. Furthermore, the 60/40 cross-shareholdings of the two joint holding companies would be unwound.[66] The restructuring was seen to be necessary in the wake of the reserves over-valuation crisis in 2004, which was blamed in part on the unwieldiness of the firm's internal organization, and as a result of Shell's failure to take advantage of the merger wave in the industry which led to the unification of Exxon and Mobil and BP with Amoco.[67]

A dual holding company approach was taken by Agfa Gevaert when this company was formed by Agfa, the German parent, and Gevaert, the Belgian parent, in

[64] For details of the unification scheme, see Royal Dutch Petroleum Co and Shell Transport and Trading Co 'Announcement of Final Proposals for the Recommended Unification of Royal Dutch and Shell Transport' (19 May 2005) at <http://www.unification.shell.com/shell_proposal/general/launch/announcement/2005-05-19_full.pdf>.

[65] Royal Dutch Shell plc has two classes of shares, 'A' and 'B' shares. 'A' shares and 'B' shares have identical rights except in relation to the source of dividend income where 'A' shares have a Dutch source and 'B' shares are intended to have a UK source. 'A' and 'B' shares trade on both the London Stock Exchange and Euronext Amsterdam and in the form of ADRs on the New York Stock Exchange: <http://www.unification.shell.com/>. Considerable unhappiness was generated among the UK shareholders who were exposed to capital gains tax on the transfer scheme 'Royal Dutch Shareholders Face a Capital Gains Tax Penalty When Group Converts' *Financial Times* 2/3 July 2005 Money and Business M3. HM Revenue & Customs advised in October 2005 that when making a capital tax calculation it valued the shares disposed of on 20 July 2005 as £35.325 per share. Similarly, the value of the Royal Dutch Shell plc 'A' shares acquired by such Royal Dutch shareholders on 20 July 2005 would be taken as £17.6625 per share acquired: <http://www.unification.shell.com/shell_proposal/entry/announcements/2005-10-18/>.

[66] See Royal Dutch Shell Announcement of 20 September 2005 available at <http://www.unification.shell.com/shell_proposal/entry/announcements/2005-09-20/>.

[67] 'Marriage After a Century of Cohabitation: Shell Prepares for the Next Merger Round' *Financial Times* 28 June 2005 at 21.

1964. Each parent owned 50 per cent of the shares in the two national holding companies. In 1981 the group was 100 per cent owned by Bayer AG of Germany, which divested itself of its remaining shares in 2002. Agfa-Gevaert is now listed on the Brussels and Frankfurt stock exchanges and is run as a unified MNE organized around two main business groups.[68] The twin holding company approach has also been adopted by Eurotunnel, which consists of jointly held French and English holding companies, Eurotunnel SA and Eurotunnel plc, each of which owns respectively the French and English concessionary companies France Manche SA and the Channel Tunnel Group Ltd.[69] This is an example of the twin holding company approach being used to establish a new transnational enterprise as opposed to the case of a merger between two existing enterprises.

Secondly, the aim of the merger is usually the achievement of greater economies of scale and scope than the founding companies could achieve by themselves. This will lead to an international divisionalization of the firm and to the creation of new transnational management structures, such as, for example, a joint management committee composed of senior managers from each of the founding firms. This approach was taken by Unilever in the 1920s when the UK consumer products company, Lever Brothers, joined with the Dutch margarine producer, Margarine Uni, to create one of the first transnational mergers.[70] The current approach is to have identity of board members for both Unilever plc, the UK parent, and Unilever NV, the Dutch parent. This identical composition of the board is achieved through a nomination procedure operated by the boards of NV and plc, acting upon the recommendation of the Nomination Committee or by shareholders in subsidiaries.[71] On the other hand, the merger in 1999 of Reckitt-Benckiser, the Anglo-Dutch food and domestic products group, was based on a single holding company from the outset. This prompted the mooting of company unification at rival Unilever, although it has not yet occurred.[72]

Thirdly, the dividend rights of shareholders must be protected. This may lead to a share equalization agreement, whereby the founding firms agree to equalize any differences in dividends payable to shareholders in each home state. Such an

---

[68] See Agfa-Gevaert *Annual Report 2005* at 4 and see 101–103 for full list of subsidiaries <http://www.agfa.com/en/binaries/agfa_annualreport_2005_en_tcm133-24874.pdf>.

[69] See Eurotunnel *Shareholder Guide* at <http://www.eurotunnel.com/NR/rdonlyres/9F744 D1C-9273-4A6A-8842-5DEF9F0EE8BC/0/UK_Guide_actionnaire_VERSION_0305051.pdf>.

[70] Schmitthoff in Hahlo, Smith, and Wright (eds) above n 37 at 34. For a full organizational history of Unilever, see Geoffrey Jones *Renewing Unilever: Transformation and Tradition* (Oxford: Oxford University Press, 2005).

[71] See Unilever *The Governance of Unilever* approved 4 May 2005 (amended 13 September 2005, 2 November 2005, 8 February 2006, and 2 August 2006) at <http://www.unilever.com/Images/ The%20Governance%20of%20Unilever_tcm13-14045.pdf> para 1.3 and see too Unilever articles of association 2006 art 19.5 at <http://www.unilever.com/Images/Articles%20of%20Association %20Unilever%20N%20V%20%202006%20-%20English_tcm13-11949.pdf>.

[72] 'Unilever House Gets Modern Facelift, Old Corporate Structure May Be Next' *Financial Times* 5/6 February 2005 Money and Business M3; 'Unilever to Keep Dual Structure' *Financial Times* 20 December 2005 at 19.

agreement was pioneered by Unilever. This is a unique arrangement that other firms have not chosen to adopt.[73] For example, the Anglo-Dutch publishing group, Reed Elsevier, whose merger took effect on 1 January 1993, chose a 50-50 joint ownership structure, without any premium or cash payment to either set of shareholders and with the retention of separate stock market listings. The operating subsidiaries were grouped under a UK holding company, while finance subsidiaries are grouped under Elsevier Reed Finance, a Dutch company.[74] However, this structure led to considerable in-fighting between the UK and Dutch interests. This was resolved not by the legal unification of the company but through a merger of the two boards and the creation of a single headquarters in London.[75]

Finally, the merger must take account of its fiscal consequences. Indeed, the structure adopted by Reed Elsevier was prompted in large measure by such considerations. It offers tax saving effects as the Dutch holding company is in a better position to benefit from tax havens, in that it is entitled to earn tax-free interest on such deposits.[76] The fiscal barriers to transnational mergers may have distorting

[73] According to para 3 of the Unilever Equalization Agreement: 'If the current profits of one Company shall be insufficient to provide in full the dividends (and arrears if any) on its Preference Shares in respect of any financial period or if there be no current profits the other Company shall to the extent of its own current profits for the same financial period after providing for the dividends (and arrears if any) on its own Preference Shares be under obligation to make good any loss incurred by the former Company during that period together with any amount by which the deficiency (if any) on profit and loss account at the commencement of the period exceeds the open reserves at that date and to make up the current profits of that Company to the amount of the dividends (and arrears if any) on that Company's Preference Shares to the close of such financial period. If after such contribution has been received by the former Company the current profits (including the amount so received) of the former Company are still insufficient for the purpose the deficiency shall in so far as the free reserves of that Company have been utilised but are not sufficient for the purpose be met by a further contribution from the other Company to the extent of its free reserves. Any contribution so made shall in so far as not utilised for making good any such loss and/or deficiency on Profit and Loss Account as aforesaid be distributed by the Company to whom such payment is made but if not so distributed shall be repaid forthwith to the Company by whom the contribution was made': consolidated text of an agreement dated 28 June 1946 between UNILEVER NV (hereinafter called 'the Dutch Company') and UNILEVER plc (hereinafter called 'the English Company') as amended by Supplemental Agreement dated 20 July 1951, Second Supplemental Agreement dated 21 December 1981 and Third Supplemental Agreement dated 15 May 2006 available at <http://www.unilever.com/Images/Equalisation%20Agreement%20-%20FINAL%20May%2006_tcm13-44490.pdf>.

[74] See Reed Elsevier website at <http://www.reed-elsevier.com/index.cfm?articleid=1186> and 'Overlapping Umbrellas' *Financial Times* 18 February 1993 at 34.

[75] 'Unilever Turns to Reed for Structural Advice' *Financial Times* 5/6 February 2005 Money and Business M1 and 'From Rivalry to Mergers: A Brief History of the Anglo-Dutch Business Model' *The Economist* 12 February 2005 at 64–65. According to Reed Elsevier: 'The boards of Reed Elsevier PLC, Reed Elsevier NV and Reed Elsevier Group plc are harmonised. Subject to approval by the respective shareholders, all the directors of Reed Elsevier Group plc are also directors of Reed Elsevier PLC and of Reed Elsevier NV. No individual may be appointed to the boards of Reed Elsevier PLC, Reed Elsevier NV or Reed Elsevier Group plc unless recommended by the joint Nominations Committee, although members of the Committee abstain when their own re-appointment is being considered. The Reed Elsevier PLC and Reed Elsevier NV shareholders maintain their rights to appoint individuals to their respective boards, in accordance with the provisions of the Articles of Association of those companies' at <http://www.reed-elsevier.com/index.cfm?articleid=1157>.

[76] 'Overlapping Umbrellas' *Financial Times* 18 February 1993 at 34.

effects on international competition, preventing the development of efficient transnational groups. Within the EC, this has been identified as a possible source of competitive disadvantage as between companies based in one Member State, and companies from more than one Member State, that wish to merge. To remedy the situation the EC Council has adopted a Directive on a common system of taxation applicable to mergers, divisions, transfers of assets, and exchanges of shares concerning companies of different Member States.[77]

Despite the above mentioned successes in transnational mergers, such entities are subject to intense centrifugal forces that may lead to their breakdown.[78] In particular, if the merger does not develop a suitable internal control and coordination system it is likely to fail. The differing corporate cultures and national backgrounds of the participating firms may prevent such an organizational development from taking place. Equally, if one of the firms involved is economically weaker, it may disappear into the stronger firm. This may not be acceptable to the home state of the weaker partner, which may act to prevent the merger from taking place. The difficulties involved were graphically illustrated by the failure of the proposed merger in 1992 between British Airways and KLM Royal Dutch Airlines. Considerable fears were expressed at the time that BA would overwhelm the smaller Dutch airline.[79] The merger negotiations came to a standstill over the profit shares that each airline would take from the merged company. KLM had insisted on a 40 per cent stake which proved unacceptable to the larger British airline.[80] KLM eventually merged with Air France on 5 May 2004. It is organized around a single holding company which owns each national carrier as a wholly owned subsidiary.[81]

The European transnational merger organized around a joint holding company, or companies, may be an increasingly outmoded form of legal structure for MNEs operating within Europe. The legal and market environments have become more uniform in part due to the effect of increased harmonization through EC law and in part due to the integrating effects of MNE activity itself. In addition, the more integrated character of international equity markets, offering the capacity to float a new company globally, makes access to international sources of finance less of a problem. On the other hand taxation remains a decentralized national function and such considerations may still play an important role, as the

---

[77] Council Directive 90/434/EEC of 23 July 1990 OJ [1990] L225/1 as amended by Council Directive 2005/19/EC of 17 February 2005 consolidated text at <http://eur-lex.europa.eu/LexUriServ/site/en/consleg/1990/L/01990L0434-20050324-en.pdf>.

[78] See Bayer 'Horizontal Groups and Joint Ventures in Europe: Concepts and Reality' in K Hopt (ed) *Legal and Economic Analysis on Multinational Enterprises Vol.II: Groups of Companies in European Laws* (Berlin and New York: Walter de Gruyter, 1982) ch 1. A classic example of the breakdown of a transnational merger is the defunct Dunlop-Pirelli union, described by Bayer at 12.

[79] 'BA Looks at Going Dutch with KLM' *Financial Times* 20 November 1991 at 25.

[80] 'The Airline Deal That Did Not Fly' *Financial Times* 28 February 1992 at 17.

[81] See <http://www.airfranceklm-finance.com/air-france-klm-group.html>. The French Government has also reduced its shareholding in Air France as part of the merger process: 'Paris to Halve Air France Stake' *Financial Times* 4 May 2004 at 28.

Reed Elsevier case shows. Equally, tax considerations remain a major reason behind Unilever's reluctance to give up its dual structure.[82] However, given the experience of Royal Dutch Shell, it would appear that the joint holding company concept may be a phase in the process of full legal and managerial integration. These firms were pioneers of the transnational merger structure and it would appear that organizational inertia has played a part in maintaining the old structures for such a long time after many of the regulatory grounds for their adoption had disappeared. It is significant that the more recent trans-European mergers of Reckitt-Benckiser and Air France KLM have adopted a single holding company structure from the start. On the other hand the joint holding company structure may still be of value in cases such as Eurotunnel, where the separate nationalities of the participating companies need to be maintained for policy reasons.

(iii) The Japanese 'Keiretsu'

The legal character of Japanese corporate groups has been strongly influenced by the requirements of the Law on Prohibition of Private Monopoly and Ensuring of Fair Trade (Anti-Monopoly Law) of 1947.[83] This law was introduced by the allied occupying powers through the Supreme Commander for Allied Powers (SCAP), as part of a wider programme for the decentralization of economic power in Japan.[84] Prior to the Second World War, the Japanese economy was dominated by major business groups, the *zaibatsu*, headed by a family holding company, each with its own bank and international trading house.[85] These groups were dissolved by law in 1945 and 1946.[86]

The Anti-Monopoly Law sought to prevent the re-emergence of *zaibatsu* by the prohibition, in Article 9, on the creation of a holding company, which was defined as a company whose primary business is to control the business activities of another company by holding its shares. This did not prohibit the holding of shares by one company in another provided that the parent company was also engaged in some form of business activity.[87] Furthermore, large joint stock companies engaged in business other than financial services whose assets exceeded 30 billion yen or which had a capital of more than 10 billion yen were prohibited from acquiring or holding shares in other companies beyond set limits. Companies engaged in financial services were prohibited from owning more than 5 per cent

---

[82] 'Unilever to Keep Dual Structure' *Financial Times* 20 December 2005 at 19.

[83] Law No 54, 1947 available at <http://www.jftc.go.jp/e-page/legislation/ama/amended_ama.pdf>.

[84] See T Blakemore and M Yazawa 'Japanese Commercial Code Revisions Concerning Corporations' 2 Am.Jo.Comp.L. 12 (1953).

[85] The major *zaibatsu* were Mitsubishi, Mitsui, Sumitomo, and Yasuda.

[86] Imperial Ordinances No 65 of 1945 and No 23 of 1946.

[87] See M Matsushita *International Trade and Competition Law in Japan* (Oxford: Oxford University Press, 1993) 124–26; Executive Office, Fair Trade Commission of Japan *The Anti-monopoly Act Guidelines Concerning Distribution Systems and Business Practices* 11 July 1991, ch 7 available at <http://www.jftc.go.jp/e-page/legislation/ama/distribution.pdf>.

(10 per cent in the case of insurance companies) of the outstanding stocks of other companies.[88]

As a result of these provisions Japanese groups have evolved unique structures which seek to avoid the prohibitions in the Anti-Monopoly Act. These groups, or *keiretsu*, are characterized by small, intra-group cross-shareholdings coupled with strong coordinated management organized around inter-company management conferences. Thus control over satellite companies of the *keiretsu* is not exercised by means of formal voting powers, but by means of managerial coordination. The *keiretsu* may be divided into two principal types.[89] The first consists of the post-war descendants of the *zaibatsu* (Mitsubishi, Mitsui, and Sumitomo) and the three original post-war *keiretsu* centred on banks (Fuji Bank, Sanwa Bank, and the Daiichi Kangyo Bank). These have been reduced in number with the merger of Sumitomo Bank and Sakura Bank combining the Sumitomo and Mitsui *keiretsu* and the merger of Daiichi Kangyo Bank with Fuji Bank and the Industrial Bank of Japan to form Mizuho, the world's largest bank.[90] The second type consists of the industrial *keiretsu* and contains at least 100 groups, including major groups such as Toyota.[91] These have a structure more akin to a 'pyramid' group, with a controlling holding company and subordinate subsidiaries. In order to comply with the 1947 Act, the principal holding company should carry on its own business and restrict its holdings in subsidiaries and associated companies to a maximum of 50 per cent of its assets and had to restrict its dividend income to a similar extent. Thus, controlling holdings were possible, although 100 per cent ownership was unusual. This allowed for substantial external shareholdings in group companies.[92]

As a result of the flexibility offered by the *keiretsu* system for the creation of joint ventures, Japanese companies have been more ready to use such an approach to overseas establishment. When investing abroad, a number of firms from the group may join together into a joint venture, which may also include partners from the host state. This approach was widely used by the textile and steel industries when setting up production facilities abroad. By contrast, the electrical and electronics industries developed their own sales and service subsidiaries followed by manufacturing subsidiaries in which the Japanese parent retained a higher share of ownership, with local joint venture partners restricted to distribution or agency functions. This approach was required to retain control over the parent company's technology and to protect the brand name.[93]

---

[88] Article 11 Anti-Monopoly Law above n 83.

[89] See T Hadden 'Regulating Corporate Groups: An International Perspective' in McCahery et al (eds) above n 39 at 343 at 352–54. See further M Hayakawa 'Zum Gegenwartigen Stand des Konzernrechts in Japan' in EJ Mestmacher and P Behrens (eds) *Das Gesellschaftsrecht der Konzerne im Internationalen Vergleich* (Baden-Baden: Nomos, 1991); R Clark *The Japanese Company* (New Haven, Conn: Yale University Press, 1979) 73–87; K Miyashita and D Russell *Keiretsu: Inside the Hidden Japanese Conglomerates* (McGraw Hill, 1994).

[90] 'Undone. Whither Japan's Corporate Groups?' *The Economist* 22 March 2003 at 72.

[91] See Hadden above n 89 at 354.   [92] ibid at 353.

[93] See Y Yoshino 'The Multinational Spread of Japanese Manufacturing Investment since World War II' 48 Bus.Hist.Rev. 357 (1974).

In 2002, Article 9 was amended. Its contemporary purpose is to control the excessive concentration of market power through the holding of stock, rather than imposing a general ban on holding companies. The Act will control only those cases in which the statutory asset thresholds have been exceeded by the group. Thus smaller concentrations of this kind are not regulated.[94] A number of cases are now completely excluded: where a company establishes subsidiaries solely through the process of splitting off its operational divisions, venture capital companies meeting the asset thresholds listed by the Fair Trade Commission in its Guidelines, the entry of financial companies into another business sphere through the establishment of a new company, and where the total assets of the company and its subsidiaries are 600 billion yen or less on a consolidated basis.[95] This change was originally introduced in 1997 as part of Japan's policy to free up the financial services sector.[96] This approach shows that concern for smaller group concentrations has receded over the years. Indeed there are also signs that the *keiretsu* structure is itself slowly changing, with a marked decline in the overall number of long-term cross-shareholdings between firms, so as to encourage greater competitiveness among firms and to allow for the growth of a market for corporate control.[97]

(iv) Changes in Business Organization and Effects on Equity Based Structures

The above mentioned equity structures have developed around groups that were initially national firms but which expanded abroad either through internal expansion, foreign acquisition, or transnational merger. As such they represent the legal forms of developing MNEs, in which centralized managerial control may be facilitated by the concentration of voting rights at the level of the parent through closely held subsidiaries. However, once firms have become established as integrated

---

[94] See Article 9(5) of the Anti-Monopoly Act and the illustrative cases in the Fair Trade Commission of Japan (FTC) *Guidelines Concerning Companies which Constitute an Excessive Concentration of Economic Power* (12 November 2002) at <http://www.jftc.go.jp/e-page/legislation/ama/Company_Concentration.pdf>. Only groups whose assets exceed 15 trillion yen possessing large scale enterprises of over 300 billion yen in five or more principal fields of business need to notify their concentration to the FTC. Additional rules apply to financial companies and companies in interrelated fields: paras 2(1)–(4).   [95] ibid para.2(5).

[96] See 'Japan to Lift Ban on Holding Companies' *Financial Times* 26 February 1997 at 4. The Republic of Korea has also introduced controls on the amounts that the controlling companies of the Korean equivalent of the *keiretsu*, the *chaebol*, can invest in affiliate companies: 'South Korea Restricts Investments by Chaebol' *Financial Times* 3 December 2004 at 15 See Monopoly Regulation and Fair Trade Act Law No 3320 31 December 1980 as amended by Law No 7315 of 31 December 2004 Chapter 3 arts 7–18, and ADDENDUM 31 December 2004 available at <http://www.ftc.go.kr/eng/>.

[97] See *The Economist* above n 90. See also 'Capitalism with Japanese Characteristics' in 'The Sun Also Rises: A Survey of Japan' *The Economist* 8 October 2005 at 6: in 1992 46 per cent of all listed equities were held by cross-shareholding between related companies and 6 per cent by foreign investors. By 2004 cross-shareholdings accounted for 24 per cent and foreign ownership had risen to 22 per cent. See further Yoshiro Miwa and J Mark Ramseyer 'The Fable of the Keiretsu' 11 Journal of Economics & Management Strategy 169 (2002) who dismiss the *keiretsu* as an invention of Marxist inspired economists and journalists, in early 1960s Japan, who wished to show the domination of the economy by 'monopoly capital'.

international businesses, the major pressures are, as noted in section 1, towards the maintenance of global competitiveness through increased international coordination and local responsiveness. This may lead, in appropriate cases, to a degree of decentralization in the business structures of the firm, with smaller business units and some demerging of activities. In legal terms, this process could result in the gradual replacement of closely held subsidiaries with free-standing companies linked to the parent by contract. While not representing a return to arm's length legal relations between former affiliates, this process entails an increased incidence of what were earlier referred to as 'control contracts', arrangements whereby economic integration between a dominant and subordinate enterprise is achieved by contractual rather than equity links. Indeed, the experience of Japanese MNEs suggests that equity based links can co-exist with looser forms of legal relation such as joint ventures between jointly managed firms and with local partners, although such links may be harder to achieve in states with strict controls over anti-competitive agreements or concerted practices.

Nevertheless, it would be wrong to consider that such developments herald the end of legal linkages based on equity in MNEs. Certain industry sectors may continue to require a high level of integrated control over subordinate enterprises which make the use of parent/subsidiary relations preferable to 'control contracts'. This may be the case where the use, by the subordinate enterprise, of innovative and highly valuable technology belonging to the parent is involved. Here contract may be an inadequate method for ensuring compliance with parent company demands for quality and confidentiality. Equally, the preservation of an international equity based network can offer advantages in relation to the limitation of liability, or the avoidance of regulatory requirements and the manipulation of earnings flows across borders through transfer pricing transactions that would be harder to achieve through 'control contracts'. Thus there may be significant benefits from the equity group form that will ensure its continued use by MNEs.

(c) Joint Ventures

The term 'joint venture' has no precise legal meaning. It can refer to any agreement or undertaking between two independent firms.[98] However, certain features are commonly associated with the concept.[99] In particular, the joint venture involves the cooperation of two or more otherwise independent parent undertakings which are linked, through the venture, in the pursuit of a common commercial, financial, or technical activity.[100] Unlike a parent-subsidiary relationship,

---

[98] See J Brodley 'Joint Ventures and Antitrust Policy' 95 Harv.LR 1523 at 1525–27 (1982). Brodley includes the creation of significant new enterprise capability in terms of new productive capacity, new technology, a new product, or entry into a new market as part of his definition of a joint venture for competition law purposes.

[99] For a fuller discussion, see Edgar Herzfeld and Adam Wilson *Joint Ventures* (Jordans, 3rd edn, 1996).

[100] Joint ventures may be established between affiliates belonging to the same group. As noted above, this is not uncommon among Japanese companies when setting up foreign operations.

in which there is control by a single dominant undertaking, the joint venture normally involves shared control by the parent undertakings, and is often treated as an associated undertaking for accounting purposes. Nevertheless, one undertaking may exercise a dominant influence over the venture, as where it holds 51 per cent or more of the equity (or of the contribution, in the case of a contractual joint venture). In such cases the joint venture may be treated as a subsidiary for accounting purposes by the dominant undertaking.

The precise nature of control, the proportionate contributions of the joint venture partners, their respective participation in profits and losses, the legal form of the venture, including its legal relation to its parent undertakings, and the conditions for dissolution are matters for determination in the joint venture agreement between the parent undertakings. The agreement is subject to the requirements of the law governing the joint venture. The joint venture itself will be subject to regulation under the relevant system of competition law applicable to it.[101]

The joint venture may take the legal form of a contract, partnership, or limited liability company. In some legal systems, such as that of England, each alternative is freely available. In others more limited choices may be available. As will be seen in chapter 5, in certain states, notably, the former socialist states of Eastern Europe and the former USSR, entry and establishment by direct foreign investors had been permitted only through the adoption of a joint venture between the foreign undertaking and a local joint venture partner, in accordance with the local law on joint ventures involving foreign capital participation. However, such laws are now less common as the liberalization of entry conditions for foreign investors has become more generalized.

The incidence of international joint ventures between firms from more than one country is common. Some joint ventures have acquired a permanence which is hard to distinguish in economic terms from an integrated group. However, full merger in legal terms has been avoided for reasons of policy. Examples can be found in many industries including steel, electrical engineering, aero-engines, and pharmaceuticals, to name but a few. A recent example from the auto industry is the Renault-Nissan Alliance. It is organized around a 50 per cent jointly owned strategic management company, Renault-Nissan BV, incorporated in the Netherlands. This company is not a traditional holding company, in that it does not hold the corporate assets of the two parents, and both partners remain legally independent entities. Renault holds 44 per cent of the shares in Nissan while Nissan holds 15 per cent in Renault. This structure has been adopted for the specific purpose of coordinating strategic cooperation while preserving the distinct corporate culture and brand identity of each partner.[102]

---

[101] On which see Brodley above n 98 and ch 10 at 394–97.

[102] Renault-Nissan *Renault-Nissan Alliance Booklet* (September 2005) available at <http://www.renault.com/renault_com/en/images/Alliance_Booklet_Sept_2005_GB_tcm1120-297154.pdf> and Renault *Annual Report 2005* at 54–57 at <http://www.renault.com/renault_com/en/images/Renault%20Annual%20Report%202005%20%20EN%20290306%20V3_tcm1120-353236.pdf>.

A unique joint venture structure is furnished by Scandinavian Airline Systems (SAS).[103] In order to capture economies of scale and scope which would be unavailable to the parent companies individually, the major national airlines of Sweden (AB Aerotransport), Norway (Det Norske Luftfartselskap A/S), and Denmark (Det Danske Luftfartselskab A/S) entered into an agreement, in 1951, to establish an international joint venture in the provision of civil aviation services. The consortium agreement was renewed in 2001 and runs until 2020. The agreement sets up the 'SAS Consortium' owned by the three parent companies in the following proportions: 3/7ths Swedish, 2/7ths Norwegian and 2/7ths Danish. The parent airlines have transferred responsibility to the Consortium for scheduled air services. The Consortium is managed by the Assembly of Representatives, composed of the parent companies' boards of directors. This body appoints the Consortium's boards of directors, approves financial statements, and decides on the amount of profit to be transferred to the parent companies. The SAS Consortium has no legal personality separate from the parent companies.

In 1996 a programme was introduced so as to improve comparability between the parent companies and strengthen the position of SAS on the financial markets. The accounts and names of the parent companies were harmonized. The parents are now SAS Sverige A/S, SAS Danmark, and Norge ASA, which became SAS Braathens in 2001 after the takeover of the Norwegian carrier Braathens. Also in 2001, a new unified parent company, SAS AB, was incorporated. Its shares are 50 per cent owned by private interests and 21.4 per cent by the Swedish State, 14.3 per cent each by the Danish and Norwegian States. In 2004 the parent airline companies were incorporated in their own right creating a two-tier holding structure for the airline businesses of SAS AB. By Article 3 of the SAS AB articles of association: '[q]uestions of amending or terminating the Consortium Agreement between SAS Danmark A/S, SAS Norge AS and SAS Sverige AB regarding SAS, as amended on May 8, 2001, shall be dealt with by the Company's General Meeting and decisions in this regard require the consent of shareholders with two-thirds of the votes cast as well as of the shares represented at the General Meeting.'[104] In many ways, the SAS Consortium is unique, combining as it does elements of a contractual and equity joint venture with integrated group management, and public sector involvement. Yet it is less than a full transnational merger. It continues on the basis of a renewable agreement between the parent companies, and thus fits better into the joint venture classification.

---

[103] See Scandinavian Airlines System 'SAS Group Legal Structure' at <http://www.sasgroup.net/ SASGroup/default.asp>. For the original structure see Angello above n 53 at 494–95. SAS AB is a member of the Star Alliance of international airlines and has a majority shareholding in four subsidiary airlines (Spanair, Air Baltic, Wideroe, Blue 1) and a 49 per cent holding in Estonian Air.

[104] SAS AB articles of association adopted at the annual general shareholders' meeting 20 April 2006 available at <http://www.sasgroup.net/SASGROUP_IR/CMSForeignContent/ Articlesofassociation_eng_aug06.pdf>.

(d) Informal Alliances between MNEs

Thus far the legal forms of inter-corporate alliance have been considered from the perspectives of contractual links, transnational mergers, and joint ventures. The reasons behind the choice of these various legal forms depend on, inter alia, the degree of integration required for the realization of the alliance's objects, and on the regulatory burdens associated with each form. Thus, an inter-corporate alliance will take the form of a transnational merger where the parent firms wish fully to integrate their business operations, and where the joint holding of group assets requires the use of equity based structures to facilitate the international integration of ownership and to ensure the benefits of limited liability. The contractual route is most likely where the alliance is set up for a specific commercial aim, such as distribution or R&D, which does not involve a high level of integration between the parties and where the risks are small enough not to require limited liability. A contractual relationship is more rarely used for the joint production of a specific product or the joint provision of a service, where the level of integration and risk may be higher. Thus, cases such as the original Airbus Industrie or SAS consortia may be seen as exceptional in this respect. In such cases a joint venture company is more likely to be established, so as to give the parent companies a measure of insulation from the venture, although a measure of limited liability can be achieved through contract by the apportionment of liability between the parent companies on a joint and several basis. On the other hand, a contractual joint venture may avoid duties of corporate disclosure and allow for less transparency than an equity joint venture. Indeed, prior to its incorporation in 2001, Airbus was frequently accused by US critics of concealing the true measure of public subsidy that it received because of the more limited disclosure requirements imposed by French law on a GIE, as compared with a joint stock company.[105]

By contrast to the above mentioned legal forms some inter-corporate alliances may, in fact, lack clear legal structures. Tricker describes these as 'federations of companies'. He gives the following simplified example, based on actual practice:

Three PLCs, each quoted on different stock exchanges around the world, have cross-holdings of each other's shares between 27 and 30%. This is sufficient to provide inter-locking directorships, but the companies are not subsidiaries or associates that would make any member a subordinate company.[106]

Tricker concludes that in this situation the common directors and chief executives of the various subsidiaries in the three groups can exercise joint influence over areas of common concern such as bids, tenders, pricing, products, research, and financial strategy. Thus, collective decisions affecting shareholders and outsiders can be made in the absence of any legal form that identifies the federated area of

---

[105] See n 44 above.   [106] Tricker above n 10 at 148–49.

concern, and through which the regulatory requirements of the relevant law would be imposed. In such a case, it would appear that managerial structures operating across the federation are not legally accountable. This raises two questions: first, whether there should be a duty on the participating companies to establish a legally identifiable joint entity, such as a consortium or joint venture company and, secondly, whether such a structure should be struck down by competition law as tending towards a reduction of normal commercial risks between otherwise independent firms.

(e) Publicly Owned MNEs

No classification of MNE structures would be complete without reference to public ownership. Despite the contemporary emphasis on privatization, there remain sufficient numbers of significant MNEs that are either partly or wholly state-owned. Indeed, some of the examples used in preceding sections involve firms with a measure of public ownership. Publicly owned MNEs can arise through one of two routes: either a state-owned enterprise adopts a strategy of international expansion, or an existing MNE is nationalized.[107] The former is more likely to occur in developing home states, where private capital and entrepreneurship are in short supply, making state entrepreneurship the only option for international expansion. This is occurring in a number of industrial sectors. For example the national petroleum companies of a number of developing countries are evolving international investment strategies.[108] The state-owned Russian energy and natural resources companies Gazprom and Rosneft are extending their international operations. They are seen by some as instruments of Russian foreign policy.[109] Similarly, Embraer of Brazil established itself as an international aerospace company while in state ownership.[110] By contrast, the nationalization route has been taken mainly in developed countries, as the principal home states of major MNEs.

---

[107] J-P Anastassopoulos, G Blanc, and P Dussauge *State-Owned Multinationals* (Wiley/IRM, 1987) at 12–13.

[108] Examples include: Petrobras (Brazil 51 per cent state owned); Pemex (Mexico 100 per cent); Kuwait Oil Company (100 per cent) ; Petroleos de Venezuela (100 per cent): See OPEC 'Member Countries National Oil Companies' at <http://www.opec.org/home/links/links.htm>; Anastassopoulos et al above n 107 at 183–84; 'Oils Dark Secret Special Report: National Oil Companies' *The Economist* 12 August 2006 at 66; Louis Turner *Oil Companies in the International System* (London: RIIA/George Allen & Unwin, 3rd edn, 1983) at 237–39. The China National Offshore Oil Corporation (CNOOC) is majority state owned. Its state ownership was one of the reasons that the US Congress was concerned about its aborted takeover proposal for the US oil company Chevron. See further ch 5 at 182. See also James Boxell and Kevin Morrison 'A Power Shift: Global Oil Companies Find New Rivals Snapping at Their Heels' *Financial Times* 9 December 2004 at 171. See also UNCTAD *World Investment Report 2007* (New York and Geneva: United Nations, forthcoming).

[109] See *The Economist* above n 108 at 67; 'Ivan at the Pipe: Special Report: Russian Energy Firms' *The Economist* 11 December 2004 at 73.

[110] Embraer was founded by the Brazilian Government in 1969. It was privatized on 7 December 1994: see Embraer website at <http://www.embraer.com/english/content/empresa/history.asp>.

In particular, the French nationalizations of 1982 brought some very large multi-national groups into public ownership.[111]

The principal question affecting the legal structures of publicly owned MNEs is the relationship between the state and the enterprise, and, in particular, the degree of control that the former wishes to exercise over the latter.[112] Normally, the enterprise will be incorporated as an entity separate from the state, with the state as the majority or exclusive shareholder. In some states ownership is achieved through a state holding company, rather than by direct shareholding.[113] The state may have directors on the board, and may impose obligations of direct reporting to the minister responsible for the industrial sector concerned. Additionally, or in the alternative, accountability may be ensured as a result of the state's control over the financing of the company. The position of the state as principal shareholder makes the enterprise dependent on grants from the state, offering the latter a powerful weapon of control.[114]

A further significant element in the control system is the setting of objectives for the enterprise. This can be done by way of statements of objects in the legislation establishing the corporation. In France, following the 1982 nationalizations, the government effected this aim through separate 'planning contracts' with the 11 nationalized groups. These were to last for four years. They set agreed obligations and targets for the group concerned in relation to its strategic options, employment trends, financial requirements, and as to its future financial commitments. By this means the French Government sought to harmonize state policy with the strategy of the major publicly owned groups.[115] However, despite such contractual controls, the French Government continued to respect the managerial autonomy of the nationalized groups, which were free to pursue their commercial and international strategies as they saw fit.

Even with a limited role in active management, the presence of a state interest in a MNE may be counterproductive. Limits on available finance could undermine a commercially necessary policy of internationalization, and the fact of state ownership could create the perception that the enterprise is no more than

---

[111] These included St Gobain (reprivatized in 1986); Pechiney (taken over by Alcan in 2003); Rhône-Poulenc (merged in 1999 with Hoechst to form Aventis which merged with Sanofi to form Sanofi-Aventis in 2004); Thomson (reprivatized in 1999); Cie Generale d'Eléctricité (reprivatized in 1987). See further J Savary *French Multinationals* (IRM/Frances Pinter, 1984) Supplement 155–91; Anastassopoulos et al above n 107 at 121–24. For an analysis of the nationalization and subsequent privatization programme, see Vivien A Schmidt *From State to Market? The Transformation of French Business and Government* (Cambridge: Cambridge University Press, 1996).

[112] See further Khan 'Some Legal Considerations on the Role and Structure of State Oil Companies: A Comparative View' 34 ICLQ 584 (1985); Thomas Waelde 'Restructuring and Privatization: Viable Strategies for State Enterprises in Developing Countries?' Utilities Policy (October 1991) 412–17.

[113] For example, in Italy the oil company Agip was controlled by Ente Nazionale Idrocarburi (ENI) prior to privatization. ENI continues to act as the parent company after privatization, which took place in four phases between November 1995 and June 1998: <http://www.eni.it>.

[114] See further Anastassopoulos et al above n 107 at 69–72.

[115] See Savary above n 111 at 161–62; Anastassopoulos above n 107 at 40.

an emanation of the home government. Thus the reduction, if not the removal, of state involvement may be required for internationalization to succeed.[116] However, the state may be a useful partner where the private sector is virtually non-existent, as in developing countries,[117] or where it provides insufficient capital for the expansion of a business. Indeed, the French nationalizations provided much needed new capital and credit to France's MNEs, and can be seen as a positive step in their international strategies.[118] Therefore, a role for continued state ownership in MNEs is foreseeable but, perhaps, not inevitable.

(f) Supranational Forms of International Business

The final category in this classification of MNE legal structures involves entities that are formed under laws adopted by regional organizations of states, aimed at the furtherance of cooperation between firms from more than one member state. It also distinguishes the 'public international corporation' from the publicly-owned MNE, so as to avoid confusion between these two distinct international business forms.

(i) Forms Adopted by the European Community

The EC established a Statute for the European Company in 2001.[119] This permits the establishment of a European level company known as the 'Societas Europea' (SE). The SE can be set up in one of four ways: by the merger of two or more existing public limited companies from at least two different Member States; by the formation of a holding company promoted by public or private limited companies from at least two Member States; by the formation of subsidiary companies from at least two different Member States; by the transformation of a public limited company which has had a subsidiary in another Member State for at least two years.[120] The SE must be registered in the Member State where it has its administrative head office and will be governed by its law.[121] It can set up subsidiaries as

---

[116] For example, Fu Chengyu, the chair and chief executive of CNOOC has suggested that a reduction in the Chinese Government's holding would combat claims that the company was an instrument of government energy policy rather than a commercial company: 'CNOOC Chief Willing to Ask For a Cut in Beijing Stake' *Financial Times* 27 October 2005 at 28.

[117] Developing countries may retain public ownership where the alternative is domination of an industry by foreign capital. However, in the long term the pressures of state control may force privatization to occur. Short of privatization, reforms aimed at increasing managerial efficiency may be taken. See *World Bank Annual Report 1983* ch 8. See also, for a study of state involvement in promoting the computer industries in Brazil, India, and Korea in the 1970s and 1980s; Peter Evans *Embedded Autonomy: States and Industrial Transformation* (Princeton University Press, 1995) and, more generally, Atul Kohli *State-Directed Development: Political Power and Industrialization in the Global Periphery* (Cambridge: Cambridge University Press, 2004).

[118] Anastassopoulos et al above n 107 at 181.

[119] Council Regulation (EC) 2157/2001 of 8 October 2001 OJ [2001] L294/1 and Council Directive 2001/86/EC of 8 October 2001 supplementing the Statute for a European Company with regard to the involvement of employees OJ [2001] L294/22.   [120] Reg 2157/2001 art 2.

[121] ibid arts 7 and 3(1).

SEs.[122] It will pay tax in accordance with the applicable rules in all the Member States in which it operates and will be subject to national competition, intellectual property, and insolvency laws.[123] The establishment of a SE will require the negotiation of an agreement on employee involvement with employee representatives in accordance with the requirements of the Directive supplementing the European Company Statute.[124]

According to the EC Commission, the principal advantage of the SE is to permit the cross-border merger of two or more companies on the basis of a single set of rules and a unified management and reporting system. This should lead to a significant reduction of administrative and legal costs.[125] However, few companies have taken advantage of the new legislation. The Commission has blamed this on the slow implementation of the Statute in national laws.[126] Companies themselves are uncertain about the tax consequences of the SE and aspects of corporate governance. In addition, given the liberalization of the law relating to rights of establishment by the European Court of Justice in recent years, it may be possible to obtain all the benefits of the SE through the cheaper expedient of incorporating a limited company under English law which offers a liberal regulatory environment to any enterprise from another EU Member State that wishes to operate throughout the Community.[127] So far the largest European company to opt for the SE structure is Allianz, the German insurer. It did so in order to take over and integrate RAS, a 55.4 per cent owned insurance subsidiary in Italy, into its European operations.[128] Other firms have been noted as expressing interest in conversion to a SE, but few have as yet done so.[129]

Of greater immediate significance is the European Economic Interest Grouping (EEIG), which was introduced by regulation in 1985.[130] Based on the French GIE,

---

[122] ibid art 3(2).   [123] ibid preamble recital 20.

[124] See Directive 2001/86/EC above n 119. See also ch 9 at 357–58.

[125] EC Commission 'The European Company Frequently Asked Questions' Press Release MEMO/01/314 Brussels, 8 October 2001 at <http://europa.eu/rapid/pressReleasesAction.do?reference=MEMO/01/314&format=HTML&aged=1&language=en&guiLanguage=en>.

[126] EC Commission 'Company Law: European Company Statute in Force, but National Delays Stop Companies Using It' Press release IP/04/1195 Brussels, 8th October 2004 at <http://europa.eu/rapid/pressReleasesAction.do?reference=IP/04/1195&format=HTML&aged=0&language=en&guiLanguage=en>.

[127] See 'Pan-European Companies: Limited Appeal' *The Economist* 17 September 2005 at 72 and see ch 6 at 242–47.   [128] ibid.

[129] See further Patrick Jenkins and Tobias Buck 'On the Move: Why European Companies May See Benefits in a Corporate Situation with Fewer Limitations' *Financial Times* 11 October 2005 at 19 and Christophe Brown-Humes 'Conversion Broadens Eloteq's Horizons' ibid explaining the Finnish electronics company Eloteq's decision to convert into a SE on the basis of greater freedom to move its domicile out of Finland, should it wish and to merge its subsidiaries in other EU Member States.

[130] Council Regulation 2137/85 of 25 July 1985 OJ [1985] L199/1 <http://eur-lex.europa.eu/LexUriServ/LexUriServ.do?uri=CELEX:31985R2137:EN:NOT>. This regulation has been implemented into UK law by means of Statutory Instrument SI 1989: 638; SI 1989: 216 (N Ireland). For analysis, see Frank Wooldridge *Company Law in the United Kingdom and the European Community* (Athlone Press, 1991) at 103–17; S Israel 'The EEIG – A major Step Forward for Community Law' 9 Co.Law 14 (1988); M Anderson *European Economic Interest Groupings* (London: Butterworths, 1990). See also

but nonetheless distinct, the EEIG seeks to create a supranational form of business association that will facilitate cross-border cooperation between business entities operating within the EC. It is of limited commercial scope, its purpose being:

[t]o facilitate or develop the economic activities of its members and to improve or increase the results of those activities; its purpose is not to make profits for itself. Its activity shall be related to the economic activities of its members and must not be more than ancillary to those activities.[131]

Consequently the EEIG is disqualified from certain commercial activities. These include: the exercise of a power of management over the activities of its members or of another undertaking; the holding of shares in a member undertaking (though it may hold shares in any other undertaking where this is necessary for the attainment of its objects and the shares are held on its members' behalf); the use of the EEIG for the making of intracorporate loans to directors or transfers of property between a company and a director or connected person, save to the extent allowed by the company laws of Member States; and membership of another EEIG.[132] It is clear, therefore, that the EEIG is not to be used as a management or holding company for the members, nor as a conduit company for the members' benefit. Furthermore, the EEIG must not employ more than 500 persons. Thus it is unlikely to be used for large scale manufacturing operations. Indeed, the EEIG is most likely to be used for joint R&D or distribution, or for other forms of smaller scale inter-corporate cooperation. It has also proved popular as a method of creating transnational legal practices, given that the membership of an EEIG extends not only to companies but also to natural persons providing inter alia professional services.[133]

The EEIG is formed by the conclusion of a contract by the participants,[134] who must be either companies with their central administrations in different Member States, or natural persons carrying on their principal activities in different Member States, or a combination of companies and natural persons from different Member States.[135] Upon registration and establishment in accordance with the regulation in a Member State,[136] the EEIG shall have full legal capacity. However, the legal personality of the Grouping falls to be determined by the laws of the Member States.[137] The internal organization of the EEIG is governed by the law of the Member State in which the official address is situated.[138]

Companies House *European Economic Interest Groupings* (London: Companies House GB 04, February 2005) available at <http://www.companieshouse.gov.uk/about/pdf/gb04.pdf>.

[131] ibid art 3(1).   [132] ibid art 3(2).

[133] ibid art 4(1). See 'EC Framework Finally Comes Into its Own' *Financial Times* 19 June 1989 at 27.

[134] ibid art 1(1). The law governing the formation contract is the law of the Member State in which the official address is situated: art 2.   [135] ibid art 4(2).

[136] On which see ibid arts 6–12.   [137] ibid art 1(2) and (3).   [138] ibid art 2(1).

The EEIG is run by the members acting collectively and the manager or managers.[139] Each member shall have one vote although more than one vote may be given in the constitutive agreement provided that no member holds a majority of the votes.[140] The profits shall be deemed to be those of the members and shall be shared among them in the proportions laid down in the contract.[141] They shall be taxed in accordance with national tax laws.[142] The members shall have joint and unlimited liability, the consequences of which fall to be determined by national law.[143]

(ii) The Andean Multinational Enterprise[144]

In the early 1980s ANCOM introduced the 'Andean Multinational Enterprise' (AME) as a means of creating supranational regional enterprises aimed at the furtherance of joint industrial development.[145] The legal form of the AME is that of a company with capital contributions from national investors from more than one member state that together exceed 60 per cent of the capital of the company.[146] It is domiciled in the territory of one of the member countries or in the country where the enterprise is transformed into a AME, through the sale of part of its stock to sub-regional investors, or created through merger between two or more national or mixed companies.[147]

According to Article 7 of the Law on Andean Multinational Enterprises (the Code), the laws governing the enterprise are, in descending order of importance, its articles of incorporation, which must be in accordance with the Code; the Code in respect of matters not stipulated in the articles; in respect of matters not governed either by the articles or the Code, the legislation of the country of principal domicile, which would normally be the country of incorporation. In certain cases, not listed by the Code, the legislation of the country where the AME establishes a legal relationship or in which the legal acts of the enterprise will take effect in accordance with the applicable rules of private international law.

AMEs are entitled to special treatment under the laws of the member countries. In particular, they are entitled to national treatment (art 9); free circulation of capital contributions (art 10); free import and export of goods constituting part of the capital contribution (art 11); access to export incentives (art 12); freedom to participate in sectors reserved for national enterprises under member countries' laws (art 14); rights to establish branches in other member countries (arts 15–16); freedom for foreign participants to repatriate earnings (art 17); national treatment

---

[139] ibid art 16(1).   [140] ibid art 17(1).   [141] ibid art 21(1).
[142] ibid preamble, recital 14.   [143] ibid art 24(1).
[144] On ANCOM investment policy see further ch 17 at 656–58.
[145] Andean Commission Decision on Andean Multinational Enterprises (16–18 March 1982): 21 ILM 542 (1982) as amended by ANCOM Decision 292 (21 March 1991): 30 ILM 1295. All references in text are to the 1991 decision. The official Spanish term is 'Empresa Multinacional Andina' (EMA).   [146] ibid art 1.
[147] ibid and arts 5–6.

in taxation matters and freedom from double taxation (arts 18–20); free choice of
personnel and free movement of investors, promoters, and executives (arts 21–22);
and privileged application of technology transfer rules (art 23).

(iii) Public International Corporations

Finally, it is necessary to distinguish between a publicly owned MNE and a public
international corporation.[148] The latter is an entity set up by two or more states
through an international treaty. It will perform a specific economic function that is
of importance to the public policy of the founding states, and which can be better
carried out by means of inter-governmental cooperation. Such corporations have
been set up inter alia in the atomic energy field,[149] transportation,[150] and satellite
communications.[151] The concept of a joint inter-governmental corporation has
been used by the Yemen Arab Republic and the People's Democratic Republic of
Yemen to develop oil reserves lying along the border between the two states.[152]

The legal regimes of corporations identified by lawyers as public international
corporations are many and varied. Some are no more than joint ventures between
publicly owned corporations from more than one country, and may be better seen
as publicly owned MNEs (for example SAS above), while others are close in character to inter-governmental organizations. There is little conclusive agreement on
the precise border between these two types of public sector enterprise.[153] According
to Kahn, the crucial question revolves around the legal regime that governs the
enterprise.[154]

The essential difference between a public international corporation and a
publicly owned MNE is that the former will be governed by a regime based on its
constitutive treaty rather than on any system of national law. Although a public
international corporation may have a seat in one of the participating states, the
law of the seat will not apply where a matter is dealt with by the treaty. Thus, for
example, the Treaty establishing Eurofima, the inter-governmental corporation
set up to administer the common servicing of rolling stock among 14 European
railway companies, states in Article I:

The Governments which are party to the present Convention approve the Company's
constitution which will be governed by the Statutes attached to the present Convention

---

[148] See further I Brownlie *Principles of Public International Law* (Oxford: Oxford University Press,
6th edn, 2003) at 65–6; D Ijalaye *The Extension of Corporate Personality in International Law* (Dobbs
Ferry, New York: Oceana, 1978) ch III; CM Schmitthoff 'The International Corporation' 30
Trans.Grot.Soc. 165 (1944); Kahn 'International Companies' 3 JWTL 498 (1969); FA Mann
'International Corporations and National Law' in Studies in International Law (Oxford: Oxford
University Press, 1973) 553 or in (1967) BYIL 145.   [149] Eg Eurochemic: see Khan ibid at 504.
[150] Eg Air Afrique: see Ijalaye above n 148 at 81–84.
[151] Eg INTELSAT: Ijalaye ibid at 91–96.
[152] See Onorato 'Joint Development in the International Petroleum Sector: The Yemeni Variant'
39 ICLQ 653 (1990).
[153] As is revealed by a comparison of approaches taken by the authorities cited in n 148 above.
[154] Above n 148 at 503–511.

(hereinafter called "the statutes") and, residually, by the law of the Headquarters' State in so far as the present Convention does not derogate therefrom.[155]

Accordingly, although Eurofima's headquarters are in Switzerland, and it is established as a corporation under Swiss law, Swiss law will be subordinated to the Treaty regime. This is reinforced by Article II(a) which gives effect to any variations in the Statutes notwithstanding that these may contradict the law of Switzerland as the Headquarters State.

In addition, a public international corporation may be identified where it is closely administered by governmental officials from the participating states rather than by commercial managers, where it enjoys a measure of diplomatic immunity not normally given to a commercial corporation, and where the dispute settlement provisions in the constitutive treaty envisage international rather than national procedures. This may involve a special tribunal set up by the participating states or, as in the case of Eurofima, by recourse to the International Court of Justice.[156]

(3) Business and Legal Forms and the Control of MNE Activities

In section 1 of this chapter, it was seen that, in common with most large multilocation enterprises, MNEs have outgrown the simple managerial structure of the entrepreneurial corporation and have reorganized along divisional lines of control based on managerial functions, products, and areas of operation. However, unlike a multiplant domestic company, a MNE will organize itself along divisional lines whose managerial reach crosses national frontiers, and through which, for business purposes, the national identity of the various operating companies in the group disappears. At the same time, in legal terms, the group remains a collection of commonly held companies possessing the nationality of their country of incorporation. Similarly, in the case of a transnational network (TNN), control over the operations of a local enterprise, and participation in the creation of the products or services offered by it, may involve several associated entities both within and outside the jurisdiction, linked by contractually based managerial control systems.

From the regulator's perspective the major question is whether the resulting legal structure corresponds with the firm's decision-making structure, and places it within the organizational presumptions underlying the legal form from which its legal duties stem. It is clear that existing legal forms of business organization, essentially contract and corporation, were simply not designed to correspond with such extensive business structures as MNEs. Contract assumes an arm's length relationship between otherwise independent entities of equal bargaining

---

[155] Convention of 20 October 1955: 378 UNTS 159. See Eurofima *Annual Report 2005* at <http://www.eurofima.org/Annual_Report_2005_E.pdf>.   [156] ibid art XIV.

power, while the corporation assumes a single unit enterprise owned and controlled by its members. Neither form contemplates the linking of legally separate entities into unified business structures, whether through 'control contract' or divisional management.

Regarding contractual structures, the possibility of managerial control by one firm over another raises the question whether the contract should be disregarded for regulatory purposes: whether the 'contractual veil' be lifted so that the dominant undertaking can be made liable for the acts of the subordinate undertaking, regardless of the contractual allocation of risk between them. Similarly, in relation to equity based structures the question arises: when should the regulator be free to disregard the corporate separation between parent and subsidiary and lift the 'corporate veil' so as to allocate responsibility with the ultimate decision-maker along the line of management in the group? As will be shown in detail in chapter 8, these questions may prove inadequate as methods of dealing with MNE regulation. What may be needed is a radical rethinking of the very legal forms themselves and their replacement with new legal forms better able to correspond with the decision-making boundaries of firms.

For the present it is enough to outline some possible answers to these problems. First, as regards the legal structures in equity based multinational corporate groups, two broad approaches to reform can be identified. The first, favoured by Hadden, is structural. The corporate entity should be reformed in a way that more closely corresponds to its business organization, and ensures the existence of a relevant unit for accounting, fiscal and other regulatory purposes. In this Hadden favours the retention of the most useful characteristic of the corporate legal form, the creation of an identifiable legal representation of the underlying business activity, and adapting it to modern realities.[157] This may entail new group enterprise forms for equity based groups, and raises the question whether informal alliances should be forced to adopt corporate legal form. The structural approach will be considered in greater detail in chapter 8.

The second approach, favoured by Tricker, is operational. He advocates leaving the present version of the company legal form intact, but increasing the obligations placed directly upon establishments or divisions within the group. In particular, Tricker favours the introduction of greater divisional disclosure through the concept of an 'accountable business activity', whereby managers would be responsible to disclose information according to the actual lines of decision-making in the enterprise, rather than relying on the limits of the legal obligation to disclose which is attached to incorporated entities only.[158] Issues of improved disclosure and governance will be considered in chapter 9.

As regards the limits of control in contractual situations, possible responses are to be found in the idea of 'network liability' put forward by Teubner,[159] which will

---

[157] Hadden *Control of Corporate Groups* above n 53 at 44–45.
[158] See Tricker above n 10 at 156–59.   [159] See writings cited in n 39 above.

be considered in chapter 8, and in the use of competition laws to protect the business independence of the weaker contracting party, and third parties that may be denied access to markets controlled by network organizations. These matters will be considered in chapter 10.

The above questions arise mainly in relation to privately owned groups, as publicly owned groups may be presumed to have stronger public controls over their decision-making, at least so far as the home state is concerned. In relation to regulation by the host state, however, publicly owned MNEs may create not only the regulatory problems associated with the limits of contract and corporation, but also the problem of dealing with the home state as the ultimate owner and controller of the enterprise. Thus further problems of a highly political nature may emerge in such cases, possibly requiring negotiated diplomatic solutions. These are beyond the scope of the present work.

Concluding Remarks

This chapter has sought to explain the internal characteristics of MNEs, concentrating on their business and legal forms. The interrelationship between these aspects of MNE organization is central to an understanding of what a MNE is and how to regulate its activities. The business and legal forms of MNEs are many and varied and no simple models can be used as catch all explanations. Rather what has been presented here should be used as a basic map against which the actual organization of particular firms can be compared. It is not possible to speak of dominant universal trends in this connection as each firm represents a unique response to its market and wider environment. Some are better at this than others. The internal culture of the firm will be a factor. However, from a regulatory perspective it is necessary to develop legal responses that serve to further the proper aims of accountability and, where necessary, liability. These will be considered in further chapters. For now attention will turn to the external effects of MNEs on the countries in which they operate and how those countries might respond through the development of a regulatory agenda.

3

Regulating Multinationals

The preceding chapters have offered certain building blocks for understanding the nature of MNE regulation. The focus has been, first, on the reasons for MNE growth, including the role, if any, of legal factors in its promotion and, secondly, on the relationship between the business and legal forms of MNEs, as an introduction to the problems of control through legal forms of business association. However, a developed understanding of the regulation of MNEs requires a further dimension. This stems from the interaction of MNEs with the political communities in which they operate. In the first edition of this book these were identified simply as nation states, given their role as the main source of formal legal regulation. A state-centric approach is no longer adequate for at least two reasons.

First, it fails to reflect the full range of regulatory actions and responsibilities to which MNEs may be subject, or indeed voluntarily undertake, in a complex globalizing environment. For example, it does not permit a proper appreciation of the interaction between formal 'command and control' regulation and informal 'self-regulation'. Secondly, it does not allow an adequate examination of the full range of parties that may seek to exert regulatory influence upon these firms. In particular, it leaves out informal regulation, carried out by non-state actors who monitor the activities of MNEs, such as campaigning non-governmental organizations (NGOs). This has become increasingly significant in the shaping of the regulatory agenda. That said, the nation state and its regulatory emanations, regional and multilateral inter-governmental organizations (IGOs), remain the central focus of regulatory action. As noted in chapter 1, these 'sites' of formal regulation couple with the 'sites' of informal regulation by non-state actors and self-regulating MNEs to form a pluralistic regulatory environment.[1]

In order to analyse this process more fully, it is proposed, first, to map out the variety of actors involved in MNE regulation and to identify their respective roles and interests. Secondly, it is necessary to explain how the substantive content of any regulatory agenda is to be ascertained. This can be done in the light of the perceived effects of MNEs on home and host communities and economies. Such an analysis is incapable of value-free discussion. Therefore, this section of the chapter will also elaborate upon certain ideological themes that have influenced the development of the regulatory debate, both historically and as regards the present. Thirdly, the

---

[1] See n 215 at 43 above and the citations of Snyder's work in this regard.

principal levels and methods of regulation will be considered. Here, the relationship between formal regulation by state bodies and informal regulation by non-
state actors will be discussed, the available sources of regulatory rules and practices
outlined, and the choices of legal jurisdiction between national, bilateral, regional,
and multilateral regulation will be considered.

(1) The Principal Actors

The discussion of relations between MNEs and the communities in which they
operate has involved a significant shift in international relations theory away from
a state-centred 'balance of power' paradigm, in which the objects of study are
nation states and their respective political, diplomatic, and military interactions,
towards a 'transnational relations' analysis, which allows for the recognition of
non-state transnational actors in the international system, and emphasizes that
the actions of such actors may increase international economic interdependence.[2]
MNEs figure most prominently among such non-state actors. Indeed, MNEs
have been seen as participants in a tripartite system of international interactions in
an increasingly global economy involving the relations of governments to governments, governments to corporations, and corporations to corporations.[3]

In particular, MNEs may be said to be at the heart of legal developments in this
field.[4] Their role as a special interest group, that seeks to influence the development of the law in a manner conducive to the furtherance of their interests as
investors, cannot be ignored. There is little doubt that MNEs lobby governments
and IGOs to ensure that normative development is business friendly.[5] How successful they may be is another issue, as the case of the failure of the Multilateral
Agreement on Investment (MAI), or of the adoption of investment rules in the
WTO, may suggest.[6] Nonetheless, it is not possible to see the development of this

---

[2] See generally Robert O Keohane and Joseph S Nye *Transnational Relations and World Politics*
(Cambridge, Mass: Harvard University Press, 1972); Susan Strange *States and Markets* (London:
Pinter Publishers, 2nd edn, 1994) ch 1.

[3] See further John Stopford and Susan Strange *Rival States, Rival Firms* (Cambridge: Cambridge
University Press, 1991).

[4] The following paragraphs draw on and develop the author's manuscript that forms the basis of the
International Law Association (ILA) Committee on the International Law on Foreign Investment,
First Report, Toronto, June 2006 in ILA *Report of the Seventy-Second Conference – Toronto* (London:
2006). The author is Co-rapporteur of the Committee.

[5] See, for example, Ian H Rowlands 'Transnational Corporations and Global Environmental
Politics' in Daphne Josselin and William Wallace (eds) *Non-State Actors in World Politics* (Basingstoke:
Palgrave Publishers, 2001) 133 and Andrew Walter 'Unravelling the Faustian Bargain: Non-state
Actors and the Multilateral Agreement on Investment' in ibid 150. See further Dale D Murphy *The
Structure of Regulatory Competition: Corporations and Public Policies in a Global Economy* (Oxford:
Oxford University Press, 2004) and Geoffrey Jones *Multinationals and Global Capitalism: From the
Nineteenth to the Twenty-first Century* (Oxford: Oxford University Press, 2005) at 224–27.

[6] On which see ch 17 at 666–74. On the other hand, the influence of MNEs on domestic
legal developments may be more successful. See further Peter Muchlinski '"Global Bukowina"

area without taking account of the role of these important actors as a formative influence in the law. In addition, given the increased calls for the extension of legally binding international standards of corporate social responsibility, MNEs may become subject to new duties under international instruments, which reflect standards already accepted in many national laws.

Apart from MNEs, another significant group of non-state actors are the NGOs that seek to influence the development of rules and procedures in the wider area of international business regulation. While the activities of such organizations are, perhaps, best known to lawyers in the field of human rights protection,[7] NGOs have been increasingly active in the field of foreign investment, as the apparent voices of so-called 'civil society'.[8] With the growth of economic globalization, the activities of such bodies can be expected to grow. Indeed, aided by the internet, NGOs are filling a gap in regulatory order by placing certain ideas and issues on the political agenda, and contesting the very future of that regulatory order, by their actions.[9] This process will be examined in more detail in chapter 14, where the influence of NGOs on the development of environmental regulation of MNEs will be considered, as a prime illustration of this trend.

Together, MNEs and 'civil society groups' may be seen as the informal initiators of regulatory actions seeking to further their respective policy interests. Alongside them are the established formal regulators, states, and IGOs. In the field of FDI regulation the host state has been the central focus of regulatory action. It is the main controller of MNE activity within its borders and it is also the main holder of obligations to protect investors and their investments under international investment agreements (IIAs) concluded with the home states of MNEs.[10] Much of the early legal literature on MNE-state relations concentrated on the host country, as has much of the international relations literature.[11] More recently, this concentration on the host state has been questioned.[12]

Examined: Viewing the Multinational Enterprise as a Transnational Law Making Community' in Gunther Teubner (ed) *Global Law without a State* (Aldershot: Dartmouth Publishing, 1997) 79.

[7] See A Cassese *Human Rights in a Changing World* (Cambridge: Polity Press, 1994) 171–74; Henry J Steiner and Philip Alston *International Human Rights in Context: Law Politics Morals* (Oxford: Oxford University Press, 2nd edn, 2000) ch 11.

[8] 'Civil society' may be defined as 'the space for uncoerced human association and also the set of relational networks – formed for the sake of family, faith, interest and ideology – that fill this space': M Walzer (ed) *Toward a Global Civil Society* (Providence, Rhode Island: Berghan Books, 2nd edn, 1998) at 7 adopted by Daphne Josselin and William Wallace (eds) above n 5 at 20 n 5. On 'international civil society' see Holly Curren and Karen Morrow 'International Civil Society in International Law: The Growth of NGO Participation' 1 Non-State Actors and International Law 7 (2001).

[9] See Sylvia Ostry 'The Multilateral Trading System' in Alan M Rugman and Thomas L Brewer *The Oxford Handbook of International Business* (Oxford: Oxford University Press, 2000) 232 at 244–50.

[10] See ch 17.

[11] See, for example, Cynthia Day Wallace *Legal Control of the Multinational Enterprise* (The Hague: Martinus Nijhoff Publishers, 1983); Detlev Vagts 'The Multinational Enterprise: A New Challenge for Transnational Law' 83 Harv.LR 739 (1970).

[12] See UNCTAD *World Investment Report 2003* (New York and Geneva: United Nations) at 155.

As noted above, the bulk of international obligations have hitherto fallen upon host states. By contrast, investors and home states have few, if any, international obligations. It has already been mentioned that increasing attention is being paid to the duties of investors towards the countries in which they invest under the rubric of 'international corporate social responsibility'. Equally, it is possible to expect home states to undertake certain responsibilities. In particular, given that the majority of home states are developed, while many host states are developing or less developed, it may be valuable, as a stimulus for investment, to extend certain duties on home states to facilitate outward investment to developing countries, such as the provision of incentives or the encouragement of technology transfer.[13] In addition, the home states' legal and regulatory system might be used to ensure that MNEs based there conform to certain standards of good corporate citizenship through the sanction of home country laws and regulations, and through the provision of legal redress for claimants from outside the home country who are in dispute with the parent company for the acts of its overseas subsidiaries.[14]

In addition to states and non-state actors, the IGOs comprise a further set of influential participants in the development of foreign investment law. IGOs are organized around the constitutive instrument establishing the organization to which the member states have consented. They have an existence rooted in the sovereign acts of states, but they exist over and outside those states. Equally, each IGO creates a legal sub-system based on its constituent instrument, which, in turn will also be governed by a sub-system of public international law, the law of international institutions.[15] Furthermore, an IGO may have a quasi-legislative power to develop substantive international rules and procedures governing its substantive field of activity. This specialized legal order may be said to constitute a tool for the pragmatic development of responses to the regulation of the phenomena of globalization.[16] That this power has been used in relation to the development of norms of international foreign investment law cannot be doubted, notwithstanding the history of frequent failure in relation to the adoption of international rules in this area. In particular, the contributions of the OECD,[17] the ILO,[18] the UN Sub-Commission on Human Rights,[19] and UNCTAD[20] should be taken into

---

[13] ibid at 161–63.

[14] ibid at 156. See further Peter Muchlinski 'Corporations in International Litigation: Problems of Jurisdiction and the United Kingdom Asbestos Case' 50 ICLQ 1 (2001); Philip Blumberg 'Asserting Human Rights Against Multinational Corporations Under United States Law: Conceptual and Procedural Problems' 50 AJCL 493 (2002); and M Kamminga and S Zia-Zarifi (eds) *Liability of Multinational Corporations Under International Law* (The Hague: Kluwer Law International, 2001) especially Section III.

[15] See Philippe Sands and Pierre Klein *Bowett's Law of International Institutions* (London: Sweet & Maxwell, 5th edn, 2001) para 1–030 at 17.

[16] See Peter T Muchlinski 'Globalisation and Legal Research' 37 Int'l Law 221 at 226 (2003).

[17] See ch 6 at 248–251; ch 17 at 658–60.　　[18] See ch 12.　　[19] See ch 13.

[20] See ch 10 on the UNCTAD code on restrictive trade practices, and see further Torbjorn Fredriksson and Zbygniew Zimny 'Foreign Direct Investment and Transnational Corporations' in UNCTAD *Beyond Conventional Wisdom in Development Policy: An Intellectual History of UNCTAD 1964–2004* (New York and Geneva: United Nations, 2004) 257.

account as regards standard setting and research in this area, while the World Bank has, through the International Centre for Settlement of Investment Disputes (ICSID) established the leading investor-state dispute settlement body, which is handling an increased caseload that has an increasingly significant influence on the development of norms in this area.[21] The World Bank Group also contains the Multilateral Investment Guarantee Agency (MIGA), which is discussed in chapter15, and the International Finance Corporation (IFC), which provides strategic finance and advice for FDI projects.[22]

(2) Developing a Regulatory Agenda

The above mentioned actors each have distinctive interests that they seek to further. As already noted MNEs, and NGOs, representing business, will seek a business friendly environment that offers as few unnecessary regulatory hurdles as possible to the free choice of operating means. Public interest NGOs will seek to control what they perceive as excesses of corporate power and strive for greater accountability of firms in relation to the public interest goals the NGOs support. Host countries will seek to attract and benefit from the investment that MNEs offer, while home countries will encourage outward investment that brings useful economic and political returns to those countries. IGOs will seek to further the policy aims of their members as expressed in the constitutive instrument and as result from the political contestation of their agendas.

Although each state's policy should be viewed as unique, certain generalizations are possible as to the broad regulatory goals of home and host states respectively. Turning to host states, their regulatory priorities stem from the fact that, regardless of their level of economic development, inward direct investment may be needed to supply new capital, technology, goods, or services that no locally based firm can supply at equivalent or lower cost. Thus, host states will generally encourage the entry of firms that can bring these factors into the economy.[23] However, host states will wish to guard against some of the difficulties that can result if inward direct investment is permitted.[24] Thus, conditions may be imposed on the entry of a foreign firm. These may relate to the legal form that the local enterprise must take, the level, if any, of local ownership in the new enterprise, and any performance requirements that the enterprise must fulfil regarding, for example, import levels, technology and skills transfer, job levels, export levels, or long-term investment strategy. Alternatively, foreign firms may be prohibited completely from certain sensitive sectors of the host economy. Apart from entry requirements, the host may impose

---

[21] See on substantive legal developments chs 15 and 16 and, on procedural issues, ch 18.
[22] See further the ICF website: <http://www.ifc.org/ifcext/about.nsf/Content/WhatWeDo>.
[23] See *World Investment Report 2003* above n 12 at 86–88.
[24] See generally UNCTAD *World Investment Report 1999* (New York and Geneva: United Nations, 1999) Part Two 'Foreign Direct Investment and the Challenge of Development'.

measures to ensure adequate revenue from the investment by way of taxation. It will also normally subject the local affiliate of the MNE to the general system of business regulation in force within the host state, including competition, company, labour, and intellectual property law.

As regards home states, their traditional concerns have centred on inter alia: the protection of domestic labour against the export of jobs abroad, adequate revenue from the repatriation of dividends earned by overseas subsidiaries of home-based parent companies, the promotion and protection of technological leads enjoyed by home-based MNEs, and access to raw materials in short supply in the home state.[25] These concerns have prompted unilateral action designed to preserve the conditions of the national economy in the face of outward investment,[26] notably through the use of exchange controls,[27] or through restrictions on foreign tax credits.[28]

New concerns have emerged for home states as a result of the increased integration of the international economy. In particular, as the principal home states have also become leading host states, they have had to consider the need for the equal and reciprocal treatment of inward and outward investment. This has led to the gradual acceptance of policies aimed at the progressive liberalization of entry conditions and the harmonization of treatment standards, as evidenced by OECD Codes in these fields.[29] The leading home states are concerned to extend these principles to all host states, as shown by their willingness to conclude investor protection treaties with such states, and their support for multilateral investment rules.[30]

That home states should do so indicates an increasing willingness on their part to use their political and economic power to protect the global interests of their corporations. It is an important feature in the emerging new international regulatory framework, which will be considered in Part IV. In addition, home states may increasingly adopt policies that seek to strengthen the competitiveness of home based MNEs. This could range from the giving of political and diplomatic support for new investment opportunities by way of improved relations with potential host states, to the monitoring of host state policies that give rise to discrimination

---

[25] See eg the discussion of US interests in C Fred Bergsten, T Horst and T Moran *American Multinationals and American Interests* (Washington DC: Brookings Institution, 1978); on UK interests: JM Stopford and L Turner *Britain and the Multinationals* (Chichester: John Wiley/IRM, 1985) ch 8; on Swedish interests: E Hornall and J Vahlne *Multinationals: The Swedish Case* (Croom Helm, 1986); on Japanese interests, see JH Dunning *Multinational Enterprises and the Global Economy* (Wokingham: Addison-Wesley, 1993) at 568–69.

[26] See further Gardner 'The Transnational Corporation and the Home Country' 15 Col. J.Transnt.L. 369 (1976). Jones asserts that home country and MNE interests may not always coincide and the gains to the home economy are not always positive: above n 5 ch 9. See also 'Decoupled: The Health of Companies and the Wealth of Economies No Longer Go Together' *The Economist* 25 February 2006 at 81.

[27] As under the now repealed UK Exchange Control Act 1947, on which see Neil Hood and Stephen Young *The Economics of Multinational Enterprise* (London: Longman, 1979) at 307–310.

[28] See ch 7 at 265.   [29] See n 17.   [30] See ch 17.

against home firms, and to more general matters, such as the improvement of education and infrastructure in the home state, that act as a means of preserving the competitive advantage of home based firms.[31]

From the preceding discussion, the implication for policy-makers in nation states is that, when developing national economic policy, they must evolve approaches to the operations of MNEs which serve to increase the benefits that their state can obtain from interactions with such firms. This raises the question of what those benefits may be. At this point difficulties of evaluation arise. In terms of economic theory, a broadly beneficial effect is predicted from increased flows of direct investment, in that these may make available a wider range of goods at lower cost than would be possible in a world of closed national markets.[32] Nonetheless, examples of economic gains from foreign direct investment can often be met by counter-examples of losses caused by the same process. The point can be illustrated by reference to four factors commonly mentioned in discussions of the costs and benefits of direct investment by MNEs, namely, employment levels, balance of payments considerations, technology and skills transfer, and competitive effects in the local economy.[33]

Regarding employment effects, it is argued that MNEs can enhance employment levels in a host state by importing new jobs. However, this must be weighed against possible job losses in less competitive domestic firms. Equally, the stability of the imported job must be taken into account. Is the job likely to be long term, or is it merely a short-term job given the extent of the foreign firm's commitment to the local economy? Furthermore, from the home state perspective, it is arguable that local jobs may be lost as domestic MNEs relocate employment to more advantageous foreign locations.[34] On the other hand, the creation of overseas jobs

---

[31] On which see further M Porter *The Competitive Advantage of Nations* (London: Macmillan, 1990). See also, on the power of MNEs to influence the economic policy agenda of home states by way of their 'embeddedness' in the state-finance-industry-labour policy networks of the home state, Razeen Sally 'Multinational Enterprises, Political Economy and Institutional Theory: Domestic Embeddedness in the Context of Internationalisation' in 1 Review of International Political Economy 161 (Spring 1994) and his book *States and Firms* (London: Routledge, 1995).

[32] See M Brech and M Sharp *Inward Investment: Policy Options for the United Kingdom* (RIIA/RKP, 1984) at 30.

[33] For an extensive discussion of the economic effects of MNEs on these four variables see JH Dunning above n 25 Part 3 'The Impact of MNE Activity'; Stopford and Turner above n 25 chs 6 and 7; UNCTAD *World Investment Report 1999* above n 24 which also discusses further social issues including environmental protection and corporate social responsibility. See Jones above n 5 ch 10 for a rather gloomy assessment of the historical effects of MNEs on host economies: 'If there is one lesson of history, it is that multinationals are not the panacea for economic growth ... Multinationals have not made the whole world rich. Their emergence and growth over the last 150 years has coincided with growing income disparity between countries, and within them': at 283–84.

[34] See, for a UK based study along these lines, F Gaffikin and A Nickson *Jobs Crisis and the Multinationals: De-industrialisation in the West Midlands* (Birmingham Trade Union Group for World Development, 1983). More recently the closure, in 2006, of the Peugeot plant in Coventry has brought back concerns over the durability of jobs in the plants of foreign owned firms in the UK. See James Arrowsmith 'Peugeot Announces Closure of Coventry Plant' (European Foundation for the Improvement of Living and Working Conditions, May 2006) available at <http://www.eiro.eurofound. eu.int/about/2006/05/articles/uk0605029i.html>.

may stimulate job creation in the home state as the MNE's international linkages develop.

Turning to balance of payments considerations, a host state's balance may be improved by the inflow of new capital represented by a direct investment. However, this initial effect must be weighed against the longer term outflow of capital through repayments of loans and through dividend remittances. Should these exceed the initial investment, then a net loss to the balance of payments will result. A similar result may occur if the local affiliate is highly integrated into the international production network of the MNE and is obliged to purchase inputs from affiliates in other states to an amount that exceeds the initial inflow of capital. However, such effects may be offset by a positive export performance from the MNE affiliate. The temptation may be for the host state to impose export requirements on the foreign firm as a condition of entry. Similarly, costly imports of inputs may be controlled by requiring the local affiliate to use locally produced inputs. As will be seen in chapter 6, such performance requirements have become objects of considerable dispute between capital-exporting and capital-importing states.

On the question of technology and skills transfer, it is argued that MNEs, as the principal holders of advanced productive technology and managerial skills, can enhance a host economy through the transfer and dissemination of such competitive benefits. This argument depends on the willingness of the MNE to share its competitive advantages with local firms and workers. If the technology and know-how involved are unique, it is unlikely that the MNE will readily give up its lead by disseminating its knowledge. It would be most likely to set up a wholly owned subsidiary in the host state, so as to control the use of its technology and skills. Alternatively, it might enter into licensing agreements that impose restrictive terms on the licensee as to the use and dissemination of the technology. In either case employees using the technology may be subjected to restrictive covenants as to subsequent employment with competitors. These issues will be considered further in chapter 11.

Finally, on the question of the competitive effects of foreign direct investment on the host economy, it is often asserted that MNEs will spur domestic firms into greater efficiency by exposing them to new competition. However, as Brech and Sharp point out, in the absence of significant spill-over effects that make new techniques available to local firms, and in the absence of adequate investment capital for local firms to develop, the net result may be that the foreign firm will crowd the local competition out. Given the highly concentrated nature of many of the markets in which MNEs operate, significant anti-competitive effects may result.[35]

In the light of the uncertainty over the actual effects of FDI by MNEs, and attendant ideological and social factors, regulatory responses to the operations of MNEs have been uneven over time.[36] They have oscillated between open policies

---

[35] Above n 32 at 37–38.

[36] See A Edward Safarian 'Host Country Policies Towards Inward Foreign Direct Investment in the 1950s and 1990s' 8 Transnational Corporations 93 (No 2 1999); Jones above n 5 ch 8. See also on

in the 1950s to restrictive policies in the 1960s and 1970s. This culminated, in the mid-1970s, with the adoption of UN resolutions calling for the establishment of a New International Economic Order (NIEO), with its emphasis on sovereign rights to regulate and control foreign investors and their investments, and on the recognition of permanent national sovereignty over natural wealth and resources.[37] More recently, in the 1980s and 1990s, such sovereignty-oriented challenges appear to have been mitigated and replaced by a more open door to FDI and the acceptance of international treaty based standards of treatment as the benchmark for national regulation.[38] This can be explained by a number of factors: first, the demise of the Socialist Bloc, which brought to an end the Cold War, with its attendant clash of ideologies and alliances, and which gave rise to the process of transition to market based economies in the states of the former Soviet Union and Central and Eastern Europe; secondly, the effects of the debt crisis of the early 1980s upon the availability of public and private sector loan capital, which rendered FDI the major source of capital especially in developing countries;[39] thirdly, the increased acceptance by governments of market based approaches to economic development, in both developed and developing countries, resulting in the processes of liberalization, privatization, and gradual deregulation of national economies.[40] This last factor may be said to arise directly out of the underlying process of economic globalization that is being driven by increased transnational economic integration through the growth of transnational production chains dominated by MNEs or through interlinked alliances of free-standing firms.[41] To be successful such modes of production will require large areas of economic and regulatory uniformity across national boundaries. Hence it may be said that economic globalization contains a built in 'bias' in favour of liberalized national economic policies and pro-investor approaches to international business regulation, such as the conclusion of Bilateral Investment Treaties (BITs). This 'bias' will stimulate increased cross-border investment flows and allow for deeper integration. Such integration, it is said, will allow for the further growth of the global economy and will ensure the increased participation within that economy of developing as well as developed countries.[42] It may also require limits upon the sovereign right of states to regulate, as they please, economic activity within their borders.

---

the case of Korea William A Stoever 'Attempting to Resolve the Attraction-Aversion Dilemma: A Study of FDI Policy in the Republic of Korea' 11 Transnational Corporations 49 (No 1, 2002).

[37] See further below at 119–20.

[38] UNCTAD has noted a regular rise in national and treaty based liberalization measures in successive issues of the annual *World Investment Report* commencing in 1991. See, for example, the *World Investment Report 2005* (New York and Geneva: United Nations, 2005) at 22–23. See further chs 5 and 6.

[39] See UNCTAD *World Investment Report 1992* (New York: United Nations, 1992) at 101; see further JH Dunning above n 25 ch 2.

[40] See generally Robert Gilpin *The Challenge of Global Capitalism* (Princeton: Princeton University Press, 2000) ch 2 'The Second Great Age of Capitalism'.   [41] See ch 1.

[42] See further Martin Wolf *Why Globalization Works: the Case for the Global Market Economy* (New Haven and London: Yale University Press, 2004). For evidence that BITs can lead to an increase in FDI see Jeswald W Salacuse and Nicholas P Sullivan 'Do BITs Really Work? An Evaluation of

(3) The Role of Ideology

Given the uncertainties that surround the evaluation of MNE effects on home and host states' economies, there has evolved a significant ideological conflict over this issue, resulting in differing conceptions of the political economy of foreign investment, and in distinct policy prescriptions. The evolution of this debate can be organized around two main periods. The first reflects the 'building blocks' of the policy debate on MNEs and covers the original ideological inputs that were key from the 1960s to the 1990s. The second begins with the advent of discussions surrounding the idea of 'globalization' during the 1990s to the present.

(a) The Ideological 'Building Blocks': 1960–1990

In the first period, four major ideological strands can be identified. These are: the 'neo-classical market analysis' of the MNE, the 'regulated market perspective', the 'Marxist' perspective, and the 'nationalist' perspective.[43] They have each made significant contributions to the development of MNE policy and still retain significant influence.

(i) The 'Neo-Classical Market' Perspective

This starts from the assumption that the market, as the most efficient allocator of resources, should be allowed to operate with as little regulatory interference as possible. In the sphere of international economics, this leads to a preference for an 'open' international economy with minimal state or international regulation.[44] States should then be free to specialize in the production and sale of those commodities which they can make most efficiently, and to trade them for other

---

Bilateral Investment Treaties and their Grand Bargain' 46 Harv.ILJ 68 (2005); Eric Newmayer and Laura Spess (2005) 'Do Bilateral Treaties Increase Foreign Direct Investment to Developing Countries?' 33 World Development 1567 (2005) available online at <http://eprints.lse.ac.uk/archive/00000627/>, and see Kenneth J Vandevelde 'Investment Liberalization and Economic Development: The Role of Bilateral Investment Treaties' 36 Col.J.TransnatL. 501 (1998). A study by UNCTAD suggests that the influence of such treaties may be marginal to investment flows: UNCTAD *Bilateral Investment Treaties in the Mid-1990s* (New York and Geneva: United Nations, 1998) ch IV. See also *World Investment Report 2003* above n 12 at 89–90.

[43] 'Neo-classical market analysis' refers to theories based on classical market theory of value; 'regulated market perspective' refers to the dominant economic theories used by post-Second World War governments in the 1950s to 1970s to direct their economic policy, based on Keynesian cost-of-production theories; 'Marxist perspective' refers to theories based on the Marxist concepts of labour surplus value and monopoly; the 'nationalist perspective' refers to economic policies designed to strengthen national wealth and sovereignty. For a fuller analysis of the ideological dimension of international political economy and its contribution to earlier debates on MNE policy see Chris Edwards *The Fragmented World* (London: Methuen, 1985) and Hood and Young above n 27 ch 8.

[44] See, for a useful introduction to 'neo-classical' or 'neo-liberal' theories of international economic organization, Razeen Sally *Classical Liberalism and International Economic Order* (London: Routledge, 1997).

commodities made more cheaply by other states. This should lead to a globally efficient economy and to a rational international division of labour. In this process the MNE is an important 'medium for integrating and organising resource utilisation on a global scale'.[45] It acts as a means by which different national economies, with different comparative advantages in skills, labour, raw materials, and know-how, can be integrated through the international division of labour within the enterprise. Crucial to this is a world economy in which the MNE is free to set up affiliates whenever and wherever it wishes, to engage in uninhibited intrafirm trade, and trade with third parties. Given such conditions the MNE's operations are presumed to improve global welfare.

Although many states have pursued an 'open door' approach to foreign investment,[46] MNEs do not operate in a world free from restrictions on their activities even in so-called 'open door' economies. This fact has prompted neo-classical economists to dismiss intervention in the form of restrictions on foreign investment as being very wasteful of resources both nationally and internationally. Furthermore, they argue that such restrictions would fail to achieve the major economic objective of foreign direct investment, namely, the transfer and acquisition of productive knowledge.[47] However, such views have been criticized as failing to appreciate the difficulties involved in securing an equal international spread of benefits from foreign direct investment. This issue is taken up by the 'regulated market' school on policy towards MNEs.

(ii) The 'Regulated Market Perspective'

This approach goes beyond the neo-classical perspective's faith in a free and unregulated market as the ultimate source of economic efficiency and human welfare. Rather, this perspective argues that markets can cause imperfect allocations of resources because they are distorted by the costs of technology and the costs associated with the distribution of resources and products. This leads to a non-coincidence in the market between the supply of, and demand for, products and services, resulting in distributional conflicts. Such conflicts must be diminished or, if possible, eradicated by selective public sector intervention in the economy.

The large, managerially controlled corporation is identified as a major source of market failure. Through its size and technological capability the large corporation can monopolize and distort product markets, undermine consumer choice through advertising, avoid stock market regulation by becoming self-financing through reinvestment of profits, and avoid making losses that smaller firms cannot avoid. Thus, the corporation must be regulated to prevent these consequences. Such regulation could take a 'low intervention' or 'high intervention' perspective. At the

---

[45] Hood and Young above n 27 at 327.   [46] See ch 6 for examples.
[47] See, for example, HG Johnson 'The Efficiency and Welfare Implications of the International Corporation' in C Kindleberger (ed) *The International Corporation* (Cambridge, Mass: MIT Press, 1970) 35.

low end the so-called 'managerialists' suggest that corporate managers could be expected to take public interest, as well as profit orientated, decisions, thereby ensuring that firms act in a socially responsible way.[48] On an intermediate level the state itself can direct corporate policy through legal reforms of corporate structures and duties, ensuring that the interests of groups affected by corporate decisions will be taken into account. This is the idea of 'corporate governance'. Finally, at the 'high intervention' end there is the policy of 'corporatism' where the interests of capital, labour and society interact through public bodies, composed of governmental, business and labour interests that are dedicated to national economic planning. At this point the market is greatly curtailed as the major source of economic organization.

During the late 1960s and early 1970s many of the ideas developed by this school formed the basis of the mainstream critique and policy response to the rise of MNEs.[49] MNEs are seen as carrying the monopolistic and anti-competitive tendencies identified in large national corporations onto an international stage. There they can reproduce the same dangers of market failure. This requires selective and flexible state intervention for the minimization of the costs of MNE operations. Furthermore, should state control be ineffective, measures of supranational control through regional and universal international organizations may be required.[50] However, it is accepted that MNEs may bring net benefits to the world economy along the lines suggested in neo-classical analysis. Thus over-restrictive controls are seen as self-defeating. The result is a policy of accommodation between the MNE and the nation state. Thus, regulated market analysis has had a marked influence upon the evolution of MNE control policy. In some respects its more radical recommendations (such as nationalization or strict entry controls over foreign investors) are hard to distinguish from those advocated by adherents of the 'Marxist' school.

(iii) The 'Marxist' Perspective

This approach centres on the exploitative aspects of capitalism in the international economy.[51] Building upon Marx's theories of the concentration of capital, labour exploitation, and the division of labour in society,[52] subsequent writers have developed theories of 'monopoly capitalism' and 'imperialism' to explain the operation of international capitalism.[53] The thesis is that the tendency of national capitalist

---

[48] See eg A Bearle and G Means *The Modern Corporation and Private Property* (Harvest Books, 1968) 309–313; JK Galbraith *The New Industrial State* (London: Pelican, 1972).

[49] See, for example, the UN Group of Eminent Persons Report of 1974 discussed below at 119–20 and the various codes of conduct discussed in ch 17.

[50] See Raymond Vernon *Sovereignty at Bay* (London: Pelican, 1973) at 260–71.

[51] For a full discussion see Anthony Brewer *Marxist Theories of Imperialism* (Routledge & Kegan Paul, 2nd edn, 1990).

[52] See Karl Marx *Capital Vol I* (London: Lawrence & Wishart 1970) 350–68 and ch XXV.

[53] The connection between 'monopolies' and 'imperialism' was explained by R Hilferding in *Finance Capital* (1910, published in English by Routlege & Kegan Paul, 1981). See also N Bhukarin

industry to move towards 'monopoly' (used here to denote not single firm dom-inance but market concentration in general) prompts the export of capital. The character of the capital exported is significant. It is described as 'finance capital', a term denoting the merger between 'financial capital' (money capital dealt with by banks and other financial enterprises) and 'industrial capital' (capital employed by productive enterprises). This fusion of concepts, introduced by Hilferding, permits the view that, for the purposes of international investment, the functions of finan-cing and controlling the investment can be united in a single enterprise. As Anthony Brewer notes, 'if this generalisation of the concept is accepted, it opens the way to regarding the large multinational companies of today as part of finance capital',[54] since such companies engage in both of the above mentioned functions.

The early Marxist model of capitalist imperialism does not address certain modern concerns. In particular, it has little to say about the impact of capitalism on underdeveloped countries, other than offering a vague expectation of capitalist development within them. Nor does it consider in detail the role of MNEs in the world economy, although, as noted above, the concept of 'finance capital' could extend to such enterprises. More recent writings of Marxists from Western and Southern states have attempted to fill the gap.[55] Their starting point is the concept of a division in the world economy between the advanced 'core' countries of the capitalist North and the underdeveloped 'periphery' countries of the economically dependent South. The latter are said to be in a position of permanent disadvan-tage due to the particular way in which they have been linked to the advanced cap-italist economies.

The MNE has been fitted into this 'centre/periphery' model of underdevelop-ment. By means of its international integration the MNE is said to act as an agent of underdevelopment. It has the power to control both the flow of commodities and products out of developing countries and the degree of inward investment, because of its monopolistic control of the market(s) concerned. Furthermore, Hymer has argued that the MNE reproduces 'centre/periphery relations' within itself through the hierarchical division of authority in the firm between the high-est levels of management in the home country of the parent, intermediate man-agement in regional sub-centres, and the lowest levels of management in the branch plants located in developing countries. This management structure re-emphasizes 'core country' control through the increasing exclusion of 'peripheral country' nationals from managerial posts higher up the corporate hierarchy. At the lower

Imperialism and World Economy (1917, published in English by Merlin, 1972). Their theories were made popular by VI Lenin in his pamphlet *Imperialism: The Highest Stage of Capitalism* in VI Lenin *Selected Works* (English edn Moscow 1952 Vol 1 Part 2 or Foreign Languages Press, Beijing, 1975).

[54] Above n 51 at 93.

[55] Among the leading works in this context are P Baran *The Political Economy of Growth* (Pelican, 1973; first published 1957); AG Frank *Capitalism and Underdevelopment in Latin America* (Modern Reader Paperbacks, 1969; first published 1967); S Amin *Unequal Development* (Monthly Review Press, 1976; originally in French, 1973). For full discussion see Brewer above n 51.

levels, managers in the developing countries form a local interest group that can influence national economic policy in favour of the MNE, at the expense of the host state's real interests.[56]

These views have been the subject of extensive critical writing since the early 1970s. Two major strands of criticism are worth noting. First, some writers felt that the conventional Marxist analysis presented above underestimated the extent to which capitalist penetration of the 'peripheral' countries had in fact led to economic growth.[57] Secondly, others criticized this approach as paying too much attention to relations between states. In the process the 'new international division of labour', which serves to internationalize the class conflict between capital and labour, is ignored. Furthermore, this division of labour occurs not only through the medium of the MNE but also through transnational sub-contracting between firms.[58] Thus a MNE orientated model of international capital exploitation is seen as incomplete.

In the early 1970s the monopolistic and imperialistic theory of the MNE held sway on the left and with it a nationalistic policy response was recommended. In particular, the extensive nationalization of the 'commanding heights' of the national economy was recommended, with the result that the parent companies of the leading home-based MNEs and the major subsidiaries of foreign-owned MNEs would be brought into public ownership.[59] This approach will now be contrasted with other theories of nationalism as a theoretical foundation for MNE regulation.

(iv) The Influence of Nationalism[60]

The debate on MNEs cannot be regarded in exclusively economic terms. It contains the further issues of national independence, self-determination, and cultural autonomy. The underlying fear is that large foreign firms have sufficient power, first, to undermine the host state's political and economic independence[61] and, secondly, to threaten cultural identity by displacing locally created tastes and values with imported substitutes, spurred on by advertising through the transnational

[56] Stephen Hymer 'The Multinational Corporation and the Law of Uneven Development' in H Radice (ed) *International Firms and Modern Imperialism* (London: Pelican, 1975) 37 or in J Bhagwati (ed) *Economics and World Order From the 1970s to the 1980s* (1972) 113.

[57] See Bill Warren 'Imperialism and Capitalist Industrialisation' New Left Review 81 (1973) 3, *Imperialism: Pioneer of Capitalism* (New Left Books, l980). See also J Petras and D Engbarth 'Third World Industrialisation and Trade Union Struggles' in R Southall (ed) *Trade Unions and the Industrialisation of the Third World* (London: Zed Books, 1988) 81.

[58] See Olle and Scholler 'Direct Investment and Monopoly Theories of Capitalism' 16 Capital and Class 41 (1982); K Cowling and R Sugden *Transnational Monopoly Capitalism* (Brighton: Wheatsheaf Books, l987); F Frobel, J Heinrichs, and O Kreye *The New International Division of Labour* (Cambridge: Cambridge University Press, 1980).

[59] See Stuart Holland *The Socialist Challenge* (Quartet Books, 1976). This book represents the thinking that influenced the British Labour Party's Alternative Economic Strategy in the 1970s.

[60] See Peter T Muchlinski 'Economic Nationalism and the Regulation of Multinational Enterprises' in A Carty and H Singer (eds) *Conflict and Change in the 1990s* (London: Macmillan, 1993) 138.

[61] Through, for example, the manipulation of markets, employment, and sympathetic social groups and politicians.

media corporations.[62] Consequently, states may impose controls on MNEs that are not justifiable in economic terms, at least on a neo-classical analysis.

According to neo-classical economists, it remains to be shown that it is valuable to have certain kinds of production controlled by resident nationals rather than foreigners.[63] The return on transferring or preserving national investment is the availability of high-income jobs for members of the national or ethnic groups in question, when such jobs are transferred from foreigners to that group. This is accompanied by a non-monetary reward in terms of pride or a sense of identity.[64] Such nationalism may risk damaging the competitiveness of the economy, through the replacement of highly skilled foreigners by less skilled nationals, excessive numbers of employees, excessive stress on 'prestige' manufacturing industries at the cost of industries in which the country has a genuine comparative advantage, and through undue stress on state planning in place of the market.[65]

The neo-classical approach to economic nationalism may be contrasted with the pronationalistic sentiments of 'dependency theory'. This label covers a wide range of writings and in no way reflects a common ideological position.[66] Rather, it is an expression bringing together writers of differing political and economic backgrounds who agree on the basic thesis that the underdeveloped nations of the 'Third World' are in a relation of economic dependency towards the rich nations of the North, and can only achieve true economic development by greater national control over the economy, whether by means of the greater regulation of foreign trade and investment within the capitalist system, or, as recommended by Marxists, through withdrawal from that system.[67]

The aspiration towards economic and political sovereignty has been a continuous theme throughout the MNE debate. It serves to explain why an 'economically inefficient' response has been taken in certain cases. Furthermore, 'nationalism' informs state policy in both capitalist and non-capitalist states and regions. It cuts across the traditional 'left/right' axis of political economy, and introduces a complementary 'national/international' axis.[68] It can produce curious alliances. For

---

[62] On which see further A Mattelart *Transnationals and the Third World: The Struggle for Culture* (Massachusetts: Bergin and Garvey Inc, 1983); Leslie Sklair *Globalization: Capitalism and its Alternatives* (Oxford: Oxford University Press, 2002) ch 5 'Transnational Practices: Corporations, Class and Consumerism'.

[63] See Albert Breton 'The Economics of Nationalism' LXXII Journal of Political Economy 376–86 (1964). [64] ibid at 379.

[65] HG Johnson 'A Theoretical Model of Economic Nationalism in New and Developing States' LXXX Political Science Quarterly 169 (June 1965).

[66] For a full analysis of 'dependency' theories, see Gabriel Palma 'Dependency and Development: A Critical Overview' in D Seers (ed) *Dependency Theory: A Critical Reassessment* (Frances Pinter, 1981) 20.

[67] The foreign investment policy of the Andean Common Market (ANCOM) offers a good example of a policy based on the non-Marxist version of 'dependency' analysis. See the original version of the Andean Foreign Investment Code: 11 ILM 126 (1972) revised text 16 ILM 138 (1977), discussed in ch 17. The Andean Pact represents what Dudley Seers called 'extended nationalism': see Dudley Seers *The Political Economy of Nationalism* (Oxford: Oxford University Press, 1983).

[68] See further Seers ibid ch 2.

example, in Chile, during the early 1950s, not only the political left, informed by ideas of 'neo-colonialism', supported the increase of control over US copper companies but also the political right, who felt that without greater national control over the economy, they could never enjoy the benefits of capitalism to the full. Indeed, by the late 1960s, a broad political spectrum favoured the outright nationalization of the copper companies. The process began in the mid-1960s with the 'Chileanization' of these companies through increased public share-ownership and state control initiated by the centre-right government of Eduardo Frei. Salvador Allende's Marxist government brought this process to its logical conclusion when the US copper companies were fully nationalized in 1970–71.

The preceding discussion should not be interpreted as saying that all controls over MNEs are inspired by nationalism. Equally, not all states have pursued restrictive policies on MNEs as an outcome of nationalistic planning. Some have chosen to follow the neo-classical prescription that an 'open door' to foreign firms is the best way to serve the national interest. Significant examples exist of spectacular economic growth, and rising living standards for the mass of the population, in developing countries in South East Asia that have followed this approach.[69] Indeed, such states pose a challenge to the traditional prediction of 'dependency theory' that peripheral economies are doomed to permanent underdevelopment, and suggest that state-inspired entrepreneurship can produce growth.

(b) The Influence of the Debate on 'Globalization'

More recently, new perspectives have emerged as part of the redefinition of earlier debates in the context of the contemporary concern over globalization, itself an ideologically contested concept.[70] Two approaches appear to have long-term significance. These are a developing concept of 'global consumerism' and the increasingly discussed 'international corporate social responsibility' perspective. Before these are considered in more detail, the concept of globalization and how it has influenced the debate on MNE regulation will be briefly discussed.

(i) Globalization and MNE Regulation[71]

The parameters of the debate on globalization have distinct echoes in the debate over the content and future direction of investment law. Held et al have identified three major positions in the debate:[72] first, the '*hyperglobalists*' who stress the

---

[69] For example: Singapore, Taiwan, Hong Kong. See further M Smith et al *Asia's New Industrial World* (Methuen, 1985); L Turner and N McMullen (eds) *The Newly Industrializing Countries: Trade and Adjustment* (RIIA/George Allen & Unwin, 1982).

[70] On which see further Peter T Muchlinski 'Globalization and Legal Research' above n 16.

[71] This section draws upon the author's ILA manuscript above n 4 and upon Peter T Muchlinski 'Globalization and Legal Research' ibid at 223–25.

[72] David Held et al *Global Transformations: Politics Economics and Culture* (Cambridge: Polity Press, 1999) at 2–10.

displacement of national economies by transnational production, trade and financial networks, operating in an increasingly liberal global market order;[73] secondly, the '*sceptics*' who doubt whether the economic evidence shows any real increase in international economic activity as compared with the period up to 1914, or that production chains are as global as some have asserted,[74] and, thirdly, the '*transformationalists*' who see the levels of transnational economic integration as unprecedented, and who feel that globalization is giving rise to a fundamental restructuring of power in a world where there is no longer a clear distinction between local, national, or international affairs. However, they do not share the 'hyperglobalist' view that this is leading inexorably towards a global free market. A further distinction should be drawn between those who see globalization as a real phenomenon, whether they agree with the 'hyperglobalist' faith in global free markets or not (as in the case of the so-called 'anti-globalization' movement[75]) – the '*globalists*' – and those who deny the reality of globalization – the '*anti-globalists*'.[76] Views belonging to the latter group can range from the above mentioned 'sceptics', who assert that globalization is a myth generated to support neo-liberal policies, aimed at the deregulation of trade, investment, and financial flows, to outright nationalists, or religious fundamentalists, who reject the very notion of an integrating global economy as 'a good thing'.[77]

From this brief review of positions on globalization, the major strands in the debate on foreign investment law can be identified. Thus a 'hyperglobalist' perspective can be seen among those who favour the full liberalization of investment barriers, leading to a more open and competitive global market for FDI, and the application of state-of-the-art protection for investors in international investment agreements (IIAs). This may be said to constitute the contemporary response of neo-liberals to the globalization issue. On the other hand, a 'sceptical' position is

---

[73] See, for example, Kenichi Ohmae *The End of the Nation-State* (New York: Free Press, 1995).

[74] See also David Hurst and Grahame Thompson *Globalisation in Question* (Cambridge: Polity Press, 2nd edn, 1999). Held et al dispute the empirical basis of Hurst and Thompson's thesis, arguing that the changes in productive processes that MNEs have instituted do enhance the structural power of corporate capital at the expense of the nation state creating new issues of governance: see Held et al above n 72 at 281–82.

[75] See, for example, Naomi Kline *No Logo* (London: Flamingo Harper-Collins, 2000) who does not reject the notion of global integration of production as such, but rather calls for stronger regulation, by IGOs, of corporate abuses. By contrast some do reject the very process of global economic integration and wish to reverse it. See, for example, Colin Hines *Localisation: A Global Manifesto* (London: Earthscan, 2000).

[76] Jan Aart Scholte *Globalization: A Critical Introduction* (Basingstoke: Palgrave, 2000) at 17–18.

[77] See Vincent Cable *Globalization and Global Governance* (London: RIIA, 1999) ch 7. The ideas of the late Sir James Goldsmith, founder of the UK Referendum Party perhaps come closest to exemplifying the nationalist perspective: see his book *The Trap* (London: MacMillan, 1996). Equally, the politics of ethnic or religious identity can act as a spur to anti-globalist perspectives. See, for example, the effect of the rise of Islamic fundamentalism discussed by Ankie Hoogvelt in *Globalization and the Postcolonial World* (Basingstoke: Palgrave, 2nd edn, 2001) ch 9. 'Islamic Revolt'. Arguably Islamic fundamentalists argue for an Islamic form of global order and are not strictly 'anti-globalists'. However, their opposition to the currently dominant Western model of globalization permits them to be so classified.

taken by those who remain to be convinced that full liberalization is necessary, and who wish to retain a high degree of state discretion in policy formation and control. It may be said that a number of leading developing countries take such a position, as is evidenced by discussions in the WTO Working Group on Trade and Investment, and by the opposition, on the part of such countries to the commencement of negotiations over investment issues at Cancun in 2003.[78] In addition some, but by no means all, civil society groups and NGOs, that are concerned about the adverse effects of economic globalization, may follow this position. They are not inheritors of the traditional anti-capitalist perspectives of Marxism, although they may share some of its concerns over the adverse consequences of untrammelled capitalist production.[79]

A middle way between these positions may be said to be emerging from the work of UNCTAD. This may be said to have elements of a 'transformationalist' perspective, in that the reality of globalization is accepted and the need for some fundamental reconsideration of its regulatory consequences is required. In relation to investment issues, the fundamental starting point is an acceptance that FDI is, in general, beneficial to national economies, including those of developing countries.[80] Thus, on the whole, a policy of liberalization and protection of investors can be welcomed and appropriate obligations in IIAs can be undertaken. On the other hand, such an approach may have to be mitigated in IIAs to allow for the preservation of 'national policy space' in the development of national economic policy, and the 'right to regulate' economic activity within national borders.[81] This is especially the case for developing countries that may have greater difficulties than developed countries in opening up their economies to the full force of global competition. According to UNCTAD, in order to reap the full benefits from FDI, the developing host country may need to supplement an open approach to inward investment with further policies. In particular, it may need positive measures to increase the contribution of foreign affiliates to the host country through mandatory measures such as, for example, performance requirements and through the encouragement of desired action by affiliates through, for example, incentives to transfer technology and to create local R&D capacity. Such policy measures entail a degree of regulation. This may involve some measure of intervention in the freedom of action of the foreign investor and controls over the manner in which the investment can evolve. In turn this balance needs to be

---

[78] On the wider issues behind this scepticism, see Stephen Young and Ana Teresa Tavares 'Multilateral rules on FDI: Do We Need Them? Will We Get Them? A Developing Country Perspective' 13 Transnational Corporations 1 (No 1 2004).

[79] For a collection of essays written from a Marxist perspective see R Burbach, O Nunez, and B Kagarlitsky *Globalization and its Discontents: The Rise of Postmodern Socialisms* (London: Pluto Press, 1997).

[80] See *World Investment Report 2003* above n 12 at 85–88. The UN Global Compact is also in essence pro investment: see <http://www.globalcompact.org>.

[81] See *World Investment Report 2003* ibid ch V; UNCTAD *Right to Regulate* (forthcoming).

maintained in IIAs which should offer a degree of flexibility for development.[82] As such the UNCTAD position can be seen as a restatement of the 'regulated market' approach to FDI policy placed in the context of a globalizing economy.

(ii) 'Global Consumerism'[83]

This concept seeks to identify the social and cultural effects of the expansion of global firms producing goods for private consumption. It posits the creation of an emergent global culture based on the goods and services offered by MNEs, which form a lifestyle distinct from that traditionally experienced by the population in a host state. Of particular significance is the role of transnational media and advertising corporations as the creators of images that encourage the development of consumer tastes which fit with the products and services offered by MNEs.[84]

In response to the threat of foreign cultural domination, many states have seen fit to protect their cultural industries – in particular the mass media – from foreign control, either by means of restrictions or by outright prohibitions on foreign ownership. On the other hand, as consumer choices move towards the acquisition of globally marketed products, policy-makers may be more concerned about the satisfaction of such wants, rather than their curtailment, especially if the consumers in question form a politically influential section of the community.[85] This will be the case in lower income societies, where only the more affluent and more influential may be in a position to buy such goods and services.[86]

The emerging ideology of 'global consumerism' has continued faith in economic growth and increasing consumption as a valid goal of economic and social policy. It is, in effect, the ideological justification for the neo-liberal economic order that is currently ascendant. In this it fits well into the increasingly individualized culture of identity and lifestyle politics that has arisen since the 1960s. This has

---

[82] See further UNCTAD *International Investment Agreements: Flexibility for Development* (New York and Geneva: United Nations, 2000).

[83] See Sklair above n 62 ch 7 'The Culture-Ideology of Consumerism', Jones above n 5 at 278–82. See further Yiannis Gabriel and Tim Lang *The Unmanageable Consumer* (Sage Publications, 2nd edn, 2006).

[84] See David Korten *When Corporations Rule the World* (West Hartford, Conn: Kumarian Press, 1995) ch 11 'Marketing the World'.

[85] See Kenichi Ohmae *The Borderless World: Power and Strategy in an Interlinked World* (London: Fontana, 1991) at x–xi.

[86] See UNCTC *Transnational Corporations in World Development* (New York: United Nations, 1988) at 222–25. See also Bennett and Sharpe 'Agenda Setting and Bargaining Power: The Mexican State Versus Transnational Automobile Corporations' 32 World Politics 57 at 76 (1979–80). Bennett and Sharpe argue that, in relation to consumer tastes in cars, the Mexican middle classes 'wanted what they had become accustomed to: modern, US style products. A Mexican car would not have been acceptable. The relationship of the Mexican state to its national bourgeoisie thus demanded that Mexico needed the sort of automobile industry that only transnational firms could provide'. In the former communist states of Eastern Europe, increased access to globally branded goods is popularly seen as a yardstick for measuring the success of the transition to market economies. Again it is the newly rich entrepreneurial classes that are in the best position to satisfy their wants. See Guy de Jonquieres 'From Bare Shelves to Blue Jeans' *Financial Times* 10 June 1992 18.

had the effect of supplementing, if not actually subordinating, traditional debates about economic distribution and class conflict, characteristic of the left/right split that dominated the 20th century, with the more personal issues of race, gender, sexual orientation, youth culture, and the concerns of the affluent elderly.[87]

The rise in concern over the socially responsible corporation is another example of this perspective. The desire of the 'ethical consumer' to purchase products and services from an 'ethical corporation' may be seen as an identity and lifestyle statement. As noted above, MNEs are purveyors of lifestyles and identities through their products and services. Consumers select their lifestyles and identities through their patterns of consumption. The 'ethical consumer' has thus become a target for the 'ethical corporation'. In effect, a market for socially responsible products and services has resulted.[88] Whether such a market can be said to be truly global remains to be seen. It appears at present to be a phenomenon in predominantly affluent societies. In developing countries the problem remains one of uneven access to consumer goods produced by MNEs with consumption favouring the privileged.[89]

The social responsibility element of 'global consumerism' raises a possible contradiction. As a growth and consumption oriented ideology it may clash with the rising concern for environmental protection and sustainable development, which is usually treated as an aspect of ethical business practice. This paradox has been resolved by business initiatives which suggest that environmental concerns can be compatible with growth and consumption provided that firms produce recyclable products, replace renewable resources, conserve non-renewable resources and move to full environmental costing, allowing the market to dictate environmentally sound choices in terms of products and processes. This is known as 'eco-efficiency'. The concept will be studied in more detail in chapter 14 as will its regulatory implications.

(iii) 'International Corporate Social Responsibility'

The 'international corporate social responsibility' (ICSR) of MNEs can be seen as a response to popular perceptions concerning the loss of corporate accountability

---

[87] See Peter T Muchlinski 'Human Rights and Multinationals: Is There a Problem?' 77 International Affairs 31 at 34–35 (2001). See further Eric Hobsbawm in *Age of Extremes: the Short History of the Twentieth Century* (London: Abacus, 1995) ch 11; Mark Mazower *Dark Continent: Europe's Twentieth Century* (Harmondsworth: Penguin, 1999) 356–63; Manuel Castells *The Information Age: Economy Society and Culture Volume II: The Power of Identity* (Oxford: Blackwell Publishing, 2nd edn, 2004) chs 1, 3, and 4.

[88] Perhaps the best illustration is the rapid rise of the organic food industry. See, for the rise of this industry in the US, Samuel Fromartz *Organic Inc: Natural Foods and How they Grew* (Orlando, Fla: Harcourt Books, 2006). As demand grows the industry has begun to concentrate around major food multinationals: Michael Sligh and Carolyn Christman *Who Owns Organic? The Global Status, Prospects, and Challenges of a Changing Organic Market* (Rural Advancement Foundation International-USA, 2003) at <http://www.rafiusa.org/pubs/OrganicReport.pdf>.

[89] See Sklair above n 62 at 204.

as an effect of economic globalization.[90] It may be said to rest on the obligations that corporations owe to the societies in which they operate. This may be justified philosophically by appeals to a 'social contract' and to the need of all actors, including non-state actors, to observe the preservation of human dignity through adherence to fundamental human rights.[91] There remains a great deal of disagreement over the precise extent of this issue. Indeed, there are equally strong voices arguing that the whole question of ICSR is much exaggerated and may well lead to policies that will harm the beneficial effects of international business activity.[92]

Thus, the precise content of the ICSR discourse remains open to ideological contest. There are at least three main contemporary positions that can be discerned from the literature.[93] The first, a 'hard libertarian' position, adheres strictly to a Lockean version of the social contract and limits the ethical agenda to the protection of private property and basic market freedoms. It seeks no wider social duties to be observed by corporations and, indeed, sees such wide duties as being illegitimate. The second position, that of the 'neo-liberals' emphasizes the benefits of an 'economic constitution', based on international free trade and investment, but, unlike the libertarian position, it is not opposed to the protection of fundamental rights or the environment.[94] The precise role to be played by such standards is not fully explained, although there is a clear rejection of the 'right to development'. The third position, that of the 'regulatory functionalists', which includes both pro-market and (so-called) anti-capitalist positions,[95] sees serious problems in the unrestrained operation of MNEs in an increasingly deregulated (or under-regulated) global economy and seeks, in response, to develop a global

[90] See Korten above n 84 and Kline above n 75. For a more alarmist account see Noreena Hertz *The Silent Takeover: Global Capitalism and the Death of Democracy* (Arrow Books, 2002).

[91] See further Thomas Donaldson *The Ethics of International Business* (Oxford: Oxford University Press, UK paperback edn, 1992) and Peter T Muchlinski 'International Business Regulation: An Ethical Discourse in the Making?' in Tom Campbell and Seumas Miller (eds) *Human Rights and Moral Responsibilities of Corporate and Public Sector Organisations* (The Hague: Kluwer Law International, 2004) 81. See also ch 13.

[92] See, from a neo-liberal perspective, David Henderson *Misguided Virtue: False Notions of Corporate Social Responsibility* (Wellington: New Zealand Business Roundtable, 2001). For a critical development perspective, see Michael Blowfield and Jedrzej George Frynas (eds) 'Critical Perspectives on Corporate Social Responsibility' 81 International Affairs 3, May 2005.

[93] See Peter T Muchlinski 'Human Rights, Social Responsibility and the Regulation of International Business: The Development of International Standard by Intergovernmental Organizations' 3 Non-State Actors and International Law 123 at 124–26 (2003) on which the next two paragraphs draw.

[94] On which see further John H Jackson *The Jurisprudence of the GATT and WTO* (Cambridge: Cambridge University Press, 2000) ch 21 'World Trade Rules and Environmental Policies: Congruence or Conflict?' and E-U Petersmann 'Human Rights and International Economic Law in the 21st Century: The Need to Clarify Their Inter-relationships' 4 JIEL 3 (2001).

[95] See Donaldson above n 91 and Kline above n 75 as examples of each approach. The term 'regulatory functionalists' is borrowed from Martin Loughlin's *Public Law and Political Theory* (Oxford: Clarendon Press, 1992). It seeks to denote a tendency, which encompasses many shades of political opinion, with the common feature of an acceptance of governmental regulation, and a degree of scepticism towards the market as an appropriate method of social and economic organization. It is in essence the same as the 'regulated market' approach outlined earlier in the chapter.

code of corporate social responsibility. The current debate on ICSR is, in essence, a reformist debate rooted in an acceptance of some form of global market economy, not its rejection.[96]

The three main positions noted above are contesting the agendas of IGOs. Here it is important to note that different IGOs have different cultures that respond more or less sympathetically to each of the above positions. For example, it is hard to envisage UNCTAD ever denying the existence of a right to development as such, although it would be open to debate on what that right means in practice.[97] On the other hand, the WTO is often, perhaps not entirely accurately, seen as a purveyor of 'hard libertarianism'. It is, in fact, closer in detail to the 'neo-liberal' position, and in practice it is willing at least to hear out alternative social positions, as witnessed by the informal access now given to NGOs to WTO dispute settlement panels.[98] The World Bank, too, is engaged in dialogues with governments, development institutions, the business world, and NGOs as to the meaning, content, and operationalization of ICSR. So far, these have gone furthest in relation to the environmental monitoring of project proposals.[99]

ICSR obligations may be seen as the quid pro quo for the protection of investors and investments under international investment protection agreements and international economic rules such as those of the WTO.[100] Such obligations can be drawn rather widely.[101] For example, the OECD Guidelines for Multinational Enterprises contain a section on 'General Policies' which is worth reproducing in

---

[96] Henderson above n 92 sees this reformist process as motivated by a misunderstanding of the market mechanism and hostility to capitalism, especially on the part of certain NGOs. This is itself open to dispute.

[97] See further UNCTAD *International Investment Agreements: Flexibility for Development* above n 82.

[98] See J Dunoff 'The Misguided Debate Over NGO Participation at the WTO' 1 JIEL 433 (1998)

[99] See World Bank Group 'Corporate Social Responsibility and the World Bank Group' (Washington DC: Business Partnership and Outreach Group, Briefing Note 6, November 2000) and S Schlemmer-Schulte 'The World Bank and Human Rights' 4 Austrian Review of International and European Law 230 (1999).

[100] For a discussion of the concept of social responsibility and its implications for international standard setting and investment protection see UNCTAD *The Social Responsibility of Transnational Corporations* (New York and Geneva: United Nations, 1999); UNCTAD *World Investment Report 1999* (New York and Geneva: United Nations, 1999) ch XII; UNCTAD *World Investment Report 2003* (New York and Geneva: United Nations, 2003) ch VI. See also UNCTAD *Social Responsibility* UNCTAD Series on issues in international investment agreements (New York and Geneva: United Nations, 2001) all available online at <http://www.unctad.org/iia>.

[101] For instance, the Draft United Nations Code of Conduct on Transnational Corporations lists the obligations of transnational corporations (TNCs) across a wide range of issues dealing with such matters as respect for the sovereignty of the host state and its political system, respect for human rights, abstention from corrupt practices, refraining from using the economic power of the TNC in a manner damaging to the economic well-being of the countries in which a firm operates, including observance of tax and anti-monopoly laws, and ensuring full disclosure concerning the activities of the firm. See UNCTAD *International Investment Agreements: A Compendium* (New York and Geneva: United Nations, 1996) vol I at 161.

full as it offers what appears to be an emerging consensus on the social obligations of MNEs:[102]

Enterprises should take fully into account established policies in the countries in which they operate, and consider the views of other stakeholders. In this regard, enterprises should:

1. Contribute to economic, social and environmental progress with a view to achieving sustainable development.

2. Respect the human rights of those affected by their activities consistent with the host government's international obligations and commitments.

3. Encourage local capacity building through close co-operation with the local community, including business interests, as well as developing the enterprise's activities in domestic and foreign markets, consistent with the need for sound commercial practice.

4. Encourage human capital formation, in particular by creating employment opportunities and facilitating training opportunities for employees.

5. Refrain from seeking or accepting exemptions not contemplated in the statutory or regulatory framework related to environmental, health, safety, labour, taxation, financial incentives, or other issues.

6. Support and uphold good corporate governance principles and develop and apply good corporate governance practices.

7. Develop and apply effective self-regulatory practices and management systems that foster a relationship of confidence and mutual trust between enterprises and the societies in which they operate.

8. Promote employee awareness of, and compliance with, company policies through appropriate dissemination of these policies, including through training programmes.

9. Refrain from discriminatory or disciplinary action against employees who make bona fide reports to management or, as appropriate, to the competent authorities, on practices that contravene the law, the Guidelines or the enterprise's policies.

10. Encourage, where practicable, business partners, including suppliers and subcontractors, to apply principles of corporate conduct compatible with the Guidelines.

11. Abstain from any improper involvement in local political activities.[103]

As may be apparent from this wide-ranging list of issues, the precise classification of ICSR standards is difficult as, potentially, the phrase could cover all aspects of corporate regulation. By contrast, the UN Global Compact contains a more specific set of standards. The Ten Principles on which the Global Compact is founded concern the areas of human rights, labour, the environment, and anti-corruption. These are said to enjoy universal consensus and are derived from a number of significant international instruments.[104] From the above, it is clear that social

---

[102] The remaining chapters include: 'Disclosure, Employment and Industrial Relations, Environment, Combating Bribery, Consumer Interests, Science and Technology, Competition and Taxation'.

[103] OECD Guidelines for Multinational Enterprises, 27 June 2000, 3–4 available at <http://www.oecd.org/dataoecd/56/36/192248.pdf>.

[104] See further <http://www.unglobalcompact.org>. These are: The Universal Declaration of Human Rights; The International Labour Organization's Declaration on Fundamental Principles

responsibility may take both an economic and a social and ethical dimension in that MNEs are expected to conduct their economic affairs in good faith and in accordance with proper standards of economic activity, while also observing fundamental principles of good social and ethical conduct. The implications of this new dimension to the regulation of MNEs will be discussed in Part III.

(4) Bargaining Power, Sources and Sites of MNE Regulation

This section considers the boundaries and modalities of effective regulatory action. The discussion will commence by considering the issue of bargaining over controls between states and MNEs, seeking to identify how far each participant may enjoy the power to structure a regulatory environment favourable to their concerns. It will go on to outline the principal sources of regulatory standards, making the distinction between informal, non-binding, and formal, mandatory, sources. The discussion will end by considering the choice of 'sites' for regulation, distinguishing between self-regulation by MNEs, informal regulation by non-state actors, unilateral regulation at the national level, bilateral interstate regulation through a treaty regime, regional regulation through supranational organizations of states, and global regulation by multilateral treaty and/or through intergovernmental organizations.

(a) Bargaining Between States and MNEs

The discourse on bargaining between states and MNEs over deals, and the regulations that underpin them, has undergone a number of phases. The earliest accounts centre on bilateral negotiations between the host country and the MNE. This is still the most significant relationship. However, limiting analysis to this alone risks missing out on the importance of wider interactions between states and firms in the global market. In particular, the outcome of individual bilateral bargains cannot be properly assessed in isolation from the competitive situation in the given market. This will involve the need to understand the actions of the MNE's

---

and Rights at Work; The Rio Declaration on Environment and Development; and The United Nations Convention Against Corruption. The Global Compact asks companies to embrace, support, and enact, within their sphere of influence, a set of core values in the areas of human rights, labour standards, the environment, and anti-corruption: 'Human Rights: Principle 1: Businesses should support and respect the protection of internationally proclaimed human rights; and Principle 2: make sure that they are not complicit in human rights abuses. Labour Standards: Principle 3: Businesses should uphold the freedom of association and the effective recognition of the right to collective bargaining; Principle 4: the elimination of all forms of forced and compulsory labour; Principle 5: the effective abolition of child labour; and Principle 6: the elimination of discrimination in respect of employment and occupation. Environment: Principle 7: Businesses should support a precautionary approach to environmental challenges; Principle 8: undertake initiatives to promote greater environmental responsibility; and Principle 9: encourage the development and diffusion of environmentally friendly technologies. Anti-Corruption: Principle 10: Businesses should work against all forms of corruption, including extortion and bribery.'

competitors, the home states of all the market participants, and third states that may be active as competing locations for investment in the market in question. All these interactions will affect the bargaining power of the parties to the bilateral transaction.[105] In addition, the relocation of the state from its traditional position as the sole arbiter of regulation, and its relative weakening of certain regulatory functions as a response to the demands of global integration, has opened up the bargaining process with MNEs to non-state actors such as NGOs.[106] Their influence is not as strong as that of the MNE and state participants but, nonetheless, they possess a capacity for highlighting the need for certain parameters to be drawn around that process, consistent with public policy goals that no investment relationship should transgress.

Turning, first, to the bilateral relationship between the host state and MNE, the bargaining process between them will involve a consideration of the content of the host state's laws and regulations. This should be viewed as a starting point for negotiation, as an initial statement of the host's regulatory goals. How far that system is actually applied in a given case will depend on the outcome of bargaining at the stage of entry. This, in turn, depends on the relative bargaining strength of the host state and the MNE. Although generalization on such a case-specific issue is difficult, certain theories have emerged concerning the relativity of bargaining power between MNEs and host states. Earlier in this chapter one such theory, the 'dependency' theory, was described. It predicts that less developed host states are in a permanently weaker bargaining position in relation to MNEs as a result of the unequal conditions of trade and investment in the international economy, and because of the willingness of local ruling elites to submit to the interests of foreign capital. Thus, dependency theory posits a picture of exploitation of less developed host states by MNEs which cannot easily be remedied.

In contrast to the pessimism of dependency analysis, the 'bargaining' theory of host state-MNE relations posits that there can be situations in which even a developing host state has the stronger bargaining position. This approach was first developed, in the context of the copper industry in Chile, by Theodore Moran.[107] Having examined the continuing relationship between US copper companies and the Chilean state between 1945 and the overthrow of Salvador Allende's government in 1973, Moran concluded that a slow shift in the balance of power had occurred in favour of the host state, which led to the eventual nationalization of

---

[105] See Stopford and Strange above n 3.

[106] On this intentional weakening of regulatory functions, see further Peter T Muchlinski 'Globalization and Legal Research' above n 16 at 229–33 and Boaventura de Sousa Santos *Toward a New Legal Common Sense* (London: Butterworths, 2nd edn, 2002) ch 5.

[107] Theodore H Moran *Multinational Corporations and the Politics of Dependence: Copper in Chile* (Princeton University Press, 1974). See also Moran 'Multinational Corporations and Dependency: A Dialogue for Dependistas and Non-Dependistas' 32 Int.Org. 79 (1978); Leonard 'Multinational Corporations and Politics in Developing Countries' (1980) World Politics 454; Dunning above n 25 at 551–54; Donald Lecraw 'Multinational Enterprises and Developing Countries' in Peter J Buckley (ed) *New Directions in International Business* (Aldershot: Edward Elgar, 1992) 28.

the copper companies by President Allende's government in 1970. Moran suggested that the bargaining power of the MNE was at its strongest on entry, because of the uncertainties surrounding the future prospects of a natural resource investment, but that it weakened over time as the actual profitability of the investment became apparent and as the host state moved up the learning curve of negotiating, operating, and supervisory skills. However, the balance of power would shift back to the MNE on those occasions when the host state needed new investment in production or processing facilities, the technology for which was owned and controlled by the MNE. Furthermore, in determining whether the host state was likely to use its theoretical bargaining power to the full, account had to be taken of certain local variables. In particular, these included: the prominence of the targeted industry in the national economy; the setting for negotiations, especially the host state's perception of the costs and benefits of the investment as compared with the cost of replacing or of doing without it; the process of policy formation, taking into account the value of retaining or removing the foreign investment to various interest groups and their ability to influence public policy in line with their interests.[108]

Moran's initial work was restricted to the natural resources industry. In relation to manufacturing industries a different pattern of bargaining power appears to apply.[109] First, the MNE may be in a weak position at the point of entry given the host state's control over terms of access to the local market. However, once admitted, the firm may gain in power over time as it forges alliances with local suppliers, distributors, and creditors.[110] Secondly, where the industry concerned is characterized by continuous technological change and/or dynamic markets, the MNE is likely to possess a lasting bargaining advantage over the host state. This is because the firm is in a better position to control access to the relevant technology and international markets. However, even where the host state acquires an independent technological base it may find itself in a situation of technological dependency given that new developments vital to the well-being of the national industry will happen outside its borders. Thus, the host state may have to attract foreign firms possessing the latest technology even where it has a domestic presence in the field.[111]

To conclude, in manufacturing industries, the host state appears to be in a weaker position than the foreign firm, unless the firm is operating in a mature industry that is not reliant on new technology. In such cases the foreign firm may be vulnerable as

---

[108] *Copper in Chile* at 217. See, for example, Bennett and Sharpe above n 86.

[109] See generally Theodore H Moran (ed) *Multinational Corporations: The Political Economy of Foreign Direct Investment* (Lexington, 1985).

[110] See further Garry Gereffi *The Pharmaceutical Industry and Dependency in the Third World* (Princeton University Press, 1983) at 159–60.

[111] See, for example, the cases of the Indian and Brazilian computer industries: Greico 'Between Dependency and Autonomy: India's Experience with the International Computer Industry' 36 Int. Org. 609 (1982); Adler 'Ideological Guerillas and the Quest for Technological Autonomy: Brazil's Domestic Computer Industry' 40 Int.Org. 673 (1986); Evans 'State, Capital and the Transformation of Dependence: The Brazilian Computer Case' 14 World Development 791 (1986). On the legal details behind these policies, see ch 11 below.

its contribution to the host economy may be easy to replicate locally. Given the fore-going emphasis on technology as the major source of bargaining power, the distinction between manufacturing and natural resources industries may not be so great in that technological dependency can also arise in the latter. As already noted, when Chile needed technology and investment for new mining ventures in the copper industry the bargaining power of the US copper companies increased. Furthermore, after nationalization the Chilean copper industry remained vulnerable to pressure from US firms by means of an embargo on spares and new technology.

As regards service industries, host states appear to be in a relatively strong position, given the traditionally high degree of prudential regulation in such sectors. Furthermore, many states have instituted public monopolies in the provision of services, to the exclusion of foreign firms. Certain services, deemed vital to the national economy, may in addition be classified as sectors restricted to foreign investors. In this area, liberalization by way of privatization, and the reduction of entry barriers, may have to occur before the issue of host state-MNE bargaining can be considered in the light of extensive experience. At present, the liberalization of investment in services is still in its infancy but is rapidly increasing, due in part to the adoption of the General Agreement on Trade in Services (GATS Agreement) in the WTO but also to the increased tradability of knowledge based services across borders.[112] It may be predicted that host state power will remain strong wherever the host country offers a major market opportunity for services-based FDI, although, as with natural resources and manufacturing, where the service in question is dependent on imported technology controlled by the MNE then the same inequality of bargaining power will persist as in those sectors.

The above comments should not be taken as anything more than broad general propositions. They arise from specific studies of countries and/or industry sectors, concentrating on natural resources and manufacturing. This empirical work is far from complete as the case of services shows. Moreover, much of it is concerned with a rather inconclusive debate over the continuing relevance, if any, of dependency analysis, offering evidence both in support of and against this position. However, as Stopford and Strange point out, the traditional concern of dependency theory with the unequal economic situation of less developed states may have been supplanted by a more complex dependency that affects both developed and less developed states alike. This rests on the constraint of governmental policy choices, in an increasingly integrated global economy, through the independent decisions of the dominant firms in industry sectors regarding such matters as the location of production or R&D, product development and marketing and choice of technology.[113] In a world where all governments suggest that they are committed to increasing the welfare of their citizens, responding to these decisions while

---

[112] See UNCTAD *World Investment Report 2004* (New York and Geneva: United Nations, 2004) ch V 'National Policies'.   [113] Above n 3 at 229.

attempting to meet these social objectives may entail a significant limitation of state power.[114]

On the other hand, this should not imply that cooperative approaches to MNE-host state relations are impossible. Indeed, Stopford and Strange suggest that such cooperation is not only desirable but possible, given that firms are themselves in a weaker bargaining position as a result of increased international competition between firms, which offers host states 'the opportunity to trade firms off against one another.[115] Of significance in this respect would be access on the part of host states to information about firms and the international markets in which they operate. Here states with more developed databases and professional analytical skills will be at an advantage. Inevitably, the poorer states will be at a relative disadvantage.[116] Thus 'neo-dependency' may manifest itself in the inability to formulate an effective bargaining position due to a lack of relevant information. This dimension of state power should not be overlooked. It may be remedied by the use of multilateral rather than unilateral approaches to regulation, a matter to be considered further below.

Beyond the interactions of states and MNEs, the role of NGOs needs to be taken into account as a relatively new participant in the process of bargaining over regulatory controls. The most comprehensive analysis of this role to date can be found in Braithwaite and Drahos's *Global Business Regulation*.[117] The authors present a complex methodology that shows the full range of interactions which contribute to the development of global regulatory norms and practices. Having identified the principal significant actors,[118] they go on to distinguish between the

[114] Thus, for example, the UK Government was constrained in its bargaining, during the 1970s, with the Chrysler Corporation over the latter's investment in the Linwood car manufacturing plant in Scotland because of the pressure to maintain employment in what was a region of high unemployment. See N Hood and S Young *Multinationals in Retreat: The Scottish Experience* (Edinburgh University Press, 1982) 61–80; L Grunberg *Failed Multinational Ventures* (Lexington, Mass: DC Heath, 1981) ch 5.

[115] Above n 3 at 214–27. See also John M Kline 'The Role of Transnational Corporations in Chile's Transition: Beyond Dependency and Bargaining' 1 Transnational Corporations 81 (No 2 August 1992) and *Foreign Investment Strategies in Restructuring Economies: Learning From Corporate Experiences in Chile* (Westport, Conn: Quorum Books, 1992).

[116] See, for an example of how such problems might be overcome with the assistance of international organizations, Fui S Tsikata (ed) *Essays From the Ghana-Valco Renegotiations 1982–85* (Accra: Ghana Publishing Corporation, 1986).

[117] John Braithwaite and Peter Drahos *Global Business Regulation* (Cambridge: Cambridge University Press, 2000). This summary is taken from Peter T Muchlinski 'Globalization and Legal Research' above n 16 at 231–32.

[118] ibid ch 20. These include: the nation state, which has hitherto been the most important actor but is now being decentred; inter-governmental organizations, whose influence varies according to how the dominant powers – the United States in particular – perceive them; business itself through lobbying efforts; individuals who have significant personal influence arising from their positions as leaders of corporations or industries, or as leading intellectuals or activists; non-governmental organizations (NGOs), and mass publics as repositories of popular views on matters germane to business regulation and epistemic communities of experts who, through their interactions inter se and with other types of actors, can create dialogues from which policies, and policy consensus, can emerge. Though more complex than the set of actors presented in section 1 it follows much the same range of public and private actors.

traditional concept of the 'rule of law', with its seemingly impartial emphasis on individual autonomy of action in the context of rules enacted by a neutral state, and what they term the 'rule of principles', which informs the reality of international business regulation through the continuing contest between competing principles upon which the conduct of such business should be based. They do so to avoid what they see as the false objectivity of 'rule of law' analysis, pointing out that this doctrine, when applied in the international business sphere, is used as an instrumental tool for the furtherance of a neo-liberal version of freedom.[119] The authors then consider the mechanisms of globalization of which 'modelling' is seen as the most important. It rests on 'observational learning with a symbolic content, not just the simple response mimicry implied by the term "imitation"'[120] and on 'conceptions of action portrayed by words and images'. Its main function is to spread specific types of regulatory regimes by reason of their use as 'models' for wider adoption. This can occur through coercion, as in the case of the spread of Western notions of property, contract, and legal order through the process of colonialism, or it can occur through webs of dialogue and persuasion.[121] In particular, the authors argue that concerned NGOs can, through the use of alternative policy models, shift the debate away from industry-specific concerns towards a more socially responsive agenda from the perspective of what they term 'popular sovereignty' which, they feel, still remains a powerful source of opinion even where national and parliamentary sovereignties may be weakened by globalization.[122]

Braithwaite and Drahos provide an analytical model that owes much to the social action programmes and strategies followed, in the recent past, by the feminist and environmental movements and, to a lesser extent, by the consumer movement.[123] They also offer an aspiration that through the process of dialogue, persuasion, and conflicts of principles, based on the use of oppositional regulatory models, a more democratically formed system of international business regulation will emerge.[124] However, one is left with the feeling that this approach assumes so much that is absent in many of the countries engaged in the process of economic globalization. In particular, the effectiveness of the 'modelling' principle must surely depend on a relatively good level of general education, access to relevant information, access to the media especially for weaker groups, a liberal and tolerant political order, and finally, educational and campaigning institutions that are

---

[119] ibid at 531. For the contrary position advocating a liberal international 'rule of law' in the regulation of international economic activity, aimed at the control of state power in relation to the economic freedoms of other states and non-state actors, see John Jackson 'Global Economics and International Economic Law' 1 JIEL 1 (1998). [120] ibid at 580.

[121] On which see further ibid ch 23.   [122] ibid ch 26.

[123] The present work details this process in relation to environmental regulation of MNEs in ch 14.

[124] In a similar vein see the discussions of deliberative democracy in George A Bermann, Matthias Herdegen and Peter L Lindseth (eds) *Transatlantic Regulatory Co-operation* (Oxford: Oxford University Press, 2000), by Robert Howse 'Transatlantic Regulatory Cooperation and the Problem of Democracy' 470 at 478–80, and Sol Picciotto 'North Atlantic Cooperation and Democratising Globalization' 495. For the potential of the internet as a tool for furthering deliberative democracy see Peter Strauss 'The Challenges of Globally Accessible Process' in ibid at 547.

sufficiently free and unbiased that they can become credible sources of alternative policy making. Such conditions may only exist in the Western liberal democracies, and even here this may be doubted. Thus while this approach offers much in terms of highlighting the range of variables that an understanding of emerging global business regulation requires, it emphasizes, by reason of its omissions, the relative powerlessness of NGOs in relation to bargaining processes occurring outside democratic and relatively affluent states.

(b) Sources of Regulatory Standards

This section seeks to highlight a theme in the sources of regulatory controls which has emerged, in particular, in relation to the social dimension of MNE regulation.[125] Although not an all embracing generalization, it is fair to say that the regulation of MNEs tends to be based on formal, mandatory sources of regulation such as national laws, administrative rules, and binding international agreements, where the commercial organization of the firm and the protection of its investments are involved. On the other hand, the vast bulk of sources concerning ICSR are non-binding voluntary codes or declarations.[126] These include codes of conduct developed by individual companies or industry sectors,[127] NGO codes,[128] codes drawn up by governments,[129] or IGOs of which the codes of conduct developed by the International Labour Organization (ILO) are of especial importance.[130] On the other hand, some sources are legally binding as they take the form of binding conventions on specific issues. The 1997 OECD Convention on Combating Bribery of Foreign Officials in International Business Transactions is the most prominent

[125] This section is based on Peter T Muchlinski 'Human Rights, Social Responsibility and the Regulation of International Business' above n 93 at 127–30.

[126] See Ans Kolk, Rob van Tulder and Carlijn Welters 'International Codes of Conduct and Corporate Social Responsibility: Can Transnational Corporations Regulate Themselves?' 8 Transnational Corporations 117 (No 1 1999) and the articles in 14 Transnational Corporations (No 3 2005). Further readings on corporate codes of conduct can be found in ch 12 n 103 at 488–89.

[127] See further UNCTAD *Social Responsibility* UNCTAD Series on issues in international investment agreements (New York and Geneva: United Nations, 2001) especially at 37–40. See also UNCTAD *Employment* Series on issues in international investment agreements (New York and Geneva: United Nations, 2000); UNCTAD *Environment* UNCTAD Series on issues in international investment agreements (New York and Geneva: United Nations, 2001); Peter T Muchlinski 'The Social Dimension of International Investment Agreements' in J Faundez, M Footer and JJ Norton (eds) *Governance, Development and Globalisation* (London: Blackstone Press, 2000) 373 at 386–88 and sources cited therein. For a full inventory of corporate codes of conduct, see OECD Working Party of the Trade Committee *Codes of Corporate Conduct: An Inventory* (OECD Doc TD/TC/WP(98)74/FINAL 3 May 1999) available at <http://www.olis.oecd.org/olis/1998doc.nsf/c16431e1b3f24c0ac12569fa005d1d99/c125692700622425c12569a40038da6c/$FILE/04E95110.pdf>.

[128] See, for example, the NGO codes reproduced in UNCTAD *International Investment Agreements: A Compendium* (New York and Geneva: United Nations, 2000) Part Four. See, in particular, the Amnesty International UK Business Group *Human Rights Guidelines for Companies* (London: Amnesty International, 1998).

[129] For example, the UK Ethical Trading Initiative: <http://www.ethicaltrade.org>.

[130] See further ch 12.

example,[131] as are the numerous ILO conventions on labour standards. Such inter-national standard setting conventions acquire the force of binding international treaties among the membership of the sponsoring IGO, or among the signatory states, if membership of the convention is permitted to any country including non-members of the sponsoring IGO.

However, the majority of the above mentioned sources are legally non-binding 'soft law' instruments. They offer little more than moral force, in that the major method of enforcement is through the shame of non-adherence. That does not imply that such codes are doomed to complete legal ineffectiveness. At the inter-national level 'soft law' can 'harden' into positive law, where it is seen as evidence of emergent new standards of customary international law. For these purposes the origin of the legal principle in a 'soft law' instrument, such as a voluntary code of conduct or a non-binding resolution of an international organization, is of little consequence if a consensus develops that the principle in question should be viewed as an obligatory standard by reason of subsequent practice.[132] Given that many of the most important international expressions of welfare values tend to be in such form[133] the 'hardening process' may be of especial importance here. On the other hand, it should not be forgotten that even in 'hard law' agreements, provisions con-cerning controversial social issues have been put into very general, and probably meaningless, hortatory language, simply to show that something has been done, but where there is little intention to see these provisions having any real legal effect.[134]

Equally, at the level of national law, a non-binding code of conduct can acquire legal force in private law. Private law suits can be brought against the firm or orga-nization adopting a voluntary code by other firms or organizations, consumers, or other members of the community. Such claims may allege that a failure to comply with the code is evidence that the sponsoring firm or organization is not meeting industry standards of conduct and is, therefore, not exercising reasonable care or due diligence. Furthermore, failure to follow the terms of a voluntary code could be evidence of a breach of contract, where such adherence is an express or implied term of the agreement, or of an actionable misrepresentation, as where a firm alleges that its adherence to a code of conduct entitles it to be regarded as qualify-ing for a governmental standard setting *marque* of approval, but where in fact it fails to meet such standards. In such cases, consumers can bring an action if they

---

[131] This convention entered into force on 15 February 1999. See OECD Doc DAFFE/IME/BR(97) 20 8 April 1998 or <http://www.oecd.org/dataoecd/56/36/192248.pdf>.

[132] See, for example, OA Elias and CL Lim *The Paradox of Consensualism in International Law* (The Hague: Kluwer Law International, 1998) at 230–32.   [133] ibid.

[134] See, for example, the discussion of Article 19 of the Energy Charter Treaty (environmental aspects) by Thomas Waelde in 'Sustainable Development and the 1994 Energy Charter Treaty: Between Pseudo-Action and the Management of Environmental Investment Risk' in F Weiss, E Denters, and P de Waart (eds) *International Economic Law with a Human Face* (The Hague: Kluwer Law International, 1998) 223–70; and see T Waelde 'Non-conventional Views on "Effectiveness": The Holy Grail of Modern International Lawyers: The New Paradigm? A Chimeria? Or a Brave New World in the Global Economy?' 4 Austrian Review of International and European Law 164 (1999).

claim to have been attracted to purchasing the firm's products or services in the light of such assertions of good conduct. Also the relevant government agency might bring an action for abuse of its certification scheme.[135]

Therefore, to dismiss voluntary sources of international or national corporate social responsibility standards as irrelevant seems to fail to appreciate how formal rules and principles of law emerge. The very fact that an increasing number of non-binding codes is being drafted and adopted in this area, suggests a growing interest among important groups and organizations – corporations, industry associations, NGOs, governments, and IGOs – and is leading to the establishment of a rich set of sources from which new binding standards can emerge. No doubt this process can, and is being, criticized as one in which corporate interests are trying to capture the agenda through code making. It is fair to say that non-business NGOs are attempting the same with their codes. The real issue is when and how will all this 'codification' turn into detailed legal standards which can act as fully binding benchmarks for the control of unacceptable lapses in corporate conduct at the international level. That is, as noted earlier, an issue of ideological contest, but one which seems to be veering slowly towards an acceptance of some kind of articulated set of minimum international standards for corporate social responsibility, as a trade-off for greater corporate freedom in the market.[136]

(c) 'Sites' of Regulation

The international scope of MNE operations offers, in theory, a range of regulatory 'sites'. These will begin with informal self-regulation by firms, informal regulation by NGOs, and unilateral formal governmental regulation at the local, sub-national, and national levels. Beyond national borders regulation can arise out of a bilateral treaty concluded between home and host states, at the regional level, involving a supranational regulatory authority established by a group of states sharing common economic interests in a defined geographical area; and the international level, involving regulation by a substantial majority of the world's states acting through multilateral inter-governmental organizations.[137] Each level will be considered taking into account the economic interests that it may be able to serve and the legal problems that may be associated with it. Of course these 'sites' are not mutually exclusive. To the contrary, regulation will often occur on the basis of a mix of

[135] See Government of Canada *Voluntary Codes: A Guide for their Development and Use* (Ottawa, March 1998) at 27, also available at <http://strategis.ic.gc.ca/volcodes>; Kernaghan Webb 'Voluntary Initiatives and the Law' in R Gibson (ed) *Voluntary Initiatives: The New Politics of Corporate Greening* (Peterborough Ont: Broadview Press, 1999) 32–50.

[136] This is precisely what Henderson fears. He would deny that such a trade-off is possible and that it would lead to over-regulation and loss of market freedom. See Henderson above n 92.

[137] See generally Siqueiros 'The Juridical Regulation of Transnational Enterprises' in *New Directions in International Trade Law Volume I* (UNIDROIT, 1978) 281; Detlev Vagts 'The Multinational Enterprise: A New Challenge for Transnational Law' 83 Harv.LR 739 (1970).

'sites' acting upon the corporation simultaneously, as will be shown empirically in the environment chapter below.[138]

(i) Self-Regulation

Since the 1980s the concept of corporate self-regulation has become increasingly advocated as part of the business friendly climate created by the neo-liberal ascendancy. It is clear that the withdrawal of the state from high levels of mandatory regulation in the business sphere will require alternative approaches to regulation. In this regard corporate self-regulation may be used to fill the regulatory gap. This may lead to transnational systems of informal regulation based on the practices of MNEs, beyond the positive law of the nation state or of international law, resulting in order maintenance systems that are unconnected with any particular territory. These systems exist wherever networks or groups operate across borders and create their own system-specific internal proto-legal orders.[139] The application of commercial customs and practices by firms may be one example creating a system that develops new contract regimes and dispute settlement systems outside formal state or international laws. Another might be the internal management systems of multinationals which may be used to determine the resolution of internal disputes and issues without reference to outside laws.[140]

The key to this new level of law is its distance from the existing centres of law-making – national parliaments, global legislative institutions, and inter-governmental agreements.[141] In Teubner's words: '[t]he new world law is primarily peripheral, spontaneous and social law. Private government, private regulation and private justice are becoming central sources of law.'[142] A similar empirical foundation has been used by De Sousa Santos in his work on globalization and the creation of post-modern legal relations.[143] Like Teubner, De Sousa Santos also accepts that formal state-centred law is being supplemented by new informal legal orders ranging, in his work, from the practices of Brazilian urban squatters to those of global business groups.[144] Thus, for De Sousa Santos, globalization is leading towards a recasting

---

[138] Ch 14. See also Peter Utting *Rethinking Business Regulation: From Self-Regulation to Social Control* (Geneva: UNRISD Technology Business and Society Paper No15, September 2005).

[139] See Gunter Teubner ' "Global Bukowina": Legal Pluralism in the World Society' in Gunter Teubner (ed) *Global Law Without a State* (Aldershot: Dartmouth, 1997) 3. See further Sol Picciotto 'Networks in International Economic Integration: Fragmented States and the Dilemmas of Neo-Liberalism' 17 NW J. Int'l Law & Bus. 1014 (1996/97) and 'The Regulatory Criss-Cross: Interaction Between Jurisdictions and the Construction of Global Regulatory Networks' in W Bratton, J McCahery, S Picciotto, and C Scott (eds) *International Regulatory Competition and Cooperation* (Oxford: Clarendon Press, 1996) 89.

[140] See Peter T Muchlinski above n 6 and Jean-Philippe Robe 'Multinational Enterprises: The Constitution of a Pluralistic Legal Order' in Teubner (ed) ibid at 45.   [141] ibid at 3.

[142] ibid at 4.

[143] De Sousa Santos above n 106 ch 5. For a valuable summary and critical assessment of this difficult work, see William Twining *Globalisation and Legal Theory* (London: Butterworths, 2000) ch 8.

[144] Thus De Sousa Santos also cites inter alia the 'new *lex mercatoria*' (on which see ch 15 n 20 at 581) and the emergence of global human rights issues as evidence of legal globalization: ibid at 208–215; 257–301.

of legal theory in which the state is no longer a central pillar, although not a defunct element.

(ii) Regulation by NGOs

Connected to the relative decline of formal state centred regulation is informal regulation through NGO action. This has been termed 'civil regulation'. It encompasses both cooperative approaches, under which NGOs and MNEs act in partnership to further certain social responsibility goals, and more critical approaches, such as the highlighting of corporate malpractice in the course of a campaign, as well as monitoring compliance with voluntary and/or mandatory standards. This type of regulation has been widely used in relation to environmental issues and will be considered in more detail in chapter 14.

(iii) National Regulation

Notwithstanding the above mentioned shift away from exclusive governmental regulation, this still remains the most significant level of regulation.[145] Emergent regional and multilateral regulatory orders remain insufficiently developed to replace the nation state as the principal focus for the regulation of MNEs, while informal regulation by non-state actors is likely to be selective and probably self-serving. As noted above, the main aim of regulation at the national level is to secure the greatest economic and social benefits from the activities of MNEs, whether as a home or host state. In economic terms this unilateral approach may result in 'beggar-thy-neighbour' policies.[146] In the pursuit of their national interests states will not consider the impact of their regulatory policies on the economic welfare of other states.

Unilateral national regulation tends to create a global market divided by different policy regimes, leading to distortions in investment patterns caused by the extensive adoption of second-best policies based on state intervention. Each state will seek to attract the greatest advantages from relations with MNEs, resulting in competition over investment incentives which can act as a form of protectionism. Equally, states may use their legislative power to establish 'regulatory havens' specifically designed to attract internationally mobile investment on the basis of a more lax regulatory regime.[147] This may add to the welfare of the haven jurisdiction but reduce global welfare by distorting the allocation of resources and profits across the international system. Unilateral regulation may lead to a system in

---

[145] See Stephen J Kobrin 'Sovereignty@bay: Globalization, Multinational Enterprise and the International Political System' in Rugman and Brewer (eds) above n 9 at 181.

[146] See Hood and Young above n 27 at 244. A similar problem can emerge within the nation state where different sub-national entities, regions, or communities compete over mobile inward FDI.

[147] On 'flag of convenience' states and offshore finance and tax havens, see Sol Picciotto 'Offshore: The State as Legal Fiction' in Mark P Hampton and Jason P Abbott *Offshore Finance Centres and Tax Havens: The Rise of Global Capital* (London: MacMillan, 1999) 43; Murphy above n 5 Part II.

which the weaker states will be increasingly disadvantaged and in which much public expenditure may be wasted in attracting MNEs. Furthermore, differences in regulatory regimes can be exploited by MNEs to their benefit, without any necessary corresponding gain being transmitted to the states in which they operate, as already outlined in chapter 1. In this process, firm lobbying over regulatory controls becomes a significant variable.[148]

The principal legal problem attached to unilateral regulation by the state arises from the fact that the MNE operates across the limits of national legal jurisdiction. The integrated character of its business activities will result in a mismatch between, on the one hand, the managerial and operational reach of the firm and, on the other, the jurisdictional reach of the state that seeks to regulate the MNE. This may result in situations where regulation exclusively within the territorial jurisdiction of the regulating entity may be ineffective.[149] The response of the state may be to extend the operation of its laws outside its territorial jurisdiction, that is, to apply its laws extraterritorially.

Thus, the legislature may wish to prescribe laws that apply to the whole of the MNE group regardless of its presence in another jurisdiction. For example, the home state may seek to protect its strategic interests by prohibiting companies possessing its nationality from trading with potential enemy powers. Such a prohibition would apply to the parent by reason of its nationality of incorporation. It could be made to extend to its overseas subsidiaries by reason of the nationality of the parent, on the basis of the control that it exercises over its subsidiaries. This disregards the legal nationality of the subsidiary as a juristic person incorporated under the law of the host state, and extends the law of the home state to its actions. To take another example, where the home state of a MNE imposes disclosure requirements on the parent, whether for the purposes of company law or taxation, the latter may seek to avoid those requirements by locating the relevant information abroad with a subsidiary incorporated under a legal system that protects the confidentiality of commercial information. In these circumstances the home state will order the production of the information only if it is prepared to extend the reach of its court orders into the host country of the subsidiary.[150] Equally, where a foreign parent company incorporates an operating subsidiary in the host country, and that subsidiary eventually becomes insolvent as a result of negligent decisions made by the parent, the liquidator of the subsidiary may only be successful if

---

[148] According to Murphy (above n 147) a clear correlation exists between large firm size, the possession of valuable firm-specific assets, market concentration, and the ability to influence regulatory outcomes. Murphy shows that firms will not always seek to reduce regulation. Where they possess significant assets, MNEs may actually seek to increase regulation as a means of protecting their market position: ibid Part III.

[149] See further, on the relationship between the MNE's business organization and its amenability to control by the state, Louis Wells Jr 'The Multinational Business Enterprise: What Kind of International Organisation?' in Keohane and Nye (eds) above n 2 at 97.

[150] See eg *Lonrho v Shell Petroleum* [1980] 1 WLR 627 (HL).

he can persuade the courts of the host state to issue process out of the jurisdiction against the parent corporation in an action for negligence.[151]

In each of these cases the court must be prepared not only to pierce the corporate veil between parent and subsidiary to establish liability, but, first, to pierce the 'jurisdictional veil' between them and seek to make the law of the forum apply to the foreign based unit of the enterprise. Furthermore, in each of the above mentioned cases, the regulating state seeks to make the overseas unit of the MNE act in accordance with the law that governs the activities of the unit present within the regulating state. In the home state, that will involve the regulation of an overseas subsidiary through the imposition of legal duties on the parent to direct the acts of the subsidiary in the required manner. In the host state, that will involve the imposition of legal duties on the foreign parent through the physical presence of the subsidiary within the jurisdiction. This may have the effect that obedience to one legal system will result in a violation of the law of the other, or, at least, in the imposition of legal standards not accepted under the law of that other.

The extraterritorial application of law can have serious political effects. First, it can be seen as an attempt by the regulating state to impose its policies upon others, disregarding the interests of the target state. Secondly, the target state's exclusive territorial sovereignty will have been infringed. This can lead to diplomatic conflict and to retaliatory measures against the regulating state. The perception that the target state's sovereignty has been disregarded can escalate the seriousness of the conflict, regardless of the actual damage inflicted on the economic interests of the target state.[152] Relations between the regulating and target states may deteriorate.

Attempts to exercise extraterritorial jurisdiction are a manifestation of the regulating state's power and confidence in the validity – if not superiority – of its policies. Generally, weak states do not attempt such an exercise. Indeed, the history of extraterritoriality disputes is closely related to the history of American power. Attempts by the US, since the Second World War, to extend the reach of its laws have led to the majority of such disputes.[153] Such disputes have occurred between the US and its principal trading partners from within the OECD. They have not involved the developing countries. These states are more likely to accept the extraterritorial operation of foreign laws as a price to be paid for foreign aid and investment. Furthermore, as the evolution of international direct investment involves increased cross-investment between the US, Europe, and Japan, conflicts over the right to regulate the activities of MNEs are more likely to emerge among the developed market economies. It is mainly a problem of the developed countries coming to terms with the emergence of an integrated global economy.[154]

---

[151] This is a simplified version of the facts that occurred in the English case of *Multinational Gas and Petrochemical Co v Multinational Gas and Petrochemical Services Ltd* [1983] Ch 258, [1983] 2 All ER 563 (CA).

[152] See IA Litvak and CJ Maule 'Conflict Resolution and Extraterritoriality' 13 Journal of Conflict Resolution 305 (1969).   [153] See further ch 4.

[154] See Sol Picciotto 'Jurisdictional Conflicts, International Law and the International State System' 11 Int'l.Jo.Soc.L 11 (1983).

On the other hand, developing host states may seek to engage the protection of their interests through a process of 'reverse extraterritoriality' where the laws of the home state impose higher standards of regulation over the parent company than those imposed on the locally incorporated subsidiary. Thus, during the American proceedings in the *Bhopal* case,[155] the private plaintiffs and the Indian Government argued that the US was the appropriate forum for the conduct of the litigation, and that US law was the applicable law, on the grounds inter alia that Indian law was procedurally and substantively incapable of dealing with such complex issues of liability. By comparison, US law offered the prospect of less delay and greater damages. The US courts rejected this argument. The host state should not be permitted to invoke US law in preference to its own law in the case of an accident that occurred on its own territory. US law would not apply globally to the overseas subsidiaries of US companies, in determining liability for tortious acts.

The emergence of extraterritoriality conflicts has led to calls for greater coordination between states in the development and enforcement of regulatory and procedural standards. It is an issue that underlies many of the regulatory techniques to be considered in this book. Accordingly, the next chapter will consider these matters in more detail as an introduction to Part II.

(iv) Bilateral Regulation

Some of the problems of regulatory diversity between states can be solved on a bilateral level through the use of treaties based on reciprocity between the parties. Bilateral treaties have been concluded to control numerous commercial matters of direct concern to the signatory states, including double taxation,[156] recognition of corporations, and transportation. Increasing numbers of states have concluded Bilateral Investment Treaties (BITs) or Free Trade Agreements (FTAs) with investment protection provisions, which establish minimum standards of treatment for investors and/or traders from the other contracting state in the territory of the host state. Such treaties may limit the absolute discretion of the host state in setting the standards by which foreign investors and/or traders are to be regulated. According to Siqueiros, such bilateral regimes can work only if entered between states of broadly similar economic development. Otherwise the reciprocity on which the treaty is based will be illusory.[157] In such cases the treaty may in fact impose the regime favoured by the stronger party onto the weaker party. This may be particularly true of BITs, bearing in mind that these are usually based on a standard form model developed by the capital-exporting party. On the other hand, it may be in the interests of the capital-importing party to show that it will uphold the minimum standards of treatment contained in the BIT as a signal of commitment to attracting FDI and treating investors well. In any case, bilateral treaties

---

[155] *In Re Union Carbide Gas Plant Disaster at Bhopal India* 634 F Supp 842 (SDNY 1986), 25 ILM 771 (1986); *aff'd as modified* 809 F 2d 195 (2d Cir 1987), 26 ILM 1008 (1987); *cert den* 108 S Ct 199 (1987).   [156] See further ch 7.
[157] Above n 137 at 288.

offer no more than a limited solution to problems of regulatory diversity, as they represent specific regimes applicable only to the signatory states.

(v) Regional Regulation

One alternative to unilateral state regulation is for states with common economic interests in a coherent geopolitical region to form a joint economic organization for the coordination of their economic policies. This may take the form of a free trade area, in which customs duties between the participating states are progressively removed, or of a developed common market, in which not only free trade but full economic integration are pursued. Such policies may or may not involve the broader aim of full political union. In relation to MNE operations, such a development has the advantage of creating a harmonized economic policy area in which MNEs can organize their international network without having to confront differences in regulatory regimes. This should result in greater economic efficiency.

In relation to MNE regulation, the regional approach should increase the bargaining power of individual states through collective action (on the assumption that a common policy on direct investment is pursued), and reduce the mismatch between the territorial limits of jurisdiction and the geographical scope of MNE operations, at least as regards firms operating exclusively within the territory of the participating states. However, in relation to firms operating both within and outside the territory of the regional organization, the problem of jurisdictional limitation will re-emerge. Indeed, the regional organization may have to apply its own laws extraterritorially in order to ensure effective regulation over firms operating across its borders. In jurisdictional terms it is no more than a 'super-state'.

Further problems may emerge in the evolution of a common policy on MNEs. The participating states may disagree over the content of such policy.[158] The organization may not even have a comprehensive policy in this area. Thus the success of such an approach depends on political agreement about regulatory goals. Nevertheless, as noted in chapter 1, the regional approach to regulation is growing in significance as a means of integrating policies among regional groupings of states. On the other hand, it may lead to an altogether different result, particularly if the global economy succumbs to the protectionist pressures created by economic recession, to damaging international competition between MNEs from different home regions and to political instability. The resulting model may involve a world of competing, self-contained regional and interregional economic blocs, which increase economic interdependence within their boundaries while decreasing interdependence with other blocs.[159]

---

[158] See, for example, the case of ANCOM discussed in ch 17.

[159] See further Lester Thurow *Head to Head: The Coming Economic Battle Among Japan, Europe and America* (London: Nicholas Brealey Publishing, 1994). For a contrary view see Paul Krugman *Pop Internationalism* (Cambridge, Mass: MIT Press, 1996).

(vi) Multilateral Regulation

Neo-classical economic analysis points to the development of multilateral regulation as the most efficient solution to the control of MNEs.[160] The area of control
would coincide with the global market, allowing for the progressive removal of
national regulatory barriers to foreign investment and intrafirm trade. Competition
would be ensured by the establishment of global competition regulation, while
externalities could be regulated internationally through universal environmental
and resource transfer laws. Incentives for MNEs to exploit differences in national
regulations could be removed by the harmonization of tax laws, disclosure standards, labour regulations, and corporate liability regimes. International incorporation for MNEs could be instituted as well as a universal standard for the protection
and promotion of investment. The system would require the establishment of multilateral institutions that would police and develop the system. This model requires
the restriction of state sovereignty in the economic sphere through the acceptance
of the right of the international system to regulate matters previously within the
exclusive domain of state jurisdiction. Such a system has been periodically promoted, as under the abortive Havana Charter of 1948, which sought to set up the
International Trade Organization as part of the post-war multilateral economic
order.[161] Its most recent manifestation comes with the above mentioned initiatives
of the OECD and the World Bank in the field of foreign investment, and in the
establishment of the WTO and the extension of its mandate to investment related
trade issues.[162]

The 'neo-classical' model was challenged in the past by an international model
which sought to protect host state sovereignty in the control of national economic
policy, including control of MNEs. Such was the purpose behind the now defunct
UN programme for the creation of a New International Economic Order (NIEO)
of the 1970s, which was briefly mentioned in chapter 1 as one of the motivating
factors in the development of concern over the activities of MNEs.[163] The UN
Secretary General's Group of Eminent Persons, which produced its influential
report on the role of MNEs on development and international relations in 1974,
helped to lay down UN policy in the field of MNEs.[164] The Group recommended
the setting up of what would become the UN Commission on Transnational
Corporations and UN Centre on Transnational Corporations (UNCTC).[165] These

---

[160] Hood and Young above n 27 at 238–39.   [161] On which see further ch 17 at 654–55.
[162] See further chs 6, 11, and 17.
[163] The principal UN General Assembly Resolutions on the New International Economic Order are:
Res 3201 (S–VI) of 9 May 1974 *The Declaration on the Establishment of a New International Economic
Order*; Res 3202 (S–VI) of 16 May 1974 *The Programme of Action on the Establishment of a New
International Economic Order* both reproduced in 13 ILM 715–766 (1974). These were followed by Res
3281 (XXIX) of 15 January 1975 *The Charter of Economic Rights and Duties of States* reproduced in 14
ILM 251–65 (1975).   [164] UN Doc E/5500/Add 1 (Part I) 24 May 1974: 13 ILM 800 (1974).
[165] See Peter T Muchlinski 'Attempts to Extend the Accountability of Transnational Corporations:
The Role of UNCTAD' in Menno T Kamminga and Sam Zia-Zariffi (eds) *Liability of Multinational
Corporations Under International Law* (The Hague: Kluwer Law International, 2000) 97.

were designated as the bodies responsible for the conclusion of a UN Code of Conduct on TNCs, and for the furtherance of research and consultancy in the field of TNC activities. In relation to the principal substantive issues, the Group adopted a philosophy that was not opposed to investment by MNEs in developing countries, but which required the regulation of MNEs so that they could become instruments of development. The vision was one of a cooperative, rather than a conflictual relationship, coupled, however, with recognition that powerful foreign firms could act in an abusive manner towards a developing host state, and, to that extent, they had to be controlled.

It was a position very much within the 'regulated market' perspective. In particular, the Group accepted that the global organization, size and technological superiority of the MNE could threaten the sovereignty of the host state through the ability of the MNE to evade national regulation and taxation, to abuse its competitive power by distorting market conditions, and to exploit the lack of technological know-how of the host where the latter needed modern technology to ensure the growth of its economy. Furthermore, certain undesirable non-economic abuses were singled out for control. These included subversive political intervention in the host state, the introduction of alien cultural values and lifestyles, and the generation of inter-governmental confrontations between home and host states. All these abuses were to be controlled through national regulation backed up by international controls, based on the contents of an internationally agreed code of conduct. This would lay down clearly what MNEs could and could not do, and also the principles upon which the host country should formulate its policy towards MNEs.[166]

The UN has not taken a leading role in the most recent international initiatives on FDI and MNEs owing, in part, to the suspicion generated towards the UN from capital-exporting countries as a result of their experience during negotiations on the Draft Code of Conduct.[167] In 1992, the UNCTC was reorganized and renamed as the Transnational Corporations Management Division (TCMD), one of eight divisions of the United Nations Department of Economic and Social Development. This was moved, in 1993, from New York to Geneva and reformed as the Division on Investment Technology and Enterprise Development (DITE) of UNCTAD. Unlike the UN Commission and Centre for TNCs, UNCTAD/DITE is not a body for the negotiation of new international rules on the regulation of MNEs. Rather, it acts as a development-oriented think tank and technical

---

[166] For a full discussion of negotiations over the Draft UN Code of Conduct on TNCs and the reasons for its non-adoption, see ch 17 at 660–62.

[167] See Braithwaite and Drahos above n 117 at 567: 'The UN Centre on Transnational Corporations was abolished under US pressure, the most extreme example of forum shifting we have seen in our case studies'. The UN Global Compact initiative (see n 104), and the growing willingness of the UN to enter into partnerships with business to carry out its work, may be seen as an attempt to improve the UN's standing among US political circles and international business. For a critical appraisal, see Ann Zammit *Development at Risk: Re-thinking UN-Business Partnerships* (Geneva: The South Centre/UNRISD, 2003).

assistance centre, seeking out policies that ensure developing countries attract and benefit fully from inward FDI. In addition, as noted earlier, UNCTAD/DITE advocates a flexible approach to investor protection standards in international investment agreements so as to balance the host state's right to regulate in the public interest with the need to create a transparent, secure and predictable environment for investors. This is a far cry from the large scale discretionary interventionism that was understood to form a part of the NIEO. It manifests an acceptance of market based development policy coupled with selective and targeted regulation.[168] DITE has also acted in cooperation with the WTO in relation to trade and investment issues during the existence of the WTO Working Group on Trade and Investment.[169]

Concluding Remarks

This chapter has traced the major elements contributing towards an understanding of how MNE regulation works. It has examined the main actors, their interests, the ideological and bargaining power aspects of determining regulatory priorities, and the sources, methods, and levels of regulation. It has shown that changes in the organization of international production, with greater emphasis on integrated global production chains dominated by MNEs, have led to changes in international and national regulatory environments. The trend has been away from 'investor control' towards 'investor promotion and protection', among both developed and less developed countries espousing free market or mixed economies. At the same time, with the end of the Cold War and the disintegration of the socialist system, there appears to be no serious alternative to the corporate capitalism espoused by MNEs backed up by the 'neo-classical' system of market liberalization and the legitimating ideology of 'global consumerism'.

The new political environment no longer places 'right/left' issues of ownership and control at centre stage. Rather, there has been a transformation in political discourse which challenges not the legitimacy and value of free private enterprise as such, but its legitimacy as a polluter, an abuser of market power, a corruptor of state officials, an exploiter of workers, and a potential accomplice to violations of fundamental human rights. Thus regulation as such has not ended and it is taking the shape of 'international corporate social responsibility'. In this new investment environment, new regulatory issues, of the kinds listed above, emerge.[170] It may be said that the economics of the 'neo-classical' model are again being challenged

[168] See further Fredricksson and Zimny above n 20 and Peter T Muchlinski in Kamminga and Zia-Zariffi (eds) above n 165. [169] See ch 17.
[170] On which see further AA Fatouros 'International Investment Agreements and Development – Problems and Prospects at the Turn of the Century' in G Hafner, G Loibl, A Rest, L Sucharipa-Berman, and K Zemanek (eds) *Liber Amicorum Professor Seidl-Hohenveldern – in Honour of His 80th Birthday* (The Hague: Kluwer Law International, 1998) 115.

by a 'regulated market' perspective of a relatively mild type. Whether this will lead to a swing back to 'corporatist' approaches remains to be seen. The examples of the rising new economies such as Brazil, Russia, India, and China, all of which have a significant and powerful state-owned enterprise sector, and have long traditions of high discretion economic intervention policies, suggest that this is not impossible.

The opening chapters of this work have laid the conceptual ground for the study of the legal phenomena surrounding the operations of MNEs. The significance of particular issues to the more detailed analysis that follows has been highlighted by way of cross-referencing. It remains to explain the sequence of chapters in Parts II, III, and IV. Part II will begin with a detailed analysis of the legal limits of national jurisdiction in chapter 4. Chapter 5 will then go on to discuss controls over entry and establishment, followed by chapter 6 which deals with 'open door' policies and incentives for investors. It also considers attempts at the bilateral, regional, and multilateral levels to liberalize conditions for the entry and establishment of foreign investors. Chapters 7 to 11 will then discuss specific issues of post-entry economic regulation that have become objects of concern in relation to MNEs. These are taxation and tax avoidance, group liability and the liability of directors, corporate governance and disclosure, competition, and technology transfer. Part III introduces the social dimension of MNE regulation through consideration, in chapter 12, of labour relations followed by human rights and environmental issues in chapters 13 and 14. Part IV will discuss the questions surrounding the international law relating to foreign investment by MNEs. Chapters 15 and 16 deal with the regulation of investment risk under international law through the development, by arbitral bodies, of international treaty based protection standards in the fields of takings of property, non-discrimination, fair and equitable treatment, and full protection and security. Chapter 17 will follow with a discussion, in an historical context, of attempts to codify the substantive international law applicable to foreign investor/host state relations. It contains a detailed examination of the principal types of provisions found in IIAs, focusing on BITs as the most common form of this type of agreement. Finally, chapter 18 will consider the settlement of investor-state disputes through international dispute settlement methods. In particular, it will examine the procedures of ICSID and selected regional bodies using its facilities.

PART II

ECONOMIC REGULATION BY HOME AND HOST COUNTRIES

4

The Jurisdictional Limits of Regulation Through National or Regional Law

In the previous chapter, it was seen that the principal jurisdictional level for the regulation of MNEs remains the nation state. Given the international nature of MNE organization and management, this situation creates the problem of extraterritoriality. The present chapter will consider in more detail the main legal issues that have emerged from attempts to exercise extraterritorial jurisdiction over MNEs. This issue has been extensively documented in legal literature.[1] However, this work would be incomplete without an analysis of the principal trends in legal and diplomatic practice that have emerged in this area. The chapter will begin with an overview of the legal bases for the exercise of extraterritorial jurisdiction. These are based on the rules of public international law concerning state jurisdiction. It will then go on to consider state practice in this area, examining how the various bases of extraterritorial jurisdiction have been used in the fields of prescriptive, personal, and enforcement jurisdiction. In relation to enforcement jurisdiction, particular attention will be given to the problem of the disclosure of evidence in proceedings involving a MNE. The chapter will conclude with an analysis of how extraterritoriality conflicts can be limited by way of legal and diplomatic initiatives.

(1) The Legal Bases for the Extraterritorial Regulation of MNEs

The legal regulation of state jurisdiction is covered by rules of public international law. These are based on the exclusive sovereignty of each state over the territory it controls. Given that all states are equal in the eyes of international law, this power is to be enjoyed without let or hindrance from another sovereign state. Therefore,

---

[1] See further D Rosenthal and W Knighton *National Laws and International Commerce: The Problem of Extraterritoriality* (London: Chatham House Papers No 17 RIIA/RKP 1982); A Neale and M Stephens *International Business and National Jurisdiction* (Oxford: 1988); PM Roth 'Reasonable Extraterritoriality: Correcting the Balance of Interests' 41 ICLQ 245 (1992); Upendra Baxi 'Mass Torts, Multinational Enterprise Liability and Private International Law' 276 Hague Receuil 301 (1999).

each state has a reserved domain of domestic jurisdiction. This has as its corollary a duty of non-intervention on the part of other states.[2]

Should the territorial principle of state jurisdiction be observed to the letter, any assertion of extraterritorial jurisdiction by a state would amount to a violation of international law. Such a view might be unduly restrictive of a state's legitimate interest in the effective enforcement of its laws against MNEs. This raises the question of whether the territorial principle can be modified to justify a measure of extraterritorial jurisdiction. According to Brownlie, international law is developing in the light of the need to modify the territorial principle.[3] Consequently, alternative bases of jurisdiction have been put forward as exceptions to the territorial principle of jurisdiction, subject to the reservation that these must preserve a substantial and genuine connection between the subject-matter of jurisdiction and the territorial base, and reasonable interests, of the state seeking to exercise jurisdiction.[4] Of the various exceptions put forward three are of particular relevance to the regulation of MNEs: the nationality, protective, and objective territorial principles.[5]

(a) Nationality

It is accepted that in certain cases a state can assert jurisdiction over its nationals abroad.[6] In accordance with this principle, the home state of a MNE could seek to justify jurisdiction over the activities of an overseas unit in a number of situations. First, the managers of an overseas subsidiary, by reason of their home country nationality, could be subjected to home country legal requirements. Secondly, where there are no home country nationals on the board of the subsidiary, or they are in a minority, the home state could require the parent company to order its

---

[2] See further I Brownlie *Principles of Public International Law* (Oxford: 6th edn, 2003) chs 14 and 15; DP O'Connell *International Law* (London: Stevens 2nd edn, 1970) vol II ch 19; Akehurst 'Jurisdiction in International Law' 46 BYIL 145–257 (1972–73); FA Mann *Studies in International Law* (Oxford: Oxford University Press, 1973) ch I or 111 Hague Recueil 1 (1964 I).

[3] Brownlie n 2 above at 297.   [4] ibid.

[5] The principle of universal jurisdiction may also acquire relevance in civil as well as criminal cases, should the practice of subjecting MNEs to actions for violations of human rights, arising outside the forum jurisdiction, become more widespread. Currently such civil actions are possible under the US Alien Tort Claims Act (ATCA). Their jurisdictional basis has been challenged in amicus briefs presented before the US Supreme Court in the case of *Sosa v Alvarez-Machain* 542 US 692 (2004). In their joint amicus brief, Australia, Switzerland, and the UK, required an appropriate connection to the US, or activities involving US nationals, to found such jurisdiction. In a separate brief, the European Commission argued for the restriction of universal civil jurisdiction to those areas already covered by universal criminal jurisdiction. See further Donald Francis Donovan and Anthea Roberts 'The Emerging Recognition of Universal Civil Jurisdiction' 100 AJIL 142 (2006).

[6] For example, under English law, a British subject can be prosecuted before the English courts for a number of offences committed abroad, including treason and murder: *R v Casement* [1917] 1 KB 98 (treason); Offences Against the Person Act 1861 s 9 (murder). See further DJ Harris *Cases and Materials on International Law* (London: Thomson Sweet & Maxwell, 6th edn, 2004) 267–68; O'Connell n 2 above vol II 824–26.

overseas subsidiaries to act in compliance with home country laws, by reason of the nationality of the parent company as the principal shareholder in the foreign subsidiary. This effectively disregards the foreign nationality of incorporation of the subsidiary. Such an assertion of jurisdiction has caused difficulties in practice, as will be seen in the context of US trade embargoes addressed to the overseas subsidiaries of US firms. Thirdly, where the parent company operates abroad through unincorporated branches, these will retain the nationality of the parent and could, therefore, be subjected to the direct jurisdiction of the home country by reason of their corporate nationality. This has been a matter of significance in the extraterritorial regulation of the overseas branches of US banks.[7]

(b) Protective Jurisdiction

Nearly all states accept the right of a state to exercise extraterritorial jurisdiction over acts done abroad which adversely affect the vital interests of the regulating state.[8] For example, in relation to customs, fiscal immigration, or sanitary regulations, a coastal state is entitled to exercise the control necessary to enforce such regulations over a zone on the high seas contiguous to its territorial waters.[9] On an analogy with the contiguous zone concept, it might be possible to argue that the exercise of jurisdiction over the foreign units of a MNE is acceptable when required to secure vital national interests in areas of public governmental regulation. A convincing example would be the control of tax avoidance by the parent company through the use of transfer price manipulations between itself and its foreign subsidiaries.[10] On the other hand, it is debatable whether the mere protection of economic advantage on the part of the regulating state, at the expense of the target state, could be seen as the protection of 'vital interests'. It may be necessary to draw a distinction – not unlike the distinction between sovereign and commercial acts in the context of state immunity – between acts pursued in the genuine public interests of the regulating state and those designed to favour its commercial interests at the expense of other states.

(c) Objective Territorial Jurisdiction

The question of a modification to the strict territorial principle of jurisdiction arises where the elements of a criminal offence are commenced in one state and are

---

[7] See references at n 22 below.

[8] See eg *DPP v Joyce* [1946] AC 347 (acts of treason committed by an alien abroad are within the jurisdiction of the British courts); *Molvan v Attorney-General for Palestine* [1948] AC 351 (PC) (an alien involved in acts of illegal immigration committed on the high seas is subject to British jurisdiction). See also *Attorney-General of the Government of Israel v Eichmann* 36 ILR 5 (1961)(District Court Jerusalem).

[9] See the Geneva Convention on the Territorial Sea and the Contiguous Zone 1958 art 24 (UKTS 3 (1965); Cmnd 2511; 516 UNTS 205; UN Convention on the Law of the Sea 1982 art 33 (UN Doc A/CONF 62/122); 21 ILM 1261 (1982).   [10] See ch 7.

completed in another. This has given rise to the assertion by states of an objective territorial jurisdiction over offences initiated abroad and completed within the jurisdiction.[11] The objective principle was accepted as a valid basis for the exercise of state jurisdiction in criminal matters by the Permanent Court of International Justice (PCIJ) in the *Lotus* case.[12] In that case, the Turkish courts had convicted, on a charge of involuntary manslaughter, the officer of the watch on a French ship that had collided with a Turkish ship on the high seas, causing the death of Turkish nationals on board the Turkish ship. The PCIJ held that Turkey was entitled to exercise its criminal jurisdiction on the basis that the effects of the offence were produced on the Turkish vessel. The Turkish vessel could be regarded as a place assimilated to Turkish territory, and that, therefore, the offence was committed within Turkish territory, even though the perpetrator was, at the relevant time, aboard the French ship. The PCIJ held that the territoriality of criminal law was not an absolute principle of international law and by no means coincided with territorial sovereignty.[13] The Court further held that states retained a wide measure of discretion in respect of the application of their laws and the jurisdiction of their courts to persons, property, and acts outside their territory.[14]

The Court did not clarify the limits of this discretion, leaving the precise scope of the objective territorial principle unclear and open to interpretation by states. On the other hand, subsequent decisions of the International Court of Justice (ICJ) have laid stress on the need for a genuine connection between the subject-matter of the jurisdiction and the territory of the state seeking to exercise its jurisdiction.[15] Therefore, an unlimited discretion on the part of states to assert jurisdiction on the basis of the objective principle cannot be presumed. Furthermore, according to Neale and Stephens,[16] the application of the objective principle gives rise to at least two main areas of dispute. First, the conduct involved may be regarded as criminal in the state where it is completed but not in the state where it was initiated. Such differences in the law may be particularly common in the areas of economic and business regulation. Secondly, there is the problem of establishing a sufficient causal connection or nexus between the initiation and completion of the crime to justify applying the objective principle. A state determined to extend the scope of its laws will give a broad interpretation to the relevant chain of causation, taking remote rather than immediate causes as the justification for its action.

Having considered the main exceptions to the strict territoriality principle in international law, the remainder of the chapter will describe how state practice has

---

[11] See Brownlie n 2 above at 299–301. See further *Harvard Research Draft Convention on Jurisdiction with Respect to Crime 1935*: 29 AJIL Supp 443 at 484–87.   [12] (1927) PCIJ, Ser A No 10, 23.
[13] ibid at 20.   [14] ibid at 19.
[15] See *Nottebohm* case ICJ Reports (1955) at 4 (Jurisdiction to confer nationality on individuals must be exercised in the light of effective links between the individual and the state); *Anglo-Norwegian Fisheries* case ICJ Reports (1951) at 116 (Jurisdiction to delimit territorial sea must be exercised in the light of a genuine connection between the land domain and the sea). These cases lay the basis for Brownlie's opinion on the development of international law in this area referred to at n 4 above.
[16] Above n 1 at 15.

evolved in relation to the extraterritorial regulation of MNEs. A state's legal juris-diction can be divided between the jurisdiction to prescribe laws, to adjudicate disputes and to enforce legal orders and judgments.[17] Each area of claims to juris-diction will now be considered.

(2) Jurisdiction to Prescribe

The United States has led attempts to extend its laws to non-resident units of MNEs.[18] This has been justified on the basis of the need for regulatory effective-ness in major fields of economic and public policy. For example, in relation to US antitrust laws: '[t]he reach of the U.S. antitrust laws is not limited, however, to conduct and transactions that occur within the boundaries of the United States. Anticompetitive conduct that affects U.S. domestic or foreign commerce may violate the U.S. antitrust laws regardless of where such conduct occurs or the nationality of the parties involved.'[19] Similarly, under US securities laws, pre-scriptive jurisdiction exists over transactions occurring outside the US which have, or can be expected to have, a significant effect on the US securities market.[20] Furthermore, the US has, over the years, asserted the power inter alia:[21] to restrict exports of goods by the overseas subsidiaries of US firms operating in third coun-tries so as to prevent the avoidance of US trade embargoes against unfriendly powers; to freeze the assets of unfriendly powers held in bank accounts located in the overseas branches of US banks;[22] and to criminalize the making of corrupt

---

[17] See *The Third Restatement of the Foreign Relations Law of the United States* (American Law Institute 1987) s 401. The author favours the use of the American classification as the clearest con-ceptualization of the questions involved. In practice, however, issues of jurisdiction usually involve a mix of the heads of jurisdiction mentioned in the text.

[18] See further Rosenthal and Knighton n 1 above.

[19] US Department of Justice Antitrust Division *Anti-trust Enforcement Guidelines for International Operations* (April 1995) s 3.1 available at <www.usdoj.gov/atr>.

[20] See US Restatement n 17 s 416 at 295–96 and see Comment (a) at 297.

[21] See US Restatement ibid s 414 and Reporter's Notes 3–8 at 269–82.

[22] See US Restatement ibid s 414 Reporter's Note 6 279–80; Heininger 'Liability of US Banks for Deposits Placed in Their Foreign Branches' 11 Law & Pol.Int'l Bus. 903 (1979). According to the Restatement, two groups of issues have emerged in litigation in the US and elsewhere:

(i) to what extent may the US courts or government agencies require production of records of for-eign branches of banks whose headquarters are situated in the US or restrict the transfer of funds deposited at such branches;

(ii) to what extent are home offices liable for obligations entered into or deposits made at branch banks in foreign states.

The first issue will be considered below. See text at n 166–68 below. The second issue is extensively discussed by Heininger and need not be further discussed. On the response of the English courts to attempts by the US authorities to freeze the assets of foreign governments held in the UK branches of US banks, see *Libyan Arab Foreign Bank v Bankers Trust Co* [1988] 1 Lloyd's Rep 259, [1989] 3 All ER 252; *Libyan Arab Foreign Bank v Manufacturers Hanover Trust Co* [1988] 2 Lloyd's Rep. 494 [1989] 1 Lloyd's Rep 608.

payments to foreign government officials by US companies under the Foreign Corrupt Practices Act 1976–77.

In 1996 the Helms Burton Act and the Iran and Libya Sanctions Act introduced new powers to impose sanctions on non-US investors in Cuba, Iran, and Libya.[23] In particular, the Helms Burton Act introduced the controversial concept of 'trafficking' in property confiscated by Cuba from US nationals.[24] Should an investor from a third country be found to benefit from the use of such property, the US courts would be empowered to entertain a suit by the former owner for civil damages from that third party, on the ground that they were trafficking in illegally obtained property. This would be so even if the non-US investor had acquired good title to the property in question under Cuban law. The claim could extend not only to the property itself but also to the proceeds of that property, thereby exposing US based assets of the non-US investor to the risk of such action. The concept of 'trafficking' in confiscated property was widely condemned as going beyond acceptable principles of jurisdiction in international law.[25] It is perhaps not surprising that no US President has brought the relevant part of the Helms Burton Act into operation. A further notable extension of US jurisdiction in recent years has been the passage of the Sarbanes-Oxley Act in 2002 which extends regulatory jurisdiction to overseas based auditors, where they act as auditors to US-listed companies, and requires non-US based firms to comply with the accounting and auditing standards contained in the Act and its implementing regulations.[26]

Throughout these areas there runs a common theory of jurisdictional competence, which is seen, at least by American lawyers, as being compatible with international law.[27] According to this theory, a state has jurisdiction to prescribe on the basis of territorial control, effects within the jurisdiction, the nationality of the person or entity subject to control, and under the protective principle. In relation to the regulation of MNEs the nationality and effects principles have been of particular

---

[23] The Cuba Liberty and Democratic Solidarity (Libertad) Act (Helms Burton Act) US Public Law 104–114 of 12 March 1996, 35 ILM 357 (1996); Iran and Libya Sanctions Act US Public Law 104–172 of 5 August 1996, 35 ILM 1273 (1996).   [24] Helms Burton Act Title III ss 301–3.

[25] See EU *Demarches Protesting the Cuban Liberty and Democratic Solidarity Act* (5 and 13 March 1996), 35 ILM 397 (1996); OAS Inter-American Juridical Committee *Opinion Examining the US Helms Burton Act* (27 August 1996) 35 ILM 1322 (1996); for academic discussion, see the exchange of views between Andreas Lowenfeld and Brice Claggett in 'Agora: The Cuban Liberty and Democratic Solidarity (Libertad) Act' 90 AJIL 419–40 and 641–44 (1996). The US legislation gave rise to retaliatory legislation in the EU to protect potential target investors: see Council Regulation 2271/96 22 November 1996 protecting against the effects of the extraterritorial application of legislation adopted by a third country and actions based or resulting therefrom OJ [1996] L309/1, 36 ILM 125 (1997). In addition national laws were adopted seeking to combat Helms Burton: Cuba: 36 ILM 472 (1997); Canada: 36 ILM 111 (1997) see also Canada-Cuba Declaration on Co-operation: 36 ILM 210 (1997); Mexico 36 ILM 133 (1997). In 1997 the US and EU entered into an understanding that Helms Burton was not to apply in return for the EU withdrawing its threatened WTO challenge to the Act *EU-US Memorandum of Understanding* (11 April 1997): 36 ILM 529 (1997).

[26] Sarbanes-Oxley Act 2002 HR 3763 23 January 2002 discussed in ch 9 at 349–50.

[27] See s 402 of the *Third Restatement* n 17 above.

importance as justifications for the assertion of US jurisdiction. Their application in controversial cases will be considered first, followed by an analysis of the limitations on the exercise of extraterritorial prescriptive jurisdiction developed under US law in response to resulting inter-state conflicts. This section will then end with a consideration of how prescriptive jurisdiction could be asserted over a non-resident parent of the MNE by reason of the presence of a subsidiary within the jurisdiction.

(a) Nationality Links

The nationality principle was applied by the US in the *Fruehauf* case.[28] During the 1960s the US restricted trade with the People's Republic of China (PRC) under its Trading with the Enemy legislation. Fruehauf France SA, a company two-thirds owned and controlled by its American parent, Fruehauf International, entered into a major contract to supply the French truck maker, Berliet, with trailers that would be exported along with Berliet tractor units to the PRC. The US Treasury Department ordered the American parent company to stop the sale. An order to this effect was passed on to the French subsidiary. Berliet refused to accept the termination of the contract and threatened to sue the French subsidiary. Thereupon, the French directors of the subsidiary, who were in a minority of three to five in relation to the American nominees, applied to the courts claiming that, under French law, the purported termination was an abuse of rights (*abus de droit*) by the majority of American directors, whose decision had been motivated by the threat of personal liability under US law, and was not in the company's best interests, given the large potential liability for the breach. The Paris Court of Appeal affirmed the decision of the commercial court of Corbeil that a temporary administrator should be appointed to oversee the performance of the contract, as the decision of the board not to perform was indeed not in the interests of the company. Thereupon the US Treasury Department accepted that the French subsidiary was not under the control of its US parent and withdrew the order.[29]

The US Government again sought to exercise extraterritorial jurisdiction on the basis of inter alia the nationality principle in the Soviet gas pipeline affair.[30] On 22 June 1982 the US Department of Commerce, at the direction of the President,

---

[28] *Société Fruehauf v Massardy* [1968] D S Jur 147 [1965] JCP II 14 274 bis (Cour d'appel, Paris), English translation: 5 ILM 476 (1966). See CD Wallace *Legal Control of the Multinational Enterprise* (The Hague: Martinus Nijhoff, 1983) 100–103; Craig 'Application of the Trading with the Enemy Act to Foreign Corporations Owned by Americans: Reflections on *Fruehauf v Massardy*' 83 Harv.LR 579 (1970).   [29] See Rosenthal and Knighton n 1 at 63.

[30] For a chronology of the affair, see G Hufbauer and J Schott 'The Soviet-European Gas Pipeline: A Case of Failed Sanctions' in T Moran (ed) *Multinational Corporations: The Political Economy of Foreign Direct Investment* (Lexington Books, 1985) 219 at 225–39. For analysis, see D Morse and J Powers 'US Export Controls and Foreign Entities: The Unanswered Questions of Pipeline Diplomacy' 23 Va.J.Int'l.L 537 (1983); H Moyer and L Marby 'Export Controls as Instruments of Foreign Policy: The History, Legal Issues and Policy Lessons of Three Recent Cases' 15 Law & Pol.Int'l Bus. 1 (1983); Ellicott 'Extraterritorial Trade Controls – Law, Policy and Business' Private Investors Abroad – Problems and Solutions in International Business in 1983 1 (1983).

extended existing controls on the export and re-export of goods and technical data relating to oil and gas exploration, exploitation, transmission, and refinement.[31] The regulations prohibited the export of oil and gas equipment and technical data needed for the construction of a new gas pipeline from the Soviet Union to Western Europe. To the extent that the regulations prohibited direct exports of such equipment and data from the US they were unobjectionable. However, they extended the prohibition to the re-export of such goods and data, where these were of US origin, by persons in third countries. Furthermore, the re-export of non-US goods and data by a person 'subject to the jurisdiction of the United States' was conditional on permission from the US Office of Export Administration. Finally, no person in the US or in a foreign country could export or re-export to the USSR foreign products based on US technical data where any person subject to the jurisdiction of the US received royalties for, or had licensed the use of, the technical data concerned. The effect of the regulations was to extend the operation of US export controls to companies not possessing US nationality but using US technology under licence, and to the overseas subsidiaries of US companies by reason of their US ownership or control.

According to the Commission of the European Communities, these regulations went beyond what was acceptable under international law,[32] on the grounds, first, that they violated the territorial principle of jurisdiction in that they purported to regulate the activities of companies in the EC, not under the territorial competence of the US[33] and, secondly, because there could be no support for the scope of the regulations under the nationality principle. As regards the EC-based subsidiaries of US companies, the regulations purported to impose US nationality on companies contrary to their nationality of incorporation and place of registered office, these being the tests of corporate nationality accepted as general principles of international law by the ICJ in the *Barcelona Traction* case.[34] As regards the companies whose only tie to the US was through the use of licensed technology, or the possession of US origin goods, the Commission stated that: '[g]oods and technology do not have any nationality and there are no known rules under international law for using goods or technology situated abroad as a basis for establishing jurisdiction over the persons controlling them.'[35] These violations of the nationality principle were seen by the Commission as exacerbating the infringement of the territoriality principle. The US regulations elicited widespread protests from European states. Some European states applied blocking measures that required the companies covered by the US orders to fulfil their contracts.[36] In

---

[31] The relevant regulations appear in 21 ILM 864 (1982).

[32] See Commission of the European Communities 'Comments on the US Regulations Concerning Trade with the USSR' 12 August 1982: 21 ILM 891 (1982).   [33] ibid para 5 at 3.

[34] ICJ Reports 1970 3 at 43. Cited ibid para 7 at 4.   [35] ibid para 8 at 4.

[36] See eg United Kingdom: The Protection of Trading Interests (US Re-export Control) Order 1982 SI 1982: 885 30 June 1982 made under the Protection of Trading Interests Act 1980 rendering the US regulations measures which were damaging to UK trading interests. On 2 August 1982, the

response, in November 1982, President Reagan rescinded the regulations and the 'sanctions' that had been imposed on companies that had continued to perform their contracts.

(b) The 'Effects' Doctrine

This doctrine evolved in the context of US antitrust law to deal with overseas cartels which interfere with the US market to the detriment of the US consumer in violation of s 1 of the Sherman Act.[37] By s 1 of the Sherman Act 'every contract, combination in the form of trust or otherwise, or conspiracy in restraint of trade or commerce among the several states or with foreign nations ... ' is illegal and a felony. By s 2 of the Act: 'every person who shall monopolize, or attempt to monopolize any part of the trade or commerce among the several states or with foreign nations, shall be deemed guilty of a misdemeanour.' The wide language of these provisions suggests that they apply not only to impugned transactions or conspiracies within the US but also to such activities when they occur outside the US.

Initially, the US Supreme Court observed the limits of US territorial jurisdiction in this area.[38] This did not, however, prevent the application of the Sherman Act to a conspiracy which, while involving the acts of a foreign sovereign, also involved deliberate anti-competitive acts by the conspirators within the US.[39] The most significant American case in this area is *US v Alcoa*,[40] decided in 1945. There, the US Court of Appeals for the Second Circuit established the principle that the Sherman Act extended to the activities of non-nationals abroad where this produced anti-competitive effects within the US. The case concerned antitrust proceedings that had been instituted against the Aluminum Company of America (Alcoa) and Aluminum Limited (Limited), a Canadian corporation. Limited had been incorporated in 1928 to take over all the non-US assets of Alcoa. By 1935 the two corporations had become completely separate. In 1931 Limited joined an international cartel in the aluminium market, which, by 1936, included imports into the US market. The trial court held that Alcoa itself had no part in these agreements. The remaining question was, therefore, whether Limited could be held to have violated the Sherman Act.[41]

Secretary of State for Trade and Industry, Lord Cockfield, issued directions under s 1(3) of the Protection of Trading Interests Act to four British companies forbidding them to comply with the American embargo.

[37] Given the extensive and instructive literature on this subject it is unnecessary to offer more than an introductory account in this work. For more detailed analysis, see Rosenthal and Knighton above n 1 ch 2; Neale and Stephens n 1 chs 3–8; J Atwood and K Brewster *Antitrust and American Business Abroad* (2nd edn, Colorado Springs: McGraw-Hill, 1981 and 1993 supplement); Wilbur L Fugate *Foreign Commerce and the Antitrust Laws* (New York: Aspen Publishers, 5th edn, and supplements).

[38] See *American Banana Company v United Fruit Co* 213 US 347 (1909).

[39] See *US v Sisal Sales Corporation* 274 US 268 (1927). For comment, see Rosenthal and Knighton, above n 1 at 24 and Neale and Stephens n 1 above at 87.   [40] 148 F 2d 416 (1945).

[41] In personam jurisdiction had been established over Limited because it ran an important administrative office in New York. This could have been its actual headquarters.

The Appeal Court held that Limited could be held liable under the Sherman Act. The Court's opinion was delivered by Judge Learned Hand. On the question of jurisdiction the judge said:

'It is settled law ... that any state may impose liabilities, even upon persons not within its allegiance, for conduct outside its borders that has consequences within its borders which the state reprehends; and that these liabilities other states will ordinarily recognize.'[42]

On its true construction, the Sherman Act was held to impose liability on the conduct of persons not in allegiance to the US for conduct occurring outside its territory. The jurisdiction of the US under the Sherman Act was limited to those cases in which an anti-competitive agreement made by non-US parties outside US jurisdiction was intended to affect US imports or exports, and its performance was shown actually to have had some effect upon them.[43] On this issue, as soon as the intent to affect imports or exports had been established, on the basis of the foreseeability of the effects of the agreement in question, the burden of proof shifted to the defendant to show that no appreciable effects had in fact occurred.

This case laid the foundations for the more extensive application of the Sherman Act to foreign cartels which was to lead to the first major conflicts over US extraterritorial jurisdiction. However, since *Alcoa*, US antitrust enforcement policy has been such that applications of the 'effects doctrine' have been rare.[44] Most cases have involved American companies, as participants in illegal cartels, over whom jurisdiction was never in doubt. Furthermore, foreign companies have not usually been named as defendants in suits initiated by the US authorities unless the express purpose of the restrictive agreement concerned had been to divide up world markets, with the US market being preserved for the US party in return for its exclusion from overseas markets. Direct interference with the US market is clear in such cases.[45]

Major conflicts over the application of the 'effects doctrine' did occur in two leading cases, each of which involved a direct challenge to the economic policy of the target state.[46] The first was the *Swiss Watchmakers* case.[47] In that case, the US courts attacked the Swiss watch industry's government sponsored cartel whose aim was the protection of the industry against damaging competition both from within and outside Switzerland. The court held that the conduct of the Swiss

---

[42] ibid at 443.   [43] ibid at 444.

[44] See M Sornarajah 'The Extraterritorial Enforcement of US Antitrust Law: Conflict and Compromise' 31 ICLQ 127 (1982).

[45] See further Neale and Stephens n 1 above ch 5 and their discussion of *US v National Lead Co* 63 F Supp 513 (SDNY 1945), 332 US 319 (1947); *US v General Electric Co* 82 F Supp 753 (1949), 115 F Supp 835 (1953); *US v United States Alkali Export Association Inc* 86 F Supp 59 (1949); *Timken Roller Bearing Co v US* 83 F Supp 284 (1949), 341 US 593 (1951).

[46] See also *US v ICI* 100 F Supp 504 (SDNY 1951) and 105 F Supp 215 (SDNY 1952), as reviewed by the English courts in *British Nylon Spinners v Imperial Chemical Industries* [1953] 1 Ch 19 (CA) and [1955] 1 Ch 37.

[47] *US v Watchmakers of Switzerland Information Center Inc* 1963 Trade Cases CCH, para 70600, 1965 Trade Cases CCH, para 71352.

industry in Switzerland was itself a violation of US antitrust laws and ordered changes in the organization of that conduct. That resulted in diplomatic protest from Switzerland, leading to the intervention of the State Department, and to a modification of the court's order so as to exclude actions undertaken by Swiss defendants that were not contrary to Swiss law.[48] Similarly, in *Zenith Radio Corp v Hazeltine Research Inc*[49] a private treble damages action was successfully brought by the plaintiff corporation against the defendant on the ground that the latter, along with other US firms supplying the Canadian domestic appliances market, had entered a patent pool in Canada which had the effect of hampering competition from imports into Canada. The patent pool had been encouraged by the Canadian government as part of its domestic economic policy favouring the local production of consumer goods for the Canadian market. The decision engendered protest from the Canadian Government.[50]

An apparent change of direction occurred in the case of *Timberlane v Bank of America*[51] where the US Court of Appeals for the Ninth Circuit restated the effects doctrine in the light of the need to take account of the legitimate interests of foreign states. According to the judgment of the Court, delivered by Judge Choy, 'a tripartite analysis seems to be indicated'.[52] The antitrust laws require:

in the first instance that there be *some* effect – actual or intended – on American commerce before the Federal courts may legitimately exercise subject matter jurisdiction under those statutes. Second, a greater showing of burden or restraint may be necessary to demonstrate that the effect is sufficiently large to present a cognizable injury to the plaintiffs and, therefore, a civil violation of the antitrust laws ... Third, there is the additional question which is unique to the international setting of whether the interests of, and links to, the United States – including the magnitude of the effect on American foreign commerce – are sufficiently strong vis-a-vis those of other nations, to justify an assertion of extraterritorial authority.[53]

The elements to be weighed in this process include the degree of conflict with foreign law or policy, the nationality or allegiance of the parties and the locations or principal places of business of corporations, the extent to which enforcement by either state can be expected to achieve compliance, the relative significance of effects on the US as compared with those elsewhere, the extent to which there is an explicit purpose to harm or affect American commerce, the foreseeability of such effect, and the relative importance to the violations charged of conduct within the US as compared with conduct abroad.

In *Mannington Mills v Congoleum Corp*,[54] the Third Circuit Court of Appeals added four further factors that should be considered in the balancing process. These were the possible effect on foreign relations if the court exercises jurisdiction and grants relief; if relief is granted, whether a party will be placed in the position of

---

[48] See 1965 Trade Cases, para 71352 and Neale and Stephens n 1 above at 156–57.
[49] 395 US 100 (1969).   [50] Rosenthal and Knighton n 1 above at 31.
[51] 549 F 2d 597 (1976 Ninth Circuit). See further Neale and Stephens n 1 above ch 6.
[52] ibid at 613.   [53] ibid.   [54] 595 F 2d 1287 (1979).

being forced to perform an act illegal in either country or be under conflicting requirements by both countries; whether an order for relief would be acceptable in the US if made by a foreign nation under similar circumstances; and whether a treaty between the affected nations has addressed the issue.[55]

The balancing test laid down in *Timberlane* and *Mannington Mills* is further supplemented by the doctrines of sovereign immunity and 'foreign sovereign compulsion' as a means of reducing conflicts over the extraterritorial application of antitrust laws.[56] Thus, in *International Association of Machinists v The Organisation of Petroleum Exporting Countries*[57] an antitrust action brought against the member states of OPEC failed on the ground that the defendants were sovereign states entitled to immunity from suit for their actions as members of the said organization, in that these actions were undertaken in pursuit of sovereign purposes. As regards 'foreign sovereign compulsion' the US Department of Justice will not prosecute conduct that has been compelled by a foreign sovereign in circumstances where a refusal to comply with the foreign sovereign's command would give rise to the imposition of significant penalties or to the denial of specific substantial benefits. Foreign government measures short of compulsion do not suffice for this defence, although they can be relevant in a comity analysis.[58]

Finally, mention should be made of the Foreign Trade Antitrust Improvements Act 1982 (FTAIA). This limits the operation of the Sherman Act to conduct involving trade or commerce, other than import trade or commerce, with foreign nations unless such conduct has a direct, substantial, and reasonably foreseeable effect on US domestic trade or commerce, or on import trade or commerce with foreign nations, or on US exporters.[59] The effect of this provision is to reduce the number of antitrust cases involving foreign defendants through its exclusion of import commerce, although its effect on the balancing test may be to narrow its scope in cases where the statute applies.[60] In *F Hoffmann-La Roche v Empagran SA* the US Supreme Court held that the FTAIA did not apply to cases where the foreign plaintiff's claim is based solely on independent foreign harm. On the facts the plaintiffs, distributors of vitamins based in Ukraine, Australia, Ecuador, and Panama, alleged that they had been harmed by the anti-competitive price fixing practices of Hoffman-La Roche, acting in concert with other pharmaceutical companies, in relation to certain classes of vitamins. They failed to pass the jurisdictional hurdle under FTAIA as the claim rested solely on harm they had suffered on imports outside the US.[61] This prompted

---

[55] ibid at 1297–98.

[56] See further Neale and Stephens n 1 above ch 7; Sornarajah n 44 above at 138–47.

[57] 649 F 2d 1354 (Ninth Circuit 1981).

[58] US Department of Justice, *Antitrust Enforcement Guidelines* n 19 above para 3.32. See further *Continental Ore Co v Union Carbide and Carbon Corp* 370 US 690 (1962); *Interamerican Refining Corp v Texaco Maracaibo Inc* 307 F Supp 291 (D Del 1970); *Matsushita Electric Industrial Co v Zenith Radio Corp* 475 US 574 (1986).

[59] 15 USC s 6a. See too US Department of Justice *Antitrust Enforcement Guidelines* n 19 above at paras 3.11–3.122.   [60] Roth n 1 above at 259.

[61] *F Hoffmann-La Roche Ltd v Empagran SA* (US Sup Ct 14 June 2004) 542 US 155; 124 S Ct 2359; 159 L Ed 2d 226; 2004 US LEXIS 4174.

the plaintiffs to try another argument before the US courts. They alleged that the harm they had suffered outside the US was causally connected with the pharmaceutical firm's pricing practices within the US, which caused higher prices worldwide and, without which, the global price fixing cartel would have broken down. This was rejected by the US Court of Appeals for the District of Colombia on the ground that it involved a 'but for' test of causation. That was insufficient to link the foreign harm with the US market. The FTAIA required proximate cause between the US and foreign conduct that led to the injury.[62]

It is notable that US law has evolved its own doctrines to meet the criticism of an excessive assumption of extraterritorial jurisdiction.[63] The above mentioned developments in US antitrust law have been reflected and generalized beyond the field of antitrust in s 403 of the Third Restatement.[64] By s 403(1): 'even when one of the bases of jurisdiction listed in s 402 is present, a state may not exercise jurisdiction to prescribe law with respect to a person or activity having connections with another state when the exercise of such jurisdiction is unreasonable.' This principle has been applied by some US courts as a requirement of comity, that term being understood not merely as an act of discretion and courtesy but as reflecting a sense of obligation among states.[65] Whether the exercise of jurisdiction is unreasonable depends on an evaluation of all the relevant factors including those listed in s 403(2)(a)–(h).[66] These considerations are not exhaustive nor are they listed in any order of priority.[67]

---

[62] *Empagran SA v F Hoffmann-La Roche* (USCA DC Cir 28 June 2005) 417 F 3d 1267, 2005 US App LEXIS 12743. A similar argument, involving markets in certain chemicals, was dismissed in *Latino Quimica-Amtewx SA v Akzo* (US DC SDNY 7 September 2005) 2005 US Dist LEXIS 19788. The plaintiffs did succeed on such an argument in *In Re Monosodium Glutamate Antitrust Litigation* (US Dist Ct Minn 2 May 2005) 2005 US Dist LEXIS 8424. Here the plaintiffs alleged direct injury from the US market as they had been prohibited by the defendants from purchasing supplies at lower cost from US sources.

[63] The extent to which this balancing approach can be effective in avoiding conflict will be considered at the end of this chapter. By contrast, the German system of antitrust law, which also espouses an 'effects doctrine' modelled on US precedents, has approached the issue of excessive jurisdictional claims by way of a two-tier test. First, there must be clear proof of harm to the domestic competitive system within Germany that amounts to a violation of the particular substantive provisions involved. Secondly, the compatibility of the proposed exercise of jurisdiction will be tested by reference to the principles of international law. Thus German law has evolved in the context of an explicit reference to the controlling authority of international law. See further Gerber 'The Extraterritorial Application of the German Antitrust Laws' 77 AJIL 756 (1983).   [64] Above n 17 at 244.

[65] ibid Comment (a) at 246.

[66] The factors listed are: '(a) the link of the activity to the territory of the regulating state i.e. the extent to which the activity takes place within the territory, or has substantial, direct and foreseeable effect upon or in the territory; (b) the connections, such as nationality, residence, or economic activity, between the regulating state and the person principally responsible for the activity to be regulated, or between that state and those whom the regulation is designed to protect; (c) the character of the activity to be regulated, the importance of regulation to the regulating state, the extent to which other states regulate such activities, and the degree to which the desirability of such regulation is generally accepted; (d) the existence of justified expectations that might be protected or hurt by the regulation; (e) the importance of the regulation to the international political, legal or economic system; (f) the extent to which the regulation is consistent with the traditions of the international system; (g) the extent to which another state may have an interest in regulating the activity; and (h) the likelihood of conflict with regulation by another state.'   [67] ibid Comment (b) at 246.

Conflicting exercises of jurisdiction by two states are dealt with by s 403(3). This recommends that where two states could each reasonably exercise jurisdiction over a person or activity, but the prescriptions by the two states are in conflict, each state is obliged to evaluate its own as well as the other state's interest in exercising jurisdiction in the light of all the relevant factors. A state should defer to the other state where that state's interest is clearly greater. The scope of s 403(3) was reviewed by the US Supreme Court in the case of *Hartford Fire Insurance Co v California*.[68] Certain London based reinsurers were alleged to have engaged in unlawful conspiracies with US based primary insurers and reinsurers to affect the terms upon which reinsurance for commercial general liability cover would be available on the US domestic market. The London reinsurers argued that the claims against them should have been dismissed as improper applications of the Sherman Act to foreign conduct. The US Supreme Court dismissed this argument. It held that a US court should only decline to exercise Sherman Act jurisdiction on the grounds of international comity where there was a true conflict between the requirements of domestic and foreign law. According to s 403(3) such a conflict did not exist, 'where a person subject to regulation by two states can comply with the laws of both'.[69] Following this prescription, the Supreme Court held that the London reinsurers were subject to US jurisdiction in that they did not argue that British law required them to act in some fashion prohibited by US law, or that their compliance with the laws of both countries was otherwise impossible. Thus there was no relevant conflict with British law. In so holding the Supreme Court rejected the argument of the UK Government, as *amicus curiae*, that it had established a comprehensive regulatory regime over the London reinsurance market and that the conduct of the London reinsurers was perfectly consistent with British law and policy. The fact that their conduct was lawful in the UK was not, in itself, a bar to the application of US antitrust laws.[70]

The *Hartford Insurance* case gave rise to considerable criticism. The majority of the US Supreme Court was seen to be reviving a 'pure effects' approach to extraterritorial jurisdiction that effectively diminished the comity based balancing process developed in earlier cases and in the US Restatement.[71] That could

---

[68] 509 US 764; 125 L Ed 2d 612; 113 S Ct 2891(1993).

[69] Third Restatement above n 17 s 403 comment (e) at 247.

[70] The majority opinion was met with a dissenting opinion, led by Scalia J, which asserted that, although the Sherman Act undoubtedly had extraterritorial scope, the balancing analysis required under s 403 of the Third Restatement pointed to the conclusion that the UK had a heavy interest in regulating the activity in question under s 403(2)(g). The US should defer to that overriding interest, especially as the activity relevant to the counts in issue took place primarily in the UK, the defendants were British corporations and British subjects having their principal place of business or residence outside the US (see s 403(2)(a) and (b)). Furthermore, the majority's interpretation of s 403(3) was contrary to earlier case law and would bring the Sherman Act and other laws into sharp and unnecessary conflict with the legitimate interests of other countries.

[71] See further Andreas Lowenfeld 'Conflict, Balancing of Interests, and the Exercise of Jurisdiction to Prescribe: Reflections on the Insurance Antitrust Case' 89 AJIL 42 (1995); for a view supporting the majority Phillip R. Trimble 'The Supreme Court and International Law: The Demise

only harm US economic relations with major trading partners and allow for an exercise of US jurisdiction in all but the clearest cases of conflict, as where conduct required under the law of the US would be prohibited under the law of the target jurisdiction.[72] Nevertheless, this approach was endorsed in the 1995 revision of the US Department of Justice Antitrust Enforcement Guidelines for International Operations.[73] In addition, more recent cases have extended the operation of the *Hartford* approach from private party civil suits to criminal suits brought by the US Government.[74] On the other hand, to obtain jurisdiction under the *Hartford* approach, the claimant must show a substantial effect on US commerce arising for the foreign conduct in question.[75] Thus the potential scope of this ruling can be limited in given cases. Equally, since the decision in *Hartford Fire*, there have not been any major disputes over the extraterritorial application of US antitrust law, comparable to those of the past. This may be due, in part, to the adoption, by the US, of bilateral antitrust cooperation agreements with major trading partners, which will be briefly discussed below.

(c) Links of Ownership and Control

Finally, the possibility of asserting prescriptive jurisdiction over a foreign parent company based on the presence of its subsidiary within the host state should be considered. Such a basis for prescriptive jurisdiction is suggested in the US Restatement.[76] The assertion of jurisdiction on this basis involves disregarding the corporate separation between parent and subsidiary. Consequently, often difficult enquiries would have to be made regarding the extent of control exercised by the overseas parent over the acts of its subsidiary, to determine whether the two corporations can be regarded as a single entity for the purposes of legal regulation by the state seeking prescriptive jurisdiction. The issue of disregarding corporate

---

of Restatement Section 403' 89 AJIL 53 (1995); Larry Kramer 'Note: Extraterritorial Application of American Law After the Insurance Antitrust Case: A Reply to Professors Lowenfeld and Trimble' 89 AJIL 750 (1995). See further Roger P Alford 'The Extraterritorial Application of US Antitrust Laws: A Postscript to *Hartford Fire Insurance Co v California*' 34 Va.J.Int'l L. 213 (1993); James P Rhatican '*Hartford Fire Insurance Co v California*: A Mixed Blessing for Insurance Antitrust Defendants' 47 Rutgers LR 905 (1995). For UK comment, see Roth 'Jurisdiction, British Public Policy and the US Supreme Court' 110 LQR 194 (1994); Robertson and Dimitriou 'The Extraterritorial Application of US Antitrust Laws and the US Supreme Court' 43 ICLQ 417 (1994).

[72] See Kenneth Dam 'Extraterritoriality in an Age of Globalization: The Hartford Fire Case' (1993) Sup Ct Rev 289.   [73] Above n 19 at para 3.1.

[74] See *United States of America v Nippon Paper Industries Co* (US CA 1st Cir decision of 17 March 1997), 109 F 3d 1, 1997 US App LEXIS 4939.

[75] See *DEE-K Enterprises Inc v Hevafil* 299 (US CA 4th Cir Decision of 30 July 2002) 299 F 3d 281; US App LEXIS 15256.

[76] See Third Restatement n 17 above s 414 comment (h) also at 273. See *Commonwealth v Beneficial Finance Co* 275 NE 2d 33 (Sup Ct Mass 1971) cert denied 407 US 914 (1972). In this case, the Supreme Court of Massachusetts held that prescriptive and adjudicatory jurisdiction over an out-of-state (although not alien) parent company could exist where the subsidiary within the jurisdiction has committed an offence within the jurisdiction as an agent of the parent: 275 NE at 56–57.

separation between resident and non-resident units of a MNE has arisen mainly in relation to the question of personal jurisdiction over the non-resident unit, and will be further considered in that context.

(3) Personal Jurisdiction

The starting point for the assertion of personal jurisdiction is the presence of the defendant within the jurisdiction for the purpose of issuing process against him or her.[77] However, every advanced legal system accepts a power to issue process against a non-resident defendant, provided that there are sufficient factors connecting that defendant with the forum, which can justify the assertion of personal jurisdiction over him, her, or it.[78] In certain common law jurisdictions, notably the US, even if a sufficient connection is found to justify the exercise of personal jurisdiction over the non-resident unit of the MNE, the courts of the forum may consider whether, taking into account the interests of the parties to the proceedings and the implications for international comity between states, they should in fact do so. Thus, in such legal systems, the analysis of personal jurisdiction over non-resident units of MNEs can involve not only questions of fact concerning the existence of relevant connecting factors, but also questions of discretion regarding the appropriateness of the forum as the place for determining the dispute before it. Each will be considered in turn.

(a) Establishing a Sufficient Connection Between the Forum and the Non-Resident Unit of the MNE

In relation to the service of process against non-resident units of a MNE, the major question is whether the non-resident unit can be brought before the courts of the forum despite its absence from their territory. As noted above, this depends on the establishment of sufficient links between the non-resident unit and the actions that are the subject-matter of proceedings before the forum jurisdiction. Clearly, where the non-resident unit has acted directly on its own behalf within the jurisdiction, no difficulty should arise in exercising jurisdiction over it. More problematic is the case where the non-resident unit acts outside the jurisdiction, but those acts have damaging effects on persons within the forum jurisdiction. At this point the assertion of jurisdiction over the non-resident unit will have to be based either on the presence of an affiliated enterprise within the forum jurisdiction and, in particular, on the links of ownership and control between the resident

---

[77] See eg under English law *Sirdar Gurdyal Singh v Rajah of Faridkote* [1894] AC 670 at 683–84 per the Earl of Selborne LC; under US law *Pennoyer v Neff* 95 US 714 at 717 (1878), *Hanson v Denkla* 357 US 235 at 250–51 (1958). See further Phillip I Blumberg, Kurt A Strasser, Nicholas Georgakopoulos, and Eric J Gourvan *Blumberg on Corporate Groups* (New York: Aspen Publishers, 2nd edn, 2005) vol 1 para 23.02.   [78] See eg s 421 US Restatement above n 16 at 305–306.

and non-resident affiliates, or upon other significant business contacts with the jurisdiction, such as the presence within the forum jurisdiction of officers of the non-resident entity, or of products made by that entity.

(i) Corporate Links Between Resident and Non-Resident Units of the MNE

The mere presence of an affiliate within the jurisdiction may not be sufficient, of itself, to establish personal jurisdiction over the non-resident entity. The crucial question is whether the relations between the resident and non-resident entities are such that the two can be regarded as a single unit for the service of process. This involves, first, an analysis of the legal form of the entity within the jurisdiction and, secondly, an ascertainment of the way in which business activities between the two entities are organized.

The legal form of the entity within the forum jurisdiction may be crucial in determining the amenability of the non-resident unit to suit. In particular, the legal distinction between establishment through a branch or a subsidiary may be of considerable practical importance given that a branch does not possess separate legal personality from that of its parent whereas a subsidiary does. For example, under the English Companies Act 1985, where a company incorporated outside the United Kingdom (an oversea company) establishes an unincorporated place of business within the UK,[79] it will be amenable to suit before the English courts so long as it has an identifiable place of business within the jurisdiction to which process may be served or sent.[80] The effect is 'to protect a foreign company's British creditors by obtaining for them ab initio the means of serving process in this country, free from the inconvenience of seeking out the foreign company in its country of incorporation'.[81] In this respect the foreign company is placed on the same footing as an English company. In striking contrast, where a foreign parent chooses to incorporate an English subsidiary, rather than operate through a branch or office, the English courts will look first and foremost to the English

[79] See Companies Act 1985 s 691 (as amended by Companies Act 1989 s 145), s 695 preserved by Civil Procedure Rules 1998 (CPR) Part 6, Rule 6.2(2) (b). See also Companies Act 2006 Part 34 ss 1044–1059.

[80] For the meaning of 'a place of business' under s 695 see *South India Shipping Corporation v Export Import Bank of Korea* [1985] 2 All ER 219 (CA); *Re Oriel* [1985] 3 All ER 216 at 223 per Oliver LJ (CA). On what constitutes valid service under s 695(1), see *Rome v Punjab National Bank* [1989] 1 WLR 1211. See also the alternative procedure, introduced in s 694A Companies Act 1985 (inserted by SI 1992/3179, preserved by CPR 1998 Part 6, Rule 6.2(2)(c)), applicable to branches registered under the Eleventh Company Law Directive (Council Directive 89/666 OJ [1989] L395/36) which provides for service at the British registered branch of any limited company incorporated abroad in respect of the carrying on of the business of the branch. This requirement has been widely interpreted and is fulfilled if the service under s 694A (2) is in part in respect of carrying on of the business of the branch: *Saab v Saudi American Bank* [1999] 4 All ER 321 (CA). See also the Companies Act 2006 n 79 above Part 34 which introduces revised rules for registration of particulars, company names, and disclosure requirements for oversea companies and their UK branches.

[81] *South India Shipping* ibid per Ackner LJ at 224a–b.

subsidiary as the relevant corporate unit, respecting the corporate separation between the parent and subsidiary. Thus service of process on the local subsidiary will not normally amount to service on the foreign parent company.[82]

On the other hand, US law will normally accept as valid the service of process on the foreign parent company through its US subsidiary.[83] There is no requirement to the effect that the foreign defendant should be served under the procedures established by the Hague Convention of 1965 on the Service Abroad of Judicial and Extra-judicial Documents in Civil and Commercial Matters, which is only one of a number of methods of service authorized by US Federal Procedure Rules.[84] On the other hand, it was held in *Federal Trade Commission v Compagnie de Saint Gobain Pont à Mousson*[85] that where a subpoena effecting compulsory process is served by direct mail on a foreign company in a foreign jurisdiction, the failure to use established channels of international judicial assistance will render such service invalid under US law, as it violates accepted principles of territorial sovereignty at international law. More recently, the US Court of Appeal for the Ninth Circuit has accepted service on a foreign corporate defendant by way of the internet at the defendant's internet address, where service had been attempted at the address of the defendant's US attorney, but the attorney declined to accept service and where normal postal service had failed. However, this was an exceptional means of service abroad and could only be effected by court order. In this instance the district court had acted properly to authorize such service, within its discretion under Rules 4(h)(2) and 4(f)(3) of the Federal Rules of Civil Procedure, as the defendant was an internet-based business and other more usual methods of service had failed.[86]

---

[82] See Companies Act 1985 s 725(1) and CPR 1998 Part 6 Rule 6.2(2)(a). In order for the foreign parent to become a party to English proceedings, where the parent is domiciled outside the EC, it must be shown that the parent is a proper party to be served in accordance with one or more of the heads of CPR 1998 Rule 6.20. Where the parent company is domiciled within the EU, service of process will be subject to the provisions of the Brussels Convention on Jurisdiction and Enforcement of Judgments in Civil and Commercial Matters 1968 incorporated into English law by the Civil Jurisdiction and Judgments Act 1982. The Brussels Convention has now been superseded, for EU Member States, by Council Regulation (EC) 44/2001 of 22 December 2000 on Jurisdiction and the Recognition and Enforcement of Judgments in Civil and Commercial Matters: OJ [2001] L12/1. It entered into force on 1 March 2002 by the Civil Jurisdiction and Judgments Order 2001 (SI 2001/3929). For the main changes introduced by the Judgments Regulation see Oliver Parker 'Developments in Judicial Co-operation in Civil Matters in the EU' New Law Journal 15 February 2002 at 227. See generally Adrian Briggs and Peter Rees *Civil Jurisdiction and Judgments* (London: Lloyds of London Press, 4th edn, 2005). In addition, the service of judicial and extra-judicial documents in civil and commercial matters within the EU is governed by Council Regulation 1348/2000 of 29 May 2000 OJ [2000] L160/37.

[83] See *Volkswagenwerk AG v Schlunk* 468 US 694 (1988); 27 ILM 1092 (1988) and *Blumberg on Corporate Groups* above n 77 ch 36.

[84] ibid. The convention came into effect on 10 February 1969. For text, see 4 ILM 341 (1965). See further US Federal Rules of Civil Procedure, Rule 4(f)(1) which requires use of 'any internationally agreed means reasonably calculated to give notice, such as the means authorised by the Hague Convention' and Rule 4(f)(3) which allows the use of 'other means not prohibited by international agreement as may be directed by the court'.   [85] 636 F 2d 1300 (DC Cir 1980).

[86] *Rio Properties Inc v Rio International Interlink* (US CA 9th Cir decision of 20 March 2002) 41 ILM 987.

Having considered the legal form of the relationship between parent and local affiliate the business relationship between them must be analysed to determine whether the acts of the affiliate within the jurisdiction can be attributed to the non-resident parent. Where a local branch is involved this should not be difficult. However, where a local subsidiary is involved an analysis of fact will have to be undertaken which is not dissimilar to a 'lifting the corporate veil' for the purposes of establishing the liability of the parent company for the acts of its subsidiary.[87] This involves consideration of the extent to which the parent controls the acts of its subsidiary within the jurisdiction, so that the acts of the latter can be seen as, either, the direct acts of the foreign parent, with the subsidiary acting as the 'alter ego' of the parent, or as acts which create parent company responsibility on the basis of agency.[88] However, it seems well settled that the mere ownership of shares in the subsidiary is not a sufficient connecting factor between the parent and the jurisdiction. A further connection must be found.[89] The burden of proof falls on the party seeking personal jurisdiction over the non-resident parent. The standard of proof may be lower than that required to establish the substantive liability of the non-resident parent.[90] In relation to a non-resident affiliate other than the parent company, the major question is whether the degree of economic integration between itself and the entity within the forum is sufficient to see the latter as the agent or 'alter ego' of the former for the purpose of the actions that are subject to legal proceedings. In this respect US courts have been relatively liberal in establishing the requisite economic links between affiliates,

[87] See further ch 8.

[88] See Fawcett 'Jurisdiction and Subsidiaries' [1985] JBL 16. See, for the US position, *Wells Fargo & Co v Wells Fargo Express Co* 556 F 2d 406 (9th Cir 1977); *Doe v Unocal Corporation* (US CA 9th Cir, 27 April 2001) 248 F 3d 915; 2001 US App LEXIS 769; *Dole Food Company v Watts* (US CA 9th Cir, decision of 10 September 2002) 303 F 3d 1104; 2002 US App LEXIS 18524; *Harris Rutsky and Company Insurance Services v Bell and Clements Limited* (US CA 9th Cir, decision of 12 May 2003) 328 F 3d 1122; 2003 US App LEXIS 8842 and *Blumberg on Corporate Groups* above n 77 chs 23–32. In antitrust cases, the US courts have applied the same general principles of jurisdiction as apply in other cases. In doing so the courts act under the statutory authority granted by s 12 of the Clayton Act and s 7 of the Sherman Act to bring antitrust proceedings against a corporation in any district in which it is 'found' or 'transacts business'. It is enough to show that the corporation transacted business within the jurisdiction, either from abroad, or through a US subsidiary: *US v Scophony Corporation of America* 333 US 795 (1948). There must be some evidence of control going beyond the mere existence of the parent/subsidiary relationship. However, as was pointed out in *Akzona v Du Pont* 607 F Supp 227 at 238–240 (Dist Ct Del 1984) the standards of jurisdiction under s 12 of the Clayton Act are more leniently applied, so as to give effect to the policy of the antitrust acts. Thus the presence of separate corporate formalities will not prevent jurisdiction from being exercised where, in fact, the US subsidiary is controlled by the foreign parent for the purposes of antitrust violations. See further *Blumberg on Corporate Groups* above n 77 para 31.02.

[89] See eg the US case *Cannon Manufacturing Co v Cudhay Packing Co* 267 US 333, 45 S Ct 250, 569 L Ed 634 (1925) discussed in *Blumberg on Corporate Groups* above n 77 ch 25. See also *Walker v Newgent* 583 F 2d 163 (5th Cir 1978); *Product Promotions Inc v Cousteau* 495 F 2d 483 (5th Cir 1974); 36 Am Jur 2d s 347; *Harris Rutsky and Co Insurance Services v Bell and Clements* above n 88 where the court held that even 100 per cent ownership of stock does not make a subsidiary an 'alter ego' of the parent without more.

[90] See *Hargrave v Fireboard Corp* 710 F 2d 1154 at 1161 (5th Cir 1983).

although approaches may vary between different State Courts and among the Federal Circuits.[91]

By contrast to US law, English law has been highly territorial in its approach to personal jurisdiction over MNEs. Thus in *Multinational Gas and Petrochemical Services Co v Multinational Gas and Petrochemical Services Ltd*,[92] the Court of Appeal refused to accept jurisdiction over American, French, and Japanese parent companies, the sole shareholders in a joint venture operating within the jurisdiction through an agent company, in a claim brought against them by the liquidator of the joint venture. The Court of Appeal held inter alia that the foreign parent companies could not be regarded as proper parties to the action, in that the joint venture was a separate enterprise for whose acts the parent companies had no responsibility in accordance with the doctrine established in *Salomon's*[93] case and culminating in *Re Horsley & Weight Ltd*.[94] In any case, were the foreign parent companies to be joined in the action, they 'would ... be faced with an action in this country involving novel propositions of law as well as lengthy and expensive investigation of the facts'.[95] That weighed against the granting of leave to serve process outside the jurisdiction. This decision illustrates the difficulties of taking litigation to the 'centre' of a MNE located outside the jurisdiction. The liability to suit of the non-resident parent company can be avoided by reference to traditional doctrines of company law, which fail to disclose a cause of action. It is an instance of allowing the logic of the single unit enterprise to shield the directing units of a corporate group from potential liabilities which were, arguably, created by their mismanagement of the joint venture.

That said, more recent developments in English law, driven in part by the influence of EC law, appear to show a greater willingness to extend jurisdiction to foreign incorporated companies. For example, in *Re BRAC Rent-A-Car International* it was held that an administration order, under the EC Regulation on Insolvency Proceedings,[96] could be made against an entity not incorporated in an EC Member State, but in the US, if the centre of that company's main interests was in the Member State making the order.[97] In *The Deichland* the Court of Appeal held that a company incorporated in Panama, whose central management and control

---

[91] See, for example, *Frummer v Hilton Hotels International Inc* 227 NE 2d 851 (1967); affirmed but distinguished in *Delagi v Volkswagenwerk* AG 29 NY 2d 426, 278 NE 2d 895, 328 NYS 2d 653 (1972). See, more recently, *Wiwa v Royal Dutch Petroleum Co* 226 F 3d 88 at 95 (US CA 2d Cir 2000); 2000 US App LEXIS 23274 at 14; *Victor Meier v Sun International Hotels* (US CA 11th Cir, decided 19 April 2002) 288 F 3d 1264; 2002 US App LEXIS 7239; *Simeone v Bombardier Rotax GmbH* (US Dist Ct E Dist Penn, decided 9 March 2005) 360 F Supp 2d 665; 2005 US Dist LEXIS 3601.

[92] [1983] Ch 258; [1983] 2 All ER 563; [1983] 3 WLR 492 (CA). The tort law aspects of this case will now be governed by Part III of the Private International Law (Miscellaneous Provisions) Act 1995: see further David McLean and Kisch Beevers *Morris: The Conflict of Laws* (London: Thomson, Sweet & Maxwell, 6th edn, 2005) at 375–89. Note too the draft EC Regulation on the law applicable to non-contractual obligations discussed in *Morris* at 389–91.   [93] [1897] AC 22.

[94] [1982] Ch 442.   [95] [1983] 2 All ER 563 at 588(f).

[96] Regulation (EC) 1346/2000 OJ [2000] L160/1.

[97] [2003] EWHC (Ch) 128; [2003] 2 All ER 201 (ChD).

was exercised in Germany, had its seat in Germany, and so the Brussels Convention on Civil Jurisdiction and Judgments could apply allowing that company to insist on jurisdiction of the courts of its domicile, Germany, rather than the English courts.[98] In both of these cases incorporation in the non-Member State was a formality, with the substance of the activities of the company occurring in the EC. Thus a significant territorial nexus still existed between the foreign incorporated entity and the European jurisdiction. While these cases show a greater willingness to look at the substance rather than the form of corporate nationality for jurisdictional purposes, it is open to debate whether this will allow for an extension of jurisdiction to a foreign parent company of a UK based subsidiary in a situation such as that seen in *Multinational Gas*.[99]

The question of extending forum jurisdiction to non-resident units of MNEs has also arisen under EC law, in the context of Articles 81 (formerly 85) and 82 (formerly 86) of the Treaty of Rome, which are the foundations of Community competition law.[100] The issue arises where a non-EC based parent company, operating within the EC through a subsidiary, is suspected of participating in anti-competitive conduct occurring within the territory of the Community that has an adverse effect on EC trade and competition. In order to establish jurisdictional authority over non-EC based parent companies in competition matters, the EC Commission and the European Court of Justice (ECJ) initially applied an 'enterprise entity' test to prove a territorial connection between the non-EC parent and the jurisdiction through the presence of its subsidiary within the Community.[101] The early dicta of the Commission and the Court suggest that the very existence of a parent subsidiary relationship is prima facie sufficient to establish jurisdiction over the non-resident parent, although, as Merkin and Williams point out, it is unclear from the early judgments of the ECJ whether the true basis of extraterritoriality is 'the notion that the conduct of EEC subsidiaries is imputed to their foreign parents or that all companies within the same group are treated as a single "economic entity"'.[102]

The approach taken in the early leading cases was confirmed by the Commission in the *Wood Pulp*,[103] *Zinc Producer Group*,[104] and *Aluminium Imports From Eastern*

---

[98] [1989] 2 All ER 1066; [1990] 1 QB 361 (CA).

[99] The appropriateness of bringing a company law claim before an English court will also be a consideration: see *Konamaneni v Rolls Royce Industrial Power (India) Ltd* [2002] 1 All ER 979 (ChD) where India was seen as the appropriate forum for a derivative action on the part of shareholders in an Indian company.

[100] See further R Whish *Competition Law* (London: Lexis Nexis Butterworths, 5th edn, 2003) ch 12; R Merkin and K Williams *Competition Law: Antitrust Policy in the United Kingdom and the EEC* (Sweet & Maxwell 1984) at 471–73; Whatstein 'Extraterritorial Application of EC Competition Law – Comments and Reflections' 26 Israel LR 195 (1992).

[101] See *Re Cartel in Aniline Dyestuffs* (Commission Decision 69/243, 24 July 1969) [1969] CMLR D23. Upheld in Case 48/69 *ICI v Commission* [1972] CMLR 557, [1972] ECR 619; Case 61/72 *Continental Can v Commission* [1973] ECR 215, [1973] CMLR 199; Case 6 & 7/73 *Commercial Solvents v Commission* [1974] 1 CMLR 309.   [102] Above n 100 at 472.

[103] *Re Wood Pulp* [1985] 3 CMLR 474.

[104] *Re the Zinc Producer Group: The Community v Rio Tinto Zinc Corporation plc and Others* [1985] 2 CMLR 108.

Europe[105] cases. In addition, these cases extended the scope of EC competition jurisdiction. In particular, the reach of EC competition law was extended to non-EC firms that exported directly to, or did business within, the Community, irrespective of whether they had an established corporate presence within the Community. This extension of jurisdiction was approved by the ECJ in the appeal against the Commission's decision on jurisdiction in the *Wood Pulp* case.[106] In the course of its judgment, the ECJ noted that the conclusion of an agreement which had the effect of restricting competition in the Common Market consisted of conduct made up of two elements, the formation of the agreement and its implementation. The applicability of EC competition law could not be made to depend on the place where the agreement was formed but on whether it was implemented within the Common Market. Otherwise undertakings would have an easy way of evading the law. On the facts the wood pulp producers had implemented their pricing agreement (which had been concluded outside the Community) although selling to purchasers within the Community at coordinated prices. The Court concluded that: 'it is immaterial in that respect whether or not they had recourse to subsidiaries, agents, sub-agents, or branches within the Community in order to make their contacts with purchasers within the Community.'[107]

This decision caused some commentators to believe that the Community has accepted a broad 'effects doctrine', similar to that espoused in the US.[108] However, it appears that the Community's jurisdiction is limited only to non-EC firms with direct or indirect trading links within the EC. Thus, in the *Zinc Producer* case, the Commission noted that where a restrictive agreement involved firms that would make no significant contribution to improving competition in the Community in the absence of the agreement, such firms were outside the scope of Community law. On the other hand, under the EC Merger Regulation, the Commission appeared to have applied a pure effects test in the case of *Gencor/Lonrho*, when it prohibited a merger between two South African undertakings, on the ground that this would lead to the creation of a collective dominant position in the platinum and rhodium markets, significantly impeding competition in the Common Market.[109] On appeal, the Court of First Instance (CFI) upheld the Commission.[110] Although the merger had been approved by the South African Government, this was a case in which EC jurisdiction could be legitimately exercised. The criterion of implementation in the *Wood Pulp* case was satisfied by 'mere sale within the Community,

---

[105] [1987] 3 CMLR 813.   [106] Case 89/85 [1988] 4 CMLR 901.
[107] ibid para 17 at 941.
[108] See eg A Hermann 'EC Joins Extraterritoriality Club' *Financial Times* 13 October 1988 at 39. This view was criticized by Sir Alan Neale, co-author of Neale and Stephens n 1 above, in a letter to the *Financial Times* published on 23 November 1988 at 29. He sees the case as offering a stricter test, requiring proof of anti-competitive acts within the Community. This view appears to be borne out by other cases discussed in the text below.   [109] OJ [1997] L11/30, [1999] 4 CMLR 1076.
[110] *Gencor Limited v EC Commission* Case T–102/96 [1999] ECR II 753, [1999] 4 CMLR 971 Comment Eleanor Fox 'The Merger Regulation and its Territorial Reach: *Gencor Ltd v Commission*' 20 ECLR 334 (1999) and Whish above n 100 at 439–40.

irrespective of the sources of supply and the production plant. It is not disputed that Gencor and Lonrho carried out sales in the Community before the concentration and would have continued to do so thereafter'.[111] The CFI added that 'application of the Regulation is justified under public international law when it is foreseeable that a proposed concentration will have an immediate and substantial effect within the Community.'[112] The CFI then applied a comity analysis and held that there was no violation of the principles of non-interference or proportionality on the facts.[113]

The reasoning of the CFI in *Gencor* sounds very like that of the effects doctrine used by the US courts.[114] On the other hand, this is not a pure effects case given the finding of a substantial business presence, by reason of sales, within the Community. In addition, the CFI was at pains to consider the effects issue as one of public international law and not Community law. Thus, according to Richard Whish, '[a]s in the case of the ECJ's judgments in *Dyestuffs* and *Wood Pulp*, the CFI avoided the adoption of the effects doctrine'.[115] It may be added that any further extension of extraterritorial jurisdiction by the ECJ or CFI is unlikely given the difficulties of enforcing EC law against non-EC companies, and the lack of any procedure for compelling disclosure of relevant information from such firms.[116] In addition, the application of the economic entity doctrine or the *Wood Pulp* case should cover most situations. A pure effects doctrine may only be needed in the rare case where an anti-competitive agreement is formed and implemented outside the EC, but has economic effects within the Community, and none of the participants has any commercial ties there.[117]

From the above examples, it is clear that different legal systems will take different positions on the extent to which they will 'lift the corporate veil', disregard the legal separation between resident and non-resident units of a MNE, and establish personal jurisdiction over the non-resident unit by virtue of the presence of its affiliate within the jurisdiction. Much depends on the legal culture involved and, in particular, on the extent of its support for the territorial principle of jurisdiction in the face of the potential ineffectiveness of its laws in relation to MNEs.

A further factor is whether the legal system is prepared to go beyond the logic of corporate separation between affiliated enterprises in a MNE and adopt the 'economic entity' principle, making the MNE group as a whole subject to the personal jurisdiction of the forum. Here, a presumption of control by the parent over the subsidiary is involved. Such a presumption can serve as notice to the foreign parent, that on setting up a subsidiary within the host state's jurisdiction, it is subject to all the liabilities that a locally incorporated parent company may bear. For

---

[111] ibid at para 87.   [112] ibid at para 90.   [113] ibid at para 102.
[114] See Fox above n 110 at 335–36.   [115] Whish above n 100 at 440.
[116] Merkin and Williams above n 100 at 472–73.
[117] Whish above n 100 at 437. According to Roger Alford, when such a case reaches the ECJ it will apply a full effects doctrine: 'The Extraterritorial Application of Antitrust Laws: The United States and European Community Approaches' 33 Va.J.Int'l.L 1 (1992). So far this has not occurred, unless one reads the *Gencor* case in this way.

example, Article 10 of the Argentinean Draft Code of Private International Law states:

Multinational Enterprises, such as conglomerates or holding companies, operating within the jurisdiction of several countries, despite the pluralistic nature of their legal personality, shall be considered economic units, and their activities shall be evaluated in the light of economic realities respecting their subjection to Argentine law.[118]

This provision makes clear that the activities of MNEs shall be regulated in accordance with Argentine law, on the basis of their economic unity and regardless of the legal separation between the various companies within the group.

Similarly, in the case of a parent company incorporated in the forum jurisdiction, a presumption of control may serve as notice of its responsibility before the courts of its home state for the acts of its overseas subsidiaries, where these would give rise to liability if they occurred locally. Such reasoning appears to be implicit in the US case law in various fields on establishing jurisdiction over the foreign subsidiaries of US corporations. Although the courts have not departed from the language of corporate separation, the fact of such separation has not been allowed to interfere with the reach of US law to the subsidiary. Equally, in the UK *Cape Asbestos* case such a possibility was not ruled out. In the first Court of Appeal decision jurisdiction was asserted over the UK based parent company on the ground that it was domiciled in the UK and that it was alleged to have controlled the operation of the mines and mills in South Africa from which the claimants' injuries were alleged to have arisen. In these circumstances the alleged breaches of duty may be said to have occurred in England, although their effects were felt by the claimants in South Africa.[119] On appeal the House of Lords would not determine this question but Lord Bingham, in giving the judgment of the House, did not consider this assessment to be unreasonable or wrong.

(ii) Links Based on Other Business Contacts With the Forum Jurisdiction

Apart from links based on ownership and control between the resident and nonresident units of the MNE, other possible bases of personal jurisdiction include the presence of officers of the non-resident unit within the jurisdiction, and/or the presence of products manufactured by the non-resident unit within the jurisdiction, whether as a result of direct sales from abroad or of trade through third parties within the jurisdiction. In addition, more recent years have seen the rise of transnational business transactions conducted through the internet. The question

---

[118] The full text of the code can be found in 24 ILM 269 (1985). For background, see Goldschmidt (1972) II Hague Receuil 201.

[119] *Lubbe v Cape* plc [1998] CLC 1559 (CA 30 July 1998); Schalk Willeam Burger Lubbe v Cape plc [2002] 2 Lloyd's Rep 383 at 390–91, [2004] 4 All ER 268 at 276j (HL). See further Peter T Muchlinski 'Corporations in International Litigation: Problems of Jurisdiction and the United Kingdom Asbestos Cases' 50 ICLQ 1 (2001). A presumption that a wholly owned subsidiary will

arises whether a provider of goods or services through the internet is present within the jurisdiction in which they do business, for the purposes of legal action, even if they are located outside the jurisdiction.

Presence of Corporate Officers

Under English law, it would appear that the temporary presence, within the jurisdiction, of officials of a foreign firm carrying on business on its behalf will suffice to establish personal jurisdiction over it.[120] Under US law, the question has arisen whether it is within the principle of due process to issue proceedings against a defendant who is temporarily present in the jurisdiction. This has been answered to the effect that transient presence is a sufficient basis for the exercise of personal jurisdiction.[121] This approach has since been upheld by the US Supreme Court, albeit in a non-commercial case.[122] These cases show a varied approach to the question whether a non-resident corporation can be validly subjected to jurisdiction through the temporary presence of its officers in the jurisdiction. However, where such an officer is within the jurisdiction on the business of the foreign entity, it may be possible to serve that entity through him or her, despite the tentative nature of the contact involved, provided that the subject-matter of the suit has a sufficient connection with the forum jurisdiction.

Presence of Products Manufactured by a Non-Resident Corporation

In recent years, courts in various jurisdictions have been asked to assert personal jurisdiction over non-resident manufacturing enterprises on the basis of the presence of their products within the jurisdiction. The issue has arisen in the context of actions for personal injuries caused by accidents occurring within the jurisdiction involving foreign manufactured products.[123] This is likely to become a more frequent phenomenon in litigation, as the manufacture of consumer products becomes increasingly internationalized. A number of situations can be distinguished.

---

carry out the parent company's instructions is accepted in EC law. It is for the parent to rebut that presumption. See *Stora Kopparbergs Bergslags AB v Commission* Case T–354/94 [1998] ECR II–2111 (CFI) and [2002] ECR II–843, [2002] 4 CMLR 1397 (CFI). Rebuttal may take the form of evidence that the subsidiary failed to follow the instructions of the parent Case 32/78 *BMW Belgium SA v Commission* [1979] ECR 2435, [1980] 1 CMLR 370.

[120] See *Dunlop Pneumatic Tyre Co Ltd v AG für Motor und Motorfahrzeugbau vorm Cudell & Co* [1902] 1 KB 342 (CA).

[121] See *Amusement Equipment v Mordelt* 779 F 2d 264 (5th Cir 1985).

[122] *Burnham v Superior Court of California* 110 S Ct 2105 (1990) (a New Jersey resident was validly served by his wife, who was resident in California, with a court summons and divorce petition in California, while he was there on a temporary visit for business purposes and to see his children).

[123] See further Campbell McLachlan and Peter Nygh (eds) *Transnational Tort Litigation: Jurisdictional Principles* (Oxford: Oxford University Press, 1996) and *Blumberg on Corporate Groups* above n 77 ch 30.

The first involves finished goods that have been imported into the jurisdiction by the foreign manufacturer and distributed through a local sales subsidiary. In such a case, as noted above, personal jurisdiction could be asserted on the basis of presence through the subsidiary. Secondly, there is the case where the goods enter the jurisdiction through an independent third party distributor. It may be desirable to sue the manufacturer where the third party excludes liability for defects in the goods, or where it has insufficient assets to compensate the claimant under the contract of sale. Under English law the foreign corporation will be amenable to suit in such a case only if the distributor within the jurisdiction has been carrying on the foreign corporation's business, and not merely its own business, through the introduction of the foreign corporation's products into the jurisdiction. This demands an analysis of the functions the distributor has been carrying out and all aspects of the relationship between it and the foreign corporation. Significant questions include: whether the distributor has acquired business premises to enable it to act on behalf of the foreign corporation; whether the foreign corporation pays for the distributor's business overheads or only pays a contractual commission; the extent to which the foreign corporation controls the distributor in the conduct of its business; whether the distributor is allowed to display the foreign corporation's name and/or trademark; whether the distributor enters contracts of sale on its own behalf or as agent of the foreign company and, if so, whether the distributor is capable of binding the foreign company contractually.[124] Under US law such contracts may also be sufficient to establish personal jurisdiction over the non-resident company.[125]

Thirdly, a more difficult situation arises where there is no direct or indirect business presence on the part of the manufacturer in the jurisdiction and the product is brought in by the consumer. A still harder case arises where an accident is caused by the failure of a component manufactured by a non-resident company which is then incorporated into the finished product by another independent foreign company. If national laws are to protect the consumer effectively in such cases, then jurisdiction over foreign manufacturers may have to be asserted on the basis of the presence of their products alone.

Although certain US judges appear to be sympathetic to this view, as witnessed by the vigorous dissenting judgments in the US Supreme Court in *Worldwide Volkswagen Corporation v Woodson*[126] and *Asahi Metal Industry Co v Superior Court of California*,[127] US law has not gone quite so far. The current state of US law is summarized in *Asahi*. Relying on the long established US test of personal jurisdiction over foreign corporations, first laid down by the US Supreme Court in the

[124] See *Adams v Cape Industries plc* [1991] All ER 929 at 1014–1015 per Slade LJ (CA).

[125] See *International Shoe v Washington* 326 US 310; 90 L Ed 95 (1945); *Waters v Deutz Corporation* 460 A 2d 1332 (Del Sup Ct 1983); *Worldwide Volkswagen Corporation v Woodson* 444 US 286 (1980). See, in the context of antitrust actions, *Hoffman Motors Corp v Alfa Romeo* 244 F Supp 70 (SDNY 1965); *US v Aluminum Company of America* 20 F Supp 13 (1937) *Akzona Inc v EIDu Pont de Nemours & Co* 607 F Supp 227 especially at 236–40 (Dist Ct Del 1984).

[126] 444 US 286 (1980).

[127] 107 S Ct 1026, 74 L Ed 2d 92 (1987) and 26 ILM 702 (1987) (Slip Opinion).

leading case of *International Shoe Co v Washington*,[128] as interpreted in the *Worldwide Volkswagen* case, and on the authority of *Burger King Corp v Rudzewicz*,[129] the Supreme Court held:

> The placement of a product into the stream of commerce, without more, is not an act of the defendant purposefully directed toward the forum State. Additional conduct of the Defendant may indicate an intent or purpose to serve the market in the forum State, for example, designing the product for the market in the forum State, advertising in the forum State, establishing channels for providing regular advice to customers in the forum State, or marketing the product through a distributor who has agreed to act as the sales agent in the forum State. But a defendant's awareness that the stream of commerce may or will sweep the product into the forum State does not convert the mere act of placing the product into the stream into an act purposefully directed towards the forum State.[130]

On balance, the policy of US courts appears to be to allow jurisdiction save in the most exceptional cases. Where the defendant is a MNE with a business presence in the US, this seems reasonable. For, if the corporation enters the 'stream of commerce' within US jurisdiction, and enjoys the protection of US law, this privilege carries with it a responsibility to respond to suits which are brought against the corporation as a result of its activities within the jurisdiction.[131] The line to be drawn is between a fortuitous, albeit theoretically foreseeable, presence of products in the forum jurisdiction – whether brought about by the acts of consumers after purchase or through incorporation into other products by intermediate manufacturers who then bring the finished product into the jurisdiction – and a purposeful strategy of market penetration, whether involving the presence of a local affiliate or not.[132] The above mentioned American cases offer excellent illustrations of the jurisdictional problems involved in transnational product liability litigation, and of possible solutions to them which stretch, but ultimately do not destroy, the concept of a connection between the territory of the forum jurisdiction and the subject-matter of the claim against the non-resident manufacturer.

Supply of Goods and Services Through the Internet

Increasingly, MNEs operate their businesses by means of the internet. In particular, the use of a website that can be accessed by clients throughout the world raises issues as to the jurisdictional presence of the firm operating that site. Transactions

---

[128] 326 US 310, 90 L Ed 95 (1945).   [129] 471 US 462 (1985).

[130] 26 ILM 702 (1987) Slip Opinion at 8. See, for a more recent application of this principle, in relation to internet based firms: *Rio Properties v Rio International Interlink* above n 86. See also *Progressive Northern Insurance Co v Fleetwood Enterprises* (US Dist Ct WD Wash, 18 October 2005) 2005 US Dist LEXIS 25669; *Simeone v Bombardier Rotax GmbH* above n 91.

[131] See *Galle v Allstate Insurance Co* 451 SO 2d 72 at 75 (Lo 4th Cir 1984).

[132] On the other hand, the isolated contacts of an alien corporation with the US jurisdiction, such as a single contract negotiating session, or the purchase of products for use abroad, or the training

on the internet have to come out somewhere and they can be regulated, as the decision of the Tribunal de Grande Instance de Paris in the case of *LICRA & UEJF v Yahoo! Inc & Yahoo France* shows. In that case, the French court ordered Yahoo! Inc to prevent web surfers in France from accessing Nazi artefacts via its website. It rejected Yahoo! Inc's argument that the site was located in California and intended for use by an American audience, and that, therefore, any French order was ineffective as an unwarranted extraterritorial extension of French jurisdiction. The French court held that it was entitled to make its decision on the basis that the harm was suffered in France. While Yahoo! Inc was in no way committing an intentional wrong it was enough that by:

permitting the visualisation in France of these objects and eventual participation of a surfer established in France in such an exposition/sale Yahoo! Inc . . . committed a wrong on the territory of France.[133]

Thus Yahoo! Inc was unable to say that it only operated from the US and so had no actual presence in France. In addition, the fact that it operated a French website through its French subsidiary was not considered relevant. The French court did not see this separate corporate presence as a bar to holding Yahoo! Inc directly responsible for the harm caused by the accessing of information available on its US site.[134]

Although it is not easy to determine which country has the right to regulate – several other countries apart from France could equally have said they had such a right – it is clear that a state can regulate if it sees fit. This was reaffirmed in the Australian case of *Dow Jones and Co Inc v Gutnick*, where the High Court of Australia held that a defamatory statement, contained in an article posted on the appellant's website in New Jersey, could found an action on the part of the respondent, who could read the article in Victoria, Australia, and who was domiciled there.[135] The High Court reasoned that as the damage was suffered in Victoria by

---

of personnel within the jurisdiction for employment abroad is not a contact of a continuous and systematic nature within the principle of *International Shoe*. See *Helicopteros Nacionales de Colombia v Hall* 466 US 408, 104 S Ct 1868, 80 L Ed 2d 404 (1984).

[133] First Decision of 22 May 2000 (unofficial English translation at <http://www.gyoza.com/lapres/html/yahen.html>). Decision affirmed 20 November 2000 (unofficial English translation at <http://www.gigalaw.com/library/france-yahoo-2000-11-20-lapres.html>. See further Uta Kohl 'Eggs, Jurisdiction and the Internet' 51 ICLQ 555 (2002); Jack Goldsmith 'Yahoo! Brought to Earth' *Financial Times* 27 November 2000 at 27. See also Financial Law Panel *Report on Jurisdiction and the Regulation of Financial Services on the Internet* (London: October 1998).

[134] Yahoo sought to prevent the enforcement of the French court's order in California on the ground that the First Amendment of the US Constitution, protecting free speech, precluded enforcement within the United States. The US District Court for the Northern District of California upheld this argument: *Yahoo! Inc v La Ligue Contre le Racisme et L'Antisemitisme* 169 F Supp 2d 1181 at 1194 (ND Cal 2001). However, that decision was overturned on the ground that the case was not yet ripe for decision, given Yahoo's substantial apparent compliance with the French court's order, which cast doubt on whether its First Amendment rights had in fact been infringed: *Yahoo! Inc v La Ligue Contre Le Racisme et L'Antisemitisme and L'Union des Etudiants Juifs de France* (US CA 9th Cir 12 January 2006) 433 F 3d 1199; 2006 US App LEXIS 668.

[135] [2002] HCA 56, 10 December 2002, 42 ILM 41 (2003).

a resident of that state, jurisdiction was possible. The alternative was to apply the jurisdiction of the place where the website existed. That would allow for an exorbitant American jurisdiction, given that the majority of websites was located in the US. Furthermore, as noted by Callinan J:

There is nothing unique about multinational business, and it is in this that the appellant chooses to be engaged. If people wish to do business in, or indeed travel to, or live in, or utilise the infrastructure of different countries, they can hardly expect to be absolved from compliance with the laws of those countries. The fact that publication might occur everywhere does not mean that it occurs nowhere. Multiple publication in different jurisdictions is certainly no novelty in a federation such as Australia.[136]

Thus the founding of jurisdiction, on the basis of the effects of doing business through a website located outside the jurisdiction, can be accepted in national courts. Indeed, in the US such a justification has been used in relation to the control of offshore gambling and banking services offered through the internet.[137] Equally, personal jurisdiction will be asserted under the *International Shoe* doctrine where the offshore website is used actively to enter the stream of commerce in the US or its States. Thus, while the operation of a passive website, which only informs consumers about products and services, will not constitute purposeful availment, where the website does something more, such as request money, or make representations to induce consumers into making a purchase, or where it is accompanied by advertising in the local media, this will show a clear intent to do business with consumers in the jurisdiction.[138] Whether such an approach will be taken in all jurisdictions remains open to debate.[139]

(b) The Doctrine of *Forum Non Conveniens* as Applied to Non-Resident Units of MNEs

Even where the non-resident unit of the MNE is amenable to the personal jurisdiction of the forum in accordance with the above mentioned principles, in a common law jurisdiction, the court may conclude, under the *forum non conveniens* doctrine, that the exercise of jurisdiction is inappropriate, in view of the inconvenience that the proposed litigation would cause to the parties and to the proper administration of justice. In relation to litigation involving the activities of MNEs

---

[136] ibid at para 186.

[137] See *The People v World Interactive Gambling Corp* 714 NYS 2d 844 (1999).

[138] See *Rio Properties v Rio International Interlink* above n 86; *Zippo Manufacturing Co v Zippo Dot Com* Inc 952 F Supp 1119 (WD Pa, 1997).

[139] The EC Judgments Regulation above n 82, by art 15.1(c), allows jurisdiction over consumer contracts in cases where inter alia the supplier directs 'by any means' commercial or professional activities into the consumer's Member State of domicile. This would appear to allow for a variant of the US approach but it is not certain that this is how the law will develop. See further Joakim ST Oren 'International Jurisdiction over Consumer Contracts in e-Europe' 52 ICLQ 665 (2003); Oren Bigos 'Jurisdiction over Cross-Border Wrongs on the Internet' 54 ICLQ 585 (2005).

this question will be of particular significance where the facts leading to the dispute have occurred in a foreign host jurisdiction, at the hands of a subsidiary, but the plaintiff is seeking the procedural advantage of litigating before the forum jurisdiction of his or her choice, whether the home jurisdiction where the parent company is present, or a third jurisdiction where an affiliate is present.[140] This is known as 'forum shopping'.

Historically, the American courts were favoured in cases where an American made product or industrial process had caused injury abroad to a non-US claimant. The hope was that the US forum would be made available to the foreign plaintiff against the US corporation responsible for the product or process, thereby giving the plaintiff the advantage of US personal injuries litigation with low legal costs based on the contingency fee system,[141] liberal rules of pre-trial discovery, trial by jury, and the prospect of a high damages award. However, in the 1980s US courts restricted the availability of US jurisdiction in such cases.[142] As a result the US courts will not normally entertain a claim where an appropriate foreign forum exists, even though it may be less advantageous to the plaintiffs than a US forum. Where an adequate alternative forum exists, the American court will weigh the relevant private and public interest factors to determine whether dismissal is appropriate.[143] Furthermore,

---

[140] Under US law, even where the cause of action does not arise out of or relate to the foreign corporation's activities in the forum state that corporation can be subjected to the personal jurisdiction of the forum when there are sufficient contacts between the foreign corporation and the forum, as where the foreign corporation maintains an office within the jurisdiction. See *Perkins v Benguet Consolidated Mining Co* 342 US 437 (1952); *Barbara Bauman v Daimler Chrysler AG* (US Dist Ct ND Cal, 22 November 2005) 2005 US Dist LEXIS 31929 (insufficient links with forum through US based sales subsidiary).

[141] Whereby the claimant's US attorney will not take fees for his or her services but will be remunerated only on the basis of a percentage of any award of damages.

[142] See the leading case of *Piper Aircraft v Reyno* 454 US 235 (1981). See further Peter T Muchlinski 'The Bhopal Case: Controlling Ultrahazardous Industrial Activities Undertaken by Foreign Investors' 50 MLR 545 at 553–54 (1987). But see *Dow Chemical Co and Shell Oil Co v Castro Alfaro* 786 SW 2d 974 (Tex 1990) *cert den* 111 S Ct 671 (1991). In that case, the Texas Supreme Court asserted jurisdiction in death and personal injury cases, brought by foreign plaintiffs, based on the Texas long-arm statue which excluded *forum non conveniens* from such cases. The Texas law has since been revised to come into line with the more restrictive general US practice. For comment see Baxi above n 1 at 333–34. On *forum non conveniens* and its application to MNEs under US law see *Blumberg on Corporate Groups* above n 77 ch 33 and Sarah Joseph *Corporations and Transnational Human Rights Litigation* (Oxford: Hart Publishing, 2004) ch 4.

[143] See *Gulf Oil v Gilbert* 330 US 501 (1947). On the English doctrine of *forum non conveniens*, see *MacShannon v Rockware Glass* [1978] AC 795; *The Abidin Daver* [1984] AC 398; *Spiliada Maritime Corporation v Cansulex Ltd 'The Spiliada'* [1986] 3 WLR 972 per Lord Goff at 985F: 'The basic principle is that a stay will only be granted on the ground of forum non conveniens where the Court is satisfied that there is some other forum having competent jurisdiction, which is the appropriate forum for the trial of the action, i.e. in which the case may be tried more suitably for the interests of all the parties and the ends of justice.' The factors to be weighed in the exercise of the court's discretion are summarized by Lord Goff at 895G–987G and 991D–992E. Lord Goff's judgment was cited and summarized with approval by Bingham LJ in *Du Pont de Nemours & Co and Endo Laboratories Inc v IC Agnew KW Kerr and Others* [1987] 2 Lloyd's Rep 585 at 588 (CA). See also *Ronleigh Ltd v MII Exports Inc* [1989] 1 WLR 619 (CA). However, as will be discussed in the text below at nn 157–67, this doctrine appears to have been severely limited by the application of EC law on jurisdiction.

where the plaintiff is foreign his or her choice of forum deserves less deference, as the very object of the inquiry is to ensure that the trial is convenient.[144]

The above mentioned principles were applied in the *Bhopal* case to deny US jurisdiction to the Indian victims of the gas leak disaster of 2–3 December 1984 at Union Carbide's pesticides plant in Bhopal.[145] The Indian plaintiffs, with the Government of India, had argued for US jurisdiction against Union Carbide Corporation (UCC), the parent company of Union Carbide of India (UCIL), on the grounds, first, that the Indian legal system was inadequate to meet the demands of such complex litigation,[146] secondly, that UCC, 'a monolithic multinational, controlled the design, construction and operation of the Bhopal plant through its global network of corporate planning, direction and control',[147] and was therefore responsible for the acts of its Indian subsidiary at the plant and should be sued in the US, because the relevant evidence as to its liability lay in the US, and, thirdly, that there was an overwhelming US public interest in retaining the case, in view of potential dangers to the American public from similar industrial processes used at Bhopal's sister plant at Institute, West Virginia, and because America, as the world's foremost industrial nation, had an interest in encouraging, 'American multinationals to protect the health and well being of peoples throughout the world'.[148]

At first instance Judge Keenan rejected these arguments on the grounds that India was an adequate forum, possessing a legal system and remedies based on the English law of tort; that India was a proper forum on private interest considerations, in that the accident had occurred there, and all the principal witnesses could be found there; and that the overriding public interest in the litigation lay with the Indian jurisdiction as the jurisdiction possessing the superior regulatory interest in the case.[149] Therefore, Judge Keenan dismissed the case to India. He was upheld on this finding by the US Court of Appeals for the Second Circuit.[150]

Judge Keenan saw the *Bhopal* case as one of an accident whose locus was in India, and so refused to characterize the issues in the case as arising out of the control exercised by the US parent over its Indian subsidiary. Therefore, it was

---

[144] See *Piper Aircraft* n 142 above at 256.

[145] *In Re Union Carbide Gas Plant Disaster at Bhopal India* (Opinion and Order 12 May 1986) 634 F Supp 842 (SDNY 1986), 25 ILM 771 (1986). For analysis, see Peter T Muchlinski above n 142; Indian Law Institute *Inconvenient Forum Convenient Catastrophe: The Bhopal Case* (1986); Baxi above n 1 at 354–64.

[146] On which see further Marc Galanter 'Legal Torpor: Why So Little Has Happened in India After the Bhopal Tragedy' 20 Texas J. Int'l L. 273 (1985).

[147] Plaintiff's Executive Committee Memorandum in Opposition to Union Carbide Corporation's Motion to Dismiss on Grounds of Forum Non Conveniens, 6 December 1985 at 3.

[148] ibid at 88.　　　[149] See, for full discussion, Peter T Muchlinski above n 142 at 555–60.

[150] 809 F 2d 195 (USCA 2d Cir), 26 ILM 1008 (1987), *cert denied* 108 S Ct 199 (1987). The USCA rejected two conditions that Judge Keenan had attached to his dismissal of the case, concerning the monitoring of due process before the Indian courts by the US District Court, and the application of Federal pre-trial discovery to UCC alone. The Court of Appeals upheld the condition that UCC voluntarily submit to Indian personal jurisdiction, without which India would not have provided an adequate alternative forum. For discussion see Peter T Muchlinski above n 142 at 560–63. As Baxi points out, the inclusion of this condition appears to render the argument, that there was an alternative forum in India, incorrect: n 1 above at 362.

inevitable that he should conclude that the balance of interests pointed to the Indian forum. This decision suggests that there may be little purpose in a foreign plaintiff, who has suffered an injury at the hands of an overseas subsidiary of a US MNE, seeking to sue the parent in the US, unless there is clear proof of the direct involvement of the parent company in the wrongdoing, and there is a clear US interest in the litigation. On both issues the foreign plaintiff will have a hard burden to discharge. The US courts are not willing to become a global forum for litigation brought against US MNEs.

One exception to this appears to be emerging in relation to claims based on violations of fundamental human rights under the Alien Tort Claims Act (ATCA) or the Torture Victim Protection Act (TVPA).[151] In the case of *Wiwa v Royal Dutch Petroleum Company and Shell Transport and Trading Company plc*[152] the US Court of Appeal held that the US interest in pursuing claims for torture under the Alien Tort Claims Act and the more recent Torture Victim Prevention Act[153] was a significant factor to be taken into account when determining whether an action brought on such grounds before a US court against a foreign MNE should be removed to a foreign jurisdiction on the basis that it was a more suitable forum for the litigation.[154] On the facts, the USCA held that an action brought against the defendant corporation for allegedly supporting the Nigerian state in its repression of the Ogoni people through inter alia the supply of money, weapons, and logistical support to the Nigerian military which carried out the alleged abuses, could be heard in the United States. This case was brought by US resident plaintiffs. It is not certain that US jurisdiction will be so readily accepted where the plaintiffs are from outside the US.

Indeed, in *Aguinda v Texaco* the US Court of Appeal for the Second Circuit upheld the decision and the reasoning of the District Court for the Southern District of New York that rejected US jurisdiction over a claim under ATCA, brought by Ecuadorian and Peruvian citizens against Texaco, alleging that the company had polluted rain forests and rivers in those two countries causing environmental damage and personal injuries.[155] The district court had reviewed the *Wiwa* decision and concluded that it did not introduce a different test of jurisdiction

---

[151] Alien Tort Claims Act 1789: 28 USC s 1350. ATCA states: 'The district courts shall have original jurisdiction of any civil action by an alien for a tort only, committed in violation of the law of nations or a treaty of the United States' Torture Victim Protection Act 1991: 28 USC s 1350 App. See generally Joseph above n 142 at 87–99.

[152] USCA 2d Cir 14 September 2000: 2000 US App LEXIS 23274.

[153] 28 USC s 1350 App (1991).

[154] In other cases the absence of a claim equivalent to ATCA in the possible alternative forum has been held to show the absence of an adequate alternative forum: *Sarei v Rio Tinto Zinc* 221 F Supp 2d 1116 (2002) (Australia); *Presbyterian Church of Sudan v Talisman Energy* 244 F Supp 2d 289 (SDNY 2003) (Canada).

[155] 945 F Supp 625 (2001) upheld on appeal 303 F 3d 470 (USCA 2nd Cir, 16 August 2002). See also for a similar outcome, requiring the plaintiffs to sue in Peru: *Flores v Southern Peru Copper* 253 F Supp 2d 510 (SDNY 2002) upheld 343 F 3d 140 (US CA 2d Cir, 2003). For a Canadian approach to jurisdiction over human rights claims see *Recherches Internationales du Quebec v Cambior Inc* 1998 Q J No 2554 (QL).

under ATCA to that generally applicable to cases where the issue of whether the US, or a foreign forum, was more appropriate as the place in which the claim should be heard (the *forum non conveniens* doctrine). Given that the balance of the private and public interest factors used to determine the appropriate forum pointed overwhelmingly to Ecuador the district court held that this claim should be heard there. In any case, the corporate links between the US parent and the Ecuadorian operating affiliate were of a kind that it could not be said that any wrong had been committed by the parent in the US such as would justify a claim under ATCA. Thus it may be difficult for a foreign claimant to assert the jurisdiction of the US courts over US-based MNEs for alleged violations of human rights where there exists an appropriate alternative forum in the host country and where there is little evidence of direct involvement by the parent in the acts leading to the alleged harm. The only possible exception may be where the plaintiff is claiming to be a victim of torture, although even in such cases, the choice of US forum will not be decisive under the *forum non conveniens* doctrine. In addition, one factor that may point decisively to US forum is the possibility that the plaintiffs will be subjected to great personal risk by bringing an action in the host country forum.[156]

In recent years the English courts have also sought to control the practice of 'forum shopping'.[157] However, the approach of the English courts to the question of *forum non conveniens* appears to have been constrained by the Brussels Convention on Jurisdiction and the Enforcement of Civil and Commercial Judgments 1968, now Council Regulation 44/2001 (the Judgments Regulation).[158] Section 49 of the Civil Jurisdiction and Judgments Act 1982 (which incorporates the Brussels Convention into English law) states that: 'Nothing in this Act shall prevent any court in the United Kingdom from staying, sisting, striking out or dismissing any proceedings before it, on the ground of *forum non conveniens* or otherwise, where to do so is not inconsistent with the 1968 Convention.' The scope of s 49 has been the subject of litigation. It was held, in two first instance decisions involving insurance claims arising out of policies entered into in the London market by foreign insurers covering foreign risks, that where the convention points to the English forum as a mandatory forum, it would be contrary to the purposes behind the convention to permit any residual discretion over forum in the English courts, even though the facts of the case may point to the forum of a non-contracting country as the appropriate forum.[159]

[156] See *Presbyterian Church of Sudan v Talisman Energy* above n 154 (Sudan not an adequate alternative forum due to likelihood that the plaintiffs would be put at great personal risk); *Sarei v Rio Tinto Zinc* above n 154 (risk of persecution of plaintiffs by the government in Papua New Guinea favoured retention in the US); *Luis Alberto Galvis Mujica v Occidental Petroleum Corp* (US DC Cent Dist Cal decided 28 June 2005) 381 F Supp 2d 1134; 2005 US Dist LEXIS 21470.
[157] See R Schuz 'Controlling Forum Shopping: The Impact of *MacShannon v Rockware Glass Ltd*' 35 ICLQ 374 (1986); *Smith Kline & French v Bloch* [1983] 2 All ER 72 (CA); *SNI Aerospatiale v Lee Kui Jak* [1987] 3 All ER 510 (PC). [158] Above n 82.
[159] See *S & W Berisford plc v New Hampshire Insurance Co* [1990] 2 QB 631, [1990] 2 All ER 321 (Com Ct); *Arkwright Mutual Insurance Co v Bryanston Insurance Co Ltd* [1990] 2 QB 649, [1990] 2 All ER 335 (Com Ct).

The Court of Appeal restricted the scope of these rulings in *Re Harrods (Buenos Aires) Ltd*.[160] In an action between the two Swiss corporate shareholders of Harrods (Buenos Aires), a company incorporated in England, but whose business as a department store was carried on exclusively in Argentina, the Court of Appeal held that Article 2 of the Brussels Convention did not mandate English jurisdiction over the dispute simply because the Harrods company was domiciled in the UK. On the facts Argentina was clearly the more appropriate forum. This case has been strongly criticized as being contrary to the true meaning of the Brussels Convention.[161] Its authority was challenged in argument before the courts in the *Cape Asbestos* cases but no determination upon its correctness or otherwise was made by the House of Lords.[162] Their Lordships preferred to rule in favour of English jurisdiction on the basis of the *Spiliada* doctrine.[163]

In the light of recent European case law, it now appears highly likely that the earlier cases were correct and that *Re Harrods (Buenos Aires)* will need to be overruled. In particular, in *Owusu v Jackson*, the ECJ has suggested that the doctrine of *forum non conveniens* is incompatible with the Brussels Convention (now the Judgments Regulation).[164] The case was brought by a UK domiciled claimant against a UK domiciled defendant and several Jamaican defendants. Article 2 of the Brussels Convention renders mandatory jurisdiction based on the domicile of the defendant. This is subject to the various exceptions provided for in the convention. As regards the *forum non conveniens* doctrine, the ECJ held that legal certainty demanded its exclusion from the scheme of the convention. The authors of the convention had not provided for such an exception and, if it were accepted, the wide discretion it offered was liable to undermine the predictability of the rules of jurisdiction laid down by the convention. It would also undermine the legal protection of persons established in the Community as a defendant could generally better conduct their defence before the courts of their domicile. In addition, the doctrine was recognized in a limited number of contracting states, whereas the objective of the Brussels Convention was to lay down common rules to the exclusion of derogating national rules. As for inconvenience to the Jamaican

---

[160] [1992] Ch 72, [1991] 4 All ER 334 (CA).

[161] See PM North and JJ Fawcett *Cheshire and North's Private International Law* (London: Butterworths, 13th edn, 1999) at 264–66.

[162] Above n 119. For discussion see Peter T Muchlinski above n 119 at 12–14.

[163] See *Lubbe v Cape plc* [2000] 2 Lloyd's Rep 383 at 391–94, [2000] 4 All ER 268 at 275A–E to 276A–J, 279J–80A, 282F–H and 287F. The *Spiliada* doctrine (described at n 143 above) requires, inter alia, that an appropriate alternative forum allows substantive justice to be obtained. On the facts, it was clear that South Africa did not allow for substantive justice to be obtained by the claimants, in that it had no legal aid and few, if any, practitioners able to take on mass tort litigation. See also *Connelly v Rio Tinto Zinc* [1997] 4 All ER 335 (HL).

[164] *Owusu v Jackson* [2001] QB 68 (CA) before the ECJ: Case C–281/02 judgment of 1 March 2005 available at <http://curia.eu.int>. The ECJ has also ruled that the Brussels Convention applies to give jurisdiction against a defendant, domiciled in an EC Member State, to claimants domiciled in a country that is not a party to the convention: Case C–412/98 *Société Group Josi Reinsurance Company SA v Compagnie d'Assurances Universal General Insurance Company* ECJ Opinion of 13 July 2000 available at <http://curia.eu.int>.

defendants, this was not seen as sufficient to call into question the mandatory nature of Article 2 of the Brussels Convention. Accordingly, the ECJ concluded that the Brussels Convention precluded a court of a contracting state from declining the jurisdiction, conferred upon it by Article 2 of the convention, on the ground that a court of a non-contracting state would be a more appropriate forum for the trial of the action, even if the jurisdiction of no other contracting state was in issue or the proceedings had no connecting factors to any other contracting state.[165] In the light of this ruling, it is unlikely that a future English court would apply the *forum non conveniens* doctrine in any case to which the Judgments Regulation applies.[166] Thus, English law appears to be moving away from the discretionary approach of common law doctrine, and to be coming closer to European doctrine under which no discretion over the exercise of jurisdiction by a national court is recognized.[167]

However, it would be misleading to say that the common law speaks with one voice on *forum non conveniens* in cases involving MNEs. For example, Australia takes a more robustly pro-plaintiff position and allows forum choice to stand unless this is so inappropriate as to be vexatious or oppressive to the defendant.[168] This is so despite that fact that the current Australian Rules of the Supreme Court only require that the choice of Australian forum be 'inappropriate' whereas case-law speaks of the forum having to be 'clearly inappropriate'. As noted by the majority of the High Court of Australia, in *Regie National des Usines Renault SA v Zhang*, the rules encapsulate a judicial discretion and that is to be defined by judicial decision.[169] However, Kirby and Callinan JJ dissented on the ground that they believed the Rules had altered the scope of judicial discretion and that an 'inappropriate' forum would be easier to show than a 'clearly inappropriate' one. In addition, Kirby J felt that the English doctrine in the *Spiliada* case was more in tune with the realities of international litigation and the limits of extraterritorial jurisdiction under applicable principles of international law, while Callinan J supported the English doctrine on the ground that globalization, the need to deter forum shopping and the need for consistency between common law jurisdictions pointed towards its adoption in Australia.[170]

Equally, at least one common law jurisdiction has enacted legislation that effectively abolishes the *forum non conveniens* doctrine in certain tort cases. In 1997 the

---

[165] ibid at paras 37–46.

[166] For a discussion of situations in which *forum non conveniens* remains available, see Morris *The Conflict of Laws* above n 92 at 126–27 paras 5–045 and 5–046; Graeme Halkerston 'A Funny Thing Happened on the Way to the Forum …' New Law Journal 25 March 2005 at 436.

[167] See the *Berisford* case at [1990] 2 All ER 332A–E citing the Schlosser Report on the 1968 Convention: OJ [1979] C 59 at 97–99 paras 76 and 78. See also for a critical appraisal of this tendency, including a scathing critique of *Owusu v Jackson* Trevor C Hartley 'The European Union and the Systematic Dismantling of the Common Law of Conflict of Laws' 54 ICLQ 813 (2005).

[168] See *Voth v Manildra Flour Mills* (1989) 15 NSWLR 513; *Oceanic Sun Line Special Shipping Co Inc v Fay* (1988) 165 CLR 197 (High Court of Australia); Peter Prince 'Bhopal Bourgainville and OK Tedi: Why Australia's *forum non conveniens* Approach is Better' 47 ICLQ 573 (1998).

[169] [2002] HCA 10 (14 March 2002) at paras 22–23.

[170] ibid. Kirby J at paras 94, 144, 162; Callinan J at paras 193–94.

Dominican Republic passed the Transnational Causes of Action (Product Liability) Act, to allow easier access to Dominican courts in cases involving a transnational product liability action, where that action had been dismissed in a foreign forum on *forum non conveniens* grounds.[171] The statute imposes strict liability and punitive damages on foreign manufacturers and distributors who are defendants in such cases and who have successfully invoked the *forum non conveniens* doctrine to remove the case from the foreign forum. Thus any procedural advantage obtained through the stay of proceedings in the foreign forum is thereby removed under the Act. Other countries in Latin America have also adopted similar blocking statutes.[172]

(4) Jurisdiction to Enforce[173]

Where a legal system has accepted jurisdiction to prescribe laws concerning the activities of non-resident units of MNEs, the effectiveness of such a policy must ultimately depend on its ability to enforce any judgments made against the non-resident. At this point the problem of extraterritoriality is at its most acute, as the judgment against the non-resident entity attempts to regulate its conduct within the territory of another sovereign state. The exercise of extraterritorial enforcement jurisdiction can take place, either, where the enforcing jurisdiction makes direct orders against the foreign units of the MNE, or takes non-judicial measures within its jurisdiction against the assets of the foreign entity, or denies to it certain privileges usually accorded to enterprises engaged in the same business such as import licences, tax credits, or access to government tenders.[174]

The most serious disputes over exorbitant US claims to enforcement jurisdiction have arisen in antitrust cases.[175] As seen above, in certain such cases, the US courts have been forced to amend the extraterritorial aspects of their orders after diplomatic intervention by the foreign state concerned.[176] Attempts to enforce

---

[171] Act No 16 of 1997. See, for analysis, Zanifa McDowell '*Forum non Conveniens*: The Caribbean and its Response to Xenophobia in American Courts' 49 ICLQ 108 (2000).

[172] See Henry Saint Dahl '*Forum Non Conveniens* and Latin America and Blocking Statutes' 35 U. Miami Inter-Am.L.Rev. 21 (2003–2004) covering Ecuador, Guatemala, Dominica, Nicaragua, Costa Rica, and the PARLATINO Model Law on the International Jurisdiction and Applicable Law to Tort Liability 1998. English translations of these laws and other relevant documents are appended to this article. See also Organization of American States, Inter-American Judicial Committee 'Proposal for an Inter-American Convention on the Effects and Treatment of the *Forum Non Conveniens* Theory' OEA/Ser Q CJI/doc 2/00, 3 March 2000.

[173] Enforcement jurisdiction includes the issue of jurisdiction to apply measures to entities that enjoy sovereign immunity. Such a question may conceivably arise where a state trading enterprise is involved, but it is not relevant in cases concerning privately owned corporations. It is therefore not discussed.

[174] See further US Restatement above note 17 s 431; Comment c at 321, 322. Under US law, non-judicial enforcement measures are subject to judicial review for fairness: ibid Comment e.

[175] See, for example, *British Nylon Spinners v Imperial Chemical Industries* [1953] 1 Ch 19 (CA); [1955] 1 Ch 37 (Dankwerts J).

[176] See the *Swiss Watchmakers* and *Zenith Radio* cases above n 47 and 49 and Neale and Stephens above n 1 at 156–57.

US judicial decisions against non-resident entities of MNEs have been met not only with diplomatic measures of opposition from target states but also with legal responses. Thus numerous countries have passed so-called 'blocking statutes' which have the effect inter alia of refusing recognition to foreign judgments that adversely affect the trade or commercial policy of the legislating state,[177] or principles of international law or comity.[178]

Equally, the corporate separation between parent and subsidiary in a multinational corporate group could be used as a justification by the courts of the home state for refusing to enforce a judgment issued against a subsidiary in a foreign host jurisdiction, with the aim of holding its parent company liable. Thus in *Adams v Cape Industries plc*,[179] the Court of Appeal refused to 'lift the corporate veil' between a British parent company and its American sales subsidiary, or to treat the two companies as a single 'economic entity', so as to permit the enforcement, in the UK, of a US default judgment given against the parent. However, this case should not be interpreted as laying down a principle that corporate separation is an absolute bar to the enforceability of a foreign judgment against a UK based parent company. On the facts, the judge in the American proceedings had not assessed the defendants' liability to each individual plaintiff, but had merely awarded a total sum to be divided among the plaintiffs by their counsel. This constituted a breach of natural justice under English law, making the award unenforceable before the English courts. In these circumstances, the refusal of the Court of Appeal to 'lift the corporate veil', or to see the presence of affiliated companies in the US as the presence of the British parent, is understandable.

(a) The Disclosure of Evidence in Proceedings Involving a MNE

A particularly contentious issue in the field of extraterritorial jurisdiction has been the assertion, again by US courts, of powers to order the disclosure of evidence located abroad with the foreign affiliates or associates of companies operating within US jurisdiction.[180] By contrast, the English courts have been unwilling to 'lift the corporate veil' and to order the disclosure of documents located in the overseas subsidiaries of British firms.[181]

The general principles observed by US courts in this respect have been summarized in s 442(1) of the Third US Restatement on Foreign Relations Law.[182] The

---

[177] See eg UK: Protection of Trading Interests Act 1980 (c 11) ss 5 and 6; Canada: Combines Investigation Act as amended by Stats Can 1974/75 c 76 s 12 ss 31.5, 31.6; Australia: Foreign Antitrust Judgments (Restriction of Enforcement) Act 1979 No 13 of 1979 s 3.

[178] See Australia: ibid.

[179] [1991] 1 All ER 929 (CA) affirming Scott J (ChD). Leave to appeal refused by Appeal Committee of the House of Lords 24 October 1989.

[180] See eg *In re Grand Jury Subpoena Duces Tecum* 72 F Supp 1013 (1947); *In Re Investigation of World Arrangements with Relation to . . . Petroleum* 13 FRD 280 (1952); and see US cases on disclosure by banks of records held by branches in foreign jurisdictions at nn 206–211 below.

[181] See *Lonrho v Shell Petroleum* [1980] 2 WLR 367 (CA) *aff'd* [1980] 1 WLR 627 (HL); *Re Tecnion Investments Ltd* [1985] BCLC 434 (CA). [182] Above n 17 at 348–49.

Restatement states that a court or agency of the US, when authorized by statute or rule of court, may order a person subject to its personal jurisdiction to produce documents, objects or other information relevant to an action or investigation, where the information or the person in possession of the information is outside the US.[183] In deciding whether to make such an order the court or agency should take into account:

the importance to the investigation or litigation of the documents or other information requested; the degree of specificity of the request; whether the information originated within the United States; the availability of alternative means of securing the information; and the extent to which non-compliance with the request would undermine important interests of the United States, or compliance with the request would undermine important interests of the state where the information is located.[184]

Failure to comply with an order to produce the requested information may subject the person to whom the order is addressed to sanctions including a finding of contempt, dismissal of a claim or defence, or default judgment, or may lead to a determination of fact favourable to the opposing party.[185] These general principles have been applied in numerous areas. However, orders for the discovery of documents in antitrust cases, and in areas covered by foreign secrecy laws, have engendered the greatest hostility from target states and deserve closer scrutiny.

(i) Disclosure of Evidence in US Antitrust Proceedings

In this area, foreign defendant corporations have been subjected to the broad requirements of US antitrust investigations and pre-trial disclosure rules on numerous occasions since the late 1940s.[186] Of particular significance were attempts, in the early 1960s, to control the use of liner conferences on routes between the US and Europe,[187] and the uranium cartel litigation of the 1970s.[188] Each series of cases led to the adoption of 'blocking statutes' by several target states, aimed at restricting compliance with wide-ranging US disclosure orders by companies located within their respective jurisdictions.

The experience of the uranium cartel litigation led to the adoption of the UK Protection of Trading Interests Act 1980.[189] By this Act the Secretary of State for

---

[183] ibid s 442(1)(a).   [184] ibid s 442(1)(c).   [185] ibid s 442(1)(b).

[186] For early controversies in the antitrust field, see the cases cited in n 180 above.

[187] On the liner conferences dispute and blocking legislation, see Sol Picciotto 'Jurisdictional Conflicts, International Law and the International State System' 11 Int'l Jo.Soc.L. 11 at 19–21 (1983); Neale and Stephens above n 1 at 110–14. The UK passed the Shipping Contracts and Commercial Documents Act 1964 (c 87) to block US measures in this area. Other states passed similar legislation during the mid to late 1960s. These included Germany, France, Norway, Belgium, and Sweden. For full references to these laws, see US Restatement above n 17 s 442 Reporter's Note 4 at 358.

[188] See *In re Westinghouse Uranium Contract* [1978] AC 547 (HL); *Re Westinghouse Electric and Duquesne Light Co* (1977) 78 DLR (3d) 3 (Ont HC). See also *Gulf Oil Corporation v Gulf Canada Ltd* (1980) 111 DLR (3d) 74 (Sup Ct Can).

[189] For analysis of the Act, see Vaughan Lowe 'Blocking Extraterritorial Jurisdiction: The British Protection of Trading Interests Act 1980' 75 AJIL 257 (1981) and A Lowenfeld's reply in ibid 629;

Trade and Industry can issue orders to persons carrying on business in the UK not to comply with measures taken, or to be taken, by any overseas country for the regulation or control of international trade, where it appears to the Secretary of State that those measures apply extraterritorially to persons carrying on business in the UK, and are damaging, or threaten to damage, the trading interests of the UK.[190] The Secretary of State is further empowered to issue orders prohibiting compliance, by a person in the UK, with a request made by any court, tribunal or authority of an overseas country to produce before it any commercial document that is not within the territorial jurisdiction of that country or to furnish any commercial information to any such court, tribunal, or authority.[191]

These powers were reviewed by the House of Lords in *British Airways Board v Laker Airways Ltd*.[192] This case arose out of the collapse, in 1982, of Laker Airways (Laker), which had been running a low-fare transatlantic air service between the UK and US. Shortly after going into liquidation, Laker commenced US antitrust proceedings before the Federal District Court in Washington DC against a number of airlines who were members of the International Air Transport Association and others, alleging a conspiracy between them to eliminate Laker by charging predatory air fares which forced Laker out of business, and claiming treble damages and punitive damages of more than $2 billion. In the course of the US proceedings, Laker sought extensive pre-trial discovery of documents and answers to far reaching interrogatories from British Airways (BA) and British Caledonian (BCal). The latter applied to the English courts for an injunction to restrain the US proceedings. The judge refused to grant the relief sought and BA and BCal appealed. Before the appeal could be heard the Secretary of State for Trade and Industry issued an order, in June 1983, under ss1 and 2 of the 1980 Act prohibiting BA and BCal from complying with any request or prohibition imposed upon them under the US antitrust laws as a result of a judgment in the US action, and prohibiting compliance with any request for the production of documents or commercial information in the US action without the Secretary of State's consent. Laker sought to challenge this order on judicial review. The Court of Appeal allowed the appeal against the refusal of injunctions restraining the US proceedings, on the basis of the Secretary of State's order, but dismissed Laker's application for judicial review.[193] Both issues were appealed to the House of Lords.

G. Marston 14 JWTL 461 (1980). See also the annotated version of the Act in Current Law Statutes 1980 (c 11). For examples of similar blocking statutes in other jurisdictions, see Australia: Foreign Proceedings (Prohibition of Certain Evidence) Act 1976 replaced by Foreign Proceedings (Excess of Jurisdiction) Act 1984, Austl Acts No 3; Canada: Foreign Extraterritorial Measures Act, Stat Can 1984 c 49; France: Law No 80–538 of 16 July 1980 [1980] *Journal Officiel* 1799, English translation: 75 AJIL 382 (1981); South Africa: Second General Law Amendment Act 94 1974 ss 2, 12 Stat S Africa 602.

[190] ibid s 1.   [191] ibid s 2(1).

[192] [1984] 3 WLR 413, [1984] 3 All ER 39 (HL). For analysis, see Neale and Stephens above n 1 at 117–27.   [193] [1983] 3 All ER 375 (QBD and CA).

The House of Lords rejected Laker's application for judicial review. Their Lordships also rejected the appeal of BA and BCal. An injunction against the US proceedings would not be issued on the ground that to do so would deprive Laker of a remedy against these airlines under US antitrust law, which fell within the jurisdiction of the Federal District court in Washington DC, within whose territory both BA and BCal had premises and carried on business. No equivalent remedy was available under English law and so this was not like a *forum non conveniens* action. Either the US proceedings could continue or Laker would have no cause of action. Furthermore, contrary to the view expressed by the Court of Appeal, the House of Lords held that the Minister's order was not decisive in favour of granting an injunction.

This decision shows that the English courts will respect the right of a foreign court to determine a cause of action arising under its law against a UK based defendant, where that cause of action arises out of activities carried on by the defendant within the foreign jurisdiction. In such a case an order under the Protection of Trading Interests Act 1980 will not be construed as an absolute bar to those proceedings. In this respect the House of Lords' decision in *Laker* conforms to a territorial conception of jurisdiction, in that it avoids giving to the order of the Secretary of State the power effectively to terminate proceedings legitimately brought by the plaintiff before the courts of a foreign country.[194]

On the other hand, where such proceedings are sought against a defendant who has no relevant connection with the foreign jurisdiction, the English courts will enjoin the foreign proceedings. Thus, in *Midland Bank v Laker Airways Ltd,*[195] the mere existence of a parent/subsidiary relationship between an enterprise based in the UK and its foreign affiliate was held not to be sufficient to prove the presence of the UK based company in the foreign jurisdiction for the purposes of adjudication. Consequently, the Court of Appeal issued an injunction against antitrust proceedings that were to be brought against the Midland Bank by Laker Airways. The British Airways case could be distinguished on the grounds that Midland's connection with Laker arose out of banking transactions in England governed by English law and intended to be so governed; there was no connection between Midland and any of the airlines operating in the US; Midland had done nothing in the US that could have been governed by the US antitrust laws; the Midland Bank's subsidiary bank in California had a separate legal existence, was not managerially controlled by its parent and had no connection of any kind with the airlines involved in the liquidator's antitrust suit; and such banking activities as were carried on in the US by Midland's subsidiary, Thomas Cook, were incidental

---

[194] This objection was raised by Judge Wilkey in *Laker Airways Ltd v Sabena* 731 F 2d 909 at 930 (DC Cir 1984), over the effect of the Court of Appeal's ruling in the *Laker* case, in the course of his judgment restraining two European airlines, Sabena and KLM, from seeking recourse to foreign courts against the US antitrust proceedings. That judgment was given before the House of Lords decision in *Laker*, which meets many of Judge Wilkey's objections against the restraining injunction granted by the Court of Appeal.   [195] [1986] 1 All ER 526 (CA).

to the group's tourist business and had no relevance to the facts in issue. It followed that the Midland Bank had not submitted itself to the jurisdiction of US antitrust legislation in the same way as BA and BCal had done.

The above cases show that an antisuit injunction can be a significant means of control over transnational litigation as it has the effect of requiring a person subject to the jurisdiction of an English court not to begin, or to continue existing proceedings, in a foreign jurisdiction. The Protection of Trading Interests Act 1980 offers a special case for the application of such an order. Normally the question of an antisuit injunction will arise in the context of the personal jurisdiction of the court. Such an injunction will be issued where the parties have agreed in advance to the exclusive jurisdiction of the English courts, or to English arbitration, in a commercial contract. Not to do so would condone a breach of contract.[196] In addition, an antisuit injunction will be issued where proceedings are commenced in another jurisdiction so as to pre-empt English jurisdiction in circumstances that amount to a vexatious or oppressive choice of forum. However, such an injunction should be issued only where justice requires it and with a view to comity.[197] Furthermore, there should be an element of unconscionability in the bringing of the foreign proceedings.[198] The discretion of the English courts in this area has also been restrained by EC law. Thus the first court seized of the dispute within the EC has the right to verify whether it has jurisdiction, even if the courts of another Member State are specified in an exclusive jurisdiction agreement, or the proceedings in the first court were brought by the claimant in bad faith.[199] The uniformity of the Judgments Regulation takes precedence in these circumstances and the courts of the Member States must follow its provisions.[200]

---

[196] See *Sabah Shipyard (Pakistan) Ltd v Islamic Republic of Pakistan* [2002] EWCA Civ 1643 (CA); *West Tankers Inc v Ras Riunione Adriatica Di Sicurta: The Front Comor* [2005] EWHC 454 (Comm). See also, for the circumstances under which an exclusive jurisdiction clause could be ignored, *Donohue v Armco* [2001] UKHL 64, [2002] 1 All ER 749 (HL).

[197] See *Airbus Industrie GIE v Patel* per Lord Goff [1999] 1 AC 199 at 138, [1998] 2 All ER 257 (HL) at 269A–B. In that case a personal injuries claim was brought in Texas by Indian plaintiffs against the French manufacturer of Airbus aircraft, arising out of a crash of one such aircraft in India. An antisuit injunction was sought before the English courts by Airbus on the grounds that neither party had any connections with Texas, no cause of action arose there, nor was any loss suffered, and the law of Texas was inapplicable to the dispute. However, although the House of Lords accepted that the action in Texas was oppressive, the injunction was refused as it would offend international comity for the English court, which itself had no connection with the dispute, to restrain proceedings in Texas. See also *SNI Aerospatiale v Lee Kui Jak* [1987] AC 871. Here it was held that trial in Texas would be oppressive when the proper forum for the personal injuries litigation was Brunei. These cases arose when Texas did not accept the principle of *forum non conveniens*.

[198] See *Laker Airways* [1984] 3 All ER at 57C (per Lord Scarman).

[199] See *Gasser v MISRAT* [2004] 1 Lloyd's Rep 222; *Turner v Govit and Haranda Ltd and Changepoint SA* [2004] 1 Lloyd's Rep 216.

[200] See further Philip Ember 'Controlling Proceedings Abroad' New Law Journal 26 September 2003 1430; Louis Flannery 'The End of Anti-suit Injunctions?' New Law Journal 28 May 2004 798; Nathalie Burn 'ASIs – The Tide Has Turned' New Law Journal 10 September 2004 1330. For a critical perspective, see Hartley above n 167 at 815–23. See also Jonathan Harris 'Stays of Proceedings and the Brussels Convention' 54 ICLQ 933 (2005) examining the effect of *Owusu v Jackson* (above

(ii) US Disclosure Orders and Foreign Secrecy Laws

Another significant source of conflict between the US and other states has arisen in cases where the US authorities seek evidence located abroad with the affiliates or associates of litigants, or with third parties (often the litigant's foreign bank), and that evidence is subject to secrecy laws in force in the target jurisdiction. The applicable principles are summarized in s 442(2) of the US Restatement on Foreign Relations Law, which draws upon the leading decision of the US Supreme Court in *Société International v Rogers*.[201] By s 442(2):

If disclosure of information located outside the United States is prohibited by a law, regulation, or order of a court or other authority of the state in which the information or prospective witness is located, or of the state of which a prospective witness is a national,

(a) a court or agency in the United States may require the person to whom the order is directed to make a good faith effort to secure permission from the foreign authorities to make the information available;

(b) a court or agency should not ordinarily impose sanctions of contempt, dismissal, or default on a party that has failed to comply with the order for production, except in cases of deliberate concealment or removal of information or failure to make a good faith effort in accordance with paragraph (a);

(c) a court or agency may, in appropriate cases, make findings of fact adverse to a party that has failed to comply with the order for production, even if that party has made a good faith effort to secure permission from the foreign authorities to make the information available and that effort has been unsuccessful.[202]

This provision applies not only to cases involving foreign secrecy laws but also to cases where a 'blocking statute' prohibits disclosure in accordance with the trading interests of the target state.

The US courts have interpreted the *Société* decision, as requiring a 'balancing approach'.[203] This involves taking account of the factors listed in s 442(1)(c) of the Restatement and, in particular, comparing the importance of the US interest in disclosure against the interest of the target state in retaining the confidentiality of the information or documents in question. This approach has been applied in cases involving requests for information from both US- and foreign-based MNEs by the US Internal Revenue Service (IRS), where that information is located in overseas subsidiaries, or in the foreign parent company, and is subject to commercial secrecy

---

n 164) on the discretion to grant stays of proceedings in the case of a foreign exclusive jurisdiction clause. Harris notes that in *Konkola Copper Mines plc v Coromin* ([2005] EWHC 898 (Comm) judgment of 10 May 2005) it was held that the court could stay English proceedings, in favour of a non-contracting state forum, where that forum was designated in an exclusive jurisdiction clause. The decision in *Owusu* did not preclude this (at 944–45).

[201] 357 US 197, 78 S Ct 1087, 2 L Ed 2d 1255 (1958).

[202] US Restatement above n 17 at 348–49.

[203] See eg *In Re Westinghouse Electric Corp Uranium* 563 F 2d 992 at 997 (1977).

laws.[204] The US courts have generally held that the US interest in disclosure out-weighs the target state's interest in preserving commercial confidentiality. These cases can be justified on the ground that, in the absence of strong extraterritorial disclosure requirements, MNEs can use their international network of companies to avoid not only the payment of tax but also to resist legitimate investigations by the IRS. Arguably, had the relevant records remained within the US jurisdiction, no issue of extraterritorial law enforcement would have arisen.

However, such decisions have met with protests from foreign governments. For example, the Government of Japan made such a protest when a US District Court in California held that a summons for information issued by the IRS, against the US sales subsidiary of the Japanese Toyota Corporation, was sufficient to effect service on the Japanese parent company.[205] According to the Japanese Government such service violated international law. However, the Court held that service was effected within the bounds of international law, it having applied the require-ments of the Third Restatement to conclude that there was a strong American interest in obtaining the information and there was no reasonable alternative means of obtaining it.

Harder to justify are cases where the order for disclosure is made against an innocent third party, such as a bank, which holds information relevant to an investigation by US agencies. Here too, the US courts have resorted to a balancing test.[206] However, the precise limits of permissible discretion have not been clearly drawn. Much depends on the nature of the investigation involved and on the weight to be given to good faith efforts at disclosure in the face of penal confiden-tiality laws. For example, in the area of grand jury investigations into drug related crimes, the discretion to require disclosure from third parties operating in 'secrecy havens' has been widely interpreted.[207] No doubt a finding that the third party has not acted in good faith is a significant consideration. However, even where the third party does act in good faith it can face impossible choices. The courts of other jurisdictions have often refused to give effect to US extraterritorial disclos-ure orders.[208] Nonetheless, the US courts may still require compliance with the US order. For example, in *US v Chase Manhattan Bank*[209] the US District Court

---

[204] See *US v Vetco Inc* 644 F 2d 1324 (9th Cir 1981) *cert den* 454 US 1098 (1981); *Marc Rich & Co AG v US* 707 F 2d 663 (2nd Cir 1983).

[205] *US v Toyota Motor Corporation* 569 F Supp 1158 (1983).

[206] See eg *First National City Bank v IRS* 271 F2d 616 (2nd Cir 1959) (taxation); *In re Application of Chase Manhattan Bank* 297 F2d 611 (1960) (taxation); *US v First National City Bank* 396 F 2d 897 (2nd Cir 1968)(antitrust); *SEC v Banca della Svizzera Italiana* 92 FRD 111 (SDNY 1981) (insider dealing).

[207] See *US v Bank of Nova Scotia II* 740 F 2d 817 (11th Cir 1984) *cert den* 469 US 1106 (1985). See also *US v Bank of Nova Scotia I* 691 F 2d 1384 (11th Cir 1982) *cert den* 103 S Ct 3086 (1983).

[208] See eg England: *XAG and Others v A bank* [1983] 2 All ER 464 (QBD Com Ct); Germany: *Krupp Mak Maschinenbau GmbH v Deutsche Bank AG* (Landgericht Kiel 6/30/82) 22 ILM 740 (1983).

[209] 590 F Supp 1160 (SDNY 1984). See, for the original order, *US v Chase Manhattan* 584 F Supp 1080 (SDNY 1984). See also parallel cases arising out of the same facts: *Garpeg Ltd v US* 583 F Supp 789 (SDNY 1984), motion to vacate denied 583 F Supp 799 (SDNY 1984) and see 588 F Supp 1237 (SDNY 1984); *Vanguard International Manufacturing Inc v US* 588 F Supp 1229 (SDNY 1984).

held the Chase Manhattan Bank to be in civil contempt for failure to comply with an order to disclose to the IRS records held by its Hong Kong branch where the disclosure of those records had been prevented by an order of the Hong Kong courts. Chase's good faith argument, based on the revised Restatement, was found to be unpersuasive in the balancing process. The Restatement did not require the court to refrain from imposing a contempt order where the bank had acted in good faith, it gave it a discretion to do so. Furthermore, the order in the present case was a court order, not a rule of law or a regulation.[210] By contrast, in *US v First National Bank of Chicago*[211] the Court of Appeals for the Seventh Circuit held that where the bank can establish with certainty that the release of information pursuant to an IRS summons would subject its employees in a foreign jurisdiction to the risk of imprisonment, this should weigh significantly in the court's application of the balancing test. However, such a finding did not bar a court from compelling production of the information where this could be obtained without endangering the liberty of the foreign employees. The bank was still obliged to undertake a good faith effort to secure the information.

Thus, US law leaves a considerable measure of discretion in the issuing of extraterritorial orders for the disclosure of evidence held by third parties. By comparison English law will not permit the issue of orders for the discovery of documents located in the foreign branches of UK or foreign banks that are doing business within the English jurisdiction. In *MacKinnon v Donaldson Lufkin & Jenrette Securities Corp*[212] Hoffmann J rejected a request for an order under s 7 of the Bankers Books Evidence Act 1879, requiring access to the banking records of the defendant corporation which were held at the head office of Citibank in New York. Such an order would infringe the sovereignty of the US. In the course of his judgment Hoffmann J specifically rejected the adoption of a balancing test to weigh the respective interests of the English and American jurisdictions, on the ground that this would carry little conviction outside the forum. However, the Bank of England may override a court order restraining a bank from disclosing documents to a foreign bank regulator, or to any third party, where it reasonably requires those documents for the discharge of its supervisory functions under s 39(3)(a) of the Banking Act 1987. This may include cases where the foreign bank regulator and the Bank of England have a shared interest in the information and the Bank of England is willing to cooperate in securing the information for itself and for the foreign regulator.[213]

---

[210] 590 F Supp at 1162.   [211] 699 F 2d 341 (7th Cir 1983).

[212] [1986] 1 All ER 653 (ChD) applying *R v Grossman* (1981) 73 Cr App R 302 (CA).

[213] See *A and Others v B Bank, Bank of England Intervening* [1992] 1 All ER 778 (QBD Com Ct Hirst J). See further, on the problems of international cooperation in international bank supervision, *Inquiry into the Supervision of the Bank of Credit and Commerce International* (Chairman Rt Hon Bingham LJ, 22 October 1992) especially ch 3; Treasury and Civil Service Committee of the House of Commons Fourth Report *Banking Supervision and BCCI: International and National Regulation* (HC Paper 177 1991–92).

(b) The Reduction of Conflicts over Demands for Disclosure of Evidence Located in a Foreign Jurisdiction

The major objection to overbroad US discovery orders has been the fact that they infringe the sovereignty of the target jurisdiction. On the other hand, the motives behind such orders are often justifiable. MNEs should not be able to take advantage of their international network of companies to evade their legal duties under US law. Thus the US authorities do have a legitimate interest to protect. The problem is not so much one of ends as of means. The US authorities have become more sensitive to this issue and numerous techniques for the reduction of conflicts over extraterritorial discovery have gradually been adopted, with, it must be said, varying degrees of success. The techniques involved can be divided between bilateral methods of cooperation, and the multilateral approach adopted by the Hague Convention on the Taking of Evidence Abroad of 1970.

(i) Bilateral Cooperation

The evolution of such cooperation is well illustrated by the experience of the US Securities and Exchange Commission (SEC) in dealing with insider trading investigations involving requests for information from Swiss banks.[214] In the early 1980s two cases arose in which SEC investigations were hampered by Swiss bank secrecy laws. The first concerned an investigation into possible insider dealing in the course of the takeover of St Joe Minerals Corporation by Joseph E Seagram and Sons in 1981.[215] The second case involved suspected insider dealing associated with the merger between Kuwait Petroleum Corporation and the *Santa Fe* International Corporation.[216] Although the SEC was successful in these cases, each resulted in less than an ideal solution from the regulator's point of view. The BSI case generated tensions between the US and Switzerland, and in the *Santa Fe* case the request for information was delayed for 30 months. These experiences led the SEC, in 1984, to advocate the enactment of a 'waiver by conduct' law, whereby the mere fact of executing a securities transaction in the US would amount to a waiver of foreign bank secrecy laws and to an implied consent to the disclosure of information and evidence relevant to the transaction for the purposes of the enforcement of Federal securities laws.[217] This proposal met with widespread criticism. It would have increased opposition to SEC investigations from foreign states. Furthermore, it would have been easy to avoid the application of the principle by use of a chain

---

[214] For a fuller account of these matters, see Baltic 'The Next Step in Insider Trading Regulation: International Cooperative Efforts in the Global Securities Market' 23 Law & Pol.Int'l Bus. 167 (1991–1992).   [215] *SEC v Banca della Svizzera Italiana* 92 FRD 111 (SDNY 1981).

[216] See *Judicial Assistance in the Santa Fe Case* First Opinion Swiss Sup Ct: 22 ILM 785 (1983); Second Opinion: 24 ILM 745 (1985).

[217] See SEC 1934 Release No 21186 File no S7–27–84 'Request for Comments Concerning a Concept to Improve the Commission's Ability to Investigate and Prosecute Persons Who Purchase or Sell Securities in the US Markets From Other Countries'.

of foreign intermediaries preventing any investigation from identifying the true facts. The 'waiver by conduct' approach was superseded in 1988 by the Insider Trading and Securities Fraud Enforcement Act 1988, which offers far-reaching assistance to foreign securities authorities which believe that information about securities violations in their country can be found in the US, in return for reciprocal cooperation being offered to the SEC.[218] This more cooperative approach became manifest in Swiss-US relations after the BSI case. On 30 August 1982 a Memorandum of Understanding to establish mutually acceptable means for improving international law enforcement and cooperation in the field of insider trading was signed on behalf of the Swiss and US governments.[219] Furthermore, Switzerland made insider dealing a crime under its law, thereby removing some of the difficulties experienced by the SEC in the *Santa Fe* case.[220]

In the field of competition, the US Government has also concluded non-binding memoranda of understanding[221] or binding agreements on cooperation with other governments,[222] and with the EC,[223] based on good faith principles of mutual assistance, as recommended by the OECD Council.[224] It has also adopted, in 1994, the International Antitrust Assistance Enforcement Act which authorizes the US to conclude further agreements on the mutual exchange of information in antitrust matters.[225] Other OECD member countries have concluded similar bilateral cooperation treaties.[226] Such agreements offer a structure for cooperation between the signatories based on comity principles. In particular, two types of comity analysis may be used. The first is 'negative comity' which entails an exercise of restraint when dealing with requests for extraterritorial cooperation. In such agreements requests for information are generally subject to a power of refusal on

---

[218] Public Law No 100–704 102 Stat 4677 (1988).

[219] See 22 ILM 1 (1983) and Note 'Insider Trading Laws and Swiss Banks: Recent Hope for Reconciliation' 22 Col.J.Transnat.L 303 (1984). Similar agreements have been concluded with the UK, Japan, the Canadian Provinces of Ontario, Quebec and British Columbia, Brazil, Italy, the Netherlands, and France: see Baltic n 159 above at 191.

[220] Insider dealing was prohibited by art 161 Swiss Penal Code enacted 1 July 1988.

[221] See eg US-Canada Memorandum of Understanding as to Notification Consultation and Co-operation with Respect to the Application of National Anti-trust Laws of March 9 1984: 4 Trade Reg Rep (CCH) s 13,503, 23 ILM 275 (1984).

[222] See eg US-Australia Agreement Relating to Cooperation in Antitrust Matters June 29 1982, TIAS No 10365 4 Trade Reg Rep (CCH) s 13,502; US-Germany Agreement Relating to Mutual Cooperation Regarding Restrictive Business Practices June 23 1976, 27 UST 1956, TIAS No 8291, 4 Trade Reg Rep (CCH) s 13,501. See further UNCTAD *Competition* Series on issues in international investment agreements (New York and Geneva: United Nations, 2004) at 40–53.

[223] European Communities-United States Agreement on the Application of Their Competition Laws: 30 ILM 1487 (1991).

[224] See OECD Council Recommendation Concerning Cooperation Between Member Countries on Restrictive Business Practices Affecting International Trade OECD Doc No C(86) 44 Final 21 May 1986 reproduced in 25 ILM 1629 (1986).

[225] Public Law 103–438 2 November 1994, 108 Stat 4597, 34 ILM 494 (1995). So far one agreement has been concluded under this power: see US-Australia Agreement on Mutual Antitrust Enforcement Assistance 1999 cited in UNCTAD *Competition* above n 222 at 44.

[226] See France-Germany Agreement Concerning Cooperation on Restrictive Business Practices 28 May 1984: 26 ILM 531 (1987).

the part of the requested state where its substantial economic or other vital interests are threatened by the communication of such information.[227] Thus something reminiscent of a balancing of interests test is present. The second approach is 'positive comity' which allows for the substitution of the competition authorities of one country for those of another in dealing with an investigation. An example of the latter is the 1991 US-EU Co-operation Agreement, as supplemented by the 1998 Agreement on the Application of Positive Comity Principles in the Enforcement of Their Competition Laws.[228] By Article III positive comity is described as follows:

The competition authorities of a Requesting Party may request the competition authorities of a Requested Party to investigate and, if warranted, to remedy anticompetitive activities in accordance with the Requested Party's competition laws. Such a request may be made regardless of whether the activities also violate the Requesting Party's competition laws, and regardless of whether the competition authorities of the Requesting Party have commenced or contemplate taking enforcement activities under their own competition laws.

These wide powers of cooperation should be seen in their context. The 1998 agreement does not oust the negative comity aspects of the 1991 agreement. Nor has it avoided conflicting approaches to given cases between US and EC competition authorities. In particular, the agreement does not apply to merger controls and this is where some major disagreements have occurred.[229] However, in most cases cooperation proceeds well. The types of confrontations seen in past years should not recur.

(ii) The Hague Convention on the Taking of Evidence Abroad in Civil or Commercial Matters 1970[230]

The Hague Convention is designed to assist in the gathering of evidence required in civil or commercial matters that is situated outside the forum jurisdiction. The judicial authority that requires evidence located in another jurisdiction, will issue a letter of request addressed to the authority in the other jurisdiction designated to receive such requests.[231] The letter of request specifies the details of the evidence required. The convention places few limits on the power to issue letters of request. Only three general qualifications appear in Article 1 of the convention. First, the

---

[227] Eg France-Germany ibid art 5 and US-EU 1991 Agreement above n 223 art VI.

[228] Agreement of 4 June 1998, 37 ILM 1070 (1998).

[229] See Whish above n 100 at 440 and 451 citing the cases of Boeing/McDonnell Douglas and GE/Honeywell.

[230] Cmnd 6727 reproduced 9 ILM 87 (1970). See too the Report of the US delegation to the preparatory conference: 8 ILM 785 (1969), Amram 63 AJIL 521 (1969); Report of Second Meeting of Special Commission on the Operation of the Convention: 24 ILM 1668 (1985); US Department of State Circular on Hague Evidence Convention Operations, *Hague Convention on Taking of Evidence Abroad in Civil or Commercial Matters*, available at <http://www.travel.state.gov/law/info/judicial/judicial_689.html>. See also, for the applicable regime within the EU, Council Regulation 1206/2001 28 May 2001 on cooperation between the courts of Member States in the taking of evidence in civil and commercial matters [2001] OJ L 174/1.   [231] ibid arts 1 and 2.

issuing authority must act in accordance with the provisions of its governing law. Secondly, a letter shall not be used to obtain evidence which is not intended for use in judicial proceedings, commenced, or contemplated. Thus general fishing expeditions unconnected with judicial proceedings are outside the convention. Thirdly, the convention does not extend to the service of judicial documents, the issuance of any process of execution or enforcement or for provisional or protective measures. These are covered by the Hague Convention of 1965 on the Service Abroad of Judicial and Extra-judicial Documents in Civil and Commercial Matters.[232] In sum, the Hague Evidence Convention is limited to requests for evidence arising in the course of actual litigation.

By Article 23 of the Convention, 'a Contracting State may, at the time of signature, ratification or accession, declare that it will not execute Letters of Request issued for the purpose of obtaining pre-trial discovery of documents as known in Common Law countries'. Numerous contracting states have made reservations to this effect.[233] In its reservation, the UK has gone further and has specified what it understands to be included in the discovery of documents. According to the UK reservation a letter of request issued for the purpose of pre-trial discovery of documents includes any letter of request which requires a person '(a) to state what documents relevant to the proceedings to which the letters of request relate are, or have been, in his possession, custody or power; or (b) to produce any documents other than particular documents specified in the letter of request as being documents appearing to the requested court to be, or to be likely to be, in his possession, custody or power'. This wording echoes s 2(4) of the Evidence (Proceedings in Other Jurisdictions) Act 1975 which implements the scheme of the convention into English law. Section 2(4) was interpreted by the House of Lords in the *Westinghouse* case as excluding general 'fishing expeditions'.[234] Thus the UK reservation clearly seeks to prevent the convention from being misused as a cover for unacceptable US pre-trial discovery procedures. Indeed, the convention as a whole, 'was intended primarily to apply to 'evidence' in the sense of material required to prove or disprove allegations at trial. It was not intended to apply to discovery in the sense of the search for material which might lead to the discovery of admissible evidence'.[235]

Against this background, the judicial controversy in the US, surrounding the relationship between the Hague Convention and US pre-trial discovery rules, will

---

[232] Above n 84.

[233] Eg Denmark, Finland, France, Norway, Portugal, and Sweden from among the original ratifying states subsequently joined by Germany. All the ratifying states except the US, Barbados, Israel, the Czech Republic, and Slovakia have made a reservation under art 23.

[234] Above n 188. For the limits of permissible requests under English law see, further *Re Asbestos Insurance Coverage* cases [1985] 1 WLR 331; *Re State of Norway's Application (Nos 1 and 2)* [1989] 1 All ER 745 (HL); *Panayiotou v Sony Music Entertainment (UK) Ltd* [1994] 1 All ER 755 (ChD).

[235] L Collins 'The Hague Evidence Convention and Discovery: A Serious Misunderstanding?' 35 ICLQ 765 at 783 (1986). This article presents convincing evidence in support of the thesis referred to and accepted in the text.

be examined.[236] The issue arose in a series of cases involving the tortious liability of European manufacturers for deaths and injuries suffered by US citizens, caused by accidents involving their products, which took place within the US jurisdiction. By the mid-1980s a disagreement had emerged among lower level US courts as to whether there was a requirement to proceed first under the Hague Convention[237] or whether the US court could proceed under US discovery rules alone, without this constituting a threat to the sovereignty of the foreign state in which the evidence is located.[238]

The issue went up to the US Supreme Court in the joined cases of *Anschuetz GmbH v Mississippi River Bridge Authority* and *Messerschmitt Bolkow Blohm v Walker*. These cases were settled after argument had been submitted and so no judgment resulted.[239] However, the Supreme Court did deliver a judgment in the case of *Société Nationale Industrielle Aerospatiale v US District Court for the Southern District of Iowa*.[240] The Supreme Court held that an American court should resort to the convention when it deemed that course of action appropriate after considering the position of the parties before it as well as the interests of the foreign state concerned. However, the Supreme Court declined to articulate specific rules to guide this 'delicate task of adjudication'. In this the Supreme Court followed the argument of the US Government in its *amicus* brief, which saw the convention as an optional method for obtaining discovery that should apply when considerations of comity and the facts of the given case warranted it. On the other hand, the Supreme Court rejected the view of the Court of Appeals that the convention simply did not apply to discovery sought of a foreign litigant subject to the jurisdiction of a US court. In arriving at this conclusion, the Supreme Court rejected the petitioner's argument that the convention should be treated as a mandatory procedure to be used

---

[236] This discussion concentrates on the issue of when a US court can request discovery under Federal Rules of Procedure in an action before it. More recently the issue has arisen whether a request by a foreign court for discovery in the US should be limited by the rules of that foreign court. In this situation the US Supreme Court has sanctioned a balancing approach under 28 USC s 1782(a): *Intel Corporation Inc v Advanced Micro Devices Inc* 542 US 241, 124 S Ct 2446, 159 L Ed 2d 355 (2004), 2004 US LEXIS 4570; *In Re Application of Imanagement Services Ltd* (US Dist Ct D NJ 28 February 2006), 2006 US Dist LEXIS 8876.

[237] As held eg by the Supreme Court of West Virginia in *Eickhoff Maschinenfabrik v Starcher* 328 SE 2d 492 (1985).

[238] As held in *Anschuetz & Co v Mississippi River Bridge Authority* 754 F 2d 602 (5th Cir 1985); *MMB v Walker* 757 F 2d 729 (5th Cir 1985); *Re Société Nationale Industrielle Aerospatiale* 788 F 2d 1408 (9th Cir 1986); *Société Nationale Industrielle Aerospatiale v US District Court for the District of Iowa* 782 F 2d 120 (8th Cir 1986).

[239] The principal briefs of the parties are reproduced in 25 ILM 803 et seq (1986). The US Government, as *amicus*, had argued that the courts had a discretion to use either the convention or US rules of discovery in the light of considerations of international comity; the petitioners, supported by *amicus* briefs from the German, French and British Governments, argued that the Hague Convention procedure should apply first and that the application of US pre-trial discovery rules was a violation of international law in that they failed to acknowledge the judicial sovereignty of foreign states in which evidence was located.

[240] 107 S Ct 2542 (1987); 26 ILM 1021 (1987). The parties' principal briefs are reproduced in 25 ILM 1475 et seq (1986).

in preference to US rules of discovery by an American court. In the Supreme Court's view, this was contrary to the language and history of the convention.

Thus, under US law, it is possible to persuade a US court that the Hague Convention procedure should be used in preference to US rules of pre-trial discovery.[241] However, as noted above, the Hague Convention was not specifically designed to provide for pre-trial discovery. Moreover, as most of the contracting states have made reservations under Article 23, refusing to recognize letters of request made for the purposes of US-style pre-trial discovery, it is hard to see how the convention can assist the US litigant. Therefore, it is likely that in cases where a US court is faced with a request for pre-trial discovery against a foreign party over which it has subject-matter and personal jurisdiction, it will conclude that US rules should apply.[242] As Collins has noted, the real problem lies not with discovery but with the consequences of the assumption of wide rules of personal jurisdiction by the US courts.[243] It is the latter that give rise to the problem of extraterritoriality which is consummated by the request for discovery. On the other hand, given the unsuitability of the Hague Convention procedure for dealing with US-style pre-trial discovery, insistence upon its use by foreign defendants is hard to justify on grounds other than the desire to deprive the US plaintiff of a legitimate procedural advantage before the US courts. Such an argument may be no more than a delaying tactic that seeks to protect a foreign manufacturer, whose products or acts have injured a US citizen, from proof of liability.[244]

Concluding Remarks

This chapter has considered the legal consequences that follow when a state or supranational organization adopts a unilateral policy of extending jurisdiction extraterritorially to the foreign units of a MNE. That the US has been the most

---

[241] See, to this effect, *Hudson v Hermann Pfauter GmbH & Co* 117 FRD 33 (NDNY 1987); *In re Perrier Bottled Water Litigation* 138 FRD 348 (D Conn 1991).

[242] This is confirmed by more recent cases, none of which accept the need for the Hague Convention to prevail even in relation to jurisdictional discovery, an issue that did not arise in *Aerospatiale*. See, for example, *Madden v Wyeth* (US Dist Ct ND Texas 12 January 2006) 2006 US Dist LEXIS 880; *In Re Automotive Refinishing Paint Antitrust Litigation* (US CA 3d Cir, 13 February 2004) 358 F 3d 288; 2004 US App LEXIS 24320; *Hagenbuch v 3B6 Sistemi Elettronici* (US Dist Ct ND Ill, E Div, 12 September 2005) 2005 US Dist LEXIS 20049; *In Re Vitamins Antitrust Litigation* (US Dist Ct DC, 20 September 2000) 120 F Supp 2d 45, 2000 US Dist LEXIS 14102. See also Cynthia Day Wallace ' "Extraterritorial" Discovery: Ongoing Challenges for Antitrust Litigation in an Environment of Global Investment' 5 JIEL 353 (2002).

[243] Above n 235 at 785. See further B Oxman 37 U.Miami L.Rev. 733 at 740–42 (1983); Jennings 33 BYIL 146 at 171 (1957) and L Collins 'International Law Aspects of Obtaining Evidence Abroad' in C Olmstead (ed) *Extraterritorial Application of Laws and Responses Thereto* (ILA/ESC, 1984) at 186.

[244] However, as Collins points out, the convention may be of use in producing evidence where eg a foreign co-defendant fails to appear and its evidence is essential to prove the case against the co-defendants, or to facilitate a site inspection: ibid at 784.

assertive state in this respect is, perhaps, not surprising. Not only has it been, until recently, the dominant political power in the international economy, but also it has a legal experience based upon the creation of a unified transcontinental economy that has conditioned its legislators, administrators, and judges towards an easy acceptance of extraterritorial jurisdiction in all its forms. However, the conflict generated by US assertions of extraterritorial jurisdiction has given rise to numerous attempts at minimizing its incidence, both on a unilateral level by the US courts, and on a bilateral and multilateral level through diplomatic agreements and initiatives. As noted earlier, on a unilateral level, US courts have adopted the 'balance of interests' approach, inspired by successive revisions of the US Restatement on Foreign Relations Law. However, the effectiveness of this approach as a means of minimizing conflicting requirements being placed upon MNEs is open to question. As Judge Wilkey stated in *Laker Airways v Sabena*:[245]

Domestic courts are created by national constitutions and statutes to enforce primarily national laws. The courts of most developed countries follow international law only to the extent it is not overridden by national law. Thus courts inherently find it difficult neutrally to balance competing foreign interests. When there is any doubt, national interests will tend to be favoured over foreign interests. This partially explains why there have been few times when courts have found foreign interests to prevail.[246]

In this respect, it has been suggested that extraterritoriality conflicts could be avoided by the adoption of a 'shared values' approach.[247] Thus, where a state wishes to apply extraterritorially a mandatory rule of its internal economic law, should that law express the shared values of both states, the courts of the target state ought to apply it. They should only prevent the application of the enforcing state's law where there is a genuine threat to the national interests of the target state in the specific circumstances of the case. The mere fact that the sovereignty of the target state has been interfered with should not be decisive, if its vital economic interests are not threatened. This approach appears to add little to the 'balancing test'. It will always be open for the court in the target state to see the existence of a threat to vital national interests where the enforcing state seeks to infringe the former's sovereignty. Moreover, it is a mistake to assume that the economic policies of the major Western states are converging, so that 'shared values' can be identified.

On the other hand, the state-centred model of international business regulation can be supplanted as states agree to develop new harmonized standards of international economic regulation, and create new conflict avoidance procedures.

---

[245] Above n 194.

[246] ibid at 951. See further Maier 'Interest Balancing and Extraterritorial Jurisdiction' 31 Am.Jo.Comp.L 579 (1983); Rosenthal and Knighton above n 1 at 25–28; Roth above n 1. Note also the views of Hoffmann J on the balancing test in *MacKinnon v Donaldson Lufkin and Jenrette Securities Corp* above n 212.

[247] See Grossfeld and Rogers 'A Shared Values Approach to Jurisdictional Conflicts in International Economic Law' 32 ICLQ 931 (1983).

Developments in the EC such as the 1968 Brussels Convention, and the various programmes for the development of a uniform substantive economic law of the Community, exemplify the alternative. In addition, the conclusion of bilateral cooperation agreements in various fields where there exist risks of extraterritorial regulatory action, and the work of the Hague Conference on Private International Law may serve to reduce future conflicts.[248] However, success in these initiatives remains tentative. For the foreseeable future the administration, by states, of competing systems of economic regulation will continue to generate the risk of conflicts of jurisdiction in cases involving the activities of MNEs where vital national interests are involved.

[248] See *Morris: The Conflict of Laws* above n 92 at 15–16 paras 1–024 and 1–025.

5

The Control of Inward Investment by Host States

This chapter deals with the principal techniques used by host states to control the entry and establishment of foreign direct investment. These techniques represent policy responses that seek to preserve national economic independence against possible threats from the activities of foreign investors. They range, at one extreme, from the complete exclusion of foreign investors to techniques of controlled access to the host state's economy. In the next chapter techniques for the encouragement of foreign direct investment will be considered both at the level of the host state and at the bilateral and multilateral levels, thereby completing the continuum of policy choices from controlled access to open access and investment incentives. Before turning to specific techniques of control, certain general points should be made concerning the possible constraints on a host state's discretion in the regulation of inward direct investment stemming from international law. This is of particular significance in view of the increased use of bilateral and regional investment protection agreements and investment related provisions in the WTO Agreements.[1]

(1) The Scope of Host State Discretion

Host state control over inward investment can be divided into three major areas. First, there may be restrictions excluding such investment from the state as a whole or from specific sectors and/or industries. Secondly, foreign direct investment may be permitted after a review process, which may or may not place conditions upon the foreign investor in return for permission to enter the host state. Thirdly, once the foreign investment has been established, the activities of the investor will be subject to the general laws of the land.

The first and second areas operate at the stage of entry. Here the host state exercises its sovereign right to control the presence of aliens within its territory. In terms of international law, the host state has an unlimited discretion at this stage, subject

---

[1] See further ch 6 and Part IV below.

only to restraints voluntarily undertaken in international economic agreements. Thus it is highly important to consider how far a given host state has accepted international obligations to guarantee access for foreign investors into its territory. It may be unlawful under the applicable international treaty regime for the host to adopt the kinds of measures to be discussed below.

The third area represents the post-entry phase, when the foreign investor has subjected itself to the laws of the host state. In general, the laws applicable at this stage are the same as those applied to domestic enterprises. However, the operation of these laws may be affected by the nature of the MNE's business organization and activities, and may result in the creation of new legal responses aimed at MNEs in particular. Again, according to established principles of state sovereignty under international law, the host state has a theoretically unlimited discretion to regulate the activities of the foreign investor.[2] However, the question arises whether international minimum standards for the treatment of foreign investors should control the extent of this discretion.[3] Not surprisingly, capital exporting countries favour such an approach. By contrast, capital importing countries have traditionally opposed the control of their discretion in this area by international law. On the other hand, more recently, many host states have submitted to international protection standards through the conclusion of bilateral investment treaties (BITs), or free trade agreements (FTAs) containing investment provisions. Where this is so, the content and effect of host state laws on the legal rights of foreign investors may be subject to review in accordance with the standards contained in the applicable treaty. The legal effects of international investment agreements (IIAs) will be discussed at length in Part IV below. It should be stressed here that IIAs do not normally restrict the host state's discretion to control the entry and establishment of foreign investors. In general, this discretion is explicitly preserved by the terms of the IIA, which will leave the matter to regulation under the applicable law of the host state.[4] However, US and Canadian BITs, certain bilateral FTAs, and regional agreements such as NAFTA, ASEAN, and MERCOSUR, extend the protection of non-discrimination standards to entry and establishment by investors from other member countries. Such provisions constitute a technique of investment liberalization extending equal protection of investors to the pre-entry stage. However, the majority of IIAs still pertain only to the post-entry stage of the investment.[5]

---

[2] See CD Wallace *Legal Control of the Multinational Enterprise* (The Hague: Martinus Nijhoff, 1983) 84.   [3] See further ch 15.

[4] See further Antonio Parra 'Principles Governing Foreign Investment, as Reflected in National Investment Codes' 7 ICSID Rev.-FILJ 428 at 429–35 (1992); UNCTAD *Admission and Establishment* Series on issues in international investment agreements (New York and Geneva: United Nations, 1999) 16–29.

[5] See UNCTAD *World Investment Report 2003* (New York and Geneva: United Nations, 2003) at 107–110.

(2) Techniques for Restricting Entry and Establishment

In the discussion of such techniques an initial problem arises over the adoption of a suitable system of classification. Some writers have distinguished between the policies of developed and developing host states.[6] This distinction is of little help when describing legal (or, indeed, economic and political) phenomena associated with the contemporary international division of labour created by economic globalization and will not be followed here.[7] In practice, given the move away from restrictive policies on inward investment by developing countries, the former socialist states of Central and Eastern Europe and remaining socialist states, such as China or Vietnam, the legal techniques used by developing and developed countries to control the entry and establishment of MNEs do not differ very much in nature. The distinction is primarily of historical value as an explanation of the motives behind legal developments in the 1960s and early 1970s. A second approach is to classify control techniques according to their ideological origins.[8] Its importance lies in stressing the need for an interdisciplinary understanding of foreign investment controls. However, excessive stress on ideology can lead to a blurring of the distinct legal questions that different degrees of control over entry and establishment create, regardless of the political motives behind them. In the light of these observations the approach adopted here is one of considering techniques of control along the continuum from total exclusion to conditional entry, identifying the policy origins of the various techniques involved, and the principal legal issues that each technique raises.

(a) Total Exclusion and Sectoral Exclusion of Foreign Investors

(i) Total Exclusion

The most restrictive legal response to foreign investors is the imposition of a complete prohibition on inward direct investment. Such a response has been advocated by the more radical forms of economic nationalism and dependency

---

[6] See AE Safarian *Governments and Multinationals: Policies in the Developed Countries* (British-North American Committee, 1983) 53–54. Safarian notes that, in the past, the less developed countries took actions which went beyond those taken by developed countries in protecting their economic sovereignty. See also, for developed host state policies in this area, AE Safarian *Multinational Enterprise and Public Policy: A Study of the Industrial Countries* (Edward Elgar, 1992).

[7] See further N Harris *The End of the Third World: Newly Industrializing Countries and the Decline of an Ideology* (Pelican, 1986).

[8] See eg Seidman 'Foreign Private Investors and the Host Country' 19 JWTL 637 (1985). Seidman, in this comparative study of LDC foreign investment laws, has distinguished between 'investor protection codes', which are inspired by a pro-capitalist economic policy and seek to offer an 'open door' to foreign investors, 'investment codes' which seek to reconcile a 'mishmash' ideology involving adherence to a market economy with a 'socialist' social welfare programme, and 'investor control codes' which seek to involve MNEs in the host state economy only under conditions of strict

theories.[9] This approach can now be viewed as obsolete, given that it isolates the host state from access to foreign capital and technology and requires the development of substitute domestic products and technology which can prove to be unattainable and/or financially ruinous. In the past, the former socialist states of Eastern Europe, led by the USSR, and the People's Republic of China (PRC) practised a total ban on private inward direct investment. Such investment was impossible until the more recent liberalization of the East European economies, first, through the introduction of joint venture laws, followed by the introduction of laws permitting direct investment through wholly owned subsidiaries and then by the eventual transition to a full market economy.[10] Similarly, China closed its doors to private direct investment after the Revolution of 1949 until 1979, when joint ventures were first permitted by law, with wholly owned foreign enterprises being permitted to invest after the introduction of new legislation in 1986.[11]

(ii) Sectoral Exclusion

Short of the complete exclusion, inward direct investment can be excluded from certain sectors of the host state's economy. Most states have adopted either total or partial restrictions in what are perceived as 'key sectors' in the economy. These areas generally encompass industries relevant to national security and defence, for example shipbuilding or aerospace, culturally significant industries, such as film and broadcasting, and public utilities.[12] The general use of such laws suggests that they pose few problems for states in their international economic relations, representing a recognized 'reserved domain' for national ownership and control. On

---

regulation as to the form and conduct of an investment, often requiring the setting up of a joint venture controlled by the partner from the host state.

[9] See ch 3 above.   [10] See further text at n 77–92 below.

[11] See further text at n 93–135 below.

[12] See David Conklin and Donald Lecraw 'Restrictions on Foreign Ownership During 1984–1994: Developments and Alternative Policies' 6 Transnational Corporations 1 (No 1 1997). On US restrictions see Phillip I Blumberg, Kurt A Strasser, Nicholas L Georgakopoulos, and Eric J Gouvin *Blumberg on Corporate Groups* (New York: Aspen Publishers, 2nd edn, 2005) vol 4 ch 152. US Federal laws restrict foreign investment in the following sectors: public broadcasting and telecommunications, coastal and internal shipping, internal air traffic (although liberalization is being considered), minerals exploitation on public lands, and atomic energy. Until recently state banking laws prohibited alien ownership or control of banks, although Washington State still maintains such restrictions. See also US, Canadian, and Mexican reservations to the North American Free Trade Agreement: 32 ILM 605 at 704–780 (1993). For example, current restrictions prohibit more than a 25 per cent foreign holding of voting stock in a US airline: Federal Aviation Act 1958 PubLNo 85–726 72 Stat 766 (1958) 49 USC ss 40101 et seq (2003). In 1993 British Airways' bid for a 44 per cent stake in US Air was blocked. However, a renewed bid for a 19.9 per cent stake in US Air was given temporary approval. British Airways increased its holding in US Air to 24.6 per cent: 'BA Buys 19.9% Stake in US Air' *Financial Times* 22 January 1993 at 15; 'BA Wins Temporary Approval for US Air link-up' *Financial Times* 16 March 1993 at 1; 'BA Buys Additional US Air Stock and Maintains 24.6% Holding' *Financial Times* 27 April 1993 at 21. BA disposed of its shareholding in US Air in 1997. More recently talks have occurred between the US and EU for an 'open skies' deal that would liberalize flying between the two parties. These have included discussions on the easing of foreign ownership rules in US airlines: 'US to Update on Airline Stakes' *Financial Times* 5 May 2006 at 25.

the other hand, as privatization, deregulation, and marketization policies are more widely used by host countries, the justification for excluding certain sectors from foreign investment becomes more tenuous. Difficulties can occur, in particular, where a host state so interprets its vital national economic and security interests as to create a discriminatory regime for the exclusion of foreign investors from sectors where national firms are under threat from foreign competition.

For example, in the US, there have been periodic calls for controls over foreign takeovers of US firms where vital commercial interests were at stake.[13] However, such pressures were resisted during the passage of the Exon-Florio amendment to the Defence Production Act 1950, which empowers the US President to prohibit the takeover of a US firm by a foreign firm where there exists, 'credible evidence that the foreign interest exercising control might take action that threatens to impair national security'.[14] Under the implementing regulations companies voluntarily notify the Committee on Foreign Investment in the US (CFIUS) of a proposed takeover of an American company. The Committee has 30 days to decide whether to undertake an investigation into the proposed acquisition. If it does investigate the inquiry must be completed within 45 days. A recommendation is then made to the President, who has 15 days to announce his decision, and from which there is no right of appeal. 'National security' is not defined in the regulations, but the General Discussion of the regulations makes clear that only transactions that involve products, services and technologies important to US national defence requirements are covered.[15] In 1993 a power of investigation was added by amendment, 'in any instance in which an entity controlled by or acting on behalf of a foreign government seeks to engage in any merger, acquisition or takeover of a US entity that could affect the national security of the United States'.[16] This has been interpreted as giving discretion to CFIUS as to whether to institute an investigation.[17]

CFIUS has used its discretion sparingly. By the end of 2005 of the 1593 notices filed with CFIUS only 25 resulted in investigations. To date only one takeover has been blocked, that of the US aircraft parts manufacturer Mamco by the China

---

[13] See generally EM Graham and PR Krugman *Foreign Direct Investment in the United States* (Washington DC, Institute for International Economics, 3rd edn, 1995); David Bailey 'US Policy Towards Inward FDI – CFIUS and Extension of the Concept of "National Security" ' 4 JWI 867 (2003).

[14] See the US Omnibus Trade and Competitiveness Act 1988 s 5021 Public Law 100–418 23 August 1988 102 Stat 1107 reproduced in 28 ILM at 460 (1989). Reinstated permanently by Defense Production Act Extension Amendments Public Law 102–99, 105 Stat 487 17 August 1991. EM Graham and DM Marchick *US National Security and Foreign Direct Investment* (Washington DC, Institute for International Economics, 2006) at 40–46. US Treasury regulations implementing this provision were introduced on 21 November 1991: 31 ILM 424 (1992). For analysis, see Holmer, Bello, and Preiss 'The Final Exon-Florio Regulations on Foreign Direct Investment: The Final Word or Prelude to Tighter Controls?' 23 Law & Pol.Int'l Bus. 593 (1992).

[15] Regulations ibid at 31 ILM 429 col 2.

[16] National Defense Authorization Act for the Fiscal Year 1993 Public Law 102–484 s 837(a) (the 'Byrd Amendment').   [17] Graham and Marchick above n 14 at 37.

National Aero-Technology Import and Export Company.[18] However, the law has resulted in several deals being restructured to meet CFIUS objections.[19] In addition, by the end of 2005, 13 transactions have been withdrawn after CFIUS began investigation. More recently, after the terrorist attacks of 11 September 2001, investigations have increased in number and intensity and have led to greater concern over foreign ownership or control of 'critical infrastructure', as exemplified by the concerns expressed in Congress, and the US media, over the decision by CFIUS to approve the takeover of the UK company P&O's port operations in the US by Dubai Ports World, subject to certain assurances on security matters.[20]

The CFIUS review process has been characterized by a reluctance to allow foreign government owned or controlled entities to take over US firms. Thus, in 1992, the French state-owned defence electronics firm, Thomson CSF, withdrew its bid for the missile division of LTV Aerospace and Defence Company, after it became apparent that a CFIUS review would have blocked the bid on the ground of foreign governmental control.[21] This reluctance has also recently been highlighted by the failed bid by the China National Offshore Oil Corporation (CNOOC) for the US oil and gas company Unocal. CNOOC took the unusual step of filing a unilateral notice to CFIUS without Unocal, which was by now committed to a takeover by US based Chevron. CFIUS did not come to any findings as CNOOC decided to withdraw its bid in response to Congressional pressure.[22]

The increased sensitivity to foreign ownership in the US has led to renewed calls for the revision of the Exon-Florio provisions. A number of bills have been introduced before Congress, all seeking to enhance the CFIUS review process.[23] For example, the Committee on Foreign Investment in the United States Reform Act,[24] revises provisions concerning presidential authority to review any mergers, acquisitions, and takeovers that could result in foreign control of persons engaged in interstate commerce in the United States. Among other matters, it introduces additional factors to be considered in an investigation, including whether the transaction affects US critical infrastructure. The role of Congress is increased through the requirement of annual and quarterly reports to Congress on reviews and investigations. Finally, the Bill re-establishes CFIUS as a multi-agency committee whereas it is currently a committee within the Department of the Treasury. However, more far-reaching proposals, including one which would have given Congress the power to overrule a decision of the President to approve a transaction, have been rejected.[25]

---

[18] *Financial Times* 6 February 1990 at 6.   [19] See Holmer et al above n 14 at 610–14.
[20] See Garaham and Marchick above n 14 at 136–41.
[21] See Graham and Krugman above n 13 at 112–13; 130–31.
[22] See Graham and Marchick above n 14 at 128–36.   [23] See further ibid at 47–56.
[24] HR 4915 IH 109th Congress 2d Session, 9 March 2006 House of Representatives available at <http://www.thomas.loc.gov>.
[25] See the Inhofe Amendment SA 1311 to S 1042, 109th Congress 1st Session (2005); Shelby Amendment SA 1467 to S 1042 109th Congress 1st Session (2005) discussed in Graham and Marchick above n 14 at 51–53. These more restrictive proposals could still be revived: 'Cfius Overhaul Back in Spotlight' *Financial Times* 24 August 2006 at 9.

Japan too has traditionally reserved certain sectors from foreign investors.[26] Such reservations were replaced by a system of discretionary screening, which subjected intended investment projects to possible revision or cancellation where these were found to be injurious or damaging to national security or public order and public safety, or were to be made in the exceptional industries of agriculture, forestry, fisheries, mining, petroleum, leather, and leather products, or where a project bypasses regulations on capital transactions.[27] These changes represented an ongoing process of liberalization in Japanese inward investment regulation, emphasized in the Japanese Cabinet's decision of 26 December 1980, that the inward investment screening procedure would be applied in conformity with the OECD Code on the Liberalization of Capital Movements.[28] More recently, Japan has carried out major reforms of its commercial and corporate laws, to allow for greater openness for foreign entry and establishment. A new Corporate Law was enacted on 29 June 2005. This requires no more than the registration of a branch or subsidiary with the Legal Affairs Bureau as the previously mandated minimum capital registration requirements have been abolished.[29] However, significant restraints on liberalization remain in the form of complex and non-transparent administrative procedures that span across departments. Indeed it may be said that Japanese officials are split between those who seek more rapid liberalization and those who prefer to maintain the status quo.[30]

The reservation of specific sectors from foreign investors has been used by developing countries to protect indigenous industries from foreign domination, on the basis of the so-called 'infant industry' and 'crowding out' arguments. According to the 'infant industry' argument, a newly established national enterprise is seen as entitled to protection from the full effect of market forces, where these could expose it to fatal competitive pressures from established foreign firms, and so deny to the country concerned an opportunity to create its own industrial base in the relevant industrial sector. This was the aim behind South Korea's originally restrictive policy on inward investment.[31] Similarly, both Brazil and India

---

[26] See MY Yoshino 'Japan as Host to the International Corporation' in I Frank (ed) *The Japanese Economy in International Perspective* (Johns Hopkins University Press, 1975) 273.

[27] See Foreign Exchange and Foreign Trade Control Law (Law No 228, 1 December 1949 as amended) Chapter V arts 26–30; Cabinet Decision Concerning Policy Applications on Inward Direct Investments (Decision of Cabinet Meeting of 26 December 1980) in *Japan: Laws, Ordinances and Other Regulations Concerning Foreign Exchange and Foreign Trade* (Chuo Shuppan Kikaku Co 1990) at (A)–20 to (A)–27 and (A)–206. See also Sakamoto 'Japan's Outward and Inward FDI' The CTC Reporter No 27(Spring 1989) 64 at 67; M Matsushita *International Trade and Competition Law in Japan* (Oxford: Oxford University Press, 1993) 241–47.

[28] See above n 27. On the OECD Code see, ch 6 at 239–42.

[29] See further Japan External Trade Organisation (JETRO) *Investing in Japan; Laws and Regulations on Setting up Business in Japan* at <http://www.jetro.go.jp/en/invest/setting-up/>; David Bailey 'FDI in Japan: An "Open Door" or a Legacy of "Non-Institutional Barriers?" ' 4 JWI 315 (2003).

[30] See David Ibson 'Japan "Must Reform" to Woo Foreign Investors' *Financial Times* 18 March 2003 14 ibid 'The Long Struggle to Remove Bureaucratic Lethargy' *Financial Times* Special Report: Investing in Japan 24 March 2004 4.

[31] See D Encarnation *Dislodging the Multinationals: India's Strategy in Comparative Perspective* (Cornell University Press, 1989) 204–13; Westphal et al 'Foreign Factors in Korea's Industrialisation'

initially restricted foreign investors from their mini- and micro-computer industries. Both have since reduced these restrictions, so as to ensure that the national industry would not be deprived of the latest foreign informatics technology. India has also liberalized its technology import controls.[32]

As regards the 'crowding out' argument, this maintains that unless local enterprises are protected from foreign competition they may disappear from the market to the detriment of local capital formation and economic independence. The actual evidence for this phenomenon is mixed and may even suggest that increased inward investment actually stimulates additional domestic investment – a 'crowding-in' impact.[33] Nonetheless, certain host countries have reserved certain industrial and commercial sectors for exclusive equity ownership by the nationals of the host state so as to develop an indigenous capital base. For example, under the now repealed Nigerian Enterprises Promotion Decrees (after 1991 redesignated as Acts) of 1972, 1977, and 1989[34] certain industrial and commercial activities, that were deemed to be within the technical and managerial competence of Nigerian citizens, were reserved exclusively for Nigerians.

(b) Laws Restricting Foreign Shareholdings in National Companies

In this context an initial distinction can be made between laws that merely require local financial participation in what would otherwise be a wholly owned subsidiary of a foreign parent company, and equity joint venture laws. The latter require not only local shareholding but also local participation in the management of a locally incorporated joint enterprise with the foreign investor. These laws seek to restrict not only foreign ownership but also foreign control over the investment and are, therefore, of particular importance to states that wish to retain direct control over the activities of the foreign investor. Joint venture laws have for this reason been especially significant in socialist states. They will be considered in more detail in section (c) below.

The present section will consider laws restricting foreign shareholdings in locally incorporated companies. In recent years, restrictions on foreign shareholding have been used for numerous purposes by host states. This section will concentrate in particular on 'indigenization' laws and on restrictions associated with privatization programmes in various countries. Of relevance too are restrictions

in Changsoo Lee (ed) *Modernisation of Korea and the Impact of the West* (East Asian Studies Center: University of Southern California, 1981); Hayward 'Foreign Investment and Licensing in Korea' 23 U.Brit.Col.LR 405 (1989).

[32] See further Greico 'Between Dependency and Autonomy: India's Experience with the International Computer Industry' 36 Int'l Org. 609 (1982); Adler 'Ideological Guerillas and the Quest for Technological Autonomy: Brazil's Domestic Computer Industry' 40 Int'l Org 673 (1986), Evans 'State, Capital and the Transformation of Dependence: The Brazilian Computer Case' 14 World Development 791 (1986). The legislative bases of Brazil's informatics policy and India's technology licensing policy, and their subsequent liberalization, are described briefly in ch 11 below at 451.

[33] See UNCTAD *World Investment Report 2003* above n 5 at 105.   [34] See n 36 below.

on the takeover of host state firms by foreign investors, based on the application of national competition laws. These will be considered in chapter 10 below.

(i) Indigenization Laws

A major purpose behind legal restrictions on foreign ownership in local companies has been to secure the 'indigenization' of foreign owned companies, that is, to transfer the ownership of shares in the company concerned to nationals of the host state. This should not be confused with 'nationalization' or 'expropriation' in that the shares of the foreign owned company are not forcibly divested in return for compensation, but are placed on the market for local investors to purchase at market prices.[35]

A leading example of such a policy is the series of now repealed Nigerian Enterprises Promotion Acts passed in 1972, 1977, and 1989.[36] These successive laws developed the Nigerian indigenization programme, setting up the institutional structure for the transfer of shares from foreign to Nigerian ownership,[37] and laying down the criteria for indigenization. The method adopted was to classify industrial sectors into separate schedules each of which specifies a different limit to foreign ownership. Under the 1977 Act there were three schedules.[38] Schedule 1 specified sectors which required little capital to set up and operate, such as cake making or hairdressing, or involved particular national interests, such as radio and TV broadcasting, and which were deemed to be within the competence of Nigerians to operate and own. These sectors were reserved for exclusive Nigerian ownership.[39] Schedule 2 listed enterprises in which Nigerians were able to participate, but where foreign capital contributions and managerial expertise were considered valuable, for example, banking, beer brewing, construction, mining, and book publishing. In these sectors Nigerian ownership could not be less than 60 per cent.[40] Schedule 3 listed enterprises involving highly complex

---

[35] On 'nationalization' and 'expropriation' see ch 15. On the distinction between these concepts and 'indigenization', see Beveridge 'Taking Control of Foreign Investment: A Case Study of Nigeria' 40 ICLQ 302 at 305–306 (1991); Akinsanya 'Host Governments' Responses to Foreign Economic Control: The Experience of Selected African Countries' 30 ICLQ 769 at 776–78 (1981).

[36] Nigerian Enterprises Promotion Act 1972 (No 4 of 1972) [1972] Official Gazette Fed Rep Nig 123 A11 (Supp Part A); Nigerian Enterprises Promotion Act 1977 (No 3 of 1977); Nigerian Enterprises Promotion Act 1989 (No 54 of 1989) [1989] Official Gazette Fed Rep Nig 76 A809 (Supp Part A); CAP 303 Laws of the Federation of Nigeria vol 23 (revised edn, 1990). For analysis of the 1972 and 1977 Decrees, see Megwa 'Foreign Direct Investment Climate in Nigeria: The Changing Law and Development Policies' 21 Col.J.Transnat.L 487 (1983); Osunbor 'Nigeria's Investment Laws and the State's Control of Multinationals' 3 ICSID Rev.-FILJ 38 (1988); Beveridge n 35 above; TJ Biersteker *Multinationals, the State, and Control of the Nigerian Economy* (Princeton University Press, 1987). For the background to the 1989 Act, see Nigerian Federal Ministry of Industries *Industrial Policy of Nigeria (Policies, Incentives, Guidelines and Industrial Framework)* (January 1989) 41–45.

[37] First through the Nigerian Enterprises Promotion Board set up by the 1972 Act ibid and then through its successors, the Nigerian Securities Exchange Commission and/or the Minister of Industries: 1989 Act ibid. Explanatory Note and ss 3–5.

[38] For analysis, see Osunbor above n 36 at 52.   [39] 1977 Act above n 36 s 4.

[40] ibid s 5.

operations for which foreign capital and know-how were essential. These included distilling and blending of spirits, pharmaceuticals, manufacture of engines and turbines, motor vehicles, and aerospace. Here Nigerian ownership could not be less than 40 per cent.[41] Under the 1989 Act these schedules were reduced to one. The sectors listed there were reserved for exclusive Nigerian ownership.[42] They encompassed broadly the same areas as Schedule 1 of the 1977 law. In 1995 Nigerian foreign investment law was fundamentally reformed in line with the new commitment to liberalization of investment conditions. Under the Nigerian Enterprises Promotion (Repeal) Decree of 1995,[43] a non-Nigerian may invest and participate in the operation of any enterprise in Nigeria, except the petroleum industry or industries included in the 'negative list' in s 32 of the decree.[44]

Comparable restrictions on foreign equity participation were introduced in India under the Foreign Exchange Regulation Act of 1973 (FERA).[45] By s 29 of the Act, as it stood in 1973, a foreign investor could own no more than 40 per cent in a branch or company incorporated in India. This provision sought, first, to contribute to the conservation of India's foreign exchange reserves by controlling the outflow of foreign currency through its limitation of foreign equity participation in Indian companies, resulting in reduced remittances of earnings abroad. Secondly, by restricting the foreign ownership of Indian companies, s 29 sought to increase indigenous participation in industrial development. The imposition of foreign ownership limits under FERA resulted, during the 1970s, in a substantial dilution of shareholding by MNEs, which had until then controlled some one-fifth of India's corporate assets.[46] Some companies, notably IBM and Coca-Cola, refused to dilute their holdings and left India.[47] However, the majority complied, fearing loss of access to a major market due to India's strict controls over imports

---

[41] ibid s 6.   [42] 1989 Act above n 36 s 1(1).

[43] Decree No 16 of 16 January 1995; see ICSID *Investment Laws of the World Vol VI* (Dobbs Ferry, New York: Oceana Publications) Release 2001–1 Nigeria (June 2001) or the Nigerian Investment Promotion Commission (NIPC) website at <http://www.nipc-nigeria.org>.

[44] ibid ss 17, 18. In addition, the screening requirements of the old legislation were abolished and replaced with a registration requirement: see s 20 as amended by s 4 of Decree No 32 of 30 September 1998 (available in ICSID ibid or the NIPC website ibid). However, a foreign investor must incorporate a local company in accordance with Nigerian companies' legislation to obtain a valid registration: s 19 as amended by s 3 of Decree No 32. The industries included in the negative list under s 32 are arms production, production and dealing in narcotic and psychotropic drugs, production of military and paramilitary wares and accoutrement, and 'such other items as the Federal Executive Council may, from time to time, determine'. The NIPC website lists only the first two in the list.

[45] Act 46 of 1973. See AIR 1973 Acts or SR Roy *The Foreign Exchange Regulation Act 1973* (Calcutta: Kamal Law House, 3rd edn, 1989) 148–97. For comment see Saxena and Kapoor 13 JWTL 170 (1979). For the Act as amended by Act 29 of 1993 see *Baharat's Foreign Exchange Regulation Act 1973* (New Delhi: Baharat Law House, 1994).

[46] See further DJ Encarnation above n 31 on which the following paragraphs are based.

[47] Coca-Cola has since returned: 'India Clears Way for Entry of Big Foreign Companies' *Financial Times* 25 June 1993 at 6. IBM returned in a joint venture with Tata Industries, Tata Information Systems, to make computer systems and to develop software: 'IBM Returns to India for Joint Computer Venture' *Financial Times* 4 February 1992 at 3.

and the possibility that a competing company would take over the existing company's market share.[48]

On the other hand MNEs were not without power in this new environment. They still retained control over the resulting jointly owned companies. In many cases local ownership was so dispersed as to provide no controlling influence against the foreign firm. Furthermore, foreign equity was often turned into foreign debt, thereby preserving both the income flow of the foreign firm and its control over the Indian company. Moreover, the control that they possessed over technology and access to foreign markets ensured that MNEs would retain a strong bargaining position. Thus, the effect of FERA was to permit the retention of MNE control over operations in 'core' areas of the economy and in the export orientated industries, while reducing overall levels of foreign ownership in the Indian economy. A further effect was the stimulation of domestic business houses to enter industries hitherto dominated by MNEs and to develop indigenous substitute technologies, thereby reducing dependence on foreign capital and technology. Nonetheless, this policy did not provide India with the kind of industrial development it had hoped for, sparking debate over whether India should retain a restrictive policy on foreign participation.[49]

That debate resulted in the Congress government of 1991 recommending the liberalization of FERA, as part of a wider programme to introduce greater deregulation and competition into the Indian economy.[50] The reforms included the amendment of s 29 of FERA, terminating any statutory control over the maximum level of foreign shareholding by a foreign investor in an Indian company.[51] That approach continues in the current regulatory regime based on the Foreign Exchange Management Act 2000.[52] Under that regime, foreign direct investment (FDI) up to 100 per cent is allowed under the 'automatic route' in all activities or sectors except those that require prior approval of the government.[53] Under this procedure, investors are only required to notify the regional office concerned of

---

[48] As happened in the computer industry after IBM pulled out and more generally in the electronics and electrical goods sectors. See Greico 'Between Dependency and Autonomy: India's Experience with the International Computer Industry' 36 Int.Org. 609 (1982); Encarnation above n 31 at 166–69.   [49] See Encarnation ibid ch 5.

[50] See Press Information Bureau, Government of India, Press Release of 24 July 1991 'New Industrial Policy 1991 Announced' reproduced in UNCTC *Foreign Direct Investment and Technology Transfer in India* (New York: UN Doc ST/CTC/117, 1992) Annex VII 128; *Financial Times* 2 July 1991 at 6. 'India Moves to Ease Industrial Controls'; *Financial Times* 25 July 1991 at 20 'India Eases Foreign Investor Rules'.

[51] See s 29(1) Foreign Exchange Regulation Act 1973 as amended by the Foreign Exchange Regulation (Amendment) Act 1993 (Act 29 of 1993) in *Baharat's Foreign Exchange Regulation Act 1973* (New Delhi: Baharat Law House, 1994).

[52] Act No 42 of 1999 (29 December 1999) entered into force 1 June 2000 available at <http://finmin.nic.in/the_ministry/dept_eco_affairs/america_canada/ac_fema_acts.htm>.

[53] This summary draws on Reserve Bank of India 'Foreign Investments in India' available at <http://www.rbi.org.in> under 'FAQs'. See further Planning Commission, Government of India, *Report of the Steering Group on Foreign Direct Investment* (New Delhi: August 2002).

the Reserve Bank of India (RBI) within 30 days of receipt of inward remittances, and file the required documents with that office within 30 days of issue of shares to foreign investors. Prior governmental approval is required for activities that require an industrial licence, proposals in which the foreign collaborator has an existing financial and/or technical collaboration in India in the same field, proposals for acquisition of shares in an existing Indian company in the financial services sector where the Securities & Exchange Board of India (Substantial Acquisition of Shares and Takeovers) Regulations 1997 apply and all proposals falling outside notified sectoral policy caps for FDI, or under sectors in which FDI is not permitted.[54] FDI activities requiring prior government approval are considered by the Foreign Investment Promotion Board (FIPB), Ministry of Finance. Indian companies having foreign investment approval through this route do not require any further clearance from RBI for receiving inward remittances and for the issue of shares to foreign investors. Such companies are required to notify the concerned regional office of the RBI within 30 days of the receipt of inward remittances and within 30 days of issue of shares to the foreign investors. FDI is prohibited under both the government and the automatic route in a specified number of sectors.[55]

Both in India and Nigeria, the principal social and economic effect of indigenization was an extension of equity ownership among the better-off sections of society,[56] without any major increase in control over the operations of the MNEs involved, and at the cost of shortages of new technology and investment capital. However, the economic nationalism of earlier years has been relaxed in favour of increased access to the national economy by MNEs as a source of new investment capital, subject to specific sectoral controls, which remain more far reaching in the case of India as compared to Nigeria.

(ii) Restrictions on Foreign Ownership in Privatized Companies

In the last 25 years numerous governments have initiated privatization programmes designed to introduce greater competition and private investment into economic

---

[54] Foreign investment caps are specified in periodically updated Foreign Exchange Management Act Circulars (AP (DIR) Series) available at <http://www.rbi.org.in/scripts/fema.aspx>. For a recent summary of Indian FDI policy caps see Ministry of Finance, Department of Economic Affairs *Report of the Committee on Liberalisation of Foreign Institutional Investment* (New Delhi: June 2004) Annex I available at <http://www.finmin.nic.in/the_ministry/dept_eco_affairs/investment_div/invest_fip.htm>.

[55] These are retail trading, atomic energy, lottery business, gambling and betting, housing and real estate business, agriculture (excluding floriculture, horticulture, development of seeds, animal husbandry, pisiculture, and cultivation of vegetables, mushrooms etc. under controlled conditions and services related to agro and allied sectors), and plantations (other than tea plantations).

[56] On India see Swamy *Multinational Corporations and the World Economy* (New Delhi: Alps, 1980) ch 1. On Nigeria see A Akinsanya 'The Indigenisation of the Economy and Power Relations in a Developing Economy: The Nigerian Experience' Paper delivered at the 13th World Congress of the International Political Science Association, Paris 15–20 July 1985; C Ake 'Indigenisation: Problems of Transformation in a Neo-Colonial Economy' in C Ake (ed) *The Political Economy of Nigeria* (Harlow: Longman, 1985) ch 9.

sectors hitherto dominated by publicly owned enterprises.[57] Given that publicly owned enterprises have predominated in strategic industries such as transport, public utilities, natural resources, energy, financial services, and defence, the unregulated sale of such enterprises to the private sector raises the possibility of their falling under foreign ownership and control, thereby threatening existing national control over vital economic interests. Consequently, privatizations of publicly owned companies have often involved restrictions on foreign ownership. To illustrate the techniques of control employed the examples provided by the UK and French privatization programmes of the 1980s will be considered.

In the UK, the government retained control over certain matters in recently privatized companies by way of the so-called 'golden share'. By this device, the government retained one special rights redeemable preference share of £1 held by itself or its nominee in the privatized company. The company's articles of association then specified that certain matters are deemed to be a variation of the rights of the special share and can only be effective with the consent in writing of the special shareholder.[58] In certain strategically significant companies the 'golden share' was used specifically to restrict foreign ownership. These restrictions raised objections from the European Commission on the grounds that they could be used as a means of discriminating against the participation of nationals from other EC Member States in the capital of the British companies, contrary to Article 221 (now Article 294) of the Treaty of Rome. In France, after the widespread nationalizations of 1981–82, the new right-of-centre government of Jaques Chirac introduced a major programme of privatization in 1986. As part of this policy, the control of foreign participation in privatized companies was enshrined in statute. By Articles 9 and 10 of Law No 86–912 of 6 August 1986,[59] no individual or corporation could acquire more than 5 per cent of the shares transferred at the time of sale of the shares by the state, and the sum total of the shares sold directly or

---

[57] On the British and French programmes, see Cosmo Graham and Tony Prosser *Privatizing Public Enterprises* (Oxford: Clarendon Press, 1991). On privatization in developing countries, see UNCTC *Transnational Corporations in World Development: Trends and Prospects* (New York: UN Doc ST/CTC/89, 1988) 264–65; VV Ramanadham (ed) *Privatisation in Developing Countries* (London: Routledge, 1989); P Cook and C Kirkpatrick (eds) *Privatisation in Less Developed Countries* (Sussex: Wheatsheaf Books, 1988). See also Peter T Muchlinski 'A Case of Czech Beer: Competition and Competitiveness in the Transitional Economies' 59 MLR 658 (1996) and Graeme A Hodge *Privatization: An International Review of Performance* (Boulder, Colorado: Westview Press, 2000).

[58] Graham and Prosser ibid 141. A full analysis of the use of the 'golden share' by the British Government can be found in Graham and Prosser at 141–51. See also AP Rutabanzibwa 'What is Golden in the Golden Share? Company Law and the Implications of Privatisation' 17 Co.Law 40 (1996). The UK Government has also controlled the build-up of foreign shareholdings in strategic British companies through its competition policy. Most notably, such a strategy was adopted after the sale of the government's holding in BP when the Kuwait Investment Office built up an unacceptably high shareholding stake in BP. This case will be considered in ch 10 below, as part of a general examination of UK policy on foreign takeovers of British companies. Under the Industry Act 1975, the Secretary of State for Trade and Industry had the power to prevent the transfer of control of 'important manufacturing undertakings' to non-residents, where they built up a share of over 30 per cent in the undertaking. See ss 11–20. However, these powers were never used.

[59] English translation in 26 ILM 1399–1401 (1987).

indirectly by the state to foreign individuals or corporations, or to those under foreign control, should not exceed 20 per cent of the capital of the enterprise. Article 10 of Law No 86–912 continued by laying down the legal regime for the creation of a governmental 'golden share' in newly privatized companies. This governed foreign shareholdings in privatized companies after the initial sale of shares by the state. For each company subject to the Privatization Law of 1986[60] the Minister of the Economy, after consultation with the privatization Commission, would determine by decree whether the protection of national interests, 'requires that a common share held or acquired by the Government be transformed into an extraordinary share bearing rights defined in this present article'. The principal right attached to the extraordinary share was that of permitting holdings by one or several individuals or corporations acting in concert to exceed 10 per cent of the capital. The extraordinary share could be converted back to a common share at any time by ministerial decree. It lapsed by operation of law after five years. The extraordinary share was less powerful than the British 'golden share' given its limited duration and the absence of powers to block disposals of assets.[61] Furthermore, it was not used as often.[62]

Other EC Member countries also adopted their own versions of 'golden shares' or imposed limits on foreign ownership in privatized industries. These laws were subjected to review by the European Court of Justice (ECJ) in a series of major cases involving Portugal, France, Belgium Spain, the United Kingdom, and Italy.[63] In these cases the EC Commission argued that golden shares and other similar statute based powers violated Articles 43 and 56 of the EC Treaty, which protect free movement of capital, by discriminating against investors from other Member States. Such restrictions could only be justified in cases where vital public policy, public security, or public health considerations applied. In none of the cases did the Commission see such considerations as existing. The ECJ ruled in favour of the Commission in all but the case against Belgium. From these decisions the following approach can be discerned. Direct investment in the form of participation in an undertaking by means of a shareholding, or by the acquisition of securities on capital markets, constitutes capital movement within the EC Treaty. As accepted by the Commission, the retention of a certain degree of influence over privatized undertakings is justifiable where these are involved in the provision of

---

[60] Law No 86–793 of 2 July 1986.   [61] Graham and Prosser above n 57 at 152.
[62] See ibid at 152–53.
[63] See *EC Commission v Portugal* (C–367/98) [2002] 2 CMLR 1213; *EC Commission v France* (C–483/99) [2002] 2 CMLR 1249; *EC Commission v Belgium* (C–503/99) [2002] 2 CMLR 1265; *EC Commission v Spain* (C–463/00) [2003] 2 CMLR 557; *EC Commission v United Kingdom* (C–98/01) [2003] 2 CMLR 598; *EC Commission v Italy* (C–174/04) judgment 2 June 2005 available at <http://www.curia.europa.eu>. See further EC Commission, Staff Working Document, *Special Rights in Privatised Companies in the Enlarged Union – A Decade Full of Developments* (Brussels 22 July 2005) available at <http://ec.europa.eu/internal_market/capital/framework/reports_en.htm>; Erika Szyszczak 'Golden Shares and Market Governance' 29 LIEI 255 (2002); Christine O'Grady Putek 'Limited But Not Lost: A Comment of the ECJ's Golden Share Decisions' 72 Fordham L.Rev. 2219 (2003–04).

services in the public interest or strategic services. However, such restrictions can only be taken in accordance with the reasons set down in Article 58(1)(b) of the EC Treaty or by overriding requirements of the general interest.[64] They have to apply equally to all persons and undertakings pursuing an activity in the territory of the host Member State. They are subject to a test of suitability in relation to the securing of the objective in question, and should not go beyond what is necessary in order to attain it so as to accord with the principle of proportionality. In addition, any restrictive measure has to conform to essential requirements of precision and clarity, and should be subject to a duty to state reasons and an opportunity for judicial review.[65] These principles do not prohibit golden shares outright but place strict limits on their use. Most of the pre-2004 EC Member Countries are now in the process of abolishing or limiting golden shares in line with these legal requirements. Nonetheless, further cases are pending against the Netherlands and Germany[66] and, given the widespread use of golden shares by some of the governments and authorities of the new Member States that joined in 2004, further cases can be expected if the measures put into place to restrict golden shares do not bear fruit.[67]

(c) Laws Regulating Equity Joint Ventures Between Foreign and Local Enterprises

A policy of integration into the international division of labour may be combined with a desire to retain local managerial control over the enterprise in which the foreign investor participates. One attempt to create such a compromise is embodied in laws regulating the establishment of equity joint ventures between foreign and local enterprises. The basic technique of control involved is to make the entry of the foreign investor into the host state conditional upon the substantial involvement of local participants in the ownership and control of the investment project in question. The local participant may be a private or public sector entity, depending on the circumstances of the case and on the prevailing economic system and policy of the host state. Such laws go beyond the indigenization laws studied in

---

[64] Article 58(1)(b) permits measures 'to prevent infringements of national law and regulations, in particular in the filed of taxation and the prudential supervision of financial institutions, or to lay down procedures for the declaration of capital movements for purposes of administrative or statistical information, or to take measures which are justified on grounds of public policy or public security'.

[65] See in particular *EC Commission v Belgium* above n 63 at paras 48–53.

[66] The Netherlands case concerns the powers of the state to nominate directors and a power of veto over strategic decisions, while the German case concerns the 20 per cent ownership limit on voting rights and the mandatory right of the Land of Lower Saxony to sit on the supervisory board of the company irrespective of the number of shares it holds: see EC Commission above n 63 at 12–13.

[67] ibid at 15–19. In particular, the Czech Republic, Hungary, and Poland all use golden share devices. All have put into place schemes for their abolition. Poland has been the slowest to abolish golden shares, and has introduced new requirements for some companies. However, the Commission accepts that the transitional economies may have special reasons to keep such devices for some time to come, though it will take proceedings if it deems these to be necessary.

the previous section in that the local participant not only owns a share of the equity in the joint venture, which by itself may be insufficient to ensure control, but also participates in its management.

Such arrangements are not, however, a guarantee of local control. First, local management may not be able to manage the project effectively. Indeed, a major reason for bringing in the foreign partner may be to enhance local managerial skills and technical knowledge. Thus the local partner is likely to be dependent on the foreign partner for major decisions, at least in the early stages of the joint venture.[68] Secondly, where the foreign partner is a MNE, the joint venture will be dependent on the international network of that partner for its success. For example, the joint venture will depend on the production and marketing organization of the MNE for supplies of inputs and access to export markets. Similarly, the foreign partner may control the know-how and technology needed for the joint venture. Consequently, the foreign partner may exercise effective business control over the joint venture, even where it holds a minority share of the equity.

Nonetheless, joint ventures have been commonly used in developing host countries and in the socialist and post-socialist states. There are significant advantages for both the MNE and the host state.[69] Briefly put, for the MNE, a joint venture offers an opportunity to enter a new market with the advantage of the local business know-how of the local partner, which may prove invaluable in an unfamiliar, if not hostile, business environment. Furthermore, the foreign nationality of the MNE can be subsumed behind the local nationality of the joint venture, thereby reducing the risk of being identified as a 'foreign' corporation and being subjected to discriminatory treatment.

For the host state, the joint venture offers a means of introducing new capital and technology into the domestic market, while at the same time retaining the legal form, if not the commercial substance, of control over the foreign investor. Consequently, joint venture laws have been of particular importance in states espousing economic development policies in a strongly nationalistic political environment. For example, in Indonesia, under a Government Policy Statement of 22 January 1974 all new foreign investment in Indonesia should have Indonesian participation of not less than 30 per cent. All new foreign investment had to be initiated as a joint venture with Indonesian participation being raised to 51 per cent within a period of 10 years.[70] In 1986 Indonesia relaxed its previously strict rules

---

[68] See further UNCTC *Joint Ventures as a Form of International Economic Co-operation* (New York: 1988 UN Doc ST/CTC/93) at 68–73; Samuel Asante 'Restructuring Transnational Mineral Agreements' 73 AJIL 335 (1979).

[69] See Wallace above n 2 at 75–77; UNCTC *Joint Ventures* ibid at 48–68; Lawrence Franko 'International Joint Ventures in Developing Countries: Mystique and Reality' 6 Law & Pol.Int'l Bus. 315 (1974).

[70] See UNCTC *National Legislation and Regulations Relating to Transnational Corporations: A Technical Paper* (New York: 1983 UN Doc ST/CTC/35) at 73–76; see further the Law on Foreign Capital Investment Law No 1 of 1967 under which joint ventures are established: ICSID *Foreign Investment Laws of the World* (Dobbs Ferry: Oceana) vol IV release 97–2 October 1997 at 1.

over majority Indonesian equity participation in joint ventures with foreign firms, allowing a more flexible period within which the requirement of 51 per cent local ownership was to be met.[71] Further measures of liberalization were introduced in 1987.[72] In 1992, 100 per cent foreign ownership was allowed for the first time since independence.[73] However, wholly foreign owned companies, known as 'Straight Investment Companies' are expected to sell a part of their shares to Indonesian citizens and/or legal entities within 15 years after commencing commercial operations.[74] Indonesia is currently planning a major overhaul of its foreign investment laws, aimed at bringing the law into line with market principles. In particular, investors shall be permitted to invest in any sector of the economy except in a small number of activities, which shall be included in a 'negative list'. There shall be no restriction on the size of the investment, the source of funds or whether the products are destined for export or for the domestic market. Existing foreign investors will be able to invest in activities other than those initially authorized, except for activities included in the 'negative list'.[75] Other countries and regions espousing joint venture policies have also progressively liberalized restrictions on foreign participation.[76]

The ability of joint venture laws to legitimate inward direct investment within a politically unfavourable environment has made them particularly attractive to socialist states, which had been opposed to foreign direct investment within their borders. Since the early 1970s the former socialist states of Central and Eastern Europe, and of the former Soviet Union, and other socialist states outside Eastern Europe passed laws permitting Western capital to enter on the basis of joint ventures with domestic state enterprises and, thereafter, as wholly owned foreign enterprises. As they lagged increasingly behind the West in technological capability and productivity, particularly in the civilian sector, the socialist states became less able to satisfy the growing demands of their populations for material consumption or to earn sufficient returns from exports. Somehow the introduction of new, Western, productive knowledge into domestic civilian production had to be

---

[71] See Sunaryati Hartono, 'Indonesia's Laws and Policies on Foreign Investment' (Mimeo, 1990) paper presented at the Singapore Conference on International Business Law: International Investment, Westin Plaza, August 1990.   [72] ibid.

[73] See further Halverson 'Foreign Direct Investment in Indonesia: A Comparison of Industrialized and Developing Country Investors' 22 Law & Pol.Int'l Bus. 75 (1991). See now Government Regulation No 20/1994 on Investment 19 May 1994 in ICSID *Foreign Investment Laws* above n 70 at 11; Decree No 15/SK/1994 on Implementation Guidelines of the Government Regulation No 20/1994 ibid 17 and Presidential Decree No 31 of 1995 Concerning the List of Sectors that are Closed for Investment ibid at 31.   [74] Decree No 15/SK/1994 art 11(1).

[75] See Indonesia Investment Co-ordinating Board *Investment Policies Statement* available at <http://www.bkpm.go.id/en/info.php?mode=baca&cat=7&t=Investment&info_id=18> (accessed 25 May 2006).

[76] See eg South Korea which in 1984 increased the number of sectors in which foreign investments are allowed: UNCTC *National Legislation and Regulations Relating to Transnational Corporations Volume IV* (New York: 1986 UN Doc ST/CTC/53) 198–200; Kim 'Legal Aspects of Foreign Investment in Korea' 15 Hastings Int'l & Comp.L.Rev. 227 (1992). See also the reform of the Andean Investment Code in ch 17 below at 656–58.

assured and, at the same time, the domestic economy had to be protected against uncontrolled capitalist penetration. This was achieved through the use of joint venture laws.[77] In these states, the incidence of joint venture laws is best seen as a transitional phase towards an open free market economy in which wholly owned subsidiaries of foreign firms are, in principle, welcome and key enterprises are privatized.[78] Indeed, with the accession of eight former Eastern Bloc countries, including three former Soviet Republics, to the EU in 2004, this process has been fully achieved in those countries.[79]

In a similar vein, the Russian Federation and its former Soviet Republics have also sought to move beyond joint venture laws towards full rights of entry for foreign investors. The former Soviet Union embarked on a transition to a market economy in 1987, commencing with a reversal of its long-standing prohibition of foreign inward investment through the enactment of a law on joint enterprises.[80] The aim behind the international aspects of Soviet economic reforms was to ensure the increased involvement of the former Soviet Union in the international division of labour.[81] The 1987 law represented the first step towards a market economy in which foreign investors were encouraged. It served as a learning experience for the Soviet authorities, who constantly sought to improve its terms through reforms. A new legal regime for foreign investment was introduced by the Russian Soviet Federated Socialist Republic Law of 4 July 1991.[82] The 1991 law permitted, for the first time, the establishment of wholly foreign-owned enterprises in the Russian Republic.[83] A Federal Law on Foreign Investment was passed in 1999, replacing the 1991 law.[84] This law determines the basic guarantees for investors' rights to their investments, and to income and profits derived therefrom, sets the terms of business activities of foreign investors and aims to attract foreign material and financial resources, technology and management experience to

[77] For a discussion of the laws of Hungary, former Yugoslavia, Poland, Romania, Bulgaria, Czechoslovakia, Ethiopia, North Korea, Cuba, Vietnam, and the former Soviet Union, see Peter T Muchlinski *Multinational Enterprises and the Law* (Oxford: Blackwell Publishers, revised paperback edn, 1999) at 187–88; 192–93. For an earlier comparative account, see D Campbell and M Miller (eds) *Legal Aspects of Joint Ventures in Eastern Europe* (Kluwer 1981); see also UNCTC *Transnational Corporations in World Development* above n 57 ch XVIII 'Joint Venture Policies of the Socialist Countries of Eastern Europe'; World Bank *Foreign Direct Investment in the States of the Former USSR* (Washington DC: 1992).

[78] See further R Frydman et al *The Privatization Process in Central Europe* (Central European University Press, 1993).

[79] These are the Czech Republic, Estonia, Hungary, Latvia, Lithuania, Poland, Slovakia, and Slovenia.

[80] Decree on Joint Enterprises with Western and Developing Countries 13 January 1987: 26 ILM 749 (1987). See further MM Boguslavskii *Joint Ventures With the USSR* (IB Tauris & Co, 1992).

[81] See further UNCTAD Consultant Study 'USSR: New Management Mechanism in Foreign Economic Relations' UNCTAD/ST/TSC/10 2 October 1987; *The Economist* 9 April 1988 'A Survey of the Soviet Economy'; Jerry F Hough *Opening Up the Soviet Economy* (Brookings Institution, 1988).   [82] English translation in 31 ILM 397 (1992).

[83] ibid art 3.

[84] Federal Law on Foreign Investment in the Russian Federation, 9 July 1999: 39 ILM 894 (2000).

Russia.[85] A notable feature of the law is that it provides a stabilization guarantee against changes in rates of import and customs duties, federal taxes, obligatory payments to the state budget funds and federal laws and normative acts that increase the cumulative tax burden on priority investment projects, which are defined as projects in which the total amount of investment is over 1 billion roubles or where the foreign investment interest or contribution is at least 100 million roubles or foreign currency equivalent.[86] More recently, draft legislation has been introduced to control foreign investment in strategic sectors of industry including defence, nuclear energy, and aerospace.[87] In such sectors foreign investors will require permission from the government to acquire a blocking minority stake of more than 25 per cent or a controlling stake of more than 50 per cent in an existing company.[88] In addition, in 2005, foreign controlled companies were barred from biding for tenders in strategic oil and metals deposits.[89] Thus alongside liberalization Russia retains sectoral restrictions in key areas of the economy.

Other former Soviet republics have enacted foreign investment laws.[90] Most require registration of foreign investments with a designated authority, usually the Ministry of Finance. In some cases several different authorities must be approached. The laws all specify certain standards of treatment. A common feature is the provision for national treatment. Transfers of capital are generally allowed in accordance with national laws and regulations. Rights of expropriation are sometimes very narrowly drawn, being limited to exceptional situations such as epidemics or natural disasters,[91] and compensation is payable for the loss suffered by the foreign investor. However, more recent laws tend to offer wider coverage and to provide compensation according to its real value or fair market value.[92] Recourse to international arbitration is generally authorized. Underlying all the laws is the

---

[85] For analysis, see Mark S Vecchio and Peter Chessick 'The New Russian Foreign Investment Law: Old Wine in New Bottles?' <http://www.russianamericanchamber.org/newsletter/new_russian_investment_law.html>.   [86] Above n 84 art 9(1) and art 2.

[87] However, Russia may ease restrictions on foreign investment in commercial aircraft projects 'Russia to Ease Rules on Foreign Investment' *Financial Times* 24 August 2006 at 6.

[88] 'Russia to Set Controls on Foreign Investment' *Financial Times* 3 March 2006 at 6.

[89] 'Russia Restricts Foreign Bids' *Financial Times* 11 February 2005 at 1.

[90] See World Bank above n 77 22–37. The study deals with the foreign investment laws of Azerbaijan, Belarus, Estonia, Kazakhstan, Kyrgyzstan, Latvia, Lithuania, Russia, Ukraine, and Uzbekistan. For more recent versions of the laws of the non-EU countries, see Azerbaijan, ICSID *Investment Laws of the World* (Dobbs Ferry: Oceana) vol I release 2004–1 (March 2004) or <http://www.economy.gov.az>; Belarus, Investment Code No 37–3 of 22 June 2001 ICSID ibid vol I release 2004–1 (March 2004) or <http://www.main.gov.by>; Kazakhstan Law No 373 of 8 January 2003 ICSID ibid vol IV release 2004–1 (March 2004) or <http://www.kazinvest.kz>; Kyrgyz Republic Law on Investments of 7 February 2003 ICSID ibid vol IV release 2005–1 (September 2005) or <http://www.mvtp.kg>; Ukraine Law On the Regime of Foreign Investment 25 April 1996 available at <http://www3.sympatico.ca/tem-ukraine/law_fir.htm>; Uzbekistan Law on Foreign Investments, 30 April 1998 ICSID ibid vol X Release 98–2 (November 1998) and see Ana Stanic 'Doing Business in Uzbekistan – A Guide to Its Foreign Investment Framework' 4 JWIT 1047 (2003).

[91] See, for example, Azerbaijan Law on Investment Activity N 952 13 January 1995 art 18(3) above n 90.

[92] See Belarus above note 90 art 12 (real value), Kyrgyz Republic above n 90 art 6 (fair market price).

controlling influence of national law in that investment is allowed in all sectors as prescribed by that law and subject to its requirements. As a result it is not possible to ascertain from the foreign investment law alone, what the permissible scope of foreign direct investment is or the regulatory permissions and requirements that will apply.

By contrast the People's Republic of China (PRC) has retained its joint venture laws, although within a unique policy environment. Since 1979 China has progressively liberalized the legal regime for foreign investment. The principal legislation affecting inward direct investment consists of the equity joint venture law,[93] the contractual joint venture law,[94] and the law on wholly owned foreign enterprises.[95] Each law is supplemented by supporting regulations.[96] The basic framework was amended in 2000–2001 so as to ensure conformity between these national

[93] Law of the People's Republic of China on Chinese-Foreign Equity Joint Ventures, adopted by the Second Session of the Fifth National People's Congress on 1 July 1979: 18 ILM 1163 (1979), revised in the Third Session of the Seventh National People's Congress on 4 April 1990: Beijing Review 7–13 May 1990 at 27–28, revised for the second time in accordance with 'Resolution on Revision of the Law of the People's Republic of China on Chinese-Foreign Equity Joint Ventures' of the Fourth Session of the Ninth National People's Congress on 15 March 2001 available at <http://www.fdi.gov.cn/Itlawpackage/index.jsp> or <http://www.english.movcom.gov.cn/topic/lawsdata.html> (accessed 21 May 2006) (EJVL). For analysis, see MJ Moser (ed) *Foreign Trade, Investment and the Law in the Peoples Republic of China* (Oxford: Oxford University Press 2nd edn, 1987); Comment: Rich 15 Int'l Lawyer 183 (1981); Topp 14 Jo.Int.Law & Econ. 133; Therowy 14 Jo.Int.Law & Econ. 185; Jaslow 31 Am.Jo.Comp.L 209 (1983) Rui Mu 22 Col.Jo.Transnat.L 61 (1983–84); Fenwick 40 Bus. Law 839 (1985); Chen 6 NYL Sch. ICL 1 (1984) Wei Beijing Review No 22 June 2 1986 4–5; Shan Wenhua 'Towards a Level Playing Field of Foreign Investment in China' 3 JWIT 327 (2002).

[94] Law of the People's Republic of China on Chinese-Foreign Contractual Joint Ventures, adopted at the First Session of the Seventh National People's Congress on 13 April 1988, Beijing Review June 20–26 1988 at 29, amended according to the Decision on Revision of the Law of the People's Republic of China on Chinese-Foreign Contractual Joint Ventures adopted at the 18th Meeting of the Standing Committee of the Ninth National People's Congress on 31 October 2000 available at <http://www.fdi.gov.cn/Itlawpackage/index.jsp> or <http://www.english.movcom.gov.cn/topic/lawsdata.html> (accessed 21 May 2006) (CJVL).

[95] Law of the People's Republic of China on Foreign-Capital Enterprises, adopted at the Fourth Session of the Sixth National People's Congress on 12 April 1986 Beijing Review No 18 5 May 1986 at 16, amended according to the Decision on Revision of the Law of the People's Republic of China on Foreign-Capital Enterprises, adopted at the 18th Meeting of the Standing Committee of the Ninth National People's Congress on 31 October 2000 available at <http://www.fdi.gov.cn/Itlawpackage/index.jsp> or <http://www.english.movcom.gov.cn/topic/lawsdata.html> (accessed 21 May 2006) (FCEL).

[96] Regulations for the Implementation of the Law on Sino-Foreign Equity Joint Ventures (2001), promulgated 20 September 1983 by the State Council: 22 ILM 1033 (1983), revised 15 January 1986, 21 December 1987 and 22 July 2001 by the State Council in accordance with the Decision of the State Council to Revise the Law of the People's Republic of China on Sino-foreign Equity Joint Ventures available at <http://www.fdi.gov.cn/Itlawpackage/index.jsp> or <http://www.english.movcom.gov.cn/topic/lawsdata.html> (accessed 21 May 2006); Rules for the Implementation of the Law of the People's Republic of China on Foreign-Capital Enterprises Approved on 28 October 1990 by the State Council, issued on 12 December 1990 by the Ministry of Foreign Economic Relations and China Economic News Supplement 1991.3.4 or SC 12/12/90 [1991] China Law and Practice 35; see also MOFERT *PRC Wholly Foreign Owned Enterprise Law Implementing Rules Explanation* 6 December 1991 [1992] China Law and Practice 30, revised according to the Decision of the State Council Regarding the Revision of Rules for the Implementation of the Law of the People's Republic

laws and China's impending accession to the WTO. This required the removal of any provisions that were inconsistent with, in particular, the national treatment requirement and the prohibition on trade related investment measures (TRIMs) contained in the WTO Agreements.[97]

Turning, first, to the contractual and equity joint venture laws, these share many features in common. Thus the following discussion will concentrate on the equity joint venture law and reference to the contractual joint venture law will only be made where there are significant differences. The purposes behind the equity joint venture law are stated in Article 1 as being inter alia the expansion of international economic cooperation, technical exchange, and enabling foreign companies and individuals to incorporate themselves within the territory of the PRC. Indeed, this was the first Chinese law to create the possibility of incorporation as an entity other than a state enterprise. The joint venture takes the form of a 'limited liability company' governed by the laws of the PRC.[98] A contractual joint venture also acquires the status of a 'legal person' in accordance with Chinese law.[99] These terms are uncertain in their scope. Limited liability is not defined under Chinese law,[100] although under the joint venture law the risks are shared by the participants in accordance with their respective contributions.[101] The term 'legal person' is defined by the General Principles of Civil Law of 12 April 1986 as including the right to own, use, and dispose of property; the right to carry on management and productive activities independently and the right to sue and be sued.[102] These difficulties

of China on Foreign-capital enterprises on 12 April 2001 available at <http://www.fdi.gov.cn/ltlawpackage/index.jsp> or <http://www.english.movcom.gov.cn/topic/lawsdata.html> (accessed 21 May 2006); Detailed Rules on the Implementation of the Law on Sino-Foreign Cooperative Joint Ventures (approved by the State Council of the People's Republic of China on 7 August 1995 and Promulgated by the Ministry of Foreign Trade and Economic Cooperation on 4 September 1995) available at <http://english.mofcom.gov.cn/aarticle/topic/lawsdata/chineselaw/200301/20030100062857.html> (accessed 10 September 2006) as clarified by Explanations of MOFTEC on Implementing Certain Articles of Detailed Rules on the Implementation of the Law on Sino-Foreign Cooperative Joint Ventures Promulgated by the Ministry of Foreign Trade and Economic Cooperation on 22 October 1996) available at <http://english.mofcom.gov.cn/aarticle/topic/lawsdata/chineselaw/200301/20030100063816.html> (accessed 10 September 2006).

[97] Shan above n 93 at 328–31.   [98] EJVL above n 93 arts 4 and 2.

[99] CJVL above n 93 art 2. An equity joint venture is also referred to as a 'legal person' in art 2 of the EJVL Regulations above n 96.

[100] See, however, the Opinions on Standards for Companies Limited by Shares of 19 June 1992 and Opinions on Standards for Limited Liability Companies promulgated by the State Commission for Restructuring the Economy of 22 June 1992 discussed in Wohlgemuth 'Joint Stock and Limited Liability Companies in the Law of the People's Republic of China' [1993] 1 ICCLR 12. See also the Company Law of the People's Republic of China 2005 (Order of the President of the PRC No 42, promulgated 27 October 2005, entered into force 1 January 2006) art 3(2): 'In the case of a limited liability company, shareholders shall assume liability towards the company to the extent of the amount of the capital contribution subscribed for by them respectively; in the case of a joint stock limited company, shareholders shall assume liability towards the company to the extent of the shares subscribed by them respectively.' (ISinoLaw Reference ID 76611–10009128).

[101] EJVL above n 93 art 4.

[102] According to Moser, there remain many uncertainties as to how this definition applies to joint ventures: above n 93 at 102.

may not have been alleviated by the passage, in 1993, of the first general Company Law in China.[103] According to Article 18 of the Company Law, this law applies to a foreign funded limited liability company. However, that provision also states that the specific rules in the three foreign investment laws will prevail in cases of difference between them and the Company Law. Given that these laws precede the Company Law, virtually all foreign investments in China have been established under them and so the Company Law may well be inapplicable.[104]

Both equity and contractual joint ventures are subject to approval by the relevant Chinese authorities before they can operate. The approval procedure involves the submission of a joint venture contract and articles of association to the reviewing authority, which must decide within a prescribed period. For equity joint ventures the relevant authority is the Ministry of Foreign Trade and Economic Cooperation of the People's Republic of China (MOFTEC).[105] In addition, the State Council is empowered to delegate the power to examine and approve the establishment of joint ventures to the people's governments in provinces, autonomous regions and centrally administered municipalities and relevant departments under the State Council where, 'the total amount of investment is within the limit of the investment examination and approval power as stipulated by the State Council, and the source of capital of the Chinese parties has been ascertained' and 'no additional allocations of raw materials by the State are required and the national balance of fuel, power, transportation and foreign trade export quotas, etc. is not affected'.[106] Approval will be denied inter alia where the proposed joint venture appears to be detrimental to Chinese sovereignty, or to violate Chinese law, to be incompatible with China's national economy, to be likely to cause environmental pollution or to contain obvious inequity in the agreements, contracts or articles of association.[107] Once approval has been given, the joint venture shall apply to the relevant authorities to register and will obtain an operating licence.[108]

An equity joint venture must contain at least 25 per cent foreign capital, although there is no upper limit on the foreign contribution. Profits are shared by the participants in proportion to their respective contributions.[109] Each party to the venture can contribute cash, capital goods, or industrial property rights. Where the foreign party contributes technology this must be advanced technology that is appropriate to China's needs. Should the foreign party intentionally provide outdated equipment or technology it shall pay compensation for any resulting losses. The Chinese party can contribute the right to use a site as part of its contribution.[110]

---

[103] The Corporation Law of the People's Republic of China enacted 29 December 1993 entered force 1 July 1994 available at <http://www.english.movcom.gov.cn/topic/lawsdata.html>. See, for analysis, Kingsley TW Ong and Colin R Baxter 'A Comparative Study of the Fundamental Elements of Chinese and English Company Law' 48 ICLQ 88 (1999).   [104] Shan above n 93 at 341.

[105] EJV Regulations above n 96 Chapter II arts 6–9. For the procedures applicable to contractual joint ventures, see CJVL art 5 which lays down a 45-day limit for the making of a decision.

[106] ibid   [107] EJV Regulations ibid art 4.   [108] EJVL art 3; CJVL Law art 6.

[109] EJVL art 4.   [110] ibid art 5.

The joint venture shall have a board of directors, with a composition stipulated in the contract and the articles of association after consultation between the parties to the venture. The chairman and the vice-chairman are determined by the parties to the venture or elected by the board of directors. The chairman may come from either party, and the other party shall assume the office of vice-chairman. In handling major problems, the board of directors shall reach a decision through consultation by the parties to the venture, in accordance with the principle of equality and mutual benefit.[111] Profits are distributed in accordance with the respective shares of the parties in the venture after payment of income tax on gross profits.[112]

The foreign exchange transactions of the joint venture shall be conducted in accordance with the regulations on foreign exchange control of the People's Republic of China. In its operating activities a joint venture may directly raise funds from foreign banks but all insurance shall be procured at the insurance companies within the territory of the People's Republic of China.[113] The joint venture can set up a foreign exchange account in its own name with a bank or any other financial institution which is permitted to handle foreign exchange transactions.[114] The remittance of net profits of the foreign party, and the earnings of foreign employees of the joint venture, is guaranteed.[115]

By Article 15 of the Equity Joint Venture Law, disputes arising between the parties to a joint venture, that the board of directors cannot settle through consultation, may be settled through mediation or arbitration by a Chinese arbitration agency, or through arbitration by another arbitration agency agreed upon by the parties to the venture. Where no arbitration clauses have been included in the joint venture contract, or no written arbitration agreement has been reached after a dispute arises, any party may bring a suit with the People's Court. This provision should now be read alongside China's bilateral investment treaties, which contemplate international arbitration.[116] Indeed, the PRC has ratified the Washington Convention on the Settlement of Investment Disputes 1965 accepting the International Centre for Settlement of Investment Disputes (ICSID) as a means

---

[111] ibid art 6 as amended. The original provision required that the chairman be appointed by the Chinese participant. Article 6 continues: 'The board of directors is empowered, pursuant to the provisions of the articles of association of the joint venture, to discuss and decide all major problems of the venture: expansion programmes, proposals for production and operating activities, the budget for revenues and expenditures, distribution of profits, plans concerning manpower and pay scales, the termination of business and the appointment or employment of the president, the vice-president(s), the chief engineer, the treasurer and the auditors, as well as their powers and terms of employment, etc. The offices of president and vice-president(s) (or factory manager and deputy manager(s)) shall be assumed by the respective parties to the venture. Contracts shall be entered into in accordance with the law to prescribe the recruitment, dismissal, remuneration, welfare, labor protection, labor insurance, etc.' In 2001, a new art 7 was inserted to protect the rights of employees to form and join trade unions.   [112] ibid art 8.
[113] ibid art 9.
[114] ibid. Under the 1979 Law such an account could only be opened with the Bank of China.
[115] ibid arts 11, 12.   [116] See further ch 17n 158 at 683 and 692.

of international arbitration and conciliation in disputes with foreign investors.[117] Furthermore, in an attempt to reinforce China's commitment to an open door policy the 1990 amendment to the Joint Venture Law introduced a new Article 2(3) whereby: '[t]he state does not practice nationalization and expropriation of a joint venture; under special circumstances, the state, in accordance with the needs of social public interest, expropriates a joint venture pursuant to legal procedures and offers corresponding compensations.' This falls far short of a comprehensive protection against expropriation. However, the very fact of its inclusion is itself a significant step.

As an alternative to a joint venture the foreign investor is able to set up a wholly owned subsidiary in accordance with the Law on Foreign-Capital Enterprises (FCEL) and its implementing regulations. Approval for such an enterprise is required from MOFTEC or other authorities designated by the State Council of the PRC.[118] By Article 3 of the FCEL: '[e]nterprises with foreign capital shall be established in such a manner as to help the development of China's national economy. The State may encourage the establishment of foreign capital enterprises that are export-oriented or technologically advanced.' This wording replaces the compulsory wording in the original version of this provision, so as to ensure conformity with the TRIMS Agreement of the WTO.[119] Regulations shall be formulated by the State Council regarding the lines of business which the state forbids enterprises with foreign capital to engage in or on which it places certain restrictions.[120] Should the enterprise fail to invest in China within a designated period after approval, its licence to operate will be revoked.[121]

Where the enterprise fulfils the conditions for being considered a legal person under Chinese law it shall be so considered.[122] While the precise meaning of this provision is unclear, given the uncertainty surrounding the application of the Company Law to entities established under the FCEL, the latter offers certain guarantees to the enterprise. Thus, by Article 4 of the Law: '[t]he investments of a foreign investor in China, the profits it earns and its other lawful rights and interests are protected by Chinese law.' Furthermore, the enterprise is protected from expropriation except 'under special circumstances when public interests require, enterprises with foreign capital may be requisitioned through legal procedures and appropriate compensation shall be made'.[123] This protection should be enhanced by the terms of investment protection treaties entered into by the PRC and by access to ICSID, given that China has agreed to the jurisdiction of the Centre in

---

[117] On ICSID, see ch 18. The PRC accepts ICSID jurisdiction only in relation to disputes over the level of compensation payable upon expropriation of foreign owned property. See further Koa 'The International Bank for Reconstruction and Development and Dispute Resolution: Conciliating and Arbitrating with China Through the International Centre for the Settlement of Investment Disputes' 24 NYUJ Int'l Law and Pol. 439 (1991).

[118] FCEL above n 95 art 6. FCEL Rules above n 96 art 7.   [119] Shan above n 93 at 334.
[120] FCEL above n 95 art 3.   [121] ibid art 9.   [122] ibid art 8.
[123] ibid art 5.

disputes over compensation resulting from expropriation and nationalization.[124] In return for these guarantees '[e]nterprises with foreign capital shall abide by Chinese laws and regulations and may not engage in any activities detrimental to China's public interests'.[125]

So long as the enterprise acts in accordance with its approved articles of association, it will be free from interference in its operations.[126] Profits legitimately earned from the enterprise may be remitted abroad.[127] The enterprise may employ Chinese workers as well as foreign workers,[128] set up account books in China and submit to independent audit,[129] pay taxes in China,[130] insure with insurers located in China,[131] and observe Chinese foreign exchange regulations.[132] Liquidation of the enterprise will be subject to regulations.

The operation of foreign investments in the PRC has been beset with problems. A major difficulty lies with the high levels of control exercised by the Chinese authorities over industrial and commercial activities, notwithstanding commitments to building a 'socialist market economy'. In particular, significant regulations are classed as 'internal' (*neibu*) and may not be revealed to foreigners.[133] Thus not all the relevant administrative rules are always accessible.[134] In addition, the extent of legal guarantees to foreign investors is very limited as compared to other countries' laws. There is no comprehensive investor protection code as such under Chinese law, making the protection offered under BITs all the more significant. The problems of transparency and effective legal protection are compounded by the potential overlap between the various foreign investment laws and the Company Law. These factors have led to calls for a fully revised foreign investment code that would cover the admission and protection of foreign investment, while leaving the corporate organization and governance for foreign investments to the Company Law alone.[135]

(d) 'Screening' Laws

'Screening laws' involve the case-by-case review of proposed foreign investments by a specialized public authority in the host state that is charged with the task of establishing whether or not a given proposal is in accordance with the economic and/or social policies of the host state. As we have seen in the foregoing sections, 'screening' procedures are often established in association with restrictive regimes regulating the ownership and control of foreign investments. On the other hand, 'screening' may be used as the sole technique of regulation, unaccompanied by any statutory requirements concerning permissible limits of foreign ownership

---

[124] See ICSID News Release of 7 January 1993; News from ICSID vol 10 No 1 (Winter 1993) 1.
[125] FCEL art 4.   [126] ibid art 11.   [127] ibid art 19.   [128] Articles 12–13.
[129] Article 14.   [130] Article 17.   [131] Article 16.   [132] Article 18.
[133] See Moser (ed) above n 93 at 102; Shan above n 93 at 340.
[134] See Moser (ed) ibid at 111–16.   [135] See Shan above n 93 at 342–43.

and/or control, and be aimed only at ensuring official scrutiny and approval of proposed investments. In many cases the 'screening' process will empower the reviewing authority, or the minister or government department to which it is answerable, to impose operational conditions, usually referred to as performance requirements, upon the investor as the price for approval. The 'screening' of foreign investments is one of the most widely used techniques for controlling the entry and establishment of MNEs in host states.[136] This approach has been favoured by states that welcome foreign owned and controlled investments, but which are concerned about the loss of economic sovereignty or adverse economic consequences that may accompany such investments in particular cases. Both economically advanced and developing countries have adopted 'screening laws'.

Certain developing countries have adopted this technique, often in association with the imposition of performance requirements and/or access to investment incentives, as an alternative to strict restrictions on foreign ownership and control of inward direct investments. Two typical examples of this approach are the laws of Mexico and Ghana.

In 1984 and again in 1989 Mexico, which had hitherto imposed strict limitations on foreign investment under the 1973 Act on Foreign Investment, liberalized its previous ceiling of 49 per cent on foreign ownership outside restricted sectors and introduced automatic approval procedures based on certain conditions that the foreign investor must fulfil.[137] The 1989 reforms were effected through regulations. This raised some uncertainty as to their legality under the regime of Federal law as reflected in the 1973 Act. Consequently, for the avoidance of uncertainty and as a further measure of liberalization, the 1989 regulations were formally codified and developed in the Foreign Investment Act of 1993 (the Act).[138] New regulations were adopted in 1998, to bring the 1993 Act into full operation.[139]

---

[136] See further M Sornarajah *The International Law on Foreign Investment* (Cambridge: Cambridge University Press, 2nd edn, 2004) ch 3.

[137] For the 1984 reforms, see Sandra F Maviglia 'Mexico's Guidelines for Foreign Investment: The Selective Promotion of Necessary Industries' 80 AJIL 281 (1986). For the 1989 reforms, see Etienne 'The New Investment Opportunity: Mexico' BIFD (September 1992) 419.

[138] Published in *Diario Oficial de la Federacion* 27 December 1993 First Section 92–99; English translation in 33 ILM 207 (1994).

[139] Regulations to the Foreign Investment Act of 1993 and to the National Register of Foreign Investments *Diario Oficial* of 8 September 1998, entered into force 20 days later (except for paragraph 4 of Article 18 which entered into force six months later). Spanish original in ICSID *Investment Laws of the World* (Dobbs Ferry: Oceana) vol V release 2000–2 (November 2000) 1. The following English summary of the 1998 regulations comes from Jose Vargas (ed) *Mexican Law: A Treatise for Legal Practitioners and International Investors* (West Publishing, 1998 and 2001) available at <http://www.mexlaw.com/recent.html> (visited 28 May 2006): 'The 1998 Regulations are composed of 49 sections (Artículos) divided into eight titles. I General Provisions (Artículos 1–4), sets forth general definitions of legal terms used in the Act; in addition, it enumerates specific industries not subject to the rules and principles of the Act, such as freight, warehousing, and some activities associated with the generation of electricity and oil. II Of the Acquisition of Real Estate, the Exploitation of Mines and Water, and of Trusts (Artículos 5–12). This title governs the acquisition of real estate in Mexico, both in the Restricted Zone and elsewhere, for commercial and residential

The Act has limited screening procedures to certain economic activities, listed in Article 8, where the foreign investor is seeking a participation of more than 49 per cent,[140] and to foreign acquisitions of over 49 per cent in Mexican corporations where the total value of the stated capital exceeds 85m New Pesos.[141] Screening is to be carried out by the National Commission of Foreign Investments.[142] In evaluating applications for approval under the above provisions, the Commission must take into account: the impact upon the employment and training of workers; the technological contribution; compliance with environmental provisions and, in general, the contribution of the proposed investment to the increased competitiveness of Mexico's factories and businesses.[143] Unlike the 1989 regulations, which imposed specific performance requirements, the 1993 Act only permits the Commission to impose requirements which will not distort international trade.[144] On the other hand, the Commission may prohibit acquisitions by foreign investment for reasons of national security.[145]

Outside those areas requiring screening by the Commission, the Act guarantees freedom of foreign investment in any proportion of capital; in the acquisition of fixed assets; in entry into new areas of economic activity or in the manufacture of new lines of products; in the opening and management of commercial entities; or in the expansion or relocation of those already in existence. This general freedom is excluded where the Act reserves certain listed activities for the state,[146] or for

purposes. Interestingly, contrary to Article 27(I) of the Federal Constitution, the new regulations detail how a Mexican corporation with foreign investment may acquire the direct ownership of real estate anywhere in Mexico, even in the Restricted Zone, when said acquisition takes place for commercial purposes. Trust contracts, known as 'Fideicomisos', and now valid for 50 years, must continue to be used for residential purposes. III Of Societies (Companies, Artículos 13–20). This title enunciates the rules foreigners must comply with to invest and participate in Mexican legal entities, in particular when the company in question does not contain the so-called 'Exclusion of Foreigners Clause' (Cláusula de Exclusión de Extranjeros). IV Of the Investment by Foreign Legal Entities (Artículo 21). This sets out the manner in which foreign corporations must register with the Mexican Government to be authorized to conduct business in Mexico. V Of Neutral Investments (Artículos 22–25). It establishes the requirements needed to obtain authorization from the Mexican Government to establish or modify neutral investments. VI Of the National Commission of Foreign Investments (Comisión Nacional de Inversiones Extranjeras, Artículos 26–29). This title enumerates the legal and administrative duties imposed upon this National Commission, including its internal rules of procedure. VII Of the National Register of Foreign Investments (Registro Nacional de Inversiones Extranjeras, Articulos 30–46), sets out the organization, activities, and basic inscriptions to be made by the Registry, whose major objective is to organize, keep and maintain an official register of all foreign investments in Mexico. The register is divided into three 'sections' 1) Foreign individuals and foreign legal entities; 2) Societies (Companies); and 3) Trust contracts (Fideicomisos). VIII Of Supplementary Provisions (Artículos 47–49).'

[140] The economic activities listed in art 8 are: port services to vessels engaged in internal navigation; shipping corporations engaged exclusively in high seas operations; administration of air traffic terminals; private education at all levels; legal services; credit information services; securities rating institutions; insurance brokers; cellular telephones; oil pipeline construction; drilling of oil and gas wells.

[141] ibid art 9 and Tenth Transitory Article. The threshold figure will be reviewed annually.

[142] ibid art 26 (II).   [143] ibid art 29.   [144] ibid.   [145] ibid art 30.

[146] See ibid art 5, which lists eg petroleum, electricity, railroads posts, and telecommunications.

Mexicans or Mexican corporations.[147] In addition, Article 7 of the Act lists several economic activities where foreign investment is limited by percentages, ranging from 10 per cent up to 49 per cent, but where approval by the Commission is unnecessary. The listed areas include inter alia domestic air transportation, cable TV, fishing, and insurance. The listed areas were previously reserved for Mexicans. The scheme of the 1993 Act ensures that national treatment is accorded to foreign investors in all fields save those specifically reserved for Mexican participation. This ensures that Mexican foreign investment law is in line with the requirements of the North American Free Trade Agreement.[148]

A similar approach to screening was adopted by the Ghana Investments Centre under the Investment Code of 1985, which liberalized the restrictive conditions of entry for foreign investors under the 1981 Investment Code.[149] The 1985 Code was replaced in 1994 by the Ghana Investment Promotion Centre Act.[150] In areas other that those reserved exclusively for Ghanaian investors,[151] or in mining or petroleum, which is subject to a separate statutory regime,[152] the centre will approve an enterprise wholly owned by a non-Ghanaian if it involves an investment of foreign capital or equivalent goods worth at least US$ 50,000 or its equivalent worth in capital goods by way of equity capital.[153] Under the 1985 Code the approval procedure required an appraisal of the capacity of the enterprise to

---

[147] See ibid art 6 which lists eg national land transportation, radio and television other than cable TV, and retail gasoline sales.

[148] See Canada-Mexico-United States North American Free Trade Agreement 17 December 1992 Part Five Investment, Services and Related Matters: 32 ILM 605 at 639–70 (1993). See further ch 6 at 239–42.

[149] Ghana Investment Code 1985 (PNDC Law 116 of 1985) summarized in UNCTC *National Legislation and Regulations Relating to Transnational Corporations Volume VII* (New York: 1989 UN Doc ST/CTC/91) 21–24; comment Laryea 39 ICLQ 197 (1990). For similar screening laws in other African countries, see Zambia: Investment Act 1993 (No 39 of 1993) ICSID *Investment Laws* above n 90 vol X release 97–1 (March 1997) or <http://www.zic.org.zm/downloads/Investment%20Law.pdf>; Uganda: Investment Code, 1991 (Statute No 1 1991 25 January 1991) ICSID *Investment Laws* vol X release 92–2 (June 1992); Tanzania: National Investment (Promotion and Protection) Act (Act No 10 of 1990) reproduced in 6 ICSID Rev-FILJ 292 (1991) or 3 RADIC 840 (1991); see also Peter 'Promotion and Protection of Foreign Investments in Tanzania: A New Investment Code' 6 ICSID Rev-FILJ 42 (1991). Tanzania passed a new Investment Act (No 26 of 1997) on 9 September 1997: ICSID *Investment Laws* vol IX release 99–1 (May 1999) and see, for a summary, the Tanzania Investment Centre website <http://www.tic.co.tz/IPA_Information.asp?hdnGroupID=28&hdnLevelID=2>. This law provides for positive investment promotion by way of a 'one stop' agency but the power to issue licences and other permissions is still retained by the relevant government departments: see s 16; Nigeria: see text at notes 43–44; Cameroon: Kofele-Kale 'Investment Codes as an Instrument of Economic Policy: A Cameroon Case Study' 25 Int'l Law 821 (1991). See also Parra n 4 above.

[150] Act 478 of 29 August 1994: ICSID *Investment Laws of the World* above n 90 vol III release 95–3 (June 1995) also available at <http://www.gipc.org.gh/IPA_Information.asp?hdnGroupID=4&hdnLevelID=4>.

[151] See ibid s 18. Reserved sectors are listed in the Schedule to s 18 as sales in a market, petty trading, hawking or selling from a kiosk, operation of taxi or car hire services unless the non-Ghanaian has at least 10 vehicles, pool betting business and lotteries except football pools, operation of beauty salons and barber shops.   [152] ibid s 17.

[153] ibid s 19(2)(b). By s 19(2)(a) a joint enterprise with a Ghanaian partner requires the non-Ghanaian to contribute at least $10,000.

contribute to any of the following objectives: development of the productive sectors of the economy; efficient utilization, expansion and diversification of the productive capacity of existing enterprises; utilization of local materials, supplies, and services; creation of employment opportunities in Ghana; real increase in national export earnings; real savings on national imports; development and transfer of advanced technology, including the upgrading of indigenous technology; country-wide distribution of viable enterprises; and such other objectives as the centre may consider relevant for achieving the objects of the code.[154] The 1994 Act replaced this detailed screening process with the simplified requirements found in sections 21 and 22. The emphasis is now on automatic registration with the centre of any foreign investment that complies with the minimum capital requirements required under s 19. The only other requirement is that the enterprise is incorporated and registered in accordance with the Companies Code of 1963. Once a proposed investment is registered the investor will be entitled to the various fiscal and other benefits that are available under the 1994 Act.[155] Certain industrial sectors that are regarded as priority investment areas are given special benefits and incentives under regulations.[156] In addition to easing entry requirements ss 27–32 of the Act also include, for the first time, guarantees to investors concerning free movement of capital, protection against expropriation, and access to dispute settlement procedures. The 1994 Act embodies a typical example of the shift from detailed screening towards more open conditions for entry and establishment, and explicit investor guarantees, which characterize many of the newer FDI laws. According to UNCTAD, the 1994 Act 'was considered at that time to be the best in Africa'.[157]

Screening laws have been frequently found in economically advanced states that do not espouse an 'open door' approach to foreign investment. Examples have included inter alia Japan,[158] France,[159] and Spain.[160] Australia[161] and

[154] Investment Code above n 149 s 22(1).

[155] Investment Act 1994 above n 150 at ss 23–26. See further UNCTAD *Investment Policy Review: Ghana* (New York and Geneva: United Nations, 2003) or <http://www.unctad.org/Templates/Page.asp?intItemID=2752&lang=1> at 29–33.

[156] ibid s 26. See further UNCTAD ibid at 40–46.   [157] ibid at 20.

[158] See text at n 26–30 above.

[159] See Law No 66–1008 of 28 December 1966 [1966] *Journal Officiel* 11621; Decree No 67–78 of 1967 [1967] *Journal Officiel* 1073 and 1074; Decrees No 71–143 and 71–144 of 1971 discussed in Wallace n 2 above at 63–65; Decree Nos 80–617 and 80–618 of 4 August 1980 concerning Community Investments. See further UNCTC *National Legislation and Regulations Relating to Transnational Corporations: A Technical Paper* (New York: UN Doc ST/CTC/35, 1983) 316–32; Safarian n 6 above.

[160] See Royal Decree 1265/1986 of 27 June 1986 Chapters II, VI, VII and VIII as amended 1991; Royal Decree 2077/1986 of 25 September 1986 Sections II, VI, VII and VIII English translation in 26 ILM 727–44 (1987).

[161] Foreign Acquisitions and Takeovers Act 1975 Act No 92 of 1975 as compiled on 1 January 2005 taking into account amendments up to Act No 120 of 2004 <http://www.comlaw.gov.au/ComLaw/Legislation/ActCompilation1.nsf/current/bytitle/AA1C2617808E9AA9CA256F89001094E6?OpenDocument&mostrecent=1>; Foreign Acquisitions and Takeovers Regulations 1989 Statutory

New Zealand[162] continue to screen major investments in land and in sensitive business sectors. The most comprehensive example of inward investment regulation through 'screening' laws in an economically developed country is to be found in the Canadian experience since the early 1970s.

Canada has long been a major location for foreign direct investment, particularly from the US. The considerable levels of investment by US firms have created a close economic relationship between the two countries, more recently manifested by their membership of NAFTA. It has also led, at times, to a sense of dependency and loss of national identity on the part of Canadians. This has periodically manifested itself in nationalistic calls for the reduction of US influence in Canada.[163] Such sentiments were prominent in the late 1960s and early 1970s in relation to the then growing debate on the effect of MNEs on Canadian society and its economy. Between 1968 and 1972 three government reports on direct investment in Canada helped to create an environment of concern over the increasing domination of MNEs, especially from the US, over the Canadian economy.[164] Of these the most important was the last, the so-called 'Gray Report'. This report recommended the setting up of a new investment screening agency which would act as a bargaining agent with MNEs and prevent monopolistic foreign ownership in Canadian industry.

In January 1973, the newly elected Liberal government led by Pierre Trudeau introduced the bill that was to become the Foreign Investment Review Act (FIRA).

Rules 1989 No 177 as amended made under the Foreign Acquisitions and Takeovers Act 1975 compiled on 1 January 2005 taking into account amendments up to SR 2004 No 401 <http://www. comlaw.gov.au/ComLaw/Legislation/LegislativeInstrumentCompilation1.nsf/06CA9C8A062F2D 6A8CA256F80007B66B4/$file/ForeignAcqTake1989.doc>. See further Australian Government, The Treasury *Summary of Australia's Foreign Investment Policy* (Canberra: January 2006) <http://www. comlaw.gov.au/ComLaw/Legislation/LegislativeInstrumentCompilation1.nsf/0/6CA9C8A062F2 D6A8CA256F80007B66B4/$file/ForeignAcqTake1989.doc>. Breit 'Australian Multinationals: Growth or Survival?' 10 JWTL 265 (1976); Ryan 'Foreign Investment in Australia and New Zealand' 54 ALJ 443 (1980); Hamilton 'New Foreign Investment Rules for Australia' 50 ALJ 574 (1976); D Flint *Foreign Investment Law in Australia* (Sydney: Law Book Co, 1985).

[162] Overseas Investment Act 2005 (082) available at <http://rangi.knowledge-basket.co.nz/ gpacts/public/text/2005/an/082.html>.

[163] See Turner 'Canadian Regulation of Foreign Direct Investment' 23 Harv.ILJ 333 at 335–37 (1983). See also Franck and Gudgeon 'Canada's Foreign Investment Control Experiment: The Law, the Context and the Practice' 50 NYULR 76 at 77–84 (1975). More recently opposition to NAFTA, and to the proposed Multilateral Agreement on Investment, in which Canadian NGOs were prominent, could be seen as similarly motivated.

[164] These were: (i) The Government of Canada Task Force Report *Foreign Ownership and the Structure of Canadian Industry* (Ottawa: Queens Printer, 1968) commonly referred to as the 'Watkins Report' after the head of the Task Force; (ii) The Eleventh Report of the Standing Committee on External Affairs and National Defence Respecting Canada-US Relations: 28th Parl 2d Sess s 3.01 (1970) commonly referred to as the 'Wahn Report'; (iii) *Foreign Direct Investment in Canada* (Ottawa: Information Canada, 1972) commonly referred to as the 'Gray Report' after Herbert Gray the head of the Governmental Working Group set up to review Canada's policy on direct investment. For a discussion of these reports, see Franck and Gudgeon above previous note at 98–105; A Rugman *Multinationals in Canada: Theory, Performance and Economic Impact* (Martinus Nijhoff, 1980) ch 9. reprinted from 10 JWTL 171–76 (1976); Leckow and Mallory 'The Relaxation of Foreign Investment Restrictions in Canada' 6 ICSID Rev-FILJ 1 at 1–11 (1991).

The Liberals had lost their overall majority in the House of Commons and had to rely on the left-wing New Democrat Party for support. Consequently, the provisions of the bill were tougher on foreign investors than the government would have liked.[165] Furthermore, it was one part of a wider policy aimed at increasing Canadian participation in the national economy.[166] The Act became law on 12 December 1973.[167] Following the recommendation of the Gray Report, the Act established the Foreign Investment Review Agency (the Agency) as a screening body for the approval of new inward investment on the basis of its being or likely to be, 'of significant benefit to Canada',[168] as defined by reference to the criteria listed in s 2(2) of the Act and subsequent regulations.[169] The Act applied to two forms of inward investment: the acquisition of control of existing Canadian enterprises and the establishment of new businesses in Canada.[170] It did not limit the internal expansion of foreign owned enterprises already operating in Canada, which, according to Rugman, accounted for most new direct investment recorded in Canada.[171]

The review procedure set up by FIRA involved an initial assessment by the Agency followed by a report to the Minister of Industry, Trade, and Commerce. The minister would then assess whether the investment represented a significant benefit to Canada. If it did, the minister would recommend to the cabinet that the investment be approved. If it did not, the investor would be given more time to provide further information and to make further representations. The cabinet would then decide whether the investment met the statutory test of significant benefit to Canada. The approval could be made conditional on the acceptance of specific commitments by the investor, which would become legally binding upon the granting of approval by the cabinet.[172] This procedure was to be completed within 60 days.[173] It was a closed procedure, involving as it did the highest executive organ in the country. This made the likelihood of judicial review more remote, given the immunity of the cabinet from such an action.[174] In practice the majority of applications under FIRA were approved.[175] However, the Act

---

[165] See Franck and Gudgeon above n 163 at 107; Rugman ibid at 129.

[166] Franck and Gudgeon, at 108–111.

[167] Ch 46, 1973–74 Statutes of Canada 620 amended by ch 52, 1976–77 Statutes of Canada 1274. For an analysis of the provisions of FIRA, see Turner above n 163 at 338–41; Franck and Gudgeon ibid at 111–142; Donaldson and Jackson 'The Foreign Investment Review Act: An Analysis of the Legislation' 52 Can.Bar.Rev. 171 (1975).   [168] ibid s 2 (1).

[169] The criteria listed included inter alia the effect of the investment on employment, resource processing, exports from Canada, productivity, competition, technological, and product development, the degree of Canadian participation, and general national industrial and economic policy goals.

[170] The Act came into operation in two phases: the first came into effect on 9 April 1974 concerning the takeover of existing Canadian firms by foreign investors, the second on 15 October 1975 concerning the setting up of new businesses in Canada.   [171] Rugman above n 164 at 129.

[172] Undertakings could be agreed with investors in five areas: the production of export goods; the location of research and development in Canada; the processing of raw materials in Canada; the hiring of Canadian managers and directors, and the purchasing of Canadian goods and services.

[173] ibid ss 10–11.

[174] RK Paterson *Canadian Regulation of International Trade and Investment* (Toronto: Carswell, 1986) at 299.

[175] See Turner above n 163 at 341; Rugman above n 164 ch 10 at 134 et seq, reprinted from 11 JWTL 322–33 (1977).

engendered opposition both from within Canada and from the US Government. Within Canada, the administrations of the provinces saw the legislation as inhibiting their power to attract inward investment.[176]

Meanwhile, in the US, the free market orientated Reagan administration adopted a policy of opposition to the Canadian legislation.[177] In 1982, the US Government made a request before the GATT Council that it set up a panel to examine matters concerning the administration of FIRA. The US complained about undertakings given by foreign investors under FIRA in relation to the purchase of Canadian goods and the maintenance of export levels. It is important to stress that the complaint did not relate to the compatibility of the screening procedure per se with the GATT, but to the adverse and discriminatory effects on international trade between the US and Canada that were allegedly created by the above mentioned undertakings. The panel concluded that Canada had violated GATT principles through the adoption of such undertakings. The Canadian Government responded by discontinuing the practice of accepting undertakings from investors which gave preferential treatment to Canadian goods and services over imported goods.

In 1984, the new Conservative administration promptly repealed FIRA and replaced it with the Investment Canada Act 1985 (the 1985 Act).[178] This introduced a less stringent screening procedure applicable only to larger investment proposals, which was conducted by lower levels of government. The new government was concerned to change the perception of foreign investors as to Canada's attitude to foreign direct investment. Thus, according to s 2 of the 1985 Act:

Recognizing that increased capital and technology would benefit Canada, the purpose of this Act is to encourage investment in Canada by Canadians and non-Canadians that contributes to economic growth and employment opportunities and to provide for the review of significant investments in Canada by non-Canadians in order to ensure such benefit to Canada.

The 1985 Act requires that non-Canadians[179] making an investment to establish a new Canadian business, or an investment to acquire control of a Canadian business in any manner specified in the Act, must provide notice of such investments to the Director of Investments (the Director) who replaces the Investment Canada

---

[176] Turner ibid at 336–37.

[177] See Turner ibid at 344–46. For a fuller account of this proceeding see Paterson n 174 at 300–304, on which the next paragraph is based.

[178] Statutes of Canada 1985 c 20 as amended: see <http://strategis.ic.gc.ca/epic/internet/inica-lic.nsf/en/home>. See further Paterson above n 174 at 316–17 for a note of the political background to this statute. For analysis of the Act, see further Paterson ibid 317–35; Glover, New, and Lacourciere 'The Investment Canada Act: A New Approach to the Regulation of Foreign Investment in Canada' 41 Business Lawyer 83 (1985); Grover 'The Investment Canada Act' 10 Can.Bus.LJ. 475 (1985); Rose 'Foreign Investment in Canada: The New Investment Canada Act' 20 Int'l Law 19 (1986); Arnett 'From FIRA to Investment Canada' 24 Alta. L.Rev. 1 (1985); Evans 'Canada for Sale: The Investment Canada Act' 21 JWTL 85 (1987); Leckow and Mallory above n 164.

[179] A 'non-Canadian' is defined by s 3 of the 1985 Act as 'an individual, a government or an agency thereof or an entity that is not Canadian'. 'Canadian' is defined by s 3. as (i) a Canadian citizen; (ii) a permanent resident of Canada who has been resident in Canada for not more than one

Agency.[180] This requirement does not apply to the exempt transactions listed in s 10(1) of the 1985 Act. The 1985 Act does not clarify the purpose of the notification procedure,[181] but it appears from the terms of s 13(3) that notification is required so that the Director can determine whether the investment is reviewable under the Act or, alternatively, is exempt from review. The Director must send a notice for review to the prospective investor within 21 days after the certified date upon which notice of the investment was given.[182]

The establishment of a new business in Canada by a non-Canadian[183] is not reviewable unless it involves the commencement of a business that falls within a prescribed specific type of business activity that is related to Canada's cultural heritage or national identity.[184] Whether a business activity is related to Canada's cultural heritage or national identity falls to be determined by regulations made under the 1985 Act. The acquisition of control of a Canadian business[185] is subject to review depending on the mode of acquisition involved and the value of the assets of the targeted Canadian enterprise. Section 28(1) of the 1985 Act designates five types of acquisition relevant to the Act:

(*a*) the acquisition of voting shares of a corporation incorporated in Canada carrying on the Canadian business;

(*b*) the acquisition of voting interests of an entity that
   (i) is carrying on the Canadian business, or
   (ii) controls, directly or indirectly, another entity carrying on the Canadian business, where there is no acquisition of control of any corporation;

(*c*) the acquisition of all or substantially all of the assets used in carrying on the Canadian business; or

(*d*) the acquisition of voting interests of an entity that controls, directly or indirectly, an entity in Canada carrying on the Canadian business, where
   (i) there is no acquisition of control, directly or indirectly, of a corporation incorporated elsewhere than in Canada that controls, directly or indirectly, an entity in Canada carrying on the Canadian business, or
   (ii) there is an acquisition of control described in subparagraph (i).

---

year after the time at which he first became eligible to apply for Canadian citizenship; (iii) a federal, provincial, or local Government of Canada or an agency thereof; (iv) a corporation, partnership, trust, or joint venture determined in accordance with s 26 of the Act to be Canadian controlled. By s 26 Canadian control is established by the existence of a Canadian voting majority in the company, or by de facto Canadian control despite a non-Canadian majority of voting shares as where the Canadian minority is the controlling group or two-thirds of the board has Canadian members.

[180] Investment Canada Act 1985 s 11. The Investment Canada Agency is set up under ss 6–9 of the Act.   [181] See Grover above n 178 at 476–77.
[182] ibid s 13(1)(b)(ii).
[183] Section 3 of the 1985 Act defines a 'new Canadian business' as a business that is not already being carried on in Canada by the non-Canadian and that, at the time it is established, is either unrelated to any other business being carried on in Canada by the non-Canadian, or is related to another business being carried on in Canada by that non-Canadian but falls within a prescribed specific type of business activity that, in the opinion of the Governor in Council, is related to Canada's cultural heritage or national identity.   [184] ibid s 15.
[185] Defined in s 3 of the 1985 Act as a business that (i) has a place of business in Canada; (ii) has an individual or individuals in Canada that are employed or self-employed in connection with that business, and (iii) has assets in Canada used in carrying on that business.

The acquisition can be effected by a chain of transactions provided one of the above results is achieved.[186] The acquisition of control is presumed, for the purposes of s 28, where a majority of the voting shares in the Canadian corporation is acquired, but not where less than one-third of the voting shares is acquired. Where more than one-third but less than a majority of the voting shares is acquired control is presumed unless it can be proved that the acquirer does not in fact control the corporation through its acquisition.[187]

Once an acquisition of control by any of the above methods has taken place the review procedure will come into operation only if the value thresholds laid down in the statute are met. By s 14 of the 1985 Act, where the investment involves the acquisition of direct control of a Canadian business or of its assets[188] review is required where the asset value of the Canadian business is C$5m or more. Where the investment involves the acquisition of indirect control over a Canadian business[189] the threshold for review is C$50m or more. These limits were removed for US investors as a result of the US-Canada Free Trade Agreement, and new thresholds have been introduced for all WTO investors.[190] It is of some significance to note that, so far as review of indirect acquisitions is concerned, this involves an extraterritorial exercise of jurisdiction. Under FIRA the Canadian courts were willing to defend the exercise of such jurisdiction.[191] The 1985 Act appears to

---

[186] ibid s 29.   [187] ibid s 28(3).   [188] ie the cases listed in s 28(1)(a)–(d)(i) above.

[189] As defined in s 28(1)(d)(ii) above.

[190] See US-Canada Free Trade Agreement 1988 Annex 1607.3: 27 ILM 281 (1988) discussed in Peter T Muchlinski *Multinational Enterprises and the Law* (Oxford: Blackwell Publishers, revised paperback 1st edn, 1999) at 239–41; Investment Canada Act 1985 s 14.1 above n 178:

'14.1 (1) Notwithstanding the limits set out in subsection 14(3), an investment described in paragraph 14(1)(*a*), (*b*), or (*c*) by

(*a*) a WTO investor, or

(*b*) a non-Canadian, other than a WTO investor, where the Canadian business that is the subject of the investment is, immediately prior to the implementation of the investment, controlled by a WTO investor,

is reviewable pursuant to section 14 only where the value, calculated in the manner prescribed, of the assets described in paragraph 14(3)(*a*) or (*b*), as the case may be, is equal to or greater than the applicable amount determined pursuant to subsection (2).

Amount for subsequent years

(2) For the purposes of subsection (1), the amount for any year shall be determined by the Minister in January of that year by rounding off to the nearest million dollars the amount arrived at by using the formula:

Current Nominal GDP at Market Prices
divided by Previous Year Nominal GDP at Market Prices
multiplied by amount determined for previous year

where

'Current Nominal GDP at Market Prices' means the average of the Nominal Gross Domestic Products at market prices for the most recent four consecutive quarters; and

'Previous Year Nominal GDP at Market Prices' means the average of the Nominal Gross Domestic Products at market prices for the four consecutive quarters for the comparable period in the year preceding the year used in calculating the Current Nominal GDP at Market Prices.'

The amount is 265 million dollars for the year 2006 published in the *Canada Gazette* Part I on 21 January 2006, 132.

[191] See *Dow Jones & Co Inc v Attorney-General of Canada* (1980) 113 DLR (3d) 395 *aff'd* 122 DLR (3d) 731 (FCA 1981); *A-G of Canada v Fallbridge Holdings Ltd* 63 NR 17 (FCA 1985) cited in

have preserved such jurisdiction in cases where the acquisition of a Canadian business forms a major part of a larger foreign takeover.[192]

After receipt of an investment notification, should the Director decide that the investment falls within a reviewable category, the application is forwarded to the minister responsible for the administration of the 1985 Act.[193] The minister will then decide whether the proposed investment is likely to be 'of net benefit to Canada'.[194] The level of decision-making is thus lowered from that of the cabinet. Furthermore, the 'net benefit' test introduces a lower requirement for approval than the 'significant benefit' test under FIRA. However, the statutory criteria for consideration of a 'net benefit' are similar to those found in FIRA in connection with the former test. Thus, the minister must consider the effect of the investment on economic activity in Canada including:

(*a*) the effect of the investment on the level and nature of economic activity in Canada, including, without limiting the generality of the foregoing, the effect on employment, on resource processing, on the utilization of parts, components and services produced in Canada and on exports from Canada;

(*b*) the degree and significance of participation by Canadians in the Canadian business or new Canadian business and in any industry or industries in Canada of which the Canadian business or new Canadian business forms or would form a part;

(*c*) the effect of the investment on productivity, industrial efficiency, technological development, product innovation and product variety in Canada;

(*d*) the effect of the investment on competition within any industry or industries in Canada;

(*e*) the compatibility of the investment with national industrial, economic and cultural policies, taking into consideration industrial, economic and cultural policy objectives enunciated by the government or legislature of any province likely to be significantly affected by the investment; and

(*f*) the contribution of the investment to Canada's ability to compete in world markets.'[195]

The minister must make the required decision within 45 days from the certified date of receipt of the application. If no decision is made within this period, the minister must notify the applicant that he or she is unable to complete their consideration of the investment. There remains a further 30-day period for decision that may be extended by mutual agreement. Should that period run out without a decision being made, the investment is automatically allowed.[196] If the minister decides that the investment does not comply with the 'net benefit' criterion the applicant may be requested to make further representations or to enter into undertakings.[197] Thereupon the minister makes a final determination as to the 'net benefit' of the investment. If the investment is disallowed the applicant shall

---

Paterson above n 174 at 324–26; see further O'Laughlin 'Extraterritorial Application of Canadian Foreign Investment Review' 8 NW J.Int'l Law & Bus. 436 (1987); Romer 'Was the Sigh of Relief Premature? The Investment Canada Act' 19 Vanderbilt Jo.Transnat. Law 613 (1986).

[192] Paterson ibid at 325.   [193] ibid s 21(1).   [194] ibid.   [195] ibid s 20.
[196] ibid s 22(2)–(3).   [197] ibid s 23(1).

not implement it or, if it has been implemented, control of the Canadian business that is the subject of the investment must be relinquished through divestment.[198]

Compared with FIRA, the Investment Canada Act allows a wider range of inward investments to be made without approval, has lowered the criterion for approval from 'significant' to 'net' benefit, has shortened the review period and has located the centre of decision-making at ministerial level. However, these changes are not as radical a departure from the spirit of FIRA as they appear to be. Although the emphasis has shifted from investment control to investment promotion,[199] it is clear that the Canadian Government did not abandon its right to review investment it considers to be 'of national sensitivity or significance'.[200] Indeed, in a rare exercise of its powers under the 1985 Act, in June 1991 the Canadian Government turned down a proposal by Aerospatiale of France and Alenia of Italy to buy De Havilland of Canada from the US aerospace company Boeing unless certain assurances as to significant Canadian participation, continued research, and as to the long-term commercial viability of the Canadian company would be given.[201] More recently, a proposed amendment to the Investment Canada Act will introduce, if passed, national security review requirements similar to those found in US law.[202] Furthermore, the 1985 Act contains little to protect the investor's rights against a decision of the minister to refuse permission for a proposed investment. First, despite removing decision-making power from the cabinet the Act has retained the confidentiality provisions of FIRA almost intact.[203] Thus disclosure to the investor remains limited. Secondly, while there is a statutory right of appeal against court orders made against the investor under s 40 of the 1985 Act, there is no corresponding right to judicial review of a ministerial decision to refuse approval for an investment. According to Paterson, the investor is left to the general law on judicial review, where it might be extremely difficult to make out a case in view of the tradition of not giving reasons for the disallowance of an investment.[204] Thirdly, the drafting and structure of the Act leaves much to be desired in terms of clarity. The giving of advice on the basis of the Act is difficult, and therefore compliance costs are likely to be high. Equally, legal planning may avoid the review process, again at cost to the investor.[205]

The above mentioned examples of 'screening laws' share certain essential features in common. They all use a specialized investment review agency, or governmental office, to deal with the administration of the host state's foreign investment policy, with final decision-making power being located either with the agency or with a higher level of government. The decision-making process tends to

---

[198] ibid s 24.

[199] The original version of the 1985 Act contained statutory duties placed upon the minister to encourage business investment in Canada: s 5(1). These were repealed in 1995.

[200] Glover et al above n 178 at 98.

[201] 'Canada Blocks de Havilland Sale to European Groups' *Financial Times* 21 June 1991 23.

[202] See House of Commons Canada Bill C–59 1st Session 38th Parliament 53–54 Elizabeth II 2004–2005.   [203] See Paterson above n 174 at 331 and s 36 of the 1985 Act.

[204] Paterson ibid at 334.   [205] See further Grover above n 178 at 480–81.

be highly discretionary, and is commonly exercised in the absence of effective judicial review against the decisions unfavourable to the foreign investor. This problem, mentioned in the context of the Canadian legislation, is common to many jurisdictions.[206]

Arguably judicial review is inappropriate in such cases. Major investment decisions may be unique given variations in the nature of the foreign investor, the size and characteristics of the proposed investment and the industrial sector involved. Thus a case-by-case approach is almost inevitable, and a clear indication as to the likelihood of a proposal being accepted may not always be possible. Nevertheless, there are few safeguards against the unreasonable exercise of ministerial or administrative discretion in national investment laws. Host states wishing to encourage inward investment, but, equally, wishing to retain a foreign investment screening procedure, could consider offering rights of judicial review to investors against unfavourable decisions by the screening authorities. Additionally, clear administrative guidelines should be issued from which investors could reasonably predict what the response of host state authorities to a particular proposal would be. The investment promotion literature of the host state should serve to fill this role. In the absence of positive national remedies, investors may use the provisions of bilateral investment agreements, where these apply to pre-entry treatment, to bring claims under their protective provisions against acts of abuse of discretion in the screening process.[207]

Concluding Remarks

This chapter has described the major techniques of inward investment control that have been used by host states to prevent the domination of their national economies by foreign investors. Such techniques were at the forefront of the policy response to MNEs in the 1970s, when levels of foreign investment in host state economies were reasonably high and considerations of economic nationalism and self-determination were at their highest. However, as the international division of labour evolves so the cost of economic nationalism is perceived to be too great to sustain, given the resulting loss of access both to investment capital and to the most modern productive technology. Increasingly, both economically advanced and less developed countries are turning away from the strict regulation of foreign ownership and control of investment and are permitting such investment on less stringent terms. The progressive liberalization of indigenization laws is perhaps the best example of this trend. Similarly, investment screening laws are being applied less restrictively. Furthermore, the policies of outright prohibition of foreign investment pursued in the past by socialist states are virtually obsolete. Given

---

[206] See, for further examples, Seidman 'Foreign Private Investors and the Host Country' 19 JWTL 637 at 651–54 (1985).

[207] See further chs 15–18 below for a full analysis of the scope of investor protection under IIAs.

the widespread adoption of privatization programmes, the range of industrial sectors reserved for public ownership is decreasing and a corresponding increase in investment opportunities is being created. While reservations and controls over levels of foreign investment in privatized companies are a common feature of such programmes, in many countries the very purpose of privatization is to increase the overall level of inward foreign investment in the economy. Thus privatization policies are clearly within the trend towards liberalization of foreign investment even though they offer good examples of controls over foreign ownership.

The remaining prohibitions on foreign investment are to be found in sectors of the national economy relevant to national security. In this connection, the question remains whether states are willing to extend the meaning of 'national security' to include 'national economic security'. This offers a possible future avenue for protectionism in an otherwise increasingly deregulated environment for foreign investment.

6

Measures for the Encouragement of
Inward Direct Investment

This chapter continues the analysis of specialized investment laws and goes beyond issues of control towards issues of promotion of foreign investment. It is arguable that the techniques used to promote inward investment are now more significant than techniques of control. Indeed, data from UNCTAD appears to confirm that most changes in investment laws are towards greater liberalization than restriction, notwithstanding the continued use of restrictions by most countries for strategic purposes.[1] Against this background the chapter looks, first, at host state techniques for ensuring open access for investors and for encouraging investment through incentives. Secondly, it goes beyond unilateral measures taken by host states and looks at bilateral, regional and multilateral initiatives for the liberalization of controls over entry and establishment by foreign investors, as expressed in various international legal agreements and instruments. These developments act as a source of restraint on the absolute sovereignty of nation states over the entry and establishment of foreign investors within their jurisdiction. They signify a voluntary acceptance of internationally sanctioned rights of entry and establishment that will bind not only the governments that accept such restrictions but also subsequent governments for so long as they choose to adhere to the international agreements in question.

(1) The Encouragement of Inward Direct Investment
by Host States

This section will consider the principal techniques used by host states seeking to ensure an 'open door' to foreign investors. The prerequisite for such an approach is the absence of onerous administrative measures for the approval of foreign

---

[1] See UNCTAD *World Investment Report 2005* (New York and Geneva: United Nations, 2005) at 22 where it is noted that, in 2004, a total of 271 measures were adopted by 102 economies of which the vast majority (87 per cent) tended to make conditions more favourable for foreign companies to enter and to operate. This general trend has continued in 2005–06 except in Latin America where more restrictive laws have been passed in a small number of countries mainly in the natural resources sector

investments and the general absence of ownership, control, or performance requirements as a condition of entry. In addition to the absence of such controls, certain states may offer investment incentives in the form of new opportunities for investment as a result of deregulation and privatization policies, fiscal, or other benefits associated with inward investment, and the creation of special economic zones for export-orientated investment. The content of national laws in areas relevant to foreign investors, such as planning regulations, corporate disclosure requirements or labour relations, may also be framed in a manner that is attractive to their interests. As noted in the previous chapter, where applicable, investment approval procedures may also be simplified and concentrated in 'one-stop' investment agencies.[2] These may also engage in investment promotion activity.[3] Finally, states may offer constitutional guarantees for the peaceful enjoyment of private property and may reinforce these by the conclusion of Bilateral Investment Treaties (BITs), or Free Trade Agreements (FTAs) with investment provisions, which subject the host contracting state's treatment of investors from the other contracting state to the international minimum standards of treatment contained in the treaty.[4] However, as shown in the previous chapter, even in states espousing an 'open door' to foreign investors, there are likely to be sectors that are excluded from foreign investment. Furthermore, in the absence of privileged concessions, foreign investors will be subjected to the principle of 'national treatment'[5] and will be expected to follow the general commercial and other applicable laws of the land. In this sense, foreign investors are never absolutely free to invest or act as they please. Finally, it should be stressed that 'open door' policies may be espoused by states following a policy of high governmental regulation in the economy. In this sense, the techniques described below are not exclusively associated with free-market economies.

(a) Host States Without Specialized Controls on Inward Direct Investment

Numerous states have adopted an 'open door' policy on inward direct investment.[6] In particular, the member states of the OECD have pledged themselves to the progressive removal of restrictions on inward investment under the Code for

---

(Venezuela, Chile, Bolivia) or as a result of economic emergency measures (Argentina): see UNCTAD *World Investment Report: 2006* (New York and Geneva: United Nations, 2006) at 23–25.

² See Alvin G Wint 'Promoting Transnational Investment: Organising to Service Approved Investors' 2 Transnational Corporations 71 (No 1, 1993).

³ See UNCTAD *The World of Investment Promotion at a Glance* (New York and Geneva: United Nations, 2002).   ⁴ See further ch 17 below.

⁵ On which see further ch 16 below.

⁶ For examples of developing countries espousing an 'open door' approach, see examples in the previous chapter and see also Seidman 'Foreign Private Investors and the Host Country' 19 JWTL 637 at 638–42 (1985). On early post-independence 'open door' policies in Nigeria, see Megwa 'Foreign Direct Investment Climate in Nigeria: The Changing Law and Development Policies' 21 Col. J. Transnat. L. 487 at 488 (1983).

the Liberalization of Capital Movements.[7] The majority of the OECD states espouse this approach, although not without reservations. Of these the UK and US have among the most liberal regimes.

The UK has traditionally welcomed inward direct investment under successive Conservative and Labour administrations.[8] Since the 1980s policy has swung decisively towards the encouragement of inward investment. In 1979, the then newly elected Conservative government suspended controls over inward capital movements under the Exchange Control Act of 1947.[9] The Exchange Control Act was itself repealed in 1987, thereby removing the most significant restrictions on inward and outward investment under English law. The only remaining powers relevant to the control of inward investment were those given to the Secretary of State for Trade and Industry under the scheme of 'golden shares' in privatized companies and under the Industry Act of 1975, both discussed in the previous chapter, and under the merger control provisions of the Fair Trading Act 1973, now superseded by the 2002 Enterprise Act, which may be used to prevent the takeover of a British company by a foreign investor where this is deemed to constitute a potential abuse of a dominant market position. These powers will be considered in chapter 10 below. The general policy of the UK Government is outlined as follows in the Department of Trade and Industry (DTI) White Paper on Trade and Investment of 2004:

Openness to foreign investment is also important. Research published in 2003 identified the UK as being the OECD country most open to foreign investment, and having the lowest number of restrictions imposed on inward investors ... Many investors cite the lack of barriers to entry as an important factor in persuading them to choose the UK over international competitors. Together with our business friendly environment, this has helped the UK to be the number one inward investment destination in the EU in recent years. With the internationalisation of business increasing, the Government is determined to maintain the UK as a top destination for inward investment. This means maintaining and building on our existing strengths, of economic stability and openness to investment, while recognising that over recent years, as with trade activity, the nature of inward investment into the UK has changed. There is now more investment in higher value activities, not exclusively but most notably in the 'knowledge driven' sectors. Inward investment also encompasses a range of activities from the physical setting up of a business, through to the various kinds of collaboration and joint venture that are now commonplace. The help and

---

[7] See further below at nn 190–207.

[8] See, for the period 1964–70 and a brief discussion of the 1970–74 Conservative government, Michael Hodges *Multinational Corporations and National Governments: A Case Study in the United Kingdom's Experience 1964–70* (Farnborough: Saxon House, 1974); for the 1974–79 Labour government and the early years of the Conservative government of the 1980s, see AM Gamble and SA Walkland *The British Party System and Economic Policy 1945–83* (Oxford: Clarendon Press, 1984) 132–40. See further M Brech and M Sharp *Inward Investment: Policy Options for the United Kingdom* (Chatham House Papers No 21 RIIA/RKP 1984); J Stopford and L Turner *Britain and the Multinationals* (IRM/Wiley, 1985) especially chs 6, 7, and 9.

[9] See Part III of the Exchange Control Act 1947; suspended by SI 1979/1333 and SI 1979/1660. See Hodges ibid at 76–86 for an analysis of the regulatory scheme under the 1947 Act.

advice the Government can offer to potential inward investors will continue to develop, to match as closely as possible the needs of individual companies.'[10]

As noted by the DTI, British policy on inward investment has involved not only the removal of regulatory barriers but also the positive encouragement of investors through the activities of public agencies. This has involved regional and national investment promotion agencies, the selective use of industrial aid, and the setting up of enterprise zones and free ports. These will be considered in more detail in the next section below.

Like the UK, the US adopts an 'open door' to inward investment on the ground that free market forces in the global circulation of capital promote economic efficiency and should be encouraged.[11] The freedom of entry and establishment into the US is enshrined in the network of Friendship Commerce and Navigation Treaties concluded since the Second World War by the US with its principal trading partners from among the developed nations.[12] This freedom is protected in FCN Treaties by the principle of 'national treatment', whereby the foreign corporation is entitled to the same treatment within the US as is accorded in like situations to US corporations.[13] This includes the right to form a locally incorporated subsidiary, which will then enjoy the same rights, and be subject to the same duties, as a US corporation. FCN treaties do not provide for treatment better than national treatment for the US subsidiaries of foreign MNEs, but merely assure to them 'the right to conduct business on an equal basis without suffering discrimination based on their alienage'.[14] Such treaties can override conflicting provisions of US law as they are generally deemed to be 'self-executing', thereby possessing the force of a superior rule of law within the US legal system.[15]

---

[10] DTI, UK Trade and Investment White Paper *Making Globalisation a Force for Good* (London: DTI, Cm 6278, July 2004) available at <http://www.dti.gov.uk/europeandtrade/trade-policy/t-i-white-paper/page23431.html>.

[11] See UNCTC *National Legislation and Regulations Relating to Transnational Corporations Volume VII* (New York: 1989 UN Doc ST/CTC/91) 280. See generally R Turcon *Foreign Direct Investment in the United States* (London: Sweet & Maxwell, 1993) and Philip I Blumberg, Kurt A Strasser, Nicholas Georgakopoulos, and Eric J Gouvin *Blumberg on Corporate Groups* (New York: Aspen Publishers, 2005) vol 4 ch 151.

[12] FCN Treaties are no longer concluded, having been superseded in relation to developing countries by BITs. See further ch 17 below.

[13] The principle is also guaranteed under the right of equal protection under US laws to resident aliens. See *Bethlehem Motors v Flynt* 256 US 421 (1921). See also D Vagts 'The United States of America and the Multinational Enterprise' in HR Hahlo et al (eds) *Nationalism and the Multinational Enterprise* (Sijthoff: Oceana, 1977) see from 3 especially 15–16.

[14] See *Sumitomo Shoji America Ltd v Avagliano* 21 ILM 970 at 976–77 (1982); 638 F 2d 552 (2d Cir 1981) *vacated* 457 US 176 (1982). For the view that this case was wrongly decided, in that the FCN treaty guaranteed the freedom to manage to Japanese investors, see Ishizuka 86 Col.LR 139 (1986).

[15] See *Kalamazoo Spice Extraction Co v The Provisional Military Government of Socialist Ethiopia* (US 6th Cir 1984) 729 F 2d 422 (1984); 78 AJIL 902 (1984); 23 ILM 393 at 398–99 (1984). However, on the basis of the *Sumitomo* case (above n 14) it appears that FCN treaties cannot override fundamental civil rights, in that case the right against discrimination in the workplace on the ground of gender. See further ch 12 at 482.

On the other hand, as seen in the previous chapter, the 'open door' principle is not unqualified under US law. Legal restrictions on foreign ownership in given sectors,[16] and the controls imposed by the Exon-Florio amendment,[17] have been introduced. Furthermore, foreign investors face not inconsiderable levels of regulation under US domestic laws in accordance with the principle of 'national treatment' and permissible exceptions thereto. Thus, the investor is subject to disclosure requirements in the areas of company law, securities regulation, and taxation.[18] Specialized disclosure requirements cover acquisitions of agricultural land by foreign investors under the Agricultural Foreign Investment Disclosure Act 1978.[19] Furthermore, foreign investors are subject to specific reporting requirements under the International Investment and Trade in Services Survey Act of 1976.[20] By this statute, a foreign national or corporate entity or other foreign person who creates buys or sells a 10 per cent or greater voting interest in a US business enterprise, or in US real estate, must submit a report to the Bureau of Economic Analysis of the Department of Commerce. The report must be filed within 45 days of the acquisition being made and must contain information as to: the legal interest established or transferred; the identity of the transferor, the transferee, and the beneficial owner of the interest; the enterprise or property in which the interest is held; the management and financial structure of the US affiliate and the composition of its debts, assets, and income; and, finally, the extent of transnational trade in goods or services conducted or to be conducted by the US affiliate.[21] In addition to such transactional reporting requirements, the 1976 Act introduced a duty to make annual reports and five yearly reports on the investment.[22] A quarterly report is required from any US affiliate exceeding an exemption level of $10m.[23] Thus, US disclosure requirements recognize the special need for information concerning the acquisition of US enterprises by foreign investors.[24] However, even with these requirements, the US remains one of the most open economies in the world.

(b) Investment Incentives

States often employ incentives to attract internationally mobile foreign investors. These may be available only after the official approval of a project by the relevant screening agency, or they may be available as of right once the foreign investor has

---

[16] Listed in ch 5 n 12 at 180.   [17] See ibid at 181–82.

[18] UNCTC above n 11 at 301–303; Scarborough 'The Foreign Investor in the United States: Disclosure, Taxation and Visa Laws' 19 Int'l Law 85 (1985). See further ch 9 (disclosure) and ch 7 (taxation).

[19] Pub L No 95–460 92 Stat 1263 (1978); 7 USC ss 3501–3508 (1994). See Scarborough ibid at 94–97; UNCTC ibid at 302.

[20] Pub L No 94–472 90 Stat 2059 (1976) 22 USC ss 3101–3108 (2003). See Scarborough ibid at 87–94; UNCTC ibid at 301.   [21] 22 USC s 3104 (b).

[22] 22 USC s 3103(b).   [23] Introduced in 1984: 49 Fed Reg 3174.

[24] The data collection process under this legislation was rationalized in 1990: see further Edward M Graham and Paul R Krugman *Foreign Direct Investment in the United States* (Washington DC: 3rd edn, 1995) Appendix A.

decided to invest. The justification for incentives is twofold. First, they may reduce risk to investors, thereby making the host state more attractive to them as a location for investment and, secondly, they may encourage investors to act in certain ways that might be desirable from the perspective of the host country, as where subsidies for local training, research and development activity, or the creation of new jobs, are offered. These goals can be achieved either through direct subsidies (eg waiver of export or import duties, concessions from indirect taxes, rates or other charges, or industrial development grants) or by way of income tax incentives.[25] Other types of incentives may be offered in the form of lower regulatory standards, infrastructure improvements and market concessions.[26] Such policies are likely to be favoured by countries that would otherwise be of marginal interest to foreign investors on purely economic grounds.

One of the pioneers of an incentive led inward investment policy has been the Republic of Ireland. Since 1958, the Republic has offered fiscal incentives to manufacturers.[27] Currently, the tax rate applicable to all corporate trading profits is 12.5 per cent. In addition, provided that a trade qualified for a 10 per cent maximum corporate tax rate for manufacturing profits before 30 July 1998, that rate can still apply until 31 December 2010. The maximum rate for non-trading profits is 25 per cent.[28] This has resulted in Ireland being used by foreign MNEs as a 'tax haven' jurisdiction. MNEs have structured their operations so as to take full advantage of the lower tax rates, either by the use of offshore holding companies controlling an unincorporated entity in Ireland, thereby allowing Irish profits to be reinvested abroad without subjection to tax in the home state of the parent company, or by using international transfer pricing manipulations to inflate the profits of Irish subsidiaries.[29] In 2004 legislation was passed to enable an Irish

---

[25] See further Y Hadari 'The Role of Tax Incentives in Attracting Foreign Investments in Selected Developing Countries and the Desirable Policy' 24 Int'l Law 121 at 125–29 (1990). A good example of a country using tax incentives to attract inward direct investment is Israel. See G Klugman *Transnational Taxation of Foreign Investments in Israel* (Yacov, Salomon, Lipschutz & Co, 1992) ch 2.

[26] See UNCTAD *Incentives* Series on issues in international investment agreements (New York and Geneva: United Nations, 2004) at 5.

[27] See the Industrial Development (Encouragement of External Investment) Act 1958.

[28] See Industrial Development Authority, Ireland, *A Guide to Tax in Ireland* (October 2005) at 2, available at <http://www.idaireland.com/uploads/documents/IDA_Publications/IDA_Tax_Brochure_2005.pdf>. On what constitutes 'trading' for tax purposes, see Irish Revenue Authority *Guidance Note* available at <http://www.revenue.ie/doc/trade.doc> (accessed 22 June 2006). In relation to corporate groups, the *Guidance Note* states: 'Where a company seeking trading status is a member of a group and another group company or companies have an involvement in the conduct of the particular trade, Revenue would need to be satisfied as to the role of the various companies. In particular the company seeking trading status in respect of an activity must establish that it carries on sufficient activity to be trading in its own right. Evidence in relation to the levels of authority and responsibility across the group will clarify where the real decision-making lies, and information in relation to the deployment of assets and personnel will clarify the business activities carried on by each company. An explanation of the commercial reasoning and the business objectives behind a particular group structure will be helpful in understanding the underlying strategic business purpose and the value added by the applicant company.'

[29] See T Hadden 'Controlling the Multinationals: Experience in Ireland and Abroad' paper read at a conference on 'Multinationals in Ireland', Faculty of Law, University College, Galway, Ireland 13 June 1986.

company to act as a European or regional holding or intermediate holding company. The changes relate to the treatment of capital gains and foreign dividends. In relation to the former, Irish holding companies are allowed an exemption from capital gains tax on the disposal of shares in their subsidiaries provided the company holds at least 5 per cent of the shares of another company. In relation to the latter, the receipt of foreign dividends is normally taxed at a rate of 25 per cent, but this liability can be reduced by the foreign underlying tax already paid on this income. There is a unilateral tax credit for underlying foreign tax provided there is a 5 per cent shareholding relationship between the companies. In addition, 'onshore pooling', allows the foreign dividends to be pooled together, before they are offset against the Irish tax liability. The tax credits do not need to be utilized in the year that the dividend is received. They can be carried forward indefinitely or offset against Irish tax on future foreign dividends.[30]

Similarly, Singapore has offered incentives to foreign manufacturers since the 1960s. At that time the government adopted a growth strategy based on an expansion of export-orientated manufacturing dominated by MNE investors.[31] To achieve this objective, the government established free zones offering tariff, tax, and regulatory reliefs to businesses located therein. These zones permitted firms to trade without restriction with the rest of the world, to process goods for export at low cost and to benefit from offshore banking facilities free from exchange controls. In addition, the government established tax incentives for so-called 'pioneer industries' to set up new capital and technology intensive projects in the country. Other tax allowances were made available as incentives for, among other things, expansion of investments or exports, for the setting up of technical service and research and development activities or for construction projects.[32]

Economically developed countries may use investment incentives to attract internationally mobile investors to the less developed regions of the country. UK policy in this field offers a good illustration. Selective assistance to foreign and domestic investors is available both on a local and regional level. The basic approach is to provide financial incentives through discretionary grants and aids to industry, as well as selective concessions on fiscal and other legal obligations that would otherwise extend to the investor. In this there is an element of industrial planning aimed at alleviating the economic and social problems caused by the decline of

---

[30] See Finance Act 2004 ss 31, 34, and 42 available at <http://www.finance.gov.ie/documents/publications/legi/financeact04.pdf> summarized at <http://www.idaireland.com/home/index.aspx?id=659> (visited 22 June 2006).

[31] See further Hafiz Mirza *Multinationals and the Growth of the Singapore Economy* (Croom Helm, 1986) ch 3.

[32] For the current incentive regime, see *Investor's Guide to Singapore* (published annually by the Singapore Chamber of Commerce); see further <http://www.sicc.com.sg/public_index.html>. See also UNCTAD *Tax Incentives and Foreign Direct Investment: A Global Survey* (New York and Geneva: United Nations, 2000) at 95–97. This study contains summaries of the tax incentive regimes for over 45 countries in all regions of the world. See also UNCTAD *World Investment Report 2002* (New York and Geneva: United Nations, 2002) at 206–207 for a summary of the Malaysian policy on targeted investment incentives.

traditional industries in certain regions and cities of the UK. These powers are subject to control under European Community rules concerning state aids to industry and should be considered alongside EU regional aid provisions.

At the local level, local authorities are empowered under s 2 (1) of the Local Government Act 2000 to promote the economic, social, and environmental well-being of their areas.[33] The power under subsection (1) includes power for a local authority to incur expenditure, give financial assistance to any person, enter into arrangements or agreements with any person, cooperate with, or facilitate or coordinate the activities of, any person, exercise on behalf of any person any functions of that person, and provide staff, goods, services, or accommodation to any person.[34] Further assistance is available to reclaim derelict land under the Derelict Land Act 1982.[35] There are also a number of schemes for inner city regeneration including local assistance in the creation of 'improvement areas' under the Inner Urban Areas Act 1978.[36] On the regional level, regional development agencies were set up in the 1970s for Scotland and Wales, following the pattern of the Industrial Development Board for Northern Ireland, to further economic development in their regions. These have since been replaced, respectively, by Scottish Enterprise,[37] the Welsh Assembly Government's Invest Wales Department,[38] and Invest Northern Ireland.[39] Each body operates its own investment incentives scheme, in accordance with national and regional legislation.[40] In this regard, Invest Northern Ireland is empowered to offer assistance which is more generous than that available for other regions of the UK, in view of the higher than average rates of unemployment in the region and the historical difficulties caused by the local political situation.[41] In 1999 the Labour government established eight new English Regional Development Agencies (RDAs), under the Regional Development Agencies Act 1998,[42] with a ninth being established in July 2000 for London

---

[33] Local Government Act 2000 (2000 Chapter 22) ss 2–5 available at <http://www.opsi.gov.uk/acts/acts2000/20000022.htm>.   [34] ibid s 2(4).

[35] Derelict Land Act 1982 (1982 Chapter 42).

[36] Inner Urban Areas Act 1978 (1978 Chapter 50).

[37] Established under the Enterprise and New Towns (Scotland) Act 1991 (1990 Chapter 35) s 1 available at <http://www.opsi.gov.uk/acts/acts1990/Ukpga_19900035_en_2.htm#mdiv1>.

[38] The powers of the Welsh Development Agency were transferred to the Welsh Assembly Government under the Government of Wales Act 1998 (1998 Chapter 38). See further the Welsh Assembly Government website at <http://new.wales.gov.uk/topics/businessandeconomy/?lang=en>.

[39] Established under the Industrial Development Act (Northern Ireland) 2002 (2002 Chapter 1) available at <http://www.opsi.gov.uk/legislation/northernireland/acts/acts2002/20020001.htm>. See also the Invest Northern Ireland website at <http://www.investni.com/index.htm>.

[40] See n 42 below.

[41] For example, pre-employment training grants of up to 50 per cent of training costs, and research and development grants of up to 50 per cent of costs are on offer, as are tailor-made grant and other support packages. See further Invest Northern Ireland 'Invest NI Services' at <http://www.investni.com/index/locate/lc-how-can-we-help/how_can_we_help_-_investni_services.htm> and PricewaterhouseCoopers *Doing Business in Northern Ireland: A Guide for Inward Investors* (2003) available at the Invest Northern Ireland website <http://www.investni.com/doingbusinessinni-aguideforinwardinvestors-3.pdf>.

[42] See the Regional Development Agencies Act 1998 (1998 Chapter 45) available at <http://www.opsi.gov.uk/acts/acts1998/19980045.htm>.

after the establishment of the Greater London Authority.[43] The RDAs were set up to ensure a more equal institutional structure for the encouragement of inward investment and local economic development in the English regions. This was motivated, in part, by the feeling that the non-English regions had an unfair advantage in this regard through the existence of regional agencies.[44]

For other regions of the UK the government offers assistance to areas, known as 'assisted areas', under s 7 of the Industrial Development Act 1982.[45] Assistance is currently provided thorough the Selective Finance for Investment in England (SFIE) scheme in England, and by the Regional Selective Assistance (RSA) scheme in Scotland and Wales.[46] Assistance is in the form of a discretionary grant made to an investor on the basis of a number of criteria, including a demonstrable need for assistance so that the project can go ahead.[47] This discretionary approach has replaced the original policy of the 1982 Act, the Regional Development Grant Scheme, which gave automatic assistance to projects located in assisted areas of up to 15 per cent of the cost of capital expenditure on new assets and £3000 for

---

[43] The nine regional development agencies are: the North West, Yorkshire, the North East, West Midlands, East Midlands, East of England, the South West, London, and the South East; see further <http://www.englandsrdas.com/home.aspx>.

[44] See further UK Government White Paper *Building Partnerships for Prosperity: Sustainable Growth, Competitiveness and Employment in the English Regions* Cm 3814 December 1997 and, for more recent developments, *RDA News* (November 1998 to present).

[45] See Industrial Development Act 1982. As a result of the devolution legislation (the Scotland Act 1998, the Government of Wales Act 1998 and SI 1999/672), from 1 July 1999 some powers under the Act have been exercised in Scotland by the First Minister of the Scottish Executive, in Wales by the First Minister of the National Assembly for Wales and, concurrently throughout the UK, by the Secretary of State for Trade and Industry.

[46] *Industrial Development Act: Annual Report 2005* (London: The Stationery Office, HC 207, 20 June 2005) at para 4.

[47] According to the *Annual Report 2005* (ibid) at para 5:

'5. Applications for both RSA and SFIE were assessed against the following criteria:

a) Location – Projects must have been undertaken in the Assisted Areas;

b) Need (additionality) – Applicants need to have demonstrated that a grant was necessary to enable the project to proceed;

c) Eligible investment – The project must have involved capital expenditure on fixed assets, such as property, plant and machinery. Expenditure could relate to expansion, modernising or the establishment of a new company;

d) Jobs – The project must have created or safeguarded sustainable long term jobs except in England where for cases below £100,000 this is optional. But projects which were likely to create overcapacity or which simply displaced jobs elsewhere in the UK, or aimed to relocate jobs from one part of the country to another, were not eligible for assistance;

e) Viability – Businesses and projects should have been viable; and the project would normally have been expected to become self sustaining within three years;

f) Quality – Four key factors were amongst those used to determine the quality of projects: wage levels, sustainable employment, value of R&D and training;

g) National and Regional benefit – All projects should have contributed positive benefits to both the regional and national economies;

h) Prior commitments – Project appraisal must have been completed and a formal offer of assistance issued before the applicant entered into a commitment to proceed with the project; and

i) Other funding – The greater part of the funding for the project should have been met by the applicant or come from other sources in the private sector.'

every new job created.[48] The application of assistance to designated assisted areas is subject to the regional aid rules of the EC.[49] The new European Commission guidelines on regional aid were adopted on 21 December 2005.[50] In the main, the new guidelines lower permitted limits on aid (as a percentage of eligible costs) compared with current guidelines. Different aid ceilings will apply in different categories of eligible areas across the Community. The guidelines also reduce the proportion of the EU population covered by areas where regional aid is permissible. They require that Member States submit regional aid maps to the Commission as soon as possible in order for a new map to be operational by 1 January 2007.

The principal danger with investment incentive policies is that they may, in fact, be ineffective in attracting useful, long-term investment. A foreign investor may be happy to take advantage of the host state's incentives, and, as soon as these run out, to disinvest. A major concern behind any investment incentive scheme should be, therefore, to avoid the encouragement of such short-term, opportunistic investment.[51] A balance must be sought between the legitimate reduction of high start-up costs for the foreign investor by means of incentives and a wasteful public subsidization of private gain. At heart, the decision to invest is still motivated by factors, such as market size and location, which cannot be altered by legislation. This should militate against over-generous incentives offered by countries that have good comparative advantages in such areas. The UK is taking such a market-orientated view through its selective approach to financial assistance and through making such assistance conditional upon the degree to which the foreign investor is willing to invest. The assistance offered to Nissan in the 1980s for its project to establish a car factory in North-East England offers the first illustration of this approach. Only if the project reached a specified output of cars would public finance become available to the Japanese firm.[52] On the other hand, the decision of

---

[48] See s 4(1)(a) Industrial Development Act 1982 as amended by the Co-operative Development Agency and Industrial Development Act 1984 s 5 and Schedule 1, and Statutory Instrument SI 1984/1845. Regional Development Grants were terminated after 31 March 1988 by the Regional Development Grants (Termination) Act 1988 (c 11 1988). The DTI's policy behind this change is explained in 'DTI: The Department for Enterprise' (Cm 278, 12 January 1988).

[49] See further State Aid Action Plan 'Less and better targeted state aid: a roadmap for state aid reform 2005–2009' (Consultation document), European Commission, 2005 and DTI *Review of the Assisted Areas Stage I Identifying Criteria* (DTI Consultation Paper 15 February 2006) available at <http://www.dti.gov.uk>.

[50] Guidelines on National Regional Aid for 2007–2013 (2006/C 54/08) OJ [2006] C54/13.

[51] The classic illustration of this was the willingness of the UK Government to offer generous grants to the late John de Lorean, to establish the De Lorean car plant in Northern Ireland. In 1978 £55 million was given by the then Labour government with a further £30 million given by the succeeding Thatcher government. The plant went bankrupt after one year of operation in 1982, having produced only 10,000 cars and most of the aid money had disappeared. See 'Maverick De Lorean Dies at 80' *The Guardian* 21 March 2005 at 1. See also, on the closure of the LG television plant in Newport South Wales, which benefited from Welsh Development Agency grants on its establishment in 1996, 'Wales Suffers as the Chips Go Down' *Financial Times* 4 September 2006 at 20.

[52] John Stopford and Louis Turner *Britain and the Multinationals* (Wiley/IRM, 1985) 239. The specified output of cars was reached and the money was provided: see *Financial Times* 15 December 1987 at 1.

the Toyota company to set up a car factory in Derbyshire attracted no assistance from the government, as this was regarded as unnecessary.[53] By contrast, countries such as Ireland or Singapore, that enjoy fewer natural comparative advantages as locations for foreign investment, can be expected to continue offering much greater incentives. However, even in such states, caution must be exercised against using public money without effect.

A further danger behind such incentive based policies is that they may lead to a distortion of the international economy. Competition over incentives to foreign investors amounts to a protectionist policy, especially when there is less internationally mobile capital to go round. Within the EC, state aids to investment will be contrary to the provisions of Article 87 of the Treaty of Rome where they interfere with trade between the EC Member States, and do not fall within the permissible categories of state aids listed in Article 87.[54] However, there exists no general international regulation of excessive public subsidies to investors. Thus, in the world economy as a whole, competition over investment incentives is likely to continue for so long as governments believe that fiscal and other incentives can compensate for the shortcomings of their states as locations for inward investment. This has an unfortunate effect on developing countries in particular. Such countries are less able to afford the foregoing of revenue or to have capital available to provide subsidies. However, they may feel compelled to undertake such strategies as part of an 'incentives race' with other potential locations for foreign investment, to their economic detriment.[55] In addition, while market distorting performance requirements are subject to international disciplines under the WTO Agreement on Trade Related Investment Measures (TRIMs), discussed below, and similar rules in other regional and bilateral agreements, investment incentives generally are not, save where export oriented trade subsidies are used to encourage export oriented investment. Such subsidies may be contrary to the WTO Agreement on Subsidies and Countervailing Measures.[56] Given that developing countries are more likely to apply performance requirements, or use export oriented trade subsidies,[57] while developed countries are more likely to apply locational and

---

[53] See 'Young Hails Investment Decision "landmark"' *Financial Times* 19 April 1989 at 12.

[54] For analysis of the applicable case law see AM Arnull, AA Dashwood, MG Ross, and DA Wyatt *Wyatt and Dashwood's European Union Law* (London: Sweet & Maxwell, 4th edn, 2000) ch 24. See also Case C–156/98 *Germany v Commission* ECJ judgment, 19 September 2000, available at <http://curia.europa.eu/> where the Court held that the tax based investment subsidies offered by the German Federal Government to investors in the Eastern *Länder* were not within the exceptions in Article 87 as they could not be directly linked to the economic disadvantage created by the earlier physical division of Germany. In the US the commerce clause of the US Constitution may help to regulate discriminatory state level incentives. However, the US Supreme Court recently denied standing to Ohio taxpayers who brought a claim under this clause; see *Daimler Chrysler v Cuno* No 04–1704 decided May 15 2006, 126 S Ct 1854; 164 L Ed 2d 589; 2006 US LEXIS 3956; 74 USLW 4233.

[55] See UNCTAD *World Investment Report 2003* (New York and Geneva: United Nations, 2003) at 128.   [56] See further UNCTAD *World Investment Report 2002* above n 32 at 208–13.

[57] UNCTAD suggests that the greater use of such export oriented subsidies by developing countries might make these countries more susceptible to countermeasures under the WTO Subsidies Agreement: ibid.

production oriented investment incentives, an imbalance in the regulation of market distorting investment policies remains, one that is more favourable to developed countries.[58]

(c) Export Processing Zones (EPZs) and Related 'Policy Enclaves' Within the Host State

The EPZ represents a specialized form of investment incentive regime that has played a significant role in the evolution of globalized production by MNEs. Accordingly, this type of policy instrument will be considered in some detail, commencing with its evolution and then concentrating on its main legal features. The economic effects of EPZs will then be briefly assessed. The section ends with a discussion of the Chinese Special Economic Zone (SEZ). This takes the EPZ concept to a higher level, in that an entire region of the country may apply the kinds of export friendly policies that EPZs use in a particular location.

(i) The Evolution of EPZs

Such a zone has been defined as 'a designated specialized industrial estate which produces mainly for export and which constitutes an enclave from the trade and customs regime of a country in which free trade applies'.[59] Thus, the EPZ is a legally defined 'policy enclave' within the host state's territory, to which a distinct regime of customs and trade regulations applies. This may be coupled with a package of investment incentives, designed to attract internationally mobile inward direct investment, preferably in the manufacturing sector.[60] Most EPZs are established and operated by public sector bodies. However, an increasing number are privately managed.[61]

---

[58] See further Thomas L Brewer and Stephen Young *The Multilateral Investment System and Multinational Enterprises* (Oxford: Oxford University Press, 1998) 191–92.

[59] ESCAP/UNCTC *An Evaluation of Export Processing Zones in Selected Asian Countries* (United Nations, ESCAP/UNCTC Publication Series B, No 8 1985) 1 (cited hereafter as ESCAP 1985). According to the ILO: 'The ILO has defined EPZs as "industrial zones with special incentives set up to attract foreign investors, in which imported materials undergo some degree of processing before being re-exported". With developments in information technology, "imported material" would also include "electronic data" today, as well as, call centres located in zones. EPZs have evolved from initial assembly and simple processing activities to include high tech and science parks, finance zones, logistics centres and even tourist resorts. Their physical form now includes not only enclave-type zones but also single-industry zones (such as the jewelry *[sic]* zone in Thailand or the leather zone in Turkey); single-commodity zones (like tea in Zimbabwe); and single-factory (such as the Export Oriented Units in India) or single-company zones (such as in the Dominican Republic).': <http://www.ilo.org/public/english/dialogue/sector/themes/epz.htm>. See also Michael Likosky *The Silicon Empire: Law Culture and Commerce* (Aldershot: Ashgate, 2005) ch 4 'Dual Legal Orders' tracing the history of policy enclaves and offering a detailed analysis of the EPZ concept. The remainder of the book assesses Malaysia's use of dual legal order strategies including, more recently, EPZ and science park policies in attracting high technology FDI in the information technology industry.

[60] See further Wall 'Export Processing Zones' 10 JWTL 478 (1976).

[61] See UNCTAD *World Investment Report 2002* above n 32 at 214 citing the example of the Philippines where 40 privately run economic zones have been established since 1995 under the

In essence, the EPZ has grown out of a compromise between two conflicting strategies of economic development pursued by developing countries. During the late 1960s and 1970s, numerous such countries adopted policies of import substituting industrial development, which aimed at the creation of an independent domestic industrial base by means of, inter alia, restrictions on imports and inward foreign investment. However, such policies were strongly biased against export activity. The result was that these countries failed to earn adequate returns on domestic investment. By way of response, in the 1970s, certain developing countries, not wishing to abandon import substituting policies entirely, introduced EPZs as a means of partial and limited liberalization.[62] The aim was to attract MNEs into the EPZ, by means of favourable customs regulations and other incentives, so that these firms would set up production facilities in the zone. From these, they would service global export markets in both finished and intermediate products. Thereby, it was believed, the host state could earn increased export earnings. Furthermore, investment in EPZs by MNEs was thought likely to bring further benefits in the form of increased employment opportunities, improved training and skills for the workforce and the transfer of modern productive technology.[63] However, as will be seen below, actual performance has not always lived up to these expectations.

The EPZ phenomenon has been viewed as an evolution of the ancient 'free port' concept.[64] This is correct so far as both approaches involve the creation of a 'policy enclave'. Nevertheless, a crucial difference between a 'Free Port' (or 'Free Trade Zone' (FTZ)) and an EPZ is that, while both are created by a special customs regime, the former aims mainly at the encouragement of free trade in finished products and commodities, while the latter is specifically concerned with encouraging export-orientated manufacturing investment. This is not to suggest that elements of a 'free port' cannot co-exist with an EPZ. Nevertheless, the aim of encouraging inward investment by MNEs has clearly been the dominant motive for setting up EPZs.

The first EPZ was established in Ireland in 1956 with the creation of the Shannon Free Zone around Shannon Airport.[65] However, the principal developments in this policy have occurred in developing countries, particularly in East Asia. Thus, inter alia, India, Taiwan, Malaysia, the Philippines, and South Korea have all adopted EPZs.[66] In Africa, the first EPZ was created in Mauritius in

---

Philippines Economic Zone Authority. For legal basis see H No 14295 S No.1061 Republic Act No 7916 Special Economic Zone Act of 1995 as amended by S No 1136 H N 5992 Republic Act No 8748: An Act Amending Republic Act No 7916 available at <http://www.peza.gov.ph/about_peza.htm>.

[62] See R Kumar *India's Export Processing Zones* (Delhi: OUP, 1989) 4–6.

[63] See further ESCAP 1985 above n 59 at 15–21.

[64] ESCAP 1985 ibid at 9–10. See also Likosky above n 59.

[65] On which see further Leslie Sklair 'Foreign Investment and Irish Development: A Study of the International Division of Labour in the Midwest Region of Ireland' Progress in Planning vol 29 at 149–217 (1988).

[66] See ESCAP 1985 above n 59 Table 1–7 at 45. See further Jean Pierre Singa Boyenge *Database on Export Processing Zones* (Geneva: ILO, Sectoral Activities Department, 2003) for a comprehensive

1970.[67] Other Sub-Saharan countries have since established EPZs.[68] In North Africa, Egypt has established similar zones as part of its *infitah* (open door) policy.[69] In Latin America Puerto Rico was the first to adopt the EPZ concept in 1962.[70] In Mexico, a unique policy based on EPZ principles has emerged as a means of stimulating industrial development along the US-Mexican border. US firms have, for some years, been taking advantage of conditions in ss 806.30 and 807 of the US Tariff Schedule. These allow for the export of goods from the US for assembly abroad and for their reimportation at favourable rates of tariff, in that import duties are only levied on the value added abroad.[71] These regulations have made it profitable for US firms to export labour-intensive production activities to low labour-cost areas. The low labour costs attract low reimportation tariffs due to the low value added. Indeed, such tariff concessions may be seen as a significant home country contribution to the growth of EPZs in developing countries. In 1965, the Mexican Government introduced the Border Industrialization Programme, so as to encourage US industrial investors to exploit this concession in US tariffs by locating labour-intensive production in Mexico. Special customs concessions were introduced for the importation of parts and raw materials required for the processing, assembly, and finishing of products destined entirely for export,

survey of EPZs around the world. On India's EPZs see Kumar above n 62 and see also the Special Economic Zones policy, which was introduced in 2000; see <http://sezindia.nic.in/>.

[67] See Mauritius Export Processing Zone Act (No 51) 1970 as amended by Acts Nos 50 of 1975 and 13 of 1980. See further PG Alter *Export Processing Zones for Growth and Development: The Mauritian Example* (1990); P Hein 'Structural Transformation in an Island Country: The Mauritius Export Processing Zone (1971 to 1988)' 1 UNCTAD Rev. 41 (No 2, 1989). See further the Enterprise Mauritius website <http://www.epzda.intnet.mu>.

[68] These include Senegal, Liberia, Ghana, Zaire, Togo and Madagascar, Cameroon, and Kenya. For details, see UNCTAD *Export Processing Free Zones of Sub-Saharan Africa* (UNCTAD/ECDC/ 225, 1992) and the *ILO Database* above n 66. See also Nigeria Export Processing Zones Decree 1991 (Decree No 34 13 June 1991) repealed and replaced by Nigeria Export Processing Zones Decree (No 63 1992) of 19 November 1992: Federal Republic of Nigeria *Official Gazette* No 62 vol 79 of 1992. This decree empowers the President of Nigeria to designate areas of the country as EPZs. It also establishes the Nigeria Export Processing Zones Authority (NEPZA) to manage, control, and coordinate all activities within the zones. The authority has control over all goods deposited or manufactured in the zones and power to demarcate areas within the zones as customs territory. The first Nigerian EPZ was set up in Calabar, the capital of Cross River State. See 'Goose with the Golden Egg' *Newswatch Magazine* 16 March 1992 at 29. See further NEPZA *Investment Procedures, Regulations and Operational Guidelines for Free Zones in Nigeria 2004* available at <http://www.nepza.org/downloads/NEPZA %20FREE%20ZONE%20REGULATIONS.pdf>.

[69] See Law No 8 of May 11 1997 Promulgating the Law on Investment Guarantees and Incentives in ICSID *Investment Laws of the World* (Dobbs Ferry: Oceana) vol II Release 97–2 issued October 1997. See, for preceding laws, Law No 230 for 1989 of 20 July 1989: unofficial English translation in 4 ICSID Rev-FILJ at 376–95 (1989); comment by Marchais ibid at 297. For a discussion of the origins and effects of the original Free Zones established under Law 43 of 1974, see L Sklair 'The Costs of Foreign Investment: The Case of the Egyptian Free Zones' in Elie Kedourie and Sylvia G Haim (eds) *Essays on the Economic History of the Middle East* (London: Frank Cass, 1988) 132. See further General Authority for Investment and Free Zones (GAFI) website at <http://www.gafi.gov.eg/ docs/freezones.htm>.   [70] ESCAP 1985 above n 59 at 10.

[71] See N Hood and S Young *The Economics of Multinational Enterprise* (London: Longmans, 1979) 207.

within a 20 kilometre strip parallel to the international border or to the coastline.[72] Since the 1960s the in-bonded factories of the so-called *maquila* industry have extended hundreds of miles inland from the border, thereby straining the 'enclave' character of the original border zone.[73]

(ii) The Principal Legal and Administrative Features of EPZs in Developing Host States

The most important legal and administrative features of an EPZ are: the applicable incentive regime and facilities offered to investors; pre- and post-entry administrative procedures; and the relationship between the EPZ and the rest of the host state referred to as the Domestic Tariff Area (DTA). Each will be considered in turn.

The major incentives offered in EPZs relate to tax exemptions and duty-free imports. These are usually supplemented by exemptions from import quotas and the freedom to import capital and to remit profits. There may also be non-fiscal financial incentives such as export allowances or subsidized interest rates.[74] Where the host country has a comparative advantage in the production of commodities for which there is a world demand, such incentives should be enough to attract the required investment. However, in certain cases it may be necessary to develop the infrastructure required for the desired industries to evolve.[75] Thus, many EPZ projects include the provision of facilities in the form of transport links, factory buildings, commercial services and housing and social services for the workforce. In areas of low population, it may also be necessary to bring in workers from other regions.[76] The development of such facilities is particularly characteristic of EPZs that are aimed at the industrialization of underdeveloped regions of the host state.[77]

Of especial significance to the evolution of EPZs is the harnessing of the major locational advantage of less developed host states, namely, low-cost labour. Thus, the legal control of labour relations within the EPZ acquires considerable importance as a means of preserving this advantage. Consequently, it is not uncommon to find that the employment rights of workers, and the right to establish trade unions or to take industrial action, are more limited within the EPZ than in the DTA.[78] This has led to debate over the benefits of EPZs for the local workforce.

---

[72] See Leslie Sklair *Assembling for Development: The Maquila Industry in Mexico and the United States* (Unwin Hyman, 1989, updated US publication by the Center for US-Mexican Studies, University of California, San Diego, 1993) 45.

[73] See Sklair ibid ch 7. The *maquila* system is governed by the decree for the Promotion and Operation of the Maquiladora Manufacturing and Export Services Industry 1 November 2006 available on payment at <http://www.mexicanlaws.com/scfi/maquiladora_decree.htm>.

[74] ESCAP 1985 above n 59 at 21–27. See also UNCTC *Transnational Corporations in World Development Trends and Prospects* (New York: 1988, UN Doc ST/CTC/89) Box XVII.2 at 274–75. (cited hereafter as UNCTC 1988).   [75] Wall above n 60 at 481.

[76] See ESCAP above n 59 at 30–32.

[77] See eg the Kandla Free Trade Zone in India described by Kumar above n 62 at 36–37; the Bataan EPZ in the Philippines described in ESCAP 1985 above n 59 at 220–45.

[78] ESCAP 1985 at 33. See further International Confederation of Free Trade Unions, Trade Unions and the Transnationals, Information Bulletin, Special Issue No 3. 'Export Processing Zones'

On the one hand, the restriction of labour rights is seen as a disadvantage, while, on the other, the compensating advantage of new employment, often at higher rates of pay than those experienced in the DTA,[79] is emphasized.[80] Further controversy has also centred on the fact that the majority of workers in EPZs are young, single, females. It has been suggested that this may depress overall wage rates and create a more docile workforce, less inclined to espouse trade union membership, which, traditionally, has been geared to male concerns. On the other hand, women may in fact have opportunities for employment and pay within the EPZ that far surpass anything they could otherwise have expected.[81]

It is common for the administrative regime of an EPZ to establish eligibility criteria for investments. Most often, these include a combination of one or more of the following: the export-orientation of the investment; limited or no local equity participation; substantial foreign capital investment; significant local content in production; employment promotion effects and possibilities for technology transfer.[82] The authorization required for entry into the EPZ will usually be within the power of a specialized agency set up to administer the EPZ on behalf of the host state government. Some countries have a central authority for this purpose.[83] Others have established separate authorities for the administration of EPZs.[84] Ideally, the relevant authority will have sufficient links with government departments to enable it to act as a 'one-stop' service for the foreign investor, thereby reducing administrative inconvenience. In this way the EPZ authority can be used to bypass bureaucratic delays. Apart from administering the entry of foreign investors, the authority will usually have responsibility for the provision of infrastructure and services within the EPZ, the promotion and marketing of investment opportunities within the zone, and the recruitment of workers. The funds for developing and operating EPZs usually come from central government. Thus, in order to be successful, an EPZ should generate returns over and

(ICFTU, Brussels, 1983) especially paras 35–55. See, for a discussion of the position in India's EPZs, Kumar above n 62 at 112–23.

[79] Per contra, Kumar shows that wage rates in the Indian EPZs are in fact only two-thirds of those in the DTA: ibid at 120–21.

[80] See further Leslie Sklair *Globalization Capitalism and its Alternatives* (Oxford: Oxford University Press, 3rd edn, 2002) at 128–32.

[81] UNCTC 1988 above n 74 Box XIII.2 at 216; however, see ILO Committee on Employment and Social Policy *Employment and Social Policy in Export Processing Zones* (ILO Doc GB.286/ESP/3 286th Session Governing Body Geneva, March 2003) at para 11: 'Export-led industrialization has been strongly female-intensive, with no developing country having increased manufacturing exports without greater recourse to women workers. 16 Zones have created an important avenue for young women to enter the formal economy at better wages than in agriculture and domestic service. Women make up the majority of workers in the vast majority of zones, reaching up to 90 per cent in some of them. However, there is a suggestion that as the nature of employment in zones evolves, with higher technology inputs, the gender profile of the workforce changes.'

[82] ESCAP 1985 above n 59 at 33–34.

[83] Eg South Korea and Thailand: ESCAP 1985 ibid at 34.

[84] See ibid at 35–38 for a comparative analysis.

above the public funds provided. Whether this is the case will be considered in sub-section (iii) below.

As noted earlier, the essential feature of an EPZ is its status as an enclave within the host state bounded by a distinct customs regime. In effect, the EPZ is outside the territory of the host state for trade and investment purposes. Thus, a common feature of EPZs is that they are bounded by two frontiers: the political, fiscal, and excise frontier between the host state and the rest of the world, and an internal fiscal and excise frontier between the zone and the rest of the host state (the DTA). This has significant effects upon the manner in which relations between the EPZ and DTA are arranged. In order to preserve the enclave status of the EPZ, certain states have, as already noted, specified the total or partial exclusion of local capital from investment in the EPZ, although the policies of individual states differ in this respect. More significantly, the local authorities must ensure that goods entering the zone are employed for the purposes of consumption or production within it, and are not smuggled into the DTA. Smuggling has proved to be one of the undesired, but perhaps inevitable, side-effects of EPZs.

In order to protect domestic producers from adverse competition, and to preserve the export orientation of the zone, firms operating in the EPZ may be prohibited or restricted from selling in the domestic market of the host state.[85] However, there may be schemes that permit sales into the local market. For example, in India, EPZ located firms are permitted to sell 25 per cent of their output on the local market provided all necessary import licences have been obtained and duties paid.[86] Similarly, the Egyptian Foreign Investment Law of 1997 states in Article 33 that 'import into the country from the free zones shall be in accordance with the general rules on import from abroad. Customs taxes shall be payable on goods imported from the free zone to the local market as though they were imported from abroad'.[87] By contrast, sales by local producers to firms within the EPZ are generally encouraged. These will be treated as deemed exports from the DTA, and may attract fiscal and/or other benefits for EPZ firms as incentives to utilize local sources of supply.[88]

Finally, it should be noted that the enclave status of the EPZ may be diluted over time. First, the geographical unity of the EPZ may be weakened if the fiscal and other advantages offered in the EPZ are extended to firms operating outside it. As noted above, this has happened in Mexico in relation to *maquila* factories. Similarly, in Egypt, firms were encouraged to locate on the outskirts of EPZs by having the benefits of the zone apply to their operations, creating individual 'Private Free Zones'.[89] Furthermore, domestic firms might be encouraged to enter the zone to take advantage of more favourable export conditions.[90] Secondly, the EPZ system can be eroded where the regime for foreign investment applicable to the DTA is liberalized. This may undermine the economic rationale behind the

---

[85] ibid at 28–29.   [86] See Kumar above n 62 at 47–48.   [87] Above n 69.

[88] ESCAP 1985 above n 59 at 29–30.   [89] See further Sklair above n 69.

[90] See UNCTAD *World Investment Report 2002* above n 32 at 215.

EPZ, and encourage firms to invest in the DTA. For example, a significant reason behind the failure of the Bataan EPZ in the Philippines appears to have been the extension of the bonded warehouse scheme, at first initiated exclusively within the zone, to other EPZs, coupled with the easier availability of investment incentives to investors outside the zone.[91]

(iii) The Performance of EPZs

As devices for attracting inward investment by MNEs, EPZs have met with considerable success. Since the 1960s such zones have become locations for the more labour intensive stages of production undertaken by MNEs. Taking advantage of the lower labour costs found in EPZs, MNEs in assembly-type industries (particularly consumer electronics, light machinery, clothing, textiles, and resource processing) have established plants therein. These investments have increased jobs in the host countries, and have contributed to export promotion, in that most of the production in EPZs has been orientated towards supplying developed country markets. According to Wall, the success of pioneering EPZs in Ireland, South Korea, and Taiwan may have led many developing countries to believe that this was attributable to the zone instrument itself and not to the inherent attractions of those countries to export-orientated investment.[92] This may explain why the idea has since been emulated by so many countries. However, the results have not been uniformly good in terms of the objectives behind such zones.

First, although much new employment has been generated in EPZs, the contribution of EPZs to resolving the labour surplus problem may be marginal in most countries.[93] Equally, the employment situation is not static and gains can be regularly offset by losses as the life cycle of the EPZ develops.[94] Secondly, although EPZs may contribute to an increase in the export of manufactured goods from a country, this may be at the cost of considerable imports that may counterbalance, and even extinguish, any resulting foreign exchange surplus.[95] Thirdly, while firms in EPZs will develop backward linkages with DTA firms, the incidence of such cooperation may be limited.[96] Fourthly, the nature of EPZ production, concentrating as it does on labour intensive, low skill, assembly work, is unlikely to ensure any significant transfer of modern technology into the host country's economy, nor to offer significant training opportunities in higher skills areas.[97] Fifthly, there have been instances in which the costs of setting up the EPZ have not been recouped due to poor decisions on location, contradictory policies, and the lack of effective marketing to potential investors.[98] As Kumar points out, a

---

[91] See ESCAP 1985 above n 59 at 240–41.   [92] Wall above n 60 at 485.

[93] ESCAP 1985 above n 59 at 71. See too UNCTAD *World Investment Report 2002* above n 32 at 216–19.   [94] ILO Committee on Employment and Social Policy above n 81 at paras 10–15.

[95] ESCAP 1985 above n 59 at 75.   [96] ibid at 81.

[97] ibid at 82–83; UNCTAD *World Investment Report 2002* above n 32 at 217.

[98] See, in particular, Kumar's analysis of the relative failure of the Kandla Free Trade Zone in comparison with the Santa Cruz Electronics Export Processing Zone in India: above n 62; and the reasons given for the failure of the Bataan EPZ in the Philippines in ESCAP 1985 above n 59 at 240–44.

major difficulty with EPZs has been that they have been given a multiplicity of incompatible goals to achieve. It may not, in fact, be possible to do more than achieve a net increase in foreign exchange and employment through the establishment of EPZs. The wider goals of developing economically backward regions should, in his view, be dropped.[99] On the other hand, according to the UNCTAD *World Investment Report 2002*, EPZs can be successful if they have coherent and comprehensive policies, provide for human resource development, have good working and living conditions, and aim to transform themselves into higher value-added industrial parks.[100]

That said, certain more fundamental weaknesses in the EPZ concept are emerging. In particular, as more developing host states liberalize investment conditions within the country as a whole, the justification for retaining special economic enclaves within the economy is weakened. As noted at the beginning of this section, EPZs were set up as exceptions to a general policy of import substituting growth through the encouragement of domestic enterprises. Once the host country abandons such a policy and the conditions prevailing in the EPZ become generalized, the need for an EPZ is less apparent. In addition, membership of the WTO entails adherence to the SCM Agreement which, as was noted above, prohibits certain export oriented subsidies. While this will not affect services oriented export subsidies, many manufacturing oriented export subsidies will fall foul of the prohibition on 'specific' subsidies covered by that agreement.[101] This will leave little room for manoeuvre in the provision of subsidies to EPZ based companies.[102] Indeed, the traditional EPZ may be a redundant concept in an open, developing, economy that is managing to attain more advanced levels of efficiency, institutional capacity, and skills upgrading.[103] However, such zones continue to attract the attention of countries and analysts and countries continue to apply laws and regulation establishing and operating EPZs.

---

[99] Kumar above n 62 at 184–85.   [100] Above n 32 at 217 and 219.

[101] By Article 1 of the SCM Agreement a subsidy is defined as a financial contribution by a government or any public body within the territory of a WTO member that confers a benefit on the recipient. Article 2 adds that subsidies must be specific to an enterprise, an industry or a region to become 'actionable' within the required procedures under the agreement, while Article 3 prohibits two types of subsidy outright: those attaching to the export of goods or to the substitution of imports. Actionable subsidies will give rise to a right to seek remedial action, by way of countervailing duties being imposed on imports from the WTO member that initiated the subsidy, where it can be shown that the subsidies have caused, or threaten to cause, material injury to the industries or enterprises of another WTO member. See further M Trebilcock and R Howse *The Regulation of International Trade* (London: Routledge, 3rd edn, 2005) at 266–75 and UNCTAD n 32 above.

[102] According to UNCTAD the options open to developing country members using EPZs are (i) to maintain EPZ subsidies but eliminate the conditionality of restricting sales on the domestic market or (ii) establish a new system of incentives for all domestic companies that is not contingent on export performance either in law or in fact. WTO rules also permit border tax adjustments, so EPZs can continue to exempt exports by companies in these zones from indirect taxes (such as sales taxes), border taxes (such as consular fees), and import charges: n 32 above at 218.

[103] ibid at 219.

(iv) The Chinese 'Special Economic Zone' Policy

The Chinese Special Economic Zone(SEZ) policy aims not only at encouraging inward direct investment by MNEs but, more importantly, at the creation of a capitalist economic enclave within the PRC, which can act as a testing ground for the creation of a new Chinese 'Socialist Market Economy'. Thus, in the PRC, the EPZ and FTZ concepts have been adapted into a new kind of administrative regime for the reorganization of socialist relations of production. This forms a pivotal part of China's wider 'Open Door' policy, leading, eventually, it is hoped, to that country's integration into the international division of labour, while at the same time preserving its socialist ideological perspective.[104]

The first SEZs were created in 1979 in the municipalities of Shenzhen, Zhuhai, and Shantou in Guangdong province in Southeast China. These were followed in 1980 by Xiamen in Fujian province. In 1983 Hainan Island in Southern China was elevated to a special administrative zone under the jurisdiction of the Guangdong Provincial People's Government, displaying many of the features of an SEZ. In May 1984 14 coastal cities were opened up to foreign trade and investment, and in 1985 three special delta economic zones were established in the Pearl River and Yangtze areas.[105] The provinces of Guangdong and Fujian were chosen as the sites for SEZs in view of their coastal locations, their traditional links with expatriate Chinese, from whom considerable investment could be expected and, because of their proximity to Hong Kong with its financial infrastructure and resources, anticipating their integration with Hong Kong in 1997.

The basic regulatory framework for the Guangdong SEZs comes from the Regulations on Special Economic Zones in Guangdong Province, adopted by the Fifteenth Session of the Standing Committee of the Fifth National People's Congress on 26 August 1980.[106] The Xiamen SEZ is governed by five regulations on the registration of enterprises, land use, labour management, the import of

---

[104] On the relationship between economic policy and ideology in the PRC's policy on SEZs, see T Chan, EKY Chen and S Chin 'China's Special Economic Zones: Ideology, Policy and Practice' in YC Jao and CK Leung (eds) *China's Special Economic Zones: Policies, Problems and Prospects* (Oxford: Oxford University Press, 1986) ch 5; V Sit 'The Special Economic Zones of China: A New Type of Export Processing Zone?' The Developing Economies vol XXIII–1 (March 1985) 68; Leslie Sklair 'Problems of Socialist Development: The Significance of Shenzhen Special Economic Zone for China's Open Door Development Strategy' 15 International Journal of Urban & Regional Research (No 2 1991) Special Issue: 'Urbanisation in the Hong Kong-South China Region' 197.

[105] See E Pow and MJ Moser 'Law and Investment in China's Special Investment Areas' in M Moser (ed) *Foreign Trade, Investment and the Law in the People's Republic of China* (Oxford University Press, 2nd edn, 1987) 199; Sklair above n 80 ch 9 'Capitalist Globalization in China'.

[106] English translation: *China's Foreign Economic Legislation* (Beijing: Foreign Language Press, 1982) vol I 193–200; or East Asian Executive Reports vol 2 No 10 (15 October, 1980) 26–28 or <http://www.novexcn.com/guangdong_regs_on_sez.html> (cited hereafter as Guangdong Regulations. The citations in the text are from the East Asian Executive Reports translation). For analysis, see K Herbst 'The Regulatory Framework for Foreign Investment in the Special Economic Zones' in Yao and Leung (eds) above n 104 at 124–37; Pow and Moser in Moser (ed) above n 105 at 205–211; S Nishitateno 'China's Special Economic Zones: Experimental Units for Economic Reform' 32 ICLQ 175 (1983).

technology and association with inland parts of China.[107] Similar specific regulations have also been passed in relation to the Guangdong SEZs.[108]

This regulatory framework does not create a distinct regime from the national laws of the PRC. Thus Article 2 of the Guangdong Regulations states that '[t]he enterprises and individuals operating in the special zones must abide by the laws, decrees and relevant regulations of the People's Republic of China'. However, Article 2 continues by making an exception to this general rule in relation to special provisions as stipulated in the regulations. Therefore, the specific provisions in the SEZ regulations supersede national law in the matters covered by them.[109] Thus, for example, the regulations permit the setting up of joint ventures in the SEZ. However, they are silent on the detailed regulation of such ventures. This must, therefore, be provided by the national law on joint ventures, except where the SEZ regulations differ as, for example, on the question of taxation. It is not possible to provide a comprehensive analysis of all the Chinese SEZ regulations. This has, in any case, been done elsewhere.[110] Rather, the Guangdong Regulations will be briefly reviewed to consider the similarities and differences between the SEZ concept and EPZs in capitalist developing countries.

The objectives of Chinese SEZs differ from those of EPZs in capitalist developing countries. While the latter are concerned mainly with the encouragement of export orientated industry, the SEZs in Guangdong are involved in 'all undertakings which have a positive meaning in international economic cooperation and technical exchange including the fields of industry, agriculture, animal husbandry, breeding, tourism, housing and other construction work and advanced technological research and manufacturing work. They may also engage in other business which is of interest to both sides'.[111] Nevertheless, there are broad similarities between SEZs and EPZs in the incentives and preferential treatment given to foreign investors.

Thus the foreign investor has the right to set up an independently owned and operated enterprise in the SEZ,[112] a right not extended to the rest of China until the passing of the Law on Enterprises Operated Exclusively with Foreign Capital of 12 April 1986.[113] Secondly, machinery and equipment, spare parts, raw, and semi-processed materials, means of transportation and other capital goods required

---

[107] English translations: *China Economic News* 25 March 1985, Registration Regulations and Labour Management Regulations; 15 April 1985, Land Use Regulations and Regulations on Economic Association Between the Xiamen SEZ and Inland Areas of China; 22 April 1985, Regulations on Technology Imports. See further Pow and Moser ibid at 211–30.

[108] ibid. See also Herbst above n 106 at 126–27. These were adopted on 17 November 1981. English translations: China's Foreign Economic Legislation (1982) vol I at 207–11 (Entry and Exit Regulations); 223–28 (Labour and Wage Regulations); 215–19 (Business Registration Regulations); 233–39 (Land Registration Regulations). In 1992 the Shenzhen SEZ was given legislative autonomy thereby allowing more localized rule-making than was hitherto possible under the regulatory powers of the government of Guangdong Province: *Financial Times* 3 July 1992 at 6.

[109] Pow and Moser above n 105 at 205.   [110] See in particular Pow and Moser ibid.

[111] Guangdong Regulations above n 106 art 4.   [112] Guangdong Regulations ibid art 10.

[113] English translation in Beijing Review No 18 5 May 1986 at 16–17.

for production imported by enterprises in the SEZ are exempt from import duties.[114] The income tax rate within the zone was set at 15 per cent,[115] as compared with 30 per cent for the taxable income of joint ventures and foreign enterprises in the rest of China.[116] Furthermore, preferential treatment was given to enterprises established within two years of the promulgation of the regulations, enterprises with an investment of US$5 million or more and enterprises involving higher technologies or having a longer cycle of capital turnover.[117] Thirdly, free remittance of profits is guaranteed after payment of income tax.[118] Fourthly, upon reinvestment of profits in the SEZ for five years, the foreign trader may apply for a reduction or exemption of income tax on profits so reinvested.[119] Fifthly, entry and exit procedures were simplified for foreigners.[120] These are now covered by the specific regulations mentioned above.

Further similarities with EPZs are contained in the requirement that the commodities produced by enterprises in the SEZ are to be sold on the international market.[121] Sales to the domestic Chinese market can only be made with the permission of the SEZ administrative committee and on payment of customs duty.[122] Thus the export enclave status of the SEZ is preserved. On the other hand, purchases by SEZ firms of raw materials and other supplies from Chinese producers are encouraged.[123] The enclave status of SEZs has been further emphasized in subsequent regulations on entry and exit. In particular, on 1 April 1986, regulations were introduced to reinforce the internal border or 'Control Line' between Shenzhen SEZ and the rest of China, so as to reduce the incidence of smuggling and black market activities.[124]

The administration of the Guangdong SEZs is carried out by the Administrative Committee of the Special Economic Zones of Guangdong Province (ADCOM). This is given broad powers of action over the operation of the zone.[125] These include the approval of proposed investments,[126] the preparation of the infrastructure[127] and the operation of personnel recruitment services either directly or through labour service companies.[128] In order to assist in the economic activities of the zone the Guangdong Provincial Special Economic Zones Company has been established. Its functions include the accumulation of funds and trust and investment work, cooperation with foreign investors in setting up joint ventures, assisting in procurement and marketing work with units in China and consultancy services.[129] Thus the principal administrative organs of the SEZs carry

---

[114] Guangdong Regulations above n 106 art 13.

[115] Guangdong Regulations ibid art 14. Income Tax Law of the People's Republic of China for Enterprises with Foreign Investment and Foreign Enterprises 1 July 1991 art 7. English translation in Beijing Review 24–30 June 1991 at 23.   [116] See 1991 Income Tax Law ibid art 5.

[117] Guangdong Regulations above n 106 art 14.   [118] ibid art 15.   [119] ibid art 16.

[120] ibid art 18.   [121] ibid art 9.   [122] ibid.   [123] ibid art 17.

[124] See Pow and Moser above n 105 at 212–14.

[125] See Guangdong Regulations above n 106 art 23.   [126] ibid.   [127] ibid. art 5.

[128] ibid art 19.   [129] ibid art 25.

out many of the same functions as their counterparts in capitalist developing countries.

In all, it can be concluded that the Guangdong SEZs share many of the operational features of EPZs. The principal differences lie in the broader range of economic activities sought to be encouraged in the SEZs and in the underlying policy objective of developing a capitalist economy within an enclave of a socialist country. Upon joining the WTO, given this broad coverage of SEZs, China would not have to dismantle many of the incentives offered in those areas. As with EPZs, only those aspects of SEZ regulations which introduce subsidies on the export of goods, or subsidies for import substitution, are prohibited. In the Accession Protocol, China makes the following commitment in respect of special economic areas:

(B) Special Economic Areas

1. China shall notify to the WTO all the relevant laws, regulations and other measures relating to its special economic areas, listing these areas by name and indicating the geographic boundaries that define them. China shall notify the WTO promptly, but in any case within 60 days, of any additions or modifications to its special economic areas, including notification of the laws, regulations and other measures relating thereto.

2. China shall apply to imported products, including physically incorporated components, introduced into the other parts of China's customs territory from the special economic areas, all taxes, charges and measures affecting imports, including import restrictions and customs and tariff charges that are normally applied to imports into the other parts of China's customs territory.

3. Except as otherwise provided for in this Protocol, in providing preferential arrangements for enterprises within such special economic areas, WTO provisions on non-discrimination and national treatment shall be fully observed.[130]

In Annex 5B to the Accession Protocol, China commits itself to phase out by 2000 the subsidies of 'the priority in obtaining loans and foreign exchange based on export performance' and 'preferential tariff rate based on localization rate of automobile production'. However, China does not commit itself to rescind the subsidies of 'preferential policies for the economic and technology development areas', 'preferential policies for the economic zone of the Pudong area of Shanghai', 'preferential policies for foreign invested enterprises', and 'preferential income tax rate for high-tech enterprises', which are contained in Annex 5A of Access Protocol and notified to WTO and its members.[131]

---

[130] WTO Accession of the People's Republic of China, Decision of 10 November 2001 (WT/L/432 23 November 2001) available at <http://www.docsonline.wto.org>.

[131] See further Wenger Vilei Belser, Beijing Office, *Special Economic Zones of China and WTO – Will the Privileges Survive?* (October 2003) at 9–12.

(2) Bilateral and Regional Measures for the Encouragement of Direct Investment

As noted at the beginning of this chapter, the encouragement of direct investment should be considered not only from the perspective of unilateral policies undertaken by host states, but also from that of inter-state initiatives. The US network of FCN treaties, which guarantee the freedom of entry and establishment for investors from each contracting party, has already been alluded to above.[132] In addition, during the 1990s, a series of bilateral accords between the US and Japan sought to ensure more open market access for investors from each country.[133] More recently, both the US and Canadian model Bilateral Investment Treaties (BITs) provide for non-discrimination against foreign investors at the pre-entry as well as the post-entry phase. This includes the right to establish an investment.[134] It remains, in this section, to consider certain selected regional initiatives for increased economic integration and investment liberalization. The discussion will concentrate on North America and Europe as illustrative cases.[135] Attention will be paid to the North American Free Trade Agreement (NAFTA) and to the European Internal Market of the European Community (EC). In theory, these initiatives illustrate two distinct approaches to trade and investment liberalization. The NAFTA sets out, in principle, to do no more than ensure freer access for trade and investment between the participating states, which retain their national powers of economic regulation subject to the principle of national treatment.[136] By comparison, the European Internal Market goes further in that the EC aims at creating a single common market, governed by harmonized supranational regulations, and aiming at eventual economic and monetary union between the Member

---

[132] See text at nn 12–15 above.

[133] See Japan-United States: Policies and Measures Regarding Inward Direct Investment and Buyer-Supplier Relationships 20 July 1995: 34 ILM 1341 (1995) where Japan commits to greater market access and to the regulation of restrictive trade practices that might impede foreign access to internal markets as well as commitments to encourage foreign participation in mergers and acquisitions. See also Japan-United States Measures on Financial Services, 13 February 1995: 34 ILM 617 (1995); Japan-United States Measurers Regarding Insurance, 1 October 1994: 34 ILM 661 (1995).

[134] For full discussion see ch 17 below.

[135] These are by no means the only initiatives among states for closer economic cooperation. Others include ASEAN (SE Asia); see Framework Agreement on Enhancing ASEAN Economic Cooperation of 28 January 1992: 31 ILM 506 (1992); ANCOM (Venezuela, Bolivia, Colombia, Chile, Ecuador: see further ch 18 below; Mercosur (Brazil, Argentina, Paraguay, Uruguay) see 30 ILM 1041 (1991); ECOWAS (W Africa) see 14 ILM 1200 (1975). Other relevant bodies include Caribbean Economic Community (CARICOM), EFTA-EEC European Economic Area (Europe), The Maghreb Association (North Africa). Space constraints prevent a full discussion of all initiatives in respect of investment taken by these bodies. See further UNCTAD *Investment Provisions in Economic Integration Agreements* (New York and Geneva: United Nations, 2006) available also at http://www.unctad.org/iia; Thomas Pollan *Legal Framework for the Admission of FDI* (Utrecht: Eleven International Publishing, 2006) ch 3.

[136] See Canada-Mexico-United States: North American Free Trade Agreement 17 December 1992 Parts One–Three: 32 ILM 289 (1993), Parts Four–Eight: 32 ILM 605 (1993) (cited as NAFTA).

States.[137] In practice, however, the two approaches may not have very different results in that they both tend towards the economic convergence of the states concerned. In particular, the NAFTA contains provisions not commonly found in a mere free trade agreement, including provisions on services, investment, intellectual property and bilateral dispute settlement mechanisms.[138] It may therefore be proper to regard the NAFTA as a' halfway house to a North American common market'.[139] Each approach will be considered in turn.

(a) The North American Free Trade Agreement (NAFTA)

The NAFTA aims at the closer integration of the economies of the US, Canada and Mexico by means of a single trilateral free trade agreement. It has been preceded by bilateral negotiations. Thus, the US and Canada ratified a bilateral Free Trade Agreement (FTA) between them in the autumn of 1988. It entered force on 1 January 1989.[140] This agreement is notable as it contained a specific chapter on investment protection and acted as a model for the investment provisions of NAFTA.[141] In addition, the US agreed a framework understanding on bilateral trade with Mexico in 1987.[142] A framework agreement between Canada and Mexico was also being negotiated.[143] These initiatives were overtaken by NAFTA after its entry into force on 1 January 1994.

Part Five of NAFTA contains essentially the same types of provisions on investment, services (including financial services), and related matters as the US-Canada FTA, and extends these to the three contracting parties.[144] Chapter Eleven of Part Five contains the provisions that deal specifically with investment. Chapter Eleven,

---

[137] See H Crookell *Canadian-American Trade and Investment Under the Free Trade Agreement* (New York: Quorum Books, 1990) at 19–21. See further Peter Robson *The Economics of International Integration* (London: Routledge, 5th edn, 2007) chs 1 and 2.

[138] See NAFTA above n 136 Parts Five, Six, and Seven.

[139] D Cameron 'Striking a Deal' in D Cameron (ed) *The Free Trade Deal* (Toronto: James Lorimer & Co, 1988) ch 2 at 23.

[140] See 27 ILM 281 (1988). For a guide to the provisions of the agreement see: JR Johnson and JS Schachter *The Free Trade Agreement: A Comprehensive Guide* (Canada Law Book Inc, 1988). For policy commentary, see Crookell above n 137; D Cameron (ed) n 139 above; JJ Schott and MG Smith (eds) *The Canada-United States Free Trade Agreement: The Global Impact* (Washington: Institute for International Economics, 1988); P Morici (ed) *Making Free Trade Work: The Canada-US Agreement* (Council on Foreign Relations 1990); M Gold and D Leyton Brown *Trade-Offs on Free Trade: The Canada-US Free Trade Agreement* (Toronto: Carswell, 1988); C Reynolds, L Waverman, and G Bueno *The Dynamics of North American Trade and Investment: Canada, Mexico and the United States* (Stanford UP, 1991).

[141] See further Raby 'The Investment Provisions of the Canada-United States Free Trade Agreement: A Canadian Perspective' 84 AJIL 394 (1990).   [142] See 27 ILM 438 (1988).

[143] Reynolds et al above n 140.

[144] Part Five is at 32 ILM 639–70 (1992). See also Part Eight Chapter Twenty-One: Exceptions: ibid at 699–702; Annex I (Reservations for Existing Measures and Liberalisation Commitments) ibid 704–748; Annex II (Reservations for Future Measures) ibid 748–59; Annex III (Activities Reserved to the State) ibid 759–60 (concerning Mexico only); Annex IV (Exceptions For Most Favoured Nation Treatment) ibid 760–61.

Section A, provides the framework of guarantees for investors and principles of state action that are designed to liberalize the North American investment environment. It provides what could be termed the 'North American Model' of investment liberalization. Thus, investors of another party and their investments are entitled to national treatment,[145] and Most Favoured Nation (MFN) treatment.[146] As between these standards the one that offers the better treatment to investors shall be applied.[147] These standards shall apply not only after the investment has been made but also to the pre-entry stage, in that both the national treatment and MFN provisions include establishment and acquisition within their scope. Thereby, NAFTA guarantees a right of non-discriminatory entry and establishment. This is subject to a 'negative list' of exceptions based on industry sectors which each contracting party has annexed to the agreement. After entry, investors shall, in addition, enjoy the protection of minimum standards of treatment under international law, including fair and equitable treatment and full protection and security, and non-discrimination with respect to measures relating to losses suffered as a result of armed conflict or civil strife.[148] Performance requirements are prohibited. Apart from the familiar list of prohibited export and import requirements, local content and procurement rules, and local sales quotas, NAFTA includes within the prohibition requirements to transfer technology, production processes or other proprietary knowledge except when this requirement is imposed by a court, tribunal or competition authority as a result of an alleged violation of competition laws, or to act in a manner not inconsistent with the agreement.[149] Thus NAFTA goes beyond the prohibitions contained in the WTO TRIMs Agreement, which will be discussed further below.

Furthermore, no nationality requirement may be imposed as to the composition of the board of directors of a local enterprise that is an investment from another contracting party, although a party may require that the majority of the board be of a particular nationality, or resident in the territory of that party, provided that this does not materially affect the ability of the investor to exercise control over its investment.[150] The parties may make reservations to the operation of national treatment and MFN standards, and to the prohibitions on performance requirements and board membership requirements, as regards any existing non-conforming measures at the levels of federal, state, or local government. Thus a 'standstill' on new restrictions is introduced.[151] Chapter Eleven continues with a guarantee on the free transfer of profits, proceeds of sale, contractual payments, compensation payments, and arbitral awards connected with the investment.[152] Regarding expropriation, this must be for a public purpose, non-discriminatory, in accordance with due process of law and international law, and must be accompanied by payment of compensation equivalent to the

---

[145] ibid art 1102. This provision includes a prohibition on minimum national equity or indigenization requirements: art 1102.4.   [146] ibid art 1103.
[147] ibid art 1104.   [148] ibid art 1105.   [149] ibid art 1106.1.
[150] ibid art 1107.   [151] ibid art 1108.   [152] ibid art 1109.

fair market value of the expropriated investment immediately before the expropriation took place.[153]

Apart from laying down standards for the treatment of investors, Chapter Eleven, Section A, also establishes certain rights of action in relation to investment for the administrative authorities of the contracting parties. Thus, the parties may adopt measures that prescribe special formalities in connection with the establishment of investments by investors from another party, provided these do not materially impair the protection given under the agreement, and to require that the investor supplies routine information concerning the investment.[154] Likewise, the agreement permits measures that are considered appropriate to ensure that investment activity in the territory of a party is undertaken in a manner sensitive to environmental concerns, so long as these measures are otherwise consistent with the agreement.[155] The parties stress that it is inappropriate to encourage investment by relaxing domestic health, safety, and environmental measures. Thus they undertake not to weaken such measures as a means of encouraging investment. Should one party feel that another is carrying out such a policy, it may request consultations with a view to avoiding such encouragement.[156] This provision is designed to meet one of the fears expressed by opponents of NAFTA, namely, that it could permit US and Canadian firms to relocate to Mexico and take advantage of the lower environmental and health and safety standards to be found there.

Chapter Eleven, Section B, establishes a detailed system for the settlement of investment disputes between a party and an investor from another party, based on the principles of international reciprocity and due process before an impartial tribunal.[157] This is discussed briefly in chapter 18. There has been a significant rise in such disputes, resulting in a substantial number of arbitral awards. These are an important source of interpretation for NAFTA. They will be considered in chapters 15 and 16 below.

The NAFTA created controversy as regards its effects on regional and international trade and investment. In particular, US labour unions were concerned that US firms would relocate to Mexico to take advantage of lower environmental standards and pay rates. This led President Clinton to call for supplementary agreements on the enforcement of labour laws and environmental standards by Mexico so as to avoid the relocation of jobs to that country.[158] Supplemental agreements in these areas were concluded as part of the NAFTA package.[159]

As regards the implications of NAFTA for the global process of trade and investment liberalization, opinion was divided. It was not clear at the time of its adoption

---

[153] ibid art 1110.   [154] ibid art 1111.   [155] ibid art 1114.1.
[156] ibid art 1114.2.   [157] ibid art 1115.
[158] 'Clinton Gets Tips on Fine-tuning Nafta' *Financial Times* 18 February 1993 at 3.
[159] For the texts of both side agreements, see 32 ILM 1480 (Environmental Co-operation), 1499 (Labour Co-operation) (1993). For discussion see Gary Hufbauer and Jeffrey Schott (Washington DC: Institute for International Economics, 1993) Addendum 157; Pierre Marc Johnson and Andre Beaulieu *The Environment and NAFTA: Understanding and Implementing the New Continental Law* (Washington DC: Island Press, 1996).

whether NAFTA would be a spur to such liberalization or a brake upon it. This issue first surfaced in the context of the US-Canada FTA. Proponents of the former view argued that the US-Canada FTA kept the momentum for liberalization going, in that the parties to the world's largest bilateral trading relationship adopted a policy of such liberalization between them, and thereby created a model for multi-lateral negotiations to follow.[160] A similar argument could be made for NAFTA, in that it would be instrumental in creating a single market for the whole of North America including, for the first time, a major newly industrializing country of the South. It could offer a new model of cooperation between developed and developing countries.

By contrast, it was also arguable that the US-Canada FTA and NAFTA represented a form of bilateral and trilateral protectionism, offering reciprocal preferential treatment for US, Canadian and Mexican traders and investors, to the exclusion of their competitors from outside North America. Significantly, a GATT working party on the US-Canada FTA reported to the GATT Council that it was unable to agree over whether the FTA was consistent with the aims of the GATT, and described it as having the potential of undermining the GATT system's credibility in that third party interests were not clearly protected.[161] The 1992 dispute between the US and Japan and Canada over North American content requirements for Honda cars produced in Ontario is a case in point.[162] However, NAFTA should act as a spur to liberalization given that non-North American firms are able to benefit from its provisions merely by reason of their presence in the region. The definition of 'investor of a party' includes an enterprise of a party, and 'enterprise of a party' is defined as, 'an enterprise constituted or organized under the law of a Party, and a branch located in the territory of a Party and carrying out business activities there'. This is wide enough to encompass a North American subsidiary or branch of a non-North American parent.[163]

(b) The European Internal Market

The Treaty of Rome (EC Treaty) ensures that restrictions on the freedom of establishment, or the freedom to supply services, are removed for natural and legal persons possessing the nationality of a Member State.[164] Consequently, as between

---

[160] Indeed, in art 1610 of the agreement, the US and Canada pledged their intention in the Uruguay Round and in other international forums, to improve multilateral arrangements and agreements with respect to investment. Although the provisions of the agreement could not be automatically transported into the GATT negotiations, they offered a statement of a common US-Canadian position. See further J Schott 'Implications for the Uruguay Round' in J Schott and M Smith (eds) above n 140 at 159.

[161] See 'FTA Could Undermine Credibility of Gatt System' *Financial Times* 13 November 1991.

[162] In 1992 the US Customs Service had ruled that Honda cars produced in Ontario did not qualify for duty-free benefits under the US-Canada FTA, as they did not contain the 50 per cent North American content required for such treatment. Accordingly a 2.5 per cent import duty was levied upon such cars. See Cantin and Lowenfeld 'Rules of Origin, The Canada-US FTA, and the *Honda* case' 87 AJIL 375 (1993).   [163] See NAFTA above n 136 art 1139.

[164] See EEC Treaty arts 43–55 (ex arts 52–66). See also, for illustrations of the types of restrictions to be abolished, General Programme for the Abolition of Restrictions on Freedom of Establishment

the Member States, existing restrictions on direct investment or on the provision of cross-border services, by nationals of Member States, are being progressively abolished and no new restrictions can be introduced.[165] In relation to the operations of companies or firms, Article 48 of the EC Treaty provides:

Companies or firms[166] formed in accordance with the law of a Member State and having their registered office, central administration or principal place of business within the Community shall, for the purposes of this chapter, be treated in the same way as natural persons who are nationals of Member States.

The right of establishment, as it applies to companies and firms, includes: 'the right to take up and pursue activities as self-employed persons and to set up and manage undertakings, in particular companies or firms within the meaning of the second paragraph of Article 48,[167] under the conditions laid down for its own nationals by the law of the country where such establishment is effected, subject to the provisions of the chapter relating to capital.'[168] Article 55 of the EEC Treaty extends Article 48 to the provision of services, ensuring that companies can also benefit from the freedoms accorded in that area to natural persons. Article 48 suggests two possible routes into another Member State: first, the establishment of a new company, or the transfer of an existing company, from one Member State to another, known as 'primary establishment'; secondly, the establishment of an office, branch or subsidiary in another Member State, termed 'secondary establishment'.[169]

Regarding primary establishment, it has been made clear by the European Court of Justice (ECJ) in *R v HM Treasury, ex p Daily Mail and General Trust plc*,[170] that a transfer of the central management and control of a company from one Member State to another, while that company retains its status as a company incorporated under the legislation of the first Member State, does not amount to 'establishment'

OJ [1974] Sp Ed 2nd Series IX 7; General Programme for the Abolition of Restrictions on Freedom to Provide Services JO 32/62; OJ [1974] Sp Ed 2nd Series IX 3. See further *Wyatt and Dashwood's European Union Law* above n 54 ch 15.

[165] Thus Spain and Portugal were bound to liberalize their restrictive foreign investment screening laws on entry into the EC, as would prospective new Member States possessing such laws. However, six of the new members from Eastern Europe, who acceded in 2004 (Czech Republic, Estonia, Latvia, Lithuania, Poland, the Slovak Republic, plus the prospective members Bulgaria and Romania) have been permitted to retain, for a transitional period, the preferential treatment for US investors granted under BITs with that country even where this is inconsistent with their membership obligations: see US-EU Bilateral Investment Understanding for Accession Countries, 22 September 2003, available at <http://useu.usmission.gov/Dossiers/EU_Enlargement/Sep2203_BITs_Signing.asp>.

[166] Article 48 goes on to define 'companies or firms' as 'companies or firms constituted under civil or commercial law, including co-operative societies, and other legal persons governed by public or private law, save those which are non-profit making'.   [167] See above n 166.

[168] EC Treaty art 43.

[169] See *R v HM Treasury, ex p Daily Mail and General Trust plc* [1989] 1 All ER 328 at 343D–G per Advocate-General Darmon.

[170] ibid. For comment, see Lever 26 CMLR 327 (1989). See also *Re Expatriation of a German Company* (Case 3Z BR 14/92, Bayerisches Oberstes Landesgericht) 7 May 1992 [1993] 2 CMLR 801. The German Court applied the *Daily Mail* case to prevent the relocation of the seat of a German company to London.

for the purposes of Articles 43 and 48.[171] Consequently, in the absence of harmonized Community law concerning the retention of legal personality in the event
of the transfer of the registered office of a company from one Member State to
another, the home state is free to introduce national laws that regulate the consequences of such a move.[172] However, the ECJ also held that the home Member
State must not hinder the establishment in another Member State of one of its
nationals or of a company incorporated under its legislation and having its registered office, central administration or principal place of business within the
Community. Otherwise the rights guaranteed by Articles 43ff would be rendered
meaningless.[173] This complements the duty on the host Member State to ensure
that foreign nationals and companies are treated in the same way as nationals of
that state. This approach has been applied to control the activities of the home
Member State in relation to the taxation of multinational groups, so that less
favourable tax treatment of the parent, as regards the profits and losses of its subsidiaries located in other Member States, will be treated as an infringement of the
right to establishment.[174]

The most common method whereby companies from one Member State enter
a host Member State is through the establishment of an office, agency, branch, or
subsidiary.[175] In these cases, the host Member State must not impose discriminatory provisions, such as tax provisions, which would limit the freedom for companies to choose the appropriate legal form for their activities within the host
Member State.[176] Where the company seeks to enter a host Member State through

---

[171] ibid at 349 paras 21–25.   [172] ibid at 348–49 paras 19–20.

[173] ibid at 348 paras 15–16.

[174] See *XAB and YAB v Riksskattevereket* Case C–200/98 [2000] 3 CMLR 1337; *Baars v Inspecteur der Belastingdienst Particulieren/Ondernemingen (Gorinchem)* Case C–251/98 [2002] 1 CMLR 1437; *Marks and Spencer plc v Halsey (Her Majesty's Inspector of Taxes)* Case C–446/03 [2006] 1 CMLR 480 and [2006] EWHC 811, [2006] 3 CMLR 229 (ChD). See also on controlled foreign corporation tax rules ch 7 at 302–304 and Case C–196/04 *Cadbury Schweppes plc, Cadbury Schweppes Overseas Limited v Commissioners of Inland Revenue* judgment of 12 September 2006 at <http://curia.europa.eu/jurisp/cgi-bin/form.pl?lang=EN&Submit=rechercher&numaff=C-196/04>.

[175] In *Baars* above n 174 at para 22, the ECJ held that for the purposes of art 43 a holding sufficient to give the shareholder influence over the activities of such an entity, and allow them to determine those activities, was required to show that such a holding was an exercise of a right of establishment.

[176] See, for example, *EC Commission v France* Case 270/83 [1986] ECR 273, [1987] 1 CMLR 401; *R v Inland Revenue Commissioners, Ex p Commerzbank AG* [1993] 3 CMLR 457, [1993] 4 All ER 37 (ECJ); *Royal Bank of Scotland v Elliniko Dimosio (Greece)* Case C–311/97 [1999] 2 CMLR 973; *Bosal Holding BV v Staatssecretaris van Financien* Case C–168/01 [2003] 3 CMLR 674; *CLT-UFA SA v Finanzamt Koln-West* Case C–253/03 [2006] 2 CMLR 743; *Finanzamt Offenbach und Main-Land v Keller* Case C–471/04 [2006] 2 CMLR 774. Other types of discriminatory provisions found to infringe art 43 include professional qualification requirements that may discourage the set-ting up of a local entity: *Payroll Data Services (Italy) SRL and Others* Case C–79/01 [2004] 3 CMLR 763; allowances against tax for research expenditure offered to domestic research enterprises only: *Société Baxter v Première Ministre* Case C–254/97 [2000] 2 CMLR 899; discriminatory refusal to regis-ter a cross-border merger where no legitimate public policy considerations exist for such differential treatment: *Sevic Systems AG* Case C–441/03 [2006] 1 CMLR 1192. The English Court of Appeal recently overruled a first instance decision to award an injunction to restrain possible strike action against a shipping company that proposed to re-flag its Finnish owned vessel to Estonia. At first

secondary establishment methods, it must show a real and continuous link with the economy of a Member State to qualify as a beneficiary of this right.[177] Thus entry into a mere contractual arrangement in the host Member State will not suffice in the absence of an established place of business.[178] However, more recent case law from the ECJ accepts that a company can be set up in any Member State, regardless of whether it pursues economic activity there, even if the main purpose of such establishment is to avoid more onerous regulatory requirements in the Member State where the economic activity is actually carried out.[179] The only circumstances where this will not be allowed is where the establishment in another Member State is designed improperly to circumvent the national legislation of the country in which the business in fact operates, or where some fraud or abuse is involved.[180] This development allows for a degree of regulatory arbitrage for investors between the company, and other laws, regulating establishment in the EU Member States. As such it is not dissimilar to the 'Delaware Effect' in US law, where the favourable conditions of Delaware state company laws have encouraged a very large number of US firms to incorporate there while doing business in other US states. No clear equivalent of Delaware has yet emerged in the EU, although the UK, Ireland, Luxembourg and, in relation to tax treatment, the Netherlands all offer favourable regimes of company establishment. By contrast, this legal development is having a major effect upon the internal laws of countries such as Germany and Austria, which recognize a 'seat' theory of corporate personality and require the establishment of a company or branch within their jurisdiction if that company carries on business there. The new freedom to establish outside the jurisdiction of actual business operations means that such requirements will be incompatible with the freedom of establishment.[181]

instance, the court held that such industrial action could infringe art 43 as it impaired the shipping line's right of establishment in Estonia after that country had acceded to the EU. The Court of Appeal requested a ruling on this issue from the ECJ: *Viking Line v International Transport Workers' Federation and Another* [2005] 2 CMLR 764 (QBD, Comm Ct) overruled [2006] 1 CMLR 693 (CA).

[177] See General Programme for the Abolition of Restrictions on Freedom of Establishment OJ Sp Ed 2nd Series IX 7 Title I; Case 79/85 *Segers* [1986] ECR 2375, [1987] 2 CMLR 247.

[178] See *Foulser and Another v MacDougall (Her Majesty's Inspector of Taxes)* [2003] 1 CMLR 1079 (English High Court ChD) at paras 78–79.

[179] See *Centros Ltd v Erhvervs-OG Selskabsstyrelsen* Case C–212/97 [1999] 2 CMLR 551. Two Danish nationals had incorporated a company in England, but carried on the substantive business of the company in Denmark. The Danish authorities refused to register the Danish branch of the company on the ground that this arrangement sought to circumvent Danish rules concerning the paying up of a minimum capital, as would be required of a principal establishment. The ECJ held that this was in breach of arts 43 and 48 even though the Danish authorities argued that the regulatory requirements were necessary to protect creditors and other contracting parties. See, for analysis, Anne Looijsteijn-Clearie 'Centros Ltd – A Complete U-Turn in the Right of Establishment for Companies?' 49 ICLQ 621 (2000). See also *Kamer van Koophandel en Fabrieken voor Amsterdam v Inspire Art Ltd* Case C–167/01 [2005] 3 CMLR 937; *Uberseering BV v Nordic Construction Company Baumanagement GmbH (NCC)* Case C–208/00 [2005] 1 CMLR 1.

[180] *Centros* ibid at para 24.

[181] See *Uberseering* above n 179 at paras 71–82. The ECJ concluded: 'where a company formed in accordance with the law of Member State (A) in which it has its registered office is deemed, under the

The benefits of the right to establishment and freedom to provide services are available subject to the derogations contained in Article 46. This permits the special treatment of foreign nationals on grounds of public policy, public security, or public health. This provision is interpreted in the same manner as the restrictions on the free movement of workers under Article 39 of the EC Treaty.[182] In should be noted that the possibility of tax avoidance and the risk of revenue loss to Member States have been considered insufficient to create an additional derogation to the above mentioned freedoms.[183]

It is clear from Articles 48 and 55 that the right to establishment and the right to provide services in another Member State can only be enjoyed by a company formed in accordance with the law of a Member State and having its registered office, central administration, or principal place of business within the Community. This is wide enough to cover the EC-based subsidiaries of non-EC parent companies. However, the EC Treaty does not guarantee these rights to companies that have no legally recognized EC presence in the sense of Article 48. Therefore, it is not possible for, say, a US or Japanese based company to invoke the EC Treaty if it is denied access to the economy of a Member State whether for the purpose of establishing a place of business or for the provision of cross-border services. In the absence of a common Community policy on inward investment from outside the EC, individual Member States retain discretion over their policy towards investors from outside the EC.[184] In general, the Member States of the EC espouse an 'open door' to non-EC investors, so there should be little real disadvantage to such investors.

However, in sensitive regulatory sectors the EC has adopted some restrictive polices. In the field of financial services, non-EC firms initially feared that new EC provisions would establish a 'mirror-image' concept of reciprocity, in that access to the Common Market for non-EC firms would depend on their home jurisdictions

---

law of another Member State (B) to have moved its actual centre of administration to Member State B, Articles 43 EC and 48 EC preclude Member State B from denying the company legal capacity ...' On the facts, the Dutch incorporated claimant company was held to have been wrongly denied legal capacity on this ground and was entitled to bring legal proceedings before the courts of Member State B (Germany) against the defendant company. In *S v Companies Register Graz* 6 Ob 124/99z [2001] 1 CMLR 995 the Austrian Oberster Gerichtshof held that the 'seat' theory, which prohibited the recognition of branches set up by companies established in Member States where the 'incorporation' theory prevailed, restricted the exercise of, and therefore conflicted with, the Community principle of freedom of establishment.

182 On which, see further *Wyatt and Dashwood's European Union Law* above n 54 at 416 and 485; Directive 64/221 of February 25 1964 OJ [1964] 850.

183 *EC Commission v France* above n 176 at para 25 and see the tax cases cited in n 176.

184 A common inward investment policy can be adopted under Article 57 of the EC Treaty. Such a policy was advocated by Art.III.217 of the Draft Treaty Establishing a Constitution for Europe (Luxembourg: Office for Official Publications of the European Communities, 2003). For analysis, see Joachim Karl 'The Competence for Foreign Direct Investment – New Powers for the European Union?' 5 JWIT 413 (2004). The latest version of the Draft Constitution is available at <http://eur-lex.europa.eu/JOHtml.do?uri=OJ:C:2004:310:SOM:EN:HTML> or OJ [2004] C 310. See now Art.III-157.

offering identical terms of access for EC-based firms. However, these fears were somewhat allayed by the adoption of a modified concept of reciprocity, based on national treatment standards. For example, in the Second Banking Directive,[185] should a non-EC state fail to grant national treatment to EC credit institutions, a subsidiary of a credit institution from that country may be denied an EC banking licence. On the other hand, lack of equivalent treatment will lead to negotiations between the state concerned and the EC Council but not to the denial of licences.[186] A similar approach was adopted in the Investment Services Directive.[187] More recently, in relation to the liberalization of services the proposed Directive on Services in the Internal Market introduces a general non-discrimination standard to host country regulation. By Article 16 of this draft:

Member States shall respect the right of service providers to provide services in a Member State other than that in which they are established.

The Member State in which the service is provided shall ensure free access to and free exercise of a service within its territory.

Member States shall not make access to or exercise of a service activity in their territory subject to compliance with any requirements which do not comply with the following principles:

(a) Non-discrimination: the requirement may be neither directly nor indirectly discriminatory with regard to nationality or, in the case of legal persons, with regard to the Member State in which they are established,

(b) Necessity: the requirement must be justified for reasons of public policy, public security, public health or the protection of the environment,

(c) Proportionality: the requirement must be suitable for securing the attainment of the objective pursued, and must not go beyond what is necessary to attain the objective.[188]

This approach replaces the original proposal to use the country of origin principle and exclude regulation by the host country altogether.[189] The proposal does not specifically mention service providers from non-EU countries and so no particular difference in treatment will arise in this context. The same principles will apply as under the EC Treaty itself.

---

[185] 89/646/EEC OJ [1989] L386/1 30 December 1989. This directive entered into force on 1 January 1993. This has been superseded by Directive 2000/12 of 20 March 2000 OJ [2000] L126/1; see arts 23–5.   [186] ibid art 23.

[187] Council Directive on investment services in the securities field 93/22/EEC OJ [1993] L 141/27 art 7. See further Cremona 'A European Passport For Investment Services' [1994] JBL 195. This directive has been superseded by Directive 2004/39 of 21 April 2004 OJ [2004] L145/1; see art 15.

[188] See European Commission Amended Proposal for a Directive of the European Parliament and Council on Services in the Internal Market COM(2006) 160 final 4 April 2006 available at <http://eur-lex.europa.eu/LexUriServ/site/en/com/2006/com2006_0160en01.pdf>.

[189] On which see further Nikolai Fichtner 'The Rise and Fall of the Country of Origin Principle in the EU's Services Directive – Uncovering the Principle's Premises and Potential Implications' Essays in Transnational Economic Law (No 54/2006, Institut fur Wirschaftsrecht, Martin-Luther-Universitat, Halle-Wittenberg) available at <http://www.wirtshaftsrecht.uni-halle.de> or <http://www.telc.uni-halle.de>.

(3) Multilateral Arrangements Dismantling Barriers to Inward Investment

The major capital-exporting countries have maintained a policy inter se of progressively dismantling barriers to inward investment through multilateral arrangements. Initially, this was manifested in the OECD Codes on the Liberalization of Current Invisible Operations and on the Liberalization of Capital Movements, which were adopted by the OECD Council on 12 December 1961.[190] More recently, the major capital exporters, led by the US, sought to limit the powers of non-OECD host states in controlling the entry and establishment of foreign investors in the Uruguay Round of the GATT Negotiations, which resulted in the adoption of investment related obligations under the WTO Agreements concerning the establishment of services, intellectual property rights, and the use of performance requirements as conditions of entry for foreign investors. Each will be considered in turn.

(a) The OECD Codes of Liberalization

The two OECD Codes deal, respectively, with the progressive abolition of obstacles to trade and investment in the fields of current invisibles, covering the major service industries,[191] and capital movements, which include inter alia all other areas where direct investment may occur.[192] Thus the codes seek to liberalize transactions involving foreign investment rather than the protection of investors and their assets, which is covered, as will be discussed below, by other OECD instruments. The codes have the legal status of an OECD decision which is binding on all members. Although they cover distinct subjects, the two codes are governed by similar general principles and monitoring procedures. The Codes enshrine the principle of liberalization by means of a reciprocal duty to abolish any national restrictions upon the transfers and transactions to which the codes apply.[193] This

---

[190] *Code on the Liberalization of Current Invisible Operations* [OECD/C(61)95] (hereafter Invisibles Code); *Code on the Liberalization of Capital Movements* [OECD/C(61)96] (hereafter Capital Movements Code). The codes are regularly updated by decisions of the OECD Council to reflect all changes in the positions of members. The updated codes are periodically republished. The current editions at the time of writing are Invisibles Code (September 2004) and Capital Movements Code (October 2005) to which all subsequent references pertain. Both are available for download at <http://www.oecd.org/document/63/0,2340,en_2649_34887_1826559_1_1_1_1,00.html>. For background to the codes, see OECD *OECD Codes of Liberalization of Capital Movements and of Current Invisible Operations User's Guide* (Paris: OECD 2003) available for download at <http://www.oecd.org/document/63/0,2340,en_2649_34887_1826559_1_1_1_1,00.html>; *Forty Years' Experience with the OECD Code of Liberalization of Capital Movements* (Paris: OECD, October 2002) summary and conclusions available for download at the above website reference.

[191] See Invisibles Code ibid Annex A for list of current invisible operations covered.

[192] See Capital Movements Code above n 190 Annex A, List A(I) and (II), which deal with the freedom to make and to liquidate direct investments.

[193] See art 1 'General Undertakings' in the respective codes.

is reinforced by a positive duty to grant any authorization required for the conclusion or execution of the transactions or transfers covered,[194] and by a duty of non-discrimination in the application of liberalization measures to investors from other Member States.[195]

However, the codes permit members to lodge reservations in relation to matters on which full liberalization cannot be immediately achieved, thereby stressing the progressive nature of the liberalization involved.[196] Furthermore, the obligation to liberalize is not peremptory. It is qualified by the member's reasonable public interest concerns. Thus, Article 3 of each code states that a member is not prevented from taking action which it considers necessary for, '(i) the maintenance of public order or the protection of public health, morals and safety; (ii) the protection of essential security interests; (iii) the fulfilment of its obligations relating to international peace and security'.

The obligation to liberalize is further qualified by the preservation, in each code, of the powers of members to verify the authenticity of transactions or transfers and to take any measures required to prevent evasion of their laws or regulations.[197] Moreover, where the economic and financial situation of a member justifies such a course, the member need not take all the measures of liberalization provided for in the code.[198] Similarly, where the member has taken such measures of liberalization, it may derogate from those measures where these result in serious economic and financial disturbance or where there exists a seriously deteriorating balance-of-payments situation.[199] As in the case of reservations, the derogation provisions permit for a gradual liberalization of restrictions in situations where unconditional liberalization may be against a member's immediate interests.

The lodging of a reservation or derogation does not disentitle the member concerned from the right to benefit from measures of liberalization offered by other members, provided the notification and examination procedures laid down in the codes are complied with.[200] These procedures are administered by the Committee on Capital Movements and Invisible Transactions.[201] Under the Invisibles Code the examination is conducted in relation to subject matter, the reservations of all member countries being considered at the same time, whereas under the Capital Movements Code examinations are by each member country in turn. This reflects differences in the approach to restrictions in each field. Under the Invisibles Code, most restrictions are concentrated in a small number of unrelated service sectors, while under the Capital Movements Code restrictions are often closely related to

---

[194] ibid art 2 'Measures of Liberalization'.   [195] ibid art 9 'Non-Discrimination'.

[196] ibid These reservations are set out in Annex B to each code. They offer a good periodic indicator of how far liberalization has actually progressed among the OECD member states.

[197] Both codes art 5(a) 'Controls and Formalities'.

[198] ibid art 7(a) 'Measures of Derogation'.   [199] ibid sub-paras (b) and (c).

[200] ibid art 8 'Right to Benefit From Measures of Liberalization'. For the notification and examination procedure in relation to reservations see both codes art 12; for the notification and examination procedure in relation to derogations see both codes art 13.

[201] See both codes Part III 'Terms of Reference' for the composition and functions of the Committee.

one another and to the macroeconomic policy and performance of each country concerned.[202] Upon completing its examination, the Committee reports to the OECD Council, which may endorse a member's decision to withdraw or amend a reservation by means of a legally binding decision, or may make non-binding recommendations to a member on further measures of liberalization.[203]

In relation to direct investment and establishment, the Capital Movements Code is of primary significance. In Annex A to the code, direct investment is defined as 'investment for the purpose of establishing lasting economic relations with an undertaking such as, in particular, investments which give the possibility of exercising an effective influence in the management thereof . . .'. The code extends to both inward and outward investment effected by means of, either, the creation or extension of a wholly owned enterprise, subsidiary or branch, the acquisition of full ownership of an existing enterprise, participation in a new or existing enterprise or by way of a long-term loan of five years or longer. In 1984 the Capital Movements Code was extended to include the right of establishment.[204] Thus Annex A continues:

The authorities of the Members shall not maintain or introduce: Regulations or practices applying to the granting of licences, concessions, or similar authorisations, including conditions or requirements attaching to such authorisations and affecting the operations of enterprises, that raise special barriers or limitations with respect to non-resident (as compared to resident) investors, and that have the intent or the effect of preventing or significantly impeding inward direct investment by non-residents.

This definition of the right to establishment is wide enough to cover most policies that restrict, or make conditional, access to non-resident investors. They are subject to the above mentioned public policy exemptions to the code.

The Invisibles Code protects the right of establishment and operation for branches and agencies of foreign insurers,[205] foreign banks, and financial institutions.[206] In addition, a right of access to associations and self-regulatory bodies has been added, a right which, according to the OECD, 'in many countries is essential for anybody who wants to provide financial as well as certain professional services'.[207] While host countries remain entitled to regulate the establishment of foreign service providers in these sectors, this must be done in accordance with the general principle of equivalent treatment for national providers and those from other OECD member states, so that the latter shall not be liable to heavier burdens than those imposed on the former. Therefore, equivalent authorization provisions must apply to both.

---

[202] See *OECD User's Guide* above n 190 at 43–4.
[203] See both codes art 12(d) and 19 and *OECD User's Guide* ibid 44.
[204] See further *Introduction to the OECD Codes of Liberalization* (Paris: OECD, 1987) 22–24.
[205] See Invisibles Code Annex I to Annex A Part III.   [206] ibid Annex II to Annex A.
[207] *OCED User's Guide* above n 190 at 9.

The Liberalization Codes must be read alongside the National Treatment Instrument in the OECD Declaration on International Investment and Multinational Enterprises and the OECD Guidelines on Multinational Enterprises.[208] While the Liberalization Codes cover rights of establishment for non-resident investors, the National Treatment Instrument covers the standards applicable to already established enterprises owned or controlled by non-residents. It requires that such enterprises be treated in a manner no less favourable than that accorded to domestic enterprises in a similar situation. Unlike the Liberalization Codes it is a non-binding instrument. The National Treatment Instrument is reviewed by the OECD Committee on International Investment and Multinational Enterprises. Together, the various OECD Codes provide an integrated set of principles by which the progressive liberalization of investment and establishment can be furthered among the OECD member states. They establish the OECD members' general policy on investment, a policy which gives an indication of the kinds of regulatory principles that these states are seeking to apply to the global economy as a whole.

(b) Direct Investment and the WTO Agreements

The Uruguay Round of multilateral trade negotiations introduced, for the first time, investment related issues into the GATT agenda. New areas of negotiation were instituted concerning: the freedom of cross-border trade and rights of establishment in relation to services, the protection of intellectual property against counterfeiting and host country technology transfer measures, and the limitation of trade-related investment measures, such as performance or equity requirements, imposed by host states on foreign investors. These issues came to be on the negotiating agenda as a result of pressure from the major capital-exporting countries, and from the US in particular.[209] The underlying aim of the capital exporters was to remove what they perceived as impediments to the growth of an integrated global economy, in which the activities of MNEs would be free from restrictive regulation, enabling them to act on purely economic considerations to the presumed benefit of all states.

The Uruguay Round was launched at the Special Session of GATT contracting parties held at Punta del Este, Uruguay, between 15–20 September 1986. The meeting ended with the adoption of the Punta Del Este Declaration, which sets

---

[208] See ch 16 at 626–28 and ch 17 at 658–60. Both instruments were revised in 2000 and can be downloaded from <http://www.oecd.org/document/28/0,2340,en_2649_34889_2397532_1_1_1_1,00.html>.

[209] For a critical analysis of the background to the Uruguay Round negotiations, see C Raghavan *Recolonisation: GATT, the Uruguay Round and the Third World* (London: Zed Books, 1990) chs 1–4. See, for a critical assessment of the services and intellectual property Uruguay Round Agreements, Christopher Arup *The New World Trade Organization Agreements: Globalizing Law Through Services and Intellectual Property* (Cambridge: Cambridge University Press, 2000).

out the agenda for the Round.[210] In relation to investment issues, the declaration embodied a compromise between the capital-exporting states and the developing countries, which were concerned that excessive liberalization in the fields under review could result in their economies being swamped by foreign MNEs to the detriment of domestic firms.[211] While trade related intellectual property issues (TRIPs) and trade related investment measures (TRIMs) were included as negoti-ating items within the GATT framework, services were to be negotiated separ-ately. This was a compromise worked out to accommodate the developing countries comprising the so-called Group of Ten, led by Brazil and India,[212] who remained opposed to any extension of the GATT beyond pure trade issues.[213] The Round proceeded to a mid-term review in December 1988 and April 1989.[214] In 1990, negotiations broke down as a result of major disagreements over agriculture between the EC and the US. Negotiations continued in December 1991, after the EC and US worked out an initial compromise on the differences that separated them. In January 1992 it was hoped that the Round could be concluded on the basis of final texts drawn up by the Secretary-General of GATT in all major areas, including those of concern to this work.[215] The negotiations finally came to an end in December 1993, when the Final Act Embodying the Results of the Uruguay Round of Multilateral Trade Negotiations was drawn up for signature.[216] The Final Act was opened for signature on 15 April 1994 in Marrakesh, Morocco. The WTO came into existence on 1 January 1995. Against this background each of the three investment related areas of negotiation will be considered.

(i) Services

In recent decades trade and direct investment in services have become increasingly significant features of the world economy, a trend even more pronounced now than at the time of the Uruguay Round.[217] The principal providers of services are

[210] The declaration is reproduced in Raghavan Annex 1; or 25 ILM 1623 (1986).

[211] For a forceful statement of the LDC position, see generally Raghavan ibid. For a critical exam-ination of India's approach to the Uruguay Round negotiations see Desai 'India in the Uruguay Round' 23 JWTL 33 (No 6 1989).

[212] The other members were Argentina, Cuba, Egypt, Nicaragua, Nigeria, Peru, Tanzania, and former Yugoslavia. Argentina detached itself from the group prior to the Special Session, while Kenya and Zimbabwe joined.

[213] See Randihawa 'Punta del Este and After: Negotiations on Trade in Services and the Uruguay Round' 21 JWTL 163 at 163–64 (No 4 1987); 'Gatt Ministers Seek a Draw in Wrestling Match Over Services' *Financial Times* 18 September 1986 at 5.

[214] For the decisions adopted at the conclusion of the mid-term review, 8 April 1989, see *GATT Focus*, Newsletter No 61 of May 1989 reproduced in 28 ILM 1023 (1989).

[215] GATT Secretary-General *Draft Final Act of the Uruguay Round* (GATT Doc MTN.TNC/W/FA).

[216] See GATT Doc MTN/FA 15 December 1993 (UR-93–0246). Extracts in 33 ILM 1 (1994).

[217] See UNCTC *Transnational Corporations, Services and the Uruguay Round* (New York: 1990, UN Doc ST/CTC/103); UNCTC 'The Role of Transnational Corporations in Services, Including Transborder Data Flows' (UN Doc E/C.10/1987/11) summarized in The CTC Reporter No 23 (Spring 1987) 18–21. UNCTAD *World Investment Report 2004* (New York and Geneva: United Nations, 2004) Part Two 'The Shift Towards Services' and see the discussion in ch 1 at 424.

firms located in the major capital-exporting countries. In order to exploit the potential international market for their activities, service orientated MNEs need open access to host countries whether through cross-border trade or, where necessary, through establishment within the host country. However, the areas in which service enterprises work (eg financial services, insurance, transport, media, tourism) have been among the most highly regulated of business sectors.[218] Consequently, markets have tended to be fragmented along national lines. Business environments in host states will often favour local providers over foreign competitors, or exclude them altogether. Furthermore, national markets may be controlled by local private or public monopolies, making liberalization particularly difficult. It is against such restrictions that the capital exporting countries launched their initiative on services in the Uruguay Round. They argued that the GATT should cover all traded commodities, which must now include services as well as goods. The capital exporters partially succeeded in this aim. Although services would not be discussed under GATT, parallel negotiations leading to an eventual international agreement on services would take place.[219]

The resulting General Agreement on Trade in Services (GATS) contains a right of establishment.[220] By Article I thereof, trade in services is defined as the supply of a service inter alia through the commercial presence of a service supplier of one member in the territory of any other member.[221] Furthermore, by Article XXVIII(d) 'commercial presence' is defined as meaning 'any type of business or professional establishment, including through (i) the constitution, acquisition or maintenance of a juridical person, or (ii) the creation or maintenance of a branch or a representative office within the territory of a Party for the purpose of supplying a service'. This definition is consistent with the existence of a right of establishment. Such a right will exist where a member of the GATS makes specific commitments on market access under Article XVI of the GATS. Article XVI goes on to state that, in sectors where the member undertakes market access commitments, it is prohibited from imposing certain listed limitations on the supply of services, unless it expressly specifies that it retains such limitations. These limitations include measures that would affect access through inter alia direct investment. Thus, in the absence of express reservation, the member cannot restrict or require specific types of legal entity or joint venture through which a service could be provided, nor impose limits for the participation of foreign capital drawn up in terms of limits on maximum foreign shareholding or total value of individual or aggregate foreign investment.[222]

---

[218] See further Klodt 'International Trade, Direct Investment and Regulation of Services' 12 World Competition 49 (No 2 1988); Putterman 'Transnational Production in Services as a Form of International Trade' 16 World Competition 123 (No 2 1992).

[219] See Raghavan above n 209 ch 5.

[220] GATT Doc MTN/FA II-A1B; 33 ILM 44 (1994) available at <http://www.wto.org>.

[221] ibid art 1(c).   [222] ibid art XVI(2)(e)–(f).

The wording of Article XVI makes clear that the receiving state is entirely free in determining the extent of its market access commitments, and that it may expressly reserve powers to limit the mode of supply; there is no general obligation to remove all barriers concerning the entry and establishment of service providing firms. Each Member of GATS is obliged to do no more than set out the specific market access commitments that it is prepared to undertake in a schedule drawn up in accordance with Article XX of the GATS. Thereafter, members shall enter into subsequent rounds of negotiations with a view to achieving progressively higher levels of liberalization.[223]

This approach has been termed the 'GATS type positive list' or 'bottom-up' approach to investment liberalization. It contrasts with the NAFTA style 'negative list' or 'top down' approach, which was described earlier, and which is also used in the OECD Liberalization Codes. There is a continuing debate over which approach is better. Countries committed to progressive liberalization argue that a positive commitment to liberalization, coupled with a 'negative list' of exceptions, is more likely to result in actual liberalization of entry and establishment conditions. On the other hand, developing countries, in particular, have favoured the GATS type approach on the ground that it allows for a more considered and gradual process of liberalization, which the 'negative list' approach does not, as this requires an ex ante determination of which sectors should be excluded from the pressures of open competition with foreign investors. Such a calculation may be impossible to make at the time of entering into an international agreement, especially for a country with limited resources to assess the competitive condition of its economic sectors. By contrast the 'positive list' approach does not put immediate pressure on the country to make choices as to exclusions from rights of entry and establishment. Rather, the host country can wait and see which of its sectors evolves to a position where it can be opened to competition from foreign investors.[224] Thus, by adopting this approach, the GATS stops short of guaranteeing rights of establishment in all cases, and leaves a wide margin of discretion to the members. Indeed, a blanket abolition of national controls over services would have been impossible to negotiate. Consequently, a slower, progressive approach to liberalization has been adopted by all the participating states.[225]

The gradual nature of the GATS is further exemplified by the scope of the obligations that must be observed by receiving states in relation to those sectors in which market access commitments have been made. Thus, under Article XVII,

---

[223] ibid Art XIX(1). Currently there are negotiations over services liberalization but no conclusive results have been reached.

[224] See further *World Investment Report 2003* above n 55 at 148–9; UNCTAD *International Investment Agreements: Flexibility for Development* Series on issues in international investment agreements (New York and Geneva: United Nations, 2000) 60–64.

[225] See, for analysis of this negotiating problem, Jackson 'Constructing a Constitution for Trade in Services' 11 The World Economy 2 (1988). For a more radical, prescriptive approach see Nicolaides 'Economic Aspects of Services: Implications for a GATT Agreement' 23 JWTL (No 1 1989) 125. See also 'Slender Success in Attacking Barriers' *Financial Times* 16 December 1993 at 4.

national treatment is guaranteed to services and service suppliers of any other member in the scheduled sectors, but is made subject to 'any conditions and qualifications set out therein . . . '.[226] Any additional commitments that are not subject to scheduling under Article XVI or Article XVII, including those relating to qualifications, standards, or licensing matters, are left to negotiation between GATS members.[227] On the other hand, certain obligations attach automatically when a member makes a specific commitment. Thus, members must apply domestic regulations in sectors where specific commitments have been undertaken in a reasonable, objective, and impartial manner,[228] and establish legal procedures that will provide the service supplier with, 'prompt review of, and where justified, appropriate remedies for, administrative decisions affecting trade in services'.[229] In addition, a member must not apply restrictions on international payments and transfers for current transactions relating to its specific commitments,[230] unless there exist serious balance-of-payments and external financial difficulties or the threat thereof.[231] These obligations can only be terminated through the termination of the underlying specific commitment.

Apart from specific commitments made under the above mentioned provisions, the GATS introduces certain general obligations binding upon members as a result of signing the agreement. Thus members are bound inter alia to extend Most Favoured Nation (MFN) treatment to all other members (Article II); offer transparency in the publication of laws and regulations pertaining to trade in services (Article III); work towards the progressive recognition of national qualifications in the field of services (Article VII); and ensure that monopoly suppliers of services act consistently with the MFN principle and with members specific commitments (Article VIII). These general obligations are subject to public order, public health, and national security exceptions (Articles XIV, XIVbis). Furthermore, members are allowed to declare exemptions lasting up to 10 years from the MFN standard.[232] Thus the general obligations are rather weak.

Finally, it should be noted that the GATS contains provisions relating to developing countries. The preamble recognizes the particular need of developing countries to exercise the right to regulate the supply of services within their territories in order to meet national policy objectives. Equally, Article IV(1) encourages the negotiation of specific commitments by different members relating to: the strengthening of the domestic services capacity of developing countries, their efficiency and competitiveness through, inter alia, access to technology on a commercial basis; the improvement of developing country access to distribution channels and information networks; and the liberalization of market access in sectors and modes of supply of export interest to developing countries. Furthermore, developed country members are encouraged, by Article IV(2), to establish contact points designed

---

[226] GATS above n 220 art XVII(1).   [227] ibid art XVIII.   [228] ibid art VI(1).
[229] ibid art VI(2).   [230] ibid art XI(1).   [231] ibid art XII.
[232] ibid art II (2) and Annex on art II Exemptions para 6.

to facilitate developing country service suppliers in obtaining relevant commercial and technological information. Thus, the GATS is cautious not to subject developing countries to immediate liberalization and offers certain general obligations to ensure that service suppliers from these countries can compete in international markets.[233] However, these are rather weak commitments which do not impose positive duties to open up markets for such suppliers.

(ii) Trade-Related Intellectual Property Measures (TRIPs)

For some years prior to the Uruguay Round MNEs pressed their home governments for increased action over the protection of their technological advantages against copyright abuses in countries where such rights had not been respected.[234] In particular, US firms from the computer, chemical, and automobile industries formed the Intellectual Property Committee to press for increased controls over international copyright 'piracy' and 'counterfeiting' of goods.[235] This led the US, supported by other capital-exporting countries, to press for the inclusion of TRIPs into the Uruguay Round. In addition, the US had added intellectual property rights infringements to its list of unfair trade practices that could result in retaliatory action under section 301 of the Trade Act 1974, as amended, leading to a number of high profile and controversial unilateral actions against alleged infringements by India, China, and Brazil among others. These were designed, in part, to put pressure upon these opponents of the new issues in the Uruguay Round, to accept them.[236]

The argument for inclusion of disciplines on intellectual property asserts that the non-observance of intellectual property rights by certain host states serves to distort trade and to impede investment in these countries. Such non-observance is said to act as a disincentive to firms that have tied up large sums in the development of new technology and products as they may be unwilling to risk that advantage being freely taken by competitors in the host state. The assumption behind

---

[233] The OECD has recommended the liberalization of services in developing countries as a positive stimulus to development. See OECD *Trade in Services and Developing Countries* (Paris: OECD, 1989).

[234] The UNCTC estimated the losses resulting from such abuses as around US$60 billion at the time of the Uruguay Round negotiations. See IK Minta 'Intellectual Property Rights and Investment Issues in the Uruguay Round' The CTC Reporter No 29 (Spring 1990) 43. See also UNCTC report on the subject to the 16th Session of the UN Commission on TNCs: UN Doc E/C.10/1990/13.

[235] See 'A Question of Patent Unfairness' *Financial Times* 8 September 1986.

[236] See s 301 Trade and Tariff Act 1974 88 Stat 1978, 19 USC s 2411 et seq as amended by the Omnibus Trade and Competitiveness Act of 1988 Public Law No 100–418 102 Stat 1107 s 1301. Under this provision the US Trade Representative (USTR) keeps a 'watch list' of countries that are identified as indulging in unfair trade practices, including intellectual property practices, that adversely affect US trading interests. Listing will be followed by bilateral negotiations, which, if unsuccessful in resolving the matter, will be followed by retaliatory measures taken by the USTR against the listed country. On s 301 generally, see further J Bhagwati and H Patrick (eds) *Aggressive Unilateralism: America's 301 Trade Policy and the World Trading System* (Harvester Wheatsheaf, 1991); Thomas O Bayard and Kimberly Ann Elliot *Reciprocity and Retaliation in US Trade Policy* (Washington DC: Institute for International Economics, 1994).

this argument is that, unless the creators of new technology are assured a monopoly rent from their innovation, technological development and investment based on the most modern technology will be impaired. However, this theoretical position may not stand up to empirical scrutiny. The level of intellectual property protection in a host state is not necessarily a determinant of investment. There are cases of high investment levels amid low levels of such protection, and cases of non-exploitation of patents when these are granted.[237] On the other hand there appears to be some positive correlation between enhanced intellectual property protection and increased levels of foreign direct investment, provided that such protection is accompanied by other polices that encourage dynamic competition and technical development, such as enhanced skills training, market access liberalization, and effective competition policy and an enhanced technology infrastructure.[238]

Notwithstanding these debates, the Punta Del Este Declaration proceeded on the basis of the capital exporters' theoretical assumptions and placed the elaboration of new rules and disciplines in the area of TRIPs on the negotiating agenda. The aim was to 'reduce the distortions and impediments to international trade . . .', and the declaration emphasized the need 'to promote effective and adequate protection of intellectual property rights, and to ensure that measures and procedures to enforce intellectual property rights do not themselves become barriers to legitimate trade . . .'. The declaration goes on to mandate negotiations for the development of a new multilateral framework to deal with trade in counterfeit goods, and stresses that the GATT negotiations shall be without prejudice to initiatives taken in the World Intellectual Property Organization (WIPO) or elsewhere.

From the outset, negotiations became embroiled in disputes over the extent of this mandate. The developing countries were opposed to any discussion of substantive standards in the GATT. Such matters should, in their view, be discussed in international organizations with competence in this area. The GATT negotiations should be limited only to a clarification of the relevant GATT provisions.[239] By the Mid-Term Review, this disagreement had not been resolved.[240] However, ministers agreed to continue negotiations in this area on specific issues.[241] The dispute over GATT jurisdiction in relation to TRIPs was resolved in the Final Act by giving the Agreement on TRIPs separate administrative status

---

[237] Minta above n 234. Minta cites case studies from the Turkish pharmaceutical industry and a survey of patent exploitation by MNEs in Nigeria to support his argument. See Kirim 'Reconsidering Patents and Economic Development: A Case Study of the Turkish Pharmaceutical Industry' 13 World Development 227 (1985); Adikibi 'The Multinational Corporation and Monopoly of Patents in Nigeria' 16 World Development 517 (1988).

[238] See further Keith E Mascus *Intellectual Property Right in the Global Economy* (Washington DC: Institute for International Economics, 2000) and ch 11 below.

[239] Raghavan above n 209 at 128.   [240] ibid at 257, 260.

[241] Mid-Term Review Decision above n 214 at ILM 1030.

from the GATT.[242] The agreement would have its own council acting under the umbrella of the new World Trade Organization. The GATT, and the GATS, would have their own administrative councils.[243]

The TRIPs Agreement accepts the principle that intellectual property rights are private rights deserving protection.[244] Thus it accords national treatment[245] and MFN/non-discrimination standards to foreign firms.[246] Patents are to be protected for 20 years,[247] and designs for integrated circuits for 10 years.[248] Computer programs will be protected as literary works under the Berne Convention.[249] The TRIPs Agreement also accepts the 'special needs of the least-developed country Members in respect of maximum flexibility in the domestic implementation of laws and regulations in order to enable them to create a sound and viable technological base'.[250] Accordingly, developing countries were allowed to delay product patent protection for up to 10 years.[251] The TRIPs Agreement has significant effects upon the policy space of WTO members in the field of technology transfer and its relationship with intellectual property rights protection. These issues will be discussed more fully in chapter 11.

(iii) Trade-Related Investment Measures (TRIMs)

The final area of investment-related WTO provisions concerns TRIMs. The capital-exporting countries sought to have TRIMs included in the Uruguay Round in the light of their belief that the investment policies of certain developing and developed host states were too restrictive to permit investment decisions from being made on purely economic grounds. The US Government was particularly willing to take a stand against TRIMs, as shown by the bringing of the GATT case against Canada concerning performance requirements agreed with investors under the Foreign Investment Review Act.[252] Furthermore, s 301 of the 1974 Trade Act, as amended in 1988, was invoked against countries that denied access to US firms on the basis of TRIMs.[253] For example, the US applied s 301 against India, in respect of what it saw as that country's excessive restrictions on foreign investment and, in particular, on the establishment of foreign service industries.[254]

---

[242] Agreement on Trade Related Aspects of Intellectual Property Rights, Including Trade in Counterfeit Goods: GATT Doc MTN/FA II–A1C; 33 ILM 81 (1994) or <http://:www.wto.org>.

[243] ibid Part VII. See also the Agreement Establishing the World Trade Organization above n 216 especially art IV.   [244] ibid preamble.

[245] ibid art 3.   [246] ibid art 4.

[247] ibid art 33. By art 27(1), 'patents shall be available for any inventions, whether products or processes, in all fields of technology, provided that they are new, involve an inventive step and are capable of industrial application'. The protection is to be available regardless of the place of invention or whether the products are imported or locally produced. Article 27(3) permits the exclusion from patentability of (a) diagnostic, therapeutic and surgical methods for the treatment of humans and animals and (b) plants and animals other than micro-organisms and essentially biological processes for the production of plants or animals other than non-biological and microbiological processes.

[248] ibid art 38.   [249] ibid art 10(1).   [250] ibid preamble.   [251] ibid art 65.

[252] See previous chapter at 208.   [253] Above n 236.

[254] See Raghavan above n 209 at 146; Bayard and Elliot above n 236 at 164–68. See also 'US Versus India' *Financial Times* 12 June 1989 at 19. India has since liberalized its foreign investment law: see previous chapter at 187–88.

The most common TRIMs to which objection had been taken included inter alia: local equity requirements restricting foreign ownership of investments; licensing requirements and technology transfer rules requiring the transfer of foreign firms' technology; remittance and foreign exchange restrictions limiting external financial transfers; manufacturing limitations restricting production levels; domestic sales, local content and manufacturing requirements that seek to displace imports; and export requirements seeking to increase the export performance of the host state.[255] Such measures have been taken mainly by less developed host states in order to secure the investments required for their development needs and priorities, to protect their balance-of-payments situation against distortions caused by profit remittances or payments for goods and services, and to control possible restrictive business practices on the part of foreign firms related to their market power and ownership of technology.[256] They have also been used by developed countries as part of their investment policies.[257]

As with the other areas of investment-related negotiating issues, the debate on TRIMs was strongly influenced by neo-classical economic analysis. Under this paradigm, perfect competition is assumed. It follows that TRIMs, as second-best economic policies, are, in principle, distortive and must be removed so as to ensure the survival of conditions of perfect competition. Failure to do so increases the costs of investment for MNEs and distorts international investment flows, which, in turn, distort international flows of trade in intermediate products. However, as noted in chapter 1, the very existence of MNEs results from the failure of perfect competition in international markets. Thus, economic policy-makers will tend to introduce measures that combat the adverse effects of imperfect competition as conducted by MNEs. In this sense TRIMs attempt to minimize the adverse effects on the host state's economy of structural imbalances in the distribution of investment and technology. The empirical evidence suggests that there is some merit in the use of TRIMs and that the neo-classical objections are overstated.[258] Although import-substituting TRIMs are likely to have adverse effects on the host state's economy if they merely shelter inefficient producers from competition, export performance TRIMs may actually benefit the host by ensuring a higher return from exports to world markets and encouraging backward and forward linkages that

[255] See Minta above n 234 Table at 45. For an explanation of the principal types of investment measures taken by developing countries see Raghavan above n 209 at 148–51. See further UNCTAD *Foreign Direct Investment and Performance Requirements: New Evidence from Selected Countries* (New York and Geneva: United Nations, 2003) chs II–V covering Chile, India, Malaysia, and South Africa. See also T Moran *The Impact of Trade-Related Investment Measures (TRIMs) on Trade and Development: Theory Evidence and Policy Implications* (UNCTC, 1991) ch II. A shorter summary can be found in Moran 'The Impact of TRIMs on Trade and Development' 1 Transnational Corporations (No 1 1992) 55–65.   [256] See Raghavan ibid at 147–48.

[257] See eg Irish and UK investment incentives described above; see also the policy behind Canada's FIRA in the previous chapter. See also UNCTAD n 255 ch VI.

[258] Minta above n 209 at 46. See further T Moran and C Pearson *Trade-Related Investment Performance Requirements* (OPIC, Washington DC: 1987); Moran and Pearson 'Tread Carefully in the Field of TRIP Measures' 11 The World Economy 119 (1988).

enhance economic development.[259] Therefore, the need for strict controls over TRIMs may have been overestimated by the capital-exporting states.

The Agreement on TRIMs is a compromise measure steering a middle way between total prohibition of all types of TRIMs and full freedom for national policy.[260] Developing countries were free to deviate temporarily from these provisions to the extent that they were allowed to deviate from Articles III and XI of the GATT under Article XVIII thereof, and to take advantage of the five-year transition period contained in the agreement.[261] The agreement specifies that certain categories of TRIMs offend the principles of the GATT 1994. TRIMs that are inconsistent with the GATT are said to be investment measures that are mandatory or enforceable under domestic law or under administrative rulings, or compliance with which is necessary to obtain an advantage. The measures in question must relate to 'investment'.[262] This is an issue of fact in each case, one that will be determined on the actual effect of the measure and not on its formal classification.[263] In addition, the measure must be related to 'trade in goods only'.[264] This too is an

---

[259]   See Moran above n 255 chs III, IV.

[260]   Agreement on Trade-Related Investment Measures: GATT Doc MTN/FA II-A1A-7 available at <http://www.wto.org>. The TRIMs Agreement is administered by a Committee whose responsibilities are assigned to it by the Council for Trade in Goods: art 7. See also Trebilcock and Howse above n 101 at 436–37. Other agreements go further than TRIMs and prohibit a wider range of performance requirements: see, for example, NAFTA art 1106; US and Canadian BITs and the proposed Multilateral Agreement on Investment (MAI): see further UNCTAD *Host Country Operational Measures* Series on issues in international investment agreements (New York and Geneva: United Nations, 2001) at 34–52; UNCTAD *Investment Provisions in Economic Integration Agreements* above n 135 at 94–97.

[261]   ibid arts 4 and 5. The transition period for developing countries ended in December 2003.

[262]   ibid art 1.

[263]   *Indonesia – Certain Measures Affecting the Automobile Industry* WT/DS 44/R Panel Report adopted 23 July 1998 paras 14.74–14.81. In this case Indonesia offered tax and customs duty benefits on 'National Cars' to car manufacturers located in that country in return for compliance with local content rules in the production of such cars. Japan the US and EC claimed that this scheme violated art 2 of the TRIMs Agreement and art III (4) of the GATT 1994. The panel upheld these claims. It concluded that the scheme in fact concerned investment even though the Indonesian Government did not designate the underlying regulations as investment regulations. In subsequent cases similar issues, pertaining to the preferential treatment of locally incorporated auto manufacturers, have been dealt with under the MFN, national treatment and quantitative restrictions provisions (Articles I, III: 4 and XI:I GATT 1994): *Canada – Certain Measures Affecting the Automotive Industry* (WT/DS139/R) panel Report adopted 11 February 2000) where the panel held that, as there was a violation of art I and art III:4 GATT, it was unnecessary to consider a possible violation of the TRIMs Agreement; *India – Measures Affecting the Automobile Sector* (WT/DS146/R) panel Report adopted 21 December 2001 where the panel found violations of art III:4 and XI:1 and held that, as a matter of judicial economy, it was unnecessary to consider whether there was also a violation of the TRIMs Agreement (both cases available at <http://:www.wto.org>). These cases have been criticized for departing from the principle, recognized in other WTO rulings, that the more specific provision is to be considered prior to the more general provision: see Dr A Jayagovind 'Shackling the Sovereignty: A Critique of the WTO Rulings on Investment Measures' in Dr A Jayagovind (ed) *Reflections on Emerging International Law: Essays in Memory of Late Subrata Roy Chowdhury* (Calcutta and Bangalore: International Law Association Calcutta Centre, Law Research Institute, Calcutta, National Law School of India University, Bangalore, 2004) 244; Trebilcock and Howse above n 101 at 456–57 and see also Mitsuo Matsushita, Thomas J Schenbaum, and Petros C. Mavroides *The World Trade Organisation: Law Practice and Policy* (Oxford: Oxford University Press, 2nd edn, 2006) at 838–44.

[264]   TRIMs Agreement above n 260 art 1.

issue of fact in each case. Thus, in the *Indonesia Autos* case, the WTO Panel held that local content requirements were necessarily 'trade related' as such requirements, by definition, always favoured the use of domestic products over imported products and therefore affected trade.[265] The panel also held that, to come within the TRIMs Agreement, investment measures do not need to be specifically targeted at foreign investors nor need they be formally designated as foreign investment measures. Thus internal tax advantages or subsidies that are tied to any measures that offend the TRIMs Agreement are covered.[266]

The TRIMs Agreement identifies two groups of TRIMs that offend GATT 1994 in an Illustrative List that is annexed to the agreement. The first consists of TRIMs that offend the national treatment principle in Article III(4). These TRIMs either require the purchase or use by an enterprise of locally produced products or impose import restrictions on the enterprise that relate the amount of imports permitted to the volume or value of local products exported by it.[267] Secondly, the TRIMs Agreement lists other TRIMs that are equivalent to quantitative restrictions prohibited by Article XI(1) of the GATT. These include: restrictions on the importation by an enterprise of products used in or related to its local production whether generally or in proportion to the amount that it exports; the achievement of such import restrictions by limiting the enterprise's access to foreign exchange; export requirements whether specified in relation to certain products, the volume or value of products, or as a proportion of local production.[268] These lists are illustrative not exhaustive. A WTO panel is free to determine whether a particular measure comes within the prohibitions in the TRIMs Agreement as an issue of fact in each case. The key question is not whether the measure in question is expressly listed but whether it violates Article 2.1 of the TRIMs Agreement because it is inconsistent with Article III(4) or Article XI(1) of the GATT. An examination of whether a measure comes within the Illustrative List merely serves to confirm that it is inconsistent with the specific GATT provision to which the list relates. Thus, in *Indonesia Autos*, the panel had little difficulty in finding that the local content requirements, which were contested in this case, came within the prohibition against such measures under Article III(4) of the GATT as they were expressly mentioned in the Illustrative List.[269]

Concluding Remarks

The present chapter has considered policies of investment liberalization and promotion both at the level of unilateral measures undertaken by host states and at the bilateral, regional, and multilateral levels. In each case, the policy aim has been

---

[265] Above n 263 at para 14.82.
[266] ibid at para 14.73. The panel concluded that the 'National Car' scheme in fact concerned investment even though the Indonesian Government did not designate the underlying regulations as investment regulations.   [267] ibid art 2 and Annex para 1.
[268] ibid art 2 and Annex para 2.   [269] Above n 263.

to remove regulatory barriers to the free flow of inward direct investment in the belief that this is likely to offer the most positive economic gains to both the national and global economy. However, the removal of host state controls cannot automatically guarantee adequate levels, or useful kinds, of inward investment. Nor will it guarantee an equitable international distribution of the benefits of such investment. Furthermore, competition over investment incentives between states may create economic distortions between them with little positive gain to their economies. Nonetheless, the reduction of barriers to direct investment and the use of investment incentives stand to benefit MNEs in that they can establish operations over a wider geographical space and can enjoy reduced investment risks.

Against this background, the leading home states of MNEs have placed the reduction of barriers to foreign direct investment onto the agendas of regional and multilateral economic organizations. In this way it is hoped to influence the content of host state policy away from restrictive controls over direct investment and towards an increasingly deregulated environment. This strategy has met with some success. Regional bodies such as NAFTA and the EC have been willing to reduce barriers to direct investment within their territories. In principle, the opening up of such regional markets has been extended not only to firms already established within the region but also to those established outside it. However, the fears remain that such regional organizations can become protectionist and introduce restrictive and discriminatory regulations against the entry and establishment of firms from outside the region. By contrast, the WTO Agreements offer few concrete commitments to liberalization. The limited rights of entry and establishment under the GATS are a case in point. On the other hand, the TRIPs and TRIMs Agreements offer some significant controls over host state discretion and allow for the removal of certain significant barriers to investment.

7

Taxation Problems Associated with MNEs

As in the case of a purely domestic company, the principal aim behind the taxation of MNEs is to collect revenue on the undistributed profits of the company and upon the distributions of profits made to shareholders, in accordance with the rules applicable to the taxing jurisdiction concerned.[1] However, the taxation of MNEs involves further issues arising out of the internationally integrated operations of the firm, the legal relations between its affiliates, and the territorial limits of national revenue laws. Of the many tax issues relevant to MNEs,[2] this chapter will concentrate on three areas that illustrate the particular difficulties faced by taxpaying MNEs and the countries that seek to collect revenue from them. The first concerns problems of international double taxation encountered by MNEs. Secondly, the ways in which home and host states can influence the location of MNE activities by use of their tax systems will be considered as a prelude to the third issue, which deals with the opportunities for tax avoidance enjoyed by MNEs as a result of their integrated international operations.

(1) International Double Taxation and MNEs

Where a domestic firm carries on business as an economically integrated unit through a network of separately incorporated companies, each company will be assessed to tax as a separate taxpayer. Thus, a subsidiary is liable to tax on its undistributed profits and the parent is liable to tax on the profits remitted to it by its subsidiary. This may result in the risk of double taxation where a subsidiary pays a dividend out of its profits to the parent company. The risk arises as the remitted profits would already have been included in the calculation of the subsidiary's own

---

[1] On the domestic tax treatment of companies, see JDR Adams and J Whalley *The International Taxation of Multinational Enterprises in Developed Countries* (London: Institute of Fiscal Studies/ Associated Business Programmes, 1977) ch 2; on UK company taxation see JH Farrar and BM Hannigan *Farrar's Company Law* (London: Butterworths, 4th edn, 1998) ch 21.

[2] For a full treatment of the taxation of MNEs, see Sol Picciotto *International Business Taxation* (London: Weidenfeld and Nicolson, 1992); Alex Easson *Taxation of Foreign Direct Investment: An Introduction* (The Hague: Kluwer Law International, 1999).

tax liability. Such a result may be avoided by use of group income provisions.[3] Secondly, trading losses occurring in one company may not be set off against profits occurring in another. To avoid this result domestic tax laws normally allow for certain group reliefs.[4] By contrast, MNEs experience further, distinctive, tax difficulties associated with their international operations. In particular, they are prone to suffer international double taxation. This differs from the double taxation to which a domestic corporate group is exposed in that the latter involves the risk of 'an income flow being subjected to more than one charge to tax within the *same* domestic tax system'.[5] International double taxation, on the other hand, arises from 'a profit being subjected to more than one charge to tax because that profit would ... be within charge to tax under the system of two or more countries'.[6] International double taxation can arise in the case of MNE operations because both the host and the home countries will claim a charge to tax on the profits of the company.[7] The host country will tax the profits of the subsidiary on the basis that these arise, or have their 'source', within the host's territory. Furthermore, the host may impose a withholding tax on dividends that are remitted out of the subsidiary's profits to the parent company. Likewise, the home country will charge the remitted profits to tax as part of the worldwide profits of the parent company, the home country's jurisdiction to tax being based on the residence of the parent company in that country.

Were this income flow to remain subject to international double taxation, companies would face considerable disincentives against the making of foreign investments. A major investment outlay might not be returned in the form of adequate net profits. It has been argued that this result would be economically inefficient, in that there would be unequal tax treatment between domestic and foreign investment, causing a distortion in international investment and resource allocation patterns.[8] The effect would be contrary to that predicted under a state of 'tax neutrality' where, ideally, tax rates for domestic and foreign investment would be the same and taxation would thereby cease to be an important factor in investment decision-making.[9]

In order to combat international double taxation, the tax laws of most capital-exporting countries include rules for its alleviation. This can be done, either, by unilateral relief measures under the state's internal tax laws, or by rules contained in bilateral double taxation conventions. Unilateral relief is granted irrespective of whether any other state grants reciprocal relief, while bilateral relief is granted

---

[3] See, for example, UK Income and Corporation Taxes Act 1988 s 240 and see further ibid ch VI ss 402–413.   [4] See ibid ss 402–403.
  [5] Adams and Whalley above n 1 at 41.   [6] ibid.
  [7] See ibid at 42–43; see also Sylvian Plasschaert *Transfer Pricing and Multinational Corporations: an Overview of Mechanisms and Regulations* (Gower: Saxon House, 1979) ch 10. Appendix 1 paras 10.4–10.5 at 112.   [8] See Adams and Whalley above n 1 at 66–68.
  [9] See further Gumpel 'The Taxation of American Business Abroad – Is Further Reform Needed?' 15 Jo.Int.Law & Econ. 389 (1981); Richard E Caves *Multinational Enterprise and Economic Analysis* (Cambridge: Cambridge University Press, 2nd edn, 1996) ch 8 especially 198–200.

under the reciprocal regime contained in the tax treaty concluded by the two signatory states.[10]

There are two principal methods of relieving double taxation, used both in unilateral and bilateral systems.[11] The first is the tax credit system. Under this method the parent company is permitted to set off the taxes paid by its subsidiary in the host state against its tax liability to the home state on its remitted worldwide profits. This has the effect of subjecting the MNE to the home country rate of tax so long as it is equal to, or higher than, the combined rate charged by the host state on the subsidiary's profits under corporation tax and on dividend remittances under withholding tax.

Thus, for example, where the subsidiary earns profits of 100 in the host state (H) and is taxed at a rate of 50 per cent, the remaining 50 per cent is remitted to the parent company. This is then 'grossed up' by the amount of tax paid in H, that is, 50 per cent + 50 per cent = 100 per cent. The grossed up figure is then subjected to home country tax, say 50 per cent, which results in a tax liability for the parent of 50 per cent. The 50 per cent paid in tax in H is credited against this liability, which in this case results in the elimination of further tax liability in the home state. If the home state tax were, say, 60 per cent, the parent company's liability to tax would be 10 per cent.[12] Such a system is used by the UK, Canada, Japan, and the US.[13] It achieves tax neutrality between domestic and outward foreign investors in the home state. However, where the host state tax rate is higher than that of the home state, the credit system will not protect the foreign investor against the higher foreign tax liability thereby incurred. It merely avoids the same income flow being taxed twice by the home and host state.[14]

The second method of double taxation relief is the exemption method. By this system, the home state exempts the profits of the foreign subsidiary from domestic taxation when they are remitted to the parent company. Only when the parent company distributes those profits as a dividend to its shareholders will the home state derive any revenue from them. Given that the profit remittance from the subsidiary will have been subjected to a withholding tax in the host state, and the shareholders will have been charged to full personal income tax on their received dividends without any relief for the host state withholding tax, this system retains an element of unrelieved international double taxation.[15]

However, the MNE as a whole will have been subjected only to the host state rate of tax. This results in a lower burden of tax on foreign investments than on

[10] Adams and Whalley above n 1 at 44–45.

[11] See Adams and Whalley ibid at 45–46; Plasschaert above n 7 at paras 10.7–10.12 at 113–14; DR Davies *Principles of International Double Taxation Relief* (London: Sweet and Maxwell, 1985) paras 1.03–1.05.

[12] For examples of the application of a foreign tax credit, see Adams and Whalley ibid at 75–76.

[13] Davies n 11 above para 1.03. On the US system see Paul R McDaniel, Hugh J Ault, and James R Repetti *Introduction to United States International Taxation* (The Hague: Kluwer Law International, 5th edn, 2005) ch 6.   [14] McDaniel, Ault, and Repetti ibid at 88–89.

[15] Adams and Whalley above n 1 at 74.

domestic investments, provided that the tax rate in the host state is lower than that applicable in the home state.[16] It is therefore an attractive method for investors who have income from low tax countries. This has led to criticisms that the exemption method encourages investment in low tax countries and the use of tax havens.[17] On the other hand, it is an easy system to administer and, unlike the credit system, which is limited to relief from foreign income taxes, capital gains taxes or corporation taxes, it permits account to be taken of foreign taxes that do not correspond to such taxes.[18] Among the countries using this method are the Netherlands, Belgium, France, and Switzerland.[19]

As noted above, apart from adopting unilateral measures, states may enter into bilateral tax treaties which regulate the incidence of international double taxation experienced by inter alia firms operating in both countries. According to Davies, given that most developed states offer unilateral reliefs against international double taxation that are virtually identical to treaty reliefs, it is arguable that tax treaties have only a minor role in relieving double taxation.[20] In his opinion, the major function of such treaties lies in the assistance of commercial relations between treaty partners by enabling them to divide between themselves tax revenues in respect of income falling to be taxed in both jurisdictions.[21] The result will reflect the relative economic strength of the parties. Thus where both parties enjoy equivalent reciprocal flows of trade and investment, each stands to benefit to a similar extent from the treaty. However, where the flow of trade and investment is from one party to the other, as is the case in relation to developed and less developed countries, the bulk of the benefits will flow to the capital-exporting state party.[22] The majority of bilateral tax treaties are between developed states and are based, in large measure, on terms similar to those found in the OECD Model Double Taxation Convention. It is not proposed to discuss these terms, save to the extent that they establish bilateral approaches to the problems of tax avoidance by MNEs.[23]

---

[16] Plasschaert above n 7 at para 10.10.   [17] Davies above n 11 at para 1.05.
[18] ibid para 1.04.   [19] ibid.
[20] Davies above n 11 para 1.06. See further Elizabeth A Owens 'United States Income Tax Treaties: Their Role in Relieving Double Taxation' 17 Rutgers LR 428 (1963).
[21] See also McDaniel, Ault, and Repetti above n 13 at 178. In addition to the avoidance of double taxation, tax treaties also frequently proclaim their purposes as including the avoidance of tax evasion and the promotion of trade and investment. See further Philip Baker *Double Taxation Conventions and International Tax Law* (London: Sweet and Maxwell, 3rd edn, 2001 loose-leaf), UNCTAD *Taxation* Series on issues in international investment agreements (New York and Geneva: United Nations, 2000).
[22] See further Charles R Irish 'International Double Taxation Agreements and Income Taxation at Source' 23 ICLQ 292 (1974).
[23] The latest revision of the OECD Model Convention is 28 January 2003 available upon payment at <http://www.oecd.org/document/17/0,2340,en_2649_33747_35035793_1_1_1_1,00.html>. It includes a comprehensive commentary. See also the UN Model Double Taxation Convention (1999 revision) at <http://daccessdds.un.org/doc/UNDOC/GEN/N00/676/65/PDF/N0067665. pdf?OpenElement>. On US practice, see United States Model Income Tax Convention 20 September 1996 at <http://www.treasury.gov/offices/tax-policy/library/model996.pdf> and Technical Explanation at <http://www.treasury.gov/offices/tax-policy/library/techxpln.pdf>; McDaniel, Ault, and Repetti above n 13 ch 11. See, for details of current UK practice, HM Revenue and Customs 'Double

(2) Location of Investments and Tax Considerations

In chapter 6 it was seen how host states may seek to influence the locational decisions of MNEs by offering tax incentives. Equally, home states may introduce tax
incentives for domestic firms to invest abroad, as where a tax credit or exemption
system operates. Alternatively, home states may introduce tax penalties against
foreign direct investment where the outflow of domestic capital is believed to
harm domestic investment, employment, and/or balance-of-payments.[24]

A foreign tax deduction system will be attractive to a home state that wishes to
discourage outward direct investment by its corporations, in that it subjects foreign
investment to a higher tax liability than domestic investment. Under this method
foreign tax is allowed as a deduction against the profit liable to tax in the home
state. Thus the tax paid in the host state is deducted from the tax base of the parent
company, unlike under the foreign tax credit system, where foreign tax is credited
against the parent company's tax liability on gross profits.

Thus, for example, where a subsidiary earns profits of 100 per cent in the host
state and is taxed at a rate of 50 per cent, the remaining 50 per cent is remitted to
the parent company. This is then subjected to home country tax, say 50 per cent,
which results in a tax liability for the parent of 25 per cent. The total tax paid is
thus 75 per cent:50 per cent in the host state and 25 per cent in the home state. By
comparison, as shown above, the same example yielded no parent company liability to tax under the foreign tax credit system, the total liability to tax being the 50
per cent paid in the host state. From this example it can be seen that a deduction
system will usually result in little or no relief from double taxation. It does no
more than prevent the total burden of home and host state taxes from exceeding
100 per cent.[25]

A deduction system was proposed in the US in the early 1970s under the Burke-
Hartke Bill.[26] It aimed to replace the foreign tax credit and to act as an incentive
for US firms to invest more in the domestic economy. However, if it had been
implemented the effect on cutting outward direct investment may not have been
very great, as US MNEs would have turned from the export of domestic capital to
foreign capital for the expansion of their overseas operations. Furthermore, the

Taxation Agreements' News Release NAT 41/06 24 July 2006 available at <http://www.gnn.gov.uk/
Content/Detail.asp?ReleaseID=216585&NewsAreaID=2>.

[24] See further Alex Easson *Tax Incentives for Foreign Direct Investment* (The Hague: Kluwer Law
International, 2004); Park 'Fiscal Jurisdiction and Accrual Basis Taxation: Lifting the Corporate Veil
to Tax Foreign Company Profits' 78 Col.LR 1609 (1978). Raymond Vernon *Storm Over the
Multinationals* (Macmillan, 1977) 123–28; Adams and Whalley above n 1 ch 12. OECD *Taxation
and International Capital Flows* (Paris: OECD, 1990). This study notes that tax incentives are relatively ineffective in attracting inward direct investment, but that more countries are using them.

[25] Adams and Whalley above n 1 at 46.

[26] S 2592 92d Cong 1st Sess (1971); H.8784 92d Cong 1st Sess (1971). See K Hughes *Trade,
Taxes and Transnationals* (Praeger, 1979) at 23–35.

abolition of the foreign tax credit would have subjected US firms to increased risks of international double taxation as compared with their foreign competitors, which would have put them at a long-term competitive disadvantage.[27]

Notwithstanding governmental policies that use tax incentives and disincentives to affect flows of foreign inward and outward investment, it would appear that tax considerations play a relatively limited part in MNE decision making in most situations. According to UNCTAD,

As a broad generalization, it seems that tax considerations play little part in the initial decision to invest abroad, may play a more important role in locational decisions, are more important for some types of investment than for others, and are growing in importance.[28]

The reasons for this are that the decision where to locate will be influenced more by factors such as the nature of the market and political conditions than by the applicable tax rates.[29] In addition, the importance of host-country taxation varies considerably according to the type of investment. Thus, market-oriented investment is normally unaffected by tax considerations whereas export-oriented FDI is far more sensitive to the host-country tax burden.[30] There is also evidence that the importance of taxation may vary according to the type of industry or activity concerned, reflecting the relative mobility of the investment and the range of possible locations.[31] Nonetheless, tax considerations are becoming a more significant factor in investment decisions than they were in the past.[32] This is an effect of the progressive elimination of barriers to foreign investment, which results in remaining obstacles, such as tax conditions, assuming an increased importance.[33]

Despite the relative unimportance of tax considerations in relation to major strategic decisions, the outcome of numerous management decisions will involve a consideration of applicable tax conditions. Examples include: the decision whether to operate through a permanent establishment that is subject to local taxation, or through a representative office or agent only company that enjoys tax advantages; whether the subsidiary in a high tax host state should have a high debt

---

[27] See C Bergsten, T Horst, and T Moran *American Multinationals and American Interests* (Brookings Institution, 1978) at 112 n 20 208–210 and 179; N Hood and S Young *The Economics of Multinational Enterprise* (Longman, 1979) at 302–305.

[28] See UNCTAD *Taxation and Technology Transfer: Key Issues* (New York and Geneva: United Nations, 2005) at 19. See also Michael P Devereux 'The Impact of Taxation on the Location of Capital, Firms and Profit: A Survey of Empirical Evidence' (European Tax Policy Forum (ETPF) Research Paper, ETPF/IFS Public Conference: *The Impact of Corporation Tax Across Borders*, 24 April 2006, London) at <http://www.etpf.org/research/Phase1/etpf_devereux.pdf>.

[29] See further J Morisset and N Pirnia 'How Tax Policy and Incentives Affect Foreign Direct Investment: A Review' in Louis T Wells Jr, Nancy J Allen, Jacques Morisset, and Neda Pirnia *Using Tax Incentives to Compete for Foreign Investment: Are They Worth the Costs?* (FIAS Occasional Paper15 2001) 69–96.

[30] UNCTAD *Taxation and Technology Transfer* above n 28 at 20.   [31] ibid.

[32] H Grubert and J Mutti (2000) 'Do Taxes Influence Where U.S. Corporations Invest?' 53 National Tax Journal 825 (2000); OECD *Corporate Tax Incentives for Foreign Direct Investment* (Paris: OECD, Tax Policy Studies No 4 2002).

[33] UNCTAD above n 28 at 20 citing WS Clark 'Tax Incentives for Foreign Direct Investment: Empirical Evidence on Effects and Alternative Policy Options' 48 Canadian Tax Journal 1139 (2000).

structure that could involve loans from tax haven finance companies affiliated to the MNE group; whether sales to affiliates or to third parties should be channelled through conduit companies located in low tax jurisdictions;[34] whether leasing, licensing, royalty, and service payments should be structured so as to channel funds to low tax jurisdictions; or whether research and development (R&D) activities should be located in the home country or overseas so as to take maximum advantage of available R&D expense allowances.[35] The transfer of technology may also be significantly affected by tax considerations.[36] Thus, tax considerations will affect the economic and legal nature of a MNE's presence in a country, and will provide the background to international tax avoidance mechanisms employed by MNEs.

(3) Tax Avoidance and MNEs

One of the most contentious issues arising from the operations of MNEs has been their apparent ability to avoid, or even to evade,[37] tax through the use of their integrated international business networks. In particular two issues have given rise to concern: the so-called 'transfer pricing' problem and the use of 'tax havens' by MNEs.

(a) The 'Transfer Pricing' Problem

In chapter 1 it was seen that, according to the proponents of the 'internalization' theory of MNE growth, one of the principal features of the MNE is its ability to replace cross-border, arm's length markets in intermediate factors of production with an intrafirm 'market'.[38] This permits the transfer of goods, services, and know-how between affiliates of a MNE without the uncertainties of arm's length transactions, under a system of planning in the allocation and pricing of such transfers. Thereby, the overall costs of production to the MNE can be reduced, enhancing its efficiency as a producer.

---

[34] On which see further OECD *International Tax Avoidance and Evasion* Issues in International Taxation No 1 (Paris: OECD, 1987) 88–106.

[35] This was a contentious issue in the US in the early 1980s when Congress instituted a moratorium on the allocation of R&D expenses to foreign source income of US firms, resulting in its allocation to US source income. This caused a reduction of revenue to the US as the reallocation of R&D expenditures from foreign to domestic income increased the amount of taxable foreign source income that could be credited against US taxation. The beneficiary firms argued that the moratorium would act as an incentive to locate R&D investment in the US. Critics saw this as special pleading for lower tax liability. On R&D incentives see further UNCTAD *Taxation and Transfer of Technology* above n 28 at 25–33.   [36] See UNCTAD ibid.

[37] According to Davies: '[t]he concepts of tax avoidance and tax evasion are notoriously difficult to define, but in general terms both involve a reduction or elimination of tax liability through either legitimate/legal means (avoidance) or through illegitimate/illegal means (evasion).' Above n 11 at para 1.09.

[38] See ch 1 28–29 above. See also Lorraine Eden 'Taxes, Transfer Pricing and the Multinational Enterprise' in Alan M Rugman and Thomas L Brewer (eds) *The Oxford Handbook of International Business* (Oxford: Oxford University Press, paperback edn, 2003) see from 591 especially 593.

When such integration of production flows occurs across national borders, not only can the MNE organize production around the more efficient internal 'market' in inputs, it can also control that market across national jurisdictions, so as to minimize the group's exposure to liability under the fiscal and excise regimes of the countries in which it operates. Thus, for example, where a subsidiary in country A is subject to a corporation tax rate of 40 per cent and a subsidiary in country B is subject to a rate of 20 per cent, the prices charged for transfers of inputs between them can be manipulated so as to ensure that the bulk of the profits earned by the two related undertakings appears in the books of the subsidiary in B. This can be done, first, by under-invoicing B for the cost of inputs bought by it from A, thereby reducing the profits made by A from sales to B, and increasing the profits of B by reason of cheaper inputs from A. Alternatively, should B supply inputs to A, A can be over-invoiced for the cost thereof, resulting in a reduction in A's profits, and in a corresponding transfer of the inflated purchase price to B's profit account.[39] From the firm's perspective this is an efficient outcome, as the group's overall liability to tax is reduced. From country A's perspective this amounts to a loss of revenue from the business activities of subsidiary A, by reason of A's profits being relocated to subsidiary B through the internal 'market' of the MNE. From country B's perspective, it is a gain to the revenue from profit-generating activities that take place outside its jurisdiction.

From this simple example it is clear that the internal administration of transfer prices by a MNE can create significant regulatory conflicts. First, country A may seek to control the manipulation of internal transfer prices by the MNE, so as to ensure that profit-generating activities carried on by the MNE within its borders are effectively and fully taxed. Secondly, country A may seek the cooperation of country B in reducing the incentive for tax avoidance that the latter's lower rate of tax offers. This may entail the opposition of country B, in that it stands to gain from such avoidance so long as country A's tax rates are higher, and on the ground that country A may be interfering with country B's sovereign power to set and administer taxation within its own jurisdiction.

In order to understand how such regulatory conflicts arise and the types of measures that have been devised to combat the problem of tax avoidance by MNEs this section will consider, first, how transfer prices are established within the internal 'market' of a MNE. Secondly, the incentives that prompt firms to engage in transfer price manipulations, and the costs of so doing, will be identified. Too often, discussion on the activities of MNEs simply assumes that because the possibility of manipulating transfer prices exists it will always be taken. However, in practice the costs may outweigh the advantages, and the firm will not engage in such manipulations. The existing empirical evidence on the incidence of transfer price manipulations by MNEs will be briefly considered in this connection. After these

---

[39] See also UNCTAD *Transfer Pricing* Series on issues in international investment agreements (New York and Geneva: United Nations, 1999) 4–5.

matters have been dealt with, the two principal approaches to the control of transfer price manipulation will be described. These are the so-called 'arm's length' and 'formula apportionment' approaches. This section will include an analysis of the 'comparable profit' method (CPM) which was introduced by the US in the mid-1990s to complement the arm's length method amid considerable controversy.

(i) Establishing Transfer Prices in MNE Networks

The pricing of transfers of goods and services within a MNE network creates considerable managerial and accounting problems. In particular, while the management of individual plants and divisions may be carried out on a decentralized basis, and is made accountable by means of separate accounts for each 'profit centre', the collective interests of the group enterprise may require the formulation of a centralized financial strategy. This often results in the centralized setting of transfer prices over which each profit centre will have no control. The ability of individual profit centres to maximize their profits could be compromised in the process. Thus, to avoid the creation of disputes over pricing between profit centres, or between central and local management, the enterprise must establish transfer prices in a rational way.[40] Furthermore, the pricing mechanism must be such as to allow for the setting of optimal prices on internal flows of goods and services. Failure to do so could result in misallocations of resources and in distortions in the final prices of products.[41]

To meet these requirements MNEs have used a variety of mechanisms to set internal transfer prices. Two basic methods are used, although there are numerous individual variations.[42] The first is the 'cost-plus' method. This starts with the basic cost of the item to be transferred, calculated according to one of a number of possible costing criteria, to which is added a percentage mark-up, allowing a margin of profit to accrue to each seller in the chain. The second is the 'sales-minus' method. Here the final price of the finished product is the starting point. From this a percentage discount is subtracted, leaving the buyer with a margin of profit on the transfer, based on the assumption that the affiliated buyer will add value to the product prior to resale at the final price.

From a purely economic perspective both approaches have been criticized.[43] The cost-plus method has been criticized as condoning avoidable high cost production techniques, for not taking into account the price a final product might fetch, and for the fact that the mark-up percentage can at best be determined by a rule of thumb. Furthermore, there is serious disagreement as to the type of costing criterion that should be adopted. One of three main criteria may be applied: first,

---

[40] See Plasschaert above n 7 at para 3.2 at 29 and 24–26.   [41] Plasschaert ibid.

[42] See J Arpan 'International Transfer Pricing' in C Nobes and R Parker (eds) *Issues in Multinational Accounting* (Philip Allan Publishers, 1988) see from 161 especially 163. See also OECD *Transfer Pricing Guidelines for Multinational Enterprises and Tax Administrations* (Paris: OECD, 2001) ch II.

[43] See Plasschaert above n 7 paras 3.10–3.11 at 33 from which the following remarks are taken.

marginal or direct costing, which charges only the direct costs of labour and raw materials to the transaction, the overheads being charged against the parent company's profit and loss account; full costing, which allocates overhead costs to the various products being transferred; and standard costing, which allocates costs based on anticipated costs per unit of output. The sales-minus approach, while acknowledging the final price of finished products, does not avoid the other above mentioned drawbacks of the cost-plus formula. Furthermore, the final price might be artificially inflated by the monopolistic position of the enterprise in its market, thereby making it only remotely connected with the true costs of production. Moreover, if the final retail price were inflated by the marketing division, its profits could rise at the expense of production division profits.

Given these drawbacks the question arises whether open market prices for the items transferred may be used. In principle, such prices should offer the most efficient and accurate valuation system. Furthermore, market prices would appear to be suitable for use in a divisionalized enterprise operating through profit centres, in that they would create incentives for profit centre managers to reduce costs and maximize profits. However, the realities of MNE operations limit the utility of open market prices. First, the use of such prices assumes that profit centres are free to purchase inputs on the open market rather than through the MNE network. This may not be the case, even for commonly available inputs. Secondly, the market pricing approach assumes that all the relevant productive inputs are freely available on open markets at arm's length prices. Where a MNE possesses specialized productive technology or managerial know-how, it is highly unlikely that comparable and/or compatible alternative inputs can be purchased in an open market. Thus no open market may exist in which an arm's length price can be established.[44]

Furthermore, it might be wrong to assume that open market prices are somehow more objective and less arbitrary than internally determined transfer prices. The existence of perfectly competitive markets in intermediate products cannot be assumed. In cases where a free market does not exist, an internally determined transfer price may be the best approximation of its value.[45] Even where a comparable free market price can be established, it will benefit the firm to use internally set transfer prices so as to achieve the various efficiency objectives that the manipulation of such prices can offer.[46] In this respect the general preference has been to use cost based methods, although market price based approaches have also had wide application.[47]

The transfer of financial payments and flows within a MNE can occur in a variety of ways. The conduit chosen for such purposes will have important implications for ensuring an efficient allocation of money payments among the component

[44] See Plasschaert ibid paras 3.7–3.9 at 31–32.   [45] Arpan above n 42 at 163–64.
[46] See further text at nn 51–53 below.
[47] Arpan above n 45. See further JS Arpan *International Intracorporate Pricing: Non-American Systems and Views* (Praeger, 1972).

companies of the MNE, given that different financial flows will incur different rates of tax liability. Therefore, MNEs will use different conduits to channel funds depending on their relative profitability to the group. For example, a subsidiary can remit profits to its parent by way of a dividend payment, which would become subject to withholding tax in the host state and to corporation tax in the hands of the parent. However, should the parent make a loan to the subsidiary, the remittance of interest by the latter to the parent may not incur the same level of tax liability. The payment of interest by the subsidiary would not normally incur liability to withholding tax in the host state, and the interest repayments would be tax deductible in the hands of the subsidiary. Furthermore, the interest rate can be set to achieve the best profit shifting effect. Consequently, the overall tax burden of the group can be reduced, provided the repayment complies with the home and host states anti-avoidance laws as a genuine repayment and not a deemed dividend, and the interest rate charged is not questioned.[48] Additionally, certain channels may be preferred over others because transfer price manipulations will be harder to detect. Thus, payments for services may be preferred to payments for goods, as arm's length prices for services rendered may be harder to ascertain.[49]

The principal conduits for transfer pricing manipulations can be classified as follows.[50] First, trade related payments may be used in the form of payments for goods and payments of interest on trade credits. Secondly, as noted in the above mentioned example, intrafirm loans can be used, as where a short or long-term loan is made to an affiliate and the interest rate is fixed for maximum profit shifting effect. Thirdly, service payments can act as conduits. These may include payment fees for use of patents and trademarks, payments of overhead costs, and payments for specific services rendered by one affiliate to another. Financial flows within the enterprise also occur through equity related payments. These may be made by the parent, through its equity contribution to the subsidiary, and by the subsidiary, through its dividend remittances to the parent. Here the MNE may have little flexibility in manipulating transfer prices due to high levels of legal regulation, but the amount of remittance and reinvestment may be controlled by the parent, thereby ensuring a more efficient distribution of finance throughout the group. These flows may be particularly important in relation to the use of tax haven holding companies.

(ii) Incentives, Disincentives and Empirical Evidence for Transfer Price Manipulations

Incentives for transfer price manipulations can be classified under two broad heads: those which maximize the present value of the MNE's overall profits and

---

[48] On the question whether a loan payment between associated enterprises in a MNE should be treated as an equity payment for tax purposes, see further OECD *Thin Capitalisation* Issues in International Taxation No 2 (Paris: OECD, 1987). See also OECD *Report on Transfer Pricing and Multinational Enterprises* (Paris: OECD, 1979) ch V 'Loans'.

[49] Plasschaert above n 7 at para 4.21.   [50] See Plasschaert ibid paras 4.15–4.22.

those which minimize the present and future risk of uncertainty about the value of profits.[51] Under the first heading come manipulations aimed at: the reduction of tax or tariff liability by taking advantage of differences in national tax and tariff rates; the avoidance of restrictions on the remittance of profits by overpricing imports into the jurisdiction; exchange rate speculation involving the removal of profits from a devaluing currency into a stronger one; and the reduction of dividends payable to local shareholders by way of reducing the profitability of a local subsidiary through the overpricing of imports.[52] Under the second heading come manipulations aimed at minimizing the exposure of the firm's profits to governmental threats of expropriation or to threats from trade union activism, or at reducing the apparent profitability of a subsidiary as a method of deterring competitors from making an entry into the subsidiary's market.[53]

As mentioned above, whether or not a MNE will take advantage of such possibilities depends upon the actual profitability of such manipulations to the enterprise. Merely because the theoretical opportunity to engage in transfer price manipulation exists, does not mean that it will take place. According to Plasschaert, given the actual operation of the international taxation system, with tax credits, exemptions, and limited deferral rules being employed by states, the actual possibilities of making significant savings to tax are relatively limited, except in the case of tax haven jurisdictions. However, even such jurisdictions may offer only temporary advantages as profits remitted there will have to be repatriated to the home country to sustain dividend payments and, as will be seen below, several home states have adopted laws controlling the use of tax havens.[54]

Furthermore, the costs of running an effective transfer pricing operation may be too great given the specialist tax and other expertise involved, the possibility of conflicts between central management and local profit centre managers,[55] and the rate at which local tax and excise conditions change, requiring complex computer modelling of the international tax situation of the firm. In such circumstances it may be better to establish stable internal transfer prices, even if this results in the loss of marginal gains against tax liability.

In addition to such internal costs, the increasing use of transfer pricing controls by national revenue authorities may increase the external limitations on transfer price manipulations.[56] This is enhanced by more recent policies that require the keeping of contemporaneous documentation of the MNE's transfer

---

[51] Sanjaya Lall *The Multinational Corporation* (London: MacMillan, 1980) 112.

[52] Lall ibid at 113–14; see also DF Channon and M Jalland *Multinational Strategic Planning* (London: MacMillan, 1978) 155–57; Arpan above n 42 at 164–71. On the use of transfer price manipulations in relation to local shareholder interests see Peter Fitzpatrick 'Transfer Pricing, Company Law and Shareholders' Interests' [1975] JBL 202.   [53] Lall ibid at 115–16.

[54] Plasschaert above n 7 at paras 5.6–5.16.

[55] But see Lall above n 51 at 118, who feels this restraint on transfer price manipulation is overstated.

[56] For information on national transfer pricing laws, see International Bureau of Fiscal Documentation (IBFD) *Transfer Pricing Database* available by subscription at <http://www.ibfd.org/portal/app?bookmarkablePage=research&plc=tp&url=Ne%3D876%26N%3D3%2B902&sortKeys=p_sort_boomId%7C0>.

pricing practices, making manipulations aimed purely at tax savings more difficult to overlook.[57] Indeed, the detection of such tax avoidance could seriously harm the reputation of the firm. Therefore, the firm must consider the likelihood of being detected before it engages in tax reducing manipulations. This depends on the extent to which the country in question can effectively operate its anti-avoidance legislation. In this respect the developed home states of MNEs are likely to be more effective than less developed host states, with their more limited resources.[58]

Finally, the extent to which MNEs actually engage in transfer price manipulations should be briefly considered. The major sources of evidence for such practices consist of a number of empirical studies,[59] whose general representativeness has been questioned,[60] and reports of cases involving transfer price abuses. Of these, the most extensive report is that of the old UK Monopolies and Mergers Commission (MMC) into the pricing practices of the Swiss pharmaceutical firm Hoffmann-La Roche during the 1960s.[61] This concerned inter alia the transfer prices charged by the Swiss company for imports of Librium and Valium to its UK subsidiary during that time. The MMC found that considerable over-pricing of the imported active ingredients had occurred. It ordered the company to reduce the prices of its final products, to repay the UK Government for earlier over-pricing of the products sold to the National Health Service and to pay some £1.58 million in additional tax.[62] This report was made in the context of a monopolies investigation and, as such, the tax avoidance issues were incidental to the major questions of market dominance and overpricing of finished products. The outcome of the investigation shows how these issues can be interrelated.[63] In one

---

[57] See Eden above n 38 at 594.

[58] See further Lall above n 51 at 146–51; Charles R Irish 'Transfer Pricing Abuses and Less Developed Countries' 5 Asian Pacific Tax and Investment Bulletin (1987) 227–37; 298–313.

[59] See in particular C Vaitsos *Intercountry Income Distribution and Transnational Enterprises* (Oxford: OUP, 1974); S Lall above n 51 at 120–27;144–46. For a summary of the principal empirical studies in this field, see JH Dunning *Multinational Enterprises and the Global Economy* (Wokingham: Addison Wesley, 1993) 516–21 and Caves above n 9 at 208–12. The pharmaceutical industry has been a major source of empirical data on transfer pricing: see G Gereffi *The Pharmaceutical Industry and Dependency in the Third World* (Princeton University Press, 1983) 193–98. On the relationship between R&D based investment and income shifting by MNEs, see Harry Grubert 'Intangible Income, Intercompany Transactions, Income Shifting, and the Choice of Location' National Tax Journal Vol LVI, No 1, Part 2 March 2003 at 221.

[60] See Raymond Vernon *Storm Over the Multinationals* (London: MacMillan, 1977) 154–58; Alan Rugman *Multinationals in Canada: Theory, Performance and Economic Impact* (Martinus Nijhoff, 1980) ch 7.

[61] The MMC has been superseded by the Office of Fair Trading and Competition Commission under the Enterprise Act 2002 Part 3. See further ch 10 below. More recently, in 2004, the Inland Revenue settled a major transfer pricing case with Nissan for £37 million and Japanese tax authorities investigated similar problems involving Honda: 'Nissan Settles Tax Dispute Over Shifting Profits' *Financial Times* 11 November 2004 at 21.

[62] Monopolies and Mergers Commission *Chlordiazepoxide and Diazepam: A Report on the Supply of Chlordiazepoxide and Diazepam* (London: HMSO, 1973).

[63] See further CR Greenhill and EO Herbolzheimer 'International Transfer Pricing: The Restrictive Business Practices Approach' 14 JWTL 232 (1980). See also *United States Steel Corp v Commissioner* 36 TCM 586 (1977), *rev'd* 617 F 2d 942 (1980).

respect, the MMC report is exceptional. So far as Inland Revenue investigations into transfer pricing abuses are concerned, it is not usual to publish any findings. The procedure is confidential and subject to strict prohibitions against disclosure.[64] Furthermore, the Inland Revenue prefers a negotiated approach to transfer pricing issues and litigation in open court has not occurred. Thus, little officially reported information on transfer pricing practices is available in the UK.[65]

By contrast, the US transfer pricing control system, with its emphasis on detailed rules and regulations, is more likely to result in litigation. Thus, a significant source of information over transfer pricing manipulations has come to light in reported US cases.[66] However, these cases concern evidence of past practices in specific industries under particular tax conditions. Thus, even these sources cannot offer conclusive general data as to the nature and incidence of transfer pricing.

Nevertheless, given the fact that the tax authorities of most of the major capital exporting countries, and not insignificant numbers of capital importing countries[67] are prepared to set up transfer price monitoring units, and to empower tax commissioners to reallocate income from transfers of value between related entities, it can be presumed that transfer price manipulations are likely to be taken up by MNEs in the absence of the deterrent effect of these regulatory structures.

[64] See Inland Revenue Press Release 26 January 1981[7] 'The transfer pricing of multinational enterprises' para 12. This does not appear to have been changed by the more recent reforms.

[65] However, a small selection of leading Tax Commissioners cases, dealing with transfer pricing issues, is summarized on the Inland Revenue website: <http://www.hmrc.gov.uk/manuals/intmanual/INTM435000.htm>.

[66] According to Judge Nims, Chief Judge of the United States Tax Court, in 1990 there were then over 200 cases before the Tax Court filed by the US Internal Revenue Service involving alleged transfer pricing manipulations with reported profit deficiencies ranging from $10 million to $6 billion: Tax Notes Today 6 November 1990, cited by DW Williams in DW Williams (ed) *Tax on the International Transfer of Information* (Longman Special Report, 1991) 3. For examples of a 'classic' instance of profit shifting between jurisdictions for tax advantages, see *El Du Pont De Nemours & Co v United States* 608 F 2d 445 (Ct Cl 1979); *Seagate Technology Inc v Commissioner* 102 TC No 9, summarized in IBFD Tax News Service TNS–139 (1994). In 2004 a total of $8.4 billion of disputed income was involved in litigation. In 2005 the Internal Revenue Service had stepped up enforcement and more litigation was expected. Major cases were pending involving Motorola ($500 million disputed tax), Glaxo Smith Kline ($7.8 billion tax demand, settled for $3.1 billion in September 2006) and National Westminster Bank causing some tension between UK and US tax authorities: 'US Revenue Service Gets Tougher on Multinational Manoeuvres to Avoid Tax' *Financial Times* 3 February 2005 at 9; 'A Taxing Battle' *The Economist* 31 January 2004 at 67; 'Glaxo Smith Kline in $3.1bn Settlement of US Tax Dispute' *Financial Times* 12 September 2006 at 1.

[67] See A Devoy 'Recent Transfer Pricing Developments Around the World' The Tax Journal 19 March 1992 at 15, where Korea, Pakistan, Mexico, and Brazil are mentioned as developing countries with controls over transfer pricing. See, for a more recent treatment of Mexico, Venezuela, Argentina, and Brazil, Richard J Hay 'Private Banking Opportunities in Latin America' 12 Jo. Int'l Trust & Corp. Planning 46 (2005).The People's Republic of China introduced transfer pricing rules, under the 1991 Income Tax Law for Enterprises with Foreign Investment and Foreign Enterprises, which require arm's length dealing between affiliated enterprises: see Notice on Implementation Measures for the Administration of Transactions Between Affiliated Enterprises 1992 (*Guo Shui Fa* 237 of 29 October 1992) noted in IBFD Tax News Service TNS–423 (1993). See also IBFD website above n 56 for further examples and updates.

(iii) The Regulation of Transfer Price Manipulations: Arm's Length and Comparable Profit Methods (CPM)

This section will describe the principal regulatory approaches to international transfer price manipulations by MNEs.[68] When considering the effects of transfer pricing transactions between related entities, tax authorities have to determine whether the allocation, between those entities, of the costs and benefits of the transaction is appropriate, given its underlying nature and the accounting methods used. The aim is to examine whether that allocation can be accepted as a proper reflection of the underlying economic transaction, or whether it is being used so as to avoid taxation. If so, then the tax authorities will be empowered to reallocate costs and benefits in a manner that allows for the true value of the transaction to be subjected to the applicable level of taxation. In an international context, as noted above, the use of transfer pricing manipulations can achieve a tax shifting effect between the jurisdictions in which the related entities operate. Thus transfer pricing reallocations will be used to restore taxable income and profits to the jurisdiction that has lost revenue as a result of the transaction in question.

In order to undertake this examination, tax authorities have used a number of approaches. The most important is the 'arm's length' method, which seeks to allocate costs and benefits between related entities as closely as possible to the allocation that would occur in an identical or comparable open market transaction between unrelated entities. As will be shown below, this approach does not always offer good results in cases involving MNEs that operate complex cross-border production and/or services networks, often trading intangible assets for which no ready open market exists. To deal with these problems tax authorities have applied a comparable profits approach, which supplements a comparable market transaction based approach with the use of economic analysis based on profit ranges in similar economic sectors or activities. In addition a non-market based approach, the formula apportionment method, has also been used in certain jurisdictions. Such approaches have been pioneered by the US authorities in particular. They have been a source of major controversy in an international tax system that treats the arm's length approach as the preferred method of allocation in transfer pricing cases. The arm's length and comparable profits methods will be discussed in this section. The next section will deal with certain common administrative problems associated with transfer pricing controls and the last section will look at the most controversial approach, that of formula apportionment.

---

[68] See further Stanley S Surrey 'Reflections on the Allocation of Income and Expenses Among National Tax Jurisdictions' 10 Law & Pol.Int'l Bus. 409 (1978); Picciotto above n 2 ch 8; Eden above n 38 at 601–15 and Lorraine Eden *Taxing Multinationals: Transfer Pricing and Corporate Income Taxation in North America* (Toronto: University of Toronto Press, 1998) ch 2; Joseph Isenbergh *International Taxation* (Aspen Publishers, 2003) vol I Part I – Elements of International Taxation, ch 27 'International Transfer Pricing: Framework of Section 482' available at *Lexis-Nexis Professional*.

The arm's length approach is the principal method used for the reallocation of income between related enterprises for tax purposes. It is the approach accepted by the OECD member states in the OECD Model Double Taxation Convention.[69] Essentially, it seeks to allocate the profits and losses on a transfer between entities under common ownership or control by reference to the prices charged in a comparable transaction undertaken by uncontrolled entities dealing at arm's length with each other. Thereby, the tax authorities can make a reallocation which reflects, as far as possible, the allocation that would have occurred if the related parties had themselves been dealing at arm's length.

The arm's length standard underlies the UK approach to transfer pricing controls.[70] For accounting periods ending on 30 June 1999, the old rules under section 770 of the Income and Corporation Taxes Act 1988 apply. This was a 'direction-led' approach which did not oblige the taxpaying enterprise to make a return on the basis of the arm's length principle. Only where the Inland Revenue directed the taxpayer to do so did such an obligation arise.[71] For accounting periods commencing 1 July 1999, and income tax years of assessment from 1999–2000 onwards, a mandatory approach to the use of the arm's length principle has been adopted.[72] Under the current system, the arm's length principle applies if an actual provision[73] has been made or imposed between any two affected persons, by means of a transaction or series of transactions, and one of those persons is directly or indirectly participating in the management, control, or capital of the other, or a third person is participating in the management, control, or capital of both the affected persons.

---

[69] See above n 23 art 9: '[When] conditions are made or imposed between … two [associated] enterprises in their commercial or financial relations which differ from those which would be made between independent enterprises, then any profits which would, but for those conditions, have accrued to one of the enterprises, but, by reason of those conditions, have not so accrued, may be included in the profits of that enterprise and taxed accordingly.' See further Baker above n 21; Davies above n 11 ch 14. OECD *Transfer Pricing Guidelines for Multinational Enterprises and Tax Administrations* (Paris: OECD, 2001 loose-leaf, revision due in Spring 2007) at paras 1.6–1.12. See also OECD 1979 above n 48 and OECD *Transfer Pricing and Multinational Enterprises: Three Taxation Issues* (Paris: OECD, 1984).

[70] A guide to the UK law and practice on transfer pricing can be accessed from the Inland Revenue website at <http://www.hmrc.gov.uk/manuals/intmanual/INTM430000.htm>.

[71] See Inland Revenue INTM436010 – Transfer pricing before CTSA at <http://www.hmrc.gov.uk/manuals/intmanual/INTM436010.htm>.

[72] See Income and Corporation Taxes Act 1988 Schedule 28AA inserted by the Finance Act 1998, s 108, Schedule 16, as amended by Finance Acts 2000, 2004, and 2005 (No 2) (ICTA 88/Sched28 AA). See Inland Revenue *Transfer Pricing* at <http://www.hmrc.gov.uk/international/transfer-pricing.htm>. See further Inland Revenue *International Manual* INTM432000 – Schedule 28AA: how it works at <http://www.hmrc.gov.uk/manuals/intmanual/INTM432000.htm>.

[73] According to the Inland Revenue, '[t]he term provision is not defined in the legislation. It is, however, broadly analogous to the phrase "conditions made or imposed" in Article 9, and embraces all the terms and conditions attaching to a transaction or series of transactions. However, although the term provision is arguably wider than the phrase "conditions made or imposed", ICTA88/SCH28AA/PARA2 means that it must never be interpreted as such. That is, the scope of Schedule 28AA can be no wider than the scope of Article 9, as informed by the OECD Transfer Pricing Guidelines.': INTM432040 – Schedule 28AA – how it works, Meaning of 'provision' in Schedule 28AA at <http://www.hmrc.gov.uk/manuals/intmanual/INTM432040.htm>.

The actual provision will be compared with the arm's length provision which would have been made between independent enterprises.[74] If the actual provision confers a potential UK tax advantage on one or both of the affected persons, an adjustment is to be made to the taxable profits of the tax-advantaged persons.[75] The amount of the adjustment is that required to bring the profits up to what they would have been if the arm's length provision had applied. Adjustments under the current provisions may only increase taxable profits or reduce a tax loss, introducing a 'one way street' approach to transfer pricing adjustments.[76] These rules are to be construed in a manner consistent with the expression of the arm's length principle in Article 9 of the OECD Model Tax Convention on Income and on Capital and the guidance in the OECD's Transfer Pricing Guidelines for Multinational Enterprises and Tax Administrations (the OECD Transfer Pricing Guidelines). Where interpretations of the basic rule conflict, the OECD material takes precedence. The legislation requires interpretation in accordance with Article 9 and the OECD Transfer Pricing Guidelines regardless both of whether there actually is a double taxation agreement between the UK and the other country in question, and of the specific wording of any individual agreement.[77]

The most comprehensive national system using the arm's length approach to income allocation has been developed by US Federal tax law. The basic power to reallocate income between related entities is set down in section 482 of the US Internal Revenue Code:

In any case of two or more organizations, trades or businesses (whether or not incorporated, whether or not organized in the United States, and whether or not affiliated) owned or controlled directly or indirectly by the same interests, the Secretary may distribute, apportion, or allocate gross income, deductions, credits, or allowances between or among such organizations, trades, or businesses, if he determines that such distribution, apportionment, or allocation is necessary in order to prevent evasion of taxes or clearly to reflect the income of any such organizations, trades, or businesses. In the case of any transfer (or license) of intangible property (within the meaning of section 936(h)(3)(B)), the income with respect to such transfer or license shall be commensurate with the income attributable to the intangible.[78]

---

[74] According to the Inland Revenue: '[t]he actual provision is that which has been made between the two connected parties ... The arm's length provision is that which would have been made between independent enterprises. If no provision would have been made or imposed between independent persons then the legislation allows the advantaged person's profits to be computed accordingly – thus reflecting the arm's length position. In comparing the actual provision with the arm's length provision it is necessary to look at all of the terms and conditions of the transactions in question and to adjust them to arm's length terms if necessary.': INTM432040 ibid.

[75] ICTA88/Sched 28AA para 5 provides that there is a potential advantage in relation to UK taxation if a person's taxable profits for a chargeable period are reduced, or losses, expenses of management or group relief are increased as a result of a non-arm's length price: Inland Revenue INTM432100 – Schedule 28AA: how it works. Advantage in relation to UK taxation at <http://www.hmrc.gov.uk/manuals/intmanual/INTM432100.htm>.

[76] See Inland Revenue INTM432000 – Schedule 28AA: how it works above n 72.

[77] ICTA 88/Sched 28 AA para 2 and Inland Revenue ibid.

[78] *US Internal Revenue Code*: 26 USCA Subtitle A, Chapter 1 Sub-chapter E Part III s 482. The first version of s 482 was adopted in 1921. It is not proposed to discuss all the principal situations in

Regulations prescribing the criteria to be used for the control of income allocations falling under section 482 were first passed in 1968, and were revised in
1994.[79] The regulations establish that: '[t]he purpose of section 482 is to ensure
that taxpayers clearly reflect income attributable to controlled transactions, and to
prevent the avoidance of taxes with respect to such transactions. Section 482
places a controlled taxpayer on a tax parity with an uncontrolled taxpayer by determining the true taxable income of the controlled taxpayer.'[80] In order to reallocate income under section 482, the Commissioner must establish, first, that the
entities involved are owned or controlled directly or indirectly by the same interests and, secondly, that the allocation of income between the related entities is
other than that which could be expected where the transaction had been effected
between uncontrolled entities dealing at arm's length. The Commissioner's discretion in these matters is broad.[81] Only where the Commissioner makes a reallocation that is arbitrary, capricious, or unreasonable will it be overruled.[82] Should the
taxpayer overcome the Commissioner's presumption of correctness and prove that
the deficiencies set forth in the notice of deficiency are arbitrary, capricious, or
unreasonable, it must go on to prove that alternative allocations it proposes satisfy
the arm's length standard. Should the taxpayer fail to do so, the Court must determine from the record the proper allocation of income between or among the controlled entities.[83] 'Controlled' for the purposes of section 482 is defined as 'any
kind of control, direct or indirect, whether legally enforceable, and however exer-
cisable or exercised. It is the reality of control which is decisive, not its form or the
mode of its exercise. A presumption of control arises if income or deductions have
been arbitrarily shifted'.[84] To come within the scrutiny of section 482, the

which an arm's length allocation is possible. The transactions not discussed are: loans (see Treas Reg
s 1.482–2(a)); performance of services for another (see Treas Reg s 1.482–2(b)); use of tangible property under lease or other arrangement (see Treas Reg s 1.482–2(c)).

[79] Treasury Regulations Section 1.482. (Treas Reg s 1.482). See for the last version to adopt a pure
arm's length approach *Federal Tax Regulations 1991* (West Publishing Co) vol 2 ss 1.482–1 and
1.482–2. The revised regulations were introduced in April 1993 on a temporary basis and were
adopted on 8 July 1994. See McDaniel, Ault, and Repetti above n 13 ch 8. The 1994 Regulations and
their introduction of the CPM are discussed below in the text at nn 105–131. For analysis of the original 1968 Regulations, see Jenks 'Treasury Regulations Under Section 482' 23 Tax Lawyer 279 (1970);
Baker and Hartline 'Recent Developments Concerning Internal Revenue Code s.482' 11 Houston LR
89 (1973); Comment: 8 Texas ILJ 219 (1973); Madere 'International Pricing: Allocation Guidelines
and Relief from International Double Taxation' 10 Texas ILJ 108 at 111–20 (1975); Note 89 Harv.LR
1202 (1976); Schindler and Henderson 'Intercorporate Transfer Pricing' 29 Tax Notes 1171 (1985).
[80] Treas Reg s 1.482–1(b)(1).
[81] See *Charles Town Inc v CIR* 372 F 2d 415 (CA Md 1967) (finding of common control will not
be reversed unless clearly erroneous); *Peck v CIR* 752 F 2d 469 (9th Cir 1985) (Commissioner has a
broad discretion to place controlled taxpayers in the same position as uncontrolled taxpayers dealing
at arm's length).
[82] *Eli Lilly & Co v CIR* 856 F 2d 855 (7th Cir 1988); *Seagate Technology Inc v CIR* (USTC) 102
TC 149; 1994 US Tax Ct LEXIS 10; 102 TC No 9.
[83] See *Sundstrand Corp & Subs v Commissioner* 96 TC 226 (1991) at 354; *American Terrazzo Strip Co
v Commissioner* 56 TC 961, 971 (1971); *Nat Harrison Associates Inc v Commissioner* 42 TC 601 (1964).
[84] Treas Reg s 1.482–1A (a)(3). See eg *Forman & Co Inc v CIR* 453 F 2d 1144 (2d Cir 1972).

controlling interest must have complete power to shift income among its subsidiaries.[85]

Under the 1968 Regulations the arm's length allocation methods to be used by the Commissioner were laid down in a strict order of application.[86] In the case of sales involving tangible property, the Commissioner was obliged to use one of three allocation methods prescribed in the regulations. He or she was first obliged to consider the transaction under the comparable uncontrolled price method.[87] However, where there were no comparable uncontrolled sales, the resale price method had to be used.[88] Where there were no comparable uncontrolled transactions and the resale price method was inappropriate, the Commissioner had to use the cost plus method. Typically, this would be appropriate where 'a manufacturer sells products to a related entity which performs substantial manufacturing, assembly or other processing of the product or adds significant value by reason of its utilization of its intangible property prior to resale in uncontrolled transactions'.[89] Should none of these methods be reasonably applicable to the facts of a particular case, the Commissioner could use some other appropriate method of pricing.[90]

In certain cases this entailed the determination of an appropriate 'profit split' between the related entities. This standard was not formally recognized in the 1968 Regulations but was a court developed standard. In *Eli Lilly & Co v CIR*, the Court of Appeals for the Seventh Circuit described the profit split method as one that 'divides combined revenues based on an ad hoc assessment of the contributions of the assets and activities of the commonly controlled enterprises'.[91] The Court of Appeals went on to criticize it as an inherently imprecise method of allocation. Indeed the outcome may be largely determined by bargaining between the fiscal authorities and the taxpaying company.[92] The profit split approach has been used in a number of cases involving the transfer of intangibles between related entities, an area in which the ascertainment of arm's length prices is often fraught with difficulty, owing to the relative absence of comparable uncontrolled transactions from which an arm's length price can be determined.[93] A profit split may be

---

[85] *CIR v First Security Bank of Utah* 405 US 394 (1972). See also *Procter & Gamble Co v Commissioner* 95 TC 323 (1990) *aff'd* 961 F 2d 1255 (6th Cir 1992); *Exxon Corp v Commissioner* (TCM 1993–616) noted IBFD Tax News Service TNS–56 (1994) TC Memo 1993–616; 1993 Tax Ct Memo LEXIS 629; 66 TCM (CCH) 1707; *DHL Corporation and Subsidiaries v Commissioner* TC Memo 1998–461; 1998 Tax Ct Memo LEXIS 461; 76 TCM (CCH) 1122; TCM (RIA) 98461. A joint venture may qualify as a controlled taxpayer: see *GAC Produce Co v Commissioner* TC Memo 1999–134; 1999 Tax Ct Memo LEXIS 183; 77 TCM (CCH) 1890; TCM (RIA) 99134.

[86] See Treas Reg s 1.482–2 (1968).

[87] Treas Reg s 1.482–2(e)(2) (1968). See, for an example of the application of this method, *Compaq Computer Corporation and Subsidiaries v Commissioner* TC Memo 1999–220; 1999 Tax Ct Memo LEXIS 254; 78 TCM (CCH) 20; TCM (RIA) 99220.   [88] ibid.

[89] Treas Reg s 1.482–2(e)(1)(ii) (1968).   [90] Treas Reg s 1.482–2(e)(1)(iii) (1968).

[91] 856 F 2d 855 at 871 (7th Cir 1988).   [92] See Plasschaert above n 7 at para 11.7.

[93] Eden above n 38 at 607. See the following cases as examples of the complexities of trying to apply the arm's length standard to transfers of intangibles: *Hospital Corporation of America v CIR* 81 TC 520 (US Tax Ct 1983) *Held:* 75/25 per cent split of income from use of intangibles; *Eli Lilly & Co v*

more appropriate in dealing with transfers of intangibles between related enterprises because, to the transferor, the income stream from the transfer will consist
not only of the consideration payable for the intangible by the related transferee
but also the enhanced value of its direct or indirect equity interest in the related
transferee. Thus an unmodified arm's length pricing approach may not show
clearly the true economic value of the transaction.[94] The profit split method has
been accepted as one of the appropriate methods in the 1994 Regulations.[95]

   The problems associated with the allocation of transfer prices for intangibles
led to the amendment of section 482 by the Tax Reform Act 1986. This added the
last sentence, which introduces the 'commensurate with income' standard to cases
involving the transfer or licence of intangible property.[96] Its effect is to require a
profit splitting approach, which looks to the actual profit generated by the intangible, and to encourage the periodic adjustment of royalty rates in licensing agreements between related parties so as to reflect its true economic value. This will
discourage an artificially low rate of royalty on intangibles whose success may have
been initially uncertain but which have subsequently become successful.[97] In
1988 the US Treasury Department issued a 'White Paper' to review the application of the 'commensurate with income' standard.[98] The White Paper introduced

Commissioner 84 TC 996 (1985) modified in part 856 F 2d 855 at 871–73 (7th Cir 1988) *Held:*
45/55 per cent split; *Ciba-Geigy Corp v Commissioner* 85 TC 172 (1985); *GD Searle & Co v
Commissioner* 88 TC 252 (1987); *Seagate Technology Inc v Commissioner* above n 82. See further
Michelle Markham *The Transfer Pricing of Intangibles* (The Hague: Kluwer Law International, 2005);
Monica Boos *International Transfer Pricing: The Valuation of Intangible Assets* (The Hague: Kluwer
Law International, 2003).

   [94] See further Staff of the Joint Committee on Taxation *General Explanation of the Tax Reform Act
of 1986* (1987) 1015–17.

   [95] See Treas Reg s 1.482–6. The current regulations provide for two methods of profit splitting:
comparable profit split which 'is derived from the combined operating profit of uncontrolled taxpayers
whose transactions and activities are similar to those of the controlled taxpayers in the relevant business activity. Under this method, each uncontrolled taxpayer's percentage of the combined operating
profit or loss is used to allocate the combined operating profit or loss of the relevant business activity':
Treas Reg s 1.482–6(c)(2)(i); *residual profit split* which allocates normal market returns to the routine
contributions made by each related party and then allocates returns from intangible assets owned by
each party on the basis of their estimated values: Treas Reg s 1.482–6(c)(3)(i)(A) and (B). See Treas
Reg s 1.482–8 Example 8 for an illustration of when the residual profit split method will be the best
method under the regulations. This approach is based on the analysis undertaken in the US Treasury
Department White Paper of 1988 discussed below at nn 98–101.

   [96] Under s 482 intangible property includes: a patent, invention, process, know-how, copyright,
trade-mark, franchise, method, system, or technical data. See Internal Revenue Code s 936(h)(3)(b); see
also Treas Reg s 1.482–2(d)(3), which omits 'know-how' from the list. The 1994 Regulations include,
under intangible property: patents, inventions, formulae, processes, designs, patterns, know-how; copy-
rights, and literary, musical, or artistic compositions; trademarks, trade names, or brand names; fran-
chises, licences, and contracts; methods, programmes, systems, procedures, campaigns, surveys, studies,
forecasts, estimates, customer lists, or technical data; other similar items: Treas Reg s 1.482–4T(b).

   [97] McDaniel, Ault, and Repetti above n 13 at 152–53.

   [98] *A Study of Intercompany Pricing Under s 482 of the Code* IRS Notice 88–123, 1988–2 CB 458. See
further DW Williams (ed) *Tax on the International Transfer of Information* (Longman Special Report,
1991) papers by Karen P Brown at 27 and Rom Watson at 75; JE Bischel 'The S.482 White Paper and
Super-royalties: Existing and Proposed Transfer Pricing Methods' BIFD (February 1990) 83.

four different approaches to the allocation of income from intangibles, each of which aimed at ascertaining a price as close as possible to an arm's length price. The first two approaches, the 'exact comparable' and the 'inexact comparable' methods, echoed the arm's length method. The price of the intangible transferred in the related party transaction would be determined by comparison with an exactly comparable transaction between unrelated parties, if such a transaction existed, or, in the absence of an exactly comparable transaction, with an inexactly comparable transaction, which was sufficiently similar in economic terms to permit reasonable comparison.[99]

Where no exact or inexact comparable transactions existed, the White Paper advocated the use of the 'basic arm's length rate of return' method (BALRM). This method involved an allocation of profits between the related entities which sought to distinguish between profit that was attributable to the use of tangible assets and that which was derived from the use of intangibles. This was achieved by ascertaining the market rate of return on the tangible assets and factors of production used by each entity, through a comparison with similar functions and assets employed by unrelated entities, and allocating that rate of return to the entity using the asset or factor of production in question. The remaining income would then be allocated to the intangible and was thereby allocated to the owner of the intangible, the related transferor.[100] In cases where the related transferee also owned intangibles that were used in exploiting the transferred intangible the 'BALRM plus profit split' method would apply. The method would operate as follows. First, each party would be allocated a return on the functions performed through the application of the BALRM method. The remaining income, representing the residual income from the use of intangibles, would then be split according to the relative value of the intangibles of each party. The White Paper recognizes that the splitting of intangible income will largely be a matter of judgment.[101]

In addition to defining the principles by which the 'commensurate with income' standard should be applied, the White Paper considered how that standard could be applied to cost-sharing arrangements. A cost-sharing arrangement was defined in the White Paper as 'an agreement between two or more persons to share the costs and risks of research and development as they are incurred in exchange for a specified interest in any property that is developed'.[102] The White

---

[99] See White Paper at 486–87 and Brown ibid at 29–30; Bischel ibid at 84–85.

[100] See Bischel ibid at 85. The following example is given in P McDaniel and H Ault *Introduction to United States International Taxation* (The Hague: Kluwer, 3rd edn, 1989) at 141: 'P has developed a patent for the manufacture of a product which will be manufactured under a licence granted to a foreign affiliate. The transaction will generate 500 of income and, at a market rate of return on the tangible assets involved, 150 of the income would be allocated to the tangible assets held by the subsidiary and 150 to the tangible assets of the parent. The remaining 200 would be allocated to P as the commensurate amount of income from the patent.'

[101] Brown above n 98 at 31 referring to White Paper at 490–91.

[102] Above n 98 at 492. For a full analysis of cost-sharing arrangements and their use as tax avoidance devices see: OECD 1979 above n 48 at paras 102–24 55–62; OECD 2001 above n 69 ch VIII 'Cost Contribution Arrangements'.

Paper concluded that bona fide cost-sharing arrangements would continue to be acceptable, so long as any new participant compensated existing parties to the arrangement for the value of any intangibles already developed. Such arrangements are covered by the 1994 Regulations on the basis that related parties can allocate the costs of developing an intangible in proportion to the reasonably expected benefits assigned to each party under the agreement.[103]

The White Paper of 1988 represents a significant attempt to tackle the inherent weaknesses of the arm's length approach, in particular, the assumption that comparable sales between uncontrolled entities exist from which an arm's length price can be determined. This leads to an air of unreality where no comparables exist. In such cases it may be unfair to the taxpayer to subject it to a comparison with inexactly comparable third party transactions, or to second guess internal transfer pricing decisions which may have been made upon commercially justifiable grounds, taking account of the competitive conditions in a particular industry and of differences in the efficiency of firms in the industry.[104] It is against the background of the White Paper that the US Internal Revenue Service (IRS) proposed, in 1992, a modification of the arm's length standard by supplementing it with the CPM which is now embedded in the 1994 Regulations.

The proposed IRS Regulations of 1992[105] sought to extend the 'commensurate with income' principle in section 482 to related party transfers of tangibles as well as to intangibles, by way of the general adoption of the CPM.[106] The proposed regulations did not seek to replace the existing methods of allocation under section

---

[103] See Treas Reg s 1.482–7 and McDaniel, Ault, and Repetti above n 13 at 151–52. See also *Xilinx and Subsidiaries and Consolidated Subsidiaries v Commissioner* Docket Nos 4142–01, 702–03. Filed 30 August 2005 available at US Tax Court website: <http://www.ustaxcourt.gov/InOpHistoric/ Xilinx55.TC.WPD.pdf>. According to the headnote, '[the Petitioner] entered into a cost-sharing agreement to develop intangibles with its foreign subsidiary. Each party was required to pay a percentage of the total research and development costs based on its respective anticipated benefits from the intangibles. The [Petitioner] issued stock options to its employees performing research and development. In determining the allocation of costs pursuant to the agreement, the Petitioner did not include in research and development costs any amount related to the issuance of stock options to, or exercise of stock options by, its employees. The [Commissioner], in his notices of deficiency, determined that for cost-sharing purposes, pursuant to sec. 1.482–7(d), Income Tax Regs, the spread (i.e., the stock's market price on the exercise date over the exercise price) or, in the alternative, the grant date value, relating to compensatory stock options, should have been included as a research and development cost. It was held that the [Commissioner's] allocation was contrary to the arm's-length standard mandated by sec. 1.482–1(b), Income Tax Regs, because uncontrolled parties would not allocate the spread or the grant date value relating to employee stock options. In addition, the Petitioner's allocation satisfied the arm's length standard mandated by sec. 1.482–1, Income Tax Regs.'

[104] Jenks above n 78 at 310. See also Bird 'Shaping a New International Tax Order' BIFD (July 1988) 292 at 294.

[105] Proposed Treasury Regulations s 1.482 57 Fed Reg 3571 (1992) (Prop Treas Regs). For analysis, see Weizman 'US Transfer Pricing: Grim Prospects for Multinational Companies' [1992] 5 ICCLR 163; BIFD (June 1992) at 271–306.

[106] See Quigley 'A Commentary on How the Proposed Regulations Affect the General Principles of Section 482 as Described in the Existing Regulations and in Case Law' BIFD (June 1992) 281 at 282–84. Quigley doubts whether s 482 authorizes the IRS to extend the 'commensurate with income' standard to transfers of tangible property.

482. The comparable uncontrolled price method would still have first priority, and the resale price, cost-plus and 'fourth' methods would remain.[107] However, where an allocation was made under any of these three latter methods, the CPM would be used to validate the resulting transfer price by showing that it produced a level of operating income for the controlled party that was within the comparable price interval.[108]

The CPM method involves a comparison of the taxpayer's allocation of profits between related entities with the range of profits that would have been earned by similarly situated uncontrolled taxpayers engaging in comparable uncontrolled transfers. It requires a complex analysis.[109] First, the controlled party whose profits are to be tested must be identified. The tested party will generally be:

the participant in the controlled transaction whose operating profit attributable to the controlled transactions can be verified using the most reliable data and requiring the fewest and most reliable adjustments, and for which reliable data regarding uncontrolled comparables can be located. Consequently, in most cases the tested party will be the least complex of the controlled taxpayers and will not own valuable intangible property or unique assets that distinguish it from potential uncontrolled comparables.[110]

Secondly, the comparable uncontrolled businesses whose profitability will be used to establish the comparable profit must be identified. This requires identification of comparable uncontrolled businesses with the most similar functions to those of the tested party.[111] Failure to identify a proper comparable will undermine the whole analysis.[112] Thirdly, the operating income of the tested party will be computed on the basis of a comparison of the profit level indicators of the uncontrolled parties and the controlled tested party. Profit level indicators are, 'ratios that measure relationships between profits and costs incurred or resources employed'.[113] These include the rate of return on operating assets, the ratio of operating profits to sales, and the ratio of gross profit to operating expenses.[114] Profit level indicators must be established for a sufficient number of years to allow for an accurate comparison to be made. Generally, such a period should encompass at least the taxable year under review and the preceding two taxable years.[115] Fourthly, the 'comparable operating profit' is calculated by 'determining a profit level indicator for an uncontrolled

---

[107] Prop Treas Reg s 1.482–2(e)(1)(ii).   [108] Prop Treas Reg s 1.482–2(e)(1)(iii), (iv).
[109] Prop Treas Regs s 1.482–2(f)(3)–(9). See now Treas Reg s 1.482–5 on which the following summary is based.   [110] Treas Reg s 1.482–5(b)(2).
[111] Comparability will be based on a number of factors including: the relevant lines of business, the product or service markets involved, the asset composition employed (including the nature and quantity of tangible assets, intangible assets, and working capital), the size and scope of operations, and the stage in a business or product cycle: Treas Reg s 1.482–5(c)(2)(i). Other relevant factors are: functional, risk, and resource comparability; varying cost structures, management experience, and business efficiency; and consistency in accounting practices between the controlled and uncontrolled taxpayer: ibid at paras (c)(2)(ii)–(iv). See also the comparability criteria in Treas Reg s 1.482–1(d)(2)–(3).
[112] Cole and Rubloff 'Proposed Transfer Pricing Regulations under s.482 of the Internal Revenue Code' BIFD (June 1992) 292 at 296.   [113] Treas Reg s 1.482–5(b)(4).
[114] ibid.   [115] ibid.

comparable, and applying the profit level indicator to the financial data related to the tested party's most narrowly identifiable business activity for which data incorporating the controlled transaction is available (relevant business activity)'.[116] Finally, the tested party's reported operating profit is compared with the comparable operating profits derived from the profit level indicators of uncontrolled comparables to determine whether the reported operating profit represents an arm's length result.[117] Such convergence around a similar level of profitability is an indication of the level of profitability that the tested party could be expected to achieve if it were operating at arm's length.

The original version of the proposed regulations was received with criticism from international business circles, on the grounds inter alia that companies would be forced to disregard actual contractual terms agreed on commercial principles and apply artificial pricing rules based on hypothetical profits. This would introduce arbitrary additional tax costs, vast amounts of detailed information would have to be amassed about the confidential affairs of US and foreign companies, this information would often be unavailable and, as a result, the IRS would have to make subjective judgments about profit comparisons; international double taxation would be increased to an unprecedented scale.[118] In January 1993, the OECD Committee on Fiscal Affairs reported on the proposed US reforms.[119] It was critical of the US for departing from the classical arm's length approach and of risking increased international double taxation if other states did not accept the new US approach. The OECD Committee expressed a preference for transaction-based or profit-split approaches, with CPM being used as a method of last resort.[120] It urged the US to make substantial amendments to this effect in the proposed regulations, and to introduce them on a temporary basis only.

In line with these criticisms the US issued new regulations, effective from April 1993, on a temporary basis which became permanent in July 1994.[121] In relation to transfers of tangible property, the 1994 Regulations abandoned the insistence, in the 1992 proposals, on the CPM as a method of priority. Furthermore, they abandoned the approach of the 1968 Regulations in that there is no longer a strict hierarchy of methods. Instead, the 1994 Regulations provide that the method that best gives the most accurate arm's length result should be applied. This is referred

---

[116] ibid para (b)(1).   [117] ibid.

[118] See the Joint Paper of the Business and Industry Advisory Committee to the OECD and the International Chamber of Commerce on the Proposed Intercompany Pricing Regulations (May 1992): (1993) Tax Notes International 103–13.

[119] OECD Committee on Fiscal Affairs 'The US Proposed Regulations Dealing with Tax Aspects of Transfer Pricing Within Multinational Enterprises' Report of 10 January 1993: see Executive Summary in BIFD (January 1993) 21–25.

[120] See further OECD 2001 above n 69 ch III especially paras 3.1–3.4.

[121] Treas Reg s 1.482–1T to 1.482–6T: TD 8470, Notices of Proposed Rule Making IL 21–91 and IL 401–88. See Ruchelman 'Transfer Pricing Regulations Issued in the United States' BIFD (April 1993) 187. A summary of the Temporary Regulations, and how they differed from the proposed Regulations of 1992, can be found in IRS Bulletin 1993–10 March 8 1993. See now the 1994 Regulations above n 79 on which the following summary is based.

to as the 'best method rule'.[122] The regulations then provide for a functional analysis in determining whether uncontrolled transactions are comparable with the transaction under investigation, taking account of the functions performed, the risks involved, contractual terms adopted, applicable economic conditions and property or services involved in the transaction.[123] They also permit for an arm's length range of prices to be considered as the basis of comparison, rather than expecting a single price to be arrived at.[124] As for pricing methods, the 1994 Regulations retain the comparable uncontrolled price, resale price and cost-plus methods used in the 1968 Regulations.[125] To these the CPM is added as a non-mandatory alternative.[126] Where none of the other methods can reasonably be applied any other method may be used provided that the taxpayer discloses that method in its tax return.[127] As already noted, the profit-split method is expressly included.[128] The 1994 Regulations go on to provide separate treatment for transfers of intangible property.[129] They retain the matching transaction and comparable adjustable transaction methods from the 1992 proposals, but no longer make the results subject to confirmation using the CPM. They also retain use of the CPM and permit another method to be used on the same terms as for transactions involving tangible property. In addition, the 1994 Regulations deal with the problem of restrictions on payments under foreign laws and their effects on IRS allocations under section 482.[130] New penalties for understatement of tax arising from a substantial valuation misstatement were also introduced in 1994.[131]

Despite these apparent concessions to the criticisms of the 1992 proposals, the 1993 Regulations were themselves criticized by the International Chamber of Commerce (ICC) Commission on Taxation.[132] The ICC Commission felt that the arm's length standard remained the only legitimate approach for determining inter-company transfer prices in cross-border transactions and that the 1993 Regulations still gave the CPM too high a status. The ICC Commission concluded that the 1993 Regulations remained essentially the same in terms of methodology as the 1992 proposals, and were open to the same objections on grounds of impracticality as well as on the grounds of incompatibility with the arm's length principle.[133] The OECD reaction was less hostile. Although it maintained the view that CPM was a method of last resort, it developed its own version in the 'transactional net margin' method. This approach centres on a transactional comparison

---

[122] Treas Reg s 1.482–1(b)(1) and (c).
[123] Treas Reg s 1.482–1(d)(1). See Ruchelman above n 121 at 189–90; McDaniel, Ault, and Repetti above n 13 at 147–48.   [124] Treas Reg s 1.482–1(e).
[125] ibid s 1.482–3(a).   [126] ibid s 1.482–5 summarized at n 109–17 above.
[127] ibid s 1.482–3(e).   [128] Treas Reg s 1.482–6.   [129] Treas Reg s 1.482–4.
[130] See Treas Reg s 1.482–1(h); see McDaniel, Ault, and Repetti above n 13 at 158.
[131] Section 6662 accuracy related penalties discussed in ibid at 159–60.
[132] (1993) Tax Notes International 103. Given the minor changes from the 1993 Temporary Regulations to the 1994 Regulations, these criticisms still appear to carry force, and are indeed reinforced by the continuing opposition from the OECD to the use of transactional profit methods other than as a method of last resort: OECD 2001 above n 69 at para 3.50.
[133] (1993) Tax Notes International ibid para 33.

rather than a firm based comparison. It examines the net profit margin relative to the appropriate base, for example costs, sales or assets, which a taxpayer realizes from a controlled transaction. In this it is deemed to be similar to the cost-plus and sales-minus methods.[134] In practice there may be little difference between the US CPM and the OECD transactional net margin approaches in that they each arrive at an arm's length range of comparable profits albeit from different starting points.[135]

(iv) Problems Relating to the Administration of Transfer Pricing Controls Using the Arm's Length Standard

Despite differences in the formal content of laws, certain common problems concerning the administration of a transfer pricing control system will emerge. First, it may be hard to identify that a MNE is engaging in tax avoidance through transfer price manipulations. The tax authorities will have to infer facts from annual tax returns. Initial indications of such practices may appear in the form of consistent losses made over a period of years in an associated enterprise. However, there may be good reasons for such a situation, such as the existence of strong political or social pressures to keep the enterprise open, or the hope that eventually it will become a profitable venture.[136] Other indications might include the receipt of goods or services from a related enterprise for little or no payment.[137] Again, the authorities must be satisfied that there are no sound commercial reasons for such a practice, and that the main purpose of the transactions is the shifting of liability to tax. To assist in the determination of appropriate arm's length prices, the tax authorities of various countries have conducted periodic industry-wide studies, thereby enhancing their general knowledge of pricing practices.[138]

Secondly, there will be problems in obtaining the relevant information from the taxpaying MNE. Once the authorities are satisfied that an investigation should be mounted, they will request further information about the MNE's commercial organization, its production and distribution systems, and any other matters that will help in determining whether the internal transfer prices used by the firm are compatible with the arm's length standard. Such information can usually

---

[134] OECD 2001 above n 69 at paras 3.26–3.28.   [135] Eden above n 38 at 609.

[136] See OECD 1979 above n 48 at para 28 p 21 and para 42 p 31.

[137] ibid para 40 p 29. See also *Hospital Corporation of America v CIR* 81 TC 520 (US Tax Ct 1983). For example, the Australian Tax Office will consider the following as indicators that a tax audit of a corporation may be necessary: financial or tax performance that varies substantially from industry patterns; significant variations in the amounts or patterns of tax payments compared with past performance and relevant economic indicators and industry; unexplained variation between economic performance, productivity, and tax performance; unexplained losses, low effective tax rates, and cases where a business or an entity consistently pays relatively low tax; a history of aggressive tax planning by the corporation, group, board members, key executives or advisers; weaknesses in the structures, processes, and approaches to tax compliance; tax outcomes that are inconsistent with the policy intent of tax reform: <http://www.ato.gov.au/large/content.asp?doc=/content/33802.htm&page=5&H5=&pc=&mnu=6568&mfp=001/009&st=&cy=>.   [138] OECD 1987 above n 34 at paras 96–97 at 41–42.

be ordered for disclosure if the firm does not supply it voluntarily.[139] Two problems bear specific mention in this respect. First, the taxpaying corporation may
not retain sufficient documented information for use by the authorities. To avoid
this difficulty the US Internal Revenue Service Regulations[140] demand annual
information returns in respect of 'reportable transactions'[141] with related persons,
from all US corporations that are 25 per cent foreign-owned, foreign corporations
engaged in a US business that are 25 per cent foreign-owned and any foreign corporation that is engaged in a US business even if it is not foreign-owned. Failure to
comply results in monetary and non-monetary penalties.[142] Other countries also
require periodic disclosure of information for transfer pricing control.[143] In the
UK the reforms to the transfer pricing legislation have introduced special documentation requirements for taxpaying firms. Firms, other than those qualifying
for the small and medium sized business exemption from the transfer pricing
rules, must comply with the record keeping requirements to be observed in relation to returns made in accordance with the arm's length principle. Specifically, all
documentation that can be used to ascertain whether transactions with related
parties have been conducted in accordance with the arm's length principle must be
made available to the Inland Revenue for inspection. The records kept must be
sufficient to enable the taxpayer to deliver a correct and complete return and the
records must be preserved until the latest of: six years from the end of the period
concerned; the date on which any enquiry into the return is completed; or the
date on which the Revenue is no longer able to open an enquiry. The records to be
kept and preserved include: records of all receipts and expenses in the course of the

[139] For example, in the UK, where the taxpayer fails to comply with voluntary information disclosures to the Inland Revenue the inspector has general information powers to deal with such cases. The
general information powers available are: Finance Act 1998 Schedule 18 paras 27 to 29 for enquiries
into company tax returns; Taxes Management Act 1970 s 19A for enquiries into other tax returns
and s 20 power to call for documents of taxpayer and others and SI 1994/1811/Reg10 or SI
1994/1812/Reg10 powers exercised by the General and Special Commissioners: Inland Revenue
INTM434020 – Schedule 28AA: enquiries and management provisions at <http://www.hmrc.
gov.uk/manuals/intmanual/INTM434020.htm>.

[140] See Treas Reg s 1.6038A [Effective for taxable years beginning after 10 July 1989] published
US Federal Register vol 56 No 118 (19 June, 1991) 28056–75, with corrections vol 56 No 164 (23
August 1991) 11792; reproduced in 30 ILM 1320 (1991) or <http://www.access.gpo.gov/nara/
cfr/waisidx_06/26cfr1m_06.html>.

[141] Including sales and purchases, rents, royalty payments, service payments, loan payments,
and transactions involving non-monetary consideration or less than full consideration: Treas Reg
s 1.6038A–2(a)(3) and (4).   [142] See Treas Reg s 1.6038A–4 and s 1.6038A–7.

[143] For example, Australia requires the periodic conclusion of special-purpose questionnaires which
are attached to the tax return: see Australian Tax Office *International Transfer Pricing: Introduction to
Concepts and Risk Assessment* (Canberra, April 2005) at 4, available at <http://www.ato.gov.au> and
Taxation Ruling TR 98/11 Income tax: documentation and practical issues associated with setting
and reviewing transfer pricing in international dealings <http://law.ato.gov.au/atolaw/view.
htm?DocID=TXR%2FTR9811%2FNAT%2FATO%2F00001>. Canada introduced reporting
requirements similar to those used by the US under the 1987 tax reforms: Borden, Elliot, Howard,
Mackie, Barristers and Solicitors *Report For Non-Residents* Vol 1 Issue at 1 Winter 1990 at 1. See also
TPM–05 Contemporaneous Documentation 13 October 2004 as amended <http://www.cra-arc.
gc.ca/tax/nonresidents/common/trans/tpm05-e.html>.

company's activities; records of all sales and purchases made in the course of any trade involving dealing in goods; and supporting documents relating to these items such as accounts, books, deeds, contracts, vouchers, and receipts.[144] These principles are applied in accordance with the OECD Transfer Pricing Guidelines.[145] The EC Transfer Pricing Forum has also introduced a code on transfer pricing documentation which will affect UK practice. It is to be read in the light of the OECD Transfer Pricing Guidelines.[146]

The possibility of jurisdictional conflicts over disclosure can be diminished, although not entirely eliminated, where a bilateral double taxation treaty exists between the home and host state of the MNE. This will usually contain a provision requiring the exchange of information necessary for carrying out the provisions of the treaty or the domestic tax laws of the contracting states.[147] However, under the OECD Model Convention the duty to exchange information does not include any obligations: to carry out administrative measures at variance with the laws and practices of one or other contracting state; to supply information that is not obtainable under the laws or in the normal course of the administration of one or other contracting state; or to supply information which would disclose any trade secrets or trade processes, or information the disclosure of which would be contrary to public policy (*ordre public*).[148] Therefore difficulties may still arise over whether the information requested is within the ambit of the duty to exchange or whether it lies outside its scope.

A third problem associated with the regulation of transfer price manipulations is that of international double taxation. This may arise where a reallocation decision results in the shifting of income from one country to another. For example, if the

---

[144] Inland Revenue INTM433020 – Schedule 28AA: Self Assessment obligations Record keeping: the general duty and transfer pricing <http://www.hmrc.gov.uk/manuals/intmanual/INTM433020. htm>. See further INTM433020 – Schedule 28AA: Self Assessment obligations Record keeping: transfer pricing documentation <http://www.hmrc.gov.uk/manuals/intmanual/INTM433020.htm>.

[145] See further OECD 2001 above n 69 Ch V especially paras 5.16 to 5.27.

[146] See Resolution of the Council of the European Union and the Representatives of the Governments of the Member States, meeting within the Council, on a Code of Conduct on transfer pricing documentation for associated enterprises in the European Union (EU TPD) Brussels, 20 June 2006 10509/1/06 REV 1 FISC 91 OC 468 at <http://ec.europa.eu/taxation_customs/resources/ documents/taxation/company_tax/transfer_pricing/forum/code_en.pdf>. According to the EC Commission: 'The documentation that multinational enterprises would have to file with tax administrations in order to report on their pricing for cross-border intra-group activities would consist of two main parts: One set of documentation (the "masterfile") should provide a "blue print" of the company and its transfer pricing system that would be relevant and available to all EU Member States concerned. It would provide information such as a general description of the business and business strategy, of the transactions involving associated enterprises in the EU and of the enterprise's transfer pricing policy. Second, a set of standardised documentation ("country-specific documentation") for each of the specific Member States concerned with the intra-group transactions. This documentation would include information such as amounts of transaction flows within that country, contractual terms and the particular transfer pricing methods used and would only be available to the relevant Member State.' Press Release IP/05/1403 10 November 2005 at <http://europa.eu/rapid/ pressReleasesAction.do?reference=IP/05/1403&format=HTML&aged=0&language=en&gui Language=en>.   [147] See OECD Model Double Taxation Convention above n 23 art 26.

[148] ibid art 26(2).

taxable income split on a transaction between the parent and its foreign subsidiary is stated by the parties as being 25/75 per cent, and the home state reallocates this to 50/50 per cent, unless the host state tax authorities make a corresponding downward adjustment of 25 per cent on the taxable income of the subsidiary, there is a risk of economic double taxation on the group as a whole. To alleviate this possibility Article 9(2) of the OECD Model Double Taxation Convention recommends that the host state makes the necessary adjustment to the tax charged on the subsidiary's profits. However, the Article 9(2) procedure is not compulsory which weakens it considerably. Where the host state refuses to make an adjustment, as where it disagrees with the application of the arm's length valuation made by the home state, the two states should enter into consultations through their competent authorities with a view to resolving their differences.[149] In addition, it may be necessary to ensure that time limits on determining corresponding adjustments are met by reducing the length of mutual agreement proceedings, and that taxpayers are informed of the applicable procedures, although they do not have any specific rights to participate in such deliberations.[150]

A more developed system of double taxation control in disputes regarding transfer price adjustments has recently been developed by the European Community (EC). In 1990 the EC adopted a convention on the elimination of double taxation in connection with the adjustment of profits of associated enterprises.[151] This introduces a compulsory procedure for the settlement of such disputes. Any taxpaying enterprise that feels it has been subjected to unrelieved double taxation as a result of an arm's length reallocation of income, may complain to the competent authority of the contracting state of which it is an enterprise or in which its permanent establishment is situated.[152] The competent authority will then seek to reach a mutual agreement with the competent authority of any other contracting

---

[149] Article 9(2) states: 'Where a Contracting State includes in the profits of an enterprise of that State – and taxes accordingly – profits on which an enterprise of the other Contracting State has been charged to tax in that other State and the profits so included are profits which would have accrued to the enterprise of the first-mentioned State if the conditions made between the two enterprises had been those which would have been made between independent enterprises, then that other State shall make an appropriate adjustment to the amount of the tax charged thereon on those profits. In determining such adjustment, due regard shall be had to the other provisions of this Convention and the competent authorities of the Contracting States shall if necessary consult each other.' Even though art. 9(2) says that the other state *shall* make the appropriate adjustment, the OECD Commentary to the Model Convention makes clear that the making of such an adjustment is discretionary and not mandatory and depends on the other state agreeing with the reallocation made by the first state: see OECD 2001above n 69 at paras 4.29–4.42; Davies above n 11 at paras 14.05–14.06; OECD 1984 above n 69; Madere 10 Texas ILJ 108 at 126–32 (1975).

[150] OECD 2001 above n 69 at paras 4.43–4.66.

[151] Convention (90/436/EEC) OJ [1990] L225/10 available at <http://eur-lex.europa.eu/LexUriServ/LexUriServ.do?uri=CELEX:41990A0436:EN:HTML>. The Arbitration Convention was in force for an initial period of five years from 1 January 1995 until 31 December 1999. It re-entered into force, with retroactive effect from 1 January 2000, on 1 November 2004. It will be automatically renewed in 2009 unless a Member State objects. See further Transfer Pricing and the Arbitration Convention at <http://ec.europa.eu/taxation_customs/taxation/company_tax/transfer_pricing/arbitration_convention/index_en.htm>. [152] ibid art 6(1).

state concerned. If the competent authorities fail to reach such agreement within two years from the date that the taxpaying enterprise first submitted its complaint, they shall set up an advisory commission charged with delivering its opinion on the elimination of the double taxation in question.[153] The commission shall consist of an independent chairman, two representatives of each competent authority concerned and an even number of independent persons of standing to be appointed by mutual agreement from a list of independent persons nominated by the contacting states.[154] The commission shall deliver its opinion not more than six months from the date on which the matter was referred to it.[155] Thereupon the competent authorities party to the dispute shall take a decision by common consent which will eliminate the double taxation complained of within six months of the date of the commission's opinion. They are free to take a decision that deviates from the commission's opinion, so long as they apply the arm's length standard.[156] However, if they fail to reach agreement within the requisite period, they shall be obliged to act in accordance with that opinion.[157] This procedure deals with double taxation only after it has occurred. In order to improve procedures under the convention a non-binding code of conduct for the implementation of the convention was adopted in 2004.[158] It covers the starting points for the review periods contained in the convention and the arrangements to be followed under the mutual agreement procedure and the arbitration procedure in the absence of agreement being reached under the first phase.

A fourth difficulty arises in tax systems that permit a credit against foreign tax, in that a reallocation may affect the entitlement of the parent company to foreign tax credit. Under US law provisions exist to ensure that foreign tax credit is not used by the US taxpaying parent as a means of reducing the tax effect of any reallocation of income to it. Only where the parent can show that all efforts by its foreign subsidiary, in seeking a repayment of foreign taxes on the reallocated income, have been exhausted without success, will any foreign tax credit be allowed against the tax already paid on the reallocated income.[159] Otherwise, any foreign taxes paid will be assumed to have been made as a voluntary contribution to the host state not eligible for foreign tax credit.

---

[153] ibid art 7(1). Under art 8 of the convention, the mutual agreement procedure need not be initiated where one of the enterprises concerned is liable to a serious penalty as a result of its transfer pricing practices, and where judicial or administrative proceedings, which may result in the imposition of such a penalty, have been instituted and are being conducted simultaneously with proceedings under the convention the latter proceedings may be stayed until the judicial or administrative proceedings have been concluded.   [154] ibid art 9(1), (4).

[155] ibid art 11(1).

[156] ibid art 12(1); art (4) which requires use of the arm's length standard in allocating profits on related party transactions.   [157] ibid.

[158] EU Council *Code of Conduct for the Effective Implementation of the Arbitration Convention* (90/436/EEC of 23 July 1990) Brussels, 31 March 2005 12695/2/04 Rev 2 Fisc 173 at <http://register.consilium.europa.eu/pdf/en/04/st12/st12695-re02.en04.pdf>.

[159] Revenue Procedure 2002–52, 2002–2 Cum Bull 242 and see McDaniel, Ault, and Repetti above n 13 at 157–58.

Inevitably, an element of uncertainty can creep in to the control of transfer pricing in related party transactions. It is in response to such uncertainty that a number of countries have followed the OECD recommendation to adopt a system of Advanced Pricing Arrangements (APAs), whereby the taxpayer can approach the tax authority for a ruling that a proposed system of internal transfer pricing meets the requirements of its transfer pricing rules.[160] According to the OECD, APAs are mostly useful when traditional mechanisms for resolving transfer pricing issues fail or are difficult to apply.[161] It is not a procedure to be used in cases where the approach to determining the transfer prices is relatively straightforward. Indeed, the UK Inland Revenue will reject requests for an APA where this is the case.[162] Given the international dimension of transfer pricing arrangements many countries will not give an APA unless it is bilateral or multilateral.[163] The main advantage of an APA is that it can eliminate uncertainty for the taxpayer in a complex situation. It introduces a non-adversarial environment and will help to avoid time-consuming investigations and possible litigation. It also provides the revenue authorities with information allowing for a saving in time for future examinations. Bilateral and multilateral APAs will assist in reducing the risk of double or non-taxation.[164] The OECD discourages the use of unilateral APAs as these may lead to disagreements with non-participating administrations and may create adjustment problems.[165] Agreements may also fail to cover all the countries in which the MNE and its affiliates operate, thereby diminishing the value of the arrangement in an international context.[166] A further problem is that increasing demand for APAs may stretch tax authorities and lead to their devoting resources to more compliant firms, while less compliant taxpayers, who will not readily use

[160] For the UK see Finance Act 1999 ss 85–87 and INTM469010 – Transfer Pricing: Advance Pricing Agreements (APAs). Background to APAs at <http://www.hmrc.gov.uk/manuals/intmanual/INTM469010.htm> and see Inland Revenue Statement of Practice SP 3/99 Advance Pricing Agreements (APAs) available at <http://www.hmrc.gov.uk/practitioners/sop.pdf> United States: Revenue Procedure 2004–40, 2004–29 IRB 50 and Rev Proc 2006–9 2006–2 IRB released 19 December 2005 available at <http://www.irs.gov/pub/irs-drop/rp-06-9.pdf> and see McDaniel, Ault, and Repetti ibid at 158–59; Canada: Information Circular 94–4R *International Transfer Pricing: Advance Pricing Arrangements (APA)* revised 16 March 2001 available at <http://www.cra-arc.gc.ca/E/pub/tp/ic94-4r/ic94-4r-e.pdf> Australia: Australian Tax Office *Advance Pricing Arrangements* (Canberra, April 2005) available at <http://www.ato.gov.au>.

[161] OECD 2001 above n 69 at para 4.124. See, for the problems of applying APAs to the transfer pricing of intangibles, Mildred A Hastbacka 'Valuation of Technology Intangibles for Transfer Pricing: Time for Industry Initiatives?' Tax Notes Int'l 20 October 2003 at 265.

[162] See INTM469010 above n 160.

[163] See OECD 2001 above n 69 at para 4.131. On 18 June 2004, the Pacific Association of Tax Administrators (PATA) members released documents about internal operational guidance in respect of mutual agreement procedures (MAP) and bilateral advance pricing arrangements (BAPA). PATA is comprised of representatives from the tax administrations of Australia, Canada, Japan, and the United States. The documents are available on member country websites: obtained from the Canada Revenue Agency website at <http://www.cra-arc.gc.ca/tax/nonresidents/common/trans/issuance-e.html>. See also the *BAPA Operational Guidance for Member Countries of the PATA* (6 February 2004) at <http://www.irs.gov/pub/irs-utl/pata_bapa_guidance_-_final.pdf>.

[164] OECD 2001 ibid at paras 4.143–4.147.   [165] ibid paras 4.148–4.151.

[166] ibid para 4.152.

APAs, will avoid investigation.[167] Other concerns may arise out of the poor administration of APAs.[168] Nonetheless, the OECD gives this procedure its support provided it is carried out mainly on a bilateral or multilateral basis, it offers equitable access to all taxpayers, and leads to closer cooperation between national tax authorities.[169]

(v) Formula Apportionment

Much of the preceding discussion has centred on the difficulties inherent in establishing appropriate arm's length prices for related party transactions. Critics of the arm's length approach argue that such an enquiry is bound to fail where the transaction occurs between affiliates of an internationally integrated MNE. The arm's length standard simply does not conform to the economic reality of the group, and imposes an artificial 'separate entity' analysis upon its operations.[170] As an alternative, the formula apportionment approach is recommended.

The formula apportionment or unitary business method has been applied to taxpaying MNEs under the laws of certain states of the US, most notably in California.[171] The essence of this approach was described by the US Supreme Court in *Container Corporation of America v Franchise Tax Board*.[172] The Court held that the unitary business/formula apportionment approach rejects geographical or transactional accounting and instead calculates the local tax base of corporations operating in more than one jurisdiction by means of a two step approach: first, the scope of the 'unitary business', of which the taxpaying enterprise's activities in the taxing jurisdiction form one part, must be ascertained; secondly, the total income of the unitary business between the taxing jurisdiction and the rest of the world must be ascertained and apportioned on the basis of a formula taking into account objective measures of the corporation's activities within and outside the jurisdiction.

The basic US constitutional requirement that entitles a state to tax income on a unitary basis is that there is some 'nexus' between the taxing state and the taxpayer. This is fulfilled by the conduct of some part of the corporation's business within the jurisdiction.[173] Assuming such a 'nexus' exists the question of whether the business involved is a 'unitary business' arises.

---

[167] ibid para 4.153.   [168] ibid paras 4.154–4.149.   [169] ibid paras 4.160–4.166.

[170] See Schindler and Henderson 'Intercorporate Transfer Pricing' 29 Tax Notes 1171 at 1172–73 (1985); Eden above n 38 at 613–5.

[171] See California Revenue and Taxation Code s 25101–25141 as amended available at <http://www.leginfo.ca.gov/cgi-bin/displaycode?section=rtc&group=25001-26000&file=25101-25108>, <http://www.leginfo.ca.gov/cgi-bin/displaycode?section=rtc&group=25001-26000&file=25110-25116>, and <http://www.leginfo.ca.gov/cgi-bin/displaycode?section=rtc&group=25001-26000&file=25120-25141>.

[172] 463 US 159 (1983); Slip Opinion reproduced 22 ILM 855 (1983). Comment: Heising 16 Law & Pol.Int'l Bus. 299 (1984). See also *Chicago Bridge and Iron Co v Caterpillar Tractor Co* 103 S Ct 3562 (1983); *Anaconda Corp v Franchise Tax Board of California* 103 S Ct 3563 (1983).

[173] See *Container Corporation of America v Franchise Tax Board* ibid at ILM 858 citing *Exxon Corporation v Wisconsin Department of Revenue* 447 US 207 at 210–20 (1980) and *Mobil Oil v Commissioner of Taxes of Vermont* 445 US 425 at 436, 437 (1980).

In determining whether a 'unitary business' exists the tax authorities must under-take an economic analysis of the activities of the MNE, and ascertain the extent to which its affiliates act as a unified business entity.[174] The approach is reminiscent of cases involving the 'lifting of the corporate veil' between parent and subsidiary, and not dissimilar criteria of analysis are employed to show that actual control over the business activities of the group is exercised by the parent company.[175] However, this is not an example of veil piercing but of the application of an enterprise analysis. The case law expressly rejects the need to resort to veil piercing techniques.[176]

In the *Container Corporation* case,[177] the US Supreme Court made two general observations on the evidence required to find a 'unitary business'. First it left open the question whether any one factor indicating control would be sufficient, by itself, to prove the existence of a 'unitary business'. Secondly, the Supreme Court held that it was unnecessary to show a substantial flow of goods between enter-prise units to prove a 'unitary business'. The prerequisite to an acceptable finding of a unitary business was a 'flow of value, not a flow of goods'.[178] Thus the Court adopted a broad approach which could include evidence of dividend flows, roy-alty fees, management charges, or intra-corporate loans in the determination of the existence of a 'unitary business'. The burden is on the taxpayer to disprove the existence of a 'unitary business' where the state's assessment is challenged.[179] This can be done by showing that the income assessed to tax was derived from activities

---

[174] The meaning of a 'unitary business' has been considered in the following US Supreme Court decisions: *Mobil Oil v Commissioner of Taxes of Vermont* 445 US 425 (1980); *Exxon Corporation v Wisconsin Department of Revenue* 447 US 207 (1980); *FW Woolworth & Co v Taxation and Revenue Department of the State of New Mexico* 458 US 354 (1982); *Asarco Inc v Idaho State Tax Commission* 458 US 307 (1982); *Container Corporation of America v Franchise Tax Board* above n 172; *Allied-Signal Inc v Director, Division of Taxation* 504 US 768, 772 (1992); *Hunt-Wesson v Franchise Tax Board* 528 US 458 (2000). See further Phillip I Blumberg, Kurt A Strasser, Nicholas L Georgakopoulos, and Eric J Gouvin *Blumberg on Corporate Groups* (New York: Aspen Publishers, 2nd edn, 2005) vol 4 paras 136.02[A]–[I]. For leading state decisions see ibid paras 136.3[A]–[E].

[175] The leading cases cited in the above n 174 establish the following conditions for a valid finding of a 'unitary business' for the purposes of liability to tax:

– It must involve substantially the same business activity. A diversified firm cannot therefore be a 'unitary business' when viewed as a whole.

– The existence of unified business activity will be determined by reference to functional business criteria. Thus mere passive ownership, or unusual potential for control, is insufficient. Evidence of actual control is required and mere economic benefit is not enough.

– Evidence of actual control involves an examination of the parent/subsidiary relationship. The fol-lowing criteria have been considered: stock ownership, the nature and identity of the management, the degree of centralization of the business, the degree of autonomy given to the subsidiary, includ-ing the extent of its financial and technical dependence on the parent, and the interchangeability and powers of personnel.

– Legal and divisional separation, as well as internal accounting procedures, can be disregarded for the purposes of establishing control.

– No one criterion is decisive and each case involves an analysis of its own facts.

[176] See *Mobil Oil Corp v Commissioner of Taxes of Vermont* above n 173 at 440–41.

[177] Above n 172.   [178] ibid ILM 865.

[179] *Mobil Oil v Commissioner of Taxes of Vermont* 445 US 425 at 439 (1980); *Exxon Corporation v Wisconsin Department of Revenue* 447 US 207 at 221 (1980).

unrelated to the taxpayer's business within the taxing jurisdiction. In adjudicating the issue the court will look to the 'underlying economic realities of a unitary business' and must be satisfied that the income derives from an 'unrelated business activity' which constitutes a 'discreet business enterprise', if the taxpayer is to succeed.[180]

Once the existence of a 'unitary business' has been established, the tax authorities will require evidence of the worldwide profits of that business, from which the proportion of profits chargeable to tax in the taxing jurisdiction will be calculated. This is done by applying a formula based on the proportion of total payroll, property, and sales of the unitary business that are located within the taxing jurisdiction. Under US law, for an apportionment to stand, it must be applied fairly by the taxing state and must not result in discrimination against interstate or foreign commerce, in breach of the US Constitution.[181] This requires that the application of the formula should not lead to double taxation. Furthermore, within the context of US state and federal relations, the application of the formula must not impair the need for federal uniformity in matters of foreign commerce.[182]

The formula apportionment method engaged considerable opposition, both from US and foreign MNEs, from the US Government and from a number of foreign states, including the United Kingdom. Indeed, the UK introduced, under section 54 of the Finance Act 1985, a power of retaliation against US companies operating in the UK, if any British company was subjected to tax on the unitary principle.[183] The major basis of opposition is that the unitary tax system inevitably leads to double taxation. Furthermore, so far as the US Government is concerned, the use of worldwide unitary taxation methods by states of the Union prevents it from speaking with one voice in matters of international trade given the wide adoption of 'water's edge', namely source based, approaches to corporate taxation by other countries and by the US in international tax treaties.[184]

As to the issue of double taxation, where a payroll, property and sales formula is used, it will tend to allocate a higher proportion of income to jurisdictions where wage rates, property values, and sales prices are higher. Thus it has an inevitable double taxation effect, in that a high proportion of income already taxed at source

---

[180] *Mobil Oil v Commissioner of Taxes of Vermont* 445 US 425 at 439 (1980).

[181] *Container Corporation* above n 172.

[182] *Japan Line Ltd v County of Los Angeles* 441 US 434 (1979). See also *Reuters Ltd* (NY State CA) noted in Tax News Service TNS–8 (1994).

[183] On US Government attitudes, see P Winship 'State Taxation of Multinational Business: The Unitary Tax Debate' [1985] JBL 179; *Alcan Aluminum Ltd v Franchise Tax Board of California* Brief Amicus Curiae of the United States: 25 ILM 683 (1986). The US Government proposed legislation banning states from applying worldwide unitary taxation; see 25 ILM 704–715; 739–759 (1986). The UK position and s 54 of the Finance Act 1985 are reproduced in 25 ILM 734–738 (1986). See further Inland Revenue and US Treasury *Unitary Tax: Review of Progress Towards Resolving the Issues* (Inland Revenue, 1991).

[184] For a summary of the principal arguments against the imposition of unitary tax on the worldwide profits of MNEs, see *Container Corporation v Franchise Tax Board of California* above n 172 dissenting opinion of Powell, O'Connor JJ, Burger CJ.

in a foreign jurisdiction will be reallocated to the taxing jurisdiction, provided it is more economically developed than the foreign jurisdiction.[185] For example, on the facts of *Container Corporation*,[186] some 13 per cent of the appellant US corporation's worldwide income from its unitary business was allocated to its operations in Latin America. This was less than half of the arm's length total. Thus profits taxed at source in Latin American host states would again be taxed in California.

In *Container Corporation* a US based company with a business presence in California sought to challenge the constitutionality of California's use of the unitary tax system in relation to its cardboard package manufacturing business, which took place in California and in several Latin American affiliates. The US company did not succeed. The Supreme Court was satisfied that the Californian tax authorities had acted constitutionally. However, the Supreme Court explicitly left open the question whether the application of worldwide unitary tax to the US subsidiary of a foreign parent company would be constitutional.[187] Indeed, cases challenging unitary tax assessments against US subsidiaries of foreign parent companies have reached US courts. In *Franchise Tax Board of California v Alcan Aluminum*.[188] the Supreme Court accepted in principle that the foreign parent of a US subsidiary, which had been subjected to a worldwide unitary tax assessment, could be said to have suffered an actual financial injury such as would give it standing to bring a case under the Foreign Commerce Clause of the US Constitution. However, the Supreme Court did not feel it necessary to offer standing before the US Federal courts on the ground that, in the first instance, any challenge against the application of state taxation laws should be made before state courts. Furthermore, it was held that the foreign parent need not have an independent right of action before the state courts. The US subsidiary could plead injury to the parent company's interests on the latter's behalf, by virtue of the control exercised by the parent over its subsidiary. Thus, while not giving an unqualified right of action to foreign parent companies, and thereby avoiding a decision as to whether this was an appropriate case for direct shareholder rights of action,[189] this case appears to have moved a little beyond earlier decisions, made in certain circuits of the US Court of Appeals, to the effect that unitary tax does not cause direct or independent harm to the foreign parent company.[190]

Significantly, in California, changes in the law moved away from the use of worldwide unitary taxation in the case of foreign parent companies and their US

---

[185] ibid.   [186] Above n 172.

[187] *Container Corporation v Franchise Tax Board* above n 172 at 189 n 26, and at 195 n 32; ILM 870, 873.   [188] 107 L Ed 2d 696 (1990).

[189] As was held by the US Court of Appeals for the Seventh Circuit in this case: 860 F 2d 688 at 696–697 (1988).

[190] See *Shell Petroleum NV v Graves* 709 F 2d 593, 595 (9th Cir) *cert.den. sub. nom Shell Petroleum BV v Franchetti* 464 US 1012 (1983); *EMI v Bennett* 738 F 2d 994, 997 (9th Cir) *cert.den.*469 US 1073 (1984); *Alcan Aluminum Ltd v Franchise Tax Board* 558 F Supp 624, 626–629 (SDNY) *aff'd* 742 F 2d 1430 (2nd Cir 1983) *cert.den.* 464 US 1041 (1984). See further Hartman 'Constitutional Limitations on State Taxation of Corporate Income from Multinational Corporations' 37 Vand. L. Rev. 217 (1984).

subsidiaries. In 1988, California allowed foreign based MNEs the option of computing their California taxes according to the 'water's edge' principle, on payment of a fee into the California Unitary Fund.[191] Furthermore, in November 1990 the California Court of Appeals held, in the case of *Barclays Bank International Limited v Franchise Tax Board*[192] that California's unitary tax law, as applied to foreign based unitary businesses, was unconstitutional, being in violation of the Foreign Commerce Clause. However, the Supreme Court of California reversed this ruling and held that the California worldwide unitary tax apportionment method was constitutional.[193] The US Supreme Court upheld this decision.[194] Equally, US based corporations have also continued to challenge the application of California's unitary tax to their international operations.[195] Alongside these developments in litigation, the UK Government stepped up the pressure on the Clinton administration by threatening to apply the retaliatory powers under the 1985 Finance Act from 1 January 1994. The US Treasury apparently put pressure upon California further to reform the law so as to meet the UK's objections. A reform Bill was passed by the Californian legislature in September 1993, although the UK was not satisfied that it met those objections.[196]

The above mentioned developments show that, on purely political grounds, the use of formula apportionment/unitary tax methods creates difficulties. In addition, there are significant policy problems created by this approach, which make it hard to say conclusively that it is a better method than the arm's length principle in dealing with the taxation of flows of value between related entities in a MNE.[197] The first problem, that of enhanced double taxation, has already been highlighted. Unless all countries agree, contrary to current practice, to abandon 'water's edge' approaches and to replace these with an agreed unitary tax formula, double taxation and confusion is bound to continue. Even if all states were agreed on the

[191] Senate Bill 85 of 1986 which entered force after 1 January 1988. See Rothschild 'California Unitary Tax Update' BIFD (February 1991) 71.

[192] Case No 325061 (Cal App Dept Super Ct 16 June 1987) Corp Counsel Weekly (BNA) 1 July 1987 at 136 *affd*. 3 Cal App 4th 1034, 275 Cal Rprtr 626 (1990).

[193] 2 Cal 4th 708, 809 P2d 279 (1992).

[194] *Barclays Bank plc v Franchise Tax Board* 512 US 298 (1994). See for background Rothschild 'California's New "Water's Edge" Election Enhances Business Opportunities for Foreign Investors: The US Supreme Court to Rule in *Barclays* Case' BIFD (January 1994) 3; McNeill 'California's Recent Legislation on Unitary Taxation and *Barclays Bank plc v Franchise Tax Board of California*' 48 Tax Law 231 (1994); Sabransky '*Barclays Bank plc v Franchise Tax Board*: California's Taxation of Foreign-based Multinational Corporations' 31 Cal W Int'l L. Rev. 317 (1995).

[195] See Rothschild above n 191 at 73.

[196] Senate Bill 671 enacted 10 September 1993 signed by Governor Wilson on 6 October 1993. See now California Revenue and Taxation Code ss 25110–25116 at <http://www.leginfo.ca.gov/cgi-bin/displaycode?section=rtc&group=25001-26000&file=25110-25116>. For analysis, see Rothschild above n 191. See also 'UK Still Unhappy With California Tax Proposals' *Financial Times* 21/22 August 1993 at 2. The principal changes enacted by SB 671 are that: firms electing to be taxed under the 'water's edge' principle shall no longer be subject to an election fee; they will no longer be required to produce a domestic disclosure spreadsheet; the election period is extended to seven years, with automatic annual renewal unless the taxpayer notifies non-renewal; and the Franchise Tax Board cannot disregard a water's edge election.   [197] See further OECD 2001 above n 69 at paras 3.58–3.74.

worldwide adoption of a uniform formula apportionment system,[198] should the currently most popular payroll, property, and sales formula be used, it would not avoid the resulting inequality of revenue distribution between developed and less developed tax jurisdictions that was pointed out by the dissenting judges in *Container Corporation*.[199] Secondly, as the OECD has stated, formula apportionment demands 'a complex analysis of the different functions of the various associated enterprises and a sophisticated weighing up of the different risks and profit opportunities in the various different stages of manufacturing, transportation, marketing and so on. Nor would the information necessary for such an assessment be readily available or, in many cases, available at all'.[200] The obtaining and analysis of the relevant information would demand considerable resources that would not be available to many countries. Furthermore, it would put MNEs to considerable expense in providing the information. The additional costs may not be justifiable in terms of the marginal improvements in profit allocation analyses that formula apportionment might offer over the arm's length approach.[201]

(b) The Use of 'Tax Havens' by MNEs

A further advantage arising out of the MNE's international network is its ability to set up and use controlled subsidiaries in 'tax haven' jurisdictions as conduits for various transactions which have the effect of channelling funds to the tax haven subsidiary. To understand the value of a tax haven to a MNE, and to appreciate the nature of regulatory responses from non-tax haven states in which the MNE operates, it is necessary, first, to describe the concept of deferral in the international tax system.[202]

In the major capital exporting countries, tax on income generated by overseas subsidiaries only becomes due when it is repatriated to the parent company in the home country. Until such time, therefore, tax on the unremitted income is deferred. Should the home country tax rate be higher than that of the host country a saving to tax results. This is equal to the unremitted income times the rate differential for the period of deferral. The deferral benefit amounts to an investment subsidy by the home country to its foreign investor, in that it offers an incentive for the reinvestment of foreign sourced profits into foreign operations. This enables firms

---

[198] For a view supporting the adoption of a new international tax order for direct foreign investment based on a uniform unitary tax system: Bird 'Shaping a New International Tax Order' BIFD (July 1988) 292. For a critical response, see Muten 'A New International Tax Order?' BIFD (November 1988) 471. An alternative may be to use a global profit split approach which is more consistent with the arm's length principle; see Jinyan Li 'Global Profit Split: An Evolutionary Approach to International Income Allocation' 50 Canadian Tax Journal 823 (2002).

[199] Above n 172; see also Muten ibid and OECD 2001 above n 69 paras 3.65–3.66.

[200] OECD 1979 above n 48 at para 14 and see also OECD 2001 paras 3.69–3.73 for more detailed analysis of the problems that MNEs would encounter in adhering to a formula apportionment system.

[201] ibid.

[202] See Plasschaert above n 7 at paras 10.12–10.14; McDaniel, Ault, and Repetti above n 13 at 113–14 and 125–28 on which this paragraph draws. See further Picciotto above n 2 ch 5.

from countries not using an exemption method of double tax avoidance to compete on equal terms with firms from such countries, in that both groups of firms then effectively pay only the host country rate until the eventual remittance of profits by the firm from the country not employing an exemption for foreign source income.[203] Tax deferral may thus achieve 'capital import neutrality' in the host country, in that all foreign firms pay the same effective rates of tax, at least until remittance to the home country.

The possibility of tax deferral has contributed to the rise of tax haven jurisdictions.[204] Tax havens are characterized by little or no taxation. They are, typically, small communities with independent tax authorities, although they are not necessarily independent states. They are usually located close to major economic areas. Their principal source of income rests in the administration charges levied for the use of tax haven facilities, such as, for example, company registration fees, and in the private income generated by the demand for specialist commercial, legal, accounting, and other services.[205] A further advantage of tax havens is their common adherence to standards of strict commercial confidentiality. This has given rise to conflicts over disclosure of evidence in litigation involving, in particular, multinational banks operating branches in tax havens.[206]

MNEs may use tax haven subsidiaries in a number of ways. First, the firm may locate an offshore holding company in a tax haven to benefit fully from deferral possibilities. Dividends will be paid into this company, which will then be free to

---

[203] Similar considerations motivated the US use of tax subsidies for export income under the Domestic Sales International Corporation (DISC) legislation which was successfully challenged by the EC as an unlawful export subsidy under GATT Article XVI:4: *DISC – United States Tax Legislation* Report of GATT Panel 12 November 1976 GATT 23rd Supp BISD 98 (1977) available at <http://www.wto.org>: see John Jackson 'The Jurisprudence of International Trade: The DISC Case in GATT' 72 AJIL 747 (1978). This was replaced in 1984 with the Foreign Sales Corporation (FSC) which encouraged the use of FSCs located in tax havens to channel export sales of products with at least 50 per cent US content. Typically these would be subsidiaries of the US exporter. FSCs were used as conduits for indirect sales to end customers, with the profit on the transaction remaining in the FSC, which enjoyed privileged tax treatment under US law. This scheme was also successfully challenged by the EU under the GATT 1994: *United States – Tax Treatment for Foreign Sales Corporations* WT/DS108/AB/R Report of the Appellate Body adopted 20 March 2000 available at <http://www.wto.org>. This law was replaced by the FSC Replacement and Exclusion of Extra-territorial Income Act 2000 (ETI) which was again successfully challenged by the EU as failing to remedy the preferential tax treatment of export income: *United States – Tax Treatment of FSCs: Recourse to Article 21:5 DSU by the EC* WT/DS108/AB/RW issued 14 January 2002 available at <http://www.wto.org>. The ETI was repealed in 2004 but with long transition periods: McDaniel, Ault, and Repetti above n 13 at 161–62. The EU again complained that the reforms were insufficient and the WTO Appellate Body upheld this position in February 2006: *United States – Tax Treatment for Foreign Sales Corporations Second Recourse to Article 21:5 DSU by the EC* WT/DS108/AB/RW2 13 February 2006 at <http://www.wto.org>.

[204] See further OECD *Harmful Tax Competition: An Emerging Global Issue* (Paris: OECD, 1998) available at <http://www.oecd.org/dataoecd/33/0/1904176.pdf> ch 2; RA Johns *Tax Havens and Offshore Finance* (Frances Pinter, 1983). See further Picciotto above n 2 ch 6.

[205] See Adams and Whalley above n 1 at 129–132; OECD *International Tax Avoidance and Evasion: Four Related Studies* Issues in International Taxation No 1 (Paris: 1987) 'Tax Havens: Measures to Prevent Abuse by Taxpayers' at paras 6–45, 21–29.   [206] See ch 4 above.

redistribute financial resources throughout the international network of the firm. This is known as 'primary sheltering' as the character of the income flow remains unaltered. The separate legal personality of the tax haven company shelters the income from home country tax. According to the OECD, this is the most common use to which tax havens are put by MNEs.[207] Secondly, the MNE may use transfer pricing manipulations involving the tax haven subsidiary to shelter income arising from sales to affiliates and to final customers. This may be achieved by means of 'cross-invoicing'. A subsidiary in a high tax jurisdiction may channel a sale to an affiliated or unaffiliated purchaser in another country through an affiliated tax haven base company. Thus what would normally have been a single sales transaction is divided into two steps. First, a sale to the tax haven company will be effected at undervalue. Secondly, a sale will be effected between the tax haven company and the eventual purchaser at the agreed contract price, as where the buyer is an unrelated entity, or, even, at overvalue where the buyer is an affiliate in a high tax country. In either case the profit on the sale accrues to the tax haven subsidiary.[208]

Thirdly, a MNE may use tax haven subsidiaries to alter the character of the income to take advantage of exemptions provided for by tax treaties or domestic laws in the home country. This is known as 'secondary sheltering'.[209] This result may be achieved in a number of ways. For example, an income flow from an overseas subsidiary may be channelled to a tax haven subsidiary which then makes a loan to the parent company, thereby altering what should have been a dividend remittance taxable at the hands of the parent into a loan, the principal and interest being repayable to the tax haven without further liability to tax in the home country. For this purpose the tax haven subsidiary may be set up as a financial services corporation. A similar result may be achieved by the use of a 'captive' insurance company. The MNE may set up a wholly owned insurance company in a tax haven, which deals with the insurance of the parent company's risks. In return the parent pays premiums to the insurance company. Not only will income be thereby diverted to the tax haven, but the parent will be able to deduct the premiums from home country tax. The premium will be set for the best possible tax saving effect.[210] Further savings may be obtained by the use of captive management services companies located in a tax haven. Profits can be shifted from affiliates in high tax jurisdictions to the tax haven as fees for services rendered by the captive service company.[211]

The control of tax avoidance involving tax haven affiliates can be carried out in at least two principal ways. First, where transfer pricing manipulations result in an artificial shifting of profits to the tax haven subsidiary from the parent company or

---

[207] OECD 1987 above n 205 at para 30, 25.
[208] See Plasschaert above n 7 para 10.18. The US FSC and ETI laws allowed US exporters to take advantage of such cross-invoicing techniques: n 203 above.
[209] OECD 1987 above n 205 para 27, at 25.   [210] OECD 1987 ibid. para 34, at 26.
[211] ibid para 38.

its affiliates, the home or host country can apply transfer pricing controls to reallocate those profits back to the company within its jurisdiction. Secondly, specialized laws that seek to control both primary and secondary sheltering may apply.
Primary sheltering is controlled by denying any deferral advantage to income that
is in the hands of a tax haven affiliate, treating it as income taxable in the hands of
its parent company as the principal shareholder. Secondary sheltering is controlled by denying the tax deductible status of a given transaction and treating any
income attributed to the tax haven subsidiary as the taxable income of its parent
company.

The original model for such legislation was developed by the US under the
so-called 'Subpart F' provisions of the Internal Revenue Code.[212] These were first
introduced in 1962. These provisions created the concept of a 'Controlled
Foreign Corporation'(CFC). This is defined as a foreign corporation in which
'United States shareholders'[213] own more than 50 per cent of the 'total combined
voting power' of all classes of stock or more than half of the 'value' of the stock.[214]
These provisions are not applied mechanically. Thus where US shareholders
devise schemes of indirect ownership, or sell stock to foreign interests so that the
US share falls below 50 per cent, the foreign corporation will nonetheless be
regarded as a CFC where the foreign shareholders are, in effect, the instruments of
the US shareholders.[215] The test is one of substance and not form.[216] Thus, relevant

---

[212] See 26 USC ss 951–964 discussed by McDaniel, Ault, and Repetti above n 13 at 114–28. Other
countries employing similar anti-avoidance provisions include France, Japan, Germany, Canada, and
the UK: OECD ibid para 62, at 32–33. The OECD report contains a comparative analysis of the principal features of these laws at para 63, at 33. A more recent OECD report is *Controlled Foreign Company
Legislation, Studies in Foreign Source Income* (Paris: OECD, 1996). Korea and Mexico adopted CFC
legislation in 1997. The UK legislation was introduced by the Finance Act 1984, c 43, ss 82–91; see Part
XVII of Chapter IV Income and Corporation Taxes Act 1988: see further Inland Revenue *International
Manual* INTM201000 – Controlled Foreign Companies: legislation – introduction and outline at
<http://www.hmrc.gov.uk/manuals/intmanual/INTM201000.htm> Baxter 'The United Kingdom and
Tax Havens: A Comparative Comment' 33 Am.Jo.Comp.L. 707 (1985); Picciotto above n 2 ch 7. The
European Court of Justice (ECJ) has held that the CFC legislation constitutes a possible infringement of
the freedom of establishment. The CFC legislation is compatible with EC law only to the extent that it
controls wholly artificial arrangements intended to circumvent national tax law; see Case C–196/04
Cadbury Schweppes plc, Cadbury Schweppes Overseas Limited v *Commissioners of Inland Revenue* judgment of 12 September 2006 at <http://curia.europa.eu>. For comment see 'Victory is Sweet but Result
Could be Bitter' *Financial Times* 13 September 2006 at 3. The French legislation can be found in Art
209B of the Code General des Impots: see further Pascal Picault *Fiscalité Française des Investissements a
l'Etranger* (Paris: Dunod, 1986) 159–85. On the New Zealand law see Prebble 'The New Zealand
Controlled Foreign Company Regime' 8 Asian Pacific Tax and Investment Bulletin (1990) 186. See
also, for a comparative study of six jurisdictions, BJ Arnold *The Taxation of Controlled Foreign
Corporations: An International Comparison* (Toronto: Canadian Tax Foundation, 1986). On Japan, see
Magnin and Rautalahti 'Japan; Tax Haven and Foreign Tax Credit Rules: 1992 Amendments and Their
Impact on Dutch Holding Companies' BIFD (May 1993) 286.
[213] Defined as a US citizen owning at least 10 per cent of the total combined voting power:
s 951(b) IRC.   [214] Section 957(a) IRC.
[215] Ownership by US shareholders includes stock held directly or indirectly through foreign corporations, partnerships, trusts, and estates: ss 957(a), 958(a)(1)(B).
[216] *CCA Inc v Commissioner* 64 TC 137 (US Tax Ct, 1975).

factors to be considered include inter alia the consideration paid by the foreign shareholders for the US shareholders' shares, the relationship between the US and the foreign shareholders, the powers of the foreign shareholders, and the incidence of dissent and debate over the future activities of the foreign corporation.[217] Even where a US parent company apparently sells a foreign subsidiary to an independently owned foreign holding company, the true relationship between the US seller and the foreign purchaser must be examined to determine whether the transaction is no more than a scheme for the retention of US control designed to avoid the burden of Subpart F.[218]

Once it is established that the foreign corporation is a CFC the Subpart F provisions require the US shareholder to report as a dividend its pro rata share of the CFC's 'Subpart F income' and its 'increase in earnings invested in United States property'.[219] Subpart F income consists of insurance income arising from premiums on policies covering risks outside the CFC's tax haven country,[220] and 'foreign base company income' (FBCI).[221] FBCI covers profits accruing to the tax haven subsidiary as a result of 'cross-invoicing' transactions or service payments. It also includes payments for shipping or other transport services, or oil related income, where the tax haven company is set up as a base for the profits accruing from these classes of activity.[222] However, if the CFC purchases property from a related party and substantially transforms it prior to sale, or includes it in a substantial manufacturing operation prior to sale, or where the company's conversion costs in connection with the use of such property account for 20 per cent or more of the total cost of the goods sold, the income derived from those sales will accrue to the CFC and will not be included in the US taxpayer's FBCI.[223] Otherwise, the US parent would be liable to tax on the earnings of its overseas subsidiaries regardless of the nature of their operations. Only transactions that are set up to avoid US tax should come within Subpart F scrutiny. Difficulties over distinguishing between genuine manufacturing activities and tax avoidance operations are likely, and adequate information over the precise nature of an activity may not always be forthcoming.[224]

The second category of CFC income relates to transactions whereby a dividend remittance to the parent is transformed into an otherwise non-taxable investment or flow of funds, the clearest example being a loan from the tax haven subsidiary to the parent. The code treats such investments or flows as a dividend in that amount paid to the US shareholder and then taxed as current income in the hands of the shareholder. 'United States property' for this purpose includes any tangible property

---

[217] *Garlock v Commissioner* 489 F 2d 197 (1973); *Kraus v Commissioner* 490 F 2d 898 (2nd Cir 1974).   [218] See *Koehring Company v US* 583 F 2d 313 (7th Cir 1978).
[219] Section 951(a)(1)(A)(i), (B).   [220] Section 952(a)(1) and s 953.
[221] Section 952(a)(2); s 954.   [222] See s 954 and Treas Reg s 1.954.
[223] See Treas Reg s 1.954–3(a)(2) and s 1.954–3(a)(4)(i)–(iii); *Dave Fischbein Manufacturing Company v Commissioner* 59 TC 338 (US Tax Ct 1972).
[224] OECD 1987 above n 205 para 108 44.

located in the US, stock in related corporations, obligations of a US person, and the right to use US patents acquired or developed by the CFC for use in the US.[225]

The overall effect of these provisions is to ensure that the genuine overseas business activities of US MNEs enjoy the deferral subsidy, while mere tax avoidance schemes are controlled. However, Subpart F provisions lose much of their relevance if the home country tax rate is significantly lowered, as the incentive to defer remittances is then much reduced.[226] On the other hand, according to the OECD, Subpart F type laws have led to an increase in taxable income in the countries using such laws.[227] Much, no doubt, depends on the relative tax rates in place at any time, upon the effectiveness of tax administrations in investigating tax avoidance schemes successfully, and upon the ingenuity of taxpaying corporations in devising new schemes to avoid the existing legislation.[228]

In more recent years the harmful effects of tax haven jurisdictions have been more openly discussed. In particular, the OECD has taken a lead against what it terms 'harmful tax practices'.[229] A harmful preferential tax regime will be characterized by a combination of a low or zero effective tax rate and one or more other factors. These include, as key indicators: 'ring fencing' of regimes whereby a country protects its own economy from the regime;[230] lack of transparency including, among other matters, favourable application of laws and regulations, negotiable tax provisions, and a failure to make widely available administrative practices; and the lack of effective exchange of information in relation to taxpayers benefiting from the operation of a preferential tax regime. Additional factors include: an artificially narrow definition of the tax base, a failure to adhere to international transfer pricing principles, the exemption of foreign source income from residence country tax, a negotiable tax base or rate, the existence of secrecy provisions, access to a wide network of tax treaties, wide advertising of preferential tax regimes, and the encouragement of purely tax driven operations or arrangements.

The OECD advocates cooperative international action to eliminate harmful tax practices. This is motivated by the view that:

Harmful preferential tax regimes can distort trade and investment patterns, and are a threat both to domestic tax systems and to the overall structure of international taxation. These regimes undermine the fairness of the tax systems, cause undesired shifts of part of the tax burden from income to consumption, shift part of the tax burden from capital to labour and thereby may have a negative impact on employment. Since it is generally considered that it is difficult for individual countries to combat effectively the spread of harmful preferential

---

[225] Section 956 IRC.   [226] McDaniel, Ault, and Repetti above n 13 at 114.

[227] See OECD 1987 above n 205 paras 99–102 at 42–43.

[228] See further ibid paras 105–111 at 43–45.

[229] See OECD 1998 above n 204 at paras 57–79 on which this account is based.

[230] According to the OECD: 'Ring-fencing may take a number of forms, including: – a regime may explicitly or implicitly exclude resident taxpayers from taking advantage of its benefits; – enterprises which benefit from the regime may be explicitly or implicitly prohibited from operating in the domestic market.' ibid para 61 Box II.

tax regimes, a co-ordinated approach, including a dialogue with non-member countries, is required to achieve the level playing field which is so essential to the continued expansion of global economic growth. International cooperation must be intensified to avoid an aggressive competitive bidding by countries for geographically mobile activities.[231]

To this end OECD members are to observe the following three guidelines when considering their tax policies: first, to refrain from adopting new legislative or administrative measures, or extending the scope of, or strengthening existing measures, that constitute harmful tax practices; secondly, to review and identify existing measures that constitute harmful tax practices; thirdly, to remove, before the end of five years starting from the date on which the guidelines are approved by the OECD Council, the harmful features of their preferential tax regimes. These will be identified in a list of measures that constitute harmful tax practices drawn up in accordance with the second guideline. These lists are to be reported to the OECD Forum on Harmful Tax Practices, set up to develop international cooperation in this area, within two years from the date on which the guidelines are approved by the OECD Council. The lists will be reviewed annually to delete those regimes that no longer constitute harmful preferential tax regimes.[232] In 2000, the Committee identified 47 preferential tax regimes in nine overall categories as potentially harmful.[233] At the time of writing,[234] 33 jurisdictions made commitments to transparency and effective exchange of information and are considered cooperative jurisdictions by the OECD's Committee on Fiscal Affairs. A small number of jurisdictions identified as tax havens in June 2000 have not yet made commitments. A number of jurisdictions, which have not yet made commitments to transparency and effective exchange of information, have been identified by the OECD's Committee on Fiscal Affairs as uncooperative tax havens.[235]

---

[231] ibid at 56 Box III. See also Reuvan S Avi-Yonah 'Globalization, Tax Competition and the Fiscal Crisis of the Welfare State' 113 Harv. LR 1573 (2000). Avi-Yonah argues that tax havens deprive developed and developing countries alike of taxable income forcing greater reliance on consumption taxes, which affect the poor disproportionately. In addition, welfare state programmes are deprived of funds. Thus economic efficiency and equity considerations require the placing of limits on international tax havens. For evidence of such a tax shifting effect, see John Plender 'Counting the Cost of Globalization: How Companies Keep Tax Low and Stay Within the Law' *Financial Times* 21 July 2004 at 15 and Dan Roberts 'Multinationals Find Tax Relief Abroad' *Financial Times* 2 February 2004 at 27.

[232] ibid.

[233] See OECD *The OECD's Project on Harmful Tax Practices: the 2004 Progress Report* (Paris: OECD, 2004) or <http://www.oecd.org/dataoecd/60/33/30901115.pdf> para 6. Switzerland and Luxembourg abstained on the Council approval of the 1998 Report which also applies to any follow-up work undertaken since 1998. In 2001 the US attempted to stop the OECD programme but has not continued its opposition: 'Bush to Scuttle OECD plan' *The Guardian* 10 May 2001 at 23; 'OECD to Defy Bush Over Tax Havens' *The Guardian* 12 May 2001 at 25; 'OECD May Have Deal to fight tax evasion' *Financial Times* 28 June 2001 at 9. The main effect of this dispute has been to limit the sanctions the OECD will take against uncooperative tax havens avoiding punitive action and relying on peer pressure and the conclusion of information exchange agreements between members and between members and third parties.   [234] August 2006.

[235] These are Andorra, Liberia, The Principality of Liechtenstein, The Republic of the Marshall Islands, and The Principality of Monaco. See <http://www.oecd.org/document/57/0,2340,en_2649_33745_30578809_1_1_1_1,00.html>.

Concluding Remarks

This chapter has sought to introduce some of the best known taxation problems surrounding the activities of MNEs. It has shown how the integrated operations of such firms can offer opportunities for efficient tax planning that may not be open to purely domestic firms, and how national tax authorities may seek to control any resulting tax avoidance. The international character of the income generating activities of MNEs, the national reach of individual tax administrations, increased international competition over attracting inward direct investment and the need to obtain sufficient revenue returns from MNEs has led, inevitably, to calls for the reform of the international tax system.[236] In addition the rise of e-commerce has challenged many of the basic assumptions of the current international tax system. In particular, it calls for a reconsideration of whether the source or residence principle should apply to such commerce and whether applying the arm's length principle to transfer prices used in such transactions between controlled entities is workable.[237] The need for greater international coordination of tax policies is clear. For the present, however, the primary locus for regulation remains with national tax authorities applying systems of taxation designed to further national policy goals.

---

[236] See Bird and Muten above n 198; Easson 'A New International Tax Order – Responding to the Challenge' BIFD (October 1991) 465.

[237] See further OECD *Taxation and Electronic Commerce* (Paris: OECD, 2001); OECD *Are the Current Treaty Rules for Taxing Business Profits Appropriate for E-Commerce: Final Report* (Paris: OECD, Technical Advisory Group on Monitoring the Application of Existing Treaty Norms for Taxing Business Profits, 19 December 2005); Kelley L Mayer 'Reform of United States Rules Governing Electronic Commerce and Transfer Pricing' 21 Thomas Jefferson L. Rev. 283 (1999). Some experts advocate a global profit split approach to e-commerce transfer pricing issues: see Jinyan Li above n 198; Reuven S Avi-Yonah *International Taxation of Electronic Commerce* 52 Tax L. Rev. 507 (1997) and see generally Richard L Reinhold 'Some Things that Multilateral Tax Treaties Might Usefully Do' Spring, 57 Tax Law 661 (2004). Reinhold advocates a multilateral convention on e-commerce taxation.

8

Group Liability and Directors' Duties

This chapter develops the themes of corporate control and liability first mentioned in chapter 2. It will examine in more detail the implications for existing principles of company law of integrated group enterprises and transnational contractual network enterprises (TNNs). This will be done by reference to the distinct issues that affect the various classes of claimants who may wish to invoke the liability of the enterprise or, indeed, of its directors. The first class of potential claimant are the minority shareholders in the subsidiaries of the MNE. Their principal interest lies in obtaining the full financial value of their investment in the subsidiary. They are dependent on the actions of the directors of the subsidiary for the realization of their gains. The second class are the voluntary creditors who enter into commercial relations with affiliates of the MNE and who depend on the ability of the affiliate to meet its contractual liabilities to them. The third class consists of involuntary creditors who are forced by circumstances not of their choosing into a claim for compensation against the enterprise, usually as victims of corporate negligence.

The specific legal principles that have been developed in the context of each relationship will be discussed in turn. The first and second sections of the chapter will deal with the general issue of the liability of the parent for the actions of its subsidiaries both in an equity based group and in a transnational network enterprise based on contract. The principles considered in this section will be of relevance to the claims of both voluntary and involuntary creditors. The approach is to describe the limits of existing law and then to consider various suggestions for reform that have been made in the context of MNE operations.

The third and fourth sections of the chapter go on to deal, respectively, with the more specialized issues surrounding the protection of minority shareholders in subsidiaries and the compensation of creditors on the insolvency of the affiliate with which they are dealing. These matters raise questions that go beyond the general principles of group liability discussed in the first section and, moreover, introduce issues as to the personal liability of directors. It is important not to limit the discussion to the liability of the corporation alone, but also to consider that of its senior officials, as in many cases such personal liability may ensure more effective compliance with good business practice. The criminal liability of MNEs is not considered, although recent developments in the law of corporate manslaughter include the possibility of parent company liability.[1]

(1) The Regulation of MNE Group Liability Under Existing Legal Principles

Group liability is a complex issue involving numerous permutations of legal organization that embody the capacity of one undertaking to control the actions of another, or to act jointly and severally with another. In particular, a basic distinction needs to be made between structures of control based on the ownership of equity by one undertaking in another and those based on contractual relations. While, at first sight, the former would appear to offer greater capacity to control, the latter may be equally effective in practice, especially where the actual economic power of one contracting party is superior to that of the other. Given the variety of legal forms that MNEs may adopt (as noted in chapter 2) a complete analysis of group liability requires both major legal methods of business association to be examined.

(a) Equity Based MNE Groups

This section will examine first the question of the direct liability of the parent company for the acts of its affiliates. In practice this is the most common means of establishing liability, as in many cases the parent will be directly involved in the acts leading to the legal claim, whether as a contracting party or as a joint tortfeasor. However, in cases where the direct involvement of the parent in the acts leading to liability cannot be established, it may still be possible to 'lift the corporate veil' and attach liability to the parent on an indirect basis. This matter is discussed in the second sub-section.

---

[1] See generally Celia Wells *Corporations and Criminal Responsibility* (Oxford: Oxford University Press, 2nd edn, 2001) and Celia Wells 'The Reform of Criminal Liability' in John de Lacy (ed) *The Reform of United Kingdom Company Law* (London: Cavendish Publishing, 2002) 291. On the criminal liability of corporate groups, see James Gobert and Maurice Punch *Rethinking Corporate Crime* (London: LexisNexis, Butterworths, 2003) ch 5; James Gobert 'Corporate Killings at Home and Abroad – Reflections on the Government's Proposals' 118 LQR 72 (2002). See also the Corporate Manslaughter Bill (Bill 53/4 March 2005) in Home Office *Corporate Manslaughter: The Government's Draft Bill for Reform* (CM 6497 March 2005) available at <http://www.parliament.uk/documents/upload/DraftBillCorporateMan.pdf>. The Home Office document makes clear at para 37: 'Under the Bill, a parent company (as well as any subsidiary) would be liable to prosecution where it owed a duty of care to the victim in respect of one of the activities covered by the offence and a gross management failure by its senior managers caused death.' The current version of the bill is the Corporate Manslaughter and Corporate Homicide Bill (Bill 220, 20 July 2006).

(i) Direct Liability of the Parent Company

In litigation involving issues of MNE liability, once the question of jurisdiction has been answered in favour of impleading the foreign parent company,[2] the extent of its responsibility for the acts of its local subsidiary or branch will depend on the applicable principles of law concerning corporate group liability.[3] In many cases concepts of contractual or tortious liability will suffice to establish the liability of the parent company, without the need to resort to liability based on control. Liability based primarily on control becomes significant in those cases where the direct liability of the parent is doubtful in the light of established legal rules, but where, for reasons of policy, it may be desirable for the parent to be answerable for losses suffered by the claimant.

In Anglo-American jurisprudence, the direct liability of the parent company can arise in both contract and tort. First, if the foreign parent company is a party to a contract entered into between its subsidiary and a third party, it can be held liable on that contract. This depends on whether the subsidiary has acted as the agent of the parent for the purposes of the contract, which can involve difficult problems of proof. In the absence of an express provision authorizing the subsidiary to act as the agent of the parent and/or establishing the parent as a party to the contract, the issue will turn on the extent to which the parent in fact controlled the acts of the subsidiary in relation to the transaction in question. Under English law, although the parent may exercise a high degree of general managerial control over the subsidiary, this may not be enough to show that, for the purposes of the transaction in issue, the subsidiary acted as the agent of the parent.[4] On the other hand, certain American cases in the New York jurisdiction suggest that an inference of 'agency' can arise simply out of the fact of common ownership between the parent and subsidiary, or between affiliates. This inference can be negated in the absence of equity links, despite the existence of contractual relations between two firms where one firm closely controls the activities of the other, as in the case of a franchising agreement.[5] However, the liability of

---

[2] On which see ch 4 above.

[3] See further Hofstetter 'Parent Responsibility for Subsidiary Corporations: Evaluating European Trends' 39 ICLQ 576 (1990); 'Multinational Enterprise Parent Liability: Efficient Legal Regimes in a World Market Environment' 15 NCJ Int'l & Com.Reg. 299 (1990); Philip Blumberg *The Multinational Challenge to Corporation Law: The Search for a New Corporate Personality* (Oxford: Oxford University Press, 1993). Professor Blumberg's views are conveniently summarized in 'The Corporate Entity in an Era of Multinational Corporations' 15 Del.J.Corp.L. 285 (1990). For an extensive survey of corporate group law see further Philip I Blumberg, Kurt A Strasser, Nicholas L Georgakopoulos, and Eric J Gouvin *Blumberg on Corporate Groups* (New York: Aspen Publishers, 2nd edn, 2005, 5 vols).

[4] See *Adams v Cape Industries plc* [1990] Ch 433, [1991] 1 All ER 929 (Scott J and CA). See further Fawcett 'Jurisdiction and Subsidiaries' [1985] JBL 16 at 20; Paul L Davies *Gower and Davies' Principles of Modern Company Law* (London: Thomson, Sweet & Maxwell, 7th edn, 2003) 187.

[5] See *Frummer v Hilton Hotels International* 19 NY 2d 533, 227 NE 2d 851, 281 NYS 2d 41 *cert.denied* 389 US 923 (1967); *Delagi v Volkswagenwerk AG* 29 NY 2d 426, 278 NE 2d 895, 328 NYS 2d 653 (1972). For analysis, see *Blumberg on Corporate Groups* above n 3 vol 1 at s 29–03[B] and see further ibid s 16.03 and vol 2 chs 66–70.

controlling and/or collaborating enterprises in TNNs was not considered relevant in these cases. Consequently, their utility as precedents in such situations may be open to doubt. This matter will be considered further in sub-section (b) below.

A further question has arisen as to the liability of the parent company as a guarantor of the subsidiary's obligations under a contract. In this connection, the English courts have held that the use of equivocal language renders the alleged guarantee too uncertain to be enforceable. There must be a clear assumption of the duties of a guarantor by the parent company.[6] A mere statement of intent will not do.[7] Nor will a guarantee made in a document that is 'subject to contract'.[8] In the absence of an express agreement to guarantee the liability of the subsidiary, the question arises whether the parent company remains liable if it has reserved the power to authorize the subsidiary to enter into the transaction in question. Here the doctrine of corporate separation will apply. A distinction must be drawn between actions undertaken on behalf of the parent in a relationship of principal and agent, where the parent will be a direct party to the contract in question, and those undertaken as part of the business of the subsidiary, albeit with the authorization of the parent. Accordingly, no inference of agency can be drawn in the latter case so as to make the parent liable for the fulfilment of the obligations undertaken by its subsidiary.[9]

Secondly, in tort, the parent company can be liable if it is shown that, by its acts or omissions, it was a joint tortfeasor with its subsidiary.[10] The decision of the US District Court in the *Amoco Cadiz* illustrates such an approach.[11] The court was faced inter alia with claims of negligence from French plaintiffs against Amoco Transport Co (Transport), Amoco International Oil Co (AIOC), and their parent, Standard Oil Co (Indiana) (now Amoco Corporation), arising out of the oil spillage caused by the grounding of their tanker, Amoco Cadiz, off the coast of Northern France in 1978. Judge Frank McGarr found, on the facts, that the proximate cause of the grounding and spillage was the failure of the ship's steering mechanism. That failure was attributable to negligence in the design, maintenance,

---

[6] See *Amalgamated Investment & Property Co v Texas Commercial Bank* [1982] QB 84 (CA) where a bank was estopped from denying that it had agreed to guarantee loans made by its wholly owned subsidiary which was set up specifically to effect the loans in question. The use of the word 'guarantee' on the document will not be conclusive: *Gold Coast Ltd v Caja de Ahorros del Mediterraneo* [2001] EWCA Civ 1806, [2005] 1 All ER (Comm) 142. The substantive effect of the document is conclusive: *Marubeni Hong Kong & South China Limited v Mongolian Government* [2005] EWCA Civ 395, [2005] 1 All ER (Comm) 289.

[7] See, in this connection, the cases on letters of comfort: *Re Augustus Barnett* [1986] BCLC 170 noted Prentice 103 LQR 11 (1987); *Kleinwort Benson v Malaysian Mining Corporation* [1988] 1 All ER 714 QBD *reversed* [1989] 1 All ER 785 (CA), leave to appeal refused HL 10 May 1989 [1989] 2 All ER xviii.   [8] See *Carlton Communications v Football League* [2002] EWHC 1650 (Comm).

[9] ibid at paras 67–72.

[10] For a detailed discussion of English law see Myfanwy Badge *Transboundary Accountability for Transnational Corporations: Using Private Civil Claims* (London: Chatham House Working Paper, March 2006) available at <http://www.chathamhouse.org.uk/pdf/research/il/ILP_TNC.pdf>. On US law see *Blumberg on Corporate Groups* above n 3 vol 2 chs 57–65.   [11] [1984] 2 Lloyd's Rep 304.

and repair of the system, and to negligent crew training, which left the latter unprepared to avoid and remedy such a failure.

Judge McGarr then undertook a detailed analysis of the organization and functioning of Standard's shipping operations.[12] He concluded that both the subsidiaries and the parent company were liable.[13] The reasons for holding the parent corporation liable were as follows:

43. As an integrated multinational corporation which is engaged through a system of subsidiaries in the exploitation, production, refining, transportation and sale of petroleum products throughout the world, Standard is responsible for the tortious acts of its wholly owned subsidiaries and instrumentalities AIOC and Transport.

44. Standard exercised such control over its subsidiaries AIOC and Transport that those entities would be considered to be mere instrumentalities of Standard. Furthermore, Standard itself was initially involved in and controlled the design construction operation and management of Amoco Cadiz and treated that vessel as if it were its own.

45. Standard therefore is liable for its own negligence and the negligence of AIOC and Transport with respect to the design, operation, maintenance, repair and crew training of Amoco Cadiz.

46. Standard therefore is liable to the French claimants for damages resulting from the grounding of Amoco Cadiz.[14]

Thus, the parent was liable on two grounds: by its own active involvement in the alleged negligence, and through its close control over the operating subsidiaries.[15] Unfortunately, no authorities were cited or discussed in the case. The finding of direct negligence on the part of the parent is consistent with general Anglo-American doctrines of liability involving joint tortfeasors. The finding of liability against the parent on the basis of integrated management suggests that the simple fact of managerial control is enough to establish a case against the parent on the basis that this allows the parent to become directly involved in the acts or omissions leading to the breach of a duty of care.

For example, in the New South Wales case of *CSR v Wren* the plaintiff successfully sued the parent company of the subsidiary in which he was employed on the ground that its negligence contributed to his contraction of mesothelioma caused by exposure to asbestos.[16] In particular, the Court of Appeal for New South Wales held that the parent was sufficiently proximate to the harm because it had taken control of the management of the subsidiary, in that all of the managers of the subsidiary were employees of the parent. Thus as they had directed the working conditions at the subsidiary the parent could be held directly responsible for any resulting negligence. In a similar vein, in the US District Court for the Northern District of California, Chevron Texaco was found to be responsible as principal

---

[12] ibid at 308–11; 319–28.

[13] For the liability of Amoco International, see ibid at 328–36; for the liability of Amoco Transport, see ibid at 337–38.   [14] ibid at 338.

[15] For the facts that were held to show Standard's control over its subsidiaries, see ibid 332–34.

[16] *CSR v Wren* (1997) 44 NSWLR 463 (CA NSW).

for the acts of its Nigerian subsidiary, Chevron Nigeria Limited.[17] This case was brought by Nigerian plaintiffs under the US Alien Torts Claims Act (ATCA).[18] They alleged that the subsidiary had acted in concert with the Nigerian military authorities to suppress protests against the operations of the subsidiary, leading to deaths and injuries amounting to violations of international human rights norms. Judge Illston held that the parent was actively involved in the conduct of its subsidiary's security policy, had engaged in a very high level of communication with the subsidiary at the time of the protests, and had a large number of parent company offices employed at the subsidiary. This amounted to more than a usual degree of direction and control and was evidence of an agency relationship between the parent and subsidiary.

However, the preponderance of authority is in the other direction, with few cases accepting that the parent will be liable even where there is a high degree of integrated management. In Australia *CSR v Wren* has not been uniformly followed. Thus in *James Hardie v Hall* the Australian Court of Appeal rejected a claim, for asbestos related illness, brought by the New Zealand based employees of the local subsidiary of the Australian parent company.[19] Although the judge at first instance had held that the New Zealand subsidiary and the Australian parent company did owe a joint duty of care to the plaintiffs, on the basis of the actual influence exercised by the Australian parent over the subsidiary, this was reversed on appeal. The Supreme Court of New South Wales held that, despite the evidence of some control and influence over the subsidiary, this was insufficient to justify lifting the corporate veil so as to create a direct duty of care on the part of the parent towards the employees of the New Zealand subsidiary.[20] In a similar vein, there are several cases from various US state jurisdictions, dating from before the *Amoco Cadiz*, suggesting that the existence of the parent/subsidiary relationship, and the integrated nature of the corporate group, is insufficient to ground parent company liability of the tortious acts of its subsidiary.[21]

More recently, in *United States v Bestfoods*, the US Supreme Court reiterated that the active participation in, and control over, the operations of a subsidiary could not, without more, render a parent liable for the acts of its subsidiary.[22]

---

[17] *Larry Bowoto v Chevron Texaco Corp* 2004 US Dist LEXIS 4603 (22 March 2004, US Dist Ct ND Cal). See further Sarah Joseph *Corporations and Transnational Human Rights Litigation* (Oxford: Hart Publishing, 2004) ch 7.   [18] See further ch13 at 527–31.

[19] (1998) 43 NSWLR 554 (SC NSW). For a discussion of the background, the official inquiry and the eventual settlement of the James Hardie asbestos claims, see John Kluver 'Entity vs Enterprise Liability: Issues for Australia' 37 Connecticut LR 765 (2005).   [20] ibid at 584.

[21] See *Moffat v Goodyear Tyre & Rubber Co* 652 SW 2d 609 (Texas CA 1983); *Liberty Financial Management Corp v Beneficial Data Processing* Corp 670 SW 2d 40 (Missouri CA 1984); *Brock v Alaska International Industries Inc* 645 P 2d l88 (Alaska Sup Ct 1982); *Grywczynski v Shasta Beverages Inc* 606 F Supp 61 (California 1984). These cases are discussed more fully in Peter T Muchlinski 'Lifting the Corporate Veil on the Western Multinational Corporate Group' in MA Jakubowski (ed) *Anglo-Polish Legal Essays Volume I* (Warsaw: University of Warsaw Faculty of Law and Administration 1986) see from 159 especially 183–84.

[22] 524 US 51, 118 S Ct 1876, 141 L Ed 2d 43, 1998 US LEXIS 3733. Compare the English court's analysis of whether a parent company is a 'proprietor' of a 'food business' operated by a subsidiary for

Under US environmental protection laws, an operator of a polluting facility could be held liable for the costs of cleaning up hazardous wastes at that facility.[23] Such a facility was owned and operated by a subsidiary of the parent. At first instance it was held that the parent was an operator of the facility on the ground that it had selected the subsidiary's board of directors and had populated the executive ranks of the subsidiary with officials of the parent, and that one such executive had been active in formulating the subsidiary's environmental compliance policy.[24] The Court of Appeal reversed in part saying that the parent could be liable under a lifting of the corporate veil analysis which had not been made out on the facts.[25] According to the Supreme Court the general principles that a parent is not liable for the acts of its subsidiaries, and that the corporate veil should only be pierced when the corporate form was being abused for wrongful purposes, should not be rejected. In any case a parent that actively participated in, and exercised control over, the operations of the facility could be held directly liable under the applicable law and so it was not necessary to approach the matter in the manner that the lower courts had done.

In the above cases, the imposition of liability on the parent can be defended on the ground that, where decision-making is so centralized, that major policies could not have been formulated or put into operation without the direct involvement of the parent company, the parent ought to be answerable. In these circumstances the parent is likely to be aware, or ought to be aware, of the risk to potential claimants of such group actions, and to be sufficiently proximate to hold a duty of care towards them. On the other hand, the inconsistent case law does not offer much guidance as to the circumstances in which the court will conclude that the parent company is liable on the basis of integrated management. The business manager is left uncertain as to the legal significance of separate incorporation in a group, making it harder for him or her to be able to plan the allocation of risk among the units of the enterprise. It is in order to ensure certainty that the majority of cases have held the parent not to be liable, even where considerable control exists over the operations of the subsidiary. This issue will be considered further below in relation to the effect of the 'enterprise entity' doctrine.

(ii) Lifting the Corporate Veil

In relation to the liability of foreign parent companies, the Anglo-American doctrine of 'lifting the corporate veil' offers a means of justifying group liability in circumstances where the subsidiary has insufficient assets to meet the claims against

---

the purposes of food safety legislation in *Greene King plc v Harlow DC* [2004] 2 All ER 102 (QBD). On the facts the parent was held to be a 'proprietor' as it had taken an active part in the management of its subsidiary's food business.

[23] Comprehensive Environmental Response, Compensation and Liability Act 1980 (CERCLA) 42 USCS 9607 (a) (2) s 107(a)(2).   [24] 777 F Supp 549.

[25] 113 F 3d 572.

it, but where the case for compensation of the claimants is hard to resist on policy grounds.[26] It was in this sense that the Indian courts applied the doctrine in the *Bhopal* case, during the course of hearings on interim measures.[27] Of particular importance is the judgment of Seth J, given in the High Court of Jabalpur, on appeal from the order of the Bhopal District Court.[28]

Judge Seth based his decision on the rule, contained in the English Rules of the Supreme Court,[29] that an interim payment could be made where, if the action proceeded to trial, the plaintiff would obtain judgment for substantial damages against the respondent.[30] The question was, therefore, whether the Union of India could get an award of substantial damages against Union Carbide Corporation (UCC) under the applicable principles of Indian tort law. This matter turned on the effect of the Indian Supreme Court's decision in *Mehta v Union of India*,[31] which concerned a leak of oleum gas from a caustic chlorine plant resulting in some 340 injuries and, possibly, one fatality. In the course of its judgment, the Supreme Court laid down a new principle of absolute liability for enterprises engaged in a hazardous or inherently dangerous industry.[32] The order of the Bhopal District Court was founded upon this new principle. The question for Seth J was whether the new doctrine indeed represented Indian law, and whether it could justify the imposition of liability against UCC.

Having held that the doctrine elaborated in *Mehta* provided the substantive law by which the final decision on the merits would be made, Seth J stated that only two questions remained to be answered before an interim payment could be ordered: first, whether it was permissible to 'lift the corporate veil' between UCC

[26] Civil law systems have achieved a similar objective through concepts of fraudulent corporate simulation, abuse of corporate personality, actio Pauliana (giving creditors powers over debtors who act in a manner prejudicial to the creditors' rights of execution) and "*abus de droit*". See Dobson 'Lifting the Veil' in Four Countries: The Law of Argentina, England, France and the United States' 35 ICLQ 839 (1986). For a general discussion see *Blumberg on Corporate Groups* above n 3 vol I Part II 'Veil Piercing Theory' and Kurt A Strasser 'Piercing the Veil in Corporate Groups' 37 Conn. LR 637 (2005).

[27] *Union of India v Union Carbide Corporation* (Gas Claim Case No 113 of 1986) Order 17 December 1987, Deo J. Upheld in part: *Union of India v Union Carbide Corporation* Civil Revision No 26 of 1988 4 April l988, Seth J (referred to hereafter as Civil Revision 4 April l988).

[28] The District Court had ordered Union Carbide to pay 3,500 million Rupees ($270m) by way of interim relief. That order was upheld by the High Court though the sum awarded was reduced to 250 crores Rupees ($190m).   [29] Order 29 rule 11.

[30] Civil Revision 4 April 1988 paras 13.01.01–13.01.07.   [31] AIR 1987 SC 965, 1086.

[32] ibid paras 31–33 at 1098–1100. The Supreme Court formulated the applicable principle as follows: 'An enterprise which is engaged in a hazardous or inherently dangerous industry which poses a potential threat to the health and safety of the persons working in the factory and residing in the surrounding areas owes an absolute and non-delegable duty to the community to ensure that no harm results to anyone on account of the hazardous or inherently dangerous nature of the activity which it has undertaken. The enterprise must be held to be under an obligation to provide that the hazardous or inherently dangerous activity in which it is engaged must be conducted with the highest standards of safety and if any harm results on account of such activity, the enterprise must be absolutely liable to compensate for such harm and it should be no answer to the enterprise to say that it had taken all reasonable care and that the harm occurred without any negligence on its part' para 31 at 1099.

and its Indian subsidiary so as to hold the former liable for the tort and, secondly, whether a prima facie case could be made out showing that UCC had real control over the Bhopal plant for purposes of liability. Seth J found no difficulty in answering both questions in the affirmative. Not only was this a proper case for lifting the 'corporate veil' in accordance with Indian and English case law,[33] but also UCC did, in fact, exercise real control over the enterprise which was engaged in carrying on the hazardous activities at the Bhopal plant, on the basis that UCC owned the majority of the equity (50.9 per cent) in the Indian subsidiary, controlled the composition of the board of directors of the Indian company and also had full control over its management. A perusal of the American corporation's 'corporate policy' document showed that it was a multinational corporation with the avowed purpose of managing and running industries like its own in other countries of the world through local subsidiaries, if necessary, over which it had full and effective control.

It is noteworthy that Seth J felt it necessary to 'lift the corporate veil' in order to decide whether UCC, as the parent company, was the 'enterprise' that 'carried on' the dangerous activity for purposes of liability under the terms of the *Mehta* doctrine.[34] It is unclear from the judgment of the Indian Supreme Court in *Mehta* whether the concept of 'enterprise' includes the 'economic entity' of the group, and hence involves the liability of the parent, where the dangerous activity is conducted by a subsidiary. Judge Seth's approach suggests that the parent may not be automatically liable, as its liability depends on the extent of control exercised by the parent over the subsidiary. This involves difficult, and often disputable, questions of fact. The disagreement between the US and Indian courts on the question whether UCC actually controlled its Indian subsidiary testifies to this.[35]

---

[33] The judge cited in support the Indian cases *Tata Engineering and Locomotive Co Ltd v State of Bihar* AIR 1965 SC 40, and *Life Insurance Corporation of India v Escorts Ltd* AIR 1986 SC 1370, and the English case *DHN Food Distributors Ltd v Tower Hamlets London Borough Council* [1976] 1 WLR 852 (CA). It should be noted that the concept of 'economic entity' used in the DHN case has not been widely followed in English law: see *Woolfson v Strathclyde Regional Council* (1978) 38 P & CR 521; *National Dock Labour Board v Pinn & Wheeler Ltd* [1989] BCLC 647. For a full discussion, see Rixon 'Lifting the Veil Between Holding and Subsidiary Companies' 102 LQR 415 (1986). For a contrasting view, see Clive Schmitthoff 'Salomon in the Shadow' [1976] JBL 305. See also Gower and Davies above n 4 at 184–87 discussing *Adams v Cape Industries* (above n 4) on this point. This case endorsed a narrow approach to veil lifting, permitting the separation between parent and subsidiary to prevail save in the most serious cases of abuse of the corporate form. This approach was upheld in *Re Polly Peck International plc (in administration)* [1996] 2 All ER 433 (ChD), *Ringway Roadmarking v Adbruf* [1998] 2 BCLC 625 and *Yukong Line Ltd v Rendsberg Investments* [1998] 2 BCLC 485. See further Janet Dine *The Governance of Corporate Groups* (Cambridge: Cambridge University Press, 2000) at 43–50.

[34] See n 31 above.

[35] See, for an analysis of the American court's reasoning on this question, in the context of argument over the appropriate forum, *In Re Union Carbide Gas Plant Disaster at Bhopal India* Opinion and Order 12 May 1986: 634 F Supp 842 (SDNY 1986), 25 ILM 771 (1986); *aff'd as modified* 809 F 2d 195 (USCA 2d Cir), 26 ILM 1008 (1987); *cert.den.* 108 S Ct 199 (1987). For analysis, see Peter T Muchlinski 'The Bhopal Case: Controlling Ultrahazardous Industrial Activities Undertaken by Foreign Investors' 50 MLR 545 at 556–58 (1987).

Furthermore, Judge Seth's analysis of UCC's control over the Indian subsidiary can be criticized on the ground that he confuses the overall strategic control of a multinational group by its parent company with the day-to-day running of its subsidiaries. In practice the two are quite distinct. This illustrates the practical difficulties of relating the legal justification for lifting the 'corporate veil' to the evidence of relevant managerial control.

(b) Liability of Transnational Network Enterprises

The major problems associated with establishing liability in TNNs rest with their unique legal character as enterprises consisting of entities that are linked by contract rather than equity, but which display systems of managerial control and productive cooperation not dissimilar to those found in equity based corporate groups. The responsibility of the controlling entity for the acts of the controlled entity may be avoided by reference to the contract between them, which may include risk-shifting clauses in the form of exemptions of liability for the controlling entity. The question arises whether the 'contractual veil' between the associated contracting parties should be lifted, so that the controlling party could be made liable along with the controlled party, for acts causing loss to third parties in which both contracting parties have participated by reason of the economic and business relationship underlying the contract between them.[36]

According to Teubner, the correct legal response is the simultaneous assignment of responsibility for the act giving rise to the claim upon 'the network, the centre, and the individual unit'.[37] The governing principle of liability should be that 'where the internal division of labour involves all the members of the system in performance of the contract, then all such members and not only those who happen to have contractual relations with third parties, should come within the ambit of the heightened duties of care'.[38] This represents a desirable principle of justice. It is the 'network' counterpart of 'lifting the corporate veil' in equity based groups. As with that doctrine, the crucial question is to establish the extent to which entities other than the one directly dealing with the claimant are involved in the impugned acts. Again detailed analysis of the economic and business reality of the enterprise is required. Again disputes over facts are likely. The contractual

---

[36] See further G Teubner 'The Many-Headed Hydra: Networks as Higher-Order Collective Actors' in J McCahery, S Picciotto, and C Scott (eds) *Corporate Control and Accountability* (Oxford: Clarendon Press, 1993) 41 (referred to hereafter as 'Many-Headed Hydra'); 'Beyond Contract and Organisation? The External Liability of Franchising Systems in German Law' in C Joerges (ed) *Franchising and the Law: Theoretical and Comparative Approaches in Europe and the United States* (Baden-Baden: Nomos, 1992) 105 (referred to hereafter as 'Franchising'); 'Unitas Multiplex: Corporate Governance in Group Enterprises' in D Sugarman and G Teubner (eds) *Regulating Corporate Groups in Europe* (Baden-Baden. Nomos, 1990) 67 (referred to hereafter as 'Unitas Multiplex').

[37] See 'The Many-Headed Hydra' ibid at 59.   [38] 'Franchising' above n 36.

allocation of risk in the enterprise may be undermined were a court minded to 'lift the contractual veil', resulting in uncertainty. Thus such a result is unlikely.[39]

(2) New Approaches to MNE Group Liability

From the above it is clear that the establishment of parent company liability for acts of its affiliates is not at all easy, given the logic of corporate separation that prevails as a cornerstone of company law. On the other hand, as noted in chapter 2, the basic organizational models used by MNEs show a significant degree of economic and commercial integration across borders. That raises the question whether the economic entity of the group as a whole should act as a source of funds for the compensation of voluntary and, especially, involuntary creditors, and whether there should be such a thing as 'multinational enterprise liability' based on the integrated nature of the transnational system of economic activities carried on by the MNE. [40] This issue will be considered, first, with a review of 'enterprise entity' theory and its limits and, secondly, through a consideration of how new legal approaches to the issue of group liability could develop.

(a) The 'Enterprise Entity' Theory and its Limitations

'Enterprise entity' doctrine differs from existing concepts of group liability in that it replaces an approach based on exceptions to the otherwise inviolable corporate separation between parent and subsidiary (whether through the lifting of the 'corporate veil' or through specialized group liability laws) with one that deduces parent company liability from the fact of economic integration between itself and the subsidiary. This recognizes the corporate group as a distinct form of business association, thereby opening the way for the evolution of a specialized legal regime going beyond the paradigm of the single unit limited liability joint stock company.

In this regard, the *Mehta* doctrine may be seen as an attempt by the Indian legal system to break out of the limitations of fault based liability in cases involving ultrahazardous industrial activities carried on by national or multinational

---

[39] See, for example, *Sinaltrainal v Coca Cola* 256 F Supp 2d 1345 (SD Fla 2003) where the plaintiffs sought to establish the responsibility of Coca Cola US and Coca Cola Colombia under ATCA for the actions of a local bottling company that was under contract with those companies. It was alleged that the owners of the local company had murdered a trade union leader who had been trying to unionize their plant and that all three companies were responsible. The district court dismissed the claim saying that the contract between the Coca Cola companies and the bottler was a typical franchise agreement which contained no duty upon the those companies to monitor, enforce, or control labour practices at the bottling company.

[40] See further Peter T Muchlinski 'Holding Multinationals to Account: Recent Developments in English Litigation and the Company Law Review' 23 Company Lawyer 168 (2002); Halina Ward 'Governing Multinationals: The Role of Foreign Direct Liability' Royal Institute of International Affairs Briefing Paper New Series No 18, February 2001.

corporate groups. However, the doctrine, as applied by Seth J, does not appear to have gone beyond the logic of corporate separation between the parent and subsidiary for the purposes of establishing liability. Judge Seth's reasoning is in line with the general state of national laws in the area of parent company responsibility. Most legal systems admit the direct liability of the parent company for the acts of its subsidiary only in special circumstances. The prevailing principle remains that of preserving the legal separation of parent and subsidiary.[41] Indeed, even the most advanced corporate group law, the German Stock Corporations Act 1965 (Aktiengesetz),[42] seeks to preserve the subsidiary as a separate enterprise in that the parent owes duties of compensation to the creditors and minority shareholders of the subsidiary in return for the power of control.[43] In this the German law remains grounded in the logic of the classical theory of the corporation.[44] It has not created a new form of business association, the 'group enterprise', as the object of rights and duties save, perhaps, in the exceptional case of the 'integrated group'. This is formed where at least 95 per cent of the shares in the subsidiary are held by the parent and a resolution for integration is approved by at least 75 per cent of the shareholders in the parent company, thereby allowing the parent to manage the subsidiary without consideration as to its legal separation, in return for the assumption of full liability by the parent for the debts and obligations of the subsidiary.[45]

Notwithstanding the dominant trend to retain corporate separation between group undertakings, there are some significant references to the idea of 'enterprise entity'. Apart from the above mentioned judgment of Judge McGarr in the *Amoco Cadiz*, there have been other instances in which the logic of the 'enterprise entity' has been adopted as a justification for the group liability of MNEs. First, as noted

[41] See OECD *The Responsibility of Parent Companies for Their Subsidiaries* (Paris: OECD, 1980) 'Summary of Comparative Findings' paras 65–70.

[42] See arts 17–18; 291–323 reproduced in English in K Hopt (ed) *The Legal and Economic Analysis of Multinational Enterprises Vol II 'Groups of Companies in European Law'* (Berlin: De Gruyter, 1982) at 265–95. For analysis, see Wiedemann 'The German Experience With the Law of Affiliated Enterprises' in ibid 21; F Wooldridge *Groups of Companies: The Law and Practice in Britain, France and Germany* (IALS 1981); Lutter 'The Liability of the Parent Company for the Debts of its Subsidiaries Under German Law' [1985] JBL 499; Sargent 'Beyond the Legal Entity Doctrine: Parent-Subsidiary Relations Under the West German Konzernrecht' 10 Can.Bus.LJ 327 (1985); Waelde 'Parent-Subsidiary Relations in the Integrated Corporate System: A Comparison of American and German Law' 9 Jo. Int.Law & Econ. 455 (1974); Hofstetter n 3 above at 579–83; Schiessel 'The Liability of Corporations and Shareholders for the Capitalization and Obligations of Subsidiaries under German Law' 7 NW J.Int'l Law & Bus. 480 (1986); Rene Reich-Graefe 'Changing Paradigms: The Liability of Corporate Groups in Germany' 37 Conn. LR 785 (2005).

[43] On which see further 329–30 and 332–33 below.

[44] See Lutter n 42, Wiedemann n 42 at 23, and Reich-Graefe n 42 at 814.

[45] German Stock Corporation Law 1965 arts 319–322. For an argument that German law has created an intermediate form of group law between the veil piercing approach and the enterprise entity approach, see Jose Engracia Atunes 'The Liability of Polycorporate Enterprises' 13 Conn. J.Int'l L 197 (1999). See further Jose Engracia Atunes *Liability of Corporate Groups: Autonomy and Control in Parent-Subsidiary Relationships in US, German and EU Law: An International and Comparative Perspective:* (The Hague: Kluwer Law International, 1994).

in chapter 4, in relation to the issue of jurisdiction, certain legal systems have asserted the right to extend their law extraterritorially on the basis of the economic unity of the MNE group.[46] Thus, in relation to non-EC firms operating through EC subsidiaries, jurisdiction has been asserted by the EC Commission in competition cases on the basis of the parent/subsidiary relationship. Secondly, in relation to substantive liability, throughout the proceedings in the *Bhopal* case, the Indian Government and the private plaintiffs argued that UCC should be liable for the acts leading to the accident, regardless of the legal separation between itself and its Indian subsidiary. Before the American courts it was argued that UCC, a 'monolithic multinational, controlled the design, construction and operation of the Bhopal plant through its global network of corporate planning, direction and control',[47] and should therefore be accountable for the acts of the subsidiary. However, it is not entirely clear from the plaintiffs' argument whether they sought to suggest that UCC's liability was strict in view of the economic unity of the enterprise, or whether the US parent was a direct wrongdoer and thus a necessary and proper defendant. Prior to the settlement of the case, the Indian Government had maintained, in its submissions to the Indian Supreme Court, that UCC was strictly liable for the accident. It is significant that the Indian Government did not see it necessary to refer to the 'lifting of the corporate veil' as an aspect of the *Mehta* doctrine. In the government's submission liability was not to be determined by way of an exception to the principle of corporate separation, but by reference to the enterprise as a whole and to the *capacity* of the parent to control the subsidiary. Clearly, the government was asserting a principle of liability based on the economic entity of the enterprise.[48]

Despite their persuasive force, these examples do not show a widespread acceptance of the logic of 'enterprise liability' for multinational corporate groups. The advantages of limited liability offered by the doctrine of corporate separation provide strong reasons for the retention of existing approaches to group liability. A radical abandonment of the traditional approach to group liability is unlikely.[49]

---

[46] See eg art 10 of the Argentinean Draft Code of Private International Law. The full text of the Code can be found in 24 ILM 269 (1985). For background see Goldschmidt (1972) II Hague Recueil 201.

[47] See the Indian Government's complaint before the US District Court, Southern District of New York *Union of India v Union Carbide Corporation* Complaint 85 CIV 2696 8 April 1985 at para 21; Plaintiff's Executive Committee *Memorandum of Law in Opposition to Union Carbide Corporation's Motion to Dismiss on Grounds of Forum Non Conveniens* 6 December 1985 at 3.

[48] See *Submissions of the Union of India in its Appeal Before the Supreme Court* paras 118–21. The author is grateful to Praveen Pavani, advocate of the Indian Supreme Court, for supplying a copy of this document.

[49] This is reinforced by the abandonment in the UK of an 'enterprise entity' approach to the lifting of the corporate veil: see cases cited in n 33 above and *Ord v Belhaven Pubs* [1998] BCC 607 at 614–615 per Hobhouse LJ and *Trustor AB v Smallbourne* [2001] 3 All ER 987 at 994–995 where Moritt VC held that the corporate veil could only be pierced where the company had been used as a device or façade to conceal the true facts and thereby to avoid the liability of the individual that controlled the company. Equally, in Germany, the extension of the 'de facto group' doctrine under the Aktiengesetz to the main type of group concern found in Germany, the GmbH, has been reversed by the German

In addition, a major practical problem underlying the evolution of an 'enterprise entity' approach rests in identifying the existence of such a business association. This requires the use of economic theories of corporate integration so as to develop a clearer concept of the type of firm in which the parent can be said to control its subsidiaries for the purposes of liability.[50] In this regard, caution needs to be exercised on how contemporary ideas on the business organization of MNEs should be used when constructing legal duties of care.[51] First, much of the more recent literature on open and flexible forms of corporate organization relates primarily to newer high technology industries such as information technology or advanced product manufacture. It does not relate to older forms of MNE organization, which might still appear before the court. Thus, when reviewing evidence of the business organization of the defendant MNE, sweeping generalizations, based on a literal reading of the academic literature, about the 'general' organization of MNEs should be avoided. At most such literature can offer models of business organization against which the defendant enterprise's actual organization may be compared. Secondly, none of the more recent literature predicts the imminent end of the hierarchical multinational corporate group, just that this form of enterprise has a specific application to specific industries.[52] Thirdly, even if it can be shown that the defendant MNE operates a devolved management system, or is part of a wider alliance of cooperating companies, this does not, of itself, deny the existence of a duty of care on the part of the MNE parent towards employees of its subsidiaries (or of cooperating firms in an alliance), or to members of the local community in the host country adversely affected by the operations of the enterprise. A direct duty of care may exist on the part of the parent (or the controlling enterprise[s] in an alliance) on the basis of general principles of tort, regardless of the precise business organization of the enterprise, where, as a matter of policy, it is thought important for the duty to exist. Equally, liability for certain ultra-hazardous activities may be strict and the need for proving the existence of a duty of care may be unnecessary.[53] Thus, the outcome of any claim based on the 'enterprise entity' theory depends on an interpretation of evidence that a lawyer may not be best educated to appreciate. Uncertainty is bound to result. In this respect the 'enterprise entity' doctrine of corporate liability does not offer a significant

---

Federal Supreme Court in 2001 and replaced by an approach akin to veil piercing in Anglo-American law: see *Bremer Vulcan* BGH (Sept 17 2001–II ZR 178/99) BGHZ 149 discussed by Reich-Graefe above n 42 and see Peer Zumbansen 'Liability Within Corporate Groups (*Bremer Vulcan*) Federal Court of Justice Attempts the Overhaul' 3 German Law Journal (No 1–1 January 2002) available at <http://www.gernamlawjournal.com/print.php?id=124>.

[50] The studies of corporate integration made by the US courts in the 'unitary tax' cases illustrate what may be required: see the cases referred to in ch 7 at nn 172–80.

[51] See Peter T Muchlinski above n 40 at 171 on which this paragraph is based.

[52] See Julian Birkinshaw *Entrepreneurship in the Global Firm* (London: Sage Publications, 2000) especially chs 1 and 8; and see ch 2 at 47–50.

[53] As in the Indian doctrine of absolute enterprise liability for ultra-hazardous activities discussed above.

practical advance over the requirements of 'lifting the corporate veil', although it does represent a conceptual shift away from the legal formalism of the doctrine of corporate personality as applied to corporate groups.

Finally, in the case of TNNs, the 'enterprise entity' doctrine has been criticized by Teubner as an inadequate response to the problems of establishing group liability. In particular, he feels that the approach is too 'hierarchical', in that it concentrates on locating responsibility with the parent, and thereby fails to appreciate the need for more decentralized systems of attributing liability in a more loosely formed 'network' enterprise.[54] As stated above, it is not clear whether Teubner's alternative will be any easier to apply in practice than the existing exceptions to the doctrines of corporate separation and contractual risk shifting. However, it does have the merit of offering more alternative combinations of liability across the enterprise than the vertical approach of 'enterprise entity' doctrine. Given that a unitary principle of group liability may not always be necessary for the achievement of regulatory goals,[55] the flexibility inherent in Teubner's analysis may be of considerable practical value in the evolution of future regulatory regimes.

(b) Towards a New Law of MNE Group Liability?

The foregoing analysis has been conditioned by the existence of two competing objectives: first, the need to ensure sufficient certainty in the law to permit the efficient allocation of risk in a corporate group, whether through the creation of subsidiaries, or through the contractual allocation of rights and duties; secondly, the need to ensure that the resulting allocation of risk in the group does not end in a failure to compensate third parties for losses caused by the activities of group members. There may be at least three distinct approaches to the reconciliation of these interests, although none is by itself capable of resolving the issue in all situations.[56]

The first is to retain the limits to liability inherent in the traditional concepts of corporate personality and contractual freedom and stability, and provide ad hoc exceptions thereto, which deal with individual abuses. This has been the broad approach of existing laws. Arguably, little more may be needed.[57] On the other hand, the manifest failure of traditional legal concepts to deal adequately with cases such as *Bhopal* suggests that some changes in legal policy are required. In response to such cases the second approach is that of developing a unitary concept

---

[54] See Teubner 'Unitas Multiplex' above n 36 at 87–92.

[55] See further T Hadden 'Regulating Corporate Groups: An International Perspective' in J McCahery, S Picciotto, and C Scott (eds) *Corporate Control and Accountability* (Oxford: Clarendon Press, 1993) 343.

[56] See Tom Hadden 'Liabilities in Corporate Groups: A Framework for Effective Regulation' in Paola Balzarini, Giuseppe Carcano, and Guido Mucciarelli *I Gruppi di Societa* (Giuffre Editore, 1996) see from 1361 especially 1385.

[57] On which, see further Hofstetter 'Multinational Enterprise Parent Liability' above n 3; DD Prentice 'Some Comments on the Law Relating to Corporate Groups' in J McCahery et al (eds) above n 55 at 371–74.

of the group liability, along the lines of the 'enterprise entity' doctrine. As noted above, the principal weakness of the 'enterprise entity' doctrine is the potential uncertainty that surrounds the identification of the relevant entity on a case-by-case basis. If the law is to offer certainty as to the type of corporate group that will be regarded as a single entity for the purposes of liability, some a priori judgment to this effect should be made. This may be achieved in either one of two ways.

First, a new type of incorporation for corporate groups, which assumes group liability as one of its consequences, can be adopted. In the case of MNEs this could be provided by some form of supranational incorporation. Indeed, the original proposal for a European Company (SE) contained provisions similar to those of the above mentioned German Aktiengesetz, which would permit for the management of the company as a single economic unit.[58] This approach was abandoned in the finally adopted European Company Statute in favour of one that leaves the protection of third parties and minorities to the national laws governing public limited companies of the Member States in which the individual units of the SE operate.[59] Secondly, a presumption of control by the parent over the subsidiary has been put forward as an alternative.[60] The presumption of control gives advance notice to the parent of the risk of liability, and places the onus on the parent to rebut the presumption with conclusive proof of the independence of the subsidiary. In the case of a highly integrated company that presumption may be almost impossible to rebut. However, it may be rebutted where it can be shown that the third party has transacted with the subsidiary in the full knowledge that the parent had expressly excluded its liability. On the other hand, where the third party has reasonably relied on the parent to underwrite the subsidiary's liability, then even the strongest proof of corporate independence should not excuse the parent. Furthermore, in line with the *Mehta* doctrine, where the claimant is the victim of a major industrial accident, and the subsidiary cannot meet the resulting liabilities, the parent company should be strictly liable to make up the outstanding amount of the claim.

A number of objections may be put against this presumption. First, it practically destroys limited liability for corporate groups. In reply, it is arguable that too much is made of the need for limited liability between parent and subsidiary when they form part of an integrated economic entity.[61] As has been pointed out by Philip Blumberg, in his germinal work *The Multinational Challenge to Corporation Law*[62]

Under entity law and limited liability, each higher-tier company of the multitiered corporate group is insulated from liability for the unsatisfied debts of the lower tier companies of

---

[58] See the Commission Proposal for a Council Regulation on the Statute for a European Company: COM(89) 268 final – SYN 218 at 42. These provisions were to be found in arts 223–240 of the 1975 Draft Statute.

[59] See Regulation 2157/2001 on the European Company Statute OJ [2001] L294/1 arts 2 and 3.

[60] See Clive Schmitthoff 'The Wholly Owned and Controlled Subsidiary' [1978] JBL 218.

[61] See Peter T Muchlinski above n 40 at 172–73 on which this passage is based.

[62] Above n 3.

which it is a shareholder. In the multitiered group, there are, thus, as many layers of limited liability as there are tiers in corporate structure. Limited liability for corporate groups thus opens the door to multiple layers of insulation, a consequence unforeseen when limited liability was adopted long before the emergence of corporate groups.[63]

When applied to involuntary creditors of the group, such as the victims of an alleged tort committed by the enterprise in the course of its operations, this extension of limited liability does little more than shift the risk of liability onto them and away from the group. Can this be a justifiable result when the victims are uninsured? Even where the claimants are insured, can such a transfer of risk from corporation to involuntary creditor be justifiable, given the risk of moral hazard implicit in such a policy? This point can be illustrated by reference to the facts of the UK *Cape Asbestos* litigation. The litigation arose out of the exposure of large numbers of employees and local residents to asbestos mining and milling operations undertaken by the subsidiaries of Cape in South Africa, with attendant consequences to the health of the claimants.[64]

It is not immediately obvious why the cost of dealing with asbestos related injuries should be borne by the local subsidiary alone, especially as it did not have the assets from which to compensate the claimants, given that Cape closed down its asbestos operations in South Africa in 1979. On the other hand, Cape enjoyed the profit stream from those overseas investments, and it would seem proper to make those proceeds available to compensate involuntary creditors where they can show that the parent controlled the operations in South Africa, and so could be held responsible for them. In any case direct liability might be possible on the ground that as Cape was aware of the dangers of asbestos mining and milling, given the state of knowledge at the time these activities were being carried on, and so any failure on its part to follow established safe practices, and, in particular, to require its South African subsidiaries to do so, would amount to a breach of a duty of care by omission.[65]

Therefore, the issues relating to the existence of a duty of care, and of its breach, could be kept separate from the wider issue relating to the extent to which the parent company could benefit from the principle of limited liability as a means of insulating itself against tort claims arising out of the actions of its subsidiaries. Indeed, the acceptance of a presumption of liability by the parent may protect the commercial interests of the group, by encouraging business confidence among outsiders dealing with the group and by generating goodwill among consumers who are increasingly concerned about good corporate citizenship.

[63] See Blumberg ibid at 139.

[64] See further Peter T Muchlinski 'Corporations in International Litigation: Problems of Jurisdiction and the United Kingdom Asbestos Case' (2001) 50 International and Comparative Law Quarterly 1.

[65] See further *Lubbe et al v Cape plc* House of Lords Claimants' Final Served Case 43–50.

Secondly, it may be objected that the presumption does not remove the need for a forensic examination of the relationship between the parent and the subsidiary. The existence of a parent/subsidiary relationship, and a causal connection between the control of the subsidiary by the parent, and the resulting harm suffered by the claimant would still need to be shown. Thus the presumption of liability may not, in fact, take us beyond the uncertainties caused by the doctrines of 'lifting the corporate veil' or 'enterprise entity'. On the other hand, given that, in the majority of cases of inward direct investment, it is clear from the outset who the parent company is, it may not be difficult in practice to identify the company upon which the onus of the presumption falls.

Furthermore, it is possible that a presumption of parent company liability for the acts of its overseas subsidiaries may remove some of the conceptual difficulties inherent in justifying an exercise of extraterritorial jurisdiction by the host or home state. In chapter 4 it was argued that, in relation to the operations of MNEs in host countries, a presumption of liability can serve as notice to the foreign parent, that on setting up a subsidiary within the jurisdiction, it is subject to all the liabilities that a locally incorporated parent company may bear.[66] However, objections from the home country may result, as shown by the New York Supreme Court's refusal to recognize the effect of the Argentine Supreme Court's judgment in the *Deltec* case, where the latter had ruled that, in view of the 'unified socioeconomic unity' of the Deltec group, the multinational group as a whole was jointly and severally liable for the debts of its Argentinean subsidiary.[67]

The third approach to reconciling the competing interests of group limitation of liability and adequate compensation of parties dealing with the group is the 'network liability' approach favoured by Teubner. As noted earlier, this approach is specifically geared to the distinct problems of non-equity networks which are more loosely connected than those based on parent/subsidiary relations. Certain problems associated with the operation of this doctrine of liability have already been considered and need not be repeated. The remaining issue is whether such an approach, with its advantage of flexibility, can be extended to equity based groups as well. In principle, the allocation of responsibility among any relevant combination of affiliates in the group, without necessarily involving the parent – unless appropriate on the facts – is attractive. In most cases, the nature of the claim and the sum involved will not require the resources of the group as a whole to ensure effective compensation. However, when an accident of the magnitude of the *Bhopal* case occurs, effective compensation can only be achieved by involving the assets of the group as a whole. In such extreme cases the 'network liability' approach could lead to an excessive decentralization of the locus of liability. Acting rather like the

---

[66] See ch 4 at 147–48.

[67] See Gordon 'Argentine Jurisprudence: The Parke-Davis and Deltec Cases' 6 Lawyer of the Americas 320 (1974); *Deltec Banking Corporation v Compania Italo-Argentina de Electricidad SA* 171 NYLJ 18 col 1 3 April 1974.

traditional doctrine of corporate separation, the 'network approach' could sub-divide the allocation of risk in the group to the entities actually connected with the harmful acts, while shielding the parent and other affiliates. However, given Teubner's insistence on joint and several liability, this argument may be a misrep-resentation of his intentions. Liability may, in fact, be joint and several across the group. If so, it is hard to see how the approach offers a truly radical advance upon 'enterprise entity' doctrine or, indeed, upon traditional notions of joint liability in tort. The required evidence of group liability would be much the same in all these cases.

More recently, the issue of group liability has been considered by the UK Company Law Review.[68] The Company Law Review Steering Group had little to say on these very important questions. Indeed, the issue of corporate groups was introduced only at a later stage in the Review process and consisted of a single chapter in the November 2000 Consultation Document *Modern Company Law for a Competitive Economy – Completing the Structure*.[69] In that chapter, there is little said by the Steering Group on the specific question of group liability for tortious acts of affiliates, let alone on the specific problems surrounding MNE accountability. More strikingly, the Final Report of the Steering Group, published on 26 July 2001, contains nothing on corporate groups. Neither the foreword, nor the opening chapter on 'Guiding Principles, Methods and Output', offers any explanation for this omission.[70]

In its 2000 Consultation Document, the Steering Group accepted that the arguments for permitting parent companies to take advantage of limited liability in relation to tort liability were less strong than in the case of liability to creditors, given that the latter could exact a price for the credit to reflect the risk, while in cases of tort liability the parent can externalize the risk without the need to com-pensate. Furthermore, it was recognized that torts could protect very important interests such as freedom from wrongful personal injury.[71] However, the Steering Group also noted that the British courts were unwilling to 'lift the corporate veil' in such cases, citing the case of *Adams v Cape Industries* in support.[72] The Steering Group continued:

However, there are circumstances in which we regard it as entirely proper for a holding company to segregate an activity in a subsidiary with the risks of liability, including tor-tious or delictual liability, in mind. Many torts are closely linked with contractual liabil-ities, for example liability for professional services and misrepresentation and product liability. We are also not aware of any jurisdiction providing for parent companies to be automatically liable for the torts or delicts of their subsidiaries. Defining the circumstances in which the use of limited liability in this way should be regarded as abusive would be

---

[68] See Peter T Muchlinski above n 40 at 173–75 on which this paragraph is based.

[69] (London, DTI November 2000) at Chapter 10; hereafter *Completing the Structure*.

[70] See The Company Law Steering Group *Modern Company Law for a Competitive Economy Final Report* (London: DTI, 2001) vol 1.　　　　[71] See *Completing the Structure* n 69 at para 10.58.

[72] [1990] Ch 433.

difficult. Nor are we aware of cases where parent companies have engaged in such abuse. The under-capitalisation of subsidiaries, and their operation in a way which creates undue risks of insolvency, are matters best dealt with by insolvency law. We do not propose any reforms in this regard.[73]

That is all the Steering Group said. It failed to confront the question whether the *Adams* case went too far in blocking veil lifting in appropriate situations, such as where involuntary creditors needed to seek out the resources of the group as a whole for adequate compensation. It also avoided investigating alternative theories such as the Indian *Mehta* doctrine, and provided a rather misleading analogy between tort and contract liabilities.[74] In all it was a missed opportunity to give full consideration to the issue of group liability at a time when this matter has been giving rise to litigation.

(3) The Protection of Minority Shareholders in the Subsidiary of a MNE

It was seen in chapter 2 that equity based MNEs will operate and control an international network of subsidiaries on the basis of integrated management. This means that the directors of the various subsidiaries will in reality be little more than line managers who carry out the group's business plans. This may create special problems in the case of subsidiaries that are jointly owned with local minority shareholders. The risk arises that the directors of the subsidiary will make decisions that are in the group's interests but that may adversely affect the interests of the minority. For example, the parent company may wish to use the assets of the subsidiary to subsidize investment elsewhere in the group. It may raise loans from the subsidiary, thereby reducing the funds available for distribution to shareholders. Equally, the subsidiary may be instructed deliberately to effect transfer pricing manipulations so as to reduce the profits available for distribution to local shareholders and thus increase the value of the group's share thereof. Furthermore, the parent may, with the full knowledge of the subsidiary's directors, divert business opportunities from the subsidiary for the benefit of other entities in the group, thereby reducing the prospects of the subsidiary. In all of these cases the minority shareholders' interests are subordinated to those of the group enterprise. This may have consequences for the liability of the directors of the subsidiary and of the parent under the applicable local law.

Under English law, the fact that a company is owned and controlled as part of a group does not remove the general principle that directors owe a duty to act in the best interest only of the company of which they are directors. Thus directors of a

---

[73] See *Completing the Structure* above n 69 at para 10.59.
[74] For full analysis, see Peter T Muchlinski n 68 above.

holding company have no duties as such to protect the interests of its subsidiaries where these have independent boards.[75] Similarly, the directors of a subsidiary owe their primary duty to the subsidiary.[76] They owe no fiduciary duties to the holding company as the majority shareholder.[77] The duties of a director include a duty to have equal regard to the interests of all the present and future members of the company, which requires them to act fairly as between different classes of shareholders. This includes a duty not to make decisions that may adversely affect one group of shareholders to the benefit of another.[78] Thus, where the directors of the UK-based subsidiary of a MNE make a decision that is in the interests of the group as a whole, they will be in breach of their duty to act in the interests of the members as a whole, unless they can show that the decision reasonably coincides with the interests of the subsidiary as well.[79] For example, on analogy with the facts of the leading English case, *Charterbridge Corporation v Lloyds Bank*,[80] if the subsidiary were to forward funds to its parent in an attempt to preserve the latter's solvency, this may be regarded as reasonably within the interests of the subsidiary where the latter depends on the parent for the services and know-how that keep the subsidiary in business. On the other hand, where the directors of the subsidiary are deliberately siphoning funds out of the jurisdiction as part of the group's corporate plan, thereby affecting the value of the subsidiary as a going concern,

---

[75] *Lindgren v L & P Estates Ltd* [1968] Ch 572. But see text at nn 108–109 below. See further Mike Lower 'The Regulation of Intra-Group Transactions' in John de Lacy (ed) *The Reform of United Kingdom Company Law* (London: Cavendish Publishing, 2002) 217; Gerard Hertig and Hideki Kanda 'Related Party Transactions' in Reiner R Kraakman et al (eds) *The Anatomy of Corporate Law: A Comparative and Functional Approach* (Oxford: Oxford University Press, 2003) 101.

[76] *Charterbridge Corporation v Lloyds Bank* [1970] 1 Ch 62 per Pennycuick J at 74E–F: 'Each company in the group is a separate legal entity and the directors of a particular company are not entitled to sacrifice the interest of that company. This becomes apparent when one considers the case where the particular company has separate creditors. The proper test, I think, in the absence of actual separate consideration, must be whether an intelligent and honest man in the position of a director of the company concerned, could, on the whole of the existing circumstances, have reasonably believed that the transactions were for the benefit of the company.' But see s 131 of the New Zealand Companies Act 1993 which permits directors of a wholly owned subsidiary to substitute the interests of the holding company over those of the subsidiary, where the subsidiary's constitution permits. Where the subsidiary is partly owned, in addition to permission in the constitution, an agreement to this effect of all the shareholders, excluding the holding company, is required: Lower, above note 75 at 274.

[77] *Bell v Lever Bros* [1932] AC 161 at 228 per Lord Atkin: 'It will be noticed that Bell was not a director of Levers and, with respect, I cannot accept the view of Greer LJ that if he was in a fiduciary relationship to the Niger Co he was in a similar fiduciary relationship to the shareholders, or to the particular shareholders (Levers) who held 99% of the shares.'

[78] See JH Farrar, NE Furey, BM Hannigan *Farrar's Company Law* (Butterworths, 4th edn, 1998) at 381–82.

[79] See the dictum of Pennycuick J in *Charterbridge Corporation v Lloyds Bank* n 47 above. Under Australian law directors must also have primary consideration for the interests of the company they direct. However, they are entitled to consider wider group interests to the extent that the prosperity or continued existence of their company depends on the well-being of the group as a whole. See *Reid Murray Holdings Ltd (in liq) v David Murray Holdings* (1972) 5 SASR 386; *Farrow Finance Co Ltd (in liq) v Farrow Properties Pty Ltd* (1997) 26 ACSR 544 at 581; *Japan Abrasive Materials Pty Ltd v Australian Fused Minerals* (1986) 16 ACLC 1172.　　　　　　　　　　　[80] Above n 76.

they would almost certainly be held liable for breach of duty.[81] This argument is borne out by reference to the statutory remedy that minority shareholders have under English law against unfairly prejudicial conduct on the part of the company.

By s 459 of the UK Companies Act 1985 any member of the company may apply to the court for an order on the ground that the affairs of the company are being or have been conducted in a manner that is unfairly prejudicial to the interests of some part of the members, of whom the petitioner is one. The right of petition extends to any actual or proposed act or omission of the company that is or would be unfairly prejudicial. The unfair prejudice arises out of a failure on the part of the company to follow the understanding arrived at with the minority as to how the company's affairs should be conducted.[82] In *Scottish Co-operative Wholesale Society v Meyer*,[83] a case decided under s 210 of the Companies Act 1948, the predecessor to s 459, the House of Lords held that the minority shareholders in a subsidiary are entitled to a statutory remedy where the directors of the subsidiary knowingly acquiesce in the parent's policy of running down the subsidiary as this constitutes a breach of their duties as directors. The acts of the parent are attributable to the subsidiary's directors as the latter's decisions are determined by the policy of the former. Thus, under English law there appears to be some protection for minorities subjected to group policies that are unfavourable to their interests.[84]

---

[81] See T Hadden *The Control of Corporate Groups* (London: Institute of Advanced Legal Studies, 1983) 32.

[82] See *O'Neill v Phillips* [1999] 2 All ER 961 (HL) and analysis in Gower and Davies above n 4 at 517–23, John Lowry 'Mapping the Boundaries of Unfair Prejudice' in John de Lacy (ed) *The Reform of United Kingdom Company Law* (London: Cavendish Publishing, 2002) 229.

[83] [1959] AC 325 (HL).

[84] The limits of this protection were considered in *Nicholas v Soundcraft Electronics* [1993] BCLC 360 (CA) where the parent company, Electronics, withheld payments to the subsidiary as part of the general control that it exercised over its affairs. According to the Court of Appeal, the non-payment of the debts due to the subsidiary related to the manner in which its affairs were conducted. However, the reason why Electronics delayed payment was to try to keep the group, which was in financial difficulties, afloat – something which was in the interests of the subsidiary – and, accordingly, this could not constitute unfair prejudice in the conduct of the subsidiary's affairs even though it did cause loss to the plaintiff, a minority shareholder in the subsidiary. In *Re Citybranch Group Ltd* [2005] EWCA Civ 815, [2004] 4 All ER 735 (CA) the Court of Appeal held that shareholders of the parent company could bring an action under s 459 against directors of a subsidiary where there were directors in common between the parent and subsidiary and the affairs of the subsidiary had been conducted in a manner unfairly prejudicial to the interests of those shareholders. See, for comment, Bree Taylor 'Piercing the Corporate Veil' New Law Journal 19 November 2004 at 1734. See also *Re Dominion International Group (No 2)* [1996] 1 BCLC 572, a case involving the Company Directors Disqualification Act 1986, where Knox J held that: 'I do not accept that it is right to categorise activities as necessarily belonging exclusively to the directorship of the company whose asset is being dealt with. I do accept that there may very well be many cases where that will be the correct analysis of the activities of a director of a subsidiary company even if he is also a director of the subsidiary company's holding company. But equally where an individual who is a director of both takes steps which seriously affect the interests of both companies, it strikes me as artificial to ignore his duties as a director of one of the two companies and attribute his actions solely to the directorship of the company whose asset is dealt with. Put baldly, the question is whether a director of a subsidiary company, who is also a director of its holding company, is in breach of his fiduciary duty to the holding company, if he improperly gets rid of an asset of significant value of the subsidiary. It is clear that that conduct inflicts harm on the holding company because it reduces the value of its investment in the subsidiary. In my

However, given the complexity of group transactions and the limited disclosure to which they are subjected, it will often be difficult for the minority to prove their case. Furthermore, the cost of bringing an action may act as a deterrent.[85] In any case, s 459 is designed to act in the context of private companies where there is no ready market for the shares. In the case of a public company a disgruntled minority will normally sell their shares as a less expensive option to litigation.[86] Indeed, if the minority succeeds under s 459 the usual remedy will be the compulsory purchase of their shares by the majority at their original market value had there been no prejudicial acts.[87]

Turning briefly to other jurisdictions, in the US, the rights of action of the minority are based on the fiduciary duty of the majority to respect their interests.[88] This duty has developed from the fiduciary duty owed by directors to the corporation. It requires fair treatment of the minority by the majority. This duty has been extended to the case of parent/subsidiary relations involving a minority shareholding in the latter.[89] In Germany the 1965 Aktiengesetz[90] provides for the protection of minority interests by imposing certain duties upon the controlling undertaking. Thus, where a 'control contract' group is formed,[91] the controlling undertaking must offer to pay a guaranteed dividend to minority shareholders,[92] or to buy out their shares at a fixed price.[93] Where a 'de facto' group exists,[94] the

view a director in such a position is in breach of his duty to both the holding company and the subsidiary company. If it were otherwise, the Disqualification Act would not apply to a director of a non-trading United Kingdom holding company with only foreign subsidiaries if he misappropriated the assets of the foreign subsidiaries of which he was also a director and thereby rendered the United Kingdom holding company insolvent' (LEXIS Report at 54).

[85] Hadden above n 81 above. In *Prudential Assurance v Newman Industries (No 2)* [1982] 1 All ER 354 the costs of a minority action at common law were put at £750,000.

[86] See D Prentice 'Groups of Companies: The English Experience' in K Hopt (ed) *The Legal and Economic Analysis of Multinational Enterprises Vol II 'Groups of Companies in European Law'* (Berlin: De Gruyter, 1982) from 99 especially 116–17.

[87] This was the remedy offered to the minority in *Scottish Co-operative Wholesale Society v Meyer* above n 83. The Companies Act 1985 s 461 gives wide powers for the court to make orders for relief. The most common order is for the purchase of the petitioner's shares by the controller: see Gower and Davies above n 4 at 525–56.   [88] See Waelde above n 42 at 457.

[89] See further cases discussed by Waelde ibid at 460–65. See also *Zahn v Transamerica Corp* 162 F 2d 36 (1947); *Sinclair Oil Corp v Levien* 280 A 2d 717 (Del Sup Ct 1971). Under Delaware law '[a] shareholder that owns a majority interest in a corporation' or exercises actual control over its business affairs, occupies the status of a fiduciary to the corporation'. Such a shareholder also 'occupies the status of a fiduciary to . . . [the corporation's] minority shareholders'. *In re MAXXAM Inc* 659 A 2d 760, 771 (Del Ch 1995) citing *Kahn v Lynch Communication Systems Inc* 638 A 2d 1110, 1113 (Del 1994)). See also *Disctronics Limited v Disc Manufacturing Corporation* 686 So 2d 1154 (Sup Ct Ala) 1996 LEXIS 499. This doctrine cannot be brought to bear in the case of a wholly owned subsidiary: *Donahue v Rodd Electrotype Co* 328 NE 2d 505 (Mass 1975).   [90] Above n 42.

[91] A 'control contract' group is formed when 75 per cent of the shareholders of the controlled company vote to adopt a control contract which entitles the controlling enterprise to give binding instructions to the management board of the controlled company in exchange for the undertaking of financial responsibilities on behalf of the controlled company: ibid ss 291–310.

[92] ibid s 304(1).   [93] ibid s 305(1).

[94] A 'de facto' group comes into existence by operation of the law where a legally independent enterprise (the dependent enterprise) is dominated by another enterprise (the dominant enterprise) which is able directly or indirectly to exercise a dominating influence: ibid s 17.

controlling undertaking is obliged to compensate the controlled undertaking for any losses suffered by it as a result of the controlling undertaking's influence over its business activities.[95] Failure to compensate will give rise to a claim for compensation from the controlled undertaking and from the shareholders for any damage apart from the damage they have suffered by the controlled undertaking being damaged.[96] In practice, however, these two approaches have not been widely used. The 'control contract' group has been used mainly as a tax shifting device,[97] while the de facto group has generated only one compensation claim in some 40 years of the law's existence.[98] In addition, in 2001, the judicial extension of the de facto group principle from the AG (public corporation) to the GmbH (private limited company), the most widely used form of incorporation for holding companies in Germany, was reversed by the German Federal Supreme Court, thereby excluding this concept from the majority of holding companies in Germany.[99] Under French and Argentinean law, the rights of minority shareholders may be capable of protection under the principle of abuse of rights (*abus de droit*), whereby the rights to control the company granted to the directors must be exercised in its interests.[100] In addition French law contains a related, but not identical concept of abuse by the majority (*abus de majorité*). This is an exceptional remedy and controlling shareholders are almost never held liable.[101]

Finally, it should be recalled that certain states may require, as a condition of entry, that a foreign investor enters into a joint venture with local shareholders. Where this is the case, either the foreign investor or the local shareholder may be in the numerical minority. However, as was shown in chapter 5, this may not necessarily reflect the balance of decision-making power between the parties. The foreign party is more likely to possess the commercial advantages required for the success of the venture. Provided that the local shareholders derive a fair return on the venture no difficulties should arise. On the other hand, where the foreign partner fails to fulfil its side of the bargain, the local authorities may intervene and require the observance of the terms of the joint venture. The law upon which entry was authorized, and the terms of the investment authorization, may allow for administrative intervention in the interests of the local partner.[102]

The preceding discussion has centred on the national laws of states concerning minority protection or the protection of local shareholders. It is not an issue that

---

[95] ibid s 311.   [96] ibid s 317(1).

[97] Any fiscal loss to the subsidiary is immediately recoverable from the parent as a compensation claim, for which the parent must establish a reserve fund. Such reserve amounts become payable to the subsidiary at the end of the fiscal year: see Reich-Graefe above n 42 at 790 and Peter Hommelhoff 'Protection of Minority Shareholders, Investors and Creditors in Corporate Groups: The Strengths and Weaknesses of German Corporate Group Law' 2 European Business Organization Law Review 61 (2001) at 65.   [98] Reich-Graefe ibid at 792 and Hertig and Kanda above n 75 at 124–25.

[99] See *Bremer Vulcan* above n 49.

[100] However, it is not clear whether the interests of the company are commensurate with the interests of the shareholders or are separate from these: see Dobson above n 26 at 854–956.

[101] Hertig and Kanda above n 75 at 126; Philippe Merle *Droit Commercial Sociétés Commerciales* (Paris: Dalloz, 10th Edn, 2005) at 691–93.   [102] See further ch 5 at 191–201.

has given rise to distinct laws for MNEs and for national equity based groups. Thus the domestic law of each state in which the firm operates must be consulted to gauge the extent of local shareholder protection. However, a problem that is unique to MNEs arises as a result of the foreign nationality of the parent. The directors of a subsidiary may be required by the parent company to make decisions that are in the interests of the parent, in that failure to effect the decision will result in the parent being in breach of home country laws, but which conflict with the interests of the local subsidiary. Here the local law protecting minority interests in the subsidiary might be invoked to prevent the decision from being made. It will be recalled that the French courts used the French law concerning abuse of rights in this way in the case of *Société Fruehauf Corp v Massardy*, discussed in chapter 4.[103] This case shows that the host state is entitled to subject a foreign-owned subsidiary to local company law. This is correct in view of the fact that, by reason of domicile, host state law is the proper law of the subsidiary.[104]

(4) Protection of Creditors Upon the Insolvency of the Subsidiary of a MNE

The final issue to be considered in this chapter relates to an aspect of creditor protection that has not been dealt with in section 1, namely, the rights of a creditor against the foreign parent of an insolvent subsidiary with which the creditor has been doing business. Under English law directors are not in general bound to have regard to the interests of creditors, although reform proposals recently accepted by Parliament may change this.[105] Under existing law, where a director of a company

---

[103] *Société Fruehauf v Massardy* [1968] DS Jur 147, [1965] JCP II 14, 274 bis (Cour d'appel, Paris); 5 ILM 476 (1966). For a summary of the case see ch 4 at 131. This case led to legislative amendments protecting the minority shareholders of MNE subsidiaries against decisions that could risk the ruin of the subsidiary: see Law No 66–537 of 24 July 1966.

[104] See PM North and JJ Fawcett *Cheshire and North's Private International Law* (Butterworths, 13th edn, 1999) 175.

[105] By s 309 of the Companies Act 1985: 'The matters to which the directors are to have regard in the performance of their functions include the interests of the company's employees in general as well as the interests of its members.' The interests of creditors are not mentioned. Judicial opinion is divided on the extent to which creditors' interests should be considered by directors. In favour of such consideration are: *Lonrho Ltd v Shell Petroleum*[1980] 1 WLR 627 at 635 per Lord Diplock; *Walker v Wimbourne* (1976) 50 ALJR 446 (Aust HC); *Nicholson v Permakraft (NZ)* (1985) NZCLC 96–032. Contra: *Multinational Gas and Petrochemical Co v Multinational Gas and Petrochemical Services* [1983] 2 All ER 563 (CA) at 585g per Dillon LJ. The Companies Act 2006 (c 46) replaces s 309 with s 172 entitled 'Duty to promote the success of the company':

'(1) A director of a company must act in the way he considers, in good faith, would be most likely to promote the success of the company for the benefit of its members as a whole, and in doing so have regard (amongst other matters) to—
   (a) the likely consequences of any decision in the long term,
   (b) the interests of the company's employees,
   (c) the need to foster the company's business relationships with suppliers, customers and others,

that has gone into liquidation knew or ought to have concluded, some time before the commencement of the winding up of the company, that there was no reasonable prospect that the company would avoid going into insolvent liquidation then he or she may be held liable for wrongful trading under s 214 of the Insolvency Act 1986. The only defence is that he or she took every step with a view to minimizing the potential loss to the company's creditors as he or she ought to have taken, assuming him or her to have known that there was no reasonable prospect that the company would avoid going into insolvent liquidation.[106]

Thus, if the director of a UK subsidiary of a foreign-owned parent is ordered to run that subsidiary without sufficient assets to meet its liabilities he or she may be exposed to personal liability under s 214. Furthermore, the parent company may be jointly liable as a 'shadow director',[107] that is as 'a person in accordance with whose directions or instructions the directors of a company are accustomed to act . . .'.[108] In the case of *Re Hydrodan* the issue of when a parent company and its directors could be held to have acted as a 'shadow director' was considered.[109] Millett J held that the parent company was a shadow director of its subsidiary where it directed the latter's directors. It was not enough for the parent merely to approve or authorize a decision made by directors of the subsidiary acting on their own independent discretion and judgment. The directors of the parent could also be shadow directors of the subsidiary but only where they gave individual and personal directions to the subsidiary. It was not enough for them to have acted as directors of the parent and to have voted on resolutions approving decisions of the subsidiary's board of directors, in which case only the parent company would qualify as a shadow director.

In other jurisdictions similar laws exist. Under French law, where a parent company acts as a de facto director of an insolvent subsidiary it may be liable where it has acted in contravention of its fiduciary duties as a director of the subsidiary and there is a causal connection between those acts and the damage caused to the subsidiary. However, this remedy may be limited by the fact that the parent's fiduciary duties will be defined in accordance with the legitimate pursuit of group interests.

    (d) the impact of the company's operations on the community and the environment,
    (e) the desirability of the company maintaining a reputation for high standards of business conduct, and
    (f) the need to act fairly as between members of the company.

(2) Where or to the extent that the purposes of the company consist of or include purposes other than the benefit of its members, subsection (1) has effect as if the reference to promoting the success of the company for the benefit of its members were to achieving those purposes.

(3) The duty imposed by this section has effect subject to any enactment or rule of law requiring directors, in certain circumstances, to consider or act in the interests of creditors of the company.'

---

[106] UK Insolvency Act 1986 s 214(3).   [107] ibid s 214(7).   [108] ibid s 251.

[109] [1994] BCC 161 (ChD). See also *Secretary of State for Trade and Industry v Deverell* [2000] 2 All ER 365 (CA) especially at paras 24–36 at 372–77 where Morritt LJ reviews the case law holding that the essence of the test was whether the shadow director held 'real influence in the corporate affairs of the company' but it was not necessary to show that such influence covered all the affairs of the company (at 376A–B). See also Lower above n 75 at 281–84.

Consequently successful actions under these rules are rare.[110] Under the German Aktiengesetz, the controlling undertaking will take on full liability for the debts and obligations of the controlled undertaking.[111] However, the provisions of the Aktiengesetz proved not to be effective as a means of creditor redress, especially in relation to the GmbH, which, as noted earlier, forms the main method of incorporation for groups in Germany. The German courts stepped in and partly remedied this situation by use of the 'qualified concern' doctrine whereby a controlling undertaking that exerted permanent and extensive involvement in the management of an insolvent subsidiary would be presumed to have failed to show concern for the interests of the controlled undertaking, and would be directly liable to the creditors of the controlled undertaking.[112] This approach has since been modified to exclude the principles of the Aktiengestz from GmbH companies. In their place a narrower principle of protection has been introduced which requires that the controlling undertaking maintains the mandatory stated capital requirements of the controlled undertaking and avoids the destruction of the autonomous existence of the latter.[113]

In New Zealand, the Companies Amendment Act 1980 introduced new powers whereby a court could, in its discretion, order any other company in the group to pay to the liquidator of an insolvent company the whole or part of any or all of the debts provable in the winding-up. This would be done in the light of evidence as to the extent that another company in the group has involved itself in the management of the insolvent company, its conduct towards creditors of the insolvent company and the extent to which the winding-up of the insolvent company is attributable to the actions of the first company. The courts could also wind up two or more companies in the group and pool their assets in the satisfaction of creditors where this was warranted by the facts.[114] In the US, creditor actions that seek redress from parent corporations for the unpaid debts of their subsidiaries will involve the piercing of the corporate veil based on arguments concerning the undercapitalization of the subsidiary, or its use as a vehicle of fraud. This involves difficult questions of proof, as the question of what constitutes undercapitalization or fraud is often unclear.[115]

The international dimension to insolvency situations in multinational corporate groups has not been adequately resolved. The success of a creditor's claim

---

[110] See Hofstetter above n 3 at 585.   [111] Aktiengesetz above n 42 ss 303, 309, 317(4), 322.

[112] See *Autokran* 95 BGHZ 330 (1985); *Tiefbau* BGH ZIP 1989, 440z; NJW 1800 (1989) summarized in Hofstetter above n 3 at 583; see also Schiessel above n 42 and *Wooldridge* [1996] JBL 627.

[113] See *Bremer Vulcan* above n 49 and the references to the literature therein.

[114] Summary taken from the Report of the Cork Committee on Insolvency Law and Practice (Cmnd 8558 1982) paras 1947–49.

[115] See further Whincup 'Inequitable Incorporation – the Abuse of Privilege' 2 Co. Law 158 (1981); Landers 'A Unified Approach to Parent, Subsidiary, and Affiliate Questions in Bankruptcy' 42 U.Chi.L.Rev. 589 (1975); Posner 'The Rights of Creditors of Affiliated Corporations' 43 U.Chi.L.Rev. 499 (1976); Easterbrook and Fischel 'Limited Liability and the Corporation' 52 U.Chi.L.Rev. 89 (1985).

against the foreign parent will hinge on the initial question of whether the latter is capable of being impleaded before the courts of the host state in insolvency proceedings.[116] Assuming personal jurisdiction is obtained, the problems of proving parent liability under local law will pose significant obstacles to success. The logic of corporate separation is as hard to defeat in this situation as in others, and, as the requirements of the sample of laws summarized above show, the legal tests imposed on the plaintiff creditor can be very onerous.

However, the present discussion should be kept within a reasonable perspective. Empirical evidence suggests that MNEs are unlikely to allow their subsidiaries to go bankrupt, and will often guarantee their debts.[117] Thus, the situation contemplated in this section can be seen as exceptional although, obviously, not unprecedented.[118] Indeed, in times of global recession the incidence of subsidiary default may increase, giving rise to more claims in insolvency. That said, the insolvency of an entire MNE group is very unlikely.[119] Thus, where part of a MNE network defaults, it may be reasonable to expect the surviving parts to compensate the creditors of the insolvent entity as a matter of commercial prudence, and so as to comply with local redundancy payments laws.[120] Furthermore, where a large MNE is in serious financial trouble, governments are unlikely to allow it to cease operations, as the social and economic costs may be too great when compared with some form of public subsidy. The US Government's subsidy to Chrysler in 1979 is a case in point.[121] Therefore, some element of (albeit informal and case based) public

[116] See, for example, EC Council Regulation 1346/2000/EC on the regulation of insolvency proceedings as interpreted in *Eurofoods IFSC Ltd* Case C–341/04 [2006] All ER (D) 20 May 2006: Gregory Mitchell QC and Richard Brent 'Insolvency Issues – Heard Here First' New Law Journal 23 June 2006 at 1014.

[117] See Stobaugh 'Financing Foreign Subsidiaries of US Controlled Multinational Enterprises' 1 J.Int.Bus.Stud. 43 (1970) who found that of 20 medium sized and large US MNEs studied, none would let a subsidiary default on its debt, even if it were not formally guaranteed, and of 17 small MNEs studied only one is reported to have been willing to contemplate such an event. See, for similar findings, 'Determining Overseas Debt/Equity Ratios' Business International Money Report 27 January 1986 at 26, cited in AC Schapiro *Multinational Financial Management* (Allyn and Bacon, 4th edn, 1992) at 462–644.

[118] See, for example, the English case law on 'letters of comfort' at n 7 above and the *Multinational Gas* case cited n 105 above. Schapiro ibid cites two cases where MNEs allowed their affiliates to go bankrupt: Raytheon in Sicily (1968) and Freeport Sulphur in Cuba (1960). He writes, 'the publicity surrounding these events makes it clear how unusual they were'. On Raytheon, see the *ELSI* case *(United States v Italy)* (1989) ICJ Reports 14 discussed fully in ch16 at 641–42.

[119] The collapse of the Bank of Credit and Commerce International (BCCI) in 1991 is perhaps the best example. See further the Bingham Inquiry into the Supervision of the Bank of Credit and Commerce International (July 1992 presented to the House of Commons 22 October 1992) and for the jurisdictional issues arising out of the liquidation proceedings *Re Bank of Credit and Commerce International (No 10)* [1996] 4 All ER 796 (ChD). See also, on the Maxwell Communications Corporation collapse in 1991, John Flood and Eleni Skordaki 'Normative Bricolage: Informal Rule Making by Accountants and Lawyers in Mega-insolvencies' in Gunther Teubner (ed) *Global Law Without a State* (Aldershot: Dartmouth Publishing, 1997) 109. See generally Ian Fletcher *The Law of Insolvency* (London: Thomson Sweet & Maxwell, 4th edn, 2007) Part 3 'International Insolvency'.

[120] On which see further ch 12 at 483.

[121] See N Hood and S Young *Multinationals in Retreat: The Scottish Experience* (1982) at 73–74; A Altshuler et al *The Future of the Automobile* (Counterpoint, 1984) at 152–53.

insurance against the default of a major MNE may be practised by the home government, assuming it can raise sufficient revenue to effect such action.

Concluding Remarks

This chapter has raised a number of basic issues relating to the establishment of group liability for the acts and defaults of individual units of a MNE. In each case the logic of existing law, based as it is on the concept of the single unit enterprise, fails to grasp the realities of interdependence between affiliated enterprises in the national or multinational corporate group. However, legal systems are responding with piecemeal reforms and by adapting existing legal doctrines to modern day phenomena. There is undoubtedly evolution in legal thought and practice in this area. Nonetheless, significant legal and practical obstacles remain for the effective protection of those who make claims against MNEs. Furthermore, the responsibilities of MNEs may be seen as going beyond those owed to creditors (whether voluntary or involuntary) and shareholders, and to encompass other classes of 'stakeholders' such as employees and the general public at large. In all these cases significant issues of accountability emerge. These can be addressed by reforms in the internal governance of MNEs and by effective duties of disclosure. These matters will be examined in the next chapter.

9

Corporate Governance and Disclosure

This chapter deals with the related issues of corporate governance and disclosure within MNEs. This has become a highly important issue in the wake of recent corporate scandals involving MNEs, most notably the Enron collapse.[1] Both home and host states may require information from a MNE about its worldwide operations for their respective regulatory purposes. In addition, there may be non-governmental stakeholders,[2] most notably investors, creditors, employees, and consumers, who need information from the firm about matters of direct concern to their interests. The resulting demand for increased disclosure has given rise to significant developments in national and regional disclosure laws and has stimulated new policy proposals. Furthermore, the same demands have given rise to calls for the enhancement of MNE accountability through changes in the internal structure of the corporation. The first part of the present chapter will focus on this issue. The second part will then consider the problems associated with MNE disclosure. Before that is done, the principal motives for increased MNE disclosure and accountability will be considered, with particular emphasis on the interests to be furthered.

(1) Principal Motives and Interests Behind Enhanced MNE Accountability and Disclosure

The concern over MNE accountability and disclosure has many diverse sources. Apart from the traditional recipients of corporate information, namely its finance providers (the shareholders, bankers, lenders, and creditors), those interested in

[1] On which see further Peter T Muchlinski 'Enron and Beyond: Multinational Corporate Groups and the Internationalization of Governance and Disclosure Regimes' 37 Conn. LR 725 (2005). The main facts of the Enron collapse are summarized at 726–35. See further for discussion of wider influences upon the series of corporate scandals of recent years John Coffee 'What Caused Enron? A Capsule Social and Economic History of the 1990s' 89 Cornell LR 302 (2004).

[2] 'Stakeholders' may be defined as 'any identifiable groups or individuals who can affect the achievement of the corporation's objectives or who are affected by such achievement': M Zubaidur Rahman 'The Local Value Added Statement: A Reporting Requirement of Multinationals in Developing Host Countries' 25 Int.J.Acctg 87 at 88 (1990). See further RE Freeman and DL Reed 'Stockholders and Stakeholders: A New Perspective on Corporate Governance' California Management Review (Spring 1983) 83–106.

disclosure and accountability now include employees, trade unions, consumers, governments, and the general public. This has resulted in calls for a wider conception of disclosure than that needed by the financiers of the corporation.[3] Responding to such demands, international organizations have produced recommendations that widen the elements which may have to be included in a firm's annual report and in supplementary statements.[4] The general approach is well illustrated by the OECD Guideline on Disclosure which deserves quotation in full:

1. Enterprises should ensure that timely, regular, reliable and relevant information is disclosed regarding their activities, structure, financial situation and performance. This information should be disclosed by the enterprise as whole and, where appropriate, along business and geographic areas. Disclosure policies of enterprises should be tailored to the nature, size and location of the enterprise, with due regard taken of costs, business confidentiality and other competitive concerns.

2. Enterprises should apply high quality standards for disclosure, accounting and audit. Enterprises are also encouraged to apply high quality standards for non-financial information including environmental and social reporting where they exist. The standards or policies under which both financial and non-financial information are complied should be reported.

3. Enterprises should disclose basic information showing their name, location and structure, the name, address and telephone number of the parent enterprise and its main affiliates, its percentage ownership, direct and indirect in these affiliates, including shareholdings between them.

4. Enterprises should also disclose material information on:
   a) The financial and operating results of the company.
   b) Company objectives.
   c) Major share ownership and voting rights.
   d) Members of the board and key executives, and their remuneration.
   e) Material foreseeable risk factors.
   f) Material issues regarding employees and other stakeholders.
   g) Governance structures and policies.

5. Enterprises are encouraged to communicate additional information that could include:
   a) Value statements or statements of business conduct intended for public disclosure including information on the social, ethical and environmental policies of the enterprise and other codes of conduct to which the company subscribes. In addition, the date of adoption, the countries and entities to which such statements apply and its performance in relation to these statements may be communicated.

---

[3] See Lee H Radebaugh, Sidney J Gray, and Ervin L Black *International Accounting and Multinational Enterprises* (New York: John Wiley, 6th edn, 2006) at 22–23.

[4] See UN Group of Experts Report *International Standards of Accounting and Reporting for Transnational Corporations* (UN Doc E/C.10/33 18 October 1977) paras 9–12 at 28 and 53–79. See also *Draft UN Code of Conduct on Transnational Corporations* text of 24 May 1990 (UN Doc E/1990/94 12 June 1990) paras 44–46 at 12–14. For a more recent reiteration of this position see UNCTAD International Working Group of Experts on International Standards of Accounting and Reporting (hereafter ISAR) *Guidance on Good Practices in Corporate Governance Disclosure* (UN Doc TD/B/COM.2/ISAR/30 26 September 2005) at paras 19–20.

b) Information on systems of managing risks and complying with laws, and on statements or codes of business conduct.

c) Information on relationships with employees and other stakeholders.[5]

The guideline offers a summary of responses to the various concerns underlying MNE disclosure. It should be read alongside the OECD Principles of Corporate Governance which offer more detailed analysis of the terms used in the Disclosure Guideline.[6] The basic starting point for disclosure in the Corporate Governance Principles is that 'the corporate governance framework should ensure that timely and accurate disclosure is made on all material matters regarding the corporation, including the financial situation, performance, ownership and governance of the company'.[7] This is deemed central to shareholders' ability to exercise their ownership rights on an informed basis and thus to allow capital markets to operate efficiently. In this regard, the financial and operating results of the company must give the 'whole picture' and, where transactions relate to the performance of the group as a whole, the accounts must include information based on the highest international accounting standards and give full information about contingent liabilities and off-balance sheet transactions.[8] Apart from shareholder interests, the Disclosure Guideline and the Corporate Governance Principles both stress the need for a broad disclosure of company objectives. These cover not only commercial objectives but also policies relating to business ethics, the environment and other public policy commitments, with the aim of better evaluating the relationship between companies and the communities in which they operate and the steps they have taken to implement their objectives.[9] The requirement to disclose major ownership and voting rights will assist not only shareholders, in having full knowledge of the structure of the group of companies and intra-group relations, but also regulators who will need such information to identify potential conflicts of interest or insider trading. Similarly, the information on key board members and their remuneration will assist in identifying conflicts of interest and monitoring the effects of remuneration schemes such as stock options and their relationship to company performance.[10]

The Corporate Governance Principles go on to consider the issue of related party transactions in some greater detail than the rather basic requirements of paragraph 3 of the Disclosure Guideline. Full disclosure of such transactions is necessary to ensure that the company is being run with due regard to the interests of all its investors. This should be done on an individual or grouped basis indicating whether the transactions in question have been made at arm's length and on normal market terms. Related parties include 'entities that control or are under

---

[5] OECD *The OECD Guidelines for Multinational Enterprises* (Paris: OECD, 2000) 20, available at <http://www.oecd.org/dataoecd/56/36/1922428.pdf>.

[6] OECD *Principles of Corporate Governance* (Paris: OECD, 2004) available at <http://www.oecd.org/dataoecd/32/18/31557724.pdf> at 22–23 and 49–57. See further Alan Dignam and Michael Galanis 'Governing the World: The Development of the OECD's Corporate Governance Principles' 10 EBLR 96 (1999).   [7] ibid at 22.

[8] ibid at 50.   [9] ibid at 50–51.   [10] ibid at 51.

common control with the company, significant shareholders including members of their families and key management personnel'.[11] The inclusion of foreseeable risk factors relates to industry or area-specific risks, financial market risks, risks related to derivatives, and off-balance sheet transactions (which were a key factor in the Enron case) and environmental liability risks.[12] The two final items for disclosure, employee and other stakeholder issues and corporate governance structures and polices, are a response to the fact that companies are now encouraged, if not actually obliged by law, in some countries, to provide information on these matters. In relation to employees, this includes any issue that may materially affect the performance of the company including relations with creditors, suppliers, and local communities. As regards corporate governance polices, this is a response to the growing requirements for companies to set down a code of corporate governance and to report on why they may have departed from such standards on a 'comply or explain' basis.[13]

From the foregoing, it is clear that the OECD approach to disclosure seeks to encourage greater openness and transparency by MNEs for public policy purposes, alongside their existing national disclosure requirements, as a means of creating a more informed environment for policy responses to be formulated. In this the OECD approach goes beyond disclosure aimed at mere investor protection, the traditional concern of corporate disclosure laws. On the other hand, the OECD Disclosure Guideline also shows sensitivity to the concerns of corporate managers, specifically mentioning confidentiality and cost as factors to be considered when contemplating the form and extent of the recommended disclosure. Finally, it should be noted that the Guideline has only persuasive and not legal force. The ultimate arbiter of disclosure requirements still remains the law of the OECD member country in which the MNE operates.

The disclosure of information will normally be required by law as part of the system of corporate governance to which the corporation must subject itself in return for the privilege of incorporation. However, the mere disclosure of information may not ensure that the user is effectively protected, let alone given all the facts that he or she requires.[14] Consequently, developments in disclosure requirements must be considered alongside moves to reform the internal organization of publicly held corporations for the sake of greater accountability, whereby the interested party becomes a part of the corporate decision-making process.

(2) Reforming the Internal Governance Structures of MNEs

Traditionally, the publicly held corporation has been perceived as an entity whose purpose is the making of profit for its members. The resulting internal legal structure has generally reflected this fact, in that it aims at the regulation of

---

[11] ibid.   [12] ibid at 53.   [13] ibid at 53–54.
[14] See further T Hadden *The Control of Corporate Groups* (London: Institute of Advanced Legal Studies, 1983) ch 6.

decision-making in the interests of the shareholders alone. Thus, in Anglo-American law, the corporation typically consists of a unitary board of directors and a general meeting of shareholders. The former undertakes the management of the company while the latter acts as the elector of the board and the general controlling body of the company.[15] In certain European legal systems, most notably that of Germany, an alternative three-tier system is found. In addition to the general meeting and the executive board of directors there is the supervisory board. Its function is to control the executive board, stressed by its distinct membership in that dual membership of both boards is prohibited.[16] Yet here too, the aim is the organization of the company in the interests of its principal investors, often represented as members of the policy-making supervisory board.[17]

This classical legal model of the corporation, whether of the single or dual board type, has been found wanting as a means of ensuring shareholder control, given the rise of a professional managerial class distinct from the principal shareholders, and by the fragmentation of corporate ownership through the rise of mass stock markets.[18] The issue of whether shareholders' interests are effectively protected by corporate structures has given rise to calls for stronger shareholder powers, including the strengthening of the powers of the general meeting and, as seen in the previous chapter, more effective remedies for minorities.[19] In addition, a major effect of the Enron scandal has been to renew emphasis on the strengthening of the internal governance structures of the corporation so as to ensure greater transparency in dealings. In particular the role of outside or non-executive directors sitting on the boards of MNEs has acquired greater significance as has the reform of auditing procedures and of the audit committee.[20] This has been accompanied by stronger external regulation of the auditing process. Furthermore, the classical Anglo-American model of the single board corporation may not give adequate voice to the interests of stakeholders other than shareholders. By

[15] See further Paul L Davies *Gower and Davies Principles of Modern Company Law* (London: Thomson Sweet & Maxwell, 7th edn, 2003, 8th edn in preparation for 2007) at 38–40 and ch 14; JH Farrar and BM Hannigan *Farrar's Company Law* (London: Butterworths, 4th edn, 1998) ch 22.

[16] Gower ibid at 317.

[17] See the paper by Reich in N Horn and J Kocha *Law and the Formation of Big Enterprises in the Nineteenth and Early Twentieth Centuries* (Gottingen, 1979) at 262–65.

[18] See A Bearle and G Means *The Modern Corporation and Private Property* (Macmillan, 1932, rev edn, 1967) and Gower and Davies above n 15 at 38–39; Janet Dine *The Governance of Corporate Groups* (Cambridge: Cambridge University Press, 2000) at 118–19. However, this fact has not diminished the modern corporate manager's commitment to the maximization of profits as the major corporate goal, especially when linked to personal share option schemes as a major source of income: see generally ES Herman *Corporate Control, Corporate Power* (Cambridge: Cambridge University Press, 1981); David C Korten *When Corporations Rule the World* (West Hartford, Conn: Kumarian Books, 1996); Frank Partnoy *Infectious Greed: How Deceit and Risk Corrupted Financial Markets* (London: Profile Books, 2003) and Coffee above n 1.

[19] See Hadden above n 14; previous chapter at 326–31.

[20] See further Lord Wedderburn of Charlton 'The Legal Development of Corporate Responsibility: For Whom Will Corporate Managers be Trustees?' in K Hopt and G Teubner (eds) *Corporate Governance and Director's Liabilities, Legal Economic and Sociological Analyses on Corporate Social Responsibility* (Berlin: Walter de Gruyter, 1985) 3.

contrast the German dual board model has been supplemented by a mandatory allocation of seats on the supervisory board for workers representatives under the co-determination laws (*Mitbestimmung*).[21] Of significance in this respect are developments in the EC which have sought to enhance workers' access to information and participation in the decision-making structures of companies operating within the Community. These issues will be examined in turn.

(a) The Use of Outside or Non-Executive Directors

The principal aim of the board is to oversee the effective conduct of the company's business. It is not principally a regulator of the executive directors, a role traditionally assigned to the general meeting of shareholders.[22] However, in the light of Enron, a greater emphasis on its regulatory and monitoring function has arisen. In turn, this has highlighted the need for non-executive directors to act as the principal internal 'watchdogs' given that they are meant to be independent of executive managers and can be expected to offer an objective oversight of the company's decision-making and accounting and disclosure processes.[23]

In the light of this assumption, the first issue to examine is the concept of 'independence' to be applied to non-executives. Both US and UK regulators have developed revised definitions of independence, along broadly similar lines.[24] Thus the definition in the UK Higgs Review of the Role and Effectiveness of Non-Executive Directors, which is contained in the revised Combined Code of Corporate Governance, stresses several key criteria for the board to consider when determining whether an individual is sufficiently independent to hold a non-executive directorship. These include, in particular, independence of character and judgment and the absence of any relationships or circumstances that could affect, or

---

[21] See the Co-Determination Act 1976 (Mitbestimmungsgesetz) BGBl 1976 1153. German version available at <http://bundesrecht.juris.de/bundesrecht/mitbestg/gesamt.pdf>. The basic principle is that, for any stock corporation with over 2000 employees, 50 per cent of the seats on the supervisory board will be allocated to employee representatives: see s 7. This system is currently under some pressure to change: Hugh Williamson 'Beware, Union on Board? Why Germany's Worker Directors Need to Justify Their Jobs' *Financial Times* 30 August 2006 11.

[22] This section is an updated version of Peter T Muchlinski above n 1 at 736–44.

[23] The ensuing discussion focuses on US and UK reforms. The EC has left this issue mainly to national reform, though it intends to establish minimum EC standards concerning independence of directors. See further EC Commission *Modernising Company Law and Enhancing Corporate Governance in the European Union – A Plan to Move Forward* COM(2003) 284 final 21 May 2003, EC Commission *Recommendation on the role of (independent) non-executive or supervisory directors* (Consultation Document 5 May 2004) Commission Recommendation 2005/162/EC OJ [2005] L52/51 all available at <http://ec.europa.eu/internal_market/company/independence/index_en.htm>.

[24] EC Recommendation 2005/162 ibid offers a general approach stating, in art 13, that 'a director should be considered independent only if he is free from any business, family or other relationship with the company, its controlling shareholder, or the management of either that creates a conflict of interest such as to impair his judgment'. The ultimate determination of independence is left to the board. Annex II of the recommendation offers a more detailed analysis of the concept that closely follows the Higgs Review approach.

appear to affect, the director's judgment.[25] In a similar vein the New York Stock Exchange (NYSE) Corporate Governance Rules (the Rules) define an 'independent director' as one whom the board affirmatively determines, in its annual proxy statement or annual report, as having no material relationship with the listed company in question. The Rules go on to provide for certain bright line tests of independence based on matters pertaining to former employment with the company, the receipt of compensation other than directors' fees for past service to the company, family ties, ties with present or former internal auditors, subjection of earnings to the decisions of a compensation committee of another company, on which directors of the company in question sit as members, and payments for property or services from the company.[26]

Independence can be further protected by way of the regular turnover of non-executives so that they do not 'go native' and increasingly accept executive management perspectives on decision-making. Thus the Higgs Review recommended that non-executive directors serve no more than two consecutive three-year terms.[27] This was criticized as allowing for the loss of a non-executive director just at the time that they were developing a strong working knowledge of the company in question, and was in effect an arbitrary period.[28] As a result the UK Combined Code of Corporate Governance takes a more flexible view and, building on the Higgs proposal, allows for further service after the two three-year terms, subject to 'particularly rigorous review' which should 'take into account the need for progressive refreshing of the board'.[29] Further terms beyond nine years are permitted subject to annual re-election by the shareholders. Any service beyond nine years may be relevant to the determination of the non-executive director's independence.

---

[25] Derek Higgs *Review of the Role and Effectiveness of Non-Executive Directors* UK Department of Trade and Industry (London: January 2003) available at <http://www.dti.gov.uk/bbf/corp-governance/higgs-tyson/page23342.html> paragraph 9.11 and box at 37 (hereafter Higgs Review); *Combined Code on Corporate Governance* (London: July 2003 revised June 2006) paragraph A.3.1. available at http://www.frc.org.uk/documents/pagemanager/frc/Combined%20Code%20June%202006.pdf>. Such relationships or circumstances include where the director is a former employee until five years have ended after the termination of employment; has, or has had within the last three years, a business relationship with the company either directly or as a partner, shareholder, director or senior employee of a body that has such a relationship with the company; has received or receives additional remuneration from a company apart from a directors fee, participates in a company share option plan or performance related pay scheme, or is a member of the company's pension scheme; has close family ties with any of the company's advisers, directors, or senior employees; holds cross-directorships or has significant links with other directors through involvement in other companies or bodies; represents a significant shareholder or has served on the board for more than 10 years (reduced to nine years in the Combined Code).

[26] New York Stock Exchange *Final NYSE Corporate Governance Rules* (3 November 3 2004 as amended) at 4–6 available at <http://www.nyse.com/pdfs/section303A_final_rules.pdf>. For background see the *Report of the NYSE Corporate Accountability and Listing Standards Committee* 6 June 2002 available at <http://www.nyse.com>.   [27] Higgs Review above n 25 at paragraph 12.5.

[28] See further Stephen Griffin 'Corporate Collapse and the Reform of Boardroom Structures – Lessons from America' Insolvency L.J. 2003, 6 (November) 214–25.

[29] Combined Code of Corporate Governance above n 25 paragraph A.7.2.

Apart from the issue of independence, recent reforms and proposals have provided for means by which the powers of oversight enjoyed by non-executives could be strengthened. Central to this aim has been the requirement that an increased number of directors be non-executives. Here the US and UK approaches differ, in that the NYSE Rules demand that a majority of the directors be independent, while the Higgs Review recommended that at least half the board be non-executives.[30] According to the NYSE Rules, '[r]equiring a majority of independent directors will increase the quality of board oversight and lessen the possibility of damaging conflicts of interest'.[31] On the other hand, the increased number of independent directors can create the risk that the unitary board structure will be undermined, in that executive directors may take a more defensive approach to decision-making, precisely the kind of reaction that led the Enron executives to encourage a policy of non-disclosure to the board.[32] In addition, the requirement that the non-executive directors meet as a group without the presence of executive directors could further enhance the risk of the weakening of unitary structures.[33] Notwithstanding this risk, the Higgs Review expressly rejected a move towards the European style two-tier board structure.[34]

Had the Higgs Review recommended a move from the traditional Anglo-American unitary board structure, it is debatable whether that would have been more likely to protect against an Enron style scandal. It is equally possible for a determined chief executive to keep a supervisory board in the dark as it is for a unitary board.[35] Furthermore, such a structure has not prevented scandals from arising. Ahold had a two-tier board structure and this did not prevent the accounting abuses that arose in the course of its operations.[36] Nor has the two-tier structure prevented the development of a culture of accommodation between the supervisory and management boards of European companies following this approach.[37] Indeed the OECD Principles of Corporate Governance assert, 'there

[30] ibid at 4; Higgs Review above n 25 at paragraph A.3.5. The EC Recommendation above note 23 is more general and demands that there should be an appropriate balance between executive/managing and non-executive/supervisory directors, 'such that no individual or small group of individuals can dominate decision making of these bodies' (art 3.1). Note the reference to supervisory directors covers the European two-tier board structure on which see text below.   [31] ibid.

[32] See further Griffin above n 28.

[33] See Higgs Review above n 25 at paragraph 8.8. The NYSE Rules (above n 26 paragraph 3) require that all non-management directors must meet at regularly scheduled executive sessions without management being present.

[34] Higgs Review above n 25 at paragraph 1.7. The two-tier board is mandatory for publicly listed companies in Germany and the Netherlands but is an option in France: JE Parkinson *Corporate Power and Responsibility: Issues in the Theory of Company Law* (Oxford: Clarendon Press, 1993) at 191 n 125.

[35] For example, when Daimler Benz and Chrysler merged in May 1998, Jurgen Schrempp, the Daimler Benz chief executive at the time, only informed the supervisory board of the German company the day before the merger was announced, while the unitary board of Chrysler learnt of the plan in February 1998 and discussed negotiations throughout: 'The Way We Govern Now' *The Economist* 11 January 2003 61 at 62.   [36] 'Europe's Enron' *The Economist* 1 March 2003 63–64.

[37] For example the recent trial in Germany of certain Mannesmann directors, revealed a willingness on the part of non-executive directors to approve pay packages for executive directors, arising out

is no single model of good corporate governance' and that, 'they do not advocate any particular board structure and the term "board" as used in this document is meant to embrace different national models of board structures found in OECD and non-OECD countries'.[38]

A further element, designed to strengthen the role of non-executive directors, has involved a reassessment of the role of the senior non-executive director and their contact with shareholders. Thus Higgs recommends the retention of this position, even though it may conflict with that of the chief executive, especially where shareholders feel that existing means of contact with the chief executive have failed to resolve their concerns and they are then encouraged to refer to the senior non-executive.[39] The role of the chief executive has been further weakened in the approach taken to the appointment of non-executive directors. Thus both the NYSE Rules and the Higgs Review place the nomination process into the hands of independent directors.[40] This is open to the criticism that the experience of the chief executive and other executive directors may be under-represented if not entirely missing from the nomination process.[41] On the other hand, it would appear necessary as a precaution against the appointment of 'insider' non-executive directors who would take a favourable approach to executive management initiatives. Finally, it is now widely recognized that, in unitary board structures, the role of chief executive and chair of the board of directors should be held by separate persons.[42]

Turning to the international context in which non-executive directors of MNEs operate, the Higgs Review recommended that all companies operating in international markets should have at least one international non-executive director

of the takeover of Mannesmann by Vodaphone, which German prosecutors regarded as illegal. The accused, of whom four were non-executive directors, were acquitted in July 2004 but the case has been taken to appeal by the prosecutors. See further 'Court Clears Bosses Over Bonuses' *Financial Times* 23 July 2003 at 28, 'Appeal Lodged Against Trial Acquittals' *Financial Times* 24/25 July 2004, Money and Business at M6.

[38] OECD *Principles of Corporate Governance* above n 6 at 13. The EC has long abandoned a policy of harmonization of company law based on the two-tier structure as advocated in the now defunct draft Fifth Directive on Company Law. This was first proposed in 1972: OJ [1972] C131/49; greatly revised after consultations following the Commission Green Paper on Employee Participation and Company Structure in the European Communities (EC Bull Supp 8/75): OJ [1983] C240/2. Second Amendment: OJ [1991] C7/4; Third Amendment: OJ [1991] C321/9, both dealing with improved voting rights for shareholders. For analysis and comment, see Frank Wooldridge *Company Law in the United Kingdom and the European Community* (Athlone Press, 1991) 80–90; J Welch 'The Fifth Directive: a False Dawn' (1983) ELR 83; J Dine 'The Draft Fifth EEC Directive on Company Law' 10 Company Lawyer 10 (1989) and 'Implications for the United Kingdom of the EC Fifth Directive' 38 ICLQ 547 (1989); JJ Du Plessis and J Dine 'The Fate of the Fifth Directive on Company Law; Accommodation Instead of Harmonisation' [1997] JBL 23.

[39] Higgs Review above n 25 at paras 7.4–7.5.

[40] NYSE Rules above n 26 at 7–8; Higgs Review ibid paras 10.9–10.35; Combined Code above n 25 para A.2.1.   [41] See Griffin above n 28.

[42] OECD Principles of Corporate Governance above n 6 at 63–64. Higgs Review above n 25 at paras 5.3–5.5.

with relevant skills and experience.[43] In principle this is no doubt a good proposal. In practice, however, as the Enron case shows, the international character of the independent directors was no bar to their failure to act. Indeed, it may have contributed to their ineffectiveness due to the problems of arranging regular meetings and ensuring efficient information access.[44] On the other hand, having a more internationally representative board may assist in the scrutiny of MNE decisions from the perspective of the countries in which the firm operates, assuming that the non-executives will be from such countries. Here a significant issue arises. It is often said that MNEs fail to take account of local interests when making their business decisions, especially in relation to developing host countries. If the firm were to have non-executive board members from such countries then, perhaps, such interests would be more fully considered.

Such a possibility is not without obvious drawbacks, including the difficulty of selecting suitably qualified persons (although the requirements for induction and information for non-executive directors included in most reform proposals should deal with this issue), and making sure they attend meetings often far from home. There is the additional problem of maintaining a reasonable limit to board membership, while providing for an adequate range of country representation on the board. One possibility is to have a proportion of non-executives drawn from specific regions, representing the countries in a geographical area in which the firm operates. There may also be room for weighted representation in favour of nationals from the most important host countries in which the firm does business.

Should the board go down this route, the issue arises of how to coordinate the views of country, or regional, non-executive directors with those of executive directors in the affiliates of the various host countries. The latter may well feel that their authority is being side-stepped at parent company level, if the non-executive from their country is given too much influence over company decisions. In addition, a system of weighted representation poses the possible danger that the interests of the most important host countries will be over-represented at the expense of the interests of smaller host countries. Clearly, more thought needs to be given to such matters. On the other hand, a very undesirable outcome would be the internationalization of the pool of potential non-executives to those possessing the nationality of the major capital-exporting countries. This must be avoided. The issue of non-executive representation from both developed and developing host countries should be considered to be as pressing as the question of gender and ethnic imbalance in the boardroom, so far as MNEs are concerned.[45]

Apart from the general role of non-executive directors, their role in the composition and conduct of the audit committee represents the second major area of

[43] Higgs Review ibid at para 10.28.

[44] See further Peter T Muchlinski above n 1 at 728–29 and 'Governance Comes Under the Spotlight' *Financial Times* 28 January 2002 at 26.

[45] The Higgs Review above n 25 addressed the issues of gender and ethnic balance in chapter 10 at paras 10.20–10.25.

internal governance reform to arise out of the Enron scandal. In the UK this has led to a major review of the audit committee system, resulting in changes to the Combined Code of Corporate Governance.[46] In the US, the Sarbanes-Oxley Act provides a legislative footing for the regulation of audit committees that has been supplemented by the NYSE Corporate Governance Rules.[47] The EC has established common minimum standards for the creation, composition and role of the audit committee.[48]

The substantive reforms are broadly similar, aiming at a higher level of institutional independence, probity, and diligence in the activities of audit committees.[49] Thus the audit committee should contain at least three members composed of independent or non-executive directors,[50] and at least one member of the committee should have significant, relevant, and recent accounting experience.[51] As to their functions, these revolve around monitoring the integrity of the company's financial statements, the company's internal financial control system and internal audit process, and monitoring the performance of the external auditors, with particular concern for their independence, objectivity, and effectiveness.[52] It is for the audit committee to stand up to the executive management and external auditors where it feels that the audit process is deficient and will result in misleading accounts and statements being issued.[53]

In one important respect the US and UK approaches differ. The US rules are, as noted, based on mandatory legislative standards,[54] while the UK approach is to encourage voluntary compliance through observance of the Combined Code on a 'comply or explain' basis, in that companies are expected to comply with the code

[46] Sir Robert Smith *Guidance on Audit Committees* submitted to the Financial Reporting Council in December 2002 and published in January 2003 available at <http://www.frc.org.uk/documents/ pagemanager/frc/The%20Smith%20Guidance%20on%20Audit%20Committees%20June%2020 06.pdf>. The principal recommendations are incorporated into *The Combined Code of Corporate Governance* above n 25 at section C.3. Thus the text will discuss the Smith Report and Guidance as the source of UK standards in this area.

[47] Sarbanes-Oxley Act HR 3763, 107th Congress Second Session, 23 January 2002 s 301, NYSE Rules above n 26 paras 6 and 7 at 10–14.

[48] See Directive 2006/43/EC on statutory audits of annual accounts and consolidated accounts OJ [2006] L157/87.

[49] See Co-ordinating Group on Audit and Accounting Issues *Final Report to the Secretary of State for Trade and Industry and the Chancellor of the Exchequer* (URN 03/567 29 January 2003) paras 2.23–26.

[50] Smith Guidance above n 46 paras 2.1 and 2.3; NYSE Rules above n 26 paragraph 7(a) and (b). Section 301 of the Sarbanes-Oxley Act makes clear that such members must be independent members of the board of directors in that they may not accept any compensation from the company, other than in their capacity as a member of the audit committee, or be an affiliated person of the company or any of its subsidiaries.

[51] See further Smith Guidance ibid para 2.17; NYSE Rules ibid para 7(a) Commentary.

[52] Smith Guidance ibid n 46 para 2.2. NYSE Rules ibid para 7(c)(i)(A) and (B).

[53] Smith Guidance ibid paras 4.1–4.4.

[54] Under s 301 of the Sarbanes-Oxley Act failure to comply with the requirements of this section will result in an SEC ruling that the securities of the issuing company shall not be listed on national securities exchanges or national securities associations.

unless there are strong reasons for not doing so.[55] Departure from the code may be explained in company reports and statements and then it is for shareholders and others to judge the effects of this action.[56]

Thus, under s 301 of the Sarbanes-Oxley Act, the audit committee has a direct statutory responsibility:

for the appointment, compensation and oversight of the work of any registered public accounting firm employed by the issuer [of securities] (including resolution of disagreements between management and the auditor regarding financial reporting) for the purpose of preparing or issuing an audit report or related work, and each such registered public accounting firm shall report directly to the audit committee

This provision makes clear that it is up to the audit committee to resolve the kinds of issues that arose between Arthur Andersen and the Enron management, over the proper approach to the reporting of the activities of the so-called Special Purpose Entities (SPEs), that were used to take losses off the Enron balance sheet, and to secure the services of a truly independent external auditor.[57] By contrast, the UK approach is more informal. The audit committee is expected merely to make 'a recommendation on the appointment, reappointment and removal of the external auditors'. Should the board reject this recommendation it must give its reasons in the annual report.[58] Whether this approach, with its emphasis on the board as the ultimate employer of the external auditor, is sufficient to secure truly independent auditing services remains to be seen. It re-emphasizes the underlying faith in the UK for self-regulation over more formal statutory approaches.[59] However, the possible shortcomings of the UK position are not lost on policymakers. Accordingly, in their Final Report, the Co-ordinating Group on Audit and Accounting Issues, while stating that the case for bringing the operations of the audit committee under formal legislative provision had not been made out, recommended that a legal requirement for listed companies to have an audit committee should be considered again if the 'best practice, market driven approach of

---

[55] The 'comply or explain' approach is also advocated by the EC in relation to the rules on non-executive directors and corporate governance in general: see Recommendation 2005/162/EC above n 23 paras 1.1–1.2. However, the approach to statutory audit of listed companies is based on mandatory standards which was subject to unsuccessful opposition from the UK Confederation of British Industries (CBI) 'UK Business Lobby Loses Fight for Brussels Climbdown Over Audit Committee Reforms' *Financial Times* 15 October 2004 at 1.

[56] Combined Code above n 25 preamble at paras 4–5.

[57] It should be noted, however, that the issue of conflicts of interest between audit and non-audit work undertaken by the auditor is covered by the Sarbanes-Oxley Act itself and is not left to the audit committee, as it is under the UK Combined Code.

[58] Smith Guidance above n 46 para 4.17.

[59] The EC Directive 2006/43/EC above n 48, art 41(3), states that in public interest entities, which include major publicly listed companies, 'the proposal of the administrative body or supervisory board for the appointment of a statutory auditor or audit firm shall be based on a selection made by the audit committee'. This endorses a consultative rather than directive role in this process for the audit committee, in that the board's selection shall be based on, but need not follow, the audit committee's view.

the Combined Code proves ineffective in delivering the changes identified in the Smith Report and endorsed by us'.[60]

The enhancement of the supervisory role of the audit committee in Anglo-American law and practice also raises the issue of whether this is compatible with a unitary board structure. This was considered in the Smith Report.[61] Like the Higgs Review, the Smith Report supports the unitary board structure, on the grounds that it encourages collective responsibility for board decisions and allows for the non-executive directors to learn about the company's business. Accordingly, an audit committee that was separate from the board would be less effective than the conventional audit committee established as a sub-committee of the board. In addition the Smith Report felt that, as the main purpose of the audit committee was to give independent oversight of executive management that depended mostly on the independence of mind of its members rather than on any rule book or formula.

(b) Enhanced External Regulation of the Auditing Function

Apart from reforms in internal governance structures, a further feature of post-Enron reform has been the establishment of a stronger regime for the oversight of auditors and of the auditing process.[62] This has been led by the Sarbanes-Oxley Act, which may be seen as setting the regulatory agenda on this issue, given the economic power of the US in the global economy and the high level of foreign direct investment by foreign corporations in the US, many of which are listed on US securities markets. It is this underlying economic reality that has led to certain problems of extraterritoriality arising out of the legislation. By imposing its regulatory requirements on US and non-US companies and their auditors alike, the law has come into conflict with the legal requirements of other jurisdictions in this area, thereby posing a direct challenge to national policy approaches outside the US.

The principal reforms that Sarbanes-Oxley brought about can be summarized as follows.[63] First, it established the Public Company Accounting Oversight Board (PCAOB) to oversee the audit of companies subject to securities laws and to further the public interest in the preparation of informative accurate and independent audit reports for such companies.[64] In order to achieve these aims the PCAOB

---

[60] Co-ordinating Group on Audit and Accounting Issues above n 49 Conclusion 16 and paras 2.27–31.

[61] Smith Guidance above n 46 para 1.5 and see the original Smith Report of December 2002 at paras 19–26 at 24–25.

[62] This is an edited and updated version of Peter T Muchlinski above n 1 at 745–51.

[63] See, for a useful summary of the Sarbanes-Oxley Act, PN Saksena 'Accounting Fraud and the Sarbanes-Oxley Act' 15 (8) ICCLR 244–51(2004). In support of greater regulation under the Act see Lawrence A Cunningham 'The Sarbanes Oxley Yawn: Heavy Rhetoric, Light Reform (And it Might Just Work)' 35 Conn. LR 915 (2003); in opposition see Larry E Ribstein 'Market vs Regulatory Responses to Corporate Fraud: A Critique of the Sarbanes-Oxley Act' 28 J. Corp. L. 1 (2002–2003).

[64] See s 101.

has the duties of registering public accountancy firms in accordance with the criteria established under the Act,[65] to establish relevant standards of auditing quality control and ethics,[66] to conduct inspections of accountancy firms to assess compliance with the Act and its requirements,[67] and to conduct investigations and disciplinary procedures on the basis of fair procedural rules.[68] Secondly, the Act extends the operation of its requirements to foreign public accountancy firms that furnish an audit report with respect to any issuer of securities subject to SEC regulation.[69] The PCAOB may also extend the Act to firms that do not issue audit reports but which play a substantial role in the preparation and furnishing of such reports, thereby allowing for the regulation of overseas associates of the lead auditor of a MNE listed on US markets.[70] Thirdly, the Act introduces a statutory prohibition on audit firms making contemporaneous provision of certain services to the company that they are auditing, where that may lead to a possible conflict of interests.[71] Fourthly, the Act introduces certain statutory requirements for the proper conduct of the audit process. Thus, all audit work must be pre approved by the audit committee of the company concerned.[72] In addition, lead audit partners must be rotated every five years,[73] clear statements as to accounting policy used in the drawing up of the accounts must be made,[74] there must be no employment ties between the audit firm and the senior staff of the company being audited,[75] and the principal executive and financial officers of the company being audited must certify that all annual and quarterly reports do not, to their knowledge, contain any untrue statements and fairly represent the financial results and operating conditions of their company.[76] Any attempt by the senior executive, or any person acting under his or her direction, to take action to fraudulently influence, coerce, manipulate, or mislead any independent public or certified accountant into undertaking an audit of the financial statements, with the purpose of rendering such statements misleading, is rendered illegal.[77] Attorneys are also placed under a duty to report evidence of a material breach of securities law to the chief legal counsel of the company or, in the absence of an appropriate response, to the audit committee or to the non-executive directors of the board.[78]

In the UK the main response to these issues can be found in the Companies (Audit, Investigations and Community Enterprise) Act 2004.[79] This Act strengthens

---

[65] See s 101(c). According to s 102 it shall be unlawful for any person that is not a registered public accountancy firm to prepare or issue or to participate in the preparation or issue of an audit report in respect of any company issuing securities on US markets.   [66] See s 103.
[67] See s 104.   [68] See s 105.   [69] See s 106.   [70] Section 106(a)(2).
[71] See s 201. This includes the following services: bookkeeping, financial information, actuarial, internal audit outsourcing, management and human resources, broker, dealer, investment adviser, investment banking, legal or other expert services, and any other service the PCAOB determines by regulation to be impermissible. The SEC has issued detailed rules covering this requirement. See *Final Rules Strengthening the Commission's Requirements Regarding Auditor Independence* SEC Release No 33–8183 [68 FR 6006] 28 January 2003.   [72] See s 202.
[73] See s 203.   [74] See s 204.   [75] See s 206.   [76] See s 302.   [77] See s 303.
[78] See s 307.
[79] 2004 chapter 27 available at <http://www.opsi.gov.uk/acts/acts2004/20040027.htm>.

the control of auditors and the audit process, first, by increasing the powers of the Financial Reporting Review Panel (FRRP) to enforce good accounting standards, to require documents and to make reports in cases of defective accounts. The Act also increases the powers of the Inland Revenue to pass information on suspect accounts to the FRRP and imposes independent auditing standards, monitoring and disciplinary procedures on the professional accountancy bodies in the UK. It requires the disclosure by companies of non-audit services provided by their auditors but does not prohibit the provision of such services. The Act creates a strengthened right to information on the part of the auditor, which extends, through a duty of information placed upon the parent company and its officers towards the auditor of the parent company, to the non-UK based subsidiaries of the company concerned.[80] To further enhance the auditor's right to information, the Act makes it a criminal offence to fail to provide information or explanations required by the auditor, subject to a defence that it was not reasonably practicable for the person charged with the offence to provide the required information of explanations, and requires a statement in the directors' report that the directors are not aware of any relevant information of which the auditor is unaware and that they have taken all the steps they ought to have taken in order to make the auditor aware of such information, subject to a criminal sanction for making a false statement of this kind.[81]

This list appears, at first sight, to be similar to Sarbanes-Oxley, especially when taken together with the reforms introduced by the Higgs Review and Smith Report. However, the UK response remains, in essence, rooted in the culture of self-regulation. The FRRP powers come nowhere near those of the PCAOB, the

---

[80] See further s 500 of the Companies Act 2006:

'Auditor's right to information from overseas subsidiaries

(1) Where a parent company has a subsidiary undertaking that is not a body corporate incorporated in the United Kingdom, the auditor of the parent company may require it to obtain from any of the following persons such information or explanations as he may reasonably require for the purposes of his duties as auditor.
(2) Those persons are—
   (a) the undertaking;
   (b) any officer, employee or auditor of the undertaking;
   (c) any person holding or accountable for any of the undertaking's books, accounts or vouchers;
   (d) any person who fell within paragraph (b) or (c) at a time to which the information or explanations relates or relate.
(3) If so required, the parent company must take all such steps as are reasonably open to it to obtain the information or explanations from the person concerned.
(4) A statement made by a person in response to a requirement under this section may not be used in evidence against him in criminal proceedings except proceedings for an offence under section 491.
(5) Nothing in this section compels a person to disclose information in respect of which a claim to legal professional privilege (in Scotland, to confidentiality of communications) could be maintained in legal proceedings.'

By s 501(4) if a parent company fails to comply with section 490, an offence is committed by the company, and every officer of the company who is in default.

[81] ibid Part I Chapter 2 ss 8–18.

provision of non-audit services by auditors is not specifically prohibited, the accounting profession still remains mostly in control of standards, the criminal penalties imposed by the Act are weak by comparison to the US penalties, and there are no equivalent rights of action for private persons or for securities class actions.[82] Equally, UK policy on audit rotation accepts the Sarbanes-Oxley standard on lead auditor rotation, but is opposed to the mandatory rotation of audit firms or the mandatory re-tendering of audit engagements, matters which the SEC had tried to include in its proposed regulations on this issue.[83] The final version of the SEC rules has retreated in part from this position but is still more demanding than corresponding UK policy.[84]

The European approach is also more restrained than that of Sarbanes-Oxley, while apparently following certain of its provisions. The essence of the EC Directive on Statutory Audit is to place such audits of annual and consolidated accounts on a stronger legal footing.[85] It aims to replace the Eighth Directive on Company Law,[86] which did not include requirements on how a statutory audit should be carried out. The approach taken is not wholly a reaction to Enron and other scandals in Europe, but grows out of the policy aim of harmonizing statutory audit that was first agreed in 1996. However, the directive makes clear that its content has been adapted to take account of the most recent scandals. In particular it requires that the auditor of a group of companies takes full responsibility for the audit report on the consolidated accounts of the group[87] (a direct response to the Parmalat case[88]) and, as noted above, the establishment of an independent audit committee for all 'public interest entities'. In addition, the directive contains an elaboration of the principle of auditor independence, including controls over the conduct of non-audit business.

At present the directive requires Member States to ensure that an auditor shall not carry out an audit if they are not independent, as where they take non-audit work.[89] The directive also requires Member States to introduce systems of quality assurance, leaving the precise approach to be taken to their discretion on the basis of the principles set down in the directive.[90] Furthermore, an element of public oversight over the accounting profession is required.[91] While following the same policy prescription as Sarbanes-Oxley, the EC proposal is much weaker, in that

[82] See J Friedland 'Sarbanes-Oxley Makes Waves in the United Kingdom' 25 Company Lawyer 162 (2004).
[83] See 'DTI Alarm Over Tough US Rules on Auditor Rotation' *Financial Times* 7 January 2003 at 3 and Co-Ordination Group on Audit and Accounting Issues above n 49 at paras 1.20–1.30.
[84] See SEC Rules above n 71.   [85] Directive 2006/43/EC above n 48.
[86] Council Directive 84/253/EEC of 10 April 1984, OJ [1984] L126/20.
[87] Directive 2006/43/EC above n 48 art 27.
[88] See Press Release IP/04/340 16 March 2004 available at <http://europa.eu.int>.
[89] Directive 2006/43/EC above n 48 art 22 and preamble at 11. If adopted this would require a similar prohibition in UK law, which, as noted above, does not at present envisage such a prohibition.
[90] ibid art 29.   [91] ibid art 32.

the standards set down in Article 32 of the directive will be a minimum requirement for effective public oversight at Member State level and not a detailed
prescriptive scheme. There will be no Europe-wide oversight body. In relation to
the substantive auditing standards that will apply, the directive follows a harmonization approach with the adoption, by the EC, of the International Standards
on Auditing (ISAs) established by the International Auditing and Assurance
Standards Board (IAASB). There is little additional discretion left to the Member
States in that they may only impose additional audit procedures if these follow
from specific requirements relating to the scope of the statutory audit.[92]

A further feature of the EC directive is its approach to the extraterritorial
effects of Sarbanes-Oxley. In response to the EC's concerns about the extraterritorial reach of Sarbanes-Oxley,[93] the directive requires the registration, in the EU, of
auditors and/or audit firms that issue audit reports in relation to securities traded
in the EU, and for these to be subject to Member State systems of oversight quality assurance, investigations, and sanctions. Only auditors or audit firms that meet
quality criteria equivalent to those in the directive can be registered.[94] Exemption
from this requirement is possible only where the auditor or audit firm is subject to
an equivalent system of registration and oversight in its home country.[95] This will
avoid regulatory overlap between the EU and the home country by permitting
home country regulation to prevail. This is offered only on strict conditions of
reciprocity, requiring equivalent treatment in the home country of auditors or
audit firms from all EU Member States. The policy behind this proposal is clear.
Given the registration requirement imposed on EU based auditors and audit
firms providing audits of US listed companies under the Sarbanes-Oxley Act, the
EU has established an equivalent system of registration, subject to an exemption
requirement based on equivalence of regulatory standards and reciprocal treatment. This will only work if the US agrees to exempt EU based auditors and firms
from registration and regulation under Sarbanes-Oxley by accepting that the EU
standards are equivalent to those in the US, and by deferring to EU home country
regulation under the oversight system of the Member State from which the auditor or firm originates, that system being based on EU-wide criteria as settled in the
directive. It is debatable whether the EC standards are in fact the equivalent of
Sarbanes-Oxley, given that they aim to harmonize Member State policy at a *minimum* level, so as to take into account different approaches to regulation and the
actual levels of development of various national capital markets. It remains to be
seen how these matters will be resolved in practice.

[92] ibid art 26(3).
[93] On which see Press Release IP/03/571 24 April 2003 available at <http://europa.eu.int>.
[94] Directive 2006/43/EC above n 48 arts 44 and 45.
[95] ibid art 45. The requirement of equivalence has caused much concern among Japanese companies 'Accounting Fears Make Japan Wary of Europe' *Financial Times* 8 December 2004 at 11.

(c) European Initiatives for Employee Consultation and Information

The European approach to corporate accountability has gone beyond the limited Anglo-American concerns that have focused on the protection of the shareholder.[96] In particular, the EC has stressed the need for a new organization of corporate structures which can inter alia accommodate the interests of workers as a distinct group of stakeholders in the corporation, building on the experience of certain Member States, particularly Holland and Germany, in the operation of 'co-determination' laws.[97] EC policy has evolved along two distinct but complementary lines. The first seeks to ensure employee access to information and decision-making through changes in internal corporate structures, while the second involves attempts to introduce general rights of information and consultation of employees into the existing structures and operations of complex transnational undertakings.

The first approach is exemplified by the now defunct draft Fifth Directive on Company Law which contained detailed rules on worker participation that sought to reconcile the 'co-determination' approach with the 'arm's length collective bargaining' approach favoured in the UK.[98] The second approach is contained in the various proposals, put forward since 1980, that sought to institute the provision of information and consultation of workers in undertakings operating in more than one Member State. The first attempt was contained in what is commonly called the 'Vredeling Directive' in 1980.[99] This required international management in the parent company of a transnational undertaking every six months to 'forward relevant information to the management of its subsidiaries in the Community giving a clear picture of the activities of the dominant undertaking and its subsidiaries as a whole'.[100] In addition, the proposal contained duties

---

[96] Wedderburn above n 20 at 18–20.

[97] See Erika Szyszczak *EC Labour Law* (Harlow: Longman, 2000) 44–46; Brian Bercusson *European Labour Law* (London: Butterworths, 1996) chs 19–20 (new edn expected 2007 with Cambridge University Press). On 'co-determination' in Europe, see F Fabricius 'A Theory of Co-Determination' in CM Schmitthoff (ed) *The Harmonisation of European Company Law* (1973) 138; S Simitis 'Workers' Participation in the Enterprise – Transcending Company Law?' 38 MLR 1 (1975).

[98] Above n 38.

[99] Proposal for a Council Directive on procedure for informing and consulting employees of undertakings with complex structures, in particular transnational undertakings (the so-called 'Vredeling Proposal'): OJ [1980] C297/3 also reproduced in 21 ILM 422 (1982); revised in 1983: see EC Bulletin Supplement 2/83, and for revised text see: OJ [1983] C217/3. See further J Pipkorn 'The Draft Directive on Procedures for Informing and Consulting Employees' 20 CMLR 725 (1983); C Docksey 'Employee Information and Consultation Rights in the Member States of the European Communities' 6 Comparative Labour Law 32 (1985) and ibid 'Information and Consultation of Employees: The United Kingdom and the Vredeling Directive' 49 MLR 281 (1986); G Hamilton *The Vredeling Proposal and Multinational Trade Unionism* Centre for Multinational Studies, Occasional Paper No 11, September 1983; T De Vos *Multinational Corporations in Democratic Host Countries: US Multinationals and the Vredeling Proposal* (Dartmouth, 1989).

[100] ibid 1980 Text art 5(1). For a list of the matters that had to be disclosed, see art 5(2).

of information and consultation on any decision which was liable to have substantial effect on the interests of the subsidiary's employees.[101] The 1980 draft produced a strong counter-reaction from both European and non-European MNEs.[102] The result was a watered down version in 1983. Adoption of the revised proposal required unanimity in the EC Council. This was not forthcoming due, in particular, to the opposition of the UK Government.[103] As a result, despite efforts to keep the proposal alive, it was shelved.[104]

The Vredeling proposal was superseded by a proposal for the establishment of a European Works Council (EWC) in Community-scale undertakings. This sought to achieve information and consultation of employees by means of a distinct institutional system, that stopped short of worker participation on managing boards, but which sought the establishment of a forum, within the firm, for such information and consultation to occur.[105] The original proposal did not achieve the unanimity required for its adoption, due in large measure to the opposition of the UK. The Commission responded by offering a watered down version of the EWC Directive, which allows for more use of voluntary arrangements agreed between workers and employers at company level.[106] The basic object of informing and consulting employees in Community-scale undertakings[107] or groups of undertakings[108] is to be achieved through the establishment, by agreement, in every such undertaking, of a EWC or a procedure for informing and consulting employees.[109] The scope, composition, competence, and mode of operation of the EWC or procedure is to be determined by means of a written agreement between the

---

[101] ibid art 6.

[102] For an account of this opposition and the resulting lobbying of the EC Commission and Parliament by MNEs, see the works by Hamilton and De Vos above n 99.

[103] See further De Vos ibid at 209–12.

[104] For detailed analysis, see further De Vos ibid at 217–40.

[105] Proposal for a Council Directive on the establishment of a European Works Council in Community-scale undertakings or groups of undertakings for the purposes of informing and consulting employees: see OJ [1991] C39/10 COM (90) 581 final; amended proposal OJ [1991] C336/11 COM(91) 345 final.

[106] Proposal for a Council Directive on the establishment of European committees or procedures in Community-scale undertakings and Community-groups of undertakings for the purposes of informing and consulting employees COM(94) 134 final-94/0113(PRT) OJ [1994] C135/8. See, for background, 'Brussels Retreat on Works Councils' *Financial Times* 4 February 1994 at 2; 'Brussels to Draft Works Directive' *Financial Times* 31 March 1994 at 3. The proposal was adopted as Council Directive 94/451/EC on 22 September 1994: OJ [1994] L254/64 as amended by Council Directive 97/74/EC extending the EWC Directive to the United Kingdom OJ [1998] L10/22. Consolidated text available at <http://eur-lex.europa.eu/LexUriServ/site/en/consleg/1994/L/01994L0045–19980205-en.pdf>.

[107] Defined as 'any undertaking with at least 1000 employees within the Member States and at least 150 employees in each of at least two Member States' ibid art 2(1)(a).

[108] Defined as 'a group of undertakings with the following characteristics:
— at least 1000 employees within the Member States,
— at least two group undertakings in different Member States, and
— at least one group undertaking with at least 150 employees in one Member State and at least one other group undertaking with at least 150 employees in another Member State.' ibid art 2(1)(c).

[109] ibid art 1(2).

central management of the Community-scale undertaking or, in the case of a Community-scale group, the controlling undertaking,[110] and a special negotiating body drawn from and elected by representatives of employees of the undertaking or group.[111] This procedure may be initiated by the central management or upon the written request of at least 100 employees or their representatives in at least two undertakings or establishments in at least two different Member States.[112] The special negotiating body may decide by a two-thirds vote not to open negotiations or to terminate negotiations already opened. A new request may be made for the renewal of negotiations after two years have elapsed since this decision.[113] In the absence of an agreement being concluded, or where the parties so decide, the subsidiary requirements laid down by legislation in the Member State in which the central management is situated shall apply. These subsidiary requirements must conform to the rules contained in the Annex to the directive.[114] The minimum standards laid down in the Annex relate to the competence, composition, and rights to information and consultation to be enjoyed by a EWC.

The EWC Directive is expressly linked to the Community Charter of the Fundamental Social Rights of Workers, in that the preamble of the directive refers to point 17 of the charter, which states:

Information, consultation and participation for workers must be developed along appropriate lines, taking account of the practices in force in the various Member States. This

---

[110] Defined in art 3(1) as an 'undertaking which can exercise a dominant influence over another undertaking ("the controlled undertaking") by virtue, for example, of ownership, financial participation or the rules which govern it'. Article 3(2) goes on to say that dominant influence will be presumed where an undertaking, directly or indirectly, owns a majority of another undertaking's subscribed capital, or controls a majority of the votes attached to that undertaking's issued share capital or can appoint more than half of the members of that undertaking's board or supervisory board. In the case where the central management of an undertaking or controlling undertaking is located outside the Community, the responsibility to set up a EWC or information and consultation procedure will lie with its representative agent or with the management of the undertaking, or group undertaking, employing the largest number of employees in a Member State: ibid art 4(2). The non-EC based controlling undertaking is under an obligation to provide all the necessary information to the representative agent or largest EU based group undertaking so as to enable it to fulfil the requirements of the EWC Directive: *Gesamtbetriebsrat der Kuhne & Nagel AG & Co KG v Kuhne & Nagel AG & Co KG* Case C–440/00 [2004] 2 CMLR 1242. The fact that a group is organized on the basis of parity between the participating companies, without any dominant undertaking or hierarchical relations between them and with central management exercised through a steering committee rather than a central controlling company, does not absolve the group from discharging its obligation to enter into negotiations for the establishment of a EWC if it meets the size and location thresholds of the EWC Directive: Case C–62/99 *Betriebsrat der Bofrost* Josef H. Boquoi Deutschland West GMBH & Co KG v Bofrost* Josef H Boquoi Deutschland West GMBH & Co KG* [2004] 2 CMLR 1223.

[111] ibid art 5(1). The negotiating body must include at least one employee from each Member State. The resulting agreement shall determine the scope and composition of the EWC, the number of members, the allocation of seats, and the method and duration of appointment or election of members; the functions and powers of the European committee; the procedure for informing and consulting the EWC; the place, frequency, and duration of meetings of the EWC; the financial and material resources to be allocated to the EWC; the duration of the agreement and the procedure for its renegotiation: ibid art 6(2).   [112] ibid art 5(1).

[113] ibid art 5(5).   [114] ibid art 7.

shall apply especially in companies or groups of companies having establishments or companies in two or more Member States of the European Community.

The aim behind the EWC is to ensure that such rights are protected in the process of international business restructuring likely to follow from the completion of the European Internal Market. It is put forward in the belief that national procedures for informing and consulting workers are 'often not geared to the transnational structure of the entity which takes the decisions affecting those employees', and that 'this may lead to unequal treatment of employees affected by decisions within one and the same undertaking, or group of undertakings'. Furthermore, the EWC is deemed necessary to ensure proper information and consultation in cases where the employees concerned are affected by a decision taken outside the Member State in which they are employed.[115] The EWC Directive became binding in all Member States, except the UK, under the social provisions of the Maastricht Treaty on 22 September 1996. Indeed, the UK remained firmly opposed to worker participation and information measures, arguing that they would do no more than undermine economic growth and employment opportunities in the EC.[116] Upon the accession of the Labour government in May 1997, one of its first acts was to remove the opt-out from the Social Chapter of the Maastricht Treaty, paving the way for the adoption of the EWC Directive, which was put into operation for the UK by the 1997 amending directive.[117]

A scheme of employee participation was also put forward in the context of the proposed Statute for a European Company.[118] In 2001, when the European Company (*Societas Europaea SE*) Statute was adopted, the issue of worker participation was covered in an accompanying directive.[119] The reason for this separate treatment is given in the directive as follows:

The great diversity of rules and practices existing in the Member States as regards the manner in which employees' representatives are involved in decision-making within companies makes it inadvisable to set up a single European model of employee involvement applicable to the SE.

---

[115] ibid preamble.

[116] See the UK Government White Paper 'Employment for the 1990s' Cm 540 (1988) at paras 2.20–2.21. The UK was excluded from any future deliberations and adopted measures concerning the social provisions of the Maastricht Treaty. However, the compromise arrived at did not rule out a reconsideration of the British position at a future date: see Maastricht Treaty 7 February 1992 Protocol on Social Policy: 31 ILM 247 at 357 (1992).

[117] Directive 97/74/EC above n 106. See 'First Steps Taken Towards Social Chapter' *Financial Times* 6 May 1997 at 10.

[118] Proposal for a Directive on Employee Participation in the European Company COM(89) 268 Final – SYN 219 25 August 1989.

[119] See Council Regulation (EC) 2157/2001 of 8 October 2001 OJ [2001] L294/1 art 1(4) and Council Directive 2001/86/EC of 8 October 2001 OJ [2001] L294/22. On the procedure for setting up an SE, see ch 2 at 72–73. See also Directive 2005/56/EC of the European Parliament and of the Council of 26 October 2005 on cross-border mergers of limited liability companies OJ [2005] L310/1 art 16 on the extension of the rules in Directive 2001/86/EC to certain classes of cross-border mergers to which national laws on worker participation do not apply. See <http://eur-lex.europa. eu/smartapi/cgi/sga_doc?smartapi!celexplus!prod!DocNumber&lg=en&type_doc=Directive&an_doc =2005&nu_doc=56>.

Nevertheless, information and consultation procedures at transnational level should be ensured in all cases of creation of an SE. Thus firms establishing an SE are urged to set up a special negotiating body as soon as possible after entering into the process of creating the SE, whether by merger or the establishment of a new holding company.[120] That body will enter into a written agreement with employee representatives on arrangements for the involvement of employees within the SE.[121] The membership of the negotiating body must comply with the rules laid down in Article 3(2), and with the applicable national laws on election of employee representatives to such a body, to ensure that there is even representation for all member states and all undertakings involved. The representative body must be set up in accordance with the standard rules contained in the Annex to the directive, and these are to be instituted in the national laws of the Member States.[122] Where the SE is a Community-scale undertaking or the controlling undertaking of a Community-scale group, it will be exempt from the provisions of the EWC Directive, unless the special negotiating body decides not to adopt an agreement on employee involvement.[123]

It is unclear how far the various EC initiatives actually result in improved consultation and information of employees. However, they do introduce a minimum requirement to consult and inform. This means that managers must provide the requisite information in accordance with the procedures laid down in the EC directives, or face the remedies imposed by the national laws into which these directives have been transposed.[124] Equally, the EWC may create an opportunity for workers' representatives to delay management decisions and thereby to secure a degree of indirect influence over them.[125] That said the use of directives leaves the process of implementation to the Member States. They only have to offer a minimal level of compliance, by ensuring that the standards set down in the directives are reflected in national laws and regulations. Given the differing traditions of employee participation in the various Member States, local variations in the nature and extent of application are likely. Indeed, it is arguable that these European level initiatives are actually weakening much stronger national 'co-determination' processes.[126] Furthermore, increased global competition, and the apparent rise of the Anglo-American market based model of corporate governance, may have an effect of further weakening traditions of 'co-determination' in Europe, though

---

[120]   Directive 2001/86/EC art 3(1).

[121]   ibid art 3(3). The content of the agreement must comply with the requirements listed in art 4.

[122]   ibid art 7(1).   [123]   ibid art 13.

[124]   The EWC Directive above n 106, art 11(1) and (3) lays down the Member State requirements in this regard including adequate administrative and judicial remedies for non-compliance. See also Directive 2001/86/EC above n 119 art 12 to the same effect, although it mentions legal rather than judicial procedures.   [125]   Bercusson above n 97 at 300–301.

[126]   See further Berndt Keller 'The European Company Statute: Employee Involvement and Beyond' 33 Industrial Relations Journal 424 (2002).

this process is an uneven one, and it is not yet possible to say that such convergence has taken place.[127]

(3) Disclosure by MNEs in Annual Accounts and Other Statements

Corporate disclosure by MNEs in annual accounts and other financial statements raises special problems not encountered by purely national enterprises. In particular, MNEs will face differing national disclosure requirements in home and host states, all of which have to be met. Furthermore, the creation of useful financial information will be more difficult than for purely national companies. Accounting practices differ considerably between states, resulting in financial information that may be hard to compare.[128] Comparability will be further hindered by the fact that MNEs will earn their profits in different currencies. Thus, the need arises to devise methods of transnational accounting and foreign currency translation, both for the drawing up of accounts within the MNE and for comparing the performance of different MNEs. Furthermore, as corporate groups, MNEs will be required to produce consolidated accounts for their worldwide profits and losses. Given the foregoing factors the difficulties surrounding this exercise are considerable. New complications are added by growing requirements for segmental reporting, and for social disclosure aimed, not at investors, but at other constituencies representing wider social and political interests as described in section (1) above. Moreover, new reporting devices, such as value-added statements, showing the economic contribution of the MNE to a given host state, and environmental audits, showing the environmental impact of the enterprise's activities, have been instituted.

In response to these problems international organizations have sought to introduce harmonized financial reporting requirements for multinational groups.[129] The greatest progress has been made by the EC through the introduction of the Fourth and Seventh Directives on Company Law, as amended, which have created, respectively, more uniform disclosure standards for single unit companies and for corporate groups operating within the EC.[130] In addition, since 1 January 2005 all

---

[127] See Tony Edwards 'Corporate Governance, Industrial Relations and Trends in Company Level Restructuring in Europe: Convergence Towards the Anglo-American Model?' 35 Industrial Relations Journal 518 (2004).

[128] For a full discussion of such differences, see Christopher Nobes and Robert Parker *Comparative International Accounting* (Harlow: FT Prentice-Hall, 8th edn, 2004) especially chs 2, 3, Part II 'Country Studies' and ch 17. See also UNCTC *International Accounting and Reporting Issues 1991 Review* (UN, New York: 1992 UN Doc ST/CTC/124) Chapter II for a review of the accounting and reporting laws and practices of 44 states.

[129] See further UNCTAD (ISAR) Review of Practical Implementation Issues of International Financial Reporting Standards UN Doc TD/B/COM.2/ISAR 28 21 October 2005.

[130] Fourth Council Directive 78/660/EEC of 25 July 1978 on the annual accounts of certain types of companies OJ [1978] L222/11; Seventh Council Directive 83/349/EEC of 13 June 1983 on

public listed companies in the EC have had to comply with the International Accounting Standards (IAS) issued by the International Accounting Standards Board (IASB).[131] Furthermore, the UN Intergovernmental Working Group of Experts on International Standards of Accounting and Reporting (ISAR) has worked, since 1982, on the harmonization of international accounting standards. It published, in 1988, its Conclusions on Accounting and Reporting by Transnational Corporations, as a contribution to the harmonization process. This stated, in the form of a code of principles, ISAR's recommendations as to the best standards of accounting practice that should be adopted in the effort to create uniform and informative disclosure requirements for MNEs.[132] Since then it has worked on more specific questions relating to the process of harmonization including: promoting small and medium sized enterprise development, qualification requirements of accountants, corporate governance, disclosure of the impact of corporations on society, environmental accounting and reporting, and capacity building for developing countries.[133]

The legal aspects of MNE disclosure will be discussed under four major subheadings. First, the problem of consolidated accounts will be considered, with particular emphasis on the provisions of the Seventh EC Directive and IAS 27 as the foremost attempts at international harmonization. This section will also consider the effects of the Enron scandal upon reform of consolidation rules. Secondly, segmented disclosure will be discussed, with emphasis on the difficulties that are inherent in the production of disaggregated information on a worldwide basis. Thirdly, the special difficulties of social and environmental disclosure will be considered. Finally, the problems of foreign currency translation will be briefly described, although these issues are more fully within the concerns of accountancy than company law.

---

consolidated accounts OJ [1983] L193/1 as amended by Directive 2003/51/EC OJ [2003] L178/16 which permits the application of IAS to the preparation of accounts under the Fourth and Seventh Directives. See further text at nn 137–77 below.

[131] See further EC Regulation 1606/2002 on the application of international accounting standards of 19 July 2002: OJ [2002] L243/1 art 4. In preparation for this major harmonization measure, the EC adopted Regulation 1725/2003 which endorsed all the IAS and their related interpretations (SICs) except IAS 32 (on disclosure and presentation of financial instruments) and IAS 39 (on recognition and measurement of financial instruments) which are still under discussion by the IASB: EC Regulation 1725/2003 endorsing International Accounting Standards of 29 September 2003 OJ [2003] L261/1 and see Press Release IP/03/1297 29 September 2003 available at <http://europa.eu.int>. See also EC Regulation 707/2004 amending Regulation 1725/2003 of 6 April 2004 OJ [2004] L111/3 which adopts International Financial Reporting Standard (IFRS) 1 designed to provide improved procedures for first time users of IFRS. On the IASB, see Nobes and Parker above n 128 ch 5.

[132] UNCTC *Conclusions on Accounting and Reporting by Transnational Corporations* (UN, New York: 1988, UN Doc ST/CTC/9).

[133] See ISAR 'Current Activities' at <http://www.unctad.org/Templates/Page.asp?intItemID=2906&lang=1>. See generally the ISAR Annual Reviews of International Accounting and Reporting Issues available at <http://www.unctad.org/Templates/Page.asp?intItemID=2911&lang=1>.

(a) Consolidated Financial Statements

Consolidated financial statements emerged with the rise of the holding company as a significant form of business organization.[134] Their aim is to provide information on the financial performance and future prospects of the group as an economic entity. Thus, consolidated statements aggregate the financial information on each legal entity in the group into a single set of data.[135] In relation to MNEs, this process will occur on an international level.

In the present legal and accounting environment, the practice of consolidating MNE accounts is still evolving. Certain national laws require consolidated information on the worldwide activities of MNEs whose parent is based in the country. The UK and US have led the way, being the first countries to have evolved consolidated disclosure rules.[136] Continental European countries began to introduce consolidated accounting rules for groups in the 1980s, spurred on by the initiative of the Seventh EC Company Law Directive.[137] The IASB has contributed through the issuing, in 1976, of International Accounting Standard No 3 (IAS 3) on consolidated financial statements. This has since been replaced by IAS 27.[138] Nonetheless, considerable national and regional disparities remain. It is not possible to give a comprehensive analysis of all the major national systems in a work of

---

[134] See Nobes and Parker above n 128 at 373–74.   [135] ibid at 374–75.

[136] Disclosure in the US is governed by the reporting requirements established by the Securities Exchange Commission under the Securities Act 1933 and the Securities Exchange Act 1934. The major reporting requirements for US firms are to be found in SEC Regulation S–X (17 CFR pt 210) available at <http://www.access.gpo.gov/nara/cfr/waisidx_06/17cfr210_06.html>. See A Gutterman *Regulatory Aspects of the Initial Public Offering of Securities* 60 CPS (BNA 1991) especially at A–65 to A–67. The presentation of consolidated and combined financial statements is governed by art 3A of Regulation S–X. This regulation has been adapted for use by foreign MNEs that issue securities within the US. In the UK consolidated disclosure is covered in ss 227–232 and Schedules 4A and 5 of the Companies Act 1985 as amended by the Companies Act 1989. These amended provisions introduce the requirements of the Seventh EC Directive on Company Law into English law. For full analysis, see N Furey and D Parkes *The Companies Act 1989: A Practitioners' Guide* (Jordans, 1990). A shorter summary can be found in Gower and Davies above n 15 at 206–209 or Wooldridge above n 38 at 54–68. See also the Companies Act 2006 ss 403–414 which introduce the requirement to use IAS in group accounts in accordance with EC provisions available at <http://www.opsi.gov.uk/acts/acts2006/ukpga_20060046_en.pdf>.

[137] See France: Law No 85–11 of 3 January 1985 JO 4 January 1985 at 101; Germany: Bilanzrichtlinengesetz 19 December 1985 BGBl1.2355; Greece: Presidential Decrees No 409/86 8 November 1986 and No 419/86 10 December 1986; Luxembourg: Law of 11 July 1988 Memorial JO A No 45 of 18 August 1988; Spain: Law 19/1989 of 25 July 1989 and Decree Law 1564l/89; Belgium: Royal Decree 90/763 of 27 March 1990 *Moniteur Belge* 27 March 1990 5675.

[138] IAS 27 Consolidated and Separate Financial Statements issued December 2003 applicable to annual periods beginning on or after 1 January 2005. See, for discussion, Nobes and Parker above n 128 ch 16 and 'Understanding the IFRS' *Financial Times* Supplement 29 September 2004. For all current versions of the IAS, see IASB *International Financial Reporting Standards* (London: Lexis-Nexis Publishers, 2006 annually updated) and the IASB website where free summaries are available and access to the text of the IAS is by subscription: <http://www.iasb.org>. Other IAS relevant to the issue of group accounting include IAS 14 on segment reporting, IAS 31 interests in joint ventures, IAS 24 related party disclosures.

this size.[139] Rather, a sense of the legal problems created by demands for consolidated disclosure by MNEs can be given through a brief examination of the genesis and evolution of the Seventh EC Directive.[140]

The original proposal, introduced in 1976, was explicit in its aims. According to the Commission's explanatory memorandum:

The harmonization of national laws on group accounts would also make a contribution to the work currently in progress at various levels to take better account of the situation relating to multinational companies and, if possible, to provide an appropriate legal framework for them. Following this process of harmonization, multinational companies having their registered offices in the Community will be required to draw up and publish clear and complete information which will ensure that their relationships with other group companies, as well as their activities, will be clearly visible. Such companies will have to publish consolidated accounts covering all their affiliated companies throughout the world and drawn up on the basis of principles and methods of consolidation which are uniformly applicable throughout the Community. These provisions also apply to multinational companies having their registered offices outside the Community as far as their activities through companies established in the Community (sub-groups) are concerned.[141]

Contrary to these initial objectives, complete harmonization did not prove possible. The Seventh Directive allows for certain important matters to be introduced at the option of the Member State in its implementing legislation, as will be seen below. Nor has the directive achieved maximum information disclosure by MNEs, given the wide-ranging exemptions from the duty to consolidate that it contains. Nonetheless, the directive represents a significant advance in that it has made the hitherto predominantly Anglo-American practice of consolidated disclosure into the Community standard to be adopted by Member States who had not, as yet, imposed legal requirements for consolidation of group accounts.[142]

The Seventh Directive seeks to ensure that the consolidated accounts of EC based groups 'shall give a true and fair view of the assets, liabilities, financial position and profit or loss of the undertakings included therein taken as a whole'.[143] To achieve this, the Seventh Directive extends the formats of accounts and valuation rules applicable to individual companies under the Fourth Directive[144] to groups of companies.[145] It also introduces prescribed consolidation techniques. These can only be listed here, as they are more appropriately discussed in specialized accounting texts.[146] Full consolidation is required for subsidiary undertakings

---

[139] On which see generally Nobes and Parker above n 128 and UNCTC 1992 above n 128.

[140] Above n 130. See Sharon M McKinnon *The Seventh Directive: Consolidated Accounts in the EEC* (Kluwer/Arthur Young International, 1984) chs 1–3; M Petite 'The Conditions for Consolidation Under the 7th Company Law Directive' 21 CMLR 81 (1984); TE Cooke 'The Seventh Directive – An Accountant's Perspective' 9 ELR 143 (1984).   [141] See Bull EC Supp 9/76 (1976) at 19.

[142] For detailed analysis of individual country positions prior to the enactment of the directive see McKinnon above n 140 chs. 4–14; see also Cooke above n 140 at 151–160.

[143] Seventh Directive above n 130 art 16(3).

[144] OJ [1978] L222/11. See further Companies Act 1985 s 226 and Schedule 4 which implement the requirements of the Fourth Directive into English law.

[145] Seventh Directive above n 130 arts 17 and 29.   [146] See eg McKinnon above n 140 ch 3.

(Articles 18 and 22); the purchase accounting (or acquisition) method is the preferred consolidation technique, but merger accounting (or pooling of interests) method is an option (Articles 19 and 20); the method used must be applied consistently (Article 25); debts and claims between undertakings included in a consolidation, income, and expenditure relating to transactions between such undertakings and the resulting profits on these transactions must be eliminated (Article 26); the consolidated accounts must be drawn up as at the same date as the annual accounts of the parent undertaking (Article 27); an extensive range of items must be disclosed in notes to the accounts (Article 34) and in the directors' report (Article 36); the consolidated accounts must be audited (Article 37), and published once approved (Article 38). The foregoing accounting provisions were not controversial, as many had already been agreed in the Fourth Directive. The most controversial provisions related to company law matters concerning the definition of the undertakings to which the duty to consolidate should apply, and the circumstances in which such a duty could be dispensed with.[147] The text of the Seventh Directive represents a series of compromises on these matters, resulting in a legal regime that has fallen short of original intentions.

The first step in any consolidation regime is to define the group of undertakings to which the duty of consolidation attaches. When this regime is to be supranational in nature, it must take into account differences in national approaches to the definition of a corporate group for disclosure purposes. In this respect the European Commission had a choice between the English approach, based on the legal control exercised by a parent over its subsidiaries, which concentrates on linkages of majority shareholdings and voting rights in the subsidiary, and the German approach, which concentrates on effective managerial control by means of control contracts or the de facto ability to exercise a dominant influence over a subordinate undertaking. Initially, the Commission's proposal favoured the German model.[148] However, after discussions in the Council of Ministers significant concessions were made to the English approach with the resulting text taking elements from both national models.

Thus, Article 1 of the directive includes, in its definition of an undertaking required to draw up consolidated accounts, linkages between parent and subsidiary undertakings that rely on the parent undertaking's majority voting rights (Article 1(1)(a)), its right to appoint or remove a majority of the members of the administrative, management, or supervisory body of the subsidiary undertaking (Article 1(1)(b)),[149] and the parent's right to exercise a dominant influence over a subsidiary either pursuant to a control contract, or to a provision in its memorandum

---

[147] For a valuable and detailed discussion of these matters, see Petite above n 140.

[148] See Petite ibid at 87–88.

[149] Where the duty to draw up consolidated accounts is founded on the basis of voting rights, or rights of appointment and removal, any such rights exercised by another subsidiary or by a person acting on behalf of the parent or another subsidiary must be added to those of the parent: Seventh Directive above n 130 art 2(1).

or articles of association, where the law governing the subsidiary undertaking permits its being subjected to such contracts or provisions (Article 1(1)(c)).[150]

In addition to the above, a parent undertaking will be obliged to draw up consolidated accounts where it is a shareholder in or member of a subsidiary undertaking and, either, the majority of the members of the administrative, management, or supervisory bodies of the subsidiary, who have held office in the previous financial year up to the time when consolidated accounts are drawn up, have been appointed solely as a result of the parent's voting rights (Article 1(1)(d)), or, the parent controls alone, in agreement with other shareholders in or members of the subsidiary, a majority of shareholders' or members' voting rights in the subsidiary (Article 1(1)(d)). The Member States must introduce measures for at least the second case and may introduce more detailed measures concerning the form and contents of such agreements.[151]

Article 1(2) of the directive gives Member States the option to impose a duty to prepare consolidated accounts on a parent undertaking which holds a participating interest in a subsidiary undertaking and it actually exercises a 'dominant influence' over the subsidiary, or where the parent and the subsidiary undertaking are managed on a unified basis by the parent. The UK has implemented Article 1(2).[152] This was done to avoid the practice of companies using controlled non-subsidiaries as a means of keeping assets or liabilities off the consolidated balance sheet.[153]

The final linkage giving rise to a duty to consolidate accounts is laid down in Article 12 of the Seventh Directive. This extends the duty to horizontal groups that are linked not by shareholding but by unified management based on a contract or provision in the memorandum or articles of association, or where the management of both companies is substantially the same in the financial year for which accounts are to be drawn up. This covers European transnational groups such as the British and Dutch parent companies of Unilever, which operate under common sets of objectives and identical management boards,[154] and the Dutch group Philips, whose US holdings are controlled by a separate trust in which its Dutch shareholders have an interest.[155]

Having established the principal types of group to which the duty to consolidate attaches, the next question concerns the extent, if any, to which exemption from that duty can be granted. In this respect the Seventh Directive has undergone substantial changes in comparison with the initial proposal, reflecting intensive

---

[150] Despite the absence of control contract arrangements in English law, the UK has accepted the linkages set down in art 1(1)(c). See s 258(2)(c) of the Companies Act 1985, inserted by the Companies Act 1989 s 21(1), which lays down the definition of a parent undertaking for accounting purposes. See also the Companies Act 2006 sections 1161–1162.

[151] The UK has provided for the second case in s 258(2)(d) of the Companies Act 1985 as inserted by s 21(1) of the Companies Act 1989.

[152] Companies Act 1985 s 258(4) as inserted by Companies Act 1989 s 21(1).

[153] See Furey and Parkes above n 136 at paras 2.11–2.12 at 8–9 and para 2.13 at 10–11.

[154] On which company see further ch 2 at 60–61.   [155] See McKinnon above n 140 at 39.

lobbying for particular corporate and national interests. The most important compromise occurred in relation to the issue of sub-consolidation, whereby a duty of consolidation is placed upon every intermediate holding company within a group. The initial version of the Seventh Directive favoured this approach.[156] It has the advantage of giving segmented information about the group's activities, in particular about the location of profits and losses. It has the disadvantage of increasing the administrative burdens and costs of the group as a whole. In a complex MNE these could be considerable.[157]

In response to such criticisms the original proposal was not followed in the final text of the directive. Instead there exist certain compulsory and optional exemptions from sub-consolidation, based on the size of the ultimate parent's shareholding in the exempted undertaking and on the applicability, to the ultimate parent, of consolidated accounting obligations that are in accordance with the requirements of the Seventh Directive.[158] A Member State need not apply these exemptions to companies the securities of which have been admitted to official listing on a stock exchange established in a Member State.[159] In addition to the conditions stated in the Seventh Directive, a Member State may make exemption conditional upon disclosure in the consolidated accounts of additional information required of undertakings governed by the national law of that Member State which are obliged to prepare consolidated accounts and are in the same circumstances as the exempted undertaking.[160] A Member State may further require disclosure of all or some of the following information from the exempted parent undertaking regarding the group of which it is the parent: the amount of fixed assets, net turnover, profit and loss for the financial year and the amount of capital and reserves, and the average number of employees in the financial year.[161] None of these compulsory or optional exemptions shall affect the Member States' legislation on the drawing up of consolidated accounts so far as these are required for the information of employees or their representatives or for administrative or judicial purposes.[162]

Finally an optional exemption is given, by Article 11 of the directive, to EC-based intermediate parent undertakings whose ultimate parent is a non-EC based company. This exemption is conditional upon the consolidation of the exempted undertaking and all of its subsidiaries in the accounts of a larger body of undertakings, those accounts being drawn up in accordance with the directive, or in an

---

[156] Bull EC Supp 9/76 above n 141.

[157] Unilever argued that the original proposal would have required it to produce over 200 additional sets of consolidated accounts. BP estimated the increased reporting burden at 36 sets: McKinnon above n 140 at 40.

[158] Space prevents a detailed analysis of these provisions. See further Seventh Directive above n 130 arts 7 and 8; UK Companies Act 1985 s 228 inserted by Companies Act 1989 s 5(3) and the Company Law Reform Bill 2006 above n 136.

[159] ibid art 7(3). The UK has elected not to apply the exemption in art 7 to this class of companies: Companies Act 1985 s 228(3) as inserted by s 5(3) Companies Act 1989.   [160] ibid art 9(1).

[161] ibid art 9(2).   [162] ibid art 10.

equivalent manner, and upon their being audited by one or more authorized auditors under the national law governing the undertaking which drew them up.[163] The absence of a definition of equivalence in the directive means that it is for each Member State that adopts the exemption in Article 11 to determine whether the consolidated accounts drawn up by the non-EC parent meet the required standards. The Contact Committee set up to consider the harmonized application of both the Fourth and the Seventh Directives may have to clarify this concept in future.[164] The UK has not introduced an exemption under Article 11.

In accordance with general practice on consolidation, the parent undertaking is given a measure of discretion under the Seventh Directive when determining which subsidiaries to include in its consolidated accounts. Thus, while a parent undertaking is obliged to include all of its subsidiary undertakings on a worldwide basis, and to include the subsidiaries of its subsidiaries,[165] undertakings whose inclusion would not be material for giving a true and fair view of the assets, liabilities, financial position, and profit and loss of the group need not be included.[166] In addition, where severe long-term restrictions hinder the parent undertaking from exercising its rights over the assets or management of a subsidiary undertaking the latter need not be included.[167] Similarly, subsidiaries may be excluded where unified management between parent and subsidiary as defined in Article 12(1) of the directive exists,[168] or where the gathering of information needed for consolidation would involve disproportionate expense or undue delay,[169] or the shares in the subsidiary undertaking are held exclusively with a view to their immediate resale.[170]

On the other hand, a subsidiary undertaking must not be included where its activities are so different that its inclusion would be incompatible with a true and fair view of the group's finances.[171] For this purpose it is not enough of a difference that the subsidiary undertaking may be partly industrial, partly commercial, and partly provide services or that it carries on different industrial or commercial activities involving different products or services.[172] The exemption is meant to apply, for example, where a manufacturing group also owns a bank or an insurance company. The assets and liabilities of the different lines of business are so distinct that any attempt to consolidate them may give a distorted view of the group's position.[173] However, much is left to the discretion of the parent company's management in determining what a different activity is.

---

[163] ibid art 11(2).

[164] See Fourth Directive art 52; Seventh Directive art 47. For fuller discussion of this issue, see Petite above n 140 at 113–14; McKinnon above n 140 at 44–45.

[165] Seventh Directive above n 130 art 3; Companies Act 1985 s 229(1) as inserted by Companies Act 1989 s 5(3).   [166] ibid art 13(1); ibid s 229(2).

[167] ibid art 13(3)(a)(aa); ibid s 229(3)(a).   [168] ibid art 13(3)(a)(bb); not applied in the UK.

[169] ibid art 13(3)(b); Companies Act 1985 s 229(3)(b) as inserted by Companies Act 1989 s 5(3).

[170] ibid art 13(3)(c); ibid s 229(3)(c) which adds the condition that the subsidiary undertaking has not previously been included in consolidated group accounts prepared by the parent company.

[171] ibid art 14(1); ibid s 229(4).   [172] ibid art 14(2); ibid.

[173] McKinnon above n 140 at 53; Petite above n 140 at 118–19.

Further exemptions from the obligation to publish consolidated accounts may be introduced by Member States. First, a Member State may exempt a parent undertaking that is not a limited liability company (Article 5(2)).[174] Secondly, exemption may be granted where a parent company is a financial holding company and it has not taken an active part in the running of a subsidiary undertaking, and has made loans only to undertakings in which it has a participatory interest (Article 5). This provision was included on the insistence of Luxembourg which acts as host to a large number of such holding companies.[175] Thirdly, a Member State may exempt a parent undertaking on the basis of the small size of the group. The exemption will apply where the latest annual accounts of the parent and its subsidiaries, if taken together, do not exceed the size threshold laid down in Article 27 of the Fourth Directive, as periodically amended, which takes account of the balance sheet total, net turnover, and average number of employees in the group.[176] This exemption has been introduced into English law by s 13(3) of the Companies Act 1989, as s 248 of the Companies Act 1985. In the Companies Act 2006 small groups are given the option to consolidate their accounts.[177]

The above mentioned provisions of the Seventh Directive are no more than guidelines to management as to the proper exercise of their discretion. In the light of the EC decision to require the use of IAS, the exercise of that discretion must be undertaken subject to the requirements of those standards. The starting point is IAS 27 on consolidated and separate financial statements.[178] It establishes the principle that a parent company will present financial statements in which it consolidates its investment in subsidiaries unless it meets certain conditions allowing it not to consolidate. The key concept, that determines whether a subsidiary should be consolidated or not, is the control that the parent exerts over that entity. By paragraph 12 of IAS 27 control is defined on the basis of majority ownership of the voting shares in the subsidiary, or by the possession of de facto power to control the operating and financial policies of that entity, where less than a majority shareholding exists.[179] IAS 27 goes on to say that a subsidiary should be excluded

---

[174] For the background to this option see McKinnon ibid at 45–46.

[175] See further ibid at 46–48.

[176] For a recent revision, see Council Directive 84/569 OJ L314/28 27 November 1984.

[177] Companies Act 2006 above n 136 sections 381–84.

[178] IAS 27 Consolidated and Separate Financial Statements above n 138. The following paragraphs edit and update Peter T Muchlinski above n 1 at 755–57.

[179] 'Control is presumed to exist when the parent owns, directly or indirectly through subsidiaries, more than one half of the voting power of an enterprise unless, in exceptional circumstances, it can be clearly demonstrated that such ownership does not constitute control. Control also exists even when the parent owns one half or less of the voting power of an enterprise when there is:

(a) power over more than one half of the voting rights by virtue of an agreement with other investors;
(b) power to govern the financial and operating policies of the enterprise under a statute or an agreement;
(c) power to appoint or remove the majority of the members of the board of directors or equivalent governing body; or
(d) power to cast the majority of votes at meetings of the board of directors or equivalent governing body.'

from consolidation when, either, control is intended to be temporary because the subsidiary is acquired and held exclusively with a view to its subsequent disposal in the near future, or it operates under severe long-term restrictions which significantly impair its ability to transfer funds to the parent. Such subsidiaries should be accounted for in accordance with IAS 39, financial instruments: recognition and measurement. In addition, a subsidiary is not excluded from consolidation because its business activities are dissimilar from those of the other enterprises within the group. According to IAS 27, '[b]etter information is provided by consolidating such subsidiaries and disclosing additional information in the consolidated financial statements about the different business activities of subsidiaries. For example, the disclosures required by IAS 14, segment reporting, help to explain the significance of different business activities within the group'. Where separate financial statements are prepared, investments in subsidiaries that are excluded from consolidated financial statements should be either carried at cost, accounted for using the equity method as described in IAS 28, accounting for investments in associates; or accounted for as available-for-sale financial assets as described in IAS 39, financial instruments: recognition and measurement.

As part of its work programme the IASB is aiming to issue a new revision of IAS 27 that will take into account the effect of special purpose entities (SPEs), following the use of such vehicles to alter the true profit and loss situation of the Enron group.[180] To this end the IASB has engaged in a series of discussions on consolidation.[181] These have been undertaken on two levels. The first deals with the question of control as the basis of consolidation in relation to entities other than SPEs,

[180] The collapse of Enron stemmed from an announcement, by its management, on 16 October 2001 that the company had incurred a $1.01 billion charge and a $1.2 billion reduction in its shareholder equity as a result of extensive off-balance sheet dealings that led to an SEC investigation. This caused Enron share prices to fall by more than 50 per cent by early November 2001 and for the firm to be downgraded by all major credit agencies. Enron filed for bankruptcy on 2 December 2001. This dramatic collapse can be attributed to a shift in Enron's activities from the operation of gas pipeline facilities (valued at some $2 billion) into energy trading occasioned by the deregulation of energy markets. This was financed by the sale of some of its existing assets and through the borrowing of new funds for expansion. In the course of this expansion, Enron shifted debt into special partnerships and trusts, the so-called 'special purpose entities' (SPEs) that could be excluded from the balance sheet under US accounting rules. These entities were set up prima facie as partnerships with outside interests, aimed at reducing the investment risk inherent in an industry such as oil and gas. In fact, they became vehicles for the hiding of losses and for personal enrichment by the senior Enron managers who oversaw their creation. They were set up in a series of transactions, between 1997 and 2001, which established a complex web of entities that could be taken off the consolidated balance sheet on the basis that they complied with the Financial Accounting Standards Board (FASB) Emerging Issues Task Force (EITF) opinion 90–15, as sanctioned by the SEC in a guidance letter of the SEC's Office of the Chief Accountant of 1991. By this guidance, which does not carry the force of law, a SPE could be treated as an independent entity for accounting purposes, by a company that does business with it, provided, first, that an owner independent of the company makes a substantive equity investment of at least 3 per cent of the SPE's assets, and that 3 per cent must remain at risk throughout the transaction and, secondly, that the independent owner must exercise control of the SPE. See further Peter T Muchlinski above n 1.

[181] See IASB Topic Summary 'Consolidation (including special purpose entities)' 3 August 2004 and Project Update April 2006 available at <http://www.iasb.org>.

while the second considers the concept in the context of SPEs. As to the first issue, the concept of control is widened from the current approach of IAS 27 and is seen as requiring the satisfaction of three major criteria: the ability unilaterally to set strategic direction and to direct operating and financing policy and strategy (the 'Power Criterion'); the ability to access benefits (the 'Benefit Criterion'); and the ability to use such power so as to increase, protect or maintain the amount of those benefits (the 'Link Criterion'). It was tentatively agreed that irrespective of the form of control, if the control criteria were satisfied, consolidation should be required. Also, no minimum shareholding requirement should be necessary as control could be achieved when an entity had less than a majority of voting shares and the balance of holdings was dispersed.

Control could be achieved not only through equity but also through contract.[182] Equally, control could arise through indirect ability to exert power through agents or other related parties as defined in IAS 24. Indeed, the IASB feels that there should be a presumption that agents will vote at the controllers direction and that, therefore, there should be a presumption of control over any entity where the controller has an indirect shareholding through agents or other 'straw men'. As to the 'benefit' and 'link' criteria, the IASB explains that the first can include potential benefit, even if not received, and is wide enough to encompass more than residual ownership interests such as access to technology, while the second should be included to distinguish between a fiduciary with broad delegated power and a true controller.

As regards control and SPEs, the IASB is yet to finalize its approach. However, it has made certain initial decisions.[183] In particular, among other matters, it has been determined that control should be the basis for the consolidation of SPEs and that the criteria for consolidating SPEs should be consistent with the criteria for consolidating other entities. However, in the absence of an ability to determine policy, control would have to be assessed by other means. In addition, the IASB has identified a specific subset of SPEs, those that have no independent strategic operating and financing policies. In such cases, the entity responsible for predetermining these policies for the SPE satisfies the power criterion and is likely to be its controller. This is a question of substance in each case. Certain indicators could assist in identifying the ultimate controller including the entity's risk exposure and whether the SPE's activities further the controller's business purposes. Were these criteria to have been applied to the Enron SPEs, it is clear that they would have to have been consolidated into Enron's accounts. They were never designed to have an independent operating or financing policy, and were used by Enron for the benefit of its enhanced share price. The substance test would ensure that the

---

[182] This is important as it can avoid manipulation of group structures by removal of a direct equity interest in an affiliate and conducting future business with it as an apparently independent entity by contract, while retaining economic and strategic control over its activities.

[183] See IASB Topic Summary above n 181 at 5.

kind of formal approach taken under the then applicable US rules could be avoided and the true economic relationship between Enron and the SPEs would have been the basis of consolidation.[184]

(b) Segmental Disclosure

While the worldwide consolidation of MNE accounts is useful when seeking to judge the performance of the enterprise as a whole, it may also serve to conceal the details of that performance. In particular, consolidated accounts will not disclose the geographical spread of the enterprise's profits, losses, and risks, nor the extent to which one line of business is performing better than another. Such disaggregated, or segmented, information may be required for a more accurate analysis of the firm's operations by investors and their advisers. Furthermore, for certain purposes, such as disclosure to the host state or the information of employees, the degree of disaggregation might have to be very high, operating at individual country and plant levels, if useful information is to be obtained. Thus degrees of disaggregation will vary with the purposes for which the information is needed.[185]

As noted above, the OECD Guideline on Disclosure and Information calls for segmental disclosure where appropriate along lines of business and geographical areas.[186] However, the most comprehensive requirements for segmental disclosure were put forward by the UN Group of Experts on International Standards of Accounting and Reporting in 1977. The Group recommended segmentation both along geographical area and line of business for the enterprise as a whole and for individual operating companies.[187] According to the UN Group of Experts the enterprise as a whole should segment and disclose geographically the following: sales to unaffiliated customers, transfers to other geographical areas that have been eliminated in consolidation, operating results, such as profit before general corporate expenses, interest expense, taxes on income, and unusual items. To the extent identifiable with a geographical area, the enterprise should also disclose: total assets or net assets or total assets and liabilities; property, plant, and equipment gross; accumulated depreciation; other long-term assets; and new investment in property, plant and equipment. Furthermore, the enterprise should describe

---

[184] It has been argued that, prior to Enron, the US system of accounting was too rule based and allowed compliance in form while ignoring the substance of transactions. However, it may not have been the rule itself but the manner of its misapplication by the auditors that contributed to the Enron collapse, see William W Bratton 'Enron Sarbanes Oxley and Accounting: Rules Versus Principles Versus Rents' 48 Vill. L. Rev. 1023 (2003) and David Kershaw 'Evading Enron: Taking Principles too Seriously in Accounting Regulation' 68 MLR 594 (2005) who argues that the UK principles-based approach would be unlikely to avoid an Enron type scandal.

[185] See further Nobes and Parker above n 128 at 437–41 and 450–57.

[186] See text at nn 5–6 above.

[187] See above n 4 at 66–67, 75. See further UNCTC *Towards International Standardisation of Corporate Accounting and Reporting* (UNCTC, New York: 1982) 72–74; Intergovernmental Group of Experts on International Standards of Accounting and Reporting *Conclusions on Accounting and Reporting by Transnational Corporations* (UN Sales No E.88.II.A.18) paras 62–66 at 19–20.

principal activities in each geographical area or country, disclose the basis of accounting for transfers between areas or countries and disclose exposure to exceptional risks of operating in other countries. The same items should be disclosed by the enterprise for discrete lines of business. In addition, individual companies in the group should disclose similar items relating to their foreign assets and operations and, where applicable, to operations in more than one line of business.

By contrast, the Seventh EC Directive[188] contains few requirements for disaggregated information. Although it was suggested during negotiations that the number of employees inside the EC and the value of sales within the EC should be disclosed, the only disaggregated disclosure requirements are that the notes to the accounts should include, first, the consolidated net turnover broken down by categories of activity and into geographical markets in so far as these differ substantially from one another and, secondly, the average numbers of employees in a financial year broken down by categories.[189] In this the provisions of the Seventh Directive reproduce the requirements placed on individual companies under the Fourth Directive.

At the level of national laws the most comprehensive system of segmental reporting for firms with foreign operations is to be found in the US. Since 1969 the Securities and Exchange Commission (SEC) has required the disclosure of line of business information in securities registration documents and, in 1970, this requirement was extended to the annual submission required from registered companies under Form 10–K.[190] Initially such disclosure was governed by the principles of Financial Accounting Standard No 14 (FAS 14) issued by the US Financial Accounting Standards Board in December 1976. Under FAS 14 the enterprise concerned would provide disaggregated information upon line of business and geographical segments including revenue from unaffiliated customers, sales or transfers between geographic areas and the transfer pricing methods used, operating profits and losses so long as a consistent measure was used in all geographic areas and in relation to the assets held by segment. Separate information was required for the foreign operations of the enterprise if these contributed 10 per cent or more of consolidated revenues or the assets identifiable with the foreign operations exceed 10 per cent or more of consolidated assets.[191] FAS No 14 did not offer much guidance on segment identification. A segment was considered significant if its revenues or identifiable assets were more than 10 per cent of the consolidated figures. The identification of geographic segments was left to the discretion of management.[192] They could report foreign operations as a single segment or as a number of segments based on individual countries or groups of countries defined by reference to their, 'physical proximity, economic affinity, the similarities in their business environments and by the nature, scale and degree of the enterprise's

---

[188] Above n 130.   [189] Seventh Directive ibid art 34(8) and (9).
[190] Nobes and Parker above n 128 at 443.   [191] FAS No 14 para 32.
[192] ibid para 12.

operations in the various countries'.[193] The approach of FAS 14 was closely followed in IAS 14 first issued in 1981.[194] IAS 14 recommends segmentation on the basis of the materiality of the segment to the business as a whole, using the 10 per cent of consolidated revenue, operating profit or total assets criterion as a guideline, although not as an exclusive guideline.[195] IAS 14 requires reporting of significant industry segments[196] and geographical areas[197] on the basis of consolidated statement information.[198]

In the UK, the first requirements for segmental disclosure were issued in 1965 by the London Stock Exchange in its listing requirements.[199] The official listing of securities is now governed by the Financial Services and Markets Act 2000, Part VI.[200] It is a condition of acceptance onto the Official List that a company publish formal details about the issuers, the company's capital, management, recent developments, and prospects in accordance with the listing particulars issued by the Financial Services Authority (FSA).[201] In addition to the information required by the FSA, the listing particulars shall contain all such information as investors and their professional advisers would reasonably require, and reasonably expect to find there, for the purpose of making an informed assessment of the assets, liabilities, financial position, profits and losses, and the prospects of the issuer of the securities as well as the rights attaching to those securities.[202] The Act reflects disclosure requirements based on an EC Directive which harmonizes the minimum listing requirements of stock exchanges in the Community.[203] These requirements include inter alia duties to disclose segmental information on lines of business and geographical activities, information on the average number of employees broken down by category of employment, and information on the geographical distribution of investments.[204]

---

[193] ibid para 34. See further SJ Gray and LH Radebaugh 'International Segment Disclosures by US and UK Multinational Enterprises: A Descriptive Study' 22 Journal of Accounting Research 351 at 352–53 (1984).

[194] See <http://www.iasb.org> for web summary or subscription download or IASB above n 138.

[195] ibid para 14.

[196] Defined as 'the distinguishable components of an enterprise each engaged in providing a different product or service, or a different group of related products or services, primarily to customers outside the enterprise': ibid para 4.

[197] Defined as 'the distinguishable components of an enterprise engaged in operations in individual countries or groups of countries within particular geographical areas as may be determined appropriate in an enterprise's particular circumstances': ibid.   [198] ibid paras 20–25.

[199] Nobes and Parker above n 128 at 445.

[200] 2000 chapter c 8 <http://www.opsi.gov.uk/acts/acts2000/20000008.htm>. See further Gower and Davies above n 15 ch 26.   [201] ibid s 75.

[202] ibid s 80.

[203] See European Parliament and Council Directive 2001/34/EC OJ [2001] L184/1 consolidated text at <http://eur-lex.europa.eu/LexUriServ/site/en/consleg/2001/L/02001L0034–20030412-en.pdf>. For background see Gower and Davies above n 15 at 650.

[204] ibid. Schedule A Chapter 4 'Information concerning the issuer's activities'.

Until 1996, segmental information was also required under the Companies Act 1985 in relation to a group's annual accounts.[205] Since 1996 segmental disclosure has been governed by the UK accounting profession's standard SSAP 25 on 'Segmental Reporting'.[206] According to the Explanatory Notes in SSAP 25, when identifying reportable segments, directors should have regard to the overall purpose of presenting segmental information and the need of the user of financial statements to be informed, where an entity carries on operations in different classes of business or in different geographical areas, that these earn a return on investment out of line with the rest of the business, or are subject to different degrees of risk, or have experienced different degrees of growth or have different potentials for future development.[207] Directors should also review their definitions of segments annually and redefine them when appropriate, bearing in mind the need for consistency and comparability between years.[208] Finally, SSAP 25 repeats the above mentioned statutory right of directors not to disclose information that would, in their opinion, be seriously prejudicial to the interests of the company, provided that the fact of non-disclosure is stated.[209]

As with the US and IASB standards, the basic approach to segmental identification in SSAP 25 rests on the significance of the segment to the business entity as a whole. A segment is significant if '(a) its third party turnover is ten per cent or more of total third party turnover of the entity; or (b) its segment result, whether profit or loss, is ten per cent or more of the combined result of all segments in profit or all segments in loss, whichever combined result is greater; or (c) its net assets are ten per cent or more of total net assets of the entity'. SSAP 25 goes on to define a separate class of business as 'a distinguishable component of an entity that provides a separate product or service or a separate group of related products or services'.[210] SSAP 25 suggests that directors should take into account inter alia the nature of the products or services involved, the nature of the relevant production processes, the markets in which the products or services are sold, their distribution channels, the manner in which the entity's business is organized, and any relevant legislative framework for business organization.[211] However, it concludes that no single set of characteristics is universally applicable nor is any single characteristic conclusive. Consequently, 'determination of an entity's class of business must depend on the judgment of the directors'.[212] A geographical segment is defined as 'a geographical area comprising an individual country or group of countries in which the entity operates, or to which it supplies products or services'.[213] SSAP 25 does not identify

---

[205] Requirements for segmental reporting by holding companies were first introduced by the Companies Act 1967. They were repealed by Statutory Instrument in February 1996: Nobes and Parker above n 128 at 445–46.

[206] See SSAP 25 on 'Segmental Reporting' (June 1990) <http://www.frc.org.uk/images/uploaded/documents/SSAP%2025.pdf>.   [207] ibid at para 8.

[208] ibid at para 10.   [209] ibid at para 43.   [210] ibid at para 11.
[211] ibid at para 12.   [212] ibid at para 13.   [213] ibid at para 14.

any general method of grouping. Instead, it asserts that a geographical analysis should help the user of the financial statement to asses the extent to which an entity's operations are subject to factors such as: expansionist or restrictive economic climates; stable or unstable political regimes; exchange control regulations; and exchange rate fluctuations. The purpose is the identification of investment risk in given areas, as well as the provision of financial information on turnover by origin, results and net assets on a geographical basis.[214]

A new approach to segmental reporting has been adopted since 1997 in the US under SFAS 131.[215] This statement requires that a public business enterprise report financial and descriptive information about its reportable operating segments. Operating segments are defined as a component of an enterprise:

a. That engages in business activities from which it may earn revenues and incur expenses (including revenues and expenses relating to transactions with other components of the same enterprise),

b. Whose operating results are regularly reviewed by the enterprise's chief operating decision maker to make decisions about resources to be allocated to the segment and assess its performance, and

c. For which discrete financial information is available.

An operating segment may engage in business activities for which it has yet to earn revenues, for example, start-up operations may be operating segments before earning revenues.[216]

Generally, financial information is required to be reported on the basis that it is used internally for evaluating segment performance and deciding how to allocate resources to segments.[217] Thus the new approach is based on managerial methods of reporting, rather than on a 'risk and return' basis. The main reportable segments are organized around enterprise-wide disclosures, information on products and services, geographical areas, and major customers.[218]

The managerial approach of SFAS 131 has been adopted to a degree in the 1997 revision of IAS 14.[219] The IASB believes that the management approach improves financial reporting on the following grounds:

6. A number of academic research studies have shown that the management approach of SFAS 131

• increases the number of reported segments and provided a greater quantity of information;

• enables users to see an entity through the eyes of management;

• enables an entity to provide timely segment information for external reporting with relatively low incremental cost;

---

[214] See ibid at para 34.

[215] SFAS 131 Disclosures about Segments of an Enterprise and Related Information (June 1997) available at <http://fasb.org/pdf/fas131.pdf>.   [216] ibid at para 10.

[217] ibid Summary at 4.

[218] See ibid paras 36–39. This approach connotes the concept of the 'accountable business activity' used by Tricker: see ch 2 at 78.

[219] See IAS 14 as applicable after 1 July 1998 at <http://www.iasb.org> and see Nobes and Parker above n 128 at 442.

- enhances consistency with the management discussion and analysis or other annual report disclosures; and
- provides various measures of segment performance

7. The Board was also aware that many users of financial statements supported the management approach of SFAS 131 for the reasons mentioned in the previous paragraph.[220]

However, the experience of SFAS 131 is not unproblematic. According to Nobes and Parker, while the amount of information disclosed for each segment and the number of segments disclosed have increased, the amount of geographical disclosure has decreased and there remain inconsistencies with other parts of the annual corporate review which contains disaggregated information.[221]

The principal characteristic of the above mentioned accounting standards is the degree of discretion left to corporate officials in determining the segments to be reported. This is not surprising, given the difficulty involved in segment identification. However, the potential for inadequate reporting resulting from the wrong identification of segments is considerable. Furthermore, the disclosure of segmental information implies that the segments reported are relatively autonomous and independent of each other. In a highly integrated MNE this may not be the case. There may be large transfers between the segments which cannot be understood in isolation from the rest of the company. However, there is no doubt that segmental reporting is of considerable value to the market and is set to develop further.[222]

(c) Social Disclosure

As noted above, the activities of large corporations attract the attention not only of financial stakeholders but also of other groups and interests. The latter may require information of an order different from that contained in the firm's financial statements. Thus, according to Choi and Mueller, social disclosure or accounting 'refers to the measurement and communication of information about a firm's effects on employee welfare, the local community and the environment. In contrast to traditional reporting methods, social responsibility disclosures embrace *non-financial* as well as financial performance measures'.[223] Social disclosure challenges the notion that a corporation is not responsible to the community at large for its actions. The demand for social disclosure places the corporation in a position more like that of a provider of public services that must explain and account for its actions in the light of broad conceptions of the public interest.

Such an approach could lead to a fundamental rethinking of how a company should report its performance. This is well illustrated by the nature and scope of

---

[220] IASB Project Update 'Segment reporting' (December 2005 at paras 6–7 available at <http://www.iasb.org>.   [221] Nobes and Parker above n 128 at 445.

[222] ibid at 458.

[223] FDS Choi and GG Mueller *International Accounting* (Prentice Hall, International Editions, 2nd edn, 1992) at 330 (emphasis in the original).

the Operating and Financial Review (OFR) proposed in the UK by the Company Law Review of 2001. According to this proposal, the OFR is to be published by all public and very large private companies (defined as having an annual turnover of more than £500 million) as part of the annual report. It is to give an account by the directors of:

the performance and direction of the business, including in all cases a fair review of achievements, trends and strategic direction, and covering other matters, including wider relationships, risks and opportunities and social and environmental impacts where these are relevant to an understanding of the performance of the business[224]

The aim of the OFR is to 'account for and demonstrate stewardship of a wide range of relationships and resources which are of vital significance to the success of modern business, but often do not register effectively, or at all, in financial accounts'.[225] Initially the OFR was to have been placed on a mandatory footing in the Company Law Reform Bill. The UK Government took the decision in November 2005 to repeal the mandatory requirement on quoted companies to prepare an Operating and Financial Review (OFR) as contained in the OFR regulations. Companies are now required to prepare a business review instead.[226] This decision was made in the light of the government's strong commitment to strategic forward-looking narrative reporting and its policy of not imposing unnecessary burdens on UK companies, and taking into account the large body of evidence from previous consultations on narrative reporting.[227] Nonetheless almost half of large UK listed companies apply an OFR informally. This may be as a result of preparations for a mandatory regime, rather than out of conviction in their utility.[228]

Demands for social reporting have given rise to the practical questions, first, as to what information should be given in addition to the usual information available through annual financial statements and, secondly, as to the instruments and structures through which this information could be intelligibly conveyed to its intended users.[229] These two related matters will be considered in the context of the three main strands of development in this field that are of especial relevance to

---

[224] See Company Law Review Steering Group *Modern Company Law for a Competitive Economy – Completing the Structure* (London: DTI, November 2000) at para 3.2. See further The Company Law Steering Group *Modern Company Law for a Competitive Economy Final Report* (London: DTI, 2001) vol 1 ch 8.   [225] See *Completing the Structure*, above n 224 at para 3.4.

[226] See Companies Act 2006 above n 136 section 417.

[227] See DTI *Consultation on Mandatory Business Reporting* (closed 24 March 2006) at <http://www.dti.gov.uk/bbf/financial-reporting/business-reporting/page27239.html>. Equally, new requirements for wider disclosure under EC rules may have prompted this change: Directive 2003/51/EC of the European Parliament and of the Council (18 June 2003) OJ [2003] L178/16 introduces a requirement that the director's report includes a 'fair review' of the company's business. See also 'Brown in Retreat on Business Red Tape' *Financial Times* 2 February 2006 at 1.

[228] See 'OFRs Published by Half of Big Business' *Financial Times* 21 August 2006 at 3.

[229] See further UNCTAD (ISAR) *Disclosure of the impact of corporations on society: Current trends and issues* UN Doc TD/B/COM.2/ISAR/20 15 August 2003 available at <http://www.unctad.org/en/docs//c2isar20_en.pdf>.

the operations of MNEs: disclosures to employees, the use of local value-added statements, and environmental disclosure.

(i) Employee Disclosure

The organizational aspects of this matter have already been discussed in the context of corporate accountability above. The remaining issue in this section is what employee disclosures should contain. Both financial and non-financial information might be of relevance to employees and trade union representatives. Thus, information on matters of employment might include not only information on its structure but also on income from such employment.[230] Furthermore, given the extensive information required by employees, it may be necessary to present special purpose reports that could present the information in an accessible and useful form.[231] The information offered might include inter alia: information about the number of employees broken down by category, line of business, country and establishment, wages and salaries paid to these various groups, working conditions in countries and establishments including health and safety conditions, training and industrial relations matters, and any other information deemed to be of value to employees. The most extensive employee information requirements are to be found in the French Labour Code, which requires each enterprise to produce an annual social report, the *Bilan Social*, covering matters of the kind mentioned. This is to be distributed to all shareholders and to the firm's works council.[232] The practice of firms in the field of employee disclosure varies from country to country. The general level of employee disclosures is low. However, individual companies have used this type of disclosure.[233]

(ii) Value-Added Statements

The value-added statement is an accounting device that seeks to show the production contribution made by the company in the course of an accounting period. Value-added statements are common in European firms' annual reports. They are

---

[230] UN Group of Experts Report 1977 above n 4 at para 52 at 37.   [231] ibid.

[232] Article L.432–1 C trav; art L.432–4 al 5 et 8.C. trav. See Philippe Merle *Droit Commercial Sociétés Commerciales* (Paris: Dalloz, 10th edn, 2005) at 559 para 474; A Brunet and M Germain 'L'information des actionnaires et du comité d'entreprise dans les sociétés anonymes depuis les lois du 28 octobre 1982, du 1er mars 1984 et du 25 janvier 1985' (1985) Revue des Sociétés at 1. See also Loi No 2001–240 sur les Nouvelles Regulations Economiques discussed in EC Commission *Corporate Social Responsibility: National Public policies in the European Union* (Directorate-General for Employment and Social Affairs Unit D.1 January 2004) at 19 available at <http://ec.europa.eu/employment_social/soc-dial/csr/national_csr_policies_en.pdf>. This study summarizes the main social disclosure rules for all the EU Member States prior to enlargement in May 2004. Portugal also employs a social balance reporting system: Law No 141/85 and Decree-Law No 9/92 require that companies with 100 or more employees issue a 'report on the social balance' every year and forward it to the Labour Ministry. The social balance report provides essential information on the organization's human resources management, and the effectiveness of social investments and of actions to improve employees' quality of life: EC Commission ibid at 32.

[233] See Nobes and Parker above n 128 at 162. See further C Roberts *International Trends in Social and Employee Reporting* (London: Chartered Association of Certified Accountants, 1990).

less common in the reports of UK and Commonwealth countries, although in the mid to late 1970s they were more common among UK companies.[234] The value added by the company is the difference between the market value of the goods or services produced by the firm and the cost of goods, materials, and services purchased from other suppliers in the course of the relevant accounting period.[235] According to the UN Intergovernmental Working Group of Experts on International Standards of Accounting and Reporting value added should normally be derived from: '(a) sales revenue less costs of material and services purchased from outside suppliers, and excise duty; (b) share of profits earned by or received from associated companies; (c) investment income; (d) surplus on realization of investments; (e) extraordinary items; (f) exchange gain or loss.'[236] Furthermore, the group recommends that information should be provided in respect of the distribution of value added to different contributors, such as employees and providers of capital, and that value added retained in the business as represented by depreciation and retained earnings should be disclosed.[237]

A local value-added statement by the subsidiary of a MNE can show the overall contribution made by it to the economy of the host state. Such a statement will be of use to the economic policy-makers in the host state government. It will also be valuable to employees by showing the worth, to the firm, of the local operation thereby indicating the firm's likely attitude to long-term investment and employment maintenance. The value-added statement may be of particular use to developing countries where the prime users of information about the operations of MNE subsidiaries are not investors but the government as principal economic planner, and other groups concerned with the impact of MNEs on national development.[238] More recently value-added statements have begun to include information as to the sustainable value added by the investment, thereby bringing this type of social disclosure closer to environmental disclosure.[239]

(iii) Environmental Disclosure

Concern about the environmental effects of the operations of MNEs has become an increasingly prominent issue. As part of the policy response to such phenomena, increasing attention is being devoted to the creation of information and reporting structures on matters of environmental concern. Thus, both the US and the EC have introduced laws requiring the disclosure, to public authorities, of

---

[234] Choi and Mueller above n 229 at 337; Burchill, Clubb and Hopwood 'Accounting in its Social Context: Towards a History of Value Added in the United Kingdom' 10 Accounting Organisations and Society 381 (1985).

[235] See Zubaidur Rahman above n 2 at 89–90; Choi and Mueller above n 229 at 333–37.

[236] UNCTC (1988) above n 132 para 153 at 40–41.   [237] ibid para 154 at 41.

[238] Zubaidur Rahman above n 2 at 87.

[239] See UNCTAD (ISAR) *International Accounting and Reporting Issues 2000 Review* (New York and Geneva: United Nations, 2000) at 34–37 and ch IV. ISAR noted that practice is still far from uniform in this regard. See further Global Reporting Initiative *Sustainability Reporting Guidelines* (Draft, 2006) available at <http://www.grig3.org/guidelines.html>.

specific information relevant to the control of industrial hazards in the fields of construction and operation of facilities, sale of products, and health and safety at work.[240] By contrast, national legal requirements for environmental accounting by firms are still relatively few on the global scale although this is increasingly common within the EU.[241]

So far, the main initiatives have occurred through the voluntary efforts of firms, which have devised internal accounting standards and have undertaken environmental audits of their activities. However international organizations are developing schemes of environmental accounting. In particular, ISAR has begun to study the problems of environmental accounting, and has put forward proposals for improved disclosure in this field.[242] Similarly, the EC has laid down new standards by way of Regulation on eco-auditing by firms operating in the Community.

The UN initiative has generated information about the practices of firms in this area, from which recommendations based on 'best practice' can be made.[243] It appears that German and Swiss firms have the most developed practices in reporting capital and current expenditures related to environmental measures.[244] In particular, the German Chemical Industry Association (Verband der Chemischen Industrie eV) has developed recommendations on the definition of environmental measures taken by firms and the appropriate manner in which to cost these. The measures concerned should be categorized according to the intended purpose of the equipment used by the firm, namely, the control of air, water, waste, and noise pollution. The calculation of expenditure should rest on, either, a general ledger account specification or, where necessary, on statistical approximations. Furthermore, the estimates must be made to reflect the fact that environmental expenditures are not exclusively related to environmental concerns. Thus, where necessary, an apportionment of expenditures must be made.[245]

A particular problem identified by ISAR is the definition of the border between environmental expenditure and the pre-estimation of environmental liabilities. It

---

[240] For a detailed analysis, see UNCTC *Transnational Corporations and Industrial Hazards Disclosure* (UN, New York: 1991, Environmental Series No 1 UN Doc ST/CTC/111).

[241] According to the EC Commission above n 232 in the EU a number of countries have mandatory environmental reporting rules. These include: Denmark, France (see n 232) and Sweden and the Netherlands for companies in the most polluting industries. In the Netherlands environmental reporting has been developed through a joint government-industry commission: see Huizing and Dekker 'The Environmental Issue on the Dutch Political Market' 17 Accounting Organizations and Society 427 (1992). The remainder have either voluntary reporting policies or no policy.

[242] See UNCTAD (ISAR) *A Manual for the Preparers and Users of Eco-efficiency Indicators* (UN Doc UNCTAD/ITE/IPC/2003/7 New York and Geneva: United Nations, 2004). Note also the Global Reporting Initiative above n 239.

[243] See *Report of the Secretary-General on Accounting For Environmental Protection Measures* UN Doc E/C.10/AC.3/1991/5 11 February 1991; reproduced in UNCTC *International Accounting and Reporting Issues 1991 Review* (UN, New York: 1992, UN Doc ST/CTC/124) ch IV.

[244] Dutch firms have also been at the forefront of such developments. See Huizing and Dekker above n 241 and 'Helping to Pull Our Planet Out of the Red: An Environmental Report of BSO/Origin' 17 Accounting Organizations and Society 449 (1992).

[245] See further UNCTC above n 243 paras 11–17.

is very difficult to quantify the latter, and firm practice in this area appears to be based on little more than 'reasonable estimates'. This is a matter closely bound up with the limits of knowable risk and is, therefore, contingent on changes in the understanding of risk and on the specific circumstances of the firm's activities. Furthermore, the estimation involved is of a long-term character, making pre-estimation still harder.[246]

Based on the above mentioned research, ISAR has developed a more advanced approach to environmental accounting. This departs with the concept of 'eco-efficiency', which is defined as a corporate strategy that 'reduces the damage caused to the environment while increasing or at least not decreasing (shareholder) value'.[247] The main accounting objective is to 'describe the method that enterprises can use to provide information on environmental performance vis-à-vis financial perform-ance in a systematic and consistent manner over periods of time'.[248] This is to be achieved through the use of eco-efficiency indicators. ISAR defines these as, 'the ratio between an environmental and a financial variable. It measures the environ-mental performance of an enterprise with respect to its financial performance'. It also noted that in constructing eco-efficiency indicators, 'there are no agreed rules or standards for recognition, measurement and disclosure of environmental inform-ation either within the same industry or across industries. Most importantly, there are no rules for consolidating environmental information for an enterprise or for a group of enterprises so that it can be used together and in line with the enterprise's financial items'.[249] Guidance on how to do this can be obtained from generally accepted international accounting standards and by reference to the standard setting work of the Global Reporting Initiative in the field of sustainability reporting.[250]

Against this background ISAR has made the following recommendations on how to achieve a balance between environmental and financial approaches to cor-porate disclosure. First, enterprises should be able to report on five generic issues relating to environmental performance: water use, energy use, the global warming contribution of the enterprise, the use of ozone depleting substances, and waste. These indicators address worldwide problems as reflected in international agree-ments or protocols. Furthermore they can be used by all enterprises across all sec-tors. Hence they are generic rather than sector-specific indicators. These indicators are not exhaustive and management can add new areas where appropriate.[251] Secondly, comparability of data is a key element:

Users must be able to compare the eco-efficiency information of an enterprise over time in order to identify trends in its eco-efficiency performance. Users must also be able to com-pare the eco-efficiency information of different enterprises in order to evaluate their rela-tive eco-efficiency performance (benchmarking). Hence, the measurement and display of

---

[246] ibid paras 37–56.   [247] See ISAR Manual above n 242 at 1 Box 1.
[248] ibid at para 1.   [249] ibid.   [250] See n 242 above.
[251] ISAR Manual above n 242 at paras 4–6.

the environmental effect of like activities and other events must be carried out in a consistent way throughout an enterprise and over time for that enterprise and in a consistent way for different enterprises. Because users wish to compare the eco-efficiency information over time, it is important that the eco-efficiency information show consistent information for the preceding Periods.[252]

Thirdly, eco-efficiency statements should convey what is generally understood as a true and fair view of, or as presenting fairly, such information.[253] Fourthly, while all financial items will be used as prescribed in international accounting standards, the concept of 'value added' needs to be adapted to this context so as to take into account the fact that inputs of goods and services bought from outside the enterprise have already had an environmental impact prior to purchase. Accordingly, depreciation on such tangible assets will be deducted from value added.[254] Finally, the question of how to consolidate eco-indicators in the reports of a group is considered. Consolidated eco-efficiency statements should be prepared using uniform accounting policies for both the environmental and the financial items for like transactions and other events in similar circumstances.[255] The consolidation method used for the consolidated financial report shall also be applied to the consolidation of the environmental items used for the eco-efficiency indicators.[256] Full consolidation is normally applied to all enterprises that are controlled by a parent enterprise, that is, where the parent enterprise owns or controls, directly or indirectly, 50 per cent or more of voting rights in its subsidiary.[257]

Turning to the EC eco-audit Regulation,[258] this introduces a voluntary scheme for environmental auditing which aims at the establishment, by firms, of effective environmental protection systems, the carrying out of regular evaluations of the performance of such systems and the provision of information about this performance to the public.[259] The evaluation of these systems is to be carried out by means of an environmental audit, defined in the regulation as 'a management tool comprising a systematic, documented, periodic and objective evaluation of the performance of the organization, management system and process designed to protect the environment with the aim of: (i) facilitating management control of practices which may have an impact on the environment; (ii) assessing compliance with the environmental policy, including environmental objectives and targets of the organisation'.[260] An environmental audit will be carried out for each organization, the identity of which is subject to agreement with the environmental verifier charged with overseeing the audit. The smallest entity that can be considered is the site upon which relevant industrial activities take place though a smaller entity can be registered in exceptional conditions.[261] The issues to be

---

[252] ibid at para 61.   [253] ibid at para 68.   [254] ibid Box 9 at 104.

[255] ibid para 317 citing IAS 27 para 21.   [256] ibid at para 319.   [257] ibid at para 324.

[258] Regulation of the European Parliament and Council (EC) No 761/2001 allowing voluntary participation by organizations in a Community eco-management and audit scheme (EMAS) OJ [2001] L114/1 replacing Regulation (EEC) No 1836/93: OJ [1993] L168/1.

[259] ibid art 1(2).   [260] ibid art 2(l).   [261] ibid art 2(s).

covered by the audit include direct environmental activities such as emissions to air, releases to water, or use of natural resources and indirect activities such as product related issues, capital investments, new markets or the activities of contractors, subcontractors, and suppliers.[262] The results of the environmental audit shall form the basis of an environmental statement, which shall be written specifically for public disclosure in a concise and non-technical form.[263] This statement shall be validated by accredited environmental verifiers.[264] Each Member State shall ensure, within 12 months of the entry into force of this regulation that systems for the accreditation of environmental verifiers and for the supervision of their activities are put into place.[265] Firms participating in the eco-audit scheme may use a special EC logo on sites owned by them that have received validated environmental statements.[266]

(d) Foreign Currency Translation

The matters covered in this section may be dealt with briefly, as they are primarily the concern of accountants rather than lawyers. However, no legally orientated discussion of the problems of MNE disclosure would be complete without a basic description of the practical problems involved in accounting for profits and losses incurred in different currencies. When consolidating their accounts, MNEs will face the problem that the component financial statements are denominated in different currencies. It is not possible to consolidate such statements without selecting a single currency in which the consolidation will appear. Thus the MNE must choose a currency in which its consolidated accounts will be drawn up. Usually, this will be the currency in which the parent operates. Then the individual financial statements of the component companies will be recast, or 'translated', into that currency. The purpose is to give a true and fair view of the MNE's business operations. Consequently, the consolidated statement should 'reflect the financial results and relationships as measured in the foreign currency financial statements prior to translation'.[267]

The major accounting problem in this area arises from the lack of fixed exchange rates. This raises the question whether translation should be based on the exchange rate in operation at the time the affiliate acquires or disposes of an asset (for balance sheet purposes) or makes a profit or loss on a transaction (for profit and loss account purposes) or whether it should be based on the rate applicable at the time the consolidated accounts are drawn up. The former approach is known as the 'historic rate', while the latter is referred to as the 'closing rate'. There has

---

[262] ibid Annex VI.   [263] ibid art 3(2)(c) and Annex III para 3.2.
[264] ibid Annex V para. 5.4.   [265] ibid art 4.
[266] ibid art 8. The logo is reproduced in Annex IV of the regulation.
[267] ICAEW SSAP No 20 'Foreign Currency Translation' (1983) para 2 available at <http://frc.co.uk/images/uploaded/documents/SSAP%2020%20cover.pdf>.

been considerable disagreement over which approach should be used.[268] However, the major national and international statements of standard accounting practice now appear to have accepted the closing rate approach as the usual method, with the historic or 'temporal' method being used in cases where the business activities of the foreign affiliate are so closely interlinked with those of the parent that they should be expressed in the currency of the parent using the exchange rate in operation at the time the relevant transactions are carried out, taking account of local levels of inflation where these are high.[269]

Concluding Remarks

This chapter has taken account of changes to the internal organization of MNEs that are designed to enhance accountability and the principal issues in MNE accounting relevant to ensuring the provision of relevant information to the principal classes of stakeholders. In each case the major legal developments are in a state of evolution, particularly in the light of recent accounting scandals. As yet it is not possible to talk of long-settled approaches to MNE accountability and disclosure. However, the main issues in this area are being examined by international organizations and by the accounting profession both on a national and international level. There can be little doubt as to the economic utility of having increasingly harmonized financial information about MNEs that is of use to investors. Developments in this area can be expected to continue. Considerable evolution and change can also be expected in the more politically contentious aspects of MNE accountability, particularly in the topical areas of environmental control and public accountability. The direction and speed of change will be dependent on the degree to which political interest in the regulation of MNEs for public purposes can be aroused, and in the willingness of policy-makers to impose new administrative and expenditure burdens on MNEs. Considerable lobbying on these matters by both civil society groups and MNEs can be expected.

[268] On which see further Nobes and Parker above n 128 at 411–15.

[269] See US Financial Accounting Standards Board Statement of Financial Accounting Standards No 52: Foreign Currency Translation (1981); SSAP No 20 above n 267; IAS 21 Accounting for the Effects of Changes in Foreign Exchange Rates (1983) discussed in Nobes and Parker above n 128 at 415–19.

10

Regulation Through Competition Law

The primary aim of competition laws (antitrust laws in US terminology) is to control competition and not to control MNEs. Nevertheless, where a MNE acts in a way that violates such laws it will be subjected to control in the same way as a local enterprise. The main jurisdictional implications of control by competition law have already been considered in chapter 4.[1] This chapter concentrates on the substantive issues of competition regulation that arise in the context of MNE operations. As will be shown below, the operations of MNEs in an increasingly global economy create new dimensions to issues that are well known in relation to the promotion of competition in national markets. As already mentioned in chapter 1, these new dimensions centre on the international market power that arises from the development, by MNEs, of international networks of production and distribution in what are often concentrated global markets. Furthermore, the expansion of MNEs creates new questions for regulators who might be intent on using competition law as a barrier to the entry and establishment of foreign firms on the ground of preserving the national economy from what they may perceive as destructive foreign competition. Finally, the global operations of MNEs, and the global nature of their markets, have given rise to calls for international competition regulation. This has met with little success, as the removal of competition issues from the WTO Doha Round of negotiations at the Cancún Ministerial of 2003 testifies. Progress in this area has so far been limited to attempts, conducted under the auspices of UNCTAD, at the harmonization of the principles by which restrictive business practices should be controlled. Each of these issue areas will be considered in turn.

(1) The Nature and Aims of Competition Regulation

The basic purpose of competition laws is to promote competition through the control of restrictive business practices.[2] It is assumed that competition between firms will enhance the overall efficiency of the economy, first, by encouraging

---

[1] Certain jurisdictional issues arising in the context of the regulation of mergers and acquisitions remain to be considered. See text at nn 88–110 below.

[2] For those unfamiliar with competition laws and enforcement procedures, useful comparative introductions can be found in the following articles: Grendell 'The Antitrust Legislation of the United

price competition, resulting in lower prices for consumers, and, secondly, by forcing firms to produce more efficiently so as to compete on price with their rivals.[3] Free competition in markets is assumed to be possible, with no single producer or buyer having the power to control supply or demand. Consequently, the market will set prices and firms will act as 'price takers'. However, in practice, markets do not conform to this model of free competition. The distribution of market power will be uneven and anti-competitive practices may result. These must be curtailed through regulation so as to restore competitive conditions in the market.

Anti-competitive practices are generally divided into three main groups. The first consists of agreements or concerted practices between otherwise independent competitors that serve to reduce competition between them.[4] These arrangements may arise between competitors at the same level of the economy, as, for example, between rival producers in the same market. These are termed 'horizontal' arrangements. Alternatively, such arrangements may be concluded between businesses at different levels of the productive process. For example, a producer may enter into a distribution agreement with a reseller. Such arrangements are referred to as 'vertical' arrangements. Some types of anti-competitive arrangements will be absolutely prohibited. In most competition law systems price fixing cartels between competitors come within such a prohibition. Other arrangements may not be subject to absolute prohibition, but will be prohibited only if their anti-competitive aspects outweigh any consequential benefits to consumers or in the improvement of

States, The European Economic Community, Germany and Japan' 29 ICLQ 64 (1980); Boyer 'Form and Substance: A Comparison of Antitrust Regulation by Consent Decrees in the USA, Reports of the Monopolies and Mergers Commission in the UK, and Grants of Clearance by the European Commission' 32 ICLQ 904 (1983). For an analysis of UK and EC law and practice see Richard Whish *Competition Law* (London: Lexis-Nexis, Butterworths, 5th edn, 2003); Piet Jan Slot and Angus Johnston *An Introduction to Competition Law* (Oxford: Hart Publishing, 2006); Maher Dabbah *EC and UK Competition Law: Commentary Cases and Materials* (Cambridge: Cambridge University Press, 2004); on EC law, see DG Goyder *EC Competition Law* (Oxford: Oxford University Press, 4th edn, 2003). On US law, see Ernest Gellhorn, Willliam E Kovacic, and Stephen Calkins Antitrust *Law and Economics* (West Publishing Co, 5th edn, 2004). On Japanese Law, see H Oda *Japanese Law* (Oxford: Oxford University Press, 2nd edn, 2001) ch 13; M Matsushita *International Trade and Competition Law in Japan* (Oxford: Oxford University Press, 1993). On German law, see DM Raybould and A Frith *Law of Monopolies: Competition Law and Practice in the USA, EEC, Germany and the UK* (London: Graham and Trotman, 1991) 382–429. This chapter concentrates on the laws of developed market economy countries, especially US and EC law. Many developing and transitional countries have passed competition laws but their experience in this field is comparatively limited. For information on competition laws in developing countries see UNCTAD *Competition Legislation* at <http://r0.unctad.org/en/ subsites/cpolicy/english/comp_leg.htm> and UNCTAD *Handbook on Competition Legislation* at <http://r0.unctad.org/en/subsites/cpolicy/english/cphandbook.htm>.

[3] See further FM Scherer and D Ross *Industrial Market Structure and Economic Performance* (Boston: Houghton Mifflin, 3rd edn, 1990) ch 2.

[4] See US Sherman Act (26 Stat 209 (1890) as amended) s 1; art 81(1) EC Treaty; Japan Anti-Monopoly Law 1947 (Law No 54, 1947) s 2(6), s 3 available at <http://www.jftc.go.jp/e-page/legislaion/ ama/amended_ama.pdf>; Germany Act Against Restraints of Competition of 27 July 1957 (1957 BGB1 I 1081 as amended) art 1 available at <http://www.bundeskartellamt.de/Englisch/download/ pdf/GWB_7_e.pdf>.

productive or distributional efficiency. This is often referred to as the 'rule of reason' standard.[5]

The second main group of anti-competitive practices stems from the acquisition of a dominant position in a market by a single enterprise. A dominant producer may emerge who will be able to determine supply because of the size of its control over output, as compared with its closest rivals. The dominant producer can increase its profits by creating scarcity through lowering output, thereby forcing consumers to pay higher prices for a commodity that they cannot substitute with other products. It may also prevent the entry of competitors onto the market. Competition law will intervene and control such an abuse of a dominant position, not only to protect consumers from unfair pricing behaviour, but also because the dominant enterprise may become inefficient in that it has no reason to innovate or to reduce costs in the absence of competitive incentives.[6] Where the dominant producer is the only supplier on a market it will enjoy a pure monopoly in that market. Such pure monopoly is rare. More commonly, a market may be dominated by a small number of major producers (oligopolists) who have little room to compete on price, as the pricing decisions of one firm will be immediately matched by those of its rivals.[7] In such cases the temptation to control the market by way of collusive arrangements may be considerable, though it is not an infallible method of reducing competition between the participants, as the threat of non-compliance with the arrangement is ever present.

The third class of regulated anti-competitive conduct relates to mergers and acquisitions. A company may expand its operations by voluntarily combining with another company to create a new company, the merged company, or it may acquire a controlling interest in another company, thereby allowing it to control that other company. A merger may be horizontal, where it takes place between competitors at the same level of the market, or vertical, where it takes place between a company and its supplier or distributor, or conglomerate, where it takes place between firms in unrelated industries. M&As can be driven by short-term financial gain, as where a finance company acquires a target company with a view to its resale. M&As can be friendly, in that all parties agree to the transaction, or hostile,

---

[5] The 'rule of reason' standard is derived from US law. See *Continental TV Inc v GTE Sylvania* 433 US 376 (1977); see further Gellhorn above n 2 at 204–14, 224–36, 259–62. Under EC law the balancing of pro- and anti-competitive effects is done under the terms of art 81(3) EEC Treaty, which lays down criteria for determining whether an agreement or practice caught by art 81(1) can nevertheless be exempted from the legal invalidity that follows from a prohibition under art 81(1). See Whish above n 2 at 124–27,150–63; *Métropole Television v EC Commission* Case T–112/99 [2001] 5 CMLR 1236 para 72 where the Court of First Instance expressly rejected a US style rule of reason and re-emphasized the role of balancing under art 81(3).

[6] See art 82 EC Treaty; Sherman Act above n 4 s 2. Clayton Act 38 Stat 730 (1914); 15 USCA ss 12–27, ss 2–4; Japan Anti-Monopoly Act 1947 above n 4 s 3; Germany Act Against Restraints of Competition above n 4 art 19.

[7] This is known as 'parallel pricing behaviour'. See further Whish above n 2 at 514–16 and *Re Wood Pulp Cartel: A Ahlström OY and Others v EC Commission* [1993] 4 CMLR 407 (ECJ).

in that the target firm does not wish to enter into the merger or acquisition.[8] Expansion through mergers and acquisitions may be pro-competitive where it results in greater economies of scale and scope, or in the replacement of inefficient management with more efficient successors. On the other hand, a merger or acquisition may result in the creation of a dominant enterprise with the potential to control competitive conditions on the market, without producing any compensating efficiency gains.[9] Where this is the case the merger or acquisition may be prohibited by the competition authorities.[10]

(2) The Incidence of Anti-Competitive Conduct on the Part of MNEs and Regulatory Responses

The operations of MNEs have given rise to regulatory responses in all three major areas of competition law. As a preliminary matter, it should be recalled that MNEs grow as a result of market failure, which stimulates the internalization of markets in intermediate products.[11] This may lead to a concentration of ownership and control over such markets in the integrated MNE. It may also lead to a concentration of competing firms in those sectors where MNEs are likely to be prevalent.[12] Thus MNEs tend to operate in oligopolistic or monopolistic markets.[13] The effect of this process is that MNEs display competitive characteristics which are identical to several significant barriers to entry into industries: they engage in high cost advertising, they operate in industries where there are high capital costs to entry and they engage in high cost research and development.[14]

However, it would be wrong to conclude that MNEs are therefore anti-competitive combinations. On the contrary, they may be the most competitive

---

[8] UNCTAD *World Investment Report 2000* (New York and Geneva: United Nations, 2000) at 100–104. UNCTAD notes that short-term financially motivated M&As are decreasing in importance as compared with other M&As.

[9] Whish above n 2 at 783–86; Scherer and Ross n 3 above at 167–74.

[10] See US Clayton Act above n 6 s 7; UK Enterprise Act 2002 Part 3; EC Council Regulation 139/2004/EC OJ [2004] L24/1; Japan Anti-Monopoly Law 1947 above n 4 s 15(1); Germany Act Against Restraints of Competition above n 4 Seventh Chapter arts 35–43.

[11] See ch 1 above.

[12] On the correlation between MNE activity and market concentration see further UNCTAD *World Investment Report 1997* (New York and Geneva: United Nations, 1997) at 136–79. The principal finding of the report is that while entry of MNEs in host developed countries may reduce concentration (although the increased incidence of entry through mergers and acquisitions may change this), their entry into developing host countries may increase concentration if it results in the 'crowding out' of local firms. However concentration per se is not the problem: the resulting market power of the investing firm, and the possibility of its abuse, is. In this regard see also Peter T Muchlinski 'A Case of Czech Beer: Competition and Competitiveness in the Transitional Economies' 59 MLR 658 (1996) at 670–72 examining the risk of concentration as a consequence of the privatization of the Czech brewing industry in the mid-1990s.

[13] See JH Dunning *Multinational Enterprises and the Global Economy* (Wokingham: Addison Wesley, 1993) at 429–30.

[14] See Richard E Caves *Multinational Enterprise and Economic Analysis* (Cambridge: Cambridge University Press, 2nd edn, 1996) at 83–84.

form of business organization available for the market in question. As noted in chapter 1, MNEs may exist in highly competitive environments. That competition will not always be over prices. It may take place in non-price areas such as the production of high quality goods or in after-sales service. Furthermore, certain types of product may be capable of being produced only by highly concentrated firms.[15] These potential benefits have been recognized in law by the fact that most competition law systems do not prohibit corporate group structures per se, and will not treat agreements between a parent and its majority owned and controlled subsidiaries as anti-competitive conspiracies, on the ground that the firms involved constitute a single economic entity in which the subsidiary has no choice but to carry out its parent's plans.[16] However, should the parent not be in actual control of its affiliate, and the latter acts as an independent party, then a conspiracy between the two entities is in principle possible.[17]

The potential benefits of inward investment by MNEs may lead some host countries to offer market-power inducements to MNEs as part of their privatization programmes. Such inducements may include the granting or transferring of exclusive establishment and/or production rights, sales or market rights, and the introduction of protective tariff and non-tariff measures.[18] In addition, a state monopoly may be sold as a going concern to a single foreign investor giving rise to a private dominant position in the host country market. Such measures may be justified on the basis of the need for a swift injection of capital into an ailing state industry, or to boost export competitiveness by allowing the investor to benefit from economies of scale.[19] However, the long-term effects may be negative in terms of enhancing competition and consumer welfare.[20] Thus the value of this policy tool may be doubted. [21]

---

[15] Dunning above n 13 at 431.

[16] See *Copperweld Corporation v Independence Tube Corp* 467 US 752 (1984): US Supreme Court overruled the 'intra-enterprise conspiracy' doctrine and held that a parent and its wholly-owned subsidiary cannot be 'conspiring entities' under the Sherman Act. The 'intra-enterprise conspiracy' doctrine has not been adopted by the European Court of Justice. Thus art 81 of the EC Treaty cannot apply to an agreement between a parent and subsidiary: *Béguelin Import v GL Import Export* Case 22/71 [1971] ECR 949, [1972] CMLR 81; *Viho v EC Commission* Case T–102/92 [1995] 4 CMLR 299 (CFI) upheld by ECJ in C–73/95 P [1997] 4 CMLR 419. However, the economic unity between parent and subsidiary will extend the operation of EC competition law to the parent even if it is not present in the EC as a result of the conduct of its subsidiaries in the Community: see ch 4 at 145–48.

[17] See *Bodson v Pompes Funèbres des Régions Libérées SA* Case 30/87 [1989] 4 CMLR 984 (ECJ).

[18] See UNCTAD *World Investment Report 1997* above n 12 at 159–62.   [19] ibid at 161–63.

[20] ibid at 163. Such arrangements may be inimical to the spirit of WTO disciplines in that a dominant position, monopoly (or export cartel) in the host country that is used mainly for export to foreign markets may reduce foreign consumer welfare by allowing for the charging of supra-competitive prices: Michael J Trebilcock and Robert Howse *The Regulation of International Trade* (London: Routledge, 3rd edn, 2005) at 592. In the absence of specific rules on competition and investment in the WTO it is hard to see how market power inducements could be challenged. They appear to fall outside the jurisdiction of the WTO Agreements in that they affect rights of entry and establishment for other foreign investors and not trade access rights. However, where trade distortion arises as a consequence of such inducements, then a WTO challenge to the underlying government policy may be possible.

[21] See further UNCTAD *World Investment Report 1997* above n 12 at 185–89.

The anti-competitive activities of MNEs will now be considered in turn, beginning with the incidence of anti-competitive agreements or concerted practices operated by MNEs, followed by discussion of abuse of a dominant position by MNEs and concluding with an analysis of international merger and acquisition activities on the part of MNEs.

(a) Anti-Competitive Agreements and Concerted Practices

MNEs have been found to have engaged in a number of anti-competitive arrangements with other firms. In particular, concern has centred on horizontal international marketing and price-fixing cartels, vertical international distribution systems established by MNEs for the sale of their products and the use of joint ventures with other firms. MNEs have also encountered competition controls in relation to restrictive terms in technology transfer licences. These will be considered in detail in chapter 11, as part of the wider issue of technology transfer regulation.

(i) International Cartels

As noted in chapter 1, prior to the Second World War international producers' cartels were commonplace. These sought to coordinate the marketing activities of MNEs by dividing global markets into exclusive spheres of influence, and to dampen price competition through resale price maintenance agreements.[22] However, since 1945 the incidence of such arrangements has decreased. This may be due to increased regulation both in the US and in Europe.[23] Indeed, the destruction of pre-war international cartels was high on the agenda of the US authorities in the early post-war period.[24] This resulted in some of the most controversial cases of extraterritorial action on the part of the US.[25] Furthermore, Japan, a number of leading European states and the EC passed new antitrust laws during the late 1940s and 1950s, acting in line with the post-war policy of economic liberalization.[26] A further factor deterring the use of cartels may be the increased incidence of competition between MNEs from the US, Europe and Japan, and a shift away from primary industries towards those producing differentiated goods in which competition is more likely.[27]

Nevertheless, cases involving international cartels have surfaced at regular intervals over the years.[28] This has prompted renewed efforts to control major

---

[22] See above at 19–24. See further Wyatt Wells *Antitrust and the Formation of the Postwar World*, (New York: Columbia University Press, 2002).
[23] Caves above n 14 at 92–93. See further JA Rahl 'International Cartels and Their Regulation' in O Schachter and R Hellawell (eds) *Competition in International Business: Law and Policy on Restrictive Practices* (New York: Columbia University Press, 1981) 240.
[24] See Haight 'The Restrictive Business Practices Clause in United States Treaties: An Antitrust Tranquillizer for International Trade' 70 Yale LJ 240 at 240–41 (1960).
[25] See ch 4 at 133–35.   [26] See n 4 above.   [27] Caves above n 14.
[28] For example the leading EC cases: *ICI v EC Commission* [1972] ECR 619, [1972] CMLR 557; *Suiker Unie v EC Commission (Sugar Cartel)* [1975] ECR 1663, [1976] 1 CMLR 295; *Compagnie*

'hard core cartels'. According to the OECD such a cartel, 'is an anticompetitive agreement, anticompetitive concerted practice, or anticompetitive arrangement by competitors to fix prices, make rigged bids (collusive tenders) establish output restrictions or quotas or share or divide markets by allocating customers, suppliers, territories or lines of commerce'.[29] It is regarded as the 'most egregious' violation of competition law that can 'injure consumers in many countries by raising prices and restricting supply, thus making goods and services completely unavailable to some purchasers and unnecessarily expensive for others'.[30] The OECD believes that closer international cooperation between competition authorities is required to control such cases, that sanctions should be adequate to act as a deterrent and enforcement procedures should be adequate to detect and remedy hard core cartels.[31] One recent feature of such enforcement is the increased incidence of the criminalization of price-fixing and the increasing willingness of the US to seek extradition of suspects under such laws.[32]

The major technical problem in cartel cases has been to distinguish genuine concerted action from the kind of parallel behaviour on prices and marketing strategies that is common in oligopolistic markets. According to the European

---

Royale Asturienne des Mines SA and Rheinzink GmbH v EC Commission [1984] ECR 1679, [1985] 1 CMLR 688; *Zinc Producer Group* OJ [1984] L220/27, [1985] 2 CMLR 108; *Re Polypropylene Cartel: SA Hercules NV v EC Commission* [1992] 4 CMLR 84 (CFI); *Wood Pulp* OJ [1985] L85/1, [1985] 3 CMLR 474 overturned on appeal: *Re Wood Pulp Cartel: A.Ahlström OY and Others v EC Commission* [1993] 4 CMLR 407. More recent reported cases include *Re the Carbonless Paper Cartel* Case COMP/E-1/36.212 [2004] 5 CMLR 1303; *Re the Plasterboard Cartel* Case COMP/E-1/37.152 [2005] 5 CMLR 1558; *Re Vitamins Cartel* Case T–15/02 [2006] 5 CMLR 27 and Case T–26/02 [2006] 5 CMLR 169; *Re Luxembourg Brewers Cartel* Joined Cases T 49–51/02 [2006] 4 CMLR 266 and *Re French Brewers Cartel* Case COMP/C. 37.750/B2) [2006] 4 CMLR 577. In 2005 the EC Competition Commission issued five final decisions against cartels in which it fined 37 undertakings a total of €683 million (compared with 21 undertakings and a total of €390 million in fines in 2004) para 174 For details of the cases see paras 182–200: EC Commission *Report on Competition Policy 2005* (Brussels, 15 June 2006 SEC(2006) 761 final) available at <http://ec.europa.eu/comm/-competition/annual_reports/2005/en.pdf>. See also for US experience International Competition Policy Advisory Committee (Antitrust Division) *Final Report* (2000) ch 4 available at <http://www.usdoj.gov/atr/icpac/chapter4.htm> and US Department of Justice Antitrust Division press releases which document numerous recent prosecutions at <http://www.usdoj.gov/atr>. On cartels and developing countries see Frederic Jenny 'Cartels and Collusion in Developing Countries: Lessons from Empirical Evidence' 29 World Competition 109 (2006).

[29] OECD Council *Recommendation Concerning Effective Action Against Hard Core Cartels* 25 March 1998 (OECD Doc C(98) 35/Final 13 May 1998) section A, para 2(a).

[30] ibid preamble.

[31] ibid Section A para 1 and Section B. This call has been acted upon by the EC Commission: 'Upon taking up office the Commissioner for Competition, Neelie Kroes, identified the fight against hardcore cartels as one of the areas in which the Competition DG must concentrate its efforts. That increased focus has manifested itself in the setting up of a new Directorate within the Competition DG devoted exclusively to anti-cartel enforcement. The Directorate became operational on 1 June [2005]. The Directorate handles the majority of cartel cases and takes a leading role, in close cooperation with the Directorate for Policy and Strategic Support, in developing policy in the area of cartel enforcement.' EC Commission *Report on Competition Policy 2005* above n 28 at para 172.

[32] Such criminal sanctions are in place in Japan, Canada, South Korea, France, and the UK: see 'Extradition Fears over US Cartel Crackdown' *Financial Times* 28 July 2006 at 1. See further for the UK Enterprise Act 2002 ss 188–202 discussed in Slot and Johnston above n 2 at 230–34, Whish above n 2 at 390–95.

Court of Justice (ECJ) in the *Wood Pulp* case,[33] parallel conduct cannot be regarded as furnishing evidence of unlawful concertation unless this is the only explanation of the conduct. If practices such as parallel price increases can be satisfactorily explained by the oligopolistic tendencies of the market then there is no proof of concertation between competitors. A similar approach has been taken in the US. There must be clear evidence of conspiracy to found a violation of the Sherman Act and this cannot be furnished by 'circumstantial evidence of consciously parallel behaviour'.[34]

(ii) Vertical International Distribution Systems

MNEs are likely to establish international distribution networks for their products either through their subsidiaries or through independent distributors. Usually, such networks will be based on agreements between the multinational producer and its controlled or independent distributor. These may include restrictive conditions. In particular, the distributor may be bound by an exclusive distribution arrangement, whereby it agrees to distribute only the products of the MNE in question and to do so only in a defined sales territory. Where such restrictions extend to an international network of sales subsidiaries or independent distributors, there arises the danger that the network will be used to partition geographical markets and to insulate them from competition originating from distributors, or third parties, operating outside the relevant sales territory.

Where significant price differences exist between the various territories, an incentive is created for distributors or third parties in a low price territory to export the contract products to customers in a high price territory by way of parallel trade. If this is prohibited by the terms of the applicable distribution agreement, consumers in the high price territory will be deprived of cheaper goods as intra-brand competition will have been restricted. On the other hand, the MNE may be unable to build up a significant international market for its products without offering its distributors the prospect of earning a reasonable return in exchange for the obligations they undertake to promote the product. Exclusivity offers such an incentive as it protects against sales by third parties ('free riders') who may benefit from the distributor's promotional efforts. Therefore a degree of territorial protection and partitioning may be acceptable for legitimate commercial reasons.

Competition authorities will not normally strike down an exclusive distribution network involving sales subsidiaries on the basis of the economic unity of the multinational group. However, such arrangements may amount to an abuse of a dominant position if the firm forecloses competition through the use of its controlled network, a matter to be considered in sub-section (b) below. In the case of

---

[33] Above n 7.
[34] *Theatre Enterprises Inc v Paramount Film Distributing Corp* 346 US 537 (1954).

independent distributors, authorities have tended to use a case-by-case analysis applying a 'rule of reason' approach.[35] Only if the network is part of a more general pattern of similar networks used by competing firms, and the market is highly concentrated and has high entry barriers, will the arrangement be subject to control.[36] However, if the network is used as a means of maintaining resale prices it will be struck down.[37]

Some systems may control distribution networks for policy reasons that go beyond the sole concern of maintaining competition. Thus, the EC Commission will strike down a distribution network that prevents single market integration by way of restrictive terms in distribution agreements.[38] Such terms may include exclusive licences of industrial property rights which are used by the licensee to prevent parallel imports from outside the contract territory.[39] In Japan, restrictive exclusive distribution networks based on *keiretsu* groups[40] have been subjected to the 1991 Guideline on Distribution Systems and Business Practices.[41] This is in part a response to criticism from foreign firms that they have been forced to enter the Japanese domestic market at a competitive disadvantage due to the need to build up distribution networks from scratch, as existing networks were prohibited from dealing in competing goods. Furthermore, considerations of maintaining good international economic relations with the US were a significant factor in these reforms, as the issue of the anti-competitive effects of *keiretsu* companies was a major topic in the US-Japan Structural Impediments Talks.[42] However, despite its findings that *keiretsu* groups have had the effect of excluding foreign competitors,

---

[35] On 'rule of reason' see n 5 above.

[36] See *GTE Sylvania* above n 5; on the EC approach see *Stergios Delimitis v Henninger Brau AG* [1992] 5 CMLR 210 (ECJ); Regulation 2790/99 OJ [1999] L336/21 and *Guidelines on Vertical Restraints* OJ [2000] C291/1, [2000] 5 CMLR 1074 and Whish above n 2 ch 16.

[37] See, on US law, *Dr Miles Medical Co v John D Park and Sons Co* 220 US 373 (1911); *GTE Sylvania* above n 5 433 US 51 n 18 On EC law, see *Guidelines on Vertical Restraints* above n 36 at paras 225–28.

[38] See, for example, *Re Po/Needles* Case F–1/38,338 [2005] 4 CMLR 792; *Re Pokemon Cards SARL La Souris Bleue v Topps Group* Case COMP/C-3/37.980 [2006] 4 CMLR 1713.

[39] See *Consten and Grundig v EC Commission* [1966] ECR 299, [1966] CMLR 418; *LTM v Machinenbau Ulm* [1966] ECR 235, [1966] CMLR 357; *Centrafarm v Sterling* [1974] ECR 1147, [1974] 2 CMLR 480; *Centrafarm v Winthrop* [1974] ECR 1183, [1974] 2 CMLR 480; *Nungesser v EC Commission (Maize Seeds)* [1982] ECR 2015, [1983] 1 CMLR 278, Regulation 2790/99 above n 36 art 2(3), *Guidelines on Vertical Restraints* above n 36 paras 30–44.

[40] On which see further ch 2 at 63–65.

[41] Executive Office Fair Trading Commission *The Antimonopoly Act Guidelines Concerning Distribution Systems and Business Practices* (11 July 1991) available at <http://www.jftc.go.jp/e-page/legislation/ama/distribution.pdf>.

[42] See *Joint Report of the US-Japan Working Group on the Structural Impediments Initiative* (28 June 1990); Paul Sheard *The Economics of Japanese Corporate Organisation and the 'Structural Impediments' Debate: A Critical Review* (Australia-Japan Research Centre, Australian National University, Canberra, Pacific Economic Paper No 205, March 1992) and '*Keiretsu* Competition, and Market Access' in J David Richardson and Edward M Graham (eds) *Global Competition Policy* (Washington DC: Institute for International Economics, 1997) ch 16.

the Japanese Fair Trade Commission has not imposed any punitive sanctions against such companies.[43] This inaction should be seen against the background of the US Department of Justice policy statement of 3 April 1992, which asserted that the department will take antitrust action against conduct occurring overseas that would be contrary to US antitrust laws and that restrains US exports whether or not there is direct harm to US consumers. This is aimed at *keiretsu* practices. However, for practical and diplomatic reasons it may not be possible for the US to put into effect the threat of extraterritorial enforcement that is explicit in the statement.[44] To date that threat has not materialized.

(iii) Joint Ventures

It was seen in chapter 2 that MNEs may use joint ventures with other enterprises as a means of developing their international operations. Joint ventures have been used as a means of effecting strategic alliances for the purposes of research and development and/or production and/or distribution of goods or services. Such joint ventures can be horizontal or vertical or combine elements of both. Although not objectionable in principle, joint ventures can be and have been used as a vehicle for anti-competitive concertation between firms. At least three main types of anti-competitive risk have been identified.[45]

First, a joint venture can be used as a vehicle for anti-competitive collusion between participants who may coordinate output decisions and exchange commercially sensitive information which enables them to reduce competition inter se and to cartelize the market in which the joint venturers operate.[46] Such collusion has been a feature of raw materials industries where competitors have established upstream joint ventures thereby creating the possibility of control over output through control over the supply of the raw material in question.[47] Secondly, the joint venture may reduce or eliminate actual or potential competition between the parents. Thus, it is unlikely that the parents will continue to operate as independent competitors in the market covered by the joint venture, should they already be

---

[43] 'Japan's Corporate Groups are Accused of Obstruction' *Financial Times* 30 June 1993 at 8.

[44] See US Department of Justice Press Release 92–117, 3 April 1992. The full text of the policy statement is reproduced in the *Financial Times* 30 April 1992 at 18. For a discussion of the legal problems associated with the policy statement, see Jason Coppel 'A Question of Keiretsu: Extending the Long Arm of US Anti-trust' 13 ECLR 192 (1995). See further Joel Davidow 'Keiretsu and US Antitrust' 24 Law & Pol'y Int'l Bus. 1035 (1993); Julie A Shepard 'Using United States Antitrust Laws Against the Keiretsu as a Wedge into the Japanese Market' 6 Transnat'l Law 345 (1993).

[45] See J Brodley 'Joint Ventures and Antitrust Policy' 95 Harv.LR 1521 at 1530–34 (1982).

[46] See eg *US v ICI* 100 F Supp 504 (SDNY) *mod.* 105 F Supp 215 (SDNY 1951); *US v Minnesota Mining and Manufacturing Co* 92 F Supp 947 (D Mass 1950) *mod.* 96 F Supp 356 (D Mass 1951).

[47] See Caves above n 14 at 107–108 discussing the oil and aluminium industries. Such anti-competitive effects can be offset by the entry of new firms. However, this may be difficult in industries such as oil where there exist high levels of vertical integration. New entrants may simply be absorbed by allowing them to join existing joint ventures.

involved in that market. Furthermore, potential competition between the parents and the joint venture is likely to be curtailed as the parents are unlikely to enter into any new market covered by the joint venture. Where such a reduction of competition is expressly agreed it may have a market dividing effect not dissimilar to a cartel.[48] The potential competition doctrine assumes that independent entry by the parents into the market covered by the joint venture is possible, and that the non-entry of the parents will significantly reduce the number of competitors in the market. These elements have not always been rigorously analysed in earlier decided cases, leading to criticism that pro-competitive joint ventures have been struck down on the basis of a purely theoretical possibility that the parents could have entered the market independently.[49] In addition to a dampening of competition in the market in which the joint venture operates, there may be a danger that the cooperation engendered by the joint venture will encourage a dampening of competition in other markets in which the parents are actual or potential competitors. Such 'spill-over' effects will be monitored by competition authorities.

Thirdly, a joint venture can be used as a means of excluding or hampering access for third party firms to raw materials or finished goods. This may act as a barrier to entry for new firms, and increase the cost of operations to existing firms. The problem can arise at the upstream end of an industry where the parents set up a joint venture to develop a new raw material supply. Should the joint venture control access to a very high proportion of the total supply of the raw material in question, then third parties will be at its mercy as regards access to that raw material. Similarly, at the downstream end, a joint distribution venture can create a monopolistic market for the goods or services in question, restricting alternative sources of direct supply from the parents and giving the joint venturers control over the market. Such an arrangement can be used as a method of partitioning markets between the parents, especially where there are few, if any, competing suppliers.[50]

---

[48] See eg *Yamaha Motor Co v FTC* 657 F 2d 971 (8th Cir 1981.) *cert.den.* 50 USLW 3799 (US 4 April 1982): discussed Brodley above n 45 at 1576–78.

[49] See eg the US case *US v Penn Ohlin Chemical Co* 378 US 158 (1964). For criticism of the potential competition theory as applied by the EC Commission, see Pathak 'The EC Commission's Approach to Joint Ventures: A Policy of Contradictions' [1991] 5 ECLR 171 discussing the EC Commission cases of *Re Vacuum Interrupters (No 1)* OJ [1977] L48/32, [1977] 1 CMLR D67; *Re Vacuum Interrupters (No 2)* [1981] 2 CMLR 217; *Re Optical Fibres* OJ [1986] L236/30; *Mitchell Cotts/Sofiltra* OJ [1987] L41/31, [1988] 4 CMLR 111. See now, for a more sympathetic view of the pro-competitive effects of joint ventures, *Re ODIN* [1991] 4 CMLR 832; *Re ECR 900* [1992] 4 CMLR 54 where the EC Commission cleared each joint venture under art 81(1); but see *BBC Brown Boveri/NGK* [1989] 4 CMLR 610; *Eirepage* OJ [1992] L306/22, [1993] 4 CMLR 64 where the EC Commission held each joint venture to be caught by art 81(1), but gave individual exemption under art 81(3).

[50] See eg *Siemens/Fanuc* [1988] 4 CMLR 945 (EC Commission) where a reciprocal exclusive distribution agreement for numerical controls (NCs) between the leading European and Japanese producers was found to have violated art 81(1) EEC on the ground inter alia that it divided world markets by denying European customers access to supplies from Japan, where the Japanese partner was selling its NCs at prices some 34 per cent below those charged in Europe by its exclusive

Despite the above mentioned dangers to competition, international joint ventures can be regarded as generally pro-competitive. First, such arrangements can create greater stability for high risk projects that one firm might find too uncertain to undertake. The pooling of technological skills, capital, and personnel may be the only way to secure an advance in research and development leading to new products or processes. As seen in chapter 2, MNEs are increasingly using joint ventures to develop and produce high technology goods. Secondly, a joint venture may be required to achieve sufficient economies of scale to make production viable without forcing the participants into a permanent union through merger. This may be an important consideration where the partners are firms from different countries, making merger a more difficult option. Thirdly, a joint venture might permit greater specialization in production allowing the partners to develop their particular competitive advantages more fully.[51] Finally, in a market with appreciable numbers of competitors, joint distribution arrangements between producers may be acceptable where the product lines of each partner are complementary and the joint distribution agreement will increase consumer access to a larger product range.[52] This may be particularly true where a smaller firm allows a larger firm with a more extensive distribution network to market its range across a territory that the smaller firm could not reach by itself. It is a means of permitting international distribution to the products of a firm that could not otherwise afford to go multinational.

In the light of such considerations competition authorities are taking an increasingly lenient approach towards joint ventures. Thus the US Department of Justice applies a rule of reason analysis which involves the following approach:

The Agencies' analysis begins with an examination of the nature of the relevant agreement. As part of this examination, the Agencies ask about the business purpose of the agreement and examine whether the agreement, if already in operation, has caused anticompetitive harm. In some cases, the nature of the agreement and the absence of market power together may demonstrate the absence of anticompetitive harm. In such cases, the Agencies do not

---

distributor. However, this case can be explained by the market dominance of the parties, especially of the Japanese partner, who was at the time the global leader in NC technology. In a less concentrated market such a horizontal joint selling arrangement might have pro-competitive effects.

[51] See further EC Commission Regulation 2658/2000/EC OJ [2000] L304/3, [2001] 4 CMLR 800 on specialization agreements which covers inter alia joint production agreements: discussed by Whish above n 2 at 566–69. A joint venture arrangement may be used to effect a restructuring between firms in an industry suffering from overcapacity: see *Re Enichem and ICI* [1989] 4 CMLR 54.

[52] See US Department of Justice and Federal Trade Commission *Antitrust Guidelines for Collaborations among Competitors* (April 2000) available at <http://www.ftc.gov/os/2000/04/ftcdojguidelines.pdf> at para 2.1 at 6: 'The Agencies recognize that consumers may benefit from competitor collaborations in a variety of ways. For example, a competitor collaboration may enable participants to offer goods or services that are cheaper, more valuable to consumers, or brought to market faster than would be possible absent the collaboration. A collaboration may allow its participants to better use existing assets, or may provide incentives for them to make output-enhancing investments that

challenge the agreement. Alternatively, where the likelihood of anticompetitive harm is evident from the nature of the agreement, or anticompetitive harm has resulted from an agreement already in operation, then, absent overriding benefits that could offset the anticompetitive harm, the Agencies challenge such agreements without a detailed market analysis.

If the initial examination of the nature of the agreement indicates possible competitive concerns, but the agreement is not one that would be challenged without a detailed market analysis, the Agencies analyze the agreement in greater depth. The Agencies typically define relevant markets and calculate market shares and concentration as an initial step in assessing whether the agreement may create or increase market power or facilitate its exercise. The Agencies examine the extent to which the participants and the collaboration have the ability and incentive to compete independently. The Agencies also evaluate other market circumstances, e.g. entry, that may foster or prevent anticompetitive harms.

If the examination of these factors indicates no potential for anticompetitive harm, the Agencies end the investigation without considering procompetitive benefits. If investigation indicates anticompetitive harm, the Agencies examine whether the relevant agreement is reasonably necessary to achieve procompetitive benefits that likely would offset anticompetitive harms. [53]

The EC Commission also takes a positive view of joint ventures, although this has not always been the case. [54] Since 1985, joint ventures in research and development (R&D) have been exempt from Article 81(1) EC Treaty, provided they conform with the requirements of the block exemption in this field. [55] This exemption applies to the joint research and development of products, the joint exploitation of results, and the joint distribution of the products of such joint R&D. It is subject to the parties retaining access to the results of the R&D for the purposes of further research or exploitation and to a requirement that joint exploitation only occurs where there has been an actual economic benefit from the joint R&D. [56] Where the parties are not actual or potential competitors exemption will last for seven years, regardless of existing market shares and, thereafter, so long as the parties combined market share has not exceeded 25 per cent at that date. [57] Where the parties are actual competitors then exemption will only be granted if their combined market shares for the products capable of being improved or replaced by the joint R&D does not exceed 25 per cent. [58]

---

would not occur absent the collaboration. The potential efficiencies from competitor collaborations may be achieved through a variety of contractual arrangements including joint ventures, trade or professional associations, licensing arrangements, or strategic alliances.'

[53] ibid para 1.2. at 4. The analysis is described in detail at paras 3.31–3.37 of the guidelines.
[54] See references in n 49 above.
[55] Commission Regulation 2659/00/EC OJ [2000] L304/7, [2001] 4 CMLR 808; see Whish above n 2 at 559–64. See also *Guidelines on Vertical Restraints* above n 36 paras 39–77.
[56] ibid art 3(2)-(4).   [57] ibid art 4(1).   [58] ibid art 4(2).

(b) 'Abuse of a Dominant Position' or 'Monopolization'

It was seen in the introduction to this section that MNEs tend to be highly concentrated firms operating in concentrated markets. Consequently, they may enjoy a measure of market power in international and national markets that purely national firms cannot match. To some extent this is inevitable and does not, of itself, create competition problems. So long as dominant MNEs do not deliberately seek the destruction of smaller competitors, or thwart the entry of new competitors, their operations are unlikely to attract the concern of competition authorities. Indeed, the presence of large internationally integrated firms may be beneficial to consumers, offering new products and services at a reasonable cost that is achieved through the greater economies of scale and scope offered by international production. It may also enhance the efficiency of the local economy through the introduction of improved product and process technologies, improved management systems, better access to global markets, and by spurring local competitors to improve their own efficiency.[59]

On the other hand MNEs may be able to use their internalization advantages in ways that abuse competition.[60] For example, the MNE may use transfer pricing manipulations to extract monopolistic profits from the host state. A notable example of such abuse was condemned in the early 1970s in the UK and Germany, when the pharmaceutical company Hoffmann-La Roche was found to have manipulated its transfer prices for Librium and Valium, resulting in the remittance of excessive profits from the UK and Germany.[61] Arguably, transfer pricing abuses are better seen as issues for tax rather than competition authorities. However, these authorities will become involved where the result of such abuses is the overcharging of customers and/or the driving out of existing competition and/or the creation of barriers to entry as a result of the greater market power enjoyed by the MNE through its increased profitability.

Similarly, a MNE can restrict competition through its exclusive ownership of proprietary technology that may be required for the operation of effective competition in the market concerned. Thus, in 1984, IBM was required by the EC Commission to make available to its competitors its System 370 products

---

[59] See UNCTAD *World Investment Report 1997* above n 12 at 150–56.

[60] The examples below are taken from EC case law, which highlights the transnational nature of certain abuses of dominant position. US case law has tended to concentrate on similar abuses effected by dominant domestic firms: see Gellhorn above n 2 ch 4.

[61] See UK Monopolies and Mergers Commission *Chlordiazepoxide and Diazepam* (HMSO, 1973); Bundeskartellamt G Beschlussabteilung 36–432190–T–37/73 both summarized in Greenhill and Herbolzheimer 'International Transfer Pricing: The Restrictive Business Practices Approach' 14 JWTL 232 (1980). In 1993 Brazil accused pharmaceutical companies of imposing abusive price increases on 150 products. This was blamed on the oligopolistic nature of the market, in that seven MNEs controlled 87 per cent of the antibiotics market: 'Brazil's Drug Companies Face Anti-trust Action' *Financial Times* 27 January 1993 at 6.

without which the latter could not upgrade their 'IBM compatible' computer products.[62] The possession of intellectual property rights could also be abused by a refusal to grant a licence to a competitor where this results in the denial of an opportunity to offer a new product or service.[63] Denial of access to an 'essential facility' owned and operated by the firm to its competitors may also amount to an abuse.[64]

Furthermore, the international integration of the MNE may serve to reduce competition to an unacceptable level. This may happen where the firm has exclusive control over a vital raw material that it alone can extract or produce.[65] Equally, the firm's control over an integrated international production, transport and distribution network may be abused. This is of particular concern where the network is significantly larger than that of its nearest competitor and is therefore insulated from inter-brand competition. Thus in *United Brands v EC Commission*,[66] the ECJ found that United Brands, one of the world's leading vertically integrated producers and distributors of bananas, had abused its dominant position on that market inter alia by charging discriminatory prices in each national market, a practice that could not be justified by local commercial conditions, and by limiting intra-brand price competition through bans on parallel trading in unripened bananas between lower and higher price sales areas.

Other marketing practices that have been condemned as abuses of a dominant position enjoyed by a MNE include: refusals to supply,[67] loyalty rebates to customers that tie them into the sales of the dominant firm,[68] target discounts for distributors which force them to purchase their requirements from the dominant firm,[69] tied sales of goods as a condition of access to the

---

[62] *The Community v International Business Machines Corporation* [1984] 3 CMLR 147. See also the Microsoft case summarized in n 70 below.

[63] See Joined Cases C–241/91 and C–242/91 P *RTE and ITP Ltd v Commission* [1995] 4 CMLR 718. The exclusive ownership of rights to TV listings by RTE, the Irish state broadcaster, the BBC and ITP, pertaining to broadcasts in Northern Ireland and the Republic of Ireland, was held to breach art 82 where they refused access to those rights for a private TV listings company. Access to the information covered by those rights was seen as essential to the development of the private TV listings market in competition with the state broadcasters own listings. However, this case is exceptional and a refusal to supply intellectual property rights will not normally be seen as an abuse of a dominant position: see Whish above n 2 at 665–66 and see also Case C–7/97 *Oscar Bronner GmbH v Mediaprint Zeitungs und Zeitschriftsverlag GmbH* [1999] 4 CMLR 112 where the RTE case was described as exceptional. See further Case C–418/01 *IMS Health GmbH & Co OHG v NDC Health GmbH & Co KG* [2004] ECR–I 5039.

[64] For example, the denial of access to port facilities by their owner to the detriment of competitors who run services out of the port alongside those offered by the owner: see *Sealink/B&I – Holyhead Interim Measures* [1992] 5 CMLR 255.

[65] See *Commercial Solvents v EC Commission* [1974] ECR 223, [1974] 1 CMLR 309.

[66] [1978] ECR 207, [1978] 1 CMLR 429.   [67] *United Brands* ibid.

[68] *Hoffmann-La Roche & Co AG v EC Commission* [1979] ECR 461, [1979] 3 CMLR 211.

[69] *Nederlandsche Banden-Industrie Michelin NV v EC Commission* [1983] ECR 3461, [1985] 1 CMLR 282.

dominant firm's products,[70] and predatory price cutting as a means of driving out competitors.[71]

The major legal issues to be determined in a case of alleged unilateral anti-competitive conduct are as follows. First, the dominance of the firm on the market must be established. This involves a two step analysis. At the outset, the relevant market must be defined.[72] This requires an often difficult analysis of the product or products involved on the basis of demand side substitutability. In essence, if the product in question is interchangeable with another then both are within the same market.[73] In some cases this analysis will be supplemented by that of the

[70] *Hilti AG v EC Commission* [1992] 4 CMLR 16 (CFI); appeal dismissed: Case C–53/92 P *Hilti v Commission, interveners: Bauco (UK) Ltd and Profix Distribution Ltd* [1994] 4 CMLR 614. See, more recently, the *Microsoft* litigation in the US and EC: *US v Microsoft* 253 F 3d 34 (DC Cir 2001) *cert den* 120 S Ct 350 (2001); case settled *US v Microsoft* F Supp 2d 144 (DDC 2002) discussed in Gellhorn above n 2 at 154–59. The EC Commission has held that Microsoft's practice of refusing to supply its competitors with certain 'interoperability information' constituted a breach of art 82 as it prevented them from using this information to develop competing products. In addition, supplying its Windows operating system with its Windows Media Player was an unlawful tying of products under art 82: *Microsoft Corporation* (Case COMP/C–3/37.792) [2005] 4 CMLR 965. Microsoft lodged an appeal against the Commission decision on 7 June 2004: OJ [2004] C179/18 (Case T–201/04) (2004/ C179/36). It argued that the Commission was wrong in relation to the interoperability information access issue, as the information in question was not indispensable to competitors to achieve interoperability with Windows operating systems, it infringed the intellectual property rights of the applicant and the EUs obligations under the WTO TRIPs Agreement. Secondly, on the tying issue, it was mere speculation to assume that the presence of the Windows Media Player would force all internet media providers to use the Windows format and so foreclose competition from other internet media formats. Thirdly, the contested decision ignored the benefits flowing from the applicant's business model. Fourthly, the Windows Media Player and the Windows software were not separate products. On 25 June 2004, Microsoft lodged an interim measures appeal at the Court of First Instance (CFI) for the decision's remedies to be suspended pending the outcome of its main appeal. On the same date, the Commission voluntarily suspended Microsoft's obligations pursuant to the decision pending the outcome of Microsoft's interim measures appeal. The application for interim relief was dismissed: Case T–201/04 R *Microsoft Corporation v EC Commission* [2005] 4 CMLR 406. Following exchanges of written pleadings, an oral hearing took place before the Grand Chamber of the CFI on 24–28 April 2006. At the time of writing (September 2006) the judgment of the CFI is pending. In July 2006 the Commission imposed a penalty payment of €280.5 million on Microsoft for continued non-compliance with the March 2004 decision: EC Commission *Press Release* IP/06/979 12 July 2006 at <http://europa.eu/rapid/pressReleasesAction.do?reference=IP/06/979&format=HTML&aged=0&language=EN&guiLanguage=en>. On 15 November 2006 the Commission again reviewed Microsoft's compliance: see EC Commission Memo (MEMO/06/430 of 15 November 2006) at <http://www.europa.eu/rapid/pressReleases>.

[71] *ECS/AKZO* OJ [1985] L374/1 [1986] 3 CMLR 273; (EC Commission) C–62/86 *AKZO Chemie BV v EC Commission* [1993] 5 CMLR 215 (ECJ); *Wanadoo Interactive* Cases COMP/38.223 [2005] 5 CMLR 120.

[72] See, for the EC approach, EC Commission *Notice on the Definition of the Relevant Market for the Purposes of Community Competition Law* [1997] OJ C372/5, [1998] 4 CMLR 177 or <http://ec.europa.eu/comm/competition/antitrust/relevma_en.html> discussed in Whish above n 2 at 24–48. For US approach see Gellhorn above n 2 at 117–28.

[73] Both US and EC law use the SSNIP test – a product is interchangeable with another if a 'small but significant non-transitory increase in price' in one product will cause customers to switch from that product to a substitute. The EC Commission Notice sets the SNIIP increase at 5–10 per cent of the existing product price: ibid para 17. In addition, the characteristics and uses of the products in question will be considered.

supply side of the market. Thus a product may be substitutable for another if the supplier of one product can switch to the production of a substitute in the short term without incurring significant costs or risks in response to small and permanent changes in relative prices.[74] Once the product market is ascertained, the geographical scope of the market must be determined on the basis of the similarity of costs and other competitive conditions in a particular area of operations.[75] Finally, the temporal scope of the market must be determined to ascertain whether there are seasonal variations in competitive conditions.[76]

Having defined the relevant market, the firm's dominance in that market must be shown. A monopoly of the market would be clear evidence of dominance. Usually, this is a very rare case, although in developing countries a MNE may be the sole operator in a particular market. In most situations the firm will coexist with other firms. Thus the main issue is whether the firm can act independently without regard for its competitors, customers or consumers and be able to prevent competition.[77] In this respect a number of factors are relevant. They include inter alia: the market share of the firm,[78] the technological advantages it possesses, the extent of vertical and/or horizontal integration, economies of scale, access to capital, product differentiation, and overall size, strength and performance.[79]

Once the dominant position of the firm has been established, then the legality of the alleged abusive conduct will be considered. Although the kinds of practices described in the introduction to this sub-section will offer strong evidence of an abuse, competition authorities will analyse the facts in the light of any objective justifications offered for the conduct.[80] Equally, where alleged abusive conduct would make no economic sense for the dominant enterprise, the theoretical possibility of such conduct might be insufficient to ground a finding to this effect. For example, in *Matsushita Electric Industrial Co v Zenith Radio Corp*,[81] the US Supreme

---

[74] EC Commission Notice above n 72 at para 20.

[75] The EC Commission Notice ibid paras 28–32. The Commission will also apply the SSNIP test to determine whether customers will react to a small permanent price increase by switching to suppliers from another area.

[76] For example, in *United Brands* above n 66 the Commission considered seasonal variations in demand for direct categories of fruit as a factor in determining the scope of the market for bananas in the EC. The ECJ did not deal with this issue: Whish above n 2 at 42.

[77] See *United Brands* above n 66 at para 38; *Hoffmann-La Roche* above n 68 at para 38.

[78] Usually, the larger the share the more likely there is to be dominance. However, even very large shares do not inevitably point to dominance. In *Hoffmann-La Roche* ibid the ECJ held that a very large share is evidence of a dominant position in the absence of exceptional circumstances and where it is held for some time (at para 41). In *United Brands* ibid the ECJ held that a market share of 40–45 per cent was enough to show the firm's dominance in the circumstances of the case. For criticism of this analysis, see Whish, above n 2 at p 182; Valgiurata 'Price Discrimination Under Art.86 EEC: The United Brands Case' 31 ICLQ 36 (1982). The US courts will not, in general, be concerned with unilateral conduct if a firm has a market share of less than 40 per cent See Gellhorn above n 2 at 137.

[79] See Whish ibid at 183–91 on EC approach; Gellhorn ibid at 140–90 on US approach.

[80] See eg *Hilti AG v EC Commission* above n 70, where the defendant company argued, unsuccessfully, that it had prohibited the use of nails manufactured by competing firms in its nail guns to protect health and safety.   [81] 475 US 574 (1986).

Court rejected a private suit brought by a group of US corporations that manufactured or sold consumer electronic products, alleging that 21 Japanese competitors were engaging in a long-term conspiracy to undercut prices on the US market so as to expand their market share, on the ground that it made no reasonable business sense for the Japanese firms to sustain losses for decades without any foreseeable profits. This case illustrates a feature of US law in this area, namely that the court will consider the reasonableness or otherwise of inferring market power from the evidence before it.[82] Indeed, in more recent years, the US courts have given a relatively broad discretion to dominant firms to implement pricing, product development, and promotional strategies.[83]

In conclusion, it should be stressed that the mere fact that MNEs may dominate certain markets, and may even be monopolists in certain jurisdictions, does not of itself indicate anti-competitive conduct. Each case should be considered on its facts, and only where the market power of the MNE is being abused should control occur. However, it should be noted that the possibility of anti-competitive effects may prompt certain states to control the entry and establishment of MNEs on the basis of preliminary screening procedures in their foreign investment laws, such as those outlined in chapter 5, or use their powers to review mergers and acquisitions to the same effect.

(c) Mergers and Acquisitions

During the 1980s and 1990s the incidence of international mergers and acquisitions (M&A) involving MNEs reached unprecedented levels. Over 24,000 such transactions took place. This occurred in two main waves, 1988–90 and since 1995. Both periods represent moments of high economic growth and widespread industrial restructuring.[84] The reasons behind the first wave lay primarily in the need for firms to expand their international operations so as to become international players in the emerging global economy.[85] Further stimulus came from

---

[82] See further *Eastman Kodak Co v Image Technical Services Inc* 112 S Ct 2072 (1992), 62 ATRR 780 (1992) (US Sup Ct).

[83] Gellhorn above n 2 at 163 and see *Verizon Communications Inc v Law Offices of Curtis V Trinko* 540 US 398 at 407, 124 S Ct 872 at 879, 157 L Ed 2d 823 at 836, 2004 US LEXIS 657 13: 'The mere possession of monopoly power, and the concomitant charging of monopoly prices, is not only not unlawful; it is an important element of the free-market system. The opportunity to charge monopoly prices – at least for a short period – is what attracts "business acumen" in the first place; it induces risk taking that produces innovation and economic growth. To safeguard the incentive to innovate, the possession of monopoly power will not be found unlawful unless it is accompanied by an element of anticompetitive *conduct*.' (Emphasis in original.)

[84] See *World Investment Report 2000* above n 8 at 106. See also UNCTAD Secretariat Report: *Concentration of Market Power Through Mergers, Take-overs, Joint Ventures and Other Acquisitions of Control and its Effects on International Markets, in Particular the Markets of Developing Countries* (UN Doc TD/B/RBP/80 22 August 1991).

[85] See UNCTC *The Process of Transnationalization and Transnational Mergers* (New York: UN Doc ST/CTC/SER.A/8, 1989) at 24–25. This study contains valuable quantitative information on

the deregulation and globalization of securities markets resulting in an internationalized market for corporate control, with shares being traded in several regional markets and shareholders and creditors being located throughout the world.[86] The second wave has further deepened these trends to the extent that the value of all M&As, both domestic and cross-border, in the world in relation to world GNP has risen from 0.3 per cent in 1980 to 2 per cent in 1990 to 8 per cent in 1999.[87] International M&A by MNEs confronts directly the national, or regional, orientations of existing regulatory systems with a commercial phenomenon that takes the global marketplace as its economic basis. This has both jurisdictional and substantive implications.

Regarding jurisdictional concerns much depends on the territorial scope for review under national competition laws. Most laws now cover both purely domestic and cross-border M&As.[88] Thus the extraterritorial application of merger controls is becoming more commonplace. Indeed, with the conclusion of cooperation agreements in the competition field, discussed in chapter 4, earlier concerns about unilateral intervention in foreign merger activity should be reduced. Today major disagreements are more likely to arise over how best to deal with the anticompetitive effects of international M&As, rather than over the right to review the foreign elements of the transaction, where these have a direct effect on the competitive situation in the regulating jurisdiction. Thus an element of extraterritorial review can be expected in certain common cases, which may be grouped as follows. First, a foreign parent may acquire a host country company. Such an acquisition may occur where the home based company has previously exported to the host country and has acquired a local competitor so as to enter the market as a local producer, or it may already have a local subsidiary and acquires the subsidiary of another local or foreign rival, so as to expand production in the host country.[89] Both cases will be of concern to host country authorities if they result in a significant reduction of the number of competitors in the local market. The host country authorities may extend their jurisdiction extraterritorially to the foreign parent to control the acquisition.[90] The home country authorities may also review the case if the level of concentration in the host country could prevent competitive exports from the home country, or monopolize supplies of imports to the home country. Secondly, two parent companies located in the home country may merge

---

international merger activity during the 1980s in the US, Western European countries and Japan. See also M Bishop and J Kay *European Mergers and Merger Policy* (Oxford: Oxford University Press, 1993).

[86] See Pinto 'The Internationalization of the Hostile Takeover Market: Its Implications for Choice of Law in Corporate and Securities Law' 16 Brooklyn J.Int'l L 55 at 61–64 (1990).

[87] UNCTAD *World Investment Report 2000* above n 8 at 106. See further 107–134 for detailed analysis of trends over the 1980s and 1990s.

[88] See UNCTAD *World Investment Report 1997* above n 12 at 193–201 on which this paragraph draws.

[89] *World Investment Report 1997* ibid at 196–97.

[90] See *Continental Can v EC Commission* [1973] ECR 215, [1973] CMLR 199. And see the practice under the EC Merger Regulation discussed below at nn 99–110.

and their affiliates in the host country may also merge as part of the merger plan.[91] The host country authorities may see this as an unacceptable concentration. They may respond by ordering the parent companies to enter into commitments, such as the divestiture of part of the merged business, so as to maintain competitive conditions in the host country market[92] However, they cannot order the dissolution of the parent company merger, as the lawfulness of that merger is for the home state authorities to determine.

From the above examples it is clear that multiple reviews of international M&A are likely. Indeed, such review may not be confined to the home and host countries alone. International M&As may have effects in third countries as well, bringing their competition authorities into the review process.[93] Multiple reviews may result in conflicting decisions. For example, in 1989, the bid for the UK company Consolidated Gold Fields by Luxembourg based Minorco was approved in the UK by the Monopolies and Mergers Commission (MMC),[94] but was seen as having potentially anti-competitive effects in the US by the US Federal courts.[95] More recently, in 1998, the merger between the two major US aerospace manufacturers, Boeing and McDonnell Douglas, was approved by the US authorities but was nearly blocked by the EC Commission, which saw significant competitive threats to Airbus Industrie, until commitments were given to modify the transaction.[96] Indeed the possibility of conflicting decisions will not, of itself, deter independent analysis where this is thought appropriate. Thus in *General Electric v EC Commission*, in response to the applicant's argument that the Commission had erred by not following an earlier factual determination of the US Department of Justice, the CFI held:

That the competent authorities of one or more non-Member States determine an issue in a particular way for the purposes of their own proceedings does not suffice per se to undermine

[91]　See *World Investment Report 1997* above n 12 at 197.

[92]　In 1970 the US Antitrust Division intervened in the merger of two Swiss firms, Ciba and Geigy, as the US affiliates of these firms were substantial competitors in the US market. By consent decree the firms agreed to sell off one of the two US affiliates: *United States v Ciba Corp* (1970) CCH Trade Cases s 73, 269 (SDNY 1970). See also the Mexican Federal Competition Commission decision in the case of the acquisition in the US of Scott Paper by Kimberly Clark requiring the divestiture of two brands of napkins and towels and three major brands of feminine hygiene products in Mexico were the merged Mexican affiliates would have over 60 per cent of the market in these areas: *World Investment Report 1997* at 198 Box V.5. More recently Poland raised objections to the Italian bank Unicredit's decision to merge its Polish affiliate with the Polish affiliate of Germany's HVB which Unicredit had bought in October 2005: 'UniCredit Broke Polish Law, Says Treasury Minister' *Financial Times* 8 March 2006 at 12. Under US law a merger between two foreign firms may create reporting requirements under the Hart-Scott-Rodino Antitrust Improvements Act 1976 (15 USC s 18a) although certain international transactions may be exempt: see 16 CFR ss 801.1 (e), 801.1(k), 802.50–802.52. See further the Federal Trade Commission website at <http://www.ftc.gov/bc/hsr/hsr.htm>.

[93]　See, for example, the effects on Kenya as an exporter of tea to Pakistan arising from the merger of Lipton and Brooke Bond based in the UK and their Pakistan affiliates: *World Investment Report 1997* above n 12 at 199 Box V.8.　　　　　　　　　　　　　　[94]　Cm 587 (1989).

[95]　See *Consolidated Gold Fields plc v Minorco* 871 F 2d 252 (2d Cir) *cert.dismissed* 110 S Ct 29 (1989).

[96]　See JD Banks 'The Development of the Concept of Extraterritoriality Under the European Merger Law and its Effectiveness Under the Merger Regulation Following Boeing/McDonnell Douglas Decision 1997' 19 ECLR 306 (1998).

a different determination by the competent Community authorities. The matters and arguments advanced in the administrative procedure at Community level – and the applicable legal rules – are not necessarily the same as those taken into account by the authorities of the non-Member States in question and the determinations made on either side may be different as a result.[97]

The CFI added that in such cases it was always open to the applicant to raise the reasoning underpinning the decision of the non-Member State authorities as a substantive argument.[98]

In the EC, the possibility of conflicting decisions has been recognized for a long time, with both national and EC merger authorities having potential control over a merger situation.[99] In order to avoid this risk – and a costly duplication of effort – the EC Merger Regulation[100] lays down a division of jurisdiction between Member States and the EC Commission. This is mirrored by national competition laws in the Member States.[101] The EC authorities have jurisdiction only in respect of a concentration[102] which has a 'Community dimension'.[103] Under Article 1(2) of the Merger Regulation, a concentration has a 'Community dimension' where the combined aggregate worldwide turnover of all the undertakings concerned is more than €5000 million, and the aggregate Community-wide turnover of each of at least two undertakings concerned is more than €250 million, unless each of the undertakings concerned achieves more than two-thirds of its aggregate Community-wide turnover within one and the same Member State. A concentration that does not meet these thresholds will nonetheless have a Community dimension where: '(a) the combined aggregate worldwide turnover of all the undertakings concerned is more than €2500 million; (b) in each of at least three Member States, the combined aggregate turnover of all the undertakings concerned

---

[97] *General Electric Company v EC Commission* Case T–210/01 [2006] 4 CMLR 686 at para 179.
[98] ibid.
[99] See eg *Guest Keen and Nettlefolds Limited, Sachs AG and the Brothers Sachs v Bundeskartellamt* [1978] 1 CMLR 66.
[100] Council Regulation (EC) 139/2004 OJ [2004] L24/1 (the Merger Regulation) replacing Council Regulation (EEC) No 4064/89 of 21 December 1989.
[101] See, for example, Enterprise Act 2002 ss 67–68 and Enterprise Act (Protection of Legitimate Interest) Order 2003 SI 2003/1592 which allows the UK authorities to proceed against a merger with a Community dimension where the UK asserts a 'legitimate interest' under art 21(3) of the Merger Regulation; Article 35(3) of the German Competition Act above n 4: 'The provisions of this Act shall not apply where the Commission of the European Communities has exclusive jurisdiction pursuant to Council Regulation (EEC) No 4064/89 of 21 December 1989 on the control of concentrations between undertakings, as amended.'
[102] A 'concentration' arises, by art 3(1) of the Merger Regulation where 'a change in control on a lasting basis results from: (a) the merger of two or more previously independent undertakings or parts of undertakings, or (b) the acquisition, by one or more persons already controlling at least one undertaking, or by one or more undertakings, whether by purchase of securities or assets, by contract or by any other means, of direct or indirect control of the whole or parts of one or more other undertakings.' The acquisition of control is a key issue in determining the existence of a concentration. See further Merger Regulation art 3(2) and the EC Commission Notice on the Concept of Concentration OJ [1998] C66/5. Joint ventures may also qualify as concentrations: see Merger Regulation art 3(4)–(5) and EC Commission Notice on the Concept of Full Function Joint Ventures OJ [1998] C66/1.
[103] ibid art 1(1).

is more than €100 million; (c) in each of at least three Member States included for the purpose of point (b), the aggregate turnover of each of at least two of the undertakings concerned is more than €25 million; and (d) the aggregate Community-wide turnover of each of at least two of the undertakings concerned is more than €100 million, unless each of the undertakings concerned achieves more than two-thirds of its aggregate Community-wide turnover within one and the same Member State.'[104] The purpose of this provision, first inserted into the Merger Regulation in 1997, is to prevent multiple national notifications that raise competition issues in a number of Member States but do not meet the thresholds of Article 1(2) of the Merger Regulation.[105] These thresholds will be reviewed in 2009.[106] Where these thresholds are met, review by the EC authorities will be final.[107]

This formula will not always eliminate dual jurisdiction problems. For example, when the Hong Kong and Shanghai Banking Corporation (HKS) bid for the UK based Midland Bank, the Commission took the view that this bid had a Community dimension, but that it raised no serious anti-competitive effects.[108] At the same time the UK based Lloyd's Bank made a competing bid for Midland. This was held to fall outside Community competence as over two-thirds of the EC business of both Lloyd's and Midland was carried out in the UK. This bid was referred to the MMC on 22 May 1992, but was set aside when Lloyd's withdrew its offer.[109] Had Lloyd's maintained its bid, it may have been at a procedural disadvantage, as it would have had to await the outcome of the MMC investigation before proceeding with its bid. Meanwhile, HKS could continue its negotiations with Midland free of any further intervention from the UK or EC merger authorities. Furthermore, given that the principal competitive effects of the Midland takeover would occur in the UK, it would not be unreasonable to allow the UK authorities to review both bids. Thus, the division of competence between the EC and national authorities is not without its difficulties.[110]

---

[104] ibid art 1 (3).   [105] Whish above n 2 at 811.

[106] Merger Regulation above n 100 art 1(4)–(5).

[107] See ibid art 21. By art 21(3): 'No Member State shall apply its national legislation on competition to any concentration that has a Community dimension.' Exclusive jurisdiction is subject to a 'legitimate interests' exception whereby the Member State in question may take appropriate measures in relation to such interests. These include 'Public security, plurality of the media and prudential rules': art 21(4).

[108] Case No IV/M.213 – *Hong Kong and Shanghai Bank/Midland*: Prior notification of a concentration: OJ [1992] C113/11; ibid. Non-opposition to a notified concentration: OJ [1992] C157/8.

[109] Whish above n 2 at 813. 'Lloyd's Gives Up Battle to Acquire Midland Bank' *Financial Times* Weekend 6/7 June 1992 at 1.

[110] See also art 9 of the Merger Regulation, which empowers the EC Commission to allow Member State authorities to take action in a case where a notified concentration threatens to affect significantly competition in a market within that Member State, which presents all the characteristics of a distinct market, or a concentration affects competition in a market within that Member State, which presents all the characteristics of a distinct market and which does not constitute a substantial part of the common market. The number of referrals under art 9 has grown in recent years; see Whish above n 2 at 819–23.

Turning to substantive issues, the main concern of the Merger Regulation is to prevent a concentration that would 'significantly impede competition in the common market, or a substantial part of it, in particular as a result of the creation or strengthening of a dominant position'.[111] This is a new test which departs from the original test of whether the concentration creates or strengthens a dominant position that would impede competition in the common market.[112] Its purpose is to catch not only concentrations that create or strengthen a dominant position which, by definition, carries a risk of significantly impeding competition, but also cases where the concentration does not lead to a dominant position and occurs in an oligopolistic market. In such a case there arises the risk of creating a collective dominant position between the concentration and the remaining independent competitors in the market, which may lead to anti-competitive behaviour by all market participants given the increased transparency created in the market by the reduction of competitors through the merger.[113]

The continuing importance of the creation of a dominant position as a significant impediment to competition requires, first, the delimitation of the relevant product and geographical market in which the concentration occurs. This is done in much the same way as for cases of abuse of a dominant position that have been discussed above. Secondly, an analysis of the degree of concentration created by the merger or acquisition must be undertaken. Under US law, this is assessed according to a mathematical index of market concentration, the Herfindahl-Hirschman Index (HHI).[114] Under EC law, an economic analysis of market shares is undertaken based on the facts of the case.[115] Thirdly, the merger or acquisition will be assessed as to its effect on existing competitors and on customers, and as to the likelihood of new entrants being deterred from the market.[116]

A concentration is likely to be struck down where it enjoys a significant increase in market share coupled with a reduction in the number and market strength of competitors, where it can act independently of its competitors and customers, and

---

[111] See Merger Regulation above n 100 art 2.

[112] See Slot and Johnston above n 2 at 167. See also *Continental Can v EC Commission* above n 90 at para 26, *BAT & Reynolds v EC Commission* [1987] ECR 4487, [1988] 4 CMLR 24 at paras 36–40.

[113] ibid at 168–69.

[114] The Herfindahl-Hirschman Index (HHI) distinguishes between unconcentrated markets (where the HHI is under 1000), moderately concentrated markets (where it is between 1000 and 1800) and highly concentrated markets (HHI above 1800). In highly concentrated markets an increase of more than 100 raises a presumption that the merger is anti-competitive, and the merger will be declared illegal in the absence of evidence showing that anticompetitive effects are unlikely. In moderately concentrated markets, intervention may occur where the post-merger HHI exceeds 1800 but this is unlikely if the concentration does not exceed 1800 by at least 50 points: US Department of Justice and Federal Trade Commission *Horizontal Merger Guidelines* (1992 as revised 1997) s 1.5 available at <http://www.usdoj.gov/atr/public/guidelines/hmg.pdf> and *Commentary on the Horizontal Merger Guidelines* (March 2006) available at <http://www.usdoj.gov/atr/public/guidelines/215247.htm#4>.

[115] See further EC Commission *Guidelines on Horizontal Mergers* OJ [2004] C31/5.

[116] See US *Horizontal Merger Guidelines* above n 114 ss 2, 3.

where there is little or no likelihood of new entrants onto the market.[117] Equally, where a concentration leads to an increased risk of collusion between the remaining firms on the market it will be struck down, as where a collective dominant position is created.[118] Further problems may arise out of the anti-competitive effects associated with conglomerate mergers.[119] On the other hand, where the concentration serves to improve competitive conditions, as where it contributes to the development of technical and economic progress that is of advantage to customers, then it may be approved.[120] It is not uncommon for the competition authority concerned to clear the concentration on the basis of legally binding undertakings being given by the parties. Failure to observe such commitments will result in clearance being withdrawn.

There are numerous problems associated with the substantive regulation of international mergers and acquisitions undertaken by MNEs. First, the relevant authority may be unable to amass and analyse all the relevant information on the likely competitive effects of a new concentration involving a MNE. Caves offers the following illustration:

One national MNE acquires a company selling the same product line in another country. If the two nations' officials detect monopolistic tendencies by watching the concentration of domestic *producers*, the usual practice, neither authority sees anything amiss. That is because producer concentration remains unchanged (at least initially). But the merger leaves one less independent firm in the world market, and so international *seller* concentration results in one or both countries if either of the now-combined firms formerly exported to the other nation. The world's interest in competitive markets is therefore not automatically tended by national authorities, even if they forswear taking monopolistic advantage of each other.[121]

---

[117] See, for example, the first case to be found incompatible with the Merger Regulation: *Aerospatiale and Alenia / De Havilland* OJ [1991] L334/42, [1992] 4 CMLR M2.

[118] See US *Horizontal Merger Guidelines* above n 114 s 2.1 'Co-ordinated Interaction'; *Nestlé / Perrier* (EC Commission) OJ [1992] L356/1, [1993] 4 CMLR M17 *Airtours v EC Commission* Case T–342/99 [2002] 5 CMLR 317.

[119] See US Department of Justice and Federal Trade Commission *Non-Horizontal Merger Guidelines* (June 14 1984) available at <http://www.usdoj.gov/atr/public/guidelines/2614.pdf> and see *Honeywell International Inc v EC Commission* Case T–209/01 [2006] 4 CMLR 652 and *General Electric Company v EC Commission* above n 97.

[120] See Merger Regulation above n 100 art 2(1)(b) and EC *Horizontal Merger Guidelines* above n 115 at paras 76–88; US *Horizontal Merger Guidelines* above n 114 s 4: 'The Agency has found that certain types of efficiencies are more likely to be cognizable and substantial than others. For example, efficiencies resulting from shifting production among facilities formerly owned separately, which enable the merging firms to reduce the marginal cost of production, are more likely to be susceptible to verification, merger-specific, and substantial, and are less likely to result from anticompetitive reductions in output. Other efficiencies, such as those relating to research and development, are potentially substantial but are generally less susceptible to verification and may be the result of anticompetitive output reductions. Yet others, such as those relating to procurement, management, or capital cost are less likely to be merger-specific or substantial, or may not be cognizable for other reasons.'

[121] Caves above n 14 at 100–101. Emphasis in original.

Much therefore depends on what the competition authority sees as the relevant market that it has to consider in relation to its activities. Without effective international cooperation it may be impossible to see the effect on the world market of a given concentration. However, this is to assume that competition authorities act to further international competition. In practice other factors may enter into account. In particular, authorities may be expected by their political masters to intervene in the competitive process so as to increase the likelihood that the given country or region will be a beneficiary of international competition, even at the expense of other countries or regions. Much depends on the dominant ideological orientation of the political system in question. In this connection, certain common issues arise.

First, there is the question whether international controls over M&As should be linked to the industrial policy of the regulating country or region. The problem was graphically illustrated by the EC Commission's first merger decision in the case of *Aerospatiale and Alenia/De Havilland*.[122] Aerospatiale of France and Alenia of Italy set up, in 1982, the joint venture Avions de Transport Regional (ATR), which became a leading designer and manufacturer of turboprop regional airliners. In May 1991 the ATR partners notified the EC Commission of their proposed acquisition of the Canadian based De Havilland division of Boeing, which specialized in the design and manufacture of regional turboprop aircraft. The Commission blocked the proposed acquisition on the ground that it would unduly concentrate the community market in regional turboprop aircraft,[123] thereby risking its monopolization by the proposed joint enterprise. This decision was strongly criticized by a dissenting minority of the EC Advisory Committee on Concentrations, at its eighth meeting on 20 September 1991, on the ground that the Commission had overestimated the market shares of the participants and underestimated the strength of competitors and customers in the market. In their opinion, the decision was 'not so much protecting competition but rather protecting the competitors of the parties to this proposed concentration'.[124] The decision was greeted with criticism from the French and Italian transport ministers who argued that it undermined EC industrial policy. The French minister M Paul Quiles said at the time: '[i]t seems to me imperative that the Commission should not content itself with looking at competition [criteria]. It's not enough'.[125]

Thus, the decision was criticized for concentrating too much on competition issues. This might have been a valid point if the European regional aircraft industry

---

[122] Above n 117. See Hawkes 'The EC Merger Control Regulation: Not an Industrial Policy Instrument: The De Havilland Decision' [1992] 1 ECLR 34. The *Boeing/McDonnell Douglas* case is another more recent illustration: see n 96 above.

[123] According to the Commission, the new entity's share of the 40–59 seat aircraft market would be about 64 per cent of the world market and 72 per cent of the EC market and in the 60 plus seat market the world share would be 76 per cent and the EC share 74 per cent.

[124] [1992] 4 CMLR M2 at M35, OJ [1991] C314/7.

[125] Quoted in 'Brussels Merger Policy Attacked' *Financial Times* 8 October 1991 at 22.

was at risk from larger foreign competitors, making the increased concentration of European firms a valuable defensive strategy. However, this was a market in which ATR was the leading firm. Allowing it to take over De Havilland would have increased the risk that other firms would leave the market, notably British Aerospace (BAE) and Fokker of the Netherlands, with serious social and economic consequences for their home countries.[126] Thus, the Commission's decision may well have served European interests better than if it had allowed the concentration to proceed. The case shows how non-competition issues may be expected to be taken into account in the course of an investigation of a merger or acquisition.

Secondly, competition authorities may be expected to protect 'national champions' against foreign takeover. In 1989, the UNCTC asserted that one consequence of international M&A strategy is that:

[i]ndustries are becoming increasingly concentrated as firms pursue the acquisition of brands which give them a leading rank or share in key markets. Therein lies the root of the major problem which international acquirors are likely to face in the future, and which has already surfaced in numerous countries ... Throughout the industrialized world, a political backlash to international takeovers is emerging. Even in nations that have prided themselves on their open door policy to foreign investors, there has been strong political opposition to foreign bidders.[127]

The issues referred to by the UNCTC are by no means of merely historical interest. More recently there has been an increase in concern over foreign takeovers in a number of EC Member States.[128] For example, France passed a decree on 31 December 2005 giving the government a right to veto or impose conditions on foreign takeovers of 'sensitive' industries.[129] It also oversaw a merger between

---

[126] See 'Competition Stirs the EC' *Financial Times* 8 October 1991 at 20. In due course Fokker went into liquidation in 1996 (see Stork Aerospace website at <http://www.fokker.com/page.html?ch=DEF&id=5814#1980>) and BAE left the regional jet manufacturing market when production of the Avro RJ series of regional aircraft ceased in 2001 (see BAE Systems Regional Aircraft website at <http://www.regional-services.com/ur_products.html>).

[127] UNCTC above n 85 at 25.

[128] The focus of discussion is with EC Member States as these are expected to espouse an open door to bidders from other EC Member States and so their concerns represent a strong departure from the dominant goal of liberalization. Concern over foreign ownership through mergers is widespread. For example the Australian Government has imposed a 35 per cent cap on foreign shareholding in the privatization of Snowy Hydro, the largest renewable energy supplier in Australia and the operator of the Snowy Mountains hydro scheme, the largest civil engineering achievement in the country's history. Similar restrictions apply in the telecoms and airline sectors: 'Australia Puts Cap on Foreign Stake in Snowy' *Financial Times* 31 May 2006 at 28.

[129] Decree No 2005–1739 of 30 December 2005 *Journal Officiel* 31 December 2005 available at <http://www.journal-officiel.gouv.fr/frameset.html>. For corporate investors from non-EU countries, protected sectors include: gambling activities such as casinos; private security services; research, development, or production of chemical or biological antidotes; activities concerning equipment for intercepting communications or eavesdropping; services for evaluation of security of computer systems; dual-use (civil and military) technologies; cryptology; activities of firms that are repositories of defence secrets; research, production, or trade in arms, munitions, explosives, or other military equipment; or any other industry supplying the defence ministry any of the goods or services described above: art 2 amending Monetary and Finance Code art R 153–2. The EC

state owned Gaz de France and Suez, the Franco-Belgian water group, thereby averting a possible bid for Suez by Enel of Italy.[130] Spain, Luxembourg, Italy, and Germany have all recently opposed foreign takeovers or attempts by the EC Commission to liberalize takeover rules.[131] Poland has gone so far as to challenge the EC Commission's decision to approve the merger between the Italian Bank UniCredit and Germany's HVB, which Poland has opposed in relation to the reorganization of the affiliates of the merged banks in that country.[132] In response the EC Commission has made a formal request for observations from Poland concerning the compatibility of a non-compete clause contained in the Bank Pekao Privatisation Agreement concluded between the Polish Ministry of State Treasury and the UniCredit banking group in 1999. According to the Commission:

The clause in principle prevents UniCredit from investing in any of Pekao's competitors in the Polish market. It has been invoked by the Polish authorities when inviting UniCredit to sell its shares in a Pekao competitor in the context of the UniCredit / HBV merger procedure. The Commission is concerned that the clause may violate EC Treaty rules on the free movement of capital (Article 56) and the right of establishment (Article 43).[133]

The EC Commission has also started a procedure against the measure under the Merger Regulation claiming that Poland's intervention in the merger was in violation of the Commission's exclusive jurisdiction over Community dimension mergers under Article 21 of the regulation.[134] The EC Commission's strong stand

---

Commission has expressed doubts as to the consistency of the decree with EC law: 'Brussels Tells Paris to Justify Takeover Decree' *Financial Times* 27 January 2006 at 7. The EC Commission issued a letter of formal notice against France on 4 April 2006 see EC Commission *Press Release* IP/06/ 438 4 April 2006 <http://europa.eu/rapid/pressReleasesAction.do?reference=IP/06/438&format= HTML&aged=0&language=EN&guiLanguage=en>.

[130] 'Blocking of Hostile Bids Angers French Investors' and 'Mandelson Warns Against EU Protectionism' both in *Financial Times* 8 March 2006 at 12. The EC Commission is also inquiring into this action.

[131] See Tobias Buck 'Protectionist Storm Shakes Foundation of EU Open Market' *Financial Times* 1 March 2006 at 6. 'The day the factories stopped' *The Economist* 23 October 2004 at 69–70 (on Commission concern over the 1960 law protecting Volkswagen from foreign bidders); 'Brussels to Scrutinise Endesa Conditions' *Financial Times* 1 August 2006 at 21 (on the Commission's unease at the conditions imposed on the bid for Endesa, Spain's largest electricity group, by Eon of Germany).

[132] See *Financial Times* above n 92 and 'Brussels Faces Rare Merger Challenge as Poland Goes to Court' *Financial Times* 7 February 2006 at 8. On the approval of the merger, see EC Commission *Press Release* IP/05/1299 18 October 2005 <http://europa.eu.int/rapid/pressReleasesAction.do?reference= IP/05/1299&format=HTML&aged=1&language=EN&guiLanguage=en>. The grounds of claim are that the Commission failed to apply art 2(1) of the Merger Regulation correctly as it failed to appraise adequately the effects of the UniCredit/HVB merger on the structure of the Polish banking market. See Case T–41/06 *Poland v EC Commission* Action brought 6 February 2006 OJ [2006] C96/ 17 (2006/C 96/33).

[133] See EC Commission *Press Release* IP/06/276 8 March 2006 <http://europa.eu/rapid/ pressReleasesAction.do?reference=IP/06/276&format=HTML&aged=1&language=EN& guiLanguage=en>.

[134] See EC Commission *Press Release* IP/06/277 8 March 2006 <http://europa.eu.int/ rapid/pressReleasesAction.do?reference=IP/06/277&format=HTML&aged=0&language= FR&guiLanguage=fr>.

against national intervention in cross-border mergers is only to be expected given its commitment to single market integration and in view of the established policy of simplifying the conditions for cross-border mergers. This has resulted in the adoption of Directive 2005/56/EC, which aims at the removal of obstacles to cross-border mergers between limited liability companies.[135]

In the UK an 'internationalist' position on mergers and acquisitions has been firmly accepted. Indeed the British Chancellor of the Exchequer, Gordon Brown, hit out in 2006 against the recent wave of protectionism in Europe, arguing that a single European market was essential for the economic success of the continent.[136] In respect of merger control, the UK approach has resulted in major legislative changes brought about by the Enterprise Act 2002 Part 3. Based on the Government White Paper *Productivity and Enterprise – A World Class Competition Regime*[137] the current law introduces the 'substantial lessening of competition' test (SLC). The Office of Fair Trading is under an obligation to refer to the Competition Commission cases of qualifying mergers which in its view have resulted or may result in a substantial lessening of competition.[138] This replaces s 84 of the Fair Trading Act 1973, which provided for a wider 'public interest' test to be applied by the MMC and the Secretary of State for Trade and Industry when acting on a recommendation from the MMC.[139]

[135] See Directive of the European Parliament and Council 2005/56/EC of 26 October 2005 on cross-border mergers of limited liability companies OJ [2005] L310/1.

[136] 'Brown Lashes Out at EU's New Wave of Protectionism' *Financial Times* 4/5 March 2006 at 1.

[137] Cm 5233 31 July 2001.

[138] Enterprise Act 2002 n 101 ss 22 and 33. See generally the Office of Fair Trading Enterprise Act home page at <http://www.oft.gov.uk/Business/Legal/Enterprise/default.htm>; Whish above n 2 ch 22, Slot and Johnston above n 2 at 174–206; Cosmo Graham 'The Enterprise Act 2002 and Competition' 67 MLR 273 (2004). Office of Fair Trading *Mergers: Substantive Assessment Guidelines* (OFT 516, 2003) available at <http://www.oft.gov.uk/NR/rdonlyres/283E1C2D-78A6-4ECC-8CF5-D37F4E4D7B22/0/oft516.pdf>; Competition Commission *Merger References: Competition Commission Guidelines* (CC 2, 2003) available at <http://www.competition-commission.org.uk/rep_pub/rules_and_guide/pdf/15073compcommguidance2final.pdf>. A qualifying merger is one where the value of the enterprise being taken over exceeds £70 million or at least 25 per cent of the supply of goods and services in the UK, or a substantial part of it, is supplied by or to the same people: s 23. Slot and Johnston point out the SLC test is not identical to the test used under the revised Merger Regulation, although they feel that there are likely to be very strong similarities between the two approaches in practice: ibid at 190.

[139] By s 84 of the Fair Trading Act 1973, in considering whether a merger operates or may operate against the public interest, the Monopolies and Mergers Commission shall take into account: 'all matters which appear to them in the particular circumstances to be relevant and, among other things, shall have regard to the desirability – (a) of maintaining and promoting effective competition between persons supplying goods and services in the United Kingdom; (b) of promoting the interests of consumers, purchasers and other users of goods and services in the United Kingdom in respect of the prices charged for them and in respect of their quality and the variety of goods and services supplied; (c) of promoting, through competition, the reduction of costs and the development and use of new techniques and new products, and of facilitating the entry of new competitors into existing markets; (d) of maintaining and promoting the balanced distribution of industry and employment in the United Kingdom; (e) of maintaining and promoting competitive activity in markets outside the United Kingdom on the part of producers of goods, and of suppliers of goods and services, in the United Kingdom.'

In practice, an economic efficiency test has been applied for many years by the UK competition authorities. This approach was outlined in 1984 by former Secretary of State for Trade and Industry, Norman (now Lord) Tebbit, and has since become known as the 'Tebbit Doctrine'. He stated:

I regard mergers policy as an important part of the Government's general policy of promoting competition within the economy in the interests of the customer and of efficiency and hence of growth and jobs. Accordingly my policy has been and will continue to be to make references primarily on competition grounds. In evaluating the competitive situation in individual cases I shall have regard to the international context: to the extent of competition in the home market from non-United Kingdom sources and to the competitive position of United Kingdom companies in overseas markets.[140]

The MMC generally followed this approach when considering whether a merger or acquisition between a UK and non-UK firm was in the public interest.[141] Thus in *Elders IXL Ltd/Allied Lyons plc*,[142] the MMC held that the proposed takeover of Allied Lyons by the Australian brewer Elders IXL was in the public interest, despite the highly leveraged nature of the bid, as the Australian company could help improve the UK company's marketing and product innovation skills, and increase exports. The fact that there was a lack of reciprocity between the then restrictive Australian controls over foreign investment and the absence of such restrictions in the UK was not held to act against the public interest.

On the other hand, the MMC did consider the employment and balance of payments effects of a foreign takeover of a UK firm.[143] Furthermore, in *Hong Kong and Shanghai Banking Corporation/Royal Bank of Scotland* the MMC laid down a rebuttable presumption that the takeover of a UK based bank by a foreign bank is against the public interest as the 'transfer and ultimate control of a significant part of the clearing bank system outside the United Kingdom would have an adverse effect of opening up possibilities of divergence of interest which would not otherwise arise'.[144] Moreover, in 1990, the Secretary of State for Trade and

---

[140] House of Commons written answer by the Secretary of State for Trade and Industry (5 July 1984) reproduced in Annex 2 of the Office of Fair Trading Guide *Mergers* (HMSO, 1987 and 1991). The Secretary of State's statement is not reproduced in the 1991 edition of the OFT guide but is referred to in para 2.7. See also Slot and Johnston above n 2 at 175. The 'Tebbit doctrine' was reaffirmed in 1992 by the Secretary of State for Trade and Industry, Mr Michael Heseltine in a Written Parliamentary Answer: see *Hansard* Wednesday 13 May 1992 col 146 and 'Heseltine Reaffirms Mergers Policy' *Financial Times* 14 May 1992 at 20. The UK Government's non-intervention in the takeover of Rover by BMW in February 1994 may be seen as an illustration of the policy in action.

[141] For a full analysis of MMC decisions in this area, see Richard Whish *Competition Law* (London: Butterworths, 4th edn, 2001) at 826–30; Raybould and Firth above n 2 at 493–511.

[142] Cmnd 9892 (1986). See also: *Weidmann/Whiteley* Cmnd 6208 (1975).

[143] See eg *Enersch/Davey International* Cmnd 8360 (1981). In this case the MMC also felt that the lengthening of the chain of management command that would result from the merger was detrimental to Davey's ability to make quick decisions about competitive overseas project bids.

[144] Cmnd 8472 (1982) para 12.39. at 92. See further paras 12.20–12.29. The Commission's thinking appears to have been influenced by the belief that the Royal Bank of Scotland was well managed and did not need more capital. Otherwise it might have concluded that the takeover was consistent with the also public interest: see para 12.40. See also the Note of Dissent by RG Smethurst

Industry, Peter Lilley, expressed the view that he would be more likely to make a reference to the MMC where a foreign state-owned company made a bid for a UK company, in that such a company was deemed less likely to operate in an efficient manner, or to compete on even terms with private firms.[145] However, the MMC did not accept as a principle that the public ownership of the foreign bidder raised a presumption that the bid was against the public interest. In 1991 five references were made by the Secretary of State involving bids by state-owned enterprises for UK companies. Only one was found to raise public interest objections.[146] One of the companies affected, Credit Lyonnais (which had two bids referred) complained to the EC Commission that the UK policy was discriminatory. After intervention by the Commission, the UK accepted that state ownership per se could not constitute sufficient grounds for the making of a reference.[147]

Returning to the current law, predominance of the SLC test does not exclude public interest considerations altogether from the Enterprise Act. The Secretary of State for Trade and Industry, though no longer in control of the merger review process, as had been the case under the old Fair Trading Act regime, retains certain powers to review mergers which contain a 'public interest' dimension. By section 58(1) of the Enterprise Act 2002 the Secretary of State may consider national security interests and, by section 58(3), any other interests that he or she has designated by order, as involving public interest concerns, through the adoption by Parliament of a statutory instrument. In addition, the Secretary of State retains the right to review newspaper mergers as a matter of public interest.[148] The procedure for dealing with public interest concerns (as defined in s 58 and subsequent orders made thereunder) requires the OFT and Competition Commission to notify the Secretary of State about decisions that may raise such matters. The Secretary of State then issues an 'intervention notice' under s 42(2) of the Enterprise Act, where he or she considers that a public interest consideration specified under s 58 is relevant to the examination of a merger situation. The OFT then produces a report covering both the competition and public interest considerations. Thereupon, the Secretary of State acquires the discretion, normally exercised by the OFT, to decide whether a reference to the Competition Commission is necessary.[149] He or

---

at 94–97 who disagreed that the transfer of control to the Hong Kong and Shanghai Bank would be detrimental to the public interest in the way outlined by the majority.

[145] DTI Press Notice, 26 July, 1990; OFT Guide *Mergers* (1991) para 3.17.

[146] The five references were: *Credit Lyonnais SA/Woodchester Investments plc* Cm 1404 23 January 1991; *Silgos SA /Signet Ltd* Cm 1450 26 February 1991 (Silgos is a subsidiary of Credit Lyonnais); *Société Nationale Elf Aquitaine/Amoco Corporation* Cm 1521 3 May 1991; *British Aerospace plc/Thomson – CSF SA* Cm 1416 30 January 1991; *Kemira Oy/ICI* Cm 1406 23 January 1991. Only the last was objected to by the MMC: *Annual Report of the Director General of Fair Trading 1991* (HMSO, 1992). A bid by Allied Irish Banks for TSB's Northern Ireland network was also cleared but this is not reported in the Director General's Annual Report: see 'Lilley Clears Three Acquisitions by Foreign Groups' *Financial Times* 31 May 1991 at 7.

[147] 'UK Gives Way on Foreign Takeover Bids' *Financial Times* 31 October 1991 at 2.

[148] Enterprise Act 2002 above n 101 s 69. See also the Communications Act 2003 ss 375–88 which give the power to review 'media mergers' as a matter of public interest.   [149] ibid s 44.

she is bound by the OFT determination on competition matters but retains a discretion to decide upon the public interest matters.[150] The Competition Commission then makes its decision. The Secretary of State is bound by its findings on competition matters but retains discretion on how to act on the public interest matters.[151]

As Slot and Johnston point out, there is as yet no practice relating to these provisions, although some guidance could be obtained by looking at the old decisions under the earlier Fair Trading Act regime.[152] That public interest concerns will arise from time to time cannot be doubted. For example, the proposed takeover, in 2006, of the UK's biggest gas supplier, Centrica, the owner of British Gas, by the Russian state-controlled gas monopoly Gazprom raised concerns in government circles. It led the then Secretary of State for Trade and Industry, Alan Johnson, to consider passing a statutory instrument under s 58 to control bids in the energy supply industry that might threaten energy security.[153] This revelation prompted a critical response from Gazprom, which threatened to divert supplies to other customers, and made the Secretary of State appear inconsistent as he had been a vocal critic of other EC Member States that had sought to control foreign bids.[154] The matter was put to rest by the then Prime Minister, Tony Blair, who pledged that any future bid by Gazprom would be handled in the normal way by the independent competition authorities.[155] This case has prompted significant discussion over the real limits of a commitment to liberalization in relation to foreign takeovers of UK firms. That concerns over Gazprom were aired should come as no surprise. On New Year's Day 2006, Russia suspended gas supplies to the Ukraine. Earlier, Vladimir Putin, the Russian President, removed the old management and brought in his own supporters, making the company even closer to the heart of the Russian state.[156] Whether Gazprom acts as a truly independent commercial entity may be open to question. In such circumstances it may be unwise to consider any bid purely on competition grounds.

The case of Gazprom, which, in effect, restates the question whether state control is a relevant public interest factor, gives rise to a wider issue. Might it not be relevant to take into account the economic, social, and political culture from which bidders come? Companies from authoritarian or undemocratic states, or those from corrupt states, with little or no tradition of corporate accountability and transparency, may bring with them a tradition of bad corporate practice which may undermine effective and open regulation. Surely there is a case for some form of review of these practices in the public interest, especially in relation to bids in

---

[150] ibid ss 45 and 46(2).   [151] ibid s 54.   [152] Above n 2 at 195.
[153] 'Centrica Threat Led to Rethink on Mergers' *Financial Times* 17 April 2006 at 1.
[154] 'Gazprom in Threat to Supplies' *Financial Times* 20 April 2006 at 1.
[155] 'Gazprom Block Over Centrica Ruled Out' *Financial Times* 26 April 2006 at 1.
[156] See Arkady Ostrovsky 'Energy of the State: How Gazprom Acts as a Lever in Putin's Power Play' *Financial Times* 14 March 2006 at 13. Terry Macalister 'Gazprom: No Bid for British Gas Owner Yet' *The Guardian* 27 April 2006 at 27.

sensitive sectors? The narrow logic of market efficiency can appear very inadequate when it comes to such questions, questions that themselves are central to the efficient, and honest, running of a market economy. It may be easier to review this matter at the bidding stage than approve of a bid on competition grounds and live with the possibility of corporate malpractice thereafter. Equally social issues, such as employment effects and regional effects, have not lost their importance and certain cultural industries may warrant protection. It may be the case that, in practice, some kind of revival of the old 'public interest' criterion will occur.[157] The political pressure for this may become irresistible in the future.

Following from this, there is general agreement that it is proper for competition authorities to protect, against foreign takeover, firms operating in sectors vital to national security. It was seen in chapter 5 that many states have passed specialized laws to achieve this aim. These may be laws designed specifically to protect national security, as in the case of the US Exon-Florio amendment, or they may be general foreign investment screening laws which give the screening authority the discretion to consider national security issues. Thus, for example, Japan has used its foreign investment law to investigate foreign bids for Japanese companies on national security grounds.[158] However, where a country does not have a specialized law that can deal with national security issues, competition law may be used instead. As noted above this is the case under the Enterprise Act in the UK and under the EC Merger Regulation.[159]

The MMC did take strategic security considerations into account when judging whether a foreign takeover of a British firm operated against the public interest under section 84 of the Fair Trading Act 1973. A notable example occurred in the case of *Kuwait/British Petroleum plc*.[160] The case arose out of the acquisition by the Kuwait Investment Office (KIO), the Kuwaiti Government's London based

---

[157] See Barry J Rodger 'UK Merger Control Policies: the Public Interest and Reform' 21 ECLR 24 (2000); Larry Elliott 'This Takeover Free-For-All is Just Not Delivering the Goods' *The Guardian* 30 March 2006 at 33.

[158] The bid by Trafalgar Holdings Ltd for Mineba in 1985 was subjected to review on this ground as Mineba supplied aircraft parts and flight instruments to the Japanese military: see Corcoran 'Foreign Investment and Corporate Control in Japan: T Boone Pickens and Acquiring Control Through Share Ownership' 22 Law & Pol.Int'l Bus. 333 at 348–49 (1991). For Japanese law on foreign investment see ch 5 at 183.

[159] Merger Regulation above n 100 art 21(3) which includes public security as a legitimate interest that the Member State can protect. See also art 296(1) EC Treaty, which gives Member States discretion to take necessary measures in matters of security related to the defence industry. According to Whish above n 2 at 827–28 the EC Commission has been taking a stricter view of mergers in defence related industries and is less willing to allow for the art 296 exception in cases of 'dual-use' civilian and military markets.

[160] Cm 477 (1988). Security considerations were also present in the findings of the MMC in the case of *GEC plc and Siemens AG/Plessey plc* Cm 676 (1989). The MMC held unanimously that the joint bid of GEC and Siemens for Plessey should be allowed to proceed subject to certain undertakings from GEC and Siemens that would serve to safeguard the public interest. Inter alia the Commission was worried that Siemens' participation could raise issues of national security because it was a German company. In order to meet this concern, the Commission proposed that all executive directors and the majority of non-executive directors of Plessey companies owned by Siemens, or jointly owned by GEC and Siemens, should be British nationals. This would be the subject of undertakings to be negotiated with

investment arm, of some 22 per cent of the stock of British Petroleum (BP) between October 1987 and March 1988. KIO had bought up large amounts of BP stock which had been offered for sale by the British Government as part of its privatization programme, but which had fallen in value drastically as a consequence of the stock market crash of 19 October 1987. The Secretary of State for Trade and Industry referred the case to the MMC, concerned that the build up of shares in BP by a government with substantial oil interests raised issues of public interest. The MMC found that the Kuwaiti stake gave it the capacity to control BP's policy in the future. The holding was some 12 times the size of the next largest beneficial holding, that of Prudential Assurance, which was 1.8 per cent followed by HM Treasury at 1.7 per cent.[161] The Kuwaiti holding was held to constitute a merger situation that was against the public interest because future conflicts of interest between Kuwait, as a member of OPEC, and BP and the British Government were foreseeable. Furthermore, Kuwait could block commercial policies of BP that were likely to compete with Kuwaiti oil interests, and BP could be prejudiced in third states, especially the US, because of its links with Kuwait. The Commission recommended that the Kuwaiti shareholding be reduced to 9.9 per cent.

By way of conclusion, the above examples illustrate the need to reconcile national economic and social priorities with the globalization of companies and industries. Protectionism through a restrictive competition policy is tempting, especially for regions with underdeveloped or uncompetitive industries. However, the approach currently favoured in most advanced states requires the maintenance of an open market coupled with investment in locational advantages, while at the same time ensuring that international competition is workable and efficient. This last element may require the development of an effective global system of competition regulation. The EC already points the way with its regional approach but, as certain views expressed in the context of the *Aerospatiale* decision suggest, in different political conditions it could become part of a system dedicated to the protection of European industry against global competition.

(3) International Developments in the Regulation of Restrictive Business Practices

Attempts to create international machinery for the regulation of restrictive business practices (RBPs) are not new. At the end of the Second World War, the US proposed that the planned International Trade Organization (ITO) should include

---

the Secretary of State: ibid para 6.85 and Appendix 6.1. More recently, the merger of BAE and Marconi was cleared after undertakings were offered: DTI *Press Release* P/2000/220 28 March 2000. The UK Government also relied on art 296(1) EC Treaty to exclude this case (Case No IV/M.1438) from review under the Merger Regulation by the EC Commission: DTI *Press Release* P/99/354 29 April 1999.

[161] ibid para 8.9.

a Commission on Business Practices which would, 'inquire into the activities on the part of private commercial enterprises which have the effect or purpose of restraining international trade, restricting access to international markets, or of fostering monopolistic controls in international trade'.[162] The Havana Charter for the ITO contained a list of prohibited business practices in Article V. These included: price fixing, exclusion of businesses from markets, discrimination against particular firms, production limits or quotas, preventing the development of technology, illegal extension of industrial property rights and any similar practices that the ITO might declare to be restrictive business practices by a majority of two-thirds of the members present and voting.[163] However, the ITO Charter was never adopted as a result of US opposition to its foreign investment provisions.[164] Thereafter, during the 1950s, the US tried to secure UN agreement on the drafting of international rules on RBPs, but without success.[165] The US also pursued a bilateral policy by including a clause on RBPs in its Friendship, Commerce, and Navigation treaties.[166] In the 1970s, the OECD set up a Committee of Experts on RBPs which led to a report on the RBPs of MNEs. The committee came out against the creation of a different substantive competition law for MNEs and national enterprises, or the abandonment of the general exemption from competition control of parent/subsidiary relations.[167] The OECD has not established any international machinery for setting standards or for investigating RBPs carried out by MNEs. However, the OECD Guidelines for Multinational Enterprises contain a Guideline on Competition.[168] Regional organizations of developing countries are also engaged in the development of cooperation and/or harmonization of standards in this field.[169] By NAFTA Article 1501 the contracting parties commit to the adoption or maintenance of measures that proscribe anti-competitive business conduct, to take appropriate action with respect thereto, and to cooperate on issues of enforcement policy.

On the other hand, attempts to place competition issues on the agenda of the WTO have borne no fruit. In 1996 the Singapore Ministerial Declaration established a Working Group on Trade and Competition. This body examined the

---

[162] Havana Charter for an International Trade Organization, 24 March 1948, US Dept of State Pub No 3206, Commercial Policy Series 114 (1948) cited in Haight above n 24 at 241. See further Knorr 'The Problem of International Cartels and Intergovernmental Commodity Agreements' 55 Yale LJ 1097 (1946); Lockwood and Schmeisser 'Restrictive Business Practices in International Trade' 11 Law and Contemporary Problems 663 (1946).

[163] See J Davidow 'The Seeking of a World Competition Code: Quixotic Quest?' in O Schachter and R Hellawell (eds) *Competition in International Business: Law and Policy on Restrictive Practices* (Columbia University Press, 1981) 361 at 362.   [164] See further ch 17 at 654–55.

[165] See Davidow above n 163 at 363–64.   [166] See further Haight above n 24.

[167] OECD *Restrictive Business Practices of Multinational Enterprises* (Paris: OECD 1977).

[168] OECD *The OECD Guidelines for Multinational Enterprises* (Paris: OECD, 2000) at 26–27 and *Commentary* at 53–54 paras 55–59.

[169] For example, MERCOSUR, CARICOM, COMESA covered in UNCTAD *Competition* Series on issues in international investment agreements (New York and Geneva: United Nations, 2004).

relationship between trade issues and competition until 2003 when competition, one of the so-called 'Singapore Issues', was removed from the negotiating agenda of the Doha Round at the 2003 Cancùn Ministerial Meeting.[170] Thus the WTO currently has no powers to deal directly with privately constructed trade barriers. It can only act in relation to governmental policies that distort market access for goods and services from other WTO members contrary to the provisions of the WTO Agreements.[171] In this regard, some cases brought before the WTO dispute settlement mechanism, as trade related cases, can be read as attempts to combat state sanctioned private anti-competitive conduct. For example, the *Bananas* case brought by the US and other Central and Latin American members against the EU can be interpreted as an attempt to protect market access into the EU, on the part of US MNEs, where they were confronted with a discriminatory scheme of preferential treatment for European based distributors of bananas.[172] Most notably, in the *Kodak–Fuji* case the US sought to challenge the system of photographic film and paper distribution in Japan, which was dominated by Fuji Film and characterized by high levels of vertical integration.[173] The US failed to make out the case on the facts, in that it could not prove that any benefits accruing from trade liberalization had been nullified or impaired by the governmental measures that were alleged to have foreclosed the market. However, the panel was clear that an action arising out of the interrelated effects of private and governmental action could be reviewable under the GATT, thereby permitting scrutiny of the

---

[170] See Trebilcock and Howse above n 20 at 608–609. See also, for an argument in favour of adopting a WTO Competition Agreement post Cancùn, Josef Drexl 'International Competition Policy After Cancun: Placing a Singapore Issue on the WTO Development Agenda' 27 World Competition 419 (2004). For the documents of the Working Group see <http://www.wto.org>. The designation of these documents is WT/WGTCP. The last report of the Working Group can be found in WTO Doc WT/WGTCP/7 17 July 2003. For a summary of the main trends of discussion in the Working Group see Mitsuo Matsushita, Thomas Schoenbaum, and Petros Mavroides *The World Trade Organisation, Law, Practice and Policy* (Oxford: Oxford University Press, 2nd edn, 2006) at 893–99.

[171] The first case of this kind is *Mexico – Measures Affecting Telecommunications Services* (WT/DS204/R) Panel Report adopted 1 June 2004 where Mexico was found to have acted inconsistently with the GATS Telecommunications Annex and the Reference Paper that contains express commitments to prevent anti-competitive practices. The Mexican state owned telecommunications company Telemex was found to have used its dominant position to cartelize the market for the supply of cross-border telephone services. See further for a critical appraisal Damien J Neven and Petros C Mavroides 'El Mess in TELEMEX: a comment on Mexico – Measures Affecting Telecommunications Services' 5 World Trade Review 271 (2006) and for a supportive appraisal Eleanor M Fox 'The WTO's First Antitrust Case – *Mexican Telecom*: A Sleeping Victory for Trade and Competition' 9 JIEL 271 (2006). A number of other WTO Agreements contain competition related provisions including: the TBT Agreement art 8:1; GATS art VIII:1; TRIPs Agreement art 40 (discussed in ch 11 at 460–61); Safeguards Agreement art 11. For discussion see Matsushita, Schoenbaum, and Mavroides ibid at 858–64.

[172] See *European Communities – Regime for the Importation Distribution and Sale of Bananas* (WT/DS27/AB/R) Appellate Body Report adopted 25 September 1997 available at <http://www.wto.org>.

[173] See *Japan – Measures Affecting Consumer Photographic Film and Paper* (WT/DS44/R) Panel Report adopted 22 April 1998 available at <http://www.wto.org>.

competitive effects of governmental measures.[174] What remains unclear is whether this extends not only to positive measures of support for anti-competitive conduct, but also to omissions to enforce competition rules. Much would depend on the particular facts.[175]

To date the most advanced international work on competition issues has occurred under the auspices of UNCTAD.[176] At its Second Session in New Delhi, UNCTAD placed RBPs upon its agenda. In 1972 at the Third Session, the possibility of drawing up guidelines for the control and elimination of RBPs adversely affecting Less Developed Countries (LDCs) was raised. This led to the establishment of an ad hoc Group of Experts with a brief to consider the issue. In 1976, at the Fourth Session in Nairobi, Resolution 96(IV) was passed. It authorized negotiations leading towards the formulation of a Set of Principles and Rules on RBPs, which covered not only LDCs but international trade in general. A fourth ad hoc group was set up in 1978. It made significant progress and, by 1979, a conference was established to negotiate and finalize a Set of Principles and Rules. The final agreed version of the code, known as the Set of Multilaterally Agreed Equitable Principles and Rules for the Control of Restrictive Business Practices (the UN Set), was adopted by UNCTAD in April 1980, and by the UN General Assembly in December 1980.[177] The UN Set is a voluntary code having the status of a non-binding UN General Assembly resolution. Thus is it hortatory in nature. However,

---

[174] The panel held:

'10.52. As the WTO Agreement is an international agreement, in respect of which only national governments and separate customs territories are directly subject to obligations, it follows by implication that the term *measure* in Article XXIII: I (b) [GATT] and Article 26.1 of the DSU, as elsewhere in the WTO Agreement, refers only to policies or actions of governments, not those of private parties. But while this 'truth' may not be open to question, there have been a number of trade disputes in relation to which panels have been faced with making sometimes difficult judgments as to the extent to which what appear on their face to be private actions may nonetheless be attributable to a government because of some governmental connection to or endorsement of those actions.

10.53. These past GATT cases demonstrate that the fact that an action is taken by private parties does not rule out the possibility that it may be deemed to be governmental if there is sufficient government involvement with it. It is difficult to establish bright-line rules in this regard, however. Thus, that possibility will need to be examined on a case-by-case basis.'

[175] See further Brendan Sweeney 'Globalisation of Competition Law and Policy: Some Aspects of the Interface between Trade and Competition' 5 Melbourne Jo. Int'l L. 375 at 401–13 (2004).

[176] See Philippe Brusick 'UN Control of Restrictive Business Practices' 17 JWTL 337 at 340–42 (1983) on which this paragraph is based. See also Greenhill 'UNCTAD: Control of Restrictive Business Practices' 12 JWTL 76 (1978); Thomas Brewer 'International Regulation of Restrictive Business Practices' 16 JWTL 108 (1982); Davidow above n 163 at 365 et seq.

[177] UNCTAD Doc TD/RBP/CONF/10 Annex: 19 ILM 813 (1980); UN Doc A/C 2/35/6 of 23 October 1980 Annex; adopted by UN GA Res.35/63, 5 December 1980, revised 2000; see <http://r0.unctad.org/en/subsites/cpolicy/docs/CPSet/rbpc10rev20en.pdf>. See also the Fourth Review Conference 2000 <http://r0.unctad.org/en/subsites/cpolicy/english/cpconf0900.htm>. The Fourth Review Conference (25–29 September 2000) adopted a resolution (TD/RBP/CONF.5/15 of 4 October 2000) in which it, inter alia: '*Reaffirms* the validity of the UN Set of Multilaterally Agreed Equitable Principles and Rules for the Control of Restrictive Business Practices, *recommends* to the General Assembly to subtitle the Set for reference as 'UN Set of Principles and Rules on Competition', and *calls upon* all member States to implement the provisions of the Set.'

it has considerable moral authority as it was adopted unanimously by the General Assembly.[178] Furthermore, according to UNCTAD, 'the [UN] Set has the same status in terms of international law as other resolutions of the General Assembly: in a litigation it can be cited as applicable law, in particular in the absence of domestic legislation dealing with the issues under discussion'.[179]

The UN Set represents an acceptance of the view that the basic norms of competition law, which have long been in use in developed countries, should extend to the operations of enterprises, including MNEs, in developing countries.[180] Thus, the Objectives section of the UN Set emphasizes that the interests of developing countries in particular should be taken into account in the elimination of RBPs that may cause prejudice to international trade and development.[181] Furthermore, the Objectives section sees the UN Set as an international contribution to a wider process of encouraging the adoption and strengthening of laws and policies in this area at the national and regional levels.[182] This objective should be seen alongside UNCTAD's work on the formulation of a Model Law on RBPs. The Model Law embodies the principles laid down in the UN Set and couples these with a scheme for a national competition authority. It is aimed at developing countries which do not as yet have a domestic system of competition regulation.[183]

Finally, Section C(iii)(7) of the UN Set lays down a principle of preferential treatment for developing countries as an aspect of the equitable application of the principles contained in the UN Set. Thus states, in particular developed countries, are to take into account in the application of their RBP controls the 'development, financial and trade needs of developing countries, in particular of the least developed countries, for the purposes especially of developing countries in: (a) promoting the establishment or development of domestic industries and the economic development of other sectors of the economy, and (b) encouraging their economic development through regional or global arrangements among developing countries'. Therefore, the UN Set envisages 'infant industry' and regional economic integration exceptions to the application of competition controls to enterprises and other organizations from developing countries. This provision was accepted by the developed countries in return for the developing countries' acceptance of the principle that 'States, while bearing in mind the need to ensure the comprehensive application of the Set of Principles and Rules, should take due account of the extent to which the conduct of enterprises, whether or not created or controlled

---

178 See Brusick above n 176 at 342.

179 'Restrictive Business Practices (RBPS) at the Crossroads of the 1990s' *UNCTAD Bulletin* No 250 February 1989 10 at 12.

180 See J Robinson *Multinationals and Political Control* (Gower, 1983) 177. For information on competition laws in developing countries, see UNCTAD above n 2.

181 UN Set above note 177 Section A(1)–(4).   182 ibid Section A(5).

183 For background references to UNCTAD documents that originally elaborated this policy, see Brewer above n 176 at 109 n 7; Thompson 'UNCTAD: Model Law on Restrictive Business Practices' 14 JWTL 444 (1980). For the most recent revised draft of the Model Law with commentary, see <http://r0.unctad.org/en/subsites/cpolicy/docs/Modelaw04.pdf>.

by states, is accepted under applicable legislation or regulations ... '.[184] Thus the UN Set accepts that states cannot interfere with another state's decision to exempt certain activities from the operation of competition laws. However, there is no mention of the issue of extraterritoriality in the UN Set.[185]

Apart from offering special concessions to developing country interests, the UN Set also deals specifically with MNEs, which are referred to in the text as transnational corporations (TNCs), in accordance with UN practice.[186] Section B(ii)(4) of the UN Set states that, '[t]he Set of Principles and Rules applies to restrictive business practices,[187] including those of transnational corporations, adversely affecting international trade, particularly that of developing countries and the economic development of those countries. It applies irrespective of whether such practices involve enterprises in one or more countries'. Of particular importance to TNCs are the contents of Section D, entitled 'Principles and Rules for Enterprises, Including Transnational Corporations'. Section D begins by exhorting enterprises to conform to the RBP laws of states in which they operate,[188] and to consult and cooperate with the competent authorities of countries whose interests are adversely affected by RBPs.[189] The principal provisions of Section D are provision 3, which deals with anti-competitive agreements or arrangements between enterprises, and provision 4, which deals with abuse of a dominant position. Both provisions refer to issues arising out of the operation of affiliated enterprises.

Section D(3) introduces the economic entity doctrine as a limitation on the applicability of RBP controls in the case of anti-competitive agreements or arrangements.[190] It states:

Enterprises, except when dealing with each other in the context of an economic entity wherein they are under common control, including through ownership, or otherwise not able to act independently of each other, engaged on the market in rival or potentially rival activities, should refrain from practices such as the following when, through formal, informal, written or unwritten agreements or arrangements they limit access to markets or

---

[184] UN Set above note 177 Section C(ii)(6). See also Davidow above n 163 at 375.

[185] See further Brusick above n 176 at 343–44.   [186] See ch 1.

[187] The UN Set defines restrictive business practices in Section B(i)(1) as: 'acts or behaviour of enterprises which, through an abuse or acquisition and abuse of a dominant position of market power, limit access to markets or otherwise unduly restrain competition, having or being likely to have adverse effects on international trade, particularly that of developing countries, and on the economic development of these countries, or which through formal, informal, written or unwritten agreements or arrangements among enterprises, have the same impact.' According to Davidow above n 163 at 373–74, this provision does not define any offence as this is done in other provisions (see below). In his view, the definition should be read as stating that an offence exists when a practice abuses a dominant position in the ways listed and such a practice has an adverse effect on trade or development. It does not, in his opinion, make the adverse effect on developing countries the sole test of a RBP. In Section B(ii)(9) the Set makes clear that it does not apply to, 'intergovernmental agreements, nor to restrictive business practices directly caused by such agreements'. Thus inter-governmental commodity cartels like OPEC are not covered.   [188] Section D(1).

[189] Section D(2).   [190] On the 'economic entity' doctrine, see text at n 16–17 above.

otherwise unduly restrain competition, having or being likely to have adverse effects on international trade, particularly that of developing countries, and on the economic development of these countries:

(a) Agreements fixing prices, including as to exports and imports;
(b) Collusive tendering;
(c) Market or customer allocation arrangements;
(d) Allocation by quota as to sales and production;
(e) Collective action to enforce arrangements, e.g. by concerted refusals to deal;
(f) Concerted refusal of supplies to potential importers;
(g) Collective denial of access to an arrangement, or association, which is crucial to competition.

The list of RBPs covered is unremarkable, though it has been criticized for being less clear than it appears, involving many fine points of law and policy.[191] What is of considerable interest is the compromise reached over parent/subsidiary issues. The wording suggests that economic unity between parent and subsidiary is an issue of fact in each case.[192] Thus, it has been said that the possibility of 'intra-enterprise conspiracy' is not ruled out.[193]

Section D(4) lists certain abuses of a dominant position committed by affiliated enterprises. It states:

Enterprises should refrain from the following acts or behaviour in a relevant market when through an abuse or acquisition and abuse of a dominant position of market power, they limit access to markets or otherwise unduly restrain competition, having or being likely to have adverse effects on international trade, particularly that of developing countries, and on the economic development of these countries:

(a) Predatory behaviour towards competitors, such as using below-cost pricing to eliminate competitors;

(b) Discriminatory (i.e. unjustifiably differentiated) pricing or terms and conditions in the supply and purchase of goods or services, including by means of the use of pricing policies in transactions between affiliated enterprises which overcharge or undercharge for goods or services purchased or supplied as compared with prices for similar comparable transactions outside the affiliated enterprises;

(c) Mergers, takeovers, joint ventures or other acquisitions of control, whether of a horizontal, vertical or a conglomerate nature;

(d) Fixing the prices at which goods exported can be resold in importing countries;

(e) Restrictions on the importation of goods which have been legitimately marked abroad with a trademark identical with or similar to the trademark protected as to identical or similar goods in the importing country where the trademarks in question are of the same origin, i.e. belong to the same owner or are used by enterprises between which there is economic, organizational, managerial or legal interdependence and where the purpose of such restrictions is to maintain artificially high prices;

---

[191] Davidow above n 163 at 380. [192] See further the *Bodson* case cited in n 17 above.
[193] Brusick above n 176 at 345.

(f) When not ensuring the achievement of legitimate business purposes, such as quality, safety, adequate distribution or service:
  (i) Partial or complete refusals to deal on the enterprise's customary commercial terms;
  (ii) Making the supply of particular goods or services dependent upon the acceptance of restrictions on the distribution or manufacture of competing or other goods;
  (iii) Imposing restrictions concerning where, to whom, or in what form or quantities, goods supplied or other goods may be resold or exported;
  (iv) Making the supply of particular goods or services dependent upon the purchase of other goods or services from the supplier or his designee.

This provision contemplates transfer pricing abuses by affiliated enterprises as a species of abuse of a dominant position. This was opposed in principle by the developed countries, who argued that such practices were better seen as taxation issues. However, these states compromised on the basis that the OECD Guidelines on Multinational Enterprises included, as an abuse of a dominant position, transfer pricing manipulations that adversely affected competition outside the affiliated enterprises.[194] The restrictions on trademark abuses by groups of companies echo similar restrictions in the laws of developed countries.[195] Section D(4) contains a definition of 'abuse' in a footnote that has implications for group enterprises. The footnote states that the determination of whether acts or behaviour are abusive should be examined 'with reference to whether they limit access to markets or otherwise unduly restrain competition ...' and to whether they are, inter alia, '[a]ppropriate in the light of the organizational, managerial and legal relationship among the enterprises concerned, such as the context of relations within an economic entity and not having restrictive effects outside the related enterprises ...'. Thus acts engaged in by related enterprises which are inappropriate to their organizational arrangements, and which result in the limitation of access or other restraints of competition outside the related enterprises, are covered where the related enterprises are in a position of market dominance. This suggests that intrafirm practices in general are subject to review under the UN Set. It is not clear how the line between legitimate and anti-competitive intrafirm practices should be drawn.

The UN Set provides a basic international system of cooperation between states in the regulation of RBPs. In Section C(i)(1) the UN Set contemplates mutually reinforcing action at the national, regional, and international levels to deal with RBPs, especially those that affect developing countries. The UN Set further

---

[194] See OECD *The OECD Declaration and Decisions on International Investment and Multinational Enterprises 1991 Review* (Paris: OECD,1992) Competition Guideline 1(e) at 106; Davidow above n 163 at 385. See further ch 7. The 2000 Revision of the OECD Guidelines has dropped any express reference to abuses of a dominant position, concentrating on hard core cartels as the main issue. However the Commentary to the 2000 Revision makes clear that abuses of market power or dominance are a part of the national competition laws that MNEs should observe. Indeed, the main change in the 2000 Revision is to emphasize the importance of national law and policy in this field: see n 168 above.

[195] See eg *SA CNL-Sucal NV v Hag GF AG (Hag No 2)* [1990] 3 CMLR 571 (ECJ); *Consten and Grundig* [1966] ECR 299, [1966] CMLR 418.

contemplates inter-governmental collaboration at bilateral and multilateral levels, including exchanges of information on RBPs and the holding of multilateral consultations.[196] The UN Set envisages that states with greater experience in the operation of systems of RBP control should share that experience with, or otherwise render technical assistance to, other states wishing to develop or improve such systems.[197] However, the primacy of national laws is preserved in that '[t]he provisions of the Set of principles and Rules should not be construed as justifying conduct by enterprises which is unlawful under applicable national or regional legislation'.[198] Thus the UN Set lays down a minimum definition of offences, leaving individual states free to expand this at the national level. It does not lay down a maximum system of control that is internationally acceptable.

On the other hand, the UN Set offers some guidance as to acceptable behaviour on the part of states when controlling RBPs. Thus Section E, entitled 'Principles and Rules for States at National, Regional and Subregional Levels', includes requirements that States, 'in their control of restrictive business practices, should ensure treatment of enterprises that is fair, equitable, on the same basis to all enterprises, and in accordance with established procedures of law. The laws and regulations should be publicly and readily available'.[199] Furthermore, states should protect the confidentiality of sensitive business information received from enterprises on the basis of reasonable safeguards normally applicable in this field.[200]

The UN Set concludes with a section on international measures to be taken under the auspices of UNCTAD for the control of RBPs, and establishes an institutional structure for the development of the UN Set by means of an Intergovernmental Group of Experts acting as a Committee of UNCTAD. Section F, entitled 'International Measures' envisages international collaboration aimed at achieving common approaches in national RBPs policies,[201] annual communications to the Secretary General of UNCTAD on national and regional steps taken to implement the principles embodied in the UN Set,[202] an annual report by UNCTAD on developments in this field,[203] the use of UNCTAD as a forum for interstate consultations over RBP issues,[204] the continuation of work on a Model Law or Laws on RBPs,[205] and the implementation within or facilitation by UNCTAD and other relevant UN organizations of technical assistance, advisory, and training programmes on RBPs particularly for developing countries.[206] This is to be funded from the UN Development Programme and from individual country contributions.[207]

As to the Intergovernmental Working Group, this has the functions of: providing a forum for multilateral consultations, discussions and exchanges of views by states on the UN Set; undertaking studies and research on RBPs; inviting studies

---

[196] The UN Set above n 177 Section C(i)(2)–(4).   [197] ibid Section E(8).
[198] ibid Section C(i)(5).   [199] ibid Section E(3).   [200] ibid Section E(5).
[201] ibid Section F(1).   [202] ibid Section F(2).   [203] ibid Section F(3).
[204] ibid Section F(4).   [205] ibid Section F(5) and see n 183 above.
[206] ibid Section F(6).   [207] ibid Section F(7).

by other UN organizations in this field; studying matters arising under the UN Set and collecting and disseminating information on such matters; the making of appropriate reports and recommendations to states on matters within its competence, including the application and implementation of the UN Set; and, finally, submitting an annual report.[208] The UN Set makes clear, however, that 'neither the Intergovernmental Group nor its subsidiary organs shall act like a tribunal or otherwise pass judgment on the activities or conduct of individual Governments or of individual enterprises in connection with a specific business transaction'.[209] Furthermore, '[t]he Intergovernmental Group or its subsidiary organs should avoid becoming involved when enterprises to a specific business transaction are in dispute'.[210] Thus, the institutional machinery set up under the auspices of UNCTAD cannot act in an investigative or adjudicatory capacity. In this the Intergovernmental Group is unlike bodies such as the EC Commission's Competition Directorate which enjoys the above mentioned powers.

The UN Set lacks the legal standing and financial resources to grow into anything like an effective multilateral competition authority.[211] Furthermore, its orientation towards the protection of developing country interests makes it incompatible with the dominant trend in competition policy that concentrates on efficiency issues rather than on the redistribution of competitive equality. However, as was pointed out at the second Review Conference on the UN Set, in a world with fewer barriers to international trade and investment, developing countries may be placed in a very vulnerable competitive position if some form of protection for local industries and against unfairly restrictive technology licensing agreements were not forthcoming. This view was justified by analogy with the fact that the competition laws of many countries allow smaller firms a measure of protection against larger firms.[212] Therefore, an international system of RBP controls, which includes special consideration for developing country interests, would be defensible, provided that exclusions and exceptions were not abused as a disguised means of protectionism.[213]

---

[208] ibid Section G (ii)(3).   [209] ibid Section G (ii)(4).   [210] ibid.

[211] A full discussion of the pros and cons of global competition regulation is beyond the purposes of this chapter. See further Maher M Dabbah *The Internationalisation of Antitrust Policy* (Cambridge: Cambridge University Press, 2003); Aditya Bhattachareja 'The Case for a Multilateral Agreement on Competition Policy: A Developing Country Perspective' 9 JIEL 293 (2006); Dr Christian A Conrad 'Strategies to Reform the Regulations on International Competition' 26 World Competition 101 (2003); Leonard Waverman, William S. Comanor, and Akira Goto *Competition Policy in the Global Economy: Modalities for Cooperation* (London: Routledge, 1997); G Bruce Doern and Stephen Wilks *Comparative Competition Policy: National Institutions in a Global Market* (Oxford: Clarendon Press, 1996); Eleanor M Fox 'Toward World Antitrust and Marker Access' 91 AJIL 1 (1997); Global Forum for Competition and Trade Policy *Policy Directions for Global Merger Review* (Global Competition Review, April 1999).

[212] See *UNCTAD Bulletin* No 6 November–December 1990, 7 at 8. See also R Shyam Khemani *Exemptions and Exceptions from the Application of Competition Law* (Geneva: UNCTAD, 2002).

[213] See UNCTAD *World Investment Report 1997* above n 12 at 229–31; W Lachman *The Development Dimension of Competition Law and Policy* UNCTAD Series on Issues in Competition Law and Policy (New York and Geneva: United Nations, 1999); Ajit Singh *Competition and Competition Policy in Emerging Markets: International and Developmental Dimensions* G–24 Discussion

Special provisions in national laws, that link competition and industrial policy concerns may also be required.[214]

Concluding Remarks

This chapter has outlined some of the major competition issues arising out of the internationalization of markets through the growth of MNEs and of international markets for corporate control. It has considered national, regional, and international responses to those issues. The emphasis has been mainly on the practice of developed countries. These countries have the most experience with the problems of competition in international markets for two reasons: first, the developed countries form the core geographical areas in which the global economy is evolving and, secondly, they have the most advanced systems of competition regulation. However, as certain major developing countries become increasingly integrated into the global economy they too engage in the progressive implementation of a competition policy, so as to ensure that economic development is not sacrificed for increased concentration of markets and the attendant risk of market abuse.[215] By contrast, other developing countries have no such regulatory systems and they experience the risks of competitive abuse in the absence of effective regulation. One answer to this situation is the development of regional competition bodies on the EC model, provided adequate resources are made available. These developments are creating a demand for greater cooperation and technical assistance.[216] They may also spur on institutional and substantive harmonization. This is likely to occur around the various emerging regional bodies.[217] On the other hand, for now, multilateral harmonization appears unattainable.

Paper Series No 18, September 2002, UNCTAD/Center for International Development, Harvard University (New York and Geneva: United Nations, 2002).

[214] See Singh above n 213.

[215] See, for example, Brazil: Paulo Correa and Frederico Aguiar *Merger Control in Developing Countries: Lessons from the Brazilian Experience* (New York and Geneva: UNCTAD, United Nations, 2002). See further the debate in China on the adoption of an anti-monopoly law: Mark Williams *Competition Policy and Law in China, Hong Kong and Taiwan* (Cambridge: Cambridge University Press, 2005) ch 5.

[216] See UNCTAD *Competition* above n 169 at 50 for examples of technical assistance in competition matters through bilateral and regional agreements. See also Fred O Boadu and Tolulope Olofinbiyi 'Regulating the Market: Competition Law and Policy in Kenya and Zambia' 26 World Competition 75 (2003). See further UNCTAD *Experiences Gained So Far on International Cooperation on Competition Policy Issues and the Mechanisms Used* (Geneva: UNCTAD, TD/COM.2/CLP/21/Rev 2 April 2003). The work of the International Competition Network is also of significance in this regard: see <http://www.internationalcompetitionnetwork.org/index.html>.

[217] See further UNCTAD *Competition* ibid at 55–57 for MERCOSUR, CARICOM, and COMESA initiatives.

11

Technology Transfer

The previous chapter considered competition issues in general. This chapter will continue the theme of competition and competitiveness by considering what is, perhaps, the most pressing issue in this regard for developing countries, namely, their ability to access, and to benefit from, the transfer of technology. This is an area in which a significant conflict between competing regulatory models has occurred. Specifically, the technology owning and exporting developed countries have favoured a market based model of transfer, arguing that this will offer the best possibilities for technological advancement to developing countries. By contrast, the predominantly technology poor developing countries have sought, in the past, to correct what they see as major market imperfections though the espousal of a regulatory model of technology transfer. That model dominated the debate during the 1970s and 1980s. However, as will be shown below, with the adoption of the WTO TRIPs Agreement, and the gradual emergence of certain technologically more advanced developing countries, the market based approach has gained ascendancy. This does not mean that the process of technology transfer is entirely free from regulation. Rather, the type of regulation involved has changed from a highly interventionist transaction control approach to an enabling, market opportunity creating, approach. The chapter will begin, first, by describing the nature of technology transfer. Secondly, it continues by considering how the market for technology shapes the interests of technology-exporting states and technology-importing states. Thirdly, it will describe the process of technology transfer as it is conducted by MNEs, and the principal legal issues that this raises. Finally, the two models of technology transfer regulation will be analysed in chronological order.

(1) 'Technology' and 'Technology Transfer'

'Technology' can be defined in various ways.[1] The present concern is to identify, for legal purposes, a definition that encompasses all forms of commercially usable knowledge, whether patented or unpatented, which can form the subject matter of

---

[1] See further M Blakeney *Legal Aspects of the Transfer of Technology to Developing Countries* (Oxford: ESC Publishing, 1989) at 1–2; Miagsam Santikarn *Technology Transfer* (Singapore

a transfer transaction. The Draft UNCTAD Code on the Transfer of Technology (TOT Code) suggests, in its definition of 'technology transfer', that 'technology' should be described as 'systematic knowledge for the manufacture of a product, for the application of a process or for the rendering of a service and does not extend to the transactions involving the mere sale or lease of goods'.[2] This is not particularly enlightening, save for the fact that it clearly excludes goods that are sold or hired from the ambit of 'technology'.

It is the knowledge that goes into the creation and provision of the product or service that is of key importance. Such knowledge should be seen as encompassing both the technical knowledge on which the end product is based, and the organizational capacity to convert the relevant productive inputs into the finished item or service, as the case may be. Thus as, Santikarn points out,[3] 'technology' includes not only, 'knowledge or methods that are necessary to carry on or to improve the existing production and distribution of goods and services', but also 'entrepreneurial expertise and professional know-how'. The latter two elements may often prove to be the essential competitive advantage possessed by the technology owner. As will be shown below, MNEs will be in a particularly advantageous position in this regard, especially in relation to services based foreign direct investment (FDI) where such advantages are particularly important.[4]

'Technology transfer' is the process by which commercial technology is disseminated. This will take the form of a technology transfer transaction, which may or may not be a legally binding contract,[5] but which will involve the communication,

---

University Press, 1981) at 3–6; C Ubezonu *The Law Policy and Practice of Technology Transfer to Nigeria* (1990) PhD Thesis, University of London, 24–39; Keith E Maskus *Intellectual Property Rights in the Global Economy* (Washington DC: Institute for International Economics, 2000) 136: ' "Transfer of technology" covers a vast array of complex transactions that can only be summarised here. At the most basic level, it means the successful learning of information and the know-how to use it by one party from another party. The transfer may be unintentional and uncompensated, intentional and fully compensated, or somewhere in between.'

[2] UNCTAD Draft International Code of Conduct on the Transfer of Technology, as at the close of the sixth session of Conference on 5 June 1985, (TD/CODE TOT/47 20 June 1985) Chapter 1 para1.2. This is the last full draft of the Code to have been published. It is available in the UNCTAD *Compendium of International Arrangements on Transfer of Technology: Selected Instruments* (UNCTAD/ ITE/IPC/Misc 5, New York and Geneva: United Nations, 2001) available at <http://www.unctad. org/en/docs/psiteipcm5.en.pdf>. See, for analysis, SJ Patel, P Roffe, and A Yusuf (eds) *International Technology Transfer: The Origins and Aftermath of the United Nations Negotiations on a Draft Code of Conduct* (The Hague: Kluwer Law International, 2001); UNCTAD *Transfer of Technology* Series on issues in international investment agreements (New York and Geneva: United Nations, 2001) at 51–62; Blakeney above n 1 at 133–61; for historical background, see UNCTAD *Beyond Conventional Wisdom in Development Policy: An intellectual history of UNCTAD 1964–2004* (New York and Geneva: United Nations, 2004) 'Technology' 165–82 and see references at n 97 below.

[3] Above n 1 at 4.

[4] UNCTAD distinguishes between 'hard' technology, for example, equipment, industrial processes, and 'soft technology' for example, knowledge, information, expertise, organizational skills, management, marketing, and technical know-how. The latter is the main form of technology transfer in services based foreign direct investment: UNCTAD *World Investment Report 2004* (New York and Geneva: United Nations, 2004) at 132.   [5] Blakeney above n 1 at 136.

by the transferor, of the relevant knowledge to the recipient. Among the types of transfer transactions that may be used, the draft TOT Code has listed the following:

(a) The assignment, sale and licensing of all forms of industrial property, except for trade marks, service marks and trade names when they are not part of transfer of technology transactions;

(b) The provision of know-how and technical expertise in the form of feasibility studies, plans, diagrams, models, instructions, guides, formulae, basic or detailed engineering designs, specifications and equipment for training, services involving technical advisory and managerial personnel, and personnel training;

(c) The provision of technological knowledge necessary for the installation, operation and functioning of plant and equipment, and turnkey projects;

(d) The provision of technological knowledge necessary to acquire, install and use machinery, equipment, intermediate goods and/or raw materials which have been acquired by purchase, lease or other means;

(e) The provision of technological contents of industrial and technical co-operation arrangements.[6]

The list excludes non-commercial technology transfers, such as those found in international cooperation agreements between developed and developing states. Such agreements may relate to infrastructure or agricultural development, or to international cooperation in the fields of research, education, employment or transport.[7] Technology transfer must be distinguished from technology *diffusion*. The latter is a benefit of technology transfer in that once technology is transferred it will create a 'demonstration effect' by raising awareness of its existence, and the possibility of a 'spill-over' to local firms in the course of time. This may be unintentional or as a result of deliberate governmental policies, including training requirements or compulsory licensing of technology for local firms. MNEs may also contribute to this process through local sourcing of inputs which may require

---

[6] Draft TOT Code above n 2 Chapter 1 para 1.3. During negotiations the Group of 77 countries wished to see these as mere examples of technology transfer transactions, while the major developed capital- and technology-exporting states, Group B, and the then socialist Group D, saw them as exhaustive. The EC Commission Regulation on technology transfer agreements (Regulation 772/2004 OJ [2004] L123/11 of 24 April 2004) defines such agreements as follows: 'a patent licensing agreement, a know-how licensing agreement, a software copyright licensing agreement or a mixed patent, know-how or software copyright licensing agreement, including any such agreement containing provisions which relate to the sale and purchase of products or which relate to the licensing of other intellectual property rights or the assignment of intellectual property rights, provided that those provisions do not constitute the primary object of the agreement and are directly related to the production of the contract products; assignments of patents, know-how, software copyright or a combination thereof where part of the risk associated with the exploitation of the technology remains with the assignor, in particular where the sum payable in consideration of the assignment is dependent on the turnover obtained by the assignee in respect of products produced with the assigned technology, the quantity of such products produced or the number of operations carried out employing the technology, shall also be deemed to be technology transfer agreements.' [7] Blakeney above n 1 at 3.

a degree of information sharing so that the latter can meet firm specifications and requirements.[8]

(2) The Generation and Use of Technology: International Technology Markets

The respective interests of technology-exporting and technology-importing states are best understood in the context of the international market for commercial technology. Although technology exists in non-proprietary forms that can be generally accessed, as, for example, in publicly available books or journals, the present concern focuses on proprietary technology, that is, technology that is capable of generating a profit for its owner. The first assumption underlying the market for commercial technology is that such technology should be treated as the private property of its owner and not as a public good capable of general use at little or no cost to its user. Commercial technology is usually commoditized through the application of intellectual property rights (IPRs), which give the owner a legally determined monopoly over the use and disposal of that right, or by way of protected and restrictive contractual transfer as in the case of non-patentable know-how that is secret. This process of commoditization may help to increase the value of the technology to its owner by creating relative scarcity through legally restricted access to it. However, not all types of useful knowledge are so treated. Thus, knowledge in agriculture, health sciences or services is relatively free from private claims based on intellectual property and should be more freely available.[9]

The generation of commercial technology is closely bound up with the technological infrastructure of a country. This includes the public and private organizations which fund the development and adaptation of technology, the public and private research and development (R&D) organizations that conduct work on new and improved technology, the intermediaries who move the technology around the country and across its borders and the users who apply the technology in their business activities or who are the end consumers of products incorporating the technology in question.[10] Consequently, the states that possess the more

---

[8] See UNCTAD *Transfer of Technology* above n 2 at 7.

[9] See GK Helleiner 'International Technology Issues: Southern Needs and Northern Responses' in J Bhagwati (ed) *The New International Economic Order: The North-South Debate* (MIT Press, 1977) from 295 especially 309. On the other hand, see further text at nn 181–87, for discussion of the issue of whether agricultural processes based on traditional knowledge and biological products and processes should be considered as possible subjects of IPRs. See further Keith E Maskus and Jerome H Reichman *International Public Goods and Transfer of Technology under a Globalized Intellectual Property Regime* (Cambridge: Cambridge University Press, 2005) and Christopher May *The New Enclosures* (Routledge, 2000).

[10] See T Anyos 'Mechanisms for Technology Transfer: The Role of the Infrastructure' in S Gee (ed) *Technology Transfer in Industrialized Countries* (Sijthoff, 1979) 195–212. See further R Van Tulder and G Junne *European Multinationals in Core Technologies* (Wiley/IRM, 1988) especially chs 6 and 7.

developed systems for generating, delivering, and using technology are likely to be the leading sources of proprietary technology. Indeed, according to UNCTAD, between 1996 and 2002 the 10 largest spenders on R&D accounted for more than 86 per cent of the world total, with a marginal increase in their share over that period. Eight of them were developed countries, with the US by far the biggest spender, and only two developing countries, China and the Republic of Korea, were among the top 10.[11] The combined share of R&D expenditure of developing economies, South-East Europe and the Commonwealth of Independent States (the Russian Federation and former USSR republics) grew slowly but by 2002 accounted for only 8.4 per cent with the greatest concentration in South, East, and South East Asia.[12]

MNEs are strongly influential in the operation of national and international technological infrastructures. They can be found operating at each stage of such a system in the most technologically advanced economies of the world. That this should be so stems from the fact, discussed in chapter 1, that one of the main ownership-specific advantages of MNEs is their ability to 'produce, acquire, master the understanding of and organise the use of technological assets across national boundaries'.[13] Consequently, MNEs are a major force in shaping international markets for technology, particularly on the supply side. Their influence on the demand side is also significant, given that increasing amounts of international technology transfers occur between related enterprises.[14]

Turning to the supply side, the world's major MNEs will seek to control commercial technology markets for maximum gain, exploiting their dominant position in such markets. However, the degree of control exercised by these firms may vary according to the type of technology involved. A distinction has been drawn between markets for 'conventional' technology, where the technology is sufficiently distributed for many firms from many countries to be able to supply it, and markets for 'high' technology, where the technology can be developed only by a few very large firms with very high R&D spending and where constant innovation

---

[11] UNCTAD *World Investment Report 2005* (New York and Geneva: United Nations, 2005) at 105. The top 10 in total R&D, in order of expenditure, were: US, Japan, Germany, France, UK, China, Republic of Korea, Canada, Italy, Sweden. [12] ibid at 106–107.

[13] JH Dunning *Multinational Enterprises and the Global Economy* (Wokingham: Addison-Wesley, 1993) at 290. Dunning observes that in the late 1980s MNEs were accounting for between 75 per cent and 80 per cent of privately undertaken R&D in the world. These figures are confirmed for the 1990s: see Oliver Gassman and Maximillian von Zedwitz 'New Concepts and Trends in International R&D Organisation' 28 Research Policy 231 (1999). According to UNCTAD in 2002 the 700 largest firms spent $310 billion on R&D. Of these at least 98 per cent were transnational corporations. Their expenditure accounted for 46 per cent of total R&D expenditure and 69 per cent of world business R&D expenditure. Over 80 per cent of these firms came from the US, Japan, Germany, the UK, and France in order of size. They were concentrated mainly in IT hardware, automotive, and pharmaceuticals/biotechnology: *World Investment Report 2005* above n 11 at 119–21.

[14] See GK Helleiner 'The Role of Multinational Corporations in the Less Developed Countries' Trade in Technology' 3 World Development 161 (1975).

is the basis for competitive success.[15] Examples of the former include: footwear, textiles, cement, pulp and paper, or food processing. Examples of the latter include: aerospace, electronics, computers, chemicals, and machinery. The supply of technology in 'conventional' industries is said to be relatively competitive, given the stable and generally non-proprietary nature of the technology involved. By contrast, in 'high' technology areas competitive supply is likely to be restricted. Owners will guard the source of their competitive advantage, making their technology available only on restrictive terms favourable to the earning of a monopoly rent. This tendency may be reinforced because of the absence of viable alternative technology suppliers that could offer competition over the terms and conditions of transfer. However, not all 'high' technology markets should be seen as uncompetitive on the supply side. For example, in the newer high technology industries, such as semiconductors or computers, the entry of smaller, innovative firms has stimulated choice in sources of technological supply, making for increased competition in that field, although in the long term concentration can be predicted to occur.[16] Furthermore, as 'high' technology matures into 'conventional' technology, new entrants into the field can be expected. The competitive situation on the supply side of a market for technology is not, therefore, a static phenomenon, and each industrial sector should be analysed on its own terms.

In addition, as the structure of international production changes, in certain industries a process of 'fragmentation' of production is observable. This arises as a result of MNEs taking advantage of differences in production and communication costs and skills to relocate processes and functions across countries. This has allowed some developing countries without a strong R&D base to leapfrog to production in high-technology industries such as electronics.[17] As a consequence these countries have been able to attract R&D investment to take advantage of the need to locate such activities close to the site of production and of locally educated science trained personnel who can be employed for R&D functions in new technologies even in the absence of industrial experience.[18] Examples include Singapore and more recently China. However, the vast majority of developing countries are not in a position to achieve this as they lack the required local capabilities.[19]

The demand side of the market will also be conditioned by the nature of the technological infrastructure present in the state where the recipient is situated.

---

[15] See D Greer 'Control of Terms and Conditions for International Transfers of Technology to Developing Countries' in O Schachter and R Hellawell (eds) *Competition in International Business* (New York: Columbia University Press, 1981) from 41 especially 48, citing W Chudson *The International Transfer of Commercial Technology to Developing Countries* (New York: UNITAR, 1971) 18. For a more recent similar analysis, see UNCTAD *World Investment Report 2005* above n 11 at 101–105 and 109–11.

[16] See Van Tulder and Junne above n 10 ch 2.

[17] UNCTAD *World Investment Report 2005* above n 11 at 109.   [18] ibid.

[19] ibid at 111–6. UNCTAD has drawn up an 'Innovation Capability Index' which ranks countries according to their capability in absorbing R&D activity. The weakest regions are South Asia, in particular Pakistan and Sri Lanka, and sub-Saharan Africa. See further ibid ch IV for more detailed analysis of R&D investment trends in developing countries.

Thus a distinction can be made between conditions in technologically advanced recipient states and those in technologically less developed states.[20] Conditions in the former are characterized by an ability to absorb technology effectively through advanced production systems, a highly trained workforce, high demand for the technology concerned and the ability to pay for it. Furthermore, technologically advanced recipients will be in a stronger position to bargain over the terms of supply. Alternative local sources of technology, which can compete with the technology on offer from outside, are more likely to exist. Moreover, there exists a greater likelihood that the purchaser will itself be in a strong position to condition the market, as where it is another major corporation operating at the same level of the market as the supplier, or where it is in a quasi-monopolistic position such as, for example, the postal and telecommunications authority of a major advanced country.[21] As will be shown in more detail below, in advanced countries the principal concern is that of ensuring the existence of workable competition even in highly concentrated technology markets. Thus competition law plays a significant role in the regulation of technology transfers to such countries.

By comparison, the absorption of proprietary technology in developing countries is more problematic. The absence of a sophisticated technological infrastructure has significant consequences for demand conditions. In particular, a high level of dependency on outside suppliers is created due to the lack of alternative, domestically generated, technology. This creates a weak bargaining position which is exacerbated by the relative lack of information about technology caused by the absence of adequate numbers of skilled specialists who could evaluate the technology on offer. In such cases the technology owner is likely to enjoy a monopolistic position in relation to the recipient market and may be able to exact excessive prices and restrictions on the utilization of the imported technology.[22]

Furthermore, as will be elaborated in the next section, it is less likely that the technology owner will be able to introduce the technology by means other than direct investment through a controlled subsidiary. In developing countries, the incidence of firms that can act as licensees of advanced technology is much smaller than in developed countries. Consequently, the conditions of technology transfer will be determined by the needs of the MNE as an integrated enterprise. These may be inimical to the interests of the importing state, to the extent that control over technology within the firm is less likely to result in its dissemination to potential competitors, if any, in that state. In addition, where local linkages are, in principle, possible MNEs will only invest in the technological upgrading of local suppliers if they have the minimum base of skills and know-how to absorb technologies and

---

[20] See further Greer above n 15 at 56–60.

[21] See eg *Re ECR 900* [1992] 4 CMLR 54. The EC Commission found that the market for new cellular telephony technology in the EC is dominated by a small number of national telecom companies which set the terms of technological innovation and conditions of supply.

[22] See, for an economic analysis of this situation, Rodriguez 'Trade in Technological Knowledge and the National Advantage' 83 Jo.Pol.Econ. 121 (1975).

management practices.[23] That said there exist significant examples of technology upgrading by MNEs to ensure good quality local inputs to production.[24]

A final issue relating to the supply side of the market for technology is whether MNEs can supply 'appropriate technology' to developing countries. During the 1970s, when the debate on technology transfer to developing countries became a significant pillar of the wider call for a New International Economic Order,[25] this issue stood out as encapsulating the inequitable situation of developing countries in the market for technology. It was argued that developing countries were disadvantaged in technology markets because the available technology was inappropriate to their real needs. The argument was put on two levels. First, the type of technology that had been generated by MNEs from the developed countries was incapable of utilizing the primary factor endowment of developing countries, namely, unskilled labour, as it was geared to capital-intensive forms of production requiring fewer, high-skilled personnel. Thus, in developing countries, MNEs tended to set up production enterprises that had little effect on local skill and employment patterns. Secondly, the types of products made by MNEs were said to be inappropriate to developing country markets. Either they were high-technology products, with highly specialized uses, or luxury products, that few consumers in developing countries could use, or they were mass consumption items geared towards the wants of Western consumer markets that distorted consumption patterns in developing countries by persuading consumers to spend what little disposable income they had on unnecessary products such as soft drinks, 'junk foods', cigarettes or cosmetics.[26] This aspect of the argument may be said to have a contemporary equivalent in the call for more sustainable consumption patterns in both developed and developing countries.[27]

The first argument has been challenged on economic grounds, in that there may be no necessary correlation between labour-intensive technologies and welfare in developing countries.[28] Indeed the opposite may be the case. Developing countries need to enhance their competitive advantages in human and other resources to attract more advanced, high value-added investments in advanced

---

[23] See UNCTAD *World Investment Report 2001* (New York and Geneva: United nations, 2001) at 142.

[24] See the examples cited in UNCTAD ibid at 144–62. Government policy may help in this regard: see ibid chs V and VI.

[25] See GK Helleiner above n 9 at 295; Hope 'Basic Needs and Technology Transfer Issues in the "New International Economic Order"' 42 Am.J.Econ. and Soc. 393 (1983); Blakeney above n 1 at 57–67.

[26] See further Helleiner n 14 above.

[27] See Leslie Sklair *Globalization: Capitalism and its Alternatives* (Oxford: Oxford University Press, 2002) at 277; see further Yiannis Gabriel and Tim Lang *The Unmanageable Consumer: Contemporary Consumption and its Fragmentations* (London: Sage Publications, 2nd edn, 2006).

[28] See Santikarn above n 1 at 17–20. Furthermore, it may be argued that this position tends towards the perpetuation of underdevelopment by assuming that the most modern capital-intensive technologies should not be exported to developing countries, thereby depriving them of the source of economic modernity. See further Arghiri Emmanuel *Appropriate or Underdeveloped Technology?* (Wiley/IRM, 1982).

technology fields. They cannot expect MNEs to do this.[29] In any case, there is considerable evidence showing that much investment by MNEs in developing countries is of a labour-intensive kind that is geared to take advantage of lower labour costs in the production of lower technology based goods for export markets.[30] This is true not only in relation to manufacture but also in relation to services, as in the case of offshore call centres.[31] The real problem may be that MNEs are uninterested in transferring any but the more mature and labour-intensive technologies to developing countries, given the limitations of local markets for advanced technology goods and processes, and the uneconomic costs of adapting existing proprietary technology to developing country conditions.[32] The major exception to this will be, as noted above, export oriented investment in cost sensitive high technology industries that will be attracted to low labour cost, high educational skills locations. The second argument can be opposed on the ground that it is based on a subjective opinion as to what is 'appropriate' as a consumer good in a developing country. In a free market economy, the fact that the demand exists is more important in economic terms than its social implications.[33] Thus, MNEs can be expected to generate demand for their products in developing countries among those who can afford them and/or who can be persuaded to buy them. Nonetheless, despite the weaknesses of the 'appropriate technology' argument, it offered an impetus for the reconsideration of policy in this area, providing a major justification for greater regulation of international technology transfers in the interests of developing countries. It continues an existence in relation to the issue of sustainable development. This has, in turn, generated calls for the transfer of environmentally sound technology, which is discussed in chapter 14 below.

(3) Technology Transfer by MNEs and its Legal Effects

Having examined the operation of markets in technology, and the role of MNEs in their operation, this section will look more closely at how MNEs manage their internal organization to transfer technology across borders. There are two principal methods of technology transfer open to the MNE. The first is to license the technology at arm's length to an independent licensee or to a joint venture with a local partner. This is known as *externalized transfer*. The second method is to

---

[29] See UNCTAD *Foreign Direct Investment and Development* Series on issues in international investment agreements (New York and Geneva: United Nations, 1998) at 41–42.

[30] Helleiner above n 14 at 170–72. See also ch 6 above at 226–37 on Export Processing Zones.

[31] See UNCTAD *World Investment Report 2004* above n 4 at 151.

[32] Blakeney above n 1 at 64–65; Richard E Caves *Multinational Enterprise and Economic Analysis* (Cambridge: Cambridge University Press, 2nd edn, 1996) at 229–31.

[33] Sanjaya Lall 'The Patent System and the Transfer of Technology to Less Developed Countries' 10 JWTL 1 at 5–6 (1976).

transfer the technology internally to a subsidiary, known as *internalized transfer*.[34] This may involve the licensing of intellectual property rights and/or know-how by the parent to the subsidiary in return for royalty payments, although informal, royalty-free transfers may also take place. The choice of methods will be determined by what will serve to maximize the MNE's income from the technology in question.

The choice is conditioned by a number of factors centred on the nature of the technology, the strategy of the seller, the capabilities of the buyer, and host government policies.[35] Assuming that a suitable licensee, or joint venture partner, exists in the host country, the MNE is more likely to consider licensing the technology, or setting up a joint venture, where the entry barriers, such as, for example, the small size of the market, are too great to make an independent direct investment viable. Indeed, in some cases, a licensing arrangement or a joint venture may be the only legally permissible from of entry. Furthermore, where the firm is a newcomer to international markets and lacks the expertise to undertake direct investment, licensing to a third party or to a joint venture may be preferable. On the other hand, licensing may create too many medium to long-term costs to be worthwhile. In particular, the MNE must consider whether licensing will increase the risk of deterioration in quality due to the licensee's misuse of the technology, and whether the licensee will pass on the technology to competitors. Such problems may be diminished by the imposition of restrictive conditions on the licensee in the licensing agreement. However, if the technology concerned is a 'core' technology with a long commercial life-span, licensing may involve too many risks. In this respect, a joint venture may serve to ensure greater operational control over the use of the technology. On the other hand, it may not protect the owner from allowing the other joint venture partner from becoming familiar with the technology and using this advantage to set up in competition with the owner. Thus, if the owner has the ability to do so, it may prefer direct investment over licensing, as this permits closer control over the use of the technology and is more likely to preserve its confidential nature.

The transfer of technology by direct investment is more likely in developing countries, given the likely absence of suitable potential licensees or joint venture partners, and because the MNE can provide the technology as part of a larger 'package' that includes capital, management, back up services, access to markets, and other associated benefits which may be in short supply. In such cases, the major question is whether the host country will in fact gain any transfer of the technology out of the firm into the wider local economy. Internalized transfers have both advantages and disadvantages. In terms of advantages, the transfer of technology

---

[34] See UNCTAD *World Investment Report 1999* (New York and Geneva: United Nations, 1999) at 230.

[35] See ibid at 204–205; Caves above n 32 at 166–72. See also ch 1 at 38–39 where this issue is addressed in the context of MNE growth strategies.

will bring associated financial resources, expand the technology base of the host country, allow for swift transfer, and provide access to the entire technological assets of the MNE.[36] In terms of disadvantages, internalized transfer may prove more expensive to the host country if it has to pay for a full 'package' of assets that may go beyond the technology itself and include IPRs, finance, skills, and management, and where these other assets are locally available.[37] In addition, the retention of technology know-how and skills within the network of the MNE may 'hold back deeper learning processes and spillovers into the local economy, especially where the local affiliate is not developing R&D capabilities'.[38] Much will depend on the willingness of the MNE to train more personnel than it needs, the surplus employees being free to apply their experience elsewhere in the local economy.[39] However, MNEs do not appear to make the training of local personnel a major priority, and it may be questionable whether there will be sufficient outlets for the application of the skills newly learnt by the local employees of MNEs.[40] If there are, then restrictive covenants in contracts of employment may seek to protect the commercial advantage of the MNE by preventing the use of such skills by former employees for the benefit of competitors.

From the above, it can be seen that the legal structure of the recipient of the technology is a significant matter influencing the extent to which the general diffusion of the technology concerned into the wider local economy is likely to occur. Direct investment through a wholly owned subsidiary is most likely to keep the technology under the control of its owner. The terms of transfer to the subsidiary are likely to restrict the use of the technology for the benefit of the MNE alone, and this aim will be enforced by managerial control from the parent. On the other hand, a joint venture or a licensing agreement may allow the local partner or licensee to gain access to the technology and to diffuse it in the wider economy, provided that the terms of the transfer are not too restrictive. Consequently, one legal issue of relevance to the regulator is whether to restrict investments involving technology transfer to legal forms that are more likely to result in technology diffusion. Hence there may be a preference, in host state law, for joint ventures or licensing arrangements over direct investment, where adequate local partners exist. This may be accompanied by technology transfer requirements and incentives, although these may be subject to regulation under investment agreements and WTO disciplines.[41]

The second major legal issue that arises in all cases of technology transfer, whether between related or independent entities, concerns the actual terms of the transfer transaction and the degree to which these affect the likelihood that the technology will be made available to those who could benefit from it. The nature

---

[36] ibid at 208–209.   [37] UNCTAD *Transfer of Technology* above n 2 at 15.
[38] ibid.   [39] Santikarn above n 1 at 12.   [40] See Caves above n 32 at 228.
[41] On which see further ch 6 at 251–61.

and content of such terms form much of the basis for technology transfer regulation, both in technology-rich and technology-poor countries. Therefore, a brief overview of the most common terms in technology transfer transactions is in order. Technology licences, whether between the affiliated undertakings of a MNE, or between an MNE and a third party, will contain terms that seek to preserve the competitive advantage of the technology owner against abusive exploitation by the technology recipient. While such terms may be unobjectionable where the legitimate interests of the technology owner are being protected, they may also be used by the owner as a means of obtaining an unfair commercial advantage over the recipient through the exploitation of its generally weaker bargaining position.[42]

In developed recipient states, such abusive behaviour by the transferor has been dealt with as a competition issue. However, in developing countries, even if even commercially legitimate restraints are placed on the recipient, the effect of these on the ability of the host country to absorb and learn from the imported technology, or to use it as a catalyst for economic development, may be too restrictive. Therefore, controls over restrictive terms based on competition law alone may be ineffective as a means of safeguarding the public interests involved.

Restrictive terms in technology transfer transactions may be conveniently classified into two main categories: those that restrict the recipient's commercial policy in respect of the conduct of business involving the transferred technology and those that seek to preserve the exclusive ownership and use of the technology by the transferor.[43]

Technology transfer agreements will usually include restrictions on the commercial policy of the recipient that are designed to maximize the profit that the transferor can earn from its inventions and know-how. These will concern inter alia restrictions on the purchasing, production, and marketing policies of the recipient. Thus, at the level of purchasing policy, transferors may insist on the recipient buying its requirements for raw materials, plant and machinery, and other goods or services from the transferor. Such 'tie-ins' may be legitimate where certain inputs, given their quality and characteristics, can only be obtained from the transferor. However, where suitable substitutes are available more cheaply on the open market, tie-ins are harder to justify on efficiency grounds. Indeed, they may be a means of extracting monopolistic profits from the recipient that go beyond what may be legitimately expected from the mere ownership of the technology. Such manipulations have been condemned under the competition laws of developed countries, although a tying arrangement will not be upset where there are genuine commercial reasons for its existence.[44] From the perspective of a developing host country,

---

[42] See Santikarn above n 1 at 24–35; Blakeney above n 1 at 35–42 and 67–70; Richard Whish *Competition Law* (London, Butterworths, 5th edn, 2003) 735–38.

[43] Santikarn ibid.

[44] See eg *Jefferson Parish Hospital District No 2 v Hyde* 466 US 2 (1984); *United States v Jerrold Electronics Corp* 187 F Supp 545 (E D Pa 1960) *aff'd* 365 US 567 (1961); and see US Department of Justice Antitrust Division and Federal Trade Commission *Antitrust Guidelines for the Licensing of*

tying arrangements may create special problems. First, such an arrangement may conceal the true cost of the technology package, in that although the royalty payments imposed on the recipient may be reasonable, they may be enhanced by the overpricing of tied inputs through transfer pricing manipulations.[45] Secondly, tying arrangements may have the further effect of preventing backward economic integration through the growth of local suppliers. Thus local economic development may be inhibited.

The recipient may be restricted further by clauses requiring the production of minimum quantities of product, which may be linked to a minimum royalty requirement, and by clauses setting the duration of the agreement. Where the agreement is of excessive duration this may force the recipient to acquire obsolete technology and to prevent it from obtaining technology from alternative suppliers.[46] The agreement may also contain field-of-use restrictions which limit the application of the technology to particular fields only. This may be reasonable as a means of giving the transferor control over the use of its inventions, but competition authorities will not normally tolerate such a restriction where it acts as a disguised method of dividing markets.[47] For a developing country, field-of-use restrictions may prevent the full exploitation of the technology in all the areas where it may be of value as a stimulus to economic development.

At the marketing level, the recipient may be restricted as to the export markets in which it can sell products incorporating the technology in question. The owner will justify such protection on the basis that it ensures an adequate return on the cost of developing the technology. It is an aspect of the monopoly right that is inherent in patented technology, or in the competitive advantage gained by the development of secret know-how. Reasonable territorial restrictions on the business of technology recipients have been accepted under the competition laws of developed states, on the basis that some restriction of intra-brand competition may be necessary to ensure the widest possible dissemination of products incorporating the proprietary technology. On the other hand, developing countries have argued that such restrictions simply inhibit their ability to earn foreign exchange through exports.[48] There is undoubtedly a danger that an integrated MNE will use technology licences with its subsidiaries to insulate geographical markets. Markets in which high prices prevail may be protected from imports of cheaper products produced in another market by an affiliate, thereby stifling price competition

---

Intellectual Property (6 April 1995) s 5.3. available at <http://www.usdoj.gov/atr/public/guidelines/0558.htm#t53>; EC Commission Regulation 772/2004/EC on the application of Article 81(3) of the Treaty to categories of technology transfer agreements OJ [2004] L123/11 available at <http://eur-lex.europa.eu/LexUriServ/site/en/oj/2004/l_123/l_12320040427en00110017.pdf> and EC Commission Notice (2004/C 101/02) Guidelines on the Application of Article 81 to Technology Transfer Agreements OJ [2004] C101/2 at paras 191–95.

[45] Santikarn above n 1 at 28–29.   [46] Blakeney above n 1 at 41.
[47] See eg *Windsurfing International v EC Commission* [1986] ECR 611, [1986] 3 CMLR 489; Regulation 772/2004 above n 44 art 2(1)(c)(i) and (ii); *Talking Pictures Corp v Western Electric Co* 305 US 124 (1938).   [48] Blakeney above n 1 at 39.

between affiliates. Where the cheaper products originate in a developing country then some loss to revenue may be predicted as a result of such export restrictions.

A similar restraint on the recipient's commercial freedom may come from price-fixing provisions. The transferor may insist that the transferee charges a high price for products incorporating the transferred technology. This may prevent price competition between the transferor and recipient, by protecting the transferor's home market against cheaper imports from the recipient. Where such price controls are imposed on a plant operating in a developing country, the opportunity to earn foreign exchange from exports to higher price areas will be lost.

Although price fixing is generally regarded as a particularly serious anti-competitive practice, in licensing arrangements a degree of price control over the licensee may be justifiable as an aspect of the licensor's monopoly rights that stem from his invention.[49] Given that the licensee is unlikely to license a direct competitor, and that the licensor has an interest in allowing the greatest exploitation of his invention, the licensee may in fact be encouraged to sell at the lowest prices possible. However, in the context of a developing country economy, this argument may not be sufficient to justify restrictions on the earning capacity of the recipient. On the other hand, where the recipient is a wholly owned subsidiary, the ability to control corporate policy may be limited, even under competition principles. It may be necessary to impose export requirements as a condition of entry.

Restrictions on the use of the technology by the recipient aim at the preservation of the confidential nature of the technology transferred and at the preservation of the owner's competitive advantage stemming from the technology. Thus, it is common to find confidentiality clauses in technology transfer agreements. These are generally unobjectionable, provided they are not of excessive duration, as where the duty continues even though the intellectual property right protecting the technology has run out, or the know-how involved has entered the public domain. Similarly, clauses preventing the recipient from entering into arrangements with competitors of the transferor, from manufacturing competing products, or from using competing technology can be justified on the basis of confidentiality. However, in the context of a developing country economy such restraints may inhibit the gaining of experience in the field where the technology is used.[50]

More problematic are clauses that inhibit the acquisition of skill and experience on the part of the recipient as a result of interaction with the technology transferred. This may allow the recipient to compete with the transferor after the expiry of the agreement, a situation that challenges the monopoly of the transferor. To counter this threat, the agreement may prohibit the use of the technology transferred after the expiry of the agreement, or permit use only upon the continued payment of a royalty. This is acceptable where the intellectual property rights involved have not yet expired, or the relevant know-how has not entered the

---

[49] Blakeney ibid at 39.   [50] ibid.

public domain. On the other hand, a blanket prohibition on post-term use where such rights have expired, or where the know-how has become public knowledge as a result of the transferor's actions, may be unduly exploitative, as would a requirement to pay further royalties in these circumstances.[51]

In addition, the recipient may be prevented from conducting its own research and development work on the transferred technology, or, in the absence of such a prohibition, it may be obliged to transfer any resulting improvements to the transferor on a non-reciprocal basis. Such strong 'grant-back' provisions have been condemned under the competition laws of developed countries.[52] For developing countries such clauses would be especially worrying as they would inhibit the learning process that can result from the use of imported technology, and lessen the likelihood of adaptation to local needs.

Thus, restrictive clauses in technology transfer transactions will have significant effects on the manner in which the technology may be used by the recipient. The extent to which the recipient can benefit in the long term from the use of the technology will depend on the limits of contractual freedom granted to the transferor for the exploitation of its innovation. In this the responses of developed and less developed states have differed, and to these attention now turns.

(4) The Two Principal Models of Technology Transfer Regulation

From the above it can be seen that the priorities of preserving workable competition in technology markets, as espoused by developed recipient states, may not always answer the priorities of ensuring economic development espoused by less developed recipient states. Thus two distinct models for the regulation of technology transfer have emerged from these two groups of states. The developed recipients follow a model that preserves the essential logic of a legally permitted monopoly right in proprietary technology based on intellectual property law and freedom of contract, tempered in its excesses by competition law. By contrast, developing countries have sought, in the past, to create a regime of technology transfer laws that went beyond the preservation of workable competition and sought to control technology transfers in the interests of development, thereby qualifying the legal effects of private property in innovation. A comparison of these models will now be made. The discussion begins with the older regulatory approach, which was dominant in the 1970s and 1980s, and moves to the currently dominant developed country market-based model.

---

[51] Regulation 772/2004 above n 44 art 2 and EC *Guidelines* above n 44 paras 54–55 and 158–59.
[52] See Regulation 772/2004 art 5(1)(a) and (b) and EC *Guidelines* at paras 109–11; US *Guidelines* above n 44 at s 5.6.

(a) The Regulatory Control Model

This model is characterized by a reserved attitude to the protection of IPRs, although not a complete dismissal of their logic and effects,[53] coupled with the adoption of specialized technology transfer laws. It is the basis upon which the draft UNCTAD TOT Code was drawn up. The model is more complex to explain than that evolved by developed recipient states. This is because it attempts to address issues of economic development against the background of the internationalization of the developed country model of technology transfer regulation, a model that is suitable for the needs of technologically mature and innovative economies, and which places considerably more emphasis on the rights of intellectual property holders than might have been the case when the developed states were themselves undergoing the process of industrialization.[54]

(i) *Reserved Approach to the Protection of Intellectual Property Rights*

Unlike the technologically advanced countries, developing countries have been less willing to accept uncritically the assumptions behind the international system of intellectual property protection. Since 1961, they have been seeking reform of that system.[55] The process started when, in 1961, Brazil introduced a draft resolution in the Second Committee of UN General Assembly calling for a study of the effects of patents on the transfer of technology. This led, in 1964, to a report by the Secretary-General, entitled 'The Role of Patents in the Transfer of Technology to Developing Countries'.[56] It concluded that reform of the system was unnecessary. Most of the states that replied to the UN questionnaire on which the report was based said that patents were an aid to their development by promoting technology transfer. Only India, Lebanon, and Cuba offered the opposite opinion. However, by the 1970s, this approach had changed. In particular, UNCTAD had taken up the issue of technology transfer.[57] In this connection, it undertook several influential studies including one on the role of patents in technology transfer,[58] and one on the role of trademarks in developing countries.[59] Furthermore, in 1974, negotiations were under way to reform the Paris Convention for the

---

[53] See Pedro Roffe and Taffere Tesfachew 'The Unfinished Agenda' in Patel, Roffe, and Yusuf (eds) above n 2, 381 at 389.

[54] See further Blakeney above n 1 at 49–50. See also Pedro Roffe 'The Political Economy of Intellectual Property Rights – An Historical Perspective' in Julio Faundez, Mary E Footer, and Joseph J Norton (eds) *Governance Development and Globalisation* (London: Blackstone Press, 2000) from 397 especially 399–400 outlining the 19th century anti-patent movement in Europe. At that time the Netherlands and Switzerland repealed their patent laws citing the need for industrial development as the reason.

[55] See Jayagovind 'The International Patent System and the Developing Countries' (1980) Ind.JIL 47 at 56–62 on which the next paragraph is based.   [56] UN Doc E/3681/Rev1 1964.

[57] See Blakeney above n 1 at 21–24; Ewing 'UNCTAD and the Transfer of Technology' 10 JWTL 197 (1976).

[58] UNCTAD *The Role of the Patent System in the Transfer of Technology to Developing Countries* (UN Doc TD/B/AC 11/19 1974).

[59] UNCTAD *The Role of Trademarks in Developing Countries* (UN Doc TD/B/C.6/AC.3/3 Rev 1 1979). Comment: Wasserman 14 JWTL 80 (1980).

Protection of Industrial Property under the auspices of the body charged with its administration, the World Intellectual Property Organization (WIPO).[60] These developments resulted in the formulation of a comprehensive critique as to the appropriateness of traditional intellectual property laws as instruments for the transfer of technology to developing countries. The basic arguments concerned the problems associated with patents and trademarks and with the principles underlying the international system of protection.

As regards patents, it was argued that the granting of patent rights in developing countries would have adverse consequences on development in that they would be taken out for reasons that had little to do with the traditional uses of patents.[61] Given that most of the world's patents were owned by foreign firms operating in developed country markets patent protection in a developing country was not aimed at encouraging local innovation. Instead, the principal reason for taking out such a patent was attributed to the desire of the firm to protect its markets and licensing rights in the country concerned, thereby preventing rivals from entering in its place. Thus the patent would give the owner an import monopoly over the market concerned. Furthermore, the patent owner would rarely, if ever, work the patent in the country concerned. Thus, the grant of the patent would retard technology transfer not only by closing off competition but also by allowing the owner to neutralize the technology concerned through nonuse. The latter problem is not unique to developing countries. The industrial property laws of most states provide for compulsory licensing of patents that are not worked, as does the TRIPs Agreement.[62] However, according to the UNCTAD

---

[60] See Vaitsos 'The Revision of the International Patent System: Legal Considerations for a Third World Position' 4 World Development 85 (1976); Blakeney above n 1 at 24–26 and 90–104. The Paris Convention is available from the WIPO website at <http://www.wipo.int/treaties/en/ip/paris/trtdocs_wo020.html>.

[61] See Vaitsos ibid at 87–88; Vaitsos 'Patents Revisited: Their Function in Developing Countries' 9 Journal of Development Studies (1972) at 73–83; Pedro Roffe 'Abuses of Patent Monopoly: A Legal Appraisal' 2 World Development 15 (1974); Edith Penrose 'International Patenting and the Less Developed Countries' 83 Econ.Jo. 768 (1973). See also the Official Report of the Revision of the Patents Law (New Delhi: Government of India, 1959 'The Aygangar Report'), for a significant early analysis of the issues facing developing countries.

[62] TRIPs Agreement art 31 at <http://www.wto.org/english/docs_e/legal_e/27-trips.pdf> (see further below). See also Paris Convention art 5A:

'(2) Each country of the Union shall have the right to take legislative measures providing for the grant of compulsory licenses to prevent the abuses which might result from the exercise of the exclusive rights conferred by the patent, for example, failure to work.

(3) Forfeiture of the patent shall not be provided for except in cases where the grant of compulsory licenses would not have been sufficient to prevent the said abuses. No proceedings for the forfeiture or revocation of a patent may be instituted before the expiration of two years from the grant of the first compulsory license.

(4) A compulsory license may not be applied for on the ground of failure to work or insufficient working before the expiration of a period of four years from the date of filing of the patent application or three years from the date of the grant of the patent, whichever period expires last; it shall be refused if the patentee justifies his inaction by legitimate reasons. Such a compulsory license shall be non–exclusive and shall not be transferable, even in the form of the grant of a sub–license, except with that part of the enterprise or goodwill which exploits such license.'

study of 1975 most developing countries did not use their compulsory licensing procedures because of the costs and delays involved.[63] Finally, it was argued that the existence of patent rights could encourage the conclusion of unduly restrictive licensing agreements, which, given the absence of competition laws in most developing countries, could not be effectively controlled.[64]

Regarding trademarks, it was argued that while such rights served the useful functions of guaranteeing quality and source, they also created adverse effects in developing country economies.[65] In particular, trademarks tended to be owned by the subsidiaries of foreign MNEs and used to enhance market power either through their promotion by intensive advertising or by licensing to local distributors. These activities would result in considerable social costs as consumers with limited incomes would pay high prices for foreign branded products. Furthermore, local distributors would bear the cost of developing market share without any guarantee of benefiting from the resulting goodwill created towards the marked product. This goodwill would accrue to the foreign trademark owner rather than to the local licensee. In the light of such views certain developing countries adopted laws to control the use of trademarks. Thus Mexico enacted a Law on Inventions and Trademarks in 1976, which required the concurrent use of the local licensee's mark with that of the foreign licensor, in the belief that the goodwill generated by the licensee would be associated not only with the foreign mark but also with the local mark.[66] In 1972, under the Generic Names Drug Act, Pakistan banned the use of trademarks in the pharmaceutical industry. This had disastrous results, leading to sales of ineffective counterfeit drugs bearing the permitted generic name and to a black market in branded drugs. This law was repealed in 1976.[67]

Finally, as regards the international system of protection, the developing countries sought to reform, in particular, the application of the national treatment standard to their national legal regimes. Thus the 1975 UNCTAD study on patents proposed the introduction of preferential treatment for developing countries.[68] This was justified on the ground that developing and developed countries were in an unequal relationship based on the fact that most of the patent rights that stood to benefit from national treatment were held by MNEs from developed countries, and because the few patents that were issued for the nationals of developing countries

---

[63] See UNCTAD above n 58 at para 339 cited in Roffe above n 61 at 26.

[64] Roffe ibid at 18–20; Mangalo 'Patent Protection and Technology Transfer in the North-South Conflict' 9 IIC 100 at 110–11 (1978).

[65] See UNCTAD 1979 above n 59; Chudnovsky 'Foreign Trademarks in Developing Countries' 7 World Development 663 (1979); Greer 'The Economic Benefits and Costs of Trademarks: Lessons for the Developing Countries' 7 World Development 683 (1979).

[66] See Ball 'Attitudes of Developing Countries to Trademarks' 74 TMR 160 at 164–66 (1984). Other countries to have used such devices in past legislation include: Brazil (Normative Act No 15 11 September 1975 art 3.5.1) and former Yugoslavia (Law for the Protection of Inventions Technical Improvements and Distinctive Signs 1981 art 134).   [67] Ball ibid at 167.

[68] Above n 58 at paras 394–412.

involved individual inventors, not MNEs, and created distinctive needs for protection.[69] In addition, developing countries sought to reform the principle of priority contained in Article 4 of the Paris Convention. By this principle, any person who has filed an application for a patent in one of the contracting states has a right to claim similar protection as a matter of priority in other contracting states for up to 12 months. The developing countries argued that this period was too long and acted as a disincentive to invention in developing countries.

All the above arguments were subjected to forceful criticism. The developing country position on patents was doubted by proponents of the developed country approach, who asserted the original justification for patent protection as lying in the provision of incentives for innovation by enterprises. According to Beier, 'it is only patent protection which gives enterprises the necessary incentive to file their important inventions abroad and converts an invention into an object of international trade that can be transferred without too great a risk'.[70] Such a position lies behind the greater controls contained in the TRIPs Agreement to be discussed below.

However, as pointed out in chapter 1,[71] a MNE may not require the possession of patent rights to protect its competitive advantage in technology. More significant are its abilities to conduct costly R&D and to integrate patented technology with non patentable know-how, without which the patented elements of the technology may be useless. Thus the true problem for developing countries is not so much that patents are taken out by foreign firms, but that the major producers of technology tend to possess considerable market power to which the protection of intellectual property is no more than a subsidiary form of protection.[72] This suggests policy responses in other fields of law, especially competition law.

The arguments relating to trademarks were criticized on the grounds that, in the absence of assured quality in the products of local firms and of effective consumer protection legislation, foreign trademarks can act as marks of quality. Furthermore, the adverse effects stemming from the link between foreign trademarks and advertising was seen as a purely theoretical argument that cannot support the view that removal of trademark rights will prevent socially inefficient consumption.[73] Furthermore, as Blakeney points out, the commercial functions that trademarks perform may lead to the creation of a marketing infrastructure in developing countries that will facilitate the distribution of goods containing transferred technology.[74]

Finally, the arguments concerning reform of the international system of protection have not led to the hoped for reforms. Given the relatively weak bargaining

[69] Vaitsos above n 60 at 90.

[70] Beier 'The Significance of the Patent System for Technical, Economic and Social Progress' 11 IIC 563 at 584 (1980).   [71] At 34 above.

[72] See further Lall above n 33.

[73] See Ball above n 66. See further Cornish and Phillips 'The Economic Function of Trademarks: An Analysis With Special Reference to Developing Countries' 13 IIC 41 (1982).

[74] Blakeney above n 1 at 109.

position of the developing countries this is not surprising. The technologically advanced countries have few incentives to modify a system that suits their needs. However, some recognition of the interests of developing and least developed countries appears in the TRIPs Agreement, in that such countries were able to postpone the patent protection contained therein for up to 10 years, and developed countries are encouraged to ensure adequate technology transfer to developing countries, a matter further discussed below.

(ii) Specialized Technology Transfer Laws

As part of the movement for greater control over the process of technology transfer, numerous developing countries began, in the 1970s, to experiment with specialized technology transfer laws. Space permits only a brief description of the common features of such laws. More detailed accounts can be found elsewhere.[75] The main thrust for these developments came from Latin America, with the adoption in 1969 of the Andean Foreign Investment Code under Decision 24 of the Cartagena Agreement,[76] and the passing of several national laws between 1971 and 1981.[77] Other developing countries from Africa and Asia followed suit,[78] as

---

[75] See further Blakeney above n 1 ch 7, who provides references to literature for 33 countries that have used such laws at 162–64; G Cabanellas *Antitrust and Direct Regulation of International Transfer of Technology Transactions* IIC Studies in Industrial Property and Copyright Law Vol 7 (Verlag Chemie, 1984) ch 2; Correa 'Transfer of Technology in Latin America: A Decade of Control' 15 JWTL 388 (1981); UNCTAD *Control of Restrictive Practices in Transfer of Technology Transactions* (New York: UN Doc TD/B/C.6/72, 1982). The laws described in these works represent policy responses of the 1970s. It should not be assumed that all the laws mentioned in these works have remained in force unamended.

[76] See 11 ILM 126 (1972); as amended, see 16 ILM 138 (1977). For analysis, see UNCTAD *Transfer of Technology* above n 2 at 47–49.

[77] See Correa above n 75, who lists Argentina Law 19,231 of 1971, Law 20,794 of 1974, Law 21,617 of 1976 and Law 22,426 of 1981 as amended available in Spanish at <http://www.inpi.gov.ar/docs/transftec_leyes.htm>; Brazil Law 4,131 of 1962, Law 5,772 and Normative Act No 15 of 11 September 1975 (see now Normative Act 135/97 and in Law 9, 279/96 available in Portuguese at <http://www.inpi.gov.br/>); Bolivia Decree 9,798 of 1971; Colombia Decree 1,234 of 1972; Ecuador S. Decree 974 of 1971; Peru incorporated Decision 24 in 1971 and Venezuela incorporated decision 24 in 1973.

[78] See, for example, Nigeria: National Office of Industrial Property Decree 1979 discussed extensively by Ubezonu above n 1. Ghana adopted technology transfer regulations under s 30 of the Investment Code 1985: Technology Transfer Regulations 9 September 1992 (LI 1547) which remain in force; China: Law on Technology Contracts 23 June 1987, Detailed Rules for the Implementation of the regulations of the PRC on the Administration of Technology Import Contracts of 20 January 1988: Vol 2, 3 China Law and practice, 28 March 1988 at 38; for background to the evolution of China's policy in this areas, see Lubman 'Technology Transfer to China: Policies, Law and Practice' in MJ Moser (ed) *Foreign Trade, Investment, and the Law in the People's Republic of China* (Oxford: 2nd edn, 1987) ch 4. China's legislation in this area began with the Interim Regulations on the Transfer of Technology: 24 ILM 292 (1985), and the Regulations Controlling Technology Import Contracts: 24 ILM 801 (1985). India has regulated technology transfer transactions by way of administrative procedures outlined in periodic policy statements: see: Industrial Policy Statement of 23 July 1980, Technology Policy Statement, January 1983 in *National Science and Technology Policy* (Lok Sabha Secretariat, 3rd edn, 1989), Statement on Industrial Policy of July 24 1991 in UNCTC *Foreign Direct Investment and Technology Transfer in India* (New York: UN Doc ST/CTC/117, 1992) Annex VII.

did a small number of Southern European and formerly Socialist East European states.[79] Of developed countries only Japan has used such laws.[80]

The essence of technology transfer laws is the screening of international technology transfer transactions by a national authority with the aim of ensuring that the technology transferred is of use to the national economy and that the terms and conditions of transfer do not amount to an abuse of the transferor's superior bargaining power. Such laws are normally limited to transactions between a foreign transferor and a local recipient. Transactions between related enterprises are not addressed in most statutes,[81] although some laws have contained strict controls over royalty payments for technology transferred between affiliated enterprises, as a means of controlling transfer price manipulations.[82] Indirect transfers between foreign transferors and local recipients effected through a local intermediary, who receives the technology under an approved contract and then transfers it subject to unacceptable terms, may also be covered.[83]

The normal procedure is for the parties to submit either a draft or an executed contract for approval. This may involve a registration of the agreement with the screening authority. The authority will then assess the contract in the light of the legal standards laid down for review. These will concern inter alia: an examination of the restrictive clauses imposed on the recipient with a view to identifying prohibited restrictions; the reasonableness of the consideration payable; the costs and benefits of the transaction in relation to the economic and social development of the recipient state; the nature of the technology involved, paying particular attention to its positive effects on local productive capacity and skills development, the ability of the local economy to develop the technology by itself, the age and effectiveness of the technology; whether the package involves excessive tie-ins and other costs; the extent of any warranties limiting or excluding the transferor's liability for the technology; and the duration of the agreement, which must not be excessive.

---

[79] Blakeney above n 75 cites as examples: Bulgaria, the former German Democratic Republic, Greece, Portugal, Spain, and the former Yugoslavia.

[80] Cabinet Order Concerning Direct Domestic Investments October 11, 1980 Ch III Conclusion etc of Agreements for Importation of Technology arts 4–6; Ordinance Concerning Direct Domestic Investment: Order No 1 20 November 1980 as amended by Order No 1 6 April 1989 art 5 2(3); Notification No 3 of 27 November 1980 all in *Japan, Laws, Ordinances and Other Regulations Concerning Foreign Exchange and Foreign Trade* (Chuo Shuppan Kikaku Co, 1990). See further Ohara 'Japanese Regulation of Technology Imports' 15 JWTL 83 (1981); Ohara 'Regulations on Transfer of Technology in Japan' 15 IIC 121 (1984). [81] Blakeney above n 1 at 167.

[82] See Andean Investment Code, Decision 24 above n 76 art 21 which prohibited the authorization of royalty payments and their deduction for tax purposes between affiliated enterprises. By Andean Commission Decision 291 of 21 March 1991 art 15 the payment of royalties between affiliated enterprises may now be authorized in the cases previously approved by the competent national authority of the recipient country. Thus this matter is referred back to national law: 30 ILM 1283 at 1293 (1991). See also Argentina Law 22,426 of 1981 arts 2 and 5: Cabanellas above n 75 at 26–27.

[83] See eg Brazil Normative Act No 15 of 11 September 1975 art 1.3.

Failure to register the agreement for approval may lead to its being nullified.[84] Other sanctions may include fines for the performance of an unapproved transaction, prohibition of payments in favour of the transferor, and the denial of fiscal benefits.[85] The approving authority may impose conditions on the parties as the price for approval. This may include amendments to the agreement itself.[86] In particular, the relevant law may require the adoption of local law as the proper law of the agreement, thereby preventing its avoidance through the choice of a foreign law.[87]

Technology transfer laws share many features in common with other areas of law applicable to MNEs. However, they fill a distinct niche in the system of MNE regulation. This can be explained by a comparison of technology transfer laws with related areas of law, in particular, with foreign investment screening laws, competition laws, and foreign exchange and tax laws. Like foreign investment screening laws, technology transfer laws introduce an administrative review procedure as a condition of entry into the local economy. Indeed, they may complement the foreign investment law of a host state by regulating non-equity forms of entry such as licensing agreements.[88] Secondly, in common with competition laws, technology transfer laws regulate restrictive practices in technology transfer agreements. However, unlike competition laws, technology transfer laws seek to intervene in the operation of commercial markets in technology and regulate them in favour of the broader national economic interest in economic development. Although the use of competition law as an instrument of national or regional industrial policy is often debated, its primary aim is to prevent anti-competitive practices in the market, not its control.[89] Thirdly, technology transfer laws may be used as an additional means for regulating balance-of-payments issues by controlling the terms on which royalties will be paid for the importation of foreign-owned technology, by regulating tying arrangements involving the importation of inputs from abroad and by controlling the total number of technology transfer transactions that may be permitted at any one time. Similarly, as noted above, such laws may close off a potential conduit for transfer pricing manipulations by MNEs based on royalty remittances.

On the other hand, technology transfer laws pose a clear challenge to the logic of intellectual property laws. First, by regulating the consideration to be paid, they do not accept the legitimacy of allowing the owner of commercial technology to obtain monopoly rents from its application in the recipient state. Secondly, such laws may impose restrictions on the use of the technology by way of performance

---

[84]   In some cases it is arguable whether the law allows for nullification. See eg the debate over the effect of non-registration under Nigeria's National Office of Industrial Property Decree 1979 Sections 4, 5 and 7: Ubezonu n 1 above at 366–75; O Osunbor 'Law and Policy on the Registration of Technology Transfer Transactions in Nigeria' 21 JWTL 18 (1987); Fagbemi 'Registration of Technology Transactions in Nigeria: Another View' 22 JWTL 95 (1988).

[85]   Cabanellas above n 75 at 20–21.   [86]   Correa above n 75 at 391–92.

[87]   Cabanellas above n 75 at 29–30.   [88]   Cabanellas ibid at 45.

[89]   For a full discussion of this issue see Cabanellas ibid ch 3.

requirements, and may include limitations on the protection afforded to foreign patents or trademarks. Thirdly, as a consequence of these characteristics, technology transfer laws question the basis of the international system of intellectual property protection in that they reject the principles of national treatment and non-discrimination between foreign and local intellectual property rights, a rejection reinforced by the mandatory requirement of local law as the proper law of the technology transfer transaction. Thus, it is not surprising that such laws have become a target for regulation in the TRIPs Agreement.

Specialized technology transfer laws have not delivered the hoped for improvements in access to modern productive technology. For example, in Nigeria the system of technology transfer regulation set up under the National Office of Industrial Property Act 1979 has been largely ignored by foreign and Nigerian businessmen when entering agreements involving the licensing of technology. Thus contracts often contain restrictive clauses that are prohibited under the law.[90] A failure to obtain modern technology has also been noted in relation to the technology transfer provisions in Nigerian petroleum legislation.[91] Indeed, it is arguable that the existence of controls over technology transfer agreements may simply act as a deterrent to the importation of technology in that the incentive for the technology owner to exploit its competitive advantage in the recipient state is reduced.

As a consequence of the relative ineffectiveness of technology transfer controls, developing host states appear increasingly to be modifying, if not abandoning, such controls. Most notably, the ANCOM countries, which pioneered technology transfer laws, abandoned their attempt to create a standardized inter-regional regime for technology transfer. The original ANCOM regime under Decision 24 required member states to screen all contracts on the importation of technology and on patents and trademarks, and prohibited the authorization of agreements containing any of the restrictive clauses listed in article 20 thereof.[92] By contrast Decision 291, the current successor to Decision 24, simply requires the registration of technology transfer agreements under the respective laws of the ANCOM member states, leaving the details of the registration process to the relevant national laws.[93] The only clear prohibition in Decision 291 relates to clauses that prohibit or limit the exportation of products produced on the basis of the technology transferred.[94] Similarly, India reformed its extensive administrative procedures for the review of technology imports,[95] while Brazil liberalized its technology transfer regime. Of particular note is the ending of the protected status of the informatics industry.[96]

---

[90] See O Osunbor above n 84 at 21–22; See also Omorogbe 'The Legal Framework and Policy for Technology Development in Nigeria' 3 RADIC 156 (1991).

[91] See: Alegimenlen 'Petroleum Development Technology Acquisition: A Synopsis of the Nigerian Experience' 3 RADIC 526 (1991).   [92] Above n 76.

[93] Above n 82 arts 12–15.   [94] ibid art 14.

[95] See UNCTC 1992 above n 78 at 135 and references at n 78 for details of the old regime.

[96] For the background to this policy, see The National Informatics and Automation Plan reproduced in English in the *Brazilian Informatics Industry Directory 1986/87* (Abicomp, 1986) at 169–76.

(iii)   The Draft UNCTAD Code on the Transfer of Technology

In order to acquire international legitimacy for the kinds of technology transfer policies outlined in the preceding discussion, developing countries sought the adoption of an international code on technology transfer under the auspices of UNCTAD, which, as noted above, was active in articulating the developing country perspective on this issue.[97] The participating states formed three interest groupings for the purpose of negotiating the TOT Code.[98] The developing countries formed the 'Group of 77'. They sought a legally binding code, that would cover all forms of technology transfer transactions, and which would give primacy to the recipient state's laws and dispute settlement procedures. The developed market economy countries formed 'Group B'. They sought a voluntary code that would balance the rights and duties of the technology transferor and recipient, and leave the parties free to decide on dispute settlement procedures. The third group 'Group D' comprised the former Eastern Bloc states and Mongolia. These states took broadly the same position as the Group of 77 although they did not take a view on the legal character of the code, nor on applicable laws and dispute settlement procedures. They stressed the equality of states and the need for non-discrimination in technology transfer transactions. Subsequently, the People's Republic of China joined the conference as an independent participant, aiming to learn from the experience and to use this in formulating its own technology transfer policy.

The process began with extensive preliminary negotiations between 1976 and 1978 which led to the formulation of a draft negotiating text.[99] Thereupon the UN General Assembly, by its resolution 32/188 of December 1977, decided to convene a UN Conference, under the auspices of UNCTAD, to negotiate a final draft and to take all the necessary decisions for its adoption. The Conference held six sessions between 1978 and 1985.[100] However, no further sessions took place,

---

An English version of the main law in this area Law No 7232 of 1984, the Informatics Law, is reproduced in this publication at 147–51. For developments in informatics policy in Latin America, see Correa 'Informatics in Latin America: Promises and Realities' 23 JWT 81 (1989). Between 1990 and 1991, the Brazilian Government, following the liberalizing policy of former President Collor, introduced legislation which dismantled this protective regime through the gradual extension of the categories of informatics goods that could be imported: see Law No 8238 of 23 October 1991.

[97] For the historical background to the TOT Code negotiations see: Blakeney above n 1 at 131–33; Patel 'Transfer of Technology and the Third UNCTAD' 7 JWTL 226 (1973); Roffe 'UNCTAD: Code of Conduct on Transfer of Technology: A Progress Review' 12 JWTL 351 (1978); Zuijdwijk 'The UNCTAD Code of Conduct on the Transfer of Technology' 24 McGill LJ 562 (1978); Thompson 'The UNCTAD Code on Transfer of Technology' 16 JWTL 311 (1982); Roffe 'UNCTAD: Transfer of Technology Code: Fifth Session of the UN Conference' 18 JWTL 176 (1984); Roffe 'UNCTAD Code of Conduct on Transfer of Technology' 19 JWTL 669 (1985).

[98] See Thompson ibid at 313–14.

[99] See Report of the Intergovernmental Group of Experts on an International Code of Conduct on the Transfer of Technology to the United Nations Conference on an International Code of Conduct on the Transfer of Technology (UNCTAD Doc TD/CODE TOT/1, 1978).

[100] See Sixth Session of the UN Conference on an International Code of Conduct on the Transfer of Technology, Background Note (UNCTAD Secretariat, UN Doc TD/CODE TOT/49 9 October 1985).

due to deadlock over several crucial issues. It is not proposed to undertake a detailed analysis of the draft code. This has been done elsewhere.[101] The present concern rests with the reasons behind the above mentioned deadlock.

The issues that remained to be settled were those where the developed and developing country models of technology transfer regulation failed to converge. The first of these concerned the regulation of restrictive business practices in technology transfer agreements, covered by Chapter 4 of the draft code.[102] The 'Group B' countries wished to control such restrictions on the basis of competition law, and emphasized that only those practices which unreasonably restrained trade should be prohibited.[103] The 'Group of 77', on the other hand, saw such practices as being inherently unfair, being a product of superior bargaining power on the part of the transferor. They favoured the prohibition of such restrictions altogether.[104] The disagreement stemmed from the fear, on the part of the developing countries, that a competition based approach would allow the avoidance of the TOT Code on the part of the supplier, given that it was not likely to be adopted as a legally enforceable instrument.[105] Further disagreement existed under Chapter 4 as to whether different standards should apply to transfers of technology between commonly owned enterprises. The 'Group B' states saw no reason for different treatment, limiting control only to those cases where the transaction amounted to an anti-competitive abuse of a dominant position. By contrast the 'Group of 77' wished to introduce a standard that permitted such transactions so long as they did not adversely affect the transfer of technology.[106]

The second major area of disagreement concerned the issues of applicable law and settlement of disputes under Chapter 9.[107] The developing countries advocated a restrictive regime on the choice of law governing technology transfer agreements. They wished to see the law of the recipient country as the mandatory proper law of the contract, thereby avoiding the 'delocalization' of technology transfer agreements. On the contrary, the 'Group B' states favoured the preservation of the parties' freedom to choose the proper law provided it had a genuine connection with the transaction.[108] As regards the settlement of disputes, the 'Group of 77' opposed an absolute right for the parties to settle their disputes by arbitration. In their view, such a right had to be determined in the light of any rules to the contrary in the law of the technology importing state. By contrast both the 'Group B' and 'Group D' states favoured free choice of arbitration. It was on this issue that the

---

[101] Above n 2 and see references there cited.   [102] See TD/CODE TOT/47 at 8–11.
[103] See TD/CODE TOT/47 Appendix D at 1.   [104] ibid.
[105] See Thompson above n 97 at 326. On the legal effect of the draft code see Blakeney above n 1 at 134–35.
[106] ibid. For further details of the negotiations on Chapter 4 at the Sixth Session see the Report of the Chairman of Working Group I (UN Doc TD/CODE TOT/SR 21) 4 paras 5–24.
[107] See TD/CODE TOT/47 at 21.
[108] See TD/CODE TOT/47 Appendix A at 10 and see the Chinese compromise proposal in ibid Appendix A at 9.

conference broke down in 1981.[109] At the Sixth Session this issue was not discussed and negotiations concentrated exclusively on the choice of law question.[110]

In order to salvage the negotiating process, the Secretary-General of UNCTAD and the President of the Conference held regular consultations with interested governments. However, significant divergences of opinion remained on the above mentioned issues.[111] Indeed, at the eighth session of UNCTAD it was recognized that 'conditions do not currently exist to reach full agreement on all outstanding issues in the draft code of conduct. Should governments indicate, either directly or through the Secretary-General of UNCTAD reporting according to General Assembly resolution 46/214, that there is the convergence of views necessary to reach agreement on all outstanding issues, then the Board should re-engage and continue its work aimed at facilitating agreement on the code'.[112] In 1992, the Secretary General of UNCTAD collected the opinions of governments as to their views on the outstanding issues. However, there was, by then, little interest in the matter, given the slow rate of response received by him.[113] A finalized code was never adopted. It was to be overtaken by developments at the WTO where the market based development model triumphed.

(b) The Market Based Development Model

The essential features of this model are, first, the recognition of the role of IPRs in the encouragement and protection of innovation and the creation of secure conditions for the transfer of technology; secondly, acceptance that the ownership of technology can bring with it market power and the risk of its abuse, requiring the intervention of competition law to ensure a rebalancing of such power; and thirdly, an acknowledgment that market based solutions, while preferable, cannot cover all aspects of technological development. This requires a degree of 'permissive' regulation aimed at the development of market supportive science and technology polices in both home and host countries. Such regulation is 'permissive' in the sense that its major aim is to encourage the process of innovation and technology transfer through governmental policy instruments undertaken by home and

---

[109] See Thompson above n 97 at 333–34.

[110] See further the Report of the Chairman of Working Group II UN Doc TD/CODE TOT/SR 21 at 5 para 25; TD/CODE TOT/47 Appendix A at 7–8.

[111] See further Report by the Secretary General of UNCTAD on Consultations Held Pursuant to General Assembly Resolution 41/166 of 5 December 1986 (UN Doc TD/CODE/TOT/51 21 October 1987); 'Further consultations on a draft international code of conduct on the transfer of technology, report by the Secretary-General of UNCTAD' (UN Doc TD/CODE/TOT/57, 1991); 'Negotiations on an international code of conduct on the transfer of technology: consultations carried out in 1992, report by the Secretary General of UNCTAD' (UN Doc TD/CODE/TOT/58 22 October 1992).

[112] UN Doc TD/CODE/TOT/58 22 October 1992 para 6 citing the Cartagena Commitment para 173.

[113] See ibid paras 7–8. Only 10 responses had been received by the time this document was published.

host countries. This is likely in cases where pure market mechanisms fail to offer sufficient incentives for innovation and technology transfer to occur, for the reasons outlined in section 2 above. Finally, the market based development model retains certain 'mandatory' regulatory interventions in exceptional cases through intellectual property law devices. These involve, in particular, compulsory licensing or the exhaustion of IPRs. Such mechanisms can help to further permissive innovation and technology development strategies, by ensuring access to products and processes covered by IPRs where these are either not worked or have been voluntarily placed outside the protection of IPRs by their owner.

(i) IPR Protection and Technology Transfer

Developed recipient countries generally accept the private property character of commercial technology through their use of patent, trademark, and copyright laws as the basis for defining the scope of that property.[114] Such rights have been given reciprocal protection between states under international conventions embodying the principles of national treatment, non-discrimination and priority thereby guaranteeing the same protection of industrial property rights to nationals and to foreign right holders.[115] This reflects the fact that most advanced states are not only purchasers of foreign technology but are also exporters in their own right, thereby giving them an interest in the reciprocal protection of intellectual property rights.

Adherence to legally protected IPRs may also prove useful to developing countries that seek to attract and benefit from technology transfer, whether through FDI or licensing. Some studies offer evidence in support of this proposition.[116] Others do not.[117] As an UNCTAD-ICTSD study puts it, 'much uncertainty remains as to the effects of IPRs on technology transfers to developing countries'.[118]

---

[114] See, for a general introduction to IPRs and their historical development, UNCTAD-ICTSD *Intellectual Property Rights: Implications for Development* Project on IPRs and sustainable development policy discussion paper (Geneva: 2003) ch 1 also available at <http://www.ictsd.org/iprsonline>; The Commission on Intellectual Property Rights *Integrating Intellectual Property Rights and Development Policy* (London: September 2002) ch 1 available at <http://www.iprcommission.org/papers/pdfs/final_report/CIPRfullfinal.pdf>.

[115] See the Paris Convention for the Protection of Industrial Property 1883 (as amended) arts 2 and 4 above n 60. For a full list of the major conventions covering patents, trade marks, industrial designs and biotechnology, see Blakeney n 1 above at 14–21; UNCTAD-ICTSD ibid ch 2 and see the WIPO website at <http://www.wipo.int/treaties/en/>.

[116] See the studies cited in UNCTAD-ICTSD above n 114 at 5–8. See further Maskus above n 1 at 136–42; E Mansfield 'Intellectual Property Protection, Foreign Direct Investment and Technology Transfer' (Washington DC: International Finance Corporation Discussion Paper No 19, 1994).

[117] See EK Kondo 'The Effect of Patent Protection on Foreign Direct Investment' 29 JWT 97 (1995); AS Kirim 'Reconsidering Patents and Economic Development: The Case of the Turkish Pharmaceutical Industry' 13 World Development 219 (1985); Linsu Kim *Technology Transfer and Intellectual Property Rights: The Korean Experience* UNCTAD-ICTSD Project on IPRs and sustainable development Issue Paper No 2 (Geneva: 2003); Nagesh Kumar; 'Technology and Economic Development: Experiences of Asian Countries' (London: Commission on Intellectual Property Rights, 2002) available at <http://www.iprcommission.org/papers/pdfs/study_papers/sp1b_kumar_study.pdf>.

[118] Above n 114 at 88.

It appears that IPR protection is only one factor in the decision of a firm to transfer technology to a developing host country. Other important factors, as already noted, include the local level of skill, the quality of the infrastructure, and the size and stability of the market. However, there appear to be certain situations in which the presence or absence of effective IPR protection will make a difference.

To understand these it is helpful to consider technological development in terms of a pyramid with the least complex technological functions at its base and the most advanced at its top.[119] At the base lie basic production techniques, followed by the significant adaptation of existing products and processes, the improvement and monitoring of technology, leading to product and process improvement, with frontier innovation at the top, which creates new technologies as a leader or follower. IPRs will interact differently with each level of technological development. It appears that IPR protection becomes more significant the higher up the pyramid the technological function rises, as the complexity and originality of that function increases.[120] In addition, different levels of technological development will be within the capability range of particular countries. It follows that, given a particular level of technological capability, a developing country will be able to engage in only some of the technological functions involved in the production or service process in question. If those functions are basic then the presence or absence of IPR protection is irrelevant. If those functions are imitative and adaptive, then a regime of strong IPR protection may actually discourage investment, as it will cut off the producer from access to the source technology from which imitation through reverse engineering occurs. This will often be available through licensing or, even, outright piracy. A number of countries have successfully industrialized by this means, including Japan, Korea, and Taiwan.[121] The rise of the Indian pharmaceutical industry is also a good example.[122] As the capacity to absorb advanced technology improves, the host country may then have good reason for introducing strong IPR protection so as to encourage product improvement, which will require the licensing of advanced technology, and finally frontier innovation, which will produce cutting edge technologies, products, and processes from which monopoly rents will be required to justify the investment.[123]

---

[119] See UNCTAD *World Investment Report 2005* above n 11 at 101–102.

[120] See Bernard M Hoekman, Keith E Maskus, and Kamal Saggi 'Transfer of Technology to Developing Countries: Unilateral and Multilateral Policy Options' 33 World Development 1587 (2005) at 1592, 'the sophistication of technologies transferred rises with the strength of IPR protection and domestic capacities to absorb and improve technology'. See also Sanjaya Lall *Indicators of the Relative Importance of IPRs in Developing Countries* (Geneva: UNCTAD-ITCSD, 2003) and <http://www.ictsd.org/iprsonline>.   [121] See Kumar above n 117.

[122] See *World Investment Report 2005* above n 11 at 235. The Indian Patent Act 1971 denied patent protection to pharmaceutical products. This allowed for imitative product development. Over time Indian pharmaceutical companies began to innovate in their own right. The passage of the Patent Act of 2005 introduced full patent protection in accordance with the TRIPs Agreement. This corresponded with calls form Indian pharmaceutical firms for enhanced protection of their new assets. See further Kumar above n 117 at 27–37.   [123] ibid.

In these circumstances it is open to debate whether the approach to IPR protection under the TRIPs Agreement represents an optimal response to the real needs of developing countries, especially those whose capabilities rest at the level of basic production or imitative adaptation.[124] Nonetheless, the TRIPs Agreement is confident in asserting, in Article 7, that:

The protection and enforcement of intellectual property rights should contribute to the promotion of technological innovation and to the transfer and dissemination of technology, to the mutual advantage of producers and users of technological knowledge and in a manner conducive to social and economic welfare, and to a balance of rights and obligations.

This is tempered by the contents of Article 8(1) which allows WTO members to 'adopt measures necessary to protect public health and nutrition, and to promote the public interest in sectors of vital importance to their socio-economic and technological development, provided that such measures are consistent with the provisions of this Agreement'. This suggests a considerable discretion over IPR policy provided it conforms to the overall level of protection under the TRIPs Agreement. In addition Article 7 is not concerned merely with the protection of IPR owners' rights but also the need to promote social and economic welfare, including that of technology users. It urges a balance of rights and obligations as a means of interpreting the TRIPs Agreement as a whole.[125] However, according to UNCTAD, it is not clear from these provisions how IPR protection is to contribute to the transfer of technology to developing countries.[126] This is reinforced by the relative paucity of the specialized provisions on technology transfer to the developing and least developed countries which are discussed in detail in subsection (iii) below.

(ii) The Role of Competition Regulation

Article 8(2) of the TRIPs Agreement introduces competition regulation as a component of the overall approach to IPR protection under the Agreement:

Appropriate measures, provided that they are consistent with the provisions of this Agreement, may be needed to prevent the abuse of intellectual property rights by right holders

---

[124] Kumar above n 117 at 37–41. See too Kim above n 117 at 5–6: '[S]trong IPR protection will hinder rather than facilitate technology transfer and indigenous learning activities in the early stage of industrialisation when learning takes place through reverse engineering and duplicative imitation of mature foreign products . . . Only after countries have accumulated sufficient indigenous capabilities with extensive science and technology infrastructure to undertake creative imitation in the later stage that IPR protection becomes an important element in technology transfer and industrial activities . . . [I]f adequate protection and enforcement of IPRs is genuinely to enhance development, policy makers should seriously consider differentiation in terms of level of economic development and industrial sectors. Otherwise, the "one size fits all" approach is a recipe for disaster for developing countries, particularly for the least developed ones.'

[125] See UNCTAD-ICTSD *Resource Book on TRIPs and Development* (Cambridge: Cambridge University Press, 2005) at 126 and see Communication from India of 10 July 1989 MTN.GNG/ NG11/W/37 sub 2 and VI.   [126] UNCTAD *Transfer of Technology* above n 2 at 29–30.

or the resort to practices which unreasonably restrain trade or adversely affect the international transfer of technology.

This provision reflects the view adopted by the Indian delegation, among others, during the Uruguay Round negotiations that TRIPs should provide a means of restraining anti-competitive abuses of IPR protection.[127] Article 8(2) provides members with a substantial discretion when applying competition rules to arrangements covered by the TRIPs Agreement. The consistency requirement suggests that this discretion cannot be abused by making competition regulation act as a disguised restriction on the rights protected under the Agreement.[128]

As noted above, the principal concerns in this area are related to the preservation of competition in industries where technology is controlled by relatively few owners. This will involve, first, the control of cooperative arrangements and concentrations between competitors that may have an adverse effect on the availability of essential technology to third parties without any compensating technological progress and/or benefits to consumers. Secondly, as already discussed in the previous section, excessive restrictions on the commercial policy and use of technology by a recipient will be regulated. In both cases the aim is to reconcile the right of the technology owner to profit from its invention or know-how, while at the same time preventing the creation of monopolistic horizontal structures and/or vertical relationships in the market concerned. This balancing of interests is achieved through the use of a 'rule of reason' approach whereby the anti-competitive effects of the technology owner's actions are weighed against the beneficial effects on the economy of protecting its proprietary rights in the technology.[129] Given the references to practices that 'unreasonably' restrain trade or technology transfer in Article 8(2) the TRIPs Agreement may be said to extend the 'rule of reason' approach to the review of competition measures taken by WTO Members under this provision. Given the manner in which national laws already regulate IPR practices, a good faith application of such rules is unlikely to infringe Article 8(2).[130]

In relation to technology transfer, competition policy will be applied so as not to stifle technological innovation. Thus, for example, in the US the National Cooperation Research Act 1984 relaxed the application of antitrust laws to joint R&D ventures.[131] The 1995 *Guidelines for the Licensing of Intellectual Property* do not regard the possession of IPRs as evidence of market power as such, though earlier case law is unclear on this point.[132] According to the Guidelines, 'market power

---

[127] See UNCTAD-ICTSD *TRIPs Resource Book* above n 125 at 127.

[128] See Frederick M Abbott 'Are the Competition Rules in the WTO TRIPS Agreement Adequate?' 7 JIEL 687 (2004) at 692. See further UNCTAD-ICTSD *TRIPs Resource Book* ibid at 546–54 for detailed interpretation of Article 8(2).

[129] On the 'rule of reason' in competition law see ch 10 at 387 n 5.

[130] Abbott above n 128 at 692.   [131] 15 USC ss 4301–4305.

[132] The *Guidelines* above n 44: compare *Jefferson Parish Hospital District No 2 v Hyde* 466 US 2, 16 (1984) (expressing the view in dictum that if a product is protected by a patent, 'it is fair to presume that the inability to buy the product elsewhere gives the seller market power') with ibid at 37 n 7 (O'Connor J concurring) ('[A] patent holder has no market power in any relevant sense if there are

(or even a monopoly) that is solely 'a consequence of a superior product, business acumen, or historic accident' does not violate the antitrust laws'.[133] The US *Guidelines* adopt three general principles in the analysis of the competitive effects of IPRs:

a. for the purpose of antitrust analysis, the Agencies regard intellectual property as being essentially comparable to any other form of property;
b. the Agencies do not presume that intellectual property creates market power in the antitrust context; and
c. the Agencies recognize that intellectual property licensing allows firms to combine complementary factors of production and is generally procompetitive.

In addition the US authorities will only intervene where the combined market shares of the parties to the licensing agreement exceed 20 per cent.[134]

Similarly the EC has exempted technology transfer agreements from the prohibition of anti-competitive agreements or concerted practices in Article 81(1) of the EC Treaty.[135] To qualify for exemption, the agreement in question must offer improvements to productivity and technical development, be of benefit to consumers, contain restrictions on the commercial freedom of the parties which are no more than necessary for the achievement of the aforementioned aims, as defined by the relevant exempting regulation,[136] and it must not create an opportunity to eliminate competition in a substantial part of the relevant market. EC law presumes that where the undertakings party to the agreement are competing undertakings, the exemption shall apply on condition that the combined market share of the parties does not exceed 20 per cent on the affected relevant technology and product market.[137] Where the undertakings, party to the agreement, are not competing undertakings, the exemption shall apply on condition that the market share of each of the parties does not exceed 30 per cent on the affected relevant technology and product market.[138] For the purposes of exemption, the market share of a party on the relevant technology market, or markets, is defined in terms of the presence of the licensed technology on the relevant product market or markets.

---

close substitutes for the patented product.') and *Abbott Laboratories v Brennan* 952 F 2d 1346, 1354–55 (Fed Cir 1991) (no presumption of market power from intellectual property right), *cert. denied*, 112 S Ct 2993 (1992) with *Digidyne Corp v Data General Corp* 734 F 2d 1336, 1341–42 (9th Cir 1984) (requisite economic power is presumed from copyright), *cert. denied*, 473 US 908 (1985) para 2.2 n 11.

[133] ibid at para 2.2 citing *United States v Grinnell Corp* 384 US 563, 571 (1966); see also *United States v Aluminum Co of America* 148 F 2d 416, 430 (2d Cir 1945) (Sherman Act is not violated by the attainment of market power solely through 'superior skill, foresight and industry').

[134] ibid para 4.3.

[135] Commission Regulation 772/2004 above n 44 and see the definition of technology transfer agreements in this regulation at n 6 above. See further Valentine Korah *Intellectual Property Rights and the EC Competition Rules* (Oxford: Hart Publishing, 2006); Steven D Anderman *Technology Transfer and the New EU Competition Rules: Intellectual Property Licensing After Modernisation* (Oxford: Oxford University Press, 2006); Maurits Dolmans and Anu Piilola 'The New Technology Transfer Block Exemption: A Welcome Reform After All.' 27 World Competition 351 (2004).

[136] See ibid arts 4 and 5.   [137] ibid art 3(1).   [138] ibid art 3(2).

A licensor's market share on the relevant technology market shall be 'the combined market share on the relevant product market of the contract products produced by the licensor and its licensees'.[139]

Notwithstanding this generally permissive approach, national laws will control abusive exercises of IPRs in technology transfer transactions. The kinds of anti-competitive provisions that may be controlled have already been discussed in section 3. This approach is reinforced by Article 40 of the TRIPs Agreement whereby,

> Members agree that some licensing practices or conditions pertaining to intellectual property rights which restrain competition may have adverse effects on trade and may impede the transfer and dissemination of technology.

In particular, Article 40(2) lists exclusive grant-back conditions, conditions preventing challenges to validity of IPRs and coercive package licensing as examples of practices that may be controlled. Members shall enter, on request, into consultations with other members in cases where such abuses of rights are suspected.[140] As with Article 8, Article 40 was adopted on the insistence of developing countries that feared the effects of certain contractual practices that they had been unable to deal with through the unsuccessful negotiations over the draft TOT Code.[141] The link between the restrictive nature of the IPR practice in question and technology transfer is of importance in delimiting the regulatory discretion of members. Article 40(1) does not recognize national measures that seek to control technology transfer transactions because of perceived negative effects that have no connection with competition.[142] Only competition based controls are recognized. This does not outlaw specialized technology transfer controls as such, but places a competition based approach above a more general regulatory approach. The latter is permissible so long as it applies in a manner consistent with the TRIPs Agreement.[143] Nor does Article 40(2) limit members' discretion in determining which practices shall be regarded as anti-competitive under national law, save to the extent that the list must be directly related to the competition effects of the practice in question.[144]

Other international agreements and guidelines also stress the need for a competition based approach to the regulation of technology transfer. Thus, Article 1704 of NAFTA states that the parties are free to specify in their national laws, 'licensing practices or conditions that may in particular cases constitute an abuse of intellectual property rights having an adverse effect on competition in the relevant market. A Party may adopt or maintain, consistent with the other provisions of this Agreement, appropriate measures to prevent or control such practices or conditions'.[145] The OECD Guidelines for Multinational Enterprises extend this approach to the obligations of MNEs themselves, requiring that enterprises should, 'when granting licenses for the use of intellectual property rights, or when otherwise

---

[139] ibid art 3(3).   [140] TRIPs Agreement art 40(3).

[141] UNCTAD-ICTSD *TRIPs Resource Book* above n 125 at 544.   [142] ibid at 557.

[143] ibid.   [144] ibid at 559.

[145] North American Free Trade Agreement: 32 ILM 605 at 671 (1993).

transferring technology, do so on reasonable terms and conditions and in a manner that contributes to the long-term development prospects of the host country'.[146] This provision admits an element of self-regulation in determining whether the terms used are reasonable. It also suggests that development concerns may be relevant when determining whether certain terms are reasonable or not.[147] The commentary attached to the guidelines adds that enterprises should consider 'the long-term developmental, environmental and other impacts of technologies for the home and host country'.[148] This includes consideration of how to improve the innovative capacity of their international subsidiaries and sub-contractors and how they may usefully contribute to the formulation of host country policy frameworks conducive to the development of dynamic innovation systems.[149] These issues may indicate what may be considered reasonable or unreasonable in a given case.[150] However, it is hard to see how such considerations could affect competition issues. As noted in section 3 above, a competition based analysis of terms in technology licensing agreements may be quite distinct form a development oriented analysis, which goes beyond a 'rule of reason' approach and prohibits absolutely certain terms and conditions on public policy grounds. That said, it may be presumed that any anti-competitive term is also likely to be anti-developmental, as its probable effect will be to raise entry barriers by denying licensees, and third parties, the opportunity to learn from exposure to technology and, eventually to compete with the licensor, or to exploit market opportunities that the licensor wishes to retain unreasonably for itself.

Finally, the competition based approach has been used in certain international investment agreements, to permit controls over anti-competitive abuses of IPRs though performance requirements. Certain Bilateral Investment Treaties (BITs), notably those of Canada and the US, generally prohibit performance requirements relating to technology transfer. This is subject to an exception where the requirement is imposed by the courts, administrative tribunals or competition authorities of the host country to remedy an alleged violation of competition laws.[151] NAFTA Article 1106 contains a similar clause as does the Canada-Chile Free Trade Agreement of 1996.[152]

(iii) 'Permissive' Regulation

In following the above mentioned formulation, the OECD Guidelines and Commentary raise a wider set of questions that go beyond narrow competitive

---

[146] OECD *OECD Guidelines for Multinational Enterprises* (Paris: OECD, 2000) Guideline VIII 'Science and Technology' para 4.   [147] UNCTAD *Transfer of Technology* above n 2 at p 78.
[148] ibid at para 54 at 52–53.   [149] ibid.
[150] UNCTAD *Transfer of Technology* above n 2 at 79.
[151] See ibid at 79–81 (referring to the 1990s versions of these BITs). For the current version of the US provision, see US-Uruguay BIT 25 October 2004; 44 ILM 268 at 275, art 8(1)(f) and (3)(b)(ii); Canada Model BIT art 7(1)(f).
[152] Article G–06(1)(f) and (2). See UNCTAD *International Investment Agreements: A Compendium Volume V* (New York and Geneva: United Nations, 2000) at 82–83.

considerations and see enterprise obligations as encompassing a requirement to apply their IPRs in the public interest. This brings forth the third aspect of the market-based development approach, that of the extent of permissive regulation. Such policies should be seen against the backdrop of attempts to stimulate competition by the deregulation of high technology industries, as exemplified by the privatization of national telecommunications monopolies in numerous countries, and the reduction of entry barriers for foreign firms in this sector.[153] Furthermore, technologically advanced countries may encourage international cooperation in technological innovation through the approval, under competition law, of technologically innovative strategic alliances between firms from more than one country,[154] and through public sector initiatives, which can act as a source of coordination and funding for the development of new technologies by MNEs from more than one state. For example, the EC has been active in this way, in the hope of stimulating EC based firms to develop technology that can compete with US or Japanese firms.[155]

Such funding can also be devoted to encouraging the transfer of technology to developing and least developed host countries. Indeed, the TRIPs Agreement specifically encourages this approach for the latter group. By Article 66(2):

Developed country members shall provide incentives to enterprises and institutions in their territories for the purpose of promoting and encouraging technology transfer to least developed country members in order to enable them to create a sound and viable technological base.

The value of this provision has been doubted.[156] It was strengthened, in 2003, through the introduction of an obligation on developed country members to submit reports on actions taken or proposed to give effect to the obligation in Article 66(2).[157] The reports are subject to the protection of business confidential information and will, provide, inter alia, the following information:

(a) an overview of the incentives regime put in place to fulfil the obligations of Article 66.2, including any specific legislative, policy and regulatory framework;

---

[153] See Van Tulder and Junne above n 10 at 201–206.   [154] See ch 10 at 394–97.
[155] For example, the European ESPRIT Programme in Information Technology and other initiatives discussed by Van Tulder and Junne above n 10 ch 7. See, for a more recent statement of EC policy, EC Commission Communication More Research and Innovation – Investing for Growth and Employment: A Common Approach SEC(2005) 1253, COM(2005) 488 final available at <http://ec.europa.eu/enterprise/innovation/doc/com_2005_488_en.pdf>.
[156] See Maskus above n 1 at 225–26.
[157] See WTO Decision of the Council on TRIPs of 19 February 2003 IP/C/28 of 20 February 2003 at <http://docsonline.wto.org/DDFDocuments/t/IP/C/28.doc>. The reports of the developed members can be accessed at <http://www.wto.org/english/tratop_e/trips_e/techtransfer_e.htm>. According to the UNCTAD-ICTSD *TRIPs Resource Book*, 'This Decision constitutes an important step forward in the attempt to operationalise Article 66.2. It considerably reduces developed Members' discretion as to their implementation of it'. Above n 125 at 734 it may be seen as a 'soft' obligation based on public censure for inadequate action. On the other hand, reports on limited programmes can be made to appear more significant then they really are. They cannot replace a 'hard' obligation to render assistance as a matter of legal commitment: see Maskus above n 156.

(b) identification of the type of incentive and the government agency or other entity making it available;
(c) eligible enterprises and other institutions in the territory of the Member providing the incentives; and
(d) any information available on the functioning in practice of these incentives, such as:
   - statistical and/or other information on the use of the incentives in question by the eligible enterprises and institutions;
   - the type of technology that has been transferred by these enterprises and institutions and the terms on which it has been transferred;
   - the mode of technology transfer;
   - least-developed countries to which these enterprises and institutions have transferred technology and the extent to which the incentives are specific to least-developed countries; and
   - any additional information available that would help assess the effects of the measures in promoting and encouraging technology transfer to least-developed country Members in order to enable them to create a sound and viable technological base.

Such reports are updated annually and new reports have to be submitted every third year. The reports are reviewed by the Council on TRIPs with a view to giving members the opportunity to put questions. This initiative is to be reviewed by the end of 2006. Other WTO and international agreements also advocate the promotion of access to technology on a commercial basis and the removal of obstacles to the transfer of technology.[158] In this regard developed countries have used a mix of tax incentives, investment risk insurance schemes, supporting technology partnerships between firms for developed and developing countries and R&D support to further innovation and technology transfer.[159] However, their activity in this regard is uneven with some countries being more supportive than others.

(iv) *Mandatory IPR Regulation*
Finally, elements of mandatory regulation based on intellectual property law remain in place under the market based approach. Five areas in particular require discussion. They are of especial importance in relation to the IPR practices of MNEs.

---

[158] See GATS art IV(a) and XIX; WTO Agreement on Subsidies and Countervailing Measures art 8; WTO Agreement on Technical Barriers to Trade arts 11 and 12.4; the Energy Charter Treaty art 8 all discussed in UNCTAD *Transfer of Technology* above n 2 at 64–65.

[159] See further UNCTAD *World Investment Report 2003* (New York and Geneva: United Nations, 2003) at 156–58; *World Investment Report 2005* above n 11 at 220–22; UNCTAD *Facilitating Transfer of Technology to Developing Countries: A Survey of Home-Country Measures* Series on technology transfer and development (New York and Geneva: United Nations, 2004). The OECD Guideline on Science and Technology, above n 146, encourages enterprises to make sure that their activities are compatible with the science and technology policies of the countries in which they operate, to adopt practices that permit the rapid transfer and diffusion of technologies and know-how, to consider local market needs, employ local personnel in a science and technology capacity and to encourage their training and to establish ties with local universities, public research institutions and participate in local cooperative research projects with local industry or industry associations.

These are the exhaustion of IPRs where the owner voluntarily places them outside the scope of legal protection, compulsory licensing including the special case of access to patented pharmaceutical products necessary to combat major health problems, the control of biotechnology based IPRs, and the role of IPRs in relation to cultural knowledge.

Turning, first, to the issue of exhaustion of IPRs, this aims to prevent abuse of the monopoly over marketing that an IPR owner enjoys as an incident of that right. The owner enjoys the right of first placement of the protected product, service or process onto the market. However, once he has done that voluntarily, he is not permitted to use the IPR to challenge parallel trade in that item by third parties who have legitimately acquired the item in the open market. This is particularly important in relation to cross-border parallel trade, which can reduce the costs of products, processes, and services to consumers in national markets where the IPR owner maintains his monopoly. The EC has been particularly strong in controlling such abuses as part of the process of European market integration.[160] In the US there is an equivalent doctrine, the first sale doctrine.[161] The TRIPs Agreement has a limited provision on exhaustion. By Article 6, '[f]or the purposes of dispute settlement under this Agreement, subject to the provisions of Articles 3 and 4, nothing in this Agreement shall be used to address the issue of exhaustion of intellectual property rights'.[162] This provision represents a compromise as it was impossible for the negotiating parties to come to an agreed international regime on parallel imports in the Uruguay Round negotiations. As a result members retain a wide discretion to apply national policy subject only to the requirement that it does not offend national treatment under Article 3 and most favoured nation treatment under Article 4.[163]

Protection against parallel imports has been vigorously pursued by the pharmaceutical industry in particular.[164] The reason lies with the high costs of product R&D which need to be recouped through the full use of first sale rights. However, an overzealous control over access to patented medicines can lead to excessive prices and market scarcity. In this regard, the issue of affordable medicines has

---

[160] See further Whish above n 42 at 765–75.

[161] See UNCTAD *Transfer of Technology* above n 2 at 19 and *TRIPs Resource Book* above n 125 at 112–13 citing *Jazz Photo v ITC* 264 F 3d 1094 (CAFC 2001).

[162] For detailed analysis, see UNCTAD-ICTSD *TRIPs Resource Book* ibid ch 5.

[163] ibid at 108. See also Maskus above n 1 at 208–16. More detailed treatment of exhaustion of rights can be found in the Protocol on the Harmonization of Norms of Intellectual Property in MERCOSUR on Matters of Trademarks Geographical Indications and Denominations of Origin Decision No 8/95 and Decision 486 (2000) of the Andean Community both discussed in UNCTAD *Transfer of Technology* above n 2 at 35–38.

[164] Indeed the majority of the EC cases in this field have involved pharmaceutical companies: see Whish above n 42. Note that US regional and free trade agreements (FTAs) have stronger protection of pharmaceutical patents than the TRIPs Agreement protecting patent holders against parallel trade; see, for example, US Singapore FTA art 16(7)(2) US-Australia FTA art 17(9)(4) cited in Meir P Pugatch 'The International Regulation of IPRS in a TRIPs and TRIPs-Plus World' 6 JWIT 430 at 456 (2005).

arisen, in particular but not exclusively, out of concerns for access by sufferers in developing countries to AIDS/HIV retroviral drugs.[165] Concerns of this kind led to a major clash in South Africa in 1997 when 39 pharmaceutical companies challenged the provisions of the Medicines and Related Substances Control Amendment Act of that year, which authorized the parallel importation of patented medicines under s 15C. It also led to protests from the EU and the US, the latter making continued transitional aid to South Africa conditional upon the removal or suspension of s 15C.[166] It is unlikely that the Act infringed Article 6 of the TRIPs Agreement, as international exhaustion of IPRs was already recognized under case law when the TRIPs Agreement was concluded and the relevant provision, s 15C, merely gave an administrative authority to the health minister to prescribe conditions for the supply of more affordable medicines in certain circumstances so as to protect public health.[167] This case provoked a global campaign by NGOs and the legal action was withdrawn in 2001.[168] Similarly, Brazilian parallel import laws, which allowed such imports where pharmaceutical patents had not been worked in Brazil, became the subject of the WTO complaint, which was subsequently withdrawn.[169]

The issue of affordable medicines has also been considered in relation to compulsory licensing of IPRs. This involves the authorization to exploit an invention given by a public authority subject to specific conditions. The purpose of such

[165] See further Commission on Intellectual Property Rights above n 114 ch 2 and Marcelo Dias Varella 'The WTO, Intellectual Property and AIDS – Case Studies from Brazil and South Africa' 7 JWIP 525 (2004).

[166] See UNCTAD-ICTSD *TRIPs Resource Book* above n 125 at 111 and *Intellectual Property Rights: Implications for Development* above n 114 at 96 and n 3 citing US Public Law 105–277 (105th Congress, 1999) which introduced this condition.

[167] UNCTAD-ICTSD ibid. Medicines and Related Substances Control Amendment Act 1997 s 10: 'The following section is hereby inserted in the principal Act after section 15B: *Measures to ensure supply of more affordable medicines 15C.* The Minister may prescribe conditions for the supply of more affordable medicines in certain circumstances so as to protect the health of the public, and in particular may— *(a)* notwithstanding anything to the contrary contained in the Patents Act, 1978 (Act No. 57 of 1978), determine that the rights with regard to any medicine under a patent granted in the Republic shall not extend to acts in respect of such medicine which has been put onto the market by the owner of the medicine, or with his or her consent; *(b)* prescribe the conditions on which any medicine which is identical in composition, meets the same quality standard and is intended to have the same proprietary name as that of another medicine already registered in the Republic, but which is imported by a person other than the person who is the holder of the registration certificate of the medicine already registered and which originates from any site of manufacture of the original manufacturer as approved by the council in the prescribed manner, may be imported; *(c)* prescribe the registration procedure for, as well as the use of, the medicine referred to in paragraph *(b).*' <http://www.polity.org.za/html/govdocs/legislation/1997/act90.pdf>.

[168] The cases were withdrawn in return for an assurance that the legislation would be used in accordance with international patent law: 'Activists Jubilant in S. Africa Drugs Case' *Financial Times* 20 April 2001 at 9. See also David Pilling and Nicol degli Innocenti 'A Crack in the Resolve of an Industry' *Financial Times* 19 April 2001 at 19 and Stephen Ward 'Pharmaceuticals Rights Under Threat' *Financial Times* 11 June 2001 at 13.

[169] UNCTAD-ICTSD *Intellectual Property Rights: Implications for Development* above n 114 at 96. See *Brazil – Measures Affecting Patent Protection* WT/DS199/1 G/L/385IP/D/23 8 June 2000 and the *Notification of a Mutually Agreed Solution* WT/DS199/4 G/L/454IP/D/23/Add 1 19 July 2001.

discretion is to discourage IPR owners from not working their patents and thereby depriving consumers and the wider economy of the opportunity to benefit from their innovations. Compulsory licensing is recognized by Article 5A of the Paris Convention and by Article 31 of the TRIPs Agreement. This places a number of conditions upon the granting of a compulsory licence, with each case being reviewed on its individual merits. A licence should be granted only if an unsuccessful attempt has been made to acquire a voluntary licence on reasonable terms and conditions within a reasonable period of time, unless there is a national emergency or a public non-commercial use. The scope and duration of the licence will be limited to the purpose for which it was authorized, and the use will be non-exclusive and non-assignable. The licence will apply predominantly to the needs of the domestic market. It will be terminated when the circumstances that led to its adoption are terminated and are unlikely to recur, subject to the legitimate interest of the licensees. The right holder is entitled to adequate remuneration in the circumstances of each case, taking into account the economic value of the licence, and decisions are to be subject to judicial or other independent review by a distinct higher authority. Certain of these conditions are relaxed where compulsory licences are employed to remedy practices that have been established as anticompetitive by a legal process. These conditions should be read together with the related provisions of Article 27(1), which require that patent rights shall be enjoyable without discrimination as to the field of technology, and whether products are imported or locally produced.

In 2001 Brazil used its compulsory licensing powers to issue a licence for Nelfinavir, sold under the Viracept mark, an AIDS drug produced by Roche of Switzerland after the firm refused to reduce its price. By contrast Merck had agreed to reduce the prices for its AIDS medicines by 65 per cent and 59 per cent. The action against Roche was justified on the basis of a 'national emergency' rather than under the pharmaceuticals law which was challenged by the US. Brazil had been spending US$88 million on Nelfinavir, representing 25 per cent of its AIDS drugs budget as part of its highly successful free drug distribution policy.[170] Roche came to an agreement with the Brazilian Government in September 2001 to cut the price of Nelfinavir by 40 per cent.[171] Similarly, Canada awarded a compulsory licence to a local manufacturer for the anti-anthrax drug Cipro against Bayer in 2001.[172] This was unusual as Canada had generally reduced reliance on its statutory scheme for compulsory licences.[173]

---

[170] 'Brazil Acts to Override Patent on Aids Drug' *Financial Times* 23 August 2001 at 9. See also Commission on Intellectual Property Rights above n 114 Box 2.2 at 43.

[171] 'Brazil and Roche Agree Deal on Aids Drug Price Cut After Threat to Patent' *Financial Times* 1/2 September 2001 at 6.

[172] 'Bayer Angry as Canada Overrides Patent Law' *Financial Times* 20/21 October 2001 at 3.

[173] See Jerome H Reichman with Catherine Hasenzahl *Non-Voluntary Licensing of Patented Innovations* (Geneva: UNCTAD-ICTSD 2003) at 20. See also *Canada – Patent Protection of Pharmaceutical Products* WT/DS 114/R Panel Report adopted 7 April 2000 available at <http://www.wto.org>. Canada argued that the special exceptions under Article 30 of the TRIPs Agreement, to

The public health problems created by patented medicines gave rise to the Doha Declaration on the TRIPs Agreement and Public Health.[174] This recognizes the members' rights to use the provisions of the TRIPs Agreement to further public health and that the Agreement should be interpreted in a manner that is permissive of such policies. In particular, by paragraph 5:

(a) In applying the customary rules of interpretation of public international law, each provision of the TRIPs Agreement shall be read in the light of the object and purpose of the Agreement as expressed, in particular, in its objectives and principles.

(b) Each Member has the right to grant compulsory licences and the freedom to determine the grounds upon which such licences are granted.

(c) Each Member has the right to determine what constitutes a national emergency or other circumstances of extreme urgency, it being understood that public health crises, including those relating to HIV/AIDS, tuberculosis, malaria and other epidemics, can represent a national emergency or other circumstances of extreme urgency.

(d) The effect of the provisions in the TRIPs Agreement that are relevant to the exhaustion of intellectual property rights is to leave each Member free to establish its own regime for such exhaustion without challenge, subject to the MFN and national treatment provisions of Articles 3 and 4.

The main unresolved problem in this connection is the rather limited effect that the Doha Declaration has in cases of the least developed countries that cannot make effective use of compulsory licensing as they lack the industrial infrastructure to undertake pharmaceutical production. Such countries may have to rely on generic imports. Unfortunately a major generic supplier, India, has recently introduced full patent protection for pharmaceuticals making access to generic substitutes harder.[175] In addition, given the requirement in Article 31(f) that a compulsory licence can only be granted where manufacture is mainly for domestic consumption, a special exemption from this provision had to be agreed, allowing for export of generic drugs to members who cannot manufacture in their own right.[176]

patent exclusivity granted under art 27, justified competing generic manufacturers to test patented pharmaceuticals and to obtain marketing approval prior to the expiry of the patent so as to be able to get regulatory approval to sell in competition with the owner as soon as the patent expired, and to stockpile these. Canada lost on the stockpiling issue and won on the regulatory review exception issue. This is generally known as a 'Bolar exception' after the US case of that name which established the legality of such a policy under US patent law: Commission on Intellectual Property above n 114 at 50.

[174] WT/MIN(01)/DEC/2 20 November 2001 at <http://www.wto.org/english/thewto_e/minist_e/min01_e/mindecl_trips_e.pdf>.

[175] See UNCTAD-ICTSD *Intellectual Property Rights: Implications for Development* above n 114 at 101; The Patents (Amendment) Act 2005 No 15 of 2005 4 April 2005 at <http://www.patentoffice.nic.in/ipr/patent/patent_2005.pdf>.

[176] *Implementation of paragraph 6 of the Doha Declaration on the TRIPs Agreement and public health* Decision of the General Council of 30 August 2003 General Council WT/L/540 and Corr 1 1 September 2003 at <http://www.wto.org/english/tratop_e/trips_e/implem_para6_e.htm> and *Amendment of the TRIPs Agreement* General Council WT/L/641 8 December 2005 Decision of 6 December 2005 at <http://www.wto.org/english/tratop_e/trips_e/wtl641_e.htm> amending art 31(f) by way of art 31 bis which excludes the operation of art 31(f) for exporting members who supply pharmaceuticals to eligible non producing members.

As regards IPRs in the field of biotechnology, concern has been expressed at the ability of MNEs to patent products that involve modifications based on living organisms, the improvement of plants or animals, or the development of micro-organisms.[177] The earliest types of biotechnologies include brewing and baking. More recent types involve microbiological processes while the most recent techniques include the use of DNA for 'gene splicing', the creation of hybrids or clones, and genetic modification. Such products and processes will be outside the protection of TRIPs where members chose to follow Article 27(3)(b) and exclude from patentability:

plants and animals other than micro-organisms, and essentially biological processes for the production of plants or animals other than non-biological and micro-biological processes. However, members shall provide for the protection of plant varieties either by patents or by an effective sui generis system or by any combination thereof.

This provision is open to many interpretations and the fear is that it will prove of little help in preventing abusive forms of patent protection that may lead to an appropriation and commoditization by MNEs of what are essential life processes and public goods found in nature, and the genetic resources of farming and indigenous communities, so-called 'biopiracy'.[178] In particular, developing countries are concerned that their natural wealth in biodiversity will be exploited to their disadvantage.

---

[177] UNCTAD-ICTSD above n 114 at 75. See further Laurence R Helfer 'Regime Shifting: The TRIPs Agreement and New Dynamics of International Intellectual Property Lawmaking' 29 Yale J. Int'l L. 1 (2004); Martin Khor *Intellectual Property Biodiversity and Sustainable Development: Resolving the Difficult Issues* (London: Zed Books, 2006); Philippe Cullet *Intellectual Property Protection and Sustainable Development* (New Delhi: Butterworths Lexis-Nexis, 2005).

[178] See Commission on Intellectual Property above n 114 at 74: 'There is no accepted definition of "biopiracy". The Action Group on Erosion, Technology and Concentration (ETC Group) defines it as 'the appropriation of the knowledge and genetic resources of farming and indigenous communities by individuals or institutions seeking exclusive monopoly control (usually patents or plant breeders' rights) over these resources and knowledge.'

The following have been described as 'biopiracy':

a) *The granting of 'wrong' patents.* These are patents granted for inventions that are either not novel or are not inventive having regard to traditional knowledge already in the public domain. Such patents may be granted due either to oversights during the examination of the patent or simply because the patent examiner did not have access to the knowledge. This may be because it is written down but not accessible using the tools available to the examiner, or because it is unwritten knowledge. A WIPO led initiative to document and classify traditional knowledge seeks to address some of these problems.

b) *The granting of 'right' patents.* Patents may be correctly granted according to national law on inventions derived from a community's traditional knowledge or genetic resources. It could be argued this constitutes 'biopiracy' on the following grounds. Patenting standards are too low. Patents are allowed, for instance, for inventions which amount to little more than discoveries. Alternatively, the national patent regime (for example, as in the US) may not recognize some forms of public disclosure of traditional knowledge ... Even if the patent represents a genuine invention, however defined, no arrangements may have been made to obtain the prior informed consent (PIC)5 of the communities providing the knowledge or resource, and for sharing the benefits of commercialization to reward them appropriately in accordance with the principles of the [UN Convention on Biodiversity]'.

The 2001 Doha Declaration made it clear that work in the TRIPs Council under the reviews of Article 27(3)(b) or the whole of the TRIPs Agreement under Article 71(1), and on outstanding implementation issues should cover: 'the relationship between the TRIPs Agreement and the UN Convention on Biological Diversity (CBD); the protection of traditional knowledge and folklore; and other relevant new developments that member governments raise in the review of the TRIPs Agreement'. It adds that the TRIPs Council 'shall be guided by the objectives and principles set out in Articles 7 and 8 of the TRIPs Agreement, and shall take fully into account the development dimension'.[179] To this end proposals have been put forward to amend the TRIPs Agreement to ensure its consistency with the Convention on Biological Diversity and to provide that:

Members shall require that an applicant for a patent relating to biological materials or to traditional knowledge shall provide, as a condition to acquiring patent rights:

(i) disclosure of the source and country of origin of the biological resource and of the traditional knowledge used in the invention;
(ii) evidence of prior informed consent through approval of authorities under the relevant national regimes; and
(iii) evidence of fair and equitable benefit sharing under the national regime of the country of origin.'[180]

The Doha Declaration mentions traditional knowledge and folklore as an aspect of the wider debate on IPR protection and the conservation of biological diversity. At stake here is the appropriation of traditional forms of knowledge based on interactions by indigenous communities with their ecosystem. It includes, among other things, the ways indigenous peoples have of generating food, other consumption goods, handicrafts, works of art and performances, their cultural practices and property, such as spiritual artefacts, and images associated with such peoples, whether these are physical characteristics or their homes, villages, and landscapes.[181] Such assets can be protected through 'positive' protection measures, allowing traditional

---

[179] *Ministerial Declaration* WT/MIN(01)/DEC/1 20 November 2001 adopted on 14 November 2001 at <http://www.wto.org/english/thewto_e/minist_e/min01_e/mindecl_e.htm>.

[180] Communication dated 21 June 2002, from the Permanent Mission of Brazil on behalf of the delegations of Brazil, China, Cuba, Dominican Republic, Ecuador, India, Pakistan, Thailand, Venezuela, Zambia, and Zimbabwe with the request that it be circulated to TRIPs Council Members WTO Doc IP/C/W/356 24 June 2002 at <http://docsonline.wto.org/DDFDocuments/t/IP/C/W356.doc>. See also communication received from the Permanent Mission of Morocco on behalf of the African Group, IP/C/W/404 26 June 2003 <http://docsonline.wto.org/DDFDocuments/t/IP/C/W404.doc>. Submission of 26 February 2004, circulated at the request of the Delegations of Brazil, Cuba, Ecuador, India, Peru, Thailand, and Venezuela IP/C/W/420 2 March 2004 available at <http://docsonline.wto.org/DDFDocuments/t/IP/C/W420.doc>. Communication, dated 29 May 2006, circulated at the request of the delegation of India also on behalf of the delegations of Brazil, China, Colombia, Cuba, Pakistan, Peru, Thailand, and Tanzania WT/GC/W/564/Rev 2 TN/C/W/41/Rev 2 IP/C/W/474 5 July 2006 <http://docsonline.wto.org/DDFDocuments/t/ip/c/w474.doc>. See further Commission on Intellectual Property above n 114 ch 3.

[181] See Graham Dutfield *Protecting Traditional Knowledge and Folklore* (Geneva: UNCTAD-ICTSD, 2003) at 19. See further Commission on Intellectual Property Rights above n 114 ch 4.

communities and their members to hold IPRs in their traditional knowledge and folklore, and 'defensive' measures that prevent IPR claims to such categories of knowledge from persons who are not authorized to make such claims.[182] The protection of traditional knowledge and folklore has since become an issue in the work of several inter-governmental organizations.[183]

Concluding Remarks

In the contemporary economic and political climate, the challenge of the developing countries to the established international technology transfer system appears to have failed. Apart from changes in national regimes, attempts at instituting reforms in the international system of intellectual property protection have not been successful. As noted earlier, the proposed reforms of the Paris Convention have not come about, the negotiations over the TOT Code failed, and a new regime aimed at the strengthening of the international system of intellectual property protection has been put in place under the TRIPs Agreement. However, it would be wrong to characterize the current approach to technology transfer as prioritizing developed country and MNE interests alone. As the debates over public health and access to drugs show, it is possible to accommodate major public interest concerns into the current international system on IPR protection and technology transfer. Equally, new issues such as the protection of biotechnology and traditional knowledge are making their way onto the agenda of international organizations. Nonetheless, issues of special and differential treatment, and technical assistance and cooperation, with the least developed countries remain unresolved. Only a few major developing countries are in the process of moving from being technology importers to becoming innovators and technology exporters in their own right. This phenomenon should not be allowed to shroud the continuing problems of equitable access to technology, products, services, and processes that developing and least developed countries may experience.

---

[182] ibid at 1–10.
[183] See further UNCTAD-ICTSD *Intellectual Property Rights: Implications for Development* above n 114 at 122–24.

PART III
THE SOCIAL DIMENSION

12

Labour Relations

This chapter deals with the development of specialized standards for the conduct of labour relations by MNEs. These are contained primarily in the OECD Guideline on Employment and Industrial Relations (the OECD Guideline),[1] and in the International Labour Organization's (ILO) Tripartite Declaration of Principles on Multinationals and Social Policy (the ILO Declaration) as supplemented by the ILO Declaration on Fundamental Principles and Rights at Work of 1998 (the 1998 Declaration).[2] Both are products of the movement, in the 1970s, for the adoption of international codes of conduct on MNEs. Moreover, both codes are based on a consensus between governments, industry, and trade union representatives and, as such, represent 'corporatist' policy responses.[3] Despite significant changes in political attitudes towards labour issues since that time, both codes remain in effect and offer a good starting point for the study of how international practice in this area has evolved since the 1970s.[4]

The structure of the present chapter follows the principal headings in the ILO Declaration. Thus the issues of employment, training, conditions of work and life, and industrial relations will each be studied in a separate section. The terms of the ILO Declaration will be discussed alongside the corresponding provisions in the OECD Guideline, given that the two codes are complementary. Indeed, as the more elaborate code, the ILO Declaration has been said to be of use in interpreting

---

[1] OECD *OECD Guidelines for Multinational Enterprises* (Paris: OECD, 2000) at 21–22 and *Commentary on the OECD Guidelines* ibid paras 19–29 at 45–48 both available for download at <http://www.oecd.org/daf/investment/guidelines>.

[2] Adopted 16 November 1977: 17 ILM 422 (1978) revised version adopted 28 March 2006 available at <http://www.ilo.org/public/english/employment/multi/download/english.pdf>. For comment, see Gunter 'The ILO Tripartite Declaration of Principles Concerning Multinational Enterprises and Social Policy' The CTC Reporter (No 12 Summer 1982) 27–29 and Bob Hepple 'New Approaches to International Labour Regulation' 26 ILJ 353 (1997); ILO Declaration on Fundamental Principles and Rights at Work 86th Session, Geneva, June 1998: 37 ILM 1233 (1998) or <http://www.ilo.org/dyn/declaris/DECLARATIONWEB.static_jump?var_language=EN&var_pagename=DECLARATIONTEXT>. [3] See ch 3 above at 91–92.

[4] Since the 1980s neo-classical economic analysis has been hostile to harmonized international labour standards, seeing these as a source of inefficiency which threatens new job creation. This position advocates a free market solution which allows countries to compete on the basis of their comparative advantage in labour terms and conditions. For a critique arguing that harmonized international standards are in fact economically useful; see Simon Deakin and Frank Wilkinson 'Rights vs Efficiency? The Economic Case for Transnational Labour Standards' 23 ILJ 289 (1994).

the OECD Guideline, although this must bear in mind their distinct follow-up procedures.[5] Reference will also be made, where appropriate, to EC law and policy. This has made significant advances in areas expressly directed at the employment consequences of MNE operations in the integrated European market. Before that is done, the scene will be set by a brief review of the reasons behind the adoption of the two codes, and of the general policies they espouse, especially their relationship to national laws.

(1) The Evolution of the ILO and OECD Codes

The ILO has been at the forefront of the movement for the international regulation of minimum labour standards since its inception in 1919 under Part XIII of the Treaty of Versailles. To this end the ILO has adopted numerous International Labour Conventions, laying down the minimum standards for the treatment of labour that are acceptable to the international community.[6] These form the background principles on which the ILO Declaration is based. Indeed, the declaration refers to the relevant ILO Conventions both in its text and in its Annex.[7] Furthermore, the ILO is a tripartite organization with representatives of governments, business and labour having access to its decision-making organs as members of national delegations.[8] For these reasons, it was natural for the ILO to be used as the vehicle for the development of new principles applicable to MNEs.

The ILO became involved in the formulation of a code of conduct in response to demands from labour representatives and developing countries that had been made since the 1960s.[9] In the early 1970s the developing countries pressed for an

---

[5] OECD *Commentary* above n 1 at para 20.

[6] See UNCTAD *Employment* Series on issues in international investment agreements (New York and Geneva: United Nations, 2000) at 3.There are now 185 ILO Conventions. The most important are the five conventions that cover the contents of the 1998 Declaration above n 2: Conventions No 87, on Freedom of Association and the Protection of the Right to Organize, No 98, on the Right to Organize and Collective Bargaining, No 29 on Forced Labour, No 105 on Abolition of Forced Labour, No 138 on Minimum Age, No 182 on Worst Forms of Child Labour, No 100 on Equal Remuneration and No 111 on Discrimination in Employment. The ILO Conventions are available at <http://www.ilo.org/ilolex/english/convdisp2.htm>. For background on the ILO, see Jean-Michel Servais *International Labour Law* (Wolters Kluwer, 2005); Bob Hepple *Labour Laws and Global Trade* (Oxford: Hart Publishing 2005) ch 2; Brown and McColgan 'UK Employment Law and the International Labour Organisation; The Spirit of Cooperation?' 21 ILJ 265 (1992); SA Ivanov 'The International Labour Organisation: Control Over Application of the Conventions and Recommendations on Labour' in WE Butler (ed) *Control over Compliance with International Law* (Kluwer, 1991) 153.

[7] This list is periodically updated and appended to the ILO's current published version of the declaration.

[8] By ILO Constitution art 3(1) member states are entitled to send four representatives: two governmental representatives and, by agreement, one each from the most representative employers' and trade union organizations in the country: <http://www.ilo.org/public/english/about/iloconst.htm#a3p5>.

[9] See G Hamilton *The Control of Multinationals: What Future for International Codes of Conduct in the 1980s?* (IRM Multinational Reports No 2 IRM/Wiley, 1984) 9–10; J Robinson *Multinationals and Political Control* (Gower, 1983) 171–73 and see the ILO website at <http://www.ilo.org>.

ILO conference which could adopt a binding international code for MNEs. This was resisted by the employers' representatives who favoured the adoption of a voluntary code. In 1972 the negotiating process started with the first 'Tripartite Meeting on the Relationship between Multinational Enterprises and Social Policy'. The meeting set up a series of research studies that were carried out between 1972 and 1976. These resulted in a recommendation that a non-binding tripartite declaration of principles concerning multinational enterprises and social policy should be drafted. The ILO Declaration was finally adopted on 16 November 1977.

The declaration did not provide for any follow-up machinery. However, in 1980, such a procedure was adopted. The governing body of the ILO established a Committee on Multinational Enterprises (the Committee). This was charged with three tasks.[10] First, states are to make periodic reports on the implementation of the declaration on the basis of questionnaires sent through governments to unions and business organizations. Secondly, it is to conduct periodic studies on labour issues involving MNEs. Thirdly, it is to interpret the declaration through a disputes procedure. This was revised in 1986.[11] Requests for interpretation are submitted to the Committee by governments and by national or international organizations of employers or workers. Workers' requests will be received only if they are not able to have these submitted through a national government. Requests are admissible if they do not conflict with or duplicate appropriate procedures at national level, in the case of issues involving national laws, and with the ILO's international procedures under ILO Conventions, in the case of convention based issues. If the request is receivable, the International Labour Office will prepare a draft reply which is considered by the Committee. The reply is then submitted for approval by the governing body and, if approved, is published in the ILO *Official Bulletin*.[12] This procedure is not judicial in nature. It serves merely to clarify the standards contained in the declaration. However, the Committee can only do so in the context of an 'actual situation'.[13] Thus the procedure may involve the ascertainment of certain facts but not a resolution of disputes over facts and laws.

The OECD Guideline on Employment and Industrial Relations is part of the more general OECD Guidelines on Multinational Enterprises. It is, therefore, less detailed than the ILO Declaration. The background to the passage of the OECD Guidelines is discussed in chapter 17 below. For present purposes it is enough to note that the OECD Employment Guideline has been the subject of extensive interpretation by the OECD Committee on International Investment

---

[10] See ILO website at <http://www.ilo.org> and see also Lemoine 'The ILO Tripartite Declaration: Ten Years After' The CTC Reporter (No 25, Spring 1988) 22; Robinson ibid at 175–76.

[11] See Procedure for Examination of Disputes Concerning the Application of the Tripartite Declaration of Principles Concerning Multinational Enterprises and Social Policy by Means of Interpretation of its Provisions, adopted by the Governing Body of the International Labour Office at its 232nd Session, Geneva, March 1986, appended to the ILO Tripartite Declaration above n 2.

[12] For a summary of the main interpretations, see <http://www.ilo.org>.

[13] ILO Doc GB.232/12/15 February–March 1985 cited in Lemoine above n 10 at 26.

and Multinational Enterprises under its powers of interpretation.[14] As with the ILO Declaration, these powers stop short of pronouncing on the outcome of a dispute. Nevertheless, in the early years of its operation, the OECD Employment Guideline was frequently used by West European trade unions to obtain general interpretations of principles from the OECD Committee, arising out of disputes involving MNE employment and industrial relations practices.[15] However, the guideline declined as a means of bringing pressure to bear on MNEs, owing largely to a shift in West European trade union strategy towards lobbying for the development of EC policies in the labour and social fields. The adoption of strengthened National Contact Points (NCP) in 2000 may have helped to revive the OECD process.[16] There is evidence from the reports of the annual NCP meetings at the OECD that the Employment Guideline is being referred to by trade unions in their communications with NCPs.[17]

(2) General Policies of the Codes and Their Relationship to National Laws

The principal difference in the general approach of each code concerns their respective addressees. The OECD Guideline is jointly addressed by the Member Countries to MNEs operating in their territories.[18] The ILO Declaration is addressed to governments, the employers' and workers' organizations in both home and host countries, and to MNEs themselves.[19] On the other hand, both codes share much in common. First, they are voluntary in nature.[20] Indeed, it is hard to envisage that binding provisions would ever have been accepted on the basis of consensus. Employers' representatives before both bodies were opposed to binding instruments. Secondly, both instruments are addressed to MNEs and

[14] The Committee's principal interpretations are reproduced in the periodic reviews of the OECD Guidelines. See 1979 Review (Paris, 1979) or 18 ILM 986 (1979) at paras 59–72; 1986 Review (Paris: OECD, 1986) paras 53–87; 1991 Review (Paris: OECD, 1992) at 43–44; 46–49; OECD Woking Party on the OECD Guidelines for Multinational Enterprises *OECD Guidelines for Multinational Enterprises: Text, Commentary and Clarifications* OECD Doc DAFFE/IME/WPG(2000)15/Final 31 October 2001 at 21–27.

[15] See further Robinson above n 9 ch 9 and R Blanpain *The Badger Case* (The Hague: Kluwer, 1977); ibid *OECD Guidelines for Multinational Enterprises and Labour Relations: Experience and Review* (The Hague: Kluwer, vol I 1979; vol II 1982; vol III 1985).

[16] See Decision of the OECD Council C (2000)96/Final 19 July 2000 and the Procedural Guidance on National Contact Points in the OECD Guidelines 2000 above n 1 at 31–37 or at <http://www.olis.oecd.org/olis/2000doc.nsf/4f7adc214b91a685c12569fa005d0ee7/c12568d1006e03f7c12569210035d2e5/$FILE/00080619.PDF>.

[17] The annual reports of the NCP meeting began in 2001. All the reports can be downloaded either in full or summary form at <http://www.oecd.org/document/53/0,2340,en_2649_34889_2512693_1_1_1_1,00.html>.

[18] OECD Guidelines above n 1 Section I, Concepts and Principles, para 1.

[19] ILO Declaration above n 2 at para 4.

[20] ILO Declaration para 7; OECD Guidelines Section I Concepts and Principles para 1.

national enterprises. They aim to reflect good practice for all, without discrimination as to nationality.[21] Thirdly, both codes envisage the primacy of national law. Thus the ILO Declaration states:

All the parties concerned by this Declaration should respect the sovereign rights of States, obey the national laws and regulations, give due consideration to local practices and respect relevant international standards.[22]

The primacy of national law is reinforced by the requirement that the above mentioned disputes procedure cannot be used to determine issues arising out of national law. Similarly, the OECD Employment Guideline begins by stating that enterprises should respect the standards it contains, 'within the framework of applicable law, regulations and prevailing labour relations and employment practices' in each of the countries in which they operate.

The reference to the primacy of national law tends to weaken the effectiveness of both codes. The codes preserve the right of each state to determine the nature, scope and effect of its national labour laws. Consequently, despite exhortations to the contrary that will be mentioned below, the codes can do little to prevent competition between states over the reduction of labour standards as a means of reducing the cost of investment in their respective territories. In this regard the ILO Declaration contains certain additional provisions of a general nature, not found in the OECD Guideline. Thus, governments which have not yet done so are urged to ratify the core ILO Conventions as listed in paragraph 9 of the ILO Declaration.[23] Furthermore, MNEs are expected to take full account of the general policy objectives of the countries in which they operate, especially the development priorities and social aims and structures of these countries. To this end, consultations should be held between the firm and the government and employers' and workers' organizations in these countries.[24] Moreover, governments of home countries are urged to promote good social practice in accordance with the ILO Declaration having regard to the social and labour law, regulations, and practices in host countries as well as to relevant international standards. Both home and host countries are encouraged to have consultations with each other on these matters.[25] This provision urges home states to ensure that home based corporations observe good practice in their overseas operations, and at all times observe host states' laws. It therefore reinforces the territorial nature of labour regulation, in that this provision does not envisage the extraterritorial application of superior home country standards to employees in host states. This suggests that bilateral arrangements may offer a way forward in ensuring the observance of higher standards throughout the network of countries in which a MNE operates. Such efforts could be conducted under the auspices of the ILO itself.[26]

---

[21] ILO Declaration para 11; OECD Guidelines ibid para 4.   [22] ILO Declaration para 8.
[23] ILO Declaration above n 2 at para 9.   [24] ibid para 10.   [25] ibid para 12.
[26] See Zimmerman 'International dimension of US fair employment laws: Protection or interference?' 131 Int'l Lab.Rev. 217 (1992).

The relative weakness of the ILO Declaration may be contrasted with the approach of the 1998 ILO Declaration on Fundamental Principles and Rights at Work. This provides what can be termed an international 'floor of fundamental labour rights' in Article 2, which states:

... all Members, even if they have not ratified the Conventions in question, have an obliga-tion arising from the very fact of their membership of the [ILO], to respect, to promote and to realize, in good faith and in accordance with the Constitution, the principles con-cerning the fundamental rights which are the subject of those Conventions, namely:

(a) freedom of association and the effective recognition of the right to collective bargaining;
(b) the elimination of all forms of forced or compulsory labour;
(c) the effective abolition of child labour; and
(d) the elimination of discrimination in respect of employment and occupation.[27]

This provision raises the question whether an ILO member can now deviate from these standards in its national laws, notwithstanding the primacy of national law under the ILO Declaration. The wording of Article 2 asserts an obligation to observe the fundamental rights listed therein. However, there is no apparent sanc-tion. The 1998 Declaration contains only a follow-up procedure designed to encourage efforts made by ILO members to promote the fundamental principles and rights enshrined in Article 2. Indeed, the ILO Constitution itself contains no formal sanctions that can be taken against a member that fails to ratify an ILO Convention in national law. The member only has an obligation to report on this situation to the Director-General of the ILO at intervals determined by the gov-erning body.[28] Thus the ILO process remains one based on good faith and best efforts, even in relation to norms that can be regarded as binding principles of international human rights law.

Finally, the codes do not address the problem of conflicting labour standards that may arise as a result of the international operations of MNEs.[29] For example, where the firm employs a national of the home state in the host state, it may wish that person's employment contract to be governed by the law of the home state. Where home state law sanctions terms and conditions that are contrary to host state law, the contract may be unlawful in the host state. Indeed, many states may have mandatory rules of employment law that cannot be avoided through the choice of a foreign law as the proper law of the contract of employment. The terri-torial principle of jurisdiction still prevails in the field of labour law, making for considerable differences in the content of laws that will govern employment issues within the MNE. This is a major reason why MNEs tend to treat employment issues on a decentralized basis.

---

[27] ILO 1998 Declaration above n 2. These fundamental rights are echoed in paragraph 1 of the OECD Employment Guideline: above n 1.
[28] ILO Constitution above n 8 art 19(5)(e).
[29] On which see further Morgenstern and Knapp 'Multinational Enterprises and the Extraterritorial Application of Labour Law' 27 ICLQ 769 (1978).

The territorial basis of labour law will create particular problems where employees are 'peripatetic', that is, where they are normally based in one country but are frequently assigned to another to carry out work there, or 'expatriate' where they are based permanently abroad though working for a home country firm. In a recent English House of Lords case, the question arose whether UK laws relating to unfair dismissal could apply to such classes of employees.[30] Their Lordships held that although the territorial principle applied in the standard case, in that such laws extended only to employees who were working in Great Britain, in the case of 'peripatetic' employees UK unfair dismissal law could apply if the employee was in fact based in the UK but ordinarily worked outside Great Britain, regardless of the formal place of work specified in the contract. In the case of 'expatriate' employees UK law would not normally apply unless the employee was working as an employee of a UK based employer and he or she was working as a representative of a business conducted at home in the UK or was operating within an extra-territorial British social or political enclave in a foreign country, such as a British military base.

(3) Employment Issues

The ILO Declaration deals with three issues under this heading: employment promotion, equality of opportunity, and treatment and security of employment. The OECD Employment Guideline contains standards pertaining to the second and third issues, but does not espouse the broader goal of employment promotion. However, paragraph 4 of the General Policies Guideline in the OECD code asserts that enterprises should '[e]ncourage human capital formation, in particular by creating employment opportunities and facilitating training opportunities for employees'.[31]

(a) Employment Promotion

The ILO Declaration asserts the governments should 'declare and pursue, as a major goal, an active policy designed to promote full, productive and freely chosen employment',[32] and that MNEs, 'particularly when operating in developing countries, should endeavour to increase employment opportunities and standards, taking into account the employment policies and objectives of the governments, as well as security of employment and the long-term development of the enterprise'.[33] To this general objective are added specific duties to consult with host country authorities and national employers' and workers' organizations in order to keep

---

[30] *Lawson v Serco Ltd, Botham v Ministry of Defence, Crofts and Others v Veta Ltd and Others* [2006] UKHL 3, [2006] 1 All ER 823 (HL). For analysis, see Thomas Linden 'Employment Protection for Employees Working Abroad' 35 ILJ 186 (2006).   [31] OECD Guidelines above n 1 at 19.
[32] ILO Declaration above n 2 para 13 and Convention No 122 and Recommendation No 122 concerning Employment Policy.   [33] ibid para 16.

manpower plans in harmony with national social development policies,[34] to give priority to the employment and promotion of host country nationals[35] and, when investing in developing countries, to use technologies which generate employment.[36] Furthermore, supply contracts with local enterprises should be concluded whenever practicable, so as to stimulate the use and the processing of local raw materials.[37]

These aspects of the declaration now appear rather dated in the light of the abandonment, by many states, of full employment policies, and in the wake of the recessions of the 1980s and early 1990s and the Asian Crisis of 1997.[38] Indeed, as long ago as 1986, the ILO Committee on Multinational Enterprises found that MNEs made little difference in the creation of employment opportunities and that such firms suffered the same employment constraints as other firms operating in the throes of recession. Furthermore, there was generally little adaptation of productive technology to the employment needs of host states.[39] In all, the declaration appears to have been based on an exaggerated belief in the ability of MNEs to act as agents of economic and social development. Thus, while it contains a sentiment that is no doubt generally accepted, the practical utility of its exhortations may be doubted. Full employment in a global high-technology economy is becoming harder to envisage, as the demand for unskilled and semi-skilled labour decreases and automation reduces the total number of jobs required for profitable operation.[40] That said it is undeniable that MNEs have a capacity to generate new employment both directly and indirectly through new investments which, in turn, may encourage other foreign investments linked to the original project, whether by other MNEs or local suppliers. However, the prerequisites for success are complex, making precise predictions impossible. These include the nature and size of the investment, the type of international production network used by the MNE and the degree of its international integration, the capacity of the host country to adapt to international competition, the quality of the labour force, and the nature of labour market regulation.[41] In addition, while the quantity of employment so generated is important, the quality of the resulting jobs must also be considered. Ideally foreign investment will allow for a rise in the technical quality of the work offered as a spur to economic growth. In this regard training is of central importance.[42] This is discussed further below.

---

[34] ibid para 17.   [35] ibid para 18.   [36] ibid para 19.   [37] ibid para 20.
[38] See UNCTAD *World Investment Report 1999* (New York and Geneva: United Nations, 1999) at 257 citing ILO figures estimating the total job losses resulting from this crisis at 20–25 million.
[39] Lemoine above n 10 at 24. This problem is confirmed by UNCTAD in the *World Investment Report 1999* above n 38 at 271, especially in relation to the limited ability of investments in export processing zones to grow beyond low skill, low wage, and employment. See further ch 6 above at 232–33.
[40] See further R Van Tulder and G Junne *European Multinationals in Core Technologies* (Wiley/IRM, 1988) ch 4.
[41] UNCTAD *World Investment Report 1999* above n 38 at 258–69. See further Douglas AF Van Den Berghe *Working Across Borders: Multinational Enterprises and the Internationalization of Employment* (Rotterdam: Erasmus Institute of Management, 2003).   [42] ibid at 273–77.

(b) Equality of Opportunity and Treatment

The ILO Declaration states that 'all governments should pursue policies designed to promote equality of opportunity and treatment in employment, with a view to eliminating any discrimination based on race, colour, sex, religion, political opinion, national extraction or social origin'.[43] MNEs should be guided by the same principles throughout their operations but without prejudice to preferential treatment for host country employees or to governmental policies designed to correct historical patterns of discrimination.[44] Equally, governments should never encourage MNEs to pursue discriminatory policies.[45] The OECD Employment Guideline echoes the ILO Declaration by recommending that enterprises should:

Not discriminate against their employees with respect to employment or occupation on such grounds as race, colour, sex, religion, political opinion, national extraction or social origin unless selectivity concerning employee characteristics furthers established governmental policies which specifically promote greater equality of employment opportunity or relates to the inherent requirements of the job.[46]

Thus, both codes accept positive discrimination, or 'affirmative action', on the basis of governmental policies. The ILO Declaration goes further and accepts the legitimacy of preferential treatment for host state employees. Neither code has raised significant issues of interpretation in this area. Most states accept non-discrimination in employment as a principle, though it is unrealistic to expect that this is always observed in practice.[47] In this respect MNEs are subject to the same requirements and pressures as national enterprises. Much depends on the internal 'management culture' and whether, regardless of legal rules, a moral principle of non-discrimination is observed.

In the context of MNE operations, it is arguable that non-discrimination laws should apply extraterritorially, thereby ensuring the same legal protection to all employees wherever they work. The issue has arisen in relation to the application of US non-discrimination laws to US employees working in the foreign subsidiaries

---

[43] ILO Declaration above n 2 para 21 and Convention No 111 and Recommendation No 111 concerning Discrimination in Respect of Employment and Occupation and Convention No 100 and Recommendation No 90 concerning Equal Remuneration for Men and Women Workers for Work of Equal Value.   [44] ibid para 22.

[45] ibid para 23.

[46] OECD Guideline above n 1 para 1(d). The Commentary to this provision explains that 'the principle of non-discrimination is considered to apply to such terms and conditions as hiring, discharge, pay, promotion, training and retirement. The list of non permissible grounds of discrimination which is taken from ILO Convention 111 of 1958 considers that any distinction, exclusion or preference on these grounds is a violation of the Convention. At the same time the text makes clear that the terms do not constitute an exhaustive list' above n 1 at para 24.

[47] See eg art 141 EC Treaty guaranteeing that men and women should receive equal pay for equal work. See further Erika Szyszczak *EC Labour Law* (Harlow: Pearson Education, 2000) ch 4. On EC Labour Law see too Brian Bercusson *European Labour Law* (London: Butterworths, 1996) (second edition expected 2007 with Cambridge University Press); Ruth Nielsen and Erika Szyszczak *The Social Dimension of the European Union* (Copenhagen: Copenhagen Business School Press, 3rd edn, 1997).

of US corporations. In 1991 the US Supreme Court held that Title VII of the Civil Rights Act 1964, which prohibits discrimination in employment on the basis of race religion or national origin, did not have extraterritorial reach so as to protect a US citizen working abroad in a US controlled company.[48] This ruling was reversed by the Civil Rights Act of 1991 ensuring that US citizens working abroad in US controlled foreign corporations did not lose the protection of Title VII.[49] Equally, Title VII applies to the US based subsidiaries of foreign corporations. This is so despite the protection of the right of free management of foreign companies in the US under US Friendship Commerce and Navigation treaties, which includes the right to hire executive and other specialized employees of the foreign firm's choice.[50]

Furthermore, when MNE employees are sent on a short-term posting to another state it is arguable that they should be entitled to benefit from the protection of host state labour rights even though their contract of employment with the MNE may be governed by the law of another state, for example, the home state. In order to ensure that such protection exists the EC has adopted legislation on the protection of posted workers in the services sector which seeks to ensure that certain employment laws generally applicable in the Member State to which the worker is posted apply to him even though the contract of employment is governed by the law of another Member State.[51]

(c) Security of Employment

The ILO Declaration recommends that governments study the impact of MNEs on employment and develop suitable policies to deal with the employment and labour market impacts of MNE operations.[52] In their turn, MNEs and national enterprises should, through active manpower planning, 'endeavour to provide stable employment for their employees and should observe freely negotiated obligations concerning employment stability and social security'.[53] Furthermore, MNEs, because of the flexibility they are assumed to have, are exhorted to assume a leading role in promoting security of employment, particularly in countries where the discontinuation of operations is likely to accentuate long-term unemployment.[54] The declaration further states that arbitrary dismissal procedures should be avoided,[55]

---

[48] *EEOC/Boureslan v ARAMCO* 113 Sup Ct 274 (1991).

[49] See Zimmerman above n 26 at 221.

[50] See *Sumitomo Shoji America v Avagliano* 457 US 176 (US Sup Ct 1982). For a critical view of this decision, see Ishizuka 'Subsidiary Assertion of Foreign Parent Corporation Rights under Commercial Treaties to Hire Employees "Of Their Choice"' 86 Col.LR 139 (1986).

[51] See Council Directive 96/71/EC OJ [1997] L 18/1. See further Paul Davies 'Posted Workers: Single Market or Protection of National Law Labour Systems?' 34 CMLRev. 571 (1997).

[52] ILO Declaration above n 2 para 24.   [53] ibid para 25.   [54] ibid.

[55] ibid para 27 and Recommendation No 119 concerning Termination of Employment at the Initiative of the Employer.

and that governments, in cooperation with MNEs and national enterprises, should provide some form of income protection for workers whose employment has been terminated.[56]

Both the ILO Declaration and the OECD Employment Guideline accept that MNEs are free to change their operations, even if this results in major employment effects, as in the case of the closure of an entity involving collective lay-offs or dismissals,[57] or in a merger, takeover or transfer of production which results in employment rationalization.[58] In such cases, MNEs should provide reasonable notice of the impending changes to the representatives of their employees,[59] and to relevant governmental authorities, and should cooperate in the mitigation, to the greatest possible extent, of any adverse effects.[60] In the *Badger* case, where a US parent closed down its Belgian subsidiary, the OECD Committee on International Investment and Multinational Enterprises stated that this obligation included assistance to the subsidiary so as to enable the payment of termination claims to be made in accordance with the national law of the host state.[61] However, in the *Philips* case the OECD Committee noted that 'once multinational enterprises have made a decision to terminate branch activities, the Guidelines do not require them to solve or improve resulting regional development problems of host countries'.[62]

In general, for notice to be reasonable, it should be sufficiently timely for the purpose of mitigating action to be prepared and put into effect. Furthermore, management should normally be able to provide notice prior to the final decision being taken.[63] However, what constitutes 'reasonable notice' may be affected by the sensitivity of the business decisions involved, which may make it commercially difficult to give early notice of impending changes. The OECD Committee on Multinational Enterprises has envizaged that such cases would be exceptional, and that early notice could be given in most situations.[64]

Within the EC significant advances have been made in the protection of employment rights that are of direct relevance to the operations of MNEs. Collective redundancies and employees' rights on the transfer of undertakings have been the

---

[56] ibid para 28.

[57] In the *Batco* case, the OECD Committee on Multinational Enterprises held that the Employment Guideline cannot be interpreted as prohibiting the closure of even a profitable subsidiary, as this remained a prerogative of management. All that the firm had to do was to follow the requirements of national law regarding the effects of the closure: Blanpain above n 15 vol I at 150–73.

[58] ILO Declaration above n 2 at para 26; OECD Guideline above n 1 at para 6.

[59] The OECD Committee on Multinational Enterprises has stated that, where the affected employees have no trade union or other bona fide representation, enterprises must take all practical steps to ensure the observance of the terms of the Guideline within the framework of national laws, regulations and prevailing labour relations practices: 1991 Review above n 14 at 43; OECD Working Party 2001 above n 14 at p 24.   [60] ibid 1991 Review.

[61] Blanpain above n 15 vol I at 125–46: Robinson above n 9 at 125–28.

[62] Cited by Robinson above n 9 at 133. See also OECD interpretations in the *Siemens* and *Litton Industries* cases in Robinson ibid at 130 and 132; and see *Hyster* case: Blanpain above n 15 vol III at 139–54.   [63] OECD Working Party above n 14 at 23.

[64] ibid.

subject of harmonization measures in the form of directives.[65] The contents of directives must be incorporated into the national laws of the Member States. Failure to do
so may result in an enforceable right to damages against the defaulting Member
State.[66] Thus EC law offers a source of developing and effective rules for the protection of employment in situations of change.

As regards collective redundancies, Council Directive 98/59/EC was passed to
ensure that existing workers' rights to information and consultation in cases of collective redundancies could not be undermined where such redundancies were
caused by decisions of undertakings, other than the immediate employer, located
in another Member State. The Commission saw this as a problem that was likely to
increase with the growing concentration of undertakings across national frontiers
in the integrated European market.[67] Directive 98/59 requires appropriate information to be given to workers' representatives so that consultation can take place
with a view to avoiding collective redundancies or to reducing the number of workers affected, and mitigating the consequences by recourse to social measures aimed,
inter alia, at aid for redeploying or retaining workers made redundant.[68] Such consultation must take place in good time and with a view to reaching agreement.[69]
The required information must be supplied in good time and must be relevant.[70] It
must specify the reasons for the projected redundancies, the numbers and categories of workers to be made redundant, the number of workers and categories
normally employed, the period during which the projected redundancies are to be
effected, the criteria of selection to be employed, and the method of calculating
redundancy payments.[71] These obligations apply whether the decision concerning
the redundancies is being taken by the immediate employer or by an undertaking
controlling the employer. The immediate employer cannot rely on the failure of the
controlling undertaking to furnish it with the relevant information as a defence to

---

[65] See Szyszczak above n 47 at ch 5. Arguably these developments have been more concerned with
the effectiveness of market integration than with the protection of workers rights: see P Davies in
W McCarthy (ed) *Legal Interventions in Industrial Relations* (Oxford: Blackwell Publishers, 1992) ch 10;
Bercusson above n 47 at 234.

[66] See *Francovich v Italy* [1993] 2 CMLR 66, [1992] IRLR 84 (ECJ) comment: Szyszczak 55
MLR 690 (1992).

[67] OJ [1998] L225/16. The original directive which harmonized standards in this area was
Directive 75 /129/EEC OJ [1975] L48/22, which was amended by EC Council Directive 92/56/
EEC OJ [1992] L245/92. For the Commission's background proposal, see COM(91) 292 Final 13
November 1991. Directive 75/129 was interpreted as requiring consultation to begin as soon as the
employer contemplates redundancies whereas the implementing provision in English law, s 188 of the
Trade Union and Labour Relations (Consolidation) Act 1992, was interpreted as applying only once
the decision to make a person redundant has been made: *R v British Coal Corporation and Secretary of
State for Trade and Industry, Ex p Vardy and Others* [1993] 1 CMLR 721 (DC). The UK was found to
have violated the requirements of Directive 75/129: Cases C–383 & 382/92 *Commission v United
Kingdom* [1994] ECR I–2479.   [68] ibid art 2(2).

[69] ibid art 2(1).

[70] This has been interpreted to mean that the consultation must take place before any contracts of
employment are terminated, as the obligation to consult and notify arises prior to any decision by the
employer to terminate contracts of employment: *Junk v Kuhnel* Case C–188/03 [2005] 1 CMLR 1070.

[71] ibid art 2(3).

non-compliance with the directive.[72] The group as a whole must ensure conformity with the terms of the directive. Employers are further obliged to inform the relevant public authorities in writing of any projected redundancies. The document concerned must contain all the relevant information supplied to workers' representatives.[73] The proposed redundancies must not take place less than 30 days after the date of notification. This period may be reduced by Member States.[74]

Turning to EC provisions relating to employees' rights on the transfer of undertakings, Directive 2001/23/EC serves to protect the rights of an employee of an undertaking that is transferred or merged.[75] The directive applies to 'the transfer of an undertaking, business or part of a business to another employer as a result of a legal transfer or merger'.[76] When this results in a change of employer from the transferor to the transferee, the latter must continue to observe the conditions of employment agreed in a collective agreement on the same terms applicable to the transferor under that agreement.[77] Furthermore, neither the transferor nor the transferee can use the transfer as grounds for dismissal, although this 'shall not stand in the way of dismissals that may take place for economic, technical or organisational reasons entailing changes in the workforce'.[78] The essence of the directive is the protection of workers terms and conditions of employment where the undertaking that is transferred retains its economic identity. This is a question of fact in each case and involves an analysis of the nature of the business undertaken both before and after the transfer, the types of assets transferred, the number of employees transferred and whether the same customers remain served by the undertaking.[79] The directive does not apply to a transfer on insolvency, or where an employment relationship does not actually exist at the date of transfer.[80] There are duties of information and consultation concerning the proposed transfer on

---

[72] ibid art 2(4).   [73] ibid art 3(1); art 2(3).   [74] ibid art 4(1).

[75] OJ [2001] L82/16 replacing and consolidating Council Directive 77/187/EEC OJ [1977] L61/26 and Council Directive 98/50/EC OJ [1998] L201/88.

[76] ibid art 1(1). The directive does not apply merely because a majority of shares in a limited company is acquired by another company. There must be a change of employer.   [77] ibid art 3(3).

[78] ibid art 4(1).

[79] See Case 24/85 *Spijkers v Benedik* [1986] ECR 1119; *Temco Service Industires SA v Imzilyen and Others* Case C–51/00 [2004] 1 CMLR 877 at paras 23–24; *Rasmusen and Others v Total E&P Norge AS* EFTA Court Case E–2/04 [2005] 1 CMLR 484 at paras 24–27; *Abler and Others v Sodexho MM Catering GmbH* Case C–340/01 [2006] 2 CMLR 89 (transfer of kitchen equipment located inside a hospital to an new caterer was sufficient to show a transfer, even where not all of the existing staff were hired by the new caterer); *Guney Gorres and Another v Securicor Aviation (Germany) Ltd and Another* Cases C–232 & C–233/04 [2006] 2 CMLR 173 (a transfer of an undertaking within Directive 2001/23 took place where aviation security services were contracted out by the state to a new contractor, even though the security equipment at the airport in question was owned and serviced by the state and did not belong to the previous contractor. The requirement of German law, that tangible assets taken over by the new contractor had to be taken for independent commercial use, did not preclude there being a transfer of assets under the directive).

[80] See further Szyszczak above n 47 at 114–21 and cases cited therein. For the application of the directive in English law, see the Transfer of Undertakings (Protection of Employment) Regulations 1981 SI 1981/1794 and John McMullen *Business Transfers and Employee Rights* (London: Lexis Nexis, Butterworths, 1998 and subsequent updates).

both the transferor and transferee.[81] The European Court of Justice has held that employees can opt out of the provisions of the directive and the consequences of so doing are for national law to determine.[82]

(4) Training of Workers

In a world economy characterized by increased industrial restructuring, training issues acquire an importance far greater than before. The ILO Declaration encourages governments to develop national policies for vocational training and guidance, closely linked with employment.[83] MNEs are encouraged to ensure that relevant training is provided for all levels of employees in the host country to meet the needs of the enterprise as well as the development policies of the country. This should develop generally useful skills and promote career opportunities.[84] Furthermore, in developing countries, MNEs should participate in special programmes aimed at encouraging skill formation and development.[85] The OECD Employment Guideline provides for much the same approach. It states that MNEs, '[i]n their operations, to the greatest extent practicable, employ local personnel and provide training with a view to improving skill levels, in co-operation with employee representatives and, where appropriate, relevant governmental authorities'.[86]

National training schemes will apply to MNEs and national enterprises without distinction. However, MNEs may offer special skills based on their international experience.[87] Thus they may be expected to provide greater assistance, particularly in developing countries. This may be reflected in incentive schemes whereby the host country will subsidize firm based training.[88] MNEs have been criticized for aiming their main training effort at their own needs rather than those of developing countries.[89] They are likely to be reluctant to invest in training if they cannot earn a sufficient return and a large part of their effort then passes to other firms. Such concerns can be overcome through devices such as loyalty bonuses for employees to stay on after completing their training and promotion incentives.[90] Equally as skill

---

[81] Directive 2001/23/EC above n 75 art 7.

[82] *Katsikas v Konstantinidis* Case C–132/91 [1993] 1 CMLR 845 (ECJ).

[83] ILO Declaration para 29 and Convention No 142 and Recommendation No 150 concerning Vocational Guidance and Vocational Training in the Development of Human Resources.

[84] ibid para 30.   [85] ibid para 31.

[86] OECD Employment Guideline above n 1 at para 5.

[87] See JH Dunning *Multinational Enterprises and the Global Economy* (Wokingham: Addison Wesley, 1993) at 372–75.

[88] One example is the Penang (Malaysia) Skills Development Centre (PSDC) launched in 1989 as a joint venture between the local university and a number of US electronics firms. Other firms followed and the scheme became mainly privately funded. Similar schemes have since been set up by the Malaysian Government in other regions: *World Investment Report 1999* above n 38 at 276–77.

[89] See Lemoine above n 10 at 25. See further ILO *Technology Choice and Employment Generation by Multinational Enterprises in Developing Countries* (Geneva: 1984).

[90] See *World Investment Report 1999* above n 38 at 274.

levels of employees become increasingly important in information based industries firms may need to engage in active training to remain competitive.[91]

(5) Conditions of Work and Life

The ILO Declaration divides the issues under this heading between wages, benefits, and conditions of work, minimum age and safety, and health matters. The OECD Employment Guideline says little on the first set of issues, simply asserting that MNEs should observe standards of employment not less favourable than those observed by comparable employers in the host country.[92] The second set of issues is expressly referred to in paragraph 1(b) of the guidelines which asserts that enterprises should 'contribute to the effective abolition of child labour'. Safety and health issues are covered in the OECD Environment Guideline, which is discussed in chapter 14 below.[93]

(a) Wages, Benefits, and Conditions of Work

Like the OECD Guideline, the ILO Declaration applies the national treatment standard to these matters. Thus:

Wages, benefits and conditions of work offered by multinational enterprises should be not less favourable to the workers than those offered by comparable employers in the country concerned.[94]

When operating in developing countries, where comparable employers may not exist, MNEs should provide the 'best possible wages, benefits and conditions of work, within the framework of government policies'.[95] These should be related to the 'economic position of the enterprise, but should be at least adequate to satisfy basic needs of the workers and their families'.[96] Where MNEs provide workers with basic amenities such as housing, medical care or food, these should be of a good standard.[97] Finally, the declaration exhorts governments, especially in

---

[91] ibid.   [92] OECD Employment Guideline above n 1 para 4(a).

[93] See ch 14 at 564–65.

[94] ILO Declaration above n 2 at para 33. In the *Warner Lambert* case, the OECD Committee on Multinational Enterprises held that the national treatment standard did not exclude the possibility that, temporarily and under exceptional circumstances, agreement may be reached on wages less favourable than those observed by comparable employers in host countries. The MNE concerned should in good faith aim at restoring wages to the national standard as soon as the specific circumstances which gave rise to such agreement no longer persisted: Blanpain above n 15 vol I at 217–18; Robinson above n 9 at 131.

[95] ibid para 34 and Recommendation No.116 concerning Reduction of Hours of Work.

[96] ibid.

[97] ibid and Convention No 110 and Recommendation No 110 concerning Conditions of Employment of Plantation Workers; Recommendation No 115 concerning Workers' Housing; Recommendation No 69 concerning Medical Care; Convention No 130 and Recommendation No 134 concerning Medical Care and Sickness.

developing countries, to endeavour to adopt suitable measures to ensure that lower income groups and less developed areas benefit as much as possible from the activities of MNEs.[98]

Thus, the declaration does not prevent MNEs from moving their operations to lower wage areas if they so choose. It preserves the ability of MNEs to scan investment locations for lower cost operating bases. All that is required is that the firm does not fall below the national treatment standard in the host state. In its 1986 review of the declaration, the ILO Committee on Multinational Enterprises found that MNEs offered wages, benefits, and conditions of work equal or comparable to those offered by local employers and, in some cases, generally superior to local terms and conditions. It found that MNEs paid according to what they could afford rather than by reference to the local labour market and local standards of living, while the payment of better than average wages depended on the technology, marketing, and competitive skills of the given firm.[99] This conclusion was confirmed by Dunning who shows that MNE affiliates may often offer higher wages, particularly for skilled workers, and that most MNEs offer world-standard working practices, which may be better than the local average.[100] However, as Dunning points out, 'it is not normally in the interest of MNEs to provide better working conditions than those necessary to ensure economic success. Consequently, they will usually be fairly close to the norm for the particular country or industry'.[101]

The approach of a MNE to wages, benefits, and conditions will depend considerably on its 'management culture'. A firm may wish to act as a 'model employer' and unilaterally monitor, if not raise, standards. This policy is not without its pitfalls. These are well illustrated by the stand of the jeans manufacturer, Levi Strauss, on workers' rights in the host countries where it seeks to operate.[102] This company was the first to adopt strict ethical guidelines covering the 'terms of engagement' that its overseas sub-contractors have to meet in order to obtain business from the company.[103] The guidelines cover environmental requirements, health and safety

---

[98] ibid para 35.

[99] See Lemoine above n 10 at 25. A recent survey by the ILO shows that MNEs pay significantly more than domestic firms in Indonesia. During the period under study (1990–1999) wage premiums for unskilled workers were in the range of 5 per cent to 10 per cent while for skilled workers they were between 20 per cent and 35 per cent. See Ann E Harrison and Jason Scorse *Do Foreign Firms Pay More? Evidence from the Indonesian Manufacturing Sector 1990–1999* (Geneva: International Labour Office, Working Paper No 98, 2005) available at <http://www.ilo.org/public/english/employment/multi/download/wp98.pdf>.   [100] See Dunning above n 87 at 375–77, 381–82.

[101] ibid at 377.

[102] See Levi Strauss & Co *Global Sourcing and Operating Guidelines* available at <http://www.levistrauss.com/Downloads/GSOG.pdf>.

[103] See further, on corporate codes of conduct, OECD Working Party of the Trade Committee *Codes of Corporate Conduct: An Inventory* (OECD Doc TD/TC/WP(98)74/FINAL 3 May 1999) available at <http://www.olis.oecd.org/olis/1998doc.nsf/c16431e1b3f24c0ac12569fa005d1d99/c125692700622425c12569a40038da6c/$FILE/04E95110.pdf> UNCTAD *World Investment Report 1994* (New York and Geneva: United nations, 1994) at 320–39; UNCTAD *World Investment Report 1999* above n 38 at 360–65; UNCTAD *Social Responsibility* Series on issues in international investment

standards, and employment practices. Levi-Strauss will not allow sub-contractors to employ child or prison labour, working hours must not exceed 60 per week and wages must at least meet local standards. Since the adoption of these standards the company withdrew from Burma (Myanmar), and refused to invest in China. In Bangladesh, the company has had to compromise on the issue of child labour. It decided not to close down its factories, despite the employment of child labourers, as the children were the sole source of income for their families, and would not find alternative employment. Accordingly, the company ensured that sub-contractors would pay full wages to the children if they attended school up to the age of 14, whereupon they could then work full-time in the sub-contractors' factories. The company would pay for their tuition, books, and uniforms.[104] In Mexico, in 2003, the company was involved in a dispute with one of its suppliers, over breaches of fundamental labour rights guaranteed under Mexican law. This ended in the supplier refusing to accept any further business from Levi Strauss, who, in turn raised the issue with the local authorities and with other manufacturers who did business with the Mexican supplier. Levi Strauss stated that it would no longer offer any further business to the supplier.[105]

(b) Minimum Age

This section of the ILO Declaration was inserted by the 2000 revision so as to incorporate ILO Conventions No 138 on Minimum Age and No 182, the Convention on the Prohibition and Immediate Elimination of the Worst Forms of Child Labour.[106] The ILO Declaration asserts that, '[m]ultinational enterprises, as well as national enterprises, should respect the minimum age for admission to employment or work in order to secure the effective abolition of child labour'.[107]

---

agreements (New York and Geneva: United Nations, 2001) at 37–40; Hepple above n 6 ch 3; Rhys Jenkins 'Corporate Codes of Conduct: Self-Regulation in a Global Economy' in UN Non-Governmental Liaison Service (NGLS) *Voluntary Approaches to Corporate Responsibility: Readings and a Resource Guide* (New York and Geneva: UNNGLS, 2002) 1; Harry Arthurs 'Private Ordering and Workers' Rights in the Global Economy: Corporate Codes of Conduct as a Regime of Labour Market Regulation' in Joanne Conaghan, Richard Michael Fischl, and Karl Klare (eds) *Labour Law in and Era of Globalization: Transformative Practices and Possibilities* (Oxford: Oxford University Press, paperback edn, 2004) 471; Bob Hepple 'A Race to the Top? International Investment Guidelines and Corporate Codes of Conduct' 20 Comp.Labour Law & Pol'y Journal 347 (1999).

[104] See Levi Strauss & Co *Case Study – Child Labour in Bangladesh* available at <http://www.levistrauss.com/Downloads/CaseStudyBangladesh.pdf>.

[105] See Ethical Trading Initiative *Addressing Labour Rights Violations at Tarrant Ajalpan, Mexico, using the Ethical Trading Initiatives Complaints Procedure* (May 2004) available at <http://www.eti2.org.uk/Z/lib/2004/05/codeviol-mex/ETI-tarrant-summ.pdf>.

[106] ILO Convention Concerning the Prohibition and Immediate Elimination of the Worst Forms of Child Labour, 17 June 1999: 38 ILM 1207 (1999) or <http://www.ilo.org/ilolex/english/convdisp2.htm>; ILO Recommendation Concerning the Prohibition and Immediate Elimination of the Worst Forms of Child Labour, 17 June 1999: 38 ILM 1211 (1999) or ILO website at <http://www.ilo.org/ilolex/english/recdisp2.htm>. [107] ILO Declaration above n 2 at para 36.

The wording refers only to 'child labour' while Convention 182 deals only with the 'worst forms of child labour'. This is defined as comprising:

(a) all forms of slavery or practices similar to slavery, such as the sale and trafficking of children, debt bondage and serfdom and forced or compulsory labour, including forced or compulsory recruitment of children for use in armed conflict;

(b) the use, procuring or offering of a child for prostitution, for the production of pornography or for pornographic performances;

(c) the use, procuring or offering of a child for illicit activities, in particular for the production and trafficking of drugs as defined in the relevant international treaties;

(d) work which, by its nature or the circumstances in which it is carried out, is likely to harm the health, safety or morals of children.[108]

This list suggests certain types of work that major MNEs, in reputable industries, are very unlikely to expect children to perform, though it is not impossible that their sub-contractors might, for example, employ debt bonded child labourers. The one area that may be of direct relevance is the reference to health and safety in (d). Thus the convention does not really help to enlighten the meaning of the ILO Declaration in this regard. It would appear that the ILO Declaration, read literally, means that MNEs must abolish *all* labour of persons under the legal minimum age for work in the host country. The OECD Guideline urges enterprises to contribute to the effective abolition of child labour and refers to Convention 182 in the Commentary.[109] The actual contribution of MNEs to this goal is expressed through the creation of high quality, well paid jobs and raising the standards of education of children living in host countries. Such a commitment could also be read into the ILO Declaration, given the complementary nature of the two codes.

(c) Safety and Health

The ILO Declaration urges governments that have not already done so to ratify ILO conventions in this field,[110] while MNEs are required to maintain the 'highest standards of safety and health, in conformity with national requirements, bearing in mind their relevant experience within the enterprise as a whole, including any knowledge of special hazards'.[111] Furthermore, MNEs should make available information on safety and health standards relevant to their local operations,

---

[108] ILO Convention No 182 above n 106 art 3.

[109] OECD Guideline above n 1 para I(b) and Commentary para 22.

[110] ILO Declaration above n 2 para 37 which specifically refers to Conventions No 119 on Guarding of Machinery, No 115 on Ionizing Radiation, No 136 on Benzene, and No 139 on Occupational Cancer. See also the further conventions and associated recommendations listed in Addendum I to the ILO Declaration, most of which apply to para 37. Para 37 adds that the ILO codes of practice and guides in the current list of publications on occupational health and safety should also be taken into account. See further *Catalogue of ILO Publications on Occupational Safety and Health* available at <http://www.ilo.org/public/english/protection/safework/publicat/iloshcat/index.htm>.

[111] ibid para 38.

which they observe in other countries, to workers' representatives in the enterprise and, upon request, to the competent authorities and to workers' and employers' organizations in the countries in which they operate.[112] In particular, special hazards and related protective measures associated with new products and processes should be made known to those concerned.[113] This part of the declaration ends with exhortations to MNEs to cooperate in the work of international organizations in the preparation of international safety and health standards,[114] and with national authorities, representatives of workers' organizations and specialist safety and health organizations.[115] Where appropriate, matters relating to safety and health should be incorporated into agreements with workers' representatives and their organizations.[116]

These provisions of the ILO Declaration relate to a matter of recent concern regarding the operations of MNEs. There is evidence that MNEs can export hazardous operations to developing countries where more lenient health and safety standards apply.[117] As noted in chapter 6 above, the problem of attracting investment to a location on the basis of lower labour and environmental standards was an issue in the negotiations leading to NAFTA, especially in relation to Mexico.[118] Furthermore, there is evidence suggesting that safety standards at Union Carbide's pesticides plant at Bhopal were very low, and may have been a significant contributing factor to the catastrophe of 1984.[119] On the other hand, in the 1986 review of the declaration, the ILO Committee stated that in most cases MNEs were found to comply satisfactorily with health and safety standards and in some cases played a leading role in setting standards.[120] It is clear that practice varies from firm to firm. Thus, in an ILO study of 1984 into the health and safety policies of eight MNEs, it was found that some firms controlled their foreign affiliates very closely while others exercised little or no control at all.[121]

The declaration suggests that all firms should standardize their health and safety operations to the firm's best practice, through intra firm exchanges of information. However, it stops short of requiring the establishment of managerial structures that would oversee this policy. In that respect the declaration may fall short of the practice adopted by the best firms. Furthermore, the declaration is weak on the responsibility of host state governments in this field. Ultimately, the

---

[112] ibid.   [113] ibid.   [114] ibid para 39.   [115] ibid para 40.   [116] ibid.

[117] See BI Castleman 'Workplace Health Standards and Multinational Corporations in Developing Countries' in C Pearson (ed) *Multinational Corporations, Environment and the Third World: Business Matters* (Duke University Press, 1987) 149. See further ch 14 below on the 'pollution havens' hypothesis.

[118] See ch 6 at 241. See further S Zamora 'The Americanisation of Mexican Law: Non-Trade Issues in the North American Free Trade Agreement' 24 Law & Pol'y.Int'l Bus. 391 (1993).

[119] See T Gladwin 'A Case Study of the Bhopal Tragedy' in C Pearson (ed) above n 117, 223 at 229–30.

[120] Lemoine above n 10 at 25.

[121] ILO *Safety and Health Practices of Multinational Enterprises* (Geneva: ILO, 1984) especially 28–42 (covering: BASF AG, Royal Dutch/Shell, Merck & Co Inc, Bechtel Companies, BICC Group, Volkswagenwerk AG, Xerox Corp, and Brown Boveri & Co).

development of adequate safety and health standards falls on the local authorities. They should not avoid this by passing the problem over to MNEs alone, or by resting on the ratification of ILO conventions without giving full effect to them in domestic law. Developing countries may argue that their limited resources prevent the operation of effective policies in these areas. That should not act as an excuse for inaction, but as a spur for greater international cooperation in this field.

(6) Industrial Relations

The ILO Declaration deals with five issues under this heading: freedom of association and the right to organize, collective bargaining, consultation, examination of grievances, and the settlement of industrial disputes. Each area is subject to the overriding general principle of national treatment in that 'multinational enterprises should observe standards of industrial relations not less favourable than those observed by comparable employers in the country concerned'.[122] The OECD Employment Guideline contains the same general principle.[123] National treatment leaves much to the discretion of the host government in the conduct of its industrial relations policy. Although recommended to observe the standards in the ILO Declaration, there is no legally binding international sanction should the host state fail to do so.[124] This considerably weakens the standard-setting function of the two codes. It is against this background that the ILO Declaration and OECD Guideline should be examined.

(a) Freedom of Association and the Right to Organize

In accordance with the most central guiding policy of the ILO, the ILO Declaration recognizes the right of workers to establish and to join organizations of their own choosing without previous authorization, and to enjoy adequate protection against anti-union discrimination in respect of their employment.[125] This right has the

---

[122] ILO Declaration above n 2 at para 41.

[123] OECD Employment Guideline above n 1 at para 4(a).

[124] See, for example, the UK's apparent disregard for ILO Convention No 87 on Freedom of Association and for the subsequent ILO Committee of Experts' Report of 1992 criticizing the UK on this matter: Brown and McColgan above n 6 and see further Keith Ewing *Britain and the ILO* (London: Institute of Employment Rights, 2nd edn, 1994). The UK strike laws remain inconsistent with ILO standards as the Labour government of 1997 did not repeal the Conservative reforms: Hepple above n 6 at 38. On the other hand, past complaints against Malaysia appear to have had more effect: see A Wangel 'The ILO and Protection of Trade Union Rights: The Electronics Industry in Malaysia' in R Southall (ed) *Trade Unions and the New Industrialisation of the Third World* (London: Zed Books, 1988) 287.

[125] ILO Declaration para 42 and Convention No 87 art 2, Convention No 98 art 1(1). The establishment, functioning, and administration of such organizations should not be interfered with by other organizations whether representing MNEs or workers in their employment: ibid para 43.

status of a fundamental human right. Thus, Article 22(1) of the International Covenant on Civil and Political Rights 1966 states:[126]

Everyone shall have the right to freedom of association with others, including the right to form and join trade unions for the protection of his interests.

Article 22(2) enumerates certain public interest exceptions to this principle. These must be prescribed by law and be necessary in a democratic society for the protection of those interests. However, Article 22(3) stresses:

Nothing in this article shall authorise States Parties to the International Labour Organisation Convention of 1948 concerning Freedom of Association and Protection of the Right to Organize to take legislative measures that would prejudice, or apply the law in such a manner as to prejudice, the guarantees provided for in that Convention.

This right is addressed primarily to states. As such MNEs are not the object of the right. It is for the government of the host state to ensure that the freedom of association is observed in law and in fact.[127] It is for the MNE to observe the law of the land. However, foreign firms may be in a position to take the lead in the removal of restrictions over the freedom of association, by encouraging trade unions in their plants, and by defending their right to exist. Again, the prevalent 'management culture' will be decisive. On the other hand, the incidence of non-unionized MNEs is growing, as technological change and the growth in service over manufacturing industries continue to erode the traditional base for mass trade unionism.[128] Thus the role of trade unions may itself be changing in ways that the declaration has not contemplated.

The ILO Declaration goes on to enumerate certain specific policies that governments should and should not follow in the furtherance of the freedom of association. On the positive side, governments are encouraged, first, to ensure that workers in MNEs are not hindered in meeting and consulting with one another.[129] Secondly, they should not restrict the entry of representatives of workers' and employers' organizations from other countries.[130] Thirdly, governments should permit workers' and employers' organizations which represent, respectively, the

---

[126] 999 UNTS 171, UKTS 6 (1977) Cmnd, 6702 61 AJIL 870 (1967). See also European Convention on Human Rights 1950 art 11.

[127] See further the reports of the ILO Committee on Freedom of Association for regular reviews of Member's practices in this area at <http://www.ilo.org/ilolex/english/cfarepsq.htm>. See also the ILO Digest of Decisions and Principles of the Freedom of Association Committee available at <http://www.ilo.org/ilolex/english/digestq.htm>.

[128] See Van Tulde and Junne above n 40 at 121–23; ILO *World Labour Report 1997–98* (Geneva: 1998) available at <http://www.ilo.org/public/english/dialogue/ifpdial/publ/wlr97/> which notes a general decline in union membership. A more recent survey was undertaken for 23 EU Member States, two prospective Members and Norway between 1993 and 2003. It found increased membership in smaller European countries and a continuing trend of decreasing numbers in the major countries and in the former Eastern Bloc Members, where membership has declined by some 60–70 per cent see European Foundation for the Improvement of Living and Working Conditions *Trade Union Membership 1993–2003* available at <http://www.eiro.eurofound.eu.int/2004/03/update/tn0403105u.html>.

[129] ILO Declaration above n 2 at para 47.   [130] ibid para 48.

workers and the MNEs in which they work, to affiliate with international organizations of workers and employers of their choosing. This may be of importance in relation to the development of international collective bargaining, as it accepts the legitimacy of entering organizational structures that can facilitate this.[131] Indeed, the OECD Employment Guideline includes, among 'other bona fide organisations of employees' International Trade Secretariats as a body entitled to represent workers.[132]

International Trade Secretariats represent affiliated national unions in the same, or similar, industries. They can offer coordinating facilities for the exchange of information and, in exceptional cases, they have acted as the organizers of international industrial action. The most notable example has been the campaign organized, since 1948, by the International Transport Workers' Federation (ITF) against the use of 'flag-of-convenience' (FOC) vessels as a means of circumventing labour standards for seamen.[133] Although not involving MNEs as such, the campaign offers a useful insight into the legal environment surrounding international industrial action, as it has resulted in litigation in numerous jurisdictions. The campaign is aimed at the improvement of the terms of employment for crews serving on FOC vessels that do not respect the terms recommended by the ITF. When a FOC vessel suspected of violating ITF terms enters a port, the ITF will request the locally affiliated docker's union to engage in sympathy action by 'blacking' the vessel. The local union members may refuse to load or unload the vessel, or to allow it to leave port, until the owner agrees to enter into an agreement regarding the crews' terms of employment that conforms to ITF standards.

Many cases have been brought in an attempt to stop such sympathy action. The response of the courts has depended on the attitude of the relevant national law to international sympathy action.[134] Thus, US courts have held that such action did not come within the National Labor Relations Act, even when the foreign ship

---

[131] On international collective bargaining, see further KW Wedderburn 'Multinational Labour Law' 1 ILJ 12 (1972); Roberts 'Multinational Collective Bargaining: a European Prospect?' 9 Brit.J.Ind.Rel. 1 (1973); HR Northrup and RL Rowan *Multinational Collective Bargaining Attempts* (Philadelphia: Industrial Research Unit, Wharton School, 1979); Northrup, Campbell, and Slowinski 'Multinational Union-Management Consultation in Europe: Resurgence in the 1980s?' 127 Int'l Lab.Rev. 525 (1988); W Cooke 'Exercising Power in a Prisoner's Dilemma: Transnational Collective Bargaining in an Era of Corporate Globalisation?' 36 Industrial Relations Journal 283 (2005); P Marginson and K Sisson 'European Dimensions to Collective Bargaining: New Symmetries within Asymmetric Processes?' 33 Industrial Relations Journal 332 (2002); L Turner and M Gordon *Transnational Cooperation among Labor Unions* (Ithaca: Cornell University Press, 2000).

[132] OECD Employment Guideline above n 1 at para 1(a) as interpreted in the 1986 Review of the OECD Guidelines (Paris: OECD, 1986) para 56 at 32. See also Blanpain above n 15 vol I at 186–87; OECD Working Party above n 14 at 21.

[133] See the ITF website at <http://www.itfglobal.org/flags-convenience/index.cfm>, the annual FOC Campaign Reports (2004 Report available for download at <http://www.itfglobal.org/files/seealsodocs/ENG/1324/FOCREPORT.pdf>, and issues of the *Seafarer's Bulletin* for more recent news. See also, for historical background, Northrup and Rowan above n 131 ch 27.

[134] See Paul Davies 'Labour Law and Multinational Groups of Companies' in Klaus Hopt (ed) *Legal and Economic Analysis of Multinational Enterprises Vol II* (Berlin: De Gruyter, 1982) from 208 especially 216–22.

was berthed in a US port, as the activities of the foreign shipowner did not affect commerce between states as federal law required. Under US law, the international dimension of the dispute was enough to remove the protection afforded to sympathy action under the law.[135] In the UK, ITF sympathy action has been treated in accordance with the applicable national law relating to such action. No distinction has been made between domestic and international sympathy action. Up to 1980, most kinds of sympathy action were held to be covered by the statutory immunity for industrial action in the Trade Union and Labour Relations Act 1974.[136] In 1980, with the accession of the Conservative government to power, statutory restrictions were placed on secondary action, motivated to a considerable extent by a desire to control the ITF campaign. This led to court decisions that restricted the rights of national unions to engage in sympathy action as part of the ITF campaign.[137] More recently the ITF campaign has been challenged by shipowners invoking the right of establishment under Article 43 of the EC Treaty. At first instance, the Commercial Court awarded an injunction to restrain possible strike action against a shipping company that proposed to re-flag its Finnish owned vessel to Estonia. It held that such industrial action could infringe Article 43 as it impaired the shipping line's right of establishment in Estonia after that country had acceded to the EU. The Court of Appeal overturned the injunction and has requested a ruling on this issue from the ECJ.[138] Under Dutch law a strike of crew members on a Saudi Arabian ship that was supported by the ITF was held unlawful as the crewmen's contracts of employment were governed by Philippine law, which rendered the strike unlawful.[139] Only under Swedish law has the ITF action been treated preferentially.[140] Most national laws will not offer such protection.[141]

---

[135] See cases cited by Davies ibid at 216 n 22.

[136] See *Camelia Tanker SA v ITF* [1976] ICR 274 (CA); *NWL v Woods* [1979] ICR 867 (HL); Davies ibid at 219.

[137] Employment Act 1980 s 17 as interpreted in *Merkur Island Shipping v Laughton* [1983] 2 All ER 189 (HL); for criticism, see Wedderburn 46 MLR 632 (1983). See now Trade Union and Labour Relations (Consolidation) Act 1992 s 224. ITF action has also been caught under the common law of economic duress, which will apply to any contract whose proper law is English law: *Universe Tankships of Monrovia v ITF 'The Universe Sentinel'* [1983] 1 AC 366, [1982] 2 All ER 67 (HL); *Dimskal Shipping Co SA v ITF 'The Evia Luck'* [1991] 4 All ER 871, [1992] 2 Lloyd's Rep 115 (HL). ITF action has been caught under the Trade Union Act 1984 which requires a ballot of the members of a union before a lawful strike can be called. See now Trade Union and Labour Relations (Consolidation) Act 1992 ss 226–34. The workers engaging directly in ITF 'blacking' action have normally been only members of their national union and not of the ITF. The ITF could not, therefore, hold a lawful ballot of the membership and any action ordered by the ITF would be unlawful: *Shipping Co Uniform Inc v ITF Allen Ross & Davies 'The Uniform Star'* [1985] 1 Lloyd's Rep 173 (QBD). The ITF has to ensure, by a change to its rules, that members of affiliated national unions are automatically members of the ITF for the purposes of lawful balloting. More recently the EC Treaty rules on rights of establishment have been used to obtain an injunction against possible blacking action.

[138] *Viking Line v International Transport Workers Federation and Another* [2005] 2 CMLR 764 (QBD, Comm Ct) overruled [2006] 1 CMLR 693 (CA).

[139] *The Saudi Independence* (Hoge Raad, 1983) noted in 16 Jo.Mart.L.& Com. 423 (1985).

[140] See Davies above n 34 at 221–22.

[141] See further James Atleson 'The Voyage of the *Neptune Jade*: Transnational Labour Solidarity and the Obstacles of Domestic Law' in Conaghan, Fischl, and Klare (eds) above n 103 at 379.

From the above examples, it can be seen that international sympathy action can be easily prevented through national laws. The secondary action need only be made unlawful under the law of the place where it occurs, regardless of the legality of the primary action. Apart from such legal obstacles, international trade union action faces serious obstacles in the form of: the relative weakness of International Trade Secretariats as conduits for such action; the often significant differences in policies and objectives among national trade union organizations, which may make agreement on an international strategy in alliance with other national organizations impossible; the differences in real interests between groups of workers in the various national affiliates of MNEs, resulting in competition for jobs between them (most obviously between higher and lower paid employees in different countries or regions); and, finally, the reluctance of MNE management to abandon local level bargaining in favour of international negotiations.[142]

Such transnational industrial relations activities as do occur are most likely within relatively homogeneous labour markets and economies. European initiatives in this area are significant. For example, the adoption of the European Works Council Directive, discussed in chapter 9, has introduced an organizational structure into MNEs capable of adaptation into a forum for collective bargaining on an MNE-wide basis, although it must be stressed that this is not the avowed aim of the directive.[143] Equally, European Monetary Union has encouraged an increasing convergence, led by the trade union side, in Europe-wide collective bargaining in certain sectors, notably automobile production, but this is offset in part by greater company driven local level bargaining both in this sector and in others.[144] On the other hand, inter-regional collective bargaining between MNEs and transnational labour unions remains an ideal that has little prospect of turning into reality, unless and until a more homogeneous global economy and society evolves.[145]

---

[142] See further Northrup and Rowan above n 131 at ch 2; Enderwick 'The Labour Utilisation Practices of Multinationals and Obstacles to Multinational Collective Bargaining' 26 Jo.Ind.Rel. 345 (1984).   [143] See further ch 9 at 354–57.

[144] See Marginson and Sisson above n 131. Of particular note is the initiative of the European Metalworkers Federation (EMF) which has, since 1998, established cross-border collective bargaining partnerships. According to the EMF: 'The first stage of setting up these partnerships is now almost completed. Regional partnerships have been created all over Europe and the participation of observers and the exchange of data and information have become a daily routine. It should be noted in particular that these partnerships do not only focus on collective bargaining issues alone but increasingly also on concrete issues with regard to company-cross-border support. Reporting in the Collective Bargaining Committee should also devote more attention to these partnerships in the future.' The EMF cross-border collective bargaining partnerships (as of July 2006): Belgium, the Netherlands, Luxemburg, Germany-North Rhine-Westphalia; Denmark, Sweden and Germany-Coast district; France and Germany-Frankfurt; Austria, Slovenia, Czech Republic, Slovakia, Hungary, Germany-Bavaria; Switzerland and Germany-Baden Württemberg. See <http://www.emf-fem.org/areas_of_work/collective_bargaining_policy/cross_border_collective_bargaining_partnerships>.

[145] The ideal of transnational trade unionism was a major feature of writings emanating from trade unionists and their supporters in the early 1970s. See, for example, UK Trades Union Congress *International Companies* (London: 1970); C Levinson *International Trade Unionism* (London: George Allen & Unwin, 1974); KW Wedderburn 'Industrial Relations' in HR Hahlo, J Graham Smith, and

On the negative side, governments are urged not to offer any limitation of the workers' freedom of association, or of the right to organize and bargain collectively, as special incentives to attract foreign investment. Thus, the ILO Declaration exhorts governments not to engage in a 'race to the bottom' over trade union rights. However, as noted in the introduction to this section, there is nothing in the declaration to prevent states from doing just that. Furthermore, MNEs need do no more than follow the policy of the host state. Consequently, a firm may acquiesce to repressive labour laws and standards of treatment if it so wishes. Again, as with the matter of employment conditions, much depends on the firm's 'management culture',[146] and on whether the firm can withstand the possible economic losses that a 'model' industrial relations strategy might entail. Indeed, competitive pressures have often been invoked as the reason why a MNE might disinvest if its plant[s] in a host state were to become unionized. In response, certain governments, especially in developing countries that are dependent on export orientated foreign investment, have sought to restrict trade union rights by law.[147] This has led to accusations that some states practice 'social dumping' as an economic policy, in that they seek to compete in the international economy by subsidizing international producers to locate on their territory by offering lower wages and working conditions coupled with controls over trade unions.

This accusation has not been confined to developing countries. In Europe, the UK has been accused of this practice by other EC Member States, who point in evidence to the UK's original reluctance to support the Social Provisions of the Maastricht Treaty. Some further support for this view can be gathered from the ILO Committee's observations on UK labour law reforms in 1992, when it found that the UK had not observed the terms of ILO Conventions on Freedom of Association.[148] However, according to Dunning, 'throughout the 1970s, the poor industrial relations environment in the UK led some UK- and foreign-based MNEs to eschew new production facilities in the UK. By contrast, in the 1980s and early 1990s, foreign firms have responded to dramatic improvement in this

---

RW Wright *Nationalism and the Multinational Enterprise* (Leiden: Sijthoff, 1977) 244. The OECD Committee on Multinational Enterprises has declined to say that the Employment Guideline sanctions international collective bargaining, given that it is virtually non-existent in practice: *International Metalworkers' Federation* case: Blanpain above n 15 vol I at 187–91.

[146] For example, Japanese firms tend to prefer single-union arrangements, as at the Nissan plant in Sunderland, while many US firms follow a non-union approach, such as IBM or McDonald's. In Europe, the latter has evolved effective management systems to limit the impact of national and European regulation on worker participation: see Tony Royle 'Just Vote No! Union-busting in the European Fast Food Industry: The Case of McDonald's' 33 Industrial Relations Journal 262 (2002).

[147] See Barnard 'Labor Law in Malaysia: A Capitalist Device to Exploit Third World Workers' 23 Law & Pol'y Int'l Bus. 415 (1991–92).

[148] See Brown and McColgan above n 6. The Trade Union Reform and Employment Rights Act 1993 was held by the ILO to include several provisions that violated ILO conventions on the freedom of association: 'ILO rebukes Britain over unfair trade union pay rules' *The Guardian* 25 June 1994 at 6. See further Simpson 22 ILJ 181 (1993); S Auerbach *Derecognition and Personal Contracts: Fighting Tactics and the Law* (Institute of Employment Rights, 1993).

environment by favouring the UK for their EC-based operations'.[149] Thus 'social dumping' appears to have benefited the UK in the short term. On the other hand, in an economic downturn, it will be easier to make UK workers redundant, which might lead to more plant closures than in EC Member States espousing stronger employee protection.[150] Furthermore, the Southern Member States and Eastern European states may be able to offer still lower wages and working conditions than the UK.[151] Thus 'social dumping' may backfire on a country espousing this policy. It may also lead to social unrest as workers in economically successful countries that repress labour rights demand a fuller share of the resulting wealth. This has been the case, for example, in Korea and Malaysia in past years.[152]

A further factor that may discourage 'social dumping' is the possibility of economic retaliation by countries whose business and employment prospects are threatened by it. For example, the US retains powers to deny to developing countries trading privileges under the Generalized System of Preferences (GSP) if they have not taken steps to afford internationally recognized workers' rights to workers' in the country, including any designated zone in that country, or to implement its commitments to abolish the worst forms of child labour.[153] However, in

---

[149] Above n 87 at 352.

[150] See David Goodhart 'Social Dumping: Hardly An Open and Shut Case' *Financial Times* 4 February 1993 at 2. The announcement, in April 2006, by Peugeot SA (PSA) of the closure of its UK plant at Ryton is a case in point. According to James Arrowsmith of the Industrial Relations Research Unit, Warwick Business School, 'The unions ... criticised the government for what they claimed to be inadequate employment protection laws. The General Secretary of Amicus, Derek Simpson, noted: "it is inconceivable that workers in France would be laid off on this scale. Weak UK labour laws are allowing British workers to be sacrificed at the expense of a flexible labour market ... Job protection similar to that enjoyed by workers in France would give British employees the opportunity to compete for investment and work on important issues like productivity and efficiency." According to the London law firm Clifford Chance, the cost of shutting a major factory in France could be almost three times as much as in Britain because of French legal requirements for a "social plan". However, PSA Chief Executive, Jean-Martin Folz, insisted that the decision had nothing to do with British or French employment law, but with the costs of running the plant.' See James Arrowsmith 'Peugeot announces closure of Coventry plant' (European Foundation for the Improvement of Living and Working Conditions, May 2006) available at <http://www.eiro.eurofound.eu.int/about/2006/05/articles/uk0605029i.html>.

[151] On North-South employment issues in the EC, see P Buckley and P Artisien *North-South Direct Investment in the European Communities* (MacMillan, 1987). The ILO hopes that the Tripartite Declaration will help improve working conditions and trade union activities in Eastern Europe. See R Morawetz *Recent Foreign Direct Investment in Eastern Europe: Towards a Possible Role for the Tripartite Declaration of Principles Concerning Multinational Enterprises and Social Policy* (Geneva: ILO 1991). See further D Vaughan-Whitehead *EU Enlargement versus Social Europe? The Uncertain Future of the European Social Model* (Edward Elgar Publishing, 2003) and 'The Next Investment Wave: Companies in East and West Prepare for the Risks and Opportunities of an Enlarged EU' *Financial Times* 27 April 2004 at 17.

[152] On Malaysia, see Barnard above n 147 and on both Malaysia and Korea see ILO *World Labour Report 1993* (Geneva: 1993) at 51.

[153] 19 USC s 2462(b)(2)(G) and (H) available at <http://www.ustr.gov/assets/Trade_Development/Preference_Programs/GSP/asset_upload_file151_8358.pdf>. The US has prohibited public bodies to acquire the products of child labour: see Executive Order 13126 of 12 June 1999 Federal Register: 16 June 1999 [Volume 64, Number 115] [Presidential Documents] [Page 32383–32385] available at the Federal Register Online via GPO Access <http://www.wais.access.gpo.gov> [DOCID: fr16jn99–137].

recent years this power has not been systematically used. This resulted in an unsuccessful lawsuit being brought by US labour unions and human rights groups against former President Bush Snr.[154] Indeed, the President retains a discretion to allow for preferential treatment even if the labour standards provisions are not met if, 'the President determines that such designation will be in the national economic interest of the United States and reports such determination to Congress with the reasons therefor'.[155] Further powers for retaliation were made available to the US Government under s 301 of the Trade Act 1974 as amended in 1988.[156] This empowers the US Trade Representative (USTR) to take action against a country which is found to pursue policies or practices that 'constitute a persistent pattern of conduct denying internationally recognised worker rights, unless the USTR determines the foreign country has taken or is taking actions that demonstrate a significant and tangible overall advancement in providing those rights and standards throughout the country or such acts, policies, or practices are not inconsistent with the level of economic development of the country'.[157] Again, strong enforcement is unlikely given the wide qualifications attached to these statutory powers.[158] Equally, unilateral import bans such as those envisaged under s 301 may fall foul of WTO obligations under the GATT unless it can be shown that they come within one of the exceptions listed in Article XX.[159] In this regard it is noteworthy that the adoption by Congress of the Burma Freedom and Democracy Act in 2003, which banned all trade with Burma, was not challenged at the WTO.

---

[154] See *Re International Labour Rights Fund* 752 F Supp 495 (DDC 1990) *aff'd* No 90-00728 (DC Cir Jan 31 1992) discussed in Barnard above n 147 at 434–36.

[155] 19 USC s 2462 (b) (2) above n 153.

[156] Section 1301 Omnibus Trade and Competitiveness Act 1988 Pub Law No 100–418, 102 Stat 1107.

[157] US Congress, Committee of Ways and Means *Overview and Compilation of US Trade Statutes* (1989 edn) reproduced in J Bhagwati and HT Patrick (eds) *Aggressive Unilateralism: America's 301 Trade Policy and the World Trading System* (London: Harvester Wheatsheaf, 1991) at 40. See also Hepple above n 6 ch 4.

[158] The US trade union organization, the American Federation of Labor – Congress of Industrial Organizations (AFL–CIO), has brought a petition requesting the USTR to act against violations of labour rights in China. See AFL–CIO s 301 Petition at <http://www.aflcio.org/issues/jobseconomy/globaleconomy/upload/china_petition.pdf>.

[159] See further Michael J Trebilcock and Robert Howse *The Regulation of International Trade* (London: Routledge, 3rd edn, 2005) at 568. In relation to labour protection measures, Article XX expressly refers only measures relating to the products of prison labour (art XX(e)). If wider labour rights measures are to be protected then these would have to be read into either art XX(a) 'necessary to protect public morals', art XX(b) 'necessary to protect human … life' or art XX(d) 'necessary to secure compliance with laws or regulations which are not inconsistent with the provisions of this Agreement'. The other grounds in art XX would be inapplicable given their subject matter. In each case the measures would have to be applied in a manner that does not constitute arbitrary or unjustifiable discrimination between countries, where the same conditions prevail, or a disguised restriction on international trade. Thus art XX is not an ideal vehicle by which to secure import bans based on labour conditions in the country of production. On the broader issue of whether the WTO should accept the legality of the 'social clause', that is a clause in trade agreements which conditions trade liberalization upon the adopting of certain minimum labour standards, see Hepple above n 6 chs 5 and 6. On unilateral imposition of the 'social clause' by states see Hepple ibid ch 4.

According to Trebilcock and Howse, '[t]his shows that there is tolerance of unilateral action by the international community where that action is preceded by a clear multilateral determination that the country concerned is an egregious violator of core labour rights and that cooperative approaches for addressing the situation have been exhausted'.[160]

More recently the US Government established a Bureau of International Labor Affairs (ILAB) to conduct research on and formulate international economic, trade, immigration, and labour policies in collaboration with other US Government agencies and to provide international technical assistance in support of US foreign labour policy objectives. In its mission statement ILAB states that it 'is working together with other US Government agencies to create a more stable, secure, and prosperous international economic system in which all workers can achieve greater economic security, share in the benefits of increased international trade, and have safer and healthier workplaces where the basic rights of workers and children are respected and protected'.[161] Furthermore, the US has included labour rights reviews, including child labour reviews, in prospective partner countries as a part of the Congressional approval procedure for free trade agreements.[162]

An alternative approach might be to challenge imports from countries that condone unfair labour practices under competition law and/or under human rights law. Such an initiative was attempted by German producers of asbestos products, who sought an injunction against imports of competing products from South Korea, on the ground that they were exposed to unfair competition contrary to section 1 of the West German Act against Unfair Competition. The plaintiffs argued that the imports had been made by workers subjected to health risks against which German workers had to be protected, in accordance with ILO Convention No 139 of 1974 on the Protection against Carcinogen Materials and Related Occupational Hazards, which had been put into effect by legislation in force in Germany since 1977. Furthermore, the plaintiffs argued that consumers were being misled by not being informed of the true circumstances behind the production of these goods, contrary to s 3 of the Unfair Competition Act. The German Supreme Court (Bundesgerichthof) dismissed the action. The products

---

[160] ibid at 568–69. Note that the US Court of Appeals, First Circuit, overruled legislation in Massachusetts, which prohibited governmental authorities from accepting tenders for contracts from multinationals that invested in Burma, on the ground that it was unconstitutional. The law was held to usurp the Federal government's foreign affairs power and to violate the commerce clause of the US Constitution. In addition, it was pre-empted by federal sanctions against Burma and so violated the supremacy clause in the Constitution: *National Foreign Trade Council v Natsios* 181 F 3d (1st Cir 1999), 38 ILM 1237 (1999).   [161] See <http://www.dol.gov/ILAB/mission_statement.htm>.

[162] See the Trade Act of 2002 (Public Law 107–210) s 2102(c) whereby the President is required to prepare several reports to the Congress related to new free trade agreements. Among these reports are a United States Employment Impact Review, Labor Rights Report, and Laws Governing Exploitative Child Labor Report. The Department of Labor, in consultation with other federal agencies, has been delegated the responsibility for preparing these three reports. The reports can be accessed at <http://www.dol.gov/ILAB/media/reports/usfta/main.htm>.

had not been made in violation of industrial health protection rules as South Korea was not at that time a member of the ILO, nor had it acceded to the relevant convention. Furthermore, the ILO Convention did not represent common standards of human rights applicable to all humanity. To be effective the convention had to be incorporated into national law. The Supreme Court further rejected the argument concerning the right of consumers to know of the conditions under which the products were made. Consumers were assumed only to be interested in information concerning the economic value of the product, and not in the employment conditions of those who produced it.[163]

This case well illustrates the weakness of ILO protection through conventions, as these are not accorded the status of fundamental rights provisions that might be binding *erga omnes* without the need for further legislative intervention by states.[164] However, it is doubtful whether consumers are as uninterested in the treatment of foreign workers as the German Supreme Court has assumed. It may be very damaging for a MNE to be associated in the public mind with the non-observance of good employment standards in its overseas plants or sub-contractors. A more significant objection to legal action such as the above is that it may be motivated by no more than protectionist sentiments, and may in fact serve to retard the growth of gainful employment in developing countries. The balance of interests is not easy to draw in such cases.

(b) Collective Bargaining and Consultation

Both the ILO Declaration and the OECD Employment Guideline assert that the employees of MNEs should have the right, in accordance with national law and practice, to have representative organizations of their own choosing recognized for the purpose of collective bargaining.[165] What constitutes collective bargaining is a matter for interpretation in the context of different national situations.[166] The ILO Declaration may offer some harmonization in this regard in that it recommends the taking of measures appropriate to national conditions for the encouragement and promotion of negotiations through collective agreements in accordance with ILO Convention No 98 Article 4.[167] The ILO Convention may provide a basis for identifying the common expectations that a system of collective bargaining should fulfil. The ILO Declaration also seeks to encourage the development of systems for consultation between employers and workers and their representatives

---

[163] BGH, 1 ZR 76/78 judgment 9 May 1980 summarized in AH Hermann *Conflicts of National Laws with International Business Activity: Issues of Extraterritoriality* (British-North American Committee, 1982) at 71–72.

[164] On which see *The Barcelona Traction, Light and Power Company Case* ICJ Reports (1970) 3 paras 33–34.

[165] ILO Declaration above n 2 at para 49; OECD Employment Guideline above n 1 at para 1.

[166] See OECD *1986 Review of the Guidelines on Multinational Enterprises* (Paris: 1986) paras 71–73 at 35–36; OECD Working Party above n 14 at 22.   [167] ibid para 50.

on matters of mutual concern. However, such consultations should not substitute for collective bargaining.[168]

According to the OECD Committee on Multinational Enterprises, employees' representatives may be entitled to negotiations not only with integrated MNEs but also with strategic alliances of national companies where certain decisions that they take in common were previously taken at national level and were discussed with employees' representatives.[169] On the other hand, where a MNE operates a policy of union non-recognition, the committee has held that the right of employees to be represented by unions depends on national laws, practices and regulations. However, the Employment Guideline suggests that management should adopt a positive approach to the activities of unions and other bona fide organizations of employees and espouse an open approach towards organizational activities within the framework of national rules and practices. In particular, MNEs should recruit personnel regardless of their union membership.[170]

Both codes expect MNEs to provide the facilities necessary for the development of effective collective agreements, and to provide workers' representatives with information required for meaningful negotiations on conditions of employment. This should give a 'true and fair view of the performance of the entity or, where appropriate, of the enterprise as a whole'.[171] The OECD Committee of Multinational Enterprises has interpreted this as requiring the provision of more specific information to employees' representatives than would be available to the general public under the OECD Disclosure Guideline, and in a form suitable for their interests and purposes. In certain cases, as where the MNE is engaged in restructuring activities, this may cover information about the enterprise as a whole, subject to considerations of business confidentiality.[172] Both codes stress that the provision of information must accord with local law and practice. Thus, it would appear that the host state is free to protect against employee disclosure through

---

[168] ILO Declaration above n 2 at para 57. The EC espouses a policy of 'social dialogue' between workers and employers: see arts 138 and 139 EC Treaty. However, this excludes collective bargaining over pay. For full discussion see Szyszczak above n 47 at 35–42.

[169] *European Airline Groupings* case: Blanpain above n 15 vol I at 229–35 and vol II at 119–135; Robinson above n 9 at 135–36. The ITF was held entitled to meaningful negotiations with the groupings of European airlines KSSU (KLM, Swissair, SAS, UTA) and ATLAS (Alitalia, Lufthansa, Air France, Sabena), as these came within the definition of a MNE in para 3 of the Guideline on Concepts and Principles. In any case, the guidelines applied to both national and multinational enterprises and represented good practice for all.

[170] *Citibank-Citicorp* case: (complaint of anti-union policy run by a multinational bank); Blanpain above n 15 vol I at 174–86 and vol II at 107–18 (further complaints concerning anti-union policies in multinational banks brought by the International Federation of Commercial Clerical and Technical Employees); Robinson above n 9 at 134–35. See also the *Norsk Hydro (USA), Quantas Airlines (USA), and NAM (USA)* cases in Blanpain ibid vol III at 75–96.

[171] ILO Declaration above n 2 at paras 51 and 55; OECD Employment Guideline above n 1 at paras 2 and 3.

[172] See OECD *1986 Review of the Guidelines on Multinational Enterprises* (Paris: 1986) paras 85–87 at 39–40; reaffirmed in the 1991 Review above n 14 at 46–48; OECD Working Party above n 14 at 23.

strict business secrecy laws. Furthermore, according to the OECD Committee on Multinational Enterprises, legal loopholes that allow the MNE to avoid its obligations as to co-determination are not the concern of the guideline but are for national legislators to deal with.[173] On the other hand, the ILO Declaration urges governments to help workers' representatives by furnishing them, where the law permits, with information about the industry in which the MNE operates. It urges MNEs to observe any requests from governments for relevant information on their operations.[174]

Both codes recognize the implications of the group structure of MNEs for effective collective bargaining. Each code demands that the authorized representatives of employees conduct negotiations with representatives of management who are authorized to take decisions on the matters under negotiation.[175] Under the OECD Guideline this requirement has been interpreted to mean that parent companies may be obliged to take the necessary organizational steps to enable their subsidiaries to observe the guidelines, inter alia, by providing them with sufficient and timely information and ensuring that local managers are duly authorized to take the decisions on matters under negotiation.[176] Alternatively, the parent company may delegate a member of the decision-making centre to the negotiating team of the subsidiary, or engage directly in negotiations, so as to achieve the same result.[177] Furthermore, employees' representatives may be entitled to information about the decision-making structure within the enterprise, but such a right of information is confined to the negotiating situations referred to in the guideline. There is no general right to be informed about the decision-making structure within the enterprise.[178] Additionally, negotiations should take place in a language understood by both sides. This may necessitate the use of an interpreter where representatives from the parent company do not speak the language of the host state.[179]

Both the matter of furnishing adequate information and the authorization of managers to take decisions can be helped by the institution of specialized structures within MNEs. Many European firms established the practice of setting up transnational works' councils during the 1980s and 1990s. Although not designed as sites for MNE-wide collective bargaining, such bodies offer a forum for regular enterprise-wide consultations and exchanges of information.[180] Furthermore,

173 *ITT (Germany)* case: Robinson above n 9 at 133–34.
174 ILO Declaration above n 2 at para 56.
175 ILO Declaration para 52; OECD Employment Guideline above n 1 at para 8.
176 OECD *1986 Review of the Guidelines on Multinational Enterprises* (Paris: 1986) paras 65–66 at 34; OECD Working Party above n 14 at 24.
177 *Firestone* case: Blanpain above n 15 vol I at 146–50; Robinson above n 9 at 136–37; *British Oxygen (Sweden)* case: Blanpain ibid vol II at 195–220; Robinson ibid at 137–38; *Phillips (Finland)* and *Ford (Amsterdam)* cases: Blanpain ibid vol II 135–95, vol III at 154–60 (further review of *Ford* case).
178 OECD *1986 Review* above n 176 at paras 80–81 at 38; OECD Working Party above n 14 at 27.
179 *Citibank (Denmark)* case: Blanpain above n 15 vol III at 97–100.
180 See Northrup, Campbell, and Slowinski above n 131 at 532–37; ILO *World Labour Report 1992* (Geneva: 1992) Box 3.1 at 57. This lists as examples: Bull's information committee established

national unions representing workers employed by the same MNE in more than one European country have established formal links with each other as a method of preparing for Europe-wide negotiations and consultations with the firm concerned.[181] Transnational works' councils may be of considerable significance in taking account of workers' interests in the planning of restructuring policies. Such policies have become more common with the advent of the integrated European market. Indeed, as seen in chapter 9, the EC Directive on European Works Councils is motivated, in part, to meet this problem. However, the creation of such bodies on a global or inter-regional basis is still far off. For now, this should be seen as a European initiative.

Finally, both codes address the problem of unfair pressure being brought to bear upon negotiations with workers' representatives by MNEs as a result of the international scope of their operations. Thus paragraph 53 of the ILO Declaration states:

Multinational enterprises, in the context of *bona fide* negotiations with the workers' representatives on conditions of employment, or while workers are exercising the right to organise, should not threaten to utilise a capacity to transfer the whole or part of an operating unit from the country concerned in order to influence unfairly those negotiations or to hinder the exercise of the right to organise; nor should they transfer workers from affiliates in foreign countries with a view to undermining bona fide negotiations with the workers' representatives or the workers' exercise of their right to organise.

The OECD Employment Guideline contains essentially the same formulation.[182] The 1991 version of the guideline added that 'bona fide negotiations may include labour disputes as part of the process of negotiation. Whether or not labour disputes are so included will be determined by the law and prevailing employment practices of particular countries'.[183] This has been removed from the 2000 version. The OECD Committee on Multinational Enterprises has stressed that an important issue arising from this provision is the distinction between the legitimate

---

in 1988 covering 12 countries; Nestlé's first meeting in 1990 with the International Union of Food Workers and national trade union officials in what were expected to become annual meetings; Volkswagen has had a European works council since 1990 with representatives from VW, Audi, and Seat (Spain) and will include its East European joint ventures such as Skoda; Elf-Aquitaine established a European information and consultation committee in 1991. See further the discussion of the Directive on the European Works Councils in ch 9 at 354–57 and associated references and note 144 above on the EMF cross-border collective bargaining initiative.

[181] See Marginson and Sisson above n 131.

[182] OECD Employment Guideline para 7: 'Enterprises should, within the framework of applicable law, regulations and prevailing labour relations and employment practices:

. . .

In the context of bona fide negotiations with representatives of employees on conditions of employment, or while employees are exercising a right to organise, not threaten to transfer the whole or part of an operating unit from the country concerned nor transfer employees from the enterprises' component entities in other countries in order to influence unfairly those negotiations or to hinder the exercise of a right to organise.'

[183] OECD 1991 Employment Guideline para 8 n 6 above n 14 at 111.

provision of information and threats designed to influence negotiations unfairly. In its view, a distinction should be drawn between giving employees information to the effect that a particular demand has serious implications for the economic viability of the enterprise, and the making of a threat. Management should be prepared to offer information that could support its claim.[184] Furthermore, the committee has noted that the guideline was drafted to consider only operations involving existing plant and equipment. Nevertheless, future investments, such as the replacement of equipment or the introduction of new technology could be crucial to the survival of the enterprise in the medium to long term and thus might be of interest in this context.[185] So, not only threats of withdrawal from current operations but also threats to run down an operation might be seen as 'unfair', in the absence of information that justifies such a decision.

The requirement not to 'import' strike-breaking employees from affiliates in other countries was absent from the original formulation of the OECD Employment Guideline. However, it was inserted in 1979 as a result of the OECD Committee's interpretation of the guideline in the light of the *Hertz* case.[186] The OECD Trade Union Advisory Committee (TUAC) brought this case to the attention of the committee on behalf of the Danish LO union confederation, which had complained that Hertz Rentacar was bringing in employees from other parts of Europe to cover for staff shortages caused by a strike at its Danish affiliate. After the strike was over, Hertz Rentacar (Denmark) took back only half of the original staff because of structural and operational changes, and continued to employ some of the foreign workers. The committee observed that the transfer of employees from foreign affiliates had unfairly influenced negotiations and was contrary to the general spirit and approach of the guidelines even if it did not contravene them. Consequently, this gap in the original formulation had to be remedied through the insertion of appropriate words.

(c) Examination of Grievances and Settlement of Industrial Disputes

These issues are dealt with by the ILO Declaration alone. Regarding workers' grievances the following principle is recommended to MNEs: 'that any worker who, acting individually or jointly with other workers, considers that he has grounds for a grievance should have the right to submit such grievance without suffering any prejudice whatsoever as a result, and to have such grievance examined pursuant to an appropriate procedure.'[187] This is seen as particularly important where the MNE operates in a country that does not abide by the principles of ILO Conventions

---

[184] 1986 Review above n 176 at para 63 at 33; OECD Working Party above n 14 at 24.
[185] 1986 Review para 62 and OECD Working Party ibid.
[186] See Blanpain above n 15 vol I at 219–28; Robinson above n 9 at 129.
[187] ILO Declaration above n 2 at para 58 and Recommendation No 130 concerning the Examination of Grievances within the Undertaking with a View to Their Settlement.

relating to freedom of association, the right to organize and bargain collectively, to discrimination, child labour and to forced labour and to forced labour.[188]

The ILO Declaration ends with a recommendation that MNEs should seek to establish, with the representatives and organizations of the workers whom they employ, voluntary conciliation machinery to assist in the prevention and settlement of industrial disputes. This machinery should include equal representation for employers and workers, and it should be appropriate to national conditions. It may include provisions for voluntary arbitration.[189]

Concluding Remarks

The ILO Declaration and OECD Employment Guideline offer a statement of desired practice on the part of governments and MNEs in the field of labour relations. They may be criticized as representing weak legal responses, given their non-binding nature. Furthermore, the pressures of international competition may be forcing some states to weaken their existing labour protection standards or to resist improvements. In these circumstances the two codes could be dismissed as relics of the 'corporatist' 1970s that have little of relevance to offer. However, they represent the minimum international labour standards that states have agreed should apply to the operations of MNEs. As such they have at least the status of 'soft law' and such law may well 'harden' as expectations concerning good corporate conduct and social responsibility rise. Furthermore, not all legal systems are retreating from the principles that the codes espouse. Most notably the EC is making advances in these areas, although some fears are being expressed that these initiatives are undermining the competitiveness of European industry. However, should the future involve a 'race to the bottom' in international labour standards, it would reflect a decline not only in morality but also in reason. The end result may be protectionist responses from states whose businesses and workers are threatened by such competition, and a retardation of economic and social development in developing countries.

---

[188] ibid.　　　[189] ibid para 59.

13

Human Rights and Multinational Enterprises

This chapter examines the role played by human rights standards in the regulation of MNE activities. To date human rights norms have been used by corporate actors to protect their vital interests against what they may view as acts of excessive state regulation. This has led to the gradual development of a protective law of human rights for corporations. This issue will be considered in the first section. However, the principal task of this chapter is to consider whether, and how far, MNEs should be required to observe fundamental human rights standards and, possibly, to be liable for their violation. Increased concern in this area may be attributed to a number of factors including increased unease at the seemingly unaccountable operations of private capital in a globalizing economy, the perception that the ability of the nation state to act in the public interest has been weakened by the effects of economic globalization, and as a result of the greater ease of communicating cases of corporate misconduct through the media, wherever this may occur.[1] In addition, the increased vigilance of non-governmental organizations (NGOs) that are concerned with such misconduct has led to greater awareness of this issue.[2]

---

[1] Cases of misconduct appear to be focused in a number of specific industries, which, by their characteristics and location, may be more likely to encounter human rights related problems. In particular, light manufacture depending on cheap labour (such as the apparel and footwear industries) and natural resource extraction industries that may operate in less developed and more remote locations, and in politically destabilized countries or regions, seem prominent in the documented cases. There are also a number of cases involving major infrastructure projects that may have serious health and environmental implications such as dams and oil and gas pipeline projects. On the latter, see Sheldon Leader 'Human Rights Risks and New Strategies for Global Investment' 9 JIEL 657 (2006) and the two Amnesty International Reports cited in ch 15 n 24 at 582. See further, for examples and analysis, Rory Sullivan (ed) *Business and Human Rights: Dilemmas and Solutions* (Sheffield: Greenleaf Publishing, 2003) Parts 2–4; International Network for Economic, Social & Cultural Rights (ESCR–NET) Corporate Accountability Working Group Joint NGO Submission *Consultation on Human Rights and the Extractive Industry* (Geneva: 9 December 2005) at <http://www.earthrights.org/files/Reports/escrnet9_dec_05.pdf>. Earthrights International *Earth Rights Abuses by Corporations in Burma Collective Summary and Recommendations* (submission to the Special Representative on the Issue of Human Rights and Transnational Corporations and Other Business Enterprises 10 November 2005) at <http://www.earthrights.org/files/Reports/eri_submission.pdf>. On the relationship between globalization, business, and human rights, see Robert McCorquodale 'Human Rights and Global Business' in Stephen Bottomley and David Kinley (eds) *Commercial Law and Human Rights* (Aldershot: Ashgate/Dartmouth Publishing, 2002). See too UNCTAD *World Investment Report 2007* (New York and Geneva: United Nations, forthcoming 2007).

[2] See further Peter T Muchlinski 'Human Rights and Multinationals – Is There a Problem?' 77 International Affairs 31 at 33–35 (2001); UN Sub-Commission on Human Rights, Working Group

This issue will be discussed in three stages. First, the conceptual problems arising out of the extension of human rights responsibilities to corporate actors will be briefly reviewed. This provides an essential background without which the current debate may be hard to understand. It emanates directly out of the debate on international corporate social responsibility that was considered in chapter 3. Secondly, the major substantive principles, that may be said to form the foundations of MNE human rights responsibilities, will be outlined, based on the most important international instruments in this field. These include, in particular, the UN Norms on the Responsibilities of Transnational Corporations and Other Business Enterprises with Regard to Human Rights (the UN Norms). The subject matter of the UN Norms continues to be discussed by the UN Sub-Commission on the Promotion and Protection of Human Rights, although the Norms themselves are unlikely to be adopted in the near future.[3] Thirdly, the practical issues of

on the working methods and activities of transnational corporations *Human Rights Principles and Responsibilities for Transnational Corporations and Other Business Enterprises: Introduction* UN Doc E/CN.4/Sub.2/2002/WG.2/WP.1/Add 1 (hereafter Introduction) at 2–4. See also International Council on Human Rights Policy *Beyond Voluntarism: Human Rights and the Developing International Obligations of Companies* (Versoix: 2002) at 1–2.

[3] Norms on the Responsibilities of Transnational Corporations and Other Business Enterprises with Regard to Human Rights (hereafter UN Norms). (UN Doc E/CN.4/Sub.2/2003/12/ Rev 2(2003) 13 August 2003, available at <http://www1.umn.edu/humanrts/links/norms-Aug2003.html>, or <http://www.business-humanrights.org>. See also Commentary on the Norms on the Responsibilities of Transnational Corporations and Other Business Enterprises with Regard to Human Rights (hereafter Commentary) (UN Doc E/CN.4/Sub.2/2003/38. Rev 2(2003) available at <http://www1.umn.edu/humanrts/links/commentary-Aug2003.html> or <http://www.business-humanrights.org>. Other relevant documents are available at <http://www1.umn.edu/humanrts/links/omig.html>. See further David Weissbrodt and Muria Kruger 'Norms on the Responsibilities of Transnational Corporations and Other Business Enterprises with Regard to Human Rights' 97 AJIL 901 (2003); David Weissbrodt 'The Beginning of a Sessional Working Group on Transnational Corporations Within the UN Sub-Commission on Prevention of Discrimination and Protection of Minorities' in MT Kamminga and S Zia-Zarifi (eds) *Liability of Multinational Corporations Under International Law* (The Hague: Kluwer Law International, 2000) 119–38; Amnesty International *The UN Human Rights Norms for Business: Towards Legal Accountability* (London: Amnesty International, 2004); Rebecca MM Wallace and Olga Martin-Ortega 'The UN Norms: A First Step to Universal Regulation of Transnational Corporations' Responsibilities for Human Rights?' 26 Dublin Univ. LJ 304 (2004); Larry Cata Backer 'Multinational Corporations, Transnational Law: The United Nations Norms and the Responsibilities of Transnational Corporations as a Harbinger of Corporate Social Responsibility in International Law' 37 Columbia HRLR 287 (2006).The UN Commission on Human Rights requested the UN Secretary-General to appoint a special representative on the issue of human rights, transnational corporations and other business enterprises who would study further the implications of the extension of such responsibilities to business enterprises: UN Commission on Human Rights (Sixty-First Session Agenda Item 17, UN Doc E/CN.4/2005/L.87) 15 April 2005, adopted 20 April 2005 by 49 votes to 3 with one abstention. Opposed by the United States, Australia, and South Africa: Amnesty International '2005 UN Commission on Human Rights: Amnesty International welcomes new UN mechanism on Business and Human Rights' (AI Public Statement 21 April 2005 IOR 41/044/2005). See also UN Commission on Human Rights Report on the Sixtieth Session Resolution 2004/116 (UN Doc E/CN.4/2004/L.11/Add 7 22 April 2004 at 81–82) requesting the UN Commissioner for Human Rights to prepare a report on the 'responsibilities of transnational corporations and related business enterprises with regard to human rights'. The report is contained in: UN Doc E/CN.4/2005/91 15 February 2005. In June 2006 the Commission was replaced by a

monitoring and implementation will be examined, including both the major practical legal issues that will arise in the context of national litigation and the possible role of inter-governmental organizations (IGOs) in the supervision of MNE adherence to human rights norms.

(1) Human Rights and the Protection of MNEs

The right of a natural person to be protected against the human rights abuses of a state actor is at the heart of human rights law. Whether this right should also extend to a legal person, such as a corporation, is open to some doubt at the philosophical level. Arguably, a corporation cannot enjoy the protection of human rights as it is not 'human'. Indeed, corporations are granted existence by the state and have no inherent natural existence. In addition, corporations are conduits for personal gain, an aim that may, or may not be, in the wider social interest at any given time. Accordingly, they can be subjected to demands for utility to society that may not be acceptable in the case of natural persons.[4] On the other hand, human rights protection for corporations can be defended on the ground that the benefits of such protection pass to the human actors associated with the corporation.[5] This argument may well justify lifting the corporate veil and allowing the affected stakeholders a direct right of action against the state, but it is not a very convincing philosophical reason for allowing the corporation itself to bring a claim in its own name. A stronger justification would appear to be that it is unacceptable to discriminate against one class of legal persons in the enjoyment of their legal rights in a legal order that accepts equality of legal subjects before the law.[6] In addition, the enjoyment of certain fundamental rights, guaranteed by law, may be essential for the successful undertaking of corporate activities deemed

new Human Rights Council: UN GA Resolution 60/251 'Human Rights Council' 3 April 2006 at <http://www.ohchr.org/english/bodies/hrcouncil/docs/A.RES.60.251_En.pdf>. At its latest session on 7 August 2006, the Sub-Commission on the Promotion and Protection of Human Rights, recalling its resolution 2005/6 of 8 August 2005, decided, without a vote, to establish a sessional working group on the effects of the working methods and activities of transnational corporations on the enjoyment of human rights: Decision 2006/104: Report of the Sub-Commission on Human Rights UN Doc A/HRC/Sub.1/58/L.11/Add 1 24 August 2006 at <http://www.ohchr.org/english/bodies/subcom/docs/58/A.HRC.Sub.1.58.L.11.Add.1.pdf>.

   [4] See Stephen Bottomley 'Corporations and Human Rights' in Stephen Bottomley and David Kinley (eds) *Commercial Law and Human Rights* (Aldershot: Ashgate Dartmouth Publishing, 2002) 47 at 62 citing *Environmental Protection Authority v Caltex Refining Co Pty Ltd* (1994) ACSR 452 and *Trade Practices Commission v Abbco Ice Works Pty Ltd* (1994) 123 ALR 503; John M Kline *Ethics for International Business: Decision Making in a Global Political Economy* (London: Routledge, 2005) 11.

   [5] See Michael Addo 'The Corporation as a Victim of Human Rights Violations' in Michael Addo (ed) *Human Rights Standards and the Responsibility of Transnational Corporations* (The Hague: Kluwer Law International, 1999) from 187 especially 188–90 and the cases cited therein.

   [6] This would appear to be the general thrust of US case law on the constitutional rights of corporations: see Philip I Blumberg *The Multinational Challenge to Corporation Law* (Oxford: Oxford University Press, 1993) ch 2.

useful to society. Furthermore, allowing corporate actors to enjoy the benefits of human rights protection may make it easier, in turn, to demand observance of human rights standards by such actors.[7] Perhaps the key issue in this debate is not so much whether, as a conceptual matter, corporations should enjoy the benefit of human rights protection, but whether, given the nature, characteristics, and functions of corporations, they should enjoy the same human rights and to the same extent as natural persons.

Clearly, some distinctions need to be made. For example, a legal person cannot suffer torture, inhuman or degrading treatment, but it can suffer damage to its goodwill and reputation that can adversely affect its profitability. These are quite distinctive issues covered by different areas of the law. They are not comparable situations. Equally, rights to a family life mean nothing in a corporate context. On the other hand, certain rights may be enjoyed by corporations and natural persons alike, although the precise nature of the right may need to be modified to take account of the realities of corporate activity. Thus rights to the protection of private corporate premises against unlawful invasion by state authorities have been recognized,[8] as have rights to corporate free speech in the context of newspaper publishing or broadcasting.[9] However, not all corporate speech will be protected. A distinction between commercial speech, aimed at improving the commercial performance of the company, and non-commercial speech has developed, with greater protection being accorded to the latter than the former.[10] Furthermore, in

---

[7] ibid at 196.

[8] See, for example, *Colas Est SA and Others v France* E Ct HR Reports 2002–III; *Hale v Henkel* 201 US 43 (1906) (US Sup Ct).

[9] See, for example, *Sunday Times v United Kingdom* E Ct HR judgment of 26 April 1979 Series A No 30 (1979–80) 2 EHRR 245; *Autronic v Switzerland* E Ct HR judgment of 22 May 1990 Series A No 178 (1990) 12 EHRR 485.

[10] Different jurisdictions vary in the extent to which they are willing to protect corporate free speech. Thus under US law very few safeguards are available for commercial, as opposed to non-commercial, speech allowing for the regulation of commercial speech against false or misleading statements. On the other hand, in the case of *Kasky v Nike* 27 Cal 4th. 939 (S Ct Cal 2002) *cert den.* US Sup Ct *Nike v Kasky* 123 S Ct 2554 (2003), the plaintiff brought a public interest action against Nike, for allegedly breaching Californian unfair competition and false advertising laws, on the ground that Nike had publicly stated that it ensured the good treatment of workers who made Nike products in overseas sub-contractors' firms, in response to allegations of abuse of workers at such sites. Nike argued that the enforcement of these Californian laws would breach its rights to free speech under the First Amendment to the US Constitution. Nike claimed that its statements were non-commercial and so deserved protection. The California Court of Appeals upheld Nike's arguments. The California Supreme Court reversed this ruling in May 2002 holding that the statements were commercial in character. The US Supreme Court dismissed the appeal from the Californian Supreme Court on procedural grounds. The case settled in September 2003 with Nike agreeing to pay US$1.5m to the Fair Labor Association without admitting liability, to be used to monitor the overseas labour practices of US companies: see further Sarah Joseph *Corporations and Transnational Human Rights Litigation* (Oxford: Hart Publishing, 2004) ch 5. By contrast the European Court of Human Rights is more willing to protect commercial speech: see *Autronic v Switzerland* above n 9. Equally, the state is responsible to ensure equal rights of access to court in cases of corporate speech. In the McDonald's libel case, the UK was found to have breached Articles 6 and 10 of the ECHR due to lack of legal aid for the defendants in that case: Application No 68416/01 *Steel and*

two areas, there appears to be little practical distinction between the operation of human rights protection for natural or legal persons. First, due process requirements generally apply without distinction as to the nature of the legal subject in question. Corporations have argued successfully for such rights to be protected in numerous jurisdictions.[11] Equally, there is little doubt that corporations can enjoy the right to peaceful enjoyment of their possessions to protect vital property interests in much the same way as natural persons. Indeed, such a reliance on human rights may reinforce the protection of foreign investors under the international minimum standard of treatment for aliens and their property.[12] However, this is not a uniform body of doctrine as the protection offered under the European Convention on Human Rights (ECHR) differs conceptually from that provided under general international law. The European Court of Human Rights does not apply the same international law standard as arbitral tribunals, relying instead on ECHR concepts to balance the right to peaceful enjoyment of possessions with the state's right to regulate property in the public interest.[13]

Having noted the extent to which substantive human rights norms may apply to corporate actors, certain practical differences between the claims of natural and legal persons need to be considered. In particular, two issues stand out: first, given the legal form of the corporation, embedding a separation between the corporate entity and its owners, who should be regarded as the 'victim' of a human rights violation?[14] Secondly, given that corporate regulation often pursues essential public policy objectives, how might this modify the extent to which a corporate person, as opposed to a natural person, can enjoy protection? In relation to the first issue, a human rights tribunal must determine whether the corporation itself

---

Morris v United Kingdom E Ct HR judgment of 15 February 2005 at <http://cmiskp.echr.coe.int>. See further Marius Emberland *The Human Rights of Companies: Exploring the Structure of ECHR Protection* (Oxford: Oxford University Press, 2006) at 117–22 (on which the following account of ECHR law draws heavily). On corporate free speech generally, see Roger A Shiner *Freedom of Commercial Expression* (Oxford: Oxford University Press, 2003).

[11] For US case law see Blumberg above n 6; for the position under the ECHR and EC law, see Janet Dine *Companies, International Trade and Human Rights* (Cambridge: Cambridge University Press, 2005) at 207–21 (on the right against self-incrimination) and for the position under the UK Human Rights Act see Alan J Dignam and David Allen *Company Law and the Human Rights Act 1998* (London: Butterworths, 2000) ch 9.   [12] On which see further ch 15.

[13] The leading ECHR cases concerning protection against regulatory taking under the ECHR will be considered in ch 15 alongside recent arbitral case law. A debate has also arisen as to whether a 'human right to free trade' should emerge to protect corporate interests in internationally liberalized markets: see, for the argument in favour, E-U Petersmann 'Human Rights and International Economic Law in the 21st Century: The Need to Clarify their Inter-relationships' 4 JIEL 3 (2001) and against: P Alston 'Resisting the Merger and Acquisition of Human Rights by Trade Law: A Reply to Petersmann' 13 EJIL 815 (2002) eliciting a rejoinder from Petersmann at 13 EJIL 845 (2002). See further Robert Howse 'Human Rights in the WTO: Whose Rights, What Humanity? Comment on Petersmann' 13 EJIL 651 (2002), Dine note 11 above at 199–207.

[14] Thus Article 34 of the ECHR allows 'applications from any person, non-governmental organisation or group of individuals claiming to be the victim of a violation by one of the High Contracting Parties of the rights set forth in the Convention or the protocols therein'.

has suffered a human rights infringement or whether it has also affected the rights of shareholders and/or other stakeholders in the company. Under general principles of company law it would be rare for the corporate veil to be lifted and for the shareholders to have direct rights of action where the corporation was the principal entity affected by the alleged harm. It would be for the corporation to bring the claim and for the shareholders to deal with the corporation itself as regards their claims.[15] However, human rights claims are different. The nature of the harm may be such that the principal victims are in fact the natural persons that stand behind the corporate form. Accordingly, in human rights cases they may be allowed to bring direct claims alongside the company or in its place. Thus, under the ECHR, the European Commission of Human Rights was ready to regard the corporation as a mere 'vehicle' through which a shareholder does business and to allow a direct claim provided that the shareholder was a majority shareholder and that he or she had a direct interest in the subject-matter of the claim.[16] However, in relation to claims made under Article 1 of the First Protocol to the ECHR, protecting peaceful enjoyment of possessions, the European Court of Human Rights has restricted this approach and has refused to lift the corporate veil in favour of the shareholders where the proprietary interests of the company itself have been harmed.[17] There is also more recent case law suggesting that, in relation to other rights protected by the ECHR, identification of corporate and shareholder claims will not be permitted.[18]

This more restrictive approach may be explained by a desire not to upset the regulatory structure of national company laws unnecessarily and so as to ensure that aggrieved shareholders (and other stakeholders) first exhaust domestic remedies related to prejudicial actions against the company.[19] It is also consistent with the rules of international law concerning the admissibility of shareholder claims as settled in the *Barcelona Traction* case.[20] However, in two cases shareholders may still bring an action. The first is where it is impossible for the company to bring a claim.[21] This will cover cases where the company is in liquidation, receivership or

---

[15] This is known, under English law, as the rule in *Foss v Harbottle* (1843) 2 Hare 461: see Dignam and Allen above n 11 at 176–78.

[16] See *Yarrow v United Kingdom* (1983) 30 DR 155; *Pine Valley Developments Ltd v Ireland* (1991) 14 EHRR 319; *Agrotexim v Greece* Case No 14807/89 Commission Report (1992) 72 DR 148, discussed in Dignam and Allen above n 11 at 180–81 and Emberland above n 10 at 99–104.

[17] See *Agrotexim Hellas and Others v Greece* E Ct HR judgment Series A No 330 (1995); (1996) 21 EHRR 250. This approach was subsequently followed by the Commission: see Dignam and Allen above n 11 at 182–83. This does not preclude claims by shareholders under Article 1 Protocol 1 where their rights as shareholders have been infringed: see Emberland above n 10 at 69–72 citing *Sovtransavato Holding v Ukraine* E Ct HR 25 July 2002 E Ct HR Reports 2002-VII; *Olczak v Poland* E Ct HR 7 November 2002 E Ct HR Reports 2002-X.

[18] See *CDI Holding AG and Others v Slovakia* E Ct HR 18 October 2001. This approach has also been applied to a claim for identification between companies in the same group: *Société Génerale de Investissement (SGI) and Others v France* E Ct HR 4 May 1999: see Emberland above n 10 at 77–79.

[19] See Emberland above n 10 at 92–4.   [20] ICJ Reports (1970) 3.

[21] *Agrotexim v Greece* above n 17 at para 66.

subject to a court order.[22] The second is where the degree of identification between the shareholder and the company is so great on the particular facts of the case that they are virtually one and the same, as where the shareholder is a sole shareholder or owns an overwhelming percentage of the shares.[23] Thus the 'vehicle' approach appears to have been retained, not as a general rule but as an exception to the general rule of not lifting the corporate veil, to be used where the demands of effective human rights protection require it. Such an approach is in line with the practice of international investment agreements to use a broad, asset-based, definition of investment which includes a shareholding interest per se and not to restrict protection to the 'enterprise' as such, although such a more restrictive definition appears in some agreements.[24]

Turning to the issue of balancing between corporate rights and the pursuit of essential public policy goals, it is arguable that, given the utilitarian nature of incorporation and of expectations as to corporate performance, the extent to which corporations should enjoy human rights protection should be modified. Under the ECHR a degree of national discretion is preserved in the application of certain human rights even in relation to natural persons. Thus Articles 8 to 11 of the convention are drafted in two paragraphs: the first states the right itself while the second delimits the government's discretion to control its enjoyment.[25] This entails that the measure of control be prescribed by law, and that it is necessary in a democratic society to ensure the protection of certain public policy goals that could be threatened by the absolute application of the right in question. In addition, the legitimacy of any restriction will be judged in accordance with a criterion of proportionality. Furthermore, the ECHR applies a general 'margin of appreciation' to determining how far a government can act without being subjected to international scrutiny by the convention organs. Key here is the notion of subsidiarity – governments are the prime actors in securing the observance of human rights and they have a discretion in determining how best to do this. The ECHR oversees that this discretion is exercised in accordance with the principles enshrined in the convention. It does not attempt to supplant national governments.[26] Applying this approach the European Court of Human Rights held, in the case of *Markt Intern Verlag Gmbh and Klaus Beerman v Germany*,[27] that, in relation to a complaint of a

---

[22] Dignam and Allen above n 11 at 190.

[23] *Ankarcrona v Sweden* E Ct HR 27 June 2000 (sole shareholder was a victim under Article 34); *GJ v Luxembourg* E Ct HR 26 October 2000, (2003) 36 EHRR 40 (applicant held 90 per cent of shares in company); *Camberrow v Bulgaria* E Ct HR 1 April 2004 (applicant company held 98 per cent of shares in another company) discussed in Emberland above n 10 at 95–96.

[24] See UNCTAD *Scope and Definition* Series on issues in international investment agreements (New York and Geneva: United Nations, 1999) at 15–32.

[25] Articles 8–11 cover respectively, the right to a private and family life, the freedom of conscience, the freedom of expression, and the freedom of association. See further DJ Harris, M O'Boyle, and C Warbrick *Law of the European Convention on Human Rights* (London: Butterworths, 1995) ch 8.

[26] See generally Yutaka Arai-Takahashi *The Margin of Appreciation Doctrine and the Principle of Proportionality in the Jurisprudence of the ECHR* (Antwerp: Intersentia, 2002).

[27] E Ct HR judgment of 20 November 1989, Series A No 165; (1990) 12 EHRR 161.

violation of Article 10, arising out of the prohibition of certain commercial reports in a trade journal on the grounds that these contravened German competition laws, the contracting state had a certain margin of appreciation. It explained:

[s]uch a margin of appreciation is essential in commercial matters and, in particular, in an area as complex and fluctuating as that of unfair competition. Otherwise the [Court] would have to undertake a re-examination of the facts and all the circumstances of each case. The Court must confine its review to the question whether measures taken on the national level are justifiable in principle and proportionate.[28]

According to Emberland, this entails a more lenient approach to the control of governmental discretion than might be encountered in claims brought by natural persons. The Court is only concerned with whether the national authorities have undertaken the necessity/proportionality test and will not judge on the substantive subject-matter of the policy, a matter within the states' margin of appreciation.[29] Although widely criticized as ignoring the needs of the business community, this approach has been widely followed in subsequent cases involving corporate human rights claims.[30] For example, in *Fontanesi v Austria* the Court held that 'a margin of appreciation is left to the Contracting States which may be broader where professional or business activities are involved'.[31] Equally, considerable deference to governmental regulation has been given in cases of interference with the peaceful enjoyment of property rights under Article 1 of the First Protocol to the convention.[32]

From the foregoing review of ECHR law, it can be seen that human rights based claims by MNEs and other business entities are possible. They need not be seen as a threat to the underlying principles of human rights law. These types of claims will, by their very character, involve only certain aspects of human rights protection. In addition, given the commercial nature of the claimant, and the public interest in governments remaining free to regulate the economy as they see fit, considerable latitude is accorded to states in this process. On the other hand, even corporate citizens should be entitled to expect due process and legality to attend the regulatory practices of the countries in which they operate. To this end, the possibility of human rights based claims would appear beneficial. Finally, as noted above, the extension of human rights to corporate actors should entail, as a corollary, the extension of human rights responsibilities, which will now be considered.

(2) The Basis of Human Rights Obligations for MNEs

The observance of fundamental human rights can be said to lie at the heart of ethical business practice.[33] However, in relation to business ethics, the use of

---

[28] ibid para 33.   [29] Emberland above n 10 at 164–71.
[30] See further Emberland ibid chs 4 and 5 and the analysis of the cases therein.
[31] E Ct HR judgment 8 February 2000 para 1(9) cited in Emberland at 176.
[32] See Arai-Takahashi above n 26 at 149–64.   [33] See Kline n 4 at 25.

human rights standards is replete with conceptual difficulties. Indeed, there are a number of strong arguments against such an extension of human rights responsibilities to MNEs.[34] First, MNEs and other business enterprises are in business. Their only social responsibility is to make profits for their shareholders. It is not for them to act as moral arbiters in relation to the wider issues arising in the communities in which they operate. Indeed to do so may be seen as unwarranted interference in the internal affairs of those communities, something that MNEs have, in the past, been urged not to do.[35] Secondly, private non-state actors do not have any positive duty to observe human rights. Their only duty is to obey the law. Thus it is for the state to regulate on matters of social importance and for such actors to observe the law. It follows also that MNEs and other business enterprises, as private actors, can only be beneficiaries of human rights protection and not human rights protectors themselves. Thirdly, which human rights are MNEs and other business enterprises to observe? They may have some influence over social and economic matters, as for example, by ensuring the proper treatment of their workers, but they can do nothing to protect civil and political rights. Only states have the power and the ability to do that. Fourthly, the extension of human rights obligations to corporate actors will create a 'free rider' problem.[36] It is predictable that not all states and not all firms will take the same care to observe fundamental human rights. Thus the more conscientious corporations that invest time and money into observing human rights, and making themselves accountable for their record in this field, will be at a competitive disadvantage in relation to more unscrupulous corporations that do not undertake such responsibilities. They may also lose business opportunities in countries with poor human rights records, in that the host government may not wish to do business with ethically driven corporations and they may not want to do business with it. Fifthly, unfairness may be exacerbated by the selective and politically driven activities of NGOs, whose principal concern may be to maintain a high profile for their particular campaigns and not to ensure that all corporations are held equally to account.

Such arguments can be answered. First, as regards the extension of social responsibility standards to corporations, it should be noted that MNEs have been expected to observe socially responsible standards of behaviour for a long time.[37]

---

[34] This section draws on Peter T Muchlinski above n 2 at 35–44 (2001). See further SR Ratner 'Corporations and Human Rights: A Theory of Legal Responsibility' 111 Yale LJ 443 (2001); Phillip Alston (ed) *Non-State Actors and Human Rights* (Oxford: Oxford University Press, 2005) Part III 'Corporations' Andrew Clapham *Human Rights Obligations of Non-State Actors* (Oxford: Oxford University Press, 2006) ch 6.

[35] See, for example, the UN Draft Code of Conduct for Transnational Corporations paragraphs 15–16 in UNCTAD *International Investment Agreements: A Compendium* (New York and Geneva: United Nations, 1996) vol I at 165.

[36] See Ray Vernon in *Business and Human Rights* (Harvard Law School Human Rights Program, 1999) at 49.

[37] See UNCTAD *The Social Responsibility of Transnational Corporations* (New York and Geneva: United Nations, 1999) UNCTAD *World Investment Report 1999* (New York and Geneva: United Nations, 1999) ch XII.

This expectation has been expressed in national and regional laws and in numerous codes of conduct drawn up by inter-governmental organizations, as will be discussed more fully below. Indeed, MNEs themselves appear to be rejecting a purely non-social role for themselves through the adoption of corporate and industry based codes of conduct.[38] Secondly, observance of human rights is increasingly being seen by MNEs as 'Good for Business'. It is argued that business cannot flourish in an environment where fundamental human rights are not respected – what firm would be happy with the disappearance or imprisonment without trial of employees for their political opinions thereby being deprived of their labour? In addition, businesses themselves may justify the adoption of human rights policies by reference to good reputation.[39] The benefit to be reaped from espousing a pro human rights stance is seen as outweighing any 'free rider' problem, which may be in any case exaggerated.[40]

Thirdly, the private legal status of MNEs and other business enterprises may be seen as irrelevant to the extension of human rights responsibilities to such entities. As Andrew Clapham has forcefully argued, changes in the nature and location of power in the contemporary international system, including an increase in the power of private non-state actors such as MNEs (which may allow them to bypass traditional state-centred systems of governance) have forced a reconsideration of the boundaries between the private and the public spheres. This, in turn, has brought into question the traditional notion of the corporation as a private entity with no social or public obligations, with the consequence that such actors, including MNEs, may in principle be subjected to human rights obligations.[41] This position coincides with the fear that these powerful entities may disregard human rights and, thereby, violate human dignity. It follows that corporations, including, in particular, MNEs, should be subjected to human rights responsibilities, notwithstanding their status as creatures of private law, because human dignity must be protected in every circumstance.[42] Furthermore, in response to the view that MNEs cannot be subjected to human rights responsibilities because they are incapable of observing human rights designed to direct state action, it may be said that, to the contrary, MNEs can affect the economic welfare of the communities in which they operate and, given the indivisibility of human rights, this means that they have a direct impact on the extent that economic and social rights, especially labour rights in the workplace, can be enjoyed. Although it is

---

[38] See, for examples, UNCTAD *World Investment Report 1994* (New York and Geneva: United Nations, 1994) ch VIII; UNCTAD *The Social Responsibility of Transnational Corporations* (New York and Geneva: United Nations, 1999) at 31–42.

[39] See, for example, Simon Williams 'How Principles Benefit the Bottom Line: The Experience of the Co-operative Bank' in M Addo (ed) *Human Rights Standards and the Responsibility of Transnational Corporations* (The Hague: Kluwer Law International, 1999) 63–68. See also Harvard Law School *Business and Human Rights* (Cambridge, MA: Harvard Law School Human Rights Program, 1999) at 19–22.   [40] See further Peter T Muchlinski above n 2 at 38–39.

[41] See Andrew Clapham *Human Rights in the Private Sphere* (Oxford: Clarendon Press, 1993) 137–38; Clapham above n 34 at 544–48.   [42] ibid at 147.

true that MNEs may not have direct control over matters arising outside the workplace they may none the less exercise important influence in this regard. Thus, MNEs may seek to defend the human rights of their employees outside the workplace, to set standards for their sub-contractors and to refuse to accept the benefits of governmental measures that seek to improve the business climate at the expense of fundamental human rights. Equally, where firms operate in unstable environments they should ensure that their security arrangements comply with fundamental human rights standards.[43] Moreover, where companies have no direct means of influence they should avoid, at the very least, making statements or engaging in actions that appear to condone human rights violations. This may include silence in the face of such violations. Furthermore, all firms should develop an internal human rights policy which ensures that such concerns are taken into account in management decision-making, and which may find expression in a corporate code of conduct. Finally, the argument that MNEs may be subjected to arbitrary and selective targeting by NGOs should not be overstated. While it is true that such behaviour can arise out of what Upendra Baxi has termed 'the market for human rights',[44] in which NGOs strive for support from a consuming public in a manner not dissimilar to that of a service industry, MNEs and other major business enterprises are big enough to take care of themselves.

Despite this strong theoretical and moral case for extending responsibility for human rights violations to MNEs, the legal responsibility of MNEs for such violations remains uncertain. Thus, much of the literature on this issue suggests ways to reform and develop the law towards full legal responsibility, rather than documenting actual juridical findings of human rights violations by MNEs, or, indeed, other non-state actors.[45] We are yet to see such an event in the courts of the world, although it should be remembered that findings of human rights violations concerning slave labour practices have been made against individual

---

[43] See Amnesty International UK Business Group *Human Rights Guidelines for Companies* (London: Amnesty International, 1998) at 8–11.

[44] Upendra Baxi 'Voices of Suffering and the Future of Human Rights' 8 Transnational Law and Contemporary Problems from 126 especially 161–69 (1998) and *The Future of Human Rights* (New Delhi: Oxford University Press, 2002) ch 7.

[45] See, for example, David Kinley and Junko Tadaki 'From Talk to Walk: The Emergence of Human Rights Responsibilities for Corporations at International Law' 44 Va.J.Int'l L. 931 (2004); Nicola Jagers *Corporate Human Rights Obligations: In Search of Accountability* (Antwerp: Intersentia, 2002); Beth Stephens 'The Amorality of Profit: Transnational Corporations and Human Rights' 20 Berkeley J Int'l L 45 (2002); Sarah Joseph 'An Overview of the Human Rights Accountability of Multinational Enterprises' in Menno Kamminga and Sam Zia-Zarifi (eds) above n 3 at 75 and Sarah Joseph *Corporations and Transnational Human Rights Litigation* (Oxford: Hart Publishing, 2004); Chris Avery 'Business and Human Rights in a Time of Change' in Kamminga and Zia-Zarifi, (eds) ibid 17; Menno Kamminga 'Holding Multinational Corporations Accountable for Human Rights Abuses: a Challenge for the EC' in Philip Alston (ed) *The EU and Human Rights* (Oxford: Oxford University Press, 1999) 558; Amnesty International and Pax Christi International Dutch Sections *Multinational Enterprises and Human Rights* (Utrecht: November 1998).

German industrialists at the end of the Second World War.[46] Against this background, the content of the main substantive human rights obligations of MNEs and other business entities will now be considered.

(3) The Major Substantive Human Rights Obligations of MNEs

The precise content of the human rights obligations of MNEs is open to considerable speculation.[47] However, it is clear that corporate actors will not carry the same responsibilities as states. Some state responsibilities are simply impossible for MNEs and other business enterprises to carry out. Examples include protecting rights of asylum, the right to take part in government, rights to nationality, and provision of rights of due process. Equally states, as public actors, do not themselves enjoy human rights protection, while, as noted above, MNEs, as private actors, can possess rights that may need to be balanced against those of other non-state actors.[48] Against this background the development of substantive obligations will require some adaptation of existing human rights standards. In addition, it may require a wider conception of what obligations may count as human rights obligations for private corporate actors, given their influence over the development of economic and social welfare in the societies in which they operate. The analysis proceeds as follows. First the relationship between state and corporate spheres of responsibility will be considered, secondly the definition of the types of corporate entities that may be subjected to human rights obligations will be assessed and, thirdly, the actual substantive content of possible standards will be briefly discussed. The discussion will be based, in large part, on the UN Norms owing to their undoubted significance in the developing debate over the nature and scope of human rights obligations for MNEs and other business actors.

Historically, the observance of human rights standards has been an obligation of the state alone. Accordingly, the first step in the evolution of substantive standards for MNEs and other business entities requires the assertion of a direct link between the obligations of states, and of non-state actors, to promote universal respect for, and observance of, human rights and fundamental freedoms. An express reference to such a link can be found in the Universal Declaration of Human Rights (UDHR). This instrument is addressed both to governments and to 'other organs of society'. Following this provision, the third recital of the preamble to the UN Norms recognizes that 'even though States have the primary

---

[46] See Andrew Clapham 'The Question of Jurisdiction Under International Criminal Law Over Legal Persons' in Kamminga and Zia-Zarifi (eds) above n 3 especially 166–71.

[47] See further Kinley and Tadaki above n 45 at 966–93; Jagers above n 45 at 51–74; Dine above n 11 at 178–87.   [48] Kinley and Tadaki ibid at 967.

responsibility to promote, secure the fulfilment of, respect, ensure respect of and protect human rights, transnational corporations and other business enterprises, *as organs of society*, are also responsible for promoting and securing the human rights set forth in the Universal Declaration of Human Rights' (emphasis added). This is a clear acceptance of the view that corporate entities do have human rights responsibilities on the basis of their social existence. However, the legal status of the UDHR remains that of a non-binding declaration, and so this reference to the UDHR wording in the UN Norms may be no more than a statement of an ethical duty at best, reinforced by the fact that the UN Commission on Human Rights regards the UN Norms as a draft proposal that has no legal standing.[49]

Although the first concern of the UN Norms is to address the obligations of transnational corporations (TNCs) and other business enterprises in respect of human rights, this instrument continues to address the obligations of governments as well.[50] Thus, paragraph 1 of the UN Norms asserts:

States have the primary responsibility to promote, secure the fulfilment of, respect, ensure respect of and protect human rights recognised in international as well as national law, including ensuring that transnational corporations and other business enterprises respect human rights. Within their respective spheres of activity and influence, transnational corporations and other business enterprises have the obligation to promote, secure the fulfilment of, respect, ensure respect of and protect human rights recognised in international as well as national law, including the rights of indigenous peoples and other vulnerable groups.

This provision places states over TNCs and other business enterprises as the principal regulators of human rights observance. In addition, it recognizes that states and businesses operate in different fields and so each has a specific set or responsibilities in their particular field of operations, thereby obviating the possibility that business enterprises could supplant the state in its obligations to uphold and observe human rights, or that the state could use the Norms as an excuse for not taking action to protect human rights.[51]

Turning to the definitional aspects of extending human rights obligations to TNCs, the discussions over the UN Norms in the UN Sub-Commission on Human Rights reflected a desire to see the application of human rights obligations to all business entities and not merely to TNCs. This avoids an otherwise unjustifiable distinction between TNCs and national firms as regards responsibilities to observe fundamental human rights standards. The focus of the debate on

---

[49] See the discussion in Kinley and Tadaki above n 45 at 948–49 and see UN Commission on Human Rights Res 2004/116 above n 3 at point (c).

[50] The United States opposed the resolution of 20 April 2005 (above note 3) inter alia on the ground that, 'human rights obligations apply to states, not non-state actors, and it is incumbent on states when they deem necessary to adopt national laws that address the obligations of private actors': United States Statement on Item 17 of the Sixty-First Session of the UN Human Rights Commission, 20 April 2005 available from <http://www.business-humanrights.org>.

[51] See Commentary above n 3 at paragraph 2(b).

international corporate social responsibility has tended to be towards TNCs given the transnational character of their operations. However, the underlying issues of principle would apply mutatis mutandis to national firms as the applicability of human rights standards to private corporate actors does not depend on the mere fact that their business operations cross borders. Such a geographically based justification for applying human rights standards to one class of corporations, rather than another, would be unprincipled. The focus on TNCs can perhaps be explained as a pragmatic choice, evolving out of their visibility in certain widely publicized cases of mass violations of human rights and from the perception that TNCs, unlike purely national firms, can take advantage of more lax legal regimes in foreign host countries, which pay scant regard to social welfare concerns, allowing unscrupulous firms to turn this to their commercial advantage.[52] On the other hand, it should be noted that TNCs are more likely than local firms, in countries where social welfare issues are either un- or de-regulated, to observe good practices in this arena. Thus, the real problem may be a lack of proper regulation in the host country of local businesses and institutions for which TNCs may not be responsible. Therefore, any programme of responsibility must take into account the relationship between local and transnational practices and the influence of TNCs thereon.

Taking this into account, the reference to both TNCs and other business enterprises may be said to avoid the risk that an inadequate definition could allow companies to use financial and other structures to conceal their transnational nature and to appear as a domestic company thereby avoiding responsibility under the UN Norms.[53] However, the definition given of what constitutes a 'transnational corporation' is rather vague. The UN Norms state that this term 'refers to an economic entity operating in more than one country or a cluster of economic entities operating in two or more countries – whatever their legal form, whether in their home country or country of activity, and whether taken individually or collectively'.[54] Unlike other commonly used definitions of TNCs (or MNEs), this definition does not refer to control, influence, or coordination of activities as a key element in determining whether the entity is indeed a TNC. This element must be inferred from the reference to economic entity. Its absence would render the instrument applicable to any type of business relationship that crosses borders. Perhaps that is the intention, given the continued reference to 'other business enterprise' which is defined as including 'any business entity, regardless of the international or domestic nature of its activities, including a transnational corporation, contractor, subcontractor, supplier, licensee or

---

[52] See further Draft Universal Human Rights Guidelines for Companies: Introduction UN Doc E/CN.4/Sub.2/2001/WG.2/WP.1 (2001) (hereafter Introduction 2001) at paras 22–26. See also Working Group of the UN Sub-Commission on Human Rights Report for 2002 (UN Doc E/CN.4/Sub.2/2002/13 15 August 2002) at 6 para 15.

[53] Introduction 2001, at paras 18–21. For an illustrative example of such a strategy, applied for the purposes of avoiding a foreign legal liability, see the facts of *Adams v Cape Industries* [1990] Ch 433 (CA).   [54] UN Norms above n 3 at para 20.

distributor; the corporate, partnership or other legal form used to establish the business entity; and the nature of the ownership of the entity'.[55] This definition continues by presuming that the instrument will apply, as a matter of practice, if the business enterprise has any relation with a TNC, the impact of its activities is not entirely local, or the activities involve violations of the right to security of persons as defined in the text of the instrument at paragraphs 3 and 4. Taking both the definition of 'TNC' and 'other business entity' together, the UN Norms are capable of covering a wide 'sphere of influence' that the activities of a corporate network, whatever its actual form, help to create.[56]

As regards the nature and scope of substantive obligations, the discussions concerning the UN Norms have given rise to a re-examination of the range of sources, from which human rights responsibilities for MNEs and other business enterprises can be drawn. The origins and legal standing of such sources has already been discussed in chapter 3.[57] Here the actual substance of the obligations contained in those sources is briefly reviewed. From the existing instruments dealing with corporate social responsibility and human rights, as synthesized into the substantive contents of the UN Norms, at least five different types of provisions can be identified. First, there are those which cover 'traditional' civil and political human rights issues, namely: the right to equal treatment;[58] the right of security of persons as concerns business engagement in, or benefit from, 'war crimes, crimes against humanity, genocide, torture, forced disappearance, forced or compulsory labour, hostage-taking, extrajudicial, summary or arbitrary executions, other violations of humanitarian law and other international crimes against the human person as defined by international law';[59] rights of workers dealing, in particular, with those rights listed in Article 2 of the ILO Declaration on Fundamental Principles and Rights at Work 1998, namely, the prohibition on forced or compulsory labour,[60] the rights of children to be protected against economic exploitation,[61] and freedom of association.[62] In addition, the

---

[55] UN Norms at para 21. Note the circuitous drafting which replicates the notion of 'transnational corporation' as a part of 'other business entity'.

[56] See Kinley and Tadaki above n 45 at 962–66 and see the Report of the UN Commissioner for Human Rights above n 3 at paras 37–39.   [57] See text at nn 202–206.

[58] UN Norms Section B para 2. See also OECD *Guidelines on Multinational Enterprises* (Paris: OECD, 2000) Guideline II 'General Policies' and Guideline IV 'Employment and Industrial Relations'; *ILO Declaration on Fundamental Principles and Rights at Work* (Geneva: ILO, 1998) Article 2(d).   [59] UN Norms Section C para 3.

[60] UN Norms Section D para 5.

[61] UN Norms Section D para 6. This formulation in the text replaces the earlier formulation which stated that 'Companies shall not use child labour and shall contribute to its abolition'. Thus the prohibition in the earlier draft has been modified so that child labour conducted in a non-exploitative manner can be used. This reflects concern that, in some developing countries, the denial of access to labour for children might actually worsen their economic situation and that of their families. In such cases the issue is to make child labour non-abusive. Business enterprises that use child labour must create and implement a plan to eliminate this: Commentary at Section D para. 6 comment (d). By comparison the 1998 ILO Declaration requires 'the effective abolition of child labour' without qualification.   [62] UN Norms Section D para 9.

UN Norms require respect for other civil and political rights, such as privacy, education, freedom of thought, conscience and religion, and freedom of opinion and expression.[63] Secondly, following the contents, in the main, of the ILO Tripartite Declaration of Principles Concerning Multinational Enterprises and Social Policy,[64] the UN Norms contain provisions reflecting the main economic social and cultural rights including: the provision of a safe and healthy working environment;[65] compensation of workers with remuneration that ensures 'an adequate standard of living for them and their families';[66] protection of collective bargaining;[67] respect for the social, economic, and cultural policies of the countries in which companies operate;[68] respect for the rights to health, adequate food and adequate housing and other economic social and cultural rights such as rights to 'adequate food and drinking water; the highest attainable standard of physical and mental health, adequate housing, . . . and refrain from actions which obstruct the realisation of those rights'.[69] No distinction is made in the UN Norms as to the relative importance of these so-called 'first' and 'second' generation human rights. Indeed, as the preamble explains, the UN Norms are based on the 'universality, indivisibility, interdependence and interrelatedness of human rights including the right to development . . . '.[70] This approach also covers the so-called 'third generation' rights of collective solidarity, as expressed through the inclusion, in the UN Norms, of the right of development[71] and the obligation on TNCs and other business enterprises to promote, respect, and protect the rights and interests of indigenous peoples and other vulnerable groups.[72]

---

[63] ibid Section E para 12.

[64] ILO Tripartite Declaration on Multinational Enterprises and Social Policy 1977 as amended at the 279th Session of the ILO Geneva, 17 November 2000: 41 ILM 186 (2002).

[65] UN Norms Section D para 7.   [66] ibid para 8.   [67] ibid para 9.

[68] ibid Section E para 10. These include transparency, accountability, and prohibition of corruption.

[69] ibid para 12. The right to drinking water was first included at the intersessional meeting of the Working Group in February 2002: Working Group 2002 above n 52 at 6 para 14.

[70] UN Norms preamble, recital 13.   [71] UN Norms Section E para 12.

[72] UN Norms Section A para 1 and Section E para 10 as explained in the Commentary at Section E para 10 comment (c). The UN Norms have dropped any explicit reference to self-determination, which was present in earlier drafts: see Draft Universal Human Rights Guidelines for Companies (UN Doc E/CN.4/Sub.2/2001/WG.2/WP.1/Add I (2001) Section E para 11. This reference was dropped in 2002. On the issue of indigenous peoples rights and TNC obligations see further the discussion in Kinley and Tadaki above n 45 at 987–93 and Jagers above n 45 at 157–60. See also *Mayanga (Sumo) Awas Tinigi Community v Nicaragua* Case No 79 Inter-American Court of Human Rights, judgment 31 August 2001 (available on <http://www.indianlaw.org/IACHR_Judgment_Official_English.doc>) which established the right of indigenous peoples to peaceful enjoyment of their traditional lands, requiring the respondent state to protect such rights in granting concessions to foreign investors. See also UN Human Rights Committee Communication No 511/1992 *I Lansman et al v Finland* and Communication No 671/1995 *J Lansman et al v Finland* discussed in Jagers above n 45 at 158–59. The African Commission in Human and Peoples Rights heard a case brought by the Ogoni people but held that it was not competent to hear claims against private companies: Fons Coomans 'The *Ogoni* Case Before the African Commission on Human and People's Rights' 52 ICLQ 749 at 760 (2003).

A fourth group of provisions can be said to deal with the special problems created by the operations of TNCs for the realization of the types of rights listed above. Thus the UN Norms deal with a specific issue that has arisen in a number of cases, namely, the operation of security arrangements for companies. Such arrangements 'shall observe international human rights norms as well as the laws and professional standards of the country or countries in which they operate'.[73] This general principle is further elaborated in the Commentary to the Norms, which requires companies to observe the emerging best practices evolving in this field through various codes of conduct, particularly the UN Principles on the Use of Force and Firearms by Law Enforcement Officials, the UN Code of Conduct for Law Enforcement Officers, the UN Convention Against Torture, and the Rome Statute of the International Criminal Court. Business enterprises and TNCs are further urged not to supplant the state military and law enforcement services but only provide for their own preventive or defensive services and not to hire individuals known to have been responsible for human rights or humanitarian law violations.[74] Other provisions that can be added to this category are the duty to recognize and respect applicable norms of international law, national laws and regulations, administrative practices and the rule of law,[75] and the final saving provision which makes clear that 'nothing in these Norms shall be construed as diminishing, restricting, or adversely affecting the human rights obligations of States under national and international law, nor shall they be construed as diminishing, restricting, or adversely affecting more protective human rights norms'.[76] Not only does this provision offer a rule of interpretation favourable to the effective protection of human rights, but it also emphasizes that the operations of business enterprises can observe higher standards than the minimum standards required by the UN Norms.

A fifth, and final, group of substantive provisions go beyond a conventional human rights based agenda and belong more to a general corporate social responsibility code. This reflects the fact that many of the sources, referred to as contributing to the Draft Norms,[77] constitute more general codes of business ethics, which, by their nature, will deal with social issues not usually described as human rights issues. Thus, for example, the UN Norms require that TNCs and other business enterprises shall act 'in accordance with fair business, marketing and advertising practices and shall take all necessary steps to ensure the safety and quality of the goods and services they provide, including observance of the precautionary principle. Nor shall they produce, distribute, market or advertise harmful

---

[73] UN Norms Section C para 4. See further the Amnesty International *Human Rights Guidelines for Companies* above n 43. [74] Commentary Section C para 3 comments (a)–(d).

[75] UN Norms Section E para 10. This principle is echoed in the OECD Guidelines and the ILO Tripartite Declaration. [76] ibid Section H. para 19.

[77] On which see Draft Universal Human Rights Guidelines for Companies with Source Materials UN Doc E/CN.4/Sub.2/2001/WG.2/WP.1/Add 2 (2001) available on <http://www1.umn.edu/humanrts/links/omig.html>.

or potentially harmful products for use by consumers'.[78] This introduces general consumer protection standards into the instrument. Other such social responsibility provisions include a prohibition against bribery[79] and obligations with regard to environmental protection.[80] Whether these are truly 'human rights' issues is open to debate. On the other hand, as the preamble to the UN Norms notes, 'new international human rights issues and concerns are continually emerging and that transnational corporations and other business enterprises often are involved in these issues and concerns, such that further standard-setting and implementation are required at this time and in the future'. In this light, it may well be that consumer and environmental protection are emergent human rights issues. It has been argued, for example, that a right to a clean and healthy environment is a human right, though this has been disputed.[81] Whether consumer protection is a human right seems rather more tenuous, as it is hard to see how elevating such issues to the status of quasi-constitutional rights makes such protection more effective. In any case other established human rights could be sufficient. For example, death or serious injury caused by unsafe products or processes could come within the right to life and the right to personal security under Article 3 of the Universal Declaration on Human Rights and Articles 6 and 9 of the International Civil and Political Rights Covenant. Loss of livelihood, due to disability, could be covered by Article 25 of the declaration. As for the prohibition against bribery, a human rights approach seems ill-conceived, as it is not entirely clear whether there is an identifiable human victim. This is an area in which the wider social undesirability of such practices is in issue, rather than any significant adverse effects on any one individual. It would thus be better dealt with as a regulatory matter under national law and specialized international conventions than a human rights oriented instrument.[82]

---

[78] UN Norms Section F para 13.   [79] ibid Section E para 11.
[80] ibid Section G para 14.
[81] See generally M Fitzmaurice 'The Contribution of Environmental Law to the Development of Modern International Law' in J Makarczyk (ed) *The Theory of International Law at the Threshold of the 21st Century* (The Hague: Kluwer Law International, 1996) from 909 especially 909–14.
[82] On the issue of corruption and bribery, see further the United Nations Convention Against Corruption 14 December 2005 at <http://www.unodc.org/unodc/en/crime_convention_corruption.html>; OECD Convention on Combating Bribery of Foreign Public Officials in International Business Transactions adopted by the Negotiating Conference on 21 November 1997 at <http://www.oecd.org/document/21/0,2340,en_2649_37447_2017813_1_1_1_37447,00.html#text>; UNCTAD *Illicit Payments* Series on issues in international investment agreements (New York and Geneva: United Nations, 2001), S Rose-Ackerman 'Corruption and the Global Corporation: Ethical Obligations and Workable Strategies' in Michael Likosky (ed) *Transnational Legal Processes: Globalisation and Power Disparities* (London: Butterworths Lexis-Nexis, 2002) 148. For further information see the Transparency International website <http://www.transparency.org>; Thomas Catan and Joshua Chaffin 'Bribery Has Long Been Used to Land International Contracts. New Laws Will Make That Tougher' *Financial Times* 8 May 2003 at 19; 'The Short Arm of the Law' Special report: Bribery and Business *The Economist* 2 March 2002 at 85. The bribery of foreign officials was made a crime under the UK Anti-Terrorism, Crime and Security Act 2001 (2001 Chapter 24) ss 108–110 at <http://www.opsi.gov.uk/acts/en2001/01en24-d.htm>.

(4) Monitoring and Enforcement

Key to any initiatives concerning the extension of human rights responsibilities to MNEs is how to ensure that any emergent substantive human rights obligations of such entities are actually upheld. This may involve a mix of informal self-regulation by firms and formal regulation by way of national and international legal approaches. Corporate self-regulation on human rights issues is far from developed, as compared with environmental self-regulation, which is discussed in the next chapter. Whether firms can, or should, engage in such activity generates controversy. Some business voices feel that this is a step too far, requiring firms to become quasi-governmental organizations that would engage in political decisions far beyond the limits of their capability. Indeed, human rights activism by MNEs might be said to undermine their position as providers of beneficial foreign investment to less developed countries that may object to such interference in their internal political affairs.[83] Equally, human rights concerns may be of such a fundamentally different magnitude, as compared with other corporate social responsibility issues (such as environmental protection or day-to-day employment and health and safety matters), that they should never be entrusted to self-regulatory responses. On the other hand, in practice, some MNEs have found themselves embroiled in situations where human rights abuses have arisen and their responses have left much to be desired in terms of avoiding further harm, using their influence with host governments to mitigate policies of human rights abuse or inadvertently, perhaps even recklessly, contributing to an escalation of harm.[84] Accordingly, firms may have little choice but to address human rights concerns as part of their business management strategy, particularly where they invest in conflict zones, politically authoritarian and/or corrupt states, or less

---

[83] See further Frans-Paul van der Putten, Gemma Crijns, and Harry Hummels 'The Ability of Corporations to Protect Human Rights in Developing Countries' in Rory Sullivan (ed) above n 1 at 82. For an account of the complex interactions between developing host countries (in this case Malaysia and its 'Multimedia Super Corridor' investment programme), MNEs and human rights activity, see Michael B Likosky *The Silicon Empire: Law Culture and Commerce* (Aldershot: Ashgate, 2005). Note also the case of China and the internet service provider Google: 'Google censors itself for China' BBC News 26 January 2006 at <http://news.bbc.co.uk/1/hi/technology/4645596.stm>. On Google's own view of this case, see <http://googleblog.blogspot.com/2006/01/google-in-china.html>. For the wider background, see Amnesty International *Undermining Freedom of Expression in China: The Role of Yahoo!, Microsoft and Google* (London: Amnesty International UK, 2006). Both cases suggest a selective and coordinated collaboration in the repression of local human rights where firm and state interests coincide, while at the same time justifying such action as in fact pro-human rights.

[84] See, for example, the situation of Unocal in Burma that was the basis of the claims discussed below, or the experience of Shell with the Ogoni people's rights, that founds the basis of the claims brought against the company by the relatives of the late writer and human rights activist Ken Saro-Wiwa, described below. See also Rory Sullivan and Nina Seppala 'From the Inside Looking Out: A Management Perspective on Human Rights' in Rory Sullivan (ed) above n 1 at 102; Simon Handelsman 'Mining in Conflict Zones' ibid at 125; Christopher McDowell 'Privatising Infrastructure Development: "Development" Refugees and the Resettlement Challenge' ibid at 155.

developed countries. Indeed, as will be seen below, the UN Norms expect TNCs and other business enterprises to develop a human rights policy and appropriate internal monitoring systems. Thus, the trend toward developing clear internal management responses may be inevitable. However, self-regulation, of the kind seen, for example, in relation to environmental matters, may well be inappropriate in the case of human rights issues, as the state remains the prime protector of such rights and it would be politically illegitimate to hand this responsibility over exclusively to the corporation.

Turning to formal legal regulation, at the national level, both standard setting, through new laws and regulations, and public interest litigation, taken against firms alleged to have broken their human rights obligations, may be used. At the international level there arises the possibility that IGOs have a monitoring role that can supplement such national initiatives, in particular, by requiring states to comply with certain obligations to ensure that their domestic regulatory structures adequately reflect the emergent norms in this area and by providing adequate and effective remedies for those who allege to have been harmed by the failure of firms to observe fundamental international human rights standards.

(a) The National Level

At the national level, there has, to date, been relatively little progress on standard setting through new laws or regulations embodying human rights standards.[85] The most significant examples in this regard may be the US and EU initiatives to link labour rights protection to the extension of trade preferences, or the UK Ethical Trading Initiative.[86] However, specialized legislation on MNEs and human rights is virtually non-existent. One example of what might be possible arose in Australia where the draft Corporate Code of Conduct Bill contained a provision that subjected the overseas subsidiaries of Australian companies to a general obligation to observe human rights and the principle of non-discrimination.[87] That Bill was never adopted. Similar proposals in the United States and the United Kingdom have also met with little success.[88]

---

[85] In this connection the UN Norms state, 'States should establish and reinforce the necessary legal and administrative framework for ensuring that the Norms and other relevant national and international laws are implemented by transnational corporations and other business enterprises': UN Norms Section H para 17.

[86] On the UK see further <http://www.ethicaltrade.org>. For the US and EU position see M Trebilcock and R Howse *The Regulation of International Trade* (London: Routledge, 3rd edn, 2005) at 575–76.

[87] *Corporate Code of Conduct Bill 2000* The Parliament of the Commonwealth of Australia draft of 28 August 2000 clause 10.

[88] US *Corporate Code of Conduct Act* HR 4596, 106th Cong (2000) *Corporate Code of Conduct Act* HR 2782, 107th Cong (2001); UK *Corporate Responsibility Bill 2003* available <http://www.parliament.the-stationery-office.co.uk/pa/cm200102/cmbills/145/2002145.pdf>. It should be noted that the UK Bill, introduced as a private member's bill and not as a governmental initiative, concerns only civil liability and does not create specific human rights obligations on companies.

On the other hand, at the level of US national law, a degree of direct responsibility for human rights violations on the part of MNEs is being recognized through litigation brought by private claimants against the parent companies of affiliates operating in the claimants' countries.[89] Thus in the United States District Court case of *Doe v Unocal*[90] it was held, for the first time, that MNEs could, in principle, be directly liable for gross violations of human rights under the US Alien Tort Claims Act (ATCA).[91] This case can be used to illustrate the conceptual problems involved in the bringing of a human rights claim against a corporation.[92] The key difficulty is to show that the corporation was in some way implicated in human rights violations. This raises the question whether there has to be evidence of direct involvement or whether some lesser degree of involvement is sufficient. In its decision of 31 August 2000, the US District Court in the *Unocal* case awarded a summary judgment to Unocal on the ground that although there was evidence that Unocal knew about, and benefited from, forced labour on the pipeline project in Burma in which it was a joint venture partner, it was not directly involved in the alleged abuses. These were the responsibility of the Burmese authorities alone. Giving the Court's judgment, Judge Ronald Lew followed a series of decisions by US Military Tribunals after the Second World War, involving the prosecution of German industrialists for their participation in the Third Reich's slave labour policies.[93] These established that, in order to be liable, the defendant industrialists had to take active steps in cooperating or participating in the forced labour practices. Mere knowledge that someone else would commit abuses was insufficient. By analogy with these cases, Unocal could not be held liable as a matter of international law and so the claim under the Alien Tort Statute failed.[94] However, the principle that a private non-state actor can be sued before the US courts for alleged violations of human rights was not questioned.[95]

---

[89] For a full discussion, see Joseph above n 10 at ch 2. See also Jagers above n 45 at 179–203.

[90] 963 F Supp 880 US Dist Ct, CD Cal, 25 March 1997 noted in 92 AJIL 309 (1998). See also *Wiwa v Royal Dutch Petroleum Company* 96 Civ 8389 (SDNY).

[91] 28 USC s 1350. ATCA states: 'The district courts shall have original jurisdiction of any civil action by an alien for a tort only, committed in violation of the law of nations or a treaty of the United States.'

[92] For discussion of human rights based claims in England, Australia, and Canada, see Joseph above n 10 at ch 6 and, for the Netherlands and England, see Kamminga and Zia-Zarifi (Eds) above n 3 Part III chs 9–12.

[93] *US v Flick* 6 Trials of War Criminals Before the Nuremberg Military Tribunals Under Control Council Law No 10 (1952); *US v Carl Krauch* ibid vol 8; *US v Alfred Krupp* ibid vol 9; *Flick v Johnson* 85 US App DC 70, 174 F 2d 983 (DC Cir 1949).

[94] *Doe v Unocal* US Dist Ct, CD Cal 31 August 2000: 2000 US Dist. LEXIS 13327. See also 'Claim Against Unocal Rejected: Judge Cites Evidence of Abuses in Burma but No Jurisdiction' by William Branigin *Washington Post* Friday, 8 September 2000 page E10.

[95] See also in this regard *Kadic v Karadzic* 70 F 3d 232 (2d Cir 1995) where it was held that the Alien Tort Statute reaches the conduct of private parties provided that their conduct is undertaken under the colour of state authority or violates a norm of international law that is recognized as extending to the conduct of private parties.

The summary judgment was overturned in part on appeal to the United States Court of Appeal for the Ninth Circuit.[96] The USCA held that there were genuine issues of material fact to be determined as regards the possible liability of Unocal for the alleged acts of forced labour, for aiding and abetting the Myanmar military in subjecting the plaintiffs to forced labour and for aiding and abetting the Myanmar military in subjecting the plaintiffs to murder and rape occurring in furtherance of forced labour. On the other hand, there were insufficient facts to justify an examination of the allegations of liability on the part of Unocal for torture. The affirmation of the applicability of the law relating to aiding and abetting an offence to crimes or torts involving alleged violations of fundamental human rights under ATCA is of great significance.[97]

This allows for a finding that a corporation may be liable even if it has not directly taken part in the alleged violations, but has given practical assistance and encouragement to the commission of the crime or tort in question (the *actus reus* of aiding and abetting) and has actual or constructive knowledge that its actions will assist the perpetrator in the commission of the crime or tort (the *mens rea* of aiding and abetting). Thus the district judge was wrong to give the weight that he had done to the 'active participation' standard used in the Nuremberg military tribunal cases that he had relied on. In those cases this standard had been used in response to the defendant's 'necessity defence'. No such defence was invoked, nor could be invoked, by Unocal in the present case. Thus the USCA accepts that a corporate actor can be complicit in a human rights violation even where there is no direct involvement. Accordingly, different levels of complicity, both direct and indirect, can be invoked as the basis of a corporate liability claim.[98]

This leads to a further question: where is the line between indirect complicity and innocent action to be drawn? According to Sarah Joseph, mere benefit from a state's human rights abuses should not attract ATCA liability, as it lacks a clear causal connection between the activities of the company and the violation in question. In her view, 'TNCs should be held liable for aiding and abetting human rights abuse when such actions foreseeably lead to the perpetration of identifiable

---

[96] *Doe v Unocal Corp* Judgment of 18 September 2002: 2002 US App LEXIS 19263 (9th Cir 2002), 41 ILM 1367 (2002). This decision was in turn vacated on 14 February 2003 to be reheard by the *en banc* Court of Appeal for the Ninth Circuit: *John Doe v Unocal* 395 F 3d 978, 2003 US App LEXIS 2716. The case settled in December 2004: 'Unocal Settles Burma Abuse Case' *Financial Times* 14 December 2004 at 12. Since then the District Court opinion of 2000 has also been vacated by the USCA Ninth Circuit: *John Doe v Unocal* 403 F 3d 708; 2005 US App LEXIS 6070 (filed 13 April 2005).

[97] For this purpose the USCA held that the distinction between the aiding and abetting of a crime and a tort was not significant, in that similar principles applied in each situation: ibid at ILM 1376.

[98] On the issue of corporate complicity in human rights violations, see further Anita Ramasastry 'Secrets and Lies? Swiss Banks and International Human Rights' 31 Vand .Jo.Transnat'l Law 325 (1998) and ibid 'Corporate Complicity from Nuremberg to Rangoon: An Examination of Forced Labor Cases and their Impact on the Liability of Multinational Corporations' 20 Berkeley Jo. Int'l L. 91 (2002); Andrew Clapham and Scott Jebri 'Categories of Corporate Complicity in Human Rights Abuses' 24 Hastings Int'l & Comp. L.R. 339 (2001).

grave human rights abuses by another'.[99] On the other hand, continued commercial activity in the face of gross violations of human rights could be seen as complicity through inaction. This issue lay at the heart of the recent Apartheid litigation in the US where this concept was rejected.[100] The US District Court felt that such an extension of ATCA liability would have serious, if not disastrous, consequences for the flow of international commerce and was not consistent with the policy of the US, and other leading powers at the time, of constructive engagement with the Apartheid regime. It would also prevent the use of economic investment as a means of achieving greater respect for human rights by way of poverty reduction.[101]

A further difficulty in a human rights claim against a corporate actor is to determine what kinds of human rights violations can be attributed to it. In this regard the USCA judgment in *Doe v Unocal* is of particular importance in that it reaffirms the principle that, under ATCA, private actors may be directly liable for alleged violations of fundamental human rights norms that constitute *jus cogens* and to which individual liability applies. In this connection, forced labour was seen by the USCA as a modern variant of slavery, one of the crimes to which international law attributes individual liability. The incidents of rape and murder that occurred in relation to the forced labour practices of the Myanmar military were also of this type as they arose directly out of the furtherance of forced labour.[102] On the other hand, certain rights have been found by the US courts not to come within ATCA including, among others, the right to life, health, sustainable development, and environmental rights.[103]

The strategy of using ATCA as a basis for human rights claims against MNEs will be significantly affected by the US Supreme Court decision of 29 June 2004 in the case of *Sosa v Alvarez-Machain*.[104] Although not involving a corporate defendant, this case has determined that private non-state actors will only be liable for human rights abuses under ATCA where the alleged infringement of human rights law is one that has a definite content and wide acceptance among civilized nations, in other words, that it is grounded on well-established customary international law. On the facts, the claimant sought to recover damages for arbitrary arrest but failed to show that international law recognizes a general prohibition against arbitrary arrest as opposed to one against prolonged arbitrary detention. The message is clear: only the most egregious, widespread, and universally recognized violations of

---

[99] Joseph above n 10 at 50–51 and 53.

[100] *In re South African Apartheid Litigation* 346 F Supp 2d 538; 2004 US Dist LEXIS 23944. The logic of this reasoning would also be consistent with the policy underlying the voluntary Sullivan Principles of 1977, which outlined actions investors in South Africa should take to mitigate the effects of apartheid: see <http://www/revleonsullivan.org/principled/principles.htm>.

[101] 346 F Supp 2d 538 at 553–55 paras 40–44.

[102] *Doe v Unocal* above n 96 at ILM 1374–80.   [103] See Joseph above n 10 at 27–8.

[104] 124 S Ct 2739 (2004), 43 ILM 1390 (2004). See for comment Sarah Joseph 'Corporations and Human Rights Litigation' at <http://www.hartpub.co.uk/Updates/sjupdates.html> (accessed 2 August 2005).

fundamental human rights will be capable of founding a claim under ATCA. In addition, ATCA litigation will be monitored to prevent any improper intrusion into the foreign relations domain of the United States Government.[105] Lower courts were urged by the US Supreme Court to exercise 'great caution' in cases that raised risks of adverse foreign policy consequences.[106] Thus the US Supreme Court has not barred actions under ATCA against corporate defendants, as some had feared.[107] Indeed, in the case of *The Presbyterian Church of Sudan v Talisman Energy and the Republic of Sudan* the US District Court for the Southern District of New York (SDNY) held that the Supreme Court judgment does not prohibit claims against corporations and their affiliates on the ground that they are not sufficiently definite and accepted in international law, nor does it prevent claims for secondary liability on the basis of complicity in human rights abuses.[108] On the other hand, the Supreme Court has introduced a more cautious approach that should filter out all but the most extreme cases of alleged abuse.[109]

Certain additional questions need to be faced so as to make out an ATCA claim. In the case of a defendant MNE, it is necessary to determine which parts of the group enterprise should be held responsible. The local affiliate of the MNE in the host country where the alleged violation took place would be the most obvious defendant. However, the question arises whether the parent, and any intermediate holding companies, could also be held to account. Here the US courts have applied general principles of group liability in the ATCA context, requiring the plaintiff to show that the parent and/or other affiliated enterprises were directly involved in the events leading to the violation or were indirectly involved on the basis of an agency analysis.[110] In addition, the jurisdictional implications of the case have to be determined. Here the issues of personal jurisdiction and appropriateness of the forum, under the doctrine of *forum non conveniens*, will arise.[111]

Although a finding of direct responsibility on the part of a MNE for human rights violations is as yet unprecedented, there is some support for establishing the

---

[105]   124 S Ct 2739 at 2766 n 21 (2004).

[106]   ibid at 2763. See further on this issue Joseph above n 10 at 44–47 and *Sarei v Rio Tinto* 221 F Supp 2d 1116 (CD Cal 2002). The plaintiffs brought a number of claims for violations of human rights and environmental damage against the defendant arising out of the 10-year long Bourgainville uprising between 1988–98. The district court dismissed the claims on the ground that the US Government had expressed a political interest in the case, which bound the court not to proceed with the action. On appeal this finding was reversed (Judge Bybee dissenting): *Sarei v Rio Tinto* No 02–56256 CV–00–11695-MMM filed 7 August 2006 (USCA 9th Cir).

[107]   See, for example, Joseph above n 10 at 61.

[108]   Opinion of 13 June 2005: 374 F Supp 2d 331; 2005 US Dist LEXIS 11368. See per contra *In re South African Apartheid Litigation* above n 100 at 550 para 30 which rejects an aider and abettor liability under ATCA.

[109]   Indeed, as noted above, the Apartheid litigation did not survive the post-*Sosa* requirements.

[110]   See, for example, *Larry Bowoto et al v Chevron Texaco Corp* Opinion of the US Dist Ct ND Cal 22 March 2004: 2004 US Dist LEXIS 4603 discussed in ch 8 at 311–12; contrast *Alomang v Freeport McMoran Inc* 811 So 2d 99; 2002 La App LEXIS 543 where plaintiffs failed to show that the Indonesian subsidiary was the *alter ego* of the defendant parent company.

[111]   See ch 4 at 156–57 and the cases discussed there.

indirect responsibility on the part of the state for the conduct of non-state actors that amounts to a violation of the human rights of a third person. Such a responsibility could be established by international convention.[112] No such responsibility has ever been expressly provided for. Instead there is some evidence from the case law under the ECHR that the state may be under an obligation to 'secure' the rights of third persons against interference by a non-state actor. Failure to do so may result in a violation of the convention.[113] However, this case law is uncertain in its scope and too much cannot be read into it. At most, it is clear that the state cannot absolve itself of its direct human rights responsibilities by hiving them off to a privatized entity.[114]

(b) The Inter-Governmental Level

Turning to the role of IGOs in monitoring and enforcement, two sets of issues arise.[115] First, what should the legal status of any standard setting instruments be and, secondly, what kinds of procedures for monitoring and enforcement could be put in place. The discussions over the UN Norms are instructive, as these very questions have had to be faced by the participants. It is clear that the legal status of the UN Norms is yet to be settled and, for the time being, they should be regarded as non-binding.[116] There are arguments in favour of, and against, a binding code.[117] The main advantage of a voluntary instrument is that it could be used in conjunction with existing voluntary corporate codes of conduct to develop a more comprehensive system of internal values to be observed by the company.

---

[112] See Kamminga above n 45 at 559, 569.

[113] See, for example, *Young James and Webster v UK* (1981) E Ct HR Series A vol 44; *X and Y v Netherlands* (1985) E Ct HR Series A vol 91; *Arzte für das Leben* (1988) E Ct HR Series A vol 139. See further Application No 36022/97 *Hatton and Others v United Kingdom* judgment E Ct HR 8 July 2003 at <http://cmiskp.echr.coe.int> (deregulation of night flights at Heathrow Airport did not violate Article 8, right to private and family life); see Charles Bourne 'I'm Noisy Fly Me' New Law Journal 15 August 2003 at 1262. See also, on state liability for noise and environmental pollution, *Powell and Rayner v United Kingdom* E Ct HR Judgment of 21 February 1990 Series A No 172; *Lopez Ostra v Spain* E Ct HR Judgment 9 December 1994 Series A No 303–C; *Guerra and Others v Italy* E Ct HR Reports 1998–I. See generally A Drzemczewski *European Human Rights Convention in Domestic Law* (Oxford: Oxford University Press, 1983) ch 8; Clapham *Human Rights Obligations of Non-State Actors* above n 34 at 349–420; Jagers above n 45 at 36–44 and ch VI.

[114] *Costello-Roberts v UK* E Ct HR (1993) Series A vol 247.

[115] See further Kinley and Tadaki above n 45 at 995–1020 covering the possible roles of UN bodies, the World Bank, and WTO. The IMF is singled out as having suppressed any ability to act as a monitor of TNC human rights practices and as not having the necessary institutional organs to do so: see at 996.

[116] But see Weissbrodt and Kruger above n 3 at 913–15 who argue that the UN Norms are 'non-voluntary' and derive a degree of legal authority from the numerous implementation provisions they contain and from the binding sources from which they are derived.

[117] See further the 2001 version of the Introduction to the Draft Universal Human Rights Guidelines for Companies UN Doc E/CN.4/Sub.2/2001/WG.2/WP.1 (2001) at paras 34–43 on which this discussion draws. See also the UN Commissioner's Report of 2005 above n 3 at paras 20–21.

This would need to be supplemented by an effective system of accountability within the company.[118] However, the discussions on the UN Norms have tended to favour a binding instrument, bearing in mind the past history of non-binding codes, the fact that many non-binding guidelines already exist and also the need for developing practical methods for enforcing human rights standards against TNCs, especially where states might not do so given their need to focus on attracting inward investment.[119] In response, the Introduction to the second draft of the UN Norms (then known as the Draft Guidelines) offers a middle way. It asserts that 'it would be unrealistic to suggest that human rights standards with regard to companies should immediately become the subject of treaty obligations' given that only some of the standards contained in the UN Norms are binding treaty-based norms, and that the precise legal status, in the international legal order, of companies and other non-state actors remains uncertain. Indeed, even 'if the Working Group wishes to pursue a legally binding instrument or even a treaty, it would ordinarily start with some form of "soft law" exercise'.[120] This has been the normal pattern of operation in relation to the adoption of other binding human rights instruments.[121] Hence, in the absence of state opinion to the contrary (perhaps an unlikely eventuality[122]), some transition from 'soft' to 'hard' law is more likely to occur, with the Draft Norms being the first step in this process. On the other hand, as David Weissbrodt pointed out at the 54th Session of the UN Sub-Commission on Human Rights, the UN Norms are binding to the extent that they apply human rights law under ratified conventions to activities of TNCs and other business enterprises. Moreover, the language of the document emphasizes binding responsibilities through the use of the term 'shall' rather than 'should' and through the inclusion, in more recent drafts, of more comprehensive implementation measures.[123]

Connected with this issue is the question of how to give the UN Norms 'teeth' through effective implementation and monitoring procedures. In this regard the UN Norms require TNCs and other business enterprises to adopt, disseminate, and implement internal rules of operation in compliance with the Norms. In addition, they must incorporate the principles contained in the UN Norms in their contracts or other arrangements and dealings with contractors, sub-contractors, suppliers, and licensees in order to ensure their implementation and respect.[124] This represents

---

[118] Indeed a business representative at the 54th Session stressed the need for a voluntary approach and that businesses themselves should develop the draft: Working Group 2002 above n 52 at 12 para 36.

[119] Working Group 2002 above n 52 at 9 para 27, 11 paras 32, 35. On the past history of voluntary codes see Peter T Muchlinski 'A Brief History of Regulation' in Sol Picciotto and Ruth Mayne (eds) *Regulating International Business* (London: MacMillan Press/Oxfam, 1999) 47, and text in ch 17 at 654–56.   [120] Introduction 2001 above n 52 at para 40.

[121] See ibid paras 41–43.

[122] However, the UN Millennium Social Forum has indicated its support for a legally binding set of guidelines: UN GAOR, 54th Session, Agenda Item 49(b) at 11: UN Doc A/54/959 (2000).

[123] Working Group 2002 above n 52 at 6 para 14 and Weissbrodt and Kruger above n 116.

[124] Draft Norms Section H para 15.

a significant advance on the earlier drafts, which did not contain express provisions on the use of such legal measures to give force to their contents, although such measures were recommended in commentaries on those earlier drafts.[125] The UN Norms also require that TNCs and other business enterprises shall monitor and verify their compliance in an independent and transparent manner that includes input from relevant stakeholders.[126] This may be done by national, international, governmental, and/or non-governmental mechanisms in addition to internal review procedures.[127] Earlier drafts of the UN Norms focused on corporate implementation. However, the current UN Norms suggest that other actors could use the Norms to assess business practice and performance in the area of human rights responsibilities. For example, they could form the basis of industry monitoring; unions could use them as a benchmark for their expectations of company conduct, as could NGOs; and the UN's human rights treaty bodies could apply the UN Norms to create additional reporting requirements about corporate compliance with this instrument.[128] In addition, TNCs must ensure that outside stakeholders have access to information about human rights remediation efforts by firms and that workers have proper avenues by which to make complaints with regard to the violation of the Norms.[129]

In addition, the draft presented to the 54th Session of the UN Sub-Commission on Human Rights in 2002 introduced, for the first time, a provision requiring TNCs and other business enterprises to provide compensation for violations of the UN Norms.[130] The final version reads:

Transnational corporations and other business enterprises shall provide prompt, effective and adequate reparation to those persons, entities, and communities that have been adversely affected by failures to comply with these Norms through, inter alia, reparations, restitution, compensation and rehabilitation for any damage done or property taken.[131]

The UN Norms have also introduced some clarification of where such reparation is to be determined. In the words of paragraph 18 of the UN Norms: 'In connection with determining damages, in regard to criminal sanctions, and in all other respects, these Norms shall be applied by national courts and/or international tribunals, pursuant to national and international law'. By taking this approach, the UN Norms envisage a binding enforcement mechanism, centred on national courts and/or international tribunals, which offers directly effective rights of reparation for the individuals or groups affected as a consequence of a violation of the instrument. This presupposes a legally binding document that is effective within the national laws of the UN member states that adopt it. Such an effect

---

[125] See UN Doc E/CN.4/Sub.2/2001/WG.2/WP.1/Add 1 (2001) Section H para 17 Commentary at (c).   [126] UN Norms Section H para 16.
[127] ibid.   [128] Commentary Section H para 16 comments (a)–(c).
[129] ibid comments (d)–(e).
[130] See UN Doc E/CN.4/Sub.2/2002/WG.2/WP.1 29 May 2002 at 6 para 17.
[131] UN Norms Section H para 18.

could not be presumed from a non-binding declaration or recommendation of the UN, neither of which normally have the force of positive international law nor as sources of directly effective individual rights that can be invoked before national tribunals. Arguably, the UN Norms, as an instrument that contains many binding norms of international human rights law, may be enforceable by that fact alone. However, as argued above, not all the norms contained in its provisions are uncontroversial in this respect. Some of the rights that are included may not have such a legal status.[132] Therefore, if the reparation mechanism is to be real and effective it requires the adoption of an instrument that has the force of law within the legal orders of the signatory states, and which recognizes the legal effectiveness of all the norms that it contains. This would need to be something akin to an international convention, which contains an obligation to implement its contents and enforcement mechanisms into the municipal law of the signatory state. This is a far cry form a 'soft law' instrument of the kind, as discussed above, usually adopted in this field. Equally, it is unlikely that a UN framework could enforce binding rules and norms relating to the activities of TNCs.[133] In the light of these matters, there is a significant need of further clarification as to what legal form this enforcement mechanism will take and on how it is expected to work. However, given the uncertainty surrounding the status and future importance of the UN Norms in the work of the UN Human Rights Council, which replaced the UN Commission on Human Rights in June 2006,[134] and of the special representative appointed to oversee the issue of human rights and TNCs, a clear answer to this question is unlikely in the near future.[135]

A further issue that requires some comment and clarification concerns identifying the precise forum before which any claim for reparations under paragraph 18 can be brought. As it stands paragraph 18 is silent on this matter. It could, therefore, be presumed that the question of forum remains to be determined by the national laws of the jurisdiction or jurisdictions in which a claim is brought, or by reference to an international tribunal. If so, then claims brought under the UN Norms may be embroiled in lengthy and unhelpful disputes over jurisdiction, particularly in common law jurisdictions where the doctrine of *forum non conveniens* continues to apply. In such jurisdictions it may be possible for the respondent corporation, particularly if it is an MNE and the *locus* of the alleged violation

---

[132] See further 'In the Matter of the Draft Norms on the Responsibilities of Transnational Corporations and Other Business Enterprises with regard to Human Rights' Opinion of Professor Emeritus Maurice Mendelson QC (4 April 2004).

[133] See Working Group 2002 above n 52 at 7 para 17 (views of Mr Alfonso Martinez, member of the Working Group).   [134] See n 3.

[135] See further John Ruggie Interim Report of the Special Representative of the Secretary-General on the Issue of Human Rights and Transnational Corporations and Other Business Enterprises UN Doc E/CN.4/2006/97 (2006) at <http://www1.umn.edu/humanrts/business/RuggieReport2006. html>. The special representative states: 'Indeed, in the SRSG's view the divisive debate over the Norms obscures rather than illuminates promising areas of consensus and cooperation among business, civil society, governments, and international institutions with respect to human rights': para 69.

of the UN Norms is in another jurisdiction, to challenge the appropriateness of the forum chosen by the claimants and, thereby, to gain a procedural advantage either by vacating the case to another forum more sympathetic to the corporation's defence, or simply by causing delay while this issue is litigated.[136] In that process the claimants may suffer significant delay in access to justice not to mention financial loss that might undermine their ability to continue with their claim. Some legal systems are becoming sensitive to such issues[137] but others are not.[138] Thus, the UN Norms may need to establish certain basic rules of jurisdiction so that such legal techniques are not allowed to undermine legitimate claims. One solution would be to make available the jurisdiction of any state that adheres to the UN Norms on the basis of either the *locus* of the alleged violation, or the domicile of the corporation alleged to be responsible, with the claimant having the choice of forum. Equally, it might be necessary to ensure that the corporate (or contractual) separation between affiliates in an MNE group (or network)[139] is not allowed to act as a barrier to jurisdiction against related (or cooperating) entities located outside the jurisdiction where the harm is alleged to have been suffered, but which are seen as complicit in a violation of the UN Norms on the basis of their relationship with the affiliate (or network partner) located in that jurisdiction. This may prove to be rather controversial as it challenges long accepted notions of separate corporate personality (and, in the case of transnational networks or alliances, freedom of contract) as the basis for attributing liability to legal persons. However, in the absence of some clarification of this matter, national laws may well come to be used to insulate discrete entities, involved in an MNE or in a transnational network enterprise, production, or retailing chain that leads to a violation of human rights, from full responsibility.

The preceding discussion illustrates well the challenges ahead for any IGO that wishes to develop a new social responsibility agenda for MNEs and other business entities. The first point to note is that the process is a slow one and is more likely to create 'soft law' obligations. Indeed, as the special representative has pointed out, given the lack of international legal personality of corporate actors, they cannot be directly bound by international law as such, and that, apart from certain narrowly

---

[136] See further Peter T Muchlinski 'Corporations in International Litigation: Problems of Jurisdiction and the United Kingdom Asbestos Case' 50 ICLQ 1 (2001); Michael Anderson 'Transnational Corporations and Environmental Damage: Is Tort Law the Answer?' 41 Washburn LJ 399 (2002); Philip Blumberg 'Asserting Human Rights Against Multinational Corporations Under United States Law: Conceptual and Procedural Problems' 50 Am.Jo.Comp. L. 493 (2002).

[137] See, for example, the UK House of Lords decision in *Lubbe et al v Cape plc* [2000] 2 Lloyd's Rep 383, [2000] 4 All ER 268.

[138] See, for a criticism of the US system in this regard, Blumberg above n 136.

[139] It is necessary to make a distinction between equity based linkages between affiliates in a corporate group and contractual linkages between cooperating enterprises in a network enterprise or alliance for the purposes of liability as in the former case the issue of group liability involves the lifting of the corporate veil between the affiliates, whereas in the latter it involves disregarding any contractual warranties or exclusion clauses that seek to limit the liability of some or all of the participating enterprises: see further chs 4 and 8.

drawn responsibilities in the field of international criminal law, corporations have no existing international obligations in the field of human rights as most codes are voluntary in nature and are addressed to states.[140] That does not imply that the UN Norms, or any other international corporate social responsibility instrument, are doomed to complete legal ineffectiveness. As noted in chapter 3, international policies can emerge as 'soft law' and can 'harden' into positive law, where it is seen as evidence of emergent new standards of international law.[141] Equally, it is arguable that even if the UN Norms were to be adopted as a non-binding voluntary instrument, without direct effect on individual rights under national law, they could conceivably acquire legal force in private law. Private law suits can be brought against any firm or organization that holds itself out as adopting a voluntary code such as, for example, the UN Norms, by other firms or organizations, consumers, or other members of the community.[142]

Concluding Remarks

This chapter has shown that a considerable movement is under way to establish human rights responsibilities for MNEs as a corollary of their ability to bring human rights claims. Notwithstanding these developments, the prospects for human rights based approaches to corporate liability remain rather restricted. International business will not readily accept an analogy between private corporations and the state in terms of human rights responsibilities, the actual legal issues raised by such claims are still to be properly developed, and it is not clear that using human rights arguments is necessarily better than focusing on regulation and liability under established heads of law. Equally, while there is a strong basis in moral and legal thought to make private actors accountable for violations of human rights, corporations should not become scapegoats for failures of governance on the part of host country governments, which retain ultimate responsibility for human rights violations, as stressed in the opening paragraph of the UN Norms. That said, where MNEs and other business enterprises engage directly, or by way of complicity, in human rights abuses the legal means should exist both at the national and international levels to hear the claims of alleged victims and to provide redress where this is warranted. It is likely that such abuses would have to be of the most serious kind to warrant standing for the claimants and, particularly, to find a corporate defendant liable.

---

[140] Ruggie above n 135 at paras 60–65.   [141] See ch 3 at 110–12.
[142] See ibid at 111–12.

14

Environmental Issues

The globalization of production and services provision by MNEs has created a heightened sense of awareness concerning the potential for transnational environmental harm that the activities of such firms might create. On the other hand, MNEs may also be seen as the main repositories of modern, environmentally friendly, technology, and as the most advanced experts on environmentally sound management practices.[1] This chapter will consider not only issues of control and regulation, that seek to prevent environmental harm from arising out of the activities of MNEs, but also how MNEs might be encouraged to use the best technologies and managerial practices that will enhance the ability of host countries to develop their economies and societies in an environmentally friendly manner. Before these specific issues are considered it is necessary, first, to trace the basic concepts that inform the evolving context in which the environmental responsibilities of MNEs are developing.

(1) Core Concepts

The legal regulation of the environmental activities of MNEs is based on a number of core concepts. The most fundamental is that of 'sustainable development'. This is supplemented by the more specific component elements of environmental protection as a policy process. Furthermore, as regards the responsibilities of MNEs and regulators, three further concepts need to be examined, namely, the 'polluter pays', the 'preventive', and the 'precautionary' principles.

(a) Sustainable Development

This idea is hard to define with precision.[2] The most widely quoted definition is that of the Bruntland Commission which called for development that, 'meets the

---

[1] See UNCTAD *Environment* Series on issues in international investment agreements (New York and Geneva. United Nations, 2001) 9–10.

[2] The following text is a revised version of Peter T Muchlinski 'Towards a Multilateral Investment Agreement (MAI): The OECD and WTO Models and Sustainable Development' in Freidl Weiss, Erik Denters, and Paul de Waart (eds) *International Economic Law with a Human Face* (The Hague: Kluwer Law International, 1998) from 429 especially 430–31.

needs of the present without compromising the ability of future generations to meet their own needs'.[3] The emphasis is on human needs rather than wants, and on inter- and intra-generational equity.[4] The approach is based on an accommodation between economic growth, environmental concerns, and the wider social effects of economic activity. Economic growth is seen as a necessary prerequisite for environmentally sound development, but the methods and processes of economic growth must ensure the survival of a sustainable ecosystem that can last for generations. Equally, the social effects of environmental protection, or damage, as the case may be, need to be taken into account as part of the complex range of interactions that characterize the concept of sustainable development. It is in this regard that sustainable development may be seen as an aspect of human dignity and, hence, of human rights in general. Hence, the Rio Declaration on Environment and Development asserts, as Principle 1, that '[h]uman beings are at the centre of concerns for sustainable development. They are entitled to a healthy and productive life in harmony with nature'.[5]

Key to the pursuit of sustainable development is determining how far the operation of the modern global economy threatens the ecosystem. Depending on how that question is answered, resulting policy responses may be very restrictive of international trade and investment or very permissive.[6] Indeed, within the environmentalist camp, there are profound differences of opinion. Those who support the concept of sustainable development are dismissed by 'deep ecologists' for failing to appreciate that there can be no sustainable development so long as the present economic system, based on competition in deregulated markets and ever increasing consumerism, is allowed to function. For 'deep ecologists' this very system must be stopped if the ecosystem is to survive. Supporters of 'sustainable development' are criticized by 'deep ecologists' as doing no more than legitimating the economic project of globalization.[7] Nonetheless, the concept of sustainable development may be able to preserve some wider questions of equity that would otherwise go missing from the agenda of globalization. It is certainly wide enough to include issues of development in less developed countries. Indeed, this possibility led to what Daniel Esty has termed a 'pitched battle' at the 1992 Earth Summit in Rio de Janeiro over the inclusion of a 'right to development' in the Rio

---

[3] World Commission on Environment and Development *Our Common Future* (Oxford: Oxford University Press, 1987) 43.

[4] J Kirkby, P O'Keefe, and L Timberlake (eds) *The Earthscan Reader in Sustainable Development* (London: Earthscan Publications, 1995) 2.

[5] United Nations Conference on Environment and Development (UNCED) Rio Declaration on Environment and Development 1992 (United Nations, 1992) at 9 or at <http://www.un.org/esa/sustdev/documents/agenda21/english/agenda21toc.htm>.

[6] See D Esty *Greening the GATT* (Washington DC: Institute for International Economics, 1994) 41.

[7] See further E Laferriere 'Emancipating International Relations Theory: An Ecological Perspective' 25 Millenium Journal of International Studies 53 at 54–61 (1996).

Declaration. The compromise was an obligation to make development sustainable both for present and future generations.[8]

The concept may also permit some accommodation between free traders and environmentalists in that it sees economic growth, to be achieved through liberalized trade and investment, as a desirable goal. Furthermore, it does not reject market based techniques for ensuring more environmentally sensitive business and regulatory behaviour.[9] On the other hand, the concept demands recognition of the fact that unregulated industrialization and growth will create environmentally unacceptable consequences, particularly in rapidly industrializing countries. Thus a degree of control over the environmental effects of domestic and foreign investment alike will be required.[10]

(b) Environmental Protection

Following on from the concept of sustainable development is the concept of environmental protection. This is a wide concept and so cannot be exhaustively defined. It includes a number of key issues such as the preservation of the quality of the air, water, and soil; the sustainable use of natural resources; the preservation of human, animal and plant life and health, and of the ecosystem more generally.[11] These goals form the basis of environmental regulation policy, both at the national and international levels. They apply not only to states but also to private non-state actors such as corporations. The above mentioned goals have been progressively developed in various national instruments and international conventions relating to, inter alia, the atmosphere, pollution of the sea, the protection of freshwater resources, the preservation of biological diversity, the control of hazardous substances and activities, the regulation of waste creation and its disposal, and the preservation of Arctic regions.[12] Some of these instruments contain provisions relevant for MNEs as will be discussed further below. On the other hand, three general principles of environmental protection, that are of especial importance in the development of MNE responsibilities, namely, the 'precautionary', 'preventive', and 'polluter pays' principles, will now be discussed in turn. The precautionary and preventive principles operate to control the possibility of harm arising, while the polluter pays principle deals with the

---

[8] See D Esty above n 6 at 183; United Nations Conference on Environment and Development (UNCED) Rio Declaration on Environment and Development 1992 (United Nations, 1992) Principle 3: 'The right to development must be fulfilled so as to equitably meet developmental and environmental needs of present and future generations'. On the link between environment and development see further P Sands *Principles of International Environmental Law* (Cambridge: Cambridge University Press, 2nd edn, 2003) 263–66.   [9] See further Esty above n 6 at 54–59.
[10] See further Michael Carley and Ian Christie *Managing Sustainable Development* (London: Earthscan Publishers, 2nd edn, 2000).
[11] UNCTAD *Environment* above n 1 at 5. See further the Report of the United Nations Conference on the Environment Stockholm, 5–15 June 1972 UN Doc A/CONF.48/14/Rev 1 (1972) 11 LIM 1416 (1972).   [12] See generally Sands above n 8 chs 8–14.

situation where precaution and prevention have failed and those responsible or benefiting from the harm need to be held accountable, and to compensate, for the ensuing harm.

(i) The 'Precautionary' Principle

This concept, first pioneered in the domestic law of West Germany, and subsequently accepted in other national laws and in the Rio Declaration,[13] stresses that where there exists a real risk of serious and irreversible environmental damage, it is incumbent upon the regulator to act and to prevent that damage from arising even where there is a lack of full scientific certainty as to the threat in question. In relation to MNE activities this can lead to controls over actions that fall within this concept. The major difficulty lies in determining when there exists a sufficiently serious risk and, should such a determination be made, what action to take. This may have very serious commercial implications for enterprises subjected to such regulation. Indeed, it may lead to an overprotective approach that stifles corporate freedom to exploit potentially hazardous technologies, or to engage in other potentially hazardous forms of trade or investment, that may otherwise be economically and socially useful. It is in this regard that problems relating to regulatory taking may arise, in that an unreasonable and inflexible application of the precautionary principle by a governmental authority could lead to the effective neutralization of the economic value of an investment. This may lead to a claim that the environmental regulations in question are being applied to effect a regulatory taking, rather than to protect against environmental harm.[14] On the other hand, the fear of such litigation may itself be counterproductive, in that it may lead to so-called 'regulatory chill' whereby the risk of such litigation will, by itself, lead to less than optimal regulation on the part of the host country, in the belief that fully effective regulation might be challenged as a regulatory taking.[15]

(ii) The 'Preventive' Principle

An enterprise that is the user of the hazardous industrial process, or the disseminator of the harmful products or waste, has a responsibility to ensure that the process, product or waste, as the case may be, does no harm. This is termed the 'preventive principle'. It can apply to states as well as non-state actors. It is enacted in numerous national environmental protection laws and in Principle 11 of the

---

[13] Sands ibid at 267. See also MA Fitzmaurice *International Protection of the Environment* 293 Hague Receuil 13 (2002) at 260 n 676 for a review of national laws, regulations, and policy instruments applying this principle. See the Rio Declaration above note 5 Principle 15: 'In order to protect the environment, the precautionary approach shall be widely applied by States according to their capabilities. Where there are threats of serious or irreversible damage, lack of full scientific certainty shall not be used as a reason for postponing cost-effective measures to prevent environmental degradation.' [14] On which see further ch 15.

[15] See further UNCTAD *World Investment Report 2003* (New York and Geneva: United Nations, 2003) at p 111.

1992 Rio Declaration, which requires states to enact 'effective environmental legislation'.[16] This principle will ensure that firms will themselves become the first line of defence against environmental harm by seeking to prevent such harm from arising by reason of their adopting effective environmental management practices and technologies. Thus the preventive principle can be said to form the basis of self-regulation as well as external regulation.

(iii) The 'Polluter Pays' Principle

A key element in developing regimes of environmental protection is the requirement that, 'the costs of pollution should be borne by the person responsible for causing the pollution'.[17] Thus, according to the Rio Declaration, Principle 16:

National authorities should endeavour to promote the internalization of environmental costs and the use of economic instruments, taking into account the approach that the polluter should, in principle, bear the cost of pollution, with dues regard to the public interest and without distorting international trade and investment.

In relation to MNE responsibilities, this approach seems particularly well suited to cases in which the enterprise, by virtue of its expertise in relation to the technology that it uses, and by reason of its likely knowledge of the pollution risks that it undertakes, is in the best position to take on the duty of care not to pollute. Where it does so the enterprise will face the duty to compensate those who have suffered loss and/or injury caused by the pollution. This concept can be adapted to apply to other cases of environmental harm, such as those caused by the conduct of hazardous industrial activities or the dissemination of environmentally harmful products or waste. Where harm occurs, the enterprise must compensate on the grounds that justify the polluter pays principle. Having said this, the limits of such a principle of responsibility are not necessarily clear cut, as much will depend on the actual level of knowledge that the enterprise can reasonably be expected to possess regarding the extent of the environmental risk involved. In addition, where the enterprise is a MNE, then the types of problems of group liability that were discussed in chapter 8 will also arise, in that the actual scope of who the 'polluter' is will be in issue, as between different parts of the group enterprise.

(2) Environmental Regulation of MNEs

The remainder of the chapter will deal with the detail of environmental regulation as applied to MNEs in particular. It should be stressed that environmental regulation does not, as such, aim to distinguish between MNEs and domestic firms as a matter of principle. However, certain emerging international regimes of

---

[16] Sands above n 8 at 247.   [17] Sands ibid at 279.

environmental protection focus on MNEs specifically and, in the case of developing countries, the activities of MNEs may in some cases be the main, or only, significant area of industrial activity that can lead to environmental harm. Thus MNEs can be seen as major subjects of responsibilities in this field.

The discussion will consider, first, the main substantive themes and issues that arise out of these concerns concentrating on regulatory goals, the nature of the regulatory environment and the relevant techniques of environmental regulation. It will then proceed to a more specialized discussion of the major approaches to regulation. Here two main types of approach are identified. First, there is what may be termed 'informal' (or 'unofficial') regulation. This occurs through corporate self-regulation and through 'civil regulation' by civil society groups and environmental NGOs. Secondly, there is 'formal' (or 'official') regulation undertaken by governmental (whether at the national or sub-national level) or inter-governmental authorities (whether at the regional or multilateral levels). Such regulation involves traditional 'command and control' techniques that are based on laws, regulations and administrative or judicial decisions and which ascribe responsibilities and liabilities upon firms directly. It can also be conducted through cooperative methods, in partnership with business groups, individual firms, and/or civil society groups and/or environmental NGOs, which may be based on mandatory obligations contained in contracts or on voluntary compliance mechanisms. It is not proposed to advocate one method or approach over any other. Indeed, the better view is that, in practice, given the political constraints placed upon governments and firms by the assumptions of the globalizing market economy,[18] an eclectic mix of policy sites and techniques of regulation is most likely to be used. Thus 'command and control' methods will be useful, especially in setting benchmark standards and liability rules, and informal regulation will be of value in allowing for firm-specific expertise to be applied in solving environmental problems.[19] Equally, a mix of local, national, regional, and multilateral regulatory sites may be involved in dealing with particular issues.

(a) Main Themes and Issues

As noted in the introduction to this chapter, MNEs are key to effective transnational environmental protection in that they represent the interface between the environment and global economic integration. This is due not only to their capacity to produce high levels of pollution, but also their ability to develop new

---

[18] As discussed in ch 3 above.
[19] See OECD *Economic Globalization and the Environment* (Paris: OECD, 1997) at 9 and 29 and see further Gunther Teubner 'The Invisible Cupola: From Causal to Collective Attribution of Ecological Liability' in Gunther Teubner, Lindsay Farmer, and Declan Murphy (eds) *Environmental Law and Ecological Responsibility: The Concept and Practice of Ecological Self-Organization* (Chichester: John Wiley, 1994) 17.

environmentally friendly technologies and management practices that can be disseminated internationally, and their ability to develop environmentally friendly practices on their own regardless of actual levels of governmental regulation.[20] In particular, MNE networks can be used to disseminate environmental management practices and technologies uniformly across borders and to develop centralized decision-making and monitoring systems, thereby creating a firm-specific environmental regulatory order.[21] This can have the effect of generalizing home country standards globally, whether these are generated by national, or intrafirm, standard setting. Where such standards are high, this process will allow for an improvement of environmental practices by MNEs in host locations that have lower local standards.[22] In this light it may be said that two main regulatory goals inform this area: first, to control any environmental harm caused by MNE operations, and to render such firms accountable for it and, secondly, to encourage MNEs to act as conduits for improved transnational environmental management practices and technology transfer.

The extent to which these goals will be realized depends on the nature of the wider context in which they are to be achieved. Here it is important to understand the character of the economic and policy environment in which MNEs actually work. At the outset it is essential to examine critically the so-called 'pollution haven' hypothesis. According to this position, MNEs operating in 'dirty' industries are likely to invest in countries that have low regulatory standards, thereby allowing them to take advantage of a location-specific advantage for absorbing imported environmentally harmful practices. Whether such locations actually exist has been a matter of much controversy. The economic evidence for pollution havens appears to be weak, being based in the main on unreliable data.[23] On the other hand, case studies have been documented, showing specific instances of MNE investment in response to lower environmental costs.[24] Much depends on

---

[20] OECD above n 19 at 69. See JH Dunning *Multinational Enterprises and the Global Economy* (Wokingham: Addison-Wesley, 1993) 538.

[21] See UNCTAD *World Investment Report 1999* (New York and Geneva: United Nations, 1999) at 292–93. However, not all firms will follow this approach. Many will decentralize environmental decision-making and monitoring, leaving regulation to local affiliates based on conformity with local standards. See further Michael W Hansen 'Managing the Environment Across Borders: A Survey of Environmental Management in Transnational Corporations in Asia' 12 Transnational Corporations 27 (No 1, 2003).

[22] See Peter Utting 'Corporate Environmentalism in the South: Assessing the Limits and Prospects' in Peter Utting (ed) *The Greening of Business in Developing Countries* (London: Zed Books/UNRISD, 2002) 268 at 282–84.

[23] See *World Investment Report 1999* above n 21 at 298.

[24] See, for example, World Wide Fund for Nature (WWF) UK *Foreign Investment and the Environment: From Pollution Havens to Sustainable Development* (Godalming: 1999) which lists examples from the tanning, nitrogen and phosphate fertilizer, iron and steel, and extractive resources industries. The Mexican *maquiladora* industry (see further ch 6 above at 228–29) is also cited as another example of pollution haven investment: see further David Barkin 'The Greening of Business in Mexico' in Peter Utting (ed) above n 22 at 17. See also Charles S Pearson (ed) *Multinational*

the analytical criteria employed as the basis of the research. In particular, two criteria are open to debate: first, which industries are classified as being 'dirty', allowing some important sectors to be excluded and, secondly, what counts as an 'environmental' cost, as opposed to other types of business costs, allowing for a conflation of both types of costs, thereby avoiding the conclusion that environmental cost saving has motivated the investment.[25] Indeed, the question of whether a particular location is better for the location of environmentally harmful activities may not be answerable in purely economic terms, in that the lowering of regulatory standards may be caused by many other qualitative factors such as, for example, fear of regulatory chill,[26] or a lack of adequate knowledge of the applicable risks due to inadequate resources or, even, regulatory incompetence.

Of especial importance to defining the regulatory context in this area is the position of developing countries as hosts to environmentally related investment. The possibility of such countries acting as 'pollution havens' may be high, given the difficulties that these countries face in establishing and operating effective environmental regimes. It has been suggested that some developing countries ought to act as pollution havens, given that the cost of assimilating environmentally hazardous substances may in fact be lower in such locations, given the higher absorptive capacity of some developing countries.[27] However, this argument is less well received in present times. It is being overtaken by the view that attempts to raise developing county standards of environmental regulation to those of developed countries may be a form of protectionism. According to this position, the raising of standards in developing countries is designed to improve the competitive position of MNEs from more developed home countries with higher regulatory standards, which can meet those higher standards at the expense of firms operating from developing countries, given their lower environmental operating standards.[28]

This is known as the 'pollution halo' effect. This argument appears to be at odds with the view that investment by MNEs may help lead to improvements in environmental standards in developing countries, for the reasons outlined earlier, especially in countries with few, if any, competitive local firms. It may be

Corporations, Environment and the Third World: Business Matters (Durham: Duke University Press, 1987).

[25] See further Jennifer Clapp 'What the Pollution Havens Debate Overlooks' 2 Global Environmental Politics 11 (2002), who notes that many studies exclude highly polluting industries such as hazardous waste management, international trade in toxic waste, and raw material extraction, preferring to concentrate on manufacturing industries.   [26] Clapp ibid.

[27] See R Stewart 'Environmental Regulation and International Competitiveness' 102 Yale LJ 2039 (1993) and Patrick Low and Alexander Yeats 'Do Dirty Industries Migrate?' in Patrick Low (ed) *International Trade and Environment* (Washington DC: World Bank Discussion Paper 159, 1992) 89.

[28] Michael Hansen 'Environmental Regulation of Transnational Corporations: Needs and Prospects' in Peter Utting (ed) above n 22, 159 at 168–69.

motivated by shareholder and consumer pressure from home countries, the need to harmonize quality standards in global production chains, economies of scale from having global environmental standards, and the development of firm-specific competitive advantage in environmental performance.[29] However, even this effect may be undermined by fears of 'regulatory chill' arising out of competition for internationally mobile investment.[30] Finally, it should be noted that here, as in other areas studied in this book, the variation of regulatory regimes between jurisdictions adds to regulatory problems. Indeed, the preceding discussion is based on the existence of such variations. This has led to calls for greater harmonization through regional and multilateral standards, and to calls by WTO tribunals for the conclusion of agreements between countries on how to further environmental protection without the creation of barriers to trade.[31]

Finally, the types of regulatory techniques used in the regulation of environmental issues need to be considered. As noted above, the main distinction in techniques of environmental regulation lies between informal regulation by non-state actors and formal regulation by states and inter-governmental organizations or other arrangements. Some approaches can only be used in one or other of these contexts, while others are more general in application.[32] Thus, traditional 'command and control' regulation through laws, regulations, and administrative practices, which carry mandatory force, can only be practised by states and inter-governmental arrangements that have such powers delegated to them. The use of environmental impact assessments under national laws and international environmental arrangements would fall under this category.[33] Equally economic instruments that require legislative sanction, such as 'green' taxes and incentives designed to encourage firms to operate in a more environmentally friendly way,[34] mandatory environmental accounting and auditing requirements or legally binding eco-labelling schemes, can only be instituted by states. Furthermore, the establishment of legal liability mechanisms for firms that breach environmental standards will be within the exclusive competence of state actors as part of the

---

[29] WWF–UK above n 24 at 32.   [30] ibid at 48, 51.

[31] See, for example, *United States – Import Prohibition of Certain Shrimp and Shrimp Products* WT/DS 58/AB/R Report of Appellate Body adopted 6 November 1998 at paras 166–68. Whether an upward ratcheting of standards in developing countries by this means is necessarily the best approach may be open to debate. For a critique of harmonization for developing countries in the field of health, safety and technical barriers to trade, see Graham Mayeda 'Developing Disharmony? The SPS and TBT Agreements and the Impact of Harmonization on Developing Countries' 7 JIEL 737 (2004) and Matthias Busse 'Trade Environmental Regulations and the World Trade Organization: New Empirical Evidence?' 38 JWT 285 (2004).

[32] See further Jonathon Hanks 'Promoting Corporate Environmental Responsibility' in Peter Utting (ed) above n 22 at 187 at 191.

[33] See David Hunter and Stephen Porter 'International Environmental Law and Foreign Direct Investment' in Daniel D Bradlow and Alfred Escher (eds) *Legal Aspects of Foreign Direct Investment* (The Hague: Kluwer Law International, 1999) from 161 especially 177–78.

[34] On which see OECD *Environmental Taxes and Green Tax Reform* (Paris: OECD, 1997).

wider administration of the legal system of the country concerned. On the other hand, the adoption of voluntary codes of conduct, such as guidelines for sound environmental practices, can be undertaken by firms themselves, industry groups, partnerships between firms and environmental NGOs and/or governmental agencies or by governmental bodies themselves in an attempt to exhort firms to follow those standards without the fear of legal sanction. In addition 'co-regulation' through contracts entered into by firms and governmental bodies and/or NGOs, will involve aspects of informal self-regulation, in that the firm concerned will organize its internal operations to meet contractual targets. It will also involve command and control regulation, in that the contract will set standards that will result in legal sanction for breach of contract where these targets are not met. It should be stressed that none of the above mentioned techniques are mutually exclusive and that a mix of approaches will be used in practice.[35]

(b) Informal Regulation

This sub-section covers in more detail the forms of environmental self-regulation undertaken by firms alone, or in partnership with environmental NGOs through methods of co-regulation. In addition, the role played by NGOs in seeking to establish and monitor environmental standards to be observed by firms will be examined. This has been termed 'civil regulation' to distinguish such action from formal governmental regulation.[36]

(i) Corporate Self-Regulation

The rationale for self-regulation in this field was given in 1992 by Stephan Schmidheiny, the chair of the Business Council for Sustainable Development (BCSD), in an influential book *Changing Course: A Global Business Perspective on Development and the Environment*.[37] There, it was argued that global business had a responsibility to further sustainable development and that the best method for doing so was a combination of regulatory standards to direct performance and voluntary initiatives by the private sector. In particular, environmental harm was seen as a form of market failure that could be corrected through economic instruments that would offer incentives to firms to act in a more ecologically efficient way. In particular, full environmental cost pricing should be introduced, so as to move firms towards sound environmental management practices and the production of environmentally friendly products. The prevention and avoidance

---

[35] See further Rory Sullivan *Rethinking Voluntary Approaches in Environmental Policy* (Cheltenham: Edward Elgar, 2005) ch 2.

[36] See Jem Bendell and David F Murphy 'Towards Civil Regulation: NGOs and the Politics of Corporate Environmentalism' in Peter Utting (ed) above n 22 at 245–67.

[37] Stephan Schmidheiny with the Business Council for Sustainable Development (BCSD) *Changing Course: A Global Business Perspective on Development and the Environment* (Cambridge, Mass: The MIT Press, 1992).

of pollution would result from such 'eco-efficiency'. In addition, firms would be stimulated to innovate environmentally friendly production processes and products, thereby offering a competitive advantage in global markets and allowing for the dissemination of environmentally sound technologies. Thus, the power of business to improve the environment was stressed as part of what has been termed 'eco-modernism': the faith that technology could be used to ameliorate the environmental harm caused by earlier generations of productive technologies.[38] This approach amounted to a departure from earlier business perspectives on environmental issues, which saw environmental regulation as a barrier to the market and which sought to limit the effects of such regulation.[39]

Against this more cooperative background, firms including prominent MNEs, have explored methods for achieving 'eco-efficiency'. In particular, firms have adopted techniques such as 'life cycle analysis', whereby the design of a product is based on the capacity to salvage and reuse components or to dispose of them in an environmentally friendly manner,[40] voluntary eco-labelling and eco-audits, or a commitment to the development of environmentally friendly new technologies and products. For example, in response to concerns over the effects of climate change, in 1997 BP left the Global Climate Coalition (GCC), the major industry association opposing emission controls, and reduced its internal emissions by 10 per cent by 2003. It has also invested heavily in solar power technology, now ranking as the world's leading photovoltaics (PV) company. Similarly, Shell has accepted the need to reduce greenhouse gas emissions and has established internal emissions reduction targets. It too has made major investments in PVs and in geothermal and wind power.[41]

Of especial significance in relation to self-regulation has been the widespread adoption by MNEs of the International Standards Organization (ISO) 14000 series of environmental management standards.[42] These represent a hybrid private-public regulatory regime. It is private in that firms follow standards drawn

---

[38] For a critique of this position, see Richard Welford 'Disturbing Development: Conflicts Between Corporate Environmentalism, the International Economic order and Sustainability' in Peter Utting (ed) above n 22 at 135.

[39] See Harris Gleckman 'Transnational Corporations' Strategic Responses to "Sustainable Development"' in Helye Ole Bergesen and Georg Parmann (eds) *Green Globe Yearbook 1995* from 93 especially 95–96.

[40] Schmidheiny above note 37 at 98. See further OECD *Economic Globalization and the Environment* above n 19 at 71–72.

[41] See David L Levy 'Business and the Evolution of the Climate Regime: The Dynamics of Corporate Strategies' in David L Levy and Peter J Newell (eds) *The Business of Global Environmental Governance* (Cambridge, Mass: The MIT Press, 2005) 73 at 84–5.

[42] See Jennifer Clapp 'The Privatization of Global Environmental Governance: ISO 14000 and the Developing World' in Levy and Newell (eds) above n 41 at 223 on which the following account draws. See too UNCTAD *World Investment Report 1999* above n 21 at 302–304. The ISO 14000 series standards are available upon payment from the ISO website <http://www.iso.org>. See further R Krut and H.Gleckman *ISO 14001: A Missed Opportunity for Global Sustainable Industrial Development* (London: Earthscan, 1998) and Amy Pesapane Lally 'ISO 14000 and Environmental Cost Accounting: The Gateway to the Global Market' 29 Law & Pol'y Int'l Bus. 501 (1997–1998).

up by a non-governmental international organization that represents the 134 national standard setting bodies of its member countries. These national bodies are in part governmental departments and in part hybrid or fully private bodies. Decision-making is, however, dominated by national industry groups in that the various national bodies that work towards the formulation of ISO standards have a strong local industry membership.[43] On the other hand, the ISO is also a public regime to the extent that its standards are adopted as benchmarks for national laws and for the purposes of inter-governmental organization activities.[44]

The ISO standards emerged in the early 1990s in part as a result of the preparations for the United Nations Conference on Environment and Development (UNCED), which eventually led to the above mentioned Rio Declaration on Environment and Development and Agenda 21, the Programme of Action for Sustainable Development. Negotiations on ISO Standards started in 1993 as part of the programme for meeting the aims of Agenda 21. The first five of the new standards were adopted in 1996. The ISO 14000 series covers six main areas including environmental management systems, environmental auditing, environmental labelling, environmental performance, evaluation, life cycle assessment, and terms and definitions. Of the already adopted ISO 14000 series it is ISO 14001 *Environmental Management Systems – Specification with Guidance for Use* which allows for corporate certification. The other four standards are for guidance only.[45] To obtain certification each individual facility of the firm must apply. A corporate group as a whole cannot do so. The criteria for certification require that the facility has its own environmental policy statement indicating that it will comply with all local environmental laws and that it will be committed to the continual improvement and prevention of pollution, that the facility has in place a management system that ensures compliance with its policy statement, that it is audited to ensure such compliance either through self-certification or by a third party, and suppliers and contractors are encouraged to establish their own environmental management system in conformity with ISO 14001. The resulting certification must be made available to the public on request.[46] In November 2004 a revised ISO 14001 was adopted with the intention of making the standard conform more closely to the ISO 9001:2000 quality management system standard. This will be introduced by way of a transition period ending on 15 May 2006, by which time all facilities currently certified under ISO 14001:1996 shall conform to the revised certification standards in ISO 14001:2004.[47]

---

[43] Clapp ibid at 232–33.

[44] According to Clapp, the WTO Agreement on Technical Barriers to Trade (TBT Agreement) recognizes the ISO standards as international standards to be followed by members in their trade policies. It has in effect made these standards the international ceiling, as members following more stringent standards may be open to challenge as having introduced barriers to trade incompatible with the international standards recognized by the TBT Agreement: ibid at 237.

[45] ibid at 230.   [46] ibid at 230–31.

[47] See ISO Press Release 945 10 January 2005 'Details released of 18-month ISO 14001:2004 transition plan' available from <http://www.iso.org>.

The ISO 14000 standards have been criticized on various grounds. In particular, they are seen by some as the product of a closed system with little public participation, including that of developing countries as ISO members or civil society groups and NGOs, with the result that they fail to incorporate public interest concerns into the ISO process.[48] In addition, they do not allow for public access to data concerning corporate compliance with the standards. Furthermore, they rely too much on self-accreditation by enterprises and set low minimum standards so as to pre-empt more forceful command and control regulation and to make compliance easy.[49] Moreover, the ISO 14001 standards can only be obtained at relatively high cost from the ISO website, discouraging their widespread dissemination, a matter that ought to be of concern given the important role that they play as regulatory benchmarks.[50]

Self-regulation of environmental issues by MNEs and other types of firms should undoubtedly be encouraged, as part of a mix of approaches. Firms will best know the risks they are undertaking and are most likely to have the technical knowledge and resources to deal with them. The ability to transfer the highest environmental practices across the international network of the MNE to host countries may be desirable, provided that such practices do not 'crowd out' local firms that cannot match these higher environmental standards. On the other hand, there are limits to effective self-policing. Not all firms will have the same commitment to high standards, or may operate variable standards according to the levels of local regulation they encounter.[51] These may be wholly inadequate to deal with the actual risks firms are undertaking in such locations.[52] In addition, it is arguable that the 'eco-efficiency' and 'eco-modernism' position is no more than 'business as usual' with some environmental concerns but with little chance of the major changes in production systems that are needed to ensure genuine environmental protection. Some have called this perspective 'greenwash' – a public

---

[48] See Clapp above n 42. On the other hand, a degree of informal participation by NGOs is possible, although not mandated, under ISO procedures. See further Ecologic/FIELD *Participation of Non-Governmental Organizations in International Environmental Governance* (Berlin: 2002) section 3.3 available at <http://www.ecologic.de/download/projekte/1850–1899/1890/report_ngos_en.pdf>.

[49] See Hunter and Porter in Bradlow and Escher (eds) above n 33 at 196. For example, in a study of compliance with ISO 14001 in Singapore, it was concluded that firms offered little beyond the commitments required to comply with the certification process and with the governmental regulations based on ISO 14001: Martin Perry and Sanjeev Singh 'Corporate Environmental Responsibility in Singapore and Malaysia: The Potential Limits of Voluntary Initiatives' in Peter Utting (ed) above n 22, 97 at 106–108. For analysis of ISO 14001 application in Australia see Sullivan above n 35 ch 5.

[50] As of September 2006 ISO 14001:1996 costs 78 Swiss Francs (14 pages) and ISO 14001:2004 costs 102 Swiss Francs (23 pages), a combined total of 180 Swiss Francs or roughly £90 for two documents amounting to 37 pages!

[51] See Robert J Fowler 'International Environmental Standards for Transnational Corporations' 25 Environmental Law 1 (1995).

[52] Arguably, the Bhopal disaster was in part a result of inadequate local regulation which Union Carbide failed to correct: see Thomas N Gladwin 'A Case Study of the Bhopal Tragedy' in Charles S Pearson (ed) above n 24 at 223.

relations exercise designed to make corporations appear to be sensitive to the environment while continuing to despoil it.[53] Indeed, effective self-regulation may depend on effective standard setting and enforcement through traditional command and control regulation by host countries. Without this 'stick' firms may not act in the correct way.[54] However, increased 'official' regulation may itself cause problems. It may be overbearing, by requiring too much of firms, and may not be effective, especially in resource-limited host countries. Against this background there may be an alternative approach, based on partnership between firms and environmental NGOs, or firms and governmental bodies, or a combination of both. The first will be considered in the next sub-section while the latter will be discussed in sub-section (c) below.

(ii) 'Civil' Regulation

The term 'civil regulation' has been coined to cover an emerging response to corporate environmental activity which is neither pure self-regulation by firms, nor formal 'command and control' regulation by states. It involves the active participation of environmental NGOs in the process of policy development, implementation, and compliance monitoring.[55] This has come about as a result of a perceived 'regulatory gap' between traditional legal regulation by the territorial state and the increasingly transnational character of environmentally sensitive business activities. This 'gap' can also be attributed to the increased pursuit, by states, of market based economic policies that stress liberalization, privatization, and deregulation. Thus states may have consciously retreated from their role as environmental 'watchdogs' leaving much to self-regulation by firms. Such regulatory self-limitation will be compounded in developing countries that have little or no experience as environmental regulators, and which have few resources to devote to such tasks, but which have espoused market-based approaches to corporate regulation. The 'gap' is then filled by various civil society groups, including the major environmental NGOs, to create a sense of accountability that may have been lost in the process of deregulation.[56] Thus the role of NGOs could also be characterized as one of filling the 'democratic deficit' that increasing marketization, of public economic functions in particular, might be said to create.

---

[53] See Welford in Peter Utting (ed) above n 22 at 135. On 'geenwash' see S Beder *Global Spin: The Corporate Assault on Environmentalism* (Melbourne: Scribe Publications, 1997).

[54] This view is confirmed by Sullivan in his study of Australian voluntary initiatives. He sees the primary drivers for improved performance and increased participation in voluntary approaches as coming form regulation or the threat of regulation: above n 35 at 177.

[55] On 'civil regulation' see further Jem Bendell and David F Murphy 'Towards Civil Regulation: NGOs and the Politics of Corporate Environmentalism' in Peter Utting (ed) above n 22 at 245; Simon Zadek *The Civil Corporation: The New Economy of Corporate Citizenship* (London: Earthscan, 2003 paperback edn) ch 5.

[56] As noted in ch 3, the distinction between 'civil society' and 'NGOs' is not often very clear. However, for the purposes of partnerships with business the focus will be on environmental NGOs as such entities have been key to these developments.

According to Peter Newell, civil society groups will pursue a binary policy of 'liberal' and 'critical' governance strategies.[57] 'Liberal' strategies involve a cooperative approach to business and may lead to joint standard setting and to NGO/civil society-business partnerships devoted to the pursuit of particular environmental policy goals and/or the realization of particular projects. 'Critical' strategies involve NGOs and other civil society groups in a more familiar role as monitors of corporate activity, as expositors of corporate malpractices, and as advocates of more stringent controls over corporate excesses.

The 'liberal' cooperative approach is evident in numerous cases of NGO-business partnership, which have had varying degrees of success. Perhaps the best-known example is the Forest Stewardship Council (FSC). This is composed of environmental NGOs, forest industry representatives, community forestry groups and forest products certification groups. The FSC operates through national level groups. These ensure that only environmentally certified timber is sold by members. Such timber will be certified if it comes from well-managed, environmentally sustainable, forests and that a chain of custody from the forest to the end retailer has been established to ensure that the product is from the accredited source.[58] This mechanism has been subject to much criticism. In particular, many producers remain outside the scheme, especially logging companies from developing countries, and the major consumer of tropical timber, Japan, has not adopted a stance on sustainable timber trade. Furthermore, the scheme depends on market based voluntary techniques that may, by themselves, be inadequate to deal with the rise of tropical deforestation for commercial purposes, particularly in developing countries that rely on investment in the timber trade for national revenue.[59] Indeed, the accurate sourcing of timber is itself often difficult, with many avenues being open for unsustainably produced timber to enter the distribution chain.[60]

Partnership arrangements have also arisen in the context of industry privatizations that have environmental implications. Thus in the water industry, NGOs, MNEs, UN agencies and government bodies have formed such arrangements.[61] For example, under the auspices of the 'Business Partners for Development Program' the French water company, Vivendi Environment (Generale des Eaux),

[57] Peter Newell 'Environmental NGOs, TNCs and the Question of Governance' in Dimitris Stevis and Valerie J Assetto (eds) *The International Political Economy of the Environment: Critical Perspectives* (Boulder: Lynne Reiner Publishers, 2001) 85.

[58] David F Murphy and Jem Bendell 'New Partnerships for Sustainable Development: The Changing Nature of Business-NGO Relations' in Peter Utting (ed) above n 22, 216 at 219.

[59] ibid at 220.

[60] See further Nigel Sizer, David Downes, and David Kaimowitz 'Tree Trade: Liberalisation of International Commerce in Forest Products: Risks and Opportunities' Forest Notes (Washington DC: World Resources Institute, November 1999) and 'Down in the Woods' Special Report: The Logging Trade *The Economist* 25 March 2006 at 85.

[61] See Matthias Finger 'The New Water Paradigm: The Privatization of Governance and the Instrumentalization of the State' in Levy and Newell (eds) above n 41 at 275.

works with the international NGO WaterAid and the World Bank to provide access to water in urban areas and to the poor in developing countries.[62] In such partnerships, the state passes the obligation to provide water services to the MNE in question, while the NGO acts to oversee and legitimize the commercial activity. In the process the state effectively withdraws from the provision of water. Such schemes have been supported financially by the Work Bank, which advocates a market based approach to water resources management. Indeed, between 1990 and November 2002 the World Bank made privatization of water utilities a condition for the granting of loans in 84 out of the total of 276 water supply loans.[63] Partnerships may arise in other sectors as well, and may involve only the state and the MNE as partners. Such arrangements will be reviewed in the next section of the chapter.

Partnership arrangements have also appeared in the field of bio-prospecting.[64] This concept encompasses the activity of searching for valuable biological resources from which new commercial products can be created. In particular it relates to the effective exploitation of biological diversity. How this should be done without harming that diversity has led to the evolution of partnerships between MNEs (particularly in the pharmaceuticals industry which stands to gain most from the discovery of new biological sources for drugs) and governmental bodies or NGOs. The model for such arrangements was pioneered in Costa Rica. Costa Rica has a rich biological diversity in its tropical rainforests, a resource that the government has been eager to develop. At the same time this country has been strongly committed to the pursuit of environmental conservation and awareness, as well as to non-governmental governance solutions in view of limited public funds. Accordingly, a new approach to bio-prospecting was put in place. At the end of 1989 the government established a non-governmental body, the National Biodiversity Institute (INBio).[65] This is a legally independent, non-profit, organization whose task is to undertake the development of bio-prospecting in Costa Rica. In this connection, INBio concluded the first bio-prospecting agreement with the pharmaceutical firm Merck in 1991.[66] Under this agreement

---

[62] Another body sponsoring such partnership arrangements in developing countries is the Global Water Partnership.   [63] ibid at 285.

[64] See Silvia Rodriguez and Maria Antonieta Camacho 'Bioprospecting in Costa Rica: Facing New Dimensions of Social and Environmental Responsibility' in Peter Utting (ed) above n 22 at 58 on which this account is based. See further Stephen R Tully 'Corporate-NGO Partnerships and the Regulatory Impact of the Energy and Biodiversity Initiative' 4 Non-State Actors and International Law 111 (2004) and, for a review of policies in selected developing countries, see UNCTAD *The Biotechnology Promise: Capacity Building for Participation of Developing Countries in the Bio-economy* (New York and Geneva: United Nations, 2004). For the legal aspects of biotechnology laws in the ASEAN countries, see Sufian Jusoh *ASEAN Biotechnology Legal System* (London: Cameron May, 2006).   [65] See further <http://www.inbio.ac.cr>.

[66] Since then some 15 other major agreements have been signed with both foreign firms and universities. For current status and details see the INBio website cited in the previous note and see further Jorge Cabrera Medaglia 'Biodiversity for (Bio)technology Under the Convention on Biological Diversity: Bioprospecting Partnership in Practice' IP Strategy Today, No.11, Biodevelopments (New York: 2004).

INBio would give Merck access to the chemical extracts of plants, insects and micro-organisms from within the National System of Conservation Areas in Costa Rica, while Merck paid $1,135,000 as an advance and promised that, were a commercially viable product to be developed, it would pay royalties to INBio. The advance payment was applied to forest conservation, training and equipment needed to develop the bio-prospecting capacity of the host country. Although a highly original model of developing country NGO-MNE cooperation this agreement appears to have delivered less than was hoped for. The amount made available for conservation was in fact rather small when compared to the real conservation needs of the country, deforestation continued to rise, and the possibility of undertaking exploitation of new biological resources in a non-invasive manner was exaggerated. In addition, although a bio-prospecting agreement is, by its nature, speculative as to the future levels of royalties, given that these are contingent on the discovery of commercially viable products, the expectations surrounding the possible levels of royalty payments were excessively high.[67] Such results have led some to argue that bio-prospecting agreements are little more than 'biopiracy' in that the benefit of access to biological resources enjoyed by the MNE far outweighs the apparent benefits to the environment supposedly enjoyed by the host country. This has led some NGOs actively to oppose the further extension of bio-prospecting arrangements in developing countries, and to argue in particular for controls over the rights of MNEs to protect their newly acquired knowledge through intellectual property rights.[68]

A final, noteworthy, example of NGO-business partnership in this field arose out of concerns as to how insurers could use their risk assessment procedures to create insurance incentives for firms to act in an environmentally responsible manner. In the early 1990s, a number of environmental NGOs, led by the initiatives of Jeremy Leggett of Greenpeace International, sought to involve insurance companies in the campaign against climate change.[69] Insurers stand to lose considerable sums if the worst effects of climate change prove to be correct. Indeed, there is increasing evidence that insurers have been paying out more for catastrophic storm damage in recent years.[70] In this context it would be prudent for insurers to pay more attention to risk avoidance and to offer incentives for their corporate clients to act in ways that reduce global warming from industrial activities. To this end, in the early 1990s, Leggett persuaded a small group of concerned insurers, mainly European firms, to become involved in a new initiative with the United National Environment Programme (UNEP). This resulted

---

[67] Rodriguez and Camacho above n 64 at 65–66.

[68] ibid at 67–68. On the issue of intellectual property rights and biological resources, see further ch 11 at 468–70.

[69] See Sverker C Jagers, Matthew Patterson, and Johannes Stripple 'Privatizing Governance, Practicing Triage: Securitization of Insurance Risks and the Politics of Global Warming' in Levy and Newell (eds) above n 41 at 248, on which this account is based.

[70] See, for examples, ibid at 253–54.

in a Statement of Environmental Commitment by the Insurance Industry in 1995.[71] Signatory firms commit themselves to address key issues such as pollution reduction, the efficient use of resources, and climate change and to identify realistic and sustainable solutions. In particular, sustainable development is seen as a fundamental aspect of sound business management and the precautionary principle is recognized. The most significant commitments are to further sound environmental management both in relation to internal operations and management practices and to the development of insurance products and services. These will promote sound environmental practice through measures such as loss prevention, contract terms, and conditions requirements and through the inclusion of environmental considerations into asset management while continuing to satisfy requirements for security and profitability.[72] The actual response of the insurance industry has not lived up to these goals. In practice, although firms have developed new financial instruments, such as catastrophe bonds or options and futures, to deal with climate change disasters, they have also securitized those risks. The result has been a reduction of cover in some areas prone to hurricanes of cyclones, either through withdrawal of cover for those areas or a level of rate increases that make insurance unaffordable. This has adversely affected the cover of risks in the Caribbean in particular.[73] Thus the response of insurers to climate change related risks has been to increase the inequality of cover, affecting primarily less developed regions in climactically more dangerous locations. It is an example of a major shortcoming of privatized civil governance, namely, that market based solutions may not offer an adequate or equitable response to environmental risk.

The use of NGO-Business partnerships is likely to continue as governments pursue liberal market based economic policies and seek to withdraw from certain governance functions. There is little doubt that such initiatives can help to realize sustainable development goals if they are well informed and properly managed.[74] On the other hand, they are also subject to limitations as the foregoing examples suggest. Not only are there practical problems as to what type of policy response to an environmental problem is the best, there are also major questions about the precise division of responsibilities between the business and the NGO. For example, how far is the NGO to be integrated into the internal management structures of the business? If this is significant, can the NGO be jointly liable for losses caused by the adoption of inappropriate policies, or should it be subject to a contractual exclusion of liability so that only the business partner is liable? In addition, can the state take a back seat and not regulate the partnership to

---

[71] UNEP Statement of Environmental Commitment by the Insurance Industry (1995) available at <http://www.unepfi.org/signatories/statements/ii/index.html>.

[72] ibid para 2.5.   [73] Sverker, Matthews, and Stripple above n 69 at 264–65.

[74] See further Michael Likosky (ed) *Privatising Development: Transnational Law Infrastructure and Human Rights* (Leiden: Martinus Nijhoff Publishers, 2005); Michael Warner and Rory Sullivan *Putting Partnerships to Work* (Sheffield: Greenleaf Publishing, 2004).

ensure it carries out its tasks effectively? This raises issues of legitimacy: how far can the privatization of governance go without the loss of accountability that state institutions may be expected to have and can such private partnerships ever be fully accountable, especially if they have at their base the pursuit of gain by the business partner, with its attendant issues of rights to the enjoyment of private property? The risk of 'regulatory chill', as an aspect of governmental reaction to the encouragement of partnership strategies is real, and may well be enhanced by the belief that the NGO partner will be able to monitor the process adequately, which may not always be the case.

The last point leads to the consideration of 'critical' governance strategies by NGOs. Should the business partner not follow the advice of the NGO, and act in what the NGO perceives as an environmentally unfriendly manner, will the NGO be sufficiently independent to be able to provide criticism and protest against its partner? Critical strategies have tended to lead to the development of partnerships with business. Indeed, the FSC is a direct result of protest against the rapid deforestation of Brazil undertaken by local groups and by Western NGOs during the 1980s and early 1990s.[75] Equally, the campaign against Shell concerning its operations in the Niger Delta, and their effect upon the Ogoni People, helped that firm to focus more critically on its environmental policy.[76] However, once a partnership is established it may be very difficult for the NGO concerned to return to a critical strategy for fear of upsetting the partnership. On the other hand, there may be ways around this dilemma. One possibility is for the NGO and/or its supporters to buy shares in the business partner, and thereby acquire the right to sponsor resolutions at the general meeting. These may be used to question the senior management as to their strategies.[77] Equally, the more powerful and respected NGOs have taken a dual liberal and critical approach to some firms. Thus, while it was mounting a hostile campaign against the Monsanto food company, for developing genetically modified food organisms, Greenpeace was also engaged in dialogue with that company about developing a PVC-free credit card for its supporters.[78] Nonetheless, it is hard to see how, when NGOs and firms become increasingly integrated over specific projects and polices, they can remain truly independent of one another, especially where the partnership is encouraged by government policy. Ultimately, NGO monitoring and pressure will be of little avail without the commitment of government to set out benchmark standards

[75] See Murphy and Bendell above n 58 at 218–19.

[76] ibid at 223–30. On this case, see further Jedrzej George Frynas *Oil in Nigeria: Conflict and Litigation Between Oil Companies and Village Communities* (London: LIT/Transaction, 2000). Shell continues to be criticized for its activities in that region: see, for example, Christian Aid, Friends of the Earth, Platform and Stakeholder Democracy Network *Shell in Nigeria: Oil and Gas Reserves Crisis and Political Risks: shared concerns for investors and producer-communities (a briefing for Shell stakeholders)* (Lewes: June 2004) available at <http://www.stakeholderdemocracy.org>.

[77] Newell above n 57 at 99.

[78] ibid at 100. See also the corporates campaigns run by Friends of the Earth International at <http://www.foei.org/corporates/index.html>.

that will result in legal sanctions if not followed. This will be the case not only in relation to the establishment of basic environmental standards in general regulatory statutes but also in relation to the provision of a legal framework for the conduct of business-NGO partnerships.

(c) Formal Regulation

This section will consider in more detail the principal issues arising out of the formal legal regulation of the environmental practices of MNEs. Here, 'formal' regulation refers to mandatory requirements imposed by governments and regional organizations with law-making powers, as well as standard setting environmental agreements aimed at environmental protection and the furtherance of sustainable development, commonly referred to as Multilateral Environmental Agreements (MEAs). These various levels of formal regulation are strongly related to one another, in that much national regulation is now aimed at bringing national laws and practices into line with regional rules (especially in the EU)[79] and MEAs, while the latter have been influenced by policy developments at the national and regional levels. Equally, the interaction of International Investment Agreements (IIAs) with national regulations, and with MEAs, will be examined.

(i) National and Regional Regulation

National, and, in the case of the EU, regional, regulation are the principal sites for environmental protection.[80] It is essential for the application of MEAs to have national and regional laws and regulations that put in place the standards that these international agreements establish. Equally, these standards have themselves evolved out of national and regional laws and practices. Furthermore, it is at the national level where firms actually operate, where day-to-day administration of environmental regimes will occur, and where legal claims will be brought against firms.[81] The main issues of relevance to the current discussion concern how national and regional standard setting might impact on the behaviour of MNEs, how partnership based 'co-regulation' between MNEs and state and regional bodies can evolve, how national regulation may interact with the obligations

---

[79] On which see generally Sands above n 8 ch 15; Ludwig Kramer *EC Environmental Law* (London: Sweet & Maxwell, 5th edn, 2003); Joanne Scott *EC Environmental* Law (Harlow: Longman, 1998); Jane Holder (ed) *The Impact of EC Environmental Law in the United Kingdom* (John Wiley and Sons, 1997).

[80] Clearly it is beyond the scope of this work to outline the main features of national environmental laws. For a useful introduction see Stuart Bell and Donald McGillivray *Environmental Law* (Oxford: Oxford University Press, 6th edn, 2005).

[81] Given the central role of subsidiarity in the EU environmental regime, national regulation remains key in those areas where Community action is not deemed essential. See EC Fifth Environmental Action Programme 'Towards Sustainability' OJ [1993] C138/1 at para 32.

undertaken under international investment protection agreements (IIAs)[82] and, finally, how environmental litigation against MNEs can be used as a regulatory device and the problems that this will encounter.

As noted above, national standard setting and enforcement may be an essential element in ensuring that firms actually meet the levels of environmentally sound practice needed to protect the environment effectively. There is no doubt that clear standards, backed up by effective enforcement measures can change corporate behaviour. For example, the introduction of more stringent carbon dioxide emissions standards in national laws has led to the development of new technologies in the car industry that reduce such emissions and to the development of more fuel efficient cars.[83] Similarly, the introduction by the EC of the greenhouse emission trading scheme in January 2005, should give rise to cleaner forms of commercial activities.[84] Indeed, countries that have established high levels of pollution controls may be said to have created the basis for a comparative advantage in the rise of environmentally sound technologies and practices. This will then create an incentive for firms from those countries to ensure that similarly high standards apply in other countries.[85] Equally, the requirement of environmental impact assessment under national and regional laws has given regulators considerable capacity to determine the extent to which firms can meet environmental objectives in their activities.[86]

National laws may supplement substantive standard setting with requirements concerning sound environmental practices on the part of firms. This may be done through requiring the establishment of a corporate environmental governance

---

[82] Regional regulation is not usually covered by bilateral investment agreements (BITs). Regional bodies are not parties to such agreements, and regional agreements tend to be exempted from their provisions. However, regional rules may impact on the policy space available to member countries in the environmental field by reason of rules protecting investors and investments that need to be observed in the development and application of national policies.

[83] See Levy above n 41 at 87–89.

[84] See Directive 2003/87/EC of the European Parliament and of the Council of 13 October 2003 establishing a scheme for greenhouse gas emission allowance trading within the Community and amending Council Directive 96/61/EC OJ [2003] L 275/32 and see 'Big Business Acknowledges That Regulation Has a Role' *Financial Times* 22 June 2005 at 15.

[85] J Braithwaite and P Drahos *Global Business Regulation* (Cambridge: Cambridge University Press, 2000) at 267–69; ME Porter *The Competitive Advantage of Nations* (London: MacMillan Press, 1990) 647–49 See Fiona Harvey 'Time to Clean Up? The Climate is Looking Healthy for Investment in Green Technology' *Financial Times* 22 June 2005 at 15. Harvey notes that, in the first three months of 2005, companies in countries that have ratified the Kyoto protocol, including EU Member States, Canada and Japan saw their shares rise by an average of 21.9 per cent. Shares in companies specializing in renewable energy in Australia, a non-signatory of the protocol, rose by only 4.2 per cent, while shares in US (also a non-signatory) renewable energy companies actually fell 13.8 per cent on average. See also 'Welcome to Kyoto-land' *The Economist* 9 October 2004 at 73.

[86] See further Sands above note 8 ch 16 and EC Council Directive 85/337 as amended by Council Directive 97/11/EC on the assessment of the effects of certain public and private projects on the environment: OJ [1997] L 73/5. For analysis of national implementation of the EC scheme, see

system and/or through the imposition of liability rules on company directors, officers or managers and on parent companies. As to requirements concerning corporate environmental governance, here the EC has taken a lead. The eco-audit scheme of environmental reporting has already been discussed in chapter 9. It is part of a wider policy that also includes standards on eco-management. In this regard, Regulation 761/2001 allowing voluntary participation by organizations in a Community eco-management and audit scheme (EMAS),[87] lays down the basic management requirements for compliance with the scheme in Annex 1. By this provision, a firm that seeks verification under the regulation shall establish and maintain an environmental management system based on an environmental policy that:

(a) is appropriate to the nature, scale and environmental impacts of its activities, products and services;
(b) includes a commitment to continual improvement and prevention of pollution;
(c) includes a commitment to comply with relevant environmental legislation and regulations, and with other requirements to which the organisation subscribes;
(d) provides a framework for setting and reviewing environmental objectives and targets;
(e) is documented, implemented and maintained and communicated to all employees;
(f) is available to the public.

The policy must be effected through proper procedures and programmes, to be administered by specific management representatives appointed by top management, who shall ensure that the system is established and who shall report on its performance. The organization shall set up appropriate training procedures for employees and shall ensure that proper documentation is maintained. It must also target areas of operation that have significant environmental aspects, and have in place procedures to correct non-conforming actions. Periodic environmental management audits shall be carried out to scrutinize the system and management shall review the system at regular intervals. In addition, as regards legal compliance, organizations must be able to demonstrate that they have identified, and know the implications to the organization, of all relevant environmental legislation, provide for legal compliance with environmental legislation, and have procedures in place that enable the organization to meet those requirements on an ongoing basis. Several EU Members have adopted similar national rules.[88]

Commission Report of 23 June 2003 on the application and effectiveness of the Environmental Impact Assessment Directive: COM(2003) 334 available at <http://eur-lex.europa.eu/smartapi/cgi/sga_doc?smartapi!celexplus!prod!DocNumber&lg=en&type_doc=COMfinal&an_doc=2003&nu_doc=334>.

[87] Regulation (EC) 761/2001 of 19 March 2001 OJ [2001] L114/1.
[88] See David Ong 'The Impact of Environmental Law on Corporate Governance: International and Comparative Perspectives' 12 EJIL 685 (2001) at 707–16 discussing the laws of Austria, Germany, Belgium, and the Netherlands.

Turning to liability rules, the most exacting national law in developed countries is the United States Comprehensive Environmental Response, Compensation and Liability Act 1980 (CERCLA).[89] Under this statute, strict liability for environmental damage can extend to corporate directors, officers, lenders, and shareholders, although in practice the US courts have tended to observe traditional doctrines of corporate separation and have only found corporate offices, individual shareholders, or parent companies liable where there was evidence of wrongdoing on their part.[90] The laws of selected EC and other OECD countries show a similar trend towards increased liability for such damage. Most laws extend liability to directors and managers and some extend liability, at least in theory, to secondary parties such as the parent company, on the basis of a test of control over the environmentally damaging activity.[91] Laws in developing countries also follow the trend towards stricter liability.[92] For example, in 1991 India passed the Public Liability Insurance Act, which introduced 'no-fault' liability for industrial accidents involving hazardous activities though the compensation limit was set at Rs 25,000, with the right of the victim to claim higher damages being expressly preserved. In addition, as noted in chapter 8, the Indian courts have developed a concept of absolute liability for the escape of a hazardous industrial substance.[93]

[89] This Act is commonly referred to as the 'Superfund Act': US Pub L No 96–510, 94 Stat 2767 (1980) as amended by the Superfund Amendments and Reauthorization Act 1986 Pub L No 99–499 100 Stat 1625 (1986).

[90] See further Ong above n 88 at 692 and 702–703 and Phillip I Blumberg, Kurt A Strasser, Nicholas L Georgakopoulos, and Eric J Gouvin *Blumberg on Corporate Groups* (New York: Aspen Publishers, 2nd edn, 2005) vol 3 ss 999–03 to 99–05. See also *United States v Bestfoods et al* 524 US 51, 118 S Ct 1876, 141 L Ed 2d. 43, 1998 US LEXIS 3733 discussed in ch 8 at n 22.

[91] Such laws exist in Spain, the Netherlands, Finland, Sweden, the UK, and Switzerland. See further EC White Paper on Environmental Liability COM(2000) 66 final 9 February 2000 Annex 1 'Study of Civil Liability Systems for Remedying Environmental Damage' at 35. See EC Update Comparative Legal Study (Study Contract No 201919/MAR/B3) by Chris Clarke at 13–16 available at <http://europa.eu.int/comm/environment/liability/legalstudy.htm>. See also *Van De Walle and Others v Texaco Belgium SA* Case C–1/03 [2005] 1 CMLR 151. In this case a petroleum undertaking (T) supplied petrol to a service station that it owned, under a commercial lease and management contract entered into with the manager of that service station. Under the contract T maintained certain controls over the premises. A leak of hydrocarbons from the premises was discovered. The ECJ held that T could be liable under EC law for any loss caused by the leak where it had disregarded its contractual obligations to maintain the premises leading to the deterioration of the service station's storage facilities. This was so even though the manager was in day-to-day control of the premises. For discussion of national laws in Germany, the United Kingdom, Australia, Canada, Hong Kong, and Spain, see Ong ibid at 703–707. Ong argues that these examples 'reflect a general trend towards the imposition of strict, non-fault based, liability for corporate environmental damage' (at 702).

[92] See, for example, the Environmental Management for Sustainable Development Act 1996 of Zanzibar discussed in Hamudi I Majamba 'An Assessment of the framework Environmental law of Zanzibar' 1/1 Law Environment and Development Journal 18 (2005) at <http://www.lead-journal.org/content/05018.pdf>.

[93] See ch 8 at 314–16 above. See *MC Mehta v Union of India* AIR 1987 965, 1086. The absolute liability principle has also been adopted without limitation in s 3 of the National Environmental Tribunal Act 1995: see further Shyam Divan and Armin Rosencranz *Environmental Law and Policy in India* (New Delhi: Oxford University Press, 2nd edn, 2001) 105–111.

Absolute liability has been extended to the cost of restoring environmental degradation on the basis that this constitutes a specific application of the 'polluter pays' principle.[94]

More recently, the applicable principles for EU Member States have been laid down in the Directive on Environmental Liability of 2004.[95] This instrument applies the 'polluter pays' principle to 'operators' for environmental damage covered by the terms of the directive,[96] making them liable for the cost of remedial action where damage has occurred and obliging them to take preventive action where the threat of such damage is imminent.[97] The directive is without prejudice to more stringent Community rules and it excludes the rights of private parties to seek compensation for personal injuries and property damage. The remedy for this head of damage remains with national law, a factor emphasized by the preservation of Community legislation on conflicts of jurisdiction.[98] The definition of 'operator' appears to be wide enough to cover not only primary but also secondary actors in that it includes, 'any natural or legal, private or public person who operates or controls the occupational activity or, where this is provided for in national legislation, to whom decisive economic power over the technical functioning of such an activity has been delegated, including the holder of a permit or authorisation for such an activity or the person registering or notifying such an activity'. Thus the parent company of an affiliate, undertaking any occupational activity covered by the directive, may be liable where it can be shown that it controls that activity through the actual control of its affiliate, or (where national law provides) it possesses the decisive economic power over the technical functioning of the activity. In the latter case, it may be that possession and control over the technology used in the covered occupational activity would suffice, even if direct day-to-day control over that activity lay with the affiliate. Control is not defined in the directive. However, this is a concept familiar to other areas of EC law and

---

[94] *Indian Council for Enviro-Legal Action v Union of India* AIR 1996 SC 1446 as interpreted in *Vellore Citizens Welfare Forum v Union of India* AIR 1996 SC 2715 at 2721.

[95] Directive 2004/35/CE of the European Parliament and of the Council of 21 April 2004 on environmental liability with regard to the prevention and remedying of environmental damage OJ [2004] L143/56. See also the Council of Europe Convention on Civil Liability for Damage Resulting from Activities Dangerous to the Environment (Lugano Convention, 12 June 1993, not in force): 32 ILM 1228 (1993). This convention imposes liability on the 'operator' defined as the 'person who exercises control of a dangerous activity' art 2(5). The operator's liability is strict (Chapter II). The Lugano Convention goes beyond the EC directive in that it covers not only liability for environmental damage but also personal and property damage (art 2(7)). It includes a right of access to environmental information from public authorities (Chapter III) and rules concerning jurisdiction over compensation claims (art 19). It is unlikely that this convention will enter force, given the development of EC law in this area and the expansion of EU membership to 25.

[96] Environmental damage is defined as damage to protected species and natural habitats, water damage, or land damage caused by any of the activities listed in Annex III of the directive, and imminent damage to protected species and natural habitats caused by activities not listed in Annex III whenever the operator has been at fault or negligent: see Directive 2004/35 arts 2(1), 3(1)(a) and (b).

[97] ibid arts 4 and 5.   [98] ibid art 3(2) and (3) and preamble recital 14.

these could provide guidance.[99] A final point to note is that the directive grants certain rights to NGOs promoting environmental protection and meeting any relevant requirements under national law.[100] In particular, such bodies can submit observations to competent national authorities, set up to fulfil the duties of the directive, relating to instances of environmental damage or the imminent threat thereof.[101] In addition, NGOs can bring judicial review actions (subject to the applicable national laws regulating access to justice) against such authorities to review the procedural and substantive legality of their decisions to act, or failure to act.[102]

In addition to traditional 'command and control' approaches, national and regional regulation will also place emphasis on partnerships between business and public authorities. Such arrangements are becoming increasingly common. To exemplify, the approach of the EC will be examined. The EC Commission has called such a partnership approach 'co-regulation'. This kind of regulation involves the conclusion of an environmental agreement between private and public partners in the context of a legislative act. The means is by way of a binding agreement rather than a voluntary arrangement, with the underlying legislative act providing the framework of objectives, deadlines, and implementation mechanisms as well as monitoring and sanctions for non-compliance.[103] The EC Commission first considered environmental agreements at the national level in 1996.[104] It aimed to encourage business to enter into such agreements with public authorities on the achievement of environmental objectives. These could be bilateral or unilateral agreements. In the latter case the business partner would make independent and spontaneous commitments that would then be recognized by the public partner. This original initiative has now been supplemented by the extension of the concept to the Community level.[105] At this level the Commission does not negotiate agreements. Rather, it acknowledges agreements through an exchange of letters or through recommendations. Community level agreements can be self-regulatory in nature, if they arise out of a spontaneous commitment

---

[99] See for example the approach of the ECJ to the issue of control for jurisdictional purposes in ch 4 and how EC competition rules define control for the purposes of the Merger Regulation in ch 10.

[100] Directive 2004/35 above n 95 art 12(1). [101] ibid arts 11 and 12.

[102] ibid art 13. These provisions exemplify an important strand of EC policy in the environmental field. The Community is committed to the involvement of NGOs in its environmental programme and, in addition, has established a regime for access to information on environmental issues. See further: Council Decision 2005/370/EC of 17 February 2005 on conclusion on behalf of the EC of the Convention on Access to Information, Public Participation in the Decision-Making Process and Access to Justice in Environmental Matters OJ [2005] L 124/1. The convention in question is popularly referred to as the Aarhus Convention, 25 June 1998: 38 ILM 517 (1999).

[103] See EC Commission Communication on Environmental Agreements at the Community Level COM(2002) 412 final 17 July 2002 at 8.

[104] See EC Commission Communication on Environmental Agreements COM(96) 561 final of 27 November 1996.

[105] See EC Communication of 2002 above n 103 on which this account is based.

undertaken by business, or they can be concluded in the context of a legislative act by way of 'co-regulation'. Environmental agreements must comply with internal market and competition rules including the provisions on state aids. They need to be applied in the context of MEA requirements and multilateral trade rules. The Commission envisages a number of policy areas in which environmental agreements may prove useful. These include the PVC Strategy, the Integrated Product Policy and in the fields of waste management and climate change. Environmental agreements based on the original national level policy already exist in relation to CO_2 emissions from passenger cars concluded between European, Japanese, and Korean car manufacturing associations.[106]

A further issue arising specifically in relation to the environmental regulation of MNEs is the effect of IIAs on national policy space. Limitations on national regulatory discretion may arise in a number of ways. First, where the host country has concluded an investment protection agreement that extends both to pre-and post-entry treatment,[107] the application of environmental laws at the pre-entry stage may require that any controls over entry and establishment conform to the protection standards contained in the agreement. Thus, any screening or licensing requirement, or environmental impact assessment, made at this stage must be non-discriminatory and should comply with notions of fair and equitable treatment, as defined in the agreement. However, such obligations may need to be interpreted in the light of legitimate rights to regulate for environmental purposes, which may be most efficiently done at the point of entry in the case of FDI projects.[108]

It is at this point, too, that host countries may impose environmental performance requirements as a condition of entry. Such requirements may be prohibited

---

[106] These were acknowledged by the EC Commission through Commission Recommendations 1999/125/EC, 2000/303/EC, and 2000/304/EC.

[107] On which see ch 17 at 676–78. Agreements that apply to post-entry treatment only will require the application of general standards of treatment only to regulation after entry. At the point of entry, the host country is free to apply whatever environmental measures it wishes, although such measures could fall foul of WTO rules if they involve a trade-distorting element.

[108] In this connection Article 19 of the Energy Charter Treaty (33 ILM 360 (1995)) contains an extensive list of matters that the contracting parties should do in pursuit of sustainable development. Inter alia they should 'promote the transparent assessment at an early stage and prior to decision, and subsequent monitoring, of Environmental Impacts of environmentally significant energy investment projects'(art 19(1)(i)).This accepts a degree of screening and monitoring of foreign investment for environmental purposes, where this is used to set up such a project. However, such screening should conform to the principles of fairness and non-discrimination laid down in Article 10 of the Charter Treaty. In addition, FDI insurance agencies of home countries and the Multilateral Investment Guarantee Agency (MIGA) may also require an environmental impact assessment before offering cover. Thus MNEs will be obliged to submit a full assessment to these authorities as a condition of cover, which will of necessity be done at the pre-entry stage: *World Investment Report 1999* above n 21 at 307 and UNCTAD *Environment* above n 1 at 61. See also *Maffezini v Spain* ICSID Case No ARB/97/7 award of 13 November 2000: 16 ICSID Rev-FILJ 248 (2001) where the tribunal held that Spain could not be held liable for loss resulting to the investor arising out of the latter's deliberate failure to undertake an environmental impact assessment of its investment in a chemical works, required under Spanish and EC law as a condition for the establishment of the investment.

under applicable IIAs. For example, NAFTA prohibits the imposition of performance requirements as a condition of entry and establishment, including a requirement for technology transfer in paragraph (1)(f). However, Article 1106(2) of NAFTA provides that, 'a measure that requires an investment to use a technology to meet generally applicable health, safety or environmental requirements shall not be construed to be inconsistent with paragraph (1)(f)'. This approach is further developed in the most recent US BITs, where the imposition of performance requirements, including environmental measures, necessary to protect human, animal or plant life or health, or related to the conservation of living or non-living exhaustible natural resources, is permitted provided such measures are not applied in an arbitrary or unjustifiable manner and that they do not constitute a disguised restriction on international trade or investment.[109] This provision follows the pattern of the general exception clause in GATT Article XX. Assuming that the US BIT provision is to be interpreted in line with this WTO provision,[110] it subjects national discretion to a number of tests. In relation to the protection of human, animal, or plant life or health the measure applied must be 'necessary', which has been interpreted in WTO jurisprudence to mean that a country should take the least GATT inconsistent measure that is reasonably available, given the objective to be sought. In other words, the measure must be both reasonably necessary for the purpose of the environmental policy being pursued and be proportionate to that aim.[111] In relation to the conservation of living and non-living exhaustible natural resources the measure must be 'related to' these objectives, that is, it must have such conservation as its primary aim and is again subject to a test of proportionality.[112] In addition, both types of exception must come within the requirements of application in a non-arbitrary and justifiable manner and not as a disguised restriction on trade or investment. These have been interpreted to require a balancing process between the right of a country to invoke the exception and its obligation to respect the rights of other countries under the agreement.

---

[109] See, for example, the United States-Uruguay BIT, 25 October 2004, art 8(3)(c): 44 ILM 265 (2005).

[110] Given the virtually identical language this seems highly likely. On the effect of Article XX GATT in environmental cases see further WTO Committee on Trade and Environment 'GATT/WTO Dispute Settlement Practice Relating to GATT Article XX, Paragraphs (b), (d) and (g)' WTO Doc WT/CTE/W/203 8 March 2002 available at <http://docsonline.wto.org/gen_search_asp?searchmode=simple>.

[111] See *United States – Section 337 of the Tariff Act 1930* GATT Panel Report adopted 7 November 1983 36th Supp BISD 345 (1990) para 5.26; *Korea – Measures Affecting Imports of Fresh, Chilled and Frozen Beef* WT/DS 161 and 169/AB/R Appellate Body Report, adopted 10 January 2001, para 166. The NAFTA Tribunal in *SD Myers v Canada* stated that the NAFTA, and its accompanying Side Agreement on Environmental Protection, required the parties to apply high levels of environmental protection but to adopt the measures that were most consistent with open trade: see 40 ILM 1408 at 1431 paras 220–21 (2001).

[112] *Canada – Measures Affecting Exports of Unprocessed Herring and Salmon* GATT Panel Report adopted 22 March 1988 35th Supp BISD 98 (1989) at 114 ; *United States – Import Prohibition of Certain Shrimp and Shrimp Products (Shrimp Turtle)* WT/DS 58/AB/R 12 October 1998 adopted 6 November 1998 paras 135–42.

It introduces an element of good faith in the decision to rely on the exception.[113] This determination will be made on a case-by-case basis and will involve consideration of whether the measure in question has been applied without discrimination or arbitrariness both as to its substantive and procedural aspects.[114]

A second restriction arising out of the terms of IIAs concerns the use of a 'no lowering of standards' clause to combat the risk of host countries lowering their environmental standards as an inducement to investment. Such provisions are a response to the 'pollution haven' hypothesis, and represent an acceptance of the possibility of such a risk, notwithstanding the conflicting evidence for it. Such clauses may take a non-binding 'best efforts' approach, as does NAFTA Article 1114(2), which recognizes that it is 'inappropriate to encourage investment by relaxing domestic health, safety or environmental laws'.[115] Alternatively, a clause may place the obligation in mandatory language.[116] However, to date, no such clause has been linked up to dispute settlement provisions, possibly due to the difficulties of litigating a claim. The intent element in particular might be very problematic to prove.[117] As an alternative, the NAFTA Side Agreement on Environmental Co-operation has established institutional machinery that over-sees national legal and policy developments in the environmental field, aiming at high overall standards and providing for a complaints procedure concerning alleged failure by a contracting party to enforce its environmental law.[118] Finally, it should be noted that, in this connection, the OECD Guidelines on Multinational Enterprises assert that MNEs should refrain from seeking or accepting exemptions from environmental measures that are not contemplated in the statutory or regulatory framework.[119]

Notwithstanding the above mentioned restrictions on host country discretion, the right of a country to regulate on environmental matters may be protected by the terms of an IIA. This can be achieved through a provision that ensures that nothing shall prevent a party from regulating on environmental matters as it

---

[113] *Shrimp Turtle* at paras 158–59.   [114] ibid para 160.

[115] This has been criticized as a weak response but one which may recognize the real limits of trying to apply a stronger scheme: see further UNCTAD *Environment* above n 1 at 38–39 and see further Pierre Marc Johnson and Andre Beaulieu *The Environment and NAFTA: Understanding and Implementing the New Continental Law* (Washington DC: Island Press, 1996) 112–13. A similar approach is taken in the pre and post 2004 US BITs: see, for example, the US-Uruguay BIT 25 October 2004 above n 109 art 12(1).

[116] Thus the MAI Negotiating Text stated: 'A Contracting Party [shall] [should] not waive or otherwise derogate from, or offer to waive or otherwise derogate from, its [domestic] health, safety, environmental [measures] [standards], or [domestic] [core] labour standards, as an encouragement for the establishment, acquisition, expansion, operation, management, maintenance, use, enjoyment and sale or other disposition of an investment of an investor.' OECD *MAI Negotiating Text* (Paris: OECD, 24 April 1998) 54 (Alternative 2).   [117] UNCTAD *Environment* above n 1 at 39.

[118] North American Agreement on Environmental Cooperation, 32 ILM 1480 (1993). See further Johnson and Beaulieu above n 115 Part III.

[119] OECD Guidelines for Multinational Enterprises (Paris: OECD, 2000) Chapter II para 5 available at <http://www.oecd.org/dataoecd/56/36/192248.pdf>.

deems appropriate, and in a manner consistent with the agreement.[120] In addition, as noted in relation to performance requirements, IIAs could ensure the preservation of host country discretion in environmental matters through suitably worded general exception clauses.[121] Furthermore, as will be considered in the next sub-section, MEA provisions may override the terms of IIAs, and place environmental obligations above investment protection obligations, where this is necessary to achieve the objectives of the MEA in question.

Finally, the role of litigation as a regulatory device should be considered. In recent years, environmental litigation in the home country, against parent companies of affiliates operating particularly in developing host countries, has significantly increased. Indeed, such cases have made a major contribution to the key issues of group liability and jurisdiction, discussed in earlier chapters.[122] Home country litigation may be seen as an attempt to ensure adequate compensation, for victims of harmful environmental practices on the part of MNE affiliates, in host countries where adequate redress may not be possible due to difficulties inherent in the bringing of a liability claim. This may be due to the poor state of environmental liability law, including the applicable rules of compensation for torts, and/or to poor procedural rules.[123] In effect, it is an attempt to impose home country regulatory standards upon the overseas operations of home-based MNEs.[124] Equally, such litigation may form part of a campaigning strategy by civil society groups that seek to raise consciousness as to the plight of the victims. Even if the case is removed from the home country jurisdiction on the basis of conflicts of law rules, or settles (the most common outcome where the case is prima facie meritorious), the essential facts of the claim will become well known.[125] On the other hand, such strategies are subject to numerous limitations.[126] First, there are the inherent difficulties in making the case: it is hard

---

[120] See, for example, NAFTA Article 1114(1): US-Uruguay BIT Article 12(2).

[121] See further UNCTAD *Environment* above n 1 at 24–25.

[122] On which see chs 8 and 4 respectively.

[123] It will be recalled from ch 4 that in the Cape Asbestos litigation the inability of the legal system of South Africa to provide legal aid for the claimants was a key element in the House of Lords decision to allow English jurisdiction: see 158 n 163. On the role of tort law in environmental litigation against MNEs see Michael Anderson 'Transnational Corporations and Environmental Damage: Is Tort Law the Answer?' 41 Washburn L.J. 399 (2002).

[124] Such a motivation lay behind the Australian Corporate Code of Conduct Bill 2000 (discussed in ch 13 at 526) which was a response to the record of the Australian mining industry and, in particular, the controversy surrounding BHP's OK Tedi mine in Papua New Guinea which led to litigation that was settled in 1996. BHP had been accused of disposing mining waste from the OK Tedi mine into the surrounding river system causing widespread environmental damage to forests and fish stocks: See *Dagi v Broken Hill Proprietary Co Properties and Ok Tedi Mining Limited (No 2)* (1995) 1 VR 428; 'Ok Tedi Mine Damage Claim Settled' *Financial Times* 12 June 1996 at 33; Sullivan above n 35 at 146–47 and 159.

[125] See further Peter Newell 'Access to Environmental Justice? Litigation Against TNCs in the South' 32 IDS Bulletin 83 at 85 (2001); Alice Palmer *Community Redress and Multinational Enterprises* (London, FIELD, 2003) available at <http://www.christian-aid.org.uk/indepth/311field/field.pdf>. [126] Newell ibid at 86–88.

to prove a causal link between the alleged harm and the source pollutants, it may be very difficult to show that the parent company was itself involved in the causal chain, the highly technical nature of the evidence may be beyond the ability of the claimant and their lawyers to marshal, and the overall cost of the litigation may be prohibitive. Secondly, claimants may be intimidated by host governments not to bring their case in the home country for fear of losing much needed FDI. Thirdly, the claimants themselves may take a secondary role to the lawyers and campaigners who will be in charge of the litigation process, with resulting alienation from their cause. Finally, litigation is inherently unpredictable in outcome, given the uncertainty surrounding the applicable principles, which can raise novel issues of law, and the possibility of genuine differences of opinion among judges. Furthermore, only certain home jurisdictions are likely to prompt such litigation. Much depends on the activism of the home country legal profession, the applicable legal aid rules and the willingness of the courts to become 'world tribunals' for the settlement of grievances against their own MNEs. Accordingly, only some MNEs from some home countries may be exposed to the risk of this type of litigation, introducing a degree of chance in the application of this approach. Thus home country litigation may be a useful device in extreme cases where the liability of the parent may be in little doubt, but it is of little value in smaller claims, where the cost of mounting the action will not justify the sums at stake, or where liability is hard to show. Furthermore, as a development strategy, litigation in the home country may impede the progress of regulation and enforcement capacity in developing host countries. Accordingly home country litigation should be seen as a remedy of last resort.[127]

(ii) International Regulation

At present there are no detailed international rules, or procedures, for the environmental regulation of MNEs. Therefore, MNEs cannot be held liable for environmental harm under international law as such, only under applicable national laws. On the other hand, there exist a number of international instruments that create non-binding commitments for MNEs in this field coupled with certain mandatory provisions of MEAs which, although addressed to the state contracting parties, have regulatory consequences for MNEs.[128] In addition, the possible effects of customary international law on the environmental regulation of MNEs will be considered, as will the relationship between MEAs and the investment protection provisions of IIAs. One feature of the international environmental protection field that should be noted at the outset is the extent to

---

[127] ibid at 88.
[128] See UN Transnational Corporations and Management Division (TCMD) International Environmental Law: Emerging Trends and Implications for Transnational Corporations (New York: United Nations, 1993). See further, for a survey of the main MEAs, Patricia Birnie and Alan Boyle *International Law and the Environment* (Oxford: Oxford University Press, 2nd edn, 2002 and Sands above n 8).

which it has become an area of contestation and lobbying by both business and civil society groups. Indeed, it is arguable that MNEs have used such influence to help construct a more benign set of standards than might have otherwise been adopted.[129]

In particular, the close connection between the UN Conference on Environment and Development (UNCED) and business representatives is a case in point. Originally, the UN Centre for Transnational Corporations (UNCTC) was to have played a major role in formulating sustainable development standards applicable to MNEs (TNCs in UN parlance). However, the UNCED Secretariat, led by Maurice Strong, was keen to involve MNEs in the process of evolving standards. A new post of corporate adviser to UNCED was created and was filled by Stefan Schmidtheiny, the founder of the BCSD.[130] As a result the UNCTC proposals were not adopted and the resulting Conference instrument, the Rio Declaration (Agenda 21), to date the most influential repository of MNE responsibilities in the environmental field,[131] contained an approach to sustainable development that reflected closely the concerns of the BCSD.[132] Thus its emphasis is on the application of 'green' technology to environmental issues and upon cooperation between business and governments in the realization of sustainable development goals. In this context, investment is seen as a necessary prerequisite for sustainable development.[133] Governments are urged to encourage higher levels of foreign direct investment through national policies that promote investment and through joint ventures and other modalities.[134]

Although it is probable that business interests will have a closer relationship with their home country governments than civil society groups, and will have more resources to sustain lobbying campaigns, their overall influence should not be overstated. Environmental NGOs are also making headway in influencing the content of international instruments. In relation to investment it is fair to say that a major contributory cause to the failure of the MAI was NGO lobbying and

---

[129] See generally Ian H Rowlands 'Transnational Corporations and Global Environmental Politics' in Daphne Josselin and William Wallace (eds) *Non-State Actors in World Politics* (Basingstoke: Palgrave Publishers, 2001) 133.   [130] See Gleckman above n 39 at 95–97.
[131] UNCED Agenda 21: Programme of Action for Sustainable Development available at <http://www.un.org/esa/sustdev/documents/agenda21/english/agenda21toc.htm>.
[132] See Gleckman above n 39 at 95–97; Rowlands above n 129 at 144; Lucy H Ford 'Challenging Global Environmental Governance of Toxics: Social Movement Agency and Global Civil Society' in Levy and Newell above n 41, 305 at 310–12. Ford notes that a similar effort to keep the environmental regulation of business off the agenda was made at the follow-up to the Rio Conference, the World Summit on Sustainable Development (WSSD) in Johannesburg in 2002. The results of the Summit can be found in the United Nations Report on the World Summit on Sustainable Development Johannesburg, South Africa, 26 August–4 September 2002 (UN Doc A/CONF.199/20) (New York: United Nations, 2002). See especially Annex: Resolution 2: The Plan of Implementation of the WSSD at paras 18 at 15 (encouragement of corporate environmental and social responsibility); 49 at 38 (promotion of corporate responsibility based on the Rio Principles); 84 at 51 (encouragement of greater flows of FDI to developing countries to support sustainable development); 105 at 58 (promotion of environmentally sound technology transfer as agreed in chapter 34 of Agenda 21).
[133] Agenda 21 para 2.23.   [134] ibid para 33.15.

campaigning against an agreement that at first contained no provisions on labour or environmental issues and which appeared to be in open conflict with obligations under MEAs.[135] However, in most international negotiations NGOs are no more than observers and have little influence as compared to corporations that have greater access to national representatives.[136]

Turning to the substantive content of international instruments covering MNE responsibilities in the environmental field two voluntary codes are particularly important. These are Agenda 21, whose continuing importance in this area was reaffirmed at the World Summit on Sustainable Development (WSSD) in Johannesburg in 2002,[137] and the OECD Guidelines on Multinational Enterprises.[138] Both instruments emphasize, in essence, the furtherance of sustainable development through the transfer of environmentally sound technology and management practices.

Under Agenda 21, MNEs are seen as playing a major role in the development of environmentally sound technologies and in their transfer.[139] Following from this, Agenda 21 offers certain general commitments for both governments and MNEs in furthering a cooperative vision of sustainable development through technological improvement and transfer. In particular, governments and MNEs are urged to strengthen partnerships that will promote the use of cleaner technologies and develop new methods for internalizing environmental costs into accounting and pricing, while MNEs are urged to report annually on their environmental records, adopt codes of conduct reflecting best environmental practice, incorporate cleaner technologies into their production processes and cooperate with workers and trade unions and with other businesses for the development of knowledge and skills in the environmental field.[140] Furthermore, MNEs are

---

[135] See Nick Mabey 'Defending the Legacy of Rio: the Civil Society Campaign Against the MAI' in Sol Picciotto and Ruth Mayne (eds) *Regulating International Business: Beyond Liberalization* (London: MacMillan/Oxfam, 1999) 61. See also Jake Werksman and Claudia Santoro 'Investing in Sustainable Development: The Potential Interaction Between the Kyoto Protocol and the Multilateral Agreement on Investment' in W Bradnee Chambers (ed) *Global Climate Governance: Inter-linkages Between the Kyoto Protocol and Other Multilateral Regimes* (Tokyo: United Nations University, 1998) 59 and Gaetan Verhoosel 'Foreign Direct Investment and Legal Constraints on Domestic Environmental Policies: Striking a 'Reasonable' Balance Between Stability and Change' 29 Law and Pol. in Int'l Bus 451 (1998). [136] See Ford above n 132 at 320–24.

[137] See n 132 above.

[138] Article 19 of the Energy Charter Treaty can also be mentioned in this regard (above n 108). It includes the 'polluter pays' principle, the need to promote full environmental costing, cooperation on international environmental standards and energy efficiency, information gathering and public education on environmental impacts of energy systems, the promotion of research, development, and transfer of environmentally sound technologies, and the promotion of international awareness, and participation in, environmental programmes. These commitments are not couched in mandatory language, nor are they subjected to the dispute settlement rules under the charter. Article 19 is a 'soft' provision. See further Clare Shine 'Environmental Protection Under the Energy Charter Treaty' in T Waelde (ed) *The Energy Charter Treaty* (The Hague: Kluwer Law International, year) 520. The Draft UN Code of Conduct on Transnational Corporations also contained provisions on environmental protection in paras 41–43: see UNCTAD *Environment* above n 1 at 19–20.

[139] Agenda 21 above n 131 paras 30.1–30.4. [140] ibid paras 30.7–30.16.

specifically urged to establish worldwide policies on sustainable development, arrange for environmentally sound technologies to be made available to their affiliates in developing countries without extra charge and to modify local practices in line with local ecological needs.[141] Moreover, the transfer of environmentally useful technology to developing countries is to be encouraged.[142] Such measures should be taken to avoid abuse of intellectual property rights.[143]

Agenda 21 introduces some specific principles of regulation in the field of environmentally sustainable action. First, regulatory controls are seen as going hand in hand with market controls over environmental action involving full environmental costing through the 'polluter pays' and 'natural resource user pays' principles.[144] MNEs are to be consulted over such matters.[145] Secondly, a programme to develop systems for integrated environmental and economic accounting should be set up.[146] Thirdly, trade in environmentally damaging products, chemicals, toxic substances, and hazardous wastes can be lawfully banned.[147] Furthermore, MNEs, wherever they operate, are specifically urged to introduce policies, commitments, and standards of operation in relation to hazardous waste generation and disposal that are equivalent to or no less stringent than those in the country of origin.[148]

In 1991 a new chapter on environmental protection was introduced into the non-binding OECD Guidelines on Multinational Enterprises.[149] The guideline

---

[141] ibid paras 30.19–30.29.

[142] ibid para 34.11. On 'best efforts' provisions urging parties to encourage MNEs to transfer environmentally sound technology see, for example, the Vienna Convention for the Protection of the Ozone Layer 1985 Article 4 and Annex II: 26 ILM 1529 (1987); Basel Convention on the Control of Transboundary Movement of Hazardous Wastes and their Disposal 1989 art 10(2): UNTS vol 1673 57 (1992); Biodiversity Convention 1992 art 16(1): 31 ILM 818 (1992). See further UNCTAD *Environment* above n 1 at 44–50; Gaetan Verhoosel 'Beyond the Unsustainable Rhetoric of Sustainable Development: Transferring Environmentally Sound Technology' The Georgetown Int'l Envtl Law Review 49 (1998) See also the *Shrimp/Turtle* case above n 112 at para 175 where the WTO Appellate Body noted that the failure of the US to transfer relevant environmental technology equally to all countries covered by the US ban on imports of shrimps caught using prohibited methods, amounted to 'unjustifiable discrimination' contrary to Article XX GATT.

[143] ibid para 34.18(iv). Following this principle the 1992 Biodiversity Convention (previous note) asserts, in Article 22, that rights granted under another international convention shall not be affected by this convention 'except where the exercise of those rights and obligations would cause a serious damage or threat to biological diversity'. Thus any intellectual property rights granted under the TRIPs Agreement may be subordinated to the obligations in the Biodiversity Convention where they may give rise to such damage. However, such a clash is unlikely given the general framework nature of the convention: see Sands above n 8 at 1046 and 1052 and see also *Re Legal Protection of Biotechnological Inventions: Netherlands v European Parliament and EU Council* (Case C–377/98) [2001] 3 CMLR 1173 where the ECJ held that EC Directive 98/44 on the legal protection of biotechnological inventions was compatible with the TRIPs Agreement and with the Convention on Biological Diversity even though it authorized Member States to patent certain biotechnological inventions. [144] ibid para 8.28.

[145] ibid para 8.37. [146] ibid para 8.41. [147] ibid chs 19, 20.

[148] ibid para 20.29.

[149] The OECD Declaration and Decisions on International Investment and Multinational Enterprises 1991 Review (Paris: OECD, 1992) 52–54. See now the 2000 version above n 119 Chapter V 'Environment' on which the following text draws.

seeks to reflect the principles and objectives laid down in Agenda 21 and in the Aarhus Convention,[150] as well as in the ISO Standard on Environmental Management Systems.[151] It recommends that enterprises should take due account of the need to protect the environment, public health and safety, and generally to conduct their activities in a manner contributing to the wider goal of sustainable development within the framework of laws, regulations, and administrative practices in the countries in which they operate and in consideration of relevant international agreements, principles, objectives, and standards. The guideline goes on to specify particular duties to be observed by enterprises in relation to the establishment and maintenance of a system of environmental management appropriate to the enterprise, the provision of adequate and timely information to the public and employees as to the environmental impact of enterprise activities, and consideration of environmental impacts in decision-making and the preparation of appropriate environmental impact assessments. Enterprises are urged to apply the precautionary principle, consistent with scientific understanding of risks and cost-effectiveness of measures, and to maintain contingency plans for preventing, mitigating, and controlling serious environmental and health damage arising out of their operations. They are also expected to adopt the best available environmental technologies, develop products and services that are safe, have no undue environmental impacts, are energy efficient and recyclable. Finally, enterprises are urged to develop adequate education and training programmes and to contribute to the development of public policy including through partnerships or initiatives that will enhance environmental awareness and participation.

Apart from such 'soft' responsibilities, MNEs may find themselves subjected to 'hard' obligations arising out of the contents of MEAs, as a result of the implementation of international obligations by the states that are parties to these agreements. Certain key examples need to be briefly mentioned. Perhaps the most significant is the Clean Development Mechanism (CDM) established by Article 12 of the Kyoto Protocol to the United Nations Framework Convention on Climate Change.[152] The CDM allows for developed countries (Annex I parties) to enter into investments aimed at reducing carbon emissions in developing countries (Annex II parties) and credit these to their emission limitation and reduction commitments under Article 3 of the Protocol. Article 12(9) makes clear that participation in CDM projects may involve private and/or

---

[150] See n 102 above and see Elena Petkova with Peter Veit 'Environmental Accountability Beyond the Nation-State: The Implications of the Aarhus Convention' *Environmental Governance Notes* (Washington DC: World Resources Institute, April 2000).

[151] See *Commentary on the OECD Guidelines for Multinational Enterprises* (Paris: OECD, 2000) at para 30 available at <http://www.oecd.org/dataoecd/56/36/192248.pdf>.

[152] Kyoto Protocol to the United Nations Framework Convention on Climate Change 10 December 1997 FCCP/CP/1997/L.7/Add 1 at available at 37 ILM 22 (1998). For a full discussion, see Sands above n 8 at 357–81; PGG Davies 'Global Warming and the Kyoto Protocol' 47 ICLQ 446 (1998).

public entities and is to be subject to 'whatever guidance may be provided by the executive board of the clean development mechanism'. Thus MNEs may be directly involved in such activities and will find themselves subject to the regulatory control of the home and host country, as parties to the protocol. In addition to the CDM, other MEAs have established civil liability rules that apply directly to private actors involved in the conduct of a potentially harmful environmental activity. Thus the 1999 Protocol to the Basel Convention on Liability and Compensation for Damage Resulting From Transboundary Movements of Waste and Their Disposal provides a comprehensive regime for liability and compensation placed upon any person who is in operational control of the waste. It is yet to enter into force.[153] A further example arises out of the various conventions dealing with civil liability for oil pollution that set direct liabilities upon shipowners, subject to limits on recovery, establish funds from which compensation can be paid, and which require owners to carry adequate insurance.[154] Such government led initiatives have been shadowed by industry-based agreements establishing compensation schemes.[155] Indeed, the use of multilateral funds to further environmental policy and technology transfer in developing countries, or to establish pools of resources from which compensation can be paid to victims of environmental harm, may be a valuable additional approach to dealing with the costs associated with the environmental operations of MNEs as well as governments.[156]

The possibility of mandatory legal obligations being imposed on the activities of MNEs, through governmental regulation based on MEAs, may give rise to issues concerning the relationship between the investor/investment protection provisions of IIAs and such MEA-based obligations. Indeed, this was a much-vaunted issue during the negotiations over the MAI.[157] For example, a performance requirement to transfer environmentally sound technology might place greater burdens on foreign as compared to domestic investors, and environmental controls arising out of the CDM may well have implications for the national treatment and MFN standards where participating countries may be expected to discriminate between different categories of investors.[158] In order to avoid such clashes, IIAs may include provisions that privilege MEA obligations. Thus NAFTA Article 104 states that MEA obligations, listed in that provision, 'shall prevail', provided that where there

---

[153] See Sands above n 8 at 924–26.

[154] See the Brussels International Convention on Civil Liability for Oil Pollution Damage 1992; Brussels International Convention on the Establishment of an International Fund for Compensation of Oil Pollution Damage 1992. For analysis, see Sands above n 8 at 912–23.

[155] Of these only the Oil Companies Offshore Pollution Liability Agreement 1974 remains active: see Sands ibid at 922–23.

[156] For examples such as the Montreal Protocol Multilateral Fund and the Global Environment Facility, see Sands ibid ch 20. See further Jutta Brunnee 'Of Sense and Sensibility: Reflections on International Liability Regimes as Tools for Environmental Protection' 53 ICLQ 351 (2004).

[157] See the references at n 135 above.

[158] See Werksman and Santoro above n 135 at 64–66.

is a choice of policy options to fulfil the obligation that party chooses the least NAFTA inconsistent option. In addition, an IIA could make clear that ordinary environmental regulation based on MEA standards will not constitute a regulatory taking, building on general provisions of this kind already in existence in certain BITs. These refer only to non-discriminatory regulatory actions applied to protect legitimate public welfare objectives such as environmental protection.[159] It can be said that where an MEA requires discriminatory action this may be compatible with such a provision as this might not amount to a case of 'like circumstances' between domestic and foreign investors. The environmental threat in question may require differences in treatment between various foreign investors and/or between foreign and domestic investors.[160]

While obligations can arise for MNEs out of treaty provisions, the implications of customary international law on the regulation of the environmental activities of MNEs are less clear. Should any standard of environmental regulation amount to a principle of customary international law, then the regulating state would be bound to apply it in its legal order, and supranational systems of regulation would also have to comply. In addition, breach of such a principle might found the basis of a claim against the state for failure to regulate corporate activity. The corporate actor could also be directly liable in a legal system that recognizes its susceptibility to actions based on violations of international law. To date, the evidence for such a basis of action is weak. Although the principle of sustainable development has been held to be a principle of international law,[161] this is not a uniformly held view, given the complexity and vagueness of the concept.[162] Indeed, other concepts, such as the polluter pays and the precautionary principle, have also been doubted as rules of customary international law. For example, in the US case of *Beneal v Freeport-McMoran* the plaintiffs argued that the defendant mining corporation had inter alia violated the Alien Tort Claims Act by reason of its violation of principles of international environmental law that had become part of customary international law and could, therefore, found an action under this legislation.[163]

---

[159] See, for example, the US-Uruguay BIT above n 109 Annex B para 4.

[160] But see *SD Myers Inc v Canada* (NAFTA Arbitration, 12 November 2000) 40 ILM 1408 (2001) where Canada was found to have discriminated against a US investor contrary to Article 1102 (national treatment) by imposing a temporary trade ban on certain chemical waste products. This favoured Canadian waste processing firms in competition with the US claimant, who was unable to export the waste in question to its US waste processing facility during the ban. The tribunal held that Canada could have taken a less investment restrictive approach to achieve its environmental protection goals: para 255.

[161] See Sands above n 8 who writes at 254 '[t]here can be little doubt that the concept of "sustainable development" has entered the corpus of international customary law . . . ' citing the ICJ judgment in the *Gabcikovo-Nagymaros* case (1997) ICJ Reports 78 para 140 and the Separate Opinion of Judge Weeramantry at 92; see also the opinion of Justice Kuldip Singh in the Supreme Court of India in *Vellore Citizen's Welfare Forum v Union of India* AIR 1996 2715.

[162] See, for example, Fitzmaurice above n 13 at 47–64.

[163] See *Beneal v Freeport-McMoran* 969 F Supp 362 (EDLA 1997) *aff'd* 197 F 3d 161 (USCA, Fifth Cir 1999). On the Alien Tort Claims Act and its application to MNEs generally, see ch 13 at 527–30.

In particular, they alleged that Freeport's mining operations in Iriyan Jaya, Indonesia, had led to environmental damage that it was obliged to compensate for under the polluter pays, precautionary, and proximity principles. Judge Duval noted that environmental torts based on these principles had not acquired the status of customary law.[164] Even if they had, the judge doubted whether they could apply to a non-state corporation in the absence of a treaty provision to that effect. Equally, the precautionary principle has not been accepted as a general principle of international law that could bind a WTO panel or Appellate Body in the *EC – Beef Hormones* case.[165] The WTO Appellate Body held that this principle did not override the requirements of Articles 5.1 and 5.2 of the WTO Agreement on Sanitary and Phytosanitary Measures, which applied a cost-benefit risk assessment analysis, and a test of reasonable scientific knowledge, to the evaluation of whether the EC ban on the importation of hormone-treated beef into the EU from the US infringed the GATT.

On the other hand, it is well established that a country is liable under international law for harm caused by the trans-boundary escape of airborne pollutants originating in privately owned facilities within its borders.[166] This may offer a cause of action where it is not possible to sue the corporation that caused the harm directly.[167] The host country acts as an 'insurer of last resort' in such cases. In addition, the host country, and any neighbouring countries that are affected by the

---

[164] This finding is confirmed in other ATCA cases: see *Flores v Southern Peru Copper* 343 F 3d 140 (2d Cir 2003), 43 ILM 196 (2004); *Sarei v Rio Tinto* 221 F Supp 2d 1116 (CD Cal 2002) overturned on other grounds *Sarei v Rio Tinto* Case No 02–56256 DC No CV–00–11695–MMM. Filed 7 August 2006 (US CA 9th Cir). See further Sarah Joseph *Corporations and Transnational Human Rights Litigation* (Oxford: Hart Publishing, 2004) 28–30.

[165] *European Communities–Measures Concerning Meat and Meat Products* WT/DS 48/AB/R adopted 13 February 1998 paras 120–25. The approach of the Appellate Body in the *Hormones* case was followed by the WTO panel in the *GMO* case. See *EC – Measures Affecting the Approval and Marketing of Biotech Products* WT/DS291, 292 and 293 Panel Report circulated 29 September 2006 at paras 7.71–7.89. However, under WTO law it is possible to ban the importation of a dangerous substance in an appropriate case. Thus in *European Communities – Measures Affecting Asbestos and Asbestos Containing Products* WT/DS 135/AB/R adopted 12 March 2001, 40 ILM 1193 (2001) the Appellate Body held that France was entitled to ban the importation of asbestos containing products from Canada on the basis that they were not 'like products', as compared with domestic substitute products that were asbestos free, for the purposes of the national treatment provision in Article III:4 of the GATT, as they were dangerous to health.

[166] See the *Trail Smelter* arbitration (1938, 1941) 3 RIAA 1905. The same company that operated the trail smelter in the 1930s Teck Cominco (Cominco at the time of the arbitration) is again involved in a dispute over cross-border pollution from the smelter, this time waterborne pollution in the Columbia River basin. This had led to litigation with Native American tribes on the US side of the river who claim their lands have been harmed by the discharges into the river. See further Austen A Parrish 'Trail Smelter Déjà vu: Extraterritoriality, International Environmental Law, and the Search for Solutions to Canadian-US Transboundary Water Pollution Disputes' 85 Boston Univ. LR 364 (2005) and see *Pakootas v Teck Cominco Metals* 452 F 3d 1066; 2006 US App LEXIS 16684; 62 ERC (BNA) 1705 (US CA 9th Cir). The Court of Appeals for the Ninth Circuit held that CERCLA could apply to the facts of the case as the release of hazardous substances was a domestic, rather than an extraterritorial application of CERCLA, even though the original source of the hazardous substances was located in Canada. [167] See Hunter and Potter above n 33 at 170.

airborne pollution may seek to arrive at a cooperative solution to the underlying problem, bearing in mind not only the harm to those affected by the pollution, but also the social and economic interests associated with the polluting operation in the host country. Furthermore, the risk of responsibility may encourage the host country to undertake preventive measures which may include the passing of necessary legislation and other legal or administrative action, and international cooperation with other governments and international organizations.[168]

Concluding Remarks

The development of binding norms for environmental protection that cover the activities of MNEs represents a major challenge, bringing together not only complex issues of substantive regulation but also (as noted in chapters 4 and 8) issues of group liability, procedure, and jurisdiction. It has been seen that MNEs are a major source of potential and actual environmental harm but can also act as leading sources of technology to combat environmental problems. Thus it is not a simple matter of condemning or complementing MNEs on their environmental performance. Accordingly, the main theme of this chapter has been to expose the variety of approaches to regulation and how these interact with each other, while at the same time placing these matters into the wider context of the debates on globalization and the environment. In some respects, this is a most tentative area for corporate regulation and one in which many new approaches to regulation have been experimented with. How effective these various approaches have been, or are likely to be, remain areas of keen controversy. However, it cannot be doubted that increased regulation of MNE environmental strategies through a combination of self-regulation, co-regulation, and command and control methods (through) will continue to develop. Equally, it is likely that environmental litigation will continue to make a significant contribution to the development of standards in the field.

---

[168] See further International Law Commission Draft Articles on the Prevention of Transboundary Harm from Hazardous Activities (2001) in ILC Report of the International Law Commission 53rd Session 2001 GA Off.Recs, 56th Sess Suppl No10 (A/56/10) reproduced in I Brownlie *Principles of Public International Law* (Oxford: Oxford University Press, 6th edn, 2003) 278–81. Under the European Convention on Human Rights a state may be liable for failure to regulate pollution as an interference with the right to private and family life under art 8. See the cases cited in ch 13 n113 at 531.

PART IV

INTERNATIONAL REGULATION

15

Control of Investment Risks I: Contractual Stability, Renegotiation, Taking of Property, and Investment Guarantees

This chapter, and the next, introduce Part IV of this work by considering the major issues arising in MNE/host state relations that are regulated primarily by international law. These centre on the control of investment risks arising under international investment contracts. Originally, such matters concerned the revision or termination of an international investment contract entered into between the host state and a foreign investor,[1] and the expropriation of assets belonging to the foreign investor. Legal conflict in these situations was most pronounced in the 1970s and early 1980s, in the wake of major renegotiations and nationalizations of foreign owned natural resource operations, particularly in the oil industry.[2] In recent times the incidence of such events has been rare.[3] However, that cannot rule out the possibility of conflicts over the control and ownership of foreign investments, especially in a period where the sense of dependence on foreign investors may be reduced and nationalistic sentiments heightened.[4]

[1] See further Wolfgang Peter *Arbitration and the Renegotiation of International Investment Agreements* (The Hague: Kluwer Law International, 2nd edn, 1995) ch 1. Peter uses the term 'transnational investment agreement' which he defines as referring to 'legal relationships, whereby a state, generally a Third World country, or a state enterprise enter into an agreement with a foreign investor, usually a *transnational* company . . . , for the purpose of an investment project'. ibid at 5 (emphasis in the original).

[2] See further Korbin 'Expropriation as an Attempt to Control Foreign Firms in LDCs: Trends From 1960–1979' 28 International Studies Quarterly 329 (1984); A Akinsanya *The Expropriation of Multinational Property in the Third World* (New York: Praeger, 1980); Peter T Muchlinski 'Law and the Analysis of the International Oil Industry' in J Rees and P Odell (eds) *The International Oil Industry: An Interdisciplinary Perspective* (London: Macmillan Press, 1987) 142.

[3] See UNCTC The New Code Environment UNCTC Current Studies Series A No 16 (New York: UN, 1990) 18.

[4] See the Bolivian hydrocarbon natural resources nationalization law: Decreto Supremo No 28701 1 May 2006 (in Spanish). English translation 45 ILM 1018 (2006). Events in the Russian Federation concerning the oil company Yukos raised concerns of increased state intervention in foreign owned and operated investments: 'Yukos Sell-Off Brings Threat of Legal Action' *Financial Times* 12 December 2004 at 28 as has the more recent suspension of Shell's investment licence in the Sakhalin-2 natural gas project 'Investors Fear Economic Cold War as Kremlin Eyes Western Assets' *The Guardian* 20 September 2006 at 25. See also Max Gutbrod and Steffen Hindelang 'Externalization of Effective Legal Protection Against Indirect Expropriation' 7 JWIT 59 (2006). In 2004 four mining companies

The experience of these major expropriations prompted the establishment of national investment guarantee schemes and the setting up, in 1985, of the Multilateral Investment Guarantee Agency (MIGA). More recently, the focus has shifted to forms of indirect taking of foreign owned assets, and to the increased use of general standards of treatment, contained in international investment agreements (IIAs), for the assessment of governmental action that interferes with the operation of an investment. In particular, recent arbitral decisions have highlighted the growing importance of the national treatment and most favoured nation standards of non-discrimination, and the fair and equitable treatment standard, as benchmarks for the review of such action. The question of state responsibility for full protection and security of investments has also arisen. Each of these original, and more recent, developments will be considered in this, and the next, chapter. The present chapter will concentrate on renegotiation of investment contracts, the taking of foreign owned property, and the operation of national and multilateral investment guarantee schemes, while the next chapter will deal with the application of the other treaty based standards of treatment listed above.

However, before that is done, a preliminary question arises as to the role of international law in the regulation of investment risk. Although the internal law of the host state will usually be the proper law of the investment agreement,[5] and will therefore offer the initial legal framework for determining the legality of any governmental interference with the enjoyment and operation of a foreign investment by the investor, international law can be – and has been – invoked by foreign investors as the ultimate standard of legality in such cases. How this view is justified in terms of legal doctrine will now be considered, as a general introduction to the more specific legal questions that follow.

(1) The Restriction of State Sovereignty in the Field of Contractual Relations with Foreign Investors

Capital-exporting countries have sought to control host state sovereignty in this field by way of two principal legal techniques: first, by asserting that the proper law governing the international investment agreement is international law[6] and, secondly,

---

planned to sue the South African Government for expropriation, after the Mineral and Petroleum Resources Development Act of that year returned all mineral rights to the state: 'Foreign Mining Groups Set to Sue S. Africa for Expropriation' *Financial Times* FT Money & Business 30/31 October 2004 at M30. See also the Karaha Bodas case against Indonesia published at <http://www.transnational-dispute-management.com>.

[5] See *Serbian and Brazilian Loans Cases* PCIJ Ser ANos 20/21 (1929) at 41: 'any contract which is not a contract between states in their capacity as subjects of international law is based on the municipal law of some country'. See further DP O'Connell *International Law* (London: Stevens, 2nd edn, 1970) 978–79.

[6] On which see further FA Mann 'The Law Governing State Contracts' 21 BYIL 11 (1944); ibid 'The Proper Law of Contracts Concluded by International Persons' 35 BYIL 34 (1959). However,

by the adoption of so-called 'stabilization clauses' in international investment contracts under which 'the government party undertakes neither to annul the agreement nor to modify its terms, either by legislation or by administrative measures'.[7] This invokes the doctrine of 'sanctity of contract' as a justification for limiting the ability of the host state subsequently to alter the terms of the investment agreement by law. Both approaches are controversial as they assert a contractually based restriction upon the sovereignty of the host state over internal economic affairs.

(a) The 'Internationalization' of International Investment Agreements

The suggestion that international investment agreements are governed by international law as their proper law was discussed in a number of international arbitrations in the late 1970s and early 1980s arising out of expropriations, during the early 1970s, in the Middle Eastern oil industry. Of these, perhaps the most controversial was the *Texaco* arbitration.[8] In that case the arbitrator, Professor Dupuy, held that an oil concession agreement between a US oil company and the Government of Libya was 'internationalized', that is assimilated to international law, on two principal grounds. First, the reference to principles of international law, and to general principles of law,[9] in the choice of law clause in the concession

Dr Mann recanted on this position in his case-note on the House of Lords decision in *Amin Rasheed Shipping Corporation v Kuwait Insurance Company* [1983] 2 All ER 884; see 33 ICLQ 193 at 196–197 (1984). See also Robert Jennings 'State Contracts in International Law' 37 BYIL 156 (1961); Brown 'Choice of Law Provisions in Concession and Related Contracts' 39 MLR 6 (1976); Peter n 1 above ch 3. For a critique of the 'internationalization' theory, see Tang An 'The Law Applicable to a Transnational Economic Development Contract' 21 JWTL 95 (1987); Sornarajah 'The Myth of International Contract Law' 15 JWTL 187 (1981) and M Sornarajah *The International Law on Foreign Investment* (Cambridge: Cambridge University Press, 2nd edn, 2004) 416–29; Bowett 'State Contracts with Aliens: Contemporary Developments on Compensation for Termination or Breach' 59 BYIL 49 at 51–52 (1988); AFM Maniruzzaman 'Internationalization of Foreign Investment Agreements – Some Fundamental Issues of International Law' 1 JWI 293 (2000) and 'State Contracts in Contemporary International Law: Monist Versus Dualist Controversies' 12 EJIL 309 (2001).

[7] I Brownlie *Principles of Public International Law* (Oxford: Oxford University Press, 6th edn, 2003) 526.

[8] *Texaco v Libya* 17 ILM 1 (1978). For comment, see Bowett 37 CLJ 5 (1978); Fatouros 74 AJIL 134 (1980); Von Mehren and Kourides 75 AJIL 476 (1981); White 30 ICLQ 1 (1981); Greenwood 53 BYIL 27 (1982).

[9] General principles of law recognized by civilized nations have been included in numerous international investment agreements as the governing law. They form part of the sources of public international law as defined in art 38(c) of the Statute of the International Court of Justice. See further the following awards upon which Professor Dupuy relied as indicating that a reference to general principles was sufficient to show that the agreement was internationalized: *The Lena Goldfields Arbitration* Cornell Law Quarterly 1950 at 42, Annual Digest 5 (1929–1930) 3, 426; *Sheikh of Abu Dhabi v Petroleum Development (Trucial Coast) Ltd* 1 ICLQ 247 (1952), 18 ILR 144 (1951); *Sapphire International Petroleum Ltd v National Iranian Oil Company* 35 ILR 136 (1963); *Aramco Case* 27 ILR 117 (1963). See further McNair 'The General Principles of Law Recognised by Civilised Nations' 33 BYIL 1 (1957).

agreement was held to define the extent to which Libyan law could apply.[10] Only if Libyan law was in conformity with international law should it be applied to determine the legality of Libya's expropriation of the US company's assets. Secondly, the fact that the contract was an economic development agreement emphasized the need for internationalization. According to Professor Dupuy, such agreements justified assimilation to international law on the basis of their broad subject-matter, long duration, and the magnitude of the investment made by the foreign party. This required a measure of stability by which the investor could be protected against legislative uncertainties and governmental measures that might lead to an abrogation or rescission of the contract. Hence stabilization clauses were inserted which removed all or part of the agreement from the internal law and provided for its correlative submission to *sui generis* rules or to a system which was properly an international law system.[11]

Professor Dupuy's approach was followed in the *Revere Copper* arbitration.[12] However, it was not followed in the subsequent oil arbitrations of the early 1980s. In *Liamco v Libya*[13] the arbitrator, Dr Mahmassani, considered that the mere characterization of the concession as an 'economic development agreement' was, without more, insufficient to assimilate it to international law. However, on the basis of the express terms of the choice of law clause, Dr Mahmassani concluded that the proper law of the concession was Libyan law, excluding any part of that law which was in conflict with principles of international law.[14] In the *Aminoil* arbitration,[15] which involved an expropriation dispute between a US oil production company and Kuwait, the tribunal took a similar approach to that of Dr Mahmassani in *Liamco*. It held that the law of Kuwait applied subject to established public international law, which was found to be a part of the law of Kuwait, and to general principles of law, which were part of public international law.[16]

From the above it can be concluded that Professor Dupuy's approach, based on internationalization implied from the context of the agreement, does not find uniform support in arbitral awards.[17] The decisive factor appears to be the actual

[10] By clause 28 of the Deeds of Concession: 'This concession shall be governed by and interpreted in accordance with the principles of the law of Libya in common to the principles of international law and in the absence of such common principles then by and in accordance with general principles of law, including such of those principles as may have been applied by international tribunals.'

[11] Above n 8 at para 45, ILM 16–17.　　[12] 17 ILM 1321 (1978) or 56 ILR 258.

[13] 20 ILM 1 (1981) or 62 ILR 140. For comment see Greenwood n 8 above.

[14] Award 66–67, ILM 34–35.

[15] 21 ILM 976 (1982). For comment, see Fernando Teson 24 Va.J.Int'l L. 323 (1984); Mann 54 BYIL 213 (1983); Redfern 55 BYIL 65 (1984); Gann 23 Colum.J.Transnt'l L. 615 (1985).

[16] ibid para 6.

[17] See also the ICSID award in *Klockner v Cameroon* extracted in Paulsson 'The ICSID *Klockner v Cameroon* Award: The Duties of Partners in North-South Economic Development Agreements' 1 Jo.Int'l Arb. 145 at 157 (1984): 'We do not intend to apply new or exceptional legal principles to turn-key operations only because they concern projects affecting the economic and social development of a given country.' See further I Pogany 'Economic Development Agreements' 7 ICSID Rev-FILJ 1 (1992).

content of the agreement. Of particular importance are the terms of any express choice of law clause used by the parties and, in addition, whether there exists a stabilization clause restricting the host state's sovereign powers.[18] Furthermore, the *Liamco* and *Aminoil* awards are noteworthy for their assimilation of the national law of the host state with international law.[19] In particular, the *Aminoil* award appears to be adopting something akin to a 'transnational law' approach.[20] In that case the concession agreements themselves referred to general principles of law. However, in Article III(2) of the arbitration agreement, the parties referred to the transnational character of relations with the concessionaire and to general principles of law. The tribunal held that the different sources called upon in this article were not in contradiction with one another. Indeed, they formed a blend of sources as international law was a part of the law of Kuwait, and general principles of law correspondingly recognised the rights of the state in its capacity as protector of the general interest.[21]

This approach may serve to avoid choice of law problems by adopting an eclectic attitude to the sources of law governing international economic transactions. Instead of making a simple choice between national law, or international law supported by general principles of law recognized by civilized nations, all these sources are held to be available for the international tribunal to apply.[22] However, the adoption of this approach appears to have been made conditional upon an express acceptance of it by the parties to the dispute. This raises interesting issues concerning the relative bargaining positions of the parties, and how these may influence the content of the choice of law clause. The transnational law approach may avoid the stultification of dispute resolution procedures that might otherwise have become enmeshed in futile conflicts over the applicable law, with the host state favouring exclusive use of its law and the foreign investor insisting on the internationalization of the dispute. Where both parties are of equal bargaining power the compromise of adopting 'transnational law' may be used.

[18] See Greenwood n 8 above at 53.

[19] See further ch 18 at 737–40 below on the choice of law in ICSID arbitrations, where such assimilation also appears to have been accepted.

[20] On which see further P Jessup *Transnational Law* (New Haven: 1956); E Langen *Transnational Commercial Law* (Leiden: Sijthoff, 1973); P Lalive 'Contracts Between a State or a State Agency and a Foreign Company' 13 ICLQ 987 (1964); A Redfern and M Hunter *Law and Practice of International Commercial Arbitration* (London, Thomson Sweet & Maxwell, 4th edn, student version, 2004) paras 2–57 to 2–72. For a critical view of this concept, see Mann 33 ICLQ 193 (1984); Delaume 'The Proper Law of State Contracts and the *Lex Mercatoria*: A Reappraisal' 3 ICSID Rev-FILJ No 1 (1988). See also on the related concept of the 'New *Lex Mercatoria*' Abul FM Maniruzzaman 'The *Lex Mercatoria* and International Contracts: A Challenge for International Commercial Arbitration?' 14 Am.U.Int'l L.Rev. 657 (1999).   [21] ibid para 10.

[22] It is noteworthy that a decision of an arbitrator to decide the case before him on the basis of 'internationally accepted principles of law governing contractual relations' was endorsed by the English Court of Appeal, which refused to hold that the resulting award was unenforceable as being uncertain or as contravening public policy: *Deutsche Schachtbau-und-Tiefbohrgesellschaft GmbH v R'As Al Khaimah National Oil Company* [1987] 2 All ER 769 (CA) reversed on other grounds [1988] 2 All ER 833 (HL).

On the other hand, more recent practice has tended to place a preference on the internationalization of investment disputes, with international arbitration and international law as the proper law of the agreement being chosen. This choice can be cemented by the inclusion of an appropriately worded arbitration clause in the investment contract and supplemented by the availability of an international dispute settlement clause in any applicable investment protection treaty.[23]

(b) Sanctity of Contract and Stabilization Clauses

Following on from the 'internationalization' doctrine, the classical legal doctrine of 'sanctity of contract' has been invoked as a limitation on the absolute sovereignty of the host state over its relations with foreign investors. In this context, the legal effect of stabilization clauses in investment contracts has caused controversy.[24] Stabilization clauses can be used to exclude rules of the host state's law from the regulation of the agreement, by making international law or general principles of law the proper law of the agreement. Stabilization clauses may further exclude subsequent amendments of host state law from operating upon the investment contract. Thus the original terms of the investment agreement can be preserved from subsequent legal challenge by virtue of the stabilization clause.

Under the theory of sanctity of contract, the will of the parties must serve as the foundation of their agreement. Consequently a stabilization clause, as an expression of the will of the parties, must be upheld. This view led Professor Dupuy to hold, in the *Texaco* award, that the effect of the stabilization clause was to limit the state's sovereignty in relation to its rights over natural resources for the limited period of the concession.[25] On the other hand, in the *Liamco* award, Dr Mahmassani maintained that the principle *pacta sunt servanda* was qualified by the right of states to nationalize subject to the obligations of compensation.[26]

---

[23] This raises complex issues of the relationship between arbitration clauses in investment contracts and in investment protection treaties. These are considered in ch 17 at 696–98.

[24] See further Thomas Waelde and George Ndi 'Stabilizing International Investment Commitments: International Law Versus Contract Interpretation' 31 Texas Int'l L.Jo. 215 (1996); Abdullah Al Faruque 'The Rationale and Instrumentalities for Stability in Long-Term State Contracts - The Context for Petroleum Contracts' 7 JWIT 85 (2006). NGOs have asked whether such clauses might not unduly constrain the protection of the fundamental human rights of citizens, through the privileging of the rights of foreign investors under investment contracts and the restrictions against legal and policy change placed on governments. See, for example, Amnesty International *Human Rights on the Line: The Baku-Tiblisi-Ceyhan Pipeline Project* (London: Amnesty International UK, 2003) at <http://www.amnesty.org.uk/uploads/documents/doc_14538.pdf> and *Contracting Out of Human Rights: The Chad-Cameroon Pipeline Project* (London: Amnesty International UK, 2005) at <http://www.amnesty.org.uk/uploads/documents/doc_16423.pdf>. One solution may be to introduce human rights protection clauses into investment contracts, such as the 'Understanding on Human Rights' that amends the Baku-Tiblisi-Ceyhan Consortium Agreement: see Sheldon Leader 'Human Rights, Risks and New Strategies for Global Investment' 9 JIEL 657 (2006).   [25] See *Texaco v Libya* n 8 above at paras 71–77.

[26] See *Liamco v Libya* n 13 above at 89–113 of the award at ILM 46–56 and award 120 at ILM 61 for summary.

In *BP v Libya*[27] the sole arbitrator, Gunnar Lagergren, simply held that the concession involved constituted 'a direct contractual link between the respondent and the claimant'.[28]

In the *Aminoil* arbitration,[29] the tribunal held that the host state was in no way prevented from granting stability guarantees by contract.[30] However, the tribunal required an express provision restricting the state's power of nationalization. The contractual limitation of the state's right was 'a particularly serious undertaking which would have to be expressly stipulated for, and be within the regulations governing the conclusion of State contracts'.[31] Furthermore, the tribunal did not wish to prohibit the state's power to nationalize in the context of the great changes that had in fact come about in the agreement through a prolonged process of renegotiation.[32] The tribunal concluded that, owing to the changing nature of the concession, brought about by periodic renegotiation, the stabilization clauses had lost their absolute character. This was not a fundamental change in circumstances involving a departure from the contract, but a change in the nature of the contract itself, brought about by time, and the acquiescence or conduct of the parties.[33] Moreover, it appears from the tribunal's reasoning in *Aminoil* that the stabilization clause, on its terms, could not effectively limit the host state's power.[34] Thus, the case of a fundamental change of circumstances has been recognized in the *Aminoil* award as a justification for renegotiation. Presumably, in such cases, the existence of a stabilization clause cannot serve to justify the continuation of arrangements that were agreed before the full value of the investment was known, and which, if continued, would adversely affect the value of the project to the host state.[35]

(2) Renegotiation of International Investment Agreements

Despite the above mentioned arguments favouring the strict stability of international investment agreements, international practice in this field has increasingly favoured the periodic renegotiation of such agreements.[36] In these

---

[27] 53 ILR 297 (1974).   [28] ibid at 327.   [29] Above note 15.

[30] ibid at para 90.   [31] ibid at para 95, ILM 1023.   [32] ibid paras 97–98.

[33] ibid paras 100–101 at ILM 1024.

[34] According to Rosalyn Higgins, the tribunal's award is, in this respect, based on unpersuasive and contradictory reasoning: see Higgins 'The Taking of Property by the State: Recent Developments in International Law' 176 Hague Recueil (1982 III) 259 at 303–305. See also the Separate Opinion of Sir Gerald Fitzmaurice in *Aminoil* who felt that the nationalization of Aminoil's undertaking was irreconcilable with the stabilization clauses in the concession, although he agreed with the operative part (*dispositif*) of the award and did not dissent: above note 15 at ILM 1043–1053.

[35] According to Sornarajah it may not be possible in any case for a state to fetter its legislative discretion by contract as this may be unconstitutional: Sornarajah above n 6 at 407–410.

[36] See Asante 'Stability of Contractual Relations in the Transnational Investment Process' 28 ICLQ 401 (1979) and 'Restructuring Transnational Mineral Agreements' 73 AJIL 335 (1979); Brown 'The Relationship Between the State and the Multinational Corporation in the Exploitation of Resources' 33 ICLQ 218 (1984); ibid 'Contract Stability in International Petroleum Operations

circumstances the international legality of renegotiation per se can no longer be doubted. In order to avoid the inflexibility that a contract governed by a stabilization clause may create, the view has been put forward that investment agreements should, as a matter of standard form, include renegotiation clauses.[37] The inclusion of such a clause would clearly place renegotiation on a plane of legal acceptability and avoid arguments that taint renegotiation with illegality.[38] On the other hand, such a clause may encourage specious attempts at renegotiation by either party. Thus, relatively few agreements have a general renegotiation clause.[39]

The renegotiation of contracts at the initiation of the host may be as a result of a gradual shift in bargaining power away from the MNE towards the host state.[40] Whether the government can renegotiate successfully is, however, a matter of fact in each case. In any case, renegotiation will not always be at the instigation of the host state alone. There may be good reasons for the MNE to seek renegotiation. The MNE may welcome renegotiation initiated by the host state, especially where this might lead to a diffusion of hostility towards the firm's operations and guarantee long-term stability. Thus renegotiation may be a commercially desirable process for both parties.[41] However, if negotiations lead to unreasonable terms being imposed on the MNE, this may amount to unacceptable economic coercion by way of a diminution of corporate assets, or a partial sale thereof at undervalue, resulting from pressure in negotiations. This allows the state to achieve a result that it could not achieve lawfully through, say, nationalization without compensation. There may be a fine line between government coercion and unlawful expropriation. This raises the question whether there is a doctrine of unfair coercion in international law that can control abuses of power on the part of the host state in the renegotiating process.[42] The control of coercion on the part of the foreign corporation may also need to be subjected to such a regime, although this raises difficult questions as to the amenability of corporations to regulation by international law. Consequently, the discussion that follows may be

---

The CTC Reporter No 29 (Spring 1990) 56; Waelde 'Revision of Transnational Investment Agreements: Contractual Flexibility in Natural Resources Development' 10 Law.Am. 265 (1978); ibid 'Third World Mineral Investment Policies in the Late 1980s: From Restriction Back to Business' 3 Mineral Processing and Extractive Metallurgy Review 121 esp 161–74 (1988); Peter n 1 above especially ch 2; M Sornarajah 'Supremacy of the Renegotiation Clause in International Contracts' 5 J.Int'l Arb. 97 (1988).

[37] See references cited in above n 36.

[38] See M.Sornarajah *International Commercial Arbitration: The Problem of State Contracts* (Longman, 1990) 248–62.

[39] See further Abba Kolo and Thomas Waelde 'Renegotiation and Contract Adaptation in International Investment Projects' 1 JWI 5 at 47 (2000); see also Thomas Waelde and Abba Kolo 'Environmental Regulation, Investment Protection and "Regulatory Taking" in International Law' 50 ICLQ 811 (2001); Piero Bernardini 'The Renegotiation of the Investment Contract' 13 ICSID Rev-FILJ 411 (1998); Peter above n 1 ch 2.

[40] CD Wallace *Legal Control of the Multinational Enterprise* (Martinus Nijhoff, 1983) 236. See generally ibid 236–47.   [41] See further Kolo and Waelde above n 39.

[42] See further Vagts 'Coercion and Foreign Investment Rearrangements' 72 AJIL 17 (1978).

of relevance only to host state behaviour. The behaviour of the foreign corporation will remain to be judged in accordance with the proper law of the investment agreement, usually the law of the host state.

In the absence of established rules of international law on the matter, the control of unreasonable terms imposed on foreign investors by way of contractual renegotiation may be analysed on analogy with general principles of contract law found in modern legal systems.[43] In particular, the issues of duress and discrimination should be considered as vitiating factors in renegotiations between host states and foreign investors. Some instructive dicta on duress were given by the tribunal in the *Aminoil* award,[44] in the context of renegotiations undertaken in the light of a threat of expropriation against Aminoil. The US corporation argued that certain renegotiations of the concession agreement with Kuwait were tainted by duress in that the undertaking was threatened with 'shutdown' or a total prohibition on exports and that, accordingly, the corporation could not be bound by their outcome.[45] The tribunal rejected this argument. It made a distinction between strong economic pressure to conform to disagreeable terms and true coercion or duress that would invalidate agreement:

[i]t is necessary to stress that it is not just pressure of any kind that will suffice to bring about a nullification. There must be a constraint invested with particular characteristics, which the legal systems of all countries have been at pains to define in terms either of the absence of any other possible course than that to which the consent was given, or of the illegal nature of the object in view, or of the means employed . . . . But the illicit character of the threats against AMINOIL has not been fully proved.[46]

The tribunal went on to say that even if there were illicit threats in the circumstances they could not be said to have vitiated consent. First, Aminoil gave way without even making the qualification that the company was conscious that something illicit was being imposed upon it. It was understandable that it avoided resorting to arbitration because of costs and delays, but it entered neither reservations of position nor protests.[47] Secondly, the tribunal felt that, in truth, the company had made a choice:

[d]isagreeable as certain demands might be, it considered that it was better to accede to them because it was still possible to live with them. The whole conduct of the company shows that the pressure it was under was not of a kind as to inhibit its freedom of choice. The absence of protest during the years following upon 1973 confirms the non existence, or else the abandonment of this ground of complaint.[48]

---

[43] See further Vagts ibid; Kolo and Waelde above n 39 at 34–38.   [44] Above n 15.
[45] ibid para 40 at ILM 1007.
[46] ibid para 43 at ILM 1007; para 45 ILM 1008. On the English law of 'economic duress', see *Pao On v Lau Yiu Long* [1980] AC 614 (PC); *North Ocean Shipping Co Ltd v Hyundai Construction Co Ltd* [1979] QB 705. On US law, see Dawson 'Economic Duress – An Essay in Perspective' 45 Mich.L.Rev. 253 (1947).   [47] ibid para 44, ILM 1008.
[48] ibid.

The tribunal was thus emphasising the need for the company persistently to object to the alleged duress, for the argument to be credible. On the facts it appeared that the company had acquiesced to the new terms. In taking this stance, the tribunal shows that it would not readily interfere with the bargaining process between the parties and would not rewrite a contract simply because it contained disagreeable terms that a foreign investor had accepted where, on balance, it was commercially better to accept them, rather than to end the operation. This 'laissez-faire' approach is emphasized by the tribunal's view of the effects of the balance of negotiating power between the parties. The tribunal noted that the balance of advantage in the Gulf region had tilted in favour of governments and that Aminoil had been subjected to strong pressure to accept the repeated demands of the Kuwaiti Government. But all the tribunal had to decide was whether these constraints were of such a nature as to cause the malfunction of the interim agreement of 1973 or of certain other consents. This had not been shown.[49] Thus, the mere fact that the balance of negotiating power lay with the government did not amount to conclusive evidence of coercion.

It is not clear from the award whether the investor must persistently object to the unfair terms in all cases or whether this is unnecessary in cases where clearly it has no choice but to succumb to coercive pressure. It is submitted that the correct view should be that where it is clear that the investor has no choice but to accept (as where the alternative is confiscation) the absence of protest cannot be decisive. Indeed, the absence of protest may itself be an effect of the threat. Where, however, there is some element of choice (as where non-acceptance may result in expropriation with appropriate compensation) then acceptance of the new terms without protest would, arguably, vitiate any claim of duress. This is consistent with the view that the successful use of economic pressure by the state is not duress per se. There must be, in addition, proof of the unwillingness of the investor to accept the terms.[50]

The award leaves open the question of what evidential weight should be given to the investor's objections. Is the fact of objection, in itself, sufficient to vitiate consent, or must the tribunal consider further the question whether objection is justifiable on the facts? The latter view ought to prevail. Not every objection is with foundation. Furthermore, to decide the question on evidence of protest alone would be contrary to the view that disagreeable terms obtained as a result of economic pressure are not invalid by that fact alone. Thus the protest must be coupled with proof of some illicit action on the part of the state. Proof of the effects of the renegotiation on the corporate 'state of mind' is too subjective to be clear proof of duress.

[49] ibid para 45, ILM 1008.

[50] See, in this connection, *North Ocean Shipping Co Ltd v Hyundai Construction Co Ltd* n 46 above, where consent to a variation of contract obtained by economic duress was held to have affirmed the validity of the varied agreement.

This raises a further question: how are we to distinguish between acts of the state that are merely a legitimate exercise of economic power and those that are sufficiently coercive as to vitiate consent on the part of the investor to renegotiate terms? No absolute rules can be laid down. Each case must be judged on its own facts. However, certain guidelines can be suggested. First, threats of physical injury to the personnel of the corporation should always vitiate consent. This is a principle well known to most systems of contract law.[51] Secondly, threats of the physical destruction or legal attachment of the firm's property should have a similar effect where there is no legal justification for such interference.[52] On the other hand, threats of expropriation with the payment of appropriate compensation should not be treated as acts of duress per se, given the essential legality of such action. However, where the compensation offered is derisory when compared to the value of the foreign investor's assets, this might amount to evidence of duress in the absence of further objective justification. A further issue to be considered is whether the foreign investor has been unfairly discriminated against in the renegotiating process. The legal principles applicable to these matters are the same as those pertaining to the taking of property and are considered below.

(3) The Taking of Foreign Corporate Assets

This section of the chapter is divided into four parts. The first considers what constitutes a taking of foreign corporate assets; the second deals with the legality of takings in the law of the host state; the third examines the legality of takings in international law; and the fourth deals with the issue of compensation.

(a) What Constitutes a Taking

What constitutes a 'taking of property' is a matter of some debate. It has been argued that not only express policies of nationalization or expropriation fall to be considered, but also methods that do not involve an overt taking but which effectively neutralize the benefit of the property for the foreign owner. These have been referred to as cases of 'constructive taking' or 'creeping expropriation' or 'regulatory taking'. They may be referred to collectively as 'indirect takings' as they have the common feature of not being a specific, direct, measure that deprives the

---

[51] See eg *Barton v Armstrong* [1975] 2 WLR 1050 (PC); *Bernstein v van Heyghen Freres SA* 163 F 2d 246 (2d Cir 1947) *cert.denied* 332 US 772 (1948); *Bernstein v NV Nederlandsche-Amerikaansche Stoomvart Maatschappij* 173 F 2d 71 (2d Cir 1949); 210 F 2d 375 (2d Cir 1954); *Zwack v Kraus Bros & Co* 237 F 2d 255 (2d Cir 1956). See also *American Bell International Inc v Iran* 6 Iran-US CTR 74 (1984) which involved threats of 'serious personal consequences' for company representatives.

[52] See eg the English case on 'duress of goods' *Maskell v Horner* [1915] 3 KB 106. See further Beatson 'Duress as a Vitiating Factor in Contract' [1974] CLJ 97.

owner of its title to property.[53] To take each term in turn, a nationalization will involve the appropriation of foreign owned assets into public ownership and control by the host country. This can take place in all economic sectors, or be industry specific, depending on the policy of the taking state. An expropriation involves the compulsory taking of property belonging to another upon payment of compensation for its loss. The taker is usually a private entity acting on behalf of a public authority. Subsequently, the expropriated property may be acquired by a third party. The more general term 'taking of property' may be used to cover both cases.[54] The term is also apt to describe the incidence of 'creeping expropriation' which is defined by UNCTAD as, 'the slow and incremental encroachment on one or more of the ownership rights of a foreign investor that diminishes the value of its investment'[55] and 'regulatory taking', which is defined by UNCTAD as a taking of property that falls 'within the police powers of a State, or otherwise arise[s] from State measures like those pertaining to the regulation of the environment, health, morals, culture or economy of a host country'.[56]

In relation to indirect or regulatory takings, a distinction needs to be made between a legitimate exercise of the state's 'police power' and such a taking. Where a deprivation of property or other economic loss arises out of, for example, bona fide general taxation, regulation, or forfeiture for crime, then this is not generally compensable.[57] Thus, for example, the non-discriminatory application of

---

[53] See generally OECD *International Investment Law: A Changing Landscape* (Paris: OECD, 2005) ch 2 'Indirect Expropriation' and 'The Right to Regulate in International Investment Law'; Vaughan Lowe 'Regulation or Expropriation?' 55 CLP 447 (2002) and the articles on regulatory takings in 11 NY U Environmental Law Journal 1–316 (No 1 of 2002).

[54] See Domke 55 AJIL 585 at 588 (1961); UNCTAD *Taking of Property* Series on issues in international investment agreements (New York and Geneva: United Nations, 2000) 11. For an example of an outright expropriation, see *Wena Hotels v Egypt* ICSID Case No Arb/98/4 award of 25 May 1999 41 ILM 881 (2002).

[55] UNCTAD ibid See also W Michael Reisman and Robert D Sloane 'Indirect Expropriation and its Valuation in the BIT Generation' 74 BYIL 115 (2003) at 122–28.

[56] UNCTAD ibid at 12.

[57] See *Saluka v Czech Republic* UNCITRAL Rules Arbitration, Permanent Court of Arbitration, award of 17 March 2006 at paras 253–65 (at <http://www.ita.law.uvic.ca>). At para 262: 'In the opinion of the Tribunal, the principle that a State does not commit an expropriation and is thus not liable to pay compensation to a dispossessed alien investor when it adopts general regulations that are "commonly accepted as within the police power of States" forms part of customary international law today. There is ample case law in support of this proposition. As the tribunal in *Methanex Corp v USA* (Final Award on Jurisdiction and Merits 3 August 2005, 44 ILM 1345 (2006)) said recently in its final award, "[i]t is a principle of customary international law that, where economic injury results from a *bona fide* regulation within the police powers of a State, compensation is not required." See also American Law Institute *Restatement (Third) of the Foreign Relations Law of the United States* (St Paul, Minnesota: American Law Institute Publishers, 1987) vol I s 712(1). See further *Feldman v Mexico* ICSID Case No ARB (AF)/99/1 award 16 December 2002 available <http://www.naftaclaims.com> or 18 ICSID Rev-FILJ 488 (2003) at para 112 and *Azanian v Mexico* ICSID Case No ARB (AF)/97/2 award 1 November 1999 available at <http://www.naftaclaims.com> or 14 ICSID Rev-FILJ 538 (1999). See also *EnCana v Ecuador* UNCITRAL Rules Arbitration London Court of International Arbitration award of 3 February 2006 (at <http://www.ita.law.uvic.ca>) at para 177: 'From the perspective of expropriation taxation is a special category. In principle a tax law creates a new legal liability on a class of persons to pay money to the State in respect of some defined

competition law to an investment would be within the state's general police power.[58] On the other hand, a regulatory, taking might occur, for example, where a foreign investor is irrevocably deprived of its contractual rights in a joint venture created under an investment agreement. Such interference will give rise to a right of compensation.[59] Equally, the denial of a licence essential to the lawful operation of an investment may give rise to such a right.[60] These cases are justified in the light of the theory of property ownership: the incidents of ownership include not only possession but also use and free alienation. Any measure that irrevocably interferes with any one of these attributes of ownership deserves to be considered as a taking of property, entailing an obligation of compensation for any resulting economic loss suffered by the owner.[61] This approach assumes that the assets in question are in fact economically valuable. Thus, where a company owned by the foreign investor is no longer viable, and has no valuable assets to be expropriated, any act of regulatory intervention motivated by the need to deal with the consequences of that situation, such as a judicial reorganization of the company, will not amount to an expropriation.[62]

It has been suggested that a distinction should be made between a temporary administrative interference with property rights and the permanent deprivation of those rights.[63] Otherwise, the legitimate exercise of a state's regulatory powers could be unduly impeded by reference to international legal standards that go beyond what is generally accepted in the municipal laws of the world.[64] This

---

class of transactions, the money to be used for public purposes. In itself such a law is not a taking of property; if it were, a universal State prerogative would be denied by a guarantee against expropriation, which cannot be the case. Only if a tax law is extraordinary, punitive in amount or arbitrary in its incidence would issues of indirect expropriation be raised.'

[58] See Daniel Clough 'Regulatory Expropriation and Competition under NAFTA' 6 JWIT 553 (2005).

[59] See *Southern Pacific Properties (Middle East) Limited v Arab Republic of Egypt* Award on the Merits 20 May 1992: 32 ILM 933 paras 160–73 at 967–71 (1993); *CME (Netherlands) v Czech Republic* Partial Award 13 September 2001 at paras 591–607 available at <http://www.cetv-net.com>.

[60] See, for example, *TECMED v Mexico* ICSID Case No ARB (AF)/00/2 award of 29 May 2003 available at <http://www.worldbank.org/icsid> or 43 ILM 133 (2004) and *Metalclad v Mexico* at n 70 below.

[61] See further Higgins n 34 above especially at 267–78 and 322–54. According to the tribunal in *TECMED v Mexico* regulatory administrative actions can constitute an act of indirect expropriation, 'particularly if the negative economic impact of such actions on the financial position of the investor is sufficient to neutralize in full the value, or economic pr commercial use of its investment without receiving any compensation whatsoever'. At para 121; see further *GAMI v Mexico* UNCITRAL Rules, award of 15 November 2004, 44 ILM 545 (2005) at paras 116–33.

[62] See *Noble Ventures v Romania* ICSID Case No Arb/01/11 award 12 October 2005 available at <http://www.asil.org/illibita.law.uvic.ca> at paras 212–16.

[63] See generally Christie 'What Constitutes a Taking of Property Under International Law' 38 BYIL 307 (1962). See further *Pope and Talbot v Canada* UNCITRAL Interim Award 26 June 2000 available at <http://www.naftaclaims.com>.

[64] Indeed, the European Court of Human Rights has accepted the distinction between a legitimate administrative interference with property rights and expropriation: *Case of Sporrong and*

distinction may raise controversies. For example, the US-Iran Claims Tribunal had to address the issue in relation to emergency measures taken by Iran to preserve commercial property in the wake of post-revolutionary chaos in 1978–79, which led to claims of unlawful constructive taking by Iran.[65] Furthermore, it has been suggested that laws requiring the participation of workers in the management of a company could amount to 'creeping expropriation'.[66] It is submitted that this view is unduly restrictive of the host state's right to evolve company law in the light of its chosen policy, and ignores the distinction between the regulation and expropriation of property.

On the other hand, a partial or temporary deprivation of property could amount to a taking in certain circumstances. Thus in *SD Myers v Canada* the tribunal held that while an expropriation involved the deprivation of ownership rights, regulations could involve a lesser interference, with the consequence that 'in some contexts and circumstances, it would be appropriate to view a deprivation as amounting to an expropriation, even if it ware partial or temporary'.[67] However, on the facts of the case, a temporary restriction on the claimant's ability to conduct business within Canada was held not to constitute an expropriation within the terms of Article 1110 of NAFTA. Indeed, the tribunal felt that 'regulatory conduct by public authorities is unlikely to be the subject of legitimate complaint under Article 1110 of the NAFTA, though the Tribunal does not rule out the possibility'.[68] Thus, the precise circumstances in which a temporary interference with property rights can be held to constitute a compensable taking is not entirely clear.

Under NAFTA only one case has resulted in a finding of indirect expropriation. In relation to Article 1110 of NAFTA, which covers not only measures of expropriation but measures 'tantamount' to expropriation, 'tantamount' has been held as meaning 'equivalent to'.[69] In *Metalclad v Mexico* the tribunal held that the withholding of permits, and the adoption of an ecological decree, by the local government in whose area the claimant had invested in a landfill operation, amounted to a measure tantamount to expropriation especially as the Mexican Federal Government had already given assurances that the project was in

Lonnroth (European Court of Human Rights) judgment of 23 September 1982, Series A No 52. But see Higgins n 34 above at 343–47 and 367–68 for a strong critique of the Court's approach.

[65] See eg *Sea-Land Services Inc v Ports and Shipping Organisation of the Islamic Republic of Iran* 6 Iran-US CTR 149 (1984); *Starrett Housing Corp v Iran (Interlocutory Award)* 4 Iran-US CTR 122 (1984); 23 ILM 1090 (1984), *Otis Elevator Co v Iran and Bank Mellat* 14 Iran-US CTR 283 (1987). For analysis, see R Khan *The Iran-United States Claims Tribunal: Controversies, Cases and Contribution* (Martinus Nijhoff, 1990) 171–202. See also Hassam Sedigh 'What Level of Host State Interference Amounts to a Taking under Contemporary International Law?' 2 JWI 631 (2001).

[66] See Wallace n 40 above at 268–76.

[67] *SD Myers v Canada* UNCITRAL Award of 12 November 2000 available at <http://www.naftaclaims.com> or 40 ILM 1408 (2001) at para 283.   [68] ibid at para 281.

[69] *Pope and Talbot v Canada* UNCITRAL Interim Award 26 June 2000 at para 104: see <http://www.naftaclaims.com>. *SD Myers v Canada* above n 67 at para 286.

conformity with all regulatory requirements.[70] On judicial review before the Supreme Court of British Columbia, the finding of expropriation was overturned to the extent that the tribunal had relied on the lack of transparency on the part of the Mexican Federal Government in relation to the issuing of the appropriate permits. However, the finding of expropriation based on the passing of the ecological decree was allowed to stand.[71]

In determining the distinction between an indirect or regulatory taking and legitimate regulation, a controversial issue arises as to whether only the effect of a measure on the investor's property should be taken into account or whether, in addition, the object and purpose of the measure should be considered.[72] There is recent arbitral case law to support both an 'effect only' and an 'effect and intent' approach. In relation to the former, the leading case is that of *Compania del Desarrollo de Santa Elena SA v Costa Rica*.[73] In that case the tribunal was adamant that the object and purpose of the measure was irrelevant to the question of whether it was compensable. It stated:

While an expropriation or taking for environmental reasons may be classified as a taking for a public purpose, and thus may be legitimate, the fact that the property was taken for this reason does not affect either the nature or the measure of compensation to be paid for the taking. That is, the purpose of protecting the environment for which the property was taken does not alter the legal character of the taking for which adequate compensation must be paid ... where property is expropriated, even for environmental purposes, whether domestic or international, the state's obligation to pay compensation remains.[74]

This approach has been criticized for failing to give sufficient weight to the essential public interest purposes behind a regulatory act, which may justify its characterization as a non-compensable measure,[75] and to the risk that the threat of compensation may give rise to 'regulatory chill' and discourage entirely legitimate interference with foreign owned private property rights in the public interest.[76] One way to avoid such a consequence is to introduce a balancing approach between the effects of the measure on the investment and the public interest purposes behind it. At least two matters are relevant in this connection: the

[70] *Metalclad v Mexico* ICSID Case No Arb (AF)/97/1 available at <http://www. naftaclaims.com> or 40 ILM 36 (2001).

[71] *United Mexican States v Metalclad Corp* 2001 BCSC 664 2 March 2001.

[72] See, in particular, L Yves Fortier and Stephen L Drymer 'Indirect Expropriation and the Law of International Investment: I Know It When I See It, or *Caveat Investor*' 19 ICSID Rev-FILJ 293 (2004); Bjorn Kunoy 'Developments in Indirect Expropriation Case Law in ICSID Transnational Arbitration' 6 JWTI 467 (2005).

[73] ICSID Case No Arb/96/1 Award 17 February 2000 available at <http://www. worldbank.org/icsid/cases/santaelena_award.pdf> or 15 ICSID Rev-FILJ 169 (2000).

[74] ibid at paras 71–2. See also *Metalclad v Mexico* above n 70 at para 111. 'The Tribunal need not decide or consider the motivation or intent of the adoption of the Ecological Decree.'

[75] See Sornarajah above n 6 at 375.

[76] See UNCTAD *World Investment Report 2003* (New York and Geneva: United Nations, 2003) at 111.

legitimate expectations of the investor and the proportionality of the measure taken to the public purpose in question.

As to the role of investor's legitimate expectations, these may be said to revolve around the entitlement of the investor to rely on any assurances made to them, by the host state authorities, about the nature and extent of regulatory control that the investment will experience during its projected life. This does not exclude the risk of loss due to regulatory change where this is foreseeable, and where it has not been excluded by way of a general stabilization clause or specific representation.[77] Neither does it include the avoidance of the ordinary risks inherent in investment transactions. Investment protection agreements do not act as insurance policies against bad business judgments.[78] Accordingly, where the loss to the investor can be said to arise out of a bad investment decision, it will not be allowed to rely on any regulatory act that apparently takes away its property rights, as this is not the major cause of the loss. Only where a regulatory act is unforeseeable, and is the primary, or at least a contributory, cause of the loss to the investor, will it be able to claim compensation.[79] On the other hand, where an express representation has been made that a certain course of regulatory conduct will not be followed, or where there is a general stabilization requirement, governmental action that is not in conformity with these assurances will normally give rise to compensation.[80]

As to the issue of proportionality, an important contribution has been made by the tribunal in the case of *TECMED v Mexico*.[81] In that case the claimant complained that it had been subjected to a measure tantamount to expropriation contrary to Article 5(1) of the Spain-Mexico Agreement on the Reciprocal Promotion and Protection of Investments of 1996. In particular, the claimant argued that the refusal, by the National Ecology Institute of Mexico (INE), to renew its permit to operate the landfill site that was the subject of its investment, rendered the investment economically redundant and so amounted to an act of indirect expropriation. The tribunal held that it had to approach the matter in the light of what would amount to reasonable measures on the part of the state 'with respect to their goals, the deprivation of economic rights and the legitimate

---

[77] See *Methanex v United States* Final Award on Jurisdiction and Merits 3 August 2005 44 ILM 1345 (2005) especially Part IV-Chapter D 5 paras at 9–10; *Feldman v Mexico* above n 57 at para 112.

[78] See *Maffezini v Spain* ICSID Case No Arb/97/7 award of 13 November 2000 available at <http://www.worldbank.org/icsid> or 16 ICSID Rev-FILJ 248 (2001) at para 64; *Waste Management v Mexico* ICSID Case No Arb(AF)/00/3 award of 30 April 2004 available at <http://www.naftaclaims.com> or 43 ILM 967 (2004) at para 177.

[79] Compensation may be reduced to take into account the degree to which the investor's own conduct has contributed to the loss. See further *MTD Equity v Chile* ICSID Case No Arb/01/7 award of 25 May 2004 available at <http://www.worldbank.org/icsid> or 44 ILM 91 (2005). The award is subject to annulment proceedings.

[80] See, for example, *Metalclad v Mexico* above n 70. This principle appears to be unaffected by the judicial review of this case by the Supreme Court of British Columbia (above n 71), which turned on the relationship between different parts of NAFTA, and not on this issue of principle.

[81] Above n 60. See also for a helpful analysis Andrew Newcombe 'The Boundaries of Regulatory Expropriation in International Law' 20 ICSID Rev-FILJ 1 (2005).

expectations of who suffered such deprivation'.[82] It added: '[t]here must be a reasonable relationship of proportionality between the charge or weight imposed on the foreign investor and the aim sought to be realised by any expropriatory measure.'[83] Relevant to this calculation was the size of the ownership deprivation caused by the actions of the state and whether this was compensated or not. It should also be taken into account that foreign investors might not be entitled to take part in the decisions made unlike nationals who might have the ability to exercise political rights, such as voting for the authorities that might issue the decision that will affect foreign investors.[84] The tribunal cited case law of the European Court of Human Rights in support of these propositions.[85] On the facts the tribunal found that the aim of the measure, to protect public health and to respond to public pressure resulting from the location of the landfill, was not such as to render proportional the deprivation of the investor's rights and the negative economic impact upon the investment. Specifically, the infringements committed by the investor of the original licence were not of a kind as to warrant non-renewal, and the public pressure arose out of the location of the landfill and not the manner in which it was operated by the investor. That was an issue upon which the various Mexican authorities could have acted without denying the renewal of the permit, but by authorizing a removal of the landfill site to another location. In addition, the investor's operation never compromised the ecological balance of the site or the protection of the environment or the health of the people.[86] Finally, the denial of the permit contravened the claimant's legitimate expectation that this was a long-term investment.[87] While the particular application of this approach to the facts of the case will, no doubt, be open to discussion, it is certain that the issue of proportionality offers an important method of assessing the relationship between a governmental act, and the ensuing damage that it may cause to an investor, as a means of assessing whether its public purpose can justify such damage. Indeed, this approach has been endorsed by a more recent ICSID Tribunal in the case of *Azurix v Argentina*.[88]

Related to the issue of proportionality is the question of necessity. Specifically, according to Article 25 of the International Law Commission's Articles on State Responsibility, a state may not invoke necessity as a ground for precluding the wrongfulness of an act not in conformity with an international obligation of the state unless it is the only means by which that state can safeguard an essential interest against a grave and imminent peril and it does not seriously impair the

---

[82] ibid at para 122.   [83] ibid.   [84] ibid.

[85] Specifically the cases of *Matos e Silva Lda v Portugal* E Ct HR judgment 16 September 1996; *Mellacher and Others v Austria* E Ct HR judgment 19 December 1989; *Pressos Compania Naviera and Others v Belgium* E Ct HR judgment 20 November 1995; *James and Others v United Kingdom* E CT HR judgment 21 February 1986 all available at <http://hudoc.echr.coe.int>.

[86] Above n 60 at paras 125–51.   [87] ibid at para 149.

[88] ICSID Case No Arb/01/12 award of 14 July 2006 available at <http://www.ita.law.uvic.ca> at paras 311–12.

rights of other states or of the international community as a whole.[89] Such a plea is exceptional. In the context of an investment dispute, such a plea was made, by the Government of Argentina, in the case of *CMS Gas Transmission Co v Argentina*.[90] The case arose out of the Argentine Government's privatization programme. This included the privatization of the national gas transmission industry. The claimant acquired one of the privatized companies. Towards the end of the 1990s Argentina faced a serious economic crisis with profound political and social ramifications. In 2002 the Argentina Government passed the Emergency Law declaring a public emergency and introducing, inter alia, restrictions on the rights of licensees of public utilities to convert their tariffs to US dollars. Subsequent attempts at renegotiations with licensees failed to resolve the resulting problems. The claimant argued that, as a result of these extraordinary measures, their investment was devastated as they would not be able to repay their debts in that domestic tariff revenue had decreased by 75 per cent due to the ending of dollar based rates and their replacement with domestic currency rates. The claimant felt that these effects were an indirect expropriation of their investment, a breach of the fair and equitable treatment standard and a breach of the observance of obligations (umbrella) clause, in the US-Argentina BIT of 1991. The tribunal dismissed the expropriation claim on the ground that the claimant continued to enjoy full ownership and control of the acquired company.[91] However, it held that the fair and equitable treatment standard, and the umbrella clause, had been breached.[92] This in turn raised the question whether, despite these established breaches of the BIT, Argentina could claim exemption from liability by reason of necessity arising out of the grave and imminent peril posed to the country by the economic crisis. Having held that Article 25 of the ILC Articles on State Responsibility represented the state of customary international law, the tribunal examined whether, on the facts, a state of necessity existed. It came to the view that it did not. While undoubtedly very serious, the economic crisis did not justify extreme measures, nor were such measures the 'only way' for Argentina to safeguard its interests. The tribunal laid particular weight on the fact that successive governments, including the incumbent, had also contributed to the crisis by their polices and so there were internal, as well as external, factors that were of relevance.[93] In addition, the

---

[89] See James Crawford *The International Law Commission's Articles on State Responsibility; Introduction Text and Commentaries* (Cambridge: Cambridge University Press, 2002) 178.

[90] ICSID Case No Arb/01/8 award of 12 May 2005 available at <http://www.worldbank.org/icsid> and 44 ILM 1205 (2005). See, however, *LG&E Energy Corporation v Argentina* ICSID Case No Arb/02/1 Decision on Liability 3 October 2006 available at <http://www.ita.law.uvic.ca> The tribunal held that Argentina was entitled to take emergency measures, at least for a specific period in which the tribunal found a national emergency to exist. As a result the claimant had to bear the consequences of the measures taken and could not claim compensation for losses sustained as a result of those measures during that period: see paras 226–66.

[91] ibid at paras 262–64.   [92] ibid at paras 266–303.   [93] ibid at paras 317–31.

emergency measures clause in the BIT did not derogate from treaty rights and so could not be invoked to exclude them.[94]

This case appears to set a very high standard for the state to meet if it claims exemption from investor protection standards on the ground of necessity. Nothing short of the complete collapse of the Argentine economy, rendering any economic activity impossible, would appear to have been required. In addition, the stress laid on the decisions of successive governments would make any such defence almost impossible to use. In every case of grave and catastrophic economic collapse it will be possible to show mistakes made by governments. Thus the *CMS* Case appears to offer little by way of reassurance for host countries facing severe economic crises that their emergency measures will not fall foul of the provisions of international investment agreements. Whether it will be uniformly followed by subsequent tribunals is, however, uncertain.

Finally, in relation to the distinction between compensable takings and legitimate governmental regulation, it should be noted that much of the uncertainty surrounding this issue has arisen out of the lack of proper definitions of such terms in IIAs. While most expropriation provisions will state that a direct or indirect taking will require compensation, they do not exemplify measures that qualify as such.[95] More recent agreements are taking tentative steps to rectify this problem. Thus, the recent United States-Uruguay BIT of 25 October 2004, which is based on the 2004 US Model BIT, offers the following definition of an indirect taking in Annex B paragraph 4:

The second situation addressed by Article 6(1) [expropriation] is known as indirect expropriation, where an action or series of actions by a Party has an effect equivalent to direct expropriation without formal transfer of title or outright seizure.

(a) The determination of whether an action or series of actions by a Party, in a specific fact situation, constitutes an indirect expropriation, requires a case-by-case, fact-based inquiry that considers, among other factors:
   (i) the economic impact of the government action, although the fact that the action or series of actions by a Party has an adverse effect on the economic value of an investment, standing alone, does not establish that an indirect expropriation has occurred;
   (ii) the extent to which the government action interferes with distinct, reasonable investment backed expectations; and
   (iii) the character of the government action.

(b) Except in rare circumstances, non-discriminatory regulatory actions by a Party that are designed and applied to protect legitimate public welfare objectives, such as public health, safety, and the environment, do not constitute indirect expropriations.[96]

---

[94] ibid at para 375.   [95] For examples see further UNCTAD above n 54 at 19–24.
[96] Treaty Between the United States of America and the Republic of Uruguay Concerning the Encouragement and Reciprocal Protection of Investment 25 October 2004: 44 ILM 268 at 294 (2005).

This type of provision was first introduced into United States bilateral Free Trade Agreements (FTAs) pursuant to deliberations in Congress on the meaning of expropriation under the Trade Act of 2002.[97] It reflects the standards of review contained in US domestic judicial review case law.[98] This is a welcome development in so far as it allows for some more specific, and structured, discussion of how the scope of a state's right to regulate will be assessed in the case of regulatory acts that impair the economic value of an investment.

(b) The Legality of Takings Under the Law of the Host State

The legality of a taking is at first instance a question for the internal law of the host state. Such an act is generally taken in pursuit of a statutory or other legal authority of the host state.[99] Furthermore, host state law may provide the means by which the titleholder can challenge the taking. Local administrative law may provide for judicial review, or special provisions under the legislation governing the taking may set up a disputes procedure. Such measures can serve to control excesses of executive power, where they are applied with regard to due process.[100] Moreover, the law of the host state may provide constitutional controls over the passage of laws authorizing the taking of property.[101]

In this field, the primacy of internal review and judicial control should be stressed. Indeed, under public international law, the foreign investor is obliged to exhaust local remedies, unless they are obviously futile, before it can present a claim under international law.[102] It is likely that most takings, if carried out under legal authority, and in accordance with the requirements of procedural justice, will raise no questions of conformity with either internal or international law. Consequently, the legality of a taking of foreign owned property has become a question of international law only in those cases where local law has failed to satisfy the claims of the foreign investor to adequate compensation and to due

---

[97] See, for example, *US-Chile FTA* Annex 10–D; *US-Singapore FTA* ch 15 (exchange of letters on expropriation) available at <http://www.unctad.org/iia>.

[98] See further Gary H Sampliner 'Arbitration of Expropriation Cases under US Investment Treaties – A Threat to Democracy or the Dog that Didn't Bite?' 18 ICSID Rev-FILJ 1 at 35–42 (2003).

[99] But see cases before the Iran-US Claims Tribunal, raising issues concerning the responsibility of the host state for the acts of Revolutionary Guards or Committees that interfered with property belonging to US nationals: *William Pereira Associates, Iran v Iran* 5 Iran-US CTR 198 (1984); *Sola Tiles Inc v Iran* 14 Iran-US CTR 223 (1987). Where Revolutionary Guards acted as instrumentalities of the state in the absence of a confiscatory decree, Iran was held responsible for resulting losses of property belonging to foreign claimants.   [100] See, for example, *Azanian v Mexico* above n 57.

[101] See, for example, the background to the French nationalizations of 1981: Alison Doyle 'The French Nationalisations: Mitterand Challenges the Multinationals' in BS Fisher and J Turner *Regulating the Multinational Enterprise: National and International Challenges* (1983) 67; L Favoreu *Nationalisations et Constitution* (Paris: Economica, 1982); Linotte 'Les Nationalisations De 1982' (1982) Revue de Droit Publique 435; Juillard 'Les Nationalisations Françaises' (1982) AFDI 767.

[102] See further ch 18 at 705–706.

process. The role of international law in this area is that of an exceptional standard of control to be used only in relation to extraordinary abuses of power by the host state in its treatment of the foreign investor.[103]

(c) The Legality of Takings at International Law[104]

The legality of expropriation has been one of the most contentious problems in international law. Due to changes in the international political system during the 20th century, uncertainty arose as to the norms of international law applicable to foreign investors.[105] According to the repeated practice of the major capital-exporting powers, a taking is lawful only in cases where it is carried out for a clear public purpose, without discrimination and upon payment of 'prompt adequate and effective compensation'.[106] This is often referred to as the international minimum standard for the treatment of property belonging to aliens. On the other hand, the major capital-importing states have periodically doubted the validity of this standard, which they see as having been evolved to serve the interests of capital-exporting states and, therefore, lacking the generality of acceptance required of a norm of customary international law.[107] During the 1970s these states were active in proposing alternative standards through the UN, that centred on increased host state control over expropriation and, in particular, over levels of compensation.[108]

---

[103] This view appears has been reinforced by the refusal of the European Court of Human Rights to examine cases involving a taking by a state of the property of its own nationals by reference to international law under the European Convention on Human Rights. See *Lithgow and Others* E Ct HR judgment of 8 July 1986 paras 111–19. Confirmed by the European Commission on Human Rights in *Scott's of Greenock (Est'd 1711) Ltd and Lithgows Limited* (Strasbourg: 1989) Commission Report of 17 December 1987 at para 81.

[104] Among the extensive literature on this subject the following are recommended as valuable overviews containing extensive further references: Brownlie above n 7 ch 24; DJ Harris *Cases and Materials on International Law* (Thomson Sweet & Maxwell, 6th edn, 2004) 577–613; Higgins n 34 above; American Law Institute *Third Restatement on the Foreign Relations Law of the US* (St Paul, Minn: 1987) s 712 at 196–216.

[105] See generally Charles Lipson *Standing Guard: Protecting Foreign Capital in the Nineteenth and Twentieth Centuries* (Berkeley: University of California Press, 1985) Part I.

[106] This term is attributed to the US Secretary of State Cordell Hull, who used words to this effect in a note to Mexican Government of 21 July 1938 concerning the latter's expropriation of US agrarian interests in 1938. See 32 AJIL Supplement 181–207 (1938) or 3 Hackworth Digest of International Law 655–61 (1942). For background, see Kunz 'The Mexican Expropriations' 17 NYULQR 327 (1940).

[107] See further Lipson above n 105; Dolzer 'New Foundations of the Law of Expropriation of Alien Property' 75 AJIL 553 (1981); Schachter 'Compensation for Expropriation' 78 AJIL 121 (1984); Jimenez de Arechaga 'State Responsibility for the Nationalisation of Foreign Owned Property' 11 NYU J. Int' L. & Pol. 179 (1978); A Akinsnaya 'Host Government's Responses to Foreign Economic Control: The Experiences of Selected African Countries' 30 ICLQ 769 (1981); ibid *The Expropriation of Multinational Property in the Third World* (New York: Praeger 1980); Sornarajah 'Compensation for Expropriation: The Emergence of New Standards' 13 JWTL 108 (1979); M Sornarajah above n 6 345–49.

[108] According to the Charter of Economic Rights and Duties of States (UNGA Resolution 3281 (XXIX) 12 December 1974) 14 ILM 251 (1975) art 2(2)(c): 'Each State has the right . . . to

However, a number of factors point to the dominance of the international minimum standard in the legal analysis of the consequences of takings. First, the standard is widely accepted by capital-importing countries in bilateral and regional investment treaties as well as in free trade agreements with investment provisions.[109] Secondly, it continues to inform the expropriation policies of major capital-exporting states. For example, the French Government was concerned to conform to international law where compensation for foreign shareholders was in issue during the nationalizations of 1982. Thus, foreign banks were excluded from nationalization and foreign shareholders in the nationalized companies were promised prompt, adequate, and effective compensation. Thirdly, the courts of major capital-exporting countries may not give effect to an act of taking that does not conform to the international minimum standard, at least as regards the requirements of public purpose and non-discrimination.[110] Fourthly, although newer international investment contracts tend to be governed by the law of the host state rather than by international law, the contents of national law will often conform to the international minimum standard.[111] Thus the difference in applicable principles may not be that great where host state law accepts the international standard. Fifthly, the international minimum standard continues to be a major source of legal principle applied by international arbitral tribunals.[112]

---

nationalize, expropriate or transfer ownership of foreign property in which case appropriate compensation should be paid by the State adopting such measures, taking into account its relevant laws and regulations and all the circumstances that the State considers pertinent. In any case where the question of compensation gives rise to a controversy, it shall be settled under the domestic law of the nationalising State and by its tribunals, unless it is freely and mutually agreed by all States concerned that other peaceful means be sought on the basis of the sovereign equality of States and in accordance with the principle of free choice of means.' See also UNGA Resolution 3171 (XXVIII) GAOR 28th Sess Supp 30 52 (1973), 68 AJIL 381 (1974); Declaration on the Establishment of a New International Economic Order para (4)(e) UNGA Resolution 3201 (S–VI) 13 ILM 715 (1974).

[109] See further ch 17.

[110] See further M Sornarajah *The Pursuit of Nationalized Property* (Martinus Nijhoff, 1986). On US law, see Foreign Sovereign Immunity Act 1976 s 1605(3); *Kalamazoo Spice Extraction Co v The Provisional Military Government of Socialist Ethiopia* 24 ILM 1277 (1985); *First National City Bank v Banco Para El Commercia Exterior de Cuba* 462 US 611 (1983), 22 ILM 840 (1983); *US Third Restatement* n 57 above para 444 Comment d at 385 and see para 455(3) and Comment c at 412–13; *Banco Nacional de Cuba v Sabbatino* 376 US 398 (1964); *Banco Nacional de Cuba v Farr* 383 F 2d 166 (2d Cir 1967) *cert.den.* 390 US 956 (1968); *First National City Bank v Banco Nacional de Cuba* 406 US 759 (1972); *Banco Nacional de Cuba v Chase Manhattan Bank* 658 F 2d 875 (2d Cir 1981). On English law, see *Williams and Humbert Ltd v W and H Trade Marks (Jersey) Ltd* [1986] AC 368, [1985] 2 All ER 208 (Nourse J), [1985] 2 All ER 619 (CA), [1986] 1 All ER 129 (HL); *Settebello Ltd v Banco Totta e Acores* [1985] 2 All ER 1025, [1985] 1 WLR 1050 (CA); *Luther v Sagor* [1921] 3 KB 532; *Anglo-Iranian Oil Co v Jaffrate 'The Rose Mary'* [1953] 1 WLR 246; PM North and JJ Fawcett *Cheshire and North's Private International Law* (Butterworths, 13th edn, 1999) 116–23.

[111] In the *Aminoil* award n 15 above, the law of Kuwait was characterized as consistent with the international standard. See also *Letco v Liberia* (ICSID Tribunal) 26 ILM 647 (1987) where the law of Liberia was found to be in conformity with international law. However, this is not to say that national laws reflect a general acceptance of the principle that full compensation is always payable for a taking of property: see further Amerasinghe 'Issues of Compensation for the Taking of Alien Property in the Light of Recent Cases and Practice' 41 ICLQ 22 at 25–27 and 30–31 (1992).

[112] See further Norton 'A Law of the Future or a Law of the Past? Modern Tribunals and the International Law of Expropriation' 85 AJIL 474 (1991); Amerasinghe ibid. Note that Amerasinghe

Nonetheless, it is important to be aware of the limitations of the above mentioned factors. In particular, inroads may be made into the philosophy of 'prompt adequate and effective' compensation for practical commercial and political reasons, leading to less than full compensation in negotiated settlements or lump sum agreements. This issue will be considered in more detail in sub-section (d) below. Furthermore, investment treaties may incorporate the international minimum standard precisely because its status as customary law has often been in doubt.[113] Moreover, as regards arbitral jurisprudence, this has at times evolved in the context of factors that may limit its claim to represent an international consensus on applicable standards. These include the non-appearance of Libya in the oil arbitrations of the late 1970s and early 1980s,[114] and the persistent lodging of dissenting opinions, critical of the application of the international minimum standard, by the Iranian arbitrators sitting in the Chambers of the Iran-US Claims Tribunal.[115] As these two sets of awards are among the most cited in favour of the acceptance of the international standard, these facts should not go unnoticed. Notwithstanding these factors, the international minimum standard retains considerable force as an ordering principle for the legal discussion of takings and will be so used in the remainder of this chapter.

In that light the following elements of what constitutes a lawful taking in international law appear to be well settled: to be lawful, a taking must be for a public purpose, be non-discriminatory, and must be accompanied by compensation.[116] There is general agreement between states on the content of this aspect of the law. A taking of property is usually treated as a sovereign power that is exercised for the purposes of the state's national economic policy. That power cannot, however, be exercised arbitrarily. Thus it is subject to two qualifications: first it must be exercised for a genuine public purpose, and not for a purpose of private gain; secondly, it must conform to basic principles of justice. Hence it must be non-discriminatory and compensation must be provided.

The question of public purpose is a question of fact in each case. It is generally not in issue that a taking is undertaken for a public purpose. States enjoy a wide discretion in this respect.[117] However, certain kinds of taking would be beyond the state's lawful discretion. The clearest example arises where members of the government are using such powers as a means of obtaining private gain, rather than acting for the enrichment of the country. The same legal consequence may

---

sees the international minimum standard as being subject to exceptions in which less than full compensation may be payable for an expropriatory measure, and views the case law of international tribunals as contributing to this development of the law.

[113] This argument is elaborated in ch 17 at 701–702.

[114] Cited at nn 8, 13, and 27 above.

[115] See Norton above n 112 at 486; Khan above n 65 at 251.

[116] See further *Antoine Goetz and others v Republic of Burundi* ICSID Case No Arb/95/3 award of 10 February 1999 available at <http://www.worldbank.org/icsid/cases> or 15 ICSID Rev-FILJ 457 (2000) at paras 120–33.

[117] See *Amoco International Finance Corporation v Iran* 15 Iran-US CTR 189 (1987) at para 145.

attach where the taking is not recognized by law in effect at the time of taking as being for a public purpose.[118] Furthermore, should the property be seized in the course of committing crimes against humanity, or genocide, or other violations of human rights, the taking would be contrary to public purpose.[119] Equally, where the taking is motivated by political concerns that are not directly relevant to the state's economic policy, and is not justified by exceptional circumstances,[120] it may well be unlawful.[121]

The question of non-discrimination is closely connected to the issue of public purpose in that a discriminatory taking cannot be a taking for a public purpose.[122] The issue of discrimination involves a comparison, if any exists,[123] with the treatment afforded to domestic competitors, to other foreign investors operating in the same field and the treatment given to foreign investors in general. The basic principle of equality of treatment is in issue. Thus any difference in treatment must be objectively justifiable. In this respect, discriminatory treatment, that cannot be justified by reference to the host state's economic policy, has been presumed to be illegitimate. Thus a taking motivated by extraneous political concerns, such as, for example, retaliation against the home state of the investor for the conduct of its foreign policy, may not be acceptable.[124] On the other hand, the mere fact that different treatment is being meted out to certain corporations of foreign nationality would appear to be insufficient, in itself, to vitiate an act of taking.[125] Unless it is clear that the differentiation is without objective justification,

---

[118] Harvard Research Draft Convention on the International Responsibility of States for Injuries to Aliens art 10(1)(a): 55 AJIL 548 (1961).

[119] See *Oppenheimer v Cattermole* [1976] AC 249 (HL).

[120] Eg the existence of a state of war between the home and host state of the foreign investor.

[121] See *BP v Libya* 53 ILR 297 (1974).

[122] As stated above the principles discussed in the following paragraphs may equally apply to discrimination in cases of renegotiation. See further AFM Maniruzzaman 'Expropriation of Alien Property and the Principle of Non-Discrimination in International Law of Foreign Investment: An Overview' 8 J.Transnational.L. & Policy 57 (1998).

[123] This may be so where the foreign investor is the only enterprise engaged in a particular line of business or industry, and there is no domestic or foreign competitor.

[124] See *BP v Libya* n 121 above. In that case the sole arbitrator held that the taking of BP's property by Libya had been discriminatory. It had been motivated by the Libyan Government's opposition to the British Government's refusal to oppose Iran's occupation of the Tunb Islands in the Persian Gulf on 29 and 30 November 1972. Libya had argued that Britain was obliged to protect the islands under treaties of protection between Britain and the Trucial States (now the United Arab Emirates), which were due to end on 30 November.

[125] See *The Oscar Chinn Case* PCIJ Series A/B No 63 (1934). In this case the Belgian Government, in response to the prevailing economic recession, had reduced the tariffs to be charged by a river transportation company, operating under its control in the Congo Basin, in return for a promise of compensation. This had the result that other transportation companies could no longer compete on price with the state controlled company. The United Kingdom Government brought a claim alleging that Belgium had infringed the Treaty of St-Germain 1919, which obliged Belgium inter alia to maintain commercial freedom and equality, and freedom of river navigation, in the Congo Basin. The PCIJ rejected the UK contention on the ground inter alia that the discrimination covered by the treaty related to Belgian and non-Belgian companies, and did not extend to companies under the control of the Belgian Government. This case has been criticized as having failed to deal with the necessity of the measures adopted. See W McKean *Equality and Discrimination Under International Law*

this phenomenon cannot act as a vitiating factor, as it would render policy responses based on distinctions in corporate nationality unlawful per se.[126]

Thus, modern international law may give a certain margin of discretion to the host state in this area. However, it is not entirely clear whether this margin should be the same in all cases. Arbitral jurisprudence has mainly dealt with differences of treatment between foreign corporations possessing the same or different nationalities.[127] More problematic is the case of differing treatment between a foreign corporation and a domestic competitor that is unfavourable to the foreign entity.[128] Such treatment may violate the 'national treatment' standard, which is present in numerous bilateral investment treaties, and which is discussed further below.[129]

Should a discriminatory taking be found to have taken place, it might not be open to legal challenge, provided a just measure of compensation has been paid.[130] In this way state sovereignty and corporate interests may be reconciled. However, the issue of compensation has raised controversial questions to which attention now turns.

(d) The Issue of Compensation

There is general agreement that, to be lawful, an act of expropriation requires compensation. On the other hand, there continues to be disagreement as to how that compensation should be measured. This process involves two interrelated stages. First, the expropriated property must be valued to ascertain the actual economic loss sustained by the property owner. Secondly, the extent to which the

---

(Oxford: Clarendon Press, 1983) 194–95; but see, for the view that the PCIJ was not insensitive to the implications of greater state involvement in economic regulation, H Lauterpacht *The Development of International Law by the International Court* (Stevens, 1958) 262–65.

[126] See *Amoco International Finance Corp v Iran* 15 Iran-US CTR 189 (1987) at paras 139–42. The tribunal held that the expropriation of Amoco's interests in petrochemical joint ventures with the Iranian company NPC was not discriminatory merely because the Japanese share of a similar consortium had not been expropriated: '142. The Tribunal finds it difficult, in the absence of any other evidence, to draw the conclusion that the expropriation of a concern was discriminatory only from the fact that another concern in the same economic branch was not expropriated. Reasons specific to the non-expropriated enterprise, or to the expropriated one, or to both, may justify such a difference of treatment. Furthermore, as observed by the arbitral tribunal in *Kuwait v American Independent Oil Company (AMINOIL)* . . . a coherent policy of nationalization can reasonably be operated gradually in successive stages.' See *Kuwait v Aminoil* above n 15 at paras 84–87. Differences in treatment between Aminoil and the other remaining American concessionaire, which was not nationalized, were held to be explicable on the ground that the other concessionaire worked on offshore operations jointly run by Kuwait and Saudi Arabia, and it possessed expertise needed by Kuwait.

[127] See the cases referred to in n above 126.

[128] According to McKean above n 125 at 197: 'It is . . . generally accepted that nationalization measures are invalid under international law if they make distinctions between nationals and aliens to the detriment of the latter.' [129] See ch 16 below at 621–28.

[130] See *Third Restatement on the Foreign Relations Law of the US* above n 57 para 712. Comment f at 200.

owner is entitled to be compensated for the economic loss suffered must be determined.[131] Each stage will be considered in turn.

(i) The Valuation of Expropriated Property[132]

According to Eli Lauterpacht the value of property is, 'an objective concept with an economic content' which should be ascertained by reference to 'objectively relevant factors' before the question of the extent of compensation is addressed.[133] The choice of relevant factors is not easy. As the economists, Penrose, Joffe, and Stevens point out:

[t]here is not just *one* incontrovertible intrinsic value of any asset, but several possible values, depending not only on the purpose but also on the circumstances and the point of view; buyer or seller, public or private entities, insurance appraiser, economist or accountant. Moreover, calculations of "value" from any given point of view and using the same methods can diverge widely, depending on the assumptions on which they are based . . . It is not surprising, therefore, that there has been a considerable variety of approaches to the valuation of nationalised assets for the purpose of compensation to the private owner.[134]

Thus the approach to valuation will itself be conditioned by the purpose behind it.

In cases of expropriation the aim of the foreign investor will be to show a valuation that takes into account what Penrose et al term the 'private' value of the expropriated assets to it.[135] This may result in the use of a valuation method that will ignore the wider public costs associated with the operation of those assets. In particular, the investor may ignore the costs of externalities associated with the use of those assets, and may incorporate a calculation of expected future profits based on the degree of monopoly power that it exercises in the national and/or international market concerned.

Furthermore, where the expropriated asset is a subsidiary of a foreign parent company, the ascertainment of an appropriate value may be difficult if there is no 'market' for that company, as where it is not quoted on international stock markets. In such cases a valuation will be made by looking at the asset value of the group as a whole and effecting a profit split between the subsidiary and the other affiliates. In addition, the future profitability of the subsidiary will have to be assessed. This is done by discounting an estimated future net cash flow to produce a present value, referred to as the Discounted Cash Flow (DCF) method. This is a

---

[131] See E Lauterpacht 'Issues of Compensation and Nationality in the Taking of Energy Investments' 8 Journal of Energy & Natural Resources Law 241 at 249–50 (1990).

[132] See further R Lillich (ed) *The Valuation of Nationalized Property in International Law* (4 vols Virginia: 1972, 1973, 1975, 1987).   [133] Above n 131 at 249.

[134] Penrose, Joffe, and Stevens 'Nationalisation of Foreign-owned Property for a Public Purpose: An Economic Perspective on Appropriate Compensation' 55 MLR 351 at 359 (1992). The following paragraphs rely heavily on the valuable economic analysis developed by Penrose et al.

[135] ibid at 357.

process fraught with subjective assumptions about the future performance of the business.[136]

By contrast the expropriating state will seek a valuation that emphasizes the public interests involved. Thus, it will advocate a valuation method that reduces the actual cost of compensation by reference to the negative costs of the foreign enterprise to the host economy. This will be done in terms of the above mentioned externalities and/or monopoly profits earned or expected to be earned. This position may be justified by reference to the 'unjust enrichment' of the foreign enterprise by alleging that it has earned excess profits.[137] Habitually, host states have argued for the use of the 'net book value' method, which restricts valuation to the current replacement cost or depreciated replacement cost of the expropriated assets, with little or no allowance for estimated future profits. However, this has not been accepted by international tribunals as the appropriate method of valuation.[138]

It appears that a broader approach has been taken by certain international tribunals on the matter of valuation. This seeks to favour neither the foreign investor nor the host state but, rather, to ensure a valuation that takes reasonable account of both the private and public interests involved. The approach is exemplified by the award in the *Aminoil* arbitration, and by certain awards of the US-Iran Claims Tribunal.

In the *Aminoil* award,[139] the tribunal began by saying that a distinction had to be made between states that wished to eliminate foreign investors from their territory and that would adopt very restrictive rules as to compensation,[140] and states that welcomed foreign investment and that even engaged in it themselves. Such states could be expected to espouse an attitude towards compensation such as would not render foreign investment economically useless.[141] As Kuwait fell into the latter category there was 'no room for rules of compensation that would make nonsense of foreign investment'.[142] The tribunal then considered the

---

[136] ibid at 361–64.

[137] Such an approach was initially used by the Chilean Government in relation to the expropriation of US copper companies in 1971: see 10 ILM 1067 (1971). See further RB Lillich 'The Valuation of Copper Companies in the Chilean Nationalization' 66 ASIL Proc 213 (1972); for a critical analysis, see Orego-Vicuna 'Some International Law Problems Posed by the Nationalization of the Copper Industry in Chile' 67 AJIL 711 (1973); for argument in support see Sornarajah above n 65 above at 123–26. However, compensation was eventually set in accordance with the net book value approach: see 13 ILM 1190 (1974), 14 ILM 131 (1975). A claim based on unjust enrichment was rejected by the tribunal in *SPP v Egypt* above n 59 at paras 245–49.

[138] See eg *Kuwait v Aminoil* above n 15 at paras 155–57, where the tribunal rejected Kuwait's claim that the consistent use of the net book method by OPEC countries in their nationalizations of oil concessions in the years 1971–77 had created a legal precedent requiring its use. See also *Amoco International Finance Corp v Iran* n 117 above where Iran's valuation based on the net book method was also rejected. However, the net book value of the expropriated business was awarded by the US Court of Appeals for the Second Circuit in *Banco Nacional de Cuba v Chase Manhattan Bank* 658 F 2d 875 (2nd Cir 1981) and see comment thereon in Amerasinghe above n 111 at 46–47.

[139] Above n 15 at paras 137–178.   [140] ibid para 145.   [141] ibid para 146.

[142] ibid para 146.

notion of 'legitimate expectations' which both parties had invoked for the purpose of deciding compensation.[143] The legitimate expectations of the parties were signified by the contract itself. Thus the text should be precise and exhaustive. However, this was not only a question of the original text but also of amendments, interpretations and behaviour manifested along the course of its existence that indicated (often fortuitously) how the legitimate expectations of the parties were to be seen, and sometimes seen as modified according to the circumstances.[144]

In the light of these general pronouncements, the tribunal went on to consider the competing valuations put forward by Aminoil and Kuwait, which, respectively, relied on the DCF and 'book value' methods, and then to evaluate the 'legitimate expectations' of Aminoil. First, although they did not prohibit nationalization the stabilization clauses in the concession created a legitimate expectation that measures of a confiscatory character would be prohibited.[145] Secondly, Aminoil expected a 'reasonable rate of return', and not speculative profits, from its investment once production had reached a satisfactory level. It was in the light of this expectation that compensation had to be assessed.[146] The tribunal went on to hold that a 'reasonable rate of return' in the present case would include: a reasonable profit margin that would preserve incentives and allow for risks whether commercial or technological and allowance for reinvestment of a proportion of the profits.[147] Having considered the principles upon which compensation would be assessed on a loss of a corporation's assets, the tribunal calculated the sum of compensation owing at date of nationalization in 1977. After Aminoil's liabilities were deducted the sum owed came to $83m. In order to establish what was due in 1982 account had to be taken of a reasonable rate of interest (7.5 per cent) and of a level of inflation – fixed at 10 per cent. Thus a total annual increase of 27.5 per cent in the amount due over the amount due for the preceding year was applied. This gave a total figure of $179,750,764.

A further indication of a broader approach is given in case law emanating from the Iran-US Claims Tribunal.[148] The general value of these awards as precedents should be treated with caution. The awards made by individual chambers of the tribunal differ in their content and, as already noted, the Iranian members habitually dissented. Furthermore, it appears that, since the award in *Phelps Dodge*[149] subsequent awards were made on the basis of the Treaty of Amity between the US and Iran, rather than by reference to customary international law alone. That

---

[143] ibid para 148.   [144] ibid para 149.
[145] ibid para 159.   [146] ibid para 160.   [147] ibid para 163.
[148] For a fuller analysis than is possible here, see Khan above n 65 ch 10; Westberg 'Compensation in Cases of Expropriation and Nationalization: Awards of the Iran-United States Claims Tribunal' 5 ICSID Rev-FILJ 256 (1990); Norton above n 112 at 482–86; Amerasinghe above n 111 at 41–46 and 53–59; Hassan Sedigh 'The Contribution of the Iran-United States Claims Tribunal to the Development of the Standard of Compensation for Nationalized Property' 2 JWI 283 (2001).
[149] 10 Iran-US CTR 121 (1986 I), 25 ILM 619 (1986).

treaty contains an obligation of 'prompt payment of just compensation' which shall be in 'an effectively realizable form and shall represent the full equivalent of the property taken'.[150]

Nonetheless, as regards the issue of valuation, certain important developments occurred. In particular, in *Amoco International*[151] Chamber Three elaborated the 'going concern value' method as the appropriate means of valuation:

Going concern value encompasses not only the physical and financial assets of the undertaking, but also the intangible valuables which contribute to its earning power, such as contractual rights (supply and delivery contracts, patent licences and so on), as well as goodwill and commercial prospects. Although these assets are closely linked to the profitability of the concern, they cannot and must not be confused with the financial capitalization of the revenues which might be generated by such a concern after the transfer of property resulting from the expropriation (*lucrum cessans*).[152]

The reference to the undertaking's commercial prospects may allow for the recovery of profits by way of a 'reasonable rate of return' in all the circumstances. However, it is clear that Chamber Three did not allow for the recovery of all lost profits. Earlier in its opinion the tribunal stated:

[f]uture prospects' does not equal lost profit (*lucrum cessans*). Those are two different concepts. The first one clearly refers to the fact that the undertaking was a 'going concern' which had demonstrated a certain ability to earn revenues and was, therefore, to be considered as keeping such ability for the future: this is an element of its value at the time of the taking. The second relates to the amount of earnings hypothetically accrued from the date of the taking to the date of the expert opinion, had the enterprise remained in the hands of the former owner . . .[153]

Thus, according to Chamber Three, loss of future profits per se was not recoverable in the case of a lawful expropriation, and full restitution could not be claimed.[154] The 'going concern' approach emphasizes the real commercial prospects of the expropriated undertaking as the basis of calculating compensation. Thus, where these prospects are shown to be poor the amount of compensation awarded under this head will be considerably discounted.[155] However, other awards of the

---

[150] Article IV(2) of the US-Iran Treaty of Amity, Economic Relations and Consular Rights 15 August 15 1955 284 UNTS 93.

[151] 15 Iran-US CTR 189 (1987 II), 27 ILM 1314 (1988). See also *American International Group v Iran* 4 Iran-US CTR 96 (1983). [152] ibid para 264 (emphasis in original).

[153] ibid para 203 (emphasis in original).

[154] This led to a concurring opinion that disagreed with the tribunal's reasons by the US member Judge Brower who felt that loss of future profits was wrongly excluded from the available compensation: ibid 290 at 300–305.

[155] See, for example, *Phelps Dodge* n 149 above. See also *Sola Tiles v Iran* 14 Iran-US CTR 223 (1987); *Thomas Earle Payne v Iran* 12 Iran-US CTR 3 (1986); *CBS Inc v Iran* Award No 486–197–2 28 June 1990 (*Held*: the effects of the revolution upon the business caused it to have a negative worth at the time of expropriation and therefore no compensation was payable).

Iran-US Claims Tribunal have simply asserted that the 'full compensation' standard was applicable and that loss of full future profits could be recovered.[156]

Finally, reference should be made to awards made under the auspices of the International Centre for the Settlement of Investment Disputes (ICSID). By Article 42 of the Convention establishing ICSID[157] the parties are free to determine the law by which the dispute between them is to be determined. In the absence of such agreement, the tribunal shall apply the law of the contracting state party to the dispute (ie the host state) and such rules of international law as may be applicable. In two cases in which issues of compensation for expropriation have been considered, no stipulation as to the applicable law was made, which ensured that the law of the host state would be applied in accordance with international law.[158] In another case the parties expressly stipulated that the law of the host state (Congo), supplemented if necessary by any principles of international law, should apply.[159] In the case of *SPP v Egypt*, the parties agreed that the law of the host state (Egypt) applied but they disagreed over the extent of the role of international law. The tribunal held that Egyptian law applied subject to the corrective application of international law where the exclusive application of municipal law violated international law.[160] In more recent awards the ICSID Tribunal has applied the rules contained in the applicable IIA under which the case was brought. Thus, in all the NAFTA based arbitrations the applicable principles were those stated in NAFTA,[161] while the awards based on provisions of specific BITs would be guided by the choice contained in the expropriation clause itself. Thus ICSID awards are of some value as indications of the rules of international law applicable to expropriation cases, although they should be treated with caution given the specialized nature of these awards.[162]

ICSID Tribunals accept the right of a foreign investor to recover compensation both for the lost value of its assets and loss of non-speculative future profit.[163]

[156] See, for example, *Sedco Inc v National Iranian Oil Co and Iran* 10 Iran-US CTR 180 (1986), 25 ILM 629 (1986).

[157] The Washington Convention on the Settlement of Investment Disputes 1965: 4 ILM 524 (1965).

[158] *Benvenuti and Bonfant v People's Republic of the Congo* 21 ILM 740 at paras 4.1–4.4.(1982); *Amco Asia Corp v Republic of Indonesia* ruling of first arbitration panel: 24 ILM 1022 at para 148 (1985); vacated on grounds of improper application of Indonesian law: 25 ILM 1441 (1986); ruling of second arbitration panel: 89 ILR 580 para 40 at 594 (1992).

[159] *AGIP Company v Popular Republic of Congo* 21 ILM 726 at para 18 (1982).

[160] *Southern Pacific Properties (Middle East) Limited v Arab Republic of Egypt* Award on the Merits 20 May 1992: 32 ILM 933 para 84 at 952 (1993).

[161] All the NAFTA awards apply art 1110(2) to expropriation cases, which requires the application of the 'fair market value' principle, while other violations of NAFTA require the tribunal to apply 'a measure of compensation appropriate to the specific circumstances of the case, taking into account the principles of international law and the provisions of NAFTA'; *SD Myers v Canada* above n 67 at paras 305–309.'	[162] See Amerasinghe above n 111 at 38.

[163] See *AGIP* above n 159 at paras 95–109 (applying art 1149 of the French Civil Code incorporated into Congolese Law); *Amco Asia* above n 158 at paras 266–68 (referring to Indonesian Civil Code Art 1246, French and English law and international law); in *Benvenuti and Bonfant* there was

In *Amco Asia* the first arbitral tribunal held that the appropriate principle was the loss of a 'going concern', requiring the establishment of the net present value calculated on a DCF basis.[164] The second tribunal award expressly rejected the use of the net book value method that was favoured by Indonesia. Instead, it used two methods of valuation. The first, for the period 1980 to 1989, looked at the actual loss of contractual benefit suffered by the claimant from the date of the expropriation up to the date of the award. The second, for the period from 1990 to 1999, calculated the loss of contractual benefits from the date of the award to the end of the investment agreement by use of the DCF method.[165] However, in *Southern Pacific Properties (Middle East) Limited v Arab Republic of Egypt* (SPP case),[166] the tribunal rejected the use of the DCF method because the expropriated construction project had not been in existence for a sufficient period of time to generate the data necessary for a meaningful DCF calculation. It would result in a speculative calculation of loss. Furthermore, the application of the DCF method would have awarded *lucrum cessans* for a period that included a time during which the investment project would have become illegal under international and Egyptian law.[167] The tribunal went on to reject a confirmation of the DCF valuation by reference to private sales of shares in the project.[168] Instead the tribunal preferred a method based on the 'fair compensation' of the claimants for the amounts of capital contributions and loans made to the project and the expenditure incurred on marketing, detailed engineering designs, and the partial completion of the infrastructure and golf course that was part of the development.[169] The tribunal also added an element that represented the value of the investment in excess of the claimant's out-of-pocket expenses,[170] and interest that took account of the devaluation of the US dollar in the period since the expropriation.[171]

In *Benvenuti and Bonfant*[172] the tribunal also held that 'fair compensation' was payable. The amounts were to be determined by the tribunal *ex aequo et bono* in accordance with the earlier agreement of the parties, pursuant to Article 42(3) of

no extensive discussion of the applicable rules but a detailed analysis was made both of the loss of assets and of the alleged loss of future profits put forward by the claimant, on which see text for discussion. In *Metalclad v Mexico* above n 70 the tribunal cited with approval the *Benvenuti* and *Agip* cases stating that: 'Normally the fair market value of a going concern which has a history of profitable operation may be based on an estimate of future profits subject to a discounted cash flow analysis': at para 119.

[164] First award above n 158 at paras 271–73.
[165] Second Tribunal award ibid at paras 188–200, ILR 633–36.
[166] Above n 160.   [167] ibid at paras 188–91 at 973–74.
[168] ibid paras 192–97 at 974.
[169] ibid para 198 at 975. For the detailed application of this approach to the facts see ibid paras 199–211 975–977.
[170] ibid paras 212–18 at 978–79. This was based on a calculation of the balance between the claimant's share of the revenues from existing sales of properties completed as part of the project as against expenses incurred.   [171] ibid paras 219–44 at 979–83.
[172] Above n 158 at paras 4.73–4.79.

the convention.[173] Thus the case may not be indicative of applicable international law. Nonetheless, the tribunal's approach to determining the precise amount of lost profits is worthy of note. The claimant had made an estimation of loss on the basis of a projection over the 99 years of the investment agreement. The tribunal appointed an independent expert from another company in the same industry as the expropriated company (soft drinks). The expert stated that the projected profit was speculative as the market price for the expropriated interest had never been established, and because the host state retained full authority to fix the prices of the products made by the claimant. He advised that the more objective measure of loss was the value of the recent investment in the expropriated company. This came to a sum higher than that claimed by the company. The claimant declared that it would not insist on this higher sum and limited its petition to the lower sum originally claimed.

More recent cases have confirmed this general approach. Thus, in a number of awards, the DCF method has been rejected as being too speculative on the same grounds as those put in the SPP case, namely, that there must be a sufficient period of operation to establish a performance record and that there must be evidence of profitable operation.[174] In addition, where lost future profits are claimed, it was held in *Middle East Shipping and Handling Co SA v Egypt* that, in order for such profits to be recovered the claimant must show the actual profits lost due to the expropriation, and any legitimate expectation of future profits must be based on proof of concrete contracts missed and of the profit lost on them.[175] Furthermore, there may be a duty on the claimant to mitigate their loss if, on the facts, such a course of action is reasonably open. The burden of proof is on the respondent state to show that such a duty arises and that the claimant has failed to carry it out.[176] Where the investment fails to begin operations, preparatory expenditure may be recoverable provided that the loss to the investor arises out of the breach of the applicable investment treaty.[177] Any loss attributable to the poor business judgment of the investor that has increased their risks may be deducted from the eventual award. Thus in *MTD v Chile* the tribunal reduced damages for breach of the fair and equitable treatment standard by 50 per cent on this ground.[178] There appears to be no reason in principle why this approach should not also apply in cases of expropriation where the investor's conduct has contributed to the regulatory actions alleged to constitute the expropriation. Finally, where an asset that is essential to the profitable operation of the

---

[173] ibid at paras 4.4 and 4.63–4.65.

[174] *Metalclad v Mexico* above n 70 at para 120–22 preferring an approach based on Metalclad's actual investment in the project. See also *Wena Hotels v Egypt* above n 54 at paras 123–25.

[175] ICSID Case No Arb/99/6 award of 12 April 2002, 18 ICSID Rev-FILJ 602 (2003) at paras 112 and 128.					[176] ibid at paras 168–71.

[177] See *MTD v Chile* above n 79 at paras 240–41.					[178] ibid at paras 242–46.

investment is expropriated, the amount of compensation should reflect its fair market value, with the burden resting on the claimant to prove that value.[179]

From the above cases it is clear that no single method of valuation is preferred over the others. There is a tendency towards a middle way between claimant's and respondent's positions that is centred on the concepts such as 'legitimate expectations' or 'going concern value', assuming there is a going concern to value. On the other hand, there are some instances of 'full compensation', which includes loss of future profits, being required.[180] Furthermore, the DCF method has been used in some cases where loss of future profit has been held to be recoverable. The net book method appears to have been generally avoided. However, as Amerasinghe notes, tribunals almost never grant the amounts requested by claimants and will take all the facts of the case into account.[181] In this regard, it may be said that the award of the Stockholm tribunal, in *CME v Czech Republic*, of some $350 million, which raised serious concerns about the legitimacy of such large awards being made against host countries, may be somewhat out of line with mainstream practice.[182]

A final issue in relation to the valuation of expropriated property concerns the identification of the date of expropriation. This is key, as it will determine the precise circumstances that need to be taken into account in order to arrive at an acceptable valuation. The question is of especial importance in cases of indirect, or creeping, expropriation where the actual date at which the owner has been deprived of the economic benefit of the investment may be open to debate, given the likely absence of a clear deprivation of title and the existence of a series of governmental acts, none of which, by themselves, may be seen as an act of expropriation, but which have a cumulative effect of neutralising the value of the property.[183] According to the tribunal in the *SPP* case, the relevant date for an

---

[179] See *TECMED v Mexico* above n 60 at paras 188–90.

[180] See, for example, the *Santa Elena* case above n 73 at para 73.

[181] See Amerasinghe above n 111 at 59–61, 63. In the case of NAFTA, according to Daniel Price: 'A total of US$ 1.24 billion in damages has been claimed; a total of US$23 million in damages has been awarded. US$20 million has been claimed against Mexico; US$18 million has been awarded. US$180 million has been claimed against Canada; US$4 million has been awarded. US$865 million has been claimed against the United States; US$0 has been awarded.' Daniel M Price 'Who Wins and Who Loses in Investment Arbitration? Are Investors and Host States on a Level Playing Field: The Lauder/Czech Republic Legacy' 6 JWIT 73 at 74–75 (2005). However, the fact that most of the damages awarded have been against Mexico, the only developing country in NAFTA, ought to be a cause for concern.

[182] This award of 13 September 2001 and the parallel London award of *Lauder v Czech Republic*, of 3 September 2001, can be accessed at <http://www.cetv-net.com>. The Stockholm award was challenged by the Czech Republic before the Svea Court of Appeals in *Czech Republic v CME Czech Republic BV*. The Court of Appeals turned down the Czech challenge and upheld the award, including the approach taken to the calculation of damages based on the market value principle: SVEA Court of Appeals judgment of 15 May 2003: 42 ILM 919 (2003); see too the Introductory Comment by Thomas Waelde: 42 ILM 915 (2003).

[183] See Reisman and Sloane above n 55 at 133–34 and 140–50.

expropriation is the date of effective dispossession.[184] In relation to indirect taking that date has been held to arise 'as of the date on which the governmental "interference" has deprived the owner of his rights or has made those rights practically useless. This is a matter of fact for the Tribunal to assess in the light of the circumstances of the case'.[185] In so doing the tribunal may need to ensure that the valuation is carried out in full recognition of the need to deter illegitimate governmental action, and to ensure stability of investment regimes.[186] On the other hand, it must also ensure that sufficient weight is accorded to any legitimate policy goals that are being pursued by the host country, and which have led to the indirect taking. Thus, it would appear that the motivation of, and the actual governance techniques used by, the host country in such cases may well affect the determination of the appropriate date from which compensation is to be valued.

(ii) The Measure of Compensation

Under international law, the basic measure of compensation is restitution of the claimant to the position they were in prior to the commission of the wrongful act. This may be achieved by way of 'restitution in kind, or, if this is not possible, payment of a sum corresponding to the value which a restitution in kind would bear; the award, if need be, of damages for loss sustained which would not be covered by restitution in kind or payment in place of it'.[187] This principle has been endorsed in recent arbitral case law and leads to the conclusion that the investor should be compensated for the actual loss that they have suffered in respect of injury to their property, including capital value, loss of profits, and expenses.[188]

From the preceding section, it is clear that the choice of valuation method will have a significant bearing on the actual measure of compensation to be awarded in cases of expropriation. The most striking contrast is between cases in which some detailed attention is paid to the valuation issue, and those in which it is simplified by reference to the 'full compensation' standard. Perhaps such an approach is no more than an expression of the tribunal's belief in the illegitimacy of expropriation as a device of national economic policy, notwithstanding its formal legal validity.[189]

Such an approach makes little distinction between lawful and unlawful expropriation. The payment of 'full compensation', if it includes all future lost profits, would have the effect of neutralizing the economic objective behind the

---

[184] *SPP v Egypt* above n 160 at para 234.
[185] *Santa Elena v Costa Rica* above n 73 at para 78.
[186] Reisman and Sloane above n 55 at 150.
[187] *The Chorzow Factory Case* PCIJ Series A No 17 at 47 (1928).
[188] *CMS Gas Transmission Co v Argentina* above n 90 at para 402.
[189] Some weight for this view can be gathered from the Separate Opinion of Judge Brower in the *Sedco* case, regarding the remedies that should be available in the case of lawful and unlawful expropriation: n 156 above ILM 636 at 641–47.

expropriation, and so make a lawful policy option untenable in practice.[190] Furthermore, such an approach might encourage host states not to comply with awards of compensation, should the host state feel that an award has taken no account of its legitimate expectations, based on public interest concerns, in determining the measure of compensation. It may also lead to the eventual withdrawal of states from BITs.[191] In these circumstances, as the opinion of the Iran-US Claims Tribunal in *Amoco* notes, a clear distinction should be made between the effects of a lawful and an unlawful expropriation.[192] The tribunal highlighted the fact that *restitutio in integrum* (full restitution), or full, but not punitive, damages in lieu of restitution was the appropriate remedy in cases of unlawful expropriation, while the payment of 'fair compensation' was the appropriate remedy in cases of lawful expropriation.[193]

Full restitution for unlawful expropriation was the remedy awarded against Libya in the *Texaco* arbitration.[194] However, that approach was not followed in *Liamco*, where the arbitrator found Libya's acts to have amounted to lawful expropriation, entitling Liamco to compensation, on essentially similar facts.[195] In *BP v Libya* the sole arbitrator, Gunnar Lagergren, held that *restitutio in integrum* had been employed as a vehicle for establishing the amount of damages for breach of an obligation to perform a contractual undertaking,[196] but refused to apply it to the facts. The arbitrators in both the *BP* and *Liamco* cases noted the practical difficulties associated with full restitution, in particular, that it amounts to an intolerable interference with the sovereignty of the host state, as it demands the cancellation of the expropriatory measure,[197] and that compliance by the host state would be unlikely.[198]

---

[190] Note that in *INA Corp v Iran* 8 Iran-US CTR 373 (1985) Judge Lagergren, the chairman, said that: 'an application of current principles of international law, as encapsulated in the "appropriate compensation" formula, would in the case of lawful large-scale nationalizations in a state undergoing a process of radical economic restructuring normally require the "fair market value" standard to be discounted in taking account of "all circumstances". However, such discounting, may, of course, never be such as to bring compensation below a point which would lead to "unjust enrichment" of the expropriating state. It might also be added that the discounting often will be greater in a situation where the investor has enjoyed the profits of his capital outlay over a long period of time, but less, or none, in the case of a recent investor, such as INA': at 390. See contra Judge Holtzman at 401.

[191] For example, the Czech Republic has questioned the value of existing BITs, with their emphasis on dispute settlement as a means of resolving differences, in the light of the *CME/Lauder* cases: see Bohuslav Klein 'Who Wins and Who Loses in Investment Arbitration? Are Investors and Host States on a Level Playing Field: The Lauder/Czech Republic Legacy' 6 JWIT 65 (2005).

[192] See further Bowett n 6 above at 59–74.

[193] ibid paras 191–97. Note that the Second Tribunal in *Amco Asia v Indonesia* above n 158 held that, where there was an unlawful taking of contract rights, lost profits were in principle recoverable, but it reserved its position on the situation in a lawful taking, the taking in this case being found to have been unlawful: para 178.ILR 631.   [194] Above n 8 at paras 92–112.

[195] Above n 13.   [196] Above n 27 at 347.   [197] *Liamco* above n 13 at ILM 63–64.

[198] *BP* above n 27 at 351, 353.

Thus the actual utility of restitution as a remedy may be doubtful.[199] Indeed, the dispute between Texaco and Libya was eventually settled by an agreement to pay compensation in the form of supplies of crude oil to the value of $152 million, as were the other disputes that led to the oil arbitrations against Libya.[200] It should not be forgotten that arbitration, unlike litigation before courts, concerns the settlement of a dispute rather than the formal vindication of rights. Thus a pragmatic approach to remedies should be adopted if arbitration is not to be disregarded as an avenue of effective redress.

Given the foregoing discussion, debates as to whether international law requires the measure of compensation that reflects the 'prompt, adequate, and effective' standard, or whether it will accept something less, often described as 'appropriate'[201] or 'equitable' compensation,[202] appear increasingly obsolete and unhelpful.[203] So long as expropriation is regarded as a legitimate exercise of sovereign power, the measure of compensation payable in the case of a lawful expropriation will have to moderate the valuation of private losses in the light of broader public interest concerns. This may lead to the recovery of less than the full loss to the owner where that is objectively justifiable in the light of the political and economic realities of the case.[204] Thus, even in cases where loss of future profits has apparently not been recovered, it is arguable that adequate and effective compensation has been awarded.[205]

---

[199] See Bowett above n 6 at 60; Higgins above n 34 at 314–321 who sees restitution as promoting values important to the international community but finds 'very little evidence that restitution is perceived as a required remedy or that it is anticipated as being likely to be granted'.

[200] For details, see Von Mehren and Kourides above n 8 at 545–48.

[201] See UNGA Resolution 1803 14 December 1962 17 UN GAOR Supp (No 17) at 15 where the term 'appropriate compensation' is first used.

[202] See *Liamco v Libya* above n 13 at ILM 76–77.

[203] Indeed, even the *US Third Restatement* above n 57 has conceded the need to move away from this issue by adopting the term 'just compensation' in s 712, and by acknowledging that, while the US has consistently used the Hull Formula, other states have resisted it: Comment c at 198 and Reporter's Note 2 at 206. As to the effect of this terminological change see the debate between Robinson 'Expropriation in the Restatement Revised' 78 AJIL 176 (1984) and Schachter 'Compensation for Expropriation' ibid 121.

[204] For example, following a campaign on the part of Oxfam and *The Guardian* newspaper in the UK, Nestlé agreed to drop a $6 million claim against the Government of Ethiopia, for assets expropriated by the former military government in the 1980s, and settled for $1.5 million which was pledged to famine relief in that country. See 'Nestlé U-turn on Ethiopia Debt' *The Guardian* 24 January 2003 2.

[205] See eg Gann 'Compensation Standard for Expropriation' 23 Col.J.Transnat'l L. 615 (1985) who argues that the 'going concern' value incorporates an element for loss of future profits. Gann argues that in *Aminoil* an element for lost future profits was included in the going concern valuation, and, possibly, in an unusually high interest and inflation figure: see 638–39. Amerasinghe also feels that the compensation awarded included an element for lost profits: above n 111 at 62–63. However, FA Mann feels that the failure to award full loss of profits as expected at date of concession amounted to a failure to compensate adequately for what was, in his opinion, an unlawful taking: 'The Aminoil Arbitration' 54 BYIL 213 (1983).

(iii) Settlement of Claims Through Lump Sum Agreements

In cases involving a large number of claims of compensation for expropriation, and/or a host state that refuses to accept international minimum standards and/or international arbitration to resolve the matter, settlement has been achieved in many cases by the use of a lump sum agreement. For example, the former Soviet Union paid sums owed to Sweden in 1941 and 1946 and, in 1986, paid the UK Government a lump sum of some £45 million to compensate for the confiscation of British owned property during the Revolution of 1917.[206] In 1973, the Government of Hungary agreed with the US Government to settle outstanding claims for compensation arising out of measures of nationalization carried out against the property of US nationals.[207] In 1975 Chile agreed to pay compensation to dispossessed US firms.[208] Numerous further examples of such settlements have been documented.[209] A more recent illustration of a lump sum compensation agreement occurred in the 1980s in relation to the dispute between the US and Ethiopia over the compensation payable for the property of the Kalamazoo Spice Extraction Co (Kal-Spice) that had been expropriated by the Provisional Military Government of Ethiopia in 1975.[210] Kal-Spice sought to attach accounts payable to Ethiopia in the US under continuing supply contracts with Kal-Spice. Ethiopia argued that it had jurisdictional immunity. The issue was considered before the US District Court for the Western District of Michigan (Southern Division).[211] The action in this case was discontinued after the US and Ethiopia signed a compensation agreement on 19 December 1986 in Addis Ababa.[212]

The status of such agreements as evidence of contemporary state practice in the field of compensation for expropriation has been doubted in certain arbitral awards, on the basis that the agreed settlements are the product of non-judicial bargaining considerations which negate their value as a source of *opinio juris*.[213] This has led to criticism that a major, if not *the* major, source of state practice in this area has been ignored by international tribunals in the formulation of standards of compensation.[214] On the other hand, such settlements have arisen out of

---

[206] 'Windfall From Imperial Russia' *Financial Times* 16 July 1986 at 1.

[207] 13 ILM 407–12 (1973).   [208] 14 ILM 131–37 (1975).

[209] See G Schwarzenberger *Foreign Investment in International Law* (Stevens, 1969) 40–47; Lillich and Burns (eds) *International Claims: Their Settlement by Lump Sum Agreement* (3 vols Charlottesville, Va: 1975–1976); Dawson and Weston 'Prompt Adequate and Effective: A Universal Standard of Compensation?' 30 Fordam L.Rev. 727 at 740–57 (1962).

[210] For the main facts, see the judgment of the US District Court for the Western District of Michigan (Southern Division) in *Kalamazoo Spice Extraction Co v The Provisional Military Government of Socialist Ethiopia* reproduced in 24 ILM 1277 (1985).   [211] ibid.

[212] 25 ILM 56 (1986).

[213] See eg *Sedco v National Iranian Oil Co* above n 156 at 8 ILM 633; *Aminoil* above n 15 at paras 156–57; *Barcelona Traction Case* ICJ Reports (1970) 3 at 40.

[214] See Bowett above n 6 at 65–66; Lillich and Weston 'Lump-sum Agreements: Their Continuing Contribution to the Law of International Claims' 82 AJIL 69 (1988).

major nationalizations or expropriations and may have little relevance to the more contemporary types of indirect taking.

(4) Investment Guarantee Schemes

The threat of political risks, such as expropriation, is a factor that will increase the perceived costs of investment in a host state. However, these costs may be reduced if insurance is taken out against political risk. This kind of cover may be available through private insurers, although this has not always been easy to obtain given the difficulties of quantifying the risk involved. Thus, to ensure the availability of political risks cover, the governments of capital-exporting states have sponsored public sector or mixed public/private sector schemes. Such schemes have traditionally focused on developing host states and have been administered as part of the home state's foreign aid programme, although some schemes, such as the UK Export Credit Guarantee Department (ECGD), are directed at foreign trade and investment generally.[215] Therefore, such schemes may be more than merely an insurance service; they may be an instrument of the home state's foreign economic and development policy.

The first national scheme of this kind was introduced by the US under the Economic Co-operation Act 1948.[216] Its aim was to offer investment guarantees for the reconstruction of post-war Europe. However, it was subsequently amended to cover investment in less developed countries.[217] Under the Foreign Assistance Act of 1961 the scheme was to be run as part of the US foreign aid programme by the Agency for International Development (AID).[218] After a major review of the AID scheme, a new investment guarantee agency was proposed. This was set up in 1971 under the name of the Overseas Private Investment Corporation (OPIC).[219] The operations of OPIC came under close scrutiny in the 1970s as a result of its close involvement with the insurance of US copper and telecommunications investments in Chile at the time of their nationalization by Salvador Allende's government.[220] This resulted in a restriction of OPIC's powers in 1974 followed by further restrictions in 1978.[221] In 1981 most of these restrictions were removed

---

[215] See UK Export and Investment Guarantees Act 1991 ss 1 and 2 (1991 ch 67).

[216] 62 Stat 144 (1948).

[217] Mutual Security Act of 1954 s 413, 68 Stat 846 (1954) as amended 22 USC s 1933 (Supp III 1962).   [218] 75 Stat 424 (1961).

[219] OPIC was established under the Foreign Assistance Act of 1969 22 USC s 2191 (1970). For a summary of current practice, see OPIC *Program Handbook* (Washington DC: OPIC, 2004) available at <http://www.opic.gov>. For background, see US International Private Investment Advisory Council *The Case for a US Overseas Private Enterprise Development Corporation* (1968). See further, on the history of US investment guarantee policy, Lipson above n 105 ch 7; Brewer 'The Proposal for Investment Guarantees by an International Agency' 58 AJIL 62 at 67–70 (1964); Clubb and Vance 'Incentives to Private US Investment Abroad Under the Foreign Assistance Program' 72 Yale LJ 475 (1963).   [220] See Lipson above n 105 at 245–48.

[221] See OPIC Amendments Act 1974 (PL 93–390); OPIC Amendments Act 1978 (PL 95–268) comment Meron 'OPIC Investment is Alive and Well' 73 AJIL 104 (1979).

and the scheme was expanded to cover 'civil strife' and insurance of letters of credit.[222] OPIC will offer support for new investments, privatizations and expansions, and modernizations of existing plants, provided that such an investment arises in an eligible host country, is responsive to the development needs of that country and that it fosters private sector initiatives and competition. Projects involving anti-competitive advantages may require additional scrutiny.[223] Projects must not harm US trade benefits and not be subjected to trade related performance requirements. The environmental impact of the investment must be assessed. Support will not be granted where the project, in the judgment of OPIC, would have an unreasonable or major adverse requirement on the environment or on worker health and safety. Minimum labour rights must also be respected and the applicable national corrupt practices laws complied with.[224]

OPIC is empowered to offer investment insurance on a commercial basis backed by the full faith and credit of the US Government.[225] Cover is provided only with the agreement of the host state. To this end the US negotiates investment guarantee agreements with host states.[226] These agreements ensure that the rights of OPIC (or its successors in title or assigns) to subrogation upon payment of a claim are recognized by the host state. They also provide for international arbitration in the case of disputes that cannot be settled by negotiation. Insurance is available against expropriation, war risks, inconvertibility of currency and, as noted above, for civil strife and letters of credit. Upon the occurrence of an insured event the investor will present a claim to OPIC, which will then consider whether it comes within the terms of the cover. Should a dispute arise, the investor and OPIC may resort to arbitration.[227] After a claim has been paid, OPIC will pursue its subrogation rights against the host state under the terms of the investment guarantee agreement.

Other countries have adopted similar investment insurance schemes.[228] Thus, the UK offers insurance for overseas investments through the ECGD. By section 2

---

[222] OPIC Amendment Act 1981: 95 Stat 1021 (1981); Sampliner 'The 1981 OPIC Amendments and Reagan's "Newer Directions" in Third World Development Policy' 14 Law & Pol'y Int'l Bus. 181 (1982); Zylberglait 'OPIC'S Investment Insurance: The Platypus of Governmental Programs and its Jurisprudence' 25 Law & Pol'y Int'l Bus. 359 (1993).

[223] OPIC Programme Handbook above n 219 at 2–3.   [224] ibid at 4–5.

[225] See 22 USC ss 2191–2200a.

[226] See eg US-Equador Investment Guaranty Agreement: 28 November 1984: 24 ILM 566 (1985); US-Poland Investment Guarantee Agreement: 28 ILM 1393 (1989).

[227] 22 USC s 2197(i). See eg the arbitration between *ITT, Sud America v OPIC*: 13 ILM 1307 (1974) or, for a more recent example, *Bechtel Enterprises International(Bermuda) Ltd; BEn Dabhol Holdings Ltd and Capital India Power Mauritius I v Overseas Private Investment Corporation* AAA Case No 50 T195 00509 02, 25 September 2003 available at <http://www.transnational-dispute-management.com/>.

[228] See further ECGD *Report on the Comparison of Export Credit Agencies* (April 2004) available at <http://www.ecgd.gov.uk>. In the Netherlands, Dutch companies are offered political risks cover by NCM, a private agency owned by 13 banks, 10 insurance companies, and other corporate shareholders. The Dutch Minister of Finance sits on the Board and the government reinsures any political risks taken on for Dutch exporters. NCM took over the short-term export credit insurance functions of the ECGD in the UK. This was achieved by the sale of the Insurance Services Group, a part of the

of the Export and Investment Guarantees Act 1991,[229] any person carrying on business in the UK, whether in person or through a company controlled directly or indirectly by him, is eligible for cover in connection with any investment of resources in enterprises carried on outside the UK, or in connection with guarantees given by that person in respect of investments by others in such enterprises. Cover is given only for new direct investments in overseas enterprises against losses resulting directly or indirectly from war, expropriation, restrictions on remittances, and, where appropriate, breach of contract.[230] As a result of the 1999–2000 governmental review of its mission and status, the ECGD must now take into account the contribution of an investment to sustainable development and to the promotion of human rights and good governance.[231]

In addition to national schemes, the World Bank Convention Establishing the Multilateral Investment Guarantee Agency of 1985 (MIGA) establishes a multilateral system for investment insurance against stipulated political risks in the host state.[232] In addition, the convention offers a technical advisory and standard setting service to developing countries aimed at improving investment conditions and flows of new investment. This will be considered briefly in chapter 17. The advantages of the MIGA system are claimed to include: a more comprehensive and complete system of cover which would have the benefit of aggregating investments from many countries and enjoy access to a wider range of reinsurers and coinsurers than national systems; a depoliticized approach to underwriting decisions; consideration of the soundness of the investment and its developmental

---

ECGD, to NCM under the terms of the Export and Investment Guarantees Act 1991: *The Guardian* 11 January 1991 at 26. See also Export and Investment Guarantees Act (Commencement Order): SI 1991/2430. In Germany, investment guarantees have been available since 1959: see Budget Law of 1959 art 18(1959). Japan introduced its scheme in 1956: see Export Insurance Law 1950 as amended in April 1956 and May 1957.

[229] Above n 215.

[230] See L D'Arcy, C Murray, and B Cleave *Schmitthoff's Export Trade* (Sweet & Maxwell, 10th edn 2000) 400 at para 20–101; ECGD *Products and Services: Overseas Investment Insurance (OII)* available at <http://www.ecgd.gov.uk>.

[231] See Department of Trade and Industry *Review of ECGD's Mission and Status* Cm 4790 (London: July 2000) and ECGD *ECGD's Business Principles* (December 2000) available at <http://www.ecgd.gov.uk>.

[232] See 24 ILM 1598 (1985) or <http://www.miga.org>. For the historical background to and analysis of the Convention, see further IFI Shihata *MIGA and Foreign Investment: Origins, Operations, Policies and Basic Documents of the Multilateral Investment Guarantee Agency* (Martinus Nijhoff, 1988); Voss 'The Multilateral Investment Guarantee Agency: Status, Mandate, Concept, Features, Implications' 21 JWTL 5 (1987); Rowat 'Multilateral Approaches to Improving the Investment Climate of Developing Countries: The Cases of ICSID and MIGA' 33 Harv.ILJ 103 especially 119–34 (1992). This article contains a useful tabular comparison of the MIGA Convention system with the US, Japanese, and German systems at 139–44. The MIGA Convention has been incorporated into English law by the Multilateral Investment Guarantee Agency Act 1988 (c 8 1988) Commencement Order: SI 1988/715. As of 30 June 2006 MIGA has 167 members, 24 developed country members, and 143 developing country members. A total of $16 billion of guarantees have been issued by 30 June 2006: see MIGA *Annual Report 2006* Appendices at 112 and Highlights 2 respectively available at <http://www.miga.org>.

impact; and a broader role in the creation of a good international investment climate by offering additional specialist advisory services.[233] Together, these factors should encourage the flow of investments for productive purposes among member countries.[234]

Regarding the insurance of political risks, the basic scheme of the convention system is as follows.[235] All member states of the World Bank are eligible to join MIGA on payment of a share subscription in accordance with the number of shares required under Schedule A to the convention.[236] In return, MIGA will offer investment guarantees against loss resulting from one or more of the following types of risk: restrictions on currency transfer outside the host country, expropriation and similar measures, breach of contract, and war and civil disturbance.[237]

Regarding expropriation, cover extends to 'any legislative action or administrative action or omission attributable to the host government which has the effect of depriving the holder of a guarantee of his ownership or control of, or a substantial benefit from, his investment, with the exception of non-discriminatory measures of general application which governments normally take for the purpose of regulating economic activity in their territories'.[238] This definition makes clear that cover against 'creeping expropriation' is available. The MIGA Operational Regulations (the Regulations) state that coverage may encompass, but is not limited to, measures of expropriation, nationalization, confiscation, sequestration, seizure, attachment, and freezing of assets.[239] Coverage also extends to cases of breach of contract as where, in the case of an equity investment, the right to a dividend, or to control and the right to dispose of shares are interfered with. In the case of a non-equity investment, interference may take the form of claims against the project enterprise for agreed payments, rights to transfer such claims to third parties, or rights in participation in management.[240] Cover is excluded where the host government is acting in the public interest for the purpose of regulating economic activity in its territory. The Regulations give, as examples of such activity, 'the bona fide imposition of general taxes, tariffs and price controls and other economic regulations as well as environmental and labour legislation and measures for the maintenance of public safety'.[241] However, even such measures may come within the coverage if they are applied in a discriminatory manner and are designed to have a confiscatory effect such as causing the investor to abandon the investment or to sell at a distressed price.[242]

---

[233] See Shihata ibid at 17–21.   [234] MIGA Convention above n 232 art 2.

[235] For a full discussion, see Shihata above n 232 chs 3 and 4. See also MIGA Operational Regulations of 27 August 2002 at <http://www.miga.org/miga_documents/Operations-Regulations.pdf> and MIGA *Investment Guarantee Guide* available at <http://www.miga.org>.

[236] MIGA Convention above n 232 arts 4–10.   [237] ibid art 11(a)(i)–(iv).

[238] ibid art 11(a)(ii).   [239] MIGA Regs above n 235 at para 1.29.

[240] ibid para 1.30.   [241] ibid para 1.36. Emphasis in original.   [242] ibid.

The contract of guarantee will specify the scope of coverage.[243] The Underwriting Authority (the relevant official of MIGA charged with concluding the guarantee contract) will elect to provide either total or partial loss cover. In a case of expropriation, total loss occurs where the guarantee holder has been unable to exercise a fundamental covered right for a consecutive period of one year, or such period as the contract of guarantee may provide, or the investment project has ceased operations for such period.[244]

The inclusion of breach of contract as a covered risk protects the investor against abuses of due process. This may occur through denial of access to a judicial or arbitral forum to determine the validity of a claim of breach alleged by the host state, or by inordinate delay in the rendering of such a decision, or where such a decision cannot be enforced.[245] This is an innovative form of cover not normally found in national systems save in relation to breaches of contract associated with expropriations.[246] The coverage for currency transfer risk and for war and civil disturbance need not be commented upon here.[247] Other non-commercial risks not covered by the four categories above can be included by joint application of the investor and host country to the board which must approve by a special majority.[248] However, losses arising from acts or omissions of the host government to which the guarantee holder has consented, or for which he is responsible, or losses arising from acts or omissions occurring before the conclusion of the contract of guarantee are not covered.[249]

Investments eligible for cover include equity investments and non-equity direct investments.[250] All forms of equity investment are covered regardless of the legal form of the project or of the share held by the applicant for cover.[251] Examples of non-equity direct investments covered include production sharing contracts, profit sharing contracts, management contracts, franchising agreements, licensing agreements, turnkey contracts, operating leasing agreements, subordinated debentures, other forms that may be recommended by the President and approved by the board the remuneration for which substantially depends on the performance of the investment project and guarantees, and loans made by the person making any of the foregoing forms of non-equity investment. In all cases the investment must have terms of at least three years' duration and depend substantially on the production, revenues or profits of the investment project for repayment. In particular, projects of long duration and high developmental

---

[243] The contract will follow the standard form agreement drawn up by MIGA: MIGA Standard Contract of Guarantee and General Conditions of Guarantee for Equity Investments of 25 January 1989: 28 ILM 1233 (1989).

[244] See, for the full analysis of scope of coverage, MIGA Regs above n 235 at paras 1.39–1.41. See also MIGA Standard Contract of Guarantee ibid art 8 at ILM 1249–52.

[245] MIGA Convention above n 232 art 11(a)(iii).   [246] Shihata above n 232 at 131.

[247] See Shihata ibid at 123–24, 134–38. MIGA Regs above n 235 paras 1.23–1.28, 1.46–1.52.

[248] MIGA Convention above n 232 art 11(b).   [249] ibid art 11(c).

[250] ibid art 12(a).   [251] MIGA Regs above n 235 at para 1.04.

potential will be included.[252] Both investments in monetary form and investments in kind will be covered.[253] However, in accordance with Article 12(c) of the convention an investment is eligible for cover only if it is a new investment.[254]

Investors eligible to benefit from MIGA may be either natural or juridical persons. To qualify, a natural person must be a national of a member country other than the host country. A juridical person must be incorporated and have its principal place of business in a member country, or the majority of its capital must be owned by a member or members or nationals thereof, provided that the member in question is not the host country. In addition, the juridical person must operate on a commercial basis, whether it is privately or publicly owned.[255] Eligibility for cover may be extended to a natural person who is a national of the host country, or to a juridical person incorporated in the host country or the majority of whose capital is owned by its nationals, where the assets invested are transferred from outside the host country and the board, on a joint application from the investor and the host country, approved by a special majority.[256]

To be eligible for cover, the investment concerned must be made in the territory of a developing member country.[257] Such countries are listed in Schedule A to the convention. No contract of guarantee shall be issued before the host government has approved the issuance of the guarantee by MIGA against the risks designated for cover. In this way the host state retains a measure of sovereign authority over the operation of MIGA cover in relation to investments made in its territory. In addition, an environmental assessment will need to be made of the project in accordance with MIGA's policy on this issue.[258]

The payment of claims is made by the President of MIGA under the direction of the board, in accordance with the contract of guarantee and the board's general policies. The investor will have to seek appropriate administrative remedies under the laws of the host state before making a claim.[259] Payment of a claim will subrogate the Agency to the rights or claims of the investor against the host country and other obligors.[260] Any dispute between the Agency and the holder of a guarantee shall be submitted to arbitration in accordance with the terms of the contract of guarantee.[261] The Agency is empowered to enter into arrangements with private insurers and reinsurers to enhance its own operations and to encourage the provision of non-commercial risks coverage by such insurers.[262] This is useful as the Agency is restricted to no more than 150 per cent of its unimpaired capital and reserves in the liabilities that it may undertake.[263]

---

[252] MIGA Regs ibid paras 1.05–1.06.   [253] ibid paras 1.09–1.10.
[254] ibid para 1.11.   [255] MIGA Convention above n 232 art 13(a).
[256] ibid art 13(c).   [257] ibid art 14.
[258] See further Annex B to the MIGA Operational Regulations available at <http://www.miga.org/index.cfm?aid=18>.   [259] MIGA Convention above n 232 art 17.
[260] ibid art 18.   [261] ibid art 58.   [262] ibid art 21.   [263] ibid art 22.

Concluding Remarks

This chapter has considered what have been, historically, the first major issues of investor and investment protection in which substantive international law has been invoked as a standard for the regulation of relations between foreign investors and host states. Although considerable doctrinal conflict has existed over applicable norms, there is an underlying sense of a generally understood and accepted process for dealing with renegotiation and expropriation issues, coupled with the evolution of pragmatic approaches to the problems involved as exemplified through the use of lump sum agreements and investment guarantee systems. In the next chapter, further issues, surrounding the control of investment risk will be considered in the light of the recently emerging arbitral awards dealing with the interpretation of other investor and investment protection standards in IIAs.

16

Control of Investment Risks II: Non-Discrimination, Fair and Equitable Treatment, and Full Protection and Security

In recent years, the nature of claims made by investors, before tribunals, has changed. While expropriation claims have been historically the most important, and the issue of regulatory or indirect expropriation has given new life to such issues, a significant measure of success appears to have been had through the bringing of claims based on breaches of the national treatment or fair and equitable treatment standard.[1] In addition, the most favoured nation (MFN) standard has given rise to claims that stronger standards of protection, found in other International Investment Agreements (IIAs) entered into by the host country, should apply to the IIA underlying the dispute by way of the application of the MFN clause in that agreement. Furthermore, the responsibility of states to ensure the full protection and security of investments has given rise to some disputes. Claims based on these standards will, of course, attract compensation where they are upheld. However, the approach to compensation cannot be the same as for expropriation claims, as the nature of the loss is different. Each of these issues will now be considered.

(1) National Treatment

The national treatment standard requires that foreign investors should receive treatment no less favourable than that accorded to nationals of the host state engaged in similar business activity.[2] It seeks to ensure equality of competitive conditions between foreign investors and domestic investors in a like situation.

---

[1] This is especially true of recent NAFTA cases, where most claims that have succeeded did so on these grounds rather than on the ground of expropriation.

[2] See, for example, the OECD *Declaration on International Investment and Multinational Enterprises* 27 June 2000 'National Treatment' quoted below in text at n 22. For further examples of national treatment provisions, see UNCTAD *National Treatment* Series on issues in international investment agreements (New York and Geneva: United Nations, 1999).

It represents less than the minimum protection accepted under international law, which demands treatment of foreigners better than that given to nationals where the treatment of nationals falls below international minimum standards. On the other hand, national treatment represents the maximum protection for economic rights accorded to foreign investors under host state law. Thus there is a paradoxical element in this standard.[3] Although it aims at the elimination of discrimination between foreign and domestic investors, in the practice of capital-exporting states, national treatment does not prevent preferential treatment for foreign investors by reference to international minimum standards. In this it differs considerably from the concept of national treatment implicit in the 'Calvo Doctrine' until recently espoused by the Latin American states and some developing countries, which accepts the principle that foreign investors are to be accorded treatment no better than that given to domestic investors, regardless of whether such treatment falls below international minimum standards.[4]

Following from the above, the basis of a claim brought under the national treatment standard lies in the allegation that the investor and/or their investment have been treated less favourably than a comparable domestic investor/investment. The essential elements of the claim are as follows. The aggrieved foreign investor must show, first, that there exist domestic investors in the same economic or business sector, secondly, that the foreign investor and/or investment is being treated less favourably than its domestic counterparts and, thirdly, that the design and nature of the measures, that lead to this difference in treatment, have a discriminatory effect. This may be an express intention of the measure, or a factual effect thereof. Thus both *de jure* and *de facto* discrimination will be sufficient to found the claim. The burden of proof is usually that of establishing a presumption and a prima facie case that the claimant has been treated in a different and less favourable manner than its domestic counterpart(s), whereupon the burden shifts to the respondent state to show that no such effect has arisen.[5]

This approach has been used before NAFTA tribunals. For example, in *SD Myers v Canada*,[6] the US based claimant established a business in Canada, aimed at obtaining contracts for the treatment of hazardous PCB waste from Canada, at its US disposal facility in Cleveland, Ohio. Most such waste was located in Ontario and Quebec close to the US facility. The only comparable Canadian facility was located in Swan Hills, Alberta, in Western Canada. It was Canadian Government policy to destroy PCBs within its borders as far as was possible. However, the US Government unilaterally permitted the import of PCB wastes

---

[3] JP Laviec *Protection et Promotion Des Investissements: Etude de Droit International Economique* (PUF, 1985) 96.

[4] UNCTAD *Bilateral Investment Treaties in the Mid-1990s* (New York and Geneva: United Nations, 1998) at 59.

[5] See *Feldman v Mexico* ICSID Case No Arb(AF)/99/1 award 16 December 2002 available at <http://www.naftaclaims.com> or 18 ICSID Rev-FILJ 488 (2003) at paras 176–78.

[6] *SD Myers v Canada* UNCITRAL award of 12 November 2000 available at <http://www.naftaclaims.com> or 40 ILM 1408 (2001).

for a period from 15 November 1995 to 31 December 1997. Canada was taken by surprise and, in response to intensive lobbying by the fledgling Canadian PCB waste industry, issued an order to close the border to exports of PCB waste. This lasted from 16 November 1995 until February 1997, when the border was again opened. Thereupon, seven contracts for PCB waste removal were concluded by SD Myers. The border was again closed by US court order in July 1997.

The tribunal had no difficulty in finding a violation of the national treatment standard in Article 1102 of NAFTA. The Canadian orders that led to the closure of the border between November 1995 and February 1997 clearly favoured Canadian over non-Canadian nationals and the practical effect was to prevent the claimant from carrying out the business they had planned to undertake. They were at a clear disadvantage as compared with their Canadian counterparts. The aim of the measures was not to protect the environment but to keep Canadian industry strong so as to ensure continued domestic disposal capacity. Such an aim could have been achieved by other, less trade intrusive, means.[7] Given the fact that the Canadian operators and the claimant were in the same business sector, that the claimant could have taken away business from the Canadian operators in the absence of the measures, and given the practical impact of the measures in creating a disproportionate benefit to nationals over non-nationals, Canada had violated Article 1102 of NAFTA. In coming to its conclusion, the tribunal noted that while the intent behind a measure was important, protectionist intent was not decisive unless there was also a practical adverse effect on the claimant. In addition, such cases had to be decided in the context of all their particular facts in order to determine whether there actually had been a denial of national treatment.[8]

The approach to national treatment under NAFTA was further refined in the case of *Pope and Talbot v Canada*.[9] The tribunal was confronted with three sets of issues: the number of domestic investors with whom a comparison of treatment was to be made, the degree of differential treatment needed to show a case of de facto discrimination and the proper approach to the interpretation of 'like circumstances'. On the first question, the tribunal refused to read the reference to 'investments of investors' in Article 1102 as excluding the single foreign investor, as Canada had argued, nor did it require the investor to demonstrate that there were other similarly situated foreign investors. Furthermore, it did not require comparison with more than one domestically owned investment. Thus, there was no need for the foreign investor to show whether and how many other foreign

---

[7] Indeed, this case could be seen as a trade case rather than a true investment case as the US claimant had not established a processing facility in Canada, only a trading facility to obtain contracts for supply of waste to the Cleveland plant. However, NAFTA does not permit individual traders to bring trade claims. It may be said that the majority of NAFTA investment cases are, in reality trade, cases but that claimants are using the Chapter 11 procedure for investor-state disputes to bring such claims.   [8] ibid at paras 193–95, 252–57.

[9] Award on the Merits of Phase 2, 10 April 2001 available at <http://www.naftaclaims.com>.

investors could fall under the 'like circumstances' requirement.[10] As to the second issue, the tribunal was invited by the Government of Canada to interpret Article 1102 of NAFTA as requiring proof of a disproportionate disadvantage in cases of de facto discrimination, on the basis of GATT and WTO precedents. The tribunal refused to follow this line of reasoning, saying that the GATT/WTO case law on national treatment, and the *SD Myers* case, pointed to the opposite conclusion, namely, that any difference of treatment was sufficient to show less favourable treatment if there was some disadvantage to the investor or trader. Otherwise the national treatment standard could be effectively sidestepped through skilful drafting.[11] On the issue of 'like circumstances', the tribunal upheld the approach in *SD Myers*, that this was a matter of fact in each case, and went on to formulate a three step analysis. First, the treatment accorded to a foreign owned investment 'should be compared with that accorded to domestic investments in the same business or economic sector'.[12] Secondly, 'differences in treatment will presumptively violate Article 1102(2) unless they have a reasonable nexus to rational government policies that (1) do not distinguish on their face or de facto, between foreign owned and domestic companies, and (2) do not otherwise unduly undermine the investment liberalising objectives of NAFTA'.[13] Thirdly, once a difference in treatment is discerned, the question becomes, are the domestic and foreign owned investments in like circumstances? It is here that the issue of discrimination arises.[14]

In addition, the tribunal in *Feldman v Mexico*[15] noted two further issues of interpretation that arose out of Article 1102: the extent to which differential

---

[10] ibid at paras 36–38.   [11] ibid at paras 67, 70.

[12] ibid at para 78. This will require an analysis of the economic situation of the proposed competitors to see if they are in fact in like circumstances. See, for example, the analysis of US and Canadian based steel producers in *ADF Group Inc v United States of America* ICSID Case No Arb(AF)/00/1 award of 9 January 2003 available at <http://www.naftaclaims.com> or 18 ICSID Rev-FILJ 195 (2003) at paras 156–58. In this regard comparisons with the analysis of 'like products' in trade agreements such as the GATT are of limited value given that NAFTA Article 1102 does not refer to such a comparison but uses the term 'like circumstances'. See further the discussion in *Methanex v United States of America* award of 3 August 2005 available at <http://www.state.gov/documents/organization/51052.pdf> or 44 ILM 1345 (2005) ch IV Part B at paras 25–38. This case also adopts the view that where an identical comparator exists, that will be the best comparator to use although less 'like' but relevant comparators can be used in the absence of an identical comparator: see ibid at paras 12–19. On the other hand, the London Court of International Arbitration in *Occidental Exploration and Production Co v Ecuador* Administered Case No UN 3467 award of 1 July 2004 available at <http://ita.law.uvic.ca/documents/Oxy-EcuadorFinalAward_001.pdf>) felt able to compare the treatment accorded to a US oil company with the treatment accorded to exporters in general, rather than to Ecuadorian oil companies: see paras 173–76. For a critical assessment, see the comment by Susan D Franck in 99 AJIL 675 (2005). This would appear to be at odds with the policy of the OECD which is to encourage comparison within the same industrial sector: see text at n 24–28 below.   [13] ibid.

[14] ibid para 79.

[15] Above n 5 at para 166. A judicial review of the award and, in particular of the finding of breach of the national treatment provision, affirmed the findings of the tribunal: *In the Matter of an Arbitration Pursuant to Chapter Eleven of NAFTA Between Roy Feldman Karpa and the United Mexican*

treatment had to be a result of the foreign investor's nationality and whether a foreign investor had to receive the most favourable treatment given to any domestic investor or to just one of them. On the first issue, the tribunal rejected the Mexican argument that the claimant had to show explicitly that the discrimination had been motivated by his or her nationality. It was sufficient to show less favourable treatment for the foreign investor than for domestic investors in like circumstances.[16] On the second issue, the tribunal did not commit itself to a final view, as there was only one domestic investor in like circumstances with whom the claimant could compare his treatment. It observed that Article 1102 of NAFTA contained no 'most favoured investor' provision and that there was no language in that provision which required that the foreign investor should receive treatment equal to that provided to the most favourably treated domestic investor, if there were multiple such investors receiving differing treatment by the respondent government.[17]

These NAFTA based awards offer some guidance to the development of the national treatment standard in IIAs. However, it would be wrong to read them as definitive, in that they interpret one, specialized, agreement in which national treatment is accorded to a wider range of activities than in other agreements, including, as seen in chapter 6, a right to entry and establishment. National treatment provisions in other agreements will have to be interpreted in the light of their own wording and context. Equally, it would be wrong to read investment provisions as being interchangeable with trade based national treatment provisions. The two contexts are not alike, especially as regards the requirement that discrimination should stem from the nationality of the investor and not from the national origin of goods.[18]

Furthermore, these cases do not examine the implications of the fact that national treatment provisions may be subject to qualifications and exclusions arising out of the regulatory discretion of the host country under national law. The national treatment standard is a treaty-made standard.[19] It is not a part of the corpus of customary international law. Consequently, its content cannot be derived from international law. Rather, it is a standard defined by reference to the national law applicable to the field of economic activities covered by the treaty. As such the standard has always recognized certain exceptions based on the public

---

States (Ontario Superior Court of Justice Court File No 03–CV–23500 4 November 2003), 43 ILM 880 (2004).

[16] ibid at para 181.   [17] ibid para 185–6.

[18] See *Methanex v US* above n 12 and see further Andrea Menaker 'Standards of Treatment: National Treatment, Most Favoured Nation Treatment and Minimum Standards of Treatment' in *APEC Workshop on Bilateral and Regional Investment Rules/Agreements* (Singapore: APEC, 2002) at 102, 112.

[19] UNCTC *Key Concepts in International Investment Agreements and Their Relevance to Negotiations on International Transactions in Services* (New York: February 1990, UNCTC Current Studies Series A No 13 UN Doc ST/CTC/SER.A/13) 15.

interest of the host state. Thus restrictions required by the needs of national security and public order have been included in certain BITs.[20] In addition, some treaties contain derogations based on the development objectives of the host state. Accordingly, preferential treatment, in relation to investment incentives for nationals of the host state, may be protected by the treaty where this is required for the economic development of the host state. Often, such derogations will be subject to the condition that they do not substantially impair competition and/or investment by nationals and companies of the other contracting state.[21]

Equally, the practice of the OECD recognizes certain exceptions to national treatment. This is emphasized by phasing of the principle of 'National Treatment' in the *Declaration on International Investment and Multinational Enterprises* of 27 June 2000.[22] According to the declaration:

The adhering governments should, consistent with their needs to maintain public order, to protect their essential security interests and to fulfil commitments relating to international peace and security, accord to enterprises operating in their territories and owned or controlled directly or indirectly by nationals of another adhering government (hereinafter referred to as 'Foreign-Controlled Enterprises') treatment under their laws, regulations and administrative practices, consistent with international law and no less favourable than that accorded in like situations to domestic enterprises (hereinafter referred to as 'National Treatment').

The declaration goes on to add that adhering governments will consider applying 'National Treatment' in respect of countries other than adhering governments, and will ensure that their territorial sub-divisions apply 'National Treatment'. Finally, the declaration stresses that it does not deal with the right of adhering governments to regulate the entry of foreign investment or the conditions of establishment of foreign enterprises.[23]

The OECD Committee on International Investment and Multinational Enterprises has regularly reviewed the meaning and effect of 'National Treatment'.[24] According to its 2005 Report on *National Treatment for*

---

[20] UNCTAD above n 4 at 63 citing the German Model BIT.

[21] UNCTC *Bilateral Investment Treaties* (1988, UN Doc ST/CTC/65) paras 153–56. (mentioning the Protocol to the Papua New Guinea-Germany and Papua New Guinea-UK BITs of 1980 and 1981; Protocol to Belgium-Indonesia BIT 1970; Switzerland-Indonesia BIT 1974 Protocol No 2; Germany-Zaire BIT 1969 art 3(3)). See also UNCTAD above n 4, 64 n 79 describing German government policy in this regard.

[22] See OECD *The OECD Guidelines for Multinational Enterprises* (Paris: OECD, 2000) 11–12, available also from the OECD website at <http://www.oecd.org/dataoecd/56/36/192248.pdf>. See further OECD *National Treatment for Foreign-Controlled Enterprises* (Paris: OECD, 1985, revised 1993 and 2005). All references are to the 2005 Report, which reproduces the main interpretations of the earlier reports and updates the adhering governments' lists of exceptions to the National Treatment Instrument.

[23] In OECD practice this issue is covered by the Codes on the Liberalization of Capital Movements and Invisibles: see ch 6 at 248–51.

[24] This is done in accordance with the Third Revised Decision of the OECD Council on National Treatment (December 1991) C(91)147/ Final reproduced in Annex B to the 2005 Report.

Foreign-Controlled Enterprises, the key phrase in the declaration, 'treatment no less favourable than that accorded in like situations to domestic enterprises' has the following implications.[25] The expression, 'in like situations' means that, to be valid, comparison between domestic firms and foreign-controlled firms already established in the adhering country must be made between firms operating in the same industrial sector. National policy objectives in various fields should also be taken into account to the extent that they are not contrary to the principle of National Treatment. A key factor in determining whether the measure applied to the foreign-controlled enterprise constitutes an exception to National Treatment is whether the discrimination is motivated, at least in part, by the fact that the enterprises concerned are under foreign control. Turning to the preconditions for the application of National Treatment, these are, first, that the foreign-controlled enterprise must be operating within the territory of a member country, either through a local subsidiary or branch, with effective presence rather than legal form being decisive and, secondly, that the enterprise must be foreign-controlled, the key element being that the parent company is recognized as a national enterprise by an adhering government, provided it is effectively present in that country's area.[26]

In addition, where the provision of equal treatment for a foreign-controlled enterprise by a host country is conditional on similar treatment being extended to enterprises from the host country in the home country, this constitutes an exception to National Treatment if it results in the foreign-controlled enterprise being treated less favourably than similar domestic enterprises.[27] Finally, the declaration permits distinctions of treatment for foreign-controlled enterprises where this is consistent with the need to maintain public order, the protection of essential security interests and the fulfilment of commitments to maintain international peace and security. The interpretation of these exceptions is left to

---

[25] See 2005 Report above n 22 at 106. The 1985 Report (at 16–19) added further clarification of the circumstances in which an exception to National Treatment could be created: first, an exception to national treatment is not created by the existence of a public monopoly which results in discriminatory measures against foreign-controlled enterprises. Secondly, if a foreign-controlled enterprise already established in an adhering country receives less favourable treatment, this can constitute an exception to National Treatment if it also falls within the other criteria for determining such an exception; on the other hand, if the enterprise under foreign control receives treatment at least as favourable as that given to domestic enterprises, there can be no case of an exception to National Treatment. Thirdly, in cases where domestic enterprises do not all receive the same treatment, where a foreign-controlled enterprise already established in an adhering country is treated less favourably than the least well treated domestic enterprise, this can constitute an exception to National Treatment; if it receives treatment equivalent to that given to the best treated domestic enterprise there can be no question of an exception to National Treatment. In cases where the foreign-controlled enterprise receives treatment at least as favourable as the least well treated domestic enterprise but less favourable than the best treated enterprise, it is not certain that this constitutes an exception to National Treatment. Each such case should be reviewed on its facts, taking account of individual national characteristics and the degree to which the foreign and domestic enterprises are placed in comparable circumstances. [26] 2005 Report ibid at 105–106.
[27] ibid at 108.

the member countries, although the 2005 Report expresses the need to apply them with caution, bearing in mind the objectives of the National Treatment instrument. They should not be used as a general escape clause from the commitments under these instruments.[28]

In the light of the above mentioned considerations, the Committee on International Investment and Multinational Enterprises has considered the application of National Treatment in five main areas: official aids and subsidies, tax obligations, government purchasing and public contracts, investment by established foreign-controlled enterprises, and access to local bank credits and the capital market.[29] These are the principal areas in which the OECD member states have passed laws and regulations discriminating against foreign-controlled enterprises. The committee has also considered the area of nationality requirements, as, for example, the requirement that a certain number of members of the board of a company must possess host state nationality.[30] Under the 1991 Review of the Declaration, the application of National Treatment to the privatization of enterprises previously under public ownership was considered. Access to the areas newly opened up by such a policy should be on a non-discriminatory basis between private domestic and foreign-controlled enterprises already established in the country in question. Any restrictions applying to foreign-controlled enterprises should be reported as exceptions to National Treatment.[31]

(2) Most Favoured Nation Treatment

The MFN standard has been widely recognized in treaties by which states grant to each other reciprocal freedom of commerce. However, it is not recognized as a principle of customary international law.[32] Thus its content depends on the treaty in which it is included. The inclusion of a MFN clause in a BIT, or other type of IIA, has the effect of extending, to the home contacting state, more favourable terms of investment granted to a third state by the host contracting state. Thereby, discriminatory terms of investment, operating against investors from the home contracting state, are prevented, and the equal treatment of all foreign investors by the host state is ensured. The MFN standard thus ensures equality of competitive conditions in the host country market as between foreign investors of different nationalities.

---

[28] ibid at 112.   [29] ibid at 113–22.   [30] See 1985 Report above n 22 at para 4.1, 20.
[31] OECD *The OECD Declaration and Decisions on International Investment and Multinational Enterprises* (Paris: OECD, 1992) 27.
[32] G Schwarzenberger *International Law and Order* (Stevens, 1971) 137–38. On the MFN standard, see Schwarzenberger ibid. ch 8, and 'The Most-Favoured-Nation Standard in British State Practice' 22 BYIL 96 (1945); Report of the International Law Commission *ILC Yearbook* (1978 II) 10–83; Snyder *The Most Favoured Nation Clause* (New York: Kings Crown Press, Columbia University 1948); Sauvignon *La Clause de la Nation la Plus Favorisé* (Grenoble University Press, 1972). See also *Asian Agricultural Products Ltd v Republic of Sri Lanka* (ICSID Tribunal, Final Award,

The scope of MFN treatment is unconditional in the absence of express limitation.[33] It can be specifically excluded in relation to certain third countries.[34] However, the standard only operates in relation to the subject-matter of the IIA; it cannot be extended by implication to matters covered by other treaties, such as, for example, conventions on the protection of intellectual property.[35] The same restriction *ratione materiae* lies behind commonly found exceptions relating to privileges or benefits accorded to nationals and/or companies of third states by reason of the host contracting party's membership of any customs union, common market, free trade area or regional economic organization, or by reason of any international tax agreement entered into by the host contracting party.[36] In BITs, it is common to combine the MFN standard with the national treatment standard in the same paragraph. This has the effect of ensuring that investors can avail themselves of the MFN standard where this is more favourable than the national treatment standard, as where investors from a third state are offered treatment better than national treatment.[37] In other treaties the beneficiary country will be given the choice between the MFN and national treatment standards.[38]

Despite recent arbitral decisions, it remains uncertain how far the MFN standard can allow a claim that more favourable treatment, accorded by a host contracting party to nationals of a home contracting state under another IIA (the 'third-party agreement'), must extend to nationals of the home contracting state under the IIA pertaining to the claimant (the 'base agreement').[39] Such an argument was put by the Claimant in *Asian Agricultural Products Ltd v Republic of*

21 June 1990) 30 ILM 577 (1991) at 645 (Dissenting Opinion of SKB Asante); Jurgen Kurtz 'The MFN Standard and Foreign Investment: An Uneasy Fit?' 6 JWIT 861 (2004); Locknie Hsu 'MFN and Dispute Settlement – When the Twain Meet' 7 JWIT 25 (2006).

[33] Laviec above n 3 at 99. See further UNCTAD *Fair and Equitable Treatment* series on issues in international investment agreements (New York and Geneva: United Nations, 1999) 13–27.

[34] Eg Germany-Philippines BIT 1964 Protocol (3)(a): 'Nothing in Article 2 shall be construed to entitle nationals or companies of the Federal Republic of Germany to the special rights and privileges accorded by the Republic of the Philippines to nationals and companies of the United States of America by virtue of existing agreements.' Quoted in Laviec ibid. at 102 n 119.   [35] ibid.

[36] See eg UK-Philippines BIT artIV (3)(a) and (b) in FA Mann 'British treaties for the promotion and protection of investment' 52 BYIL 241 (1981) at 251–52. See also UNCTAD above n 4 at 63.

[37] UNCTAD ibid. at 59. See also *Siemens AG v Argentina* ICSID Case No Arb/02/8 award on jurisdiction of 3 August 2004 available at <http://www.worldbank.org/icsid> or 44 ILM 138 (2005) at para 93.

[38] Eg UK-Thailand BIT 1979 art 10(2): 'Wherever this Agreement makes alternative provisions for the grant of national treatment or of treatment not less favourable than that accorded to the nationals or companies of any third State in respect of any matter, the option as between these alternatives shall rest with the Contracting Party beneficiary in each particular case'. Quoted in Laviec above n 3 at 101 n 116; see No 99 (1979) Cmnd 7732.

[39] For a review of the case law see further Kurtz above n 32; Rudolph Dolzer and Terry Myers 'After *Tecmed*: Most-Favored-Nation Clauses in Investment Protection Agreements' 19 ICSID Rev-FILJ 49 (2004); Dana H Freyer and David Herlihy 'Most-Favored-Nation Treatment and Dispute Rev-Settlement in Investment Arbitration: Just how "Favored" is "Most-Favored"?' 20 ICSID Rev-FILJ 58 (2005). The terminology in the text is taken from Dolzer and Myers at 50.

Sri Lanka.[40] It was rejected on the ground that the claimant had failed to show that the other BIT did in fact offer more favourable treatment. However, the tribunal did not rule out such an argument in principle, and it would appear to be consistent with the aims of the MFN standard. In this light, more recent tribunals have revisited the issue. The application of the MFN clause in an IIA will depend upon its interpretation in accordance with the accepted canons of treaty interpretation under international law.[41] Given the considerable differences in the drafting of such clauses, this approach has produced significant differences of outcome in the cases. Thus, as will be shown below, some awards offer an expansive interpretation of the MFN clause while others are more cautious. In addition, a distinction has been made between the application of the MFN clause to substantive protection standards contained in an IIA and procedural standards applicable to the dispute settlement provisions of the agreement.

Turning to substantive protection standards, there is relatively little case law on this issue, perhaps because most IIAs offer similar standards of substantive protection to investors and their investments. However, in the case of *MTD v Chile*[42] the claimant did use the MFN clause in the applicable BIT (Malaysia-Chile) to argue that a more favourable substantive provision in the Croatia-Chile BIT should apply. The claimant had been denied the required planning licences to develop an investment in property development, although they had received authorization for the investment by the Chilean investment authority. Among other arguments, the claimant invoked Article 3(2) of the Croatia-Chile BIT, which states, '[w]hen a Contracting party has admitted an investment in its territory, it shall grant the necessary permits in accordance with its laws and regulations'. According to the claimant, as Chile had the discretion to amend the applicable planning laws to permit the proposed development, this clause could apply to oblige Chile to do so as a matter of international law, by reason of the application of the MFN cause in the Malaysia-Chile BIT. The tribunal was unimpressed by this reasoning. While it accepted that the MFN clause could allow this provision in the Croatia-Chile BIT to apply, the tribunal made a distinction between the right of the claimant to require the grant of a permit in accordance with the applicable national law, and a request by them to change the normative framework itself.[43] The relevant clause did not apply to the latter. Given that the claimant was in fact asking for a change in the normative framework applicable to their investment, the respondent state had not breached the BIT by refusing to change its laws.[44] A further general point applicable to the substantive protection offered under a BIT was made in the case of *TECMED v*

---

[40] Above n 32.   [41] See Freyer and Herlihy above n 39 at 62–63.

[42] *MTD Equity v Chile* ICSID Case No Arb/01/7 award of 25 May 2004 available at <http://www.worldbank.org/icsid> or 44 ILM 91 (2005).The award is subject to annulment proceedings.   [43] ibid at para 205.

[44] ibid at para 206.

Mexico. There, it was held that the time dimension of the application of the substantive provisions of a BIT was a 'core' matter. Such 'core matters' were specifically negotiated by the parties and could not be impaired by the principle contained in the MFN clause. [45] Otherwise the tribunal would be substituting the will of the contracting parties with some unbargained for result.[46] However, the tribunal did not offer any further guidance on what constituted such core matters. This is an issue for further analysis by subsequent tribunals.

By contrast, the applicability of the MFN clause to procedural issues arising out of the operation of the dispute settlement clause in IIAs, has generated more decisions. This line of cases begins with *Maffezini v Spain*.[47] There the claimant sought to avoid a provision in the Argentina-Spain BIT which required that, in the absence of an amicable settlement within six months, disputes were to be submitted to the courts of the host country, which had a period of 18 months to deal with the dispute, before they could be taken to arbitration. The claimant argued that, by reason of the MFN clause in the Argentina-Spain BIT, this provision could be replaced by the provision used in the Chile-Spain BIT, which allowed recourse to arbitration after the six-month period allowed for negotiations had expired. The tribunal accepted the claimant's position that it was being treated less favourably than a Chilean investor in Spain by reason of the additional requirement to submit disputes to a local court. It did so, first, by reference to its reading of relevant international case law, in particular the *Ambatielos* arbitration, where it was held that issues of the administration of justice came within the MFN clause in the applicable FCN treaty.[48] The tribunal went on to interpret the applicable MFN clause. By Article IV(2) of the Argentina-Spain BIT:

In all matters subject to this Agreement, this treatment shall be no less favourable than that extended by each Party to the investments made in its territory by investors of a third country.

It held that this provision was capable of including dispute settlement provisions. Given the general trend towards enhancing investor protection through international agreements, and the importance placed upon recourse to international arbitration, rather than submission to domestic courts, by traders and investors and their home countries, it was possible to extend the operation of the MFN clause to provisions in other agreements that were more favourable to the protection of the investors rights in this regard.[49] This conclusion was reinforced by the subsequent practice of Argentina, which had abandoned the local remedies requirement in

---

[45] ICSID Case No Arb (AF)/00/2 award of 29 May 2003 available at <http://www.worldbank.org/icsid> or 43 ILM 133 (2004) at para 69.

[46] Dolzer and Myers above n 39 at 59.

[47] *Maffezini v Spain* ICSID Case No Arb/97/7 Decision on Objections to Jurisdiction 25 January 2000: 16 ICSID Rev-FILJ 212 (2001).

[48] ibid at paras 49–50. See further the *Ambatioelos* arbitration (1956) RIAA 83.

[49] ibid at paras 54–56.

subsequent agreements, thus bringing it in line with Spain and Chile in this regard.[50]

The tribunal was mindful of the risks of taking an overbroad approach to the MFN clause in relation to dispute settlement. Accordingly it placed certain limits on its operation. First, the third-party treaty and the base treaty had to contain the same subject-matter, in that both should be related to the protection of foreign investment.[51] Secondly, certain public policy limitations, taken by the parties to the agreement, had to be observed.[52] Thus, if one contracting party has conditioned its consent to arbitration upon the exhaustion of local remedies, which the ICSID Convention allows, this requirement could not be by-passed. In addition, if the parties have included a 'fork-in the-road' provision in their dispute settlement arrangement, which renders the choice between submission to domestic courts or international arbitration irrevocable, this too could not be by-passed. Furthermore, any specific choice of arbitral forum could not be interfered with, nor could the choice of a highly specific institutionalized system of arbitration, such as NAFTA and similar arrangements. Other limitations could also be identified by future parties and tribunals, and a distinction had to be made between 'the legitimate extension of rights and benefits by means of the operation of the clause, on the one hand, and disruptive treaty shopping that would play havoc with the policy objectives of underlying specific treaty provisions, on the other hand'.[53]

The decision in *Maffezini v Spain* has not been uniformly followed. It was followed in four subsequent cases involving Argentina as respondent.[54] In each case the claimant successfully used the MFN clause to avoid a dispute settlement provision drafted in similar terms to that which formed the basis of the claim in *Maffezini*. All four cases accept the policy based analysis adopted in *Maffezini*, namely, that access to international dispute settlement on the part of the investor is a key element in the system of protection provided by IIAs. In the words of the tribunal in *Gas Natural v Argentina*:

The Tribunal holds that provision for international investor-state arbitration in bilateral investment treaties is a significant substantive incentive and protection for foreign investors; further that access to such arbitration only after resort to national courts and an eighteen-month waiting period is a less favourable degree of protection than access to arbitration immediately upon expiration of the negotiation period. Accordingly, Claimant is entitled to avail itself of the dispute settlement provision in the United States-Argentina

---

[50] ibid at paras 57–61.   [51] ibid at para 56.   [52] ibid at para 62.
[53] ibid at para 63.
[54] See *Siemens AG v Argentina* above n 37; *Cammuzi International SA v Argentina* ICSID Case No Arb/03/7 decision on jurisdiction 10 June 2005 available at <http://www.ita.law.uvic.ca>; *Gas Natural SDG SA v Argentina* ICSID Case No Arb/03/10 Decision on Jurisdiction 17 June 2005 available at <http://ita.law.uvic.ca>; *Suez, Sociedad General de Aguas de Barcelona SA, and Vivendi Universal SA v Argentina* ICSID Case No Arb/03/19 Decision on Jurisdiction 3 August 2006 available at <http://www.ita.law.uvic.ca>.

BIT in reliance on Article IV(2) of the Bilateral Investment treaty between Spain and Argentina.[55]

These cases appear to have come to the view that, unless the BIT clearly applies a different method for resolution of disputes, the MFN clause should be understood to be applicable to dispute settlement.[56] This is so whether the formulation is as wide as in *Maffezini* ('all matters subject to this agreement') or is narrower, as where the term 'treatment' or 'activities related to the investments' is used.[57] In addition, where a dispute settlement clause is imported into an agreement by virtue of the MFN clause, this does not entail access to all the benefits of the third-party treaty, in that the investor cannot benefit to a greater degree than the investor under the third-party treaty. Ultimately, this depends on the terms of the MFN clause and other terms of the treaties involved.[58]

Two recent cases have not accepted the conclusions in *Maffezini*. Thus, in *Salini Construttori SPA and Others v Jordan*[59] the tribunal held that the Italian claimants could not rely on the dispute settlement clauses in the US-Jordan and UK-Jordan BITs, to extend international arbitration to the dispute with Jordan. That dispute arose out of a construction contract, which was subject to a specialized dispute settlement procedure set down in the applicable investment contract. By virtue of the Italy-Jordan BIT, Article 9(2), such specialized contractual dispute settlement procedures were to apply in place of recourse to international arbitration before ICSID. This was a clear expression of intention on the part of the contracting parties to the treaty. In this, the circumstances of the case differed from those in *Maffezini*, where the wording of the MFN clause was wider, and the practice of the contracting parties to the base agreement, Argentina and Spain, generally did not require recourse to the local courts as a precondition to the submission of the dispute to international arbitration.

A similar divergence from *Maffezini* occurred in the case of *Plama Consortium Limited v Bulgaria*.[60] In that case, the dispute settlement provisions in the Bulgaria-Cyprus BIT reflected the fact that the agreement had been negotiated while Bulgaria was still a communist state. As a result, the scope of the provision was very narrow, allowing for international arbitration under the auspices of the International Court of Arbitration only regarding the amount of compensation to be paid in the event of an expropriation. On the basis of the MFN clause in the BIT, the Cypriot claimant sought to invoke the wider dispute settlement clause in

---

[55] ibid at para 31. This dispute arose out of a claim by a Spanish investor in Argentina, based on the same treaty as in *Maffezini*.

[56] See ibid at para 49. See also *Siemens v Argentina* above n 37 at para 102 and *Suez v Argentina* above n 54 at para 62.　　　　　　　　　　　[57] *Siemens v Argentina* ibid at para 103.

[58] ibid at paras 108–109.

[59] ICSID Case No/Arb/02/13 decision on jurisdiction 29 November 2004 available at <http://www.worldbank.org/icsid> or 44 ILM 573 (2005).

[60] ICSID Case No Arb/03/24 decision on jurisdiction 8 February 2005 available at <http://www.worldbank.org/icsid/cases> or 44 ILM 721 (2005). This case was distinguished in *Suez v Argentina* above n 54 at paras 64–67.

the Bulgaria-Finland BIT, which permitted recourse to ICSID arbitration. The tribunal held that the MFN provision in the Bulgaria-Cyprus BIT could not be interpreted as providing consent to submit to ICSID arbitration. As a matter of textual construction the term 'treatment' in the MFN clause could not be said to include or exclude dispute settlement provisions contained in other BITs concluded by Bulgaria.[61] In addition, the general statements in the treaty as to the creation of favourable conditions for investments were inconclusive.[62] Furthermore, the practice of Bulgaria had changed in that, after it had ceased to be a communist country it concluded BITs with more generous dispute settlement clauses. However, the renegotiation of the agreement with Cyprus failed and so did not succeed in altering the dispute settlement provision. Thus it could be inferred that the parties did not consider the MFN provision to extend to dispute settlement provisions in other BITs.[63] The tribunal added that the basis of arbitration was consent, and so any agreement offering this option had to show consent clearly and unambiguously, as was the case with the UK Model Agreement, which expressly extended MFN to dispute settlement.[64] Equally, where a specific dispute settlement procedure had been negotiated, it could not be replaced by an entirely different mechanism.[65] Agreeing with the tribunal in *Maffezini*, as to the need to avoid treaty shopping, the tribunal in the present case summarized its view as follows:

[a]n MFN provision in a basic treaty does not incorporate by reference dispute settlement provisions in whole or in part set forth in another treaty, unless the MFN provision in the basic treaty leaves no doubt that the Contracting Parties intended to incorporate them.[66]

From the above, it can be seen that there exists a difference of interpretation regarding the effect of the MFN clause on dispute settlement provisions. The cases that follow *Mafezzini* assume that dispute settlement clauses are included unless explicitly excluded, while the cases that do not establish the opposite approach. It may be said that each case turns on the specific clause before the tribunal and so it does not matter whether different outcomes arise.[67] On the other hand, the starting point in the process of treaty interpretation is significant, in that it can promote the likelihood of a particular outcome. Thus, if a tribunal assumes the MFN clause covers dispute settlement unless this is specifically excluded, the possibility of inclusion is greater and vice versa. The burden of proof will vary according to which approach is preferred. The *Mafezzini* approach places the burden on the respondent to show that it had explicitly and unambiguously excluded the MFN clause from dispute settlement issues, while the *Plama* approach places the burden on the claimant to show the absence of exceptions. In addition, it cannot be assumed that negotiating parties actually considered the

---

[61] ibid at para 189.   [62] ibid at para 193.   [63] ibid at para 195.
[64] ibid at para 204.   [65] ibid at para 209.   [66] ibid at para 223.
[67] See further Freyer and Herlihy above n 39 at 82–83.

implications of the MFN clause in this area when concluding their agreements. Such claims have only arisen very recently while most BITs were negotiated some years ago. Therefore, it may be difficult not to view these cases as revising the agreements in question, by way of judicial creativity, rather than applying them. Indeed, there is a need for sensitivity on the part of tribunals as to the wider impact of the MFN standard. In particular it may be necessary for them to address more clearly the issue of discrimination and to consider whether investors benefiting from different rights under different treaties are actually in like circumstances, so that equality of treatment is objectively justifiable. Such analysis has been conspicuously absent from the awards cited above.[68] Furthermore, it is up to the contracting parties to define more clearly the actual scope of MFN clauses and to clarify when it is not appropriate to use them for the importation of rights from other treaties.[69]

(3) Fair and Equitable Treatment[70]

The fair and equitable treatment standard is shrouded with considerable uncertainty. The concepts of 'fair' and 'equitable' are, to a large extent, interchangeable. 'Fair' is defined, by the *Concise Oxford Dictionary*, as 'just, unbiased, equitable, in accordance with rules'.[71] Thus fairness connotes, among other things, equity. It leaves open the possibility of looking not only at the conduct of the person who must act fairly but also the conduct of the person who is acted upon. Indeed, that would be the implication of the synonymous use of 'equity' in this connection. For if 'equity' means anything it suggests a balancing process and weighing up of what is right in all the circumstances. It is, after all, a word related to the idea of

---

[68] See further Kurtz above n 32 at 883–86 who notes the inclusion of a 'like circumstances' test into Article 4, the MFN provision of the 2004 Canadian Model BIT and a list of exceptions to MFN in Annex III thereof.   [69] See Dolzer and Myers above n 39 at 60.

[70] This text is an adaptation of Peter T Muchlinski '"Caveat Investor"? The Relevance of the Conduct of the Investor Under the Fair and Equitable Treatment Standard' 55 ICLQ 527 (2006). See further UNCTAD *Fair and Equitable Treatment* Series on issues in international investment agreements (New York and Geneva: United Nations, 1999); Steven Vasciannie 'The Fair and Equitable Treatment Standard in International Investment Law and Practice' 70 BYIL 99 (1999) OECD *Fair and Equitable Treatment Standard in International Investment Law* Working Papers on International Investment Law No 2004/3 (Paris: OECD, September 2004) also reproduced as ch 3 of OECD *International Investment Law: A Changing Landscape* (Paris: OECD, 2005); Patrick G Foy and Robert J Deane 'Foreign Investment Protection under Investment treaties: Recent Developments under Chapter 11 of the North American Free Trade Agreement' 16 ICSID Rev-FILJ 299 (2001); J C Thomas 'Reflections on Article 1105 of NAFTA: History, State Practice and the Influence of Commentators' 17 ICSID Rev-FILJ 21 (2002); Patrick Dumberry 'The Quest to define "Fair and Equitable treatment" for Investors under International Law – The Case of the NAFTA Chapter 11 *Pope and Talbot* Awards' 3 JWI 657 (2002); Christoph Schreuer 'Fair and Equitable Treatment in Arbitral Practice' 6 JWIT 357 (2005); Rudolf Dolzer 'Fair and Equitable Treatment: A Key Standard in Investment Treaties' 39 Int'l Law 87 (2005).

[71] *Concise Oxford Dictionary* (Oxford: Clarendon Press, 8th edn, 1990) 420.

'equilibrium' defined as 'a state of physical balance'.[72] In addition 'equity' is itself defined not only as synonymous with 'fairness' but also as 'the application of the principles of justice to correct or supplement the law'.[73] Thus the dictionary definition refers explicitly to a legal usage. Accordingly the meaning of this usage should now be briefly considered. In English law, equitable principles developed to ensure that the unjust effects arising out of a literal and inflexible application of the common law to a case could be avoided.[74] The application of equity by the Chancery was based on a willingness to review the specific facts of a case to determine whether, in that context, the application of a principle of law was proper or whether it had to be replaced by an assessment of what would be right and just on those facts. Accordingly, 'equity', in a legal sense, connotes a degree of flexibility arising out of sensitivity to the need to apply rules with discretion. This meaning of equity is accepted as an aspect of international law.[75]

A purely literal approach to the interpretation of legal terms is often very incomplete. The term in question must be reviewed in the light of the context and policy behind their use. In this connection, it should be recalled that the fair and equitable treatment standard has been described as an evolving one that is not 'frozen in time' and that it is in a constant process of development.[76] Accordingly, the meaning of the standard should be determined in the context of the value system that underlies the international investment protection treaties in which these terms can be found. The need for ensuring a good investment is one issue that will inform the content of the standard. It motivates an investor protection perspective. In addition, it will be necessary to consider the needs of the host country that is charged with the duty to regulate the entry and behaviour of aliens into its territory in the public interest.[77] This duty is based on the inherent international legal right of the sovereign state to regulate conduct that occurs upon its territory. That right pre-exists any limitation thereon created by international agreement. Accordingly, this will motivate a restrictive interpretation of

---

[72] ibid at 396.   [73] ibid.

[74] See further JH Baker *An Introduction to English Legal History* (London: Butterworths, Lexis Nexis, 4th edn, 2002) 105–11. See also FW Maitland *Equity and the Forms of Action at Common Law* (Cambridge: Cambridge University Press, 1929) 1–22.

[75] See Ian Brownlie *Principles of Public International Law* (Oxford: Oxford University Press, 6th edn, 2003) 25. In the *Tunisia-Libya Continental Shelf* case the International Court of Justice (ICJ) held that: 'Application of equitable principles is to be distinguished from a decision *ex aequo et bono*. The Court can take such a decision only on condition that the parties agree (art 38, para 2 of the Statute), and the Court is then freed from the strict application of legal rules in order to bring about an appropriate settlement. The task of the Court in the present case is quite different: it is bound to apply equitable principles as part of international law, and to balance up the various considerations which it regards as relevant in order to produce an equitable result' ICJ Reports (1982) 18 at para 71.

[76] See *ADF Group Inc v United States* above n 12 at paras 179–81, citing *Mondev International Ltd v United States* ICSID Case No Arb (AF)/99/2 award of 11 October 2002: 42 ILM 85 (2003) at paras 114–16.

[77] See generally UNCTAD *World Investment Report 2003* (New York and Geneva: United Nations, 2003) ch V.

the terms in question, as they constitute a qualification of a general principle of international law. The need to balance these two perspectives is essential if IIAs are to operate effectively and with a degree of political legitimacy. Too much investor protection will create an impression that national sovereignty has been given up to control by faceless international tribunals, whose decisions may restrict the regulatory powers of host countries, while too much discretion for the host country will raise fears of bad governance, and a resulting poor investment climate, on the part of investors. Neither outcome is intended by the terms of IIAs.

In addition, there has been much debate on whether the standard should be interpreted in the light of the international minimum standard for the treatment of aliens, or whether it is a self-standing standard.[78] This stems from the fact that IIAs do not adopt a uniform approach to the issue in that some agreements expressly link the fair and equitable treatment standard to international law,[79] while others are silent on the matter and refer only to 'fair and equitable treatment'.[80] Furthermore, arbitral awards are not uniform in this regard.[81] On the one hand, there are pronouncements to the effect that the fair and equitable treatment standard is 'additive' to the international minimum standard,[82] and that it results from an 'autonomous interpretation' of its content based on the text of the particular treaty in which it is found.[83] On the other hand, the NAFTA Free Trade Commission issued a Note of Interpretation on 31 July 2001 which rejected any notion that Article 1105 of NAFTA contained any elements that were 'additive' to the international minimum standard.[84] Moreover, the link between the fair and equitable standard and the international minimum standard has been acknowledged in a number of awards.[85] What is certain, is that some elements of the international minimum standard and the fair and equitable treatment standard overlap, such as the requirements of non-discrimination and due process. However, as UNCTAD points out, state practice indicates that states do not necessarily see the two standards as interchangeable, that the content of the

---

[78] See, for a full discussion, OCED *International Investment Law: A Changing Landscape* (Paris: OECD, 2005) 81–103 or OECD *Fair and Equitable Treatment Standard in International Investment Law* Working Papers on International Investment Law No 2004/3 (Paris: OECD, September 2004).

[79] See, for example, NAFTA Article 1105, US-Uruguay BIT 25 October 2004 in 44 ILM 268 (2005) Article 5 and Annex A. See further UNCTAD *Fair and Equitable Treatment* above n 70 at 31–34.

[80] See, for example, Netherlands-Philippines BIT 1985 Article 3 in UNCTAD *Bilateral Investment Treaties in the Mid 1990s* (New York and Geneva: United Nations) at p.54.

[81] See OECD above n 78.   [82] See *Pope and Talbot v Canada* above n 9 at para 110.

[83] See *Tecmed v Mexico* ICSID Case No Arb (AF)/00/2 award of 29 May 2003: 43 ILM 133 (2004) at para 155. However, the tribunal did not apply this approach and came to its decision by use of the international legal concept of good faith.

[84] The note of interpretation was considered to be mandatory by the tribunal sitting on the damages award in the *Pope and Talbot* case: see *Pope and Talbot v Canada* award in respect of damages, 31 May 2002, available at <http://www.naftaclaims.com> or 41 ILM 1347 (2002). This was confirmed in *Loewen v United States* ICSID Case No Arb (AF)/98/3 award of 26 June 2003: 42 ILM 811 (2003) at para 128.   [85] See *ADF v United States* and *Mondev v United States* above n 76.

international minimum standard has been a matter of controversy between developed and developing states for a considerable period, and so consensus on the interchangeability of the two standards may not be forthcoming without clear discussion, and that these considerations point to the conclusion that the two standards are not synonymous.[86]

To date, arbitral decisions have concentrated on the responsibilities of the host country in its conduct towards the investor. As a result, certain elements of an emergent standard of review of administrative action are taking shape. This standard of review reflects contemporary approaches to good governance. Thus, tribunals have noted that the original customary international law standard, with its emphasis on outrageous mistreatment of the alien, is no longer sufficient.[87] Instead, the correct question is:

[w]hether, at an international level and having regard to generally accepted standards of administration of justice, a tribunal can conclude in the light of all the available facts that the impugned decision was clearly improper and discreditable, with the result that the investment has been subjected to unfair and inequitable treatment.[88]

In the light of this contemporary perspective, it is now reasonably well settled that the standard requires a particular approach to governance, on the part of the host country, that is encapsulated in the obligations to act in a consistent manner, free from ambiguity and in total transparency, without arbitrariness and in accordance with the principle of good faith.[89] In addition, investors can expect due process in the handling of their claims[90] and to have the host authorities act in a manner that is non-discriminatory and proportionate to the policy aims involved.[91] These will

---

[86] UNCTAD *Fair and Equitable Treatment* above n 70 at 39–40.

[87] For example in *USA (LF Neer) v Mexico (Neer Claim)* (1927) AJIL 555 at 556 such treatment was defined as treatment amounting to an 'outrage, to bad faith, to willful neglect of duty, or to an insufficiency of governmental action so far short of international standards that every reasonable and impartial man would readily recognize its insufficiency'. See also *International Thunderbird Gaming Corporation v Mexico* NAFTA Arbitration under UNCITRAL Rules award of 26 January 2006 (available at <http://www.ita.law.uvic.ca>) where the majority of the tribunal suggests that under NAFTA, and the international minimum standard embodied in its fair and equitable treatment provision, Article 1105, only a gross denial of justice or manifest arbitrariness would fall below acceptable international standards (at para 194). This would appear to be more restrictive of the standard than other recent awards. See also the Separate Opinion of Professor Thomas Waelde for an extensive discussion of the scope of the doctrine of legitimate expectations in relation to the standard and its application to the particular facts of the case (available at <http://www.ita. law.uvic.ca>). For comment, see Stephen Fietta 'The "Legitimate Expectations" Principle under Article 1105 NAFTA – *International Thunderbird Gaming Corporation v The United Mexican States*' 7 JWIT 423 (2006) who considers that legitimate expectations may be becoming a self-standing basis of claim under the fair and equitable treatment standard.

[88] *Mondev International Ltd v United States* above n 76 at para 127.

[89] See *Tecmed v Mexico* above n 83 at para 154–5.

[90] See, for example, *Loewen v United States* above n 84.

[91] See *Loewen v United Sates* ibid; *Waste Management Inc v Mexico* ICSID Case No Arb (AF)/00/3 award of 30 April 2004: 43 ILM 967 (2004) at para 98; *MTD Equity v Chile* above n 42 at para 109; *Eureko v Poland* Partial Award 19 August 2005 at paras 231–35.

include the need to observe the goal of creating favourable investment conditions and the observance of the legitimate commercial expectations of the investor.[92] It is not necessary to show bad faith or a deliberate intention to injure the investment so as to show a breach of the standard, although the presence of such factors may aggravate the breach.[93] On the other hand, the standard is case specific and requires a flexible approach given that it offers a general point of departure in formulating an argument that the foreign investor has not been well treated by reason of discriminatory or other unfair measures that have been taken against its interests.[94] Such case-specific flexibility may require an examination not only of governmental but also of investor conduct in a given case.

Such a consideration may be justified by reference to the issue of investment risk. Given the international character of foreign investment it may be said to carry a higher degree of risk than purely domestic investment. Indeed, foreign investment may be characterized as a prime example of high risk-high return investment. Even large multinational enterprises can experience a high level of risk in a host country that is unfamiliar to the firm. Such risk is exacerbated where the country in question is noted for political instability, corruption, and an inefficient system of administration. In these cases it may be especially important for the investor to be able to rely on international standards of treatment, and international systems of dispute settlement, to ensure the full security of its investment. On the other hand, in a market economy, a degree of independent judgment as to the scope of an investment risk will be expected of the investor. Not all investment risks can, or should, be protected against. This may prove inimical to the efficient functioning of a market economy, where the freedom of economic actors to make informed business judgments lies at the heart of the market mechanism. It is up to the firm to determine the risks and to develop an appropriate strategy to deal with them.[95] Any assessment of regulatory fairness will need to be made in the light of this factor. Investor conduct should be considered not only because it may break the chain of causation between the governmental act and the loss to the investor, but as a matter of principle and duty, so as to balance out the emergent duties of the host country to act with proper regard to good regulatory practice. [96]

---

[92] *Tecmed v Mexico* above n 45 at para 156–7; *Saluka v Czech Republic* UNCITRAL Rules Arbitration, Permanent Court of Arbitration, award of 17 March 2006 at paras 302–9 (available at <http://www.ita.law.uvic.ca>); *Thunderbird Gaming Corporation* above n 87.

[93] *Azurix v Argentina* ICSID Case No Arb/01/12 award of 14 July 2006 at para 372 (available at <http://www.ita.law.uvic.ca>).

[94] *Mondev International Ltd v United States* above n 76 at para 118 and *Waste Management* above n 91 at para 99.

[95] See further Christopher A Bartlett, Sumantra Ghoshal, and Julian Birkinshaw *Transnational Management: Text Cases and Readings in Cross-Border Management* (Boston: McGraw Hill Irwin, 4th edn, 2004) ch 3.

[96] I am grateful to William O'Brian of Warwick Law School for raising this issue with me.

It will be said that this approach undermines the protective character of the fair and equitable treatment standard. On the other hand, it cannot be a part of the investor's legitimate expectations that they should be able to avoid losses caused by poor management, by blaming them instead on poor regulation by the host country.[97] The development of such a principle is justified by the view that IIAs 'are not insurance policies against bad business judgments'.[98] In addition, the need to consider investor conduct may arise out of the increased expectations that investors should be good corporate citizens and respect the emergent principles of international corporate social responsibility.[99] These standards can serve to inform the content of what may be regarded as ethical business practice. Failure to meet these minimum ethical standards could act as a factor in determining whether the investor's complaint of unfair and inequitable treatment is properly made out. That is not to say that, whenever the investor falls below these standards of behaviour, the host country authorities are entitled to act in any manner they like. In all cases they must act in accordance with the good governance standards that are inherent in the fair and equitable treatment standard. However, it may allow a tribunal to assess more accurately whether the regulatory action in question was proportionate and whether the nature of the investor's conduct entitled the regulator to interfere with the investor's rights.

At the substantive level, certain trends can be discerned in the decisions that point to the need for an investor to take care in how they act if they are to benefit from the full protection and security of their investment under an IIA. These may be classified around three apparently emergent duties: a duty to refrain from unconscionable conduct, a duty to engage in the investment in the light of an adequate knowledge of its risks, and a duty to conduct business in a reasonable manner. Where unconscionable conduct is found, this may have serious consequences for any claim made by the investor. Evidence of such conduct may vitiate any right to a claim, especially if the regulatory response that is being challenged arises out of the application, by the host country, of its powers to punish the conduct through an interference with the investment. On the other hand, given that the second and third duties may be said to lie in a general duty of care in the conduct of foreign investment business, rather than in a strong moral abhorrence of certain types of conduct, the consequences of a failure to comply may be less serious. Here evidence of failure to comply may result in a reduction of compensation commensurate with the causal connection between the investor's conduct and the degree of loss that can be attributed to that conduct, rather than to any

---

[97] Indeed, the legitimate expectations of the investor will be bounded by the objective state of the applicable law as the investor found it at the time of entering into the investment. In addition, the investor cannot require the host country to determine or organize the law in any particular manner See, for fuller discussion, Dozer above n 70 at 102–103.

[98] *Maffezini v Spain* Case No Arb/97/7 award of 13 November 2000: 16 ICSID Rev-FILJ 248 (2001) at para 64.   [99] On which see further ch 3 at 100–104.

alleged abuse of regulatory powers on the part of the host country. Each emergent duty is briefly discussed in turn.[100]

The principle of unconscionability recognizes that certain kinds of conduct have no place in good commercial practice. Accordingly fraud, misrepresentation, undue influence, or abuse of power on the part of an investor may all form the basis of a legitimate interference with their rights to conduct the investment. In such cases even the outright termination of the investment may be justified, provided it is a proportionate response to the impugned action.[101] Such a right may extend to cases involving corrupt practices;[102] other irregular dealings with officials;[103] misrepresentation as to competence to undertake the investment;[104] and lack of candour and transparency on the part of the investor.[105] Finally, the principle of unconscionability may require that the investor does not abuse a superior bargaining position with the host country to extract unduly beneficial promises and other advantages for the investment from it.[106]An example of this comes from the *ELSI* case.[107]

In that case, a Sicilian electronics company, ELSI, was wholly owned and controlled by two US corporations, Raytheon, which owned 99.16 per cent of the shares and Machlett, a wholly owned subsidiary of Raytheon, which owned the remaining 0.84 per cent. ELSI had ceased to be a profitable investment. Between 1964 and 1966 it had made an insufficient operating profit to cover its debts and accumulated losses. This required the company to reduce its equity under Italian law. That was done in 1966 and again in 1967. The US parent companies blamed this situation in part on over-manning and decided to embark upon a series of redundancies. Given ELSI's significance as a major employer in an otherwise economically underdeveloped region, these job losses caused considerable unrest and, eventually, led to strikes and an occupation of the plant in 1968. At the same

---

[100] For full discussion of the cases, see further Peter T Muchlinski above n 70.

[101] See, for example, *Azanian v Mexico* ICSID Case No Arb(AF)/97/2 award of 1 November 1999; 14 ICSID Rev-FILJ 538 (1999). See in particular *Inceysa Vallisoletana SL v El Salvador* ICSID Case No Arb/03/26 Decision on Jurisdiction, 2 August 2006, summary of counsel for El Salvador: held that where the claimant obtained a concession contract through fraud they could not bring a claim for breach of the applicable BIT against the termination of the concession on the ground that the concession was not obtained 'in accordance with the law' as required for the protection of the BIT to apply. The ICSID Tribunal therefore had no jurisdiction to hear the claim: <http://ita.law.uvic.ca/documents/InceysaDescription.pdf>.

[102] See for discussion rejecting this claim on the facts *SPP v Egypt* ICSID Case No Arb/84/3 award of 20 May 1992: 8 ICSID Rev-FILJ 328 (1993) at paras 127–28 and the dissenting opinion of arbitrator Mohamed Amin El Mahdi who felt there was sufficient evidence: 8 ICSID Rev-FILJ 400 at 461–72 (1993). See also *Olguin v Paraguay* ICSID Case No Arb/98/5 award of 26 July 2001 available at <http://www.worldbank.org/icsid/cases> or 18 ICSID Rev-FILJ 143 (2003).

[103] *Feldman v Mexico* dissent of Judge Bravo: 18 ICSID Rev-FILJ 580 (2003).

[104] *Azanian v Mexico* above n 101; *SPP v Egypt* above n 102 at paras 113–25.

[105] *Genin v Estonia* ICSID Case No Arb/99/2 award of 25 June 2001 available at <http://www.worldbank.org/icsid> or 17 ICSID Rev-FILJ 395 (2002).

[106] On the question of coercion of the investor by the host country, see ch 15 at 585–87 above.

[107] *Elettronica Sicula SpA (ELSI) United States v Italy* [1989] ICJ Reports 15.

time, the US parents planned an orderly liquidation of the company under Italian law, while also trying to save the plant by way of negotiations with local and national authorities in Italy. The US parents had hoped that an Italian public sector partner could enter into ownership of the company and that regional aid could be obtained. According to the majority of the ICJ, this dual track policy had a 'Janus-like character' as the management of ELSI hoped that 'the threat of closure and dismissal of the workforce might bring such pressures to bear on the Italian authorities to persuade them to provide what Raytheon had long hoped for: an influential Italian partner, new capital and Mezzogiorno benefits'.[108] While not amounting to a finding of actual coercion on the part of the investors, the attention paid by the ICJ to the context of negotiations suggests that, in appropriate cases, the conduct of the investor during negotiations with the host country could be taken into account when determining whether their claim against the host country is valid. Although the investment in ELSI was unprofitable, it can be said that the US parents still had a stronger bargaining position in that they could afford to walk away from the investment, while the Italian authorities were faced with a major regional economic and social catastrophe that they had to remedy.[109]

A duty to assess reasonably the risk of the proposed investment in the proposed host country, entails that the investor has realistic expectations as to its actual profitability,[110] and to be on notice of both the prospects and pitfalls of an investment voluntarily undertaken in a high risk-high return location. Thus in *Generation Ukraine v Ukraine*[111] the tribunal noted that:

The Claimant was attracted to the Ukraine because the possibility of earning a rate of return on its capital in significant excess to other investment opportunities in more developed countries. The Claimant thus invested in the Ukraine on notice of both prospects and potential pitfalls. The investment was speculative . . . the Claimant had undoubtedly experienced frustration and delay caused by bureaucratic incompetence and recalcitrance in various forms. But equally, the Claimant had managed to secure a 49-year leasehold over prime commercial property in the centre of Kyiv without having participated in a competitive tender and without having made any substantial payment to the Ukrainian authorities.[112]

As for the duty to conduct the business in a reasonable manner, international tribunals have made a distinction between loss caused by regulatory taking, and/or unfair and/or inequitable governmental action, and that caused by bad

---

[108] ibid at para 81.

[109] One issue that may need to be determined is how negotiations at the pre-entry stage might affect subsequent negotiations between the investor and the host country.

[110] *Olguin v Paraguay* above n 102; *Genin v Estonia* above n 105; *MTD Equity v Chile* above n 42 where the compensation for the breach of the fair and equitable treatment standard was reduced by 50 per cent on this ground.

[111] ICSID Case No Arb/00/9 award of 16 September 2003 available at <http://www.worldank.org/icsid> or 44 ILM 404 (2005).   [112] ibid para 20.37.

business management. The leading example is the *ELSI* case.[113] The United States alleged inter alia a breach of the US-Italy FCN Treaty on the ground that the response of the Mayor of Palermo to the impending closure of the plant, by requisitioning it, amounted to a violation of Article III(2), in that this deprived Raytheon and Machlett of the right to control and manage their investment as protected under that provision. The ICJ held that this claim had not been made out because, by the time the plant had been requisitioned, the parent companies had become unable to control, or to manage, the investment in a way that could lead to an orderly liquidation under Italian law.[114] In particular, no causal link had been established between the requisition and the effects on ELSI attributed to it by the United States. There were numerous causes acting together leading to what the ICJ termed the 'disaster at ELSI'. However, the underlying cause was held to be 'ELSI's headlong course towards insolvency; which state of affairs it seems to have attained even prior to the requisition'.[115] The Court continued:

There was the warning loudly proclaimed about its precarious position; there was the socially damaging decision to terminate the business, close the plant and dismiss the work-force; there was the position of the banks as major creditors. In short the possibility of the solution of orderly liquidation, which Raytheon and Machlett claim to have been deprived of as a result of the requisition, is purely a matter of speculation.[116]

This is a clear indication that the ICJ was strongly influenced by the evidence of management conduct when coming to its conclusion. In particular, the Court emphasizes the socially damaging effects of the closure, apparently suggesting that wider stakeholder interests may be relevant in determining how management is conducted. Such an approach would be consistent with recent guidelines on corporate responsibility.[117] This, coupled with the Court's highlighting of the 'arm-twisting' of the Italian authorities to assist in the continued operation of a plant that was never economically self-sufficient and never paid any dividends,[118] suggests that the real problem with ELSI was not only that the parent companies failed to manage the plant profitably, but that they also contributed to its ultimate

[113] Above n 107.

[114] This conclusion was strongly opposed by Judge Schwebel, who held, in his dissenting opinion, that the parent companies had not lost their ability to manage but had that ability thwarted by the acts of the Italian authorities.   [115] Above n 107 at para 101.

[116] ibid.

[117] For example, the OECD *Guidelines for Multinational Enterprises* would support such an approach by reference to Guideline II 'General Policies' which includes in para 4 an obligation to '[e]ncourage human capital formation, in particular by creating employment opportunities and facilitating training opportunities for employees'. However, the guidelines, as interpreted, do not prevent the closure of unprofitable facilities provided that such closure is undertaken in accordance with local laws and practices, that reasonable notice is given the employees and government authorities and that firms co-operate to the greatest possible extent in the mitigation of any adverse social effects: see ch 12 at 483–84.

[118] See text at n 108 above. See also the discussion of the case in Andreas F Lowenfeld *International Economic Law* (Oxford: Oxford University Press, paperback edn, 2003) 435–38.

downfall and to the major social consequences that this entailed. In these circumstances the act of requisition could not be said to have violated the FCN Treaty as being unreasonable or capricious. Indeed, even though the Italian courts had overruled the act of requisition on the ground of excess of powers, the Court did not find any arbitrariness in that act.[119]

The approach, taken by the ICJ in the *ELSI* case, has been endorsed by a recent ICSID Tribunal in *Noble Ventures Inc v Romania*.[120] On facts reminiscent of the *ELSI* case, the tribunal held that the claimant could not make out a claim that Romania had breached the fair and equitable treatment standard, or the expropriation provision, under the US-Romania BIT. The claimant had invested in the privatization of a major iron and steel works (CSR) located in the Resita region, which employed some 4000 workers. The claimant alleged, inter alia, that the respondent country had undermined the economic viability of the investment, through the failure of the relevant privatization authorities to secure the restructuring of CSR's debts, and by reason of its subsequent legal proceedings to effect a judicial reorganization of the company. The tribunal rejected these claims by reference to the investor's conduct. It held that Noble Ventures was as much to blame for this situation as the state privatization authority. If the claimant had believed that the restructuring was a mere formality then the claimant's assumption was fundamentally flawed.[121] On the evidence, it was clear that without the restructuring, the collapse of CSR was 'all too readily foreseeable'.[122] In addition, the claimant refused to invest any of its own funds in the restructuring process, and had defaulted on repayments on a loan facility provided by a consortium of Spanish banks, which could have provided finance for the restructuring. As a result, the claimant had failed to fulfil its promises to pay the workforce, whose wages were in serious arrears. In the circumstances, as in the *ELSI* case, the judicial reorganization of the works could be seen as the only short-term solution to the 'social crisis' that had engulfed Resita as a result of the claimant's inability to pay the workforce.[123] Given that, in addition, the judicial reorganization of CSR had been carried out without arbitrariness or discrimination, and had not been aimed at rescinding the Privatization Agreement between the parties, it was neither a breach of the fair and equitable standard, nor was it an expropriation of the claimant's investment.

In addition, as part of the general duty to conduct investment in a reasonable manner, tribunals expect investors to be aware of the regulatory environment and the possibility of regulatory change in the absence of assurances to the contrary,[124]

---

[119] But see the dissent of Judge Schwebel, who held that the act of requisition was arbitrary as the parent companies had not lost their ability to manage.

[120] ICSID Case No Arb/01/11, award of 12 October 2005, available at <http://www.ita.law.uvic.ca>.   [121] ibid at para 147.

[122] ibid at para 152.   [123] ibid para 177.

[124] See *Methanex v United States*, n 12 above. Contrast *Occidental Exploration and Production Co v Ecuador* n 12 above at paras 183–85 where a change in the regulatory framework, that was known to

to comply with local regulatory requirements affecting the admission of the investment, such as an environmental impact assessment,[125] and to take relevant professional advice.[126]

Finally, a duty of good management may require that legal disputes be taken before effective national dispute settlement bodies. Thus, in the *Feldman* case, the tribunal suggested that, as part of the process of clarification of the applicable tax measures, the claimant should have availed himself of local procedures.[127] Similarly, in the *Generation Ukraine* case the tribunal, citing the *Feldman* case, stressed the need for the investor to make a reasonable effort to obtain the legal correction of an administrative fault. Failure to do so could not turn the alleged fault into a breach of the BIT. In the absence of any per se violation of the BIT arising out of the conduct of the local authorities, the only possible violation of the BIT would be a denial of justice before the host country courts.[128] Such awards raise the possibility that the local remedies rule, a principle of international law that has been deliberately omitted from most BITs and other types of IIA, is being introduced by the back door.[129] This view may be strengthened if the duty to take effective legal measures for the review of local administrative and judicial action is built into the substantive standards of protection in BITs and other IIAs. Thus in the *Waste Management* case, the tribunal, while acknowledging that the procedural requirement to exhaust local remedies had been dispensed with by NAFTA Chapter 11, went on to say that 'the availability of local remedies to an investor faced with contractual breaches is nonetheless relevant to the question whether a standard such as Article 1105(1) has been complied with by the

the investor at the time they entered into the investment, was held to violate the fair and equitable treatment standard.

[125] *Maffezini v Spain* above n 98 at paras 70–71.

[126] *Feldman v Mexico* above n 5 at paras 25–132; *ADF v United States* above n 12.

[127] ibid para 134.

[128] Above n 111 at para 20.30. See also *Compania de Aguas del Aconquija SA and Compagnie Générale des Eaux (Vivendi) v Argentine Republic* ICSID Case No Arb/97/3 award of 21 November 2000 available at <http://www.worldbank.org/icsid> or 40 ILM 426 (2001) at para 80. Award annulled for manifest excess of powers for not examining the merits of the case: Decision on Annulment available at <http://www.worlkbank.org/icsid> or 41 ILM 1135 (2002). The Annulment Tribunal held: 'Claimants should not have been deprived of a decision, one way or another, merely on the strength of the observation that the local courts could conceivably have provided them with a remedy, in whole or in part. Under the BIT they had a choice or remedies.' (at para 114).

[129] See Christoph Schreuer 'Calvo's Grandchildren: The Return of Local Remedies in Investment Arbitration' 4 Law and Practice of International Courts and Tribunals 1 at 13–16 (2005). See also UNCTAD *Dispute Settlement: Investor State* Series on issues in international investment agreements (New York and Geneva: United Nations, 2003) at 32–34; P Peters 'Exhaustion of Local Remedies: Ignored in Most Bilateral Investment Treaties' vol XLIV Netherlands International Law Review 233 (1997); for a defence of the need to exhaust local remedies where a BIT is silent on the issue see M Sornarajah *The International Law on Foreign Investment* (Cambridge: Cambridge University Press, 2nd edn, 2004) 253–55. Note that in the *ELSI* case the ICJ held that the US-Italy FCN Treaty, which was silent on the need to exhaust local remedies, did not thereby oust the local remedies rule: above n 107 at para 50. However, that case involved a state-to-state dispute not an investor-state dispute.

State'.[130] It went on to examine the legal proceedings that had taken place in Mexico and concluded that there had not been a denial of justice in violation of the fair and equitable treatment standard.[131]

This approach may create a number of problems.[132] First, it is not clear whether recourse to domestic remedies is a general prerequisite of the fair and equitable treatment standard (or any other substantive standard, for that matter) or an element in proving that the standard has been violated due to a denial of due process before local tribunals. Secondly, to introduce such a substantive requirement may weaken the aim of providing for delocalized dispute settlement procedures under an IIA, as an inducement for investment promotion under the agreement. The exclusion of local remedies may also extend, in certain exceptional circumstances, to agreements that have an exhaustion of local remedies requirement by virtue of the application of the most favoured nation (MFN) treatment clause.[133] Such an application of the MFN principle might not be possible if the substantive requirement gathers pace in arbitral case law. It would be nonsense to require the use of local remedies as a substantive element of the fair and equitable treatment standard while, at the same time, excluding it through the MFN principle. Thirdly, it is unclear how a requirement to use local remedies would combine with a 'fork-in-the-road' provision, requiring the investor to choose between domestic tribunals and international arbitration. According to Professor Schreuer, once the investor has taken the dispute to the national courts that would rule out subsequent access to the international forum.[134] On the other hand, it would appear that such a choice would not preclude the investor from bringing an international claim for breach of fair and equitable treatment under an IIA, if the national procedure fails to meet the minimum due process standard demanded by that principle. In such a case, it is not the underlying investment dispute that founds the international case but the very fact that the national procedures, charged with its resolution, have failed to meet international treaty standards. Equally, it is not open to a tribunal to avoid examining the merits of a case merely because local remedies might be available, as it is charged with the specific task of examining whether or not the applicable IIA has been violated. To do otherwise is to deprive the claimant of their rights under the applicable agreement.[135]

On the other hand, the inclusion of the need to use local remedies can help to strike a balance between the rights of the investor and the right of the host country to regulate the investment, including through the provision of adequate national

---

[130] Above n 91 at para 116.　　　[131] See also, to similar effect, *Azanian v Mexico* above n 101.

[132] See Schreuer above n 129 at 15–16 on which this discussion draws.

[133] See *Maffezini v Spain* ICSID Case No Arb/97/7 decision on objections to jurisdiction 25 January 2000: 16 ICSID Rev-FILJ 212 (2001).　　　[134] Above n 129 at 16.

[135] See *Compania de Aguas del Aconquija SA and Compagnie Générale des Eaux (Vivendi) v Argentine Republic* Decision in Annulment above n 128 above.

remedies for investors.[136] In addition, in settling disputes, it is wise to use the procedure that is least likely to damage long-term goodwill between the disputants, assuming that they wish to continue with their relationship. Thus, in the case of investment disputes, an ascending order of dispute settlement techniques may be called for beginning with negotiation and other alternative dispute resolution methods, national arbitral and/or judicial dispute settlement and, finally, international dispute settlement. Provided the host country can offer reliable and effective dispute settlement systems it may be in the long-term interests of both parties to have recourse to local courts and tribunals first. The giving of precedence to international dispute settlement as a first option may serve only to escalate disputes, increase legal costs, and to lessen the chances of the investment relationship surviving, especially if the host country community perceives the delocalization of the dispute as being politically illegitimate. By way of conclusion on this point, it may be said that recent case law developments suggest that investors should have a duty to use local remedies as an aspect of good corporate citizenship and good management practice, in return for the host country providing proper and effective means of redress, with international dispute settlement remaining available, as an option of last resort, to determine whether essential due process standards have been observed at the national level.

This discussion has deliberately stressed the role of investor conduct rather than rehearse the decisions on governmental conduct, which have been summarized above. Ample literature already exists analysing the tribunal decisions from this perspective and it would be futile to add yet another rendition of the same points here.[137] Instead, the aim is to move the discussion of the fair and equitable standard forward by asking some fundamental questions about the balance between governmental and investor duties. This would appear especially important given the increasing role of private investors in public-private partnerships, where the investor has taken on roles that were previously within the exclusive domain of a public service provider. Indeed, many of the arbitral awards cited in this, and the preceding sections, have arisen in the context of such partnerships and it would appear, from the reasoning adopted by tribunals, that investor conduct is a significant factor to be taken into account alongside governmental conduct.

---

[136] It should be remembered that the deliberate exclusion of the local remedies rule from IIAs is based on the concern that national dispute settlement bodies, in developing host countries in particular, may be unable to deal adequately or impartially with investor-state disputes (but see the *Loewen* case above n 84 which involved the apparently developed legal jurisdiction of the State of Mississippi). As national legal systems evolve to meet the challenges of attracting investors, such a concern may become less important over time.　　　　[137] See the references in n 70 above.

(4) Full Protection and Security

Most BITs and other IIAs contain clauses providing for the compensation of the investor for losses due to armed conflict or internal disorder. These do not establish an absolute right to compensation. Rather, they lay down that the investor shall be treated in accordance with the national treatment and/or MFN standard in the matter of compensation. Some treaties, for example the German model treaty, deal with such compensation in a single provision, which also deals with compensation for expropriation.[138] Others deal with these two types of compensation in separate provisions.[139] This may be preferable as compensation for expropriation is not measured by reference to national treatment or MFN standards, but by reference to the standard of 'prompt, adequate and effective compensation'.[140] Most BITs guarantee the free transfer of compensation to the investor's home country.[141]

The scope of the host country's responsibility for such losses has been the subject of a number of ICSID arbitrations. The first was *Asian Agricultural Products Ltd v Republic of Sri Lanka*, [142] where the terms of the UK-Sri Lanka BIT of 13 February 1980, relating to the destruction of the claimant's property, were considered. The tribunal rejected the claimant's argument that the treaty established a 'strict liability' standard for such damage, preferring an approach based on customary international law, whereby the liability of the host state should be determined by reference to a 'due diligence' standard.[143] However, the tribunal established that the respondent state was liable to pay some compensation on the basis of Article 4(1) of the treaty, which applied the national treatment and MFN standards to compensation for losses owing to war or other armed conflict, in that the respondent was obliged under general international law to compensate for such loss where a failure to meet the due diligence standard was involved. This decision was met with a strong dissenting opinion from Dr SKB Asante, who felt that the majority had misunderstood Article 4(1), that they could not apply its terms in the absence of consideration as to whether the respondent

---

[138] See art 4.

[139] Eg UK-Philippines BIT note 36 above art V (compensation for expropriation), art VI (compensation for loss due to war, other armed conflicts, revolution, national emergency, revolt, insurrection, or riot).

[140] See *Asian Agricultural Products Ltd v Republic of Sri Lanta* n 32 above at 653–54.(dissenting opinion of Dr SKB Asante).   [141] UNCTC 1988 above n 21 para 201 at 47.

[142] Above n 32.

[143] See also *Wena Hotels v Egypt* ICSID Case No Arb/98/4 award of 8 December 2000 available at <http://www.worldbaank.org/icsid> or 41 ILM896 (2002) at para 84; *Saluka v Czech Republic* above n 92 at paras 483–84: 'Accordingly, the standard obliges the host State to adopt all reasonable measures to protect assets and property from threats or attacks which may target particularly foreigners or certain groups of foreigners. The practice of arbitral tribunals seems to indicate, however, that the "full security and protection" clause is not meant to cover just any kind of impairment of an investor's investment, but to protect more specifically the physical integrity of an investment against interference by use of force.'

had in fact paid compensation to its nationals or to nationals of third states under its laws, and that, in any case, the facts did not justify a holding that the respondent had failed to act with due diligence.

More recently the tribunal in *AMT v Zaire*[144] reviewed the basis upon which a claimant could recover for loss and damage to its property. In that case American Manufacturing and Trading (AMT) claimed that Zaire had violated its rights under the US-Zaire BIT by failing to compensate it for property damage and losses caused by the irregular activities of members of the Zairian armed forces in 1991 and 1993. AMT sought the fair market value of the losses, which it put at $14.3 million, with additional sums for lost profits and 8 per cent interest plus costs. The Government of Zaire argued that it had discharged its obligations by reason of the fact that it did not treat AMT any less favourably than it treated other investors, whether nationals or from other countries. The tribunal rejected this defence. It found that Zaire had violated Article II of the BIT, in that it had failed to observe its obligation of vigilance in protecting the property of the claimant.[145] Indeed, Zaire had taken no measures to ensure the protection and security of AMT's investments. Its omission to do so amounted to a case of *res ipsa loquitur*. The fact that it had also failed to protect the investments of investors from third states was irrelevant.[146] The losses were caused by members of the Zairian armed forces, acting individually, and not in their official capacity. Thus, the losses did not fall under the combat operations exception to the full peace and security standard. The fact that they had been pardoned by the President of Zaire acting on his own was also irrelevant.[147] Turning to the question of compensation, the tribunal noted that this was not a case of expropriation, but one of loss and damage to property. Thus the method of assessing compensation could not be assimilated to that used in cases of expropriation. Accordingly, the claimant's basis of calculation, using the fair market value method, was rejected.[148] Instead, the actual loss, based on the actual market value of the damaged and lost property, would apply, taking into account the realities of the political and economic risks faced by the claimant in a country like Zaire.[149] In the end the tribunal awarded AMT a total sum of $9 million excluding lost profits, which were held to be too uncertain to offer a solid basis for measurement.[150]

---

[144] ICSID Case No Arb/93/1 award of 21 February 1997 available at <http://www.worldbank.org/icside> or 36 ILM 1531 (1997). See also *Wena Hotels v Egypt* above n 143 where the seizure of the claimant's two hotels, by the Egyptian partner in the investment, was seen to violate the full protection and security standard as Egypt had failed to discharge its duty of vigilance and due diligence in protecting the hotels, despite knowledge of the intention to seize them, and by subsequently failing to restore them to their owners with suitable reparations: see paras 85–95. In *Saluka* n 92 above, the tribunal held that the suspension of trading of the claimant's shares, the prohibition of transfers of its shares; and the police searches of premises occupied by the claimant's parent did not constitute violations of the standard in the circumstances of the case as these actions were motivated by legitimate regulatory concerns and the police searches were the subject of judicial review proceedings.
[145] ibid at para 6.05. [146] ibid at para 6.09–6.10. [147] ibid at paras 7.10–7.11.
[148] ibid at para 7.03. [149] ibid at paras 7.13 and 7.16–7.17.
[150] ibid at paras 7.14 and Point 4 of the decisions of the tribunal.

(5) Compensation in Cases Other Than Expropriation

The basis of compensation for breach of the full protection and security standard has already been discussed in the previous section. Here it remains to consider the approach taken to the measurement of compensation in cases of discrimination and breach of fair and equitable treatment. In such cases, the damage suffered is not usually related to contractual types of loss, such as loss of market value or going concern value, for which an expropriation would have to occur.[151] It relates to the difference between the legitimate expectations of the investor as to the treatment he shall receive and the actual treatment he has experienced at the hands of the host country authorities and which amounts to a breach of the relevant treatment standard.[152]

In such cases, the proper measure of compensation is the amount of loss or damage that is adequately connected with the breach or that is required to satisfy the claim.[153] In all cases the tribunal must be mindful of the general principle of full indemnification for the international wrong that underlies international law in this regard.[154] The tribunal has a measure of discretion, especially as most BITs and other agreements, such as NAFTA, offer no guidance, outside the expropriation provision, as to the appropriate measure of damages or compensation.[155] In some cases, this may lead to the adoption of the fair market value standard as where the result of the breach is akin to an expropriation, in that the investor sustains important long-term losses.[156] In other cases, it will be the difference between the actual value of the investment, had the governmental authority acted properly, and the degree to which that has been damaged by the act of discrimination or unfairness. Thus, for example, in the case of *Feldman v Mexico*, the tribunal found that the claimant's only proven head of loss was the amount of unpaid tax rebates that would have been granted had the tax authorities not acted in a discriminatory manner. However, the claims for lost profits were rejected for lack of proof and the claim for loss of going concern value was held to be inappropriate, as it required a finding of expropriation.[157] Certain further general principles will apply to such cases. In particular, the burden will be on the claimant to prove the quantum of losses in respect of which it puts forward its claims, compensation will only be paid for harm that is proved to have a sufficient causal link to with the specific treaty provision that has been breached, the

---

[151] See *Feldman v Mexico* above n 5 at paras 194–98.

[152] See Thomas Waelde 'Damages in Investment Arbitration: Are the Standards Different from Commercial Arbitration? The Need for Consistency' 6 JWIT 51 at 54–55 (2005).

[153] ibid.

[154] See *SD Myers v Canada* above n 6 at paras 310–11 citing the *Chorzow Factory* case on which see text in ch 15 at 610.

[155] *CMS Gas Transmission Co v Argentina* ICSID Case No Arb/01/8 award of 12 May 2005: 44 ILM 1205 (2005) at para 409.   [156] ibid at para 410.

[157] *Feldman v Mexico* above n 5 at paras 198–207.

resulting economic losses must be proved to have arisen out of that breach and not from other causes, and damages for breach of one treaty provision must take into account any damages already awarded under another treaty provision so as to prevent double recovery.[158]

Concluding Remarks

This chapter has reviewed recent developments in the interpretation of specific investor protection standards other than expropriation. These have been based on the surge in arbitral decisions, especially under the NAFTA dispute settlement system and as a result of the Argentine economic crisis.[159] The findings of the tribunals have generated concern that governmental actions, that may be entirely legitimate from a public policy perspective, are being subjected to undue international review. On the other hand, it may be said that these decisions are the beginning of an international law on the review of administrative action that seeks to ensure better governance in the field of foreign investment, to the benefit not only of the investor and their investments, but also to the host country by ensuring an improved investment climate. Whichever position is taken, there can be little doubt that the first generation IIAs, that form the basis of these claims, will need to be reconsidered by contracting parties in the light of arbitral developments, and in the light of the legitimate regulatory interests of host countries. The implications of such a possible reconsideration will be examined further in the next chapter, as part of the wider discussion of the contents and drafting issues surrounding IIAs.

---

[158] *SD Myers v Canada* above n 6 at para 316.
[159] See UNCTAD *IIA Monitor No 4 (2005)* 'Latest Developments in Investor-State Dispute Settlement' (UNCTAD/WEB/ITE/2005/2) at 3–4.

17

The Codification of International Standards
For the Treatment of Foreign Investors

The aim of this chapter is to consider attempts at the codification of agreed international standards by which relations between MNEs and host states can be regulated. Such attempts have been made in the context of conflicts between states over the content and legal validity of international minimum standards for the treatment of aliens and their property, already briefly discussed in chapter 15.[1] The result of these conflicts has been uncertainty as to the content of customary international law in the field of foreign investment. Indeed, in the *Barcelona Traction* case, the ICJ maintained that there was no single accepted body of international law that laid down universally accepted standards for the treatment of foreign investors by host states.[2] The Court saw the reason for this as lying in a period of 'an intense conflict of systems and interests' between states, from which no generally accepted rules of international law in the field could emerge on the basis of an *opinio juris* among states. Such standards as applied were the product of bilateral agreements between states and, therefore, could not bind other states.

Against this background numerous attempts have been made over time to develop an agreed international code for the regulation of foreign investor/host state relations. To date, however, no universal codification of the international law on foreign investment exists. Nonetheless, significant numbers of bilateral investment treaties (BITs), bilateral free trade agreements with investment provisions (FTAs), and regional economic integration agreements with investment provisions (REAs) are in place.[3] In addition, as seen in chapter 6, certain OECD and WTO agreements also seek to cover investment issues as regards the liberalization of market access. Thus it would be wrong to say that there are no authoritative international legal instruments that point to the content of international investment law norms. In order to cover this issue, this chapter will be divided

---

[1] See above at 597–99. See further Charles Lipson *Standing Guard: Protecting Foreign Capital in the Nineteenth and Twentieth Centuries* (University of California Press, 1985).

[2] *The Barcelona Traction, Light and Power Company, Limited* (New Application: 1962) (*Belgium v Spain*) second phase, judgment of 5 February 1970, ICJ Reports 1970 3 at 46–47 paras 89–90.

[3] According to UNCTAD by the end of 2004 some 2392 BITs had been concluded of which 70 per cent had been signed. By the end of April 2005 some 212 bilateral, regional and inter-regional trade and investment agreements had also been concluded, most of which had been concluded after 1990: *World Investment Report 2005* (New York and Geneva: United Nations, 2005) 24–30.

into two main parts. The first will trace the development of standard setting initiatives in this field, so as to build up a clearer historical picture of the norm creation process. The second part will then analyse the principal types of provisions that are commonly found in international investment agreements (IIAs). The third part will then consider the legal effect of IIAs within national legal systems.

(1) The Development of International Standards

Initially, attempts at the codification of international standards for the treatment of investors sought the conclusion of a multilateral convention under the auspices of an international organization. Such attempts were made periodically between the 1920s and the early 1960s.[4] Thus, in 1929, the League of Nations held a diplomatic conference for the purpose of concluding an international convention on the treatment of foreigners and foreign enterprises.[5] This was followed in 1930 by the Hague Conference on the Codification of International Law, which included the subject of the responsibility of states for damage caused in their territory to the person or property of foreigners.[6] Neither initiative met with success, due to the refusal of Latin American, East European, and ex-colonial states to accept the traditional international minimum standards of treatment insisted upon by the capital-exporting states.[7]

After the Second World War attempts at a general multilateral treaty, that included a code on the protection of foreign investment, were revived.[8] The major attempt was the Charter of the International Trade Organization signed at Havana, Cuba, on 24 March 1948. The charter contained a number of provisions relevant to the regulation of foreign investment by corporations, including proposals for the control of restrictive business practices,[9] provisions protecting the security of foreign investments,[10] and an assertion of the right of capital-importing

---

[4] See generally AA Fatouros 'An International Code to Protect Private Investment – Proposals and Perspectives' 14 U of Toronto LJ 77 (1961); Miller 'Protection of Private Foreign Investment by Multilateral Convention' 53 AJIL 371 (1959); Snyder 'Protection of Private Foreign Investment: Examination and Appraisal' 10 ICLQ 469 (1961); Boyle 'Some Proposals for a World Investment Convention' [1961] JBL 18,155.

[5] See Cutler 'The Treatment of Foreigners in Relation to the Draft Convention and Conference of 1929' 27 AJIL 225 (1933); Kuhn 'The International Conference on the Treatment of Foreigners' 24 AJIL 570 (1930); Potter 'International Legislation on the Treatment of Foreigners' 24 AJIL 748 (1930). For the proceedings of the conference, see League of Nations Doc C.97 M.23 1930 II; for the text of the draft convention under discussion, see League of Nations Doc C.174 M.53 1928 II.

[6] See Hackworth 'Responsibility of States for Damages Caused in Their Territory to the Person or Property of Foreigners' 24 AJIL 500 (1930).   [7] See Lipson above n 1 at 75–76.

[8] See Fatouros above n 3 at 79–81.

[9] Havana Charter art V. See further ch 10 above at 417–18. Lockwood 'Proposed International Legislation with Respect to Business Practices' XLI AJIL 616 (194).

[10] Havana Charter art 11(1)(b): '. . . no member shall take unreasonable or unjustified action within its territories injurious to the rights and interests of nationals of other Members in the enterprise, skills, capital, arts or technology which they have supplied.'; ibid art 12(2)(a)(i): provision

states to control the conditions of entry and establishment for inward investment.[11] The inclusion of this right, and the absence of any unequivocal provision
for compensation in the case of expropriation, caused widespread opposition to the
Havana Charter among business interests and led, ultimately, to its demise when
the United States and other signatory states did not ratify it.[12]

Thereafter, attempts at stimulating interest in a multilateral convention on
foreign investment were made mainly by private sector bodies, including the ICC
and various pressure groups.[13] In particular, in 1957, the German Society to
Advance the Protection of Foreign Investments published a draft code entitled
'International Convention for the Mutual Protection of Private Property Rights in
Foreign Countries'.[14] In early 1958, another privately inspired draft convention on
foreign investments came from a group of European international lawyers headed
by Sir Hartley Shawcross.[15] These two initiatives were combined into a single draft
convention in 1959.[16] This convention was taken up by the then OEEC (now
OECD) for consideration. It led to the OECD Draft Convention on the
Protection of Foreign Property.[17] However, this draft convention failed to achieve
sufficient support to be opened for signature, owing to the reluctance of the less
developed members of the Organization (such as inter alia Greece, Portugal, and
Turkey) to bind themselves to some of the proposed provisions, in view of their
heavy leaning towards the interests of capital exporters.[18] Instead, the Council of
the OECD, by a resolution adopted on 12 October 1967, commended the draft

of reasonable security for existing and future investments; art 12(2)(a)(ii): the giving of due regard to
the desirability of avoiding discrimination as between foreign investments; art 12(2)(b): entry into
consultation or negotiations with other governments to conclude bilateral or multilateral agreements
relating to foreign investments.

[11] Havana Charter art 12(1)(c): '. . . . without prejudice to existing international agreements to
which members are parties, a Member has the right (i) to take any appropriate safeguards necessary to
ensure that foreign investment is not used as a basis for interference in its internal affairs or national
policies; (ii) to determine whether and to what extent and upon what terms it will allow future foreign
investment; (iii) to prescribe and give effect on just terms to requirements as to the ownership of existing or future investments; (iv) to prescribe and give effect to other reasonable requirements as to the
ownership of existing or future investments;'. For a critical comment on this provision, see Woolsey
'The Problem of Foreign Investment' XLII AJIL 121 at 126–28 (1948).

[12] Fatouros above n 4 at 80; Lipson above n 1 at 86–87.

[13] Apart from these initiatives certain states also made proposals to international organizations for
the adoption of a multilateral convention for the protection of foreign investments. Thus at the 14th
Session of the UN Economic Commission for Asia and the Far East (ECAFE) in March 1958, the
Prime Minister of Malaya suggested the conclusion of an international investment charter; also in
1958 both the German and Swiss Governments submitted draft investment conventions to the
OEEC. In 1957 discussions took place under the auspices of the Council of Europe for an investment
convention between the Member States of the Council and certain African states.

[14] For an analysis of this code, see Miller n 4 above.

[15] See Brandon 'An International Investment Code: Current Plans' [1959] JBL 7 at 12–15.

[16] The text of this draft can be found in 9 J.Pub.L. 116–118 (1960).

[17] See OECD Publication No 1563[6]7/Dec 1962 reproduced in 1–2 ILM 241 (1962–1963).
The last revision of the draft convention can be found in OECD Publication No 232081/Nov 1967
reproduced in 7 ILM 117 (1968).

[18] See Snyder 'Foreign Investment Protection: A Reasoned Approach' 61 Mich.LR 1087 at
1112–13. (1963); UNCTC *Bilateral Investment Treaties* (1988, UN Sales No. E.88.II.A.I) para 20 at 7.

convention to member states as a model for investment protection treaties and as a basis for ensuring the observance of the principles of international law which it contained.[19] Thus the OECD draft, while failing to contribute towards a general codification of the international law relating to foreign investments, has provided 'important guidelines for some of the more fundamental provisions on the treatment and protection of investments included in bilateral investment treaties'.[20]

Although not aimed at the regulation of MNEs as such, these earlier attempts at codification are significant as examples of the problems involved in achieving consensus on the rules that govern the relationship between foreign investors (including MNEs) and host states. They are also significant in their emphasis on investor protection, a theme that has been a consistent factor both in moves towards the conclusion of codes of conduct on MNEs and in relation to the content of BITs and other IIAs.

Since the early 1970s concern about the activities of MNEs prompted the negotiation and/or adoption of codes of conduct on the subject by various international organizations. It is intended to focus only on those aspects of selected major codes which offer insights into the role of traditional international standards of treatment in the regulation of MNEs, and which illustrate the evolution and decline of the 'codification movement' as a means of regulating host state/MNE relations. Discussion will centre on the ANCOM Code, as the sole example of a supranational approach to MNE regulation undertaken by a group of developing countries, on the OECD Guidelines on Multinational Enterprises, and on the now shelved draft UN Code of Conduct for Transnational Corporations. The most recent code of conduct, the World Bank Guidelines on the Treatment of Foreign Investment of 1992, and the standard setting provisions of the Multilateral Investment Guarantee Agency Convention (MIGA) will also be briefly considered. This section will end with a consideration of why two recent initiatives, aimed at the establishment of multilateral investment rules, have failed. These are the Multilateral Investment Agreement (MAI), negotiated under the auspices of the OECD, and the attempt to bring investment rules into the WTO.

(a) The Andean Common Market (ANCOM)

The ANCOM states[21] were the first to promulgate an interstate code on the regulation of foreign investment when they adopted the Andean Foreign Investment Code, contained in Decision 24 of the Commission of the Cartagena Accord of 21 December 1970.[22]

[19] UNCTC ibid. Denza and Brooks 'Investment Protection Treaties: United Kingdom Experience' 36 ICLQ 908 at 910 (1987).   [20] UNCTC ibid.

[21] Bolivia, Columbia, Chile, Ecuador, and Peru. Venezuela joined the organization in 1973.

[22] The full title of the code is, 'The Common Regime of Treatment of Foreign Capital and of Trademarks, Patents, Licences, and Royalties'. An English translation appears in 11 ILM 126 (1972). The final amended version of Decision 24, as of 30 November 1976, appears in 16 ILM 138 (1977). All references to the code in the text are to the 1976 amended version.

This was repealed and superseded by a revised Code contained in Commission Decision 220 of 11 May 1987,[23] which has in turn been repealed and replaced by Decision 291 of 21 March 1991.[24] The effects of the original and revised codes on the evolution of international standards for the regulation of MNE/host state relations are instructive, as the changes in the Andean Code are a microcosm of the changing attitude of capital importing states towards the treatment of foreign investors over the last three decades. The Andean Code, in its 1970s version, introduced a restrictive screening and technology transfer control regime for the regulation of foreign investments in the sub-region. It was ambiguous on the applicability of international minimum standards concerning the treatment of foreign investors. Although its provisions could not be said to violate any such standards, Decision 24 may have excluded the international minimum standard of treatment through the terms of Article 50, which accorded no more than national treatment to foreign investors, and Article 51 which limited dispute settlement procedures to those of the host state.[25] Furthermore, the code was silent on the question of expropriation. Thus it would be difficult not to see the original Andean Code as standing in opposition to traditional international standards for the treatment of foreign investors.

The consensus upon which the original code was based proved to be fragile and short lived with a number of the member countries distancing themselves from its terms in their national laws and policies.[26] In the circumstances, Decision 24 was becoming a dead letter. It had to be fundamentally revised. The result was Commission Decision 220.[27] This decision substantially liberalized the terms of Decision 24. However, as regards general standards of treatment, Decision 220 retained the principle that member countries should not grant foreign investors more favourable treatment than that granted to national investors.[28] On the other hand, in the field of dispute settlement, member countries were free to adopt international minimum standards under their local law, if they so chose.[29]

---

[23] English version in 27 ILM 974 (1988).

[24] Andean Commission: Decision 291 – Common Code for the Treatment of Foreign Capital and on Trademarks, Patents, Licences and Royalties: 30 ILM 1283 (1991).

[25] See Oliver 'The Andean Foreign Investment Code: a New Phase in the Quest for Normative Order as to Direct Foreign Investment' 66 AJIL 763 (1972). By art 50: 'Member Countries shall not grant to foreign investors any treatment more favourable than that granted to national investors.' By art 51: 'In no instrument relating to investments or the transfer of technology shall there be clauses that remove possible conflicts or controversies from the national jurisdiction and competence of the recipient country or allow subrogation by States to the rights and actions of their national investors.'

[26] See Horton 'Peru and ANCOM: a Study in the Disintegration of a Common Market' 17 Texas Int'l LJ 39 at 45–47 (1982); Comment: 'Chile's Rejection of the Andean Common Market Regulation of Foreign Investment' 16 Colum. J. Transnat'l L. 138 (1977); 'Introductory Note' to the Venezuelan Foreign Investment and Licensing Regulations and Related Documents of 1986–87 by John R Pate 26 ILM 760 (1987).

[27] Above n 23. For analysis, see Preziosi 'The Andean Pact's Foreign Investment Code Decision 220: An Agreement to Disagree' 20 U.Miami Inter-Am.L.Rev. 649 (1989); Esquirol 'Foreign Investment: Revision of the Andean Foreign Investment Code' 29 Harv. Int'l LJ 171 (1988).

[28] Article 33.   [29] Article 34.

Decision 220 was replaced by Decision 291 in 1991.[30] This effectively abandoned any common policy on foreign investment. As regards standards of treatment, by Article 2 of Decision 291, 'foreign investors shall have the same rights and obligations as pertain to national investors, except as otherwise provided in the legislation of each Member Country'. Thus, the member countries are left entirely free, if they wish, to adopt national laws and policies that protect international minimum standards of treatment. Furthermore, as regards dispute settlement, by Article10 of Decision 291, 'Member Countries shall apply that provided in their domestic legislation with respect to the solution of controversies or conflicts deriving from direct foreign investment or sub-regional investment or the transfer of foreign technology'. Therefore, the answer to the question whether international minimum standards apply to the treatment of a foreign investment in an ANCOM member state can be found in the content of each respective national law.[31]

(b) The OECD Guidelines on Multinational Enterprises[32]

The origins of the guidelines lie in the response of the major industrialized countries to the economic and political changes of the early 1970s.[33] This was a time when the developing countries were demanding a change in the balance of world economic power, through the adoption of a New International Economic Order under the auspices of the UN. Within this process the 'MNE Issue' was placed on the international political agenda, resulting in the decision of the UN Economic and Social Committee, in 1974, to set up a Commission on Transnational Corporations charged with the goal of formulating a binding Code of Conduct

---

[30] Above n 24.

[31] See E Wiesner 'ANCOM: A New Attitude Toward Foreign Investment?' 24 U.Miami Inter-Am.L.Rev. 435 (1993).

[32] The original version of the Guidelines, and the accompanying Communiqué and Council Decisions on Inter-governmental Consultation Procedures on the Guidelines, National Treatment and International Investment Incentives and Disincentives, are reproduced in 15 ILM 961–80 (1976). For comment, see Schwamm 12 JWTL 342 (1978). The current version at the time of writing (September 2006) is that of 27 June 2000 available at <http: www.oecd.org/dataoecd/ 56/36/192248.pdf> or *The OECD Guidelines for Multinational Enterprises* (Paris: OECD, 2000). See further OECD Working Party on the OECD Guidelines for Multinational Enterprises *The OECD Guidelines for Multinational Enterprises: Text, Commentary and Clarifications* OECD Doc DAFFE/IME/WPG(2000)15/Final 31 October 2001 (cited as Working Party 2001); Steven Tully 'The 2000 Review of the OECD Guidelines for Multinational Enterprises' 50 ICLQ 394 (2001); Jill Murray 'A New Phase in the Regulation of Multinational Enterprises: The Role of the OECD' 30 ILJ 255 (2001); Pia Acconci 'The Promotion of Responsible Business Conduct and the New Text of the OECD Guidelines for Multinational Enterprises' 2 JWIT 123 (2001). The Guidelines and accompanying Council Decisions are periodically reviewed by the OECD Committee on International Investment and Multinational Enterprises. See further *The OECD Guidelines for Multinational Enterprises* (Paris: OECD, 1986) (cited hereafter as the 1986 Review); *The OECD Declaration and Decisions on International Investment and Multinational Enterprises* (Paris: 1992). (cited hereafter as the 1991 Review); *The OECD Guidelines for Multinational Enterprises* (Paris: OECD, 1994).

[33] See J Robinson *Multinationals and Political Control* (Aldershot: Gower, 1983) 113–20.

for Transnational Corporations (TNCs).[34] This was followed in 1976 by the decisions of UNCTAD IV to start negotiations on Codes of Conduct in the areas of Transfer of Technology and Restrictive Business Practices, and of the ILO to draft a set of principles on MNE behaviour in the field of social policy.[35] The threat of increased host country control over the activities of MNEs was further accentuated by the waves of nationalizations in the 1960s and early 1970s, and by the oil crisis precipitated by the activities of OPEC in 1973. To counter these developments the OECD ministers, urged on by the US Government, decided to adopt their own policy on MNEs, which it was hoped would influence the UN's attempts at 'codification' to move away from a highly regulatory position of 'MNE control'.[36]

A second reason for the move towards the adoption of OECD Guidelines on MNEs was to meet demands from within the OECD countries for greater control over MNEs. Canada, Holland, and the Scandinavian states supported such controls.[37] Furthermore, demands for controls over MNEs were articulated by the trade unions through the Trades Union Advisory Committee (TUAC) of the OECD. The above mentioned Member Countries and the unions wanted a legally binding code. This was counterbalanced by calls from the representatives of the business community, articulated through the Business and Industry Advisory Committee to the OECD (BIAC), for greater emphasis on the removal of obstacles to foreign direct investment. Thus the guidelines can be seen as a 'corporatist' initiative.[38]

To achieve its objectives the OECD set up, in January 1975, the 'Committee on International Investment and Multinational Enterprises'.[39] After 18 months of negotiations the guidelines were adopted as an Annex to the 'OECD Declaration on International Investment and Multinational Enterprises' passed by the governments of the member countries on 21 June 1976, with the exception of Turkey, which abstained. In addition to the guidelines, three further council decisions were passed on the same day concerning, respectively, the principle of 'National Treatment', 'International Investment Incentives and Disincentives', and 'Intergovernmental Consultation Procedures on the Guidelines for Multinational Enterprises'. Together, these form a comprehensive system for the development of standards on the regulation of MNE/host state relations. As to the role of international minimum standards, by paragraph 7 of the Introduction to the Guidelines:

Governments have the right to prescribe the conditions under which multinational enterprises operate within their jurisdictions, subject to international law. The entities of a

---

[34] On which see the next section of this chapter.   [35] See further chs 10, 11, and 12 above.

[36] Robinson above n 33 at 117.

[37] See G Hamilton *The Control of Multinationals: What Future for International Codes of Conduct in the 1980s?* (John Wiley & Sons, IRM Multinational Reports No 2 October–December 1984) 6. See further P Levy 'The OECD Declaration on International Investment and Multinational Enterprises' in S Rubin and GC Hufbauer (eds) *Emerging Standards of International Trade and Investment* (Rowman & Allanhead, 1983).   [38] See Robinson above n 33 at 118–19.

[39] See Council Resolution C(74) 247 Final of 21 January 1975.

multinational enterprise located in various countries are subject to the laws applicable in these countries.

This is an unequivocal acceptance of the controlling role played by international minimum standards over the extent of a member country's sovereign power to regulate the operations of a MNE, once it has been admitted into the jurisdiction. Indeed, in the context of the question whether a host state can control by law the circumstances in which a MNE decides to disinvest, the requirements of paragraph 7 demand that any such law must be subject to international law and international agreements, and must respect contractual obligations to which the country has subscribed. Furthermore, such laws and policies must be carried out consistently with the member country's responsibilities to treat enterprises equitably.[40] Paragraph 7 shows that the guidelines are not intended to act as a substitute for national laws. They do no more than introduce supplementary standards of behaviour of a non-legal character with respect to the international operations of MNEs.[41]

(c) The Draft UN Code of Conduct on Transnational Corporations[42]

As already noted, the origins of the draft UN Code of Conduct lie in the claim of the newly independent and less developed member states of the UN, formed together as the 'Group of 77', for a New International Economic Order.[43] This would include inter alia the legal recognition of the right of a state to control the activities of TNCs operating within its borders. In 1972 the Economic and Social Council of the UN requested the Secretary General of the UN to establish a group of eminent persons to study the impact of MNEs on world development and international relations. As noted in chapter 3, that group recommended the setting up of a UN Commission on Transnational Corporations. It further recommended that the Commission should set about the task of formulating a Code of Conduct for TNCs. This was made a priority objective of the Commission at its first session in March 1975.[44] At its second session, the Commission decided to establish an Intergovernmental Working Group which would prepare a draft text

[40] 1979 Review para 44; reproduced in 1986 Review above note 32 para 11. at 20.

[41] Working Party 2001 above n 32 at 9.

[42] The term 'Transnational Corporation' (TNC) will be used in this section in conformity with UN practice. No distinction is intended from the term 'Multinational Enterprise' used elsewhere in this book. For a fuller discussion of the debates surrounding the Draft UN Code, see the first edition of this work *Multinational Enterprises and the Law* (Oxford: Blackwell Publishers, revised paperback edn, 1999) at 592–97.

[43] See further Robinson above n 33 at 163–66; Nixson 'Controlling the Transnationals? Political Economy and the United Nations Code of Conduct' 11 Int'l Jo.Soc.L. 83 (1983); WJ Field *Multinational Corporations and UN Politics: The Quest for Codes of Conduct* (New York: Pergamon, 1982).

[44] See Commission on Transnational Corporations *Report on the First Session 17–28 March 1975* (E/5655; E/C.10/6 Economic and Social Council Official Records 59th Session Supplement No 12) para 9 at 2.

of the code on the basis of proposals or views put to it by states.[45] The negotiations over the draft code were beset with major disagreements, particularly on whether there should be an express reference to international law in the draft code. The capital-exporting countries wished to see such a reference included, so that the international minimum standards of treatment favoured by them would be incorporated into the code, while the Group of 77, and the then socialist countries, questioned the validity of these standards on the ground that they were established by the practice of the major capital-exporting states at a time when most developing countries were under colonial rule and that, therefore, they did not command the consent of the majority of the contemporary international community.[46] These countries favoured a compromise proposal referring to 'international obligations' rather than to 'international law'.[47]

A number of revised drafts of the code were examined, culminating in the proposed text of 31 May 1990, submitted by the chairman of the reconvened special session of the Commission to the Economic and Social Council.[48] This represents the last version of the draft code. Finally, in July 1992, negotiations over the code were suspended.[49] The period of negotiations was marked by a shift away from a strongly regulatory approach towards TNCs and its gradual replacement in successive drafts of the code with formulations closer to those favoured by the capital-exporting countries.[50] It can be said that the history of the draft code represents a growing compromise by those states advocating TNC control of their original objectives. The economic and political conditions which gave rise to the initial calls for a universal code laying down obligations for TNCs

[45] See Commission on Transnational Corporations *Report on the Second Session March 1–12 1976* (Economic and Social Council Official Records 61st Session Supplement No 5 May 1976) paras 10–17 and 47–51; reproduced in 15 ILM 779 at 782–83 and 790 (1976).

[46] For a full statement of the developing country position, see Patrick Robinson *The Question of a Reference to International Law in the United Nations Code of Conduct on Transnational Corporations* (New York: July 1986, UNCTC Current Studies, Series A No 1 UN Doc ST/CTC/SER.A/1).

[47] UNCTC *Transnational Corporations, Services and the Uruguay Round* (New York: 1990 UN Doc ST/CTC/103) at 180–81. For an attempt to reconcile these conflicting positions, see Detlev Vagts *The Question of a Reference to International Obligations in the United Nations Code of Conduct on Transnational Corporations: A Different View* (New York: September 1986, UNCTC Current Studies, Series A No 2 UN Doc ST/CTC/SER.A/2).

[48] The 1990 proposed text can be found in UN Doc E/1990/94 of 12 June 1990 or in Annex IV of the UNCTC Publication *Transnational Corporations, Services and the Uruguay Round* (New York: 1990 UN Doc ST/CTC/103). This text supersedes the 1988 text which can be found in UN Doc E/1988/39/Add. 1 of 1 February 1988. The text of the code as it stood in the summer of 1986 can be found in Annex I to UNCTC Publication *The United Nations Code of Conduct on Transnational Corporations* (New York: September 1986, UNCTC Current Studies Series A No 4 UN Doc ST/CTC/SER.A/4) also available at <http://www.unctad.org/en/docs/dtci30vol1_en.pdf>. Earlier formulations of the draft code can be found in UN Doc E/C.10/1984/S/5 of 29 May 1984, reproduced in 23 ILM 602 at 626–40 and UN Doc E/C.10/1983/S/2 of 4 January 1983, reproduced in 22 ILM 177 at 192–206. This reproduces the first draft code submitted by the Intergovernmental Working Group in 1982. [49] International Chamber of Commerce *Annual Report 1992* 24.

[50] See, for example, the preamble to the draft code and UNCTC *The United Nations Code of Conduct on Transnational Corporations* (New York: September 1986 UNCTC Current Studies Series A No 4 UN Doc ST/CTC/SER.A/4) 2–3.

changed.[51] Developing countries were now faced with an acute shortfall of invest-ment by comparison to the days of the early 1970s. While investment by TNCs in developed countries had increased, it had stagnated in developing countries.[52] According to the UN Centre on Transnational Corporations, this raised new policy questions, leading to what it called a 'New Code Environment'. No longer was the control of the potentially negative impacts of TNCs the major issue; rather it was how best to reintegrate developing countries into the global economy in a manner that would ensure inflows of new investment capital. Given that TNCs were a primary vehicle for such integration, any future code should be geared to the realization of this goal.[53]

(d) The Contribution of the World Bank: The 1992 Guidelines on the Treatment of Foreign Direct Investment and Standard Setting by MIGA

The development of international standards for the treatment of foreign investors has become part of the agenda of the World Bank Group (the International Bank for Reconstruction and Development, the International Finance Corporation and the Multilateral Investment Guarantee Agency (MIGA)). In particular, the 1992 World Bank Guidelines on the Treatment of Foreign Direct Investment (the 1992 Guidelines)[54] and the standard-setting provisions of the MIGA Convention are worthy of study.

The 1992 Guidelines were prepared at the initiative of the Development Committee, a Joint Ministerial Committee of the Boards of Governors of the International Monetary Fund (IMF) and of the World Bank. In April 1991, the Development Committee, working on a proposal from France, requested that MIGA prepare a 'legal framework' to promote foreign direct investment. A working group, consisting of lawyers from each of the World Bank Group insti-tutions, was set up to prepare a report. This was submitted to the Development Committee in April 1992. The resulting guidelines were approved by the

---

[51] See UNCTC *The New Code Environment* (New York: 1990); summarized in UN Doc E/C.10/1990/5 of 29 January 1990. See Report of the Secretary-General 'Transnational Cor-porations in the New World Economy: Issues and Policy Implications'(UN Doc E/C.10/1992/5 5 February 1992); Report of the Secretary-General 'International Arrangements and Agreements Relating to Transnational Corporations' (UN Doc E/C.10/1992/8 18 February 1992).

[52] E/C.10/1990/5 paras 16–20 at 8.   [53] ibid paras At 39–41.

[54] World Bank Report to the Development Committee and Guidelines on the Treatment of Foreign Direct Investment 21 September 1992 published as *Legal Framework for the Treatment of Foreign Direct Investment (Volume II: Guidelines)* (Washington DC: World Bank, 1992) reproduced in 31 ILM 1363 (1992). See also, for the background surveys and reports on which the Guidelines are based: *Legal Framework for the Treatment of Foreign Direct Investment (Volume I)* (Washington DC: World Bank, 1992). Both volumes are reproduced with updated surveys in the Fall 1992 issue of ICSID Rev-FILJ. The guidelines, their detailed drafting history, the Report to the Development Committee and all the above mentioned supporting documentation are brought together in IFI Shihata *Legal Treatment of Foreign Investment: The World Bank Guidelines* (Martinus Nijhoff, 1993).

Development Committee in September 1992 for circulation among the member states of the World Bank Group.[55] Given that the World Bank could not issue binding rules, the guidelines do not codify existing international law. Their aim is to set down emerging rather than settled standards, and, in the process, to emphasize what the World Bank Group sees as desirable practice in the field of direct foreign investment. Furthermore, the guidelines are addressed to host states alone, covering only their activities and policies towards foreign investors. There are no provisions concerning the behaviour of foreign investors towards host states. Thus, the coverage of the 1992 Guidelines is narrower than that of the OECD Guidelines or the draft UN Code of Conduct. The 1992 Guidelines are divided into five headings: I Scope of Application, II Admission, III Treatment, IV Expropriation and Unilateral Alteration or Termination of Contracts, and V Settlement of Disputes (referred to as Guideline I, II etc). Their form is either normative or that of a policy recommendation, depending on the degree to which the standard concerned is reconcilable with general principles of contemporary international law.[56]

The 1992 Guidelines offer a clear statement on the policy preferences of the World Bank Group in the field of foreign investment. However, the report attached to the guidelines is at pains to stress the limits of their purpose and effects:

To the extent that the practice of States conforms to these recommended guidelines in a constant manner and reflects a general conviction of their binding character, the guidelines may then positively influence the development of customary international law in so far as they do not already reflect its rules. While the guidelines could serve these important purposes, they are clearly not intended to constitute part of World Bank loan conditionality or to assume for the Bank a legislative role which it does not have.[57]

Therefore, departure from the standards contained in the guidelines will not have any financial implications for states seeking a loan from the World Bank. This may serve to allay fears that the guidelines will be used as a means of intervening in the domestic policies of countries in need of such assistance.

However, the pressure on states to conform to the policies advocated in the guidelines should be seen in the context of the standard-setting conditions which may be attached to investment guarantees issued by MIGA. By Article 12(d) of the MIGA Convention, in guaranteeing an investment, MIGA (the Agency) shall satisfy itself as to inter alia the 'investment conditions in the host country, including the availability of fair and equitable treatment and legal protection for

[55] See I Shihata 'Introductory Note' to the guidelines of 25 September 1992 previous note ILM 1367 and 'The World Bank Group's New "Guidelines on the Treatment of Foreign Direct Investment"' News from ICSID (vol 10 No 1 Winter 1993) 4.

[56] Shihata News from ICSID above n 55 at 5. For a full analysis of the Guidelines, see 'The Report to The Development Committee' in *Legal Framework for the Treatment of Foreign Investment Volume II* above n 54 reproduced at ILM 1368–79. For a summary of the contents of the guidelines, see the first edition of this work Peter T Muchlinski *Multinational Enterprises and the Law* (Oxford: Blackwell Publishers, revised paperback edn, 1999) 599–602.   [57] Above n 54 para 6 at ILM 1369.

the investment'.[58] Article 12(d) makes the provision of adequate standards of
investment protection a condition precedent to the issuance of a MIGA investment guarantee, as this helps to reduce the investment risk. The Agency itself
must assess whether the host country's legal system meets the standard in Article
12(d). Guidance is offered in the MIGA Operational Regulations.[59] By paragraph
3.16 thereof:

An investment will be regarded as having adequate legal protection if it is protected under
the terms of a bilateral investment treaty between the host country and the home country
of the investor. When there is no such treaty, adequate legal protection should be ascertained by the Agency in the light of the consistency of the law and practice of the Host
Country with international law. Such assessment shall be conducted in strict confidentiality and its outcome shall be shared only with the government concerned with a view to
enabling it to improve the investment conditions in its territory.

The emphasis on BITs coincides with the Agency's general duty to 'promote and
facilitate the conclusion of agreements, among its members, on the promotion
and protection of investments'.[60] In most cases this requirement should be met,
as the majority of MIGA's developing member states have concluded BITs with
capital-exporting member states.[61] However, in the absence of a BIT, the Agency
must compare the law and practice of the host state with international law. As the
leading commentator on MIGA points out, given the absence of well-defined
international law in this area, the Agency is in fact mandated to develop standards
of this law for the purposes of its operations. This would be relevant to the general
development of customary international law, but could not substitute for the will
of states in the matter.[62] Indeed, MIGA is placed in a difficult position as an
arbiter of the content of international law. It is against this background that the
initiative which led to the adoption of the 1992 World Bank Guidelines should be
seen.[63] They offer a non-binding statement of policy in a field where general
agreement on binding international standards would be impossible. As such they
can be seen as the starting point for negotiations between MIGA and a host country over the legal standards that the latter should offer to investors if it is to benefit
from MIGA guarantees.

The result of such negotiations may be the conclusion of an investment guarantee agreement between the Agency and the host country as a precondition for a

---

[58] MIGA Convention 1985 art 12(d)(iv). The convention is reproduced in 24 ILM 1598 (1985)
or at <http://www.miga.org/sitelevel2/level2.cfm?id=1107>. For detailed analysis of the standard-
setting aspects of the MIGA Convention, see I F I Shihata *MIGA and Foreign Investment* (Martinus
Nijhoff, 1988) ch 6.
[59] MIGA Operational Regulations of 27 August 2002 <http://www.miga.org/miga_
documents/Operations-Regulations.pdf>.   [60] MIGA Convention above n 58 art 23(b)(iii).
[61] Shihata above n 58 at 233.   [62] Shihata ibid.
[63] See also Shihata ibid who floats the idea of non-binding guidelines at 244–47. Mr Shihata was
instrumental in the adoption of the 1992 Guidelines, being General-Counsel of the World Bank,
Secretary-General of ICSID and the chairman of the World Bank working group that drew up the
guidelines.

MIGA guarantee.[64] The authority to conclude such agreements is given by Article 23(b)(ii) of the MIGA Convention, which states that the Agency shall:

[e]ndeavour to conclude agreements with developing member countries, and in particular with prospective host countries, which will assure that the Agency, with respect to investment guaranteed by it, has treatment at least as favourable as that agreed by the member concerned for the most favoured investment guarantee agency of State in an agreement relating to investment, such agreements to be approved by special majority of the Board . . .

Thus MIGA has a role in the development of international standards through the conclusion of specific agreements, whose content will undoubtedly be influenced by the terms of the 1992 Guidelines.

On a more general level, the Agency can be expected to take an active part in developing international standards through its research, information, technical advice, and assistance and consultation programmes.[65] These are all aimed at the improvement of the environment for foreign investment flows to developing member countries. In performing these activities the MIGA Convention specifies that the Agency shall be guided by relevant investment agreements among member countries; it shall seek to remove impediments, in both developed and developing member countries, to the flow of investment to developing member countries and coordinate with other agencies concerned with the promotion of foreign investment, and in particular with the International Finance Corporation.[66] These considerations point to the possibility of further work in the area of standard-setting. Furthermore, the Operational Regulations make clear that '[t]he Agency's technical programs shall support its guarantee operations by strengthening assurance of fair and stable treatment of guaranteed investments in individual host countries . . . .'[67] Clearly, the development of investor protection standards would fall within this broad mandate. In conclusion, although the work of the Agency in the area of standard-setting is, like the 1992 Guidelines, only of a persuasive nature, the Agency's view of those standards is likely to influence state practice. Host states run the risk of having their access to its guarantee facilities restricted if they do not adhere to the Agency's preferred standards of treatment. In this respect the contribution of MIGA to standard-setting is of considerable importance.

---

[64] By para 3.17 of the Operational Regulations (n 59 above): 'If the Underwriting Authority is not satisfied as to the availability of fair and equitable treatment and legal protection for the investment, it shall only issue coverage after the Agency has concluded an agreement with the host country under Article 23(b)(ii) of the Convention and Paragraph 3.33(i) below.' Para 3.33(i) states: 'With a view to enhancing its ability to issue guarantees, the Agency may agree with the host country on: (i) the treatment of guaranteed investment in accordance with Article 23(b) (ii) of the Convention . . .'

[65] See MIGA Convention above n 58 art 23(a) and (c).   [66] ibid art 23(a)(i)–(iii).

[67] Operational Regulations above n 59 at para 7.01.

(e) The Failure of Recent Initiatives to Adopt Multilateral Investment Rules

In recent years two significant attempts have been made to adopt a multilateral investment code. However, like earlier attempts, neither has been successful. The first was the OECD based MAI.[68] The second was the WTO initiative, centred on the Working Group on the Relationship between Trade and Investment (WGTI), and the call in the Doha Declaration to consider the inclusion of investment rules in the Doha Development Round of WTO negotiations.[69] The history of discussions regarding the rights of investors and their protection has raised a number of hitherto unresolved issues concerning multilateral investment rules, for example: should these tend towards investor protection alone, or towards a balance between protection and regulation; should they be binding or voluntary; should investors be offered privileged treatment based on international minimum standards or only the same treatment as national investors? [70] It has been argued that these debates have been overcome by events, in that the contemporary environment is more suited to the successful creation of a new multilateral regime for investor protection, as a result of shifts towards liberalization, privatization, and the recognition of the utility of inward direct investment by MNEs as a source of capital and technology.[71]

[68] On the MAI see further MAI Negotiating Text and commentary (as of 24 April 1998) available at <http://www.unctad.org/iia>. For background, see OECD *Towards Multilateral Investment Rules* (Paris: OECD, 1996); Peter T Muchlinski 'The Rise and Fall of the Multilateral Agreement on Investment: Where Now?' 34 Int'l Law 1033 (2000); AA Fatouros 'Towards an International Agreement on Foreign Direct Investment?' 10 ICSID Rev-FILJ 181 (1995); Frans Engering 'The Multilateral Investment Agreement' 5 Transnational Corporations 147 (1996); S Picciotto and R Mayne (eds) *Regulating International Business: Beyond Liberalisation* (London: Macmillan/Oxfam, 1999); Sol Picciotto 'Linkages in International Investment Regulation: The Antinomies of the Draft Multilateral Agreement on Investment' 19 U.Pa.J.Int'l Econ.L. 731 (1998); Steven J Canner 'The Multilateral Agreement on Investment' 31 Cornell Int'l L.J. 657 (1998); UNCTAD *Lessons from the MAI* Series on issues in international investment agreements (New York and Geneva: United Nations, 1999); David Henderson *The MAI Affair: A Story and its Lessons* (London: RIIA, 1999); Tony Clarke and Maude Barlow *MAI: The Multilateral Agreement on Investment and the Threat to Canadian Sovereignty* (Toronto: Stoddart Books, 1997).

[69] See Bill Dymond and Michael Hart 'The Doha Investment Negotiations – Whither or Wither' 5 JWIT 263 (2004); Soongjoon Cho 'A Bridge Too Far: The Fall of the Fifth WTO Ministerial Conference at Cancun and the Future of Trade Constitution' 7 JIEL 219 (2004); Jurgen Kurtz 'Developing Countries and Their Engagement in the World Trade Organization: An Assessment of the Cancun Ministerial' 5 Melb.J.Int'l L. 280 (2004); Consumer and Unity Trust of India (CUTS) *We've Been Here Before: Perspectives on the Cancun Ministerial* (Jaipur: CUTS, 2004). For the background to WTO discussions on trade and investment, see the reports of the Working Group on the Relationship Trade and Investment available at <http://www.wto.org>. The documents of the Working Group are classified under the designation WT/WGTI/. See also Pierre Sauve 'Multilateral Rules on Investment: Is Forward Movement Possible?' 9 JIEL 325 (2006).

[70] The following account of the MAI negotiations is taken from Peter T Muchlinski above n 68.

[71] See Thomas Waelde 'Requiem for the New International Economic Order: The Rise and Fall of Paradigms in International Economic Law' in N Al Nauimi and R Meese (eds) *International Legal Issues Arising Under the United Nations Decade of International Law* (The Hague: Kluwer, 1995) 1301.

The MAI was undoubtedly a product of this conviction.[72] According to the Report of the Committee on International Investment and Multinational Enterprises and the Committee on Capital Movements and Invisible Transactions:

The MAI would build on the achievements of the present OECD instruments, consolidating and strengthening existing commitments under the Codes of Liberalisation and the 1976 Declaration and Decisions on International Investment and Multinational Enterprises. The aim of the negotiations is to conclude an agreement incorporating rollback, standstill, national treatment and non-discrimination/most favoured nation (MFN) as well as new disciplines to improve market access and to strengthen the basis of mutual confidence between enterprises and states. The liberalization obligations would be complemented by provisions on investment protection. The obligations under the agreement would need to be reinforced by effective dispute settlement procedures ... The agreement would be comprehensive in scope, covering all sectors under a broad definition of investment focusing mainly on [foreign direct investment]. The MAI would aim to raise the level of existing liberalization based on a 'top-down' approach under which the only exceptions permitted are those listed when adhering to the agreement and which are subject to progressive liberalization.[73]

Thus, the draft MAI was based on earlier models of binding investor protection standards leading it to be crafted as an investor and investment protection and promotion agreement, similar in type to the first generation of BITs, but incorporating the Western Hemisphere model of protection and market access.[74] This was so notwithstanding the proposed inclusion of the OECD Guidelines on Multinational Enterprises in a non-binding Annex coupled with a 'no lowering of standards' clause in relation to labour and environmental issues. While these provisions would offer some indication of the types of obligations MNEs had towards the states in which they operated, and of the need for host states not to compete for inward FDI on the basis of lowering regulatory standards in the above mentioned areas, the essential leaning of the MAI towards investor rights and protection could not be disputed. It would prove to be a major cause of the failure of the negotiations.

At the outset, significant obstacles to the successful conclusion of such an instrument were identified.[75] Of the many obstacles encountered in the negotiating process the following are worthy of highlighting. First, the negotiating environment, being based at the OECD, excluded most key developing countries. Secondly, the contents of the draft MAI were deemed too restrictive of the host country's 'right to regulate' including provisions extending investor protection standards to the pre-entry stage, a wide asset based definition of covered investment, prohibitions on performance requirements, the inclusion of indirect takings in the expropriation provisions and wide ranging dispute settlement

---

[72] See OECD *Towards Multilateral Investment Rules* above n 68 at 9 and ibid William Witherill 'Towards an International Set of Rules for Investment' at 17–30.   [73] ibid at 10–11.
[74] On which see further text at nn 123–27 below.
[75] See Guy de Jonquieres 'Rocky Road to Liberalisation' *Financial Times* 10 April 1995 at 17.

provisions. Thirdly, other 'deal breakers' were added to the negotiations as they progressed. These included: draft clauses seeking to prevent secondary boycotts of investors such as those proposed under the US Helms-Burton Act,[76] the need to make an exception to the most favoured nation (MFN) standard for regional economic integration organizations, the inclusion of a cultural industries exception, and labour and environmental standards.[77]

The problems described above proved fatal to the aim of concluding the MAI. On 14 October 1998 the French Prime Minister, Lionel Jospin, stated that France would take no further part in the negotiations, on the ground that the MAI, as currently formulated, represented an unacceptable threat to national sovereignty.[78] A week later, on 22 October, the senior representatives of the OECD members and the European Commission convened in the Executive Committee of the Special Session of the OECD in Paris. They announced that they would now proceed with further consultations on the controversies that the negotiating process had raised, thereby effectively ending the negotiations on the MAI.[79]

There is much debate on the actual causes of this failure. [80] The political opposition to the MAI generated by the NGO community undoubtedly made a significant contribution by raising awareness of its one-sided nature and by offering an organized critique based on the unaccountability of MNEs and of the multilateral economic organizations that were trying to introduce the MAI. This view of events continues to make the adoption of future multilateral rules in this area politically difficult. However, the principal reason lies in the conception of the agreement as a pure investor and investment protection instrument. This made it an anachronism from the start. The MAI was based on fundamental misconceptions as

[76] On which see ch 4 at 130–31.

[77] See further Peter T Muchlinski above n 68 at 1039–48.

[78] 'France Quits Investment Accord talks' *Financial Times* 15 October 1998 at 5; Henderson above n 68 at 30–1. For the full debate, see Assemblee Nationale, Session Ordinaire de 1998–1999, 8ème jour de séance, 18ème séance, 1ère séance du Mardi 13 Octobre 1998. The Prime Minister's official statement followed the recommendations of a special commission appointed in May 1998 to examine the MAI, under the chair of Catherine Lalumiere MEP and Jean-Pierre Landau Inspector General of Finances. This body concluded that, while France should continue to press for new negotiations, this should only be done on the fulfilment of at least seven major conditions:

– that the definition of FDI excluded portfolio investment and financial market operations;
– the dispute settlement provisions be confined to inter-state disputes;
– the deletion of the words 'full and constant protection and security' under the heading 'General Treatment of Investments';
– the deletion of the words 'measures having equivalent effect' in the draft expropriation clause;
– the restrictions on performance requirements to be limited to an extension of the TRIMs provisions to services;
– the right to bring back reservations subject to compensation for other contracting parties as in the WTO;
– final agreement to be conditional on the accession of a sufficient number of non-OECD countries.

[79] OECD News Release Paris, 23 October 1998 'Chairman's Statement Under Secretary of State Stuart Eizenstat (USA) Executive Committee in Special Session'. The negotiations were formally ended in a further informal OECD Meeting in December 1998: Henderson above n 68 at 32.

[80] The following text is adapted from Peter T Muchlinski above n 68 at 1048–50.

to the nature of transnational economic interactions in an era of increased privatization and deregulation at the national level. Thus it started from the false premise that governmental power to control business had to be curtailed. It lived in a world dominated by old political agendas signified by the 'right/left' axis of Cold War politics, in which the principal concerns of foreign direct investors were to preserve existing investments in recently decolonized and/or increasingly politically assertive host countries. As noted in chapter 3, the current political environment no longer places 'right/left' issues of ownership and control at centre stage. Rather, there has been a transformation in political discourse which challenges not the legitimacy and value of free private enterprise as such, but its legitimacy as a polluter, an abuser of market power, a corruptor of state officials, an exploiter of workers, and a potential accomplice to violations of fundamental human rights. Thus, the correct starting point should have been an acknowledgement that, in this new investment environment, new regulatory issues, of the kinds listed above, emerge.[81] It was the complete failure to address these new questions that undermined the MAI, based as it was on models of IIAs that were, in effect, a response to increased state intervention and control over the national economy through nationalizations and highly interventionist national economic plans.

Turning to the failure to include investment negotiations in the Doha Negotiating Round of WTO, this too can be attributed in part, as will be seen below, to the fear, among developing countries in particular, that their right to regulate foreign investment would be unduly curtailed. However, there may be further institutional factors at play in the WTO that render it an unlikely forum for the development of general multilateral investment rules.[82] To understand this perspective it is useful to consider how the issue of investment was placed on the agenda of the WTO. In 1996, at the Singapore Ministerial Meeting, it was agreed that a working group should be set up to study the relationship between trade and investment. So as to avoid the creation of uncertainty among developing countries in particular, its work was expressly said not to prejudge whether negotiations on the issue would be instituted in the future.[83] Then, in 2001, the Doha Ministerial Declaration placed the question of investment on a more explicit footing. Members of the WTO agreed on a work programme on investment.[84] The declaration recognizes, in paragraph 20, 'the case for a multilateral framework to secure transparent, stable and predictable conditions for long-term cross-border

---

[81] On which see further the interesting paper by AA Fatouros 'International Investment Agreements and Development – Problems and Prospects at the Turn of the Century' in G Hafner, G Loibl, A Rest, L Sucharipa-Bermann and K Zemanek (eds) *Liber Amicorum Professor Seidl-Hohenveldern – in Honour of his 80th Birthday* (The Hague: Kluwer Law International, 1998) 115.

[82] As noted in ch 6, the WTO already contains significant rules that cover market access and foreign investment.

[83] Singapore Ministerial Declaration WTO Doc WT/MIN(96)/DEC 18 December 1996 at para 20 available at <http://www.wto.org> or 36 ILM 218 (1997).

[84] Doha Ministerial Declaration WTO Doc WT/MIN(01)/DEC/W/1, 14 November 2001 at paras 20–22 available at <http://www.wto.org> or 41 ILM 746 (2002).

investment, particularly foreign direct investment, that will contribute to the expansion of trade'. However, the declaration also recognizes the need for enhanced technical assistance and capacity-building in this area for developing and least-developed countries and for enhanced support for technical assistance and capacity-building in this area, including policy analysis and development so that such countries 'may better evaluate the implications of closer multilateral cooperation for their development policies and objectives, and human and institutional development'.[85] To this end, the WTO committed itself to work in cooperation with other relevant inter-governmental organizations, including UNCTAD, and through appropriate regional and bilateral channels, to provide strengthened and adequately resourced assistance to respond to these needs. This part of the Doha Declaration explains well a major difficulty in attempting to negotiate investment rules within a multilateral forum such as the WTO. It was uncertain that the developing and least developed countries could sustain such negotiations, given their resource and capacity constraints. In addition, given the more sensitive nature of investment (as compared with trade[86]) rules for the preservation of the national policy space of members, it would be impossible to impose negotiations without unanimous agreement. Accordingly, the Doha Declaration states that negotiations would only take place after the Fifth Session of the Ministerial Conference on the basis of a decision to be taken, by 'explicit consensus' at that session 'on modalities of negotiations'.[87]

A further limitation in the WTO mandate on investment in the Doha Declaration concerned the substantive scope of any future negotiations. According to paragraph 22 of the declaration:

In the period until the Fifth Session, further work in the Working Group on the Relationship Between Trade and Investment will focus on the clarification of: scope and definition; transparency; non-discrimination; modalities for pre-establishment commitments based on a GATS-type, positive list approach; development provisions; exceptions and balance-of-payments safeguards; consultation and the settlement of disputes between Members. Any framework should reflect in a balanced manner the interests of home and host countries, and take due account of the development policies and objectives of host governments as well as their right to regulate in the public interest. The special development, trade and financial needs of developing and least-developed countries should be taken into account as an integral part of any framework, which should enable Members to undertake obligations and commitments commensurate with their individual needs and circumstances. Due regard should be paid to other relevant WTO provisions. Account should be taken, as appropriate, of existing bilateral and regional arrangements on investment.

It was a mandate to achieve far less than could already be done under bilateral investment protection agreements. For example, the Doha Declaration is silent on such substantive issues as the taking of property, incentives, performance requirements

[85] ibid at para 21.   [86] On which see further Dymond and Hart above n 69.
[87] ibid at para 20.

and transfer of technology and contains no reference to dispute settlement. The inclusion of these most sensitive substantive issues would be opposed by developing countries as a direct assault upon their regulatory discretion.[88] The exclusion of dispute settlement is not surprising, given the exclusively state-to-state nature of the WTO dispute settlement system, and the absence of any support for its extension to investor-state disputes. Furthermore, the protection accorded to investors (the usual home country interest) would be 'balanced' by the host country interest to further their pursuit of development policies and objectives and their right to regulate. No such concessions are made in existing BITs. Equally, the reference to the GATS amounts to a rejection of the approach, favoured by the United States and Canada in their investment agreements, towards liberalization of entry and establishment conditions by way of a negative list of exceptions to a general right of entry. The GATS favours limited, sector-by-sector, liberalization of entry without any general commitment to such a policy.[89]

Thus, it is not altogether clear what would be gained, on the part of investors, by having more restrictive investment rules at the multilateral, as opposed to more protective rules at the bilateral and regional levels. One possibility is that a multilateral code could replace the multiplicity of bilateral and regional agreements and so avoid the 'spaghetti bowl' effect of having numerous agreements that may contain dissimilar terms and so cause confusion. However, uniformity at the price of weaker protection standards might not have been attractive enough to displace the existing agreements. Equally, given the continuing concerns over sovereignty and the right to regulate, it is not clear why developing countries should have been expected to accept such rules at all. On the other hand, it may appear puzzling that opposition to multilateral rules is prevalent at a time when most developing countries are happy to conclude bilateral investment agreements. This may be accounted for by the belief that, in entering a bilateral or regional agreement, the country in question retains a larger measure of independent discretion to tailor the agreement to its particular policy needs. By contrast multilateral rules are inflexible and apply to all cases, thereby presenting a stronger impediment to regulatory discretion.[90]

In the face of developing country scepticism, the EU, supported by Japan, Canada, the Republic of Korea, Switzerland, and Taiwan, pressed for the inclusion of a commitment to start investment negotiations at Cancún.[91] At the last

---

[88] For a discussion of the major development orientated issues in IIAs, and their resultant policy implications, see UNCTAD *World Investment Report 2003* (New York and Geneva: United Nations, 2003) ch IV. [89] See further ch 6 at 253–55.

[90] On the relative pros and cons of concluding investment agreements at the bilateral, regional, and multilateral levels see further UNCTAD *World Investment Report 2003* above n 88 at 93–96.

[91] The EU had championed the commencement of negotiations on investment rules in the WTO even before the MAI negotiations, believing it to be a better forum due to the larger and more representative membership and the binding dispute settlement procedure. See EC Commission 'A Level Playing Field for Direct Investment Worldwide' COM(95) 42 final 1 March 1995; Sir Leon Brittan 'Investment Liberalisation: The Next Great Boost to the World Economy' 4 Transnational Corporations 1 (No 1 1995).

meeting of the WGTI before the Cancún Ministerial Meeting, Canada, Costa Rica, and the Republic of Korea argued that the time had come for negotiations to begin and that this would benefit developing and least developed countries.[92] The subsequent discussion revealed a polarization of views with some countries accepting this position, some keeping an open mind, and others opposed to negotiations due to the continuing lack of preparedness and familiarity with the issues on the part of developing countries.[93] The concerns of the developing countries in the WGTI were echoed before the Trade Negotiations Committee, the body charged with preparations for Cancún.[94] Nonetheless, preparations continued through the use of informal consultations conducted by so-called 'Friends of the Chair', referring to the chair of the WTO General Council. The 'Friend of the Chair' dealing with foreign investment issues (Brazilian Ambassador Luiz Felipe de Sexias, chair of the WGTI) held separate meetings with members who advocated negotiations, known opponents and the undecided. However, no meeting had taken place where the various groups had been brought together.[95] Indeed, the first draft of the Ministerial Declaration, of 18 July 2003, remained uncommitted to negotiations, being little more than a restatement of the Doha Declaration.[96]

Notwithstanding this situation the EU and the other 'demandeurs' (as the supporters of negotiations became known) pressed on. They believed that the Doha Declaration had already mandated the start of negotiations and, to this end, they produced a draft text on the modalities of negotiations on investment.[97] This had a considerable influence on the revised draft of the Ministerial Text of 24 August 2003. Paragraph 13 thereof offered two alternatives. The first was the setting out of the modalities for negotiations, that had been taken from the 'demandeurs' draft text, in Annex D of the draft. The second was a statement that the situation did not provide the basis for the commencement of negotiations and that further

[92] See Joint Communication of 4 June 2003 WTO Doc WT/WGTI/W/162 of 5 June 2003. For a critique of the claimed development benefits of multilateral investment rules in the WTO, see World Development Movement and Friends of the Earth Briefing *Investment and the WTO – Busting the Myths* (London, June 2003). See further Americo Beviglia Zampetti and Torbjorn Fredriksson 'The Development Dimension of Investment Negotiations in the WTO: Challenges and Opportunities' 4 JWIT 399 (2003).

[93] See WGTI Report of the Meeting Held on 10 and 11 June 2003 WTO Doc WT/WGTI/M/22 17 July 2003.

[94] See Communication from Argentina (and 25 other members) 'The Doha Agenda: Towards Cancún' WTO Doc TN/C/W13 6 June 2003.

[95] Third World Network 'Same differences among countries maintained in "informal consultations" on Singapore Issues. But will these be reflected in draft Cancun Declaration?' (Report by Martin Khor, 16 July 2003).

[96] 'Preparations for the Fifth Session of the Ministerial Conference, Draft Cancún Ministerial Text' WTO Doc JOB(03)/150 18 July 2003 para 13: 'Taking note of the work done by the Working Group on the Relationship between Trade and Investment under the mandate we gave at Doha, and the work on the issue of modalities carried out at the level of the General Council, we [adopt by explicit consensus the decision on modalities set out in document ...] [decide that ...].'

[97] Contribution by the European Communities, Japan, Republic of Korea, and Switzerland 'Modalities on Investment' (Room Document, no date, on file with the author).

clarification of the issues should be undertaken by the WGTI.[98] This formulation attracted criticism form the developing countries opposed to negotiations. Led by India, a group of 16 such countries submitted a Communication to the General Council of the WTO calling for further discussions on issues (which in fact went beyond the terms of the Doha Declaration) where there remained a wide divergence of views including: scope and definition, transparency, non-discrimination, exceptions for balance-of-payments safeguards, special and differential treatment, performance requirements, investor's obligations and home government measures, regulation of incentives, and protection standards on expropriation and compensation.[99] The delegations went to Cancún without any prior resolution of this impasse. The revised draft of 24 August stood, with the final decision being left to ministers at Cancún. It may be said that the inclusion of the 'demandeurs' draft text as Annex D created bad feeling. There was, surprisingly, no alternative text based on the communication of the opponents.

At Cancún the process for negotiation on the so called 'Singapore Issues', of which investment was one, was carried out as follows. The chair (Mexican Foreign Minister Luis Ernesto Derbez) invited five ministers to act as 'facilitators' on the various issues. For the 'Singapore Issues' he chose the Canadian International Trade Minister, Pierre Pettigrew. This choice was open to criticism, given that Canada was one of the 'demandeurs'. The facilitator would conduct consultations with the various groups and delegations. He then reported to the chair and full negotiations would start with an informal ministerial meeting, scheduled for Day 2 (11 September 2003). The opposition of developing countries was re-emphasized at Cancún in a number of communications.[100] In the course of negotiations a revised text on investment was produced on 13 September. This contained a commitment to intensify the clarification process concerning the Doha Declaration, and the elements identified by the India/Bangladesh Communication, and to convene a special session of the WGTI to work out procedural and substantive modalities. The controversial Annex, based on the 'demandeurs' draft text was dropped.[101] Subsequently, on the last day of the meeting, the EU offered to drop investment and competition from the WTO agenda.[102] However, this was to no effect, as the

---

[98] Draft Cancún Ministerial Text, revision, WTO Doc JOB(03)/150/Rev 1 24 August 2003.

[99] Communication from the Permanent Mission of India to the General Council WTO Doc WT/GC/W/514 28 August 2003.

[100] See Communication from Bangladesh (on Behalf of the LDC Group) Ministerial Conference Fifth Session Cancún 10–14 September 2003 (WTO Doc WT/MIN(03)/W/4 4 September 2003, reproducing the text of WT/GC/W/514 above n 99); ACP Declaration on the Fifth Ministerial Conference of the WTO (WTO Doc WT/MIN(03)/4 21 August 2003) at para 39; Caribbean Declaration on the Fifth Ministerial Conference of the WTO (WTO Doc WT/MIN(03)/6 29 August 2003) at para 19.

[101] Draft Cancún Ministerial Text 12 September 2003 at para 14 available at <http://www.wto.org>.

[102] See Larry Elliott, Charlotte Denny, and David Munk 'Blow to World Economy as Trade Talks Collapse' *Guardian Unlimited* 15 September 2003 available at <http://www.guardian.co.uk/international/story/0,3604,1042269,00.html>; Guy de Jonquieres 'WTO Talks Collapse Without Agreement' *FT.Com* 15 September 2003 <http://news.ft.com>.

chair decided there was no consensus, and he brought the meeting to a close.[103] Investment issues were now left for further discussion at a special meeting of the General Council on 15 December 2003.[104] At that meeting, investment issues were again left for further discussion. They were, in effect, dropped from the WTO agenda.[105]

From the above, it may be concluded that the institutional context of the WTO, especially the manner in which the preparations for Cancún, and the subsequent discussions, were carried out, left much to be desired. It is perhaps not surprising then, that the developing countries were not open to persuasion. In any case, the support for investment rules on the part of the EU was more apparent than real, as testified by the willingness to drop investment at Cancún, and by the fact that some EU Member State ministers were already prepared to make concessions over investment prior to the Cancún meeting.[106] Indeed, investment may have been no more than a bargaining counter with the developing countries over agriculture, the main issue at Cancún.[107] Accordingly, the failure to agree on investment at the WTO can be said to have arisen both as a result of traditional opposition to multilateral investment rules on the part of host countries, eager to guard their sovereignty and regulatory discretion, and as a result of the peculiarities of WTO diplomacy.

(2) The Content of International Investment Agreements

Having traced the history of the development of international investment rules, this part of the chapter will now briefly analyse the most common provisions found in IIAs. The main focus will be on BITs, as they represent the most common type of IIA. It is beyond the present work to offer a comprehensive and detailed analysis of the principal provisions of IIAs. This has been done elsewhere.[108] However, a

---

[103] Whether this was due to the impasse on the Singapore Issues or not has become a matter of some controversy: see Cho above n 69 at 231–33.

[104] See Ministerial Conference Fifth Session, Cancún, Ministerial Statement, 14 September 2003 (WTO Doc WT/MIN(03)/20 23 September 2003) para 4.

[105] See WTO News 16 December 2003 'Chair wraps up: groups can restart, but still no deal on tough issues' available at <http://www.wto.org/english/news_e/news03_e/stat_gc_chair_16dec03_e.htm> where the chair does not even mention investment specifically.

[106] See Action Aid 'Chips Off the Bloc: Disunity Within the EU on Singapore Issues' (ActionAid, August 2003).   [107] See Cho above n 69 at 227–29.

[108] See in particular the UNCTAD Series on Issues in International Investment Agreements published between 1999 and 2004. All volumes have been brought together in *International Investment Agreements: Key Issues Vols I–III* (New York and Geneva: United Nations 2004) and are also available at <http://www.unctad.org/iia>. See further, for examples of major IIAs UNCTAD *International Investment Agreements: A Compendium Vols I–XIV* also available at <http://www.unctad.org/iia>. On BITs see UNCTAD *Bilateral Investment Treaties in the Mid 1990s* (New York and Geneva: United Nations, 1998) and *Bilateral Investment Treaties 1995–2005: Trends in Investment Rulemaking* (New York and Geneva: United Nations, 2007); Rudolph Dolzer and Margrete Stevens *Bilateral Investment Treaties* (The Hague: Matrinus Nijhoff, 1995); J P Laviec *Protection et Promotion des*

general analysis of the main trends in IIA practice is essential for an understanding of their role in the regulation of relations between investors and host countries. The major provisions of BITs and other IIAs are similar, although there are some significant variations in national and regional practice.[109] Most BITs, and other IIAs with investment provisions, follow the pattern used in the text below.

(a) Preamble

The preambles to IIAs set down the general objects and purposes of such treaties. Although not legally binding they may be relevant to the interpretation of the agreement. Usually, such provisions emphasize the desirability of greater economic integration between the contracting parties through improved conditions of investment as laid down in the treaty. There is little variation between the formulations used. A significant variation is where the contracting states use the preamble to define specific sectors in which investment is to be protected or promoted. For example, BITs concluded by Switzerland with Sudan and Egypt highlight investment promotion in the fields of 'production, commerce, tourism and technology'.[110]

(b) Provisions Defining the Scope of Application of the Treaty

IIAs contain provisions that define the scope of application of the treaty by reference to subject-matter, covered persons and entities, territory, and temporal effect.

Invéstissements: Etude de Droit International Economique (PUF 1985). The texts of BITs are published by ICSID in its periodically updated collection *Investment Treaties* (Oceana: Oxford University Press). There is an extensive electronic collection available through UNCTAD at <http://www.unctad.org/iia>. For analysis see further G Sacerdoti 'Recent Developments in Bilateral Treaties on Investment Protection' 269 Hague Recueil 251–460 (1997) A Akinsanya 'International Protection of Foreign Investment in the Third World' 36 ICLQ 58 (1987). For British practice, see FA Mann 'British Treaties for the Promotion and Protection of Investment' 52 BYIL 241 (1981); Denza and Brooks 'Investment Protection Treaties: United Kingdom Practice' 36 ICLQ 908 (1987). For French practice, see Patrick Juillard 'Les Conventions Bilaterales d'Invéstissement Conclues par la France' 2 JDI 274 (1979); ibid 'Les Conventions Bilaterales d'Invéstissement Conclues par la France Avec les Pays n'Appartenant pas à la Zone Franc' AFDI (1982) 760. For German practice, see Justus Alenfeld *Die Investitionsforderungsvertrage der Bundesrepublik Deutschland* (Frankfurt: Antenaum Verlag, 1970); Heinrich Klebes *Encouragement et Protection des Invéstissements Privés Dans Les Pays en Developpement - Les Traites Bilateraux de la République Federalle Allemagne dans Leur Contexte* (Thesis, Strasbourg 1983). For US practice, see Pattison 'The United States-Egypt Bilateral Investment Treaty: A Prototype for Future Negotiation' 16 Cornell Int'l Law Jo. 305 (1983), Kunzer 'Developing a Model Bilateral Investment Treaty' 15 Law & Pol'y Int'l Bus.273 (1983), Bergman 'Bilateral Investment Protection Treaties: An Examination of the Evolution and Significance of the US Prototype Treaty' 16 NYU.J.Int'l & P 1 (1983), Cody 'United States Bilateral Investment Treaties: Egypt and Panama' (1983) Ga JIL 491; Coughlin 'The US Bilateral Investment Treaty: An Answer to Performance Requirements' in BS Fisher and J Turner (eds) *Regulating the Multinational Enterprise: National and International Challenges* (Praeger, 1983) ch 7 at 129–142; Kenneth J Vandevelde *United States Investment Treaties Policy and Practice* (The Hague: Kluwer Law International, 1992).

109 UNCTAD *Investment Provisions in Economic Integration Agreements* (New York and Geneva: United Nations, 2006).   110 UNCTAD 1998 above n 108 at 31.

It is in the negotiation of these provisions that the host state can influence the effect of the treaty upon its economy, for example by restricting it to specific sectors.[111]

(i) Subject-Matter Covered

Definition of 'Investments' to Which the IIA Applies

IIAs usually commence with a provision that defines the 'investments' of the contracting parties which are covered by the treaty. More recent agreements tend to favour broad, asset based, definitions that include not only physical assets, equity, and choses in action but also intellectual property rights and contractual concessions.[112] The aim is to ensure sufficient flexibility to encompass not only equity but non-equity investments, and to allow for the evolution of new forms of investment between the parties. Furthermore, the notion of direct investment is not taken as the starting point.[113] However, certain treaties concluded by Germany contain a clause which makes clear that all the general categories of investment mentioned in the standard definition clause are to be linked to a direct investment.[114] In addition to such definitions, some agreements contain an enterprise based definition focusing on 'the business enterprise' or the 'controlling interests in a business enterprise',[115] while other agreements take a 'transaction based' definition. For example, the OECD Code of Liberalization of Capital Movements does not define 'investment' or 'capital' as such but contains a list of covered transactions in Annex A, including direct investment.[116] Limitations may be made to the definition of 'investment'. Thus some agreements exclude portfolio investment,[117] on the ground that it is less stable than direct investment and so should not be given equal protection, or limit protection to investments permitted under the law of the host country, a formulation common in Chinese and ASEAN agreements,[118] or investments of a certain size or in specific sectors.[119]

The Admission of Investments

It has already been noted that, under general international law, states have the unlimited right to exclude foreign nationals and companies from entering their

---

[111] See further UNCTAD 1998 at 32–37and UNCTAD (Key Issues) n 108 above at 119–22.

[112] See, for example, ASEAN Agreement for the Promotion and Protection of Investments, Article 1(3) in UNCTAD *Compendium Vol II* above n 108 at 294.

[113] Laviec above n 108 at 31.

[114] See eg Germany-Israel BIT 1976 Article 1(1)(a) where the general clause is preceded by a clause stating that the term investment means: '(i) investment in an enterprise involving active participation therein and the acquisition of assets ancillary thereto, or (ii) the enterprise or assets acquired as a result of such an investment' UNCTAD 1998 above n 108 at 33.

[115] See, for example, the Canada-US Free Trade Agreement 1988 cited in UNCTAD (Key Issues) vol I above n 108 at 125   [116] UNCTAD ibid at 125.

[117] See, for example, the Denmark-Poland BIT Article 1(1)(b) where investment refers to 'all investments in companies made for the purpose of establishing lasting economic relations between the investor and the company and giving the investor the possibility of exercising significant influence on the management of the company concerned' quoted in ibid at 123.

[118] ibid at 122–23.   [119] ibid at 125.

territory. There is no international standard requiring states to adopt an 'open door' to inward direct investment.[120] On the other hand, states are free to set the limits of permissible entry in their national laws as they see fit. Thus, states are free to agree to provisions in IIAs securing access to their territory by investors from another contracting party. In this regard, two main models of agreements are emerging: a 'controlled entry' model that reserves the right of the host state to regulate the entry of foreign investments into its territory and a 'full liberalization' model that extends the non-discrimination standard (both national treatment and most favoured nation (MFN) treatment) in the agreement to the pre-entry stage of the investment.[121] Such an approach is particularly favoured in the practice of NAFTA[122] and in the bilateral treaty practice of the United States and Canada.

The majority of BITs follow a 'controlled entry' approach. Therefore, the application of the treaty to an investment is made conditional on its being approved in accordance with the laws and regulations of the host state.[123] On the other hand, the US-Uruguay BIT of 25 October 2004 illustrates the 'full liberalization' approach. By Article 3(1):

Each Party shall accord to investors of the other Party treatment no less favourable than it accords, in like circumstances, to its own investors with respect to the establishment, acquisition, expansion, management, conduct, operation, and sale or other disposition of investments in its territory[124]

This is followed by Article 3(2), which extends the same protection to investments, and Article 4(1) and (2) which cover, respectively, the MFN protection of investors and investments. These provisions make entry to the host state subject to the principle of non-discrimination, and, to that extent, represent a restriction on the host state's sovereign power to regulate the entry of foreign investors. However, the application of this principle is subject to the right of the host state to exclude certain sectors from foreign investment.[125] Therefore, the US model

[120] Laviec above n 108 at 77; and chs 5 and 6 above.
[121] UNCTAD, in its study on *Admission and Establishment* (Key Issues vol I above n 108 at 142–160), identifies five models of admission and establishment clauses: investment control, which corresponds to the controlled entry approach in the text, selective liberalization, based on the GATs type 'opt-in' sectoral liberalization approach, the regional industrialization programme approach, based on certain developing country regional integration agreements, the mutual national treatment approach of the EU, and the combined national treatment MFN approach, which corresponds to the full liberalization approach in the text. See also Thomas Pollan *Legal Framework for the Admission of FDI* (Utrecht: Eleven International Publishing, 2006) ch 4 who uses a modified version of the UNCTAD classification.
[122] See NAFTA Articles 1102–08 in UNCTAD *Compendium Vol III* above n 108 at 73.
[123] See examples cited in UNCTAD 1998 above n 108 at 46–7. See also Asian African Legal Consultative Committee (AALCC) Model BIT 'Model A' art 3 which states inter alia that '[e]ach Contracting Party shall determine the mode and manner in which investments are to be received in its territory'. 'Model B' is more restrictive of investor's rights of entry in that its art 3 makes the screening of investment proposals by the host country a mandatory treaty requirement: see 23 ILM 237 (1984) or UNCTAD *Compendium Vol III* above n 108 at 115.
[124] 44 ILM 268 (2005) at 217 also available at <http://ustr.gov/assets/World_Regions?Americas/South_America/asset_upload_file440_6728.pdf>. [125] See ibid art 14(2).

accepts restrictions on entry, provided they are applied in a manner that does not discriminate against US investors.[126] Under the Russian Federation-US BIT, the contracting states agreed that, for a period of five years, the Russian Federation would be able to require permission for large-scale investments that exceed the threshold amount in the Russian Federation Law on Foreign Investments of 4 July 1991, provided that this power was not used to limit competition or to discourage investment by US companies and nationals.[127]

Applicability to Investments Made Prior to the Conclusion of the Treaty
Most BITs extend their protection to investments already made by nationals of the contracting parties prior to the conclusion of the treaty. However, not all host countries accept such a clause. Thus some treaties extend to prior investments only on condition that the host state approves a special request to that effect in each case, while others only apply to investments made at a specified date prior to the conclusion of the treaty. Some treaties contain a blanket exclusion of investments made prior to the entry into force of the treaty.[128]

(ii) Covered Persons and Entities

The protection offered by IIAs is limited to investors who invest in the territory of the host contracting state and who possess a link of nationality with the home contracting state. Consequently, the IIA must define both the persons and the corporations that are to be treated as nationals of the other contracting party for the purposes of the treaty.

The attribution of nationality to natural persons is not generally a problem. Most BITs simply refer to the country's citizenship laws as governing the matter.[129] However, further criteria might be introduced, such as a combined requirement of citizenship and residence.[130] In British practice, the right of residence has been used as an alternative to British citizenship in defining British nationals for the purpose of a BIT.[131]

---

[126] See Pattison's discussion of the US-Egypt BIT in this respect: n 108 above at 318–19. Pattison is critical of the broad exclusion of industries from the treaty which, in his opinion, created a substantial void in the protection offered. The current version of this treaty retains these exceptions: US-Egypt BIT Supplementary Protocol of 11 March 1986 para 3 at <http://www.unctad.org/sections/dite/iia/docs/bits/us_egypt.pdf>

[127] US-Russian Federation BIT 17 June 1992 Protocol para 4(a) 31 ILM 794 at 810 (1992).

[128] See UNCTAD 1998 above n 108 at 42–43 for examples of each type of provision.

[129] Eg the US-Uruguay BIT 2004 above n 124 art I 'National' of a party means a natural person who is a national of a party under its applicable law; 'investor of a Party' means 'a Party or state enterprise thereof, or a national or an enterprise of a Party, that attempts to make, is making, or has made an investment in the territory of the other Party'; 'enterprise of a Party' means 'an enterprise constituted or organized under the law of a Party, and a branch located in the territory of a Party and carrying out business activities there'. See also examples in UNCTAD 1998 ibid Table III 3 at 40.

[130] Eg Germany-Israel BIT Article I(3)(b): UNCTAD ibid at 38.

[131] See UK-Philippines BIT in Mann above n 108 art I(3)(b).

By contrast, the definition of nationality in the case of corporations is more complex. The nationality of a company may be determined by reference to one or more of the following criteria: the place of incorporation, the location of the registered office or seat of the company or by reference to the nationality of the controlling interest in the company. Each of these criteria have been used, alone or in combination, in BITs.[132] Furthermore, the term 'companies' has not been restricted to legally incorporated entities alone; often it includes references to partnerships and other forms of business association.

The most significant issue in the context of the present study is the extent to which IIAs cover the case of an investment made by a parent company from the home contracting state through a subsidiary company incorporated under the laws of the host contracting state. Can the agreement in question extend its protection to the local subsidiary of the foreign parent company notwithstanding its possession of host state nationality? The provisions of BITs have approached this problem in a number of ways.[133] First, some treaties are silent on the matter. This is the case with the majority of early BITs concluded by France and Belgium, although some more recent French agreements now include a 'control' criterion.[134] Similarly, UK practice has been not to use a test of control in determining the nationality of a locally incorporated subsidiary.[135] The legal effect of such an approach is to remove the protection of the treaty from the locally incorporated subsidiary.

However, the provision defining the nationality of the corporation should be read alongside the definition of investments covered by the treaty. This may be broad enough to cover investments carried out through foreign owned local companies. Thus the US-Uruguay BIT of 2004 defines an 'enterprise' as 'any entity constituted or organized under applicable law, whether or not for profit, and whether privately or governmentally owned or controlled, including a corporation, trust, partnership, sole proprietorship, joint venture, association, or similar organization; and a branch of an enterprise'.[136] Without more it would be unclear from this definition whether locally incorporated foreign-owned subsidiaries were within the scope of the treaty. However, the term 'investment' is defined as 'every asset that an investor owns or controls, directly or indirectly, that has the characteristics of an investment, including such characteristics as the commitment of capital or other resources, the expectation of profit, or the assumption of risk'.[137]

---

132 For examples, see, UNCTAD 1998 above n 108 at 39–41.

133 See Laviec above n 108 at 43–48 on which the following paragraphs are based.

134 See eg France-Nepal BIT 1984 Article I in ICSID *Investment Treaties Vol 2* above n 108.

135 See eg UK-Philippines BIT above n 131 art I(4): 'The term 'company' of a Contracting Party shall mean a corporation, partnership or other association, incorporated or constituted and actually doing business under the laws in force in any part of the territory of that Contracting Party wherein a place of effective management is situated.' According to DrmMann, under this definition, '[a] Philippine company cannot claim the protection of the Agreement even if all the shares are owned by a British national': ibid at 242. 136 US-Uruguay BIT 2004 above n 124 Article I.

137 ibid.

This is sufficient to protect the investment of a national or company of the home contracting state which takes the form of a company established under the law of the host contracting state. In such a case the application of the treaty is not based on the nationality of the subsidiary, but on the nationality of its controlling interest.

A second approach to this issue is for the treaty to contain a definition of corporate nationality that includes a test based on controlling interests as an exclusive or an alternative test. Treaties using this approach include those concluded by the Netherlands, Sweden, and Switzerland.[138] This ensures that locally incorporated foreign-owned subsidiaries are covered by the treaty. However, the control test is exceptional. It makes more of the links with the home country, based on capital, than of the legal links of the subsidiary company with the host country, by reason of its incorporation there. In this the test does not represent the existing state of international law.[139]

A third approach is to infer the nationality of the home country to the subsidiary incorporated in the host country by means of an agreement between the subsidiary and the host country.[140] It is reminiscent of the approach taken under Article 25(2)(b) of the Washington Convention in relation to the jurisdiction of ICSID over disputes between the host contracting state and a local subsidiary owned by investors possessing the nationality of another contracting state.

The fourth approach is one of specifically extending the protection of the BIT to subsidiaries owned by or under the effective control of nationals or companies from the other contracting state. For example, the German model treaty extends the national treatment and MFN standards to 'investments in [the territory of a Contracting Party] owned or controlled by nationals or companies of the other Contracting Party'.[141] According to Laviec, in such a case, the protection of the treaty is extended to the local subsidiary without undermining the test of corporate nationality as established under international law. The link with home country nationals is established on the basis of their economic interests in the subsidiary, without the need to designate the subsidiary as possessing home country nationality in opposition to its nationality of incorporation.[142]

Finally, some BITs provide limited protection for shareholders from the home contracting state in companies incorporated in the host contracting state, even

---

[138] UNCTAD 1998 above n 108 at 39; Laviec above n 108 at 45.

[139] Laviec ibid. See the *Barcelona Traction* case above n 2 which rejected a test of corporate nationality based on the nationality of the controlling interest favouring a test based on the nationality of the place of incorporation or principal seat of management.

[140] See eg Netherlands-Kenya Agreement on Economic Co-operation 11 June 1979 Tractatenblad 1970 No 166 art XIV: 'For the purpose of the present Agreement: .... (b) a legal person which is lawfully established in the territory of a Contracting Party shall be a national of that Contracting Party in conformity with its legislation; except where any such legal person, established in the territory of a Contracting Party is controlled by a national or nationals of the other Contracting Party and it has been agreed between the legal person, and the first mentioned Contracting Party that it should be treated for the purposes of this Agreement as a national of the other Contracting Party.'

[141] Germany-St Lucia BIT 1985 art 3(1) ICSID *Investment Treaties Vol 2* above n 108.

[142] Laviec above n 108 at 46–47.

though they do not extend their protection to locally incorporated foreign-owned companies. Thus, in the UK-Philippines BIT,[143] Article V(2) extends the protection against unlawful expropriation to cases where the assets of a company incorporated under the law of the expropriating state are taken, and in which nationals or companies of the other contracting state own shares. Furthermore, by Article X(2) companies incorporated under the law of one contracting party, in which a majority of the shares are owned by nationals or companies of the other contracting party, shall be treated, for the purposes of disputes under the Washington Convention, as companies of the other contracting party, in accordance with Article 25(2)(b) of that convention. These provisions represent departures from the law on the diplomatic protection of shareholders, as laid down in the *Barcelona Traction* case.[144] Consequently, these provisions represent specific treaty based standards of treatment and not general principles of international law.

(iii) Territorial Application

It is unnecessary to go into detail on these provisions. The territorial scope of the treaty will be defined by its terms. Usually, the treaty will apply throughout the territory of all the contracting states. However, it may contain territorial extension or restriction clauses. A particular problem that has been encountered concerns the applicability of the treaty to maritime exclusive economic zones. This may be particularly important in relation to the treatment of offshore natural resource concessions.[145]

(iv) Temporal Application

The entry into force of a treaty occurs on the date designated by the parties for this purpose. The usual practice is that the IIA enters force either upon the exchange of instruments of approval or ratification, or upon reciprocal notification that the relevant constitutional requirements of each contracting state have been fulfilled, or at a set date after such notification has been given, usually after one month.[146] The termination of the treaty is usually provided for in that the treaty is designated to last for a period of years. The usual period is ten years, although shorter terms of five years and longer terms of up to 20 years have been agreed. Some treaties are open-ended, providing for termination after the giving of the required period of notice. In addition, there may be clauses that extend the operation of the protection granted by the treaty beyond the date of termination in cases where individual investments, entered into while the treaty was in force, continue after the date of termination.[147]

---

[143] Above n 131.   [144] ICJ Reports (1970) 3 and see n 139 above.
[145] See further UNCTAD 1998 above n 108 at 41–42.   [146] ibid at 43–44.
[147] ibid at 44.

(c) Standards of Treatment

The core provisions of BITs concern the standards of treatment to be applied to investments made by nationals and companies of one contracting party in the territory of the other. The applicable standards can be classified into general standards, encompassing both international minimum standards of treatment and standards evolved in earlier Friendship Commerce and Navigation (FCN) treaties,[148] and specific standards applicable to particular incidents of investment activity, such as the transfer of funds and taxation.

(i) General Standards of Treatment

General standards of treatment have been divided into those recognised by general international law and those that have evolved out of commercial treaty practice.[149] The principal general standards of treatment referred to in IIAs are those of fair and equitable treatment, national treatment and the MFN standard. Many treaties also contain clauses protecting the observance of obligations entered into between the investor and the host state. The interpretation of these standards by arbitral tribunals has already been considered in chapter 16. Here the focus is on how these standards are drafted in IIA provisions.

Fair and Equitable Treatment

This concept is not normally precisely defined in IIAs. Usually it is simply stated either alone or in conjunction with a reference to international law. It has been suggested that fair and equitable treatment represents a classical international law standard which embodies international minimum standards of treatment.[150] According to Laviec, a reference to fair and equitable treatment should not be read as a reference to international minimum standards. If the intention is to assimilate the two

---

[148] FCN treaties were concluded primarily by the United States with its advanced trading partners, although other advanced countries also concluded such treaties. The first treaty of amity and commerce signed by the United States was a treaty of 6 February 1778 with France: see Wilson 'Postwar Commercial Treaties of the United States' 43 AJIL 262 at 277 (1949). Such treaties included provisions on the protection of corporate investments, based on the national treatment standard. See, for example, art III (2) of the US-Italy FCN Treaty of 2 February 1948; art III(3) of the US-China FCN of 4 November 1946: see Wilson at 265. Article III(2) of the US-Italy Treaty was the subject of litigation before the ICJ in *Elettronica Sicula SpA (ELSI) (United States v Italy)* judgment 20 July 1989 ICJ Reports (1989) at 15. FCN treaties are no longer being negotiated, although such treaties remain in force for a number of countries. The principal reason for their demise is that such treaties contain a breadth of provisions dealing not only with commercial matters but also with the protection of the rights of individuals and with general good relations between the signatory states. They do not have a specific business orientation. Nor do they deal in adequate detail with the most pressing problems likely to be faced by foreign investors, such as funds transfers, unfair treatment or dispute settlement. Furthermore, FCN treaties were concluded primarily between the economically advanced states. Their purpose was to further good relations between them. Such treaties were not, therefore, suited to the task assigned to BITs, namely, the control of less-developed, capital-importing states in their treatment of foreign investors.   [149] See generally Laviec above n 108 Chapter III.
[150] See UNCTAD 1998 above n 108 at 53.

concepts, this should be made explicit in the text.[151] Otherwise, the fair and equitable treatment standard should stand on its own.[152] Indeed, the US-Uruguay BIT of 2004 contains, in Article 5(1) thereof, a provision which mentions fair and equitable treatment alongside international minimum standards.[153] Article 5(2) goes further and expressly states that '[f]or greater certainty, paragraph 1 prescribes the customary international law minimum standard of treatment of aliens as the minimum standard of treatment to be afforded to covered investments'. It continues by saying that '[t]he concepts of "fair and equitable treatment" and "full protection and security" do not require treatment in addition to or beyond that which is required by that standard and do not create additional substantive rights'. This is a direct response, to the suggestion made in NAFTA arbitral decisions, that this standard is additive to the international law standard.[154] It also makes clear that the agreement applies international minimum standards of treatment as part of the fair and equitable standard.

The practice of capital-importing countries concerning consent to the fair and equitable treatment standard is uneven. It is not included in the AALCC model treaties.[155] Nor has it been accepted by certain Asian and African states in their negotiations.[156] On the other hand, it does appear in some agreements with Central and South American states.[157] Furthermore, China has accepted the standard in some, but not all, of the agreements entered into by it.[158] The standard is accepted in the ASEAN multilateral investment framework.[159]

National Treatment
National treatment provisions are drafted according to a common basic pattern, but with some significant variations.[160] Some agreements do not refer expressly to

[151] For example, agreements concluded by France relate fair and equitable treatment to the general principles of international law and require that the right this states must not be impaired de jure or de facto (Article 3: see French Model BIT in UNCTAD 1998 ibid at 254.) Agreements concluded by Belgium-Luxembourg also normally specify that fair and equitable treatment 'may in no case be less favourable than that recognized by international law'. See art 3 Belgium-Luxembourg Economic Union-Malaysia BIT 8 February 1982 *Moniteur Belge* 30 March 1982.

[152] Laviec above n 108 at 94.   [153] Above n 124.   [154] See ch16 at 637–38.

[155] Above n 123.

[156] For example most, although not all, treaties signed by Rwanda, Pakistan, Singapore, and Saudi Arabia: UNCTAD 1998 above n 108 at 54.   [157] ibid.

[158] See Belgium-Luxembourg Economic Union-People's Republic of China (PRC) BIT 4 June 1984 art 3(1): accords 'equitable treatment' to direct or indirect investments: 24 ILM 537 at 540 (1985). This is supplemented by a reference to treatment not less favourable than that provided for in the 'generally recognised principles and rules of international law adopted by the Contracting Parties'. ibid Protocol art 7 at ILM 549. France-PRC BIT 30 May 1984 art 3(1): accords 'fair and equitable treatment to the investments made by investors of the other party' ibid ILM 552. See too Australia-PRC BIT 11 July 1988 art 3(a): 28 ILM 121 at 127 (1989). Not all BITs concluded by China contain the equitable treatment standard. Thus the Japan-PRC BIT of 27 August 1988 contains only the national treatment and MFN standards: 28 ILM 575 (1989).

[159] Above n 112 art III(2). See also the 1998 Framework Agreement on the ASEAN Investment Area, Article 5(a) which requires Member States to 'ensure that all programmes are undertaken on a fair and mutually beneficial basis' and (b) which requires transparency: UNCTAD *Compendium Vol VI* above n 108 at 230.

[160] See generally *National Treatment* in UNCTAD (Key Issues) vol I at 161–81 on which this section is based. The author prepared the original manuscript for the UNCTAD paper.

national treatment so as to avoid extending preferential treatment reserved for national enterprises to their foreign counterparts. This was the policy of China in its early agreements, although references to national treatment appear in its more recent agreements usually with the qualification that such treatment will be accorded subject to national laws and regulations. More recent Chinese agreements contain an unreserved national treatment provision.[161] On the other hand, the majority of IIAs do contain a national treatment clause. This covers a number of specific matters.

First the scope of application will be defined. As noted above, agreements such as NAFTA and the US and Canadian Model BITs apply the standard both to pre- and post-entry treatment, while BITs concluded by European capital-exporting countries tend to apply only to post-entry treatment. By contrast, as seen in chapter 6, the GATS has a hybrid approach allowing national treatment under Article XVII only in those sectors that the members have included in their schedules under Article XVI, and subject to any restrictions reserved by the member in question in their schedule to Article XVII. In addition some agreements, notably again the North American regional and bilateral agreements, specify that national treatment will apply to the political sub-divisions of the contracting parties. However, silence on this point does not mean that such sub-divisions are excluded from the standard. It is implicit in the standard itself that it applies to all forms of discriminatory treatment unless expressly excluded.

The national treatment clause will then determine the factual situations to which it applies. Some agreements refer to the 'same' or 'identical' circumstances to limit the application of the standard, or designate specific sectors or activities to which it applies.[162] The greatest subject-matter coverage will be available under clauses that refer to 'like circumstances' or 'similar circumstances'. Here the factual comparison to be made does not need to be as exact as under the more precise formulations. It was seen in chapter 16 that this comparison should be limited to genuine likeness, as where the domestic and foreign investor operate in the same economic sector. The widest scope for comparison will come with clauses that do not refer to any factual comparisons, but merely state the standard. This approach is favoured among Chilean, French, German, Swiss, and United Kingdom BITs, although the latter also retains a functional delimitation formula in relation to investors.[163]

The national treatment clause will then define the standard of treatment itself. While some agreements, notably earlier regional economic integration agreements between developing countries, included a 'same' or 'as favourable as' standard, allowing for treatment no better than that accorded to domestic investors, the majority of agreements use the 'no less favourable' standard. This permits treatment more favourable than that accorded to domestic investors, where the host country so chooses, and for the application of international

---

[161] ibid at 187 n 6.   [162] See ibid at 171 for examples.   [163] ibid at 173.

minimum standards of treatment where national standards fall below this. In addition, some agreements extend the standard to both de jure and de facto discrimination.[164] Where the provision is silent on the matter, it is possible to interpret the standard to include both types of discrimination, as was seen in relation to NAFTA in chapter 16.

Finally, the national treatment provision may be a 'stand alone' provision or be combined in one clause with the Most Favoured Nation standard and/or fair and equitable treatment. It may also be subject to exceptions. These may be of a general kind such as national security, public health and public morality exceptions, subject-specific exceptions, industry-specific exceptions and, possibly, development exceptions.[165]

Most Favoured Nation (MFN) Standard

The MFN standard presents few drafting issues. As noted in chapter 16, it is a treaty based standard that may be conditional or unconditional, though the latter formulation is now the norm. It will be subject to exceptions, especially in relation to taxation and regional economic integration commitments entered into by the contracting parties under other agreements. It may appear on its own or be combined with the national treatment standard in a single provision. There may also be provision for the more favourable of the two standards to prevail in any given case.[166]

The Observance of Obligations

BITs usually contain provisions that ensure the observance of laws and regulations, which provide for more favourable treatment of investors than the standards contained in the treaty, and of obligations entered into under investment agreements or authorizations.[167] The former preserves any benefits owed to investors under host state laws, regulations, or other international agreements that go beyond the standards of treatment provided for in the treaty, thereby avoiding the use of the BIT as a statement of the maximum possible protection that the investor can enjoy. The latter ensures that the observance of any obligations entered into by the host state towards the foreign investor, either under a state contract or within the terms of an authorization for the admission of the investment, becomes an obligation under the treaty.[168] Such a provision, known as an 'umbrella clause', ensures an additional measure of contractual stability by making the observance of obligations owed to the investor a treaty standard, thereby reinforcing the existing contractual duties owed to the investor.

---

[164] See, for example, GATS Article XVII(2) and (3).
[165] See UNCTAD above n 160 at 177–80.
[166] See, for example, NAFTA Article 1104 above n 122 at 74.
[167] See UNCTAD 1998 above n 108 at 56, 86–87; US Uruguay BIT 2004 above n 124 Article 16.
[168] ibid at 56 n 66.

'Umbrella clauses' have been the subject of some controversial arbitral decisions before ICSID. In particular two decisions, interpreting, respectively, the Swiss BITs with Pakistan and the Philippines, sought to determine whether the umbrella clause in those agreements provided jurisdiction for an international arbitral tribunal to determine the effects of an alleged breach of the underlying investment agreement between the investor and the host country.[169] Each case was brought by the same claimant, the Swiss based Société Générale de Surveillance (SGS), and covered the same question, namely, whether the applicable BIT could be used to found a claim against the host country for alleged breaches of the investment contract between the disputing parties, concerning the provision of pre-shipment customs inspection services. In *SGS v Pakistan*,[170] Pakistan argued that the claim could not be heard under the BIT as it arose entirely out of the contract between the parties, and Article 11 of that contract provided for all disputes to be heard before a local arbitral tribunal in the host country. Pakistan relied on the decision of the Annulment Committee in the *Vivendi* case[171] where it was held that where the basis of the claim is a breach of contract, the tribunal will give effect to any valid choice of forum clause. The tribunal upheld Pakistan's objection to jurisdiction. It followed the *Vivendi* case and accepted that contract based and treaty based claims were not identical.[172] Accordingly, contract claims stood to be determined by the tribunal selected under the forum selection clause in the contract. This did not, however, oust the jurisdiction of the international arbitral tribunal to hear claims based on the BIT, especially as the dispute settlement clause in the BIT, Article 9, did not state that the jurisdiction of the tribunal to determine claims in violation of the BIT was not exclusive.[173] The tribunal then turned its attention to the claimant's argument that the umbrella clause in the Swiss-Pakistan BIT gave the tribunal jurisdiction over the contract claims, noting that this was the first time an international arbitral tribunal had been asked to examine the legal effect of such a clause. Article 11 of the BIT states:

Either Contracting Party shall constantly guarantee the observance of the commitments it has entered into with respect to the investments of the investors of the other Contracting Party.

[169] See, for detailed analysis, Christoph Schreuer 'Travelling the BIT Route – Of Waiting Periods, Umbrella Clauses and Forks in the Road' 5 JWIT 231 (2004); Thomas Waelde 'The 'Umbrella' Clause in Investment Arbitration – A Comment on the Original Intentions and Recent Cases' 6 JWIT 183 (2005); Anthony Sinclair 'The Origins of The Umbrella Clause in the International Law of Investment Protection' 20 Arb. Int'l 411 (2004); Stanimir A Alexandrov 'Breaches of Contract and Breaches of Treaty: The Jurisdiction of Treaty-Based Arbitration Tribunals to Decide Breach of Contract Claims in *SGS v Pakistan* and *SGS v Philippines*' 5 JWIT 555 (2004); Yuval Shany 'Contract Claims vs Treaty Claims: Mapping Conflicts Between ICSID Decisions on Multisourced Investment Claims' 99 AJIL 835 (2006).

[170] ICSID Case No Arb/01/13 decision on objections to jurisdiction 6 August 2003 available at <http://www.worldbank.org/icsid> or 18 ICSID Rev-FILJ 307 (2003).

[171] *Compania des Aguas del Aconquija SA and Vivendi Universal (Formerly Compagnie Générale des Eaux) v Argentina* ICSID Case Arb/97/3 decision on annulment 3 July 2002) available at <http://www.worldbank.org/icsid> or 41 ILM 1135 (2002). On the relationship between contract claims and treaty based claims, see further ch 18 at 722–23.   [172] Above n 170 at para 147.

[173] ibid at para 152.

The tribunal rejected the claimant's argument, both on a textual basis and for policy reasons. The term 'commitments' was potentially susceptible to almost infinite expansion and the claimant's interpretation went against the generally accepted view that a breach of contract alleged by an investor in relation to a contract concluded with a state was a matter of municipal law and could not automatically be elevated into a breach of international law. The clause had to show that the contracting parties intended it to cover breaches of contract and the text of Article 11 did not do so. Nor was any other evidence of such an intention adduced by the claimant.[174] Furthermore, the consequences of adopting such an interpretation pointed against it. It would incorporate unlimited numbers of state contracts and municipal law instruments and render the substantive protection provisions in Articles 3 to 7 of the BIT superfluous. It could also nullify any freely negotiated dispute settlement clause in a state contract and would allow the investor to dictate the choice of forum, leaving the state at a procedural disadvantage.[175] Finally, the tribunal noted that Article 11 was placed at the end of the treaty and not among the main substantive obligations. It was thus not meant to project a substantive obligation. This did not mean that it was devoid of meaning. It could be invoked, for example, to ensure that the host country enacts any rules and obligations necessary to give effect to the investment, or where it interferes with the ability of the investor to pursue an international claim once consent to international arbitration has been given by the host country.[176]

By contrast, in *SGS v Philippines*[177] an umbrella clause was held to cover the contractual dispute between the parties, notwithstanding the presence of an exclusive jurisdiction clause in favour of local trial courts for such disputes. The tribunal considered that it was clear from the general language of Article 25(1) of the ICSID Convention that jurisdiction may extend to disputes of a purely contractual character, and Article 42(1), which covers the issue of applicable law, did not preclude such jurisdiction. However, the umbrella clause in the Swiss-Philippines BIT was phrased differently from the clause in the Pakistan case. Article X(2) of the Swiss-Philippines BIT states:

Each Contracting Party shall observe any obligation it has assumed with regard to specific investments in its territory by investor of the other Contracting Party.

This was a crucial point of distinction between the two cases. The tribunal noted that the language of Article X(2) was mandatory and it applied to any legal obligation undertaken for a specific investment. Thus it was unlike the formulation on the Pakistan BIT which applied to 'all commitments' and was less clear.[178] The tribunal continued by saying that, given the aim of the BIT, any uncertainty should be resolved in favour of the further protection of the covered investment.

---

[174] ibid paras 164–67. [175] ibid at para 168. [176] ibid at paras 169–72.
[177] ICSID Case No Arb /02/6 decision on objections to jurisdiction 29 January 2004 available at <http://www.worldbank.org/icsid>. [178] ibid at paras 116–17 and 121.

Thus the umbrella clause ought to be effective within the BIT and there was no presumption against the inclusion of contractual issues under international law. It all depended on the interpretation of the actual clause before the tribunal. In the present case the clause was effective in bringing a binding legal obligation within the framework of the BIT, given its object and purpose.[179] Having thus given effect to the umbrella clause, the tribunal then backed away from applying it to allow the claimant to bring their claim.[180] It held that the exclusive jurisdiction clause was not rendered ineffective by the umbrella clause. The BIT was a framework agreement that could not override the specific provisions of particular contracts freely negotiated by the parties to the dispute. Nor could a later BIT replace an earlier investment contract as these were legal instruments of differing types. In addition, although an exclusive jurisdiction clause could not affect the jurisdiction of a tribunal over a contractual claim, it could affect admissibility. In the present case SGS had to comply with the exclusive jurisdiction of the Philippine's courts in relation to contract based claims.[181] Finally, the tribunal inquired whether there were any independent claims based on the breach of the BIT as such. It held that there were not as the dispute was only about money owed under a contract. There was no expropriation claim raised on the facts and the fair and equitable treatment claim, like the claim under the umbrella clause, was premature as it had to await the resolution of the amount payable under the contract before it could be addressed under the BIT.[182]

The above awards offer little guidance on the precise scope of the umbrella clause, other than the obvious fact that the effect of the clause depends on its actual wording.[183] Given the absence of a doctrine of precedent in international arbitral jurisprudence, neither decision is conclusive or binding.[184] Which approach is preferred will depend on the degree to which the discretion of the host country is sought to be controlled. A wider discretion for the host country flows from the approach of the *Pakistan* case while the *Philippines* case takes a more investor centred approach.[185] Given the aim of BITs, and other IIAs, to create a

---

[179] ibid paras 116–22.   [180] See, for critical analysis, Waelde above n 169.
[181] Above n 177 at paras 141–55.   [182] ibid at paras 159–63.
[183] According to Shany above n 169 the differences in the decisions can also be explained by different ideological positions taken by tribunals on the issue of how to resolve competition between different norms applicable to an investment dispute. The *Pakistan* case is described as 'disintegrationalist', seeking to limit harmonization of norms by reference to limiting jurisdictional rules, while the *Philippines* case is seen as 'integrationalist' seeking harmonization of different rules before a widened ICSID jurisdiction.
[184] See *SGS v Philippines* above n 177 at para 97 where the tribunal explains that it is not bound to follow the interpretation of the umbrella clause in the Pakistan case.
[185] See UNCTAD *State Contracts* Series on issues in international investment agreements (New York and Geneva: United Nations, 2004) at 23 and Schreuer above n 169 at 255 who feels the umbrella clause would be rendered devoid of effect if the *Pakistan* case approach is taken. But see, for an opposite view, *Pan American Energy LLC v Argentina* ICSID Case No Arb/03/13 Decision on Preliminary Objections 27 July 2006 at <http://www.ita.law.uvic.ca> and *El Paso International Company v Argentina* ICSID Case No Arb/03/15 Decision on Jurisdiction 27 April 2006 at <http://www.ita.law.uvic.ca>. In both cases the ICSID Tribunals felt that such a reading of the umbrella clause would allow any

good investment climate, and to control excesses of governmental abuse of power in relation to investors, the correct approach may be to use the umbrella clause to cover only those breaches of contract that stem from such an abuse of power, and not from ordinary commercial breach.[186] This distinction may not resolve satisfactorily the issue of venue for the dispute. The investor may try to colour any breach of contract in the language of maladministration, in order to convert the commercial breach of contract into a breach of the applicable IIA, so as to secure international arbitration over any local dispute settlement procedures stipulated in the contract. This was precisely the fear expressed by the tribunal in the *Pakistan* case when it referred to the risk of unequal procedural advantages accruing to the investor under an expansive reading of the umbrella clause. Nor is it clear what such a reading of the umbrella clause would add to existing protection available to the investor under the expropriation, fair and equitable, treatment, and non-discrimination provisions of the applicable BIT or other IIA, which would appear to cover most, if not all, foreseeable types of maladministration on the part of the host country. If the umbrella clause means anything, it must mean that contractual obligations are protected as obligations under the BIT.[187] If so, then the inexorable conclusion must be that all substantial breaches of contract are justiciable as breaches of the BIT, unless the parties to the investment contract expressly exclude them from admissibility in their contract, as suggested in the *Philippines* case. Clearly tribunals must offer greater clarity and uniformity of approach on this issue.

(ii) Specific Standards of Treatment

BITs contain standards on specific aspects of the treatment of a foreign investment by the host state. In particular, the following matters have been commonly dealt

minor contract claim to become a BIT claim, in their view an inappropriate remedy that ICSID Tribunals had to control. See *Pan American* para 110 and *El Paso* para 82.

[186] See Waelde above n 169 at 235–36.

[187] See Schreuer above n 169 at 255. But see *Salini Construction v Jordan* ICSID Case No Arb/02/13 decision on jurisdiction 29 November 2004, 44 ILM 573 (2005) or <http://www.icsid.org> at paras 123–26 where the umbrella clause in art 2(4) of the Italy-Jordan BIT was held incapable of incorporating contractual obligations into the BIT, only obligations protective of a legal framework favourable to investors. See also *Pan American Energy LLC v Argentina* above n 185 where the tribunal endorsed the *SGS v Pakistan* decision and held that: 'it is especially clear that the umbrella clause does not extend its jurisdiction over any contract claims when such claims do not rely on a violation of the standards of protection of the BIT, national treatment, MNF [sic] clause, fair and equitable treatment, full protection and security, protection against arbitrary and discriminatory measures, protection against expropriation or nationalisation either directly or indirectly, unless some requirements are respected. However, there is no doubt that if the state interferes with contractual rights by a unilateral act, whether these contractual rights stem from a contract entered into by a foreign investor with a private party, a state autonomous entity or the state itself, in such a way that the state's action can be analysed as a violation of the standards of protection embodied in a BIT, the treaty-based arbitration tribunal has jurisdiction over all the claims of the foreign investor, including the claims arising from a violation of its contractual rights': para 112. See also, on identical terms *El Paso International v Argentina* above n 185 at para 84.

with by provisions in BITs: the free transfer of payments relating to the investment out of the host country; compensation for losses due to expropriation, armed conflict or internal disorder; the promotion of investments; the rights of entry and sojourn of individuals in connection with the investment and performance requirements. Taxation is not dealt with under BITs, save in the North American models which extend the protection against expropriation to tax measures.[188] Some treaties contain provisions expressly excluding this area from their scope.[189]

Free Transfer of Payments

Provisions on the free transfer of currency are among the most important ones in BITs.[190] They seek to ensure that the investor can transfer the income from its investment out of the jurisdiction of the host state and repatriate its capital on the termination of the investment. At the same time, such provisions may include limits on the free transfer of currency in the interests of the balance-of-payments position of the host country. Thus a balance is generally struck between the interests of the investor and of the host state. The right to transfer currency is usually subject to the requirements that it shall be made without delay, in convertible currency and at the official rate of exchange at the date of transfer.[191] Some treaties go on to specify the types of transfers protected, often by way of a non-exhaustive list,[192] while others simply refer to transfers 'in respect of investments'.[193]

Most BITs contain restrictions on free transfer based on the interests of the host state. Thus the UK-Philippines BIT states, in Article VII(1):

Each Contracting Party shall in respect of investments permit nationals or companies of the other Contracting Party the free transfer of their capital and of the earnings from it, subject to the right of the former Contracting Party to impose equitably and in good faith such measures as may be necessary to safeguard the integrity and independence of its currency, its external financial position and balance of payments, consistent with its rights and obligations as a member of the International Monetary Fund.[194]

---

[188] See US-Uruguay BIT 2004 above n 124 Article 21; Canada Model BIT Article 16 at <http://ita.law.uvic.ca/documents/Canadian2004-FIPA-model-en.pdf>.The US BIT applies non-discrimination provisions to indirect taxation as well. Both contain procedural requirements that must be complied with by the investor before any dispute relation to tax treatment can be brought under these agreements. On taxation issues under the US-Argentina BIT of 1991 see further *Pan American v Argentina* above n 185 at paras 117–39 and *El Paso v Argentina* above n 185 para 101–16.

[189] UNCTAD 1998 above n 108 at 63.   [190] UNCTAD ibid at 75.

[191] Eg US-Uruguay BIT 2004 above n 124 Article 7; Netherlands-Philippines BIT 1985 Article 7 UNCTAD ibid at 77.

[192] The US-Uruguay BIT 2004 Article 7(1) lists: contributions to capital; profits, dividends, capital gains, and proceeds from the sale of all or any part of the covered investment or from the partial or complete liquidation thereof; interest, royalty payments, management fees, technical assistance, and other fees; payments under a contract, including a loan agreement; compensation for losses due to armed conflict or civil strife or for expropriation of property, payments arising out of a dispute.

[193] Eg UK-Philippines BIT above n 131 art VII(1): 'Each Contracting Party shall in respect of investments permit nationals or companies of the other Contracting Party the free transfer of their capital and of the earnings from it …'   [194] Above n 131.

The reference to the rights and obligations of the host state as a member of the IMF introduces by implication the standards of the IMF Articles of Agreement into the BIT regime.[195] These aim at the progressive elimination of restrictions on the free transfer of funds arising from current transactions, while accepting the right of states to impose restrictions on the free movement of capital where this is necessary in the interests of that state.[196] However, should the BIT provide for a greater freedom of transfer for the investor than the IMF articles of agreement, it is arguable that the terms of the BIT should prevail, as these represent a specialized regime of investor protection that is more elaborate than the IMF regime on the transfer of funds and capital.[197] Where the BIT does not mention the IMF regime, the presumption is that it is ousted by the regime of the bilateral treaty.

Many BITs provide for the progressive phasing out of the repatriation of capital where this is warranted by the host state's foreign exchange situation. Thus, the UK-Hungary BIT provides that while each contracting party has the right, in exceptional balance of payments difficulties and for a limited period to exercise equitably and in good faith powers conferred by its laws, '[s]uch powers shall not however be used to impede the transfer of profit, interest, dividends, royalties or fees; as regards investments and any other form of return, transfer of a minimum of 20 per cent a year is guaranteed'.[198] The AALCC Models also introduce restrictions on the free transfer of capital and returns. Model 'A' contains provisions similar to the UK provisions cited above, permitting 'reasonable restrictions' and allowing for a 20 per cent guaranteed minimum right of transfer in any year period where exceptional financial or economic conditions are experienced.[199] Model 'B' leaves the repatriation of capital and returns subject to the terms set out by the host state at the time of the reception of the investment. These shall be set out in the letter of authorization issued by the host state on the approval of the investment and will remain unchanged throughout the period of the investment unless the investor and the host state agree to any alterations.[200]

Compensation for Losses Due to Armed Conflict or Internal Disorder

Most BITs contain clauses providing for the compensation of the investor for losses due to armed conflict or internal disorder. These have been discussed in chapter 16 above.

Compensation for Expropriation

As seen in chapter 15, one of the most contentious disputes between capital-exporting and capital-importing states over international minimum standards of treatment has been that relating to compensation for expropriation. To ensure that their preferred approach prevails, capital-exporting states have embodied their

---

[195] Laviec above n 108 at 142   [196] ibid at 138–42.   [197] ibid at 143.
[198] UK-Hungary BIT Treaty Series No 3 (1988) Cm 281. Article 7(1). See too UK-Jamaica BIT Article 7(a) and (b) cited in UNCTAD 1998 above n 108 at 79.   [199] Above n 123 at art 6.
[200] ibid at art 6.

understanding of the applicable rules of international law into the expropriation provisions of BITs.[201] Thus, practically all BITs contain a provision that permits expropriation or nationalization of assets owned by the investor from the other contacting state only where this is done for a public purpose, under due process of law, without discrimination and upon the payment of 'prompt, adequate and effective', 'adequate' or 'just' compensation in accordance with the fair market value of the assets immediately before expropriation.[202]

However, variations from this model do exist. For example, while the AALCC Model 'A' BIT accepts this formulation,[203] Model 'B' refers to 'principles for the determination of appropriate compensation'.[204] Furthermore, the UK-People's Republic of China BIT specifies a standard of 'reasonable compensation' which is defined as the real value of the expropriated investment immediately before the expropriation became public knowledge.[205] This amounts to a derogation from the usual British practice which specifies the market value of the assets expropriated, or, in the absence of a determinable market value, the actual loss sustained, on or immediately before the date of expropriation.[206] It was necessitated by the refusal of China to accept a reference to 'market' in the treaty in view of its command economy.[207] China has adopted a similar stance in treaties with other capital-exporting countries. Thus the treaty with the Belgium-Luxembourg Union speaks of compensation amounting to 'the value of the property and assets invested on the date immediately preceding the date of expropriation, or on the date on which the expropriation was made public'.[208] In the BIT with France the amount of compensation payable 'shall reflect the true value of the investments in question'.[209] In the BIT with Japan the standard of compensation is different again. Here the compensation payable 'shall be such as to place the nationals and companies in the same financial position as that in which the nationals and companies would have been if the expropriation, nationalization or any other measures the effects of which would be similar to expropriation or nationalization ... had not been taken'.[210] Thus a restitutionary standard is adopted. It can hardly be said that China has taken a uniform attitude to this question. However, she does not accept the traditional formula of 'prompt, adequate and effective' compensation.[211]

---

[201] For a full analysis, see UNCTAD 1998 above n 108 at 65–73; Laviec above n 108 ch V.

[202] See eg US-Uruguay BIT above n 124 at art 6(1). The US model also adds due process, fair and equitable treatment and observance of international minimum standards of treatment as requirements for a lawful expropriation.   [203] Above n 123 art 7.

[204] ibid art 7 Alternative 1. Note that Alternative 2 refers to the 'prompt, adequate and effective' formula.   [205] Article 5. See Denza and Brooks above n 108 at 919.

[206] Eg UK-Philippines BIT above n 131 art V(1).   [207] Denza and Brooks n 205 above.

[208] Protocol to the Belgium-Luxembourg-PRC BIT 4 June 1984 art 2: 24 ILM 537 at 546 (1985).   [209] France-PRC BIT Annex para 2. ibid at 561.

[210] Above n 158 art 5(3).

[211] According to Sornarajah the fact that the 'prompt, adequate and effective' formula is not used consistently in treaty practice weakens the argument that it represents the applicable international standard of compensation: 'State Responsibility and Bilateral Investment Treaties' 20 JWTL 79 at 91–92 (1986).

Concerning the modalities of payment, most BITs provide for the payment of interest and for payment without delay in fully realizable and transferable form. Furthermore, many treaties provide for judicial review, before the courts and tribunals of the host state, of the legality of the expropriation and of the amount of compensation being offered.[212] Finally, as noted in chapter 15, the majority of BITs cover not only direct expropriation but also indirect measures that have the effect of neutralizing the value of the investor's assets, while leaving their formal ownership intact.[213]

Other Specific Standards

Among other, less common, specific standards to be found in BITs are: general statements committing the home and/or host state to providing investment promotion incentives;[214] provisions protecting the right of entry and sojourn of individuals in connection with the investment, subject to the laws of the host state and the hiring of local personnel;[215] restrictions on the imposition of performance requirements on investors by the host state;[216] and transparency obligations.[217] In addition, the most recent US BITs contain provisions asserting that it is inappropriate for host countries to seek investment through the lowering of environmental or labour standards, while the Canadian counterpart applies to health, safety, and the environment.[218] The Canadian model is also notable for the inclusion of a general exceptions clause protecting the rights of the contracting parties to regulate in the fields mentioned by its terms. The clause follows the general pattern of Article XX GATT 1994 by listing areas in which regulation is consistent with the provisions of the BIT and adds a 'chapeau' requiring such regulation not to be arbitrary, discriminatory or a disguised restriction on trade and investment.[219] By contrast, the US model reserves only measures aimed at the maintenance or restoration of international peace or security, or the protection of essential security interests.[220] Finally, it should be noted that the extension of future BITs and other IIAs to include obligations upon investors and home countries has been proposed.

---

212 Eg UK-Philippines BIT above n 131 art V(1); Japan-PRC BIT above n 158 art 5(4).
213 For examples of the formulations used, see UNCTAD 1998 above n 108 at 65–66 and see ch 15 at 587–96.   214 UNCTAD 1998 ibid at 50–51.
215 ibid at 83–84.
216 ibid at 81–82 and see US-Uruguay BIT 2004 above n 124 at art 8. See, for a full discussion, UNCTAD *Host Country Operational Measures* Series on issues in international investment agreements (New York and Geneva: United Nations, 2001).
217 See, for example, US-Uruguay BIT 2004 arts 10–11. See, for a full discussion, UNCTAD *Transparency* Series on issues in international investment agreements (New York and Geneva: United Nations, 2004).
218 US-Uruguay BIT 2004 arts 12, 13, Canadian Model BIT art 11 above n 188. The areas covered are: protection of human animal and plant life and health, compliance with laws not inconsistent with the agreement, the conservation of living or non-living exhaustible natural resources, prudential financial regulation, monetary credit and exchange rate policies, essential security interests, the upholding of UN obligations and international peace and security interests, confidentiality laws, cultural industries, and measures taken in conformity with WTO decisions.
219 Above n 188 at art 10.   220 US-Uruguay BIT 2004 above n 124 at art 18.

This is seen as a means of ensuring a fair balance of rights and duties between the investor, the host and home country, thereby ending the prioritization of investor rights and host country obligations characteristic of existing agreements.[221]

(d) Dispute Settlement Clauses

Dispute settlement clauses in BITs, and other types of IIAs, can be divided between those dealing with disputes between the contracting states as to the observance and interpretation of the treaty, and those dealing with disputes between the investor and the host state.

(i) Disputes Between the Contracting Parties

Two settlement procedures are used in all BITs, namely, negotiation and ad hoc arbitration.[222] The usual procedure is for a dispute to be settled by negotiation between the contracting states, or, if this is not possible, to go to arbitration. The arbitration procedure most commonly followed is that of a three member tribunal, each contracting party appointing one member, with the chairman being appointed by these two from among nationals of third states.[223] There is usually a time limit specified within which such choices must be made. If they are not then recourse may be had to the President of the International Court of Justice, the Secretary-General of the United Nations, the Secretary-General of ICSID, or to some other specified international figure, to make the necessary appointments.[224] The decision of the tribunal is reached by majority vote and is binding on the parties. The tribunal fixes its own rules of procedure although the US model treaty specifies the use of the UNCITRAL Arbitration Rules in the absence of agreement between the parties.[225] As to the applicable law, few BITs contain specific clauses on this matter. Those that do tend to refer to 'international law' or to 'general principles of law'.[226]

A particular provision found in virtually all BITs, which can give rise to disputes between the contracting states, concerns the subrogation of the investor's claims against the host state to the home state, after that investor has been compensated for its losses out of 'political risks' insurance taken out with the investment insurance agency of the home state.[227] In such a case, the home state is

---

[221] See, for example the IISD Model International Agreement on Investment for Sustainable Development (April 2005) in 20 ICSID Rev-FILJ 91 (2005) and Howard Mann 'Introductory Note' ibid at 84. See also UNCTAD *World Investment Report 2003* (New York and Geneva: United Nations, 2003) ch VI.

[222] UNCTAD 1998 above n 108 at 100. See, for a full discussion, UNCTAD *Dispute Settlement: State-State* Series on issues in international investment agreements (New York and Geneva: United Nations, 2003).

[223] See eg UK-Philippines BIT above n 131 above art XI; Japan-PRC BIT above n 158 art 13.

[224] UNCTAD 1998 above n 108 at 101.

[225] See, for example, US-Uruguay BIT 2004 above n 124 at art 37(1).

[226] UNCTAD 1998 above n 108 at 101–102.

[227] ibid at 88–89. The US does not use such a clause in its BITs as it concludes special investment guarantee agreements with host countries as part of its overseas investment insurance programme. See further ch 15 at 614–15.

entitled to benefit from any compensation that the host state is liable to pay to the investor, up to the amount that has been paid out to the investor under the insurance cover. The normal formulation excludes any acceptance of liability on the part of the host state merely by virtue of its recognition of the home state's rights of subrogation, a right that arises from the insurance contract between the home state and the investor, and not from any delictual conduct on the part of the host state.[228]

(ii) Disputes Between the Host State and the Foreign Investor

Early BITs did not cover the issue of disputes between the host state and the investor. However, the conclusion of the Washington Convention of 1965, setting up ICSID, prompted the inclusion of ICSID jurisdiction clauses in BITs.[229] All the model agreements in their current versions include an ICSID clause.[230] Earlier treaties refer to ICSID as the only system of dispute settlement to be used between investors and host states,[231] while more recent ones offer a choice between ICSID and other systems of international arbitration.[232] More recently the US and Canadian model BITs have included detailed provisions of dispute settlement that seek to tailor procedures to the specific concerns of these countries for more effective and transparent arbitral procedures in the investment field.[233] As with dispute settlement between the contracting parties, virtually all investor-state dispute settlement clauses require that the dispute be settled first by amicable means including consultation, negotiation, and other non-binding third party means.[234]

---

[228] Eg UK-Philippines BIT above n 131 art VIII(1): 'If either Contracting Party makes payment under an insurance or guarantee agreement with its own nationals or companies in respect of an investment or any part thereof in the territory of the other Contracting Party, the latter Contracting Party shall recognise the assignment of any right or claim arising from the indemnity paid, by the party indemnified to the former Contracting Party, and that the former Contracting Party is entitled by virtue of subrogation to exercise the rights and assert the claims of such nationals or companies. This does not necessarily imply, however, a recognition on the part of the latter Contracting Party of the merits of any case or the amount of any claim arising therefrom.'

[229] See generally UNCTAD *Dispute Settlement: Investor-State* Series on issues in international investment agreements (New York and Geneva: United Nations, 2003) and see ch 18.

[230] UNCTAD 1998 above n 108 at 94–95.

[231] This is true in UK practice: Denza and Brooks above n 108 at 920; and see UK-Philippines BIT above n 131 at art X.

[232] Eg AALCC Model 'A' above n 123 at art 10 (iii)–(v) which offers ICSID as the first choice for the parties to the dispute, with the UNCITRAL Arbitration Rules 1976 applying where ICSID procedures are inapplicable. See also the ASEAN Agreement on Promotion and Protection of Investments of 15 December 1987 above n 112 art X(2) which offers a choice of ICSID, UNCITRAL, the Regional Centre for Arbitration at Kuala Lumpur, or any other regional centre for arbitration in ASEAN. For further examples, see UNCTAD 1998 above n 108 at 95–96 and UNCTAD *Dispute Settlement: Investor-State* above n 229 at 37–44.

[233] See US-Uruguay BIT 2004 Section B above n 124; Canadian Model BIT Section C above n 188.

[234] See, for example, US-Uruguay BIT 2004 ibid art 23 and UNCTAD *Dispute Settlement: Investor-State* above n 229 at 23–25.

Where a BIT refers to ICSID arbitration the precise wording of the clause is important. If the wording shows complete and unconditional consent on the part of the contracting state to the use of ICSID arbitration, this can amount to a unilateral offer of such arbitration to investors from the other contracting state, which can be turned into a binding consent to ICSID jurisdiction where the investor requests such arbitration in writing.[235] On the other hand, where the clause is conditional on further agreement to submit the dispute to ICSID it will be ineffective, on its own, to found the jurisdiction of the Centre. The host state will then retain the choice whether or not to consent to ICSID jurisdiction. In order to avoid disputes over the effect of clauses purporting to establish ICSID jurisdiction, ICSID has drawn up model clauses for BITs.[236] However, these have not been widely used and consent clauses have grown up in a rather haphazard fashion, requiring interpretation of their precise terms.[237]

In more recent years the question has arisen whether choice of dispute settlement clauses in investor-state agreements can operate to prevent the institution of international dispute settlement procedures where an option to use domestic dispute settlement procedures is available and the investor makes a choice to that effect.[238] Such 'fork-in-the-road' clauses have been the subject of recent arbitral interpretation before ICSID.[239] The key issue concerns whether the dispute submitted by the investor to the national courts or tribunals is one that invokes a

[235] Thus by art X(1) of the UK-Philippines BIT n 131above:

'The Contracting Party in the territory of which a national or company of the other Contracting Party makes or intends to make an investment shall assent to any request on the part of such national or company to submit, for conciliation or arbitration, to the Centre established by the Convention on the Settlement of Investment Disputes between States and Nationals of Other States opened for signature at Washington on 18 March 1965 any dispute that may arise in connection with the investment.'
By art X(2) access to ICSID arbitration is extended to,
'A company which is incorporated or constituted under the law in force in the territory of one Contracting Party and in which before such a dispute arises the majority of shares are owned by nationals or companies of the other Contracting Party', provided that the requirements of art 25(2)(b) of the Washington Convention are complied with. See also UK-Sri Lanka BIT 13 February 1980 art 8(1) which formed the legal basis for the ICSID arbitration in *Asian Agricultural Products Ltd v Republic of Sri Lanka* ICSID Case No Arb/87/3 award of 21 June 1990: 30 ILM 577 (1991). On the requirements of Art 25(2)(b), see ch 18 at 726–31.

[236] See ICSID/6 (1969): 8 ILM 1341 (1969).

[237] See Christoph Schreuer *The ICSID Convention: A Commentary* (Cambridge: Cambridge University Press, 2001) 210–21 and see ch 18 at 719–24.

[238] An example of such a choice is found in Article 8 of the China-Vietnam BIT 1992 cited in UNCTAD 1998 above n 108 at 91. See also Argentina-France BIT 1991at art 8(2): 'Once the investor has submitted the dispute either to the jurisdictions of the Contracting Party involved or to international arbitration, the choice of one or the other of these procedures shall be final' cited in Schreuer above n 169 at 240; Spanish original is in ICSID *Investment Treaties Vol 3* (Dobbs Ferry, New York: Oceana Publications, Release 92–4, March 1993); US-Uruguay BIT 2004 above n 124 Annex C(2): 'For greater certainty, if an investor of the United States elects to submit a claim [under Section B, the investor-State dispute settlement provisions of the Treaty] to a court or administrative tribunal of Uruguay, that election shall be definitive, and the investor may not thereafter submit the claim to arbitration under Section B.'

[239] See the discussion in Schreuer above n 237 at 239–49.

claim of a breach of the applicable BIT, or whether it is an independent cause of action that raises no such issue.[240] If the national claim is identical to the international claim made before the ICSID Tribunal then the jurisdiction of the latter body has been excluded by the investor's choice under the fork-in-the-road provision. However, questions that can only be determined under the applicable national law of the host country, such as whether a licence has been properly refused or a tax properly charged, can only be considered before national courts or tribunals in the first instance. Such determinations do not, of themselves, raise any issues as to the breach of a BIT, or other applicable IIA. Accordingly a choice of national tribunal by the investor in such a case will not operate to oust ICSID jurisdiction where the investor subsequently brings a separate claim alleging breach of the applicable BIT or IIA.

The reference of an issue of national law to the relevant national dispute settlement body should not preclude a subsequent international claim being brought under the treaty for an alleged violation of its protection provisions, on the ground that such a claim relates to the investment protected under the applicable treaty and is separate from the underlying national legal dispute. In such a case there can be no fork-in-the-road, as there is no identity of subject-matter in the two legal proceedings. In addition, it is not open to the host country to avoid its responsibility under international law by relying on an exclusive jurisdiction clause in a contract with the investor if the national claim is not one based exclusively on the investment contract but also raises issues as to the conformity of governmental action with the BIT.[241]

A second factor that emerges from recent ICSID decisions is that the dispute brought before the national courts or tribunals, and the international claim, must be brought by the same claimant for the 'fork-in-the-road' provision to preclude international jurisdiction.[242] Thus, separate national and international claims brought by different affiliates in a corporate group, or by the parent, or ultimate owner, and their affiliates, will not be regarded as definitive choices of national over international jurisdiction, binding all members of the group to that choice. Corporate groups will not be seen as a single entity for these purposes.[243] This

---

[240] See *Genin v Estonia* ICSID Case No Arb/99/2 award of 25 June 2001 available at <http://www.worldbank.org/icsid> or 17 ICSID Rev-FILJ 395 (2002) at paras 331–33.

[241] See further *Compania de Aguas Aconquija SA and Compagnie Génerale des Eaux (Vivendi) v Argentina* ICSID Case No Arb/97/3 award of 21 November 2000 available at <http://www.worldbank.org/icsid> or 40 ILM 426 (2001) at paras 53–55 upheld by the Ad Hoc Annulment Committee above n 171 at paras 38–42 but see paras 93–115 where the Committee concluded that having accepted jurisdiction over the claimant's claims the tribunal manifestly exceeded its powers for failing to determine those claims on their merits.

[242] See *Lauder v Czech Republic* Final Award 3 September 2001 available at <http://www.mfcr.cz/Arbitraz/en/FinalAward.doc> at paras 162–63.

[243] See *CMS Gas Transmission Company v Argentina* ICSID Case No Arb/01/8 decision on jurisdiction 17 July 2003 available at <http://www.worldbank.org/icsid> or 42 ILM 788 (2003) at para 80. See also *Azurix v Argentina* ICSID Case No Arb/01/12 decision on jurisdiction 8 December 2003 available at <http://www.worldbank.org/icsid> or 43 ILM 262 (2004) at paras 86–90.

raises concerns that the group as a whole might seek to use its ability to bring multiple claims as a means of putting pressure on the host country to admit liability.[244] On the other hand, different entities in the group will have different interests to protect. Thus, the local affiliate is most likely to bring claims under national law relating to the application of legal rules and administrative decisions to the investment, while the parent, or ultimate owner, may be more likely to bring claims based on the BIT. To assimilate these parties and these claims may well deprive MNEs of important legal rights that ensure the proper operation of the investment.[245]

(3) The Effect of IIAs in the National Legal Systems of the Parties

The effect of a BIT, or other IIA, within the legal systems of the contracting states depends on the applicable rules of national law concerning the domestic effect of treaties. Under English law the conclusion and ratification of a treaty is seen as an act within the prerogative of the Crown. Consequently, if a treaty were to be directly effective within the English legal system, without the need for further legislative enactment, the Crown could bypass the sovereignty of Parliament as the supreme legislature. To avoid such a consequence a treaty can only become a part of English law if an enabling Act of Parliament has been passed.[246] Therefore, a BIT can create no directly effective legal rights within the English legal system without such transforming legislation. As it has not been the practice to pass such legislation, the legal authority of BITs concluded by the United Kingdom remains solely within the international legal system, unless the law of the other contracting state accords the status of municipal law to the treaty. Should the law of the other contracting state accord such status to the BIT, it is at least arguable that its provisions can be invoked before an English court as part of the law governing the investment, given that the governing law will be the law of the other contracting state as the *situs* of the investment. Furthermore, it may be possible to accord some domestic legal force to the BIT by incorporating its terms into a contract governed

---

[244] This point has been made in relation to the bringing of multiple claims against the Czech Republic by Netherlands based CME and its owner Ronald Lauder. However, in that proceeding the Czech Republic decided against arguing for a consolidation of the claims. See further 'Who Wins and Who Loses in Investment Arbitration? Are Investors and Host States on a Level Playing Field? – The Lauder/Czech Republic Legacy' in 6 JWIT 59–77 (2005); Charles Brower and Jeremy Sharpe 'Multiple and Conflicting International Arbitral Awards' 4 JWI 211 (2003).

[245] See Schreuer above n 237 at 249.

[246] I Brownlie *Principles of Public International Law* (Oxford: Oxford University Press, 6th edn, 2003) 45. See *The Parlement Belge* [1880] 5 PD 197; *A-G for Canada v A-G for Ontario* [1937] AC 326 at 347 per Lord Atkin. See further F A Mann 'The Enforcement of Treaties by English Courts' 44 Transactions of the Grotius Society (1958–59) 29 reproduced in F A Mann *Studies in International Law* (Oxford: Oxford University Press, 1973) ch VIII; F A Mann *Foreign Affairs in English Courts* (Oxford: Oxford University Press, 1986) ch 5.

by English law. The English court may be willing to apply the terms of the treaty as a matter incidental to the construction of the intent of the parties.[247] Indeed, in the case of *Occidental Exploration and Production Company v Republic of Ecuador*[248] the Court of Appeal accepted the right of a party to an arbitration brought under a BIT to challenge the jurisdiction of the arbitral tribunal under the UK Arbitration Act 1996, even though the treaty was not incorporated into English law. English law was chosen as the applicable procedural law by reason of the choice of London as the place of arbitration by the arbitrators. The state party, Ecuador, sought to have the award made against it set aside under sections 67 and 68 of the Act. Occidental argued that the challenge required the English courts to interpret provisions of the BIT between the US and Ecuador, in contravention of the rule that such an issue was 'non-justiciable'. The Court of Appeal rejected this position on the basis that the agreement to arbitrate made under the BIT was an autonomous agreement, and not a part of the BIT, and that the BIT conferred direct rights upon the investor. Not to allow the parties to seek their procedural remedies in these circumstances would undermine the protection afforded by BITs to investors, even if one party was a sovereign state. The Court of Appeal concluded:

And we consider that the fact that the States party to the Treaty deliberately chose to provide for a mechanism for dispute resolution which invokes consensual arbitration, with its domestic legal connotations, is a factor which should make the English Court hesitate long about subjecting such arbitration proceedings to special principles of judicial restraint developed in relation to international transactions or treaties lacking any foundation or incorporation in domestic law.[249]

The Court of Appeal highlighted that the ICSID system of international investment arbitration would not come within this approach. No recourse to an English court was currently possible given the terms of the Arbitration (International Investment Disputes) Act 1966 section 3(2). However, that did not point to the need to refrain from exercising jurisdiction under the Arbitration Act 1996 in respect of an investment arbitration conducted under the dispute settlement provision of a BIT where UNCITRAL Rules had been chosen.[250]

Unlike the United Kingdom, a number of countries adhere to the principle that treaties made in accordance with the constitution bind the courts without any specific act of incorporation.[251] However, each system must be carefully examined to see whether it imposes additional conditions before the treaty can be invoked as a source of rights under municipal law. Thus, for example, under French law the treaty must be ratified and duly published before it has the force of law.[252] By Article157 of the Sri Lankan Constitution BITs are given the force of law in

---

[247] See eg *Philippson v Imperial Airways* [1939] AC 332; *Lively Ltd v City of Munich* [1976] 1 WLR 1004.   [248] [2005] EWCA Civ 116, 45 ILM 249 (2006), [2006] 2 All ER 225 (CA).
[249] ibid at para 47.   [250] ibid at para 38.   [251] Brownlie above n 246 at 47–48.
[252] Constitution of the Fifth Republic 1958 art 55.

Sri Lanka, and no executive or administrative action can be taken in contravention of the treaty, save in the interests of national security.[253] Under US law the issue turns on the question whether the treaty is 'self-executing', that is whether it is intended to be effective as domestic law without the need of implementing legislation. If it is, then by Article VI of the US Constitution, it has the force of law, subject to modification or repeal by subsequent Act of Congress.[254]

As a general rule, the US courts, in common with other jurisdictions, will not entertain a claim arising out of an expropriatory measure taken by a foreign state, on the ground that such action constitutes an act of state which cannot be subjected to review before the US courts.[255] However, this doctrine recognizes an exception based on the terms of 'a treaty or other unambiguous agreement regarding controlling legal principles'.[256] This exception to the act of state doctrine was considered in the context of FCN treaties by the US Court of Appeals for the Sixth Circuit in *Kalamazoo Spice Extraction Co v The Provisional Military Government of Socialist Ethiopia*.[257] In that case the plaintiff corporation sought damages from the defendant government for the expropriation of its share in an Ethiopian joint venture company. The question for the US court was whether it had jurisdiction to hear the claim. The answer depended on whether the terms relating to expropriation in the US-Ethiopia Treaty of Amity and Economic Relations of 1953 came within the 'treaty exception' to the act of state doctrine, as setting down the 'controlling legal principles'. The Court of Appeals held that it did saying that the treaty was a 'controlling standard in the area of international law'. Furthermore, a similar formulation in the Treaty of Amity between the United States and Iran was held to have come within the 'treaty exception', and to have grounded jurisdiction in the case of *American International Group Inc v Islamic Republic of Iran*.[258] The Court of Appeals then referred to Article VI of the US Constitution. Having noted that this provision made treaties concluded under the authority of the United Sates the supreme law of the land, the Court held that the failure to recognize a properly executed treaty would be 'an egregious error because of the position that treaties occupy in our body of laws'.[259]

In the light of the *Kalamazoo* case, it is arguable that BITs could also come within the 'treaty exception' to the act of state doctrine, given that they contain a similar standard of compensation for expropriation to that found in US FCN treaties. However, in the more recent case of *Gulf Resources of America v Republic of Congo*[260] the US District Court for the District of Columbia rejected an argument

---

[253] See *Asian Agricultural Products Ltd v Republic of Sri Lanka* above n 235 at 632.

[254] *Head Money Cases: Edye v Robertson* 112 US 580 (1884) US Supreme Court; *Sei Fuji v California* 242 P 2d 617 (1952).

[255] This principle was affirmed by the US Supreme Court in *Banco Nacional De Cuba v Sabbatino* 376 US 398 (1964).   [256] 376 US at 428 per Harlan J.

[257] 729 F 2d 422 (1984), 23 ILM 393 (1984).   [258] 493 F Supp 522 (DDC 1980).

[259] 23 ILM 399.

[260] Civil Action No 98–2978 (TPJ) 29 July2003, US Dist Ct DC 276 F Supp 2d 20; 2003 US Dist LEXIS 13904.

that sought to give direct effect to a BIT within US law. Gulf contended that s 1605(a)(1) of the US Foreign Sovereign Immunities Act 1976 did not require a formal instrument of waiver of sovereign immunity on the part of the respondent state, with a recitation of both the name of the beneficiary and an explicit submission to the jurisdiction of US courts. If a formal instrument was necessary, Gulf argued that Congo had explicitly waived its immunity under the BIT between the United States and the Republic of Congo of 12 February 1990.[261] The Court noted that under the BIT Congo would waive sovereign immunity if an 'investment dispute' arises between 'a Party [ie Congo] and a national or company of the other party [ie the United States]'. under Article VI of thereof. This would then result in consent to ICSID arbitration or to ad hoc arbitration should recourse to the Centre be unavailable. According to Gulf the interest it acquired in Congo's royalty oil was an 'investment' and its grievances with Congo were 'disputes' subject to the provisions of the Treaty. Congo replied that the treaty did not apply to Gulf, and even if it did, the treaty's only effect would be to offer Gulf the right to compel arbitration before the ICSID, not the right to proceed with its claims before the US Court. The Court agreed with Congo's position and concluded that the US-Congo BIT 'affords no basis upon which this Court may assume jurisdiction to proceed with the case'.[262]

It is arguable that if BITs, or other IIAs, were to create new rights that were directly effective before the courts of the contracting states, this could be done by means of a specific provision in the treaty obliging the contracting states to transform the treaty into their domestic law. In particular, recourse to the courts of the home contracting state could be permitted, in default of a satisfactory hearing before the courts of the host contracting state, under the provisions guaranteeing due process in cases of expropriation or other treaty breach. However, such clauses have not been included. They would probably be unacceptable to host contracting states, as they would amount to a subjection to the extraterritorial application of home contracting state's laws. Instead BITs have tended to offer a choice between local dispute settlement in the host state, which may have incorporated the terms of the BIT into its national law, or international dispute settlement.

Concluding Remarks

The development of codified standards in IIAs has gone through a number of major phases. However, no agreed multilateral investment rules have resulted. Instead, there is a patchwork of voluntary non-governmental, and inter-governmental, codes and guidelines and legally binding BITs and other IIAs. The latter provide an increasingly settled content which has lead some to argue that these now represent

---

[261] *Treaty of Reciprocal Encouragement and Protection of Investment* 12 February 1990, US – Congo, S Treaty Doc 102–1 (1991).   [262] 276 F Supp 2d at 28; 2003 US Dist LEXIS 13904 at 24.

customary international law.[263] Although compelling, this view has itself been subjected to criticism, not least because such treaties are the outcome of individual bargaining relationships which cannot act as a source of general legal obligation.[264] Given this objection, the elevation of certain treaty based standards of treatment to norms of customary international law may be mistaken. BITs and other IIAs constitute a special juridical regime designed to restate, in treaty form, international minimum standards of treatment of foreign investors as accepted by the capital-exporting states, and to merge these with established, treaty based standards of commercial conduct that do not possess the character of customary international law, despite their widespread usage over many centuries. The result is an integrated system of norms for the international regulation of investment relationships between, primarily, developed capital-exporting states and less developed capital-importing states, in a manner conducive to efficient capital accumulation by investors from the capital-exporting states. Thus BITs and other IIAs represent a particular legal instrument seeking to solve a specific problem of international economic relations, and creating an effective *lex specialis* between the parties. They are not the equivalent of a codifying convention. On the other hand, it could be argued that the increased use of BITs between developing countries themselves[265] shows that they have an impact upon the legal regime now favoured by the traditional opponents of binding international minimum standards of treatment. Perhaps the key question is what might be gained by elevating treaty based standards to customary law? In effect, it would bind all countries to what may remain contested international minimum standards of treatment, regardless of whether such countries have signed IIAs. This would prevent freedom of choice for countries as to the extent and nature of their commitments in relation to foreign investment law. Given the widespread application of otherwise contested standards as treaty based obligations, it would appear unnecessary to do so and, in this very sensitive policy area, it could produce an unfavourable political response, retarding economic integration and development. Of far greater significance is the fact that BITs and other IIAs have introduced the choice of international investment dispute settlement, to which the next chapter turns.

---

[263] See, for example, FA Mann 'British Treaties for the Promotion and Protection of Investment' 52 BYIL 241 (1981); Patrick Juillard 'Les Conventions Bilaterales d'Invéstissement Conclues par la France' 2 JDI 274 (1979); ibid 'Les Conventions Bilaterales d'Invéstissement Conclues par la France Avec les Pays n'Appartenant pas à la Zone Franc' AFDI (1982) 760. For a more recent restatement of this position, see S Hindelang 'Bilateral Investment Treaties, Custom and a Healthy Investment Climate – The Question of Whether BITs Influence Customary International Law Revisited' 5 JWIT 789 (2004); S Schwebel 'The Influence of Bilateral Investment Treaties on Customary International Law' 98 ASIL Proceedings 27–30 (2004); Dominique Carreau and Patrick Juillard *Droit International Economique* (Paris: Dalloz, 2nd edn, 2005) Part II Title II ch 3.

[264] See M Sornarajah *The International Law on Foreign Investment* (Cambridge: Cambridge University Press, 2nd edn, 2004) at 204–17.

[265] See *World Investment Report 2003* above n 88 at 89.

18

The Settlement of International Investment Disputes

This chapter concentrates on the procedural issues associated with international dispute settlement as a method of resolving differences between MNEs and host states. It is primarily concerned with the leading system for the settlement of international investment disputes set up by the World Bank, under the Washington Convention on the Settlement of Investment Disputes Between States and Nationals of Other States 1965 (the ICSID Convention), which established the International Centre for Settlement of Investment Disputes (ICSID).[1] As noted in the previous chapter, most BITs refer to ICSID arbitration as the sole, or an optional, method of dispute settlement. Investor-state dispute settlement systems established under other types of IIAs also make use of ICSID. These include, in particular, the NAFTA, the Energy Charter Treaty, MERCOSUR and the ASEAN Agreement for the Promotion and Protection of Investments 1987, as amended. How these systems use ICSID will be considered as well. However, the ICSID system cannot be fully appreciated without a preliminary introduction to the weaknesses of traditional methods of international dispute settlement when

---

[1] The Washington Convention on Settlement of Investment Disputes Between States and Nationals of Other States 1965: 4 ILM 524 (1965), 575 UNTS 159. For detailed analysis, see Christoph Schreuer *The ICSID Convention: A Commentary* (Cambridge: Cambridge University Press, 2001); Emmanuel Gaillard *La Jurisprudence du CIRDI* (Paris: Editions Pedone, 2004). For further references to the ICSID Convention, see ICSID *ICSID Bibliography* (Doc ICSID/13/Rev 2, 1 March 1992, and subsequent revisions available at <http://www.worldbank.org>). For a definitive list of cases brought before ICSID, and of cases that have been settled or concluded, see <http://www.worldbank.org/icsid>. (All cases referred to below will be available on this site and so only printed copy references will be given.) ICSID awards are not published unless the parties give their consent. However, awards are often published in ICSID Rev-FILJ and ILM and will often first appear on the American Society of International Law website at <http://www.asil.org> (members only). Another very useful website is the Investment Treaty Arbitration site at the University of Victoria, British Columbia, see <http://www.ita.law.uvic.ca>. ICSID publishes an *Annual Report* available at <http://www.worlkbank.org/icsid,/i>. and a bi-annual News from ICSID available at <http://www.worldbank.org/icsid>. ICSID should be considered alongside MIGA as part of the World Bank's system of institutions dealing with foreign investment: see IFI Shihata 'Towards a Greater Depoliticisation of Investment Disputes: The Roles of ICSID and MIGA' 1 ICSID Rev-FILJ 1 (1986) updated version published by ICSID in 1992; Rowat 'Multilateral Approaches to Improving the Investment Climate of Developing Countries: The Cases of ICSID and MIGA' 33 Harv.ILJ 103 (1992).

applied to MNE/host state relations. Accordingly, the chapter begins with a brief overview of those weaknesses.

(1) The Limitations of Traditional International Dispute Settlement Mechanisms in MNE/Host State Relations

Under the classical theory of public international law only states have the capacity to bring international claims as they are the only subjects of that law.[2] A private person, natural or legal, lacks the legal personality at international law to pursue a claim in their own right.[3] Consequently, MNEs are not regarded as subjects of international law. 'In principle, corporations of municipal law do not have international legal personality.'[4] Nonetheless, leading jurists in the field of international law have argued for the treatment of corporations as subjects of international law to the extent that they enter into agreements with foreign governments.[5] There is some authority in international arbitral jurisprudence for the view that an investment agreement between a state and a foreign corporation is an international contract subject to international law.[6] This has been read as acknowledging at least a qualified international legal personality for the foreign corporation. However, all that can be said with certainty is that the parties to a state contract retain the right to choose the governing law of the contract.[7] This is insufficient to show that the corporate party acts like a full subject of international law.

Given the absence of international personality for the MNE, the only means open, under international law, for the bringing of a claim against the respondent state is through the intervention of the state entitled to exercise diplomatic protection on behalf of the MNE. This is the state of which the MNE is a national.[8]

---

[2] See DP O'Connell *International Law* (London: Stevens, 2nd edn, 1970) vol 1 106–107.

[3] See, in relation to the status of natural persons under human rights treaties, Peter T Muchlinski 'The Status of the Individual Under the European Convention on Human Rights And Contemporary International Law' 34 ICLQ 376 (1985). For a discussion of the need to extend international personality to individuals as the scope of international law expands, see Higgins 'Conceptual Thinking About the Individual in International Law' 4 Brit.J.Int.Stud. 1 (1978). On the artificiality of excluding the individual from international personality, see DP O'Connell ibid vol I 107–108.

[4] Ian Brownlie *Principles of Public International Law* (Oxford: Oxford University Press, 6th edn, 2003) 65.

[5] See W Friedmann *The Changing Structure of International Law* (1964) 221–231; 127 Hague Recueil (1969, II) 121–24; W Jenks 'Multinational Entities and the Law of Nations' in W Friedmann (ed) *Transnational Law in a Changing Society* (1972) 70; DA Ijalaye *The Extension of Corporate Personality in International Law* (Oceana, 1978) 221–46.

[6] See the *Texaco* arbitration 17 ILM 1 (1978).

[7] See *LIAMCO v Libya* 20 ILM (1981) 1 at 34–35; *AMINOIL v Kuwait* 21 ILM (1982) 976 paras 6–10 at 1000–1001.

[8] See, for the legal background to this issue, M Diez de Velasco 'La protection diplomatique des societes et des actionnaires'141 Hague Recueil (1974 I) 87–86; P de Visscher 'La protection diplomatique des personnes morales' 102 Hague Recueil (1961 I) 427–62; Feliciano 'Legal problems of private international business enterprises' 118 Hague Recueil (1966 II) 284–95; Staker

However, the possibility of diplomatic protection by the national state of the MNE is a remedy so replete with pitfalls that it is unlikely to be of much practical value as a means of settling an investment dispute with the host state. These difficulties stem from the discretionary nature of the remedy and from several restrictions as to its availability which are exacerbated in the case of a MNE claimant.

If the state takes up the claim of its subject, the claim becomes in effect the claim of the state.[9] This may be regarded as a legal fiction, given that the primary right giving rise to the claim is a right of the individual protected by international law.[10] However, behind this legal fiction lies the fact that international law endows the national state with discretion.[11] That state has no obligation to pursue the claim or to vindicate the rights of its subject. At all times the claim will be subject to considerations of interstate relations and may be subordinated, in certain cases, to other, more important, political goals pursued by the protecting state.[12] Furthermore, the protecting state need not even pay over to the claimant any reparations received from the respondent state, although there may be a strong moral duty to do so.[13] Consequently, there is no guarantee that, once started, an international claim brought by the protecting power of the individual will act as an effective remedy for the claimant.

Secondly, before any right to diplomatic protection can arise, the claimant must exhaust all effective local remedies within the national legal system of the respondent state. Only where such remedies are ineffective will the claimant be excused from this requirement.[14] This rule emphasizes the contingent nature of diplomatic protection, and the supplementary role that international law in fact plays in the regulation of disputes between individuals, including foreign corporations, and host states.

'Diplomatic Protection of Private Business Companies: Determining Corporate Personality for International Law Purposes' 61 BYIL 155 (1990).

[9] See *Mavromatis Palestine Concessions Case (Jurisdiction) Greece v United Kingdom* (1924) PCIJ Reports, Series A No 2 at 12. See, to the same effect, the *Panevezys-Saldutiskis Case Estonia v Lithuania* (1939) PCIJ Reports, Series A/B No 76 at 4.

[10] As Brownlie puts it, 'The subject-matter of the claim is the individual and his property: the claim is that of the state' above n 4 at 459.   [11] See O'Connell above n 2 at 109.

[12] See Raymond Vernon 'The Multinationals: No Strings Attached' 33 Foreign Policy 121 at 126–27 (1978–79).   [13] O'Connell above n 2 at 111.

[14] For analysis of the local remedies rule, see Brownlie above n 4 at 472–81; O'Connell above n 2 at 1053–59. An exhaustive analysis of the applicable principles can be found in Cancado Trindade *The Application of the Rule of Exhaustion of Local Remedies in International Law* (Cambridge: Cambridge University Press, 1983). See also, in relation to the effect of the local remedies rule on claims brought under an FCN Treaty *The ELSI Case (United States v Italy)* (1989) ICJ Reports p.15 discussed, in relation to IIAs, in UNCTAD *Dispute Settlement: Investor State* Series on issues in international investment agreements (New York and Geneva: United Nations, 2003) at 32–34. Notwithstanding the support given to a presumption in favour of including the local remedies rule in the US-Italy FCN Treaty in the *ELSI* case, even though that treaty was silent on the point, the local remedies rule is presumed to be inapplicable to an IIA unless expressly included. See further discussion of Article 26 ICSID Convention below at nn 157–75.

A further difficulty concerns the establishment of a link of nationality between the claimant and the protecting power. In the absence of such a link the protecting power has no right in international law to intervene on behalf of the claimant. This causes particular difficulties where the claimant is a MNE, given that it will be linked to more than one country by reason of the international character of its operations and given the differing nationalities of the parent company and its overseas subsidiaries. These difficulties have been increased by the decision of the International Court of Justice (ICJ) in the *Barcelona Traction* case.[15] The ICJ held that, for the purposes of diplomatic protection, the nationality of a company should be established by reference to its place of incorporation and its principal seat of management, and not by reference to the nationality of the controlling shareholders through a lifting of the corporate veil. Thus, the Court was unwilling to accept that the corporate veil should be lifted as between a local subsidiary and its foreign parent. Only where the local subsidiary had ceased to exist as a legal entity could this course of action be permitted. The result is that where a MNE takes the very common course of organizing its investment in the host state as a locally incorporated company, possessing the nationality of the host state, there is no guarantee of diplomatic protection. The effect of the *Barcelona Traction* case is, therefore, to deny the existence of any general rule of international law, or of equity, which confers a right of diplomatic protection on the national state of shareholders in a foreign company where that company is injured by the acts of a third state. The protection of shareholders demands recourse to treaty stipulations or to special agreements directly concluded between the foreign investor and the state in which the investment is placed.[16]

Arguably, the very idea of extending diplomatic protection to the MNE might be inappropriate, given that its interests may not be precisely identifiable with any

---

[15] *The Barcelona Traction, Light and Power Company, Limited* (New Application: 1962) (*Belgium v Spain*) second phase, judgment of 5 February 1970, ICJ Reports 1970 at 3. For critical comment, see FA Mann 'The Protection of Shareholders' Interests In The Light of the *Barcelona Traction* Case' 67 AJIL 259 (1973); R Higgins 'Aspects of the Case Concerning the Barcelona Traction, Light and Power Company, Ltd' 11 Virg.Jo.I.L. 327 (1971); R Lillich 'The Rigidity of Barcelona' 65 AJIL 522 (1971); Metzger 'Nationality of Corporate Investment Under Investment Guaranty Schemes – The Relevance of Barcelona Traction' 65 AJIL 532 (1971). But see, for a defence of the Court's approach, Briggs 'Barcelona Traction: The *Jus Standi* of Belgium' 65 AJIL 327 (1971); Abi-Saab 'The International Law of Multinational Corporations: A Critique of American Legal Doctrines' 2 Annals of International Studies 97 (1971). For earlier international arbitral case law and state practice on the nationality of corporations for the purposes of diplomatic protection, see Kronstein 'The Nationality of International Enterprises' 52 Col.L.R. 983 (1952); Ginther 'Nationality of Corporations' 16 Osterreichische Zeitschrift Fur Offentliches Recht 27 at 29 (1966); Jones 'Claims on Behalf of Nationals who are Shareholders in Foreign Companies' 26 BYIL 225 (1949); Harris 'The Protection of Companies in International Law in the Light of the Nottebohm Case' 18 ICLQ 275 (1969). For more recent UK practice, see Foreign and Commonwealth Office *Rules Applying to International Claims* 37 ICLQ 1006–8 (1988) reproduced in DJ Harris *Cases and Materials on International Law* (Sweet and Maxwell, 6th edn, 2004) 623–24, 644–45. On US practice, see The American Law Institute's *Third Restatement of the Foreign Relations Law of the United States* (American Law Institute Publishers, 1987) vol 2 s 713, Comment e at 219.
[16] *Barcelona Traction* at 47 para 90; Briggs ibid at 327.

particular state.[17] Furthermore, it amounts to a rather limited and anachronistic method for the resolution of investment disputes. Invoking the protection of the national (ie the home) state of the MNE in its dealings with the host state is reminiscent of 'gunboat diplomacy'. Moreover, it may make little business sense, particularly where the corporation and the host state intend to continue their economic relationship with one another, but have encountered difficulties requiring the use of some means of dispute settlement. In the overwhelming majority of cases a method other than diplomatic protection will be used to settle investment disputes.[18] These will involve the MNE and host state directly without the intervention of the home state. The most important alternatives are negotiation and, should negotiation fail, conciliation and/or arbitration. These are now considered in turn.

(2) Alternatives to Diplomatic Protection: International Dispute Settlement Mechanisms Involving the MNE and Host State

Disputes between the MNE and the host state will normally arise under the terms of an international investment contract, as described in the preceding chapters. Disputes between the MNE and a private entity within the host state – for example, a partner under a management cooperation agreement or a licensee under a technology transfer contract – will not normally be subject to international methods of dispute settlement. In such a case the MNE will usually rely on the law of the host state for the protection of its rights. As regards investment disputes between the MNE and the host state, from the corporation's perspective the major problem is to find a means of dispute settlement which will act as a reliable method for protecting the corporation's commercial interests. This may require the avoidance of subjection to the host state's legal system, should that system be perceived as an inadequate means of protection. In such cases the corporation may prefer the use of a 'delocalized' dispute settlement mechanism that has limited connections with the host state's legal system. A system based on international law may be preferred, given that system's traditional support for the protection of foreign investors' rights in their relations with host states.[19]

---

[17] See AA Fatouros 'Transnational Enterprise in the Law of State Responsibility' in R Lillich (ed) *State Responsibility for Injuries to Aliens* (Charlottesville: University Press of Virginia, 1983) 361.

[18] A notable exception being the *ELSI* case (above n 14) where the US espoused the claims of the US corporation Raytheon, and its subsidiary Matchlett, against Italy under the applicable FCN Treaty, some years after their investment in ELSI had been terminated by the actions of the local Italian authorities in Sicily, where the investment had been located. See further Sean D Murphy 'The ELSI Case: An Investment Dispute at the International Court of Justice' 16 Yale J.Int'l L. 391 (1991) at 405–406.

[19] See further Christopher Dugan, Donald Wallace Jr, and Noah Rubens *Investor State Arbitration* (Dobbs Ferry: Oceana, 2005). For a critical appraisal of the use of international arbitration as a means

From the host state's perspective, the major problem is to retain control over the dispute. Ideally, this would entail the complete exclusion of international methods of dispute settlement and the restriction of the foreign investor to local remedies alone.[20] However, the desire for foreign direct investment may prompt the host state to accept international methods of dispute settlement as a means of displaying concern for the rights of the foreign investor, thereby helping to create a 'good investment climate'. Consequently, in practice, the majority of host states have accepted international methods for the settlement of disputes with foreign investors operating within their jurisdiction, thereby giving direct rights of international action to investors that are independent of their protecting national state.[21]

Assuming that the host state and the MNE agree to the use of international methods of dispute settlement, the following choices are open. At the most basic level there is negotiation. As noted in the previous chapter, most dispute settlement clauses in BITs and other IIAs specify this as the first step in the settlement process. Beyond negotiation lie methods of dispute settlement involving third party intervention, either in the form of conciliation[22] or arbitration.[23] Conciliation and/or arbitration procedures may be instituted on an ad hoc basis by the agreement of the parties themselves. Alternatively, they may choose to avail themselves of one of the institutional systems of conciliation and/or arbitration. Furthermore, the United Nations Commission on International Trade Law (UNCITRAL) has sought to improve ad hoc arbitration through its efforts at establishing internationally acceptable rules, and through the evolution of internationally agreed standards for national arbitration laws. Each approach will be considered in turn, with emphasis on its utility in relation to investment disputes.

---

of controlling host country policy space, see Y Dezalay and B Garth *Dealing in Virtue: International Commercial Arbitration and the Construction of a Transnational Legal Order* (Chicago: University of Chicago Press, 1996).

[20] Latin American States espousing the Calvo Doctrine sought to do so in the past. By this doctrine a foreign investor was required to agree not to claim diplomatic protection as a means of settling an investment dispute with the host state but to rely on local remedies. See D Shea *The Calvo Clause* (Minneapolis: University of Minnesota Press, 1955); Freeman 'Recent Aspects of the Calvo Doctrine and the Challenge to International Law' 40 AJIL 121 (1946). The original statement of the doctrine can be found in the work of its creator: C Calvo *Le Droit International Théoretique et Pratique* (5th edn, 6 vols 1896).

[21] See further Zachary Douglas 'The Hybrid Foundations of Investment Treaty Arbitration' 74 BYIL 151 (2004).

[22] Conciliation is defined as: 'a method for the settlement of international disputes of any nature according to which a Commission set up by the Parties, either on a permanent basis or an ad hoc basis to deal with a dispute, proceeds to the impartial examination of the dispute and attempts to define the terms of a settlement susceptible of being accepted by them, or of affording the Parties, with a view to its settlement, such aid as they may have requested': art 1 of the *Regulations on the Procedure of International Conciliation* adopted by the International Law Institute in 1961 cited in JG Merills *International Dispute Settlement* (Cambridge: Cambridge University Press, 4th edn, 2005) 64.

[23] See generally Alan Redfern and Martin Hunter with Nigel Blackaby and Constantine Partasides *Law and Practice of International Commercial Arbitration* (London: Thomson Sweet & Maxwell, 4th edn, 2004, student version).

(a) Ad Hoc Arbitration and Conciliation

Ad hoc arbitration or conciliation depend upon the initiative of the parties for their success. The parties must make their own arrangements regarding the procedure, the selection of arbitrators, or conciliators, as the case may be, and as to administrative support.[24] The principal advantage of ad hoc dispute settlement is that the procedure can be shaped to suit the parties.[25] However, there are numerous problems associated with ad hoc arbitration. First, the process is governed by the arbitration agreement between the parties. Its content will depend on the relative bargaining power of the parties. The stronger party may therefore obtain an arrangement advantageous to its interests. Secondly, it may be impossible to agree on the exact nature of the dispute, or on the applicable law. Thirdly, there may be difficulties in selecting acceptable arbitrators who can be relied on to act impartially and not as 'advocates' for the side that had selected them. Fourthly, the proceedings may be stultified by inordinate delay on the part of one side or both, or through the non-appearance of a party.[26] Finally, there may be a problem in enforcing any award before municipal courts should they decide that the award is tainted with irregularity, or because the state party to the proceedings enjoys immunity from execution under the laws of the forum state.[27] These difficulties have led to the use of institutional systems of arbitration.

Before going on to consider institutional systems of investment arbitration it is important to note the contribution of UNCITRAL to the improvement of ad hoc arbitration. Although they are not institutional systems for international dispute settlement, the UNCITRAL Arbitration Rules 1976, the UNCITRAL Conciliation Rules 1980, and the UNCITRAL Model Law on International Commercial Arbitration 1985 should be considered as improvements to ad hoc international arbitration or conciliation.[28] In relation to foreign investment

---

[24] Markham Ball 'Structuring the Arbitration in Advance – The Arbitration Clause in an International Development Agreement' in J Lew (ed) *Contemporary Problems in International Arbitration* (London: Queen Mary College Centre for Commercial Law Studies, 1986) 297 at 300.

[25] Redfern and Hunter above n 23 at 58.

[26] The non-appearance of the respondent state party to the arbitration can occur. See, for example, the Libyan Oil Arbitrations: *BP v Libya* 53 ILR 297; *Texaco v Libya* 17 ILM 1 (1978); *Liamco v Libya* 20 ILM 1 (1981).

[27] On which see the chs 28–33 in J Lew (ed) n 24 above at 313–73. While immunity from execution may still be enjoyed by the foreign sovereign, there is a growing national case law which holds that submission to international arbitration with a foreign corporation constitutes an implicit waiver of immunity from suit at the time of recognition proceedings following the making of an award against the state: *Société Européene D'Etudes et D'Entreprises v Yugoslavia* (France: Cour de Cassation 18 November 1986) 26 ILM 377 (1987); see also for other cases in France, the Netherlands, and the United States G Delaume *Transnational Contracts* Chapter XIV para 14:08 (October 1986).

[28] For a detailed analysis of the UNCITRAL Arbitration and Conciliation Rules, and of the Model Law on International Commercial Arbitration, see Isaak I Dore *Arbitration and Conciliation under the UNCITRAL Rules: a Textual Analysis* (Martinus Nijhoff, 1986). The United Nations Commission on International Trade Law (UNCITRAL) does not provide an institutional system of conciliation or arbitration. However, it has made major contributions to the development of unified rules of conciliation and arbitration. Thus, UNCITRAL has been concerned with international

disputes, the UNCITRAL Rules can remove some of the difficulties associated with ad hoc arbitration by basing it on internationally acceptable procedures. However, the success of the resulting award still depends to a great degree on the parties' acceptance of their obligation to observe it. There is no legal basis for the automatic recognition or enforcement of the award. Furthermore, the award is subject to the possibility of pleas of sovereign immunity by the state party, should the award be unfavourable to it. As for the UNCITRAL Model Law on International Commercial Arbitration, its purpose is to promote the harmonization of national laws relating to arbitral procedures. It does so by providing accepted international standards of arbitral procedure that can be adopted by a national legal system, thereby converting them into binding rules of law. This process may be of particular value in the context of investment disputes. Should the host state adopt the Model Law into its legal system, it would offer internationally acceptable standards of arbitral procedure within its domestic arbitration system. This should go some way towards alleviating fears that the foreign investor might have as to the adequacy of the host state's arbitration laws and procedures.

(b) Institutional Systems for International Dispute Settlement

An institutional system of arbitration/conciliation may prove to be a more reliable means of resolving a dispute than an ad hoc approach. Once the parties have consented to its use they have to abide by the system's procedures. These are designed with a view to ensuring that, while the parties retain a large measure of control over the arbitration or conciliation, they are constrained against any attempt to undermine the proceedings. Furthermore, an award made under the auspices of an institutional system is more likely to be consistent with principles of procedural fairness and so is more likely to be enforceable before municipal courts. Indeed, recognition may be no more than a formality. A number of institutional systems have been used to resolve investor-state disputes. Originally, ICSID and

commercial arbitration since its opening session in 1968. At its eleventh session, in June 1978, it included international conciliation in its work programme. These initiatives have resulted in the adoption of the UNCITRAL Arbitration Rules in 1976: UN GA Resolution 31/98 of 15 December 1976; for the text of the Rules see UN publication Sales No E.77.V.6; Dore ibid Appendix 2 or <http://www.uncitral.org>. The Rules are likely to be revised in the near future. The Conciliation Rules were adopted in 1980: see UNCITRAL, Report of 13th Session 35 UN GAOR Supp (No 17), UN Doc A/35/17 (1980) 32–38; Dore ibid Appendix 1 or <http://www.uncitral.org>. In 1985 these Rules were supplemented by the UNCITRAL Model Law on International Commercial Arbitration: UN GA Resolution 40/72 of 11 December 1985; for the text of the Model Law see Annex I to the Report of the UNCITRAL 18th Session GAOR, 40th Session Supp No 17 UN Doc A/40/17; 'UNCITRAL – The United Nations Commission on International Trade Law' (UN publication Sales No E.86.V.8.) 157; Dore ibid Appendix 4 or <http://www.uncitral.org>. For a full commentary on the Model Law and its drafting history, see Howard M Holtzmann and Joseph E Neuhaus *A Guide to the UNCITRAL Model Law on International Commercial Arbitration Legislative History and Commentary* (TM Asser Instituut & Kluwer, 2nd edn, 1995); A Broches *Commentary on the UNCITRAL Model Law on International Arbitration* (Deventer: Kluwer, 1990). See also the UNCITRAL Secretariat's Information Note on the Model Law UN Doc A/CN.9/309 25 March 1988.

the International Chamber of Commerce Court of Arbitration (ICC) were available.[29] These have now been joined by other systems under NAFTA, the Energy Charter Treaty, MERCOSUR, and ASEAN, all of which apply ICSID procedures adapted to the regime in question.[30] Each will be briefly described in this section, while ICSID will be considered in the next section. In addition, the existence of regional commercial arbitration centres, established under the auspices of the Asian African Legal Consultative Committee should be noted. These centres could be used in investor-state disputes. Space precludes any discussion here, although that has been done elsewhere.[31]

(i) The ICC Court of Arbitration

ICC arbitration clauses have been used in international investment agreements, resulting in ICC arbitration in the event of a dispute.[32] One of the criticisms lodged against the ICC Court of Arbitration as a forum for the resolution of foreign investment disputes is that, being primarily a centre for the resolution of commercial disputes between private traders, it has relatively little experience in the complexities of long-term investment agreements involving a state as a party.[33] This may account for the observation that ICC arbitration clauses appear to be used relatively infrequently in international economic development agreements.[34] However, the evidence of the actual use of the ICC Court of Arbitration in

[29] The ICC Court of Arbitration procedures are governed by the ICC Arbitration Rules. The ICC also offers Rules of Optional Conciliation. For the current version of the Rules (1 January 1998), see <http://www.iccwbo.org>. For a full discussion of the history and workings of the ICC Court of Arbitration, see W Lawrence Craig, Williams F Park, and Jan Paulsson *International Chamber of Commerce Arbitration* (Dobbs Ferry: Oceana, 3rd edn, 2000). See also Yves Derains and Eric A Schwartz *A Guide to the ICC Rules of Arbitration* (The Hague: Kluwer Law International, 2nd edn, 2005); Richard R Graving 'The ICC International Court of Arbitration: Meeting the Challenges?' 15 ICSID Rev-FILJ 417 (2000).

[30] See Antonio Parra 'Provisions on the Settlement of Investment Disputes in Modern Investment Laws, Bilateral Investment Treaties and Multilateral Instruments on Investment' 12 ICSID Rev-FILJ 287 at 344–56 (1997). Parra also discusses the provisions in the Cartagena Free Trade Agreement which is omitted for reasons of space.

[31] See further Amazu A Asouzu *International Commercial Arbitration and African States* (Cambridge: Cambridge University Press, 2001) Part 2.

[32] See, for example, *Southern Pacific Properties Limited v The Arab Republic of Egypt and the Egyptian General Company for Tourism and Hotels* 22 ILM 752 (1983); *Westland Helicopters Limited v Arab Organisation for Industrialisation, and United Arab Emirates, and Kingdom of Saudi Arabia, and State of Quatar, and Arab Republic of Egypt, and Arab British Helicopter Company* 23 ILM 1071 (1984). See also *Klockner v Cameroon* extract from award of 21 October 1983 cited in Paulsson 'The ICSID *Klockner v Cameroon* Award: The Duties of Partners in North-South Development Agreements' 1 J.Int.Arb. 145 at 149 (1984), where an ICC arbitration clause was held capable of ousting ICSID jurisdiction in relation to disputes arising exclusively from the contract containing the ICC clause. More recently ICC arbitration was used in the long-running dispute over the Dabhol Power project: see *Capital India Power Mauritius and Energy Enterprises (Mauritius) v Maharashtra Power Development Corporation Limited* ICC Case No 12913/MS award of 27 April 2005 available at <http://www.transnational-dispute-management.com>.

[33] See Peter Sutherland 'The World Bank Convention on the Settlement of Investment Disputes' 29 ICLQ 367 at 371 (1979). [34] Markham Ball above n 24 at 302.

disputes involving governments or state owned enterprises is by no means negligible.[35] Therefore this criticism of the ICC should not be overstated.

(ii) NAFTA

Chapter Eleven, Section B of NAFTA establishes a detailed system for the settlement of investment disputes between a party and an investor from another party, based on the principles of international reciprocity and due process before an impartial tribunal.[36] An investor may make a claim on its own behalf, or on behalf of an enterprise owned and controlled by it, against the host party on the basis of a violation by the host party of any of the guarantees or protective principles in Chapter Eleven, Section A, or where a state enterprise or state sanctioned private monopoly is alleged to have acted in violation of those standards.[37] The claim should first be settled by consultation or negotiation.[38] Where this fails the claim may be submitted for arbitration under the terms of the agreement. Arbitration can take place under the ICSID Convention, where both the disputing party and the party of the investor are parties to the convention. Where only one of the parties concerned is a party to the ICSID Convention, the Additional Facility Rules of ICSID can be used. The UNCITRAL Arbitration Rules can be used as an alternative in such a case or where neither disputing party is a party or a national of a party to the ICSID Convention.[39] The agreement provides detailed rules for the submission of a claim, the composition of the arbitral tribunal, the conduct of proceedings, the place of arbitration, the governing law, evidence, interim measures, and the finality and enforcement of the award.[40] In order for a dispute to be heard the claimant must comply with these procedural prerequisites and waive any rights to the use of other dispute settlement proceedings other than those for injunctive or extraordinary relief not involving an award of damages.[41] Both

---

[35] See Craig, Park, and Paulsson above n 29.

[36] North American Free Trade Agreement 1992, Article 1115: 32 ILM 605 at 642–47 (1993). See further Patrick G Foy and Robert JC Deane 'Foreign Investment Protection under Investment Treaties: Recent Developments under Chapter 11 of the North American Free Trade Agreement' 16 ICSID Rev-FILJ 299 (2001); JC Thomas 'Investor-State Arbitration under NAFTA' 11 Can.YBIL 99 (1999); HC Alvarez 'Arbitration under the NAFTA' 16 Arb.Int'l 395 (2000); Celine Levesque 'Investor-State Arbitration Under NAFTA Chapter 11: What Lies Beneath Jurisdictional Challenges' 17 ICSID Rev-FILJ 320 (2002); Barton Legum 'Lessons Learned from the NAFTA: The New Generation of US Investment Treaty Arbitration Provisions' 19 ICSID Rev-FILJ 344 (2004); Patrick G Foy 'Effectiveness of NAFTA's Chapter 11 Investor-State Arbitration Procedures' 18 ICSID Rev-FILJ 44 (2003); David A Ganz 'The Evolution of FTA Investment Provisions: From NAFTA to the United States-Chile Free Trade Agreement' 19 Am. U. Int'l Rev. 679 (2004).

[37] ibid arts 1116 (claim by investor on its own behalf), 1117 (claim by investor on behalf of an enterprise). [38] ibid art 1118.

[39] ibid art 1120. Mexico and Canada are not yet parties to the ICSID Convention.

[40] See ibid arts 1119, 1121–38.

[41] See *Waste Management v Mexico* ICSID Case No Arb(AF)/98/12 Decision on Jurisdiction 2 June 2000 available at <http://www.naftalw.com> or 40 ILM 56 (2001) at paras 10–13; *Waste Management v Mexico* ICSID Case No Arb(AF)/00/3 Mexico's preliminary objection concerning previous proceedings 26 June 2002, 41 ILM 1315 (2002): Article 1121 did not bar a new claim with corrected prerequisites notwithstanding the existence of the first decision in these proceedings (para 37).

Canada and Mexico have excluded from the scope of the dispute settlement provisions a decision following a review, under the relevant national laws, as to whether or not to permit an acquisition that is subject to review.[42]

(iii) Energy Charter Treaty

Article 26 of the Energy Charter Treaty (ECT) establishes an investor choice based system of dispute settlement for use in disputes concerning a breach of an obligation under Part III of the ECT (Investment Promotion and Protection) between a contracting party and an investor of another contracting party.[43] As is common in IIA provisions of this type, the first resort is to amicable settlement. Should such an outcome not materialize after three months, the investor party to the dispute may choose to submit it for resolution to: (a) the courts or administrative tribunals of the contracting party, party to the dispute, (b) to any previously agreed dispute resolution procedure, or (c) in accordance with the procedures set down in Article 26. Subject to specific exceptions taken by any contracting party under Annex 1D of the ECT, not to allow an investor to resubmit disputes to international arbitration where its has opted for submission to procedures under (a) or (b) above, each contracting party gives unconditional consent to the submission of a dispute to international arbitration or conciliation in accordance with the provisions of Article 26.[44] The only exception is a dispute concerning the breach of an obligation undertaken towards the investor under an investment contract, which may be subject to a contractual exclusive jurisdiction clause.[45] In accordance with the Article 26 procedure, the investor will give consent either to ICSID arbitration or conciliation, where both the contracting party of the investor and the contracting party in dispute are parties to the ICSID Convention, or to the ICSID Additional Facility where only one of the above mentioned contracting parties is a party to the ICSID Convention.[46] In the alternative, the investor may choose a sole arbitrator or ad hoc arbitration under the UNCITRAL Arbitration Rules or an arbitral proceeding under the Arbitration Institute of the Stockholm Chamber of Commerce.[47] The consent of the investor must be in writing. That coupled with the unilateral consent given by the contracting party in dispute under Article 26(3) (a) suffices to comply with the consent requirements under ICSID Rules or the concept of 'agreement in writing' under the New York Convention on the Recognition and Enforcement of Foreign Arbitral Awards and the UNCITRAL Arbitration Rules.

---

[42] ibid Annex 1138.2.

[43] See Energy Charter Treaty (ECT) 1994, Article 26 in UNCTAD *International Investment Agreements: A Compendium Vol II* (New York and Geneva: United Nations, 1996) 568–71. For analysis, see Thomas Waelde (ed) *The Energy Charter Treaty: An East-West Gateway for Investment and Trade* (The Hague: Kluwer Law International, 1996) ch 18. Kenneth J Vandevelde 'Arbitration Provisions in the BITs and the Energy Charter Treaty, and ch 19 Jan Paulsson 'Arbitration Without Privity'.

[44] See art 26(3)(a).   [45] See art 26(3)(c).   [46] Article 26(4)(a).

[47] Article 26 (4)(b) and (c).

A tribunal established under Article 26(4) shall decide the issues in dispute in accordance with the ECT and applicable rules and principles of international law.[48] In this the ECT follows NAFTA, where a tribunal is also limited to application of NAFTA and any applicable rules of international law.[49] By contrast, as will be seen below, an ICSID Tribunal can apply any rules chosen by the parties to the investment, rules of the domestic law of the respondent state, and international law. Article 26 goes on to extend Article 25(2)(b) of the ICSID Convention, to ensure that locally incorporated entities of an investor from another ECT contracting party can be treated as nationals of another contracting party for the purposes of the dispute settlement provisions of the ECT.[50] Awards made under Article 26 are final and binding on the parties to the dispute. Awards are to be carried out without delay and each contracting party shall make provision for the effective enforcement of such awards.[51] Furthermore, in relation to sub-national entities an award of damages may be made against the contracting party in question so as to ensure compliance with the ECT.[52]

(iv) MERCOSUR

The most significant feature of the MERCOSUR system of investor-state dispute settlement is the distinction made between investors from MERCOSUR member countries and those from non-member countries. The former is covered by the Protocol of Colonia for the Promotion and Protection of Investments Between Member States (MERCOSUR Decision 11/93), while the latter is covered by the Protocol for the Promotion and Protection of Investment Originating in States non-Members of MERCOSUR – Protocol of Buenos Aires (MERCOSUR Decision 11/94).[53] In relation to investors from within the region, Article 9 of the Colonia Protocol follows the same pattern as other dispute settlement provisions in IIAs and urges settlement through 'friendly consultations'. If the dispute is not settled within six months then, at the investor's request, it shall be submitted to the competent courts of the contracting party in whose territory the investment was made, or to international arbitration before either ICSID, the ICSID Additional Facility where a state not party to the ICSID Convention is involved or to ad hoc arbitration under the UNCITRAL Rules, or to the permanent system for the settlement of disputes with private persons established under the framework of

[48] Article 26 (6).
[49] See NAFTA art 1131(1): 'A Tribunal established under this Section shall decide the issues in dispute in accordance with this Agreement and applicable rules of international law' and *Feldman v Mexico* ICSID Case No Arb(AF)/99/1 available at <http://www.naftalaw.com> or 40 ILM 615 (2001) at para 62. See also *Methanex v USA* Final Award 3 August 2005, 44 ILM 1345 (2005) Part II, Chapter B, paras 1–23.   [50] ECT above n 43 art 26(7).
[51] Article 26(8).   [52] ibid.
[53] See Marta Haines Ferrari (ed) *The MERCOSUR Codes* (London: British Institute of International and Comparative Law, 2000) 233–52. See further Thomas Andrew O'Keefe 'Dispute Resolution in Mercosur' 3 JWI 507 at 508–10 (2002); Christian Leathley 'The Mercosur Dispute Resolution System' 4 JWI 787 (2003).

the MERCOSUR Treaty under the Protocol of Brasilia as amended by the Protocol of Olivos. In practice the submission of a dispute to arbitration under Article 9 will offer greater protection to the investor, as it permits recourse to ICSID or UNCITRAL procedures, and is not confined to the challenge of affirmative state acts only as is the Protocol of Brasilia, which was not amended in this regard by the Protocol of Olivos.[54] Compared to the NAFTA and ECT, the arbitral tribunal under the Colonia Protocol will be able to apply a wider range of laws including the provisions of the Protocol, the law of the contracting party that is a party to the dispute, including its rules of conflict of laws, the terms of any agreements concluded in relation to the investment and principles of international law.[55] This will introduce more variation of the applicable law from case to case than in those other systems.[56] In relation to investors from non-member states, the main difference is that they do not have a positive right to opt for investment arbitration, in that Article 2(2)(H)(2) of the Buenos Aires Protocol, states that where the dispute is not settled by friendly consultations within an appropriate period it *may* be submitted to international arbitration at the request of the investor. Accordingly, it would appear that consent to international arbitration has been given in advance by the contracting parties under the Colonia Protocol, but not under the Protocol of Buenos Aires, where consent to international arbitration of the contracting party that is a party to the dispute is specifically required.[57]

(v) ASEAN

Article X of the ASEAN Agreement for the Promotion and Protection of Investments of 1987 also provides for international arbitration.[58] Here the provision for amicable settlement prescribes six months before resort may be had to arbitration or conciliation at the election of either the investor or the contracting party in dispute.[59] The dispute may be brought before ICSID, UNCITRAL, the Regional Centre for Arbitration at Kuala Lumpur or any other regional centre for arbitration in ASEAN, whichever body the parties to the dispute mutually agree to appoint for this purpose.[60] Should the parties fail to agree on one of the above then, within two months of agreeing to form an arbitral tribunal, an arbitral tribunal consisting of three members shall be established, two arbitrators being appointed by each party who, in turn, then appoint the chair from a third contracting party within a further month, subject to the approval of the disputing parties.[61] Should this procedure fail either party to the dispute may request the President of the International Court of Justice to make the necessary appointments.[62] An award shall be made by a majority

[54] See Protocol of Olivos art 39: 42 ILM 2 (2003) at 13; O'Keefe ibid at 510–11, 516–17; Leathley ibid at 792–93, 799.   [55] Colonia Protocol art 9(5).

[56] See Parra above n 30 at 347.   [57] See Haines Ferrari (ed) above n 53 at 35.

[58] ASEAN Agreement for the Promotion and Protection of Investments 1987, Article X in UNCTAD above n 43 at 297–98. See also, on Singapore's FTA dispute settlement provisions, Locknie Hsu 'Dispute Settlement Systems in Recent Free Trade Agreements of Singapore: ANZSCEP, JSEPA, and ESFTA' 4 JWI 277 (2003).   [59] ibid art X(2).

[60] ibid.   [61] Article X(3).   [62] Article X(4).

and shall be binding. The disputing parties shall bear their own costs and share equally the costs of the chair and other relevant costs. In all other respects the tribunal shall determine its own procedures.[63] Article X is effective to create mutuality between the investor and the host contracting party, even where the dispute arises out of a contract made by the investor with an entity other than the state itself, and it is not subject to any requirement to exhaust domestic remedies. It extends the dispute settlement procedure to all investments that are made in accordance with the approval requirements present in Article II of the 1987 ASEAN Agreement.[64]

(3) The International Centre for Settlement of Investment Disputes

Despite the existence of alternatives, ICSID represents the most advanced institutional framework for the settlement of investment disputes.[65] This accounts for its use by regional dispute settlement systems and the ECT. The procedures for conciliation and arbitration offered by ICSID are specifically designed for the settlement of disputes between foreign investors and host states, whereas the ICC and UNCITRAL are mainly concerned with traditional commercial disputes. In addition to arbitration, ICSID offers a conciliation procedure and an Additional Facility for conciliation and arbitration, where one of the parties to the dispute is not a contracting party or a national of a contracting party under the Washington Convention, and/or where the dispute does not relate to investment, and for fact-finding which is not provided for under the ICSID Convention. It is not proposed to deal with the conciliation or the Additional Facility procedures.[66] The focus will be on arbitration as the most significant function of ICSID.

(a) The Aims of ICSID

The Washington Convention on the Settlement of Investment Disputes between States and Nationals of Other States was adopted by resolution of the Executive

---

[63] Article X(5).

[64] See *Yaung Chi Oo Trading Pte Ltd v Government of the Union of Myanmar* ASEAN Arbitral Tribunal ASEAN ID Case No Arb/01/1 award 31 March 2003 42 ILM 540 (2003).

[65] See further Branson and Tupman 'Selecting an Arbitral Forum: A Guide to Cost-Effective International Arbitration' 24 Virg.Jo.IL 917 (1984). For a comparison of ICSID and UNCITRAL Rules, see Georgio Sacerdoti 'Investment Arbitration under ICSID and UNCITRAL Rules: Prerequisites, Applicable Law, Review of Awards' 19 ICSID Rev-FILJ 1 (2004).

[66] On which see the Washington Convention on Settlement of Investment Disputes Between States and Nationals of Other States 1965 arts 28–35: 4 ILM 524 at 536–38(1965) or ICSID *ICSID Convention, Regulations and Rules* (ICSID/15, 10 April 2006 available at <http://www.worldbank.org/icsid>). See further ICSID *ICSID Additional Facility Rules* (ICSID/11, April 2006 available at <http://www.worldbank.org/icsid/facility/facility.htm>). The Additional Facility procedure has been of importance in relation to NAFTA arbitrations involving Canada and Mexico, neither of which are parties to the ICSID Convention.

Directors of the World Bank on 18 March 1965. It entered into force on 14 October 1966.[67] As of 25 January 2006 it had 155 signatories and 143 ratifications.[68] Initially, the case-load submitted to ICSID, established by the Convention as the principal organ for the Convention's system of dispute settlement,[69] was meagre. Prior to 1999 there were fewer than 10 such cases brought in any year. However, in the early years of the present century this has grown considerably. According to recent UNCTAD figures, at least 42 new investor-state cases were launched in the first 11 months of 2005, bringing the cumulative number of known treaty based investor-state arbitrations to 219 by November 2005. Of these, 132 have been brought before ICSID.[70] Much of this increase can be attributed to the bringing of over 30 cases against Argentina in the aftermath of its financial crisis in 2001/2002, and in the extension of the ICSID Additional Facility Rules to NAFTA arbitrations.[71]

The Washington Convention developed out of proposals made by the World Bank's general counsel following the bank's previous experiences in the provision of good offices for the solution of investment disputes.[72] In their report on the convention, the executive directors of the bank stated that the convention would offer an international method of settlement which was designed to take account of

---

[67] Note 1 above.

[68] See ICSID List of Contracting States and Signatories of the Convention (as of 26 January 2006) available at <http://www.worldbank.org/icsid>.

[69] The principal organs of ICSID are:

(i) *the Administrative Council*, the governing body of ICSID, comprised of one representative from each contracting state, and chaired *ex officio* by the president of the World Bank. Its principal functions, outlined by art 6 of the Convention, are to adopt financial and administrative regulations, rules of procedure for the institution of conciliation and arbitration proceedings and rules of procedure for the conduct of conciliation and arbitration proceedings (ICSID Convention arts 4–8);

(ii) *the Secretariat*, the principal administrative organ consisting of the Secretary-General, one or more deputy Secretaries-General and their staff. The Secretary-General is charged with the initial review of applications for conciliation or arbitration. He acts as registrar in conciliation and arbitration proceedings (ICSID Convention arts 9–11).

(iii) *the Panels of Conciliators and Arbitrators*; these are separate panels of experts in the fields of law, commerce, industry, or finance who are charged to act in ICSID proceedings in the exercise of independent judgment (ICSID Convention arts 12–16). Each contracting state designates four members to a panel. They need not be nationals of the appointing state. The chairman of the Administrative Council may designate 10 persons to each panel, each of whom must be of a different nationality and who must represent the major legal systems and major forms of industrial and commercial activity. See further Schreuer above n 1 at 12–63.

[70] UNCTAD *IIA Monitor* (No 4 2005) 'Latest Developments in Investor-State Dispute Settlement' (UNCTAD/WEB/ITE/IIT/2005/2) available at <http://www.unctad.org/iia>.

[71] On the Argentine cases see Carlos E Alfaro and Pedro M Lorenti 'The Growing Opposition of Argentina to ICSID Arbitral Tribunals: A Conflict Between International and Domestic Law?' 6 JWIT 417 (2005). On NAFTA arbitrations see further <http://www.naftaclaims.com> and for critical background see IISD/WWF *Private Rights, Public Problems A Guide to NAFTA's Controversial Chapter on Investor Rights* (Winnipeg: IISD 2001).

[72] See Sutherland above n 33 at 374–78. For example, the bank acted in a conciliatory role between shareholders and the Egyptian Government following the latter's nationalization of the Suez Canal Company in 1956. See also Schreuer above n 1 at 1–4 for a chronology of events leading to the adoption of the ICSID Convention.

the special characteristics of investment disputes, and of the parties to whom it would apply. It would provide facilities for conciliation and arbitration by specially qualified persons of independent judgment carried out according to rules known and accepted in advance by the parties. In particular, once the parties to the dispute had given their consent to arbitration or conciliation under the auspices of ICSID, such consent could not be unilaterally withdrawn. A most important feature of the ICSID Convention is its 'delocalized' system of dispute settlement operating independently and exclusively of domestic legal systems.[73] The role of domestic courts is limited to that of judicial assistance in the recognition of ICSID awards.[74] The executive directors believed that adherence to the convention by a country would provide an additional inducement for, and stimulate a larger flow of, private international investment into its territory. This was, in their opinion, the primary purpose of the convention.[75] Thus the ICSID Convention should not be seen merely as a means of dispute settlement. It is also 'an instrument of international policy for the promotion of economic development'.[76]

The response was the creation of a system which seeks to ensure authoritative, final, and effective dispute resolution in the context of a permanent international institution. In so doing the convention can be placed firmly within the 'investor protection' approach to foreign investment. By acceding to the ICSID Convention, the host state accepts that its sovereign power to regulate disputes with foreign investors is to be subjected to review in accordance with the international procedures set out under the convention and the rules promulgated under its authority. It is thus a mechanism for the control of governmental discretion and not merely a system of international commercial dispute settlement. It raises important public law issues as to the proper extent of delocalized control over what are often vital economic development projects and investment policies of host countries. Thus it would be wrong to see ICSID arbitration in purely commercial terms.[77] Against this background consideration will turn to how far the ICSID dispute settlement system is likely to impact upon the contracting states' power to regulate investment disputes.

---

[73] See arts 26 and 53 of the ICSID Convention. See, for a discussion of 'delocalization' in international commercial arbitration, Redfern and Hunter above n 23 at 105–109.

[74] By art 54 of the ICSID Convention each contracting state is required to enforce the 'pecuniary obligations' imposed by an ICSID award within its territory as if the award were 'a final judgment of a court in that state'. See further text at n 743 below.

[75] 4 ILM 524 (1965) 525 at paras 11–12.

[76] Georges Delaume 'ICSID Arbitration' in JDM Lew (ed) *Contemporary Problems in International Arbitration* (London: Queen Mary College, Centre for Commercial Law Studies, 1986) ch 4 at 23; Schreuer above n 1 at 4–5.

[77] See, for the development of this issue in relation to NAFTA arbitrations using ICSID Additional Facility Rules, Gus Van Harten 'Judicial Supervision of NAFTA Chapter 11 Arbitration: Public or Private Law?' 21Arb. Int'l 493 (2005) and see further Gus van Harten and Martin Loughlin 'Investment Treaty Arbitration as a Species of Global Administrative Law' 17 EJIL 121 (2006).

(b) The ICSID Convention and Its Effect on State Regulation of Investment Disputes

This section will consider, first, the extent of the personal jurisdiction of the Centre, and the extent of the contracting state's ability to control such jurisdiction; secondly, the Centre's subject-matter jurisdiction; thirdly, the precise means by which the ICSID Convention seeks to 'delocalize' the resolution of investment disputes brought before it; fourthly, the extent to which a party to a dispute can challenge an award made against it; fifthly, how far other contracting states will recognize and enforce ICSID awards made against the respondent contracting state and, finally, the procedures for bringing a case before the Centre and the costs thereof.

(i) The Contracting State's Ability to Control Jurisdiction[78]

The cornerstone of the jurisdiction of ICSID is Article 25(l) of the convention:

The jurisdiction of the Centre shall extend to any legal dispute arising directly out of an investment between a Contracting State (or any constituent subdivision or agency of a Contracting State designated to the Centre by that state) and a national of another Contracting State, which the parties to the dispute consent in writing to submit to the Centre. When the parties have given their consent, no party may withdraw its consent unilaterally.

Article 25(1) makes consent in writing of both parties the basis of ICSID jurisdiction. This will usually be given in an ICSID arbitration clause contained in an investment contract.[79] Consent may be deduced from a series of agreements of which only some mention ICSID arbitration. This is an issue to be decided on the facts in each case.[80] Furthermore, consent has been held to exist where the host state accepts an investment application containing a clause obliging the host state

---

[78] It is not possible to review every issue pertaining to the jurisdiction of ICSID here. See further the articles on ICSID jurisdiction by Amerasinghe in 5 J. Mar. L. & Com. 211 (1974); 47 BYIL 227 (1974–75); 19 Indian J. Int'l L 166 (1979); Tupman 'Case Studies in the Jurisdiction of the International Centre for Settlement of Investment Disputes' 35 ICLQ 813 (1986); Lamn 'Jurisdiction of the International Centre for the Settlement of Investment Disputes' 6 ICSID Rev-FILJ 462 (1991); Omar E Garcia-Bolivar 'Foreign Investment Disputes under ICSID – A Review of Decisions on Jurisdiction' 5 JWIT 187 (2004); Schreuer above n 1 at 82–344.

[79] ICSID has devised model clauses by which consent can be unambiguously given in a manner that fulfils the jurisdictional requirements of the convention: see ICSID *Model Clauses* (Doc ICSID/5/Rev 2 1 February 1993) 8 ICSID Rev-FILJ 134 (1993) available at <http://www.worldbank.org/icsid/model-clauses-en/main.htm>. For analysis, see Amerasinghe 'How to Use the International Centre for the Settlement of Investment Disputes by Reference to its Model Clauses' 13 Indian J. Int'l L 530 (1973); ibid 'Model Clauses for Settlement of Foreign Investment Disputes' 28 Arb. J. 232 (1973); Schreuer above n 1 at 196–98.

[80] *Holiday Inns and Occidental Petroleum Corp v Morocco* (Settlement 17 October 1978) discussed by Pierre Lalive in 'The First World Bank Arbitration (*Holiday Inns v Morocco*) – Some Legal Problems' 51 BYIL 123 (1980) at 159–160; see also *CSOB v Slovakia* ICSID Case No ARB/97/4 further decision on jurisdiction 1 December 2000: 15 ICSID Rev-FILJ 544 (2000) at paras 26–32.

and the investor to put disputes before ICSID.[81] Consent may also be made conditional on the fulfilment of a future contingency such as the acceptance of the ICSID Convention by the home and/or host country or the future registration of a company that will operate the investment.[82] Apart from an agreement to use ICSID arbitration in an investment contract, it is possible for the contracting state to make a unilateral offer of ICSID arbitration in its foreign investment law, or in a BIT or other IIA dispute settlement clause. This will amount to consent for the purposes of Article 25 if the foreign investor accepts the offer by choosing ICSID arbitration in writing, usually by filing a claim with ICSID.[83] This approach to consent has been termed 'arbitration without privity' in that the host country makes an offer to all foreign investors which can be subsequently accepted by any investor involved in a dispute with that country, thereby obviating the need for a prior arbitration agreement between them.[84]

The possibility of 'arbitration without privity' raises the key issue of whether the language used by the host country in its national law, or in any applicable investment protection treaty, is capable of being construed as a genuine offer of ICSID jurisdiction. As regards investment laws, ICSID has classified such laws into two broad categories, based on the nature of the reference to ICSID. The first includes laws containing a unilateral and express consent to refer investment disputes to ICSID.[85] This type of provision amounts to a unilateral offer by the host state which needs to be accepted by the investor either in an investment

---

[81] *Amco-Asia v Republic of Indonesia* Award on Jurisdiction 25 September 1983; 23 ILM 351 (1984), 89 ILR 379 (1992).

[82] See *Holiday Inns* case, Lalive above n 80 at 142–46: 'No. 20 The Tribunal is of the opinion that the Convention allows parties to subordinate the entry into force of an arbitration clause to the subsequent fulfilment of certain conditions, such as the adherence of the states concerned to the Convention, or the incorporation of the company envisaged by the agreement'; *Cable Television of Nevis Ltd and Cable Television of Nevis Holdings Ltd v The Federation of St Kitts and Nevis* ICSID Case Arb/95/2 award of 16 December 1996, 13 ICSID Rev-FILJ 328 (1998) at paras 4.09, 6.34. citing the *Holiday Inns* case; *Generation Ukraine Inc v Ukraine* ICSID Case No Arb/00/9 award of 16 September 2003, 44 ILM 404 (2005) at paras 12.6–12.8.

[83] This was accepted in the Report of the Executive Directors on the Washington Convention, para 24: see 4 ILM 524 (1965) at 527. See further Schreuer above n 1 at 198–221.

[84] See Jan Paulsson 'Arbitration Without Privity' above n 43 and in 10 ICSID Rev-FILJ 232 (1995).

[85] See, for example, art 4 of Law No 85–03 of 29 January 1985 of the Republic of Togo: 'Tout different qui pourrait surgir entre le Gouvernement Togolais et l'investisseur au sujet de l'une ou plusieurs clauses de la presente loi est reglé a l'amiable. En cas de désaccord persistant, le conflit est soumis a l'arbitrage du Centre International pour le Règlement des Différents Relatifs aux Investissements (CIRDI) pour règlement definitif' reproduced in News From ICSID (vol 3 No 2 Summer 1986) 8. In *Tradex v Albania* ICSID Case No Arb/94/2 Decision on Jurisdiction 24 December 1996 14 ICSID Rev-FILJ 161 (1999). The tribunal held that Article 8(2) of the Albanian Law on Foreign Investment 1993 gave unambiguous consent to ICSID arbitration: ' . . . the foreign investor may submit the dispute for resolution and the Republic of Albania hereby consents to the submission thereof, to the International Centre for Settlement of Investment Disputes' (at 187). In that case the tribunal also interpreted the consent in the 1993 law as being capable of applying to a dispute which arose before the entry into force of the law given that it was a continuation of existing government policy to improve the protection of investors, and the fact that the investor had not elected to use UNCITRAL procedures available under the previous foreign investment law.

agreement, a statement contained in an investment application, a simple statement by the investor that it agrees to refer a particular investment dispute to
ICSID, or in a request for arbitration submitted to ICSID after a dispute has
arisen.[86] The second category includes laws that refer to the possibility of ICSID
arbitration as one of several means of settling investment disputes.[87] In such a case
the host government and the investor would have to accept ICSID jurisdiction by
subsequent agreement. In the absence of such agreement the law cannot, by itself,
make ICSID jurisdiction applicable. Thus references to ICSID arbitration in
national investment laws should be treated with caution. Each law must be
interpreted to see whether it constitutes an unconditional offer by the state to use
ICSID arbitration, which becomes binding on acceptance by the investor, or
whether the law simply regards ICSID as an optional procedure, leaving the
question of its use to bargaining between the parties. Furthermore, the precise
jurisdictional scope of the law must be taken into account so as to ascertain the
limits of any unilateral consent, if such exists, on the part of the host state.[88]

As regards references to ICSID arbitration in BITs and other IIAs, these too
should be approached with caution. Such references occur in an agreement
between states. At most there may be a commitment, on the part of the states party
to the investment agreement, to accept ICSID arbitration as the principal means of
dispute settlement with investors from the other state party, should the investor so
request.[89] Here, the BIT, or other IIA, achieves the same as the first category of
national investment laws mentioned above, a clear unilateral offer of ICSID arbitration. Again the text of the investment agreement must be interpreted to see
whether such an offer is in fact made, or whether ICSID arbitration is simply an
option available to the state party to the investment agreement in its relations with

---

[86] News from ICSID (vol 3 No 2 Summer 1986) 8.

[87] See, for example, art 33 of the Investment Code of the Democratic Republic of Madagascar
1989: 5 ICSID Rev-FILJ 151 (1990). This offers three alternative means of settling disputes between
Madagascar and foreign investors: (i) under the provisions of the Malagasy law itself; (ii) the ICSID
Convention or (iii) the Additional Facility administered by ICSID. See for a similar provision:
Tanzania: National Investment (Promotion and Protection) Act 1990 (Act No 10 of 1990) s 29(2)
(dispute may be submitted to ICSID as one of three alternative methods of arbitration). See also
Uganda: Investment Code 1991 (Statute No 1, 1991) s 30(2)(a) (ICSID may be mutually agreed by
the parties); Zambia: Investment Act 1991 (No 19 of 1991) s 40(6)(c) (dispute may be referred to
ICSID).

[88] Such an issue arose at the Hearings on Jurisdiction in *Southern Pacific Properties (Middle East)
Limited v Arab Republic of Egypt* Decision on Jurisdiction of 27 November 1985, 16 YB Com.Arb. 19
(1991) (excerpts); Decision on Jurisdiction of 14 April 1988, 16 YB Com.Arb. 28 (1991) (excerpts).
See also Award on Merits of 20 May 1992, 32 ILM 933 at paras 8–24 at 938–40 (1993) or 8 ICSID
Rev-FILJ 328 (1993); note Dissenting Opinion of Arbitrator El Mahdi 32 ILM at 1026–29 or 8
ICSID Rev-FILJ at 472–75.

[89] See the previous chapter at 695–98 above for a discussion of investor-state dispute settlement
clauses in BITs and other IIAs. See also 'ICSID and Bilateral Investment Treaties' in News From
ICSID (vol 2 No 1 Winter 1985) 12 at 13–14 for examples of clauses containing such a binding com-
mitment: art 11 of the Netherlands-Indonesia Treaty of July 7 1968; art VIII of the Egypt-Yugoslavia
Treaty of June 3, 1977; art 8 (l) of the UK-Bangladesh Treaty of June 19, 1980; art 6 of the France-
Senegal Treaty of 8 September 1975; art VII of the US-Senegal Treaty of 6 December 1983 and see
Schreuer above n 1 at 212–16.

foreign investors.[90] Ultimately, the availability of ICSID arbitration is still conditional upon agreement between the host state and foreign investor, although the reference to ICSID in the BIT or other IIA may be taken as an indication of the host state's willingness to use ICSID procedures. In this regard it is clear that no consent can be implied on the part of the host state where the alleged violation of the BIT occurs before the date of its entry into force.[91] Nor can consent be implied where the parties to the dispute have failed to negotiate, or to seek an amicable settlement, and this is a condition precedent to the election of international arbitration in the dispute settlement provision of the applicable investment treaty.[92]

As already noted in the previous chapter, consent to ICSID arbitration will be excluded where the BIT or other IIA contains a 'fork-in-the road' clause and the investor has chosen domestic dispute settlement procedures over ICSID arbitration. The selection made by the investor under the 'fork-in-the-road' clause will be decisive as the investor is free to waive his or her rights to international arbitration if he or she so wishes.[93] On the other hand, where the underlying investment contract between the investor and the host state, or its agents, contains an exclusive jurisdiction clause, referring disputes arising under the contract to domestic dispute settlement procedures alone, this may be effective to oust ICSID jurisdiction only if the dispute is purely contractual in nature.[94] Where the dispute concerns

[90] For examples of bilateral treaties which show a willingness, but not a duty, to consent to ICSID arbitration upon request of the investor, see News from ICSID ibid 14; art 5 Treaty Between France-Malaysia of 24 April 1975; art 6 Treaty Between Sweden-Malaysia 3 March 1979. Other treaties merely note that the host state shall give 'sympathetic consideration' to the possibility of consent to ICSID arbitration: see ibid 14; art XI Netherlands-Kenya Treaty of 11 September 1970. Some treaties simply list ICSID arbitration as one option should the parties fail to settle their dispute amicably: see ibid 16 UK-St Lucia Treaty of 18 January 1983. See further Schreuer above n 1 at 216–18.

[91] See *Tradex v Albania* above n 85 at para 180; *Maffezini v Spain* ICSID Case No Arb/97/7 Decision on Jurisdiction 25 January 2000, 40 ILM 1129 (2001) at paras 90–98; *Generation Ukraine v Ukraine* above n 82 at paras 11.2–11.4. In this case the tribunal added that it makes no difference to the temporal requirement of consent that certain standards in BITs are also principles of customary international law, as the tribunal is not given a general jurisdiction over state obligations arising out of customary law (para 11.3). However, acts of the respondent state that occurred before the entry into force of the BIT, and which would have constituted breaches of the BIT, may be considered by the tribunal if they are 'a constituting part, concurrent factor or aggravating or mitigating element of conduct or acts or omissions of the Respondent which took place after such date' and which were themselves breaches of the BIT. This was particularly the case where the claimant could not reasonably have assessed the significance and effects of those earlier acts or omissions when they took place: *TECMED v Mexico* ICSID Case No Arb (AF)/00/2 award of 29 May 2003, 43 ILM 133 (2004) at para 68. The time when the investment was made is irrelevant so long as the dispute arose after the date of entry into force of the BIT: *Jan de Nul v Egypt* ICSID Case No Arb/04/13 Decision on Jurisdiction 16 June 2006 at <http://www.ita.law.uvic.ca> para 111. In *Lucchetti v Peru* ICSID Case No Arb/03/4 award of 7 February 2005, 19 ICSID Rev-FILJ 359 (2004) the tribunal considered that there was no new dispute after the entry into force of the BIT when 'the facts or considerations that gave rise to the earlier dispute continued to be central to the later dispute' at para 50.

[92] Generation Ukraine ibid at paras 14.3–14.4.

[93] See further Ole Spierman 'Individual Rights, State Interests and the Power to Waive ICSID Jurisdiction under Bilateral Investment Treaties' 20 Arb.Int'l 179 (2004).

[94] See *Compania des Aguas del Aconquija SA and Vivendi Universal (Formerly Compagnie Génerale des Eaux) v Argentina* ICSID Case No Arb/97/3 Decision on Annulment 3 July 2002, 41 ILM 1135

claims arising out of the investment contract, that also create claims based on the applicable BIT, or where the dispute involves only issues arising under the BIT, ICSID Tribunals have regularly accepted jurisdiction to deal with the claims brought under the relevant treaty regardless of the exclusive jurisdiction clause.[95] In addition, where the dispute settlement clause in the investment contract requires recourse to procedures that are mandatory under national law, such as a reference for judicial review of administrative action against the state party to the investment contract, this will not count as a choice of forum excluding ICSID jurisdiction under the relevant BIT provision, as the election of domestic procedures is not freely made by the investor. In such a case investors remain free to make their choice of forum in accordance with the international treaty.[96]

The approach of ICSID Tribunals on this matter is justified by the possibility that a breach of an investment contract may be the result of an abuse of governmental powers and so will come within the protection of the applicable investment treaty. It would not be in accordance with the aims and purposes of investor protection treaties to allow the fact of a breach of contract to exclude ICSID jurisdiction in such a case. On the other hand, as discussed in relation to the scope of the umbrella clause in the previous chapter, unless a clear distinction can be drawn between purely commercial breaches of contract and breaches induced by maladministration, there is a risk that the freely negotiated intention of the parties to an investment contract, to use only local dispute settlement procedures in the host country, may be unduly interfered with, giving investors a procedural advantage that may appear too one-sided. As noted by Paulsson, 'arbitration without privity is a delicate mechanism. A single incident of an adventurist arbitrator going beyond the proper scope of jurisdiction in a sensitive case may be sufficient to generate a backlash'.[97] Thus a balance may need to be struck, in any given case, between protection of the investor and the right of the host state to regulate economic activity and, in that process, to determine the extent of its actual consent to international dispute settlement mechanisms in investment contracts.

That said there is no warrant for interpreting strictly the requirement of consent on the part of the state party to the dispute simply because such consent may

---

(2002) at para 103; *SGS v Philippines* ICSID Case No Arb /02/6 Decision on Objections to Jurisdiction 29 January 2004 available at <http://www.worldbank.org/icsid> at paras 141–48.

[95] See *Vivendi* ibid at para 102; *Salini v Morocco* ICSID Case No Arb/00/4 Decision on Jurisdiction 23 July 2001, 42 ILM 609 (2003) at paras 61–63; *Salini v Jordan* ICSID Case No Arb/02/13 Decision on Jurisdiction 29 November 2004, 44 ILM 573 (2005) at paras 154–56; *Joy Mining v Egypt* ICSID Case No Arb/03/11 Award on Jurisdiction 6 August 2004, 44 ILM 73 (2005) at paras 75–78 where the tribunal held that the non-release of a bank guarantee was a clear commercial issue that could not raise an issue under the BIT given that a contingent liability could not be the subject of an expropriation; *CMS Gas Transmission Company v Argentina* ICSID Case No Arb/01/8 Decision on Jurisdiction 17 July 2003, 42 ILM 788 (2003) at paras 70–76.

[96] See *Lanco v Argentina* ICSID Case No Arb/97/6 Decision on Jurisdiction 8 December 1998, 40 ILM 457 (2001) at para 26; *Salini v Morocco* ibid at para 27.

[97] Above note 84, 10 ICSID Rev-FILJ at 257.

amount to a restriction on state sovereignty.[98] Should the host state be concerned about the extent of its consent to ICSID arbitration, Article 25(4) of the convention empowers any contracting state to 'notify the Centre of the class or classes of disputes which it would or would not consider submitting to the jurisdiction of the Centre'. This can be done at the time of acceptance or approval of the ICSID Convention or at any time thereafter, although any subsequent change in the contracting state's initial consent to ICSID jurisdiction has only prospective, and not retroactive, effect. Consequently, a contracting state is unable to use the Article 25(4) procedure to remove, from the jurisdiction of ICSID, proceedings to which it has already consented.[99] Article 25(4) affords to the contracting state a wide discretion to exclude such classes of investment dispute as it sees fit from its consent to ICSID jurisdiction. However, if the Article 25(4) notification is ambiguous it would fall to the ICSID Tribunal to determine its meaning and scope.[100] Thus, the contracting state must ensure that its notification is clear if it wishes to preserve its sovereign rights in particular areas of inward foreign investment. In this connection the notification is seen as an aid to interpreting the scope of the parties consent to ICSID arbitration, but it is not a reservation to the ICSID Convention. Thus the state is free not to adhere to the terms of the notification if it so wishes. Equally, if the state wishes to give legal force to the notification it must embody this in its investment agreements or treaties.[101]

In addition to consent, a further requirement of jurisdiction is that the parties to the dispute are proper parties to appear before ICSID. As regards the state party to the dispute, only a state that has become a contracting state to the ICSID Convention can be a party to ICSID proceedings. A contracting state is one which has confirmed its signature of the convention at least 30 days prior to the bringing of the dispute by depositing an instrument of ratification, accession or approval with the World Bank.[102] The state party to the dispute need not be a

---

[98] *Amco-Asia* case above n 81 para 14 at 359. Equally, in *Noble Ventures Inc* v *Romania* award of 12 October 2005 ICSID, Case No Arb/01/11, available at <http://www.investmentclaims.com/decisions/Noble-Ventures-Final-Award.pdf> the tribunal held: 'it is not *permissible, as is* too often done regarding BITs, to interpret clauses exclusively in favour of investors' para 52 (underlined in the award). In *Pan American Energy LLC v Argentina* ICSID Case No Arb/03/13 Decision on Preliminary Objections 27 July 2006 at <http://www.ita.law.uvic.ca> at para 99: 'This Tribunal considers that a balanced interpretation is needed, taking into account both the State's sovereignty and its responsibility to create an adapted and evolutionary framework for the development of economic activities, and the necessity to protect foreign investment and its continuing flow.'

[99] *Alcoa Minerals of Jamaica v Government of Jamaica* (decision of 5–6 July 1975) summarized by Schmidt in 17 Harv. ILJ 90, 96 et seq (1976); 4 YB Com.Arb. 206 (1979) (excerpts).

[100] See Delaume above n 76 at 796.

[101] See *PSEG Global Inc v Turkey* ICSID Case No Arb/02/5 Decision on Jurisdiction 4 June 2004, 44 ILM 465 (2005) at paras 139–46. The tribunal noted that the People's Republic of China inserted the terms of its Article 25(4) notification in its BITs.

[102] Washington Convention arts 68, 70, and 73. See further IBRD 'Memorandum on Signature and Ratification, Acceptance or Approval of the Convention on the Settlement of Investment Disputes between States and Nationals of Other States' (reprinted, May 1991).

contracting party at the time a clause consenting to ICSID arbitration is concluded. However, such consent is insufficient to ensure the jurisdiction of ICSID. The state must become a contracting state by the date that a request is submitted to the Secretary-General of ICSID if such contingent consent is to become binding upon the state party to the dispute.[103]

The reference, in Article 25(1) of the convention to the 'constituent sub-division' of a contracting state may be interpreted to cover a range of sub-divisions including federal states, semi-autonomous dependencies, and municipalities.[104] The reference to an 'agency' of a contracting state creates greater problems of interpretation. It seeks to include within the jurisdiction of the convention a wide range of bodies operating as state agencies, including not only departments of government but perhaps even government-owned or government-controlled corporations. It may, however, exclude entities in which the government merely owns shares and the entity carries out essentially commercial functions.[105] In each case the test is twofold: at the formal or structural level, if the entity is directly or indirectly owned or controlled by the states, this gives rise to a rebuttable presumption that it is a state entity and, secondly, where the entity performs functions that are governmental in nature a similar presumption will arise.[106] Such definitional problems may be considerably reduced given the requirement, in Article 25(1) of the convention, that constituent sub-divisions or agencies must be 'designated' to the Centre by the contracting state. Such designation would raise a strong presumption in favour of granting the sub-division or agency locus standi before the Centre.[107] Furthermore, Article 25(3) of the convention demands that consent by a constituent sub-division or agency of a contracting state requires approval by the contracting state unless that state notifies the Centre that such approval is not required.[108]

The other party to the dispute must be the national of a contracting state other than the host state. This party may be a natural or a juridical person.[109] A natural

---

[103] Amerasinghe 'Jurisdiction *Ratione Personae* under the Convention on the Settlement of Investment Disputes Between States and Nationals of Other States' 48 BYIL 227 at 232 (1974). See also the cases cited in n 82 above.

[104] Amerasinghe ibid at 233. See further *Cable Television of Nevis v St Kitts and Nevis* above n 82 at para 2.27 where the tribunal held that the federal state cannot be a party to the proceedings where only the constituent sub-division of that state is a party to the investment agreement, and where it has not been designated as a proper party to ICSID proceedings under the procedure described in the text below.

[105] Amerasinghe ibid at 234. See further *CSOB v Slovakia* ICSID Case No Arb/97/4 First Decision on Jurisdiction 24 May 1999, 14 ICSID Rev-FILJ 251 (1999) at para 16–27; *Jan de Nul v Egypt* above n 91 at paras 83–89 where the tribunal noted that the rules of attribution under international law applied to determine whether an entity was a state entity for the purposes of jurisdiction under the ICSID Convention.   [106] See *Maffezini v Spain* above n 91 at para 77.

[107] Amerasinghe ibid at 234.

[108] On what constitutes approval of consent for the purposes of art 25(3) see Amerasinghe ibid at 236–38; Schreuer above n 1 at 334–39 and the *Cable Television of Nevis* case above n 82.

[109] Sutherland above n 33 at 383. See further Stanimir A Alexandrov 'The "Baby Boom" of Treaty-Based Arbitrations and the Jurisdiction of ICSID Tribunals' 6 JWIT 387 (2005).

person must possess the nationality of a contracting state upon the date on which the parties consent to submit the dispute to the Centre and on the date that the request is registered by the Secretary-General of ICSID. This does not include any person who on either date also has the nationality of the contracting state party to the dispute.[110] As regards a juridical person, the nationality requirements are not as strict. By Article 25(2)(b) the term 'national of another contracting state' means, for the purposes of Article 25(l):

[a]ny juridical person which had the nationality of a Contracting State other than the State party to the dispute on the date on which the parties consented to submit such dispute to conciliation or arbitration and any juridical person which had the nationality of the Contracting State party to the dispute on that date and which, because of foreign control, the parties have agreed should be treated as a national of another contracting state for the purposes of this Convention.

This provision covers two cases. The first is that of a juridical person possessing the nationality of a contracting state other than that of the contracting state party to the dispute. Unlike the case of natural persons, there is no requirement for such nationality to continue at the date of registration of the request with the Secretary-General of ICSID. In the context of a MNE group, ICSID Tribunals will take a flexible approach and allow the consent to ICSID arbitration, given by a subsidiary, to be considered to have been given by its parent, the actual investor, whose subsidiary is merely an 'instrumentality'.[111] However, where the parent possesses the nationality of a non-contracting party, this approach will have to be limited, and the bringing of a claim by the subsidiary in the host country, even if the latter possesses the nationality of a contracting party, will not suffice to found jurisdiction.[112] Where the foreign parent possesses the nationality of a contracting party, and assigns its rights under an investment agreement to another foreign-incorporated subsidiary, it has been held that the host state may not be permitted to circumvent the jurisdiction of ICSID by denying the recognition of the assignee as an investor under its investment laws, where such recognition may be a condition for the host state's consent to ICSID jurisdiction, and where, on the

---

[110] ICSID Convention art 25(2)(a). For detailed analysis, see Amerasinghe, n 103 above at 246–53. For examples of the application of this principle, see *Champion Trading Company v Egypt* ICSID Case No Arb/02/9 Decision on Jurisdiction 21 October 2003, 19 ICSID Rev-FILJ 275 (2004) at 288 and *Soufraki v United Arab Emirates* ICSID Case No Arb/02/7 award 7 July 2004 at para 83.

[111] See *Banro American Resources v Congo* ICSID Case No Arb/98/7 award of 1 September 2000 (excerpts), 17 ICSID Rev-FILJ 382 (2002) at paras 11–12.

[112] Thus, in *Banro American Resources v Congo* ibid a Canadian parent company sought diplomatic protection, as a national of a non-contracting state, against the Congo, and its US subsidiary, which undertook the actual investment in that country, sought to file a claim before ICSID. The tribunal rejected jurisdiction on the ground that it was not open to the group to neutralize the nationality requirements of the ICSID Convention in this way and to undermine the fundamental consensual characteristic of the convention between the host contracting state and the home contracting state of which the foreign investor is a national.

facts, the host state knew of the proposed assignment and acquiesced in it.[113] However, the assignment must be to an entity that possesses the nationality of a contracting party to the ICSID Convention. An investor from a non-contracting party cannot perfect their standing by assigning the claim to an affiliate possessing the nationality of a contracting party.[114]

The second case is that of a juridical person possessing the nationality of the contracting state party to the dispute at the date on which the parties consented to ICSID arbitration. The purpose of this part of Article 25(2)(b) is to ensure that foreign investments carried out by means of a locally incorporated subsidiary or joint venture are not excluded from the ICSID Convention. If that were so, then a major category of investments would fall outside the scope of the convention, causing it to lose much of its utility. Thus, the ICSID Convention goes beyond the limitations laid down in the *Barcelona Traction* case, concerning the protection of foreign shareholders in a locally incorporated company.[115] The host contracting party is given discretion over whether to extend ICSID arbitration to locally incorporated entities. The extent of this discretion has been clarified to in the decisions of ICSID Tribunals.[116]

First, the agreement to treat the locally incorporated entity as the national of another contracting state should normally be express and explicit.[117] However, implied agreement can be found if the circumstances of the case would exclude any other interpretation of the intention of the parties.[118] Such circumstances do not arise in the case where the local entity is created after the investment agreement containing the ICSID arbitration clause has been concluded, and where the creation of that entity was not contemplated at the time of conclusion by the foreign parent company and the host state.[119] By contrast, where it is at all times contemplated by both the foreign investor and the host state that the investment will take the form of a locally incorporated entity, and the host state acknowledges the foreign ownership of that entity in the course of approving the investment application, there is no need for a separate agreement on the nationality of the entity for the purposes of ICSID jurisdiction.[120]

Furthermore, where a host state enters into an investment agreement containing an ICSID arbitration clause with a foreign controlled juridical person possessing the same nationality as the host state, it may be presumed, in the absence of cogent evidence to the contrary, that the host state has agreed to treat that entity as

---

[113] See *Southern Pacific Properties (Middle East) Limited v Arab Republic of Egypt* award of 20 May 1992: 32 ILM 933 (1993) at paras 133–44.
[114] See *Mihaly v Sri Lanka* ICSID Case No Arb/00/2 award of 15 March 2002, 41 ILM 867 (2002) at paras 22–26. [115] Above n 15.
[116] See further Amazou Asouzu 'A Review and Critique of Arbitral Awards on Article 25(2)(b) of the ICSID Convention' 3 JWI 397 (2002). [117] Schreuer above n 1 at 295 para 507.
[118] *Holiday Inns v Morocco* (decision of 1 July 1973) para 33 cited in Lalive above n 80 at 141.
[119] ibid.
[120] *Amco Asia v Republic of Indonesia* at n 81 above paras 14–15 at ILM 359–63; ILR 382–88.

a 'national of another contracting state'.[121] In addition, the granting of privileges normally reserved for foreign investors, such as currency convertibility, tax holidays, the recruitment of foreign nationals, and customs duty exemptions may indicate recognition as a national of another contracting state.[122] It is clear from these principles that ICSID Tribunals have taken a broad view of the circumstances in which the consent of the host contracting state exists to treating a locally incorporated entity as the 'national of another contracting state' for the purposes of ICSID arbitration. Thus, if a host state wishes to restrict ICSID arbitration only to disputes between the parent company and itself this should be made explicit.

The existence of an agreement to treat the locally incorporated entity as a national of another contracting state serves only to raise a presumption as to foreign control. In each case the tribunal will confirm that presumption by reviewing the actual evidence of foreign control. In the early cases this did not pose an issue, as in each instance foreign control was clear from the ownership and management structures between the local and foreign entities.[123] However, in *Vacuum Salt v Ghana*[124] the tribunal held that agreement to treat a claimant as a foreign national does not *ipso facto* confer jurisdiction. The requirement of 'foreign control' in Article 25(2)(b) sets an objective limit beyond which jurisdiction cannot be granted.[125] Accordingly, a 20 per cent holding by a Greek national in Ghanaian incorporated Vacuum Salt was, in the circumstances, insufficient to show foreign control, given that he did not exercise anything other than a technical advisory function and that the remaining 80 per cent of the equity, and actual managerial control, was in Ghanaian hands.[126]

In *Vacuum Salt* the fact that the majority of the controlling interests possessed the nationality of the host country party to the dispute was sufficient to dispose of jurisdiction. However, in the more recent case of *Tokios Tokeles v Ukraine* this factor appears to have been diluted.[127] By a majority, the tribunal held that a

---

[121] *LETCO v Liberia* award of 31 March 1986, 26 ILM 647 (1987) at 652–54; *Klockner v Cameroon* ICSID Case No Arb/74/3 award 21 October 1983, 2 ICSID Reports 9 (excerpts) at 16.

[122] See *Cable Television of Nevis* case above n 82 at paras 5.17–5.18.

[123] See the *Amco Asia* case above n 81 at ILM 362–63; *Klockner v Cameroon* above n 121 at 15–16; *SOABI v Senegal* ICSID Case No Arb/82/1 Decision on Jurisdiction 1 August 1984, 2 ICSID Reports 175 at 182–83; *LETCO v Liberia* above n 121 at ILM 652–53.

[124] ICSID Case No Arb/92/1 award of 16 February 1994, 9 ICSID Rev-FILJ 72 (1994).

[125] ibid at para 36.

[126] ibid at para 53. See also *Aguas del Tunari SA v Bolivia* ICSID Case No Arb/02/3 Decision on Jurisdiction 21 October 2005 20 ICSID Rev-FILJ 450 (2005) at paras 206–323 for a detailed analysis of the meaning and application of the term 'controlled directly or indirectly' in the Netherlands-Bolivia BIT, where the question of actual control by Netherlands nationals of the Bolivian claimant company was in issue for the purposes of jurisdiction. Bolivia claimed that the Netherlands holding companies were mere shells and that the real nationality of control was that of the ultimate US parent. The tribunal held that the Netherlands companies were in actual control of the Bolivian claimant company and so it was an entity under control from the Netherlands for the purposes of the BIT.

[127] ICSID Case No Arb/02/18 Decision on Jurisdiction 29 April 2004, 20 ICSID Rev-FILJ 205 (2005).

company incorporated in Lithuania, but owned and controlled by Ukrainian nationals (who owned 99 per cent of the shares and comprised two-thirds of the management), was a Lithuanian national for the purposes of Article 25(2)(b). As this provision was aimed at expanding, and not restricting, the jurisdiction of ICSID so long as the formal nationality of incorporation was that of another contracting party the tribunal would not 'lift the corporate veil'.[128] This conclusion was reinforced by the fact that the BIT defined an 'investor' of Lithuania under Article 1(2)(b) as an 'entity established in the territory of the Republic of Lithuania in conformity with its laws and regulations'. This method of defining corporate nationality was found by the tribunal to be consistent with modern BIT practice and that it satisfied the requirements of Article 25.[129] In addition, the company had been incorporated six years before the BIT between Ukraine and Lithuania had entered into force, showing that the incorporation was not undertaken to gain access to ICSID arbitration.[130]

This decision engendered a strong dissent from the president of the tribunal, Professor Prosper Weil, who held that this finding undermined the object and purpose of the ICSID Convention, which required that the investor be a national of a contracting party other than the respondent contracting party.[131] There is much to be said for this position, given the history of the convention. It is also supported by academic opinion.[132] Against this the majority justifies its view by reference to the intention of the parties as expressed in the BIT. It may be said, in response, that the jurisdiction of ICSID cannot be determined by the subjective intention of the parties to a BIT but by the convention organs themselves.[133] Perhaps it is better to see the majority decision as a pragmatic response to the reality of the mobility of capital in a globalizing economy, which cannot be given a specific 'nationality'.[134] In this it is in line with recent case law in the EC which permits an increasingly flexible approach to rights of establishment in different Member States, even where this may result in a jurisdictional advantage such as the avoidance of regulatory requirements in the country where the enterprise actually operates.[135]

---

[128] ibid at paras 45–51. See also *Saluka Investments BV v Czech Republic* UNCITRAL Arbitration partial award 17 March 2006 available at <http://www.ita.law.uvic.ca> where the tribunal held that a formal legal definition of 'investor' is effective to determine corporate nationality and that, in the absence of a specific treaty provision, a tribunal does not have the power to look behind corporate structures unless these have been used to perpetrate fraud or other malfeasance: at paras 229–30.

[129] ibid at para 52.   [130] ibid at para 56.

[131] 20 ICSID Rev-FILJ 245 (2005). Professor Weil resigned from the tribunal in protest.

[132] Thus, Schreuer asserts: 'the better approach would appear to be a realistic look at the true controllers thereby blocking access to the Centre for juridical persons that are controlled directly or indirectly by nationals of non-Contracting States or nationals of the host State' above n 1 at 318 para 563.

[133] Weil Dissent above n 131 at para 16.

[134] See Robert Wisner and Nick Gallus 'Nationality Requirements in Investor-State Arbitration' 5 JWIT 927 (2004) at 942–45. See further Anthony C Sinclair 'The Substance of Nationality Requirements in Investment Treaty Arbitration' 20 ICSID Rev-FILJ 357 (2005).

[135] See ch 6 at 244–45. See also *Aguas del Tunari SA v Bolivia* above n 126 at paras 156–80 where the tribunal does not rule out the possibility of corporate 'migration' between countries where both legal systems permit this. It notes that this is 'relatively rare': para 174.

On the other hand, the decision in *Loewen v United States* suggests that, under NAFTA, for an international claim to be sustainable, diversity of nationality must exist between the claimant investor and the respondent state from the date of the inception of the claim to the date of resolution. Accordingly, where, as in that case, the reorganization of the claimant company, due to its bankruptcy, caused it to lose its original Canadian nationality and to acquire US nationality, the international character of the claim disappeared.[136] The absence of any evidence that its controller, a Canadian national, retained any shares in the reorganized company was fatal to any personal claim he might have had under NAFTA.[137] It should be noted that this is a NAFTA case and is not binding upon an ICSID Tribunal determining jurisdiction under any other IIA. In addition, as noted above, under Article 25(2)(a), diversity of nationality need only exist under the ICSID Convention at the date the parties consent to the claim being brought and not at the date of its resolution. However, the decision in *Loewen* does stress the need to maintain a distinction between disputes of a purely national character, which should be settled before national bodies, and genuine international disputes.

The pragmatism of ICSID Tribunals on issues of corporate nationality may also be seen in cases involving intermediate holding companies as the immediate controllers of the local subsidiary in the host contracting party. It has been held that where the nationality of the immediate controller of the local subsidiary is that of a non-contracting party, by reason of its incorporation in such a country, but where the ultimate parent is incorporated in a contracting party, ICSID will have jurisdiction over a claim brought by the parent. The nationality of the intermediate holding company will not be decisive.[138] Equally, as held in the case of *Autopista v Venezuela*, where the directly controlling parent is a national of a non-contracting party, and this fact is known to the host country, a subsequent transfer of a majority of its shares in the local subsidiary to an intermediate holding company possessing the nationality of a contracting party, will not be fatal to ICSID

---

[136] ICSID Case No Arb(AF)/98/3 award of 26 June 2003, 42 ILM 811 (2003) at paras 223, 255, and 232–34.

[137] ibid at para 239. In *EnCana v Ecuador* (UNCITRAL Arbitration Award of the London Court of International Arbitration 3 February 2006 available at <http://www.ita.law.uvic.ca>) it was held that continuous nationality of ownership of the subsidiary is not required where the parent makes a claim in its own right and not on behalf of its subsidiary. So long as the nationality of the parent remains that of another contracting party then it qualifies as an investor of that party (para 128).

[138] See *SOABI v Senegal* above n 123. *Company X v State A* in News from ICSID vol 2 No 2 Summer 1985 at 3–6. State A objected to ICSID jurisdiction based on the fact that, notwithstanding its apparent consent to jurisdiction under art 25(2)(b), the immediate controller of the local subsidiary, Company X, had the nationality of a state not party to the convention and so the requirements of art 25(2)(b) were not met. The tribunal rejected this argument on the ground that since the immediate controller was itself controlled by nationals of a contracting state, Company X was entitled to bring ICSID proceedings, it having the nationality of those foreign controllers for the purpose of art 25(2)(b). A similar position has been taken in relation to NAFTA claims: see *Waste Management v Mexico* ICSID Case No Arb(AF)/00/3 award of 30 April 2004, 43 ILM 967 (2004) at paras 77, 80, and 85.

jurisdiction, where the host contracting party is aware of the situation and has applied a formal test of nationality to the local subsidiary.[139]

To summarize, the host contracting state has control over ICSID jurisdiction by means of its power to withhold consent to such jurisdiction. It also retains an important power of refusing to treat a locally incorporated entity as the national of a foreign contracting state under Article 25(2)(b). However, ICSID Tribunals will be willing to find either type of consent where possible. The tribunals have the task of applying the ICSID Convention in accordance with its meaning and intent. This has resulted in an approach that will not readily accept objections to the jurisdiction of the Centre. The extension of jurisdiction in cases such as *Tokios Tokeles* and *Autopista* suggests a risk that ICSID jurisdiction may be granted in future cases of blatant 'treaty shopping'. Investors, who are otherwise disentitled from access to ICSID by reason of nationality, may set up corporate structures, aimed at obtaining such an advantage, under BITs that apply formal tests of corporate nationality. Clearly, one response is to ensure that the dispute settlement provisions of BITs expressly apply only to investors of the other party (or parties) by use of a 'denial of benefits' clause coupled with a control test of corporate nationality, rather than a formal incorporation test.[140] However, some states may see it as being in their interests to become 'investment treaty havens' and to encourage the registration of shell companies for purposes of ICSID jurisdiction under their BITs. Whether ICSID Tribunals will accept such formal arrangements, remains to be seen, notwithstanding dicta to the effect that such 'treaty shopping' may be a ground for denying jurisdiction.[141]

(ii) Subject-Matter Jurisdiction

Article 25(1) of the convention imposes two subject-matter requirements on the jurisdiction of ICSID: first, that the dispute must arise directly out of an 'investment' and, secondly, that the dispute must be a 'legal' dispute.

---

[139] ICSID Case No Arb/00/5 Decision on Jurisdiction 27 September 2001, 16 ICSID Rev-FILJ 469 (2001). Venezuela had permitted a Mexican parent to transfer 75 per cent of its shares in its local subsidiary to a US affiliate, which now became the direct owner of the subsidiary. The tribunal held that it had jurisdiction to hear a claim brought by the US affiliate as Venezuela had applied a simple majority shareholding test for determining foreign nationality, and it was not open to it to challenge this choice by reference to economic criteria even if they would better reflect reality (paras 117–22). There was no evidence that the US affiliate was a corporation of convenience. The transfer was necessary to ensure access to adequate capital during the Mexican Peso crisis (paras 123–26). The fact that Mexico, a non-contracting party, had taken an interest in the dispute at the diplomatic level was not fatal to the claim by the US affiliate (paras 135–40). The *Banro* case above n 111 was distinguished as the transfer of the shares in that case was not subject to the approval of the government and the parties had not defined the test of foreign control (para 143).

[140] See the *Tokios Tokeles* case above n 127 at paras 32–36. Such a clause exists in the ECT. See further *Plama Consortium Limited v Bulgaria* ICSID Case No Arb/03/24 Decision on Jurisdiction, 8 February 2005, 44 ILM 721 (2005) at paras 128–31, 149. Denial of benefits will often be an issue going to the merits only unless it is clear the clause covers dispute settlement as well.

[141] See, for example, *Saluka Investments BV v Czech Republic* above n 128 at para 240. For further discussion of the link of nationality as applied to foreign investors, based on a comparison of decisions

Turning first to the notion of 'investment', this is not defined in the convention. According to George Delaume, this deliberate lack of definition has enabled the convention to accommodate both traditional types of investment, in the form of capital contributions, and new types of investment, including service contracts and transfers of technology.[142] For a long time no disputes over the meaning of this term were brought before ICSID Tribunals. It appeared that so long as the arrangement between the parties involved a long-term outlay of capital on the part of at least one party, there would be no doubt that this constituted an 'investment'.[143] More recently, a number of jurisdictional objections to ICSID arbitration have been made on this ground, possibly as a response to the more complex nature of international investment project structuring and as a result of the inclusion of wide, asset based, definitions of 'investment' in BITs.[144] It is now clear that a minority shareholding in the enterprise operating the investment will be sufficient.[145] In addition, certain types of contractual arrangements will be regarded as 'investments'.[146] For an arrangement to qualify as an 'investment' it should have 'a certain duration, a regularity of profit and return, an element of risk, a substantial commitment and that it should constitute a significant contribution to the host State's development'.[147] Accordingly, contingent liabilities, such as bank guarantees,

from a number of international dispute settlement bodies, see Pia Acconci 'Determining the Internationally Relevant Link Between a State and a Corporate Investor: Recent Trends Concerning the Application of the "Genuine Link" Test' 5 JWIT 139 (2004). See also *Pan American v Argentina* n 98 above at paras 202–22 and *Suez, Sociedad General de Aguas de Barcelona SA, and Vivendi Universal SA v Argentina* ICSID Case No Arb/03/19 Decision on Jurisdiction 3 August 2006 paras 49–51 at <http://www.ita.law.uvic.ca>. Both decisions stress that shareholders have rights to bring claims under BITs, which include the protection of shareholdings in their scope and definition clause, notwithstanding the decision in *Barcelona Traction* (above n 15) as such provisions constitute a *lex specialis* exception to the corporate nationality rule applied in that case.

[142] Above n 76 at 26; Delaume 'ICSID Arbitration and the Courts' 77 AJIL 784 at 795 (1983); ibid. 'Le Centre International pour le Règlement des Différends Relatifs aux Invéstissements (CIDRI)' 109 JDI 775 at 800–808 (1982).

[143] See, for example, *Liberian Eastern Timber Corp (LETCO) v Government of Liberia* 26 ILM 647 (1987). See also *Maffezini v Spain* above n 91 at paras 67–70.

[144] On which see ch 17 at 676.

[145] See *Lanco v Argentina* above n 96 where a shareholding of 18.3 per cent in the local subsidiary was sufficient; *CMS Gas Transmission Co v Argentina* above n 95 at paras 42–51; *Gami Investments Inc v Mexico* UNCITRAL Arbitration Award 15 November 2004, 44 ILM 545 (2005) extends NAFTA protection to minority shareholders in cases of expropriation where their derivative benefits have been interfered with.

[146] See *Fedax v Venezuela* ICSID Case No Arb/96/3 Decision on Jurisdiction 11 July 1997, 37 ILM 1378 (1998), *held*: Article 25 not limited to direct investment so promissory notes issued by the investor to fund public works in the host country were 'investments'; *LESI DIPENTA v Algeria* ICSID Case No Arb/03/8 award of 10 January 2005, 19 ICSID Rev-FILJ 426 (2005) and *Salini v Morocco* above n 95 *held*: construction contracts can be an 'investment'; *CSOB V Slovakia* above n 80 *held*: loan agreement can in certain circumstances be an 'investment'; pre-shipment inspection services contract; *SGS v Philippines* above n 94; dredging contract is an 'investment' being a protected 'contribution in services' under the applicable BIT: *Jan de Nul v Egypt* above n 91.

[147] *Joy Mining v Egypt* above n 95 at para 53, *Salini v Morocco* above n 95 at para 52; *Bayindir v Pakistan* ICSID Case No Arb/03/29 Decision on Jurisdiction 14 November 2005 at <http://www.ita.law.uvic.ca> paras 122–38. The contribution to development requirement may be open to criticism as it introduces an element of motivation into the definition. This may not be relevant if the

will not be regarded as 'investments'.[148] Nor will mere sales transactions.[149] More controversially, pre-investment expenditure has been held not to constitute an 'investment', although each such case will depend on its particular facts and, in particular, on the question whether the parties have agreed that such expenditure should be recoverable in the case of non-completion of the investment.[150] In addition, an investment contract may be held to exist even if certain terms remain to be agreed at a later date and where there is a possibility of renegotiation.[151]

As regards the requirement that the dispute be a 'legal' dispute, in the drafting stages of the convention an attempt was made to define a 'legal dispute' for the purposes of the convention. This proved to be impossible and the definition was left open. The executive directors of the World Bank explained, in their report on the convention, that while conflicts of rights were within the jurisdiction of the Centre, mere conflicts of interest were not. The dispute had to concern either 'the existence or scope of a legal right or obligation, or the nature or extent of the reparation to be made for breach of a legal obligation'.[152] This statement was cited with approval by the tribunal in *Fedax v Venezuela* which held that a disagreement over the effects of certain promissory notes constituted a 'dispute' for the purposes of ICSID jurisdiction.[153] In *Empresas Lucchetti v Peru* the tribunal added that a dispute 'can be held to exist when the parties assert clearly conflicting legal or factual claims bearing on their respective rights or obligations or that "the claim of one party is positively opposed by the other" '.[154]

A prime example of such a dispute is a disagreement over the interpretation of an investment contract or of an investment authorization.[155] On the other hand, the accepted definition will rule out disagreements over the general economic policy of the host country, in that tribunals cannot pass judgment upon whether a country's economic choices are right or wrong, only on whether investors' rights are violated by measures taken in pursuit of those policies. So long as the investor shows a prima facie adverse effect of national measures upon their rights, that is enough to ground jurisdiction on the merits.[156] In the case of a dispute over facts, for jurisdictional purposes the claimant will only have to show a prima facie case

given definition of 'investment' in the BIT is asset based: see the *Saluka* case above n 128 at paras 209–11.

[148] ibid at para 45. In *X (United Kingdom) v The Republic (Central Europe)* (SCC Case 49/2002 available at <http://www.transnational-dispute-management.com>) a 'best efforts' agreement to secure necessary licences for the investment did not have a financial value and so could not be an 'investment' under the applicable BIT.   [149] ibid at para 52.

[150] *Mihaly v Sri Lanka* n 114 at paras 51–60. See also separate concurring opinion of Mr David Suratgar, who felt that precontractual expenditure by a subsidiary in a build operate transfer (BOT) contract should in principle be seen as an 'investment', even if it is not incurred by reason of a signed contract but in anticipation of such signature ibid at ILM 878–80.

[151] *PSEG V Turkey* above n 101 at para 88.   [152] 4 ILM 524 at 528 (1965).

[153] Above n 146 at paras 15–16.

[154] Above n 91 at para 48 citing the *South West Africa* case (Preliminary Objections) ICJ Reports (1962) 319 at 328.   [155] *PSEG v Turkey* above n 101 at para 124.

[156] *CMS Gas Transmission Co v Argentina* above n 95 at paras 27–29, and 35. See also *Pan American v Argentina* above n 98 at paras 63–70; *Suez v Argentina* above n 141 at paras 31–32 and

and the tribunal will usually assume that the claimant's assertions are true and need not be examined. However, this is not an absolute rule and where significant divergences exist between the parties as to the meaning of the dispute, the tribunal can look more closely at the claimant's contentions.[157]

(iii) The Delocalized Character of ICSID Arbitration

The delocalized character of ICSID arbitration is emphasized by the principles contained in Articles 26 and 27 of the convention. By Article 26:

[c]onsent of the parties to arbitration under this Convention shall, unless otherwise stated, be deemed consent to such arbitration to the exclusion of any other remedy.

By Article 27 (1) of the convention:

No Contracting State shall give diplomatic protection, or bring an international claim in respect of a dispute which one of its nationals and another Contracting State shall have consented to submit or shall have submitted to arbitration under this Convention, unless such other Contracting State shall have failed to abide by and comply with the award rendered in such a dispute.

Thus Article 26 excludes other national remedies, while Article 27 excludes other international remedies, for the duration of ICSID proceedings. Once those proceedings are concluded, if they end in an award against the respondent contracting state, then the courts of that state and of the other contracting states must give effect to any 'pecuniary obligations' thereby imposed on the respondent. Only if the respondent state fails to honour such obligations do the international remedies of the foreign investors' national state revive.

However, there are certain limits placed upon the principle of delocalization. The first is under Article 26 itself. It continues:

A Contracting State may require the exhaustion of local administrative or judicial remedies as a condition of its consent to arbitration under this Convention.

Thus, the host contracting state retains some control over the point at which ICSID arbitration becomes available. Only one state has ever made a notification under Article 26 to require the exhaustion of local remedies and this was withdrawn in 1991.[158] Given that few, if any, contemporary BITs or other IIAs any longer contain an express agreement to include the domestic remedies rule, and given the presumption against the inclusion of a requirement to exhaust domestic remedies in such agreements, this ground of restriction for ICSID jurisdiction appears to be something of a dead letter.[159] That said, the NAFTA arbitration in

para 37 where the tribunal held that a claim based on the rights contained in the applicable BIT was a legal claim.

[157] *Joy Mining v Egypt* above n 95 at paras 29–30; *PSEG v Turkey* above n 101 at paras 63–65.

[158] Israel on ratification of the ICSID Convention in 1983: Schreuer above n 1 at 391 para 101.

[159] See further on the presumption against the domestic remedies rule UNCTAD *Dispute Settlement: Investor State* above n 14 and P Peters 'Exhaustion of Local Remedies: Ignored in Most

Loewen v United States appears to have reintroduced an element of the local remedies rule into investor-state arbitration.[160] In that case, the claimant company, and its owner, settled a lawsuit in Mississippi on the basis that an appeal against a manifestly unfair first instance decision, that had gone against them (and which the tribunal held had violated the fair and equitable treatment standard in Article 1105 of NAFTA),[161] would have been highly expensive due to the requirements of Mississippi State law for the losing party to raise a bond equivalent to 125 per cent of the damages awarded against it, which, in this case, amounted to $625 million.

The tribunal held that Article 1121 of NAFTA did not sweep away the international law requirement that, in the context of an alleged judicial violation of international law, the judicial process in the respondent state must be carried on to the highest level, so that the respondent is not exposed to international liability when a domestic review might have avoided such liability.[162] In the circumstances, the claimant had not discharged the burden of showing that the settlement was the only course of action that could reasonably have been taken and so the tribunal concluded that domestic remedies had not been exhausted by the failure to pursue an appeal to the Mississippi Supreme Court.[163] This reasoning appears questionable. It is inconsistent with the finding that the fair and equitable treatment standard had been violated. The very high award made against the claimant, some $500 million, was itself an outcome of the bias it had suffered in the first instance court. To conclude that the need to raise a resulting bond of $625 million did not constitute a real bar to appeal proceedings is simply unrealistic, especially as the claimant could not afford to risk such a high sum in the circumstances surrounding the case. The tribunal's award should not be followed in this regard. It is inconsistent with the object and purpose of investor protection treaties, and allows too much deference to domestic remedies and procedures where these have been, in the tribunal's own opinion, a source of abuse.

Once made available, the consent of the parties to ICSID arbitration brings the principle of exclusivity into operation.[164] Notwithstanding this fact, the effectiveness of Article 26 depends on the willingness of the national courts of the contracting states to refrain from adjudicating in disputes that have been taken to ICSID by consent of the parties. The response from national courts has, in this respect, been uneven.[165] For example, in the case of *MINE v Republic of*

Bilateral Investment Treaties' XLIV Neth.Int'l.LR. 233 (1997). See also *Generation Ukraine v Ukraine* above n 82 at paras 13.1–13.6: 'The United States and Ukraine have elected to omit any requirement that an investor must first exhaust local remedies before submitting a dispute to ICSID arbitration in the BIT. In any case, once the investor has accepted the state's offer to arbitrate in the BIT by filing its notice of arbitration, no further limitations or restrictions on the reference to arbitration can be imposed unilaterally, whether by the State or by the investor' (para 13.5).

[160] *Loewen v United States* ICSID Case No Arb (AF)/98/3 award of 26 June 2003: 42 ILM 811 (2003). See Todd Weiler 'Dodging Bullets: A First Look at the Final Award in the Loewen Group and *Raymond Loewen v USA*' 4 JWI 659 (2003).   [161] ibid at para 137.

[162] ibid at paras 161–62.   [163] ibid at paras 215–17.

[164] See Schreuer above n 1 at 347 paras 2–4.   [165] ibid at 369–87.

Guinea,[166] when faced with the question whether an American arbitration award could be enforced under US law while proceedings were pending before ICSID, the US courts answered, at first instance, that it could,[167] while, on appeal, that it could not, on the grounds that the Republic of Guinea had not waived its right to sovereign immunity before the US courts.[168] At neither instance was the exclusivity of ICSID proceedings accepted as a reason for not recognizing the American arbitral award.[169] By contrast, the Belgian courts did recognize the primacy of ICSID proceedings in the *MINE* case, when they were called upon to recognize the American award,[170] as did the Swiss courts.[171]

In another case involving ICSID proceedings, this time between the Republic of Guinea and Atlantic Triton, the French courts had the opportunity to consider the effect of Article 26. The Court of Appeal at Rennes upheld the exclusivity of ICSID proceedings in the course of an appeal challenging measures of attachment taken by Atlantic Triton against Guinean ships present within French jurisdiction. In the Court's opinion, not only did such exclusivity pertain to consideration of the merits of the dispute, but also to all provisional measures. If local tribunals were able to impose provisional measures while ICSID proceedings were pending, the task of ICSID arbitrators would be unduly complicated and the effectiveness of any eventual award could be prejudiced.[172] This decision was overturned by the Court of Cassation, which took the position that the exclusive character of ICSID arbitration set forth in Article 26 did not prevent a party to an ICSID proceeding from seeking provisional measures of attachment before the French courts. The Court of Cassation felt unable to pronounce upon the effect of the ICSID Convention, which was a matter for the French Government. Furthermore, the power of national courts to order pre-emptive measures could only be excluded by express consent of the parties or by implied convention resulting from the adoption of arbitral rules calling for such waiver.[173] Clearly, therefore, the Court of Cassation was not satisfied that the jurisdiction of national courts could be ousted by Article 26 without any clearer indication to this effect that was accepted by the French Government.

In response to the uncertainty surrounding the question of provisional measures before national courts, a new paragraph was added to the revised Arbitration

---

[166] See 20 ILM 666 (1981).   [167] ibid at 669 or 505 F Supp 141–44 (1981).

[168] (USCA DC Cir) 21 ILM 1355 (1982) and 22 ILM 86 (1983) or 693 F 2d 1094 (1982).

[169] See Delaume's criticism of the US Court of Appeals decision above note 142 77 AJIL 784 at 789–92.

[170] *Republic of Guinea v MINE* 24 ILM 1639 (1985) (Court of First Instance, Antwerp, 27 September 1985).

[171] *Guinea v MINE* 26 ILM 382 (1987) (Swiss Surveillance Authority 7 October 1986).

[172] *SOGUIPECHE v Atlantic Triton Co* 24 ILM 340 (1985) (Court of Appeal, Rennes, 26 October 1984).

[173] *SOGUIPECHE v Atlantic Triton Co* 26 ILM 373 (1987) (Cour de Cassation 18 November 1986). For a view supporting this decision on the ground that the ICSID convention was never intended to prevent national courts from imposing provisional measures of attachment while ICSID proceedings were pending: see Gaillard 114 JDI 125 (1987).

Rule 39 which came into force on 26 September 1984. The paragraph states:

Nothing in this Rule shall prevent the parties, provided they have so stipulated in the agreement recording their consent, from requesting any judicial or other authority to order provisional measures, prior to the institution of the proceeding, or during the proceeding, for the preservation of their respective rights and interests.[174]

However, in the absence of such express agreement, the convention prevents parties from seeking provisional measures other than those that may be recommended by the tribunal under Article 47 of the convention and Arbitration Rule 39.[175]

A second limit on delocalization concerns the law applicable to the merits of the dispute as laid down in Article 42(1) of the convention:

The Tribunal shall decide a dispute in accordance with such rules of law as may be agreed by the parties. In the absence of such agreement, the Tribunal shall apply the law of the Contracting State party to the dispute (including its rules of the Conflict of Laws) and such rules of international law as may be applicable.

This provision lays down a hierarchy of applicable laws with the law chosen by the parties being the most important, followed by the law of the contracting state party to the dispute (or the law of some other state if that applies as a result of the contracting states rules on conflict of laws) and then rules of international law.

If the host contracting state is concerned to ensure that investment disputes are decided by reference to its domestic law then it can hold out for an agreement to this effect from the investor. This, in turn, poses the question of the suitability of an ICSID Tribunal as a body charged with the interpretation and application of the host state's law. Should the tribunal manifestly fail to apply the law of the host state to the disadvantage of either party, a finding of nullity on the grounds of manifest excess of powers by failure to apply Article 42(1) of the convention is possible.[176]

A further question that arises is whether the ICSID Tribunal must apply the host contracting state's law even where this is inconsistent with the rules of international law. In *LETCO v Liberia*[177] the tribunal noted that, although the law of the contracting state was paramount within its own territory, it was subject to control by international law. However, no such problem arose in that case as the applicable rules of Liberian law were in conformity with international law.[178]

---

[174] ICSID Arbitration Rules above n 66 Rule 39(6).

[175] See further *Victor Pey Casado and President Allende Foundation v Chile* ICSID Case No Arb/98/2 decision on provisional measures 25 September 2001, 16 ICSID Rev-FILJ 567 (2001) at paras 1–27. See also News from ICSID vol 2 No 1 Winter 1985 at 6.

[176] See the decision of the ad hoc committee on annulment of the award of the tribunal in *Klöckner v Cameroon* 1 ICSID Rev-FILJ 89 at 110–13 (1986) where the committee held that the tribunal had not applied 'the law of the Contracting State', by reason of its assumption that the principle of good faith was a principle of Cameroonian law without referring to the rules and conditions under which it was implemented or to the limits of its operation. However, the first ad hoc Committee in *Amco Asia* above n 81 in 89 ILR (1992) at 521–22 held that the mere misconstruction of the applicable law was insufficient to warrant annulment.   [177] 26 ILM 657 (1987).

[178] ibid at 658.

Furthermore, it is open to the parties to the dispute to choose international treaty standards as the governing law. Thus, in *Asian Agricultural Products Ltd v Republic of Sri Lanka*[179] the tribunal found that both parties had acted in a manner that demonstrated their mutual agreement to consider the provisions of the Sri Lanka/UK Bilateral Investment Treaty as being the primary source of the applicable legal rules.[180]

Similarly, where no agreement is made on the choice of law, the host contracting state's law applies subject to any applicable rules of international law. In the *Amco Asia* case the first ad hoc committee held that the role of international law was restricted only to the filling of '*lacunae* in the applicable domestic law' and to ensuring 'precedence to international law norms where the rules of the applicable law are in collision with such norms'. The role of international law was thus 'supplemental and corrective' under Article 42(1).[181] However, the tribunal in the resubmitted case of *Amco Asia v Indonesia*[182] rejected this narrow approach and affirmed that:

Article 42(1) refers to the application of host state law and international law. If there are no relevant host state laws on a particular matter, a search must be made for the relevant international laws. And, where there are applicable host state laws, they must be checked against international laws, which will prevail in case of conflict. Thus international law is fully applicable and to classify its role as 'only' 'supplemental and corrective' seems a distinction without a difference.[183]

This formulation shows that international law provides a guarantee to the foreign investor against the unfair operation of national law, especially where fundamental norms of international law are in conflict with national laws.[184] For example, it would not be open to the host state to exclude the international law relating to expropriation, as embodied in a BIT, by reference to an inconsistent national law.[185]

More recently, the ad hoc Annulment Committee in the case of *Wena Hotels v Egypt* went a step further and held that, in an appropriate case, a tribunal could apply the law of the BIT, to the exclusion of national law, under the terms of Article 42(1) in the absence of agreement as to the proper law between the parties.

---

[179] 30 ILM 577 (1991).

[180] ibid para 20. The tribunal noted that by art 157 of the Sri Lanka Constitution the treaty had become part of Sri Lankan law. It went on to hold that the treaty applied as a *lex specialis* which was part of a wider source of rules, from both international and domestic sources, which helped to define the applicable treaty norms: ibid paras 21–24. See, however, the dissenting opinion of SKB Asante ibid at 630–32 for a critique of the majority opinion.

[181] *Amco Asia Corp v Indonesia* (decision of Ad Hoc Committee 16 May 1986) 25 ILM 1439 (1986) paras 19–22 at ILM 1445–46, 89 ILR (1992) at 519–20; see also *Klöckner v Cameroon* (decision of Ad Hoc Committee 3 May 1985) n 176 above.   [182] 89 ILR 580 at 593–94 (1992).

[183] ibid para 40 at 594.

[184] Alan Redfern 'ICSID – Losing its Appeal?' 3 Arb. Int'l 98 at 106 (1987); see also W Michael Reisman 'The Regime for *Lacunae* in the ICSID Choice of Law Provision and the Question of its Threshold' 15 ICSID Rev-FILJ 362 (2000) at 375.

[185] See *Compania del Desarrollo de Santa Elena v Costa Rica* ICSID Case No Arb/96/1 award of 17 February 2000, 15 ICSID Rev-FILJ 169 (2000) at para 64.

The tribunal stated:

The law of the host State can indeed be applied in conjunction with international law if this is justified. So too international law can be applied by itself if the appropriate rule is found in this other ambit ... In particular, the rules of international law that directly or indirectly relate to the State's consent prevail over domestic rules that might be incompatible with them. In this context it cannot be concluded that resort to the rules of international law under the Convention, or under particular treaties related to its operation, is antagonistic to that State's national interest[186]

The tribunal noted that in this case Egypt had a positive policy towards the use of BITs and that such agreements had the force of law and, in a case of conflict with national law, international law prevailed. Thus in applying the BIT exclusively the tribunal could not be said to have applied rules alien to the domestic system of the host country.[187] Arguably, this decision goes beyond the earlier cases, with their emphasis on the filling of lacunae in the national law of the host country, and gives tribunals the freedom to apply international law where this is the more appropriate system.[188] That said, the tribunal in *Wena Hotels* was at pains to stress that the circumstances of each case will justify whether a tribunal should highlight rules of national or international law, and that the inclusion of the word 'may' in Article 42(1) second sentence, did not draw a sharp distinction between the scope of international and national law but left the tribunal a certain margin and power for interpretation.[189] Accordingly, this decision should not be read as subordinating national laws completely to international rules, but as reaffirming the need to use international law where appropriate in the absence of party choice. Equally, the emphasis placed upon the law and practice of Egypt in relation to BITs would suggest that a tribunal will examine the constitutional position of international rules under the applicable national system. Here it is fairly certain that countries, such as Egypt, that adopt a monist approach to international law, and see it as part of their internal legal order, provide a *renvoi* to international law under national law.[190] Countries espousing a dualist approach, requiring an act of transformation to international law for it to be effective within the national legal order, will not offer a similar solution. In such cases the wider principle that a state cannot use an inconsistency with national law to justify non-observance of an international obligation will apply.

This relationship between national and international law is in keeping with the scheme of the ICSID Convention, which envisages recognition and enforcement of awards in all contracting states under Article 54(1) and restricts the national

---

[186] ICSID Case No Arb/98/4 decision of the ad hoc Committee 28 January 2002, 41 ILM 933 (2002) at paras 40–41.   [187] ibid at paras 42–44.
[188] See Emmanuel Gaillard and Yas Banifatemi 'The Meaning of "and" in Article 42(1) Second Sentence, of the Washington Convention: The Role of International Law in the ICSID Choice of Law Process' 18 ICSID Rev-FILJ 375 (2003).   [189] Above n 186 at para 39.
[190] ibid. See also *Middle East Shipping and Handling Co SA v Egypt* ICSID Case No Arb/99/6 award of 12 April 2002, 18 ICSID Rev-FILJ 602 (2003) at paras 85–87.

state of the investor from invoking its right of diplomatic protection under Article 27. Only an award that does not violate applicable principles and rules of international law is consistent with these provisions.[191] Therefore it is clear that even when the parties agree to use host state law the dispute will be effectively internationalized in that the ultimate standard of decision will be provided by international law. The host state's apparent control over the applicable law under Article 42(1) is thus quite substantially curtailed.[192] That this is so should come as no surprise. As already noted, an international tribunal cannot accept a plea from the respondent state that provisions of its own law or deficiencies in that law are an answer to a claim against it for an alleged breach of international law.[193] This principle was affirmed by the tribunal in *Southern Pacific Properties (Middle East) Limited v Arab Republic of Egypt*,[194] where a determination that certain acts of the Egyptian authorities, which resulted in the expropriation of the claimant's investment, were null and void under Egyptian law, was held not to exclude the operation of international law as the standard by which the responsibility of Egypt for the unauthorized acts of its officials would be ascertained, even though Egyptian law was held to be the applicable law under Article 42(1).

(iv) Annulment of Tribunal Awards

By Article 52(1) of the ICSID Convention, either party may request annulment of the award by an application in writing addressed to the Secretary-General on one or more of the following grounds:

(a) that the Tribunal was not properly constituted;
(b) that the Tribunal has manifestly exceeded its powers;
(c) that there was corruption on the part of a member of the Tribunal;
(d) that there has been a serious departure from a fundamental rule of procedure; or
(e) that the award has failed to state the reasons on which it is based.

The nature of the power to annul under this provision was described as follows by the ad hoc Committee in the case of *CDC Group v Seychelles*:

As the ordinary meaning of the terms of Article 52(1) indicates, the ICSID annulment procedure is concerned with determining whether the underlying proceeding was fundamentally fair: Article 52(1) looks not to the merits of the underlying dispute as such, but rather is concerned with the fundamental integrity of the Tribunal, whether basic procedural guarantees were largely observed, whether the Tribunal exceeded the bounds of the

---

[191] *AMCO Asia Corp v Indonesia* above n 181 first ad hoc Committee para 21 ILM 1446; ILR 521.
[192] Compare Professor Dupuy's Theory of the 'internationalization' of economic development agreements in *Texaco v Libya* 17 ILM 1 (1978) at para 45.
[193] By Article 27 Vienna Convention on the Law of Treaties 1969: 'A party may not invoke the provisions of its internal law as justification for its failure to perform a treaty . . . ' Similarly, by art 3 of the International Law Commission Articles on State Responsibility 2001: 'The characterization of an act of a State as internationally wrongful is governed by international law. Such characterization is not affected by the characterization of the same act as lawful by internal law' (ILC Report of 53rd Session ILC (2001) GAOR 56th Session, Supp 10).
[194] Award on the Merits 20 May 1992: 32 ILM 933 (1993).

parties consent, and whether the Tribunal's reasoning is both coherent and displayed. To borrow Caron's terminology, annulment is concerned with the ' "legitimacy" of the process of decision' rather than with the 'substantive correctness of the decision'. Because of its focus on procedural legitimacy, annulment is an 'extraordinary remedy for unusual and important cases'. That annulment is not the same thing as appeal is a principle acknowledged, although applied unevenly, in the various decisions of ad hoc Committees. Additionally, the Convention specifically recognises this distinction by rejecting, in Article 53, any right to appeal.[195]

This power to annul the awards of ICSID Tribunals was subjected to severe criticism in the light of the first annulment decisions in *Klöckner v Cameroon*,[196] and *AMCO Asia Corporation v Indonesia*.[197] These annulment awards were heavily criticized not only on their reasoning but also on their broader implications for the ICSID system.[198] In each case the ad hoc Committee was said to have acted as a de facto court of appeal on matters of fact and law, which goes beyond the limited grounds of annulment available under Article 52(1). Furthermore, the requirement laid down in the *Klöckner* case, that the tribunal must deal with every matter put before it, would expose most ICSID awards to the risk of annulment. The procedure of submitting 'memorials' and 'counter-memorials' to the tribunal, although useful in giving the factual background to the dispute, does not define the issues as precisely as a set of pleadings before a court. Thus there is always a risk of an issue not being dealt with by a tribunal.[199]

---

[195] *CDC Group v Seychelles* ICSID Case No Arb/02/14 (decision of ad hoc Annulment Committee 29 June 2005 available at <http://www.asil.org/ilib/2005/12/ilib051216.html#j5>) at para 34. On the annulment of ICSID awards in general, see further Emmanuel Gaillard and Yas Banifatemi (eds) *Annulment of ICSID Awards* (Huntington, New York: Juris Publishers, 2004).

[196] Above n 176.

[197] Above n 181. A third early case was *MINE v Guinea Ad hoc* Committee Decision of 22 December 1989: 5 ICSID Rev-FILJ 95 (1990). The ad hoc Committee annulled an award of US$12.3 million against Guinea but upheld the finding of breach of the investment contract. The parties requested the resubmission of the dispute to a new tribunal, but agreed a settlement on 20 November 1990. A further ad hoc Committee was set up in the case of *SPP v Egypt* but the case settled before a decision was given: Schreuer above n 1 at 897 para 21. An annulment decision was given in the *Wena Hotels* case above n 186. The decision of the ad hoc Annulment Committee in the *Vivendi* case is examined below. At the time of writing (September 2006), annulment proceedings had been instituted in *Philippe Gruslin v Malaysia* ICSID Case No Arb/99/3 (discontinued 2 April 2002 for lack of payment); *Joy Mining v Egypt* above n 95 (settled 16 December 2005); *CDC Group v Seychelles* above n 195. Three annulment proceedings are pending: *MTD v Chile* ICSID Case No Arb/01/7; *Soufraki v United Arab Emirates* above n 110; *CMS v Argentina* above n 95 and Decision to Stay of Enforcement of the Award of 1 September 2006: see List of Pending Cases <http://www.worldbank.org/icsid.. Further cases involving stays of enforcement pending an annulment decision can be found in 20 ICSID Rev-FILJ 581–643 (*Patrick Mitchell v Congo* ICSID Case No Arb/99/7; *MTD v Chile* above; *Repsol Ecuador v Petroecuador* ICSID Case No Arb/01/10).

[198] See Redfern above n 184; Feldman 'The Annulment Proceedings and Finality of ICSID Arbitral Awards' 2 ICSID Review – Foreign Investment Law Journal 85 (1987); Schatz 'The Effect of the Annulment Decisions in *Amco v Indonesia* and *Klöckner v Cameroon* the Future of the International Centre for Settlement of Investment Disputes' 3 Am.U.J.Int'l L. & Pol'y 481 (1988); Reisman 'The Breakdown of the Control Mechanism in ICSID Arbitration' (1989:4) Duke LJ 739.

[199] Redfern ibid at 109.

These concerns prompted the Secretary-General of ICSID to propose an amendment to the Arbitration Rules clarifying the exceptional nature of the annulment procedure.[200] In the event, subsequent practice appears not to have undermined the effectiveness of ICSID arbitration. Indeed, given the large rise in cases submitted to the Centre in recent years, it would appear that confidence in its procedures has never been higher. On the other hand, when the policy implications of ICSID awards are taken into account, and given the progressive development of arbitral 'case law' as the number of awards rendered increases, the need for some system of appeal, rather than mere annulment, may become more pressing, so as to give greater legitimacy and consistency to ICSID awards. The Centre itself has considered this idea, although, at present, a reform along these lines is unlikely.[201]

The function of the annulment procedure was recently reviewed by the ad hoc Committee in the *Vivendi* case.[202] As in the *CDC* case, the committee stressed that it was not a court of appeal and that its competence extended only to annulment based on one or more of the grounds expressly set out in Article 52. In this there was no presumption either in favour or against annulment. However, such an outcome could only arise in serious cases of inconsistency with Article 52, as stressed by its language. In relation to a failure to state reasons, this meant a failure to state any reasons with respect to all or part of an award, not a failure to state correct or convincing reasons. In such a case annulment should only occur in a clear case. That required two conditions: that the failure to state reasons left the decision on a particular point essentially lacking in any expressed rationale and that the point itself had to be necessary to the tribunal's decision. This did not include the presence of conflicting considerations in the decision, as tribunals might often struggle to balance conflicting considerations. Finally, even if an annullable error was found the ad hoc Committee had flexibility in determining whether annulment should be ordered, and on whether to annul the whole, or only a part, of the decision. In this regard certain findings would annul the award as a whole, as where the tribunal was improperly constituted, while other grounds may only affect part of the award. As stated in Article 52(3) the ad hoc Committee is empowered to annul an award 'in whole or in part'. The ad hoc Committee went on to assert that it was not open to the requesting party to determine the extent of the annulment as this was a matter exclusively of the committee to determine.

[200] Report of the Secretary-General to the Administrative Council ICSID Doc No AC/86/4, 2 October 1986 Annex A at 3; ICSID *Annual Report 1988* at 4. See also K Jacob 'Reinvigorating ICSID with a New Mission and with Renewed Respect for Party Autonomy' 33 Va.J.Int'l Law 123 (1993).

[201] See ICSID Secretariat *Possible Improvements of the Framework for ICSID Arbitration* (Discussion Paper, 22 October 2004) at 14–16 and Annex; ICSID Secretariat *Suggested Changes to the ICSID Rules and Regulations* (Working Paper, 12 May 2005) at para 4.

[202] *Compania de Aguas del Aconquija and Vivendi Universal (formerly Compagnie Générale des Eaux) v Argentina* ICSID Case No Arb/97/3 Decision on Annulment 3 July 2002, 41 ILM 1135 (2002) at paras 61–70 on which this account is based. See also David Williams 'International Commercial Arbitration and Globalization: Review and Recourse Against Awards Rendered Under Investment Treaties' 4 JWI 251 (2003) at 266–72.

(v) Enforcement of ICSID Awards

By Article 54 of the ICSID Convention:

Each Contracting State shall recognise an award rendered pursuant to this Convention as binding and enforce the pecuniary obligations imposed by that award within its territories as if it were a final judgment of a court in that state ...

The party seeking recognition or enforcement need only present a copy of the award certified by the Secretary-General of ICSID.[203] The execution of the award should be governed by the laws concerning the execution of judgments in force in the state where execution is sought.[204] This includes the applicable law relating to a foreign state's immunity from execution.[205] Thus the respondent state still enjoys the protection of the law of sovereign immunity as applied in the enforcing state.[206] In practical terms, therefore, the enforceability of an ICSID award is subject to the overriding principle of protecting the property belonging to a foreign sovereign, which is used for sovereign rather than commercial purposes, against execution, this being the most commonly applicable rule found in national laws.[207]

(vi) Procedure and Costs

Both the ICSID conciliation and arbitration procedures begin with a request to the Secretary-General of ICSID.[208] The party wishing to institute proceedings sends a request in writing to the Secretary-General, who shall send a copy of the request to the other party. The request must contain information concerning the matters in dispute, the identity of the parties and their consent to arbitration or conciliation in accordance with the rules of procedure for the institution of conciliation and arbitration proceedings.

The Secretary-General thereupon undertakes a preliminary investigation of the jurisdictional admissibility of the request. He or she may refuse the request if it

---

[203] Article 54(2) ICSID Convention.   [204] ibid art 54(3).   [205] ibid art 55.

[206] See, for example, the US case *LETCO v Government of Liberia* 650 F Supp 73 (SDNY 1986), 26 ILM 695 (1987) *aff'd* memo No 86–9047 (2d Cir 19 May 1987). See also Georges Delaume 'Sovereign Immunity and Transnational Arbitration' in J Lew (ed) n 24 above at 313. In *SOABI (SEUTIN) v Senegal* (France, Cour de Cassation, 11 June 1991), 30 ILM 1167 (1991), it was held that a foreign state that has consented to ICSID arbitration has thereby agreed that the award may be granted recognition (*exequatur*) which, as such, does not constitute a measure of execution that might raise issues pertaining to the immunity from execution of the state concerned. The ICSID Convention provided an autonomous and simple system of recognition which excluded domestic rules concerning recognition of foreign awards. The award in *SOABI v Senegal* is reproduced in 6 ICSID Rev-FILJ 125 (1991).

[207] See, for example, *AIG Capital Partners Inc and Another v Republic of Kazakhstan (National Bank of Kazakhstan intervening)* [2005] EWHC 2239 (Comm), [2006] 1 All ER 284 (QBD) where it was held that the property of a state's central bank or monetary authority was subject to state immunity under s 14(4) of the State Immunity Act 1978 and so could not be used to satisfy an ICSID award, even if such property was being held by third parties on behalf of the central bank or monetary authority.

[208] See for conciliation Article 28 ICSID Convention; for arbitration see Article 36 ICSID Convention.

appears to him or her, on the basis of the information contained in the request, that the Centre is not competent to admit the dispute. If the dispute appears to be within the jurisdiction of the Centre the Secretary-General registers the request in either the conciliation or arbitration register, notifying the parties of the registration on the same day. The proceedings are deemed to have commenced from the day of registration. The Secretary-General's powers in this respect are not final. The ICSID Tribunal is the ultimate judge of admissibility.[209] The registration of a dispute does not, therefore, prevent the tribunal from rejecting it for lack of competence. Should a request for registration be refused, the claimant may submit a second request but must ensure that the dispute falls prima facie within the jurisdiction of the Centre.

The conciliation commission or arbitral tribunal shall be constituted as soon as possible after the registration of the request.[210] Each body shall consist of a sole member or any uneven number of members appointed as the parties shall agree. In the absence of the agreement of the parties the conciliation commission or arbitral tribunal shall consist of three members.[211] Should no appointment be made within 90 days of registration, or such time as the parties agree, the chairman of the body in question shall appoint the conciliators or arbitrators, as the case may be.[212] At this point the conciliation and arbitration procedures diverge.

As to the conciliation procedures, conciliators may be appointed from outside the panel of conciliators, provided they possess the qualities required of a member of the panel.[213] The Conciliation Commission, being satisfied that it has the competence to proceed,[214] has the duty to clarify the issues between the parties and to endeavour to bring about agreement between them on mutually agreeable terms. It may recommend terms of settlement to the parties at any time during the proceedings.[215] If the parties reach agreement, the Conciliation Commission must draw up a report noting the issues in dispute and recording that the parties have reached agreement. If the parties fail to agree the commission must draw up a report recording the failure of the proceedings.[216] Failure by one party to appear terminates the proceedings and a report to this effect must be drawn up by the commission.[217] After the conciliation proceedings have ended each party is bound by a duty of confidentiality regarding the matters discussed and offers of settlement made during the course of those proceedings.[218]

As regards the proceedings of the arbitral tribunal, the majority of the arbitrators must be nationals of states other than the state party to the dispute and the state whose national is a party to the dispute, unless the parties agree jointly to the appointment of a sole arbitrator or to each member of a larger tribunal.[219] The arbitral tribunal will consider whether it has jurisdiction over the dispute in accordance with the standards laid down in Article 25 of the convention, and in the

---

[209] See art 41 ICSID Convention.   [210] ibid art 29(1) (conciliation); art 37(1) (arbitration).
[211] ibid art 29(2); art 37(2).   [212] ibid art 30 (conciliation); art 38 (arbitration).
[213] ibid art 31.   [214] ibid art 32.   [215] ibid art 34(1).   [216] ibid art 34(2).
[217] ibid.   [218] ibid art 35.   [219] ibid art 39.

light of the applicable law determined in accordance with Article 42 of the convention, as discussed above. Unlike conciliation proceedings, arbitration proceedings will not become invalidated by the non-appearance of a party. The tribunal may continue at the request of the other party and render an award.[220] In doing so the tribunal must follow the procedures laid down in the Arbitration Rules regarding the notification of the defaulting party and the granting of a period of grace before continuing with the arbitration.[221] The tribunal shall render its award in accordance with the requirements contained in the convention as to form and content.[222] The award is then subject to the annulment and enforcement provisions discussed above.

The costs of ICSID proceedings are determined by reference to regulations adopted from time to time by the Administrative Council.[223] Each conciliation commission and each arbitral tribunal shall determine the fees and expenses of its members within the limits established from time to time by the Administrative Council and after consultation with the Secretary-General.[224] However, the parties may agree in advance with the commission or tribunal concerned upon the fees and expenses of its members.[225] In the case of conciliation proceedings the costs shall be borne equally by the parties.[226] In the case of arbitration proceedings the tribunal shall decide, unless the parties otherwise agree, the amount of expenses incurred by the parties and how and by whom those expenses, the fees and expenses of the members of the tribunal and the charges for the use of the facilities of the Centre shall be paid.[227] Generally, the costs of ICSID proceedings are lower than those conducted under ICC procedures.[228] Administrative charges are assessed on the basis of the Centre's actual expenses,[229] and arbitrator's fees are on a reasonable per diem basis.[230]

Concluding Remarks

In adopting the aims and methods outlined above, the ICSID Convention attempts to remedy a number of problems that were identified, at the time of its conclusion, as hindering the effective resolution of disputes between foreign investors and host states. In particular these were: the risk of bias in national arbitral and judicial tribunals of, particularly, the host state; the ineffectiveness of diplomatic protection as a means of vindicating the rights of the foreign investor; the problems associated with ad hoc international arbitration, in particular, the

---

[220] ibid art 45.
[221] See *Liberian Eastern Tree Corp (LETCO) v Government of Liberia* 26 ILM 647 at 654–57 (1987). See ICSID Arbitration Rules Rule 42 in ICSID *ICSID Convention Regulations and Rules* above n 66.   [222] See ICSID Convention arts 48–49.
[223] ibid art 59.   [224] ibid art 60(1).   [225] ibid art 60(2).   [226] ibid art 61(1).
[227] ibid art 61(2).   [228] Markham Ball above n 24 at 303.
[229] ICSID Administrative and Financial Regulations, reg 14(3) ICSID *ICSID Convention Regulations and Rules* above n 66 at 61.   [230] ibid reg 14(1).

risk of non-recognition before national tribunals and the possibility that the arbitral agreement would favour the party with greater bargaining power, both matters rendering the authority and finality of the award less certain.[231] In answering these challenges ICSID provides an international dispute settlement body whose philosophy is firmly rooted in the desirability of delocalized conciliation and arbitration. It is seen as a means of encouraging foreign investment by guaranteeing its legal security. This characteristic has led increasing numbers of states, once firmly opposed to such methods of dispute settlement, to accept ICSID jurisdiction in their BITs.[232] However, certain key capital-importing states remain outside the membership.[233] Equally, the increased case-load suggests a shift in awareness as to the availability of ICSID as a source of redress against host countries.

This rise in international investor-state arbitration is not without its attendant problems. In particular, given the policy sensitive nature of the decisions made by ICSID, and other investor-state dispute settlement bodies, some have come to question the legitimacy of subjecting governmental regulatory powers to delocalized, democratically unaccountable, international bodies.[234] This has led ICSID itself to consider reforms including prompt publication of awards where the parties exercise their right to permit such publication, more open procedures allowing access to proceedings for interested third parties, and a possible ICSID appeals facility.[235] Some of these reforms have been instituted in the latest changes to the Arbitration Rules in 2006, allowing, in particular, for third party participation in ICSID arbitration at the discretion of the tribunal after the consultation of both parties.[236] This is a move towards greater openness. However, much remains to be done. The need is to ensure a balance between the rights of investors to seek international dispute settlement and the rights of host countries not to be subjected to excessive review of their policy actions and to have this done in an open, transparent, and accountable procedural setting.

[231] Sutherland above n 33 at 370–73.

[232] This is particularly true of the smaller Latin American countries that have abandoned the Calvo Doctrine (on which see n 20 above). China is also a major former objector to internationalized dispute settlement that is now a member.

[233] Key outsiders include Canada and Mexico (although both have accepted the Additional Facility jurisdiction for NAFTA disputes), Brazil, India, South Africa, and Russia, which signed the convention in 1992 but has yet to ratify it.

[234] See, for example, IISD/WWF above n 71 and William Greider 'Invalidating the 20th Century: How the Right is Using Trade Law to Overturn American Democracy' The Nation vol 273 No 11 15 October 2001 at 21. Both focus on NAFTA dispute settlement in particular, displaying how much this has caused anxiety in North American political circles.

[235] See ICSID Secretariat Discussion Paper 2004 above n 201; ICSID Secretariat Working Paper 2005 above n 201.   [236] See Arbitration Rules above n 66 Rule 37(2).

Index